LEADING ORGANIZATIONS

THIRD EDITION

*To the memory of my dear mother-in-law, Eva Hickman Bell—a warm,
witty, and wonderful mother and friend. I will be forever grateful for her love.*

and

*To the memory and legacy of James MacGregor Burns—a remarkable scholar,
mentor, and friend. The warmth of his caring spirit and friendship will always be in my heart.*

LEADING ORGANIZATIONS

Perspectives for a New Era

THIRD EDITION

Edited by

Gill Robinson Hickman
University of Richmond

Los Angeles | London | New Delhi
Singapore | Washington DC | Boston

Los Angeles | London | New Delhi
Singapore | Washington DC | Boston

FOR INFORMATION:

SAGE Publications, Inc.
2455 Teller Road
Thousand Oaks, California 91320
E-mail: order@sagepub.com

SAGE Publications Ltd.
1 Oliver's Yard
55 City Road
London EC1Y 1SP
United Kingdom

SAGE Publications India Pvt. Ltd.
B 1/I 1 Mohan Cooperative Industrial Area
Mathura Road, New Delhi 110 044
India

SAGE Publications Asia-Pacific Pte. Ltd.
3 Church Street
#10-04 Samsung Hub
Singapore 049483

Printed in the United States of America

A catalog record of this book is available from the Library of Congress.

ISBN 978-1-4833-4669-4

This book is printed on acid-free paper.

Acquisitions Editor: Maggie Stanley
Editorial Assistant: Nicole Mangona
Production Editor: Bennie Clark Allen
Copy Editor: Matthew Sullivan
Typesetter: C&M Digitals (P) Ltd.
Proofreader: Laura Webb
Indexer: Maria Sosnowski
Cover Designer: Glenn Vogel
Marketing Manager: Liz Thornton

15 16 17 18 19 10 9 8 7 6 5 4 3 2 1

Contents

Preface

My intent for the design and content of this book is to increase the reader's understanding of concepts and practices that facilitate shared responsibility for leadership and fluid roles among leaders and participants in new era organizations. The third edition of *Leading Organizations* has been restructured and revised to include many new and updated chapters throughout the book.

The central organizing feature of the book is an overarching framework (depicted in the Introduction) that outlines the components of leadership in organizations. This framework is repeated at the beginning of each Part with highlighted sections that indicate the focus of a section. The book features current chapters by many prominent scholars in the field of leadership studies and a variety of other disciplines.

This edition incorporates new chapters in every section of the book. It features a selection of chapters about global issues in organizations and contains work from a number of authors outside the United States as well as chapters by practitioners. New readings in the beginning section focus on the dynamic global contexts in which new era organizations function. Classic leadership theories remain in the volume, and shared leadership continues as a primary emphasis with new chapters on the state of research in the field. The section on shared leadership emphasizes the increasing need for leadership by participants throughout an organization.

Organization culture and inclusion have been combined into one section. There is more emphasis on ethics, which has a separate section and an expanded number of readings. The section on organizational change incorporates new readings on strategic leadership, open strategy, and big data. Sections on capacity building and social responsibility remain in this edition with new articles in each category.

The book is intended for those who study leadership in organizations *and* those who serve in roles of leaders and members. These are the individuals who can make a difference in the processes and outcomes of organizations and the people to whom we entrust the future of new era organizations.

Acknowledgments

I wish to thank the many colleagues and students who have embraced the framework and concepts in this book and continue to use the volume in their teaching and research. I am thankful to the editors and staff of SAGE Publications for their expertise and support during the editing and publication of the book, especially Maggie Stanley, acquisitions editor; Nicole Mangona, editorial assistant; and MaryAnn Vail, publishing associate.

I truly appreciate the thorough review by James Burke at Virginia Commonwealth University who provided detailed feedback on revisions for the third edition. Your review was tremendously helpful as a guide for updates and improvements. Finally, I owe deep gratitude to my husband, Garrison Michael Hickman, who carefully read and commented on all the overview sections and kept me going with food, tea, laughter, and love so that I could complete this edition of *Leading Organizations*.

SAGE Publications would like to thank the following reviewers:

Ted J. Takamura, PhD, CPA, CFE, CGMA
Eastern Oregon University – Gresham Campus

Dr. Miguel A. Cardenas
San Diego Global Knowledge University

Bruce Winston, PhD
Regent University

G. K. Cunningham
U.S. Army War College; Duquesne University

Priva Fischweicher
Barry University

Charles A. Kramer
University of La Verne

James M. Burke
Virginia Commonwealth University

Dr. Yvonne Styles
The Chicago School of Professional Psychology

SAGE was founded in 1965 by Sara Miller McCune to support the dissemination of usable knowledge by publishing innovative and high-quality research and teaching content. Today, we publish more than 750 journals, including those of more than 300 learned societies, more than 800 new books per year, and a growing range of library products including archives, data, case studies, reports, conference highlights, and video. SAGE remains majority-owned by our founder, and after Sara's lifetime will become owned by a charitable trust that secures our continued independence.

Los Angeles | London | Washington DC | New Delhi | Singapore | Boston

Introduction

Most of us spend a large portion of our lives in organizations. Face-to-face or electronically, we are educated in and work for organizations that matter a great deal. Leadership makes a meaningful difference in every aspect of these organizations. We want and expect leadership that is purposeful and intelligent, effective and competent, caring and moral. The purpose of this book is to provide an integrated perspective for facilitating good (effective and ethical) leadership of organizations so that they are well suited to meet our expectations and the demands of this new era.

The fast pace and rapidly changing environment in which current organizations function require leadership that is substantially different from Max Weber's solitary executive at the top of a bureaucratic hierarchy. Organizations require leadership that is fluid, not simply positional, dispersed rather than centralized, and agile not inflexible. The external environment and continuous advancements in technology are major driving forces underlying change in organizational leadership. A single leader or executive leadership team rarely has enough knowledge, information, expertise, or ability to understand and respond quickly, effectively, and ethically to the dynamic changes in the environment, and adapt or transform the organization and its participants.

This book focuses on concepts and practices that facilitate shared responsibility for leadership and fluid roles among leaders and participants[1] in organizations. A primary assumption underlying the book is that new era organizations can become better able to meet the challenges of their environment through dedication to a compelling and deeply held common purpose by the organization's members and the development of their capacity to share responsibility for leadership of the organization. A further assumption is that leadership of these organizations can become increasingly more trustworthy, concerned about the effect of their decisions or actions on others, and more resilient when leaders and participants base their decisions and actions on a foundation of ethics. A final assumption is that organizations will need to align their leadership and organizational processes to respond effectively to changes in the external and internal environment.

Given these assumptions, organizational participants will need to choose and cultivate their leadership philosophy, processes, and actions thoughtfully and deliberately. An organization's leadership philosophy is more than a style. It is the essence of the organization's integrity—a clear demonstration of its beliefs in action. Determining the tenets of organizational philosophy requires the combined efforts of leaders and participants. Accordingly, leadership concepts and theories are incorporated in the book to advance purposeful choices of leadership philosophy, concepts, processes, and practices.

Figure I.1 depicts a holistic framework for understanding and analyzing the role of leadership in new era organizations. The first component of this framework represents the larger external context in which organizations function. Leaders and members must understand and access this external environment for the purpose of transforming or adapting the organization to a rapidly changing context. The center of the Venn diagram represents core leadership processes,

Figure 1   Leading Organizations Framework

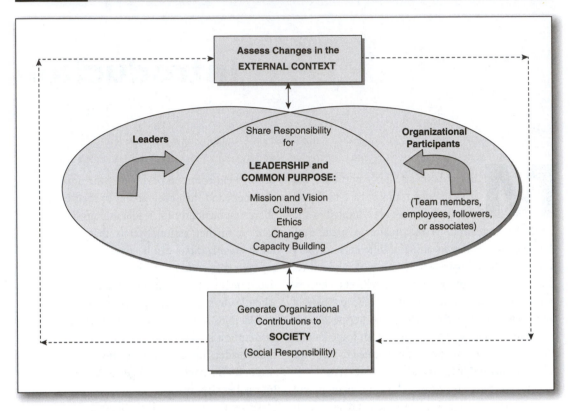

practices, and actions that permeate and guide all components of organizational life. As depicted in the framework, shared responsibilities for leadership by organizational leaders and members consist of generating and advancing the organization's common purpose, vision and mission, culture, ethics, organizational change, capacity building, and social responsibility.

This shared responsibility for leadership and the fluidity of leader and member roles represent a fundamental shift in the philosophy and functioning of leadership in organizations. Robert Kelley points out that leaders and participants play different but equal roles in carrying out core processes and actions; yet both leaders and participants do leadership.[2] Though executive leaders are designated formal responsibility and authority by a board of directors or government regulations—that is, legitimate power to act on behalf of the organization, responsibility for accomplishing the organization's purpose, accountability

for performance of its members to meet organizational goals, financial and resource accountability, and organizational structure or design—the complex realities of contemporary organizations call for leadership roles that are more fluid than in past eras. The concept of leadership as a process of initiation, and involvement does not negate formal authority. Participants share formal authority broadly in contemporary structures. Individuals move from participant to leader or leader to participant based on capabilities, expertise, motivation, ideas, and circumstances, not solely on position or formal authority. In new era organizations, leadership can start with formal leaders (appointed authorities) in concert with other organizational participants and stakeholders, and leadership can originate with participants without formal authority.

The final component of this framework emphasizes the organization's social responsibility to contribute to the well-being of society. It emphasizes the organization's commitment to care for people, communities, and the physical environment as an integral part of its double or triple bottom line.

In its entirety, the framework provides an approach to conceptualizing and guiding leadership in new era organizations. The book follows this framework throughout, and the selected readings provide meaning and depth to each component. The text contains several parts with an overview by the editor on leadership and organizational issues for each segment. Part I identifies several major changes in the external context that effect 21st century organizations and provides perspective for the long term. Part II examines current theories and concepts of leadership and followership that remain viable in many contemporary organizations. Part III focuses on one of the primary themes of this text—shared leadership. It begins with an emphasis on the organization's common purpose and presents some of the latest concepts and research on various forms of shared leadership. Part IV considers the central core of an organization—its culture. This section examines the effect of leadership on an organization's culture and the inclusion of organizational participants that represent a wide range of cultural, national, global, racial, gender, sexual orientation, and generational pluralism. Part V addresses an essential component of leadership in organizations—ethics. This section emphasizes the role of ethical leadership in shaping behavior and decision making in organizations and the challenge of averting or counteracting harmful or unethical forms of leadership. Part VI focuses on change; strategic leadership, including vision and mission; and structure or design in connection with the organization's external environment.

Part VII looks at capacity building as a means for developing the abilities of organizational members to advance their leadership capacity, work in teams, and share leadership in a rapidly changing global and local context. Finally, Part VIII explores the new responsibility of organizational leadership to contribute to society through social and environmental activism. Even though organizations in previous eras were expected to generate contributions to society, the expectations of today's organizations are considerably more extensive and challenging. Society requires more than job creation and employment. People want organizations to give time, human capital, and monetary resources to advance the well-being of society and protect the environment. Organizational leaders and participants are expected to take active roles to tackle issues such as education, the environment, health, housing, and poverty in addition to traditional forms of philanthropy. They are in highly advantageous positions to facilitate unprecedented advances for society and resolve complex problems based on their collective capacity to mobilize human, technological, and economic resources.

This book strives to provide more than a collection of engaging readings. It intends to frame a way forward for the study and practice of leadership in new era organizations.

Notes

1. This text uses the terms *participants*, *members or team members*, *employees*, *followers*, and *associates* interchangeably throughout.

2. Kelley, R. (1988). In praise of followers. *Harvard Business Review, 88*(6), 142–148.

PART I

The Context of New Era Organizations

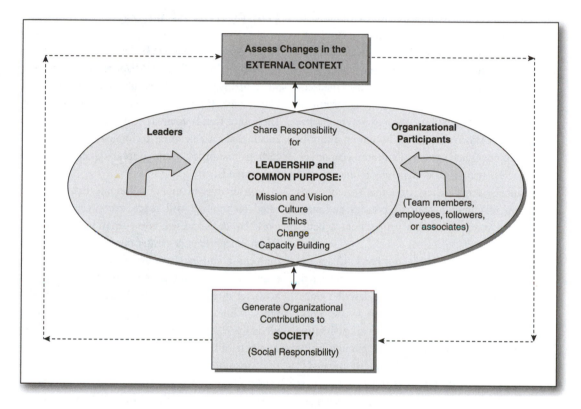

Overview

A world of global changes, shifting demographics, environmental challenges, and innovative technology characterize the context of new era organizations. Leaders and members must stay well informed of these dynamic changes and assess the potential impact on their products, services, stakeholders, and the environment. Chapters in this section explore several major contextual factors and provide a broad perspective on the complex ecosystem where organizations function.

Global Trends

Jerome Glenn, Theodore Gordon, and Elizabeth Florescu (Chapter 1) present the broadest context for organizations in their overview of the *State of the Future* report concerning the global situation for humanity and the environment. The Millennium Project collects data on 30 variables to determine where we, as a global society, are winning and losing, and where there is unclear or little progress. The results of their study show that we are winning on the human front but losing in the environmental arena.

Around the world people are healthier, wealthier, living longer, better educated, more peaceful, and increasingly connected. These results, however, are not evenly distributed. For example, poverty is being reduced globally, but the divide between the rich and poor is widening. The number of transnational war-related deaths has decreased while social instability and violence increases within some countries due to internal conflicts.

Environmentally, each of the last three decades is warmer than the last due to greenhouse gas levels and CO_2 emissions from fossil fuels, which continue to persist at higher levels than the oceans can absorb them. Half the world's topsoil is destroyed, glaciers are melting, and ocean dead zones continue to increase.

Many factors in the global context affect the leadership and functioning of business, nongovernmental, and public organizations. The authors emphasize, "Humanity is slowly but surely becoming aware of itself as an integrated system of cultures, economies, technologies, natural and built environments, and governance systems." They stress that society needs leadership, imagination, courage, policies, and management on a scale that can bring about a better future for humanity.

Martha Riche and Michàlle Mor Barak (Chapter 2) address a subset of the larger context characterized by Glenn, Gordon, and Florescu. They describe global demographic trends that influence a diverse workforce today and in the future. The world's population has grown from 1.7 billion at the beginning of the 20th century to 7 billion in 2011, and is estimated to pass 8 billion by 2025. Advances in health care have contributed to a decrease in childhood diseases and infant mortality and an increase in life span among adults. While the developing world has large numbers of young people (especially in Asia, Africa, and Latin America), developed countries such as the United Kingdom face lower birth rates and an increasing number of adults with longer healthier life expectancies. Employers and governments in developed countries are beginning to reexamine retirement policies and expect to see older adults remain in the workforce longer.

Riche and Mor Barak suggest that the global workforce will become more diverse due to many of these demographic issues. Individuals in countries with excess numbers of working-age populations will immigrate in search of employment in other countries. Developed countries with workforce deficits will need to supplement their labor force through diversity by increasing the number of immigrants, LGBT members, and people with disabilities, continuing to enhance the representation of women at all levels, and keeping or bringing in older workers.

The Future of Work

Lynda Gratton (Chapter 3) details her research to identify the forces that will shape work in 2025 with 50 companies and 400 executives in the Future of Work consortium at the London Business School. The future trends emanate from current conditions and include accelerating technology, globalization, carbon resources, demographic challenges, and social trends.

Consortium members anticipate that sophisticated technology will reach every corner of the world by 2025 and will allow small businesses and micro-entrepreneurs greater opportunities for open innovation and involvement in complex intellectual property. Work will become increasingly shaped by artificial intelligence, avatars, and cognitive assistants, while employees will perform more work virtually. These technologies will replace rising numbers of low- and medium-skilled jobs. Consortium members expect low-cost and frugal innovations to be led increasingly by developing markets. These innovations will be exported to developed markets in the West resulting in the globalization of innovation. Concerns about the price of oil and growing concern about sustainability could lead to widespread use of energy efficient ways of working. Members believe that consumers will judge companies by their record on environmental sustainability, and young workers will select and assess future employers on the same basis.

Like Riche and Mor Barak (Chapter 2), consortium members view demographic trends such as progressively older workers in Western countries or an abundance of younger workers in India and Singapore as forces that will be equally challenging but will affect these regions differently. China's one-child policy places the country in a quandary about where to find future leadership and managerial talent. Employers and governments with older workers must grapple with changing attitudes about older workers, finding work for them, and paying for pension provisions. Employers in countries with numerous younger workers and sustained growth have little concern about pension provisions, while countries with many younger workers and limited economic growth struggle with providing sufficient employment opportunities. Added to these trends are the expectations of Generation Y, as they take their place in positions of authority, for more flexibility by employers regarding work/family balance and meaningful work.

Consortium members identified three social trends moving toward 2025: rapid urbanization, the balanced man, and the rise of reflexivity. Many Western countries are already highly urbanized, and this trend will continue. They expect urbanization and migration to accelerate in innovative, creative clusters around the world, especially in cities such as Rio, Shanghai, or Singapore. In mega-cities, the outer rings of slums will see greater increases in migrant populations. These trends will play a role in where employers choose to locate and influence their relationship with the wider community.

The balanced man trend reflects a growing perception by younger men that their roles and choices are changing with regard to balancing work, career, wealth, and spending time with family and children. Unlike fathers of previous generations, they express more concern about balance and flexibility and less willingness to put work ahead of family and other priorities.

The rise of reflexivity refers to a change in the way both men and women look at their own lives and the choices they make about their personal life and work. This trend will lead individuals to "think more deeply about what is important and about the way working lives can be constructed." People are thinking more deliberately about how they want to rearrange, structure, and negotiate family. Their insights are broadening due to greater opportunities to interact with diverse people at work, and these factors are expanding their views. Consortium members believe this reflexivity at home and work will provide people with the energy and courage to make difficult decisions and trade-offs.

Technology

Erik Brynjolfsson and Andrew McAfee (Chapter 4) describe the advances in information technology—computer hardware, software, and networks—and the advantages of competing by *combining* human abilities with "ever-smarter machines." They explain that digital improvements double about every 18 months, and computers are gaining ground in areas that were never thought possible such as pattern recognition tasks used in driverless cars, and complex communication used in personal assistants such as Siri or Cortana.

Brynjolfsson and McAfee argue convincingly that we are in an era where organizational innovations are fostered best by 1) creating processes that combine the speed of technology with human insight; 2) letting humans be creative and using technology to test their ideas; 3) leveraging IT to enable new forms of human collaboration and commerce; 4) using human insight to apply IT and IT-generated data to create more effective processes; and 5) using IT to propagate new and improved processes once humans develop them. The possibilities are endless for new products, processes, and services resulting from humans working with technology to create value for organizations in this new digital economy. Certain human skills will remain in demand even with advances in technology. These entail applied math and statistics (knowing which analysis to conduct and how to interpret the results), negotiation and group dynamics, good writing, framing problems and solving open-ended problems, persuasion, and human interaction and nurturing.

Leadership for the Long Term

The last chapter in this section by Daniel Goleman (Chapter 5) provides a thought-provoking piece on leading with our long-term future in mind. He contends that humans often default to short-term wants and needs in every aspect of life from economic gains to ecological crises. In the federal government, for instance, there is no agency, office, or position charged with acting for the long term even though myriads of information and reports about environmental issues, the economy, and threats to human well-being are available from many reliable sources.

Goleman urges us to examine the consequences of our actions by asking, "How will what we do today matter to the grandchildren of our grandchildren's grandchildren?" Leadership in all sectors needs a long view for decision making built on a systems perspective. Accordingly, some business leaders have started to engage in a process called *conscious capitalism* (also discussed in Part VIII) where they position their company's performance to benefit all stakeholders, not just investors; and they think beyond the next quarter's earnings. Unilever, for example, sources its raw agriculture from small farms in several countries. The company's action lowers risks for Unilever by diversifying its food supply and security in a turbulent world and provides a range of benefits to farm communities; the famers earn better profits that, in turn, stimulate economic development and reduce poverty in rural areas. Good decisions allow organizations to meet present needs and simultaneously attend to the long view for future generations.

New era organizations have an interdependent relationship with their larger context. The active forces in this context shape organizations and, in turn, their output contributes to changes in the larger context. These dynamic forces challenge organizational leaders and members to consider the short- and long-term consequences of their actions on a broad array of stakeholders and the natural environment. Leaders and members must imagine and experiment with new ways to innovate and create value within and beyond the organization's usual boundaries

Part I — Chapters

CHAPTER 1

The Millennium Project

2013–14 State of the Future (Executive Summary)

Jerome C. Glenn
The Millennium Project

Theodore J. Gordon
The Millennium Project

Elizabeth Florescu
The Millennium Project

The global situation for humanity continues to improve in general, but at the expense of the environment. People around the world are becoming healthier, wealthier, better educated, more peaceful, and increasingly connected, and they are living longer. The child mortality rate has dropped 47% since 1990, extreme poverty in the developing world fell from 50% in 1981 to 21% in 2010, primary school completion rates grew from 81% in 1990 to 91% in 2011, only one transborder war occurred in 2013, nearly 40% of humanity is connected via the Internet, and life expectancy has increased ten years over the past twenty years to reach 70.5 years today.

However, water tables are falling on all continents, intrastate conflicts and refugee numbers are increasing, glaciers are melting, income gaps are increasingly obscene, coral reefs are dying, ocean acidity is increasing, ocean dead zones have doubled every decade since the 1960s, half the world's topsoil is destroyed, youth unemployment has reached dangerous proportions, traffic jams and air pollution are strangling cities, $1–1.6 billion is paid in bribes, organized crime takes in twice the money per year as all military budgets combined, civil liberties are increasingly threatened, and half of the world is potentially unstable.

Massive transitions from isolated subsistence agriculture and industrial economies to an emerging

Source: From *The Millennium Project: 2013-14 State of the Future: Executive Summary* by Jerome C. Glenn, Theodore J. Gordon, and Elizabeth Florescu. Reprinted with permission.

global Internet–connected pluralistic civilization is occurring at unprecedented speed and uncertainties. Monitoring major indicators of progress from health and education to water and energy shows we are winning more than we are losing—but where we are losing is very serious. After seventeen years of continuous monitoring of global change as documented in the annual *State of the Future* reports, it is clear that humanity has the ideas and resources to address its global challenges, but it has not yet shown the leadership, policies, and management on the scale necessary to guarantee a better future. It is also clear from The Millennium Project's global futures research over all these years that there is greater agreement about how to build a better future than is evident in the one-way media that holds audiences by the drama of disagreement, which is reinforcing polarization. When you consider the many wrong decisions and good decisions not taken—day after day and year after year around the world—it is amazing that we are still making as much progress as we are.

The IMF expects the global economy to grow from 3% in 2013 to 3.7% during 2014 and possibly 3.9% in 2015. With world population of 7.2 billion growing at 1.1% in 2013, the global per capita income is increasing at 2.6% per year. The world is reducing poverty faster than many thought was possible, but the divide between the rich and poor is growing faster than many want to admit. According to Oxfam, the total wealth of the richest 85 people equals that of 3.6 billion people in the bottom half of the world's economy, and half of the world's wealth is owned by just 1% of the population. We need to continue the successful efforts that are reducing poverty, but we also need to focus far more seriously on reducing income inequality if long-term instability is to be avoided.

Because the world is better educated and increasingly connected, people are becoming less tolerant of the abuse of elite power than in the past. Because youth unemployment is growing, more people have more time to do something about this abuse. Unless these elites open the conversation about the future with the rest of their populations, unrest and revolutions are likely to continue and increase. The executive summary of the *2008 State of the Future* stated:

> Half the world is vulnerable to social instability and violence due to rising food and energy prices, failing states, falling water tables, climate change, decreasing water-food-energy supply per person, desertification, and increasing migrations due to political, environmental, and economic conditions.

Unfortunately, these factors contributing to social instability have continued to worsen over the past five years, leading to the social unrest we see today in many parts of the world. The number of wars and battle-related deaths has been decreasing, however. Yet worrisome territorial tensions among Asian countries continue to slowly escalate, cyber attacks and espionage are rapidly increasing, and overlapping jurisdictions for energy access to the melting Arctic will be tests of humanity's maturity to see if these can be peacefully resolved. The U.S. and Russia argue about how to stop the bloodshed in Syria while a third of Syria's 21 million people are displaced in their country or refugees in neighboring countries. The number of nuclear weapons is falling and nation-state transborder wars are rare, yet conflicts within countries are increasing, and the world ignores 6 million war-related deaths in the Congo.

At the same time, the world is increasingly engaged in many diverse conversations about the right way to relate to the environment and our fellow humans and about what technologies, economics, and laws are right for our common future. These great conversations are emerging from countless international negotiations, the evolution of standards established by the ISO, the preparations for the post-2015 UN Development Goals and other UN gatherings, and thousands of Internet discussion groups and big data analyses. Humanity is slowly but surely becoming aware of itself as an integrated system of cultures, economies, technologies, natural and built environments, and governance systems.

These great conversations will be better informed if we realize that the world is improving better than most pessimists know and that future dangers are worse than most optimists indicate. Better ideas, new tech, and creative management approaches are popping up all over the world, but the lack of imagination and courage to make serious change is drowning the innovations needed to make the world work for all.

Meanwhile, the world is beginning to automate jobs more broadly and quickly than during the industrial revolution and initial stages of the information age. How many truck and taxicab drivers will future self-driving cars replace? How many will lose their jobs to robotic manufacturing? Or telephone support people to AI telephone systems? The number of employees per business revenue is falling, giving rise to employment-less economic growth. New possibilities have to be invented, such as one-person Internet-based self-employment, for finding markets worldwide rather than looking for local jobs. Successfully leapfrogging slower linear development processes in lower-income countries is likely to require implementing futuristic possibilities—from 3D printing to seawater agriculture—and making increasing individual and collective intelligence a national objective of each country.

The explosive, accelerating growth of knowledge in a rapidly changing and increasingly interdependent world gives us so much to know about so many things that it seems impossible to keep up. At the same time, we are flooded with so much trivial news that serious attention to serious issues gets little interest, and too much time is wasted going through useless information.

The Millennium Project has gathered the insights from creative and knowledgeable people around the world to identify and update prospects for 15 Global Challenges to provide a framework for understanding what is important to know about global change. Chapter 1 presents distilled overviews of each of these challenges so that readers can save time and more easily improve their understanding of our common future compared with more narrowly focused sources scattered around the Internet. Chapter 1 is continually updated online in the Global Futures Intelligence System. GFIS can be thought of as a global information utility from which different readers can draw different value for improving understanding and decisions. In addition to succinct but relatively detailed descriptions of the current situation and forecasts, recommendations to address each challenge are also included. Some examples suggested in Chapter 1 include:

- Establish a U.S.-China 10-year environmental security goal to reduce climate change and improve trust.
- Grow meat without growing animals, to reduce water demand and GHG emissions.
- Develop seawater agriculture for biofuels, carbon sink, and food without rain.
- Build global collective intelligence systems for input to long-range strategic plans.
- Create tele-nations connecting brains overseas to the development process back home.
- Establish trans-institutions for more effective implementation of strategies.
- Detail and implement a global counter-organized crime strategy.
- Use the State of the Future Index as an alternative to GDP as a measure of progress for the world and nations.

The world is in a race between implementing ever-increasing ways to improve the human condition and the seemingly ever-increasing complexity and scale of global problems. So, how is the world doing in this race? What's the score so far?

A review of the trends of the 30 variables used in The Millennium Project's global State of the Future Index (see Box 1.1) provides a score card on humanity's performance in addressing the most important challenges.

The State of the Future Index is a measure of the 10-year outlook for the future based on historical data for the last 20 years. It is constructed with key variables and forecasts that, in the aggregate, depict whether the future promises to be better or worse. The SOFI is intended to show the directions and intensity of change and to identify the factors responsible. It provides a mechanism for studying the relationships among the items in a system. It has been produced by The Millennium Project since 2000.

BOX 1.1: VARIABLES USED IN THE 2013–14 STATE OF THE FUTURE INDEX

1. GNI per capita, PPP (constant 2005 international $)

2. Economic income inequality (share of top 10%)

3. Unemployment, total (% of world labor force)

4. Poverty headcount ratio at $1.25 a day (PPP) (% of population)

5. Levels of corruption (0=highly corrupt; 6=very clean)

6. Foreign direct investment, net inflows (BoP, current $, billions)

7. R&D Expenditures (% of GDP)

8. Population growth (annual %)

9. Life expectancy at birth (years)

10. Mortality rate, infant (per 1,000 live births)

11. Prevalence of undernourishment

12. Health expenditure per capita (current $)

13. Physicians (per 1,000 people)

14. Improved water source (% of population with access)

15. Renewable internal freshwater resources per capita (thousand cubic meters)

16. Ecological Footprint / Biocapacity ratio

17. Forest area (% of land area)

18. CO_2 emissions from fossil fuel and cement production (billion tones [$GtCO_2$])

19. Energy efficiency (GDP per unit of energy use (constant 2005 PPP $ per kg of oil equivalent))

20. Electricity production from renewable sources, excluding hydroelectric (% of total)

21. Literacy rate, adult total (% of people ages 15 and above)

22. School enrollment, secondary (% gross)

23. Number of wars (conflicts with more than 1,000 fatalities)

24. Terrorism incidents

25. Number of countries and groups that had or still have intentions to build nuclear weapons

26. Freedom rights (number of countries rated free)

27. Voter turnout (% voting population)

28. Proportion of seats held by women in national parliaments (% of members)

29. Internet users (per 100 people)

30. Prevalence of HIV (% of population age 15 and 49)

The variables included in SOFI were selected from a set of indicators rated by an international Delphi panel for their capacity for showing progress or regress on the 15 Global Challenges and the availability of at least 20 years of reliable historical data. The variables were submitted several times to an international panel selected by The Millennium Project's Nodes to forecast the best and worst values for each variable in 10 years. These were used for the normalization and integration of all the variables into a single index[1] and for computation of the State of the Future Index. The index shown in Figure 1.1 indicates a slower progress since 2007, although the overall outlook is promising.

The World Report Card

Each of the 30 variables can be examined to show where we are winning, where we are losing, and where there is unclear or little progress, producing a report card for the world. Figures 1.2, 1.3, and 1.4 show the indicators with their historical data and projections grouped by progress criterion.

Some Factors to Consider

A great brain race has begun! The EU, U.S., Japan, and China have announced programs to understand how the brain works and apply that knowledge for better computers and to improve our relation to them. Google also is working to create artificial brains to be your personal artificial intelligence assistant. Another great race is on to make super-computer power available to the masses with advances in IBM's Watson and with cloud computing by Amazon and others. About 85% of the world's population is expected to be covered by high-speed mobile Internet in 2017. China already has nearly twice as many Internet users as the entire population of the U.S., and 81% of its Internet users gain access via mobile phones. Over 8 billion devices are connected to the "Internet of Things," which is expected to grow to 40–80 billion devices by 2020. According to the ITU, nearly 40% of humanity uses the Internet now. The global nervous system of humanity is nearing completion, making a de facto global brain(s) of humanity—partly by design and partly spontaneously. So what happens when the entire world has access to nearly all the world's knowledge and instantaneous access to artificial brains able to solve problems and create new conditions like geniuses, while blurring previous distinctions between virtual realities and physical reality?

We have already seen brilliant financial experts augmented with data and software making short-term, selfish, economic decisions that led to the 2008 global financial crisis, continued environmental degradation, and widening income disparities. It is

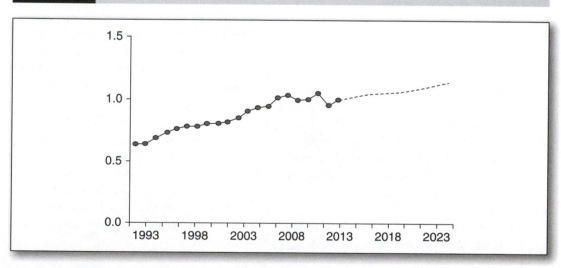

| **Figure 1.1** | **2013 State of the Future Index** |

Figure 1.2   Where Are We Winning?

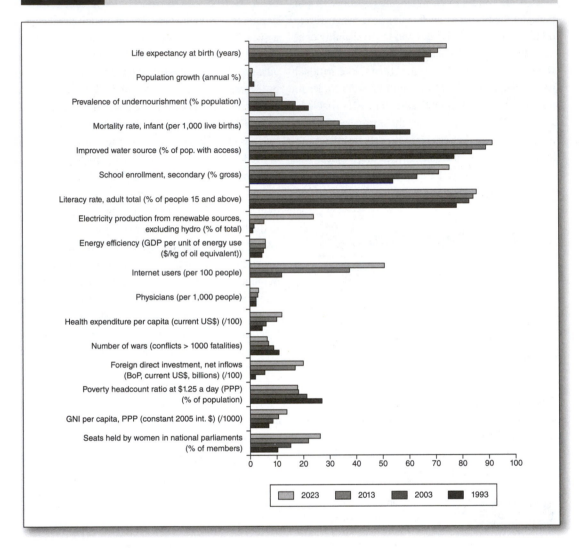

not yet clear that humanity will grow from adolescent short–term, me–first thinking to more adult longer–term, we–first planet–oriented decisionmaking. Humanity seems to be evolving from ideologically driven central decisionmaking to more decentralized pragmatic evidence–based decisionmaking. Yet multi–way interactive media that is one of the greatest forces for good also attracts individuals with common interests into isolated ideological groups, reinforcing social polarization and conflict and forcing some political systems into gridlock.

Humanity may become more responsible and compassionate as the Internet of people and things grows across the planet, making us more aware of humanity as a whole and of our natural and built environments. It also makes it increasingly difficult for conventional crimes to go undetected. Unfortunately, cyberspace has become the new media for new kinds of crimes. According to Akamai, there were 628 cyber–attacks over 24 hours on July 24, 2013, with majority targeting the U.S. Cyber–attacks can be thought of as a new kind of guerrilla warfare. Prevention may just be an endless intellectual arms race of hacking and counter-hacking software, setting cyber traps, exposing sources, and initiating trade sanctions.

Figure 1.3 Where Are We Losing?

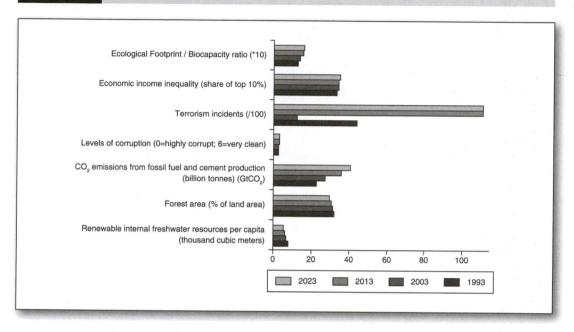

Figure 1.4 Where Is There Unclear or Little Change?

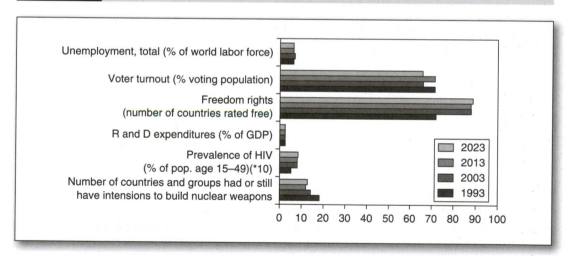

Although the long–range trend toward democracy is strong, Freedom House reports that world political and civil liberties deteriorated for the eighth consecutive year in 2013, with declines noted in 54 countries and improvements in just 40 countries. At the same time, increasing numbers of educated and mobile phone Internet–savvy people are no longer tolerating the abuse of power and may be setting the stage for a long and difficult transition to more global democracy.

Meanwhile, the Fifth Assessment Report of the Intergovernmental Panel on Climate Change found that greenhouse gases grew from an average of 1.3% per year between 1970 and 2000 to an average of 2.2% between 2000 and 2010. Each decade of the past three was warmer than the previous decade.

The past 30 years was likely the warmest period in the northern hemisphere in the last 1,400 years.

Even if all CO_2 emissions are stopped today, the IPCC report notes that "most aspects of climate change will persist for many centuries." Hence, the world has to take adaptation far more seriously, in addition to reducing GHG emissions by better conservation, higher efficiencies, changes in food and energy production, and new methods to reduce the GHGs that are already in the atmosphere.

Without dramatic changes, UNEP projects a 2° C (3.6° F) rise above pre–industrial levels in 20–30 years, accelerating changing climate, ocean acidity, changes in disease patters, and saltwater intrusions into freshwater areas worldwide. FAO reports that 87% of global fish stocks are either fully exploited or overexploited. Typhoon Haiyan that devastated the Philippines in November 2013 had gusts reaching 235 miles per hour and a storm surge of water swelling as high as 20 feet, making it the most powerful tropical storm on record to make landfall. Oceans absorb about 33% of human–generated CO_2, but their ability to continue doing this is being reduced, with changing acidity and dying coral reefs and other living systems.

In just 36 years (by 2050) the world needs to create enough electrical production capacity for an additional 3.7 billion people. There are 1.2 billion people without electricity today (17% of the world), and an additional 2.4 billion people will be added to the world's population between now and 2050. Compounding this is the requirement to decommission aging nuclear power plants and to replace or retrofit fossil fuel plants. The cost of nuclear power is increasing, while the cost of renewables is falling. Wind power passed nuclear as Spain's leading source of electricity. However, fossil fuels (coal, oil, and natural gas) will continue to supply the vast majority of base-load electricity past 2050 unless there are major social and technological changes. About 3 billion people still rely on traditional biomass for cooking and heating. If the long–term trends toward a wealthier and more sophisticated world continue, our energy demands by 2050 could be more than

| Figure 1.5 | Carbon Emission Trends Among Major Emitters |

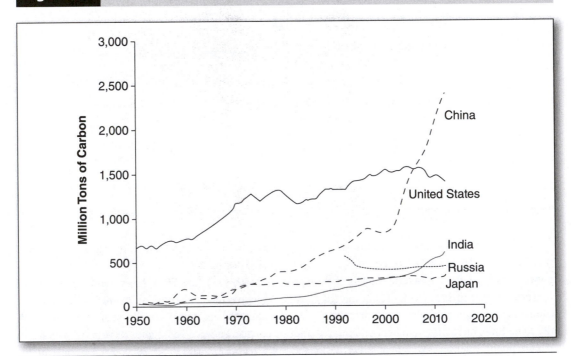

Source: Earth Policy Institute with data from CDIAC, BP.

expected. However, the convergences of technologies are accelerating rapidly to make energy efficiencies far greater by 2050 than forecast today.

Because of falling water tables around the world, climate change, various forms of water pollution, and an additional 2.4 billion people in just 36 years (the majority in Asia), some of the people with safe water today may not have it in the future unless significant changes are made. Major progress was made over the past 25 years that provided enough clean water for an additional 2 billion people, but then water tables were higher, climate change was slower, and pollution was less. According to the OECD, half the world could be living in areas with severe water stress by 2030.

The UN's mid-range forecast is that the current 7.2 billion people will grow to 9.6 billion by 2050 and there will be as many people over 65 as under 15, requiring new concepts of retirement or work. Average life expectancy at birth has increased from 48 years in 1955 to 70.5 years today. Future scientific and medical breakthroughs could give people longer and more productive lives than most would believe possible today. For example, uses of genetic data, software, and nanotechnology will help detect and treat disease at the genetic or molecular level. As a result, people will work longer and create many forms of tele-work, reducing the economic burden on younger generations and maintaining a better quality of life. In the meantime, because people are living longer, health care costs are increasing, and the shortage of health workers is growing, telemedicine and self-diagnosis via biochip sensors and online expert systems will be increasingly necessary.

The continued acceleration of S&T is fundamentally changing what is possible, and access to this knowledge is becoming universally available. But little news coverage, educational curricula, or the general public who elect political leaders seem aware of the extraordinary changes and consequences that need to be discussed. For example, China's Tianhe-2 supercomputer is the world's fastest computer at 33.86 petaflops (quadrillion floating point operations per second)—passing the computational speed of a human brain (though not its cognitive abilities). Individual gene sequencing is available for $1,000 that will lead to individual genetic medicine, while human

pancreatic cells have been change into liver cells and skin cells into heart cells. Synthetic biology is creating new life forms from computer designs. Nano-scale robots are being developed that should be able to manage nano-scale building processes for novel materials. A Higgs-like particle has been discover that could explain the fundamental ability of particles to acquire mass. Quantum entanglement of billions of particle pairs could revolutionize communications and possibly transportation, and quantum building blocks (qubits) have been embedded into nanowires to lead to quantum computers. Although seemingly remote from improving the human condition, such basic science is necessary to increase the knowledge that applied science and technology draws on to improve the human condition.

Yet the acceleration of scientific and technological change seems to grow beyond conventional means of ethical evaluation. Is it ethical to clone ourselves, to bring dinosaurs back to life, or to invent thousands of new life forms through synthetic biology? Is it ethical to implement new S&T developments without proper safety testing or to develop new forms of weapons without human control over their use and safe disposal? Should basic scientific research be pursued without direct regard for social issues and the society that funds it? Might social considerations impair progress toward a truthful understanding of reality? Since journalists have to "hype" to be read in such an information noisy world, truth can be distorted, resulting in a cynical public. We need a global collective intelligence system to track S&T advances, forecast consequences, and document a range of views so that all can understand the potential consequences of new and possible future S&T.

Although the empowerment of women has been one of the strongest drivers of social evolution over the past century, violence against women is the largest war today, as measured by death and casualties per year. Globally, 35% of women have experienced physical and/or sexual violence, and 38% of all murders of women are committed by intimate partners. While the gender gaps for health and educational attainment were closed by 96% and 93% respectively, according to the 2013 Global Gender Gap by the World Economic Forum, the gap in economic participation has been closed by only 60% and the gap in political outcomes by only 21% globally. Women account for 21.3% of the membership of national legislative bodies worldwide, up from 11.3% in 1997.

It is not reasonable to expect the world to cooperatively create and implement strategies to build a better future without some general agreement about what that desirable future is. Such a future should not be built on unrealistic fantasies unaware of the global situation. It should also be aware of the extraordinary possibilities. The overviews of the 15 Global Challenges in Chapter 1 gives a framework for understanding the current situation and prospects that have been systematically updated over the past seventeen years and with the accumulative participation of over 4,500 creative and knowledgeable people. The Global Challenges can be used as input to strategic development processes and university courses and can help the general public to understand what is important about future possibilities. This work is continuously updated with much greater detail in the Global Futures Intelligence System at www.themp.org.

Chapter 2, Hidden Hunger: Unhealthy Food Markets in the Developing World, shares an international assessment of the causes of and solutions to the increasing problem of hidden hunger: the intake of sufficient calories but with little nutritious value, vitamins, and minerals. Although the share of people in the world who are hungry has fallen from over 30% in 1970 (when world population was 3.7 billion) to 15% today (with world population at over 7 billion)—the vast majority of whom are in Africa and Asia—concerns are increasing over the variety and nutritional quality of food. FAO estimates that some 30% of the population (2 billion people) suffers from hidden hunger. Some researchers argue that industrial agriculture reduces the nutrient content of crops, thus escalating the risk of hidden

hunger. The International Food Policy Research Institute's Global Hunger Index report notes that many of the unhealthy food conditions in the developing world are related to poor government social policies, income inequalities, inefficient farming, post–traumatic stress following civil wars, and the low status and educational level of women.

Chapter 3, Vulnerable Natural Infrastructure in Urban Coastal Zones, shares an international assessment of the causes of and solutions to the increasing deterioration of the natural infrastructure along the urban coastal zones around the world. This deterioration diminishes nature's ability to reduce the impacts of hurricanes, tsunamis, and pollution, as it also negatively affects ecosystem services essential to livelihood. Over half the people in the world live within 120 miles of a coastline. Hence, without appropriate mitigation, prevention, and management of the natural infrastructure within urban coastal zones, billions of people will be increasingly vulnerable to a range of disasters.

Chapter 4, SIMAD and Lone Wolf Terrorism Prospects and Potential Strategies to Address the Threat, shares an international assessment of the increasingly destructive power of individuals acting alone. The number of terrorism incidents increased over the past 20 years, reaching 8,441 in 2012 and more than 5,000 in the first half of 2013. Of all terrorism, the lone wolf type is the most insidious, because it is exceedingly difficult to anticipate, given the actions and intent of individuals acting alone. The average opinion of the international panel participating in this study is that nearly a quarter of terrorist attacks carried out in 2015 might be by a lone wolf and that the situation might escalate: about half of the participants in the study thought that lone wolf terrorists might attempt to use weapons of mass destruction around 2030.

Chapter 5, Global Futures Intelligence System, explains an approach to bringing important information about the future together with expert judgments and decision support software in new structures for continuous updating and improvements to create collective intelligence and wisdom about the future. Throughout Chapter 1, references are made to GFIS as the online location at www.themp.org for more detailed information on a subject that is continually updated. Each of the 15 Global Challenges features a menu that includes the following: both a short and a detailed report; a situation chart of the present and desired situation, as well as potential policies for progress; news aggregated from selected RSS feeds; a scanning system with annotated information; and key related web resources, books, papers, models, discussions, questionnaires, and lists of edits to these items. The collective intelligence emerges in GFIS from synergies among data/information/ knowledge, software/hardware, and experts and others with insight that continually learn from feedback to produce just–in–time knowledge for better decisions than any of these elements acting alone. Figure 1.6 is a graphic illustration of these interactive elements.

Figure 1.6   Graphic Illustration of a Collective Intelligence System

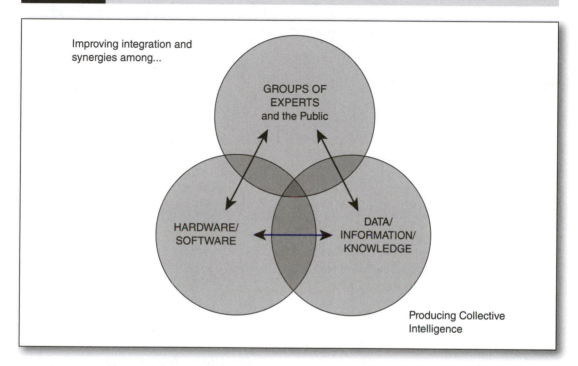

Improving integration and synergies among...

GROUPS OF EXPERTS and the Public

HARDWARE/ SOFTWARE

DATA/ INFORMATION/ KNOWLEDGE

Producing Collective Intelligence

The accelerating rates of changes discussed in the *State of the Future* will eventually connect humanity and technology into new kinds of decisionmaking with global real–time feedback. GFIS is an early expression of that future direction, as is the *2013–14 State of the Future*.

Note

1. See "State of the Future Index" in GFIS's Research section for details of the construction of SOFI, annual global SOFIs since 2001, and several national applications.

CHAPTER 2

Global Demographic Trends

Impact on Workforce Diversity

Martha Farnsworth Riche

Cornell University

Michàlle E. Mor Barak

University of Southern California

> *No more shall there be an infant that lives but a few days, or an old person who does not live out a lifetime; for one who dies at a hundred years will be considered a youth, and one who falls short of a hundred will be considered accursed.*
>
> —Isaiah 65:17–25

Global demographic trends echo this ancient prophecy, as more-developed countries are undergoing an unprecedented demographic transition,[1] one which calls into question traditional assumptions about the characteristics of the working-age population.[2] First, in countries where more adults live a full working life on the one hand and have fewer children on the other, working-age populations, as traditionally defined, are aging. Second, with increasing value put on education, increasing numbers of young people enter the workforce later than the traditional ages. Third, as the amount of time people spend in retirement lengthens, the traditional ages for leaving the labor force are coming under scrutiny. For instance, some demographers have estimated that the average baby girl born in the United States, France, or many of the most economically developed countries has a life expectancy of as much as 100. (See, for example, Vaupel, 2001; Vaupel et al., 1998.) With similar improvements projected for most developed countries, many are questioning whether their economies can afford to lose workers to retirement at the traditional ages, let alone afford to fund them in doing so.

At the same time, the working-age population in the least developed countries is growing rapidly and in the traditional pattern—among youth. This growth is particularly pronounced because here as worldwide, more children than ever before are living to adulthood and having children of their own. Though fertility rates have fallen somewhat in these countries, they are generally higher than elsewhere so births continue to drive population growth.

Thus, as economic integration and societal globalization diversify the world's workforce in new ways, global demographic trends amplify this development. On the one hand, the working-age population is surging in the least-developed countries. Their rapidly growing numbers of young people will continue to increase the supply of new workers in the developing world as their children, born and yet to be born, eventually reach working age. On the other hand, the world's more-developed countries are experiencing slowing rates of population growth, even population declines. Their static or declining numbers of young people, combined with improved health in mid- and later life, is tilting their working-age populations toward mature age groups.

Meanwhile, global economic integration, based in part on differences in labor costs, is amplifying the role of migration in balancing labor demand and supply. As in the past, workers continue to migrate to find employers; with global integration, however, employers also migrate to find workers. As a result, people from diverse backgrounds, with diverse human capital and diverse expectations, are increasingly encountering one another in the workplace. This diversity is accentuated by changes within national populations that are increasing the proportion of the workforce that is made up of nontraditional native-born workers—particularly women but also older people, people with disabilities, and people with nontraditional sexual orientations.

This chapter provides an overview of global demographic trends that contribute to increasing workforce diversity throughout the world. We begin with international population trends—trends in the working-age population in different regions and migration trends across borders. We then describe some national population trends specifically related to gender, age, race and ethnicity, disability, and sexual

orientation that contribute to increased diversity in the workplace.

International Population Trends

The world's population, virtually static throughout most of history, has grown to unprecedented size over the past two centuries, largely due to advances in health care that developed in the industrialized world, then spread to the developing world (see Figure 2.1). At the beginning of the 20th century, the world had 1.7 billion people. By 1960, after health advances had become widespread in the industrialized countries but before they became common in the developing countries, the world had 3 billion people. Then various aid programs took the new advances around the world, and its population surged past 6 billion by the century's end (Haub & Riche, 1994). It reached 7 billion in 2011 and is slated to surpass 8 billion by 2025 (United Nations, 2011a). Thanks to advances in curing infectious childhood diseases, sanitation, and public health, in most countries children now live to adulthood and to have healthy children of their own.

At the beginning of the 21st century, the world had about 1 billion adolescents and 1 billion more young children: the parents of the next generations of workers. If fertility rates continue to decline at their current pace, these young people will grow the world population to over 9 billion as they have their own children during the first half of the century (United Nations, 2011a). If rates do not decline, the United Nations sees the world's population growing more than a billion more, reaching nearly 11 billion in total. Thus, the childbearing decisions of today's young people will determine how large the world's population becomes, as well as the size and locus of the workforce of the future.

The developing world already has unprecedented numbers of young people, many of whom would have died at young ages before the public health advances of the last half century. From an employment perspective, the primary challenge is absorbing the 3 billion people who doubled the world's population during the last 40 years of the 20th century. Age 49 or under in 2010, the workforce of the next two decades is either

Figure 2.1 Worldwide Population Trends

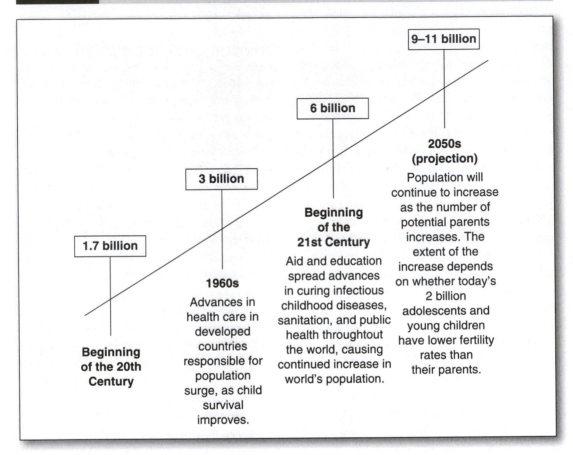

working, looking for work, or looking for the education that will help them when they reach working age.

More than 60% of the world's population ages 15 to 49 was in Asia in 2010, compared with only 4% in North America.[3] Africa had 18%, whereas Latin America (including the Caribbean) had 9% and Europe 8% (United Nations, 2011a). Looking at the population under age 15 in 2010, the source of young workforce entrants in this and the next decade, Africa had 21%, and the shares of all other regions were smaller than they had been. Asia clearly represents the center of gravity of the world's labor force now and in the future, whereas Africa increasingly accounts for net growth in the world's labor supply.[4]

Meanwhile, a second health-related trend is progressing in developed countries and beginning to show up in developing countries. Once more, science/medicine, public health, and public education have combined—this time to lengthen life expectancy. For the world as a whole, life expectancy at birth has grown by more than 20 years—to 70—just since 1950 (Population Reference Bureau, 2011). Of course, there is still a wide gap in life expectancy between developed and developing countries, and it is not converging as neatly or as rapidly as the gap in fertility reduction (C. Wilson, 2011). Currently, Japanese life expectancy is 83, compared with an average of 58 in all of Africa, where life expectancy at birth is also improving (from 38 as recently as 1950). However, demographers expect this gap to continue to narrow, and the United Nations incorporates this assumption in projecting global populations (United Nations, 2011a).

The great improvements in life expectancy during the 20th century largely resulted from successfully combating infectious childhood diseases—this is the source of the explosive growth in the world's current labor force, as more children survive to working age. Newer trends, however, are growing the labor force in a different way, by lengthening the number of working-age years for most individuals. This trend is measured by the years of life expected at age 45 (United Nations, 1999). Although the data are sparse for developing countries, the trend toward more years after age 45 is occurring around the world, albeit at different rates (R. Edwards, 2011).

Some people focus on the role that longer life expectancy plays in growing the numbers of people who are no longer working. However, the same trend plays a role in growing the numbers of people who stay involved in the workforce into older age. In the United States, for instance, the numbers of Americans ages 60 to 65 in 2010 had diminished only slightly compared to the numbers ages 50 to 55 ten years earlier, and those numbers were very close to the numbers ages 40 to 45 ten years before that (U.S. Census Bureau, 2001, 2012). In previous decades, there was a considerable falloff in the numbers of people at each 10-year marker after age 45.

Recent research in several more-developed countries suggests that this trend is not only growing the numbers of people who are surviving to the end of normal work life but pushing old age and disability back.[5] This is because active life expectancy (sometimes called healthy life expectancy) has been growing too, such that people at a given age, say 60 or 65, are healthier than people that age were a few decades earlier in terms of their activity levels (Manton, Corder, & Stallard, 1997; Manton & Gu, 2001). They also have higher educational attainment, which is directly correlated to better health in old age. The result is that "old age" is occurring at older ages for many, and the ability to work, if necessary, is commensurately extended.

This is good news for individuals, though it contains new challenges for societies. Perhaps the most important challenge is that for the first time in history, a country whose fertility rate is around replacement level (2.1 children to replace both parents in the population) is beginning to experience roughly equal numbers of people in each living generation, except the oldest. The age composition of the U.S. population is a good example of this change (see Figure 2.2). As recently as 1970, the U.S. age picture represented the classic "population pyramid," in which each younger generation outnumbered the next older generation.[6] In a revolutionary change, the U.S. population pyramid is turning into a "population pillar," with roughly equal-sized generations into older ages.

Meanwhile, the contrast between less-developed countries, which manifest the classic youth-dominated population picture, and the developed countries as a whole is stark. This is because developed countries whose fertility rates have been below replacement level for a considerable time are looking at a population that contains more older people than younger ones. This is particularly so in Europe, whose population is currently projected to decline slightly between 2000 and 2050 (United Nations, 2011a). This slight absolute decline masks a stunning reversal of the relative size of the older and younger populations. Europeans under age 15 are projected to be 10% fewer by 2050, while Europeans age 60 and older are expected to be more than 60% more numerous. Put another way, the older population in Europe is expected to be more than twice the size of the younger population by mid-century.

Of course, the situation varies from country to country, depending on both fertility rates and net migration. But in the industrialized world overall, increases in the workforce will depend more than ever on employing a higher proportion of people whose good health makes them capable of working. This essentially means employing a higher proportion of older people, thus increasing age diversity within the workforce; it also means increasing the labor force participation rates of women in countries where it has traditionally been low as well as tapping the work skills of otherwise disabled people.

Trends in the Working-Age Population

The United Nations regularly assesses the outlook for world population in response to these changing patterns in births and deaths (United Nations, 2011a). Worldwide, between 2000 and 2025, the United Nations expects the working-age population, defined internationally as ages 15 to 64, to increase by more than one third.

Figure 2.2 Historic and Projected Age Composition, 1970 and 2050

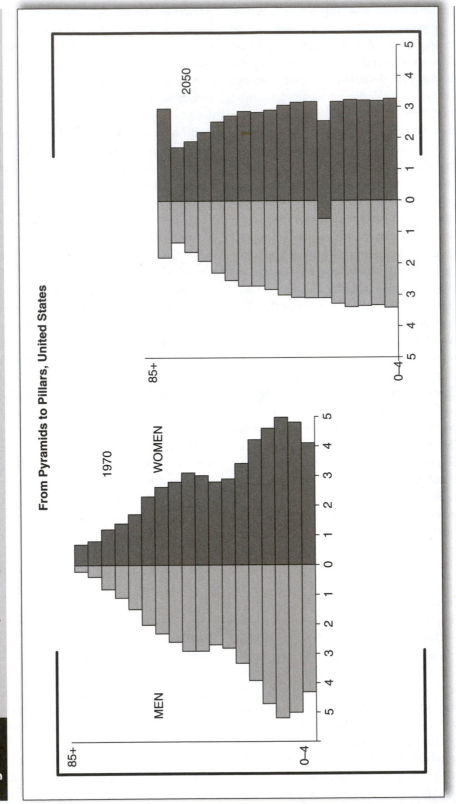

From Pyramids to Pillars, United States

Source: U.S. Census Bureau (2000).

However, the United Nations expects that the working-age population of the more-developed countries (as currently defined) will barely grow (see Table 2.1). In countries such as Germany, Italy, Japan, or the Russian Federation, the United Nations expects there to be fewer people ages 15 to 64 (see Table 2.2). Even if fertility rates increase in these countries, the current deficit in young people cannot be replaced, except by immigration. Other developed countries, such as the United States, will have more people in those ages but not enough to keep up with the pace of rapid population growth throughout the developing world as today's "youth explosion" enters the working ages.

Given these contrasting growth rates, today's more-developed countries can expect their share of the world's working-age population to drop from over 20% to 15% over the first quarter of the century (see Table 2.1). In contrast, working-age populations will continue to swell in other regions, as the substantial youth bulges produced by high fertility rates in earlier decades reach working age.

In most countries, people have become accustomed to having children survive, and fertility rates have declined. So over the next two decades, this bulge should be absorbed virtually everywhere except in Africa, which may contain more than one in four of the world's children in 2025 (see Table 2.3). Consequently, Africa may be the last frontier of "excess" labor available for low-wage competition in their home countries or to fill jobs in developed countries that have fewer working-age people.

The potential impact of HIV/AIDS on population growth injects some uncertainty into this overall picture. This impact is difficult to estimate, given the lack of reliable statistics about its prevalence in most countries. Estimates from the U.S. Census Bureau have suggested that although deaths from AIDS have dampened population growth rates in Africa, fertility is so high there that populations will continue to grow in most though not all countries (Stanecki, 2002). Population growth will also be dampened slightly in Asian countries such as Burma, Cambodia, and Thailand (Stanecki, 2002). Probably the most significant effect of HIV/AIDS on workforce demographics will not be on the numbers of workers but on the age structure of the workforce, particularly in countries where the pandemic has been severe. As people tend to contract AIDS relatively young, an estimated median survival rate of around 10 years means that the effect is felt among men in their 40s and women in their 30s. This dynamic works against the worldwide trend toward longer life expectancy and thus to increasing shares of older workers (C. Wilson, 2011).

Migration Trends

Migration is the other element in population change in addition to births and deaths. One aspect of the new demographic transition is the important role

---

Table 2.1 World Population, Ages 15–64 (in 1,000s)

	2000	*Percentage*	*2025*	*Percentage*
World	3,851,820	100.0	5,248,599	100.0
More-Developed Regions	801,117	20.8	806,671	15.4
Africa	441,765	11.5	831,950	15.9
Latin America and Caribbean	325,365	8.4	455,007	8.7
Asia	2,364,591	61.4	3,218,065	61.3

Source: United Nations (2011a).

Note: Table excludes Oceania.

Table 2.2 Population Ages 15–64, Selected Countries (in 1,000s)

	2000	Percentage of World	2025	Percentage of World	2050	Percentage of World
World	3,843,548	100.0	5,262,050	100.0	5,887,808	100.0
Europe	491,749	12.8	466,715	8.9	411,512	6.9
France	38,448	1.0	39,864	0.8	41,633	0.7
Germany	55,835	1.4	49,542	0.9	40,839	0.7
Italy	38,419	1.0	37,757	0.7	31,350	0.5
Japan	86,354	2.2	71,652	1.4	55,446	0.9
Republic of Korea	33,344	0.9	33,527	0.6	25,424	0.4
Russian Federation	101,846	2.6	87,394	1.7	75,705	1.2
United Kingdom	38,379	1.0	42,141	0.8	43,090	0.7
United States	190,190	4.9	227,147	4.3	241,725	4.1

Source: United Nations (2011a).

Table 2.3 Trends in the Population Under Age 15 (in 1,000s)

	2000	Percentage	2025	Percentage
World	1,849,266	100.0	1,914,241	100.0
More-Developed Regions	217,154	11.7	213,449	11.2
Africa	342,541	18.5	525,253	27.4
Latin America and Caribbean	165,956	9.0	153,261	8.0
Asia	1,138,850	61.6	1,033,548	53.4

Source: United Nations (2011a).

Note: Table excludes Oceania.

of migration in offsetting, fully or partially, population declines caused by unprecedented low rates of fertility (Lestaeghe, 2010). UN demographers have calculated how many migrants it could take to keep the working-age population the same size in various industrial countries over the first half of this century (United Nations, 2000a). Given the relatively lower numbers of children being born there, they calculated that Europe as a whole would need to receive a net 3.2 million migrants a year to keep its working-age population from declining. In contrast, the United States continues to have enough births to keep its working-age population constant; so immigration serves to grow that population.

Economic and demographic imbalances have increased the numbers, though not necessarily the proportion, of international migrants in recent decades, as well as their relative impact in specific countries (Massey et al., 2005; Organisation for Economic Co-operation and Development [OECD], 2009; Sassen, 1988, 1999; United Nations, 2012; World Bank, 1995; Zlotnick, 1994); This impact has been particularly pronounced in Western Europe (Table 2.4)—at least until the 2007–2008 financial crisis. Although annual migration flows may be small relative to the size of world population, social and cultural differences tend to make migrants particularly visible.

| Table 2.4 | Percentage of the Labor Force That Is Foreign-Born in Selected Countries |

	1997 Percentage	*2006 Percentage*
Austria	9.9	11.9
Belgium	8.6	9.2
Czech Republic	2.5	3.6
Germany	8.9	8.5
Italy	2.9	5.9
Japan	0.2	0.3
Korea	0.5	1.3
Norway	2.8	7.4
Spain	1.1	8.5
Sweden	5.2	4.3
Switzerland	20.5	21.0
United Kingdom	3.6	6.3

Sources: OECD (2009, Table A.2.3.); OECD (2011, Table A.2.3).

Note: These data are still the best available as only a few countries have updated their numbers more recently.

Migration data are generally imperfect for workforce analysis because they are typically derived from records kept by countries as they "control" their borders (i.e., monitor and record entries) (Zlotnick, 1994). Tourists often become workers, as do students who stay beyond their schooling. Others enter by avoiding border controls altogether, while some countries, notably members of the European Union (EU), have modified and even abolished such controls for member nations. At the same time, countries are much less likely to monitor and record exits.[7] Thus, the extent of return migration, particularly circular migration, is widely ignored, even though migration experts consider it of prime importance. The migration of workers from Eastern to Western Europe during the early part of the 21st century, and then their return home in the global economic crisis that began in 2007, is a notable example. This and other evidence suggests that globalization allows many international migrants to reinvent long-standing patterns of seasonal and temporary movement for work rather than choosing permanent settlement in a new country. However, this aspect of the global labor force is largely unmeasured.[8]

Although migration ebbs and flows in line with economic activity, international agencies generally estimate that the level of transborder migration of people seeking work has not increased relative to world population size. Instead, economic integration has transformed the international division of labor. In the 1960s, developing countries exported primary commodities; just a few decades later, they began exporting labor-intensive manufactures, under either national or global ownership (Sassen, 1988; World Bank, 1995).

In addition, the direction of migration flows has changed. Since the 1960s, migration flows from less-developed countries—to both developed and developing countries alike—have replaced the flows of Europeans in the opposite direction. Essentially, population stabilization or decline in Europe has replaced several centuries of European population explosion, which fueled European colonization of most of the rest of the world (Chesnais, 2000). In the meantime, population has exploded in the developing world. In search of work and livelihood, many leave their home countries for the developed countries (see, for example, Box 2.1). Certain migrants' need to find work sometimes meets demands in the host countries for their specific skills. For example, women from the Philippines have found a large international demand for their services as caregivers to children and to the elderly (see, for example, Box 2.2). Thus, slow population growth in most developed countries and rapid growth in developing countries has been causing the foreign-born share of the population in developed countries as a whole to rise (World Bank, 1995) (see Figure 2.3). And it is becoming more diverse (OECD, 2009).

BOX 2.1: THE WOMEN WHO LEAVE, THE CHILDREN WHO FOLLOW: ENRIQUE'S STORY

In search of work and escape from poverty and hunger, many mothers from Central America and Mexico enter the United States illegally and leave their young children behind in the care of relatives. Every year an estimated 48,000 youngsters from Central America and Mexico enter the United States illegally in an effort to reunite with their mothers. They travel any way they can, and thousands ride the tops and sides of freight trains. They leap on and off rolling train cars. They forage for food and water. Bandits prey on them. So do street gangsters, who have made the train tops their new turf. These trains have gained the nickname *los trenes del muerte*—the trains of death. None of the youngsters have proper papers. Many are caught by the Mexican police or by *la migra*, the Mexican immigration authorities, who send them back to their home countries. Enrique's story is a typical one:

Enrique was 5 years old when his mother, Lourdes, left him in his hometown Tegucigalpa, in Honduras, to immigrate illegally to the United States. Left by her husband, Enrique's father, and without any means to support her son; her older daughter, Belky; and herself, Lourdes decided to go to the United States, make money, and send it home until she could afford to bring her children to be with her. When she left, she promised to come back for them soon. She never returned. Throughout his childhood, moving from one family member to the other, Enrique dreamed of reuniting with his mother. At age 17, after six failed attempts to travel to the United States illegally, he was finally reunited with his mother in North Carolina. A few months later, he learned that Maria Isabel, the girlfriend he left back in Honduras, had given birth to their daughter. Enrique sent money to bring Maria Isabel to the United States. In an ironic twist of fate, both Enrique and Maria Isabel decided to leave the baby behind with Maria Isabel's mother until they have enough money to send for her (Nazario, 2002, 2007).[9]

BOX 2.2: THE PRICE OF MIGRATION FOR WOMEN FROM THE PHILIPPINES

Since she migrated from the Philippines 10 years ago, Marie has worked in the United States illegally as a caregiver to elderly people. When she works in a private home, room and board are provided, enabling Marie to send over 75% of her earnings to her family in the Philippines.

She is expected to be on call 24 hours a day without overtime pay. From her meager wages, Marie cannot afford the trip back home to see her family. When she left the Philippines, her youngest child was 6 years old. That same child will be 18 by the time Marie sees her again (Tung, 2000).

Filipina women have found a large international demand for their services as caregivers to children and to the elderly. However, their experiences vary widely depending on the destination country. Filipinas work as caregivers most commonly in Saudi Arabia, Hong Kong, Japan, the United Arab Emirates, and Taiwan (Kang & Tran, 2003). Other countries such as the United States also employ a large number of Filipinas. However, most of the women live and work illegally in these countries, making it difficult to accurately estimate their numbers. Canada has been a popular destination since the introduction of Canada's Live-in Caregiver Program under which foreign workers have an opportunity to incorporate into the social structure and can live comfortably, have a chance to bring their families to Canada after 2 years, and be eligible to apply for citizenship (Baga-Reyes, 2003; Cristaldi & Darden, 2011; Fudge, 2011).

However, most countries' policies are not as generous as Canada's. For example, Taiwan, which is now the fifth most popular destination for Filipina women, has significantly less desirable economic conditions. Taiwan has set a minimum monthly wage of $TND 15,840 (Taiwanese new dollars; US$480), for a 40-hour workweek. However, after factoring in the cost of mandatory payments for food, accommodations, and monthly broker fees, the women are left with $TND 10,040 to $TND 11,840 (US$304 to US$359). Further, in order to obtain a job in Taiwan, most of the women had to pay a broker's placement fee. That fee can be as high as $TND 100,000, which is usually borrowed from the broker and paid later from the woman's wages (Kang & Tran, 2003). With all of the fees associated with the legal work opportunities in Taiwan, it is little wonder that many of the women head to countries such as the United States to work illegally for wages as little as $3 per hour, with no pay for overtime.

Mexicans, for instance, now account for the greatest share of foreign-born in the current U.S. population; but as recently as 1970, people born in Italy, Germany, and the United Kingdom, as well as in Canada, each outnumbered the Mexican-born (OECD, 2000). Today's large immigrant groups in the United States include people from the Philippines, Korea, and India, leading Chesnais (2000) to remark that the United States "is no longer primarily a European country." Or take Sweden, once a major contributor to the U.S. population. Migration into Sweden turned positive (i.e., more people entered than left) during the 1960s (Council of Europe, 2000). Now there are more Swedes who were born in Iran than in Norway, more born in Iraq than in Germany, and more born in Turkey or Chile than in the United States or the United Kingdom (OECD, 2000).

In short, population movement from the Southern Hemisphere to the Northern one has been the main driver of global migration in recent decades, growing by 85% between 1990 and 2010 (United Nations, 2012). As a result, South-to-North migrants outnumbered North-to-South migrants for the first time in 2010—the former accounted for an estimated 35% of the global migrant stock, the latter for an estimated 34%. Still, while the role of migration in increasing diversity in developed countries gains attention, it continues to be important in developing countries. The difference is that migration-produced diversity in the latter countries tends to involve people from within the region, who may be less "different." For instance, while most international migrants born in Latin America and the Caribbean reside in the United States, the rest have stayed within the region (United Nations, 2012).

| **Figure 2.3** | International Demographic Trends |

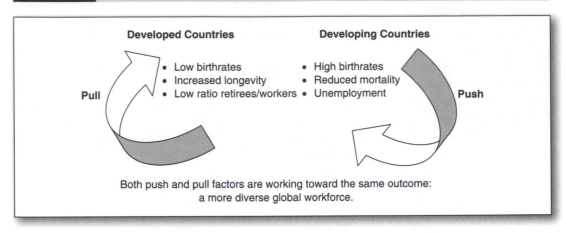

Both push and pull factors are working toward the same outcome:
a more diverse global workforce.

This process continues to evolve, as countries that have been supplying migrants develop, economically, relative to the countries that have been traditional destinations for their unemployed or underemployed workers. For instance, migration to the United States from Mexico slowed so much starting in 2005 that it ceased to exceed return migration. As a result, net migration from Mexico was essentially zero between 2005 and 2010, for the first time in several decades (Passel, Cohn, & Gonzalez-Barrera, 2012). In part, this slowdown could be attributed to poor economic conditions in the United States, but in part it reflected decreasing birth rates and expanding opportunities in Mexico (Cave, 2011). In addition, heightened border enforcement and increased deportations by the U.S. authorities contributed to this trend (Passel et al., 2012).

National Trends

Diversity in the workplace is a growing concern in many countries, and this concern extends well beyond the ramifications of international population trends. Simply put, shifts in the nature and location of economic activity are combining with social and demographic trends to increase the role of nontraditional workers, particularly women, in the paid workforce in all but the least developed countries. At the same time, international support for human rights—reinforced by messages delivered through global communications and entertainment networks—is blurring traditional patterns of workplace discrimination on the basis of religion; social class; caste, race, or ethnic origin; disability; sexual orientation; or age and gender.

Gender Diversity

Increasing numbers and shares of women in the workplace may be the most important component of diversity at the national level in most of the world not only because of their strengthened presence but also because their changing roles have a simultaneous effect at home and work. Historically, only a small proportion of women could afford to remain outside the labor force, no matter what their family responsibilities, but they tended to work as unpaid family labor, particularly in agriculture or the informal economy. This is still the case for women in some countries, mostly in sub-Saharan Africa. However, women's share of the paid labor force has become large, particularly in economies where higher educational attainments are allied with higher earning prospects in the formal economy. Thus, a country's scale of development is a major determinant of women's presence in the work place (International Labour Organization [ILO], 2011).

Globally, a large increase in women's labor force participation in recent decades took place during the

1980s and 1990s. This trend is well illustrated by its evolution in Latin America. In 1980, little more than one quarter of the measured workforce was female in Central and South America; by 1997, women made up one third of the workforce in Central America and nearly two fifths in South America (United Nations, 2000b). Women's share of the workforce also grew significantly in Western Europe and the other developed regions during those two decades. More recently, in many regions where women have traditionally been discouraged from working outside the home, they have come to make up an increasing share of the measured labor force (United Nations, 2000b, 2011a).[10]

Whether women's participation rates are high or low, the gap between women's and men's rates is narrowing in most regions (Table 2.5) (ILO, 2011). This results from two intersecting trends—(a) increased rates of participation for women and (b) decreased rates for men—especially where pension schemes have encouraged early retirement. Changes in the age composition of the working-age population also may change women's share of the labor force. For instance, the share of women in the labor force may increase even more in countries where populations are growing older, as women tend to live longer than men. Many women need to support themselves in the absence of a husband; others seek paid activity outside a home that no longer contains children. In either circumstance, where women's educational attainment equals men's (or exceeds it), employers in most countries can expect challenges to practices that favor men at all levels of the workforce, including supervisory or executive positions.

In sum, women have been increasingly active economically in most regions, especially in regions

Table 2.5	**Labor Force Participation Rates**					
	1998		2008		2011	
	Women	Men	Women	Men	Women	Men
North Africa	24.6	75.1	23.7	74.1	24.2	74.1
Sub-Saharan Africa	59.6	81.6	64.4	76.2	64.5	76.2
Latin America and Caribbean	45.6	80.2	52.1	80	53.5	79.7
East Asia	70.7	82.4	67.2	80	66.7	79.6
Southeast Asia and the Pacific	57.3	81.6	58.7	81.9	58.7	81.8
Southern Asia	35.1	83.2	33.9	82.1	31.8	81.3
Middle East	21.5	75.6	17.7	72.7	18.4	74
Developed Economies and the European Union (EU)	49.2	69.2	53	69.0	53.1	67.9
Central and Southeastern Europe (non-EU) and CIS	50.2	69.5	49.2	69.5	49.8	70.3
World	51.4	78.6	51.7	77.5	51.1	77.1

Source: ILO (2011).

Note: The 2007–2008 financial crisis also affected labor force participation trends, but the effect was uneven across regions.

where they had been relatively less active a quarter century ago. As a result, women's economic activity rates are increasingly similar around the world, except in Middle Eastern and North African countries where society invests less in girls' education and constrains women's roles outside the home.

Women's increased participation in the labor force is the product of several social and economic changes. In most countries outside Africa, large numbers of women have achieved control over their fertility, thus expanding their opportunities for education and employment. As a result, both advocates and policy makers are addressing employment-related barriers such as negative attitudes toward employed women and unfavorable public policies regarding family and child care, part-time employment, maternity benefits, and parental and maternal leave. Meanwhile, both economic growth and expansion of services and other sectors that tend to employ large numbers of women contribute to increased employment of women.

Indeed, global economic development policy now makes fostering women's employment opportunities a priority in developing countries. World Bank economists have concluded that countries that limit women's employment lose as much as a percentage point of potential annual growth through inefficient allocation of productive resources (World Bank, 2001). Low investment in female education is also costly to poor countries. One influential study estimated that decreasing the already low gender gap in school enrollment in East Asia boosted its annual economic growth rate by 0.5% to 0.9% over South Asia, the Middle East, and sub-Saharan Africa between 1960 and 1992 (Klasen, 1999). Another study estimated that in developing countries, closing the joblessness gap between girls and boys yields an increase in gross domestic product (GDP) of up to 1.2% in a single year (Chaaban & Cunningham, 2008).

In addition to the economic benefits of turning dependents into producers, researchers have shown that women's paid employment increases human capital investment in children and thus in the future labor force.[11] Women who have other choices for their lives also tend to limit their childbearing, bringing fertility rates down so that the future labor force is of

a size that the national economy can more readily absorb. This important development ensures that diversity issues regarding gender in the workplace will be increasingly salient in most countries, not just the more developed ones.

Both demographic and social changes are altering the pattern of economic activity over women's lives, creating new challenges for diversity management. Until recent decades, women in industrialized countries typically entered the labor force as soon as they completed their formal education, leaving within a few years to bear and raise children. Now, with secondary and higher education more common, participation rates are high for women in their 20s, rising through their 30s and 40s. Higher education simply makes it more costly for women to leave the labor force, as more education qualifies them for better-paying jobs and for jobs that provide advancement. This change has been most visible in Europe and North America where patterns of economic activity for women have come to resemble patterns for men (United Nations, 1999).

In these countries as well, relatively low levels of fertility mean that women whose children are grown are an increasingly important part of the labor force. In the United States, for instance, participation rates rose for older women as the well-educated baby boomers aged, and in 2008, the female workforce became roughly evenly divided between women under age 45 (generally considered the boundary between women's fertile and nonfertile years) and over it (U.S. Bureau of Labor Statistics, 2009). With two children or fewer and an increasing life expectancy, women in the more industrialized countries are spending a much smaller share of their adult life in parenting.[12] Thus, once women reach their 40s, most have effectively completed their conventional, gender-based responsibilities in the home.[13] Seeing the prospect of extended work lives after their children have grown, younger women may be less willing to accept inferior access to skill development during the early years of their careers.

Trends in Latin America and the Caribbean parallel women's participation trends in the developed regions, but here, as in other regions, women's participation rates have increased even more in the past decade. This suggests that women in less-developed regions may be less likely to afford to withdraw from the labor force to raise children, compared to women in more-developed countries. In Africa, where agriculture remains the primary industry, women have generally been active (though not usually in the paid labor force) throughout their lives, including their childbearing years, and little has changed. Indeed, in a few African countries, notably Equatorial Guinea and Mozambique, but also Benin, Burundi, Rwanda, and Togo, female participation rates have been slightly higher than men's (ILO, 2011). Asia is much more heterogeneous, and economic activity rates by age differ widely among countries (ILO, 2009; United Nations, 1999). However, outside of countries where women face educational, cultural, and institutional barriers, with women increasingly in the paid labor force during their childbearing and child-rearing years, employer work-family policies are now an important aspect of diversity management around the world.

Age Diversity

Demographic change is increasing diversity in national workforces in yet another way as longer life expectancies expand the population of older people. Few people realize the important contribution of mortality improvement to population growth. Yet, throughout the 20th century, for instance, mortality improvement added more people to the U.S. population than did the significant amount of immigration the country experienced.[14] Current U.S. population growth derives as much if not more from "postponed" deaths as from immigration.

In developing countries, most women and men who survive into old age must remain in the labor force. In developed countries, economic activity at older ages decreased in recent decades—mainly due to effective pension schemes that tended to allow or even encourage early retirement. The shift of employment away from agriculture has also had an effect, as older people traditionally found useful work on family farms. However, in many countries, this downward trend is now slowing or even reversing as workers consider how to fund a lengthening postemployment

life, and governments worry about the sustainability of pension systems.

Developed or developing, most countries can expect to see larger numbers of older people in the workforce simply because improvements in mortality continue to increase the proportion of the working-age population that lives to the end of the normal work life, however that is defined. (This is the meaning of the term *population aging*—that fewer individuals die before they reach old age.) At the same time, the workforce contains a smaller proportion of young people if only because more of them are extending their education. These two shifts have the general effect of making the workforce more diverse in terms of workers' ages.

In the United Kingdom, for example, the working-age population in 2010 (using the broad, international definition—ages 15 to 64) contained slightly more people age 40 and older as under age 40. Japan's working-age population was even larger at older ages. Even in South Korea, almost 44% of the working-age population was estimated to be age 40 or older in 2010. In contrast, less than a third were 40 or older in Pakistan, where high fertility rates continue to grow the youth population (United Nations, 2011a).

In countries that are experiencing workforce aging, some age-related diversity issues are obvious, such as those related to pay and benefits. For instance, rewarding workers for years they've spent on the job can produce disruptive inequities in the absence of visible skill differences. Or skewing benefits to people who are raising children can cause trouble with those whose later life needs are quite different.

Other issues are less obvious. In cultures where older people are accustomed to higher status at work, larger numbers of older people mean that not all can be included among the relatively smaller numbers in the upper ranks of the workforce, even if employers are willing to delay promoting younger people and younger employees are willing to go along.[15] Family issues are also changing for workers in all parts of the life cycle. For instance, smaller families often mean that working men or women at any age may need to care for family members as there are fewer people available at home. As longer life expectancy does not ensure longer marital life expectancy, workers may acquire and lose family members through marriage and divorce as well as births and deaths, further diversifying the set of work-family issues.

Racial and Ethnic Diversity

Similar issues surround the inclusion of racial and ethnic groups who have historically been allotted a subservient status in the national workplace. In many countries, such populations are growing even without significant migration because their fertility rates are high relative to the historically favored population.[16] (Higher fertility is generally associated with lower socioeconomic status.) Growth in numbers is combining with attitude change to promote attention to issues of inclusion, particularly in the workplace.

Around the world, the latter part of the 20th century saw a widespread change of attitude toward historically excluded populations—from discrimination and exploitation to tolerance and even inclusion. Granted, neither this change nor concomitant changes in policies and behavior have occurred rapidly or uniformly. Still, civil and human rights movements continue to work toward equalizing educational and employment opportunities across racial and ethnic lines. In the context of an integrated world economy, this advocacy increases the demand on employers to introduce and manage harmonious human relations policies in the workplace.

In the past few decades, immigration and differential fertility trends have made racial and ethnic diversity in the workforce an important issue in many industrialized countries. For example, U.S. economist William Darity Jr. (1999) asserts that "Germany's Turkish and other immigrant workers, France and the UK's African, Middle Eastern and South Asian workers, Japan's Korean workers, and Canada's non-White workers are in the same position as minority workers in the United States" (p. 81). However, many national workforces have long featured one or more varieties of excluded groups: castes and tribal groups in India, Blacks and "Coloureds" in South Africa, and Catholics in Northern Ireland are examples.

In some countries, the excluded group may actually be more numerous, as in Malaysia where native Malays outnumber people of Chinese origin and thus dominate the government (see Box 2.3). Or they may be equally numerous, as in Ghana, where citizens of East Indian and African origin each have their own political party, and the electoral cycle determines which one can influence the workplace (Darity & Deshpande, 2000). So diversity issues in the workplace are not necessarily a question of numbers; nor are they a question of degree of economic development. According to Darity and Deshpande (2000), "The universal persistence of racial and ethnic discrimination in labor markets in countries at all levels of development is a striking stylized fact of the modern world in the presence or absence of programs of redress for groups with inferior status" (p. 81).

Even when outright discrimination on the basis of group membership does not exist, educational differences tend to build a concrete barrier between workers of different racial and ethnic origins. Though individuals from minority populations may not have been deliberately excluded from the educational system, their relative poverty has generally hindered them from taking full advantage of it. Consequently, a country's efforts to overcome educational disparities generally herald efforts to improve representation in the workforce—particularly at higher levels. However, employers may need to undertake leadership if educational efforts are lagging workplace needs and workplace inequalities are hampering their ability to maximize workforce productivity.

BOX 2.3: ETHNIC DIVERSITY IN MALAYSIA

With a political majority of native-born Malays, or bumiputra, Malaysia made a commitment to use economic development to narrow the income gap with the ethnic-Chinese Malays via a set of affirmative action policies. These policies have had some success in reducing the income gap, partly because of programs to increase company ownership among native Malays. Thanks to substantial economic growth, even the Chinese-origin Malaysians have done well with only foreign owners losing from this diversity program (Darity & Deshpande, 2000).

However, programs to close the income gap among workers have been constrained by lower levels of education, especially English language education, among Malays of rural origin (H. Lee, 2012). Meanwhile, the government has acknowledged that the policies, although successful in creating a Malay middle class, have also created a culture of entitlement (W. Arnold, 2002) and marginalization of non-Malay groups (Daniels, 2010). Reporting the fallout from a corporate scandal, the *New York Times* quoted local executives as saying that "too often . . . managers win promotions because of their ethnic background and connections rather than their ability" (Arnold, 2002, p. W1). And those who prove competent are reportedly rewarded with more responsibility until it eventually overwhelms or even corrupts them.

The growing importance of the market in many countries is making private workplaces a particular focus of diversity concern because governments have tended to focus inclusion efforts on public education, government jobs, and political representation. For instance, India made a commitment in its constitution to address the sustained social and economic backwardness of its tribal groups and the groups at the bottom of its caste system. However, these groups are still vastly underrepresented among middle- and higher-income groups. In large part, this is due to the recent liberalization and privatization of much of the economy, which has both created funding problems for public education and constrained the growth of government employment (Darity & Deshpande, 2000). These trends limit the impact of government efforts, turning reformers' attention toward the private sector.

Ability and Disability Diversity

Global data are truly sparse in relation to people with disabilities. Some countries gather data through their census, but it tends to be unreliable (census methods are designed to count people, not collect information about their characteristics). Disability data reported as part of a program, rather than self-reported, tend to be more reliable—but that presupposes the existence of programs. Most existing programs produce data on work-related disabilities and compensation for them, not on people who can't get work because they have disabilities. Still, modern medicine is doing a better job of saving people's lives and may thus be indirectly growing the numbers of those with physical disabilities who not only survive longer but are also employable.

Developed countries generally provide benefits to people who have had disabilities from childhood. In some countries, these benefits are constructed in such a way as to discourage people with disabilities from finding paid employment because they would lose allowances that help them cope with costs they incur as a result of their disability. In other countries, this disincentive does not exist (ILO, 2010). However, it is probably safe to say that in no case are these benefits sufficiently lavish to substitute for paid employment. In developing countries, according to the ILO, people who "have disabilities which prevent them from supporting themselves are usually unable to receive any benefit, except, possibly, social security where it exists"—and where it exists, it usually excludes most low-income earners, whether self-employed or wage earners (ILO, 2000).

Thus, people with disabilities have a strong interest in removing barriers to potential employment. In countries with little or no population growth, people with disabilities can swell the labor supply. And, if for no other reason, longer life expectancies are likely to make governments less willing to provide lifetime support, however parsimonious, to people who incurred their disabilities as adults. These and other factors suggest that people with disabilities are likely to be a factor in increasing workforce diversity.

Sexual Orientation Diversity

The civil rights movement has fostered a continued striving for fairness toward all population groups in the workplace, including people with nontraditional sexual orientations. Similar to disability, global data on sexual orientation are hard to come by, and any information on sexual orientation that is collected through census data tends to be less reliable than other data. (If people aren't willing to tell census takers their income—generally the least reported item—they may have concerns about reporting their sexual orientation too.)

Absent data, sheer population growth probably means that the number of people with nontraditional sexual orientations is growing. Moreover, other trends suggest that these groups may be growing relative to populations as a whole. Public opinion polls report that younger people in developed countries are becoming more accepting of an array of sexual orientations; thus, more people may be willing to acknowledge their membership in these population groups.

Countries where labor is in short supply are likely to address barriers to full employment of all working-age adults, including those with nontraditional sexual orientations. This is all the more likely in that today's smaller families provide less economic shelter for people unwilling to confront hostility in the workplace.

Summary and Conclusion

Broad demographic trends spell more diversity in the global workplace as the world adapts to a new age in which most children survive to adulthood and most adults survive to old age. In more-developed countries, the biggest impetus for workforce diversity will

come from population stabilization and population aging. Countries will choose between growing the labor force through immigrants or through employing more nontraditional workers. Either choice will increase diversity in the workplace. In less-developed countries, diversity will come from population growth—foreign employers will continue to tap an underemployed and presumably less demanding workforce, and governments will seek new forms of employment to provide jobs for their growing numbers.

These trends interact, sometimes reinforcing, sometimes counteracting one another in relation to workforce diversity. Age diversity is a particular example, as older workers have been accustomed to excluding different others from the workplace, and may have difficulty accepting them. To the extent that younger workers have grown up in an environment of inclusion, such as attending school with members of the opposite sex or people from different religious or ethnic backgrounds, diversity is much less problematic. One implication is greater difficulty adjusting to differences among workers in established industries and businesses, compared to newer ones.

Aside from these demographic dynamics, widespread improvement in education over the last century has created a more highly educated and thus more aspiring workforce around the world. In the more-developed world, working-age people are knowledgeable about their rights and about how to make sure they are observed. In the developing world, awareness of individual and group rights is one more lesson being learned from the advanced economies. This trend alone is probably sufficient to ensure that issues related to diversity will touch more and more workplaces in the years to come.

Notes

1. For a comprehensive account of the transition, see Lestaeghe (2010).

2. We discuss the working-age population, rather than the working population, to avoid culturally based differences between countries in terms of who may join the workforce, because these differences are subject to change

as economies evolve. For instance, as recently as the 1950s, American women were expected to leave the workforce when they married and/or had children, but this is no longer the case.

3. The quantitative comparisons made in this chapter use varying time periods and age groups. This is unavoidable given the relative paucity of comparable international data. Indeed, only recent initiatives on the part of international agencies and research institutions make such comparisons possible at all.

4. How well African governments tame the AIDS epidemic will, of course, affect the future size of the region's workforce.

5. James Vaupel, the leading demographer in this line of research, has a number of instructive publications.

6. The factors that slightly distort the lower half of this "pyramid"—the small Depression and the large baby boom generations—are not unique to the United States.

7. Zlotnick (1996) offers a concise summary of the problems in accounting for migration flows, including problems of classification and problems of comparability. As she points out, migration is politically sensitive along a variety of dimensions, and countries often prefer not to know the realities.

8. Sociologist Saskia Sassen has written extensively of the ways in which globalization calls for new ways of thinking about migration, especially in a workforce context. For instance, circular migration is common, in which people prefer to work in one country to earn higher wages but to maintain their personal, cultural, and political interests by returning home on a regular basis. This migration can be temporary, just to earn a certain amount of money or acquire a certain amount of experience, knowledge, or credentials. It can be also be recurring, whether seasonally or simple commuting. See Sassen (1999) for an introduction to these and related issues.

9. Enrique's story was compiled by Sonia Nazario (2002), a writer for the *Los Angeles Times,* from interviews with Enrique, his mother, and several of his family members in Honduras. The writer and the photographer also documented his ordeal by retracing his journey riding trains and joining groups of immigrants crossing the borders illegally. The resulting story, documenting a typical journey of a child yearning to be reunited with his mother, appeared in six installments in the *Los Angeles Times.* It can

also be located on the Internet (www.latimes.com/news/specials/enrique).

10. Women's work for household consumption is not included in labor force statistics, and their unpaid labor for family enterprises, including farms, also tends to be overlooked, although their products are sold or traded. Underreporting is particularly common in countries where the culture frowns on women's economic participation (Bloom & Brender, 1993). Moreover, in less-developed countries, the bulk of women working for pay are in the informal sector (where street vending is a typical activity). This sector also poses problems for measurement.

11. World Bank and other researchers have traced how poor people in developing countries spend additional income and found that women are more likely than men to spend it on food, clothing, medical care, and education for their children (World Bank, 2001).

12. In the United States, men and women each currently spend, on average, an estimated 35% of the years between ages 20 and 69 raising children (King, 1999).

13. People who are uncomfortable with the idea of women without gender role constraints like to assume that women's responsibility for children is followed directly by a responsibility to care for aging parents. However, to the extent that such care is needed (it is often shared with other siblings and is generally short term where it is needed at all), increases in life and healthy life expectancy in industrialized societies are delaying it until later in the life of both parent and adult child. Consequently, women whose children are grown are more likely to have a significant number of work years with few or no caregiving responsibilities.

14. Demographers estimate that about half of the 2000 U.S. population would not have been alive had mortality rates remained at 1900 levels throughout the century (White & Preston, 1996).

15. At an international meeting of experts on aging populations in the late 1990s, one author heard representatives from Japan and China reject the possibility of extending the work life to ease pressure on old-age benefit systems because, they said, "How can we promote young men if older ones don't leave?"

16. Data are not readily available to make comparisons across national boundaries—in large part because the definition of excluded populations varies so much. Generally, population groups are excluded on the basis of caste, religion, language, race, or national origin.

CHAPTER 3

Workplace 2025— What Will It Look Like?

Lynda Gratton

London Business School

Introduction

These are exciting times. There are forces at work that over the coming decades will fundamentally shift much of what we take for granted about employees, work and organizations. We live at a time when the schism with the past is of the same magnitude, perhaps even greater than that last seen in the Industrial Revolution of the late 18th century. A schism of such magnitude that work—what we do, where we do it, how we work and with whom—will change, possibly unrecognizably in our lifetime. In the late 18th century, the drivers of this change were the development of coal and steam power. This time around it is not the result of a single force, but rather a subtle combination of forces that will fundamentally transform much of work.

Many of the ways of working that we have taken for granted are disappearing—working 9-to-5; aligning with only one company; spending time with family; taking weekends off; working with people we have known well; working in offices we go to every day.

And the same is happening for companies—the idea that hierarchy is the best way to manage information flows; that most people will work with team members in the same office; or that the majority of talent will be held within the boundaries of the company. All of this is shifting, and what's coming in its place is much less knowable and less understandable—almost too fragile to grasp.

The Future of Work Research Consortium

Understanding the extent and velocity of this shift has been at the center of the research agenda of the Future of Work consortium (FoW) at the London Business School. In October 2009, the first phase FoW1 was launched—led by a research team at London Business School and a membership of 21 companies, each of which nominated at least five people to participate in the consortium—in total about 200 executives from around the world. Many of these executives were from the human resource function, but others came from innovation centers, the communication function or business strategy. The major business sectors were represented by a wide array of firms, including Absa (the South African bank), Nokia, Nomura, Tata Consulting Services (TCS), Shell, Thomson Reuters, Novartis and Novo Nordisk, SAP, BT and Singapore's Ministry of Manpower, as well as two not-for-profit organizations, Save the Children and World Vision. In October 2010, a second phase FoW2 was launched, this time with 45 companies and a wider global representation, for example from Wipro, TCS and Infosys in India; Sing-Tel and DBS in Singapore; Cisco and Manpower in the USA, and Henkel and Swisscom from continental Europe. This global focus is crucial, since so many of the forces of change are taking place on a global scale. Over a period of two years, more than 50 companies and 400 executives have been actively involved in thinking about the future of work.

The consortium was built in the spirit of co-creation and in order to build deep collaboration between the companies, the research team developed a research community portal in which ideas could be shared and information posted. The portal became the site of a series of "peer assist" groups in which communities of up to 20 people focused on a specific topic and shared ideas. The conversation between the members of the community and the research team was also shaped through monthly webinars and a series of workshops in London, Singapore and Mumbai. At the same time, deep insight was created through the development of a series of surveys, through the preparation of detailed thought pieces on each of the external forces, and in the collection of a portfolio of what was called future-proofed case studies.

The Five Forces That Are Shaping Work

It is impossible to think about work—either now or indeed in the future—without understanding the external forces that are shaping and will continue to shape where and how work takes place. In order to build a deeper understanding of these external forces, in FoW1 the research team embarked on a detailed

analysis of the forces that have and will continue to shape work. In consultation with the consortium members and through a detailed analysis of the wide literature on future forces, five broad themes were identified: technology, globalization, societal trends, demography and carbon.

For each of these five broad themes a series of more detailed specific trends were identified and described. For example, in the case of the broad technology theme, 10 specific trends were identified: The exponential increase in technological capability; five billion people connected; The Cloud becomes ubiquitous; continuous productivity gains; social participation increases; the world's knowledge becomes digitalized; mega-companies and micro-entrepreneurs emerge; ever present avatars and virtual worlds; the rise of cognitive assistants and, technology replaces jobs. In total 32 trends were identified that had the capacity to significantly impact on business and work.

Once these trends were identified we developed a research survey to understand how these external trends are currently shaping work and to build a deeper understanding of how they will shape work in the future. In the spring of 2010, we surveyed a total of 3,200 executives from the consortium companies about their perceptions of the changing nature of work. Executives first rated each trend with regard to the extent they believed the trend was currently shaping their business, and then rated each trend with regard to the extent to which they believed the trend would shape their business by 2025. This second rating allowed a deeper understanding of accelerating trends.

The Trends That Are Shaping Work In 2011

There are a number of trends that executives around the world believe are currently shaping their business and how work gets done. These trends are a dynamic combination of three of the forces—technology, globalization and carbon.

Technology

One of the current shapers of work is the technology that has caused the rapid and continuous fall in the cost of computing. This has impacted the ease with which work has been outsourced to low-cost economies, and has also seen some work replaced by complex data analytics and robotics. The second technological trend that executives believe is currently shaping work is the extent of connectivity across the world. This connectivity, combined with the trend of rapid digitalization of the world's knowledge, has created the opportunity for billions of people in both megacities and rural areas to share ideas and to begin to create the possibility of a "global consciousness" that has never before been seen.

Globalization

This force is also rapidly changing the face of work. The emerging markets are playing a key role in shaping consumer preferences, while the emergence of a global talent pool following China and India's decades of growth will increasingly influence talent development and acquisition. Since the Cultural Revolution in China, and the liberalization of markets in India, both countries have experienced massive growth—fueled by a joint domestic market of over two billion consumers and the capacity to become the "back office" and "factory" of the world. Moreover, as the goods and services created by workers in these countries move up the value chain—so, too, the global aspirations of local companies increases. China and India, with a joint population of 2.6 billion in 2010 predicted to rise to 2.8 billion in 2020 and 3 billion in 2050, will rapidly become key to the talent pools of the world. Add to that, in these regions there is a propensity to study the "hard" scientific subjects. Even by 2008, India and China had each produced twice as many people with advanced degrees in engineering or computer sciences as the U.S.A. In the same year, 40 percent of Master's degrees and 60 percent of Ph.D.'s in engineering in the U.S.A. were awarded to foreigners, most of them members of the Indian and Chinese diasporas. Back in China and India, ever greater investment is being made by local companies in talent development. For example Wipro, Infosys and Tata in India are developing world-class knowledge and leadership capabilities,

while the Chinese government has set tough goals for the number of patents it expects its engineers and scientists to file over the coming decades.

Carbon: The Price of Oil

Executives around the world are aware that right now the price of oil is shaping their business, and over the coming decades the easily available energy resources of the world will be depleted. At the same time, countries such as Brazil, Russia, China and India will increase their resource requirements significantly. This was an important topic in the research consortium with members from oil companies such as Shell, describing the impact the rising cost of resources will have on the movement of goods and transportation of people. Already many companies in our consortium, such as BT, Cisco and Unilever, are piloting schemes to encourage workers to reduce commuting by working at home and to use virtual communications such as video conferencing to reduce air travel.

The Accelerating Trends That Will Shape Work in 2025

Although these current trends will continue to be crucial, as executives looked forward to 2025, they imagined a raft of other accelerating trends that will increasingly shape work. So while the forces of technology, globalization and the price of oil will continue to be crucial, they are joined by other emerging forces of demography and society.

Accelerating Technology

From a technological perspective, the trends that shape work in 2011—communications and connectivity—are joined by a more advanced relationship between technology and work. In most of the companies we studied, rapidly developing Cloud technology is under development, and the view is that this will create a global infrastructure upon which will be held services, applications and resources. At Cisco for example, Cloud technology will play a key role in the further globalization of research and development. We can also anticipate that Cloud technology (which will allow anyone with a computer or handheld device to "rent" services on a minute-by-minute basis) will have a profound impact on micro-entrepreneurs. As these become more advanced, we can expect more of the talent of a company to be held in the "ecosystem" of the myriad of small businesses, some of which will be involved in complex IP (intellectual property) development. Cloud technology has enormous potential to bring sophisticated technology to every corner of the world and this will impact both where work takes place and how work takes place. Low-cost, ubiquitous connectivity will certainly reduce barriers to the emergence of micro-entrepreneurs, while also creating ever more opportunities for open innovation. The idea of frugal innovation—developed around the world and focusing on low-cost innovation—will be increasingly crucial to the strategy of companies.

Over the coming decades, executives across the world also predict that work will be increasingly shaped by AI (artificial intelligence), avatars and cognitive assistants. At Shell, this development is already well underway in the downstream business, as complex AI and business analytics analyze enormous amounts of data to pinpoint likely oil fields. There is also an expectation that more work will be performed virtually, as workers hook up with each other across the world. Many of the global companies in the consortium are already trialling virtual communication systems, and we can anticipate that as the next generation of technology in the shape of avatars and holograms comes on stream, these will also be used across the world. At the same time, bundling and priority mechanisms, such as cognitive assistants, will act as a buffer between ever-increasing content and the needs of workers to arrange their knowledge and tasks. While these bundling mechanisms are in their infancy with the analytics of Google and Amazon, there is a perception that this rapidly developing technology will replace growing numbers of low and medium-skilled jobs. While executives believe that high-end, cognitively complex work such as strategic planning and leading will remain crucial, more and more of the productivity increases in the coming decades will come as robots

and cognitive assistants play a central role in the world of work, from manufacturing to caring for an increasingly aging population.

Accelerating Globalization

The forces of globalization will continue to shape work. In particular, rising standards of education in the emerging markets, combined with the growth of multinational companies, will see innovation move from a Western phenomenon to a global phenomenon. This was very clear in our consortium members, of whom 15 were located in Asia. Companies such as Wipro and Infosys, through their Bangalore campus, are increasingly reaching out into the community to provide education and work skills to the population. Their value-added skills are also rising sharply, from being a low-cost provider to an equal partner in the developments, for example, of the Boeing wing structures. Over the coming decades there is a belief by many executives that the developing markets will increasingly lead the world in low-cost and frugal innovations that will be exported to the developed markets of the West. This will have a profound impact on the globalization of innovation over the coming decades.

Accelerating Carbon Resources

Looking to the future, the consortium members acknowledged that the world will continue to be shaped by the price of oil. However, over time there is an expectation that values around sustainability will become ever more important, with the dwindling of easily accessed energy resources. This will create greater interest in sustainability and could lead to a widespread adoption of more energy-efficient ways of working. For example, already BT and Cisco are piloting the development of hubs—locally based centers designed to reduce commute time to major cities while providing opportunities for people to work in convivial surroundings. There are also many energy-efficient office spaces being piloted, Infosys for example has just built and is now operating two office buildings in Bangalore in parallel to see the impact of different working and cooling arrangements on resource requirements. There is also a growing belief that young people will increasingly be interested in the environmental record of a company, both as consumers and potential employees.

Accelerating Demographic Challenges

The general view of executives around the world is that while it is not yet a shaping force, demography will increasingly shape work and businesses. However, it is important to note that the impact of these demographic and longevity trends are very specific to regions and cannot be seen as generalizable global trends. What is clear, however, is that rapid advances in longevity in many regions of the world will enable millions of people to continue to make a productive contribution to the workplace into their 70s and 80s. For many companies, the challenge will be changing attitudes about the employment of older workers and creating work for them. At the same time pension provisions—particularly in the aging west, could well become a growing source of tension between the generations. For those companies located in the aging countries of Europe—such as Novartis and Unilever—these are important and shaping trends. For those located in India and Singapore, with a younger population, pension provisions are not seen as so important—since people believe they are looking forward to living in a period of sustained growth. The case of China, with its one-child policy, is particularly interesting and will certainly impact the shortage of managerial and leadership talent that is already an issue in the country.

With regard to demographic trends, there was a great deal of interest across the consortium members in the likely motivational and inspirational patterns of Generation Y. By 2025, this cohort of men and women will begin to make their needs and hopes felt in the workplace, as they assume positions of authority and responsibility. There is an expectation that for both men and women their aspirations for a work/life balance and for interesting and meaningful work could profoundly impact the design of work and the development of flexible working conditions. Debates

between members of the consortium suggested that for many of these companies, interest in work/life balance is as strong in the graduates in Mumbai (many of whom face extraordinarily long commutes into the city) as it is for European or U.S. graduates.

Accelerating Social Trends

Interestingly, none of the social trends we looked at featured high as current shapers in today's work. However, when executives look forward to 2025, they saw three social trends really beginning to shape work as they accelerate in importance: rapid urbanization of the population; the balanced man; and the rise of what we term "reflexivity."

The impact of urbanization was seen as a major accelerating trend. From 2008 onward, the proportion of the world's population living in urban centers outweighed those in rural centers. By 2010, in many Western countries more than 75 percent of people already lived in an urban region, and the trend is likely to continue. Executives acknowledged that this urbanization and the migration that accompanies it would not be equal around the world. The expectation is that innovative, creative "clusters" around the world will attract a disproportionate number of the most talented and educated people. In the past these have been in places such as San Francisco and London—but increasingly they could be Rio, Shanghai or Singapore. Moreover, for many of the world's megacities such as Mumbai, the gigantic slums that ring them will become home to an ever greater proportion of the population. Executives believe that in an ever more global and mobile world, these trends will ultimately have profound implications on where a company chooses to locate and the relationship it has with the wider community of which it is a member.

The second societal trend that executives believed could accelerate was the "balanced man"—the idea that men's perception of their roles and the choices they make could also be changing. There was a lively debate within the community portal about this. Some of the male executives believed that faced with the consequences of their Baby Boomers fathers' choices to put work before family, an increasing proportion of men will decide to make a tradeoff between work, career and wealth, and spending time with their family and children. Our own research at London Business School with M.B.A. students substantiates this. However, while this may be important for young Gen Y men, what is more difficult to predict is whether over time they will indeed make the tough choices they now say they are prepared to make. What is clear is that if more men choose a more balanced life, this will increasingly move the flexibility agenda from an issue for women—to an issue for both men and women.

Finally, one of the societal trends that was a heated topic of debate on the community portal was the potential change in the way people look at their own lives and the impact this will have on the way they make choices in their life and work. What is clear is that across many countries of the world, family structures are becoming increasingly rearranged and negotiated, with more choices about their trajectory and outcome. At the same time, employee insight increases as work groups become increasingly diverse and people have an opportunity to work with a variety of people. So we can expect that there is a trend to think more deeply about what is important, and about the way working lives can be constructed. This reflexivity at home and at work could become a crucial engine to driving a deeper understanding of choices and also provide the energy and courage to make tough decisions and trade-offs.

What is clear from the perceptions of these executives around the world is that, although work is profoundly shaped by external forces at present, we can expect this process of shaping to accelerate. Moreover, while the current forces have been primarily those of technology and globalization—over the next two decades other, more personal forces, such as those created through changing demographic patterns and shifting societal norms will also play a significant role.

The Impact of These External Forces on Work

What impact will these external forces have on work over the coming decades? In the second phase of the research consortium, the research team identified the ways in which these external forces could potentially impact on work. These were categorized under five sources of leverage.

- Shaping the values and behaviors of leaders and the way in which leadership development and succession planning takes place.
- Readjustment of the structure and architecture of the company in terms of how work is organized (e.g., the use of project teams, matrix structures, or joint ventures).
- Reshaping the dominant organizational norms and values (e.g., the extent to which collaboration is valued, or the norms around sustainability developed).
- Redesigning the people practices and processes (e.g., reward practices, performance management and development practices).
- Supporting the acquisition and development of specific skills and competencies (e.g., the extent to which people are capable of working in virtual teams or building high value networks).

For each of these points of leverage (leadership, structure, norms and values, people practices and processes, and people skills and competencies) the research team developed a list of four specific areas that could be important for the future, and for each developed a brief description. For example, with regard to leadership and leadership development, we identified four areas that could be important for the future: authentic and transparent leadership (The executives and leaders of this company behave in a transparent and authentic manner. They are true to themselves and I can trust what they say.); diverse and valuable executive networks (The executives in this company have highly developed, strong, diverse, and valuable global networks into other companies and suppliers.); focus on global and community issues (The executives in this business take the lead in focusing on global issues and the role of the company in the community.); and deep executive collaboration (The executive team behaves in a collaborative way and encourages and rewards collaboration.).

Next, we asked the executives in the consortium companies to rate each of these 20 areas in two ways: the extent to which they believed them to be critical in the future, and the extent to which they believed their company was currently competent in this area. This enabled us to create a deeper understanding of how they thought work would change, and also identify the areas of work were the gap between current capability and future need was the greatest.

In autumn of 2010, over 2,500 executives from across the consortium companies completed the survey. For each company we considered each of the 20 areas with respect to its importance to the future and current competence. The difference between importance and competence was deemed to describe the areas of risk; these were then ranked with regard to the extent of risk they involved. This enabled the research team to identify both the general areas of risk across all the companies, and also to identify those companies where current practice was rated as competent. For these companies, the research team then took a closer look at their practice. If the practice did indeed appear to be future-proofed, then a short case description was written and shared with the consortium companies.

While each of the companies has its own unique risk profile, we discovered that there are two areas which in many companies are critical for the future, but where current capacity is underdeveloped.

The first area of importance and risk is Open Innovation (Item: Our company is skilled at Open Innovation—i.e., the use of social technology to pull together ideas and knowledge from people within and outside the company to focus on innovative challenges). This describes the way in which performance and work will move from being about the output of individuals to increasingly becoming more a phenomenon of collective intelligence and communities, both inside and outside the company. The external forces that are shaping the need for Open Innovation include ever more sophisticated technology, the implications of globalization and also the likelihood that more people will want to be actively involved in questions of resource allocation, design and innovation. The challenge for companies is how to shape work in a way that acknowledges that many of the best ideas and insights will be held in consumers, entrepreneurs and joint-venture partners.

The second area of risk is Generational Cohesion (Item: We are experienced at valuing the skills of all three generations—the young in Gen Y, Gen X in their 40s and the experience and talents of the Baby Boomers—those over 55). This refers to the ways in which work can be designed to take account of the widening skill and inspirational differences between the generations. This is a direct consequence of the accelerating forces of demography and longevity, combined with societal changes that have accentuated the potential differences between generations and created a number of sources of tension. The challenge for companies is to learn how best to unite the talents across the generations to ensure the wisdom of the old is captured, while allowing the technological dynamism of the young to be felt.

Open Innovation

Innovation of products, services and increasingly supply chains is central to the long-term business strategy of many of the companies in the consortium. Therefore it is perhaps no surprise that the capacity to craft innovation from sources both inside and outside the company is seen to be increasingly important to how work is designed and executed. This is particularly crucial in the future, as it enables companies to capture the possibilities that technology creates for high levels of connectivity, while enabling the company to operate across functional and national boundaries with ease.

Within the consortium we were able to identify future-proofed capabilities in Open Innovation in a number of companies, including Indian computer services company Infosys, News Corporation and the oil giant Shell. In all cases, the executive team had, over a period of time, piloted open-innovation platforms and had begun to develop deep understanding of the practices that would support both employees and consumers becoming actively involved in the creation of strategy and products.

In 2009, the executive team at Infosys decided to more actively involve employees from across the company in strategy creation and innovation, and over the period of a six-month pilot began to hone the technology and processes that would make this happen. By 2010, in the second iteration of the project, the team leading the open-innovation process was determined to increase the participation, and ended up with over 46,000 employees actively involved with over 20,000 inputs to developing the strategy. However, to create this level of voice, the steering group had to segment employees in terms of the way they preferred to interact and communicate. The strategy-development process then used a variety of informal and formal communication; from informal strategic gatherings, broadcasts from senior executives, informal presentations, strategy graffiti walls, digital whiteboards, knowledge cafes and just a minute/chat sessions. The Infosys executives focused the energy by putting igniting questions to the community and actively inviting high-performing younger employees to participate in strategic debates on a year-round basis. They discovered that to really create high value from the ideas of employees, they also needed to give them access to rich data including, for example, confidential data on industry share, profitability and comparative competition. Much of this was held on the employee portal designed specifically for innovation and co-creation. This enabled people to link to others, to gain access to relevant data, to consult experts, and indeed to submit a business case for an idea. This generated more than 549 ideas, of which 13 were shortlisted for further elaboration and research. Over time, the daily work at Infosys has been shaped to include wider association with the whole global community and deeper use of collaborative technology.

The development of this "Market of Ideas" was crucial to creating deeper understanding and cooperation and to shaping work to be put the competencies and value of collaboration at the heart. At News Corporation, a series of initiatives have been piloted and rolled out to engage many people across the company in actively sharing ideas and knowledge as part of their day-to-day work. At the heart of the endeavour is a corporate portal—"Our News"—that is the repository for virtual brainstorming, expanded online networks, established blogs, and facilitated

dialogue. Each participating employee posts his or her individual profile, including interests and capabilities. From this data, a search-engine optimization process creates links between likeminded people. This encourages groups to naturally emerge and is crucial to building the vitality of the community and indeed to shaping work for the 21st century. By 2011, "Our News" had more than 80 active groups who used the portal to converse, to store shared documents and to host discussions. The portal also attracted people through screening of live events and links with communities such as the MIT Media Lab, of which News Corporation is a sponsor. Over time, Our News has provided a corporate-wide place where people can create virtual communities beyond the boundaries of their own business and their own age group, while the "communities of practice" that arose within the portal became the site of a number of important innovations.

At Shell, the Technology Jams have created a series of short-term, high-intensity collaboration events that brought together more than 8,000 Shell employees from 117 countries to develop new methods of working and demonstrate actionable results over a three-day period.

The initial Jam followed the creation of a new Projects and Technology (P&T) business area in 2010. The Jam was used to develop a network among the employees in the new business area, by providing an online environment for sharing ideas and solving problems led by the P&T executive leadership team. They developed a number of discussion topics that included: how the business could use technology to create "time and space to do what matters;" how efforts across the organization could be aligned; and how employees could encourage each other to "unleash our energy." Executives in hub locations around the globe moderated the event in shifts, with formal hand-offs to maintain continuity. This developed connections between executives as well as giving employees a closer relationship with their leadership. The open-forum style allowed a fluid structure that did not inhibit thinking, allowing diverse ideas and opinions to influence the problem-solving process. The exchange was limited to three days to accommodate time zones and maintain a high level of engagement and motivation.

After 36 consecutive hours, the P&T Jam saw over 9900 logins and 4206 posts by employees around the world. This short-term online collaboration event created affiliation among future members of a new business and their management team, by providing a challenge for all members to attack collaboratively. It built valuable connections across a global network, developing contacts outside of the standard value-chain that can be called upon for their expertise, and it provided diverse insights to develop solutions for existing and previously unrecognized challenges.

What is clear is that over the coming decades building deeper, collaborative links that go across boundaries will become ever more important to the innovation that will sit at the heart of the business strategy of many corporations. Moreover, as technology increasingly shapes work, so the skills in managing and igniting these communities will move to the fore.

Generational Cohesion

The challenge of shaping work to make the best of the skills and aspirations of all the generations of employees is seen as significant challenge and opportunity for executives around the world, and is not simply a Western phenomenon. The potential opportunities and conflicts that are arising between generations are a relatively recent phenomenon.

Many of the companies we studied expect to have potentially five distinct generations in the workforce or engaged as consumers: The Traditionalists (born around 1928–1945); the Baby Boomers (born around 1945–1964); Generation X (born around 1965–1979); Gen Y (born around 1980–1995); and Gen Z (born after 1995).

This potential for inter-generational conflict arises at the confluence of a number of accelerating trends. The first is the accelerating force of demography in terms of falling pension provision for many Gen Xs, the enhanced longevity of the Baby Boomers and the rising influence of Gen Y. Add to this the accelerating force of technological, which has the potential to create tensions between the technological and social media preferences of generations Y and Z, raised on a diet of Facebook and Twitter. And finally, the emerging and accelerating societal trends are also creating profoundly different shaping experiences between the generations in terms of their family experiences, their attitudes to work/life balance (particularly on the part of men), the potential emergence in Gen Y of women as a powerful source of influence, and the likely preference of Gen Y and Gen Z to be "reflexive" and to make more independent choices.

Many executives are aware that these currently nascent—but rapidly accelerating demographic, technological and societal trends, could create real risks for their companies, as generations are pitted against each other in the race for resources and power. Interestingly, we discovered that some of the anxiety about intergenerational cohesion was not focused simply on employees—but also on the intergenerational tension between employees from one generation and stakeholders from another, be they suppliers or customers.

What is clear is that these sources of tension are primed to create conflict between generations that could easily erupt in a way that significantly impacts on the performance of individuals, teams and the organization. However, as we took a closer look at organizational practice, we found cases where executives have acknowledged these sources of tension and were working in ways to both reduce these tensions, and more important, to convert the tension of conflict into the tension of innovation.

While there are indeed differences between the situations and context of the generations, the stereotypes of generations (Gen Ys being work shy, Baby Boomers struggling to use technology, Gen X feeling alienated and disengaged) are rarely accurate. Moving beyond stereotypes seems to be key. Interestingly, there is a perception that the wider the generation gap, the less the conflict—with Baby Boomer and Gen Y for example, as natural partners (perhaps because Baby Boomer parents have Gen Y children).

At the tax and audit firm KPMG, over the last two years there has been a significant attempt to equip everyone in the organization with an understanding of the possible multigenerational differences, and by doing so to create a work environment that is conducive to respect between the generations. The challenge was to first to build deep understanding, and then to educate each generation about the other, and in particular to help them discover the experiences that had shaped their lives. Using the services of a creative, innovative agency, they used cartoons, role plays and video descriptions to create greater awareness of the life journeys that each of the generations had been through, and were likely to go through. This had a positive impact on the respect between generations, while enhancing empathy and cooperation.

However, while building deeper understanding between generations is crucial, we found that those companies that had converted the tension of conflict to the tension of innovation had also taken action to encourage the generations to share ideas—through, for example, cross-generation mentoring.

There are important exchanges to be made between generations: Gen Y in particular are keen to build strong functional skills and industry knowledge and insight and yearn for feedback that those more experienced can help develop; Baby Boomers want to develop their expertise in the use of social media and newly developed technology. These can be crucial issues as the Baby Boomer generation retire, taking with them valuable tacit knowledge, insights and connections.

This was the case at the Italian business of the pharmaceutical company Novartis, where the majority of the workforce are Baby Boomers planning to retire within five years. Italy has one of the lowest birth rates of any country in the world, and at Novartis this is reflected in a work group of whom 46 percent are Baby Boomers, 50 percent are Gen X and 4 percent are Gen Y. In the "Experience in Action" program, the goal was to help transfer the tacit knowledge that is so crucial to organizational success. Mentors are typically over 50, and have critical competencies that are difficult to replace. Interviews showed that many are eager to learn new skills, are no longer career-focused and yet are still very interested in being involved in business-relevant tasks. Each mentor is assigned two mentees who have been identified as having a strong potential to grow in the organization. The program begins with a workshop explaining what mentoring is, and then mentors and mentees meet. The benefits have been clear: cross-generational mentoring provides career

enrichment and potential opportunities for horizontal progression, it helps younger, high-potential staff to connect with more senior staff to develop relationship and organizational intelligence, and to move through the organization more effectively.

This not only increased knowledge sharing, but has also helped eliminate some of the hierarchical structures that can act as a barrier to learning, and has done much to transform the relationship between generations from the "parent–child" to the "adult to adult" relationship that Gen Y craves. One of the real bonuses of the Novartis program was the extent to which the exchange of competencies between generations was key to building cohesion. Gen Y and many of the younger members of Gen X want feedback and support, while older Baby Boomers and retiring Traditionalists often times want to continue to make a positive impact, and see supporting youngsters as key to this—even as they move out of full-time employment into part-time or alumni roles.

One of the challenges of working across generations is to enable people to use the technology that they most prefer. This is particularly true for the generational cohorts in a company where typically the generations work and communicate with each other differently. Typically Gen Z and Y use social media such as MySpace, Facebook, LinkedIn, and Ning to access information instantly, to multi-task, and to build valuable networks and stay connected; typically Gen X use portals; Baby Boomers are most comfortable with e-mail as their primary technological communication tool. We found that a number of companies had created intergenerational tension by banning technology such as Facebook and social media, which is the lifeblood for the youngest generations. However, others had taken the more individualized route when a review of their communication strategy had revealed they had inadvertently favored a certain group and their technology preferences. In the case of banning Facebook, they had favored the email-based working preferences of the Baby Boomers in the company. By opening up the technology space, they allowed each person to adopt the working style that enabled him or her to work as effectively as possible.

Beyond technological preferences, it is clear from the emerging societal trends, that more and more employees, whatever their age, gender or nationality will increasingly value greater flexibility in terms of where and when work takes place and how they work. For example with regard to the generations, many Gen Ys would like greater work/life balance in jobs that can be overwhelming; younger Gen Xs would like maternity and paternity leave and time off to spend with their young children, the possibilities of sabbaticals, and to temporarily step away from frontline into less demanding roles; older Gen Xs can find themselves with aging parents who need care; and Baby Boomers would like sabbatical breaks and the opportunities to work more flexibly nearer the time of their retirement through part-time and reduced hours. We found that although a significant percentage of companies in the research consortium do indeed have a policy of offering flex arrangements, in many cases these are limited to a small number of employees and have not become a widespread practice.

Not so at the U.K. telecom company BT, where flexible working has been embedded across all the corporation through home-based working, flexible and part-time work, and job sharing. BT found that the real win occurred when senior executives became role models for flexible working, and when it was conclusively shown that those who work flexibly are up to 20 percent more productive and significantly less likely to leave the company.

This wide-scale adoption began after a series of trials in which BT employees began to discover new and more flexible ways of working, with the real shift coming from measuring output instead of measuring input. At first, employees working from home or working flexible hours found it difficult to escape the engrained attendance mindset. However, once the metric of value had been explicitly inverted from time to output, then flexibility became more acceptable. A second breakthrough came when the executive team at BT decided that it was the responsibility of the employee to present a business case that illustrated the personal, collegial and organizational benefits of working flexibly. Over time, these initial experiments became custom and practice, with over 20,000 people from all generations working on tailored flexible working programs.

Implications

Executives around the world believe that, while technology and globalization have been the primary external shapers of current work, in the future a more complex mix of forces—including societal, demographic and carbon—will play a significant role. This has deep implications for the how and why of work, and also for the when and where of work. The areas that emerge as least "future-proofed" in many companies—open innovation and intergenerational cohesion—create an exciting and challenging agenda for the human resource function. These are multi-faceted challenges that require a multi-faceted approach. They create three key challenges for the HR function.

First, these challenges have important implications for the way in which the various roles within the HR functions are able to work together and indeed to reach out across the functional boundaries to a wider group of stakeholders. Those functions that are "siloed" into technical areas such as reward, development and performance management may well struggle to meet these multi-faceted challenges, unless they are prepared and able to work closely together. One of the overwhelming aspects of the future of work is the need to work collaboratively across boundaries—be these boundaries generational, national, functional, or business boundaries. This is as true for the HR function as it is for any other part of the business.

Next, this accelerating speed of change will require high levels of adaptability on the part of the business, and this has important implications for HR. In a subsequent survey in the research consortium, we examined the extent of adaptability with regard to how much executives are aware of the changing context of work, the culture of adaptability within the company, the capabilities of rapid prototyping through pilots and experiments, and finally, the extent of scaling capability through learning from pilots, rapidly expanding pilots, and providing time to innovate and adapt. We found that in many companies, executives are struggling with adapting to the future, particularly with regard to tolerance of failure, developing pilots and experiments, and creating time to innovate. The constant refrain from the HR participants in the consortium is that they are overwhelmed with the short-term needs of the business and have very little time for the longer term. What is clear is that over the next two decades the capacity of the HR function to understand the external context, to be able to build and observe experiments and pilots, and to scale rapidly will be crucial to the continuous prosperity of the business.

Finally, the challenges of the future also require the HR function to address a series of knowledge areas and skills where currently many HR functions are undeveloped. For example, skills in network analysis and deep collaboration, skills in the customization of processes, and in building and monitoring virtual teams will become ever more vital.

Our research on the future of work shows clearly that we can expect the forces that shape work to be ever more powerful in the coming decades. Meeting these challenges while at the same time benefiting from the possibilities will only take place if HR functions are able to work collaboratively to solve multifaceted challenges; to support a culture of adaptability; and to develop competencies in future facing areas.

Selected Bibliography

A more detailed description of the five forces and the 32 trends can be found in L. Gratton, *The Shift: The Future of Work Is Already Here* (London: HarperCollins, 2011).

Open Innovation has received much academic and managerial interest over the past decade as key to creating breadth of ideas and inspiration. For an introduction to the topic, see for example, H. W. Chesbrough, *Open Innovation: The New Imperative for Creating and Profiting from Technology* (Boston: Harvard Business School Press, 2003).

Intergenerational Cohesion is a topic of growing interest. The argument for conflict between generations when it comes to the distribution of power and resources is made convincingly by D. Willetts in *The Pinch: How the Baby Boomers Stole Their Children's Future* (London: Atlantic Books, 2010).

This potential conflict can be diffused by mentoring across generations. For a more detailed description of this see, for example, J. C. Meister and K. Willyerd, "Mentoring Millenials," *Harvard Business Review,* May 2010, 1–4.

The needs and aspirations of Gen Y are attracting much attention. Some of the insights from this research come from a London Business School study of Gen Ys and their career aspirations: E. Kelan, L. Gratton, A. Mah and L. Walker, *The Reflexive Generation: Young Professionals' Perspectives on Work, Career and Gender* (London Business School – Centre for Women in Business, 2008).

CHAPTER 4

Winning the Race With Ever-Smarter Machines

Erik Brynjolfsson

Massachusetts Institute of Technology

Andrew McAfee

Massachusetts Institute of Technology

Rapid advances in information technology are yielding applications that can do anything from answering game show questions to driving cars. But to gain true leverage from these ever-improving technologies, companies need new processes and business models.

I n the past fewyears, progress in information technology—in computer hardware, software and networks—has been so rapid and so surprising that many present-day organizations, institutions, policies and mind-sets are not keeping up. We used to be pretty confident that we knew the relative strengths and

---

THE LEADING QUESTION

What are the strategic implications of recent dramatic advances in information technology?

Findings

- Computers are now making surprising inroads into tasks once done only by humans.
- Digitization is not a one-time project; it's an ongoing process.
- Think about developing new business models and processes that combine workers with ever-more-powerful technology to create value.

---

weaknesses of computers vis-à-vis humans. But computers have started making inroads in some unexpected areas—and this has significant implications for managers and organizations.

A clear illustration of the dramatic increase in computing power comes from comparing a book published in 2004 with an announcement made in 2010. The book is *The New Division of Labor* by economists Frank Levy and Richard Murnane, and it's a thoroughly researched description of the comparative capabilities of computers and human workers.

In its second chapter, titled "Why People Still Matter," the authors present a spectrum of information-processing tasks. At one end are straightforward applications of existing rules. These tasks, such as performing arithmetic, can be easily automated, since computers are good at following rules.

At the other end of the complexity spectrum are pattern recognition tasks where the rules can't be inferred. *The New Division of Labor* gives driving in traffic as an example of this type of task, and asserts that it is not automatable:

> The . . . truck driver is processing a constant stream of [visual, aural and tactile] information from his environment. . . . [T]o program this behavior we could begin with a video camera and other sensors to capture the sensory input. But executing a left turn against oncoming traffic involves so many factors that it is hard to imagine discovering the set of rules that can replicate a driver's behavior. . . .
>
> Articulating [human] knowledge and embedding it in software for all but highly structured situations are at present enormously difficult tasks. . . . Computers cannot easily substitute for humans in [jobs like truck driving].[1]

The results of the first DARPA Grand Challenge, held in 2004, supported Levy and Murnane's conclusion. The challenge was to build a driverless vehicle that could navigate a 142-mile route through the Mojave Desert. The "winning" team made it less than eight miles before failing.[2]

Just six years later, however, real-world driving went from being an example of a task that couldn't be automated to an example of one that was. In October 2010, Google announced on its official blog that it had modified six Toyota Priuses to the point that they were fully autonomous cars, ones that had driven more than 1,000 miles on U.S. roads without any human involvement at all, and more than 140,000 miles with only minor inputs from the person behind the wheel, along with data previously gathered by Google about the route. (To comply with driving laws, Google had a person behind the steering wheel at all times.)[3]

Levy and Murnane were correct that automatic driving on populated roads is an enormously difficult task, and it's *not* easy to build a computer that can substitute for human perception and pattern matching in this domain. Not easy, but possible—and this challenge is being met.

The Google technologists are not taking shortcuts around the challenges listed by Levy and Murnane, but are meeting them head on. They used the staggering amounts of data collected for Google Maps and Google Street View as well as special sensors to provide as much information as possible about the roads on which their cars were traveling. In particular, their vehicles collect huge volumes of real-time data using video, radar and optical remote sensing (LIDAR) gear mounted on the car. These data are fed into software that takes into account the rules of the road; the presence, trajectory and likely identity of all objects in the vicinity; the driving conditions; and so on. This software controls the car and probably provides better awareness, vigilance and reaction times than any human driver could. So far, the Google vehicles' only accident came when one was rear-ended by another car as it stopped at a traffic light.

Creating autonomous cars is not easy. But in a world of plentiful accurate data, powerful sensors and massive storage capacity and processing power, it *is* possible. This is the world we live in now. It's one where computers improve so quickly that their capabilities pass from the realm of science fiction into the everyday world, not over the course of a human lifetime but in just a few years.

Levy and Murnane give *complex communication* as another example of a human capability that is very hard for machines to emulate.[4] Complex communication entails conversing with a human being, especially in situations that are complicated, emotional or ambiguous. Evolution has "programmed" people to do this effortlessly, but it's been very hard to program computers to do the same. For many of us, the breakthrough came when we started using Apple's Siri personal assistant. Siri, an application that runs on the latest generation of iPhones, understands human speech well enough to answer a broad range of everyday requests, from "Where's the nearest gas station?" to "Please make a lunch appointment with Sergey." It does this by linking to a variety of public and private databases. Siri resolves ambiguous queries based on context and even has a bit of personality and humor that it uses when appropriate. As a result, many tasks on the iPhone, like making an appointment or finding a restaurant, are now easier to do by speaking natural language than by working through menus and typing text.

The Google driverless car shows how far and how fast digital pattern recognition abilities have advanced recently. Apple's Siri shows how much progress has been made in computers' ability to engage in complex communication. Another technology, one that was developed at IBM's Watson Research Center and is named Watson, shows how powerful it can be to combine these two abilities and how far computers have advanced recently into territory thought to be uniquely human.

Watson is a supercomputer designed to play the game show *Jeopardy!*, in which contestants are asked questions on a wide variety of topics that are not known in advance.[5] In many cases, these questions involve puns and other types of wordplay. It can be difficult to figure out precisely what is being asked or how an answer should be constructed. In short, playing *Jeopardy!* well requires the ability to engage in complex communication. The way Watson plays it, the game also requires massive amounts of pattern matching. The supercomputer has been loaded with hundreds of millions of unconnected digital documents, including encyclopedias and other reference works, newspaper stories and the Bible. When it receives a question, Watson immediately goes to work to figure out what is being asked (using algorithms that specialize in complex communication) and then starts querying all these documents to find and match patterns in search of the answer.

What comes out in the end is so fast and accurate that even the best human players can't keep up. In February 2011, Watson played in a televised tournament against the two most accomplished contestants in the show's history. After two rounds of the game shown over three days, the computer finished with more than three times as much money as its closest flesh-and-blood competitor. One of those competitors, Ken Jennings, acknowledged that digital technologies had taken over the game. Underneath his written response to the tournament's last question, he added: "I for one welcome our new computer overlords."[6]

Where did these overlords come from? How has science fiction become business reality so quickly? Two concepts are essential for understanding this remarkable progress. The first, Moore's Law, is well-known: it is an expansion of an observation made by Gordon Moore, cofounder of microprocessor maker Intel. In a 1965 article in *Electronics* magazine, Moore noted that the number of transistors in a minimum-cost integrated circuit had been doubling every 12 months, and he predicted that this rate of improvement would continue into the future.[7] When this proved to be the case, Moore's Law was born.

Later modifications changed the time required for the doubling to occur; the most widely accepted period at present is 18 months.[8] Variations of Moore's Law have been applied to improvement over time in disk drive capacity, display resolution, network bandwidth and, most recently, energy consumption.[9] In these and many other cases of digital improvement, doubling happens both quickly and reliably.

It also seems that software can progress at least as fast as hardware does, at least in some domains. Computer scientist Martin Grötschel analyzed the speed with which a standard optimization problem could be solved by computers during 1988–2003. He documented a 43-million-fold improvement, which he broke down into two factors: faster processors and better algorithms embedded in software. Processor speeds improved by a factor of 1,000, but those gains were dwarfed by the algorithms, which got 43,000 times better over the same period.[10]

The second concept relevant for understanding recent computing advances is closely related to Moore's Law. It comes from an ancient story about math made relevant to the present age by the innovator and futurist Ray Kurzweil. In one version of the story, the inventor of the game of chess shows his creation to his country's ruler. The emperor is so delighted by the game that he allows the inventor to name his own reward. The clever man asks for a quantity of rice, to be determined as follows: one grain of rice is placed on the first square of the chessboard, two grains on the second, four on the third, and so on, with each square receiving twice as many grains as the previous square.

The emperor agrees, thinking that this reward is too small. He soon sees, however, that the constant doubling results in tremendously large numbers. The inventor winds up with 264-1 grains of rice, or a pile bigger than Mount Everest. In some versions of the story, the emperor is so displeased at being outsmarted that he beheads the inventor.

In his 2000 book *The Age of Spiritual Machines*:

When Computers Exceed Human Intelligence, Kurzweil notes that the pile of rice is not that exceptional on the first half of the chessboard:

After thirty-two squares, the emperor had given the inventor about 4 billion grains of rice. That's a reasonable quantity—about one large field's worth—and the emperor did start to take notice.

But the emperor could still remain an emperor. And the inventor could still retain his head. It was as they headed into the second half of the chessboard that at least one of them got into trouble.[11]

Kurzweil's point is that constant doubling and other forms of exponential growth are deceptive because they're initially unremarkable. Exponential increases initially look a lot like standard linear ones, but they're not. As time goes by—as we move into the second half of the chessboard—exponential growth confounds our intuition and expectations. It accelerates far past linear growth, yielding Everest-sized piles of rice—and computers that can accomplish previously impossible tasks.

So where are we in the history of business use of computers? Are we in the second half of the chessboard yet? This is an impossible question to answer precisely, of course, but a simple, if whimsical, calculation yields an intriguing conclusion. U.S. government economic statistics added "information technology" as a category of business investment in 1958, so let's use that as our starting year. And let's take the standard 18 months as the Moore's Law doubling period. Thirty-two doublings then take us to 2006 and to the second half of the chessboard. Advances like Google's autonomous cars and Watson the *Jeopardy!* champion supercomputer, then, can be seen as the first examples of the kinds of digital innovations we'll see as we move further into the second half—into the phase where exponential growth yields jaw-dropping results. (See "Technologies to Watch.")

TECHNOLOGIES TO WATCH

New technology applications always surprise—so it's almost impossible to make accurate predictions about where information technology will go next. With that caveat, here are four digital technologies that we predict will have a large impact on the business world in the coming decade:

- **Inexpensive industrial robots.** Robots are now found in warehouses, on battlefields and vacuuming our living rooms. As their sensors and programs get better, we'll see them in more and more places. We anticipate a revolution in user-friendly robotics similar to the PC revolution in corporate computing.

- **Voice recognition and translation software.** Computers used to be laughably bad at understanding us and moving between languages. Now they're pretty good at it—and rapidly improving. We're not too far away from having full-fledged personal digital assistants that can translate for us as we travel to other countries.

(Continued)

(Continued)

- **Sophisticated automated response systems.** Watson's ability to beat the best human *Jeopardy!* players showed the world how good computers have become at extracting the "right" answer from huge bodies of accumulated information. This is what diagnosticians and troubleshooters—some of them quite well-educated and well-paid—do. Such people will soon have digital helpers—and, in effect, competitors.

- **Autonomous vehicles.** Google's self-driving car is a very expensive prototype, but its costs will drop steeply over time. And even before regulations change to allow such cars on streets without humans in the front seat, we're likely to see similar vehicles motoring around mines and airports and mowing golf course lawns.

These results will be felt across virtually every task, job and industry. Economists Susanto Basu and John Fernald highlight how powerful, inexpensive information and communication technology allows departures from business as usual:

> The availability of cheap ICT capital allows firms to deploy their other inputs in radically different and productivity-enhancing ways. In so doing, cheap computers and telecommunications equipment can foster an ever-expanding sequence of complementary inventions in industries using ICT.[12]

Note that computers increase productivity not only in the high-tech sector but also in all industries that purchase and use digital gear. And these days, that means all industries; even historically low-tech American sectors like agriculture and mining are now spending billions of dollars each year to digitize themselves.

Note also the choice of words by Basu and Fernald: Computers and networks bring an *ever-expanding* set of opportunities to companies. Digitization, in other words, is not a single project providing one-time benefits. Instead, it's an ongoing process of creative destruction; innovators use both new and established technologies to make deep changes at the level of the task, the job, the process—and even the organization itself. These changes build and feed on each other, so that the possibilities offered really are constantly expanding. (This does not mean, however, that today's

rapid advances in computing are automatically beneficial for everyone; in fact, in our recent e-book *Race Against the Machine*, we argue that as digital technologies change rapidly, society faces a serious problem because millions of people are being left behind—facing either stagnant incomes or unemployment.)

Competing Using Machines

What does it mean for companies—and their workers, and the way work is organized—when machines can do a better job than humans at an increasing number of tasks? When considering this question, it's helpful to remember that the idea of humans competing against machines is not new; in fact, it's even part of American folklore. In the latter part of the nineteenth century, the legend of John Henry became popular as the effects of the steam—powered Industrial Revolution affected every industry and job that relied heavily on human strength. It's the story of a contest between a steam—powered drill and John Henry, a muscular railroad worker and former slave, to see which of the two could bore the longer hole into solid rock.[13] Henry wins this race against the machine, but loses his life; his exertions cause his heart to burst. Humans never directly challenged the steam drill again.

This legend reflected popular unease at the time about the potential for technology to make human labor obsolete. But this is not at all what happened as the Industrial Revolution progressed. As steam power advanced and spread throughout industry, more human workers were needed, not fewer. They were needed not so much for their raw physical strength (as John Henry was), but instead for other human skills: physical ones such as locomotion, dexterity, coordination and perception, and mental ones such as communication, pattern matching and creativity.

The John Henry legend shows us that, in many contexts, humans will eventually lose the head-to-head race against the machine. But the broader lesson of the Industrial Revolution is more like the Indianapolis 500 speedway race than John Henry: Over time, technological progress creates opportunities in which people race *using* machines. Humans and machines can then collaborate in a race to produce more, to capture markets and to beat other teams of humans and machines. This lesson remains valid and instructive today as machines are winning more types of head-to-head mental contests, not just physical ones. As with the Industrial Revolution, we believe things will get really interesting as more people start competing using these powerful new machines rather than competing against them.

The game of chess provides a great example. In 1997, Gary Kasparov, humanity's most brilliant chess master, lost to Deep Blue, a $10 million specialized supercomputer programmed by a team from IBM. That was big news when it happened. However, what is less well-known is that the best chess players on the planet today are not computers. Nor are they humans. The best chess players are teams of humans using computers.

In matches pitting humans against humans, consulting a computer is considered cheating. Likewise, in computer chess competitions (yes, they also exist), human intervention is also cheating. However, "freestyle" competitions allow any combination of humans and computers. As Gary Kasparov himself notes of one such competition:

The teams of human plus machine dominated even the strongest computers. The chess machine Hydra, which is a chess-specific supercomputer like Deep Blue, was no match for a strong human player using a relatively weak laptop. Human

strategic guidance combined with the tactical acuity of a computer was overwhelming.[14]

The overall winner in that competition had neither the best human players nor the most powerful computers. Instead, Kasparov observed, it consisted of a pair of amateur American chess players using three computers at the same time.

Their skill at manipulating and "coaching" their computers to look very deeply into positions effectively countered the superior chess understanding of their grandmaster opponents and the greater computational power of other participants. Weak human + machine + better process was superior to a strong computer alone and, more remarkably, superior to a strong human + machine + inferior process.[15]

This pattern is true not only in chess, but throughout the economy. In medicine, law, finance, retailing, manufacturing and even scientific discovery, the key to winning the race is not to race *against* machines, but to win *using* machines. While computers win at routine processing, repetitive arithmetic and error-free consistency and are quickly getting better at complex communication and pattern matching, computers have three failings. Computers lack intuition and creativity, they can be painfully fragile in uncertain or unpredictable environments, and they are lost when asked to work even a little outside a predefined domain. (See "Skills That Will Remain in Demand.") Fortunately, humans are strongest exactly where computers are weak, creating a potentially beautiful partnership.

Fostering Organizational Innovation

How can we implement winning "human + machine" strategies? The solution is organizational innovation: inventing new organizational structures, processes and business models that leverage ever-advancing technology and human skills. Such strategies require more than just automating existing jobs without really rethinking them. Simply substituting machines for human labor rarely adds much value or high returns; it results in only incremental productivity improvements. Instead, managers and entrepreneurs should think about developing new business models and processes that combine workers with ever more powerful technology to create value. Some companies are showing how to effectively race with machines—how to combine the relative strengths of people and digital technologies and achieve good business results. Here is a sampling of the smart ways companies are mixing human and machine capabilities:

1. **Create processes that combine the speed of technology with human insight.** Even though computers have made amazing recent progress in pattern recognition, they're still not any good at figuring out things like what teenagers will want to wear next. However, many fashion retailers still try to plan their collections far in advance, using models based on past sales to predict future trends and demand. The Zara chain of clothing stores, which is part of the Spanish company Inditex, takes a very different approach. Instead of relying on algorithms to try to determine what will sell next, Zara relies on the abilities of its store managers around the world to discern emerging fashion trends in their communities and customer bases. These managers get an electronic form twice a week showing all available garments. They fill it out and send it back, and get the clothes they ordered within a couple of days. Store managers are also regularly consulted about the trends that they're noticing so that the company can keep making the clothes young people feel they have to have. The combination of human insight and speedy technology makes Zara far more responsive and agile than its competitors.

2. **Let humans be creative—and use technology to test their ideas.** Another example of effectively combining the skills of people and technology is the way the office supply chain Staples used an application developed by Affinnova, a software and consulting company based in Waltham, Massachusetts, when determining the new packaging for its line of copy papers. People are much more creative than computers—but are too often bad at determining which of their ideas are any good, or how they should best be combined. So software now exists that quickly and accurately tests customer responses to different ideas and finds the optimal set. People came up with the elements of the Staples packaging—colors, slogans, logos and so on—and the software ran a Web-based survey to find the best mix.

3. **Leverage IT to enable new forms of human collaboration and commerce.** Machines are also providing radically new ways for people to work together to solve scientific problems. For instance, Foldit is a social game developed at the University of Washington that enlists hundreds of thousands of players who compete to fold and manipulate molecules. Recently, UW researchers credited these players with figuring out the structure of an AIDS-like virus.[16]

The Internet has also been a particularly rich breeding ground for new marketplaces and ecosystems that combine human and machine capabilities. For instance, it facilitates the operation of "micro-multinationals"—small businesses that work with customers, suppliers and partners globally to create and deliver value.[17] What's more, platforms like eBay, Apple's iTunes, Google's Android operating system and Amazon.com's marketplace have spurred thousands of people to earn their livings by selling new, improved or simply unusual or cheaper products to a worldwide customer base. Technology manages most of the matching of buyers and sellers, the mechanics of the transactions and, in some cases, even marketing and pricing decisions. For digital goods, even distribution and delivery can be automated. In the iTunes and Android marketplaces, technology leverages creativity to make it possible to deliver a "long tail" of new niche products that otherwise would likely never reach a wide market.[18]

4. **Use human insight to apply IT—and IT-generated data—to create more effective processes.** Assurant Solutions, which sells credit insurance and debt protection products, already had an operationally optimized call center where callers were automatically routed to customer service reps with expertise in the

product a customer was calling about. But when the company brought in mathematicians and actuaries to study the data the call center generated, they discovered that, for whatever reason, certain reps did much better with certain types of customers. By automatically routing calls to customer service reps more likely to develop a rapport with such customers, Assurant Solutions reported that the success rate of its call center almost tripled.

5. Once people develop new, improved processes, use IT to propagate those processes. More and more industries have a core of software. Technology thus makes it easier to replicate not just innovative digital products but also innovative business processes. For instance, when the drugstore chain CVS developed an improved prescription drug ordering process for its pharmacies, it embedded the process in an enterprise IT system. Because the process was tightly coupled with technology, CVS could assure that every clerk and pharmacist would adhere to the new process precisely as it had been designed, increasing overall customer satisfaction scores from 86 to 91. More important, CVS could rapidly propagate the innovation to over 4,000 physical locations. In effect, this one process innovation created a 4,000-fold economic impact quickly and accurately because it was embedded in easily replicated technology. This contrasts with the slow and error-prone paper-based or training-oriented procedures that were used for propagating processes a decade ago.[19]

Combinatorial Innovation

When businesses are based on bits instead of atoms, new innovations often add to the set of innovations available to the next entrepreneur, instead of depleting the stock of resources the way minerals or farmland could be depleted in the old economy. New businesses are often recombinations of previous ones. For example, an MIT student in one of our classes created a simple Facebook application for sharing photos. Although he had very little formal training in programming, he created a robust and professional-looking app in a few days using standard tools. Within a year, he had over 1 million users. This was possible because his application leveraged the Facebook user base, which in turn leveraged the broader World Wide Web, which in turn leveraged the Internet protocols, which in turn leveraged the cheap computers of Moore's Law and many other innovations. He could not have created value for his million users without the existence of these prior inventions. Because the process of innovation often relies heavily on combining and recombining previous innovations, the broader and deeper the pool of accessible ideas and individuals, the more opportunities there are for innovation.

SKILLS THAT WILL REMAIN IN DEMAND

Computers are getting much better at pattern recognition, complex communication and many other skills. That may be good for businesses—but it's not always good for individual employees, who may not be able to adapt as quickly as technology is advancing. How can you prepare yourself—and, perhaps, your children—for careers in a fast-changing economy filled with ever-faster, ever-smarter computers?

One key is realizing that there are still many things computers are no good at. They're not creative, and they can't think "outside the box." And they're not very empathic. These limitations point to some skills that people should acquire if they want to be successful using machines in the future, instead of competing against computers:

- **Applied math and statistics.** Some think that the era of "big data" and powerful software means that fewer people have to master the gritty details of statistical analysis. This is deeply

(Continued)

(Continued)

misguided. Knowing which analyses to conduct and how to interpret their results is more valuable than ever. We think Google chief economist Hal Varian was on to something when he said that "the sexy job in the next 10 years will be statisticians."[i]

- **Negotiation and group dynamics.** Management is one of the most durable professions, even as computers advance. It turns out that organizations need dedicated managers working with teams, advancing their agendas and working with their members.

- **Good writing.** Computers can only generate the simplest, most formulaic prose. While few people write for a living, lots of us do at least some writing. Getting good at it is a way to stand out from the crowd—and from the machines.

- **Framing problems and solving open-ended problems.** Computers don't know what's wrong or where the next opportunities are. Solving open-ended problems entails both perceiving the challenge and addressing it. It's a major feature of primary and secondary educational systems like Montessori, which might explain why Montessori graduates are so common among the elite of the tech industry—the masters of racing with machines.

- **Persuasion.** Does anyone seriously think that a great salesperson will be unable to find work, even in a highly digitized economy?

- **Human interaction and nurturing.** We are biologically wired to react to human attention and the human touch in a way that no machine can replicate. That means that jobs that involve human nurturing and interaction, such as child care and nursing, will continue to defy automation.

We are in no danger of running out of new combinations to try. Even if technology froze today, we have more possible ways to configure the different applications, machines, tasks and distribution channels to create new processes and products than we could ever exhaust.

Here's a simple illustration: Suppose the people in a small company write down their work tasks—one task per card. If there were only 52 tasks in the company, as many as in a standard deck of cards, then there would be $52!$ different ways to arrange these tasks. ($52!$ is shorthand for $52 \times 51 \times 50 \times \ldots \times 2 \times 1$, which multiplies to over 8.06×1067, about the number of atoms in our galaxy.) That is far, far more than the number of grains of rice on the second half of the chessboard, or even a second or third chessboard. Combinatorial explosion is one of the few mathematical functions that outgrows an exponential trend.

No central planner could imagine, let alone consider and evaluate, all the possible new products and processes latent in all the possible combinations of the building blocks that can be configured to create value in today's digital economy. Most of the combinations may be no better than what we already have, but some surely will be, and a small fraction may be "home runs" that generate enormous value. Parallel experimentation by millions of entrepreneurs and innovative managers is the best and fastest way to identify the combinations of economic building blocks that will make a positive difference. Most of the digital economy's potential for combinatorial innovation remains yet to be tapped.

References

1. F. Levy and R. Murnane, "The New Division of Labor: How Computers Are Creating the Next Job Market" (Princeton, New Jersey: Princeton University Press, 2004).

2. J. Hooper, "From DARPA Grand Challenge 2004: DARPA's Debacle in the Desert," June 4, 2004, www.popsci.com.

3. S. Thrun, "What We're Driving At," October 9, 2010, http://googleblog.blogspot.com.

4. Levy and Murnane, "The New Division of Labor."

5. To be precise, Jeopardy! contestants are shown answers and must ask questions that would yield these answers.

6. J. Markoff, "Computer Wins on 'Jeopardy!': Trivial, It's Not," *New York Times,* Feb. 17, 2011.

7. G. E. Moore, "Cramming More Components Onto Integrated Circuits," Electronics, April 19, 1965, 114–117.

8. M. Kanellos, "Moore's Law to Roll on for Another Decade," February 10, 2003, http://news.cnet.com.

9. K. Greene, "A New and Improved Moore's Law," *Technology Review,* September 12, 2011.

10. President's Council of Advisors on Science and Technology, "Designing a Digital Future: Federally Funded Research and Development in Networking and Information Technology," December 2010, www.whitehouse.gov.

11. R. Kurzweil, "The Age of Spiritual Machines: When Computers Exceed Human Intelligence" (NewYork: Penguin Books, 2000).

12. S. Basu and J. Fernald, "Information and Communications Technology as a General-Purpose Technology: Evidence From U.S Industry Data," Working Paper Series 2006-29, Federal Reserve Bank of San Francisco, San Francisco, California, 2006.

13. Railroad construction crews in that period blasted tunnels though mountainsides by drilling holes into the rock, packing the holes with explosives and detonating them to lengthen the tunnel.

14. G. Kasparov, "The Chess Master and the Computer," *New York Review of Books,* February 11, 2010.

15. Ibid.

16. F. Khatib, F. DiMaio, Foldit Contenders Group, Foldit Void Crushers Group, S. Cooper, M. Kazmierczyk, M. Gilski, S. Krzywda, H. Zabranska, I. Pichova, J.Thompson, Z. Popovic´, M. Jaskolski and D. Baker, "Crystal Structure of a Monomeric Retroviral Protease Solved by Protein Folding Game Players," Nature Structural & Molecular Biology 18 (2011): 1175–1177.

17. M.V. Copeland, "The Mighty Micro-Multinational," *Business 2.0,* July 1, 2006.

18. M. S. Hopkins and L. Brokaw, "Matchmaking With Math: How Analytics Beats Intuition to Win Customers", *MIT Sloan Management Review* 52, no. 2 (winter 2011): 35–41.

19. A. McAfee and E. Brynjolfsson, "Investing in the IT That Makes a Competitive Difference," Harvard Business Review 86 (July August 2008): 98-107.

i. S. Lohr, "ForToday's Graduate, Just One Word: Statistics," *New York Times,* Aug. 5, 2009.

Leading for the Long Future

Daniel Goleman

Consortium for Research on Emotional Intelligence in Organizations

My late uncle, Alvin Weinberg, was a nuclear physicist who often acted as the conscience of that sector. He was fired as director of oak Ridge National Laboratory after 25 years in the job because he would not stop talking about the dangers of reactor safety and nuclear waste. He also, controversially, opposed using the type of reactor fuel that produces material for weapons. Then, as founder of the Institute for Energy Analysis, he initiated one of the nation's pioneering research and development units on alternative energy—he was one of the first scientists to warn about the threat of carbon dioxide (CO_2) and global warming.

Alvin once confided to me his ambivalence about for-profit companies running nuclear power plants, fearing that the profit motive would mean they cut safety measures—a premonition of what led to Japan's 2011 Fukushima disaster Alvin was particularly troubled that the nuclear energy industry had never solved the problem of what to do with radioactive waste. He urged them to find a solution that would persist as long as the waste remained radioactive—such as an institution dedicated to guarding those stockpiles and keeping people safe from them over centuries or millennia.

Acting for the Long Term

Decisions with the long horizon in mind ask questions like: How will what we do today matter to the grandchildren of our grandchildren's grandchildren? In a century, or in 500 years?

In that far future the specifics of our actions today may well fade like distant shadows of forgotten ancestors. What could have more lasting consequence are the norms we establish, the organizing principles for action that live on long after their originators have gone.

There are independent think tanks, as well as corporate and government groups, who think deeply about future scenarios. Consider these projections for the world in 2025, made by the US National Intelligence Council:

- Ecological impacts of human activity will create scarcity of resources like farmable soil.
- The economic demand for energy, food, and water will outstrip readily available sources—water shortages loom soon.
- These trends will create shocks and disruptions to our lives, economies, and political systems.

Source: "Leading for the Long Future," by Daniel Goleman in *Leader to Leader,* Vol. 2014 Issue 72, pp. 34–39. Copyright © 2014 by The Frances Hesselbein Leadership Institute. Reprinted with permission from John Wiley & Sons, Inc.

When that report was delivered in 2008, the federal government ignored the results. There is no agency, office, or particular government position charged with acting for the long term. Instead politicians focus on the short term—what it takes to get reelected, particularly—with virtually no attention paid to what needs to be done now to protect future generations. Politicians, like business leaders, typically make decisions for the short-term gain, not the long-term reality. Saving their jobs commands more of their attention than saving the planet or the poor.

Like politicians and business people, most of us lean toward short-term success. Cognitive psychologists find that people tend to favor now in decisions of all kinds—as in, *I'll have the pie à la mode now and maybe diet later.*

This pertains, too, to our goals. "We attend to the present, what's needed for success now," says Elke Weber, a Columbia University cognitive scientist. "But this is bad for far-sighted goals, which are not given the same priority in the mind. Future focus becomes a luxury, waiting for current needs to be taken care of first."

In 2003 New York Mayor Michael Bloomberg decreed that smoking was banned in bars. It got huge opposition—bar owners said it would ruin their business; smokers hated it. He said, you might not like it, but you'll thank me in 20 years.

How long does it take before the public reaction becomes positive? Elke Weber looked at Bloomberg's smoking ban, among other such decisions, to answer that question: "We did case studies of how long it took for a change that was initially unpopular to become the new, accepted status quo. Our data shows the range is 6–9 months."

> Most of us lean toward short-term success.

"Even smokers liked it after a while," Weber adds. "They got to enjoy hanging out with other smokers outdoors. And everyone likes that bars didn't reek of stale smoke."

Another case study: The provincial government of British Columbia imposed a tax on carbon emissions. It was revenue neutral: the fees collected were distributed among the province's citizens. At first there was tremendous opposition to the new tax. But after a while people liked getting their checks. Fifteen months later the tax was popular.

"Politicians are in charge of our welfare," says Weber. "They need to know people will thank them later for a hard decision now. It's like raising teenagers—sometimes thankless in the short term, but rewarding in the long."

Reshaping Systems

In the weeks after Hurricane Sandy devastated large parts of the New York City area, Mayor Bloomberg said it straight: this hurricane is due to global warming.

Soon after, I spoke with Jonathan F. P. Rose, a founder of the green community planning movement, who was writing a book that looks at cities as systems. "We're at an inflection point about the belief that climate change is a serious long-term problem we must deal with," Rose said. "Sandy's worst hit was the Wall Street area. You don't hear any climate warming deniers down there these days. In the Wall Street culture a quarter is a long time away. But Sandy may have gotten them to think about a much longer time horizon."

> Future focus becomes a luxury.

"If we reduce our production of heat-trapping gases today, it would still take at least 300 years for the climate to begin to cool, perhaps much longer," Rose added. "We have strong cognitive biases toward our present needs, and are weak thinkers about the long away future. But at least we're starting to recognize the degree to which we have put human and natural systems at risk. What we need now is leadership. Great leaders must have the essential long view that a systems understanding brings."

Reinventing business for the long future could mean finding shared values supported by all stakeholders, from stock owners to employees and customers to communities where a company operates—to generations as yet unborn. Some call it "conscious capitalism," orienting a company's performance around benefiting all stakeholders, not just aiming for quarterly numbers that please shareholders—and studies show that companies like Whole Foods and Zappos with this broader view actually do better on financials than their purely profit-oriented competitors. For a more in-depth examination of this topic, see *Conscious Capitalism,* the 2013 book by John Mackey, chief executive officer (CEO) of Whole Foods, and Raj Sisodia, chairman and cofounder of the Conscious Capitalism Institute.

If a leader is to articulate such shared values effectively, he or she must first look within to find a genuinely heartfelt guiding vision. The alternative can be seen in the hollow mission statements espoused by executives but belied by their company's (or their own) actions.

Even leaders of great companies can share a blind spot if their time frame is too small. To be truly great, leaders need to expand their focus to a farther horizon line, even beyond decades, while taking their systems understanding to a much finer focus. And their leadership needs to reshape systems themselves.

That brings to mind Paul Polman, CEO of Unilever, who surprised me when we were both members of a panel at the World Economic Forum in Davos. He took that opportunity to announce that Unilever had adopted the goal of cutting the company's environmental footprint in half by 2020 (this was in 2010, giving them a decade to get there). That was laudable, but a little ho-hum: many socially responsible companies announce global warming goals like that.

But the next thing he said really shocked me: Unilever is committed to sourcing their raw agriculture material from small farms, aiming to link to one half million smallholders globally. The farmers involved mainly grow tea, but the sourcing initiative will also include crops for cocoa, palm oil, vanilla, coconut sugar, and a variety of fruits and vegetables. The farms involved are in areas ranging from Africa to Southeast Asia and Latin America, with some in Indonesia, China, and India.

For Unilever, this diversification of their sourcing lowers risks in a turbulent world, where food security has come on the radar as a future issue.

Unilever hopes not only to link these small farmers into their supply chain but also to work with groups like Rainforest Alliance to help them upgrade their farming practices and so become reliable sources in global markets.

For the farmers, this will mean better profits, though exactly what these might be will vary from crop to crop and season to season. This redrawing of their supply chain, Polman pointed out, would have a range of benefits, from leaving more money in local farm communities to better health and schooling. The World Bank points to supporting smallholder farming as the most effective way to stimulate economic development and reduce poverty in rural areas

"In emerging markets three out of four low-income people depend directly or indirectly on agriculture for their livelihoods," according to Cherie Tan, who heads this initiative on sourcing from small farms. Eighty-five percent of all farms are in this smallholder class, "so there are great opportunities," she adds.

If we see a company as little more than a machine for making money, we ignore its web of connections to the people who work there, the communities it operates in, its customers and clients, and society at large. Leaders with a wider view bring into focus these relationships, too.

Although making money matters, of course, leaders with this enlarged aperture pay attention to *how* they make money and so make choices differently. Their decisions operate by a logic that does not reduce to simple profit–loss calculations—it goes beyond the language of economics. They balance financial return with the public good

In this view a good decision allows for present needs as well as those of a wider web of people—including future generations. Such leaders inspire: they articulate a larger common purpose that gives meaning and coherence to everyone's work and engage people emotionally through values that make people feel good about their work, that motivate, and that keep people on course.

Focusing on social needs can itself foster innovation, if combined with an expanded field of attention to what people need. Managers at the India division of Gillette, a global consumer goods company, saw village men bloodied by barbers using rusty razors and so found ways to make new razors cheap enough that those villagers could afford them

Such projects create organizational climates where work has meaning and engages people's passions. As for the teams that developed those cheap razors and soap bars, their labor becomes "good work": where people are engaged, work with excellence, and find meaning in what they do.

Big Picture Leaders

The good-enough leader operates within the givens of a system to benefit a single group, executing a mission as directed, operating within a single level of complexity. In contrast, a great leader defines a mission, acts on many levels, and tackles the biggest problems.

Great leaders do not settle for systems as they are, but see what they could become and so work to transform them for the better, to benefit the widest circle. They take on the greatest challenges and tackle the biggest problems. That demands a shift from mere competence to wisdom.

Then there are those rare souls who operate on behalf of society itself rather than a specific political group or business. They are free to think far, far ahead. Their thinking encompasses the welfare of humanity at large, not a single group; they see people as a We, not as Us and Them. And they leave a legacy for future generations—these are the leaders we remember a century or more later. Think Jefferson and Lincoln, Gandhi and Mandela, Buddha and Jesus.

> *Think Jefferson and Lincoln, Gandhi and Mandela, Buddha and Jesus.*

One of today's wicked messes is the paradox of the Anthropocene: human systems affect the global systems that support life in what seems to be headed for a slow-motion systems crash. Finding solutions requires Anthropocene thinking, understanding points of leverage within these systems dynamics so as to reset a course for a better future. This level of complexity adds to layers of other challenges facing leaders today.

There are, of course, many other fundamental systems dilemmas. For instance, through the health and ecological impacts of our lifestyle, the world's richest people are creating pain for the world's poorest. We may need to reinvent our economic systems themselves, factoring in human needs, not just economic growth.

Then there's the growing gap between the very richest and most powerful and the poorest worldwide. While the rich hold power, as we've seen their very status can blind them to the true conditions of the poor, leaving them indifferent to this suffering. Who, then, can speak truth to power?

> *Who, then, can speak truth to power?*

Although the perks and pleasures of civilization are alluring, there are also the "diseases of civilization," like diabetes and heart disease, which are worsened by the rigors and stresses of the routines that make those lifestyles possible. This intensifies as we fail in much of the world to make medical services equally available to all.

Then there are the perennial problems of inequities in education and access to opportunity; countries and cultures that privilege one elite group while repressing others; nations that are failing, devolving into warring fiefdoms—and on and on.

Problems of such complexity and urgency require an approach to problem solving that integrates our self-awareness and our actions, our empathy and our compassion, with a nuanced understanding of the systems at play.

To begin to address such messes, we need leaders who focus on several systems: geopolitical, economic, and environmental, to name a few. But sadly for the world, the failing of so many leaders is that their focus is too narrow. They are preoccupied with today's immediate problems and so lack bandwidth for the long-term challenges we face as a species.

The president's annual State of the Union address, Columbia University's Jeffrey Sachs proposes, should frame the present in terms of the (somewhat longer) future, by explaining how actions today might matter for people in 40 years. Sachs, like so many thinkers, sees the need not just for systems thinking but for framing our thoughts around the consequences for decades or centuries hence.

Peter Senge, who teaches at the Massachusetts Institute of Technology (MIT) Sloan School of Management, developed the "learning organization," which brings a systems understanding into companies, and was introduced in his best known book, 1990's *The Fifth Discipline: The Art and Practice of the Learning Organization.* "Essential to understanding systems is your time horizon," Senge told me. "If it's too short, you'll ignore essential feedback loops and come up with short-term fixes that won't work in the long run. But if that horizon is long enough, you'll have a chance of seeing more of the key systems at play."

"The bigger your horizon," adds Senge, "the bigger the system you can see."

But "transforming large-scale systems is hard," said Rebecca Henderson at an MIT meeting on global systems. Henderson teaches on ethics and the environment at Harvard Business School and uses a systems framework to seek solutions. For instance, recycling, she points out, represents "change at the margins," whereas abandoning fossil fuels altogether would represent a system shift.

Henderson, who teaches a surprisingly popular course at the business school on "reimagining capitalism," favors transparency that would accurately price, say, CO_2 emissions. That would cause markets to favor any means that lowers those emissions.

Or, for instance, we might take to scale what's been happening for years at Ben and Jerry's Ice Cream. One of their popular flavors, chocolate fudge brownie, calls for brownies to be broken up into the ice cream. Ben and Jerry gets their truckloads of these tasty cakes from the Greyston Bakery, located in a poverty-stricken neighborhood of the Bronx. The bakery trains and employs those who struggle to find work, including once-homeless parents who, with their families, now live in nearby low-cost housing. The bakery's motto: "We don't hire people to bake brownies. We bake brownies to hire people."

Such attitudes represent the kind of fresh thinking intractable dilemmas call for. But there's a hidden ingredient in any true solution: enhancing our attention and understanding—in ourselves, in others, in our communities and societies.

"Civilizations should be judged not by how they treat people closest to power, but rather how they treat those furthest from power—whether in race, religion, gender, wealth, or class—as well as in time," says Larry Brilliant, president of the Skoll Foundation Global Threats Fund. "A great civilization would have compassion and love for them, too."

At the same MIT meeting on global systems where Henderson spoke, the Dalai Lama said, "We need to influence decision makers to pay attention to the issues that matter for humanity in the long-run"—like the environmental crisis and the inequity in income distribution—"not just their national interest."

His words apply to us all, in our personal decisions—not just to those recognized as "leaders." In the sense that leaders influence or guide people toward a shared goal, leadership is widely distributed. Whether within a family, on social media, in an organization, or society as a whole, we are all leaders in one way or another.

"We have the capacity to think several centuries into the future," the Dalai Lama said, adding, "Start the task even if it will not be fulfilled within your lifetime. This generation has a responsibility to reshape the world. If we make an effort, it may be possible to achieve. Even if it seems hopeless now, never give up. Offer a positive vision, with enthusiasm and joy, and an optimistic outlook."

Conclusion: For Whose Benefit?

We must ask ourselves: in the service of what exactly are we using whatever talents we may have? If our focus serves only our personal ends—self-interest, immediate reward, and our own small group—then in the long run all of us, as a species, are doomed.

The largest lens for our focus encompasses global systems, considers needs of the powerless and poor, and peers far ahead in time. No matter what we are doing or what decision we are making, the Dalai Lama suggests these self-queries for checking our motivation:

Is it just for me or for others?

For the benefit of the few or the many?

For now or for the future?

PART II

Current Theories and Concepts of Leadership

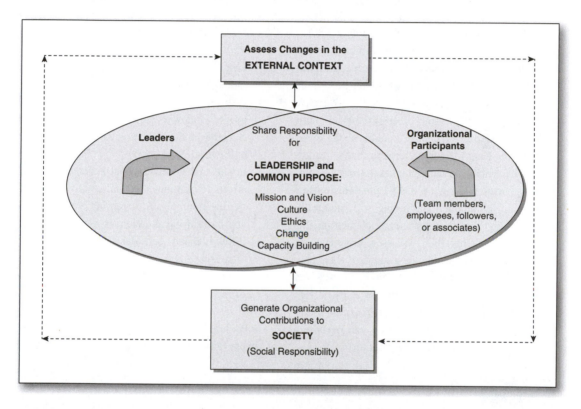

Overview

As stated in the introduction, leadership concepts and theories are incorporated in this book to advance purposeful selection of an organization's leadership philosophy, concepts, processes, and practices by its members. Parts II and III provide theories that leaders and members can use to cultivate their organization's leadership. Part II presents several leadership theories that were developed in the late 20th century and remain in use in many contemporary organizations. Several of these theories focus on the leader,

while others incorporate some aspects of followership. The final chapter concentrates exclusively on followership research.

Leadership Theories

James MacGregor Burns (Chapter 6) sparked a new era of study and practice of leadership with his groundbreaking book *Leadership*. His classic conceptualization of *transactional* and *transforming* leadership provided the foundation for revolutionary thinking about the role and purpose of leadership. Burns explains that transactional leadership takes place when one person takes the initiative in making contact with others for the purpose of an exchange of valued things. Clearly, transactional leadership can exist between leaders of two or more organizations, or between leaders and members within the same organization.

Burns contrasts this form of leadership with transforming leadership, which occurs when one or more persons engage with others in such a way that leaders and followers raise one another to higher levels of motivation and morality. Although Burns feels that transforming leadership cannot work in bureaucratic organizations, it is possible that this form of leadership can exist where organizational leaders and participants aspire to generate collective purpose and transforming processes that are ultimately linked to social change. Looking ahead to the chapters in Part VIII, many organizational leaders mobilize participants and resources to work on community, social, and environmental problems outside the organization, often partnering with nonprofit, business, or government agencies. Implementing this social mission, together with the organization's business mission, is becoming a standard leadership commitment and responsibility in many new era organizations. If this trend continues at its current rate and leaders effect real change in social conditions, then transforming leadership can become a viable form of leadership in organizations.

Bernard Bass and Ronald Riggio (Chapter 7) were the first scholars to import Burns' concepts from the political and social movement arena into the context of organizations. Bass separated Burns' link to social change from the theory of transforming leadership and adopted Burns' definition of transactional leadership to shape what he termed *transformational* leadership. Table II.1 illustrates the differences in Burns' and Bass' concepts. Bass and colleagues found that a qualitative change in performance and relationships occurs in transformational leadership to the benefit of the individual and the organization. Four critical factors, called the *Four I's*, compose this form of leadership:

- Idealized influence—serves as a positive role model for followers
- Inspirational motivation—motivates and inspires followers by providing meaning and challenge and articulating a compelling vision of the future (charisma)
- Intellectual stimulation—stimulates followers' efforts to be innovative and creative by questioning assumptions, reframing problems, and approaching old situations in new ways
- Individualized consideration—pays special attention to individual follower's needs for achievement and growth by acting as a coach or mentor

Jay Conger (Chapter 8) explores the development of theory and research on *charismatic leadership,*

Table II.I   Differences Between Transforming and Transformational Leadership Theories

	Transforming Leadership (Burns)	*Transformational Leadership (Bass)*
Purpose	To enhance the well-being of human existence	To motivate others to do more than they originally intended and often more than they thought possible
Context	Political and societal	Organizational
Influence process	Two-way (leader ⟷ follower)	One-way (leader ⟶ follower)
Requirement for social change	Yes ("real, intended change")	No

which shapes critical components of both transforming and transformational leadership. The German sociologist Max Weber was the first to identify charismatic authority in leaders who were set apart from others and endowed with exceptional powers and qualities of divine origin. Weber theorized that these uniquely gifted individuals often appeared in times of distress and that their attraction came from their acts of heroism, magical abilities, mental prowess, or remarkable ability to communicate.

In the mid-20th century, political scientists and sociologists became interested in exploring Weber's idea because of the emergence of leaders such as Churchill, Hitler, Roosevelt, Gandhi, and Kenyatta. These researchers were not able to identify a universal charismatic personality type because of the vast differences in personalities of these leaders. Researcher Ann Willner argued that charismatic leadership could be more satisfactorily understood as a relational and perceptual phenomenon based on what people see the leader as rather than what the leader is. Her concept influenced scholars in the field of organizational behavior, the next group of scholars to research charismatic leadership.

Conger identifies several distinct research topic areas for charismatic leadership in the work of behaviorists: "a) the leader's behavior; b) the followers' behavior and motives; c) the leader's and follower's psychological profiles; d) contextual influences; e) forces that institutionalize the outcomes of the leader-follower relationship; and f) liabilities of charismatic leaders." An example of this research is Conger and Kanungo's three-stage behavioral model that moves organizational members from a present state to a future state. In stage 1, charismatic leaders demonstrate their sensitivity to environmental constraints through critical evaluation of deficiencies in the status quo or poorly exploited opportunities in the environment, and demonstrate sensitivity to followers' abilities and needs. In stage 2, leaders formulate an idealized future vision and use articulation and impression management skills that set them apart from other leaders. Finally, in stage 3, these leaders use innovative and unconventional means to achieve their vision and they use personal power to influence followers.

Robert Greenleaf's (Chapter 9) concept of *servant leadership* characterizes the leader as steward or servant-first. The needs of participants are the foremost priority for servant leaders, whose role is to pave the way and provide support for participants to function at their best. Greenleaf provides several criteria for evaluating successful servant leadership: Do those served grow as persons? Do they, while being served, become healthier, wiser, freer, more autonomous, more likely themselves to become servants? And what is the effect on the least privileged in society? Will they benefit or at least not be further deprived?

Roya Ayman and Susan Adams (Chapter 10) present an overview of *contingency theories* of leadership. Contingency theorists study the effect of a leader's situation on her or his effectiveness. In general, these theories state that leadership effectiveness is maximized when leaders make their behavior "contingent" on certain situational and follower characteristics.

Ayman and Adams review several different contingency theories, including

- the contingency model, which contends effective leadership is a good fit among three variables: the leader and followers (leader–member relations), the task (degree of task structure), and the power inherent in the position (leader position power);
- cognitive resource theory, which purports that situational factors (high stress or low stress situations) will determine whether intelligence or experience predicts leadership effectiveness;
- normative model of leadership decision making, which assesses leaders' effectiveness in decision making based on their ability to balance several situational factors—decision quality (the degree to which a decision has an objectively determined better or worse outcome), time (the amount of time leaders have to make a decision), and team member acceptance (the amount of involvement needed for team members to accept the decision);
- path-goal theory, which claims the effective leader will provide or ensure the availability of

valued rewards for followers when they achieve a desired end (the "goal"), and then help them find the best way of getting there (the "path"); and

- the situational model, which looks at leaders' behavior (i.e., telling, selling, participating, and delegating) using three components: task behavior, relationship behavior, and follower readiness.

The authors argue that most previous research on contingency theory focused on the interpersonal level—contextual factors that are external to the individual such as team members' characteristics, organizational level, or industry type. They suggest that a contemporary research trend also examines contingencies at the intrapersonal level including sociodemographic characteristics (e.g., gender and culture) and psychosocial characteristics (e.g., self-monitoring, competency, or personality). Both interpersonal and intrapersonal factors are significant in contingency theory research.

Followership Theories

In contrast to the previous theories and concepts, Mary Uhl-Bien, Ronald Riggio, Kevin Lowe, and Melissa Carsten (Chapter 11) focus their attention on the other major participants in the leadership process—followers. Followership theory is a relatively recent phenomenon even though most leadership scholars consider followers and followership essential to leadership. Uhl-Bien, Riggio, Lowe, and Carsten review the research and treatment of followers in leadership research and propose a research agenda on followership for the future.

The newer perspectives on followership represent two perspective: role-based and constructionist approaches. Role-based approaches reverse the leadership lens by viewing followership as a role played by individuals in a formal or informal role as follower. These approaches consider how followers influence leader attitudes, behaviors, and outcomes. Two of the most prominent followership theories are typologies

developed by Robert Kelley and Ira Chaleff. Kelley identifies five types of followers: alienated followers, exemplary followers, conformist followers, pragmatists, and passive followers or sheep. He identifies exemplary or star followers as the most effective followers because they are independent thinkers, actively engaged, and exhibit courageous conscience. Chaleff's typology consists of four styles of follower: implementer, partner, individualist, and resource. Partners vigorously support the leader in implementing the organization's mission and vision, and they are courageous because at times they will need to challenge and confront leaders with unpleasant information and critical and honest feedback.

The researchers describe constructionist approaches as the way people come together in a social process to co-create leadership and followership. Followership is based on behaviors, rather than a role, that include claiming and granting, deferring or obeying, resisting or negotiating with another's wishes, or influencing another to go along with one's influence attempts. For instance, DeRue and Ashford propose a reciprocal identity claiming and granting process in which an individual claims an identity as either a leader or follower, and others grant that person's claimed identity. The process does not work if followers, for example, do not grant the claim of leaders. Some individuals must also claim and be granted follower identities for leadership to be constructed. Shamir calls his constructionist approach *co-production*. He proposes that leadership is co-produced by leaders and followers when they form effective leadership relationships that advance organizational goals, vision, and behaviors essential for success.

Uhl-Bien, Riggio, Lowe, and Carsten call for a formal theory of followership. They define followership theory as "the study of the nature and impact of followers and following in the leadership process." They present examples of several leadership constructs including followership characteristics, followership behaviors, and followership outcomes; and they propose two potential theoretical frameworks: the role-based approach and the constructionist approach.

Part II — Chapters

CHAPTER 6

Leadership (Excerpts)

James MacGregor Burns
Williams College

One of the most serious failures in the study of leadership has been the bifurcation between the literature on leadership and the literature on followership. The former deals with the heroic or demonic figures in history, usually through the medium of biography and with the inarticulated major premise that fame is equated with importance. The latter deals with the audiences, the masses, the voters, the people, usually through the medium of studies of mass opinion or of elections; it is premised on the conviction that in the long run, at least, leaders act as agents of their followers. The leadership approach tends often unconsciously to be elitist; it projects heroic figures against the shadowy background of drab, powerless masses. The followership approach tends to be populistic or anti-elitist in ideology; it perceives the masses, even in democratic societies, as linked with small, overlapping circles of conservative politicians, military officers, hierocrats, and businessmen. I describe leadership here as no mere game among elitists and no mere populist response but as a structure of action that engages persons, to varying degrees, throughout the levels and among the interstices of society. Only the inert, the alienated, and the powerless are unengaged.

Surely it is time that the two literatures are brought together, that the roles of leader and follower be united conceptually, that the study of leadership be lifted out of the anecdotal and the eulogistic and placed squarely in the structure and processes of human development and political action. I hope to demonstrate that the processes of leadership must be seen as part of the dynamics of conflict and of power; that leadership is nothing if not linked to collective purpose; that the effectiveness of leaders must be judged not by their press clippings but by actual social change measured by intent and by the satisfaction of human needs and expectations; that political leadership depends on a long chain of biological and social processes, of interaction with structures of political opportunity and closures, of interplay between the calls of moral principles and the recognized necessities of power; that in placing these concepts of political leadership centrally into a theory of historical causation, we will reaffirm the possibilities of human volition and of common standards of justice in the conduct of peoples' affairs.

I will deal with leadership as distinct from mere power-holding and as the opposite of brute power. I will identify two basic types of leadership: the *transactional* and the *transforming*. The relations of most leaders and followers are transactional—leaders approach followers with an eye to exchanging one thing for another: jobs for votes, or subsidies for campaign contributions. Such transactions comprise the bulk of the relationships among leaders and followers, especially in groups, legislatures, and parties. *Transforming* leadership, while more complex, is more potent. The transforming leader recognizes and exploits an existing need or demand of a potential follower. But, beyond that, the transforming leader looks for potential motives in followers, seeks to satisfy higher needs, and engages the full person of the follower. The result of transforming leadership is a relationship of mutual stimulation and elevation that converts followers into leaders and may convert leaders into moral agents.

This last concept, *moral leadership,* concerns me the most. By this term I mean, first, that leaders and led have a relationship not only of power but of mutual needs, aspirations, and values; second, that in responding to leaders, followers have adequate knowledge of alternative leaders and programs and the capacity to choose among those alternatives; and, third, that leaders take responsibility for their commitments—if they promise certain kinds of economic, social, and political change, they assume leadership in the bringing about of that change. Moral leadership is not mere preaching, or the uttering of pieties, or the insistence on social conformity. Moral leadership emerges from, and always returns to, the fundamental wants and needs, aspirations, and values of the followers. I mean the kind of leadership that can produce social change that will satisfy followers' authentic needs. I mean less the Ten Commandments than the Golden Rule. But even the Golden Rule is inadequate, for it measures the wants and needs of others simply by our own.

I propose, in short, to move from the usual "practical" questions to the most exacting theoretical and moral ones. Assuming that leaders are neither "born" nor "made," we will look for patterns in the origins and socializing of persons that account for leadership. Using concepts that emphasize the evolving structures of motivations, values, and goals, we will identify distinctive leadership roles and qualities. We will note the interwoven texture of leadership and followership and the vital and concentric rings of secondary, tertiary, and even "lower" leadership at most levels of society, recognizing nevertheless the role of "great leaders," who exercise large influences on the course of history. Searching always for the moral foundations of leadership, we will consider as truly legitimate only those acts of leaders that serve ultimately in some way to help release human potentials now locked in ungratified needs and crushed expectations.

Do skill and genius still matter? Can we distinguish *leaders* from mere power holders? Can we identify forces that enable leaders to act on the basis of common, non-culture-bound needs and values that, in turn, empower leaders to demonstrate genuine moral leadership? Can we deal with these questions across polities and across time? Can we, therefore, apply these concepts of political leadership to wider theories of social change and historical causation?

If we can do these things, we can hope to fashion a general theory of political leadership. And, when we return from moral and causal questions to ways of practical leadership, we might find that there is nothing more practical than sound theory, if we can fashion it.

***

Leadership and Followership

Leadership is an aspect of power, but it is also a separate and vital process in itself.

Power over other persons, we have noted, is exercised when potential power wielders, motivated to achieve certain goals of their own, marshal in their power base resources (economic, military, institutional, or skill) that enable them to influence the behavior of respondents by activating motives of respondents relevant to those resources and to those goals. This is done in order to realize the purposes of the *power wielders, whether or not these are also the goals of the respondents*. Power wielders also exercise influence by mobilizing their own power base in such a way as to establish direct physical control over others' behavior, as in a war of conquest or through measures of harsh deprivation, but these are highly restricted exercises of power, dependent on certain times, cultures, and personalities, and they are often self-destructive and transitory.

Leadership over human beings is exercised when persons with certain motives and purposes mobilize, in competition or conflict with others, institutional, political, psychological, and other resources so as to arouse, engage, and satisfy the motives of followers. This is done in order to realize goals mutually held by *both leaders and followers*, as in Lenin's calls for peace, bread, and land. In brief, leaders with motive and power bases tap followers' motives in order to realize the purposes of both leaders and followers. Not only must motivation be relevant, as in power generally, but its purposes must be realized and satisfied. Leadership is exercised in a condition of *conflict* or *competition* in which leaders contend in appealing to the motive bases of potential followers. Naked power, on the other hand, admits of no competition or conflict—there is no engagement.

Leaders are a particular kind of power holder. Like power, leadership is relational, collective, and purposeful. Leadership shares with power the central function of achieving purpose. But the reach and domain of leadership are, in the short range at least, more limited than those of power. Leaders do not obliterate followers' motives though they may arouse certain motives and ignore others. They lead other creatures, not things (and lead animals only to the degree that they recognize animal motives—i.e., leading cattle to shelter rather than to slaughter). To control *things*—tools, mineral resources, money, energy—is an act of power, not leadership, for things have no motives. Power wielders may treat people as things. Leaders may not.

All leaders are actual or potential power holders, but not all power holders are leaders.

These definitions of power and of leadership differ from those that others have offered. Lasswell and Kaplan hold that power must be relevant to people's valued things; I hold that it must be relevant to the *power wielder's* valued things and may be relevant to the *recipient's* needs or values only as necessary to exploit them. Kenneth Janda defines power as "the ability to cause other persons to adjust their behavior in conformance with communicated behavior patterns." I agree,

assuming that those behavior patterns aid the purpose of the power wielder. According to Andrew McFarland, "If the leader causes changes that he intended, he has exercised power; if the leader causes changes that he did not intend or want, he has exercised influence, but not power." I dispense with the concept of influence as unnecessary and unparsimonious. For me the leader is a very special, very circumscribed, but potentially the most effective of power holders, judged by the degree of intended "real change" finally achieved. Roderick Bell et al. contend that power is a relationship rather than an entity—an entity being something that "could be smelled and touched, or stored in a keg"; while I agree that power is a relationship, I contend that the relationship is one in which some entity—part of the "power base"—plays an indispensable part, whether that keg is a keg of beer, of dynamite, or of ink.

The crucial variable, again, is *purpose*. Some define leadership as leaders making followers do what *followers* would not otherwise do, or as leaders making followers do what the *leaders* want them to do; I define leadership as leaders inducing followers to act for certain goals that represent the values and the motivations—the wants and needs, the aspirations and expectations—*of both leaders and followers.* And the genius of leadership lies in the manner in which leaders see and act on their own and their followers' values and motivations.

Leadership, unlike naked power-wielding, is thus inseparable from followers' needs and goals. The essence of the leader-follower relation is the interaction of persons with different levels of motivations and of power potential, including skill, in pursuit of a common or at least joint purpose. That interaction, however, takes two fundamentally different forms. The first I will call *transactional* leadership. Such leadership occurs when one person takes the initiative in making contact with others for the purpose of an exchange of valued things. The exchange could be economic or political or psychological in nature: a swap of goods or of one good for money; a trading of votes between candidate and citizen or between legislators; hospitality to another person in exchange for willingness to listen to one's troubles. Each party to the bargain is conscious of the power resources and attitudes of the other. Each person recognizes the other as a *person*. Their purposes are related, at least to the extent that the purposes stand within the bargaining process and can be advanced by maintaining that process. But beyond this the relationship does not go. The bargainers have no enduring purpose that holds them together; hence they may go their separate ways. A leadership act took place, but it was not one that binds leader and follower together in a mutual and continuing pursuit of a higher purpose.

Contrast this with *transforming* leadership. Such leadership occurs when one or more persons *engage with others in* such a way that leaders and followers raise one another to higher levels of motivation and morality. Their purposes, which might have started out as separate but related, as in the case of transactional leadership, become fused. Power bases are linked not as counterweights but as mutual support for common purpose. Various names are used for such leadership, some of them derisory: elevating, mobilizing, inspiring, exalting, uplifting, preaching, exhorting, evangelizing. The relationship can be moralistic, of course. But transforming leadership ultimately becomes *moral* in that it raises the level of human conduct and ethical aspiration of both leader and led, and thus it has a transforming effect on both. Perhaps the best modern example is Gandhi, who aroused and elevated the hopes and demands of millions of Indians and whose life and personality were enhanced in the process. Transcending leadership is dynamic leadership in the sense that the leaders throw themselves into a relationship with followers who will feel "elevated" by it and often become more active themselves, thereby creating new cadres of leaders. Transcending leadership is leadership *engagé*. Naked power-wielding can be neither transactional nor transforming; only leadership can be.

Leaders and followers may be inseparable in function, but they are not the same. The leader takes the initiative in making the leader–led connection; it is the leader who creates the links that allow communication and exchange to take place. An office seeker does this in accosting a voter on the street, but if the voter espies and accosts the politician, the voter is assuming a leadership function, at least for that brief moment. The leader is more skillful in evaluating followers' motives, anticipating their responses to an initiative, and estimating their power bases, than the reverse. Leaders continue to take the major part in maintaining and effectuating the relationship with followers and will have the major role in ultimately carrying out the combined purpose of leaders and followers. Finally, and most important by far, leaders address themselves to followers' wants, needs, and other motivations, as well as to their own, and thus they serve as an *independent force in changing the makeup of the followers' motive base through gratifying their motives*.

Certain forms of power and certain forms of leadership are near-extremes on the power continuum. One is the kind of absolute power that, Lord Acton felt, "corrupts absolutely." It also coerces absolutely. The essence of this kind of power is the capacity of power wielders, given the necessary motivation, to override the motive and power bases of their targets. Such power objectifies its victims; it literally turns them into objects, like the inadvertent weapon tester in Mtésa's court. Such power wielders, as well, are objectified and dehumanized. Hitler, according to Richard Hughes, saw the universe as containing no persons other than himself, only "things." The ordinary citizen in Russia, says a Soviet linguist and dissident, does not identify with his government. "With us, it is there, like the wind, like a wall, like the sky. It is something permanent, unchangeable. So the individual acquiesces, does not dream of changing it—except a few, few people."

At the other extreme is leadership so sensitive to the motives of potential followers that the roles of leader and follower become virtually interdependent. Whether the leadership relationship is transactional or transforming, in it motives, values, and goals of leader and led have merged. It may appear that at the other extreme from the raw power relationship, dramatized in works like Arthur Koestler's *Darkness at Noon* and George Orwell's *1984*, is the extreme of leadership–led merger dramatized in novels about persons utterly dependent on parents, wives, or lovers. Analytically these extreme types of relationships are not very perplexing. To watch one person absolutely dominate another is horrifying; to watch one person disappear, his motives and values submerged into those of another to the point of loss of individuality, is saddening. But puzzling out the nature of these extreme relationships is not intellectually challenging because each in its own way lacks the qualities of complexity and conflict. Submersion of one personality in another is not genuine merger based on mutual respect. Such submersion is an example of brute power subtly applied, perhaps with the acquiescence of the victim.

More complex are relationships that lie between these poles of brute power and wholly reciprocal leadership- followership. Here empirical and theoretical questions still perplex both the analysts and the practitioners of power. One of these concerns the sheer measurement of power (or leadership). Traditionally we measure power resources by calculating each one and adding them up: constituency support plus access to leadership plus financial resources plus skill plus "popularity" plus access to information, etc., all in relation to the strength of opposing forces, similarly computed. But these calculations omit the vital factor of motivation and purpose and hence fall of their own weight. Another controversial measurement device is reputation. Researchers seek to learn from informed observers their estimates of the power or leadership role and resources of visible *community* leaders (projecting this into national arenas of power is a formidable task). Major questions arise as to the reliability of the estimates, the degree of agreement between interviewer and interviewee over their definition of power and leadership, the transferability of power from one area of decision-making to another. Another device for studying power and leadership is *linkage theory*, which requires elaborate mapping of communication and other interrelations among power holders in different spheres, such as the economic and the military. The difficulty here is that communication, which may expedite the processes of power and leadership, is not a substitute for them.

My own measurement of power and leadership is simpler in concept but no less demanding of analysis: *power and leadership are measured by the degree of production of intended effects.* This need not be a theoretical exercise. Indeed, in ordinary political life, the power resources and the motivations of presidents and prime ministers and political parties are measured by the extent to which presidential promises and party programs are carried out. Note that the variables are the double ones of *intent* (a function of motivation) and of *capacity* (a function of power base), but the test of the extent and quality of power and leadership is the degree of *actual accomplishment of the promised change.*

Other complexities in the study of power and leadership are equally serious. One is the extent to which power and leadership are exercised not by positive action but by *inaction* or *nondecision.* Another is that power and leadership are often exercised not directly on targets but indirectly, and perhaps through multiple channels, on multiple targets. We must ask not only whether P has the power to do X to R, but whether P can induce or force R to do Y to Z. The existence of power and leadership in the form of a stream of multiple direct and indirect forces operating over time must be seen as part of the broader sequences of historical causation. Finally, we must acknowledge the knotty problem of events of history that are beyond the control of identifiable persons capable of foreseeing developments and powerful enough to influence them and hence to be held accountable for them. We can only agree with C. Wright Mills that these are matters of fate rather than power or leadership.

We do well to approach these and other complexities of power and leadership with some humility as well as a measure of boldness. We can reject the "gee whiz" approach to power that often takes the form of the automatic presumption of "elite control" of communities, groups, institutions, entire nations. Certain concepts and techniques of the "elitist" school of power are indispensable in social and political analysis, but "elitism" is often used as a concept that *presupposes* the existence of the very degree and kind of power that is to be estimated and analyzed. Such "elite theorists" commit the gross error of equating power and leadership with the assumed power bases of preconceived leaders and power holders, without considering the crucial role of *motivations* of leaders and followers. Every good detective knows that one must look for the motive as well as the weapon.

***

The Test: Real, Intended Change

Most of the world's decision makers, however powerful they may appear in journalistic accounts, must cope with the effects of decisions already made by events, circumstances, and other persons and hence, like Khrushchev and Kennedy, must act within narrow bounds. Decision-making opportunities typically come to them in the form of a few limited options. The advisers and institutions and procedures that once upon a time might have been organized to empower them often turn out to have become sources of restraint. The main function—even of those labeled radicals or reformers or revolutionaries—is often to maintain existing political arrangements and hence to contribute to continuity, equilibrium, and stability. Such decision makers are defensive and palliative rather than creative. Occasionally they act at such critical turning points in the great affairs of nations that their tiny leverage tips affairs toward one course of action rather than another or holds matters in balance or in suspension until decisions can be made at a later time. But those later decisions may be even more constrained as a result of intervening events.

Napoleon, it is said, could look upon a battle scene of unimaginable disorder and see its coherence for his own advantage. If some decision makers seem to have enormous influence on history and are thrust into the pantheon of world heroes, this may be in part the result of miscalculation by the chroniclers of their actual impact on the shank of history and their glorification as heroes by panegyrists. Even more the reason may be a faulty or inadequate conception of the nature of change. Dramatic decision-making may lead only to cosmetic change, or to temporary change, or to the kind of change in symbols and myths that will preserve the existing order rather than transform or undermine it. Such seemed to be true of de Gaulle's regime. A realistic and restricted definition of policy and decision leadership is necessary to a serviceable concept of social change.

By social change I mean here *real change*—that is, a transformation to a marked degree in the attitudes, norms, institutions, and behaviors that structure our daily lives. Such changes embrace not only "new cultural patterns and institutional arrangements" and "new psychological dispositions," in the terms used by Herbert Kelman and Donald Warwick, but changes in material conditions, in the explicit, felt existence, the flesh and fabric of people's lives. Such changes may be a far cry from the "changes" that legislative, judicial, and executive decisions are supposed to bring automatically. The leadership process must be defined, in short, as carrying through from the decision-making stages to the point of concrete changes in people's lives, attitudes, behaviors, institutions. Even the sweep of this process is not enough, however, for we must include another dimension: *time.* Attitude and behavior can change for a certain period; as in a war, popular fads and emotional political movements change only to revert later. Real change means a continuing interaction of attitudes, behavior, and institutions, monitored by alterations in individual and collective hierarchies of values.

Leadership brings about real change that leaders *intend,* under our definition. Leaders may seem to cause the most titanic of changes—such as the human and physical wreckage left in the wake of civil war—but that wreckage itself presumably was not the central purpose of the leaders. It would be idle here to measure the extent and character of social change unless we also examine the intentions of those who make the decisions that were intended to bring about change. Such an examination is necessary if we are to find purpose and meaning, rather than sheer chance or chaos, in the unfolding of events. A definition that demands so much from leadership also requires that we consider the totality of decision-making by leaders at all levels and in all the interstices of the polity. For actions or changes that might seem errant or vagrant in relation to visible leaders may be the planned outcome of decisions by less conspicuous and less "legitimate" leaders far down the line. The test is purpose and intent, drawn from values and goals, of leaders, high and low, resulting in policy decision and real, intended change.

Social change is so pervasive and ubiquitous in the modem world, and often so dramatic and menacing, as to attract intensive scholarly investigation. It has become an intellectual growth industry. Hegel and Marx are not the only celebrated theorists who have dealt with it as a central phenomenon in social analysis and historical fact. In surveying the vast literature on change, one remarks once again on the absence of a clear concept of the role of artistic or intellectual or political or social leadership in the processes of change, on the absence in most works of references to leadership in theory or practice. Often the process of *innovation* is explored but not in a broad framework of the leadership motivations, goals, and processes within which innovation takes on meaning and direction. It is as though change took place mechanically, apart from human volition or participation. What then, in a preliminary way, can be said about the role of policy and decision-making leadership in the process of real social change?

This question can be answered only in the context of the conditions of stability, continuity, persistence, and inertia that grip most of humankind. We of the modern era hear and see so much of what is called dizzying change—the rise and fall of leaders, dynasties, and whole nations, the continuing eruptions and disruptions of technology, massive migrations, the "population explosion," rapid alterations in economic conditions, the flux of artistic, literary, and other fashions—that we tend to underplay the fixity in human affairs. "Social interaction is to be found in social fixity and persistence as well as in social change," Robert Nisbet observes. "That is why, if we are to answer the question of causation in change, we are obliged to deal with, first, *the nature of social persistence* and, then, with *variables, not constants,* when we turn to the matter of what causes the observed change in structure, trait, or idea." Systems, once established, generate countless forces and balances to perpetuate themselves.

Our very assumption of change is culture-bound. "For most of the world's people, who have known only the changelessness of history, such stress on the difficulty of change would not be necessary," according to Robert Heilbroner. "But for ourselves, whose outlook is conditioned by the extraordinary dynamism of our unique historical experience, it is a needed caution. Contrary to our generally accepted belief, change is not the rule but the exception in life." And Leonard Meyer says, at the start of a chapter headed "The Probability of Stasis": "The presumption

that social-cultural development is a necessary condition of human existence is not tenable. The history of China up to the nineteenth century, the stasis of ancient Egypt, and the lack of cumulative change in countless other civilizations and cultures make it apparent that stability and conservation, not change, have been the rule in mankind generally."

What then is all the activity? Much of it is the appearance of multitudinous readjustments as the system absorbs small variations in the basic pattern and maintains its own pace and direction. The anthropologist Alfred R. Radcliffe-Brown noted the changes within structures that did not affect the structural form of society. He made a sharp distinction between *system maintenance,* the kind of readjustment that was essentially an adjustment of the equilibrium of a social structure, and what he called *system change* or "change of type," which he defined as "a change such that when there is sufficient of it, the society passes from one type of social structure to another." The vast proportion of the decisions of decision makers, high and low, is readjustment that maintains the equilibrium of the social structure.

A system can appear dynamic in guarding its own statics. A leader who departs from system or group norms in some decision will suffer undue attention, pressure, sanctions, and perhaps rejection or exclusion. To cite one of innumerable laboratory experiments, F. Merei demonstrated that a child with evident leadership qualities was nevertheless forced to abide by the established play norms of a small kindergarten group. If a change in one part of a system seems to threaten other parts, it is sealed off; at most it is not allowed to change much faster than the others. A host of institutional safeguards, some of them vested with sacrosanct status or mystification, is built around stabilizing decision-making processes. Outsiders and outside ideas are smoothly rejected. One of the most common tendencies in the history of arms development and change has been the resistance of military decision makers to weapons innovations that much later, after being adopted in crisis or catastrophe, took on their own institutional protection.

A number of strategies have been developed to overcome resistance to change: coercive strategies, normative strategies (achieving compliance by invoking values that have been internalized), utilitarian strategies (control over allocation and deprivation of rewards and punishments), empirical-rational strategies (rational justification for change), power-coercive strategies (application of moral, economic, and political resources to achieve change), and re-educative strategies (exerting influence through feeling and thought). Coercive strategies need not detain us here, since we exclude coercion from the definition of leadership; the majority of the other strategies provide for deprivation of group support for the beliefs, attitudes, values, and concepts of self that combine to tie a person to the status quo. A common thread—perhaps the only common thread—running through these diverse strategies is their difficulty. Most seem to be aimed not so much at altering the attitudes and behavior of the ultimate targets of change—citizens in their daily lives—but at the subordinate decision makers in government or business or other collectivities who are supposed to *administer* the change. Even if top policy makers were able to exert control down the line over subordinate policy makers, a huge gap remains between their operating decisions and real change in the behavior of the greater public. "In here" is still sharply different from "out there." All this simply confirms in theory what decision-making leaders find in practice: that breaks and erosions and disturbances in the "line of command" produce attenuation of purpose and of action at the grass roots and that, even when they do not, the target publics may not respond. Decisions are rarely self-implementing. Many of the administrative devices intended to communicate command and direction from the top become means for blunting or distorting the chain of decision.

Grand policy-making and decision-making leadership, in short, can wither at the most crucial phase—that of influence over popular attitudes and behavior. Is there any way out of this dilemma?

The answer to this question ultimately turns on the nature of the goals of decision-making leadership. These, of course, vary enormously. On the most personal and individual level policy makers may seek small changes that affect only themselves. This may be a service from a government bureau, exemption from a regulation, some honor or special recognition

from the state. Frustrated by the regular bureaucratic decision-making machinery, they may "walk their papers" through the administrative labyrinth. In realizing their own specific and perhaps narrow goal, in effecting a small change for themselves, they leave the decision-making process itself hardly touched. They have "beaten the system," but the system in the long run beats them, for their very success lowers pressure to improve the machinery—at least on their part and for the short run—hence it may continue to operate poorly for the great number of persons it services. Some individual efforts, however narrowly and self-servingly motivated, may implicate others in a beneficial way, but those benefits will rarely rise above the "satisficing" level.

At the general or collective level, on the other hand, the goal of a leader may be such comprehensive social change that the existing social structure cannot accommodate it. Hence, in the eyes of certain leaders, that structure must be entirely uprooted and a whole new system substituted, probably through revolutionary means. Revolutions do not always succeed, however, and when they do succeed, revolutionary action, in disrupting existing structures and mobilizing new social forces, incidentally arouses new needs and establishes new goals. Real change may take forms very different from the revolutionary goals originally sought. The most violent revolution, no matter how far-reaching its professed desire for reconstructing society, typically falls short of complete real change. The notion of "a *complete* change in the structural form of a society is . . . incoherent," Ernest Nagel says.

Between the extremes of planning discrete individual change and planning comprehensive and drastic change lies *middle-range* planning, responding to shared needs and other motivations and aimed at collective goals that represent the main planning effort of political leadership in most societies. This kind of *planning leadership* seeks genuine social change for collective purposes, though not necessarily at the same pace, or on so wide a front, as that of revolutionary action. The task of this kind of leadership is political and governmental planning for real social change.

The critical problem concerns the implication of planned ends for planning ways and means, the demands that comprehensive real change puts on existing social and political systems (which we will label here "social structures"). We are defining planning here not only as the establishment of definite social and economic goals to meet popular wants, needs, and expectations, but as the considered and deliberate reshaping of means necessary for the realization of comprehensive real change. Lewis Coser, like Radcliffe-Brown, has made a useful distinction between changes *of* systems and changes *in* systems. He refers to a change *of* system "when all major structural relations, its basic institutions, and its prevailing value system have been drastically altered." Changes *in* system take place more slowly and affect smaller sectors of a system. Given enough time, however, changes in system, through mutual stimulation and adjustment, can produce extensive change if not fundamental transformation of system. The accumulated changes in the British political system over the past two centuries have substantially altered the political structure, but these changes (such as extension of the suffrage) appeared at the time to be changes within the system.

Changes *in* system would seem far more system transforming than changes *of* systems, if only because the latter type of change comes so hard. Yet the extent of change *of* political systems since 1800 has been remarkable. Ted Gurr has found that the incidence of "system-transforming political change" has been high and pervasive both in the Third World and in the European zone of influence. The median duration of historical Latin and Afro-Asian polities and of European nations during that period was about the same: twelve years. The incidence of abrupt political change had increased markedly from the nineteenth to the twentieth centuries, Gurr found. "Of the 150 historical polities in the sample which were established before 1900," according to Gurr, "half survived for 20 years; but for the 117 historical polities established after 1900, the 'half-life' was only nine years." The extent to which these transformations took place as a result of collective and comprehensive planning by leaders varied widely, but these findings underline the vulnerability and impermanence of social structures that may appear to be well established.

Planning for structural change, whether of the system or in the system, is the ultimate moral test of decision-making leadership inspired by certain goals and values and intent on achieving real social change; it is also the leader's most potent *weapon*. It is a test in that planning calls for thinking and acting along a wide battlefront of complex forces, institutions, and contingencies; if the planners really "mean it," they must plan for the reshaping of means as required by the ends to which they are committed. It is a weapon in that a well-conceived plan, along with available planning technology, supplies leaders with an estimate of the human, material, and intellectual resources necessary to draw up and drive through a plan for substantial social change. Planning is designed to anticipate and to counter the myriad factors that impair the line of decision and action between the policy-making of planning leaders and real change in the daily lives of great numbers of people.

Still, the best laid plans of mice and men go aft agley. Why? In part because the plans are poorly drawn or badly executed. In part because plans encounter "chance" developments no mortal could possibly predict. And in large part because most planners focus on technical and administrative factors, minimizing the psychological and the structural forces. At a certain point following the Bolshevik revolution, Alex Inkeles observes, the "political and economic development of the revolution had now run far ahead of the more narrowly 'social.' In the haste of revolutionary experiment, no systematic attention had been given to the congruence of the newly established institutional forms with the motivational systems, the patterns of expectation and habitual behavior, of the population. Furthermore, as the new institutions began to function they produced social consequences neither planned nor anticipated by the regime." The problem was exacerbated for the Bolsheviks, Inkeles adds, by a Marxist ideology that predisposed leaders to assume that basic changes in the pattern of human relations, which they viewed only as part of the "dependent" superstructure of society, must automatically follow from changes in the political and economic system.

Planners elsewhere have encountered similar problems of human motivation. A British Labour government, in nationalizing the coalmines, misconceived the reactions of the very miners whose lot it was mainly designed to ameliorate. For many miners the change seemed to amount to the substitution of one bureaucracy for another. Indian population planners miscalculated the principal motive of Indian villagers, which was to raise children who would be available for labor and for family income—a motive that overrode the effect of propaganda in favor of limited families for the sake of other goals. American political planners in 1787 shaped a superb political structure for pitting faction against faction and thus breaking the force of faction in government, but they underestimated the popular and egalitarian forces that would threaten such balanced and stabilized government from outside. In the light of planning mishaps, it is not surprising that planners often seek to isolate their new structures from unpredictable psychological forces operating through a political system. Thus the leaders of the Tennessee Valley Authority established their own planning mechanism "in the field" and resented efforts by Washington decision makers to intervene. Autonomy was a two-bladed sword, however; it protected sectoral planners against bureaucratic aggression in the central government, but it did so at the expense of contracting the scope and power of leadership planning.

To note that effective planning must consider motives and values is to return to our central emphasis on a general theory of political leadership. Planning leaders, more than other leaders, must respond not simply to popular attitudes and beliefs but to the fundamental wants and needs, aspirations and expectations, values and goals of their existing and potential followers. Planning leadership must estimate not only initial responses from the public but the extent to which successful plans will arouse new wants and needs and aims in the second and succeeding "rounds" of action. Planning leaders must perceive that consensus in planning would be deceptive and dangerous, that *advocacy and conflict* must be built into the planning process in response to pluralistic sets of values. Planning leaders must recognize *purpose*—indeed, planning is nonexistent without goals—and recognize that different purposes will inform the planning process. Plans must recognize means or model values too, especially in procedures providing for expression of majority attitudes without threatening rights of privacy and self-expression. And planning must recognize the many faces of power; ultimately the authority and credibility of planning leadership will depend less on formal position than on the capacity to recognize basic needs, to mobilize masses of persons holding sets of values and seeking general goals, to utilize conflict and the adversary process without succumbing to it, and to bring about real social change either through existing social structures or by altering them.

"Increasingly," Karl Mannheim wrote shortly before his death, "it is recognized that real planning consists in coordination of institutions, education, valuations and psychology. Only one who can see the important ramifications of each single step can act with the responsibility required by the complexity of the modern age." It is the leaders who preeminently must see in this way. But to *see* alone is insufficient; they must *act* too, and of all the tasks proposed by Mannheim, the changing of institutions is the most difficult. For institutions are encapsulated within social structures that are themselves responses to earlier needs, values, and goals. In seeking to change social structures in order to realize new values and purposes, leaders go far beyond the politicians who merely cater to surface attitudes. To elevate the goals of humankind, to achieve high moral purpose, to realize major intended change, leaders must thrust themselves into the most intractable processes and structures of history and ultimately master them.

CHAPTER 7

The Transformational Model of Leadership

Bernard M. Bass
Binghamton University

Ronald E. Riggio
Claremont McKenna College

A new paradigm of leadership has captured widespread attention. James MacGregor Bums (1978) conceptualized leadership as either transactional or transformational. Transactional leaders are those who lead through social exchange. As Burns (1978) notes, politicians, for example, lead by "exchanging one thing for another: jobs for votes, or subsidies for campaign contributions" (p. 4). In the same way, transactional business leaders offer financial rewards for productivity or deny rewards for lack of productivity. Transformational leaders, on the other hand, are those who stimulate and inspire followers to both achieve extraordinary outcomes and, in the process, develop their own leadership capacity. Transformational leaders help followers grow and develop into leaders by responding to individual followers' needs by empowering them and by aligning the objectives and goals of the individual followers, the leader, the group, and the larger organization. More evidence has accumulated to demonstrate that transformational leadership can move followers to exceed expected performance, as well as lead to high levels of follower satisfaction and commitment to the group and organization (Bass, 1985, 1998a).

Although early research demonstrated that transformational leadership was a particularly powerful source in military settings (e.g., Bass, 1985; Boyd, 1988; Curphy, 1992; Longshore, 1988; O'Keefe, 1989; Yammarino & Bass, 1990), more recent research has accumulated that demonstrates that transformational leadership is important in every sector and in every setting (Avolio & Yammarino, 2002). We soon review the components of transformational leadership, examine transactional leadership, and present the Full

Source: The Transformational Model of Leadership, by Bernard M. Bass and Ronald E. Riggio, pp. 3–16. In Transformational Leadership, 2nd ed. by Bernard M. Bass and Ronald E. Riggio (2006). Copyright © Lawrence Erlbaum Associates, Inc. Reprinted with permission.

Range of Leadership model, which incorporates all of these aspects of leadership. But first, we provide a brief discussion of the roots of transformational leadership.

Historical Background of Transformational Leadership

Historians, political scientists, and sociologists have long recognized leadership that went beyond the notion of a social exchange between leader and followers. Weber's (1924/1947) examination of charisma epitomized such study. However, both psychology and economics supported contingent reinforcement—offering a reward or compensation for a desired behavior—as the underlying concept for the study of leadership. Leadership was seen primarily as an exchange relationship (e.g., Homans, 1950). Research exemplified by Podsakoff and Schriescheim (1985), as well as much of the research with the Full Range of Leadership (FRL) model (Avolio & Bass, 1991) to be described subsequently, indicated that contingent reward is reasonably effective under most circumstances. In addition, active management-by-exception (corrective leadership for failure of a follower to comply) is more varied in effects, and passive management-by-exception ("if it ain't broke, don't fix it") is contraindicated as an effective act of leadership, for, as Levinson (1980) suggested, if you limit leadership of a follower to rewards with carrots for compliance or punishment with a stick for failure to comply with agreed-on work to be done by the follower, the follower will continue to feel like a jackass. Leadership must also address the follower's sense of self-worth to engage the follower in true commitment and involvement in the effort at hand. This is what transformational leadership adds to the transactional exchange.

Transformational leaders motivate others to do more than they originally intended and often even more than they thought possible. They set more challenging expectations and typically achieve higher performances. Transformational leaders also tend to have more committed and satisfied followers. Moreover, transformational leaders empower followers and pay attention to their individual needs and personal development, helping followers to develop their own leadership potential.

Transformational leadership is in some ways an expansion of transactional leadership. Transactional leadership emphasizes the transaction or exchange that takes place among leaders, colleagues, and followers. This exchange is based on the leader discussing with others what is required and specifying the conditions and rewards these others will receive if they fulfill those requirements. Transformational leadership, however, raises leadership to the next level. Transformational leadership involves inspiring followers to commit to a shared vision and goals for an organization or unit, challenging them to be innovative problem solvers, and developing followers' leadership capacity via coaching, mentoring, and provision of both challenge and support.

Early social science perspectives on leadership focused on the dichotomy of directive (task-oriented) versus participative (people-oriented) leadership. As we soon show, transformational leadership can be either directive or participative and is not an either or proposition.

Transformational leadership has much in common with charismatic leadership, but charisma is only part of transformational leadership. The Weberian notion of charismatic leadership was, in fact, fairly limited. More modern conceptions of charismatic leadership take a much broader perspective (e.g., Conger & Kanungo, 1998; House & Shamir, 1993), however, and have much in common with transformational leadership.

A critical concern for theories of both transformational and charismatic leadership involves what many refer to as the dark side of charisma—those charismatic leaders who use their abilities to inspire and lead followers to destructive, selfish, and even evil ends. Most often coming to mind are international leaders who wreaked havoc, death, and destruction on thousands and even millions—Adolf Hitler, Pol Pot, Josef Stalin, Osama Bin Laden. But these leaders are those who can be called pseudo transformational. They exhibit many elements of transformational leadership (the charismatic elements particularly) but have personal, exploitative, and self-aggrandizing motives. Thus, we speak at length near the end of this chapter about the notions of authenticity and authentic transformational leaders.

Components of Transformational Leadership

Transformational leaders do more with colleagues and followers than set up simple exchanges or agreements. They behave in ways to achieve superior results by employing one or more of the four core components of transformational leadership described later.

To some extent, the components of transformational leadership have evolved as refinements have been made in both the conceptualization and measurement of transformational leadership. Conceptually, leadership is charismatic, and followers seek to identify with the leader and emulate him or her. The leadership inspires followers with challenge and persuasion, providing both meaning and understanding. The leadership is intellectually stimulating, expanding the followers' use of their abilities. Finally, the leadership is individually considerate, providing the follower with support, mentoring, and coaching. Each of these components can be measured with the Multifactor Leadership Questionnaire (MLQ). Factor analytic studies from Bass (1985) to Howell and Avolio (1993), and Bycio, Hackett, and Allen (1995) to Avolio, Bass, and Jung (1997) have identified the components of transformational leadership.

Descriptions of the components of transformational leadership are presented in the following sections. *Idealized Influence (II)*. Transformational leaders behave in ways that allow them to serve as role models for their followers. The leaders are admired, respected, and trusted. Followers identify with the leaders and want to emulate them; leaders are endowed by their followers as having extraordinary capabilities, persistence, and determination. Thus, there are two aspects to idealized influence: the leader's behaviors and the elements that are attributed to the leader by followers and other associates. These two aspects, measured by separate subfactors of the MLQ, represent the interactional nature of idealized influence—it is both embodied in the leader's behavior and in attributions that are made concerning the leader by followers. A sample item from the MLQ that represents idealized influence behavior is "The leader emphasizes the importance of having a collective sense of mission." A sample item from the idealized influence attributed factor is "The leader reassures others that obstacles will be overcome."

In addition, leaders who have a great deal of idealized influence are willing to take risks and are consistent rather than arbitrary. They can be counted on to do the right thing, demonstrating high standards of ethical and moral conduct.

Inspirational Motivation (IM). Transformational leaders behave in ways that motivate and inspire those around them by providing meaning and challenge to their followers' work. Team spirit is aroused. Enthusiasm and optimism are displayed. Leaders get followers involved in envisioning attractive future states; they create clearly communicated expectations that followers want to meet and also demonstrate commitment to goals and the shared vision. A sample MLQ item for IM is "The leader articulates a compelling vision of the future."

Idealized influence leadership and inspirational motivation usually form a combined single factor of charismatic-inspirational leadership. The charismatic inspirational factor is similar to the behaviors described in charismatic leadership theory (Bass & Avolio, 1993; House, 1977).

Intellectual Stimulation (IS). Transformational leaders stimulate their followers' efforts to be innovative and creative by questioning assumptions, reframing problems, and approaching old situations in new ways. Creativity is encouraged. There is no public criticism of individual members' mistakes. New ideas and creative problem solutions are solicited from followers, who are included in the process of addressing problems and finding solutions. Followers are encouraged to try new approaches, and their ideas are not criticized because they differ from the leaders' ideas. A sample item from the MLQ that represents intellectual stimulation is "The leader gets others to look at problems from many different angles."

Individualized Consideration (IC). Transformational leaders pay special attention to each individual follower's needs for achievement and growth by acting as a coach or mentor. Followers and colleagues are developed to successively higher levels of potential. Individualized consideration is practiced when new learning opportunities are created along with a supportive climate. Individual differences in terms of needs and desires are recognized. The leader's behavior demonstrates acceptance of individual differences (e.g., some employees receive more encouragement, some more autonomy, others firmer standards, and still others more task structure). A two-way exchange in communication is encouraged, and "management by walking around" workspaces is practiced. Interactions with followers are personalized (e.g., the leader remembers previous conversations, is aware of individual concerns, and sees the individual as a whole person rather than as just an employee). The individually considerate leader listens effectively. The leader delegates tasks as a means of developing followers. Delegated tasks are monitored to see if the followers need additional direction or support and to assess progress; ideally, followers do not feel they are being checked on. A sample MLQ item from the individualized consideration scale is "The leader spends time teaching and coaching."

The Full Range of Leadership Model

In addition to the four components of transformational leadership, the Full Range of Leadership model also includes several components of transactional leadership behavior, along with laissez-faire (or non-leadership) behavior.

Transactional leadership occurs when the leader rewards or disciplines the follower, depending on the adequacy of the follower's performance. Transactional leadership depends on contingent reinforcement, either positive contingent reward (CR) or the more negative active or passive forms of management-by-exception (MBE-A or MBE-P).

Contingent Reward (CR). This constructive transaction has been found to be reasonably effective in motivating others to achieve higher levels of development and performance, although not as much as any of the transformational components. Contingent reward leadership involves the leader assigning or obtaining follower agreement on what needs to be done with promised or actual rewards offered in exchange for satisfactorily carrying out the assignment. A sample contingent reward item is "The leader makes clear what one can expect to receive when performance goals are achieved." Contingent reward is transactional when the reward is a material one, such as a bonus. Contingent reward can be transformational, however, when the reward is psychological, such as praise (Antonakis, Avolio, & Sivasubramaniam, 2003).

Management-by-Exception (MBE). This corrective transaction tends to be more ineffective than contingent reward or the components of transformational leadership. The corrective transaction may be active (MBE-A) or passive (MBE-P). In active MBE, the leader arranges to actively monitor deviances from standards, mistakes, and errors in the follower's assignments and to take corrective action as necessary. MBE-P implies waiting passively for deviances, mistakes, and errors to occur and then taking corrective action. Active MBE may be required and effective in some situations, such as when safety is paramount in importance. Leaders sometimes must practice passive MBE when required to supervise a large number of subordinates who report directly to the leaders. Sample MLQ items for management-by-exception are "The leader directs attention toward failures to meet standards" (active) and "The leader takes no action until complaints are received" (passive).

Laissez-Faire Leadership (LF). As mentioned, laissez-faire leadership is the avoidance or absence of leadership and is, by definition, most inactive, as well as most ineffective according to almost all research on the style. As opposed to transactional leadership, laissez-faire represents a nontransaction. Necessary decisions are not made. Actions are delayed. Responsibilities of leadership are ignored. Authority remains unused. A sample laissez-faire item is "The leader avoids getting involved when important issues arise."

Fundamental to the FRL model is that every leader displays each style to some amount. An optimal profile is shown in Figure 7.1. The third dimension of this model (depth) represents how frequently a leader displays a particular style of leadership. The horizontal active dimension is by self-evident definition; the vertical effectiveness dimension is based on empirical findings.

In Figure 7.1, the person with an optimal profile infrequently displays (LF) leadership. This individual displays successively higher frequencies of the transactional leadership styles of MBE-P, MBE-A, and CR and displays the transformational components most frequently. In contrast, as shown in Figure 7.2, the poorly performing leader tends toward inactivity and ineffectiveness, exhibiting LF most frequently and the transformational components least frequently.

The Effectiveness of Transformational Leadership

There is a large and growing body of evidence that supports the effectiveness of transformational leadership over transactional leadership and the other components in the Full Range of Leadership model.

The research evidence that supports this claim begins with meta-analytic findings. Transformational leadership can lead to more committed, loyal, and satisfied followers; in fact, the results suggest a hierarchy, with the four *Is*—the components of transformational leadership—at the top, followed by contingent reward, then active and passive management-by-exception, respectively, with laissez-faire leadership at the bottom as a style generally proving to be ineffective.

Clearly, there is nothing wrong with transactional leadership. It can, in most instances, be quite effective. Likewise, active, and even passive, management-by-exception can work depending on the circumstances. However, Bass (1985) proposed an augmentation relationship between transformational and transactional leadership. It was suggested that transformational leadership augments transactional in predicting effects on follower satisfaction and performance. Specifically, in statistical terms, transformational leadership should and does account for unique variance in ratings of performance (or other outcomes) over and above that accounted for by active transactional leadership.

Waldman, Bass, and Yammarino (1990) reported evidence for the augmentation effect among various samples of industrial managers and military officers, and Elenkov (2002) found it with Russian managers. The augmentation effect was also obtained by Seltzer and Bass (1990) for a sample of 300 part-time MBA students, each describing their superiors at their full-time working settings. For another sample of 130

Figure 7.1 The Model of the Full Range of Leadership: Suboptimal Profile

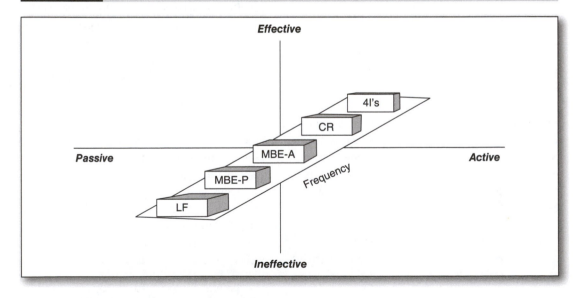

Figure 7.2	The Model of the Full Range of Leadership: Optimal Profile

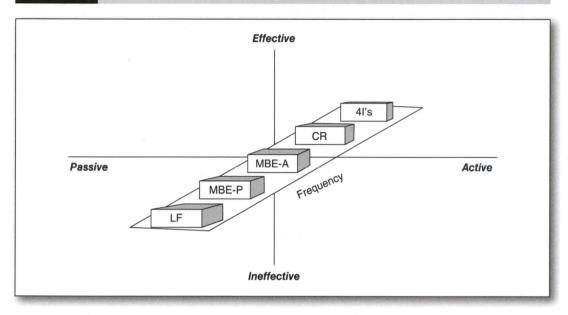

MBAs, who each asked three of their followers to complete MLQs about them, the augmentation effect held when one follower's leadership ratings and a second follower's outcomes were correlated. The same augmentation effect occurred when initiation and consideration, as measured by the Leader Behavior Description Questionnaire (LBDQ), were substituted as the measure of transactional leadership. These results demonstrate a fundamental point emphasized in the Bass (1985) theory of leadership: Transactional leadership, particularly contingent reward, provides a broad basis for effective leadership, but a greater amount of effort, effectiveness, and satisfaction is possible from transactional leadership if augmented by transformational leadership. Finally, as reported earlier by Avolio and Howell (1992), transformational leadership also augments transactional in predicting levels of innovation, risk taking, and creativity.

Transformational Leadership: Directive or Participative?

Critics perceive transformational leadership as elitist and antidemocratic. Indeed, particularly when dealing with charisma, Weber (1947) and his successors emphasized the extent that the charismatic leader directed dependent followers out of crises with radical solutions to deal with their problems; inspirational leaders were seen to be highly directive in their means and methods. The intellectually stimulating leader challenged his followers, and the individually considerate leader could rise above the demands for equality from his followers to treat them differently according to their different needs for growth. At the same time, however, such transformational leaders could share the building of visions and ideas that could be a democratic and collective enterprise. They could encourage follower participation in the change processes involved. In the same way, transactional leadership can be either directive or participative.

Table 7.1 illustrates formulaic statements illustrating that transformational and transactional leadership can be either directive or participative, authoritarian or democratic. This theory has been found useful and essential in convincing trainees that transformational leadership is not a veiled attempt at resurrecting participative leadership. It can be participative as well as more directive in orientation (Avolio & Bass, 1991).

Table 7.1	Descriptions of Participative Versus Directive Leadership and the Components of the Full Range of Leadership Model

	Participative	*Directive*
Laissez-faire	"Whatever you think is the correct choice is okay with me."	"If my followers need answers to questions, let them find the answers themselves."
Management-by-exception	"Let's develop the rules together that we will use to identify mistakes."	"These are the rules, and this is how you have violated them."
Contingent reward	"Let's agree on what has to be done and how you will be rewarded if you achieve the objectives."	"If you achieve the objectives I've set, I will recognize your accomplishment with the following reward. . . ."
Individualized consideration	"What can we do as a group to give each other the necessary support to develop our capabilities?"	"I will provide the support you need in your efforts to develop yourself in the job."
Intellectual stimulation	"Can we try to look at our assumptions as a ground without being critical of each other's ideas until all assumptions have been listed?"	"You must reexamine the assumption that a cold fusion engine is a physical impossibility. Revisit this problem and question your assumption."
Inspirational motivation	"Let's work together to merge our aspirations and goals for the good of our group."	"You need to say to yourself that every day you are getting better. You must look at your progression and continue to build upon it over time."
Idealized influence	"We can be a winning team because of our faith in each other. I need your support to achieve our mission."	*"Alea icta list* (i.e., "I've made the decision to cross the Rubicon, so there's no going back"). You must trust me and my direction to achieve what we have set out to do."

Note: From *The Full Range of Leadership Development: Basic and Advance Manuals* (pp. 5.5-5.6), by B. J. Avolio and B. M. Bass, 1991, Binghamton, NY: Bass, Avolio, and Associates. Copyright 1991 by Bass, Avolio, and Associates. Reprinted with permission.

Authentic Versus Inauthentic (Pseudotransformational) Transformational Leadership

A crucial element for James MacGregor Burns's conception of transformational leadership was his firm belief that to be transforming leaders had to be morally uplifting. Bass (1985) originally expected the dynamics of transformational leadership to be the same whether beneficial or harmful to others. As noted earlier, this notion of morally "good" and "evil"

leaders has also been a dilemma for charismatic leadership theories.

Charismatic leadership has been differentiated as socialized or personalized. Socialized charismatic leadership is based on egalitarian behavior, serves collective interests, and develops and empowers others. Socialized leaders tend to be altruistic and to use legitimate established channels of authority (House & Howell, 1992; McClelland, 1975). Personalized charismatic leadership is based on personal dominance and authoritarian behavior, is self-aggrandizing, serves the self-interest, and is exploitative of others (McClelland, 1975). Personalized leaders rely heavily on manipulation, threat, and punishment and show disregard for the established institutional procedures and for the rights and feelings of others. They are impulsively aggressive, narcissistic, and impetuous (House & Howell, 1992; Popper, 2002). For Howell and Avolio (1993) authentic charismatic/transformational leaders must be socialized leaders

This notion of personalized versus socialized leaders can apply to both charismatic and noncharismatic leaders. The defining issue is whether the leader works primarily toward personal gains as opposed to focusing also on the outcomes for followers (i.e., costs and benefits for self vs. costs and benefits for others; Bass & Steidlmeier, 1999). For example, Tyco's CEO, Dennis Kozlowski, who was prosecuted for raiding his company of $600 million to support his lavish lifestyle, represents the extreme of a personalized leader. However, a socialized leader can both achieve personal gains as well as enrich followers. An example is Bill Gates, whose Microsoft Corporation is regularly considered one of the best companies to work for and a company that made many of its employees into millionaires via generous stock options. It is important to note that for most leaders it is not clearcut. Being personalized or socialized is usually a matter of degree, being more or less selfish or selfless in one's actions (Bass, 1998b).

Originally, the dynamics of transformational leadership were expected to be the same, whether beneficial or harmful to followers (Bass, 1985), although Burns (1978) believed that to be transforming, leaders had to be morally uplifting. Since those early writings, Bass (1998b) has come to agree with Burns. Personalized transformational leaders are pseudotransformational, or inauthentic transformational leaders. They may exhibit many transforming displays but cater, in the long run, to their own self-interests. Self-concerned, self-aggrandizing, exploitative, and power oriented, pseudotransformational leaders believe in distorted utilitarian and warped moral principles. This is in contrast to the authentic transformational leaders, who transcend their own self-interests for one of two reasons: utilitarian or moral. If utilitarian, their objective is to benefit their group or its individual members, their organization, or society, as well as themselves, and to meet the challenges of the task or mission. If a matter of moral principles, the objective is to do the right thing, to do what fits principles of morality, responsibility, sense of discipline, and respect for authority, customs, rules, and traditions of a society. There is belief in the social responsibility of the leader and the organization. Thomas Paine's writings illustrated the authentic transforming leader in his appeals to reason in "Common Sense" and "Age of Reason," his appeals to principle in "Rights of Man," and his often quoted need for transcendence: "These are the times that try men's souls."

Each of the components of transformational leadership (as well as the elements of transactional leadership) can be scrutinized to determine whether they indicate authentic or inauthentic leadership. For example, the transformational components of idealized influence and inspirational motivation can be used authentically to create follower commitment and motivation to a noble cause that benefits all, or they can be used to manipulate followers and produce an unhealthy dependence on the leader. Table 7.2 displays some of the moral elements associated with components of transformational and transactional leadership to demonstrate how these can lead to authentic or inauthentic transformational leadership.

The element of transformational leadership that usually best distinguishes authentic from inauthentic leaders is individualized consideration. The authentic transformational leader is truly concerned with the desires and needs of followers and cares about their individual development. Followers are treated as ends not just means (Bass & Steidlmeier, 1999).

In recent years, scholars have begun to examine the relationship between transformational leadership and ethical leadership behavior or perceptions of leader authenticity. For example, one study examined the relationship between transformational leadership and the perceived integrity of New Zealand managers, as rated by subordinates, peers, and superiors (Parry & Proctor-Thompson, 2002). The results showed that transformational leaders were rated as having more integrity and being more effective than were nontransformational leaders. An

Table 7.2	Moral Elements of Transformational and Transactional Leadership

Leadership Dynamic	Transactional Leadership Ethical Concern
Task	Whether what is being done (the end) and the means employed to do it are morally legitimate
Reward system	Whether sanctions or incentives impair effective freedom and respect conscience
Intentions	Truth telling
Trust	Promise keeping
Consequences	Egoism versus altruism—whether the legitimate moral standing and interests of all those affected are respected
Due process	Impartial process of settling conflicts and claims
	Transformational Leadership
Idealized influence	Whether "puffery" and egoism on part of the leader predominate and whether the leader is manipulative or not
Inspirational motivation	Whether providing for true empowerment and self-actualization of followers or not
Intellectual stimulation	Whether the leader's program is open to dynamic transcendence and spirituality or is closed propaganda and a "line" to follow
Individualized consideration	Whether followers are treated as ends or means, whether their unique dignity and interests are respected or not

Note: From "Ethics, Character, and Authentic Transformational Leadership Behavior," by B.M. Bass and P. Steidlmeier, 1999, *Leadership Quarterly*, 10(2), p. 185. Copyright by Elsevier. Reprinted with permission.

interesting study of marketing managers from multinational companies in India presented these leaders with vignettes depicting certain unethical business situations (e.g., bribery, endangerment of the physical environment, personal gain, displays of favoritism) and asked the leaders how they might act in these situations. Transformational leaders, particularly those high on inspirational motivation and intellectual stimulation, were more likely to behave ethically in the tempting scenarios (Banerji & Krishnan, 2000).

In an important study, Turner, Barling, Epitropaki, Butcher, and Milner (2002) found that managers/leaders from a Canadian university and a British telecommunications company who had higher levels of moral reasoning, as assessed by a self-report, pencil-and-paper measure, were rated by their subordinates as being more transformational. Finally, Brown and Trevino (2003) found that employees of transformational leaders engaged in less employee deviant behavior than followers of leaders who were well liked but not transformational.

Clearly, and as Burns (1978) emphasized, the morality of transformational leadership is critical. Throughout our discussion of transformational leadership, we assume for the most part that we are speaking of authentic transformational leadership. Yet it is clear that much work needs to be done to better understand the dynamics of authentic leadership, in general, and authentic transformational leadership in particular.

The Universality of Transformational Leadership

Bass (1997) argued that transactional and transformational leadership can be found in all parts of the globe and in all forms of organizations. Indeed, research on transformational leadership, including the use of the MLQ has taken place in every continent and in nearly every industrialized nation. Research from the Global Leadership and Organizational Behavior Effectiveness (GLOBE) research program supports earlier notions that elements of charismatic-transformational leadership are valued leader qualities in all countries and cultures (Den Hartog, House, Hanges, Ruiz-Quintanilla, & Dorfman, 1999; Dorfman, Hanges, & Brodbeck, 2004).

Research evidence from around the world suggests that transformational leadership typically provides a positive augmentation in leader performance beyond the effects of transactional leadership. Furthermore, transformational leadership should be a more effective form of leadership globally because the transformational leader is consistent with people's prototypes of an ideal leader (Bass, 1997). Of course, there are cultural contingencies, as well as organizational factors, that can affect the impact of transformational leadership in particular instances. However, authentic transformational leadership has an impact in all cultures and organizations because transformational leaders have goals that transcend their own self-interests and work toward the common good of the followers (Burns, 1978).

References

Antonakis, J., Avolio, B. J., & Sivasubramaniam, N. (2003). Context and leadership: An examination of the nine factor full-range leadership theory using the Multifactor Leadership Questionnaire. *The Leadership Quarterly,* 14(3), 261–295.

Avolio, B. J., & Bass, B.M. (1991). *The full range of leadership development: Basic and advanced manuals.* Binghamton, NY: Bass, Avolio, & Associates

Avolio, B. J., Bass, B. M., & Jung, D. I. (1997). *Replicated confirmatory factor analyses of the Multifactor Leadership Questionnaire.* Binghamton, NY: Center for Leadership Studies, Binghamton University.

Avolio, B. J., & Howell, J. M. (1992). The impact of leader behavior and leader-follower personality match on satisfaction and unit performance. In K. E. Clark, M. B. Clark, & D.R. Campbell (Eds.), *Impact of leadership* (pp. 225–247). Greensboro, NC: The Center for Creative Leadership.

Avolio, B. J., & Yammarino, F. J. (Eds.). (2002). *Transformational and charismatic leadership: The road ahead.* Boston: JAI.

Banerji, P., & Krishnan, V. R. (2000). Ethical preferences for transformational leaders: An empirical investigation. *Leadership and Organization Development Journal,* 21, 405–413.

Bass, B. M. (1985). *Leadership and performance beyond expectations.* New York: Free Press.

Bass, B. M. (1997). Does the transactional/transformational leadership paradigm transcend organizational and national boundaries? *American Psychologist,* 52, 130–139.

Bass, B. M. (1998a). *Transformational leadership: Industrial, military, and educational impact.* Mahwah, NJ: Lawrence Erlbaum Associates.

Bass, B. M. (1998b). The ethics of transformational leadership. In J. Ciulla (Ed.), *Ethics: The heart of leadership* (pp. 169–192).Westport, CT: Praeger

Bass, B. M., & Avolio, B. J. (1993).Transformational leadership: A response to critiques. In M. M. Chemers & R. Ayman (Eds.), *Leadership theory and research: Perspectives and directions* (pp. 49–80). New York: Academic Press.

Bass, B. M., & Steidlmeier, P. (1999). Ethics, character, and authentic transformational leadership. *The Leadership Quarterly,* 10, 181–217.

Boyd, J. T., Jr. (1988). *Leadership extraordinary: A crossnational military perspective on transactional versus transformational leadership.* Unpublished doctoral dissertation. Nova University, Boca Raton, FL.

Brown, M. E., & Trevino, L. K. (2003,August). *The influence of leadership styles on unethical conduct in work groups: An empirical test.* Paper presented at the meeting of the Academy of Management, Seattle, WA.

Burns, J. M. (1978). *Leadership.* New York: Harper & Row.

Bycio, P., Hackett, R. D., & Allen, J. S. (1995). Further assessments of Bass's (1985) conceptualization of transactional and transformational leadership. *Journal of Applied Psychology,* 80, 468–478.

Conger, J. A., & Kanungo, R. N. (1988). *Charismatic leadership: The elusive factor in organization effectiveness.* San Francisco: Jossey-Bass.

Curphy, G. J. (1992). An empirical investigation of the effects of transformational and transactional leadership on organizational climate, attrition and performance. In K. E. Clark, M. B. Clark, & D. R. Campbell (Eds.), *Impact of leadership* (pp. 177–187). Greensboro, NC: The Center for Creative Leadership.

Den Hartog, D. N., House, R. J., Hanges, P. J., Ruiz-Quintanilla, S. A., & Dorfman, P. W. (1999). Culture specific and cross-cultural generalizable implicit leadership theories: Are attributes of charismatic/transformational leadership universally endorsed? *The Leadership Quarterly*, 10, 219–256.

Dorfman, P. W., Hanges, P. J., & Brodbeck, F. C. (2004). Leadership and cultural variation: The identification of culturally endorsed leadership profiles. In R. J. House, P. J. Hanges, M. Javidan, P. W. Dorfman, & V. Gupta (Eds.), *Culture, leadership, and organizations: The GLOBE study of 62 societies* (pp. 669–719). Thousand Oaks, CA: Sage.

Elenkov, D. S. (2002). Effects of leadership on organizational performance in Russian companies. *Journal of Business Research*, 55, 467–480.

Homans, G. C. (1950). *The human group*. New York: Harcourt, Brace.

House, R. J. (1977). A 1976 theory of charismatic leadership. In J. G. Hunt & L. L. Larson (Eds.), *Leadership: The cutting edge* (pp. 189–207). Carbondale: Southern Illinois University Press.

House, R. J., & Howell, J. M. (1992). Personality and charismatic leadership. *The Leadership Quarterly*, 3, 81–108.

House, R. J., & Shamir, B. (1993). Toward the integration of transformational, charismatic and visionary theories. In M. M. Chemers & R. Ayman (Eds.), *Leadership theory and research: Perspective and directions* (pp. 81–107). New York: Academic Press.

Howell, J. M., & Avolio, B. J. (1993).Transformational leadership, transactional leadership, locus of control, and support for innovation: Key predictors of consolidated business-unit performance. *Journal of Applied Psychology*, 78, 891–902.

Levinson, H. (1980). Power, leadership, and the management of stress. *Professional Psychology*, 11, 497–508.

Longshore, J. M. (1988). *The associative relationship between transformational and transactional leadership styles and group productivity*. Unpublished doctoral dissertation, Nova University, Boca Raton, FL.

McClelland, D. C. (1975). *Power: The inner experience*. New York: Irvington.

O'Keeffe, M. J. (1989). *The effects of leadership style on the perceived effectiveness and satisfaction of selected Army officers*. Unpublished doctoral dissertation, Temple University, Philadelphia.

Parry, K. W., & Proctor-Thomson, S. B. (2002). Perceived integrity of transformational leaders in organizational settings. *Journal of Business Ethics*, 35, 75–96.

Podsakoff, P. M., & Schriescheim, C. A. (1985). Leader reward and punishment behavior: A methodological and substantive review. In B. Staw & L. L. Cummings (Eds.), *Research in organizational behavior*. San Francisco: Jossey-Bass.

Popper, M. (2002). Narcissism and attachment patterns of personalized and socialized charismatic leaders. *Journal of Social and Personal Relationships*, 19, 797–809.

Seltzer, J., & Bass, B. M. (1990). Transformational leadership: Beyond initiation and consideration. *Journal of Management*, 16, 693–703.

Turner, N. Barling, J., Epitropaki, O., Butcher, V., & Milner, C. (2002). Transformational leadership and moral reasoning. *Journal of Applied Psychology*, 87, 304–311.

Waldman, D. A., Bass, B. M., & Yammarino, F. J. (1990). Adding to contingent-reward behavior: The augmenting effect of charismatic leadership. *Group and Organizational Studies*, 15, 381–394.

Weber, M. (1947). *The theory of social and economic organizations* (T. Parsons, Trans.). New York: Free Press. (Original work published in 1924)

Yammarino, F. J., & Bass, B. M. (1990). Long-term forecasting of transformational leadership and its effects among naval officers: Some preliminary findings. In K. E. Clark & M. R. Clark (Eds.), *Measures of leadership* (pp.151–169). Greensboro, NC: Center for Creative Leadership.

CHAPTER 8

Charismatic Leadership

Jay A. Conger

Claremont McKenna College

The term *charismatic leadership* has long been associated with forms of leadership based on follower perceptions of an extraordinary individual. As a leadership construct, it is far more complex than simple notions of personal charisma or charm. "Charismatic leadership" as a term appears to have been first coined by the German sociologist, Max Weber (1864–1920). In his writings on authority in society, he formulated a typology of three types—the traditional, the rational-legal, and the charismatic forms of authority. For Weber, charismatic described the forms of authority based on perceptions of a uniquely gifted individual. In contrast, the traditional and rational-legal forms of authority relied on traditions such as a lineage of kingship or else upon rules set out in constitutions and judicial systems. Charismatic authority was unique in its emphasis on an individual leader and the followers' relationship with this individual. No ordinary individual, Weber s charismatic leader was "set apart from ordinary men and is treated as endowed with . . . exceptional powers and qualities . . . [which] are not accessible to the ordinary person but are regarded as of divine origin or as exemplary, and on the basis of them the individual concerned is treated as a leader" (1947,

pp. 358–359). His construct was popularized over the twentieth century as the media and lay people used the term to describe a wide variety of leaders. At the same time, his work inspired several generations of researchers to explore in greater depth this form of leadership. In this chapter, we will explore what we have learned horn this body of research over the past 50 years, but first, we will take a deeper look at Weber's contribution.

Max Weber's Insights Into Charismatic Leadership

The word *charisma* itself comes from a Hellenistic word *kharisma*, meaning a "gift" or "divine favor or "supernatural power." In ancient times, it was believed that certain individuals such as prophets or religious leaders or healers were given gifts from the gods to help them in their earthly tasks. These were called charismata. For example, the Christians of the New Testament period used the term to describe Godly gifts given to the faithful. Borrowing from Christian texts, Max Weber applied the term more broadly to leaders in secular contexts such as government and business.

Although he pioneered the secular use of the term, Weber provided only rudimentary insights into the phenomenon. For instance, he observed that charismatic leaders often appeared in situations of distress. He theorized that the allure of these leaders came from their acts of heroism or magical abilities or mental prowess or remarkable capabilities at communicating. Successes, he felt, were critical to sustaining a leaders aura of charisma. Without success, the charismatic leader would appear to lack genuine capability or, worse be seen as a charlatan. Weber believed that the leader's charisma would eventually fade into institutional routines. Perhaps because of his sociological perspective, he offered little in the way of explaining the relational dynamics between the leader and their followers and only sketches of the leader s distinguishing personal attributes. Later generations of scholars would identify these critical dimensions.

Explorations in the Twentieth Century

In the mid-twentieth century, two critical global events unfolded that would spur scholars' interest in Weber's construct of charismatic leadership. The first was World War II and the "charismatic leaders" associated with this war. The second was the decolonization of India and African nations and the establishment of democracies. Many of the newly elected leaders of these nations were perceived as charismatic which, in turn, contributed to their appeal as elected officials.

These two events sparked the interests of political scientists and sociologists in exploring Weber's ideas in order to understand the profound influence of historical figures such as Churchill, Hitler, Roosevelt, Gandhi, Kenyatta and numerous others. Research centered on answering three central questions: Is there a universal "charismatic personality" or are there significant differences among the personalities of charismatic leaders? Where is the influence locus of "charisma"—is it to be found in the leaders extraordinary qualities, in the larger social context, or in the relationship dynamics with followers? Finally, why are charismatic leaders so attractive to their followers?

It was concluded that the search for a universal set of qualities common to all charismatic political and religious leaders would not yield decisive results (Dow, 1969; Willner, 1984). In-depth examinations led to the conclusion that the variations in individual personalities were too significant (for example, Gandhi versus Hitler versus Churchill). A universal charismatic personality type did not exist. Willner (1984), one of the more prominent researchers, argued that charismatic leadership could be more satisfactorily understood as a relational and perceptual phenomenon: "It is not what the leader is but what people see the leader as that counts in generating the charismatic relationship" (pp. 14–15). Because societies and groups differ in their definitions of what constitute "extraordinary" qualities in a leader, the content of leadership images, projected and perceived, would necessarily have to differ from group to group. It was therefore, impossible to construct a universal "charismatic personality." This line of thinking is the dominant point of view in the field to this day.

Regarding the question of where the locus of charisma resided, some (Blau, 1963; Chinoy, 1961; Friedland, 1964) argued that the social and historical context was the critical determinant in the emergence of charismatic leadership. They shared Weber's belief that times of turmoil and revolution were catalysts for charismatic leadership. In difficult rimes, people became "hungry" for charismatic leaders offering resolution to the turmoil. Others (Dow, 1969; Marcus, 1961) argued that charisma resided within the behaviors and other attributes of the charismatic leader—for example, with their communications and influence skills or their visions or ideologies. They believed that a context of distress was neither a necessary requirement nor the primary catalyst. Using case-based research on twentieth-century charismatic leaders, Willner (1984) showed that few of the situations involving charismatic leadership were associated with a turbulent environment. She identified four factors that, aided by the leaders personality, appeared to be catalytic in the attribution of charisma to a leader: (a) the invocation of important cultural myths by the leader, (b) performance of what are perceived as heroic or extraordinary fears, (c) projection of attributes "with an uncanny or a powerful aura," and (d) outstanding theoretical skills (1984, p. 61). Her work would later influence scholars in the field of organizational behavior, who similarly focused on the distinguishing attributes and behaviors of charismatic leaders rather than contextual or personality variables. The debate about the locus of charisma was not fully resolved. Rather, research simply moved in the direction of leader attributes and relationship dynamics with followers. That said, it became widely accepted that charismatic leadership was the product of the interplay between leader at tributes and context. It was concluded that a variety of contexts might be suitable for charismatic leadership and that the leader could be in a position to actually shape the context. In other words, context came to be seen as a potentially malleable dimension in the hands of a skillful charismatic leader.

The third research question of this era centered on the actual process of influence deployed by charismatic leaders, as researchers sought to answer why these leaders were so influential with followers. Political scientist James McGregor Burns proposed the most compelling theory. He formulated a simple typology of leaders: the "transformational" and the "transactional." In this case, the transformational leaders were essentially the same leaders described as charismatic by his academic colleagues. For Burns, leadership at its essence—no matter what forms it took—could be boiled down to the notion of an exchange. Both the leader and the follower had something to offer one another. It was in the nature of what was exchanged, however, that his typology came into play. For Burns, transformational or charismatic leaders offered a transcendent purpose as their mission—one that addressed the higher-order needs of their followers. This is what made them so appealing and influential. In the process of achieving an emotionally appealing and lofty mission, both the leaders and the led were literally transformed or actualized as individuals—hence the term *transforming*. Burns explained: "The result of transforming leadership is a relationship of mutual stimulation and elevation that converts followers into leaders and may convert leaders into moral agents" (1978, p. 4). This central notion would persist into the next generation of research on charismatic leadership.

At the other end of Burns's spectrum was transactional leadership. The far more common of the two forms, transactional leadership was based on a relationship with followers that consisted of more instrumental exchanges: "The relations of most leaders and followers are transactional—leaders approach followers with an eye to exchanging one thing for another: jobs for votes, or subsidies for campaign contributions. Such [instrumental] transactions comprise the bulk of the relationships. . . " (1978, p. 4). Although the central idea of leadership as an exchange was already present in the organizational and psychology literature (e.g. Graen & Scandura, 1987; Podsakoff, Todor, & Skov, 1982; House & Mitchell, 1974), earlier notions were missing the elements of higher-order needs being met and the elevation of both the leader and followers to a more evolved state of being. This was the critical contribution of Burns. Up to that moment in time, the notion of leaders who managed meaning, advocated ideological values, constructed lofty goals and visions, and inspired was missing from this literature of leadership exchange.

Contributions From Organizational Behaviorists

Interest in research on charismatic leadership among political scientists and sociologists waned by the 1980s. At the same time, interest was growing from another group of scholars. They were social psychologists and organizational behaviorists who resided primarily in business schools. They would undertake extensive attempts at investigating charismatic leadership. Several major theories were proposed along with dozens and dozens of empirical investigations of charismatic leadership in organizational settings. These studies involved a wide range of samples, such as middle and lower-level managers (Bass & Yammarino, 1988; Conger & Kanungo, 1994; Hater & Bass, 1988; Koene, Pennings, & Sehrender, 1991), senior executives (Agle Sonnenfeld, 1994; Conger, 1989), U.S. Presidents (House, Spangler, & Woycke, 1991), educational administrators (Koh, Terborg, & Sreers, 1991; Roberts & Bradley, 1988; Sashkin, 1988), military leaders (Curphy, 1990; Koene et al., 1991), and students who were laboratory subjects (Howell & Frost, 1989; Kirkparrick, 1992; Puffer, 1990; and Shamir, 1992). In addition, the subject was explored using a wide variety of research methods from field surveys (Conger & Kanungo, 1992, 1994; Hater & Bass, 1988; Podsakoff, MacKenzie, Moorman, & Fetter, 1990), to laboratory experiments (Howell & Frost, 1989; Kirkpatrick, 1992), to content analyses of interviews and observation (Conger, 1989; Howell & Higgins, 1990), to analyses of historical archival information (House, Spangler, & Woycke, 1991).

What is remarkable about this flowering of research is the relative uniformity of findings despite some differences in theoretical approaches. As Shamir, House, and Arthur (1993) noted, findings across the board demonstrate that leaders who engage in the behaviors that are theorized to be charismatic actually produce the charismatic effects that the theory predicts. In addition, many of these studies have shown repeatedly that leaders who are perceived as charismatic receive higher performance ratings, are seen as more effective leaders than others holding leadership positions, and have more highly motivated and more satisfied followers than others in similar positions.

The research of this era can be organized into distinct topic areas of charismatic leadership: (a) the leader's behavior, (b) the follower's behavior and motives, (c) the leaders' and followers' psychological profiles, (d) contextual influences, (e) forces that institutionalize the outcomes of the leader–follower relationship, and (f) liabilities of charismatic leaders. We will take a look at each topic.

The Distinguishing Behaviors of Charismatic Leadership

Both the greatest amount of theoretical development as well as empirical research to date has been in the area of leader behaviors. This is due in large part to the backgrounds of the researchers. Most have a strong behavioral orientation. Essentially, there are three groups of researchers who have carved out their own models—though each has a measure of overlap with the others in the attributes they identify. They are also the ones who have built the most comprehensive theories as well as conducted the greatest amount of empirical research in the field. They are (a) Bernard Bass, Bruce Avolio, and their colleagues, (b) Jay Conger and Rabindra Kanungo, and (c) Robert House, Boas Shamir, and their colleagues.

Bass and his colleague Avolio would borrow from Burns the notion of "transformational leadership" and develop a similar model for organizational settings. Their model goes further conceptually than Burns' original model. Bass conceptualized the transactional and transformational dimensions as separate, whereas Burns defined them as two ends of a spectrum. For Bass, therefore, a leader could be both transformational and transactional. In addition, Bass was determined to more precisely identify the actual behaviors that these leaders demonstrated, whereas Burns was content with more of a "big picture" overview.

Bass and Avolio (Bass, 1985; Bass & Avolio, 1993) built their model of transformational leadership around four behavioral components of the leader: (a) charisma or idealized influence, (b) inspiration, (c) intellectual stimulation, and (d) individualized consideration. Charisma is seen as a separate component and is defined in terms of both leader's behavior (such as articulating a mission) and followers' reactions (such as trust in the leader's ability). The model focuses on charismas role in enabling the leader to influence followers by arousing strong emotions and identification with the leader. Identifying with the leader reduces follower resistance to change, whereas emotional arousal creates a sense of excitement about the mission. Bass (1985) argued, however, that charisma alone is insufficient for transformational leadership: "Charisma is a necessary ingredient of transformational leadership, bur by itself it is not sufficient to account for the Transformational process" (p. 31). At the same time, in empirical studies, charisma generally has the strongest correlation of any of the models dimensions with subordinates' ratings of leadership effectiveness and their own satisfaction. It *is* clearly the most influential.

Although Bass and Avolio originally treated inspiration as a subfactor of charisma, later writings described it as a separate component designed to motivate. Much of this dimension centers on communication, in that the transformational leader: "Communicates high expectations, uses symbols to focus efforts, and expresses important purposes in simple ways" (1990, p. 22).

The component of individualized consideration is similar to the early Ohio State notions of consideration. As a behavioral construct, it includes providing encouragement and support to followers, assisting their development by promoting growth opportunities, and showing trust and respect for them as individuals. Its role is to bond the leader and the led and to build follower self-confidence and heighten personal development.

Intellectual stimulation, the final dimension, increases follower awareness of problems by challenging them with new ideas and perspectives and by influencing followers to creatively rethink their traditional ways of approaching organizational tasks.

Conger and Kanungo's model builds on the idea that charismatic leadership is an attribution based on followers' perceptions of their leader's behavior. For example, most social psychological theories consider leadership to be a by-product of the interaction between members of a group. The leadership-role behaviors displayed by a person make that individual (in the eyes of followers) not only a task leader or a social leader and a participative or directive leader but also a charismatic or noncharismatic leader.

The Conger and Kanungo (1999) framework is built around a three stage model of leadership that involves moving organizational members from an existing present stare toward some future state. This dynamic is also described as a movement away from the status quo toward the achievement of desired longer-term goals. In the initial stage, the leader must critically evaluate the existing situation or status quo. Deficiencies in the status quo or poorly exploited opportunities in the environment lead to formulations of future goals. However, before devising appropriate organizational goals, the leader must assess what resources are available and what constraints stand in the way of realizing future goals. In addition, the leader must assess the inclinations, the abilities, the needs and level of satisfaction experienced by followers. This evaluation leads to a second stage: the

actual formulation and conveyance of goals. Finally, in stage three, the leader demonstrates how these goals can be achieved by the organization. It is along these three stages that behavioral components unique to charismatic leaders can be identified. Conger and Kanungo do note that in reality the stages rarely follow such a simple linear flow. Instead, most organizations face ever changing environments, and their leadership must constantly be revising existing goals and tactics in response to unexpected opportunities or other environmental changes.

In terms of actual behaviors, Conger and Kanungo distinguish charismatic leaders from noncharismatic leaders in stage one by their sensitivity to environmental constraints and by their ability to identify deficiencies and poorly exploited opportunities in the status quo. In addition, they are sensitive to follower abilities and needs. In stage two, it is their formulation of an idealized future vision and their extensive use of articulation and impression management skills that sets them apart from other leaders. Finally, in stage three, it is their deployment of innovative and unconventional means to achieve their vision and their use of personal power to influence followers that are distinguishing characteristics. A more detailed explanation of each stage follows.

Charismatic leaders are very critical of the status quo. They tend to be highly sensitive to both the social and physical environments in which they operate. When leaders fail to *assess* properly constraints in the environment or the availability of resources, their strategies and actions may not achieve organizational objectives. They, in turn, will be labeled ineffective. For this reason, it is important that leaders be able to make realistic assessments of the environmental constraints and resources needed to bring about change within their organizations.

In the assessment stage, what distinguishes charismatic from noncharismatic leaders is the charismatic leaders' ability to recognize deficiencies in the present context. In other words, they actively, search out existing or potential shortcomings in the status quo. For example, the failure of firms to exploit new technologies or new markets might be highlighted as a strategic or tactical opportunity by a charismatic. Likewise, a charismatic entrepreneur might more readily perceive marketplace needs and transform them into opportunities for new products or services. In addition, internal organizational deficiencies may be perceived by the charismatic leader as platforms for advocating radical change.

Because of their emphasis on shortcomings in the system and their high levels of intolerance for them, charismatic leaders are always seen as organizational reformers or entrepreneurs. In other words, they act as agents of innovative and radical change. However, the attribution of charisma is dependent not on the outcome of change but simply on the actions taken to bring about change or reform.

After assessing the environment, charismatic leaders can be distinguished from others by the nature of their goals and by the manner in which they articulate them. They are characterized by a sense of strategic vision. Here the word *vision* refers to an idealized goal that the leader wants the organization to achieve in the future. In order to be perceived as charismatic, leaders not only need to have visions and plans for achieving them, but they must also be able to articulate their visions and strategies for action in ways so as to influence their followers. Here, articulation involves two separate processes: articulation of the context and articulation of the leaders motivation to lead. First, charismatic leaders must effectively articulate for followers the following scenarios representing the context: (a) the nature of the status quo and its shortcomings, (b) a future vision, (c) how the future vision, when realized, will remove existing deficiencies and fulfill the hopes of followers, and (d) the leaders' plans of action for realizing the vision.

In articulating the context, the charismatic's verbal messages construct reality such that only the positive features of the future vision and only the negative features of the status quo are emphasized. The status quo is usually presented as intolerable and the vision is presented in clear specific terms as the most attractive and attainable alternative. In articulating these elements for subordinates, the leader often constructs several scenarios representing the status quo, goals for the future, needed changes and the ease or difficulty of achieving goals, depending on available resources and constraints. In his or her scenarios, the charismatic leader attempts to create among followers a sense of disenchantment or discontentment with the status quo, a strong identification with future goals, and a compelling desire to be led in the direction of the goal, in spite of environmental hurdles.

Besides verbally describing the status quo, future goals, and the means to achieve them, charismatic leaders must also articulate their own motivation for leading their followers. Using expressive modes of action, both verbal and nonverbal, they manifest their convictions, self-confidence, and dedication to materialize what they advocate. Charismatic leaders' use of rhetoric, high energy, persistence, unconventional and risky behavior, heroic deeds, and personal sacrifices all serve to articulate their high motivation and enthusiasm, which then become contagions among their followers. These behaviors form part of a charismatic leader's impression management.

In the final stage leadership process, effective leaders build in followers a sense of trust in their abilities and expertise. The charismatic leader does this by building trust through personal example and risk taking and through unconventional expertise. Generally, leaders are perceived as trustworthy when they advocate their position in a disinterested manner and demonstrate a concern for followers' needs rather than their own self-interest. However, in order to be charismatic, leaders must make these qualities appear extraordinary. They must transform their concern for followers' needs into a total dedication and commitment to a common cause they share and express in a disinterested and selfless manner. They must engage in exemplary acts that are perceived by followers as involving great personal risk, cost, and energy (Friedland, 1964). In this case, personal risk might include the possible loss of personal finances, the possibility of being fired of demoted, and the potential loss of formal or informal status, power, authority, and credibility. The higher the manifest personal cost or sacrifice for the common goal, the greater is the trustworthiness of a leader. The more leaders are able to demonstrate that they are indefatigable workers prepared to take on high personal risks or incur high personal costs in order to achieve their shared vision, the more they reflect charisma in the sense of being worthy of complete trust.

Finally, charismatic leaders must appear to be knowledgeable and experts in their areas of influence. Some degree of demonstrated expertise, such as that reflected in successes in the past, may be a necessary condition for the attribution of charisma (Weber, [1924] 1947). These leaders demonstrate an expertise in devising effective but unconventional strategies and plans of action (Conger, 1985).

In one of the field's earliest writings on charismatic leadership in organizations, Robert House (1977) published a book chapter entitled "A 1976 Theory of Charismatic Leadership." It outlined not only the leader behaviors that were possibly associated with charismatic leadership but also certain personal traits and situational variables. In it, House argued that these leaders could be distinguished from others by their tendency to dominate, a strong conviction in their own beliefs and ideals, a need to influence others, and high self-confidence. Through emotionally appealing goals and the demonstration of behaviors that aroused followers' own needs for achievement, affiliation, and power, the charismatic leader was able to motivate high levels of task accomplishment.

Since that time, House, along with a series of colleagues (House & Shamir, 1993; House, Spangler, & Woycke, 1991; Shamir, House, & Arthur, 1993) made important revisions to his earlier theory. The most significant revision was by Shamir, House, and Arthur (1993) in an article entitled "The Motivation Effects of Charismatic Leadership: A Self-Concept Based Theory." Focused on explaining the profound levels of motivation typically associated with charismatic leadership, they postulated that these motivational effects could best be explained by focusing on the self-concept of the followers. They argued that, as human beings, we behave in ways that seek to establish and affirm a sense of identity for ourselves (known as the self-concept). What charismatic leaders do is to tie these self-concepts of followers to the goals and collective experiences associated with their missions, so that they become valued aspects of the followers self-concept.

In terms of details, their theory hypothesizes that charismatic leadership achieves its motivational outcomes through at least four mechanisms: (a) changing follower perceptions of the nature of work itself, (b) offering an appealing future vision, (c) developing a deep collective identity among followers, and (d) heightening both individual and collective self-efficacy.

Charismatic leaders transform the nature of work (in this case, work meant to achieve the organization's vision) by making it appear more heroic, morally correct, and meaningful. They, in essence, de-emphasize the extrinsic rewards of work and focus instead on the intrinsic side. Work becomes an opportunity for self- and collective-expression. The reward for individual followers as they accomplish mission tasks is one of enhanced self-expression, self-efficacy, self-worth, and self-consistency. The idea is that, eventually followers will come to see their organizational tasks as inseparable from their own self-concepts—that "action is not merely a means of doing but a way of being" (Strauss, 1969, p. 3) (Yukl, 1994).

To accomplish this change in perceptions of work, the charismatic leader uses several means. One of the most important mechanisms as described by Shamir et al. (1993) is the leader's vision that serves to enhance follower self-concepts through three ways. By offering an optimistic and appealing future, the vision heightens the meaningfulness of the organization's goals. Second, the vision is articulated as a shared one that promotes a strong sense of collective identity. Presumably the vision is also unique and, by stressing that the vision is the basis for the group's identity, the charismatic leader distinguishes his or her followers from others and further encourages followers to transcend their individual self-interests for the collective's. Thirdly, the leader's expression of confidence in followers' abilities to achieve the vision heightens their sense of self-efficacy. They feel capable of creating a reality out of what is currently a lofty and utopian set of ambitions.

Integral to the theory is the charismatic leader's ability to create a deep collective identity. As just noted, the shared vision is one of the principle means. In addition, the charismatic leader actively promotes perceptions that, only by banding together, can group members accomplish exceptional feats. Further, the leader uses his or her own behaviors to increase identification with the collective through the deployment of rituals, ceremonies, slogans, symbols, and stories that reinforce the importance of a group identity. The significance of creating this collective identity is in the follower outcomes that it is able to produce. Specifically, the authors cite research (Meindl & Lerner, 1983) indicating that a shared identity among individuals increases the "heroic motive" and the probability that individual self-interests will be abandoned voluntarily for collective and altruistic undertakings. As a result, as charismatic leaders cultivate a collective identity in their followers' self-concepts, they are heightening the chances that followers will engage in self-sacrificial, collective-oriented behavior. The group identification, in essence, strengthens the shared behavioral norms, values, and beliefs among the members. All this ensures a concerted and unified effort on the part of followers to achieve the mission's goals.

Finally, Shamir et al. (1993) argued that charismatic leaders achieve their extraordinary levels of follower motivation by focusing their efforts on building follower self-esteem and self-worth. They accomplish this by expressing high expectations of their followers and simultaneously great confidence in the followers' abilities to meet these expectations (Yukl, 1994). This in turn enhances the perceived self-efficacy of followers. From the research of Bandura (1986), we do know that the sense of self-efficacy can be a source of strong motivation. For example, it has been shown that individuals with high self-efficacy are more willing to expend greater work effort and to demonstrate persistence in overcoming obstacles to achieve their goals. By also fueling a collective sense of self-efficacy, the charismatic leader feeds perceptions of the group that they together accomplish tremendous feats. In addition, when collective self-efficacy is high, members of an organization are more willing to cooperate with each other in joint efforts to realize their shared aims (Yukl, 1994).

Follower Dynamics Under Charismatic Leadership

Early research by political scientists and psychoanalysts (e.g., Downton, 1973; Kets de Vries, 1988) on the follower dynamics under charismatic leadership proposed that the followers of charismatic leaders were more likely to be those who were easily molded and persuaded by such dynamic leaders because of an essentially dependent character. Followers were drawn to the charismatic leader because he or she exudes what they lack self-confidence and conviction. For example, in study of the charismatic religions leader Reverend Sun Moon, Lodahl (1982) found that followers had greater feelings of helplessness, cynicism, distrust of political action, and less confidence in their sexual identity than a sample of college students. Other studies (e.g., Freemesser & Kaplan, 1976; Galanter 1982) found followers of charismatic political and religions leaders to have lower self-esteem, a higher intolerance for indecision and crisis, and more experiences of psychological distress than others.

However, these studies were almost entirely conducted on populations of individuals disaffected by society or in contexts of crisis in which individuals are needy by definition. In the corporate world, the situation is likely to be quite different. For example in a large corporation, the subordinate of a charismatic leader may not have chosen voluntarily to belong to that leaders unit. More commonly, bosses are hired or promoted into positions, and the subordinates are already in place. So for subordinates, there is often little freedom to select who will lead them. Likewise, a leader may find him- or herself inheriting a staff of confident, assertive employees. In the case of entrepreneurial companies founded by charismatic leaders, followers may be drawn to such contexts because of the challenge and opportunity. They may be seekers of the risk and uncertainty associated with a new venture—quite in contrast to followers who are dependent seekers of certainty.

We can summarize the field's general conclusions about follower attraction to a charismatic leader around two explanations. The first centers on psychoanalytic notions of the ego. Essentially, the argument goes that followers are attempting to resolve a conflict between who they are and what they wish to become. They accomplish this by substituting their leader as their ideal, or in psychoanalytic terms, their ego ideal. Some psychoanalysts (e.g. Downton, 1973) trace this type of need back to an individual's failure to mature in adolescence and young adulthood. Because of absent, oppressive, or weak parents, individuals may develop a state of identity confusion. Associating emotionally with the charismatic leader is a means of coping with this confusion and achieving maturity. Given that the leader becomes a substitute parent and model, a powerful emotional attachment is naturally formed by followers. Wishing to garner the leader's attention and affection, followers enthusiastically comply with his or her wishes. The assumption underlying this scenario of follower-leader dynamics is that followers are fulfilling a pathological need rather than a healthy desire for role models from whom to learn and grow

The second school of thought is that followers are attracted to the charismatic leader because of a more constructive identification with the leader's abilities, a desire to learn from them, a quest for personal challenge and growth, and the attractiveness of the mission. This, of course, is what the theories in the previous section have largely argued. With Bass (1985), it is the opportunity to fulfill higher-order needs. In the Shamir et al. theory (1993), it is an opportunity to have one's self-esteem, self-worth, and self-efficacy enhanced.

Conger (1989) found, in his study of charismatic leaders in business, that subordinates often described the importance of an attraction to their leader's self-confidence, their strong convictions in the mission, their willingness to under take personal risks, and their history of prior accomplishment. As a result, subordinates often felt a sense of fulfilling their own potential as they met their leaders' high expectations. In addition, as others have found (e.g. Bass, 1985; Avolio & Bass, 1987), the leaders vision offered attractive outcomes that were motivating in themselves. However, Conger felt that simple identification and an attractive vision did not fully explain the commitment and motivation that followers demonstrated for their charismatic leaders.

Instead, Conger discovered that the personal approval of the charismatic leader became a principal measure of a subordinate's self-worth. A dependency then developed to the point that the leader largely defined one's level of performance and ability. As

Shamir et al. (1993) have also noted, the leader's expression of high expectations set standards of performance and approval, and a continual sense of urgency and the capacity to make subordinates feel unique further heightened motivation. Taken together, these actions promote a sense of obligation in followers to continually live up to their leader's expectations. As the relationship deepens, this sense of obligation grows. The leader's expression of confidence in subordinates' abilities in essence creates a sense of duty and responsibility. Subordinates can only validate the leader's trust in them through exceptional accomplishments.

Over the long term, a dilemma naturally occurs for many followers. As the subordinates' self-worth is increasingly defined in their relationship to the leader, a precarious dependence is built. Without the leader's affirmation, subordinates can feel that they are underperforming and even failing. In addition, there are fears of being ostracized. As one subordinate explained to Conger: "There's a love/hate element [in our relationship]. You love him when you're focused on the same issues. You hate him when the contract falls apart. Either you're part of the team or not—there's a low tolerance for spectators. Over the course of a career, you're in and out. A lot depends on your effectiveness on the team. You have to build up a lot of credibility to regain any ground that you've lost." The dark-side dynamics of this dependence will be discussed further in a later section.

In addition to follower attraction, there have also been studies of follower performance under charismatic leadership. One study (DeGroot, Kiker, & Cross, 2009) applied meta-analysis to assess the relationship between charismatic leadership style and leadership effectiveness, subordinate performance, subordinate satisfaction, subordinate effort, and subordinate commitment. Results indicated that the relationship between leader charisma and leader effectiveness is much weaker than reported in the published literature when leader effectiveness is measured at the individual level of analysis and when common method variance is controlled. Results also indicated a smaller relationship between charismatic leadership and subordinate performance when subordinate performance is measured at the individual level $(r = 0.31)$ than when it is measured at the group level (r = 0.49 and robust across studies). The researchers found an effect size at the group level of analysis that is double in magnitude relative to the effect size at the individual level. This suggests that the effects of charismatic leadership are stronger when the leader has similar relationships with each subordinate or uses a single style to relate to each group member. When the leader exhibits variable amounts of charisma to subordinates, or at least when the effect is measured at the individual level, the extent of effective leadership is reduced. These results also suggest that charismatic leadership is more effective at increasing group performance than at increasing individual performance. Other moderators were tested, but they did not account for a significant portion of variance in the observed distribution of correlations, suggesting a need for further research into other potential moderators. Meta-analysis examining the effects of charismatic leadership on subordinate effort and job satisfaction revealed lower correlations when multiple methods of measurement were used, with little convergence toward stable population estimates. If charismatic leadership behavior is to produce higher performance outcomes from subordinates, further research is needed to examine how this occurs.

The Interplay Between Context and Charismatic Leadership

Up until very recently, interest in the role of context and situational factors has been limited. This is due largely to the backgrounds of those researching leadership. "Microtheorists" (those with a psychological or social psychological orientation) have dominated the field to date. Few researchers with a more "macro" or sociological perspective have been active in studying leadership. As a result, environmental or contextual investigations have rarely been applied to leadership studies outside of the fields of political science and religion. As such, our knowledge in this area remains poor, and what does exist is largely theoretical and speculative.

The most common speculation has been that periods of stress and turbulence are the most conducive

for charismatic leadership (this argument is derived from the work of political scientists looking at charismatic leadership in political and religious contexts: see Cell, 1974; Toth, 1981). Max Weber (1968), for example, specifically focused on times of "crisis" as facilitating environments. The basic assumption is that times of stressful change either encourage a longing among individuals for a leader who offers attractive solutions and visions of the future or that charismatic leaders have an easier time of promoting a transformational vision during times of uncertainty when the status quo appears to no longer function (Bryman, 1992).

To date, the most important empirical study to examine situational factors in organizational contexts was conducted by Roberts and Bradley (1988). Using a field study, they looked at a school superintendent who was appointed a state commissioner of education. In her role as superintendent, she was perceived by her organization as a charismatic leader, yet, as commissioner, that perception failed to convey. In Roberts and Bradley's search to explain why the individual's charisma did not transfer, they discovered several essential differences between the two contexts.

In terms of the larger environment the individual's first context, a school district, was one in crisis—confirming the hypothesis that crisis may indeed facilitate the emergence of charismatic leadership. In contrast, the leader's second context at the state level was not in a similar state of distress. The public's perception was that their state schools were basically sound and simply in need of incremental improvements. The individual's authority also differed in the two situations. As a superintendent, she had much more control and autonomy. At the state level as commissioner, quite the opposite was true. Her number-one priority was political loyalty to the governor. She no longer possessed the freedom to undertake actions as she deemed necessary. Instead, they had to be cleared through the governor's office. Her relationships were also different. Whereas the district organization had been small, with limited stakeholders and localized geographically the situation at the state level was at the opposite end of the spectrum. The agency was far greater in size, complexity and bureaucracy.

The numerous committees and associations in which she had to participate meant that she had little time to build the deep, personal bonds that she had established at the district level. As a result, her impact at the state level was no longer personal and perceptions of her as a charismatic leader did not materialize.

From the Roberts and Bradley study, we might conclude that context shapes charismatic leadership in at least two ways. One, an environment in crisis is indeed more receptive to leadership in general and is more likely to be open to proposals common to charismatic leaders for radical change such as those embodied in the superintendent's vision. Second, there are structural and stakeholder characteristics of organizations that influence an individual's latitude to take initiative and to build personal relationships that determine perceptions of charismatic leadership. The superintendent's position provided structurally far more autonomy to act than the commissioner's. The less geographically dispersed and more limited number of stakeholders fostered deeper working relationships at the district level and also inspired affection and trust in her leadership. These, in turn, heightened perceptions of her charisma.

With findings like Roberts and Bradley's study in mind, we can think of the contexts of organizations as divided into an outer and an inner context—the outer being the environment beyond the organization and the inner including the organization's culture, structure, power distribution, and so on (Pettigrew, 1987). Using this simple framework, it is useful to divide our discussion around these two contextual dimensions. We will start with the external environment.

On the issue of whether crisis is the critical external condition, Conger (1993) hypothesized that there could actually be much more variability in environmental conditions than we might think. He argued that charismatic leadership is not necessarily precipitated by conditions of crisis and distress. In earlier research looking at charismatic business leaders (Conger, 1989), he found charismatic leaders who were entrepreneurs operating in environments not so much of crisis but of great opportunity, munificence, and optimism. Instead of crisis being the sole contextual condition, there may instead be at least two conducive environments: one demanding a major

reorientation of the existing order because of a perceived state of distress, and the other involving the emergence or creation of a new order based on a "munificence entrepreneurial" context.

In addition, Conger argued that more of interplay exists between the leader and the context. In other words, context is not the key determinant, but rather that the leader and the context influence one another—the relative weight of one's influence varying from situation to situation. For example, Willner (1984) found that, while examining charismatic leaders in the political arena, some were able to induce or create through their own actions the necessary contextual conditions of a crisis. We might be able to find charismatic leaders who are similarly able to foster perceptions of munificence and great entrepreneurial opportunity

Conger also went on to propose that the more conducive the contextual conditions, the less the magnitude or the fewer the number of charismatic attributes perhaps required for a leader to be perceived as charismatic. Similarly the greater the intensity or number of "charismatic attributes" of the leader, the need for an existing context, say, of extreme crisis or entrepreneurial opportunities, may diminish as the leader is able to create these perceptions through his or her own actions. For example, the ability to articulate unforeseen opportunities or looming problems in a credible manner may facilitate perceptions of a crisis and/or great opportunity. However, this is still an area of great speculation in need of research attention.

Beyond the limited efforts focusing on the external environments of charismatic leadership just described, there has been only one major theoretical work focusing on contextual conditions within organizations that may influence charismatic leadership. Pawar and Eastman (1997) proposed four factors of organizations that might affect receptivity to transformational leadership. Given our earlier discussion of the overlap between transformational and charismatic forms of leadership, it is worth examining their hypotheses, as they may relate to charismatic leadership.

The four factors that Pawar and Eastman identified include: (a) the organizations emphasis on efficiency versus adaptation, (b) the relative dominance of the organizations technical core versus its boundary-spanning units, (c) organizational structures, and (d) modes of governance. Their model is built around the central notion that transformational or charismatic leadership is essentially about leading organizational change. Organizational contexts that are more conducive to change are, therefore, more favorable for charismatic leadership.

They began with the notion that organizations are seeking one of two basic goals—efficiency or adaptation. The challenge is that the goals of efficiency and adaptation have conflicting purposes—the former requiring organizational stability, whereas the latter is centered on change. In reality, as we know today, most business organizations are attempting both simultaneously, and this highlights one of the dilemmas of Pawar and Easmans' theory. It was built around idealized polarities that provide a simple elegance in terms of theory building but may not reflect the complexities of reality. Nonetheless, they hypothesized that an efficiency orientation requires goal stability and necessarily administrative management or transactional leadership to achieve its goals. During adaptation periods, on the other hand, the leader's role is to overcome resistance to change and to align the organization to a new environment through a dynamic vision, new goals and values. Therefore, organizations with adaptive goals are far more open to charismatic leadership. The authors cautioned, however, that although adaptive periods are more receptive to leadership, there must be a *felt need by* organizational members for transformation, otherwise they may accept more administrative management.

The second contextual factor—the relative dominance of the technical core versus boundary-spanning units—refers to the fact that an organization's task systems are either more inwardly oriented or more externally oriented. Thompson (1967) argued that organizations divide their task systems into two parts: (a) a technical core that performs the work of input processing through the operation of technology, and (b) boundary-spanning functions that interface directly with the external environment. Isolated from an ever-changing external world, the technical core develops routines and stability in how it approaches its tasks (Thompson, 1967). In contrast, the boundary-spanning functions are forced to adapt continually to environmental constraints and contingencies and as a result can never develop highly standardized or routine approaches (Thompson, 1967). Pawar and Eastman postulated that organizations in which boundary-spanning units dominate over the technical core will be more open to transformational and charismatic leadership because they are more receptive to change.

Employing Mintzberg's (1979) typology of organizational structures, Pawar and Eastman proposed that only certain structures will be receptive to leadership. Mintzberg's five "ideal type" structures include: (a) the adhocracy, (b) the simple structure, (c) the machine bureaucracy, (d) the professional bureaucracy, and (e) the divisional structure. Of these five, two in particular may be conducive to charismatic leadership. They are the simple structure and the adhocracy. Specifically, both are more receptive to organizational change through the promotion of a vision—an outcome associated with charismatic leadership. The three other forms have internal forces that mitigate against openness to more innovative forms of leadership. For example, the machine bureaucracy is dominated by standardized tasks and work processes. Senior managers are obsessed by a control mind-set, and lower-level managers are intent only on implementing operational directives from above. As such, there is little concern with innovation and change that are potentially threatening to a tightly orchestrated status quo. In the professional bureaucracy, professionals dominate to such an extent that leadership may be marginalized to the role of facilitation. As well, the professionals in these systems are far less committed to the organization than to their own work and profession. The divisional structure is also not conducive. Built around two layers in which a headquarters operation governs quasi-autonomous divisions, the focus of the corporate headquarters is to specify operational goals and to monitor the divisions' accomplishment of them. The divisions then are concerned with attaining operational goals. Because divisional structures are concerned with operational goals, neither group is likely to show great interest in developing a vision.

The final factor influencing receptivity to charismatic leadership in the Pawar and Eastman model is the mode of internal governance. They start with the assumption that membership in organizations is built around furthering individual members' self-interests (Burns & Stalker, 1961; Thompson, 1967). Yet the aim of transformational and charismatic forms of leadership is for followers to transcend their own self-interests for collective goals. Under Wilkins and Ouchi's (1983) three modes of governance (the market, the bureaucratic, and the clan) the nature of transactions between an organization and its members will differ. Under the market mode transactions based on the exchange of commitments between the organization and its members are determined by market or price mechanisms. Because an external market shapes commitments, the organization has little incentive to socialize its members to defer self-interests. In the bureaucratic mode, a contract for commitments is built around employees accepting organizational authority in return for wages. The organization then monitors compliance through formal monitoring and exchange-mechanisms. These become the devices that curb members' self-interests. Under the clan mode, organizational members are socialized in such a way that their own interests and the organization's are aligned as one. In other words, employees still hold their self-interests, but they believe they can fulfill them through achieving the collective's interests. It is, therefore, the clan mode that is most receptive to transformational and charismatic leadership, because it allows for a merging of individual self-interests with the collective's goals.

Can Charismatic Leadership Institutionalize Itself?

When an organization possesses a charismatic leader, it creates what Wilson (1975) has called a "charismatic demand." The dilemma is that it is unlikely that a charismatic leader will be found to replace the original one. Though Bryman (1992) has found one example in a study of a transportation company, such situations appear extremely rare. Instead, what often happens is that a charismatic leader is replaced by a more managerial-oriented individual. Examples of this would be Steven Jobs who was succeeded by John Sculley and Michael Spindler, the succession of Lee Iacocca at Chrysler by Robert Eaton (Bryman, 1992), and Walt Disney's replacement by Roy Disney (Bryman, 1992). Biggart (1989) noted that, among direct selling organizations, we often see an attempt to overcome succession problems by either promoting a national sales executive into the leadership role or to "invest the mission in one's children" (p. 144). Looking at Amway and Shaklee, Biggart discovered that the founder's children assumed active roles in the company, in turn fostering a "charismatic presence." However, he also found that their roles were largely bureaucratic and that the companies had done little to institutionalize the founder's charisma beyond the presence of their children. Given the enormous demands for continual adaptation due to competition and strong needs to develop rational and formalized structures, business organizations may simply not be conducive to long-term institutionalization of a leader's charisma.

In general, institutionalization of charismatic leadership is a topic for which little research has been conducted in the organizational literature. The topic was an issue that intrigued Max Weber greatly. He believed that charisma was essentially an unstable force. It either faded or was institutionalized as the charismatic leader's mission was accomplished:

> If [charisma] is not to remain a purely transitory phenomenon, but to take on the character of a permanent relationship forming a stable community, it is necessary for the character of charismatic authority to be radically changed . . . It cannot remain stable, but becomes either traditionalized or rationalized or both. (Weber, [1924] 1947, p. 364)

He argued that there were strong incentives on the part of charismatic leaders and their followers to transform their movements into more permanent institutions. With successes, the followers achieve positions of authority and material advantage. The desire would naturally arise to institutionalize these, and so traditions and rules would grow up to protect the gains of the mission.

The only in-depth study on institutionalization was conducted by Trice and Beyer in 1986. They examined two charismatic leaders: in one case, charisma had routinized, and in another, it had not. Their conclusions were that five key factors were largely responsible for the successful institutionalization of charisma. They were: (a) the development of an administrative apparatus separate from the charismatic leader that put into practice the leader's mission, (b) the incorporation of the leader's mission into oral and written traditions, (c) the transfer of charisma through rites and ceremonies to other members of the organization, (d) a continued identification by organizational members to the original mission, and (e) the selection of a successor who resembles the charismatic leader and is committed to the founder's mission. For the case in which charisma did not routinize, these factors were largely missing.

From the standpoint of the business world, however, it does appear that charisma is a relatively fragile phenomenon in terms of institutionalization. There are several examples from the management literature where succession dilemmas prevented the routinization of charismatic leadership (e.g., Bryman, 1992 and 1993; Conger, 1989). The charismatic leaders in Conger's 1989 study have all since departed from their original organizations due to either promotions, moves to new organizations, retirement, or in one case, death. From informal observations, it is clear that there is little indication of any significant routinization of their charisma in their various organizations. In a 1993 article, Conger noted that one member of his research sample—an entrepreneur—had had some success insofar as elements of his original mission, values, and operating procedures did institutionalize. However, that individual has since left that organization, and a few years ago it was acquired by a much larger firm that superimposed its own mission, values, and procedures. Today, there is little evidence of that initial routinization of the leader's charisma. The leaders in Congers study who were acting as change agents in large, bureaucratic organizations had practically no long-term impact in terms of institutionalizing their charisma.

Even if routinization were to be successful, it is no guarantee of continued performance success for the leader's organization. As Conger (1993) noted, part of the dilemma is that successors may possess neither the strategic skills nor the abilities crucial to the firm's future leadership requirements. For example, although the retailer Walmart has apparently institutionalized Sam Walton's values and operating beliefs, a critical question is whether it can institutionalize his visionary insights into the world of retailing. Just as importantly Walton's vision was time bound. So even if his strategic competence were to be institutionalized, it is the product of a specific era in retailing. His predecessors, steeped in Walton's strategic paradigm, are, therefore, unlikely to produce the next revolution in mass merchandising. It is highly unlikely, therefore, that the visionary capacity of the charismatic leader can be institutionalized in a manner that keeps the organization highly adaptive.

Even elements as simple as institutionalized rituals may themselves become counterproductive over time. Conger (1993) cited the example of IBM, which very effectively institutionalized many of Thomas Watson Sr.'s values and traditions. Several of these would prove maladaptive only decades later. For instance, Watson's original strong emphasis on sales and marketing would ensure that future company leaders were drawn from these ranks. The price, however, would be in terms of senior leaders' failure to adequately understand the strategic importance of certain new technologies and software systems. A tradition of rewarding loyalty through internal promotions added to the problem. It encouraged inbreeding around the company's worldview and simply reinforced notions of IBM's mainframe mentality and its arrogance. Even simple traditions would lose their original meaning and transform themselves into bureaucratic norms. For example, IBM's traditional corporate dress code of dark suits and white shirts is illustrative. This requirement was intended by Watson to make his salespeople feel like executives. If you dressed like an executive, you would feel like one, was Watson's original thinking. Indeed the dress code did build pride in the early days of IBM. Many decades later, however, this norm would transform into a symbol of rigidity and conformity. It bureaucratized itself, as Weber would have guessed.

In conclusion, we have limited knowledge about this crucial area of charismatic leadership. A limited number of case studies and no systematic longitudinal research have offered us, at best, tantalizing tidbits of insight. The primary insight is that institutionalization of the leader's charisma is a fragile affair and, therefore, rare.

What Are the Liabilities of Charismatic Leadership?

Although the literature has been largely positive about the effects of charismatic leadership in organizations, there has been some interest in the negative outcomes associated with this form of leadership. In his study of the hiring and firing of CEOs at over 850 of America's largest companies, Khurana (2002) found that corporate board members and executive search consultants placed a strong emphasis on the charisma of CEO candidates. As a result, both groups artificially limited the number of candidates considered, to their companies' detriment. The CEO labor market proved to be a closed ecosystem in which selection decisions were based on highly stylized criteria that often had little to do with the problems a firm was confronting. As a result, the charismatic candidates often failed once in the CEO role. At the same time, the charismatic candidates possessed extraordinary leverage to demand high salaries and power. Because the pool of high-profile charismatic CEOs is limited, such scarcity naturally drove up wages.

To distinguish between the positive and negative outcomes associated with charismatic leadership, Jane Howell (1988) proposed a simple, dichotomous model of socialized and personalized charisma. In conjunction with Robert House (Howell & House, 1993), the theory was refined to propose a set of personality characteristics, behaviors, and effects that distinguished the two forms. Specifically, socialized charismatic leaders are described as articulating visions that serve the interests of the collective. They govern in an equalitarian, non-self-aggrandizing manner, and actively empower and develop their followers. They also work through legitimate established channels of authority to accomplish their goals. On the other hand, personalized charismatic leaders are authoritarian and narcissistic. They have high needs for power, driven, in part, by low self-esteem. Their goals reflect the leader's own self-interests, and followers' needs are played upon as a means to achieve the leader's interests. In addition, they disregard established and legitimate channels of authority as well as the rights and feelings of others. At the same time, they demand unquestioning obedience and dependence in their followers. Although they portray these two forms as dichotomous, Howell and House do acknowledge that a charismatic leader might, in reality, exhibit some aspects of both the socialized and the personalized characteristics. This latter view is probably closer to reality than their ideal model.

Drawing on actual examples of charismatic leaders, Conger (1989, 1990) examined those who had produced negative outcomes for themselves and their organizations. He found that problems could arise with charismatic leaders around (a) their visions, (b) their impression management, (c) their management practices, and (d) succession planning. On the dimension of vision, typical problems occurred when the leaders possessed an exaggerated sense of the market opportunities for their vision or when they grossly underestimated the resources necessary for its accomplishment. In addition, visions often failed when they reflected largely the leaders' needs rather than constituents or the masterpiece, or when the leaders were unable to recognize fundamental shifts in the environment, demanding redirection.

In terms of impression management charismatic leaders appear prone to exaggerated self-descriptions and claims for their visions, which can mislead. For example, they may present information that makes their visions appear more feasible or appealing than they are in reality. They may screen out looming problems or else foster an illusion of control when things are actually out of control. From the standpoint of management practices, there are examples of overly self-confident and unconventional charismatic leaders who create antagonistic relations with peers and superiors. Some, such as Steven Jobs, are known to create "in" and "out" groups within their organizations that promote dysfunctional rivalries. Others create excessive dependence on themselves and then alternate between idealizing and devaluing dependent subordinates. Many are ineffective administrators "preferring big picture" activities to routine work. Finally, charismatic leaders often have a difficult time developing successors. They simply enjoy the limelight too much to share it. To find a replacement who is a peer may be too threatening for leaders who tend to be so narcissistic.

Daniel Sankowsky (1995) has written about the dilemma of charismatic leaders who are prone to the pathology of narcissism. Specifically, he has proposed a stage model showing how dark-side charismatics implicate their followers into a cycle of exploitation. First, these leaders offer a grandiose vision and confidently encourage followers to accomplish it. Followers, however, soon find themselves in an untenable position. Because of their leader's optimism, they have underestimated the constraints facing the mission as well as the resources they need but currently lack. As a result, performance inevitably falls short of the leader's high expectations. Wishing to comply with their leader's aspirations, however, followers continue to strive. Soon their performance appears substandard as they fall behind. Although, initially, the leader will blame the outside world for undermining the mission, his or her attention will eventually turn to the followers. Conditioned to accept their leader's viewpoint and not to challenge it, followers willingly receive the blame themselves from their leader. The reverse of the many benefits ascribed to charismatic leaders then occurs. Instead of building their follower's self-worth and self-efficacy, they gradually destroy it and create highly dependent individuals.

Conclusion

As a field, charismatic leadership has made significant strides since the rudimentary theory proposed by Max Weber at the start of the twentieth century. It is clear that there are behaviors associated with charismatic leaders that distinguish them, to a degree, from other forms. We also know that charismatic leadership is not always associated with positive outcomes. Certain charismatic leaders have produced extreme negative outcomes for organizations and even for societies. As a field of research, our knowledge of the phenomenon still has important gaps. There are many opportunities for future researchers. These include the need to deepen our understanding of followed dynamics, institutionalization, and the interplay between context and the leader.

References

Agle, B. R., & Sonnenfeld, J. A. (1994). Charismatic chief executive officers: Are they more effective? An empirical test of charismatic leadership theory. *Academy of Management Best Papers Proceedings, 2–6.*

Avolio, B. J., & Bass, B. M. (1987). Charisma and beyond. In J. G. Hunt (Ed.), *Emerging leadership vistas* (pp. 29–49). Elmsford, NY: Pergamon Press.

Bandura, A. (1986). *Social foundations of thought and action: A social-cognitive view.* Englewood Cliffs, NJ: Prentice Hall.

Bass, B. M. (1985). *Leadership and performance beyond expectations.* New York: Free Press.

Bass, B. M., & Avolio, B. (1993). Transformational leadership: A response to critiques. In M. M. Chemers & R. Ayman (Eds.), *Leadership theory and research: Perspectives and directions* (pp. 49–80). New York: Academic Press.

Bass, B. M., & Yammarino, F. J. (1988). *Leadership: Dispositional and situational* (ONR Tech. Rep. No. 1). Binghamton, NY: State University of New York, Center for Leadership Studies,

Biggart, N. W. (1989). *Charismatic capitalism: Direct selling organizations in America.* Chicago: University of Chicago Press.

Blau, P. M. (1963). *Exchange and power in social life.* New York: Wiley.

Bryman, A. (1992). *Charisma and leadership in organizations.* London: Sage.

Burns, J. M. (1978). *Leadership.* New York: Harper.

Burns, T., & Stalker, G. M. (1961). *The management of innovation.* London: Tavistock Publications.

Cell, C. P. (1974). Charismatic heads of state: The social context. *Behavioral Science Research, 4,* 255–305.

Chinoy, E. (1961). *Society.* New York: Random House.

Conger, J. A. (1985). *Charismatic leadership in business: An exploration study.* Unpublished doctoral dissertation, School of Business Administration, Harvard University.

Conger, J. A. (1989). *The charismatic leader: Beyond the mystique of exceptional leadership.* San Francisco: Jossey-Bass.

Conger, J. A. (1993). Max Weber's conceptualization of charismatic authority: Its influence on organizational research. *Leadership Quarterly, 4*(514), 277–288.

Conger, J. A., & Kanungo, R. N. (1992). Perceived behavioural attributes of charismatic leadership. *Canadian Journal of Behavioural Science, 24*, 86–102,

Conger, J. A., & Kanungo, R. N. (1994). Charismatic leadership in organizations: Perceived behavioural attributes and their measurement. *Journal of Organizational Behavior, 15*, 439–452.

Conger, J. A., & Kanungo, R. N. (1999). *Charismatic leadership* in organizations. Thousand Oaks, CA: Sage.

Curphy, G. J. (1990). An empirical study of Bass, (1985) theory of transformational and transactional leadership. Unpublished doctoral dissertation, the University of Minnesota.

DeGroot, T., Kiker, D. S., & Cross, T. C. (2009). A meta-analysis to review organizational outcomes related to charismatic leadership. *Canadian Journal of Administrative Sciences, 17*(4), 356–372,

Dow, T. E. (1969). A theory of charisma. *Social Quarterly, 10*, 306–318.

Downton, J. V. (1973). *Rebel leadership.* New York: Free Press.

Freemesser, G. F., & Kaplan, H. B. (1976). Self-attitudes and deviant behavior: The case of the charismatic religious movement. *Journal of Youth and Adolescence, 5*(1), 1–9.

Friedland, W. H. (1964). For a sociological concept of charisma. *Social Forces, 43*, 18–26.

Galanter, M. (1982). Charismatic religious seas and psychiatry: An overview. *American Journal of Psychiatry, 139*(2), 1539–1548.

Graen, G., & Scandura, T. (1987). Towards a psychology of dyadic organizing. In B. M. Staw & L. L. Cummings (Eds.), *Research in organizational behavior* (Vol. 9, pp. 175–208). Greenwich, CT: J AI Press.

Hater, J. J., & Bass, B. M. (1988). Superiors' evaluations and subordinates' perceptions of transformational and transactional leadership. *Journal of Applied Psychology, 73*, 695–702,

House, R. J. (1977). A 1976 theory of Charismatic leadership. In G. Hunt & L. L. Larson (Eds.), *Leadership: The cutting edge* (pp. 189–204). Carbondale, IL: Southern Illinois University Press.

House, R. J., & Mitchell, T. R. (1974). Path-goal theory of leadership. *Contemporary Business, 3*, 81–98.

House, R. J., & Shamir, B. (1993). Toward the integration of transformational, charismatic, and visionary theories. In M. Chemmers & R. Ayman (Eds.), *Leadership theory and research perspectives and directions* (pp. 577–594). Orlando, FL: Academic Press.

House, R. J., Spangler, W. D., & Woycke, J. (1991). Personality and charisma in the U.S. presidency: A psychological theory of leader effectiveness. *Administrative Science Quarterly, 36*, 364–396.

Howell, J. M. (1988). Two faces of charisma: Socialized and personalized leadership in organizations. In J. A. Conger & R. N. Kanungo (Eds.), *Charismatic leadership: The elusive factor in organizational effectiveness* (pp. 213–236). San Francisco: Jossey-Bass.

Howell, J. M., & Frost, P. (1989). A laboratory study of charismatic leadership. *Organizational Behavior and Human Decision Processes, 43*, 243–269.

Howell, J. M., & Higgins, C. A. (1990). Champions of technological innovation. *Administrative Science Quarterly, 35*, 317–341.

Howell, J. M., & House, R. J. (1993). *Specialized and personalized charisma: A theory of the bright and dark sides of leadership.* Working paper. London, Ontario: University of Western Ontario.

Kers de Vries, M. F. R, (1988). Origins of charisma: Ties that bind the leader and the led. In J. A. Conger & R. N. Kanungo (Eds.), *Charismatic leadership: The elusive factor in organizational effectiveness* (pp. 237–252). San Francisco: Jossey-Bass.

Khurana, R. (2002). *Searching for a corporate savior: The irrational quest for charismatic CEOs.* Princeton, NJ: Princeton University Press.

Kirkpatrick, S. A. (1992). *Decomposing charismatic leadership: The effects of leader content and process on follower performance attitudes and perceptions.* Unpublished doctoral dissertation, University of Maryland, College Park.

Koene, H., Pennings, H., & Schrender, M. (1991). *Leadership, culture, and organizational effectiveness.* Boulder, CO: Center for Creative Leadership.

Koh, W. L., Terborg, J. R., & Steers, R. M. (1991). *The impact off transformational leaders on organizational commitment, organizational citizenship behavior, teacher satisfaction and student performance in Singapore.* Paper presented at Academy of Management Meeting, Miami, FL.

Lodahl, A. (1982). *Crisis in values and the success of the Unification Church.* Unpublished doctoral dissertation, Cornell University, Ithaca, NY

Marcus, J. X. (1961). Transcendence and charisma. *Western Political Quarterly 14*, 236–241.

Meindl, J., & Lerner, M. J., (1983). The heroic motive: Some ƒ experimental demonstrations. *Journal of Experimental Psychology 19,* 1–20.

Mintzberg, H. (1979). *The structuring of organizations.* Englewood Cliffs, NJ: Prentice Hall.

Pawar, B. S., & Eastman, K. K. (1997). The nature and implications of contextual influences on transformational leadership: A conceptual examination. *Academy of Management Review, 22,* 80–109.

Pettigrew, A. M. (1987) Context and action in the transformation of the firm. *Journal of Management Studies, 24,* 649–670.

Podsakoff, P. M., MacKenzie, S. B., Moorman, R. H., & Fetter, R. (1990). Transformational leader behaviors and their effects on followers' trust in leader, satisfaction, and organizational citizenship behaviors. *Leadership Quarterly, 1,* 107–142.

Podsakoff, P. M., Todor, W. D., & Skov, R. (1982). Effects of leader contingent and noncontingent reward and punishment behaviors on subordinate performance and satisfaction: *Academy of Management Journal, 25,* 810–821.

Puffer, S. M. (1990). Attributions of charismatic leadership: The impact of decision style, outcome, and observer characteristics. *Leadership Quarterly 1,* 177–192.

Roberts, N. C., & Bradley, R. T. (1988). Limits of charisma. In J. A. Conger & R. N. Kanungo (Eds.), *Charismatic leadership: The elusive factor in organizational effectiveness* (pp. 252–275). San Francisco: Jossey-Bass.

Sankowsky, D. (1995). The charismatic leader as narcissist: Understanding the abuse of power. *Organizational Dynamics, 23*(4), 57–71.

Sashkin, M. (1988). The visionary leader. In J. A. Conger & R. N. Kanungo (Eds.), *Charismatic leadership: The elusive factor in organizational effectiveness* (pp. 122–160). San Francisco: Jossey-Bass.

Shamir, B. (1992). Attribution of influence and charisma to the leader: The romance of leadership revisited. *Journal of Applied Social Psychology, 22*(5), 386–407.

Shamir, B., House, R., & Arthur, M. B. (1993). The motivation effects of charismatic leadership: A self-concept based theory. *Organization Science, 4*(4), 577–594.

Strauss, A. L. (1969). *Mirrors and masks.* London: M. Robertson.

Thompson, J. D. (1967). *Organizations in action.* New York: McGraw-Hill.

Toth, M. A. (1981). *The theory of the two charismas.* Washington, DC: University Press of America.

Trice, H. M., & Beyer, J. M. (1986). Charisma and its routinization in two social movement organizations. *Journal of Occupation at Behavior, 7,* 125–138.

Weber, M. (1925/1968). *Economy and society: An outline of interpretive sociology* (G. Roth & C. Wittich, Eds., 3 Vols.). New York: Bedminster.

Weber, M. (1947). *The theory of social and economic organizations.* (A. M. Henderson & T. Parsons, Trans.; T. Parsons, Ed.). New York: Free Press.

Wilkins, A. L., & Ouchi, W G, (1983). Efficient cultures: Exploring the relationship between culture and organizational performance. *Administrative Science Quarterly, 28,* 468–481.

Willner, A. R. (1984). *The spellbinders: Charismatic political leadership.* New Haven, CT: Yale University Press.

Wilson, B. R. (1975). *The noble savages: The primitive origins of charisma and its contemporary survival.* Berkeley, CA: University of California Press.

Yukl, G. (1994). *Leadership in organizations* (3rd ed.). Englewood Cliffs, NJ: Prentice-Hall.

CHAPTER 9

Servant Leadership

Robert K. Greenleaf

Greenleaf Center for Servant Leadership and Indiana State University

Servant and leader—can these two roles be fused in one real person, in all levels of status or calling? If so, can that person live and be productive in the real world of the present? My sense of the present leads me to say yes to both questions. This chapter is an attempt to explain why and to suggest how.

The idea of the servant as leader came out of reading Hermann Hesse's *Journey to the East*. In this story we see a band of men on a mythical journey, probably also Hesse's own journey. The central figure of the story is Leo, who accompanies the party as the *servant* who does their menial chores, but who also sustains them with his spirit and his song. He is a person of extraordinary presence. All goes well until Leo disappears. Then the group falls into disarray and the journey is abandoned. They cannot make it without the servant Leo. The narrator, one of the party, after some years of wandering, finds Leo and is taken into the Order that had sponsored the journey. There he discovers that Leo, whom he had known first as *servant*, was in fact the titular head of the Order, its guiding spirit, a great and noble *leader*.

One can muse on what Hesse was trying to say when he wrote this story. We know that most of his fiction was autobiographical, that he led a tortured life, and that *Journey to the East* suggests a turn toward the serenity he achieved in his old age. There has been much speculation by critics on Hesse's life and work, some of it centering on this story which they find the most puzzling. But to me, this story clearly says that *the great leader is seen as servant first*, and that simple fact is the key to his greatness. Leo was actually the leader all of the time, but he was servant first because that was what he was, *deep down inside*. Leadership was bestowed upon a person who was by nature a servant. It was something given, or assumed, that could be taken away. His servant nature was the real man, not bestowed, not assumed, and not to be taken away. He was servant first.

I mention Hesse and *Journey to the East* for two reasons. First, I want to acknowledge the source of the idea of the servant as leader. Then I want to use this reference as an introduction to a brief discussion of prophecy.

Fifteen years ago when I first read about Leo, if I had been listening to contemporary prophecy as intently as I do now, the first draft of this piece might have been written then. As it was, the idea lay dormant for eleven years until, four years ago, I concluded that we in this country were in a leadership crisis and that I should do what I could about it. I became painfully aware of how dull my sense of contemporary prophecy had been. And I have reflected much on why we do not hear and heed the prophetic voices in our midst (not a new question in our times, nor more critical than heretofore).

I now embrace the theory of prophecy, which holds that prophetic voices of great clarity, and with a quality of insight equal to that of any age, are speaking cogently all of the time. Men and women of a stature equal to the greatest of the past are with us now addressing the problems of the day and pointing to a better way and to a personality better able to live fully and serenely in these times.

The variable that marks some periods as barren and some as rich in prophetic vision is in the interest, the level of seeking, the responsiveness of the hearers. The variable is not in the presence or absence or the relative quality and force of the prophetic voices. Prophets grow in stature as people respond to their message. If their early attempts are ignored or spurned, their talent may wither away.

It is *seekers*, then, who make prophets, and the initiative of any one of us in searching for and responding to the voice of contemporary prophets may mark the turning point in their growth and service. But since we are the product of our own history, we see current prophecy within the context of past wisdom. We listen to as wide a range of contemporary thought as we can attend to. Then we *choose* those we elect to heed as prophets—*both old and new*—and meld their advice with our own leadings. This we test in real-life experiences to establish our own position.

Some who have difficulty with this theory assert that their faith rests on one or more of the prophets of old having given the "word" for all time and that the contemporary ones do not speak to their condition as the older ones do. But if one really believes that the "word" has been given for all time, how can one be a seeker? How can one hear the contemporary voice when one has decided not to live in the present and has turned that voice off?

Neither this hypothesis nor its opposite can be proved, but I submit that the one given here is the more hopeful choice, one that offers a significant role in prophecy to every individual. One cannot interact with and build strength in a dead prophet, but one

can do it with a living one. "Faith," Dean Inge has said, "is the choice of the nobler hypothesis."

One does not, of course, ignore the great voices of the past. One does not awaken each morning with the compulsion to reinvent the wheel. But if one is *servant*, either leader or follower, one is always searching, listening, expecting that a better wheel for these times is in the making. It may emerge any day. Any one of us may find it out from personal experience. I am hopeful.

I am hopeful for these times, despite the tension and conflict, because more natural servants are trying to see clearly the world as it is and are listening carefully to prophetic voices that are speaking *now*. They are challenging the pervasive injustice with greater force, and they are taking sharper issue with the wide disparity between the quality of society they know is reasonable and possible with available resources, and, on the other hand, the actual performance of the whole range of institutions that exist to serve society.

A fresh critical look is being taken at the issues of power and authority, and people are beginning to learn, however haltingly, to relate to one another in less coercive and more creatively supporting ways. A new moral principle is emerging, which holds that the only authority deserving one's allegiance is that which is freely and knowingly granted by the led to the leader in response to, and in proportion to, the clearly evident servant stature of the leader. Those who choose to follow this principle will not casually accept the authority of existing institutions. *Rather, they will freely respond only to individuals who are chosen as leaders because they are proven and trusted as servants.* To the extent that this principle prevails in the future, the only truly viable institutions will be those that are predominantly servant led.

I am mindful of the long road ahead before these trends, which I see so clearly, become a major society shaping force. We are not there yet. But I see encouraging movement on the horizon.

What direction will the movement take? Much depends on whether those who stir the ferment will come to grips with the age-old problem of how to live in a human society. I say this because so many, having made their awesome decision for autonomy and independence from tradition, and having taken their firm stand against injustice and hypocrisy, find it hard to convert themselves into *affirmative builders* of a better society. How many of them will seek their personal fulfillment by making the hard choices and by undertaking the rigorous preparation that building a better society requires? It all depends on what kind of leaders emerge and how they—we—respond to them.

My thesis, that more servants should emerge as leaders, or should follow only servant-leaders, is not a popular one. It is much more comfortable to go with a less demanding point of view about what is expected of one now. There are several undemanding, plausibly argued alternatives to choose. One, since society seems corrupt, is to seek to avoid the center of it by retreating to an idyllic existence that minimizes involvement with the "system" (with the "system" that makes such withdrawal possible). Then there is the assumption that since the effort to reform existing institutions has not brought instant perfection, the remedy is to destroy them completely so that fresh new perfect ones can grow. Not much thought seems to be given to the problem of where the new seed will come from or who the gardener to tend them will be. The concept of the servant-leader stands in sharp contrast to this kind of thinking.

Yet it is understandable that the easier alternatives would be chosen, especially by young people. By extending education for so many so far into the adult years, normal participation in society is effectively denied when young people are ready for it. With education that is preponderantly abstract and analytical it is no wonder that there is a preoccupation with criticism and that not much thought is given to "What can I do about it?"

Criticism has its place, but as a total preoccupation it is sterile. In a time of crisis, like the leadership crisis we are now in, if too many potential builders are taken in by a complete absorption with dissecting the wrong and by a zeal for instant perfection, then the movement so many of us want to see will be set back. The danger, perhaps, is to hear the analyst too much and the artist too little.

Albert Camus stands apart from other great artists of his time, in my view, and deserves the title of *prophet* because of his unrelenting demand that each of us confront the exacting terms of our own existence, and, like Sisyphus, *accept our rock and*

find our happiness in dealing with it. Camus sums up the relevance of his position to our concern for the servant as leader in the last paragraph of his last published lecture, entitled "Create Dangerously":

One may long, as I do, for a gentler flame, a respite, a pause for musing. But perhaps there is no other peace for the artist than what he finds in the heat of combat. "Every wall is a door," Emerson correctly said. Let us not look for the door, and the way out, anywhere but in the wall against which we are living. Instead, let us seek the respite where it is—in the very thick of battle. For in my opinion, and this is where I shall close, it *is* there. Great ideas, it has been said, come into the world as gently as doves. Perhaps, then, if we listen attentively, we shall hear, amid the uproar of empires and nations, a faint flutter of wings, the gentle stirring of life and hope. Some will say that this hope lies in a nation, others, in a man. I believe rather that it is awakened, revived, nourished by millions of solitary individuals whose deeds and works every day negate frontiers and the crudest implications of history. As a result, there shines forth fleetingly the ever-threatened truth that each and every man, on the foundations of his own sufferings and joys, builds for them all.

One is asked, then, to accept the human condition, its sufferings and its joys, and to work with its imperfections as the foundation upon which the individual will build wholeness through adventurous creative achievement. For the person with creative potential there is no wholeness except in using it. And, as Camus explained, the going is rough and the respite is brief. It is significant that he would title his last university lecture "Create Dangerously." And, as I ponder the fusing of servant and leader, it seems a dangerous creation: dangerous for the natural servant to become a leader, dangerous for the leader to be servant first, and dangerous for a follower to insist on being led by a servant. There are safer and easier alternatives available to all three. But why take them?

As I respond to the challenge of dealing with this question in the ensuing discourse, I am faced with two problems.

First, I did not get the notion of the servant as leader from conscious logic. Rather, it came to me as an intuitive insight as I contemplated Leo. And I do not see what is relevant from my own searching and experience in terms of a logical progression from premise to conclusion. Rather, I see it as fragments of data to be fed into my internal computer from which intuitive insights come. Serving and leading are still mostly intuition based concepts in my thinking.

The second problem, related to the first, is that, just as there may be a real contradiction in the servant as leader, so my perceptual world is full of contradictions. Some examples: I believe in order, and I want creation out of chaos. My good society will have strong individualism amid community. It will have elitism along with populism. I listen to the old and to the young and find myself baffled and heartened by both. Reason and intuition, each in its own way, both comfort and dismay me. There are many more. Yet, with all of this, I believe that I live with as much serenity as do my contemporaries who venture into controversy as freely as I do but whose natural bent is to tie up the essentials of life in neat bundles of logic and consistency. But I am deeply grateful to the people who are logical and consistent because some of them, out of their natures, render invaluable services for which I am not capable.

My resolution of these two problems is to offer the relevant gleanings of my experience in the form of a series of unconnected little essays, some developed more fully than others, with the suggestion that they be read and pondered separately within the context of this opening section.

Who Is the Servant-Leader?

The servant-leader *is* servant first—as Leo was portrayed. It begins with the natural feeling that one wants to serve, to serve *first*. Then conscious choice brings one to aspire to lead. That person is sharply different from one who is *leader* first, perhaps because of the need to assuage an unusual power drive or to acquire material possessions. For such, it will be a later choice to serve—after leadership is established. The leader-first and the servant-first are two extreme types. Between them there are shadings and blends that are part of the infinite variety of human nature.

The difference manifests itself in the care taken by the servant-first to make sure that other people's highest priority needs are being served. The best test, and difficult to administer, is this: Do those served grow as persons? Do they, *while being served*, become healthier, wiser, freer, more autonomous, more likely themselves to become servants? *And*, what is the effect on the least privileged in society? Will they benefit or at least not be further deprived?

As one sets out to serve, how can one know that this will be the result? This is part of the human dilemma; one cannot know for sure. One must, after some study and experience, hypothesize—but leave the hypothesis under a shadow of doubt. Then one acts on the hypothesis and examines the result. One continues to study and learn and periodically one reexamines the hypothesis itself.

Finally, one chooses again. Perhaps one chooses the same hypothesis again and again. But it is always a fresh, open choice. And it is always a hypothesis under a shadow of doubt. "Faith is the choice of the nobler hypothesis." Not the *noblest*; one never knows what that is. But the *nobler*, the best one can see when the choice is made. Since the test of results of one's actions is usually long delayed, the faith that sustains the choice of the nobler hypothesis is psychological self-insight. This is the most dependable part of the true servant.

The natural servant, the person who is *servant-first*, is more likely to persevere and refine a particular hypothesis on what serves another's highest priority needs than is the person who is *leader-first* and who later serves out of promptings of conscience or in conformity with normative expectations.

My hope for the future rests in part on my belief that among the legions of deprived and unsophisticated people are many true servants who will lead and that most of them can learn to discriminate among those who presume to serve them and identify the true servants whom they will follow.

CHAPTER 10

Contingencies, Context, Situation, and Leadership

Roya Ayman

Illinois Institute of Technology

Susan Adams

Northeastern Illinois University

I n leadership studies, we have observed two general lines of research proceeding in parallel. On one hand, many studies on the relationship between leader traits or behaviors and organizational outcomes find themselves invoking contingencies, context, and situation to explain their findings (e.g., Judge, Bono, Ilies, & Gerhardt, 2002; Judge & Piccolo, 2004). This demonstrates that despite efforts to find simple explanations for leadership, there is a more complex picture to consider. On the other hand, some scholars continue to focus on context and contingencies (e.g., Liden & Antonakis, 2009; Porter & McLaughlin, 2006), demonstrating the importance of these factors in the study of leadership. As Fiedler (1992) commented, life exists within a pretzel-shaped universe and therefore needs pretzel-shaped theories

to explain it. This is especially the case in the field of leadership research.

Historically, the 20th-century psychological exploration of leadership research started with the "great man" theory, which focused on leadership as a quality within the individual (e.g., Ayman, 1993; Chemers, 1997; Zaccaro, Kemp, & Bader, 2004). This philosophical school dominated the majority of the subsequent theoretical developments and empirical investigations and the practice of selection of leaders in organizations. On the other hand, Marx and Engels's Zeitgeist or "spirit of time" philosophical paradigm proposed that leadership is not within the person who becomes the leader, but rather in the situation and the time surrounding the person who becomes the leader. Thus, this approach focused more on the situational

Source: Contingencies, Context, Situation, and Leadership by Roya Ayman and Susan Adams, pp. 218–255. In *The Nature of Leadership,* 2nd ed. by David V. Day and John Antonakis (2012). Copyright © SAGE Publications, Inc. Reprinted with permission.

AUTHORS' NOTE: Please address correspondence concerning this chapter to Roya Ayman, College of Psychology, Illinois Institute of Technology, 3105 South Dearborn, 2nd floor, Chicago, IL 60616, USA. Phone: 312–567–3516. e-mail: ayman@iit.edu.

impact on leadership and leadership effectiveness (Ayman, 1993; Chemers, 1997) and was the backdrop of the contingency approaches to leadership in the 20th century. However, the dominant focus on the person of the leader within the leadership process is prevalent even after the introduction of contingency approaches. This is evident in the influential works of Big Five personality and leadership (Hogan, Curphy, & Hogan, 1994), full range of leadership theory (Antonakis, Avolio, & Sivasubramaniam, 2003), and leader–member exchange (Graen & Uhl-Bien, 1995). Despite this research, the empirical evidence attests that interest in contingencies and context persists (Porter & McLaughlin, 2006).

In this chapter, we first review the theories and models known within the contingency approaches of leadership. Subsequently, we analyze the definitions of contingencies, context, and situation present in leadership research, acknowledging the various variables and methodological approaches. In so doing, we present a conceptualization of these variables at the interpersonal and intrapersonal levels to assist model building regarding contingencies, context, and situation. In addition, methodological issues that facilitate the role of these concepts in understanding leadership will be discussed.

Contingency Models and Theories of Leadership

Historically, the models and theories of leadership developed in the late 1960s through the 1970s demonstrated that leadership effectiveness is a result of the interaction between the characteristics of the leader and the situation (Fiedler, 1978). Some models focused on the leader's internal state and traits, such as the contingency model of leadership effectiveness and the cognitive resource theory (Fiedler, 1978; Fiedler & Garcia, 1987). Others focused on the leader's perceived behaviors, such as the normative decision-making model (Vroom & Jago, 1978; Vroom & Yetton, 1973), path-goal theory (House, 1971; House & Mitchell, 1974), and situational leadership theory (Hersey & Blanchard, 1969). More recently, leadership categorization has been presented as another contingency theory. Its placement in our

scheme of the trait and behavioral contingency approaches to leadership is not as transparent; however, it seems that the focus is on both leader traits (e.g., Offermann, Kennedy, & Wirtz, 1994) and leader behaviors (Lord, Foti, & DeVader, 1984). As we explain later, this approach demonstrates how expectations about leaders vary due to their role or the situation. In the following subsections, we briefly describe each of these models and present a matrix to compare the models and theories based on their approach to assessing the leader, the situation, and leadership effectiveness (see Table 10.1).

Leader Trait Contingency Models

Contingency model of leadership effectiveness. Fiedler (1964) was the first to formulate a trait contingency model of leadership effectiveness, which became known as the contingency model of leadership effectiveness. In this model, Fiedler (1978) predicted leader or group success from the interaction of the leader's orientation with the leader's situation. A leader's orientation is an internal state and is not directly related to observed behaviors (Ayman, 2002). Thus, this orientation is fairly stable and comparable to other personality traits. The model uses the Least Preferred Coworker (LPC) scale (e.g., Ayman & Romano, 1998) to measure a leader's orientation toward the work setting. Most initial studies in this paradigm were experimental. Additionally, participants were chosen to act as leaders based on whether their LPC score was in the top one-third (relationship-oriented) or the bottom one-third (task-oriented). Using extreme categories allowed for an easier assessment of the effect of this trait on its interaction with the situation and the outcome of the group.

Many procedures were used to substantiate the task orientation of those with low LPC scores and the relationship orientation of those with high LPC scores. To clarify these labels further, two studies (Chemers & Ayman, 1985; Rice, Marwick, Chemers, & Bentley, 1982) examined the impact of LPC scores on the relationship between job satisfaction and performance evaluation. They found that when

| Table 10.1 | A Matrix Comparing Contingency Models' Treatment of the Leader, the Situation, and Outcomes | | | | |

	Contingency model of leadership effectiveness	Cognitive resource theory	Normative model of leadership decision-making	Path-goal theory	Situational leadership theory
The Leader					
Source	Leader	Leader	Mostly the leader some from the subordinates	Subordinates	Subordinates
Characteristic	Trait (LPC scale): task and interpersonal orientation	Intelligence and experience	Decision strategies (five styles): autocratic I & II, consultative I & II, and group II	Supervisory behavior: participative, supportive, achievement-oriented, and directive	Supervisory behavior (LEAD): selling, telling, participating, and delegating
The Situation					
Source	The leader and experimenter	The leader	The leader and experimenter	The subordinate	The leader or experimenter
The variables	Leader-member relationship; task structure; position power	Stress with boss; stress with coworkers; stress with task	Availability of information; team support and cohesion; time available (these are simplified representations of 11 conditions)	Subordinates' needs, values and abilities; subordinates task structure and difficulty	Subordinates' willingness and ability (follower maturity index)
Outcomes					
Group	Performance satisfaction (with leader and subordinates)	Actual performance	Performance satisfaction	General satisfaction	General satisfaction
Individuals	Leader's stress			Team member stress	

compared with leaders with high LPC scores, leaders with low LPC scores showed a significantly higher correlation between their satisfaction with work and their performance evaluation. This could be an indication that those with low scores seem to be task-focused individuals and those with high scores on the LPC scale could be considered relationship oriented. Based on these findings, the LPC scale was further substantiated as a measure of the

individual's focus and self-worth based on accomplishment of the task.

The contingency model of leadership effectiveness, based on the leader-match concept, predicts that leaders who are more relationship oriented will be more effective in moderate situational control than will task-focused leaders, whereas leaders who are more focused on task than on interpersonal relationships will be more effective in both high- and low-control situations. When leaders are in the situation where the model predicts their greatest effectiveness, they are considered in-match leaders. When they are in situations where the model predicts they will be less effective, they are referred to as being out-of-match leaders (Ayman, 2002).

Based on this model, Fiedler and Chemers (1984) designed a leadership-training model, which was generally supported in subsequent research (Burke & Day, 1986). Furthermore, three separate meta-analyses (Peters, Hartke, & Pohlman, 1985; Schriesheim, Tepper, & Tetrault, 1994; Strube & Garcia, 1981) found support for the general predictions of the model and called for further development and extension (Ayman, 2002). A detailed review of this model and a discussion of its strengths and weaknesses are presented elsewhere (Ayman, 2002; Ayman, Chemers, & Fiedler, 1998).

The leader's situational control in this model refers to the leader's ability to predict group performance and is based on three aspects of the situation: team climate, leader-task structure, and leader-position power. The situation defines the leader's ability to influence the accomplishment of the group's task. The team's climate, better known as the leader–member relationship, assesses the cohesion of team members and their support of the leader. The task structure includes two aspects of the leader's task: the task-structure dimensions and the leader's background (i.e., the leader's experience and training). The final task-structure score is determined by adjusting the task's structure with the level of the leader's experience and training. Position power reflects the leader's legitimacy, as well as the authority for punishing and rewarding the team members (Ayman, 2002; Fiedler, 1978). The order of importance of the situational aspects is based on their contribution to the leader's sense of control and prediction in a situation. During decades of research, Fiedler (1978) concluded that leader–member relationship is twice as important as task structure. Furthermore, task structure is twice as important as position power (Ayman, Chemers, & Fiedler, 1995, 1998). Subsequently, Ayman (2002) argued that a sense of control in a situation gives a person power. The order of importance of situational control aspects, as proposed by Fiedler, are closely representative of the relative importance associated

with French and Raven's (1959) sources of power (Podsakoff & Schriesheim, 1985).

Finally, the leader-effectiveness criterion in this model has been primarily defined as group performance (Fiedler, 1978). In response to some criticisms that the model predicts only performance, Rice (1981) suggested that the model could also predict team satisfaction, which was subsequently supported empirically (Ayman & Chemers, 1991). In addition, Chemers, Hays, Rhodewalt, and Wysocki (1985) found that if the leaders were out of match, they experienced high levels of stress and reported extreme clinical symptoms of illness.

The model has been validated mostly at the group level of analysis (Ayman et al., 1995, 1998). However, these authors noted that the design of the model allows for it to function at other levels, such as the individual and the dyadic levels of analysis. For example, in Chemers et al. (1985), the analysis was at the level of the individual leader. Results of two other studies, one laboratory (Chemers, Goza, & Plumer, 1978) and one field (Tobey-Garcia, Ayman, & Chemers, 2000), tentatively supported a dyadic level of analysis. These studies showed that in moderate situational-control conditions, relationship-oriented leaders with task-oriented subordinates yield the highest satisfaction and performance. But in these same situations, task-oriented leaders with task-oriented subordinates who have important but conflicting information seemed to do the worst. This could be partially due to the lack of match experienced in this situation by task-oriented leaders, who therefore may be stressed and not open to new ideas. In this situation, if the subordinate negates the task-oriented leader's structure and/or ideas, the leader by nature may feel further threatened and thus will likely reject the information that is vital and, potentially, lose the opportunity to succeed.

Cognitive resource theory. Cognitive resource theory (CRT) is the second contingency model based on leader traits and characteristics (Fiedler & Garcia, 1987) where the leader's effectiveness can be predicted based on the interaction of two individual, internal characteristics—intelligence and experience—with the situation. Intelligence has been one of the most frequently studied characteristics of leaders (Stogdill, 1974). However, the findings regarding its predictive validity have been somewhat inconsistent. Furthermore, although Lord, DeVader, and Alliger (1986) found intelligence to be strongly predictive of perceived leadership, it should be noted that the outcome variable was leadership emergence, not effectiveness.

In CRT, the core proposition states that situational factors will dictate whether leader intelligence or experience predicts leadership effectiveness. Fiedler (2002) incorporated Sternberg's (1995) explanations of (a) intelligence referring to "fluid" intelligence versus (b) experience being akin to "crystallized" intelligence. The first refers to cognitive ability to deal with novelty, and the second refers to automatization of responses reflective of experiences and mastery. The situation in this theory is defined by the leader's level of stress. A leader can experience job stress in various ways, such as role conflict and overload, as well as from various sources, such as coworkers, the task, or the leader's own superior (Fiedler, 1993). Empirical studies testing this theory have used stress with the leader's superior as the situational constraint (see Table 10.1 for a list of stress sources).

Fiedler (1993, 1995) summarized the findings of several studies in both the laboratory (e.g., Murphy, Blyth, & Fiedler, 1992) and the field (Potter & Fiedler, 1981) where, under stressful conditions, the leaders' performances were positively related to their experience and negatively related to their intelligence. In low-stress situations, conversely, a leader's intelligence was positively related to performance, and experience had less of an effect. Fiedler (2002) further concluded: "People can be experienced and bright or experienced and stupid. But the performance of a particular job requires the leader to give priority either to experience or to analytical or creative analysis in solving the particular problem" (p. 102).

A combination of the contingency model of leadership effectiveness with CRT could demonstrate that out-of-match leaders are stressed. These leaders then may need to rely more on their experience than their intelligence in order to perform well. Zaccaro (1995) considered CRT a promising starting point, and encouraged theorists to consider the roles of multiple traits, such as ego resilience and social intelligence.

Recently, in their quantitative review, Judge, Colbert, and Ilies (2004) provided some support for this model.

Leader Behavioral Contingency Approaches

Normative model of leadership decision making. Vroom and Yetton (1973) and later Vroom and Jago (1988) proposed a contingency model of leader decision making. This prescriptive model of leader decision-making processes is narrower in focus than other leadership-contingency approaches (Vroom & Jago, 1998). The model goes by multiple names, such as the participative leadership model, Vroom and Yetton's normative model, and the Vroom-Jago model. Vroom acknowledged that the model is more focused on situations and how leaders respond (Sternberg & Vroom, 2002) than on leader characteristics and how they interact with the situation (e.g., Fiedler's contingency model). Although Vroom and colleagues do not use the term "contingency," they nevertheless propose that a leader's choice of decision style or strategy is guided by the situation.

Overall, the normative model focuses on the interaction between a leader's decision-making strategy choices and the decision situation. Vroom and Jago (1998) identified five leadership strategies for decision making (see Table 10.1). The strategies range from decision making by the leader, to the partial inclusion of the subordinates, to full involvement of the subordinates. The decision heuristics describe the situation based on four criteria: improve the quality of the decision, improve subordinate involvement, reduce the time spent, and develop the subordinates (Vroom & Jago, 1998). These criteria are also the basis for measuring the effectiveness of the decision. The leader is presented with a decision-making tree with yes/no responses reflecting the heuristics. The full representation of this decision-process flowchart is available for review in other sources (e.g., Vroom & Jago, 1998).

If decision quality is critical, the leader has to assess his or her knowledge level, the degree of problem structure, the degree of subordinate's agreeableness, and knowledge pertaining to the decision at hand. For example, group involvement is the advised strategy when subordinates are more knowledgeable on the issue than the leader. When time is of concern, the involvement of the group becomes less practical. In time-pressured situations, therefore, it seems most leaders use more autocratic decision-making strategies. Lastly, if development of subordinate interest, acceptance, and commitment are critical for the decision to be implemented favorably, then greater subordinate involvement is advised. In such situations, the leader may have to pay the cost of increased time and perhaps even sacrifice decision quality to ensure team support and cohesion. The goal of achieving a balance between quality, time, and maintenance of team support will affect whether the leader prioritizes the goal of reaching a high-quality decision over that of high acceptance by the team members, or vice versa.

Based on the normative model, one can assess a leader's decision-style tendencies by having the leader choose an appropriate behavior across 30 different situational conditions. The model is mostly prescriptive: helping a leader learn how to respond in a given situation. In descriptive studies, it appears the situation affects responses to a greater extent more strongly than does the leader's decision style (Vroom & Jago, 1998). As the authors of the model have stated, the situation drives the model more than the leader's characteristics do.

Research has shown that subordinates' involvement is critical in gaining their commitment to feeling ownership of and implementing the decision (Vroom & Jago, 1995). However, if the criterion is quality of the decision or efficiency in the decision-making process, then subordinates' involvement in the decision-making process may not be consistently appropriate, especially when the subordinates do not have the necessary information. Therefore, the styles that will be recommended to the leader will vary according to the criteria chosen for leadership effectiveness.

Some scholars have voiced that a concern about using some of the variations of the model is the extent to which the leader can comply with the prescriptive style (Jago & Vroom, 1980). Leaders with less skill in facilitation may need training in group problem solving and team facilitation. With such training, the leader can judge the appropriate

decision-making strategy and determine the best method of implementing that strategy.

Two reports have supported that participative style was perceived positively for both genders (Heilman, Hornstein, Cage, & Herschlag, 1984; Jago & Vroom, 1983). However, Jago and Vroom (1983) also found that whereas male leaders perceived as autocratic were evaluated as modestly positive, female leaders seen as autocratic were rated negatively. Therefore, there seems to be a potential gender contingency in the relationship between the decision-making styles and outcomes.

Cross-cultural studies testing the model have shown that the cultural values in a social environment also affected the leaders' decision-making strategies. In one study, the findings were compared from before and after the fall of communism in Poland. The data show a trend for more participative practices after market economy reforms (Jago, Maczynski, & Reber, 1996). When the Polish managers were compared with Austrian and U.S. managers in another study, though, the results showed that the Polish managers had a harder time agreeing with the model's prescriptions. As the importance of the problem increased, they used a more autocratic style (Maczynski, Jago, Reber, & Boehnisch, 1994).

The effect of the perceiver's role and the perception of decision-making effectiveness were investigated across several studies (Field & House, 1990; Heilman et al., 1984). The results of these studies demonstrated that the description of the leader's decision-making style and the favorableness of the strategy vary depending on the role of the perceiver (i.e., leader or subordinate). For example, those assuming a leader role are more inclined to favor autocratic styles of decision making (Heilman et al., 1984). Field and House (1990) concluded that the model is supported when data were collected from a leader's perspective but not when collected from the subordinates' perspectives. Therefore, perceiver role appears to be a relevant contingency factor.

The participative leadership model or normative model of leadership decision making has received support. Based on the evidence, the model demonstrates that the level of participative decision making should be gauged based on the situation and the effectiveness criteria used. Additionally, there seem to be other contingencies (e.g., gender, cultural values) that appear to monitor the effectiveness of the leader's choice of decision-making style.

Path-goal theory. Inspired by Evans (1970), who further expanded the work of Georgopoulus, Mahoney, and Jones (1957), House (1971) proposed a path-goal theory of leader effectiveness (see House, 1996). The genesis of this theory was based in the Ohio State leader-behavior approach (Stogdill & Coons, 1957) and the expectancy theory of motivation (Vroom, 1964). In response to Korman (1966), House (1971) and House and Mitchell (1974) developed propositions in an attempt to reconcile inconsistent results from the leader-behavior studies. House (1971) identified directive, achievement-oriented, supportive, and participative leadership behaviors as the theory's independent variables (see Table 10.1). It should be noted that the first two are more task focused (e.g., assigning tasks, scheduling, emphasizing deadlines) and the latter two are more considerate (e.g., making people feel at ease, being open to suggestions, encouraging team members).

According to Evans (1996), the majority of the studies on path-goal theory included measures of instrumental/directive and supportive/considerate leadership styles. Schriesheim and Neider (1996) stated, "The need for such leadership [behavior] is moderated by characteristics of the environment as well as by characteristics of the subordinates" (p. 317). Schriesheim and Neider (1996) cited two meta-analyses that have been conducted to validate path-goal theory (Indvik, 1986; Wofford & Liska, 1993). Wofford and Liska (1993) included 120 studies covering the span of two and a half decades and stated: "The analysis indicated that much of the research testing path-goal theories has been flawed" (p. 857).

The most frequently studied work-environment moderator in this paradigm has been subordinates' task structure (Evans, 1996). Wofford and Liska (1993) did not find support for the moderating effect of task structure on the relationship between leader-initiated structure and subordinate satisfaction, performance, and role clarity. Also, across studies, the moderating effect of task structure on the relationship between considerate leader behavior and subordinates' satisfaction was not supported (Indvik,

1986; Wofford & Liska, 1993). However, subordinate task structure was found to have a positive effect on the relationship between considerate leader behavior and performance. When the task was unstructured, as compared with when the task was structured, a stronger relationship was found between considerate leader behavior and effectiveness.

Few studies have examined the personal characteristics of the subordinates as moderators (e.g., ability, locus of control). Schriesheim and Schriesheim (1980) demonstrated that the subordinates' need for affiliation, their authoritarianism, and their ability and experience moderated the relationship between leader behaviors and outcomes. A study demonstrated that subordinates with an external locus of control were more satisfied with participative than with directive leaders, and they were more productive under these leaders (Algattan, 1985). However, subordinates with an internal locus of control were more productive and happier when the leader's behavior was task oriented. Overall, the results of the Wofford and Liska (1993) meta-analysis demonstrated that ability was the only subordinate characteristic that moderated the relationship between leader behavior and outcomes. Subordinates with low ability, as compared with those with high ability, preferred leaders who engaged in structuring and task-related behaviors.

Various authors have highlighted notable limitations of path-goal theory. One issue seems to be related to the instruments used to measure leader behavior (Fisher & Edwards, 1988; Schriesheim & Von Glinow, 1977). Another is that most studies have examined either task or subordinate characteristics. Furthermore, Stinson and Johnson (1975) as well as Wofford and Liska (1993) recommended testing of a multiple-moderator model. Finally, Wofford and Liska (1993) also expressed concern that the majority of the studies testing the theory suffered from same-source bias (i.e., common-methods variance). To conclude, Evans (1996) stated, "In light of the absence of studies testing the critical motivational hypothesis of the theory, it is hard to argue that the theory has undergone reasonable testing. It has not" (p. 307).

On a positive note, path-goal theory can be seen as an important development in leadership theory that encouraged the evolution of new leadership conceptualizations. It was the basis of the development of theories of charismatic leadership and substitutes for leadership (House, 1996) and potentially an impetus for the development of a vertical dyad linkage model (Dansereau, Graen, & Haga, 1975). Although the empirical support for the model is mixed, it helped drive new thinking about leadership.

Situational leadership theory. Hersey and Blanchard (1969) proposed that the effectiveness of four leadership behaviors—selling, telling, participating, and delegating—depends on whether they complement the subordinates' task-related characteristics (e.g., ability, education, experience) and psychological maturity (e.g., willingness, self-esteem, motivation). Although the theory does have a measure to assess the leader's style—the Leadership Effectiveness and Adaptability Description (LEAD)—many of the empirical studies on this model seem to use the Leader Behavior Description Questionnaire (LBDQ) in measuring the leader's behaviors (e.g., Case, 1987; Vecchio, 1987; Vecchio & Boatwright, 2002).

Based on the major tenets of the theory, the leader should "delegate" (i.e., exhibit low consideration and low-structuring behaviors) in situations where subordinates are able and willing, having both the ability and the motivation to perform effectively. When subordinates are willing and unable, the appropriate leader behavior is to "sell" (i.e., engage in high-consideration and high structuring behaviors). In situations where the subordinates are unwilling but able, the leader should engage in "participative decision-making" (i.e., show high consideration but low-structuring behaviors). When the subordinates are unwilling and unable, the leader needs to "tell" them what to do (i.e., demonstrate low consideration but high-structuring behaviors). Although situational leadership theory has intuitive appeal, it has undergone only limited empirical examination. Unfortunately, most reviews have been very critical of the model and have not found much empirical support for it (e.g., Fernandez & Vecchio, 1997; Graeff, 1997; Vecchio, 1997; Vecchio & Boatwright, 2002; York, 1996).

The leadership contingency models and theories presented in this section have shown that while all are models of leadership effectiveness that acknowledge the role of the situation, they are distinctly different. The path-goal theory and situational leadership theory are different from the normative model of leadership decision making on the basis of the scope of the leader's behavior. In the normative model, the focus is on the leader's decision strategy, whereas in the path-goal and situational leadership theories, the leader's supervisory behaviors are key. The difference between the contingency model of leadership effectiveness and the path-goal theory is based on how the leader is assessed and how the situation is approached, among other factors. In path-goal theory, the perceived leader behavior is the focus, whereas in the contingency model of leadership effectiveness, the leader's traits and internal state are the focus. In the path-goal theory, the situation is assessed according to subordinates' perceptions, but in the contingency model of leadership effectiveness, the situation is described from the leader's point of view. Finally, Evans (1996) differentiated the theories according to how they were derived. He noted that Fiedler's model was empirically driven and that House "was led to the contingency aspects of his theory by both inconsistent empirical findings and theoretical insight" (p. 307).

Implicit leadership theory and leadership categorization. With the introduction of informational processing perspectives on leadership, a new paradigm grounded in implicit leadership theory (ILT) gained momentum (Eden & Leviantan, 1975). Initial research showed that expectations about a leader affect the perceptions of that leader's behavior (Lord & Emrich, 2001; Lord & Maher, 1991). The next phase of this research program focused on the content of expectations about a leader and that content's universality. Fischbein and Lord (2004) acknowledged that when examining factors that affect ILT, we need to consider the particular leadership context (e.g., political, business, military) as well as the perceiver's personal characteristics (e.g., gender, personality traits). Additionally, although some researchers believe that ideal images are the same as typical leader images (Epitropaki & Martin, 2004), others have suggested that people's image of an ideal and a typical leader have major distinctions. For example,

Heilman, Block, Martell, and Simon (1989) found that when different groups of perceivers described their images of (a) the typical woman manager, (b) the typical male manager, and (c) the successful manager, the latter two descriptions shared many of the same characteristics. The image of the typical woman manager, however, did not share characteristics with either the image of the typical male manager or that of the successful manager. The gender difference disappeared, though, when the comparison was between a successful (ideal) woman manager and successful (ideal) man manager.

In cross-cultural studies, two main approaches are recognized (e.g., Ayman & Korabik, 2010): the imposed-etic approach, in which the measures and concepts of one culture are used in another, and the emic approach, in which the measures and concepts are developed from within the culture.

Two studies examining ILT across cultures used the imposed-etic approach (Epitropaki & Martin, 2004; Gerstner & Day, 1994). Gerstner and Day (1994) implemented a measure developed in the United States by Lord et al. (1984), and they examined the mean ratings of people from different cultures (e.g., China, France, Germany, Honduras, India, Japan, Taiwan) on their ideas of a typical leader. Differences were found that were consistent with the cultural values espoused in the various countries' cultures. On the other hand, Epitropaki and Martin (2004), who conducted their study in England, showed an overall similar factor structure to Offermann et al.'s (1994) original study.

In examining the effect of perceivers' characteristics on ILT, the factor analysis studies have shown some agreement on high-level structure of ILT across cultures, age, levels in the organization, and organization type (Den Hartog, House, Hanges, Ruiz-Quintanilla, & Dorfman, 1999; Epitropaki & Martin, 2004; Offermann et al., 1994). In all these studies, the differences across perceivers' categories were at the specifics that defined the factors. For example, Epitropaki and Martin (2004), using Offermann et al.'s (1994) measure, found universal structure for ILT among British participants regardless of age, organizational level, and type. However, they found that women described "their ideal leader

as more understanding, sincere, and honest, and less domineering, pushy, and manipulative than did men" (p. 307). This shows the variance between British men and women on their ideal leader.

The above studies have used an imposed-etic approach when studying ILT across countries. When approaching the topic from an emic cross-cultural approach, we find a different result. Two lines of studies are presented here to make this point. One was a series of studies with children (Ayman-Nolley & Ayman, 2005), across gender and country, who were asked to draw a leader leading. The studies on children's ILT provided the opportunity to understand how early these ideas are formed, opening the way for potential interventions. The other series of studies replicated Offermann et al.'s (1994) methodology in China and Iran (Bassari & Ayman, 2009; W. Ling, Chia, & Fang, 2000).

The studies on children took place across three different countries: China (Liu, Ayman, & Ayman-Nolley, 2009), Costa Rica (Ayman-Nolley, Ayman, & Leone, 2006), and the United States (Leffler, Ayman, & Ayman-Nolley, 2006). The results showed that the majority of children had drawn a male image of the leader, with U.S. girls drawing more women as leaders compared with children in other countries.

Leffler et al. (2006) also showed that although the Caucasian children primarily left the leader's color blank (i.e., White, as the paper was white), the African American children tended to draw images representing shades of Brown and Black. The results for the African American girls favored neither the "similar to me" image of the leader nor the image of the leader as male. This finding needs further investigation to generalize the finding that the gender and the ethnicity of the perceiver can interact in affecting her or his image of a leader.

Also, one of the main roles that Chinese children drew for their leader leading was a manager (Liu et al., 2009), which was not present in the Costa Rican or U.S. drawings. Costa Rican children drew more military leaders as compared with U.S. children (Ayman-Nolley et al., 2006). This is interesting in light of the fact that Costa Rica does not have a military force. One explanation could be that joining mercenaries to fight in various militaries is an occupational choice, which may pay well, and the number of people who wear military fatigues in the streets is very noticeable. These findings depict the impact of culture on the content of ILT of children across countries when they are free to express themselves. Thus, not all children across countries have the same image of a leader.

Regarding adult's ILT, two studies applying a similar methodology to Offermann et al. (1994) found both similar and differing results (Bassari & Ayman, 2009; W. Ling et al., 2000). For example, in China the factors describing the leaders included morality, goal effectiveness, interpersonal competence, and versatility (W. Ling et al., 2000). This last factor was not present in previous studies of ILT and referred to the concept of a "renaissance man" or a person with wide knowledge and skills, well rounded and well read, someone who knows about the arts and sciences and is multilingual.

Bassari and Ayman (2009), with a preliminary factor analysis of data collected in Iran, showed the ILT structure for a leader and boss are somewhat different. The factors describing the leader were confident, goal oriented, considerate, and severe. The factors describing the boss were confident, goal oriented, considerate, and sensitive. Examining the factor loading for the boss showed that "severe," which was an independent factor in describing a leader, loaded on the confidence factor when describing the boss (Bassari & Ayman, 2009). These findings, while they showed some similarity to Offermann et al.'s (1994) ILT content (i.e., sensitivity, dedication, tyranny, charisma, attractiveness, masculinity, intelligence, and strength), also demonstrated differences unique to the various cultures and roles. Therefore, the concept of leadership exists in the eye of the beholder. Thus, the image of the leader is highly affected by the contingencies and situations defined from the perspective of both the leader and the perceiver, each influenced by his or her own characteristics (e.g., gender, ethnicity, culture).

Contingencies, Context, and Situation Defined

In the previous section we presented traditional contingency leadership models and theories, which propose that leadership occurs in context. In most of those models, the operationalization of contingency is similar to Johns's (2006) concept of context. Johns stated that context, which can include constraints and opportunities for behavior, surrounds a phenomenon and is external to the individual. Scholars who have written about leadership contingencies have a similar conceptualization of these contingencies that is focused on context (Antonakis et al., 2003, 2004; Avolio, 2007; Chemers, 2000; Diedorff, Rubin, & Morgeson, 2009; Liden & Antonakis, 2009).

Some researchers have considered the gender of the leader as a contingency variable (Antonakis et al., 2003; Eagly, Johannesen-Schmidt, & van Engen, 2003). The gender of the leader is not an external situation or context, though, so the definition of contingency in this case seems to include a more intrapersonal level. At the intrapersonal level, contingencies could be aspects of the leader (traits or characteristics) that enhance or inhibit each other, as they relate to the behavior and effectiveness of the leader. In this section, we argue that contingencies in leadership can be at interpersonal and intrapersonal levels. Most research has focused on the interpersonal level, but we believe there is a place for future research additionally to consider intrapersonal-level contingencies.

Interpersonal Level

At the interpersonal level, the contingencies for leadership effectiveness have been defined as context assessed mainly through the subordinates' perspectives (e.g., path-goal, situational leadership, substitutes-for-leadership). Research has also assessed context using organizational level and type of industry, as well as subordinates' characteristics (e.g., Antonakis et al., 2003; Lowe, Kroeck, & Sivasubramaniam, 1996) and leader's distance from the followers (e.g., Antonakis & Atwater, 2002). Before we present the various factors that have gained recognition as contextual factors in leadership within the present framework, we will briefly review the substitutes-for-leadership theory. This theory expanded the classic work of the contingency models by developing a more inclusive list of contextual factors of leadership and by providing a framework for the contextual factors that hinder or enhance a leader's impact.

Substitutes-for-leadership theory. Based on Jermier and Kerr's (1997) discussion, a leader's behavior typically accounts for less variance in predicting relevant leadership outcomes than do situational factors (i.e., substitutes for leadership). Kerr and Jermier (1978) proposed a taxonomy of 14 situational contingencies divided into three classes: (a) characteristics of subordinates, (b) the nature of the subordinates' tasks, and (c) organizational characteristics. Podsakoff, Mackenzie, and Bommer (1996) also concluded "on average, the substitutes for leadership uniquely accounted for more of the variance in the criterion variables than did leader behaviors" (p. 380).

The key point to remember in this work is that the contingencies were originally conceived as substitutes for or neutralizers of a leader's behaviors. To further clarify these concepts, Schriesheim (1997) described substitutes as factors that were directly related to the employee's outcomes and that replaced the need for leader behavior. Neutralizers were those factors that inhibit the leader's behavioral influence on the outcome. The distinction between the two factors is based on the relationship the situational factor has with the leader's behavior. In the substitutes-for-leadership condition, the situational factors and the outcome variables are positively related regardless of the leader's behavior. However, neutralizers are correlated with neither the leader's behavior nor the outcome, but they will nullify the effect of the leader's behavior on the outcome.

As Podsakoff and Mackenzie (1997) have argued, research on the substitutes-for-leadership theory supports the notion that leader behavior does not have a universal effect on outcomes. The results of empirical tests of the substitutes-for-leadership theory are mixed. Podsakoff et al. (1996), through a meta-analysis, tested 22 studies and found support for this theory; whereas Dionne, Yammarino, Atwater, and James (2002) did not find similar support for this finding. Dionne et al. (2002) argued that the positive findings for the effects of substitutes for leadership on outcomes may be due to common-source ratings bias. Although the support

for this model has been questioned, it has arguably contributed to a clearer conceptualization of the contingency variables from subordinates' perspectives. This model contributed to the study of moderators and mediators in leadership research.

Context in leadership. Since the 1970s, contextual factors have played a role in leadership research; however, the conceptualization of them has not been well developed. It has been argued (Sternberg & Vroom, 2002) that "We need a taxonomy of the situation, or at least dimensions on which the situations vary. Fiedler is one of the few psychologists to offer a language for describing both context and individual difference" (p. 317). Fiedler (1978) presented a taxonomy (Ayman, 2002; Sternberg & Vroom, 2002) focusing on the leader's situation. Through the level of clarity in the situation, a leader gains control and power in a small-group context. In path-goal and subsequently substitutes-for-leadership theories, the focus is on the subordinates' situation.

The early contingency theories focused primarily on leadership in the work group or in a small-group paradigm. Substitutes-for-leadership theory considered leadership in the context of a dynamic organizational and cultural milieu. Most authors seem to agree with the three main categories of context: characteristics of the subordinates, the nature of the subordinates' tasks, and organizational characteristics. This description focused more on the space surrounding the leadership process. However, in this space, most of the research primarily focused on face-to-face contact. With the evolution of information technology and virtual teams, the concept of space has expanded to include "leader distance." This concept includes both psychological and physical distance between the leader and his or her subordinates (Antonakis & Atwater, 2002).

Porter and McLaughlin (2006) argued that not only has the concept of space been expanded, but the concept of time and its impact on leadership has gained attention in leadership research. The theories that made reference to the concept of time include transactional leadership, transformational leadership, and leader–member exchange. Yet, the role of time in leadership needs further research support, both through cross-sectional studies and, more critically, through research examining development over time using longitudinal methods.

More recently, Ayman (2004) argued that culture and leadership have a symbiotic relationship, in which one cannot exist without the other; thus, leadership is culture bound. In this line of research, culture refers to both company and societal levels, incorporating values, policies, and norms (Liden & Antonakis, 2009). Some authors have further examined the concept of relationship and the social context of leadership. Historically, Fiedler (1978) was the first to highlight this concept through his group atmosphere or leader–member relationship construct. More recently, Liden and Antonakis (2009) expanded this notion to include social networks and demonstrated the role of the larger societal culture on the dynamics of group relationships. This opens the door for more research on the interaction among different contextual factors.

In the remainder of this section, we use a systems approach to groups—namely the input-process-output (I-P-O) model (Hackman & Morris, 1975)—as a heuristic for conceptualizing the contextual factors. We chose the model of team effectiveness proposed by West, Borrill, and Unsworth (1998) as a guide for this section, in part because they hold a dynamic process perspective, which allows for reciprocal effects between inputs and processes and between processes and outputs. For the purpose of our discussion, leadership process is the focus of interest. An additional reason we used the model by West and colleagues (1998) is their pronounced effort to incorporate the organizational context within the I-P-O framework of team effectiveness. As part of the inputs to the group, their definition of organization context includes reward structure, available support for the team in the form of feedback and training opportunities, location of group members, medium of communication, and time allotted to get the job done. This model also recognizes that output or outcomes can be either attitudinal (e.g., satisfaction, stress) or behavioral (e.g., turnover, performance, organizational citizenship), and can occur at leader, individual subordinate, or group levels. From a leadership perspective, both the input variables and outcomes have an important impact on the leader's characteristics and choice of action to achieve success. Each of the four input factors (cultural context, organizational context, group composition, and task features) within the West et al. (1998) team effectiveness model may be considered as moderators, and thereby, they establish the contingencies between leadership and organizational outcomes. We used this model of team effectiveness to stimulate consideration of a wide variety of interpersonal-level context variables for the study and model development of leadership and context. To further demonstrate the impact of these four input factors on leadership, the following section will highlight empirical examples for the role of organizational climate, group composition, and the nature of the task on leadership traits and behaviors.

Cultural context. Ayman and Korabik (2010) acknowledge the wide diversity of definitions provided for culture. However, for the operationalization of culture in leadership research, they identify two different categories: first, visible indices of culture as reflected by such differences between groups as country boundaries; and, second, invisible indices of culture as reflected by the values and norms that a social group has agreed on over time.

Scholars have argued that culture has more impact on individual behavior if it is strong (Mischel, 1977) or if it is tight (Pelto, 1968). Mischel (1977) stated that strong settings—such as in military organizations—where the latitude for self-expression is limited, as compared with weak settings—such as civilian organizations—have norms and demands that can control the individual's behavior. Similarly, Pelto (1968) defined cultures as being tight or loose. The more explicit the cultural norms, the tighter the culture and the less chance there is for the expression of individual differences in responses and behaviors.

Hall and Hall (1990) further explained that culture impacts communication. In some cultures, communication can either be high- or low-context. For example, in high-context cultures—such as Japan or the Middle East—where people interact with a very close social network, there is less need to provide detailed information when they interact. Thus, individuals rely on the common knowledge of the context they share. In contrast, in low-context cultures—such as Germany, Scandinavia, or the United States—individuals tend to compartmentalize their social interactions between work and personal life and thus have a greater need to explain background information when communicating. Such norms of conduct can have an impact on a leader's communication habits or expected style of social exchange with her or his team-members.

Such projects as the GLOBE studies have provided further evidence and popularity as to the impact of culture on leadership (House, Hanges, Javidan, Dorfman, & Gupta, 2004) by demonstrating similarities and differences across country boundaries and global regions on the manifestation of various leader behaviors. Additional scholars have recognized the impact of culture in understanding leadership through social cognition (Ayman, 1993; Chemers, 2000; Hanges, Lord, & Dickson, 2000).

Avolio (2007), Ayman (2004), and Chemers (2000) have offered ideas on how to integrate culture in theories and models of leadership. Three potential roles can be examined for culture in leadership: It can be considered (a) as an antecedent to leadership behavior, where leaders from different cultures may be perceived as acting differently; (b) as a moderating effect of culture on the relationship between leadership (trait or behavior) and outcomes, such as employee engagement or performance; and (c) in terms of the impact that the cultural diversity of the team and leader has on their relationship and effectiveness. In their review, Ayman and Korabik (2010) demonstrated how culture has been neglected in leadership research and theory development. They showed that most of our leadership models have not fully integrated culture in their design and conceptualization, though they have shown some validation across cultures. The complexity of the role of culture in leadership at multiple levels was further discussed in their article. Their final conclusion argues for a symbiotic relationship between leadership and culture, in which theories of leadership are evolving into a more inclusive cultural image of leadership.

Thus, it appears that the situation as a context plays an important role. For example, it is possible that in some cultures, leaders do not have the flexibility to express their personal values and beliefs because situational demands dictate their behavior. Cultural context provides restrictive norms that may not allow for a full representation of an individual leader's behavioral choices. The significance of this is that leadership needs to be considered within a cultural context because the context influences how individual leaders can behave (Rousseau & Fried, 2001).

Organizational context. Organizational context surrounds the work team and its leader. Organizational climate is reflective of organizational context, which includes normative social interactions and policies and procedures. Organizational climate can be defined objectively, such as a tall and flat hierarchy of the organization, as well as through its size. It can also be defined subjectively through shared beliefs and norms of interactions (Dennison, 1996).

The impact of organizational norms on leadership has been established across a number of studies. For example, Shartle (1951) illustrated the importance of workplace norms on how leaders behave in demonstrating that the best predictor of a leader's behavior in organizations is the behavior of his or her boss, not the leader's personality. Lowe et al. (1996) showed no effect associated with a leader's position in the hierarchy on their respective leadership styles or effectiveness. On the other hand, Lowe et al. did find that transformational leader behavior is more effective in public-sector organizations than in the private sector. This shows that although level in the organization did not affect the leader's behaviors, type of organization did.

Within the West et al. (1998) team effectiveness model, organizational context variables included, among others, physical conditions and affective reactions both to work groups and to the organization as a whole. In leadership research, though, only a few of these variables have been considered as moderators. To elaborate on the effect of space and physical conditions, earlier research on communication patterns (Leavitt, 1951) and seating arrangements (Howells & Becker, 1962) showed that these situational factors influenced leader identification and emergence. The main rationale behind such findings may be that greater eye contact gives more control and that, thereby, they are more likely to be identified as the leaders (Chemers, 1997; Shaw, 1981).

Contemporary leaders may not always engage in face-to-face interaction if work is conducted via computer-mediated environments. Along with the expansion of the virtual workplace, e-leadership has gained greater attention (Antonakis & Atwater, 2002; Avolio, Kahai, & Dodge, 2000). More recently, therefore, researchers are viewing the medium of communication as an organizational contextual factor relevant to e-leadership. Some research has shown there to be no major differences between face-to-face and computer-mediated conditions in terms of leadership emergence (e.g., Adams, Ayman, & Roch, 2010). Overall, where differences arise, they are in regard to leadership perceptions. For example, Puranova and Bono (2009) demonstrated that although transformational leaders were valuable in both face-to-face and computer-mediated conditions, the impact was stronger in virtual teams. Furthermore, Hoyt and Blascovich (2003) demonstrated that face-to-face conditions increased team members' satisfaction with a leader who was either transformational or transactional. More research is needed to better understand the impact of distance and modes of interaction on leadership and outcomes.

Group composition. The input variable of group composition (West et al., 1998) covers research that examines both the size of the work group and the effects of the heterogeneity of group membership on competitive group advantage. In today's diverse workforce, studies examining the role of group composition on leadership are of great value. Group composition can be examined at a group level or a dyadic level.

A small number of studies showed the effect of group size and composition on the relationship between leadership and outcomes. For example, to demonstrate the effect of organization or work group size on leadership and outcomes, Y. Ling, Simsek, Lubatkin, and Veiga (2008) found that the impact of transformational leadership on the

objective performance of the organization was higher in smaller organizations than in larger ones. On the other hand, the cultural and gender composition of the group could affect group atmosphere and moderate the impact of a leader.

The following findings are examples across various leadership models on the role of group interaction and leadership effectiveness. At the group level, Fiedler (1978) reported poorer leader–member relationships, or group atmosphere, when the leader and group members were from different cultures, which impedes leader effectiveness. Similarly, Bass, Avolio, Jung, and Berson (2003) demonstrated that platoon potency and cohesion partially mediated the relationship between the leadership style of the superior officers and simulated platoon performance. To the extent that leader–member relationship and group cohesion may be related to group composition, these findings can be examples of how a group's social interaction may affect the relationship between the leader's behavior and group performance. At this point, there are not that many studies that have examined group composition as a context to leadership. However, Jung and Avolio (1999) demonstrated that transformational leaders were more effective in collectivist cultures and transactional leaders were more effective in individualistic cultures. Thus, the group's diversity and tension may affect how a particular leadership style relates to a given outcome.

At a dyadic level, Ayman, Korabik, and Morris (2009) demonstrated that dyad gender composition moderated the relationship between leaders' transformational leadership and their leadership performance. Male subordinates devalued female transformational leaders as compared with male transformational leaders. Ayman, Rinchiuso, and Korabik (2004) also found that men with female subordinates who had moderate leader–member exchange (LMX) relationships had the least satisfied subordinates. These findings show that the gender dyad of leaders and followers moderates the effect of the leadership behavior and outcomes. Additionally, Polyashuk, Ayman, and Roberts (2008) found that leader-subordinate dyads with ethnic similarities or differences showed different levels of LMX. Other than the African American dyads, where quality of relationship continued to strengthen, those who were in a relationship more than five years described a lower quality of LMX. These examples show how the composition of dyads or groups can significantly affect leadership and its relationship to outcomes.

Nature of the task. The nature of the group task holds implications for the process and outcome of the work completed. The nature of a task may be assessed in many ways (for more information on task typologies, refer to Hackman, 1968, and McGrath, 1984). For example, tasks may vary in type, difficulty, degree of dependence on communication for task completion (Hollingshead & McGrath, 1995), or even gender orientation (Wentworth & Anderson, 1984).

The nature of the task alone can influence leadership. As an example, the gender orientation of a task—i.e., whether it is feminine or masculine—has been found to influence whether a man or a woman emerged as a leader (e.g., Wentworth & Anderson, 1984), and some support (e.g., Gershenoff & Foti, 2003) has been found for the effect of the role of gender and intelligence on leader emergence being moderated by the nature of the task (e.g., initiating-structure task, consensus-building task). In their meta-analysis, Eagly and Karau (1991) found men tended to emerge as overall or task leaders and women were more likely to emerge as social leaders. However, the nature of the task and the length of time for leadership affected the role of leadership emergence in mixed-gender small groups. That is, when tasks required greater social interaction or allowed for longer time periods to identify the emergent leader, the tendency for males to emerge as leaders was reduced (Eagly & Karau, 1991). Lastly, Eagly, Karau, and Makhijani (1995) demonstrated across studies that female leaders in masculine-task conditions were devalued. More specifically, Becker, Ayman, and Korabik (2002) found that female leaders who worked in educational organizations had more agreement with their subordinates on their leadership behaviors than did female leaders in business organizations. The task environment did not have as much impact for male leaders. Thus, gender

congruency of the task affects the leader and how the leader can function and be effective.

The complexity of the task and its effect on leadership were examined in various contingency models from the leaders' and the subordinates' perspectives (e.g., contingency model of leadership effectiveness, path-goal theory). In addition, the complexity and certainty of the organization's task environment as perceived by top management moderated the impact of the charismatic leadership of CEOs on financial outcomes of (Waldman, Ramirez, House, & Puranam, 2001). Thus, we can see that regardless of how we define leadership, the nature of the goal at hand or the task can affect the success of that leader.

Organization and group outcomes. As previously mentioned at the start of this interpersonal subsection, the West et al. (1998) model of team effectiveness recognizes that outcomes can be either attitudinal (e.g., satisfaction) or behavioral (e.g., turnover), and can occur at leader, individual subordinate, or group levels. The importance of the relationship between the leadership and outcome may also be affected by the organizational outcome under investigation. As Table 10.1 shows, some of the contingency models use more subjective measures of outcomes, such as satisfaction, commitment, and stress (e.g., path-goal theory, normative model, contingency model of leadership effectiveness); others have used more objective measures, like meeting goals, hitting the target (e.g., contingency model of leadership effectiveness). Thus, the actual definition of the outcome may be considered a contingency for the leadership and effectiveness relationship.

Overall the team effectiveness model provides a theoretical group perspective to the potential substitutes or enhancers for leadership, in addition to stimulating researchers to consider other contingencies, such as cultural context. Additionally, researchers need to focus on the contextual factors that are most relevant today, such as the medium of communication, the effects of leadership behavior across hierarchical levels (e.g., Kane & Tremble, 2000), and the effects of distal (indirect) and proximal (direct) leadership (e.g., Avolio, Zhu, Koh, & Puja, 2004).

Intrapersonal Level

At the intrapersonal level, relevant contingencies include different leader characteristics that may affect each other and thereby influence the person's ability to lead. For example, in reviewing individual differences, we can consider sociodemographic and psychosocial characteristics. For a more detailed discussion on various traits and personal characteristics of the leader, please refer to Chapter 6 by Timothy Judge and David Long. However, as an example, we argue that a leader's gender and self-monitoring level are two characteristics that may act as contingencies within the leadership process.

Gender is a complex phenomenon. Korabik and Ayman (2007) showed how sociodemographic gender and sex role have demonstrated different effects on leadership processes. For example, Eagly and Carli (2007) provided evidence challenging the results of the Big Five for female and male leaders and their effectiveness. Ayman and Korabik (2010) presented an intrapersonal model of leadership, and they provided evidence of how gender and culture affect leadership behavior and can moderate the relationship of some traits with leadership behaviors or of some traits and behaviors with outcomes. Although men and women may not differ on various leadership styles, feminine and masculine individuals of both genders do differ in their leadership behaviors and effectiveness.

From a multitrait perspective, Zaccaro (2007) demonstrated that different aspects of a person's personality and competency might have reciprocal influence in shaping the resultant effectiveness of a leader. His proposed model has provided an enhancement to a traditional linear bivariate approach. Zaccaro's (2007) model addresses the role of such mediators as proximal skills and behavior but does not include moderators.

A trait that may play a moderating role in the intrapersonal characteristics of a leader is self-monitoring. Gangestad and Snyder (2000) have suggested, based on a deep program of research, that higher scores on an 18-item self-monitoring scale reflect a greater alignment of a person's attitude and behavior. This can have implications on the relationship between traits, leader behavior, and performance. Ayman and Chemers (1991) explored this concept by studying the moderating impact of self-monitoring on leader match and effectiveness. They demonstrated that leaders who were low self-monitors and in match did perform better than the high self-monitors who were in match. However, high self-monitor leaders compensated when they were out of match. For example, a high self-monitor and task-oriented leader with moderate situational control performed better than the low self-monitor leader. That is, the task-oriented leader who is a high self-monitor, when out of match, will be more attentive to situational cues and manage his or her responses so as to be more appropriate. More research exploring the role of self-monitoring in moderating the effect of personality and leader behavior would be informative.

Methodological Issues Within Contingency Research

Uncovering the patterns of relationship between leader characteristics, outcomes, and contingencies is challenging. Various complex designs and methods are needed to test for such relationships. Within this section, we caution researchers and consumers of such research on the potential impact of several issues, such as research design, data source, and levels of analysis.

Research Design

With regard to research design, we encourage researchers to seek opportunities for longitudinal research. The majority of research on leadership is cross-sectional in that the information about the leader, context, and outcomes are collected at the same time and often from the same source. Longitudinal designs and experimental studies allow for stronger causal inferences to be drawn but, unfortunately, are relatively uncommon in the leadership literature. Time has an enormous potential impact on leadership processes, yet the timing of effects in terms of when things occur remains theoretically underspecified (Mitchell & James, 2001).

We consider time to include both the timing of when a leadership outcome is measured in relation to other variables and the length of the relationship between leader and follower. Next, the focus will be on the explanation of time as a critical contingency.

The timing of outcome measurement refers to the amount of time between the measurement of the leaders' trait and/or behavior and the measurement of the relevant leadership outcome. Such consideration can provide predictive validity of the relationship between leaders' characteristics and contingencies. The question then becomes: What is the appropriate time lag? This was evidenced by the work of Schneider and Hough (1995), who argued that when the task is simple, a short time is sufficient to yield the related outcome. However, if the task is complicated, then criterion measures may not be immediately predictable. Being a relational phenomenon, the impact of leadership may require extensive time before it is manifested in certain outcomes. For example, Waldman et al. (2001) argued that they needed to examine net profit margin across five years in order to establish the relationship between charismatic leadership, environmental uncertainty, and financial outcome of the organization. Day and Lord (1988) demonstrated that the relationship between CEO leadership as measured through succession and organizational performance was considerably stronger when a two-year time lag was considered as compared with no time lag.

As previously mentioned, though the number of leadership studies examining length of time or tenure in the leadership position is relatively small, some studies in the LMX paradigm have argued that the leadership relationship can only mature over time (Graen & Uhl-Bien, 1995). However, in a recent study on African American and Caucasian leaders and followers, Polyashuk et al. (2008) found that only African American leader–subordinate dyads showed an increase in trust and LMX beyond five years. Other ethnic combination dyads showed an increase in trust between the leader and follower until five years, beyond which the relationship quality decreased. From this data, the reason for this discrepancy is not clear at this point. Still, there are two important points: (a) the length of time and dyad composition may interact in moderating the effect of a leader's trustworthiness and (b) it is an oversimplification to assume that the longer a leader and subordinates are together, the more mature their relationship is. The impact of time on leadership clearly needs further investigation.

Data Source

Yukl and Van Fleet (1992) identified single-source bias as an endemic issue in leadership research. That is, information gathered about the leader, context, and outcome should not be collected from the same source (e.g., the subordinate), as this leads to artificial inflation of estimated relationships. Source of data seems to play a role in the relationship between trait and behavior or between behavior and outcome. Examples of the impact of this issue can be seen throughout leadership research. As mentioned, Field and House (1990) examined Vroom and Jago's model and found that the self-descriptions of the leader's decision strategy and the subordinates' description of the leader's decision strategy yielded differing results. This is a challenge facing all efforts in leadership research when the investigator is using survey methods as the sole tool for data collection. Thus, a more careful design of studies on leadership is warranted.

Levels of Analysis

Appropriate multilevel analysis is needed when leadership researchers include multilevel variables, such as organizational context (e.g., Porter & McLaughlin, 2006), in their research. The researchers must decide whether they are examining leadership at the individual, the dyadic, or the group level. This will affect the design of the study and the data collection strategy. Klein and Kozlowski (2000), expanding on this analytical approach, edited an influential volume that helps researchers both conceptualize and analyze multilevel data appropriately. Researchers pursuing a focus on context, situation, or contingencies need to be familiar with multilevel design and analyses issues to better examine the complexity of these relationships (Kozlowski & Klein, 2000; see also Rousseau, 2000).

Yammarino and Dansereau (2009) addressed multilevel issues pertaining to leadership and organizational behavior. There is evidence that leadership models function at multiple levels (Dansereau & Yammarino, 1998a; 1998b). They provided evidence in support of the presence and importance that levels of analysis hold in all approaches to leadership. The question remains: Is leadership best conceptualized as a group, dyad, or individual phenomenon? For example, Mumford, Dansereau, and Yammarino (2000) discussed how individualized consideration in leadership could be studied across levels. In the context of examining CEO leadership, Waldman and Yammarino (1999) argued that the inclusion of contingencies of organizational level and subordinates' perceptions call for cross-level analyses and model building. Similarly, Schyns and Van Veldhoven (2010) demonstrated that both level and strength of leadership climate affected employees' individual climate perceptions. After controlling for individual-level climate for leadership, the variability and level of leadership climate had an impact on employees' commitment. Their study showed that supportive leadership is not only dyadic but may be affected by the leaders' resources and the culture in which they are working.

In examining contingencies and context, levels of analysis become more important when a study examines the role of organizational climate on the relationship between leadership and outcomes, with each variable potentially occurring at differing levels of analysis. To examine such relationships, it is critical either to consider cross-level analysis or to align the analysis at one level. In leadership research, the relationship and nature of variables do not function at the same level. Recent promising methodological directions taken by researchers include cross-level moderation (e.g., Chen & Bliese, 2002; Chen, Kirkman, Kanfer, Allen, & Rosen, 2007) and moderated mediation models. For example, Chen et al. (2007) studied multilevel empowerment and found that leadership climate, as measured at the team level, positively moderated the relationship between LMX and individual empowerment. In addition, the use of moderated mediation techniques is becoming more accessible (e.g., Edwards & Lambert, 2007; Preacher, Rucker, & Hayes, 2007). As scholars unravel the complexity of leadership, methodologies are needed to test these assumptions and theories.

Summary and Conclusion

To address the contingency and contextual approach to leadership, this chapter has two main sections. The first part consists of a review of classical contingency models. The second part offers a conceptualization of the type of variables used to test contingencies in leadership research, as well as methodological issues related to this approach. In our review of classic contingency theories of leadership, we classified the theories into two types:

(a) those based on the relationship between the leader's traits and the outcomes (i.e., contingency model of leadership effectiveness and cognitive resource theory) and (b) those that related the leader's behavior to the outcome (i.e., the normative decision-making model, situational leadership theory, and path-goal theory).

In most of the earlier research, the contingencies were generally conceptualized in terms of aspects of the situation that is the context for the leadership process. In this chapter, we recommended considering two different type of contingencies: intrapersonal (interaction of various aspects of the leader's traits and values) and interpersonal (interaction at dyad or group level within a social context). For intrapersonal contingencies, we proposed such concepts as leaders' gender, self-monitoring, and cultural values. For the interpersonal category of contingencies, we recommended considering the West et al. (1998) model of team effectiveness, advocating the consideration of group inputs and group outcomes as potential contextual factors.

In addition, we proposed that contingencies can also be discussed from a methodological perspective. The study's design as it relates to the role of time, source, and method of data collection was emphasized. Furthermore, we offered the analytical models that test patterns of relationship between contingencies and leadership through the use of such models as level of analysis, moderation, and mediation tests. Thus, we demonstrated the evolution of and maturity in understanding the role of contingencies in leadership. The various theoretical approaches reviewed and the new methodologies attest to the omnipresent complexity in leadership and its relationship with contingencies.

The key issue to consider when thinking of contingency approaches to leadership is to remember that this approach is based strongly in a person–situation fit concept. The models in this approach have demonstrated that effective leaders respond to the situation in multiple ways: by changing their behaviors, by being perceived as behaving differently, or by choosing and managing their situation. This position is similar to Sternberg's (1988) definition of intelligent functioning, which refers to the individual's "purposive adaptation to, selection of and shaping of real-world environment relevant to one's life and abilities" (p. 65).

Finding an optimal match is what Chemers (1997) referred to as mettle. As noted by Chemers, "Mettle captures the sense of a confident and optimistic leader whose perceptions, thoughts and mood provide a reservoir of enthusiasm and energy for meeting the challenges presented by the leadership task" (p. 166). This state is somewhat similar to Csikszentmihalyi's (1990) concept of "flow," referring to when an individual's skill and knowledge is neither more nor less than the situational needs. In this state, leaders manifest the height of their potential, expressing optimism and feeling efficacious (Chemers, 2002). Fiedler (1978) referred to this state as a leader being in-match. When the situation is congenial to the leader's characteristics, the leader functions optimally and with ease.

At first glance, some may perceive a contradiction in the concept of leaders being stable and consistent as well as being flexible to meet situational needs. In essence, however, there is no difference between the two. In either case, the leader's persona does not change. For example, a high self-monitoring leader does not become a low self-monitor; nor does a high LPC leader become a low LPC leader. Instead, leaders engage in behaviors and strategies that bring them closer to being in match with the situation and experience flow or mettle.

So for example, a low LPC leader in a moderate control situation (out of match) may realize that she or he needs to include other team members in the decision-making process, as recommended by Vroom's decision-making tree. The leader may then use a nominal group technique to have a structured method of managing the situation. The other alternative is to use a consultative style, rather than a group decision-making strategy, so as to still maintain some of the control over the outcome, which is demanded by the leader's personality trait. Thus, a simple matter of accepting drop-ins versus meeting only by appointment may seem a small issue, but it may have implications in the situational match of a leader. Therefore, when we talk about flexibility, it is in reference to behaviors that manage the situation, not to changing one's trait and personality.

In many of the previous works, the ability to adjust and be flexible is recognized as an important competency for a leader (e.g., Lord et al., 1986). This competency is also present in social/emotional intelligence (Van Rooy & Viswesvaran, 2004) and cultural intelligence (Triandis, 2006). Flexibility can be considered an intraperson contingency. Leaders facing a diverse workforce frequently find themselves in situations and contexts that need to be managed by adjusting their behaviors.

Future Research

With such strong and consistent evidence that situation, context, and contingencies matter in understanding and studying leadership, is there a place for direct impact of a leader's traits and behavior on organizational and personal outcomes related to leaders and followers? In the future, scholars may consider this issue when exploring new paradigms of leadership behaviors, such as authenticity or servant leadership. The trait researcher may want to consider the situational factors when examining the relationship between traits and outcomes to enhance the meaning of these findings.

Implication for Practitioners

Practitioners use leadership knowledge either for training and development or for evaluation processes in selection and in performance review. To consider the situation, job analysis prior to identification of competencies and abilities may clarify the nature of the job and the scope of the position, which are the contingencies. Thus, this procedure may allow for a more accurate prioritization of competencies, skills, and abilities (Dierdorff, Rubin, & Morgeson, 2009). Practitioners assessing leaders' performance may need to be mindful of other contingencies, such as gender or ethnicity. Results of some studies demonstrated that competencies considered for the manager's performance vary based on the gender of the leader (Frame, Roberto, Schwab, & Harris, 2010; Ostroff, Atwater, & Feinberg, 2004). The case offered at the end of this chapter offers the reader an opportunity to explore the practical implications of the approach on the daily life of leaders and practitioners in the workplace.

Overall, the contingency approach to leadership has alluded to the fact that leaders consciously or unconsciously try to reach their optimal level of performance by being aware of their situation and responding accordingly. Therefore, such leadership training programs as leader match (Fiedler & Chemers, 1984) and situational leadership (Hersey and Blanchard, 1982) facilitate leaders to become more sensitive, responsive, and flexible. Additionally, the practice of 360-degree feedback, as a means to develop leaders, gives leaders a chance to see themselves through the eyes of others (i.e., in an interpersonal context). Training outcomes can be attained either by the behavior adjustment of the leader, as described by the subordinates, or through the leader's description of how he or she managed the situation.

To conclude, contingencies, context, and the situation are important factors to consider when we train and select leaders. In our leadership theories, we need to integrate and conceptualize these factors more effectively. A combination of skills and competencies—such as sensitivity, responsiveness, and flexibility—may help a leader reach mettle (Chemers, 2002). These competencies can be manifested in various ways through particular traits, skills, or behaviors depending on the person, the method of assessment, and the leadership situation. Therefore, contingencies in leadership cannot be ignored, as they are inevitably connected to fully understanding leadership processes.

Discussion Questions

1. Knowing the role of contingencies and context, what should be considered when selecting leaders? Use both trait and behavioral approaches in your discussion.

2. How should leadership studies be designed so as to be attentive to contingencies? What are the options and strategies?

3. Consider a leader of your choice. Describe how her or his personality and behaviors in various situations could lead to success or failure.

Supplementary Readings

Hannah, S. T., Uhl-Bien, M., Avolio, B. J., & Cavarretta, F. L. (2009). A framework for examining leadership in extreme contexts. The Leadership Quarterly, 20, 897–919.

James, E. H., & Wooten, L. P. (2005). Leadership as (un) usual: How to display competence in times of crisis. Organizational Dynamics, 34, 141–152.

Kaplan, R. E., & Kaiser, R. B. (2003). Developing versatile leadership. MIT Sloan Management Review, 44(4), 19–26.

Sally, D. (2002). Co-leadership: Lessons from republican Rome. California Management Review, 42(4), 84–99.

Snowden, D., & Boone, M. (2007). A leader's framework for decision making. Harvard Business Review, 85(11), 68–76.

Case Study

Sims, H. P., Jr., Faraj, S., & Seokhwa, Y. (2009, March 15). When should a leader be directive or empowering? How to develop your own situational theory of leadership. Harvard Business Review. Available from http://

www1.hbr.org/product/when-should-a-leader-be-directive-or-empowering-ho/an/BH318-PDF-ENG?N=516191%204294934782&Ntt=leadership

References

Adams, S., Ayman, R., & Roch, S. (2010, August). Communication frequency and content on leader emergence: Does communication medium matter? Paper presented at the annual Academy of Management Conference, Montreal, Canada.

Algattan, A. R. A. (1985, August). Test of the path-goal theory of leadership in the multinational domain. Paper presented at the annual Academy of Management Conference, San Diego, CA.

Antonakis, J., & Atwater, L. (2002). Leader distance: A review and a proposed theory. *The Leadership Quarterly, 13,* 673–704.

Antonakis, J., Avolio, B. J., & Sivasubramaniam, N. (2003). Context and leadership: An examination of the nine-factor full range leadership theory using the Multifactor Leadership Questionnaire. *The Leadership Quarterly, 14,* 261–295.

Antonakis, J., Schriesheim, C. A., Donovan, J. A., Gopalakrishna-Pillai, K., Pellegrini, E. K., & Rossomme, J. L. (2004). Methods for studying leadership. In J. Antonakis, A. T. Cianciolo, & R. S. Sternberg (Eds.), *The nature of leadership* (pp. 48–70). Thousand Oaks, CA: Sage.

Avolio, B. J. (2007). Promoting more integrative strategies for leadership theory building. *American Psychologist, 62,* 25–33.

Avolio, B. J., Kahai, S., & Dodge, G. E. (2000). E-leadership: Implications for theory, research, and practice. *The Leadership Quarterly, 11,* 615–668.

Avolio, B. J., Zhu, W., Koh, W., & Puja, B. (2004). Transformational leadership and organizational commitment: Mediating role of psychological empowerment and moderating role of structural distance. *Journal of Organizational Behavior, 25,* 951–968.

Ayman, R. (1993). Leadership perception: The role of gender and culture. In M. M. Chemers and R. Ayman (Eds.), *Leadership theory and research: Perspectives and directions* (pp. 137–166). New York: Academic Press.

Ayman, R. (2002). Contingency model of leadership effectiveness. In L. L. Neider & C. A. Schriesheim (Eds.), *Leadership* (pp. 197–228). Greenwich, CT: Information Age.

Ayman, R. (2004). Culture and leadership. In C. Spielberger (Ed.), *Encyclopedia of applied psychology* (Vol. 2, pp. 507–519). San Diego, CA: Elsevier.

Ayman, R., & Chemers, M. M. (1991). The effects of leadership match on subordinate satisfaction in Mexican organizations: Some moderating influences of self-monitoring. *Applied Psychology: An International Review, 44,* 299–314.

Ayman, R., Chemers, M. M., & Fiedler, F. (1995). The contingency model of leadership effectiveness and its levels of analysis. *The Leadership Quarterly, 6,* 147–168.

Ayman, R., Chemers, M. M., & Fiedler, F. (1998). The contingency model of leadership effectiveness and its levels of analysis. In F. Yammarino and F. Dansereau (Eds.), *Leadership: The multi-level approaches* (pp. 73–96). New York: JAI Press.

Ayman R., & Korabik, K. (2010). Leadership: Why gender and culture matter. *American Psychologist, 65,* 157–170.

Ayman, R., Korabik, K., & Morris, S. (2009). Is transformational leadership always perceived as effective? Male subordinates' devaluation of female transformational leaders. *Journal of Applied Social Psychology, 39,* 852–879.

Ayman, R., Rinchiuso, M., & Korabik, K. (2004, August). Organizational commitment and job satisfaction in relation to LMX and dyad gender composition. Paper presented at the International Congress of Psychology, Beijing, China.

Ayman, R., & Romano, R. (1998). Measures and assessments for the contingency model of leadership. In F. Yammarino and F. Dansereau (Eds.), *Leadership: The multi-level approaches* (pp. 97–114). New York: JAI Press.

Ayman-Nolley, S., & Ayman, R. (2005). Children's implicit theory of leadership. In J. R. Meindl and B. Schyns (Eds.), *Implicit leadership theories: Essays and explorations, A volume in the leadership horizons series* (pp. 189–233). Greenwich, CT: Information Age.

Ayman-Nolley, S., Ayman, R., & Leone, C. (2006, July). Gender differences in the children's implicit leadership theory: Costa Rican and American comparison. In R. Littrell (Convener), Empirical studies: Qualitative and quantitative analyses of leadership and culture. Symposium conducted at the International Congress of Cross-Cultural Psychology, Isle of Spetses, Greece.

Bass, B. M., Avolio, B. J., Jung, D. I., & Berson, Y. (2003). Predicting unit performance by assessing transformational and transactional leadership. *Journal of Applied Psychology, 88,* 207–218.

Bassari, A., & Ayman, R. (2009, May). Implicit leadership theory of Iranians. Paper presented at the meeting of the Leadership Trust Symposium, Ross-upon-Rye, UK.

Becker, J., Ayman, R., & Korabik, K. (2002). Discrepancies in self/subordinates' perceptions of leadership behavior: Leader's gender, organizational context, and leader's self- monitoring. *Group & Organizational Management, 27,* 226–244.

Burke, M. J., & Day, R. R. (1986). A cumulative study of the effectiveness of managerial training. *Journal of Applied Psychology, 71,* 242–245.

Case, B. (1987). Leadership behavior in sport: A field test of the situation leadership theory. *International Journal of Sport Psychology, 18,* 256–268.

Chemers, M. M. (1997). *An integrative theory of leadership.* Mahwah, NJ: Lawrence Erlbaum.

Chemers, M. M. (2000). Leadership research and theory: A functional integration. *Group Dynamics: Theory, Research, and Practice, 4,* 27–43.

Chemers, M. M. (2002). Efficacy and effectiveness: Integrating models of leadership and intelligence. In R. E. Riggio, S. E. Murphy, & F. J. Pirossolo (Eds.), *Multiple intelligences and leadership* (pp. 139–160). Mahwah, NJ: Lawrence Erlbaum.

Chemers, M. M., & Ayman, R. (1985). Leadership orientation as a moderator of the relationship between performance and satisfaction of Mexican managers. *Personality and Social Psychology Bulletin, 11,* 359–367.

Chemers, M. M., Goza, B., & Plumer, S. I. (1978, August). Leadership style and communication process. Paper presented at the annual meeting of the American Psychological Association, Toronto, Canada.

Chemers, M. M., Hays, R., Rhodewalt, F., & Wysocki, J. (1985). A person–environment analysis of job stress: A contingency model explanation. *Journal of Personality and Social Psychology, 49,* 628–635.

Chen, G., & Bliese, P. D. (2002). The role of different levels of leadership in predicting self and collective efficacy: Evidence for discontinuity. *Journal of Applied Psychology, 87,* 549–556.

Chen, G., Kirkman, B. L., Kanfer, R., Allen, D., & Rosen, B. (2007). A multilevel study of leadership, empowerment, and performance in teams. *Journal of Applied Psychology, 92,* 331–346.

Csikszentmihalyi, M. (1990). Flow: *The psychology of optimal experience.* New York: Harper Perennial.

Dansereau, F., Graen, G. B., & Haga, W. (1975). A vertical dyad linkage approach to leadership in formal organizations: A longitudinal investigation of the managerial role-making process. *Organizational Behavior and Human Performance, 13,* 46–78.

Dansereau, F., & Yammarino, F. J. (Eds.). (1998a). *Leadership: The multiple-level approaches—Classical and new wave.* Stamford, CT: JAI Press.

Dansereau, F., & Yammarino, F. J. (Eds.). (1998b). Leadership: *The multiple-level approaches—Contemporary and alternative.* Stamford, CT: JAI Press.

Day, D. V., & Lord, R. G. (1988). Executive leadership and organizational performance: Suggestions for a new theory and methodology. *Journal of Management, 14,* 453–464.

Den Hartog, D. N., House, R. J., Hanges, P. J., Ruiz-Quintanilla, S. A., & Dorfman, P. W. (1999). Culture specific and cross-culturally generalizable implicit leadership theories: Are attributes of charismatic/transformational leadership universally endorsed? *The Leadership Quarterly, 10,* 219–256.

Dennison, D. R. (1996). What is the difference between organizational culture and organizational climate? A native's point of view on a decade of paradigm wars. *Academy of Management Review, 21,* 619–654.

Dierdorff, E. C., Rubin, R. S., & Morgeson, F. P. (2009). The milieu of managerial work: An integrative framework linking work context to role requirements. *Journal of Applied Psychology, 94,* 972–988.

Dionne, S. D., Yammarino, F. J., Atwater, L. E., & James, L. R. (2002). Neutralizing substitutes for leadership theory: Leadership effects and common-source bias. *Journal of Applied Psychology, 87,* 454–464.

Eagly, A. H., & Carli, L. L. (2007). *Through the labyrinth: The truth about how women become leaders.* Boston, MA: Harvard Business School Press.

Eagly, A. H., Johannesen-Schmidt, M. C., & van Engen, M. L. (2003). Transformational, transactional, and laissez-faire leadership styles: A meta-analysis comparing women and men. *Psychological Bulletin, 129,* 569–591.

Eagly, A. H., & Karau, S. J. (1991). Gender and the emergence of leader: A meta-analysis. *Journal of Personality and Social Psychology, 60,* 685–710.

Eagly, A. H., Karau, S. J., & Makhijani, M. G. (1995). Gender and leader effectiveness: A meta-analysis. *Psychological Bulletin, 117,* 125–145.

Eden, D., & Leviantan, U. (1975). Implicit leadership theory as a determinant of the factor structure underlying supervisory behavior scales. *Journal of Applied Psychology, 60,* 736–741.

Edwards, J. R., & Lambert, L. S. (2007). Methods for integrating moderation and mediation: A general analytical framework using moderated path analysis. *Psychological Methods, 12*, 1–22.

Epitropaki, O., & Martin, R. (2004). Implicit leadership theories in applied settings: Factor structure, generalizability, and stability over time. *Journal of Applied Psychology, 89*, 293–310.

Evans, M. G. (1970). The effects of supervisory behavior on the path-goal relationship. *Organizational Behavior and Human Performance, 5*, 277–298.

Evans, M. G. (1996). R. J. House's "a path-goal theory of leader effectiveness." *The Leadership Quarterly, 7*, 305–309.

Fernandez, C. F., & Vecchio, R. P. (1997). Situational leadership theory revisited: A test of an across-jobs perspective. *The Leadership Quarterly, 8*, 67–84.

Fiedler, F. E. (1964). A contingency model of leadership effectiveness. In L. Berkowitz (Ed.), *Advances in experimental social psychology* (Vol. 1, pp. 149–190). New York: Academic Press.

Fiedler, F. E. (1978). The contingency model and the dynamics of the leadership process. In L. Berkowitz (Ed.), *Advances in experimental social psychology* (Vol. 11, pp. 59–112). New York: Academic Press.

Fiedler, F. E. (1992). Life in a pretzel-shaped universe. In A. Bedeian (Ed.), *Management laureates: A collection of autobiographical essays* (Vol. 1, pp. 301–334). Greenwich, CT: JAI Press.

Fiedler, F. E. (1993). The leadership situation and the black box in contingency theories. In M. Chemers and R. Ayman (Eds.), *Leadership theory and research: Perspectives and directions* (pp. 2–28). New York: Academic Press.

Fiedler, F. E. (1995). Cognitive resource and leadership performance. *Applied Psychology: An International Review, 44*, 5–28.

Fiedler, F. E. (2002). The curious role of cognitive resources in leadership. In R. Riggio, S. Murphy, & F. Pirozzolo (Eds.), *Multiple intelligences and leadership* (pp. 91–104). Mahwah, NJ: Lawrence Erlbaum.

Fiedler, F. E., & Chemers M. M. (1984). *Improving leadership effectiveness: The leader match concept* (2nd ed.). New York: John Wiley.

Fiedler F. E., & Garcia, J. E. (1987). *New approaches to effective leadership: Cognitive resources and organizational performance.* New York: John Wiley.

Field, R. H. G., & House, R. J. (1990). A test of the Vroom-Yetton model using manager and subordinate reports. *Journal of Applied Psychology, 75*, 362–366.

Fischbein, R., & Lord, R. G. (2004). Implicit leadership theory. In G. Goethale, G. Sorenson, & J. McGregor-Burns (Eds.), *Encyclopedia of Leadership* (Vol. 2, pp. 700–705). Thousand Oaks, CA: Sage.

Fisher, B. M., & Edwards, J. E. (1988). Consideration and initiating structure and their relationships with leader effectiveness: A meta-analysis. *Academy of Management Best Paper*, 201–205.

Frame, M. C., Roberto, K. J., Schwab, A. E., & Harris, C. T. (2010). What is important on the job? Differences across gender, perspective, and job level. *Journal of Applied Social Psychology, 40*, 36–56.

French, J. R., & Raven, B. (1959). The basis of social power. In D. Cartwright (Ed.), *Studies in social power* (pp. 150–167). Ann Arbor, MI: Institute for Social Research, University of Michigan.

Gangestad, S. W., & Snyder, M. (2000). Self-monitoring: Appraisal and reappraisal. *Psychological Bulletin, 126*, 530–555.

Georgopoulus, B. S., Mahoney, G. M., & Jones, N. W., Jr. (1957). A path-goal approach to productivity. *Journal of Applied Psychology, 41*, 345–353.

Gershenoff, A. B., & Foti, R. J. (2003). Leader emergence and gender roles in all female groups: A contextual examination. *Small Group Research, 34*, 170–196.

Gerstner, C. R., & Day, D. V. (1994). Cross-cultural comparison of leadership prototypes. *The Leadership Quarterly, 5*, 121–134.

Graeff, C. L. (1997). Evolution of situation leadership theory: A critical review. *The Leadership Quarterly, 8*, 153–170.

Graen, G. B., & Uhl-Bien, M. (1995). Relationship-based approach to leadership: Development of leader-member exchange (LMX) theory of leadership over 25 years: Applying a multi-level multi-domain perspective. *The Leadership Quarterly, 6*, 219–247.

Hackman, J. R. (1968). Effects of task characteristics on group products. *Journal of Experimental Social Psychology, 4*, 162–187.

Hackman, J. R., & Morris, C. G. (1975). Group task, group interaction process, and group performance effectiveness: A review and proposed integration. In L. Berkowitz (Ed.), *Advances in experimental social psychology* (Vol. 8). New York: Academic Press.

Hall, E. T., & Hall, M. R. (1990). *Understanding cultural differences.* Yarmouth, ME: Intercultural Press.

Hanges, P. J., Lord, R. G., & Dickson, M. W. (2000). An information-processing perspective on leadership and culture: A case for connectionist architecture. *Applied Psychology: An International Review, 49*, 133–161.

Heilman, M. E., Block, C. J., Martell, R. F., & Simon, M. (1989). Has anything changed? Current characterizations of men, women, and managers. *Journal of Applied Psychology, 74*, 935–942.

Heilman, M. E., Hornstein, H. A., Cage, J. H., & Herschlag, J. K. (1984). Reaction to prescribed leader behavior as a function of role perspective: The case of the Vroom-Yetton model. Journal of Applied Psychology, 69, 50–60.

Hersey, P., & Blanchard, K. (1969). Life cycle theory of leadership. *Training and Development Journal, 23*, 26–34.

Hersey, P., & Blanchard, K. (1982). *Management of organizational behavior* (4th ed.). Englewood Cliffs, NJ: Prentice Hall.

Hogan, R., Curphy, G. J., & Hogan, J. (1994). What we know about leadership: Effectiveness and personality. *American Psychologist, 49*, 493–504.

Hollingshead, A. B., & McGrath, J. E. (1995). Computer-assisted groups: A critical review of the empirical research. In R. A. Guzzo, E. Salas, & Associates (Eds.), *Team effectiveness and decision-making in organizations* (pp. 46–78). San Francisco: Jossey-Bass.

House, R. J. (1971). A path-goal theory of leadership effectiveness. *Administrative Quarterly, 16*, 312–338.

House, R. J. (1996). Path-goal theory of leadership: Lessons, legacy, and a reformulated theory. *The Leadership Quarterly, 7*, 323–352.

House, R. J., Hanges, P. M., Javidan, M., Dorfman, P., & Gupta, V. (2004). *Culture, leadership, and organizations: The GLOBE study of 62 societies.* Thousand Oaks, CA: Sage.

House, R. J., & Mitchell, T. R. (1974). Path-goal theory of leadership. *Journal of Contemporary Business, 9*, 81–97.

Howells, L. T., & Becker, S. W. (1962). Seating arrangement and leadership emergence. *Journal of Abnormal and Social Psychology, 64*, 148–150.

Hoyt, C. L., & Blascovich, J. (2003). Transformational and transactional leadership in virtual and physical environments. *Small Group Research, 34*, 678–715.

Indvik, J. (1986). Path-goal theory of leadership: A meta-analysis. Proceedings of the Academy of Management Meeting, Chicago, IL (pp. 189–192).

Jago, A. G., Maczynski, J., & Reber, G. (1996). Evolving leadership styles? A comparison of Polish managers before and after market economy reforms. *Polish Psychological Bulletin, 27*, 107–115.

Jago, A. G., & Vroom, V. H. (1980). An evaluation of two alternatives to the Vroom/Yetton normative model. *Academy of Management Journal, 23*, 347–355.

Jago, A. G., & Vroom, V. H. (1983). Sex differences in the incidence and evaluation of participative leader behavior. *Journal of Applied Psychology, 67*, 776–783.

Jermier, J. M., & Kerr, S. (1997). "Substitutes for leadership: Their meaning and measurement"—Contextual recollections and current observations. *The Leadership Quarterly, 8*, 95–102.

Johns, G. (2006). The essential impact of context on organizational behavior. *Academy of Management Review, 31*, 386-408.

Judge, T. A., Bono, J. E., Ilies, R., & Gerhardt, M. W. (2002). Personality and leadership: A qualitative and quantitative review. *Journal of Applied Psychology, 87*, 765–780.

Judge, T. A., Colbert, A. E., & Ilies, R. (2004). Intelligence and leadership: A quantitative review and test of theoretical propositions. *Journal of Applied Psychology, 89*, 542–552.

Judge, T. A., & Piccolo, R. F. (2004). Transformational and transactional leadership: A meta-analytic test of their relative validity. *Journal of Applied Psychology, 89*, 755–768.

Jung, D. I., & Avolio, B. J. (1999). Leadership style and followers' cultural orientation on performance in group and individual task conditions. *Academy of Management Journal, 42*, 208–218.

Kane, T. D., & Tremble, T. R. (2000). Transformational leadership effects at different levels of the Army. *Military Psychology, 12*, 137–160.

Kerr, S., & Jermier, J. M. (1978). Substitutes for leadership: Their meaning and measurement. *Organizational Behavior and Human Performance, 22*, 375–403.

Klein, K. J., & Kozlowski, S. W. J. (Eds.). (2000). *Multilevel theory, research, and methods in organizations: Foundations, extensions, and new directions.* San Francisco: Jossey-Bass.

Korabik, K., & Ayman, R. (2007). Gender and leadership in the corporate world:A multiperspective model. In J. C. Lau, B. Lott, J. Rice, and J. Sanchez-Hudes (Eds.). *Transforming leadership: Diverse visions and women's voices* (pp. 106–124). Malden, MA: Blackwell.

Korman, A. K. (1966). Consideration, initiating structure, and organizational criteria—A review. *Personnel Psychology, 19*, 349–361.

Kozlowski, S. W. J., & Klein, K. J. (2000). A multilevel approach to theory and research in organizations: Contextual, temporal, and emergent processes. In K. Klein & S. Kozlowski (Eds.), *Multilevel theory, research, and methods in organizations: Foundations, extensions, and new directions* (pp. 3–90). San Francisco: Jossey-Bass.

Leavitt, H. J. (1951). Some effects of certain communication patterns on group performance. *Journal of Abnormal and Social Psychology*, 46, 38–50.

Leffler, H., Ayman, R., & Ayman-Nolley, S. (2006, July). Do children possess the same stereotypes as adults? An exploration of children's implicit leadership *theories*. Poster session presented at the 26th International Congress of Applied Psychology, Athens, Greece.

Liden, R. C., & Antonakis, J. (2009). Considering context in psychological leadership research. *Human Relations*, 62, 1587–1605.

Ling, W., Chia, R. C., & Fang, L. (2000). Chinese implicit leadership theory. *Journal of Social Psychology*, 140, 729–739.

Ling, Y., Simsek, Z., Lubatkin, M. H., & Veiga, J. F. (2008). Impact of transformational CEOs on the performance of small to medium firms: Does organizational context matter? *Journal of Applied Psychology*, 93, 923–934.

Liu, L., Ayman, R., & Ayman-Nolley, S. (2009, May). Children's implicit leadership in China. Paper presented at the meeting of the Leadership Trust Symposium, Ross-upon-Rye, UK.

Lord, R. G., DeVader, C. L., & Alliger, G. M. (1986). A meta-analysis of the relation between personality traits and leadership: An application of validity generalization procedures. *Journal of Applied Psychology*, 71, 402–410.

Lord, R. G., & Emrich, C. G. (2001). Thinking outside the box by looking inside the box: Extending the cognitive revolution in leadership research. *The Leadership Quarterly*, 11, 551–579.

Lord, R. G., Foti, R. J., & DeVader, C. L. (1984). A test of leadership categorization theory: Internal structure, information processing, and leadership perceptions. *Organizational Behavior and Human Performance*, 34, 343–378.

Lord, R. G., & Maher, K. J. (1991). *Leadership and information processing: Linking perceptions and performance*. Boston: Routledge.

Lowe, K. B., Kroeck, G., & Sivasubramaniam, N. (1996). Effectiveness correlates of transformational and transactional leadership: A meta-analytic review of the MLQ literature. *The Leadership Quarterly*, 7, 385–425.

Maczynski, J., Jago, A. G., Reber, G., & Boehnisch, W. (1994). Culture and leadership styles: A comparison of Polish, Austrian, and U.S. managers. *Polish Psychological Bulletin*, 25, 303–315.

McGrath, J. E. (1984). *A typology of tasks. Groups, interaction and performance* (pp. 53–66). Englewood Cliffs, NJ: Prentice Hall.

Mischel, W. (1977). The interaction of person and situation. In D. Magnusson and D. Endler (Eds.), *Personality at the crossroads: Current issues in interactional psychology* (pp. 333–352). Hillsdale, NJ: Lawrence Erlbaum.

Mitchell, T. R., & James, L. R. (2001). Building better theory: Time and the specification of when things happen. *Academy of Management Review*, 26, 530–547.

Mumford, M. D., Dansereau, F., & Yammarino, F. Y. (2000). Followers, motivations, and levels of analysis: The case of individualized leadership. *The Leadership Quarterly*, 11, 313–340.

Murphy, S. E., Blyth, D., & Fiedler, F .E. (1992). Cognitive resource theory and the utilization of the leader's and group members' technical competence. *The Leadership Quarterly*, 3, 237–255.

Offermann, L. R., Kennedy, J. K., Jr., & Wirtz, P. W. (1994). Implicit leadership theories: Content, structure, and generalizability. *The Leadership Quarterly*, 5, 43–58.

Ostroff, C., Atwater, L. E., & Feinberg, B. J. (2004). Understanding self-other agreement: A look at rater and ratee characteristics, context, and outcomes. *Personnel Psychology*, 57, 333–375.

Pelto, P. J. (1968, April). The influence between "tight" and "loose" societies. *Transactions*, 37–40.

Peters, L. H., Hartke, D. D., & Pohlmann, J. F. (1985). Fiedler's contingency theory of leadership: An application of the meta-analysis procedures of Schmitt and Hunter. *Psychological Bulletin*, 97, 274–285.

Podsakoff, P. M., & Mackenzie, S. B. (1997). Kerr and Jermier's substitutes for leadership model: Background, empirical assessment, and suggestions for future research. *The Leadership Quarterly*, 8, 117–125.

Podsakoff, P. M., MacKenzie, S. B., & Bommer, W. H. (1996). Meta-analysis of the relationships between Kerr and Jermier's substitutes for leadership and employee job attitudes, role perceptions, and performance. *Journal of Applied Psychology*, 81, 380–399.

Podsakoff, P. M., & Schriesheim, C. A. (1985). Field studies of French and Raven's bases of power: Critique, reanalysis, and suggestions for future research. *Psychological Bulletin*, 97, 387–411.

Polyashuk, Y., Ayman, R., & Roberts, J. L. (2008, April). Relationship quality: The effect of dyad composition diversity and time. Poster session presented at the meeting of the Society of Industrial and Organizational Psychology, San Francisco, CA.

Porter, L. W., & McLaughlin, G. B. (2006). Leadership and the organizational context: Like the weather? *The Leadership Quarterly*, 17, 559–576.

Potter, E. H., III, & Fiedler, F. E. (1981). The utilization of staff members' intelligence and experience under high and low stress. *Academy of Management Journal, 24,* 361–376.

Preacher, K. J., Rucker, D. D., & Hayes, A. F. (2007). Addressing moderated mediation hypotheses: Theory, methods, and prescriptions. *Multivariate Behavioral Research, 42,* 185–227.

Puranova, R. K., & Bono, J. E. (2009). Transformational leadership in context: Face to face and virtual teams. *The Leadership Quarterly, 20,* 343, 357.

Rice, W. R. (1981). Leader LPC and follower satisfaction: A review. *Organizational Behavior and Human Performance, 28,* 1–25.

Rice, W. R., Marwick, N. J., Chemers, M. M., & Bentley, J. C. (1982). Task performance and satisfaction: Least Preferred Coworker (LPC) as a moderator. *Personality and Social Psychology Bulletin, 8,* 534–541.

Rousseau, D. (2000). Multilevel competencies and missing linkages. In K. Klein & S. Kozlowski (Eds.), *Multilevel theory, research, and methods in organizations: Foundations, extensions, and new directions* (pp. 557–571). San Francisco: Jossey-Bass.

Rousseau, D., & Fried, Y. (2001). Location, location, location: Conceptualizing organizational research. *Journal of Organizational Behavior, 22,* 1–13.

Schneider, R. J., & Hough, L. M. (1995). Personality and industrial/organizational psychology. In C. L. Cooper and I. T. Robertson (Eds.), *International review of industrial and organizational psychology* (Vol. 10). New York: John Wiley.

Schriesheim, C. A. (1997). Substitutes-for-leadership theory: Development and basic concepts. *The Leadership Quarterly, 8,* 103–108.

Schriesheim, C. A., & Neider, L. L. (1996). Path-goal leadership theory: The long and winding road. *The Leadership Quarterly, 7,* 317–321.

Schriesheim, C. A., & Schriesheim, J. F. (1980). A test of the path-goal theory of leadership and some suggested direction for future research. *Personnel Psychology, 33,* 349–370.

Schriesheim, C. A., Tepper, B. J., & Tetrault, L. A. (1994). Least preferred coworker score, situational control and leadership effectiveness: A meta-analysis of contingency model performance predictions. *Journal of Applied Psychology, 79,* 561–573.

Schriesheim C. A., & Von Glinow, M. A. (1977). The path-goal theory of leadership: A theoretical and empirical analysis. *Academy of Management Journal, 20,* 398–405.

Schyns, B., & Van Veldhoven, M. J. P. M. (2010). Group leadership climate and individual organizational commitment: A multilevel analysis. *Journal of Personnel Psychology, 9,* 57–68.

Shartle, C. L. (1951). Studies of naval leadership, part I. In H. Guetzkow (Ed.), *Groups, leadership and men: Research in human relations* (pp. 119–133). Pittsburgh, PA: Carnegie Press.

Shaw, M. E. (1981). *Group dynamics: The psychology of small group behavior* (3rd ed.) New York: McGraw-Hill.

Sternberg, R. J. (1988). *The triarchic mind: A new theory of human intelligence.* New York: Penguin Books.

Sternberg, R. J. (1995). A triarchic view of "cognitive resource and leadership performance." *Applied Psychology: An International Review, 44,* 29–32.

Sternberg, R. J., & Vroom, V. (2002). The person versus situation in leadership. *The Leadership Quarterly, 13,* 301–323.

Stinson, J. E., & Johnson, T. W. (1975). The path-goal theory of leadership: A partial test and suggested refinement. *Academy of Management Journal, 18,* 242–252.

Stogdill, R. M. (1974). *Handbook of leadership.* New York: Free Press.

Stogdill, R. M., & Coons, A. E. (1957). *Leader behavior: Its description and measurement.* Columbus, OH: Ohio State University, Bureau of Business Research.

Strube, M. J., & Garcia, J. E. (1981). A meta-analytical investigation of Fiedler's contingency model of leadership effectiveness. *Psychological Bulletin, 90,* 307–321.

Tobey-Garcia, A., Ayman, R., & Chemers, M. (2000, July). Leader-subordinate trait dyad composition and subordinate satisfaction with supervision: Moderated by task structure. Paper presented at the XXVII International Congress of Psychology, Stockholm, Sweden.

Triandis, H. C. (2006). Cultural intelligence in organizations. *Group & Organizational Management, 31,* 20–26.

Van Rooy, D. L., & Viswesvaran, C. (2004). Emotional intelligence: A meta-analytic investigation of predictive validity and nomological net. *Journal of Vocational Behavior, 65,* 71–95.

Vecchio, R. P. (1987). Situational leadership theory: An examination of a prescriptive theory. *Journal of Applied Psychology, 72,* 444–451.

Vecchio, R. P. (1997). Situational leadership theory: An examination of a prescriptive theory. In R. P. Vecchio (Ed.), *Leadership: Understanding the dynamics of power and influence in organizations* (pp. 334–350). Notre Dame, IN: University of Notre Dame Press.

Vecchio, R. P., & Boatwright, K. J. (2002). Preferences for idealized styles of supervision. *The Leadership Quarterly,* 13, 327–342.

Vroom, V. H. (1964). Work and motivation. New York: John Wiley.

Vroom V. H., & Jago, A. G. (1978). On the validity of the Vroom-Yetton model. *Journal of Applied Psychology,* 63, 151–162.

Vroom, V. H., & Jago, A. G. (1988). *The new leadership: Managing participation in organizations.* Englewood Cliffs, NJ: Prentice Hall.

Vroom, V. H., & Jago, A. G. (1995). Situation effects and levels of analysis in the study of leader participation. *The Leadership Quarterly,* 6, 169–181.

Vroom V. H., & Jago, A. G. (1998). Situation effects and levels of analysis in the study of leader participation. In F. Yammarino and F. Dansereau (Eds.), *Leadership: The multi-level approaches* (pp. 145–159). Stamford, CT: JAI Press.

Vroom, V. H., & Yetton, P. W. (1973). *Leadership and decision-making.* Pittsburgh, PA: University of Pittsburgh Press.

Waldman, D. A., Ramirez, G. G., House, R. J., & Puranam, P. (2001). Does leadership matter? CEO leadership attributes and profitability under conditions of perceived environmental uncertainty. *Academy of Management Journal,* 44(1), 134–143.

Waldman, D. A., & Yammarino, F. J. (1999). CEO charismatic leadership: Levels-of-management and levels-of-analysis effects. *Academy of Management Review,* 24, 266–285.

Wentworth, D. K., & Anderson, L. R. (1984). Emergent leadership as a function of sex and task type. *Sex Roles,* 11, 513–524.

West, M. A., Borrill, C. S., & Unsworth, K. L. (1998). Team effectiveness in organizations. In C. L. Cooper & I. T. Robertson (Eds.), *International review of industrial and organizational psychology* (pp. 1–48). Chichester, UK: Wiley.

Wofford, J. C., & Liska, L. Z. (1993). Path-goal theories of leadership: A meta-analysis. *Journal of Management,* 19, 857–876.

Yammarino, F. J., & Dansereau, F. (Eds.) (2009). *Multi-level issues in organizational behavior and leadership* (Vol. 8 of Research in multi-level issues). Bingley, UK: Emerald.

York, R. O. (1996). Adherence to situational leadership theory among social workers. *Clinical Supervisor,* 14, 5–26.

Yukl, G., & Van Fleet, D. D. (1992). Theory and research on leadership in organizations. In M. D. Dunnette and L. M. Hough (Eds.). *Handbook of industrial and organizational psychology* (2nd ed., Vol. 3, pp. 147–198). Palo Alto, CA: Consulting Psychologist Press.

Zaccaro, S. J. (1995). Leader resource and the nature of organizational problems. *Applied Psychology: An International Review,* 44, 32–36.

Zaccaro, S. J. (2007). Trait-based perspectives of leadership. *American Psychologist,* 62, 6–16.

Zaccaro, S. J., Kemp, C., & Bader, P. (2004). Leader traits and attributes. In J. Antonakis, A. T. Cianciolo, & R. J. Sternberg (Eds.) *The nature of leadership* (pp. 102–124). Thousand Oaks, CA: Sage.

CHAPTER 11

Followership Theory

A Review and Research Agenda[1]

Mary Uhl-Bien
University of Nebraska, Lincoln

Ronald E. Riggio
Claremont McKenna College

Kevin B. Lowe
University of Auckland

Melissa K. Carsten
Winthrop University

1. Introduction

We have long known that followers and followership are essential to leadership. However, despite the abundance of investigations into leadership in organizational studies (Yukl, 2012), until recently little attention has been paid to followership in leadership research (Baker, 2007; Bligh, 2011; Carsten, Uhl-Bien, West, Patera, & McGregor, 2010; Kelley, 2008; Sy, 2010). When followers have been considered, they have been considered as recipients or moderators of the leader's influence (i.e., leader-centric views, Bass, 2008) or as "constructors" of leaders and leadership (i.e., follower-centric views, Meindl, 1990; Meindl, Ehrlich, & Dukerich, 1985). The study of followers as key components of the leadership process through their enactment of followership has been largely missed in the leadership literature.

We suggest that this oversight is due in large part to confusion and misunderstanding about what followership constructs are and how they relate to leadership. This confusion happens because we have not

[1]Author acknowledgment: Thanks to Emily Chan and Claudia Raigoza for assistance.

understood leadership as a process that is co-created in social and relational interactions between people (Fairhurst & Uhl-Bien, 2012). In this process, leadership can only occur if there is followership—without followers and following behaviors there is no leadership. This means that following behaviors are a crucial component of the leadership process. Following behaviors represent a willingness to defer to another in some way. DeRue and Ashford (2010) describe this as granting a leader identity to another and claiming a follower identity for oneself. Uhl-Bien and Pillai (2007) refer to it as some form of deference to a leader: "if leadership involves actively influencing others, then followership involves allowing oneself to be influenced" (p. 196). Shamir (2007) argues that following is so important to leadership that it negates the construct of shared leadership altogether: "leadership exists only when an individual (sometimes a pair or a small group) exerts disproportionate non-coercive influence on others" (p. xviii).

The significance of following for leadership means that our understanding of leadership is incomplete without an understanding of followership. For research in followership to advance, however, we need to identify followership constructs and place them in the context of followership theory. We address this by identifying followership theory as the study of the nature and impact of followers and following in the leadership process. It investigates followership from the perspective of (a) formal hierarchical roles (e.g., followers as "subordinates") and (b) followership in the context of the leadership process (e.g., following as a behavior that helps co-construct leadership). The former focuses on studying followership behaviors from a subordinate position. The latter focuses on studying following behaviors as they combine with leading behaviors to co-construct leadership and its outcomes.

***

2. An Emerging Field of Followership Research

Although our review shows that most research on leadership recognizes the follower in some way, the focus on followership as a research area in its own

right has not occurred until very recently (Carsten et al., 2010; Collinson, 2006; Hoption, Christie, & Barling, 2012; Sy, 2010). Followership approaches are distinct from prior approaches in that they privilege the role of the follower in the leadership process. They identify followership as a topic equally worthy of study to leadership (Uhl-Bien & Pillai, 2007). A basic assumption of a followership approach is that leadership cannot be fully understood without considering how followers and followership contribute to (or detract from) the leadership process (Carsten et al., 2010; Dvir & Shamir, 2003; Hollander, 1993; Howell & Shamir, 2005; Sy, 2010).

2.1. Defining followership

The study of followership involves an investigation of *the nature and impact of followers and following in the leadership process.* The leadership process is a term used to signify a connectionist view (Lord & Brown, 2001) that sees leadership as a dynamic system involving leaders (or leading) and followers (or following) interacting together in context (Hollander, 1992a; Lord et al., 1999; Padilla et al., 2007; Shamir, 2012; Uhl-Bien & Ospina, 2012). This definition identifies followership through two lenses: followership as a rank or *position* (i.e., role), and followership as a *social process.*

The first, a role theory approach (Katz & Kahn, 1978), sees followership as a role played by individuals occupying a formal or informal position or rank (e.g., a "subordinate" in a hierarchical "manager-subordinate" relationship; a follower in a "leader-follower" relationship). The second, a constructionist approach (Fairhurst & Grant, 2010), views followership as a relational interaction through which leadership is co-created in combined acts of leading and following (DeRue & Ashford, 2010; Fairhurst & Uhl-Bien, 2012; Shamir, 2012). Whereas role-based views investigate followership as a role and a set of behaviors or behavioral styles of individuals or groups, constructionist views study followership as a social process necessarily intertwined with leadership.

Role-based approaches are consistent with Shamir's description of "reversing the lens" in leadership research (Shamir, 2007). In contrast to leader-centric approaches examining how leaders influence follower attitudes, behaviors, and outcomes, role-based followership approaches consider *how followers influence leader attitudes, behaviors, and outcomes.* These approaches identify followers as the causal agents—i.e., follower characteristics and behaviors are the independent variables, and leader characteristics and behaviors are the dependent or moderator variables (Shamir, 2007). The focus in these approaches is on follower characteristics and style, followership role orientations, implicit theories of followership, follower identities, and how follower identities and behaviors shape leader attitudes, behaviors and effectiveness (Collinson, 2006; Lord & Brown, 2004).

Constructionist approaches see followership and leadership as co-constructed in social and relational interactions between people (DeRue & Ashford, 2010; Fairhurst & Uhl-Bien, 2012; Shamir, 2007). A constructionist approach considers that leadership can only occur when leadership influence attempts or identity claims are met with followership granting behaviors (e.g., deference) or identity claims (DeRue & Ashford, 2010; see also Uhl-Bien & Ospina, 2012; Shamir, 2012). Followership is seen in "following behaviors" that can include leader and follower claiming and granting (DeRue & Ashford, 2010), deferring or obeying (Blass, 2009; Burger, 2009; Milgram, 1965, 1974), resisting or negotiating with another's wishes or influence attempts (Tepper, Duffy, & Shaw, 2001; Tepper et al., 2006), or trying to influence another to go along with one's influence attempts (Fairhurst & Uhl-Bien, 2012). In this way followership is not tied to a role but to a *behavior.* This approach allows us to recognize that managers are not always leading—they also defer to subordinates, which means they also engage in "following behaviors" (Fairhurst & Hamlett, 2003; Larsson & Lundholm, 2013).

2.1.1. Issues of semantics

These differing views are the reason behind much of the confusion in discussions of followership, and why we have had so much trouble understanding what followership is. The negative connotations of the words "follower" and "following" come from the role-based, leader-centric view that has traditionally dominated leadership research (Hoption et al., 2012). This view romanticizes leadership and subordinates followership (Uhl-Bien & Pillai, 2007). From the role-based view, the term follower has been controversial because it conjures up images of passive, powerless individuals who automatically do the leader's bidding (Kelley, 2008). It also creates confusion when those we identify as "followers" act inconsistently with the role (e.g., the Arab Spring). As a result, some have argued for the use of the term "constituents" to signify the members of a leader's collective (e.g., Gardner, 1990; Rost, 1993). Others have suggested terms such as "collaborators," "participant" and "member/team member," and some scholars have even advocated eliminating the term follower altogether due to its negative connotations (e.g., Rost, 2008).

As Shamir (2007, 2012) indicates, however, eliminating "followers" from the leadership equation means we are no longer studying leadership. Instead we are studying social phenomena more generally, such as collaboration and teamwork. As articulated by Shamir (2007), for a social phenomenon to count as leadership it must involve "disproportionate social influence" (i.e., leading and following behaviors or identities). Shamir (2012) is careful to note that this does not mean that roles and identities of leaders and followers are fixed. Nor does it mean that leadership research should center on the leader. Rather, it means that leadership *cannot* be fully "shared" (Pearce & Conger, 2003): "If it is fully shared, I suggest we don't call it *leadership* because the term loses any added value" (Shamir, 2012, p. 487).

For a social phenomenon to qualify as leadership, therefore, we must be able to "identify certain actors who, at least in a certain. . .time, exert more influence than others on the group or the process" (Shamir, 2012, p. 487). The clear implication is that *followers and followership are central to leadership,* and that *the leadership process is constituted in combined acts of leading and following.* Paraphrasing Shamir (2012), we can conclude that for a phenomenon to be called leadership we must be able to identify certain actors who are willing to defer to others (i.e., to be followers or engage in following). From a followership lens, we could even argue that *it is in following that leadership is created* (Uhl-Bien & Ospina, 2012).

Returning to the distinction between role-based and constructionist approaches, role-based approaches study the follower in a hierarchical context (i.e., as a subordinate). These approaches associate leadership and followership with holding formal hierarchical positions (e.g., manager and subordinate). Constructionist approaches study followership as part of a dynamic relational process. These approaches do not start from the assumption of hierarchical position but instead consider how leadership and followership are enacted in asymmetrical relational interactions between people, which *might or might not* coincide with formal hierarchical roles (i.e., managers might not lead and subordinates might not follow).

2.2. Role-Based Views

Role-based views consider how individuals enact leadership and followership in the context of hierarchical roles. The primary interest of role-based approaches is in advancing understanding of how followers (e.g., subordinates) work with leaders (e.g., managers) in ways that contribute to or detract from leadership and organizational outcomes (Oc et al., 2013; Carsten et al., 2010; Sy, 2010). As such, these approaches focus on issues such as follower role orientations, follower schemas, and implicit followership theories (Carsten et al., 2010; Sy, 2010). They also investigate how follower (i.e., subordinate) traits, characteristics and styles influence leaders (i.e., managers) and leadership outcomes (Dvir & Shamir, 2003; Howell & Shamir, 2005). Role-based approaches are interested in the question: "What is the proper mix of follower characteristics and follower behavior to promote desired outcomes?" (Graen & Uhl-Bien, 1995, p. 223).

2.2.1. Follower characteristics and styles (typologies)

The earliest role-based views are provided in typologies that identify follower characteristics and styles. The first such typology was provided by Zaleznik (1965). Focusing on the dynamics of subordinacy, Zaleznik distinguished followers according to two axes: dominance-submission and activity-passivity. Dominance-submission ranges from subordinates who want to control their superiors to those who want to be controlled by superiors. Activity-passivity ranges from subordinates who "initiate and intrude" to those who do nothing. The resulting typology identifies four categories of followers: (1) impulsive subordinates, (2) compulsive subordinates, (3) masochistic subordinates, and (4) withdrawn subordinates. This typology of subordinates/ followers is introduced both as a means of helping leaders better understand how to deal with followers, but also as providing direction to followers who aspire to positions of leadership. As Zaleznik and Kets de Vries (1975) state, ". . .the person who aspires to leadership must negotiate the risky passage between dependency and assertiveness" (p. 167).

Although Zaleznik provided the first typology, clearly the most cited early work on followership is that of Robert Kelley (1988). Kelley defined the ideal follower as participating in a joint process of achieving some common purpose (Kelley, 1988, 1992, 2008). He ascribed to "effective followers" an array of positive qualities, such as being self-motivated, independent problem-solvers, and committed to the group and organization. Effective followers "are courageous, honest, and credible" (Kelley, 1988, p. 144). Kelley's typology uses dependent-independent and passive-active as the quadrants (i.e., alienated followers, exemplary followers, conformist followers, passive followers, and a "center" group, midway on the two dimensions who are labeled pragmatist followers). These quadrants range from the stereotypical "sheep," which are passive and dependent, to "yes people" who are active, but dependent—the classic stereotype of followers who blindly follow whatever the leader dictates (Bjugstad, Thach, Thompson, & Morris, 2006; Hoption et al., 2012; Townsend & Gebhardt, 1997). Kelley advocated turning all followers into "exemplary followers," arguing that the best followers are anything but passive sheep—they are actively engaged and exhibit courageous conscience (Kelley, 1992).

Following Kelley, in 1995 Ira Chaleff published a practitioner book called *The Courageous Follower*. His premise was that the key to effective leadership is effective followership, which occurs when followers "vigorously support" leaders in pursuing the mission and vision of the organization. Effective followership requires followers who are accountable and willing to "stand up to and for leaders." He calls this courageous because followers at times will have to challenge and confront leaders with unpleasant information and critical and honest feedback. Effective followers are partners with leaders who contribute to satisfying and productive work environments by being accountable and taking a proactive approach to their role. Using axes ranging from low-high support and low-high challenge of the leader, Chaleff identifies four different follower styles: implementer, partner, individualist, and resource (1995, 2003, 2008). His foundational premise is that "leaders rarely use their power wisely or effectively over long periods unless they are supported by followers who have the stature to help them do so" (Chaleff, 2003, p. 1).

Coming from a political science perspective, Kellerman's (2008) focus on followership divides followers into five categories based on the level of engagement of the follower. Her typology, ranging from "feeling and doing nothing" to "being passionately committed and deeply involved," results in five types of followers: isolate, bystander, participant, activist, and diehard. Kellerman's goal in this simple typology is to suggest that the critical element in followership is engagement. For example, isolates are completely detached, bystanders observe but do not participate, participants are in some way engaged, activists feel strongly about their leaders and act accordingly, and diehards are deeply committed and prepared to die for their causes. She uses this framework to argue that followers have more power and influence than they are traditionally accredited. Her interest is in focusing on how engaged followers can act as agents of change.

Jean Lipman-Blumen (2005) in her discussion of why followers so willingly obey toxic leaders suggests that there are three general categories of followers, and that these followers actually enable and support bad leaders. The first category, "benign followers," is comprised of followers who are gullible and go along unquestioningly with what a toxic leader is saying.

These followers follow for pragmatic reasons, such as keeping their jobs. The second category, labeled "the leader's entourage," serves as the toxic leader's alter ego. They do this by committing to the leader's agenda. The final category, labeled "malevolent followers," includes those driven by greed, envy, or competitiveness. These followers work against the leader, and may actually have their sights set on unseating the leader to become the leader themselves.

Another typology is presented in Howell and Mendez (2008). They propose that there are different types of follower role orientations and that these influence the effectiveness of the leader-follower relationship. The first is followership as an *interactive role* that supports and complements the leadership role. This interactive role orientation can be a highly effective and dedicated follower, a relatively ineffective (Kelley's "sheep") follower, or even part of a toxic leader's loyal entourage. The second is followership as an *independent role*. This role orientation involves high levels of autonomy, and, in a positive vein, high levels of competence that complements the leader's role (e.g., high-level professionals such as engineers, physicians, university professors who work independently but contribute to the organization's goals). The third type is more negative, and comprises an *independent role* orientation that may involve a follower who works at cross-purposes to the leader. The final follower role orientation is a *shifting role,* in which the individual alternates between the leader and follower role. For example, in collaborative teams members may feel obligated to step up into a leadership role or feel that a less visible followership role is appropriate, depending on the circumstances.

2.2.2. Carsten's followership role orientations

The idea that followers can hold different types of role orientations can also be seen in newly emerging work on followership being advanced by Carsten and colleagues (Carsten, Uhl-Bien, & Jaywickrema, 2013; Carsten et al., 2010). Carsten et al. (2010) offer the first formal empirical investigation of *followers'* views of followership. Using an exploratory qualitative approach, they investigate how followers describe their beliefs regarding the ways they view and enact their roles, as well as the personal qualities and contextual characteristics they see as facilitating or impeding their ability to be successful as a follower. Their findings identify different follower schema. Some followers report more passive views, seeing their role as being obedient and deferent (e.g., "sheep," Kelley, 1992). Others report holding a proactive schema, viewing their roles as partnering with leaders by taking ownership and accountability for achieving organizational objectives (e.g., active co-contributors, Chaleff, 1995; Kellerman, 2008; Shamir, 2007).

Whether followers are able to act on their schema depends on the context (Carsten et al., 2010). Followers report that authoritarian or empowering leader style and bureaucratic or engaged climate are key factors in whether followers can enact their roles in accordance with their role orientation. When followers' schemas do not match the context, they report stress and dissatisfaction. For example, passive followers in empowering climates report stress from being asked to operate in ways inconsistent with their beliefs and style. Proactive followers with authoritarian leaders report frustration and dissatisfaction from being stifled by bureaucratic climates and procedures.

2.2.3. Sy's implicit followership theories

Sy's (2010) approach differs from that of Carsten et al. (2010) in that it investigates subordinates' as well as *managers'* views of followership. Paralleling research on implicit leadership theories, Sy (2010) advances understanding of implicit followership theories (IFTs). Managers were asked to report traits and behaviors they believe characterize followers. These were then formed into a measure of implicit followership theories (IFTs). Findings show that IFTs are most accurately represented by a first-order six-factor structure involving Industry, Enthusiasm, Good Citizen, Conformity, Insubordination and Incompetence. IFTs are also accurately represented by a second-order two-factor structure consisting of Followership Prototype (Industry, Enthusiasm, Good

Citizen) and Followership Antiprototype (Conformity, Insubordination, Incompetence).

Sy's research has explored IFTs from both the leader (i.e., LIFTs) and follower (i.e., FIFTs) perspectives (however, there is more research on the former than the latter). LIFTs are important because they are associated with interpersonal outcomes of relationship quality, liking, trust and satisfaction (Sy, 2010). As shown in Whiteley, Sy, and Johnson (2012), positive LIFTs are associated with higher performance expectations, liking and LMX, which are subsequently associated with follower performance (i.e., naturally occurring Pygmalion effects). Furthermore, recent research has also found an associative relationship between affect and LIFTs in that leaders who demonstrate negative state or trait affect tend to endorse more negative LIFTs (Epitropaki, Sy, Martin, Tram, & Topakas, 2013; Kruse & Sy, 2011). Although less attention has been paid to FIFTs, Sy's research suggests that LIFTs and FIFTs interact to affect relationship quality (Sy, 2013) and follower performance (Sy, 2011).

2.2.4. Followers as shapers of leaders' actions

A view of followers as shapers of leaders' actions can be seen in the work of Shamir and colleagues (Dvir & Shamir, 2003; Howell & Shamir, 2005; Shamir, 2007). This approach is based on the premise that a key role of followers is in influencing the leader and facilitating leader emergence: "Much of the literature on the study of leadership neglects to acknowledge or even recognize the important role of followers in defining and shaping the latitude of leader's action" (Hollander, 1993, p. 29). Using this premise, Dvir and Shamir (2003) investigate how follower developmental characteristics are associated with followers' ability and inclination to actively contribute to the emergence of transformational leadership. Their findings show that followers' initial developmental level (e.g., self-actualization needs, collectivist orientation, critical-independent approach, active engagement in the task, self-efficacy) positively predicts transformational leadership among indirect followers, but these relationships were negative among direct followers.

Howell and Shamir (2005) provide a conceptual framework that depicts followers as having a more active role than that assumed in traditional leadership research. Similar to Chaleffs (1995) argument that powerful leaders need to be counteracted by powerful followers, Howell and Shamir (2005) indicate that it is naive for leadership scholars to believe that charismatic leaders can engage in self-reflection, self-monitoring and feedback seeking in ways that can manage the deleterious impact of charisma. Instead, followers need to recognize and play a more active role in avoiding the pitfalls and abuses of power that can come with charismatic leadership. "In our view, understanding followers is as important as understanding leaders" (Howell & Shamir, 2005, p. 110).

2.2.5. Followership behaviors

Role-based views also consider the kind of behaviors individuals use as they enact their follower roles (Carsten & Uhl-Bien, 2012, 2013). The most classic view of followership behavior is that associated with the obedient and deferent subordinate (Kelley, 1988; Zaleznik, 1965). However, the dynamic nature of the workplace, as well as a shift from production economies to knowledge economies, has called attention to both resistance and proactive behaviors among followers (Grant & Ashford, 2008; Tepper et al., 2001, 2006).

2.2.5.1. Obedience and subordination. Traditional stereotypes of followers as passive, deferent and subordinate come from long established assumptions in the management literature that leadership is grounded in hierarchy and authority (Barnard, 1938; Taylor, 1947). This hierarchical view, rooted in the belief that hierarchy legitimizes some individuals as "authority figures" more capable and effective than others (Weber, 1968), leads to the parallel assumption that the follower role is to carry out orders without question (Heckscher, 1994). Followers demonstrate obedient and subordinate behaviors in response to common beliefs that leaders are responsible for making decisions, solving problems, gathering information, and setting goals (De Cremer

& Van Dijk, 2005; De Vries & Van Gelder, 2005; Ravlin & Thomas, 2005). This view can be seen in Carsten et al.'s (2010) findings of followers describing their job as "carrying out orders" and "doing things the leader's way."

The belief that those in follower positions are largely ineffectual is a powerful one (Courpasson & Dany, 2003). Lab studies have shown that the mere assignment of an individual to a subordinate role causes them to report less positive affect (Hoption et al., 2012), see themselves as ineffectual, and view leaders as having greater capability and agency (Gerber, 1988). Milgram's (1965, 1974) classic research on obedience shows a frightening picture of the lengths people will go to in obeying authority. As described by Milgram (1965), he was shocked at the extent to which people would "heedlessly accept" the commands of authority.

Replications of Milgram (e.g., Burger, 2009) and subsequent evidence from other studies (see Blass, 2009 for a review) suggest that the pull to follow orders from an authority figure is a powerful one, and represents a deep psychological phenomenon that is still in effect today. Burger (2009) interprets the high rate of obedience in his study as evidence of the powerful situational forces of hierarchical contexts of individuals in follower roles (see also Passini & Morselli, 2009). In followership research, Hinrichs (2007) and Carsten and Uhl-Bien (2013) link this propensity to follow to crimes of obedience, showing that individuals who hold more traditional views of followers as passive and obedient are more likely to be complicit in unethical actions of leaders by being more willing to go along with unethical requests.

Van Vugt and colleagues (King, Johnson, & Van Vugt, 2009; Van Vugt, 2006; Van Vugt, Hogan, & Kaiser, 2008) theorize that this propensity to follow may be rooted in natural selection. Using an evolutionary psychology perspective, they argue that certain traits and behaviors (e.g., leadership and followership) are selected and retained because they helped solve adaptive problems of our ancestors. Natural selection, then, predisposes individuals with genotypes for leadership and followership. This explains why some people act as followers and voluntarily subordinate themselves to others—our ancestors learned that in certain situations it is better to defer to a central command. Because evolutionary analysis suggests that the formal bureaucratic leadership structures are comparatively recent in human history, these structures may actually conflict with our evolved leadership psychology. This may shed light on why many individuals in modern organizations struggle with issues of dominance hierarchies and the powerlessness they create (Ashforth, 1989).

2.2.5.2. Resistance. The dominant view of followers as passive and obedient has resulted in much less attention being paid to other types of followership behavior, particularly resistance. Leadership research is highly normative (Padilla et al., 2007) and leader-centric (Hollander & Julian, 1969), resulting in little attention being given to the actuality that not all "followers" follow.

Early theory recognized this reality with Barnard's (1938) "acceptance theory of authority" and Hollander's (1958) idiosyncrasy credits. But formal study of follower resistance in leadership research did not occur until more recently, with Tepper and colleagues' focus on resistance behaviors (Tepper et al., 2001, 2006).

In a natural extension of abusive supervision research, Tepper et al. (2001) asked the question of how subordinates will respond to abuse from their supervisors. Arguing that they will be unlikely to reciprocate, Tepper et al. (2001) focused their investigation on two types of resistance behaviors: constructive and dysfunctional. Constructive resistance involves well-intended efforts to open a dialog with the supervisor (e.g., ask for clarification or negotiate). Dysfunctional resistance involves passive-aggressive responses in which subordinates might act as if they are too busy to complete the request, pretend they did not hear it, or say they forgot. Tepper et al. (2001) predicted and found that both types of resistance approaches are used more often in the presence of abusive supervision, and that how this occurs is partially dependent on subordinate conscientiousness and agreeableness.

In a follow-up study, Tepper et al. (2006) took the next step of examining managers' reactions to subordinate resistance. They began by suggesting that

managers view subordinate resistance as either uniformly dysfunctional (all manifestations of resistance are bad) or multifunctional (some manifestations of resistance are more functional than others). Predicting LMX as a moderator, findings showed that the uniformly dysfunctional perspective characterizes low quality LMX relationships and the multifunctional perspective is found in high quality relationships. Managers rated low LMX subordinates unfavorably *regardless* of the resistance strategy they used, but high LMX subordinates were rated favorably when they used a constructive resistance strategy (i.e., negotiating). What was most interesting about this finding was that both low and high LMX subordinates were likely to use negotiation, but managers were only receptive to it from high LMX subordinates.

In an empirical investigation of resistance behaviors related to followership beliefs, Carsten and Uhl-Bien (2013) sought to determine whether a follower's belief in co-production would be associated with their willingness to engage in constructive resistance in the face of an unethical request by a leader. Findings show that followers with weaker co-production beliefs (based on Carsten et al., 2010; Shamir, 2007) demonstrate greater intent to obey a leader's unethical request, while followers with stronger co-production beliefs are willing to constructively resist the leader. This effect is moderated by romance of leadership, such that followers with stronger co-production beliefs who romanticize leaders report a stronger intent to obey the leader's unethical request.

2.2.5.3. Proactive behaviors. Proactive behaviors assess the creative and deliberate ways that employees plan and act on their environment to influence, change and alter it in ways they see fit. Proactive behaviors include influence tactics (Kipnis, Schmidt, & Wilkinson, 1980), feedback-seeking (Ashford & Cummings, 1985), taking charge behavior (Morrison & Phelps, 1999), prosocial rule-breaking (Morrison, 2006), voice (Morrison & Milliken, 2000; Van Dyne & LePine, 1998) influencing work structures (Parker, Wall, & Jackson, 1997), and personal initiative taking. Integrating these various perspectives, Grant and

Ashford (2008) define proactive behavior as "anticipatory action that employees take to impact themselves and/or their environments" (p. 8). They characterize it as a process "that can be applied to any set of actions through anticipating, planning, and striving to have an impact" (p. 9). It can involve either in-role or extra-role activities.

While the parallels with trends in followership research are striking, there are some key differences between views in the proactivity literature and those in the followership domain. The concept of proactivity in the organizational literature is vast (Grant & Ashford, 2008), addressing a wide array of issues ranging from social processes to work structures to development and change processes. Proactivity addresses general work behavior and employees very broadly. Because followership behaviors necessarily occur in the context of hierarchical relationships with leaders, the issue of most relevance for followership research is how employees engage in this behavior in relation to leaders and how leaders receive and respond to followers' proactive behaviors (Whiting, Maynes, Podsakoff, & Podsakoff, 2012). This is not trivial, given research findings showing that leaders are not always receptive to proactivity from followers (Grant, Parker, & Collins, 2009; Whiting et al., 2012). Leaders may see proactivity as insubordination, a threat (Frese & Fay, 2001), an ingratiation attempt (Bolino, 1999) or overstepping bounds.

In early work examining these issues in the context of followership research, Carsten and Uhl-Bien (2012) investigated how individual differences in followership co-production beliefs would be associated with the way in which followers construct and enact their roles in relation to leaders. Findings show that followers higher in co-production beliefs reported greater voice and constructive resistance. This relationship was moderated by contextual variables (considerate leader style, overall relationship quality, and autonomous work climate) for voice, but not for constructive resistance. The interaction effect, contrary to predictions, showed that individuals with stronger co-production beliefs demonstrated fairly stable voice behavior, while individuals weaker in co-production beliefs varied in their voice behavior, reporting greater voice when leaders have a considerate style, relationship quality is high, and the work climate is more autonomous. The lack of a moderating effect for constructive resistance suggests that resistance, even when constructive, may be risky. Even perceptions of a supportive climate may not be enough to encourage followers to constructively resist. With respect to voice, however, followers with stronger co-production beliefs appear to be undeterred by context. They appear more likely to speak up even when their relationship with the manager is weak or they perceive that the leader will be unreceptive. This willingness to speak up may be beneficial in cases where a leader is making bad decisions, but the question remains as to whether leaders will be open to and/or receptive of the input.

2.2.5.4. Influence tactics. Research on influence tactics shows that followers are intentional and strategic in their use of strategies to shape and define the behaviors of leaders. Typically, upward influence tactics are designed to motivate supervisors to produce the outcomes desired by the subordinate (Higgins, Judge, & Ferris, 2003). Ansari and Kapoor (1987) found that influence tactics used by subordinates are significantly affected by the manager's leadership style and that they vary as a function of the goals the follower seeks to achieve by influencing the leader. When followers seek personal benefits (e.g., career advancement), ingratiation is the most often employed tactic, whereas when followers seek organizational goals, they invoke a combination of rational and non-rational tactics, such as blocking, upward appeal, and rational persuasion. With respect to leader style, followers have a greater tendency to use non-rational tactics—such as blocking, upward appeal, and ingratiation—when responding to an authoritarian manager, and rational strategies (i.e., rational persuasion) when responding to nurturant-task/participative managers (see also Cable & Judge, 2003). Research by Grant and Hofmann (2011) shows that followers may also seek to increase their influence through proactive measures, such as role expansion, which they perceive will be beneficial to performance ratings from supervisors.

Yukl and Falbe (1990) explored the relationship between influence tactics and influence objectives in downward, upward, and lateral influence attempts.

They found that the hierarchical direction of the influence attempt (e.g., upward, downward) had more impact on influence objectives (e.g., personal objectives, organizational objectives) than on the choice of influence tactics (e.g., coalition, ingratiation). Falbe and Yukl (1992) found that follower inspirational appeals and consultation were most effective, and pressure, legitimating and coalition tactics were least effective (with rational persuasion, ingratiation, personal appeals, and exchange tactics intermediate in terms of their effectiveness). Falbe and Yukl (1992) also found that combining two soft tactics or a soft tactic with rationality tends to lead to the greatest likelihood of success. This finding is bolstered by a more recent meta-analysis showing that ingratiation (a soft tactic) and rationality consistently have the strongest positive relationships with work outcomes (Higgins et al., 2003).

What seems clear from this cursory review is that followers consider the target of their influence tactics, the purpose of their influence attempts, and actions that can be taken to shape and define leader behaviors in order to achieve the personal and organizational goals of the follower. As research on follower influence tactics has increased, the results continue to suggest a higher level of goal, target, and context complexity than previously expected (Farmer, Maslyn, Fedor, & Goodman, 1997).

2.2.6. Summary of role-based views

Role-based views of followership are recognizable to leadership scholars, as they are in line with traditional approaches to studying leadership in the context of manager and subordinate roles. The difference is that they "reverse the lens" from leaders as causal agents to followers as causal agents (Shamir, 2007). In many ways they provide interesting twists on old questions. For example, instead of investigating leader style as antecedent to organizational outcomes, role-based views call for us to investigate follower traits and behavioral styles as antecedents to leader attitudes and behavioral outcomes.

For followership research to advance, therefore, new constructs and variables will have to be developed. Some of these may be variations on existing

measures (e.g., proactive behaviors to "proactive followership behaviors"; perceived leader support to "perceived follower support"). Some may already be developed (e.g., implicit followership theories, which is theoretically derived from implicit leadership theories). Others will require new approaches, such as follower role orientations and followership outcomes. As described by Shamir (2007):

"... while ultimately our approach to the study of leadership should be neither leader-centered nor follower-centered, at this stage, the study of leadership would benefit from a more follower-centered perspective. It is important to examine not only how followers contribute to the construction of a leadership relationship but also how they empower the leader and influence his or her behavior and what is their contribution to determining the consequences of the leadership relationship" (p. xxi).

2.3. Constructionist Views

Constructionist views describe how people come together in a social process to co-create leadership and followership (DeRue & Ashford, 2010; Fairhurst & Grant, 2010). What signifies constructionist views is that they are necessarily processual views. They see people as engaging in relational interactions, and in these interactions co-producing leadership and followership (e.g., relationships, behaviors and identities) (DeRue & Ashford, 2010; Shamir, 2007). These relational interactions do not necessarily align with formal hierarchical roles. Constructionist followership research investigates how people interact and engage together in social and relational contexts to construct (or not construct) leadership and followership (Fairhurst & Uhl-Bien, 2012).

2.3.1. DeRue and Ashford's leadership identity construction process

Drawing from research on "identity work" (Pratt, Rockmann, & Kaufmann, 2006; Snow & Anderson, 1987) and social interactionism (Blumer, 1969;

Goffman, 1959), DeRue and Ashford (2010) offer a constructionist view that identifies leadership and followership as co-constructed in an interactive and reciprocal identity "claiming" and "granting" process. Claiming occurs when an individual or individuals ascertain identity as either a leader or a follower. Granting occurs when others bestow the claimed identity and claim their own identity in support of the other (i.e., "I grant you a leader identity and claim for myself a follower identity"). The process works (i.e., leadership and followership are constructed) when claims are met with grants, and vice versa. Leadership and followership can also be *not* constructed in cases where grants and claims are not reciprocally supported. In other words, even though one might have a title of a "manager," he or she may not actually be a "leader" if subordinates do not grant them a leader identity and claim for themselves a follower identity. With respect to followership, DeRue and Ashford (2010) recognize that grants involve some individuals taking on follower roles. Without this claiming of a follower identity, leadership is not constructed.

DeRue and Ashford's (2010) model has other critical implications for the study of followership. For example, in contrast to portrayals of leader and follower identities as intrapersonal, one-way and static, the social construction process sees identities as shaping and shifting over time as individuals engage in mutual influence processes. Identifying claiming and granting processes allows us to recognize that there can be different types of constructions of leadership and followership. These constructions can take the form of a stable hierarchical role relationship or a shifting leadership structure. The latter involves a "dynamic exchange of leadership and followership that is constantly being renegotiated across time and situations... [such that] the boundaries between leader and follower identities are permeable" (DeRue & Ashford, 2010, p. 635). Returning to the discussion of semantics raised earlier, this again implies that equating leaders with "managers" and followers with "subordinates" in leadership research and practice underplays the dynamic and socially constructed processes of leadership and followership.

2.3.2. Shamir's co-production

Shamir also offers a constructionist view that comes from a relational perspective, but he calls his approach "co-production." Building from LMX theory (Graen & Uhl-Bien, 1995) and Hollander's (1993) notion of an active role of the follower, Shamir (2007) proposes that leadership is jointly produced (Dvir & Shamir, 2003) by leaders and followers when they form effective leadership relationships that help them co-produce leadership outcomes. The role of the follower is to work with the leader to advance the goals, vision, and behaviors essential for both work unit and organizational success. According to Shamir (2007), co-production positions the role of followers as "broader and more consequential" than seen in traditional leader-centric theories (p. xi). A co-production view elevates followers from passive recipients of leaders' influence to active co-contributors in the leadership process (cf. Hollander & Julian, 1969). In this way, it offers a more "balanced" view to leadership by calling for leadership researchers to investigate the role of both leaders and followers in the leadership process.

2.3.3. Collinson's post-structuralist identity view

Collinson (2006) argues for the importance of understanding follower identities through the use of post-structuralist analysis. Post-structuralist approaches assume that people's lives are inextricably interwoven with society. Therefore individuals are best understood as social selves (Burkitt, 1991; Layder, 1994). As a result, people's actions must be viewed in the context of complex conditions and consequences (Giddens, 1984), such as power/knowledge regimes that influence individuals' subjectivities (Foucault, 1977, 1979).

An interesting contribution of post-structuralist analysis is that it allows us to see how individuals collude in their own subordination (Collinson, 2006). Collinson offers examples of how this can occur by describing three types of follower identities that can be enacted in the workplace. The first, *conformist selves,* acts in accordance with prescribed ideal-type behaviors. "Conforming individuals tend to be preoccupied with themselves as valued objects in the eyes of those in authority" (Collinson, 2006, p. 183). The second, *resistant selves,* focuses on our "oppositional selves" that engage various dissent strategies. These strategies are enacted to deal with dissonance we experience in response to organizational and managerial control systems (with recognition that resistance will be subject to discipline and sanctions). The third, *dramaturgical selves,* recognizes that people are "under the gaze of authority. . . aware of themselves as visible objects" (Collinson, 2006, p. 185). When this self is enacted individuals experience heightened self-consciousness that leads them to become skilled manipulators of self and information (e.g., impression management; see also Goffman, 1959). By recognizing these selves, Collinson (2006) argues that we can better understand the complex ways followers invoke and enact identities in interaction with leaders.

2.3.4. Fairhurst and Uhl-Bien's relational (discursive) approach

Fairhurst and Uhl-Bien (2012) offer a discursive approach to leadership that positions followers as "actors" who "engage, interact and negotiate" with leaders to influence organizational understandings and produce outcomes. Leadership is viewed as a "relational process co-created by leaders and followers in context" (p. 1024). Discursive approaches study this process by examining the micro-dynamics of communication in interpersonal interactions. They look for co-construction by examining, for example, sequential patterns of control among leadership actors (i.e., acts of leading and following), influential acts of organizing (e.g., influence attempts and responses) and the "language games" played by those acting in leader and follower roles (e.g., how individuals position themselves to one another and how patterned redundancies get institutionalized into roles, identities and systems, cf. DeRue & Ashford, 2010).

While Fairhurst and Uhl-Bien (2012) do not privilege followership in their discussion, the critical role of following is implicit in this process. Followership and leadership can be seen in how individuals act and respond in relational control moves, in mobilizing moves, in language games (e.g., in acts of claiming and granting, DeRue & Ashford, 2010). It can be studied by analyzing how those who occupy subordinate roles engage with those occupying manager roles to see if they are constructing or not constructing leadership (e.g., through "one-up" assertions of control, "one-down" acquiescence, or "one-across" neutral moves) (Fairhurst, Green, & Courtright, 1995; Fairhurst, Rogers, & Sarr, 1987; see also Larsson & Lundholm, 2013).

2.3.5. Summary

Our review shows that the role of followers and following is essential to leadership, so much so that it is hard to disentangle followership from leadership. This is particularly true in constructionist views, which see followership as a necessary element in the co-construction of leadership, although it also applies to role-based approaches. One of the biggest challenges for the emerging study of followership is semantics that emanate from reductionist logics that cause us to immediately hone in on the "follower" as an individual or role, overlooking the fact that "following" behavior is crucial in the construction of (or failure to construct) leadership.

Following is a particular form of behavior that involves recognizing and granting legitimacy to another's influence attempt or status (DeRue & Ashford, 2010). If there are no following behaviors, there is no leadership. *In fact, it is probably easier to recognize leadership in following behaviors than it is in leadership behaviors,* since individuals attempting to be leaders are only legitimized in the responses and reception of those willing to follow them.

This creates obvious challenges for leadership scholars. It means that if we are going to study the leadership process we need to stop relying on our broad labels of leader and follower and better understand the nature of leading and following. Bedeian and Hunt (2006) call this the "truth-in-advertising" claim in leadership: We study managers ("leaders"), but do we really study leadership? This concern is also raised in Fairhurst and Antonakis (2012), who describe the problem as coming from our observational units (individual perceptions) being out of line with our ontological units (leadership and followership behaviors and processes). If we are interested in studying leading and following then we need to adopt methodological approaches that allow us to see these behaviors in action (Fairhurst & Uhl-Bien, 2012). Some even argue that our leadership measures suffer from attributional bias that should make us question whether what we are tapping into is really a general halo effect, rather than the theoretical constructs we purport to be measuring (Martinko, Harvey, Sikora, & Douglas, 2011; cf. Phillips & Lord, 1981; Rush et al., 1977; Van Knippenberg & Sitkin, 2013).

3. A Formal Theory of Followership

Despite the obvious need to better understand the role and impact of followers and following in the co-creation of leadership, we still know little about these issues. For followership research to advance, one of the biggest needs is to clearly define and identify theoretical constructs for the study of followership. Therefore, in this section we draw from our review to introduce a formal theory of followership. In our discussion we follow established guidelines for developing theory (Bacharach, 1989; Suddaby, 2010; Sutton & Staw, 1995). We begin by providing a clear conceptual definition of the construct. We then define the boundaries of the theory, identifying what followership is and what it is not. From this we establish theoretical constructs and outline directions for future research in the study of followership using two theoretical models based on our review above: role-based and constructionist approaches.

3.1. Clear Conceptual Definition

As stated in our earlier definition, *followership theory is the study of the nature and impact of followers and following in the leadership process.*

This means that the construct of followership includes a follower role (i.e., a position in relation to leaders), following behaviors (i.e., behaviors in relation to leaders), and outcomes associated with the leadership process. If adopting a constructionist (process) approach, it involves consideration of the co-constructed nature of the leadership process.

3.2. Defining Theoretical Boundaries

Theoretical validity requires that we establish clear boundaries and a nomological network for the study of followership (Bacharach, 1989; Cronbach & Meehl, 1955). Followership *is* the characteristics, behaviors and processes of individuals acting in relation to leaders. It is *not* general employee behavior. This means that the term follower is not the same as employee. For a construct to qualify as followership it must be conceptualized and operationalized: (a) in relation to leaders or the leadership process, and/or (b) in contexts in which individuals identify themselves in follower positions (e.g., subordinates) or as having follower identities (Collinson, 2006; DeRue & Ashford, 2010).

Constructs in followership research must also be operationalized within this nomological network (Cronbach & Meehl, 1955). We list theoretical constructs and a sampling of variables that could be included in the study of followership in Figure 11.1. Examples of followership constructs are:

- *Followership characteristics:* characteristics that impact how one defines and enacts followership. (Examples may include role orientations, motivations, intellectual and analytical abilities, affect, and social constructions of followers and/or individuals identified as engaging in following behaviors.)
- *Followership behaviors:* behaviors enacted from the standpoint of a follower role or in the act of following. (Examples include the multiple expressions of overt followership including obeying, deferring, voicing, resisting, advising, etc.)
- *Followership outcomes:* outcomes of followership characteristics and behaviors that may

occur at the individual, relationship and work-unit levels. (Examples include leader reactions to followers, such as burnout or contempt; follower advancement or dismissal; whether leaders trust and seek advice from followers; and how followership contributes to the leadership process, e.g., leadership and organizational outcomes.)

In selecting variables for the study of followership, a key consideration must be whether it fits the followership domain. Followership theory is *not* the study of leadership from the follower perspective. It *is* the study of how followers view and enact following behaviors in relation to leaders. This context necessarily involves issues of power, control, motivational intentions (e.g., motivation to lead, resistance to change), personal characteristics (e.g., dominance, Machiavellianism, political skill), climate (empowering versus authoritarian), behavioral intentions, and desired outcomes of followers. *Therefore, we would not expect that because a variable has been used in leadership research it necessarily means it should be used in followership research.* Nor would *any* traits or characteristics of individuals necessarily apply to followership. Variables selected must consider the unique context and research questions associated with followership. In other words, followership research should not simply mirror or replicate leadership research. Instead we must consider the unique contexts in which following takes place and theorize and operationalize appropriately.

3.3. Conceptual Framework and Directions for Future Research

For a framework to count as a theory it must specify proposed relationships among the theoretical constructs (Sutton & Staw, 1995). Consistent with this, we identify two potential theoretical frameworks for the study of followership. The first is depicted in Figure 11.2 and represents the role-based approach. We refer to this model as "reversing the lens," since it illustrates how followers' characteristics and behaviors may affect proximal outcomes of follower and

leader behaviors, and more distal outcomes like leadership processes and organizational effectiveness. This framework highlights how followers affect followership outcomes at the individual, dyad, and work unit level of analysis.

The second framework is depicted in Figure 11.3 and represents the constructionist approach. We refer to it as "the leadership process," since it illustrates a connectionist system involving leaders (or leading) and followers (or following) interacting together in context to co-construct leadership and followership as well as their outcomes. In this sense, it highlights leadership as a dynamic process that occurs in the interactions of individuals engaged in leading and following.

These models are not the only possible frameworks for the study of followership, but we chose them to be consistent with the emerging followership approaches identified in our review. For each framework we describe the model and outline a broad agenda for future research.

3.3.1. "Reversing the lens"

The "reversing the lens" approach (see Figure 11.2) centers on investigating ways that followers construe and enact their follower role, and the outcomes associated with follower role behavior. Rather than studying leaders as the entities that "cause" outcomes, this framework focuses on studying followers' characteristics and behaviors as antecedents (i.e., causal agents) of followership outcomes (Shamir, 2007) at the individual, relationship and work unit levels of analysis.

A followership role is often ambiguous and open to interpretation (cf. Parker, 2007). As such, our framework focuses on understanding the factors that influence how one constructs their follower role (e.g., goal orientation or power orientation), the various followership role constructions or orientations that exist (e.g., passive, proactive, resistant or "non-following"), and how leadership and organizational contexts influence one's constructions (e.g., leader style, authoritarian climate) (cf. Carsten et al., 2010). Given that role perceptions and orientations directly impact role behaviors (Katz & Kahn, 1978; Selznick, 1957), these followership characteristics

Figure 11.1 Theoretical Constructs and Variables for the Study of Followership

Followership Characteristics

Follower Traits

Political Skill

Goal Orientation

Machiavellianism

Follower Motivation

Mission Consciousness

Motivation to Lead

Power Orientation

Follower Perceptions and Constructions

FIFTs

Role Orientations

Romance of Leadership

Followership Identity

Leader Characteristics

Leader Power

Dependence on Leader

Empowerment

Leader Perceptions and Constructions

Leader Identity

LIFTs

Perceived Follower Support

Satisfaction with Follower

Leader Affect

Positive and negative state and trait affect

Followership (and Leadership) Behaviors

Followership Behaviors

Proactive Behavior

Initiative Taking

Obedience

Resistance

Upward Influence

Voice

Dissent

Feedback Seeking

Advising

Leadership Behaviors

Consultation with Followers

Feedback Seeking

Democratic/ Autocratic Decision Making

Development of Followers

Followership Outcomes

Individual Follower Outcomes

Informal leadership

High Potential

Follower Effectiveness

Organizational Advancement

Individual Leader Outcomes

Energy/Burnout/Motivation

Leader Derailment

Relationship Outcomes

LMX

Trust

Leadership Process Outcomes

Higher Ethical Thinking/ Unethical Conduct

Advancing Change/ Maintaining the Status Quo

Mission Fulfillment

Goal Accomplishment

| **Figure 11.2** | Reversing the Lens |

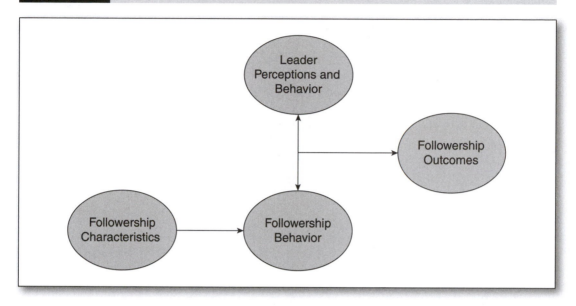

are important drivers of how followership is enacted at the individual and group levels.

In addition to understanding how individuals (or groups) construct the follower role, our framework denotes the different ways in which the follower role can be enacted, consistent with the discussion of follower typologies above. From a role perspective, they are behaviors that followers (i.e., subordinates) demonstrate while interacting with leaders (i.e., managers) in organizations. Such behaviors may serve to advance the leader or the leadership process (i.e., voice or initiative taking), derail the leader or detract from the leadership process (e.g., dysfunctional resistance), or overthrow the leader altogether (Detert & Burris, 2007; Tepper et al., 2006). Alternatively, followers may engage in behaviors that neither help nor hurt the leader (e.g., disengagement) or passively accept whatever directive the leader hands down (i.e., obedience) (Uhl-Bien & Carsten, 2007). These various followership behaviors will produce different outcomes depending on the leader, the context, and the goals to be accomplished (Carsten et al., 2010).

Followership outcomes result from followership characteristics and behaviors in the leadership process. Such outcomes can occur at the individual leader level (e.g., leader burnout), the individual

follower level (e.g., being identified as an informal leader or high potential), the relationship level (e.g., LMX), or the work-unit level with regard to leadership processes (e.g., mission fulfillment, accomplishment of goals). For example, followers can affect leaders at the individual level with regard to their motivation and energy (cf. Gooty, Connelly, Griffith, & Gupta, 2010); they can also influence the way the leader uses power and influence tactics, or the leader's ability to understand problems and priorities (cf. Yukl & Falbe, 1990). A follower's behavior is likely to be influenced by how they are treated by the leader (e.g., follower development, follower repression), whether the leader perceives them as effective, or whether they advance within the organization. At the relationship level, followership behaviors can affect LMX and the level of trust leaders have in followers. At the work unit or organizational level, followership behaviors can impact unit-level decision making, problem solving, ethical conduct, and the ability of a department or organization to adapt and change.

What is interesting about these outcomes is that they begin to explore "the leader side" of the leadership story (i.e., how leaders are affected by followers). Rather than simply agents of leadership, role-based followership approaches focus on investigating leader

Figure 11.3   The Leadership Process

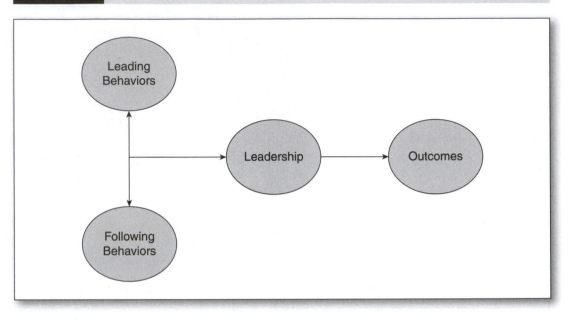

wants, needs, attitudes, motivations, emotions, and effectiveness as *outcomes* of followership characteristics, behaviors and styles. Exploring the leader side of the story makes sense, particularly in today's environment, as we know the demands on leaders are more challenging with the changing face of followership and power in the workplace (Bennis, 2000). Moreover, in most situations leaders (i.e., managers) inherit their followers (i.e., subordinates) when they enter a work unit, and those followers already have patterns of relationships and behaviors. Although leaders can try to break or influence these patterns of behavior, they cannot fully control them (Biggart & Hamilton, 1984; Streatfield, 2001). Reversing the lens causes us to think about leaders as recipients of follower behaviors and support (or lack of support), and examine issues of reverse causality raised in the literature by Lowin and Craig (1968) and Herrold (1977) but never fully explored.

3.3.2. "The leadership process"

The "leadership process" approach (see Figure 11.3) is interested in understanding how leaders and followers interact together in context to co-create leadership and its outcomes. It does not assume that leading and following are equated with one's hierarchical position in an organization. Rather, it acknowledges that managers can also follow (and might not lead), and subordinates can also lead (and might not follow). In the "leadership process" framework, the primary question of interest for followership is what characterizes following behaviors, and how do following behaviors work together with another's leading behaviors to construct leadership and its outcomes?

The basic assumption of a leadership process approach is that leadership can only occur through combined acts of leading and following. If someone makes a leadership (influence) attempt(s) but it is not responded to with following (deference) behavior(s) then it is not leadership (cf. Shamir, 2007, 2012; Uhl-Bien & Pillai, 2007). The constructionist approach to followership, therefore, studies how individuals or collectives engage in following behaviors in ways that construct leadership.

Following behaviors can be those that "grant" power and influence to another. These behaviors are associated with an individual "claiming" a follower identity or granting a leader identity (DeRue &

Ashford, 2010). Such behaviors may take the form of succumbing to the wishes or desires of another by deferring, obeying, or complying. Following behaviors could also involve "co-producing" leadership outcomes by still deferring to another and granting their leader claim, but also advising, challenging, correcting or persuading in a respectful and trusting way to generate more effective outcomes.

By thinking about followership as behaviors and relational interactions we open up possibilities for seeing leadership and followership in more meaningful ways (Uhl-Bien & Ospina, 2012). A focus on following behaviors allows us to consider how patterns of leading and following behaviors work together to construct leadership (Fairhurst et al., 1987; Fairhurst et al., 1995; Larsson & Lundholm, 2013). Questions raised by this perspective are: What do patterns of leading and following look like in effective leadership and followership? What kinds of following behaviors are effective (and ineffective) for those in formal leadership positions? Can managers follow too much or too little? How far can subordinates go with co-producing following behaviors, and when will managers accept and reject their influence attempts? Are some co-producing following behaviors more effective than others?

A leadership process approach also allows us to investigate situations of "non-following." Non-following occurs when one's leading attempts are not responded to with following behaviors. For example, non-following can occur in formal hierarchical roles when a manager's leading behaviors are responded to with subordinates' resistance behaviors. Resistance behaviors could be passive, such as ignoring or withdrawing (Tepper et al., 2001), which essentially negates a leading behavior attempt(s). Or resistance behaviors could be active, for example, when one person's (e.g., a manager's) leading attempt is met with another's (e.g., a subordinate's or group's) leading attempt, essentially constructing a power struggle (Bennett, 1988).

Right now these non-following situations are probably indicated by studies showing ineffective leadership or low quality leader-member relationships. But because our predominant approaches in leadership research have been survey data that capture individual

perspectives, we know little about the nature of actual following and non-following behaviors in the leadership process. To align with the ontology and epistemology of the leadership process model, research in this area would need to include a range of methodologies, and not just survey measures. Such methodologies could include qualitative approaches (Creswell, 2012), discursive approaches (Fairhurst & Uhl-Bien, 2012), process studies (Langley, 1999), experience based sampling (Sin, Nahrgang, & Morgeson, 2009), experimental studies (Avolio, Reichard, Hannah, Walumbwa, & Chan, 2009), etc.

4. Conclusion

Followership theory offers promise for reinvigorating leadership research in rich new ways. It:

- Moves us beyond leader-centric views to recognize the importance of follower roles, following behaviors, and the leadership process.
- Distributes responsibility for constructing leadership and its outcomes to all players (leaders and followers) in the leadership process.
- Focuses us on identifying more and less effective followership behaviors.
- Brings in context as embedded in the leadership process.
- Recognizes that leadership can flow in all directions, e.g., not only downward but also upward in a hierarchy when subordinates engage in leading behaviors.
- Allows us to understand why and how managers are not always effective leaders (i.e., when they are not able to co-construct leadership with their subordinates).
- Calls for followership development (and followership competencies), not just leadership development.

The full promise of followership theory can only be met, however, if we are disciplined to remain true to the followership construct. A temptation for leadership researchers will be to simply do what we did in leadership studies but change our causal paths and dependent variables. As we describe in our Defining theoretical boundaries section above, however, followership theory is not the mirror of leadership theory. It requires new ways of thinking, new types of theorizing, and operationalizing and testing different kinds of variables.

A very real concern we have for moving forward is that leadership researchers will flock to the role-based approach and not fully consider the leadership process approach. We tend to study what is easy (Lord & Brown, 2001). Moreover our field and journals get locked into certain methodological approaches (e.g., *Leadership Quarterly* tends toward quantitative, often at the expense of qualitative, cf. Bryman, 2004). But followership is theorized as a multi-paradigmatic framework. It calls for scholars to conduct research across a range of paradigmatic assumptions and methodological approaches: role-based approaches are more entity/postpositive and leadership process approaches are more constructionist/interpretivist (Ospina & Uhl-Bien, 2012). Moreover, it calls for theoretical models to be generated inductively (e.g., using qualitative research) as well as deductively (e.g., using quantitative research). And for true scholarly advances, followership researchers should draw insights from across all paradigmatic perspectives and findings on followership.

In moving forward with followership theory we echo Shamir's (2007) call for research that not only "reverses the lens" but also takes a "balanced" approach that views both leaders and followers as co-producers of leadership and its outcomes (see also Uhl-Bien & Ospina, 2012). In addition, we heed Van Knippenberg and Sitkin's (2013) admonishment of transformational and charismatic leadership as a strong warning call for research on followership theory: *As we advance followership theory, we must be careful not to replicate our mistakes of the past* (see Van Knippenberg & Sitkin, 2013). We suggest we can do this by paying careful attention to strong theory-building (Bacharach, 1989), adopting a range of methodological approaches (Fairhurst & Uhl-Bien, 2012), sufficiently specifying causal models with theoretically and empirically distinct paths of followership (Van Knippenberg & Sitkin, 2013), not confounding

followership with its effects (Van Knippenberg & Sitkin, 2013), and engaging in paradigm interplay among followership researchers using multiple paradigmatic perspectives (Uhl-Bien & Ospina, 2012).

In this article we set the stage for this process by offering a clear conceptual definition of followership and two general frameworks for research on followership theory based on a systematic review of the literature. We seek to spark more in-depth theorizing among followership researchers that takes into careful consideration the unique followership construct and context. By advancing a broad framework of followership that brings together scholars across multiple paradigmatic perspectives, we believe followership research can provide deep new insight into the nature of leadership and followership in organizations. In this way, we will contribute not only to our understanding of followership, but also add new understanding to what it means to be leaders and followers in the face of ever-increasing workforce demands.

References

Ansari, M. A., & Kapoor, A. (1987). Organizational context and upward influence tactics. *Organizational Behavior and Human Decision Processes*, 40(1), 39–49.

Ashford, S. J., & Cummings, L. L. (1985). Proactive feedback seeking: The instrumental use of the information environment. *Journal of Occupational Psychology*, 58, 61–91.

Ashforth, B. (1989). The experience of powerlessness in organizations. *Organizational Behavior and Human Decision Processes*, 43, 207–242.

Avolio, B. J., Reichard, R. J., Hannah, S. T., Walumbwa, F. O., & Chan, A. (2009). A meta-analytic review of leadership impact research: Experimental and quasi-experimental studies. *The Leadership Quarterly*, 20(5), 764–784.

Bacharach, S. B. (1989). Organizational theories: Some criteria for evaluation. *The Academy of Management Review*, 14(4), 496–515.

Baker, S. D. (2007). Followership: Theoretical foundation for a contemporary construct. *Journal of Leadership and Organizational Studies*, 14(1), 50–60.

Barnard, C. (1938). *The functions of the executive*. Cambridge, MA: Harvard University Press.

Bass, B. M. (1985). *Leadership and performance beyond expectations.* New York: Free Press.

Bass, B. M. (2008). *The Bass handbook of leadership* (4th ed.). New York: Free Press.

Bass, B. M., & Riggio, R. E. (2006). *Transformational leadership* (2nd ed.). Mahwah, NJ: Lawrence Erlbaum.

Bedeian, A. G., & Hunt, J. G. (2006). Academic amnesia and vestigial assumptions of our forefathers. *The Leadership Quarterly, 17*(2), 190–205.

Bennett, J. B. (1988). Power and influence as distinct personality traits: Development and validation of a psychometric measure. *Journal of Research in Personality, 22,* 361–394.

Bennis, W. G. (2000). *Managing the dream: Reflections on leadership and change.* New York: Perseus.

Biggart, N. W., & Hamilton, G. G. (1984). The power of obedience. *Administrative Science Quarterly, 29*(4), 540–549.

Bjugstad, K., Thach, E. C., Thompson, K. J., & Morris, A. (2006). A fresh look at followership: A model for matching followership and leadership styles. *Journal of Behavioral and Applied Management, 7,* 304–319.

Blass, T. (2009). From New Haven to Santa Clara: A historical perspective on the Milgram obedience experiments. *American Psychologist, 64*(1), 37–45.

Bligh, M. (2011). Followership and follower-centered approaches. In A. Bryman, D. Collinson, K. Grint, B. Jackson, & M. Uhl-Bien (Eds.), *The Sage Handbook of Leadership* (pp. 425–436). London: Sage.

Bligh, M. C., Kohles, J. C., &Meindl,J. R. (2004). Charting the language of leadership: A methodological investigation of President Bush and the crisis of 9/11. *Journal of Applied Psychology, 89*(3), 562–574.

Blumer, H. (1969). *Symbolic interactionism: Perspective and method.* Englewood Cliffs, NJ: Prentice-Hall.

Bolino, M. C. (1999). Citizenship and impression management: Good soldiers or good actors? *Academy of Management Review, 24,* 82–98.

Bono, J. E., & Judge, T. A. (2004). Personality and transformational and transactional leadership: A meta-analysis. *Journal of Applied Psychology, 89*(5), 901–910.

Bryman, A. (2004). Qualitative research on leadership: A critical but appreciative review. *The Leadership Quarterly, 15*(6), 729–769.

Burger, J. M. (2009). Replicating Milgram: Would people still obey today? *American Psychologist, 64*(1), 1–11.

Burkitt, I. (1991). *Social selves: Theories of the social formation of personality.* London: Sage.

Cable, D. M., & Judge, T. A. (2003). Managers' upward influence tactic strategies: The role of manager personality and supervisor leadership style. *Journal of Organizational Behavior, 24*(2), 197–214.

Carsten, M., & Uhl-Bien, M. (2012). Follower beliefs in the co-production of leadership: Examining upward communication and the moderating role of context. *Journal of Psychology, 220*(4), 210–220.

Carsten, M., & Uhl-Bien, M. (2013). Ethical followership: An examination of followership beliefs and crimes of obedience. *Journal of Leadership & Organizational Studies, 20*(1), 45–57.

Carsten, M., Uhl-Bien, M., & Jaywickrema, A. (2013). *"Reversing the lens" in leadership research: Investigating follower role orientation and leadership outcomes.* New Orleans, Louisiana: Presented at the Southern Management Association (SMA) Annual Meeting.

Carsten, M. K., Uhl-Bien, M., West, B. J., Patera, J. L., & McGregor, R. (2010). Exploring social constructs of followership: A qualitative study. *The Leadership Quarterly, 21*(3), 543–562.

Chaleff, I. (1995). *The courageous follower: Standing up to and for our leaders.* San Francisco: Barrett-Koehler Publishers, Inc.

Chaleff, I. (2003). *The courageous follower: Standing up to and for our leaders* (2nd ed.). San Francisco: Berret-Koehler Publishers, Inc.

Chaleff, I. (2008). Creating new ways of following. In R. Riggio, I. Chaleff, &J. Lipman-Blumen (Eds.), *The art of followership: How great followers create great leaders and organizations* (pp. 67–87). San Francisco: Jossey-Bass.

Chemers, M. M. (2001). Leadership effectiveness: An integrative review. In M. A. Hogg, & R. S. Tindale (Eds.), *Blackwell handbook ofsocial psychology: Group processes* (pp. 376–399). Oxford, UK: Blackwell.

Collinson, D. (2006). Rethinking followership: A poststructuralist analysis of follower identities. *The Leadership Quarterly, 17*(2), 179–189.

Conger, J. A., & Kanungo, R. N. (1987). Toward a behavioral theory of charismatic leadership in organizations. *Academy of Management Review, 12*(4), 637–647.

Conger, J. A., & Kanungo, R. N. (1988). The empowerment process: Integrating theory and practice. *Academy of Management Review, 13*(3), 471–482.

Courpasson, D., & Dany, F. (2003). Indifference or obedience? Business firms as democratic hybrids. *Organization Studies, 24*(8), 1231–1260.

Creswell, J. W. (2012). *Qualitative inquiry and research design: Choosing among five approaches* (3rd ed.). Thousand Oaks, CA: Sage Publications.

Cronbach, L. J., & Meehl, P. E. (1955). Construct validity in psychological tests. *Psychological bulletin, 52*(4), 281–302.

Dansereau, F., Graen, G., & Haga, W. J. (1975). A vertical dyad linkage approach to leadership within formal organizations: A longitudinal investigation of the role making process. *Organizational Behavior and Human Performance, 13*(1), 46–78.

De Cremer, D., & Van Dijk, E. (2005). When and why leaders put themselves first: Leader behaviour in resource allocations as a function of feeling entitled. *European Journal of Social Psychology, 35*(4), 553–563.

De Vries, R. E., & Van Gelder, J. (2005). Leadership and the need for leadership: Testing an implicit followership theory. In B. Schyns, & J. R. Meindl (Eds.), *Implicit leadership theories: Essays and explorations* (pp. 277–304). Greenwich, CN: Information Age Publishers.

DeRue, S., & Ashford, S. (2010). Who will lead and who will follow? A social process of leadership identity construction in organizations. *Academy of Management Review, 35*(4), 627–647.

Detert, J. R., & Bums, E. R. (2007). Leadership behavior and employee voice: Is the door really open? *Academy of Management Journal, 50*(4), 869–884.

Dinh, J. E., & Lord, R. G. (2012). Implications of dispositional and process views of traits for individual difference research in leadership. *The Leadership Quarterly, 23*(4), 651–669.

Dvir, T., & Shamir, B. (2003). Follower developmental characteristics as predicting transformational leadership: A longitudinal field study. *The Leadership Quarterly, 14*(3), 327–344.

Eden, D., & Leviatan, U. (1975). Implicit leadership theory as a determinant of the factor structure underlying supervisory behavior scales. *Journal of Applied Psychology, 60*(6), 736–741.

Ehrhart, M. G., & Klein, K. J. (2001). Predicting followers' preferences for charismatic leadership: The influence of follower values and personality. *The Leadership Quarterly, 12*(2), 153–179.

Epitropaki, O., & Martin, R. (2004). Implicit leadership theories in applied settings: Factor structure, generalizability, and stability over time. *Journal of Applied Psychology, 89*(2), 293–310.

Epitropaki, O., Sy, T., Martin, R., Tram, S., & Topakas, A. (2013). Implicit leadership and followership theories 'In the Wild:' Taking stock of leadership processing approaches in organizational settings. *The Leadership Quarterly, 24*(6) 858–851.

Fairhurst, G., & Antonakis, J. (2012). Dialogue: A research agenda for relational leadership. In M. Uhl-Bien, & S. Ospina (Eds.), *Advancing relational leadership research* (pp. 433–459). Charlotte, NC: Information Age Publishers.

Fairhurst, G. T., & Grant, D. (2010). The social construction of leadership: A sailing guide. *Management Communication Quarterly, 24*(2), 171–210.

Fairhurst, G. T., Green, S. G., & Courtright, J. A. (1995). Inertial forces and the implementation of a sociotechnical systems approach: A communication study. *Organization Science, 6*, 168–185.

Fairhurst, G. T., & Hamlett, S. R. (2003). The narrative basis of leader-member exchange. In G. B. Graen (Ed.), *LMX leadership: The series* (pp. 117–144). Charlotte, NC: Information Age Publishers.

Fairhurst, G. T., Rogers, L. E., & Sarr, R. (1987). Manager-subordinate control patterns and judgments about the relationship. In M. McLaughlin (Ed.), *Communication yearbook 10* (pp. 395–415). Beverly Hills, CA: Sage.

Fairhurst, G. T., & Uhl-Bien, M. (2012). Organizational discourse analysis (ODA): Examining leadership as a relational process. *The Leadership Quarterly, 23*(6), 1043–1062.

Falbe, C. M., & Yukl, G. (1992). Consequences for managers of using single influence tactics and combinations of tactics. *Academy of Management Journal, 35*(3), 638–652.

Farmer, S. M., Maslyn, J. M., Fedor, D. B., & Goodman, J. S. (1997). Putting upward influence strategies in context. *Journal of Organizational Behavior, 18*(1), 17–42.

Fiedler, F. E. (1967). *A theory of leadership effectiveness.* New York: McGraw-Hill.

Fleishman, E. A. (1953). The description of supervisory behavior. *Journal of Applied Psychology, 37*, 1–6.

Follett, M. P. (1927). Leader and expert. In H. C. Metcalf (Ed.), *The psychological foundations of management* (pp. 220–243). Chicago: Shaw.

Follett, M. P. (1949). *The essentials of leadership.* London: Management Publications Trust.

Foucault, M. (1977). *Discipline and punish.* London: Allen Unwin.

Foucault, M. (1979). *The history of sexuality.* London: Allen Unwin.

Frese, M., & Fay, D. (2001). Personal initiative: An active performance concept for work in the 21st century. *Research in Organizational Behavior, 23*, 133–187.

Gardner, J. W. (1990). *On leadership.* New York: Free Press.

Gerber, G. W. (1988). Leadership roles and the gender stereotype traits. *Sex Roles,* 18(11/12), 649–668.

Giddens, A. (1984). *The constitution of society.* Cambridge: Polity.

Goffman, E. (1959). *The presentation of self in everyday life.* New York: Doubleday Anchor.

Gooty, J., Connelly, S., Griffith, J., & Gupta, A. (2010). Leadership, affect, and emotions: A state of the science review. *The Leadership Quarterly,* 21(6), 979–1004.

Graen, G., Novak, M. A., & Sommerkamp, P. (1982). The effects of leader-member exchange and job design on productivity and satisfaction: Testing a dual attachment model. *Organizational Behavior and Human Performance,* 30(1), 109–131.

Graen, G. B., & Scandura, T. A. (1987). Toward a psychology of dyadic organizing. *Research in Organizational Behavior,* 9,175–208.

Graen, G. B., & Uhl-Bien, M. (1995). Relationship-based approach to leadership: Development of leader-member exchange (LMX) theory of leadership over 25 years: Applying a multi-level multi-domain perspective. *The Leadership Quarterly,* 6(2), 219–247.

Graham, P. (2003). *Mary Parker Follett: Prophet of management.* Maryland: Beard Books.

Grant, A., & Ashford, S. (2008). The dynamics of proactivity at work. *Research in Organizational Behavior,* 28, 3–34.

Grant, A. M., & Hofmann, D. A. (2011). Role expansion as a persuasion process: The interpersonal influence dynamics of role redefinition. *Organizational Psychology Review,* 1(1), 9–31.

Grant, A. M., Parker, S., & Collins, C. (2009). Getting credit for proactive behavior: Supervisor reactions depend on what you value and how you feel. *Personnel Psychology,* 62(1), 31–55.

Heckscher, C. (1994). Defining the post-bureaucratic type. In C. Heckscher, & A. Donnellon (Eds.), *The post-bureaucratic organization: New perspectives on organizational change.* Thousand Oaks, CA: Sage.

Herrold, D. M. (1977). Two-way influence processes in leader-follower dyads. *Academy of Management Journal,* 20(2), 224–237.

Hersey, P., & Blanchard, K. H. (1977). *Management of organizational behavior: Utilizing human resources.* Englewood Cliffs, NJ: Prentice-Hall.

Higgins, C. A., Judge, T. A., & Ferris, G. R. (2003). Influence tactics and work outcomes: a meta analysis. *Journal of Organizational Behavior,* 24(1), 89–106.

Hinrichs, K. T. (2007). Follower propensity to commit crimes of obedience: The role of leadership beliefs. *Journal of Leadership & Organizational Studies,* 14(1), 69–76.

Hogan, R., Curphy, G. J., & Hogan, J. (1994). What we know about leadership: Effectiveness and personality. *American Psychologist,* 49(6), 493–504.

Hogg, M. A. (2001). A social identity theory of leadership. *Personality and Social Psychology Review,* 5(3), 184–200.

Hogg, M. A., & Reid, S. A. (2006). Social identity, self-categorization, and the communication of group norms. *Communication Theory,* 16(1), 7–30.

Hogg, M. A., & Terry, D. I. (2000). Social identity and self-categorization processes in organizational contexts. *Academy of Management Review,* 25(1), 121–140.

Hollander, E. P. (1958). Conformity, status and idiosyncrasy credit. *Psychological Review,* 65(2), 117–127.

Hollander, E. P. (1971). Style, structure and setting in organizational leadership. *Administrative Science Quarterly,* 16(1), 1–9.

Hollander, E. P. (1985). Leadership and power. *The Handbook of Social Psychology,* 2, 485–537.

Hollander, E. P. (1986). On the central role of leadership processes. *Applied Psychology,* 35(1), 39–52.

Hollander, E. P. (1992a). The essential interdependence of leadership and followership. *Current Directions in Psychological Science,* 1(2), 71–75.

Hollander, E. P. (1992b). Leadership, followership, self, and others. *Leadership Quarterly,* 3(1), 43–54.

Hollander, E. P. (1993). Legitimacy, power, and influence: A perspective on relational features of leadership. In M. Chemers, & R. Ayman (Eds.), *Leadership theory and research: Perspectives and directions* (pp. 29–47). San Diego: Academic Press.

Hollander, E. P. (2012). Inclusive leadership and idiosyncrasy credit in leader-follower relations. In M. G. Rumsey (Ed.), *The Oxford handbook of leadership* (pp. 122–143). Oxford, UK: Oxford University Press.

Hollander, E. P., & Julian, J. W. (1969). Contemporary trends in the analysis of leadership processes. *Psychological Bulletin,* 71(5), 387–397.

Hollander, E. P., & Offermann, L. R. (1990). Power and leadership in organizations: Relationships in transition. *American Psychologist,* 45, 179–189.

Hoption, C. B., Christie, A. M., & Barling, J. (2012). Submitting to the follower label: Followership, positive affect and extra-role behaviors. *Journal of Psychology,* 220, 221–230.

Howell, J., & Mendez, M. (2008). Three perspectives on followership. In R. Riggio, I. Chaleff, &J. Lipman-Blumen (Eds.), *The art of followership: How great followers create great leaders and organizations* (pp. 25–40). San Francisco: Jossey-Bass.

Howell, J. M., & Shamir, B. (2005). The role of followers in the charismatic leadership process: Relationships and their consequences. *Academy of Management Review,* 30(1), 96–112.

Judge, T. A., Bono, J. E., Ilies, R., & Gerhardt, M. W. (2002). Personality and leadership: A qualitative and quantitative review. *Journal of Applied Psychology,* 87(4), 765–780.

Judge, T. A., Piccolo, R. F., & Ilies, R. (2004). The forgotten ones? The validity of consideration and initiating structure in leadership research. *Journal of Applied Psychology,* 89(1), 36–51.

Katz, D., & Kahn, R. L. (1978). *The social psychology of organizations* (2nd ed.). New York: John Wiley & Sons.

Kellerman, B. (2008). *Followership: How followers are creating change and changing leaders.* Boston: Harvard Business Press.

Kelley, R. E. (1988). In praise of followers. *Harvard Business Review,* 66(6), 141–148.

Kelley, R. E. (1992). *The power of followership.* New York: Doubleday Business.

Kelley, R. E. (2008). Rethinking followership. In R. Riggio, I. Chaleff, & J. Lipman-Blumen (Eds.), *The art of followership: How great followers create great leaders and organizations* (pp. 5–16). San Francisco: Jossey-Bass.

King, A. J., Johnson, D. D., & Van Vugt, M. (2009). The origins and evolution of leadership. *Current Biology,* 19(19), 1591–1682.

Kipnis, D., Schmidt, S. M., & Wilkinson, I. (1980). Intraorganizational influence tactics: Explorations in getting one's way. *Journal of Applied Psychology,* 65(4), 440–452.

Klein, K. J., & House, R. J. (1995). On fire: Charismatic leadership and levels of analysis. *The Leadership Quarterly,* 6(2), 183–198.

Korman, A. K. (1966). Consideration, initiating structure, and organizational criteria: A review. *Personnel Psychology,* 19, 349–361.

Kruse, E., & Sy, T. (2011). Manipulating implicit theories by inducing affect. *Academy of Management Proceedings,* 1, 1–6.

Langley, A. (1999). Strategies for theorizing from process data. *Academy of Management Review,* 24(4), 691–710.

Larsson, M., & Lundholm, S. (2013). Talking work in a bank: A study of organizing properties of leadership in work interactions. *Human Relations,* 66(8), 1101–1129.

Layder, D. (1994). *Understanding social theory.* London: Sage.

Liden, R. C., Sparrowe, R. T., & Wayne, S. J. (1997). Leader-member exchange theory: The past and potential for the future. In G. R. Ferris (Ed.), *Research in personnel and human resources management, Vol. 15.* (pp. 47–119). Greenwich, CT: JAI Press.

Lipman-Blumen, J. (2005). Toxic leadership: When grand illusions masquerade as noble visions. *Leader to Leader, 36,* 29–36.

Lord, R. G. (1985). An information processing approach to social perceptions, leadership and behavioral measurement in organizations. *Research in Organizational Behavior,* 7, 87–128.

Lord, R. G. (2013). *Four leadership principles that are worth remembering. Presentation to the Biennial Meetings of the Australian Industrial Organizational Psychology,* Perth Australia.

Lord, R. G., & Brown, D. J. (2001). Leadership, values, and subordinate self-concepts. *The Leadership Quarterly,* 12(2), 133–152.

Lord, R. G., & Brown, D. J. (2004). *Leadership processes and follower self-identity.* Mahwah, NJ: Lawrence Erlbaum Associates Publishers.

Lord, R. G., Brown, D. J., & Freiberg, S.J. (1999). Understanding the dynamics of leadership: The role of follower self-concepts in the leader/follower relationship. *Organizational Behavior and Human Decision Processes,* 78(3), 167–203.

Lord, R. G., Brown, D. J., Harvey, J. L., & Hall, R. J. (2001). Contextual constraints on prototype generation and their multilevel consequences for leadership perceptions. *The Leadership Quarterly,* 12(3), 311–338.

Lowin, A., & Craig, J. R. (1968). The influence of level of performance on managerial style: An experimental object-lesson in the ambiguity of correlational data. *Organizational Behavior and Human Performance,* 3(4), 440–458.

Martinko, M., Harvey, P., Sikora, D., & Douglas, S. (2011). Perceptions of abusive supervision: The role of subordinates' attributional styles. *The Leadership Quarterly,* 22(4), 751–764.

Meindl, J. R. (1990). On leadership: An alternative to the conventional wisdom. *Research in Organizational Behavior,* 12, 159–203.

Meindl, J. R., Ehrlich, S. B., & Dukerich, J. M. (1985). The romance of leadership. *Administrative Science Quarterly,* 30, 78–102.

Milgram, S. (1965). Some conditions of obedience and disobedience to authority. *Human Relations,* 18(1), 57–76.

Milgram, S. (1974). *Obedience to authority: An experimental view.* New York: Harper & Row.

Morrison, E. W. (2006). Doing the job well: An investigation of pro-social rule breaking. *Journal of Management,* 32(1), 5–28.

Morrison, E. W., & Milliken, F. J. (2000). Organizational silence: A barrier to change and development in a pluralistic world. *Academy of Management Review,* 25(4), 706–725.

Morrison, E. W., & Phelps, C. C. (1999). Taking charge at work: Extra-role efforts to initiate workplace change. *Academy of Management Journal,* 42(4), 403–419.

Oc, B., & Bashshur, M. R. (2013). Followership, leadership, and social influence. *The Leadership Quarterly,* 24(6), 919–934.

Oc, B., Bashshur, M. R., & Moore, C. (2013). Stooges and squeaky wheels: How followers shape leader fairness over time. *Working paper.*

Ospina, S., & Uhl-Bien, M. (2012). Mapping the terrain: Convergence and divergence around relational leadership. In M. Uhl-Bien & S. Ospina (Eds.), *Advancing Relational Leadership Research: A Dialogue Among Perspectives* (pp. xix–xlvii). Charlotte, NC: Information Age Publishers.

Padilla, A., Hogan, R., & Kaiser, R. B. (2007). The toxic triangle: Destructive leaders, susceptible followers, and conducive environments. *The Leadership Quarterly,* 18(3), 176–194.

Parker, S. K. (2007). "That is my job": How employees role orientation affects their job performance. *Human Relations,* 60(3), 403–434.

Parker, S. K., Wall, T. D., & Jackson, P. R. (1997). "That's not my job": Developing flexible employee work orientations. *Academy of Management Journal,* 40(4), 899–929.

Passini, S., & Morselli, D. (2009). Authority relationships between obedience and disobedience. *New Ideas in Psychology,* 27(1), 96–106.

Pearce, C. L., & Conger, J. A. (2003). *Shared leadership: Reframing the hows and whys of leadership.* Thousand Oaks, CA: Sage.

Phillips, J. S., & Lord, R. G. (1981). Causal attributions and perceptions of leadership. *Organizational Behavior and Human Performance,* 28(2), 143–163.

Pratt, M. G., Rockmann, K. W., & Kaufmann, J. B. (2006). Constructing professional identity: The role of work and identity learning cycles in the customization of identity among medical residents. *Academy of Management Journal,* 49(2), 235–262.

Ravlin, E. C., & Thomas, D. C. (2005). Status and stratification processes in organizational life. *Journal of Management,* 31(6), 966–987.

Rost, J. C. (1993). *Leadership for the twenty-first century.* New York: Praeger.

Rost, J. C. (2008). Followership: An outmoded concept. In R. Riggio, I. Chaleff, & J. Lipman-Blumen (Eds.), *The art of followership: How great followers create great leaders and organizations* (pp. 53–64). San Francisco, CA: Jossey-Bass.

Rush, M. C., Thomas, J. C., & Lord, R. G. (1977). Implicit leadership theory: A potential threat to the internal validity of leader behavior questionnaires. *Organizational Behavior and Human Performance,* 20(1), 93–110.

Sanford, F. H. (1950). *Authoritarianism and leadership: A study of the follower's orientation to authority.* Philadelphia: Institute for Research in Human Relations.

Schyns, B., & Meindl, J. R. (Eds.). (2005). *Implicit leadership theories: Essays and explorations.* Greenwich, CT: Information Age Publishers.

Selznick, P. (1957). *Leadership in administration.* New York: Harper & Row.

Shalit, A., Popper, M., & Zakay, D. (2010). Followers' attachment styles and their preference for social or for personal charismatic leaders. *Leadership & Organization Development Journal,* 31(5), 458–472.

Shamir, B. (2007). From passive recipients to active co-producers: Followers' roles in the leadership process. In B. Shamir, R. Pillai, M. Bligh, & M. Uhl-Bien (Eds.), *Follower-centered perspectives on leadership: A tribute to the memory of James R. Meindl* (pp. ix–xxxix). Charlotte, NC: Information Age Publishers.

Shamir, B. (2012). Leadership research or post-leadership research: Advancing leadership theory versus throwing out the baby with the bath water. In M. Uhl-Bien, & S. Ospina (Eds.), *Advancing relational leadership research: A dialogue among perspectives* (pp. 477–500). Charlotte, NC: Information Age Publishers.

Sin, H. P., Nahrgang, J. D., & Morgeson, F. P. (2009). Understanding why they don't see eye to eye: An examination of leader-member exchange (LMX) agreement. *Journal of Applied Psychology,* 94(4), 1048–1057.

Sivasubramaniam, N., Kroeck, K. G., & Lowe, K. B. (1997). In the eye of the beholder: Folk theories of leadership in an academic institution. *Journal of Leadership Studies,* 4(2), 27–42.

Snow, D. A., & Anderson, L. (1987). Identity work among the homeless: The verbal construction and avowal of personal identities. *American Journal of Sociology,* 96(6), 1336–1371.

Stogdill, R. M. (1948). Personal factors associated with leadership: A survey of the literature. *Journal of Psychology,* 25(1), 35–71.

Stogdill, R. M. (1950). Leadership, membership and organization. *Psychological Bulletin,* 47(1), 1–14.

Streatfield, P. J. (2001). *The paradox of control in organizations.* London: Routledge.

Suddaby, R. (2010). Editor's comments: Construct clarity in theories of management and organization. *The Academy of Management Review,* 35(3), 346–357.

Sutton, R. I., & Staw, B. M. (1995). What theory is not. *Administrative Science Quarterly,* 40(3), 371–384.

Sy, T. (2010). What do you think of followers? Examining the content, structure, and consequences of implicit followership theories. *Organizational Behavior and Human Decision Processes,* 113(2), 73–84.

Sy, T. (2011). *I think, therefore I do: Influence of leaders' and followers' implicit followership theories on relationship quality and follower performance.* San Antonio, TX: Presented at the Academy of Management.

Sy, T. (2013). *An indirect measure of IFTs using a projective approach.* Unpublished Manuscript.

Taylor, F. W. (1911). *The principles of scientific management.* New York: Harper & Bros.

Taylor, F. W. (1934). *The principles of scientific management.* New York: Harper & Bros.

Taylor, F. W. (1947). *The principles of scientific management.* New York: Harper & Brothers.

Tepper, B. J., Duffy, M. K., & Shaw, J. D. (2001). Personality moderators of the relationship between abusive supervision and subordinates' resistance. *The Journal of Applied Psychology,* 86(5), 974–983.

Tepper, B. J., Uhl-Bien, M., Kohut, G. F., Rogleberg, S. G., Lockhart, D. E., & Ensley, M. D. (2006). Subordinates' resistance and managers' evaluations of subordinates' performance. *Journal of Management,* 32(2), 185–209.

Townsend, P. L., & Gebhardt, J. E. (1997). *Five-star leadership: The art and strategy of creating leaders at every level.* New York: Wiley.

Uhl-Bien, M., & Carsten, M. (2007). Being ethical when the boss is not. *Organizational Dynamics,* 36(2), 187–201.

Uhl-Bien, M., Graen, G. B., & Scandura, T. A. (2000). Implications of leader-member exchange (LMX) for strategic human resource management systems: Relationships as social capital for competitive advantage. *Research in Personnel and Human Resources Management,* 18,137–186.

Uhl-Bien, M., & Ospina, S. (2012). Paradigm interplay in relational leadership: A way forward. In M. Uhl-Bien, & S. Ospina (Eds.), *Advancing relational leadership research: A dialogue among perspectives* (pp. 537–580). Charlotte, NC: Information Age Publishers.

Uhl-Bien, M., & Pillai, R. (2007). The romance of leadership and the social construction of followership. In B. Shamir, R. Pillai, M. Bligh, & M. Uhl-Bien (Eds.), *Follower-centered perspectives on leadership: A tribute to the memory of James R. Meindl* (pp. 187–210). Charlotte, NC: Information Age Publishers.

Van Dyne, L., & LePine, J. A. (1998). Helping and extra-role behavior: Evidence of construct and predictive validity. *Academy of Management Journal,* 41(1), 108–119.

Van Knippenberg, D., & Hogg, M. A. (2003). A social identity model of leadership effectiveness in organizations. *Research in Organizational Behavior,* 25,243–295.

Van Knippenberg, D., & Sitkin, S. B. (2013). A critical assessment of charismatic-transformational leadership research: Back to the drawing board? *The Academy of Management Annals,* 7(1), 1–60.

Van Vugt, M. (2006). Evolutionary origins of leadership and followership. *Personality and Social Psychology Review,* 10(4), 354–371.

Van Vugt, M., Hogan, R., & Kaiser, R. B. (2008). Leadership, followership, and evolution: Some lessons from the past. *American Psychologist,* 63(3), 182.

Vroom, V. H., & Jago, A. G. (1978). On the validity of the Vroom-Yetton model. *Journal of Applied Psychology,* 63,151–162.

Vroom, V. H., & Yetton, P. W. (1973). *Leadership and decision-making.* Pittsburgh, PA: University of Pittsburgh Press.

Weber, Max (1968). *Economy and society.* Totowa, NJ: Bedminster.

Weick, K. E. (1979). Cognitive processes in organizations. *Research in Organizational Behavior,* 1, 41–74. Weick, K. E. (1995). *Sensemaking in organizations (vol. 3).* London: Sage.

Weierter, S. J. (1997). Who wants to play "follow the leader"? A theory of charismatic relationships based on routinized charisma and follower characteristics. *Leadership Quarterly*, 8(2), 171–194.

Whiteley, P., Sy, T., & Johnson, S. K. (2012). Leaders' conceptions of followers: Implications for naturally occurring pygmalion effects. *The Leadership Quarterly*, 23(5), 822–834.

Whiting, S. W., Maynes, T. D., Podsakoff, N. P., & Podsakoff, P. M. (2012). Effects of message, source, and context on evaluations of employee voice behavior. *Journal of Applied Psychology*, 97(1), 159–182.

Yukl, G. (2001). *Leadership in organizations* (5th ed.). Upper Saddle River, NJ: Prentice Hall.

Yukl, G. (2012). *Leadership in organizations* (8th ed.). New York: Prentice Hall.

Yukl, G., & Falbe, C. M. (1990). Influence tactics and objectives in upward, downward, and lateral influence attempts. *Journal of Applied Psychology*, 75(2), 132–140.

Yukl, G., & Van Fleet, D. D. (1992). Theory and research on leadership in organizations. In M. D. Dunnette, & L. M. Hough (Eds.), *Handbook of industrial and organizational psychology* (pp. 147–197) (2nd ed.). Palo Alto, CA: Consulting Psychologists Press.

Zaleznik, A. (1965). The dynamics of subordinacy. *Harvard Business Review*, 43(3), 119–131.

Zaleznik, A., & Kets de Vries, M. F. (1975). *Power and the corporate mind*. Boston: Houghton Mifflin.

PART III

Shared or Collective Leadership

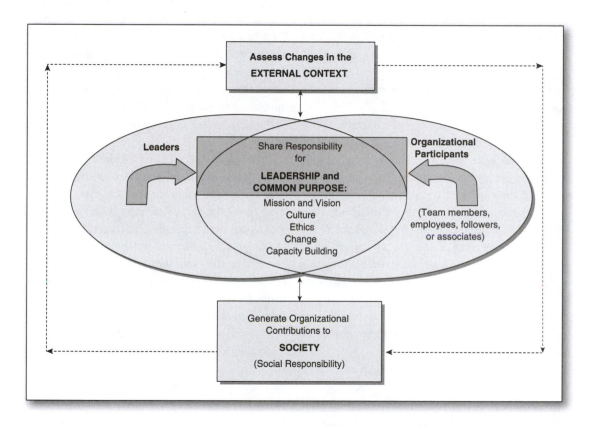

Overview

A primary assumption underlying this book is that new era organizations can become better able to meet the challenges of their complex and rapidly changing environment through shared or collective responsibility for leadership. Shared leadership in various forms from self-led teams to democratic workplaces is gaining momentum in leadership research and practice, though it is not presently as pervasive as more predominant forms of leadership. In the words

of Zander, Mockaitis, and Butler (discussed later in this section), these new forms are "surfacing more quickly than scholars are able to study them; research on global and virtual team leadership, in particular, is lagging behind." This research–practice gap is one of the main challenges for current and future research on shared leadership.

The chapters in Part III present concepts, theories, and research that contribute to the developing area of shared or collective leadership. Together organization members generate and commit to the organization's common purpose and cultivate its leadership. With the common purpose and leadership framework intact, leaders and members share responsibilities for the organization's mission and vision, culture, ethics, change, capacity building, and contributions to society.

Gill Hickman and Georgia Sorenson (Chapter 12) present a shared leadership concept called *invisible leadership* where the impetus and motivation for leadership originate from the common purpose. Invisible leadership embodies situations in which dedication to a compelling and deeply held common purpose is the motivating force for leadership. Individuals willingly use their strengths in leader or follower roles and cultivate a strong shared bond that connects participants to each other in pursuit of their purpose.

The researchers stress that purpose is more than a mission statement. It is a deeply held sense of common destiny, a life course or calling; it is aligned with a mission but resonates profoundly with people's values and their sense of themselves. It binds people together and is the reason for their shared leadership. The common purpose is often the reason people are attracted to the work of an organization; and often the reason they stay. This invisible force is the space where inspiration, interactions, and connections between the purpose and its leaders and followers ignite to bring about something extraordinary. Hickman and Sorenson refer to this phenomenon as *charisma of purpose.*

The question underlying this research was, "Can a common purpose actually inspire leadership?" To answer this question, the researchers surveyed members of 21 democratic companies and nonprofit organizations. They used an eight factor scale consisting of self-selection/attraction; commitment to or ownership of the purpose; influence/inspiration to contribute; bond among participants; self-agency; taking action (leadership) visibly or invisibly; rising above self-interest; and taking advantage of or utilizing opportunities and resources. Though the data are not reported in this chapter of their book, the researchers found the vast majority of respondents agreed or strongly agreed—they were committed to achieving their organization's common purpose; they

accepted the common purpose as their own; the common purpose inspired them to contribute their best work; they formed a strong bond or relationship among employees by working together on behalf of the common purpose; they were willing to work in either a leader or team member role to accomplish the common purpose; and they believed they had the power to act (lead) on behalf of the organization's common purpose.

Christina L. Wassenaar and Craig L. Pearce (Chapter 13) describe the shift from hierarchical to shared leadership as moving the role of leadership from one person's hand to the arms of the group as they work together toward their common objectives. They define shared leadership as "a dynamic interactive influence process among individuals in groups for which the object is to lead one another to the achievement of group or organizational goals or both."

Wassenaar and Pearce provide a historical base for shared leadership that incorporates Follett's law of the situation (follow the person in the group with the most knowledge of the situation); Hollander's leadership emergence (leaders emerge from or are selected by the group); leadership substitutes (processes or procedures that can substitute for a hierarchical leader); Manz and Sims' self-leadership (groups lead themselves without formal leaders); and empowerment (delegation of power from the top level to individuals who are responsible for the day-to-day work).

Studies to date have researched the antecedents and outcomes of shared leadership. Several antecedents were found to enable shared leadership: facilitating forces and actions of hierarchical or vertical leaders; enabling support structures such as technology, team training, and coaching; conducive organizational culture and group empowerment; relationship longevity; flow, especially in creative groups; and proximity. Studies found outcomes of shared leadership at the individual, group, and organizational levels. Individual outcomes associated with shared leadership entail individual satisfaction, self-efficacy, and mimetic effect, which means as people learned shared leadership from others, they mimetic those behaviors in their units. Group-level outcomes include cognitive advantages (team confidence and potency, motivation, social integration, group cohesion, and group empowerment); behavioral outcomes (team citizenship and networking behavior, constructive interaction, swift coordination of activities, reliability, information exchange, and intercultural fit); and group/team effectiveness and performance. Organization-level outcomes in one study demonstrated that shared leadership in multiple firms predicted the companies' financial performance. In another study, the company demonstrated increased revenues, reduced turnover, and substantially higher numbers of job applications.

Increasingly, scholars and practitioners are beginning to view leadership as a process that can be shared, distributed, and acted on collectively. Consistent with other authors in this section, Wassenaar and Pearce acknowledge the need for considerably more research in this area and better understanding of the methods used to measure shared leadership.

One rapidly developing form of shared leadership is e-leadership. Bruce Avolio, John Sosik, Surinder Kahai, and Bradford Baker (Chapter 14) review the research on e-leadership more than a decade after Avolio, Kahai, and Dodge's 2001 article on the same topic. The aim of their review is to examine how advanced information technology (AIT) and leadership interact and how their interaction affects individuals, groups, organizations, and communities. Their updated definition describes e-leadership as "a social influence process embedded in both proximal and distal contexts mediated by AIT that can produce a change in attitudes, feelings, thinking, behavior and performance."

The researchers stress that AIT is transforming the way people work, and it is actually transforming organizations. They examine the positive and negative aspects of several distinct changes in the workplace: the increasing use of AIT in organizations; greater transparency and openness; the rise of social networks; constant contact between and among organization members; and increased use of tracking devices.

There has been increased interest in the emerging concept of e-leadership but insufficient understanding of and research on the effect of technologies on leadership. Avolio, Sosik, Kahai, and Baker draw several conclusions based on their review of the leadership literature.

- The gap between the practice and implementation of AIT and what we know about its effects has grown over the last decade.
- Opportunities to examine how AIT can completely transform the way leaders are developed is barely mentioned in leadership literature, but information is beginning to appear on the use of technology to support leadership development such as online learning or development tools.
- There are many ethical issues that need to be addressed regarding how applications of the technology should and should not be used in e-leadership.
- There has been relatively little in the leadership literature on how leadership styles and orientations interact with some of the latest AIT.
- There has been relatively little attention paid to the impact of social, cultural, and physical distance that is mediated in e-leadership.
- Researchers need to examine leadership within and across all organizational levels based on the new connections made possible with AIT—including leading peer-to-peer and leading up management levels.
- How organizations are structured in the future, and how they change and transform will no doubt be affected by the appropriation of AIT.

Based on the authors' findings, much more research is needed in the vital area of e-leadership. They contend that "it may be time to totally rethink what constitutes an organization and in turn, its leadership."

Complexity leadership generates shared processes by allowing leadership to emerge from various parts of the organization in response to arising situations and needs. Mary Uhl-Bien and Russ Marion (Chapter 15) explain that complexity theory developed as organizations moved from static equilibrium to dynamic equilibrium models in response to a context of dynamic and continual changes. "Complexity leadership theory is the study of leadership based in complexity science." According to Wheatley's 1992 concept, complexity theory presumes leadership emerges from interactions and relationships among people in the organization in response to nonlinear, emergent changes and situations in the organization and its environmental context. Leadership in this setting is more fluid, responsive, and creative, more suited to the knowledge era. It enables new and creative solutions to arise from members of the organizations through interactions among people in formal and informal networks.

"Knowledge era organizations are poised at the 'edge of chaos' that exists between order and disorder, stability and instability—continuously changing, rather than giving in to equilibrium, stability-seeking tendencies." Organizations in this context operate as complex adaptive systems ready to engage people in newly emerging changes and opportunities. Uhl-Bien and Marion identify three leadership functions in these organizations: administrative functions that drive business results; adaptive functions that drive innovation (product innovation) and adaptability (process innovation); and enabling functions that operate in the interface between administrative and adaptive functions to loosen administrative systems and allow adaptive leadership to surface and advance.

Lena Zander, Audra Mockaitis, and Christina Butler (Chapter 16) discuss the current literature on global teams. Global teams are distinguished by their "national, cultural and linguistic heterogeneity and operate in a globally dispersed virtual environment." These teams differ from other teams on two dimensions: globally dispersed work environment and heterogeneity on multiple dimensions. They are multicultural in composition and virtual in action; consequently, they cross two literature streams: multicultural team research and virtual team research.

The authors review recent work on virtual team leadership, multicultural team leadership, and the team leader. Several themes for future research emerge from their review: global team leaders as boundary spanners, bridge makers, and blenders; people-oriented leadership in global teams; and leveraging global team diversity. Zander, Mockaitis, and Butler raise the compelling question, "What will

change when a multicultural team leader has to work virtually and correspondingly when a virtual team leader faces a multicultural team?" Researchers will need to investigate how global leaders enact multiple roles that involve engaging in boundary spanning between organizational units, bridging cultural and linguistic differences among team members, and blending or uniting subgroups in the team. Future research will need to explore whether people-oriented leadership (or another form) is feasible, effective, and successful in virtual, multicultural, global teams where members hold differing mental models and expectations of leadership. Finally, research studies will need to examine how these leaders can bring out the best qualities of diverse team members, in other words, leverage diversity in a virtual context.

Workplace or organizational democracy is one area of shared leadership where practice seems to be outpacing research. Traci Fenton (Chapter 17) discusses the advantages of organizational democracy in large, medium, and small companies around the world, including Zappos, Hulu, DaVita, HCL Technologies, WD-40, Brainpark, Great Harvest Bread Company, NixonMcInnes, among others. She explains that "decisions are made throughout the organization by those who have the most knowledge or will be most impacted by the decision, not just by those in the C-suite." These organizations practice 10 principles of organizational democracy: purpose + vision; transparency; dialogue + listening; fairness + dignity; accountability; individual + collective; choice; integrity; decentralization; and reflection + evaluation.

The examples provided by Fenton of organizational democracy clearly illustrate Gastil's definition in practice. Democratic leadership involves three functions: distributing responsibility among the membership, empowering group members, and aiding the group's decision-making process.[1] Most members of the group perform these functions and exchange leader and follower roles often. Workplace democracy does not mean there are no leaders. Instead, organizations become stronger because leadership is distributed throughout. These organizations experience improvements in the bottom line while becoming more efficient and productive, increasing innovation, attracting and retaining top talent, lowering absenteeism, and providing superior customer service.

Note

1. Gastil, J. (1994). A definition and illustration of democratic leadership. *Human Relations, 47*(8), 953–975.

Part III — Chapters

12. Unmasking Leadership

    Gill R. Hickman and Georgia J. Sorenson

13. The Nature of Shared Leadership *Christina L. Wassenaar and Craig L. Pearce*

14. E-Leadership: Re-Examining Transformations in Leadership Source and Transmission

    Bruce J. Avolio, John J. Sosik, Surinder S. Kahai, and Bradford Baker

15. Complexity Leadership Theory

    Mary Uhl-Bien and Russ Marion

16. Leading Global Teams

    Lena Zander, Audra I. Mockaitis, and Christina L. Butler

17. Inspiring Democracy in the Workplace: From Fear-Based to Freedom-Centered Organizations

    Traci L. Fenton

CHAPTER 12

Unmasking Leadership[1]

Gill R. Hickman
University of Richmond

Georgia J. Sorenson
University of Maryland

This book explores the idea of invisible leadership—leadership in which the common purpose, rather than any particular individual, is the invisible leader that inspires leaders and followers to take action on its behalf. It is an idea that often goes unrecognized in the study and practice of leadership. We will examine stories and organizations where invisible leadership propels groups to the highest levels of commitment, innovation, and success. We will also provide evidence of the power of invisible leadership in action.

What we will describe exists in the space between people and in their shared dreams. Although that space is completely invisible, the effect is immensely powerful. We have called this region "the space between" and compared it to American jazz great Thelonious Monk's "blue notes." An evening spent listening to Monk's jazz saxophone on "Straight, No Chaser" is an experience you will never forget. But why is his music so extraordinary? Jazz critics attribute the genius of Monk's remarkable musical

gift to the nuance, phrasing, and rhythm of the spaces between the formal notes. Indeed, it is the relationship between notes that makes the music soar, not the actual notes themselves. The score shows you the formal notes, not the blue notes, yet it is the blue notes in the performance that stir your soul and transform the musical experience.

Although it is not readily apparent, there is a lot going on that we can't see, as can be discerned from a number of scientific lenses, from the cosmic to the intrapsychic. Note the recent findings of dark holes in the universe yielding a churning cauldron of organizing dark material. NASA recently confirmed what was speculation by Fritz Zwicky in the 1930s: "Most of the stuff in clusters of galaxies is invisible and, since these are the largest structures in the universe held together by gravity, scientists then conclude that most of the matter in the entire universe is invisible." This invisible "dark matter" is the rich "space between" of our cosmos (NASA, n.d.).

Noted psychoanalyst Harry Stack Sullivan revolutionized the practice of psychotherapy by working solely within the space between the patient and thera-pist. He reasoned that whatever the patient's dysfunc-tion or unhappiness—a tragic childhood, a distant catastrophic event, a numbing malaise, or another disturbing event or condition—it would eventually show up in the developing relationship between the patient and therapist (Barton & Sullivan, 1996). The space was like a mirror to the past; if he remained still and listened carefully, the experience would be repli-cated in full in the space between him and the patient. He could then work backward toward the genesis of the original dysfunction. We can learn much in the space between ourselves and others and in our shared work toward an inspiring common purpose.

This invisible space, while subtle, is not inaccessi-ble to us, however. Sometimes we sense it in music, such as Monk's work, or in great art. Take, for exam-ple, the extraordinary photographs that short-story writer Eudora Welty made when she was young. Just out of college, Welty was hired by Franklin D. Roosevelt's Works Progress Administration to travel her native state of Mississippi. She took along her camera to photograph the people she met on the road. In an undated photograph she titled "Saturday Off," the sense of intimacy and trust between the photograph's subject—a young Jackson, Mississippi, woman—and the photographer is profoundly evi-dent. It is this utterly invisible human interaction that makes the photograph great.

Welty described her work this way: "In tak-ing. . . these pictures, I was attended, I now know, by an angel—a presence of trust" (Pleasants, 2001). The trust is the blue note, the invisible space between, the relationship between the two women that makes this photograph extraordinary. Great art emerges in the space between, that inexplicable sense of connection that goes beyond the technical abilities of the artist.

Revealing the Hidden Leader—the Common Purpose

So what do the ideas of blue notes, unseen spaces, and the space between dark matter and people have to do with leadership, the subject of this book? We

"Saturday Off," from the Eudora Welty Collection.

Source: Reprinted courtesy of the Eudora Welty Collection, Mississippi Department of Archives and History, and Russell & Volkening as agents for the author's estate. Copyright ©1936 & 1971 Eudora Welty, LLC.

think it has everything to do with a concept we call *invisible leadership*. Invisible leadership embodies situations in which dedication to a compelling and deeply held common purpose is the motivating force for leadership. This common purpose provides inspi-ration for participants to use their strengths willingly in leader or follower roles and cultivates a strong shared bond that connects participants to each other in pursuit of their purpose.

As we will see in the results of our study of award-winning innovative companies and nonprofit organi-zations, passionate commitment to and ownership of the common purpose occur when participants join together because the purpose embodies deeply mean-ingful shared experiences, beliefs, values, or goals.

The commonality of participants' experiences, beliefs, or values moves them beyond self-interest to focus on the well-being of a group, organization, or society. Participants initiate leadership for a common purpose based on a perceived opportunity to act and on their individual or collective self-agency. Opportunity occurs when resources (human, monetary, intellectual, or social capital) become available, or when a precipitating event provides the catalyst for action. Participants rely on self-agency and collective efficacy to advance the purpose and create new approaches, power structures, or institutions, or to defy existing authorities and institutions that are unresponsive or unjust.

> *Invisible leadership embodies situations in which* dedication to a compelling and deeply held common purpose *is the motivating force for leadership.*

The purpose is more than a mission statement, as many respondents in our study confirmed. Common purpose is a deeply held sense of common destiny, a life course or calling; it is aligned with a mission but resonates profoundly with people's values and their sense of themselves. It is the substance that binds people together and the aim or reason for their collective leadership. We found that it is often the reason people are attracted to the work of a business, nonprofit, community initiative, or social movement. It is also the reason they stay. This invisible force becomes the space where inspiration, interactions, and connection between a purpose and its leaders and followers ignite to bring about something extraordinary. It is more powerful than the classic Weberian charismatic personality, because it goes beyond individuals and institutions. We call this charisma of purpose.

Think about the first time you read or saw *The Wizard of Oz*. At the end of the story, you were astonished by the man behind the curtain. He looked and sounded nothing like the larger-than-life image (the great leader) that awed and intimidated Dorothy and her friends.

The story teaches us much about the essence of invisible leadership. At first we are disappointed to see the small person behind the curtain. But Dorothy and her friends show us that there is nothing as motivating and powerful as an inspiring purpose. They need committed involvement with each other to find the wizard (the common purpose, in this case). They must be willing to play leader and follower roles at different times, and even make personal sacrifices to further the group's goals. One of the most important lessons that Dorothy and her friends learn is that they have the power or self-agency to achieve their cherished goal. While meeting their collective goal, the common purpose, each character gains something different and valuable from the experience. The Tin Man finds his heart, the Lion gains courage, the Scarecrow discovers his brain, and Dorothy finds that she has the power to return to her family in Kansas. They each develop a better and stronger self and form an enduring bond of relationship, leadership, and action in the invisible space between.

Can a common purpose actually inspire leadership? Our research leads us to believe that it can. When you ask most people about leadership, they think of extraordinary individuals—their abilities, experience, traits, circumstances, and situations. Many scholars and students of leadership studies are conditioned to think of leadership in terms of the leader (like the great and powerful wizard) helping a group of followers understand and commit to an important purpose, the leader influencing and persuading followers to do the work and reach the goal. In fact, a great deal of leadership is done this way or at least characterized this way. Our work, however, and the work of other leadership scholars described in Chapter 2, led us to consider other ways that leadership can occur. Invisible leadership does not eliminate leaders. It emphasizes the idea of leader-as-role over leader-as-person, as introduced in the work of organizational behaviorist Robert Kelley (1988, 1992). The use of leader-as-role allows for a more fluid and multifaceted process where responsibility can be distributed among multiple actors or concentrated in one person. The crucial role of leaders in invisible leadership, as we describe in Chapter 6, is to create a context or environment where invisible leadership can thrive and the common purpose flourishes as lived experience among participants.

We asked our colleagues and ourselves: Does leadership involve the same dynamic when people already understand and are committed to an important purpose? When they know what needs to be done and willingly bring their talents and skills to the work? When they hold themselves responsible and accountable for achieving the common purpose? When they sometimes put the purpose ahead of their personal needs or safety?

After some work in this realm, we discovered that the idea of a common purpose inspiring people to initiate leadership is not a new concept. Mary Parker Follett, an early management scholar and practitioner in the United States, first described this concept in 1928. Instead of the accepted or classical view of leadership as people following a charismatic leader, Follett observed that in certain highly effective companies, leaders and followers are both following the invisible leader—the common purpose:

> While leadership depends on depth of conviction and the power coming therefrom, there must also be the ability to share that conviction with others, the ability to make purpose articulate. And then the common purpose becomes the leader. And I believe that we are coming more and more to act, whatever our theories, on our faith in this power of this invisible leader. Loyalty to the invisible leader gives us the strongest possible bond of union. (Follett, 1949/1987, p. 55)

Invisible leadership takes into account the people and the processes of leadership but stretches beyond these parameters into a realm of leadership and action that encompasses wholeness of purpose and the transformation of people, wisdom and values within the group, ethics of the purpose, means and ends, and limitless possibilities. Thus, "increasing shareholder value" is not antithetical to a common purpose, as highly successful entrepreneur Béla Hatvany will later

tell us. The purpose is the leader and motivating force for all aspects of the enterprise.

The Essence of Invisible Leadership

How did we happen upon this concept? We developed our initial conception of invisible leadership by analyzing situations where leadership appeared to be inspired by the purpose as much as or more than by the influence of particular leaders (Sorenson & Hickman, 2002). We probed case studies of business and nonprofit organizations; studied written accounts of social movements; and examined existing interviews with activists, initiators of change, entrepreneurs, and organizational founders. We examined how other fields (physics, psychology, management, music, and photography) and cultures (Asian, African, and Native American) use the idea of invisible processes. We also explored the concept with focus groups of leadership scholars, educators, and professionals in lectures and workshops, and engaged leadership studies students in a semester-long examination of the topic.

As we distilled our thinking, we settled on three essential points that are fundamental to invisible leadership, although there are numerous subsets of these points that we enumerate in our research design in Chapter 4:

- A compelling and deeply held common purpose,
- A readiness to use individual strengths in either leader or follower roles with or without visible recognition or personal ego, and
- A strong shared bond among participants pursuing the common purpose.

For this study, we surveyed 21 award-winning companies and nonprofit workplaces to test our concepts. The results are detailed in Chapters 4 and 5. We include the survey results in these chapters to encourage further research on invisible leadership. Indeed, our study is a starting point that we hope will lead to further scholarship on this topic.

Invisible Leadership in Action

People tell us they can easily see that compelling social causes with a common purpose, such as the civil rights movement or the environmental movement, can certainly inspire individuals to act collectively and bring about a common good. They are not convinced, however, that other contexts can generate such strong, committed leadership from most people in the process without one prominent leader motivating the group and showing the way. We believe that invisible leadership can and does exist in companies, governmental bodies, nonprofit organizations, neighborhoods, schools, communities, and grassroots and social movements. The examples that follow come from our examination of existing case studies of organizations; written accounts of social movements in autobiographies and biographies; and interviews with activists, initiators of change, and organizational founders (Sorenson & Hickman, 2002).

Illustrations From Nonprofit Organizations

In the nonprofit arena, the Orpheus Chamber Orchestra is a conductorless ensemble founded on the belief that musicians can create extraordinary music when an orchestra uses the full talents and creativity of every member (Seifter & Economy, 2001). Its purpose is to demonstrate a collaborative leadership style in which the musicians, rather than a conductor, interpret the score. Leader and follower roles are fluid and rotating, permitting members of the ensemble to share equally in the group's leadership. All the while, the group's leadership remains invisible to the public. The driving force of the orchestra is its common purpose, as Seifter and Economy (2001) make clear:

> Above all, Orpheus Chamber Orchestra is marked by our passionate dedication to our mission. That passion drives every musical and business decision that we make. Our organization's mission isn't imposed from above but is determined—and constantly refined—by the members themselves. (p. 16)

We observed the Orpheus model personally in a demonstration with several of the Czech Republic's finest chamber orchestra musicians at the International Leadership Association in Prague several years ago. The concert was truly amazing. Fascinated, we later interviewed Harvey Seifter (2009), former executive director of the Orpheus Chamber Orchestra. We learned just how radical the Orpheus model truly is: There is no conductor! Members of the orchestra share and rotate leadership roles. As Seifter and Economy (2001) described in their book, for every work that they perform, orchestra members select the concertmaster and principal players for each section. These players constitute the core group, form initial concepts of the piece, and shape the rehearsal process. At final rehearsals, all members participate in refining, interpreting, and executing the piece. Members take turns listening from the auditorium for balance, blend, articulation, dynamic range, and clarity of expression and give feedback to the group.

Another example from the nonprofit sector is C-SPAN. Brian Lamb started C-SPAN to provide direct and unfiltered broadcasts of public policy matters to the American people so that they could decide key issues for themselves (Frantzich & Sullivan, 1996). Although he retains a powerful influence on C-SPAN, in the 34 years he has been broadcasting, Lamb has never spoken his own name on the air (Farhi, 2012). Lamb along with those who fund C-SPAN and the founding members of the organization believe wholeheartedly in its purpose and persevere in their quest to bring public issues to the people. C-SPAN's approach to reporting and media competition has been credited with "transforming American politics" (Hazlett, 1996). The broadcast has gained tremendous respect and popularity since its inception in 1975. Even so, Lamb, in keeping with the role and style of invisible leadership, was determined to have increasingly less influence on C-SPAN. At the same time, when we first interviewed him, Lamb (1999) saw no particular reason to prepare for organizational succession. When Lamb did make the transition in 2012, the succession was publicly seamless. "I never thought the person on top here mattered all that much, except to keep the rhythm of the place going," he said (Farhi, 2012).

Illustrations From Public Sector (Government) Organizations

Much of the leadership in public sector agencies below the political appointee level is, by design, invisible. At its best, invisible leadership in public agencies consists of men and women who work on behalf of the public good without particular recognition or fanfare. They are quite literally "public servants."

Invisible leadership is strongest in public sector agencies when organizational members regard citizens as their central focus, truly care about citizens' well-being, and gain their inspiration from the compelling common purpose of their agency. These "servants" serve the public first, and their commitment to serve is true in the United States and in other countries around the globe.

Accenture (2006) studied public leadership in 21 countries throughout Africa, Asia, Australia, Europe, North America, and South America and discovered that leadership in high-performing public sector agencies has a "citizens-first" point of view—all necessary information is organized around the citizen, and is particularly focused on their desired outcomes, which are defined by the mission (p. 1).

A nationwide, representative telephone survey of 1,051 U.S. federal government workers and 500 private sector employees, conducted by the Princeton Survey Research Institute for political scientist Paul Light at the Brookings Institution, found federal workers were split in their motivation to join the public sector: Some joined for job security and others for their commitment to the mission of public service (typically the higher-level employees). The report concludes, "Whatever their primary motivation for coming to work each day, the key question for a healthy public service is whether employees care about their organizations' missions" (Light, 2001, p. 4).

Some tribal governments in the United States, such as the Cherokee Nation, have built their communities around purpose, mission, and service. Again, a leader whose personal style was consistent with these factors arose in the Cherokee Nation. Wilma Mankiller was the first woman to be elected chief of a major Native American tribe, which made her quite visible. Invisible leadership does not require leaders or followers to be invisible. It is the space between that is invisible—the strong bond of relationship and leadership generated by a group's shared work toward a compelling and deeply held common purpose.

Beginning with a small project—a 16-mile water line to rural homes—Mankiller turned the economy and the identity of the Cherokee Nation around. During Mankiller's term of office, the Cherokee Nation grew its net worth from $34.6 million to nearly $52 million. It funded $20 million in new construction, including job corps facilities, health clinics, an educational center, and a museum. Unemployment rates and high school dropout rates slowed dramatically, even in the face of slashed federal programs for Native Americans during the Reagan years.

What was her secret? She was a true follower of the invisible leader—the common purpose of the Cherokee Nation. Mankiller never lost this focus. Her cultural identity is central in her sense of self and purpose, she told us:

> Knowing and valuing our culture helps me keep some perspective and keeps my feet on the ground. I have to spend so much time away from the basic kind of work I started out doing, which is community organizing and Indian advocacy. Now much of my work is involved in administration, lobbying in Washington, activities of that nature. It's still development, but it's at a different level. To keep my feet on the ground, I still participate in tribal ceremonies and make sure I take the time to be involved in Cherokee culture, even if it's much less time than I'd like. I still do that because it keeps things in perspective. There is something very grounding about going to a tribal ceremony that has been celebrated since time immemorial—to sing songs and participate in dances that we have been doing forever. That's the anchor. (Mankiller, 1992)

Although Mankiller is frequently described as a visionary, she is a visionary who is very aggressive about achieving the goals she has in mind for her people, goals inspired by the group's vision rather than a personal vision:

> As a result of my experience, I came to the conclusion that everyday Indians and poor people have a lot to contribute. I wanted to try to get people to be involved in articulating their own visions. I see a lot of beauty and intelligence and sharing in our communities. I would like to build on that. (Mankiller, 1992)

Leaders like Mankiller, who practice invisible leadership, look to the true heart of the community and know that the leadership must pass on to others. "I try to make decisions that are in the interest of the Cherokee Nation after listening to a lot of people and getting input from all kinds of folks," she said. It's about their collective vision, not about her own. "I really see myself as a temporary person; I'm here for a while, and then I pass the leadership on, and somebody else continues." Mankiller, who died in 2010, left a legacy of powerful invisible leadership. She was far from invisible personally, yet she kept her focus on the tribe's core purpose and legacy.

Illustrations From Business

Colors restaurant in New York is Manhattan's first cooperatively owned restaurant. It is run by former workers from the legendary Windows on the World restaurant (in Tower One of the World Trade Center). It is a self-governing organization, founded on the idea that everyone who works there has to be an owner. Their inspiring purpose came from their desire to move forward as a tribute to the 73 workers who died at the restaurant on 9/11 (Casimir, 2006). Restaurant worker–owners decided to share their diverse cultures as American immigrants through food from their countries of origin. The staff of owners includes 44 immigrants from 22 countries. They operate under the premise that everyone has to have the same share— an equal say in the restaurant. Its purpose not only inspires and organizes the business but also attracts customers, who come for the good food as well as to support the worker–owners' purpose of honoring their lost colleagues, as can be seen in recent Yelp restaurant review postings.

Béla Hatvany is an iconic pioneer in the information industry and was cofounder in 1983 of SilverPlatter, one of the first companies to produce commercial reference databases on CD-ROMs for libraries and other users. Companies he founded have been responsible for the first online public access catalog (OPAC), the first CD-ROMs, the first networked CD-ROM, the first client-server library databases, and some of the earliest Internet library database retrieval engines (Baczewski, 1994).

Since he sold SilverPlatter in 2001 for a purported $113 million, Hatvany has had the resources to dedicate himself to buying and working with purpose-oriented businesses around the world, including Classical.com, JustGiving, Credo Reference, Productorial, Mustardseed Charitable Trust, and Coreweb. In turn, these companies have helped him to develop a business philosophy that empowers others and produces companies that are strikingly successful by any measure.

One of Hatvany's approaches is to sit with members of one of his enterprises, and listen. This may be just one or two days a year, since he does not manage his companies. "This is leadership not management. It is not directing or managing outcomes. It is inquiring deeply and thus drawing forth the joint understandings hidden in the spaces between all of the knowledge of the participants in the inquiry," he told us (Hatvany, 2012).

A bedrock criterion for his work is "to serve all constituents in a balanced way" (Hatvany, 2000). He defines constituents as the "customers, our business partners, our employees and our investors—all must be served in a balanced way" (Hatvany, 2000).

To do so, he believes that leaders have a role in holding shared values, because behind a powerful purpose are compelling and commonly held values:

> Organizations don't have values, people do, so it is up to the leader to be the persistent carrier of these values. . . reminding everyone in the organization of how they guide actions. For me these values must always be centered on the imperative of serving everyone in a balanced way. (Hatvany, 2012)

His thinking has evolved to where he sees all of the world as what he terms *corpus humanitatis,* a great human "corporation" or "body" connected by the Internet, an ecology of limitless possibilities. In his own words,

> I wish to enable an "ecology" in which all experience themselves to be wellserved. I experience a world whose abundance is made available by human collaboration. . . . Money [commerce] is made of human agreement and enables this collaboration on a world-wide scale. (Hatvany, 2012)

Recently, leadership scholar James MacGregor Burns met with Hatvany to discuss leadership, and Burns remarked that Hatvany embodied and made real in a practical way his ideas about transforming leadership (personal communication, October 9, 2010).

Illustration From Social Movements

The work of the Women's Political Council (WPC) provides an example of invisible leadership committed to achieving an inspirational goal. Prior to the Montgomery, Alabama, bus boycott, a group of black women activists, who were members of the WPC, began the fight against segregation in their city by targeting Montgomery's segregated bus-seating practices. Jo Ann Robinson played a key role in initiating the WPC-orchestrated boycott. David Garrow's description of Robinson captures the essence of invisible leadership in action:

> Mrs. Robinson remains generally hesitant to claim for herself the historical credit that she deserves for launching the Montgomery Bus Boycott of 1955–1956. Although her story fully and accurately describes how it was she, during the night and early morning hours of December 1 and 2, 1955, who actually started the boycott on its way, it is only with some gentle encouragement that she will acknowledge herself as "the instigator of the movement

to start the boycott." Even then, however, she seeks to emphasize that no special credit ought to go to herself or to any other single individual. Very simply, she says, "the black women did it." (Robinson, 1987, p. xv)

What Invisible Leadership Is Not

When people first hear the term *invisible leadership,* they often assume it means something different from the concept as we define it. We mean the common purpose is the invisible leader that inspires leaders and followers to take action on its behalf. We would like to clarify what our concept of invisible leadership is not.

It is not leadership that no one recognizes or acknowledges. Leaders and members of the organization know and value the work that others do to advance the purpose (like Jo Ann Robinson or Brian Lamb), even though much of their leadership may be internal to the organization, behind-the-scenes, quiet, unassuming, or not visible to those outside the organization.

Invisible leadership is not rendering individuals invisible. Certain groups of people in society, such as women, minorities, older people, or people with disabilities, are often made to feel invisible in their organizations. This is an important area of inquiry, which we have written about in earlier work but do not pursue here, and it is not what we mean by invisible leadership.

Invisible leadership does not mean that leaders or followers are invisible. Like Wilma Mankiller, people who use invisible leadership can be highly visible, or they can be deliberately in the background, like Jo Ann Robinson or Brian Lamb. They may choose either foreground or background leadership, and some are thrust into visibility as embodiments and advocates of their group's common purpose.

Invisible leadership is not a leadership substitute. On the contrary, there is plenty of leadership taking place by positional and nonpositional leaders at all levels of the organization. Positional leaders who engage in invisible leadership may have different functions from the leader roles in classic theories, because many organizational members are able to take action or lead based on a clear understanding of and commitment to the purpose. There are, however, essential functions for positional leaders, founders, and informal leaders. Béla Hatvany plays an essential role in the companies he is part of, as did Wilma Mankiller, Brian Lamb, and Jo Ann Robinson. All of them have personal traits of humility, emotional intelligence, and powers of listening and inquiry. But each of them understands deeply that the organization's success depends not on single leaders as much as the purpose, the group's shared work, and the relationships formed in "the space between." When leaders and members join in the invisible leadership of the organization, amazing things are possible.

Note

1. We presented portions of this chapter at the China Executive Leadership Academy Pudong Leadership Conference, October 19–20, 2007, in Shanghai, China. We also presented some of these concepts in these publications:

Hickman, G. R. (2004). Invisible leadership. In G. R. Goethals, G. Sorenson, & J. M. Burns (Eds.), *Encyclopedia of leadership* (pp. 750–754). Thousand Oaks, CA: Sage.

Sorenson, G., & Hickman, G. R. (2002). Invisible leadership: Acting on behalf of a common purpose. In C. Cherry & L. R. Matusak (Eds.), *Building leadership bridges* (pp. 7–24). College Park, MD: James MacGregor Burns Academy of Leadership.

References

Accenture. (2006). *Leadership in customer service: Building the trust*. Retrieved March 9, 2012, from http://www.accenture.com/us-en/Pages/insight-publicleadership-customer-service-building-trust-summary.aspx

Baczewski, P. (1994). *The Internet unleashed: Volume 1*. Retrieved August 22, 2012, from http://en.wikipedia.org/wiki/Béla_Hatvany#cite_note-2

Barton, E. F., III, & Sullivan, H. S. (1996). *Harry Stack Sullivan* (Makers of Modern Psychotherapy series). London, UK: Routledge.

Casimir, L. (2006, January 6). New window on taste. Colors eatery rises from WTC. *New York Daily News*, p. 21.

Farhi, P. (2012, March 19). For C-SPAN founder, a quiet exit. *The Washington Post*, p. C01.

Follett, M. P. (1949/1987). *Freedom & co-ordination: Lectures in business organization*. New York, NY: Garland.

Frantzich, S., & Sullivan, J. (1996). *The C-SPAN revolution*. Norman: University of Oklahoma Press.

Hatvany, B. (2000, February). Miles Conrad Memorial Lecture. Retrieved August 22, 2012, from http://www.nfais.org/page/46-Béla-hatvany-2000

Hatvany, B. (2012, August 20). Interview with Georgia Sorenson.

Hazlett, T. W. (1996). *Changing channels: C-SPAN's Brian Lamb on how unfiltered reporting and media competition are transforming American politics*. Retrieved January 2, 2003, from http://www.reason.com/9603/fe.LAMB.text.html

Kelley, R. E. (1988). In praise of followers. *Harvard Business Review, 66*(6), 142–148.

Kelley, R. E. (1992). *The power of followership: How to create leaders people want to follow. . . and followers who lead themselves*. New York, NY: Doubleday.

Lamb, B. (1999, November 20). Interview with G. J. Sorenson.

Light, P. C. (2001). *To restore and renew: Now is the time to rebuild the federal public service*. Brookings Institution. Retrieved October 14, 2007, from http://www.brookings.edu/articles/2001/11governance_light.aspx

Mankiller, W. (1992). Interview with G. J. Sorenson.

NASA. (n.d.) *Dark matter: Introduction*. Retrieved February 23, 2012, from http://imagine.gsfc.nasa.gov/docs/science/know_11/dark_matter.html

Pleasants, A. K. (2001). Trust and intimacy: Eudora Welty, who died July 23, captured the south in pictures as well as words. *Smithsonian, 32*(7), 38.

Robinson, J. G. (1987). *The Montgomery bus boycott and the women who started it: The memoir of Jo Ann Gibson Robinson*. Knoxville: The University of Tennessee Press.

Seifter, H. (2009). Interview with G. R. Hickman and G. J. Sorenson.

Seifter, H., & Economy, P. (2001). *Leadership ensemble: Lessons in collaborative management from the world's only conductorless orchestra*. New York, NY: Times Books.

Sorenson, G., & Hickman, G. R. (2002). Invisible leadership: Acting on behalf of a common purpose. In C. Cherry & L. R. Matusak (Eds.), *Building leadership bridges* (pp. 7–24). College Park, MD: James MacGregor Burns Academy of Leadership.

CHAPTER 13

The Nature of Shared Leadership

Christina L. Wassenaar
Claremont Graduate University

Craig L. Pearce
University of Nebraska

It is amazing how much people get done if they do not worry about who gets the credit.

—Swahili proverb

When we consider the nature of leadership, it conjures deep and profound considerations (Antonakis, Cianciolo, & Sternberg, 2004). In this regard, shared leadership theory moves us from a perspective on leadership as a hierarchical role to that of leadership as a dynamic social process (Pearce & Conger, 2003). The notion of nature in human social behavior implies that the activities that are engaged in are inherent or characterological, that our instinct takes over our decisions, or that certain attributes or behaviors are innate. It implies that the actions that we take in our daily lives are part of a predetermined character that is formed through our environment, upbringing, and cultural history. As members of a community, as parents, children, employees, and finally as leaders, our nature—the foundation of who we are—is integral to how we interact with those around us.

But is that enough? Can we rely on our personal and traditional understanding of societal rules in a world that is clearly moving in new directions, driven primarily by technology but also by demography, the rise and fall of various embedded norms, and by new geopolitical paradigms? At some level, we are part of a brave new world—but how many times have our ancestors wrestled with change? Even more relevant to the topic at hand, *who* led this change?

Source: The Nature of Shared Leadership by Christina L. Wassenaar and Craig Pearce, pp. 363–389. In *The Nature of Leadership,* 2nd ed. by David V. Day and John Antonakis (2012). Copyright © SAGE Publications, Inc. Reprinted by permission.

AUTHORS' NOTE: Please address correspondence concerning this chapter to Christina L. Wassenaar, e-mail christina.l.wassenaar@gmail.com, or Craig L. Pearce, e-mail craig.l.pearce@gmail.com.

Accordingly, the purpose of this chapter is to offer a foundational view of the theory of shared leadership. In the past few decades, this particular form of leadership—which has been present in our society for ages—has gained relevance both in its practical application through the workplace and in scientific research. Shared leadership is defined as "a dynamic, interactive influence process among individuals in groups for which the objective is to lead one another to the achievement of group or organizational goals or both" (Pearce & Conger, 2003, p. 1). In other words, shared leadership occurs when group members actively and intentionally shift the role of leader to one another as needed by the environment or circumstances in which the group operates. Although this is markedly different from the more traditional models of leadership where the influence and decision making travels downstream from the vertical leader to the followers (Day, Gronn, & Salas, 2004, 2006; Day & O'Connor, 2003; Pearce & Sims, 2000, 2002; Riggio, Chaleff, & Lipman-Blumen, 2008), it is *not* our intention to promote the idea that studying shared leadership supersede or replace the study of hierarchical leader or the more traditionally understood forms of leadership (Pearce, Conger, & Locke, 2008). Rather, with shared leadership, the role of leadership does not reside in one person's hands, but rather, in the group's arms as they move together toward common objectives.

Clearly, this type of leadership is a departure from the traditional understanding of the hierarchical leader. Our typical notion is that of a single person around whom the rest of the group circles and who is the arbiter of decisions and purpose. Throughout history, we have read about these celebrated souls (Bass & Bass, 2008; Carlyle, 1841/1894; Figueira, Brennan, & Sternberg, 2009)—and yes, we do celebrate them, for better or for worse. We aspire to achieve their status or at least, their acceptance. Because of this, the primary focus in the study of leadership has been on the attitudes, behaviors, and activities of these leaders with the hope of understanding, demystifying and, perhaps, even emulating them (Bass & Bass, 2008).

Pearce and Conger (2003) suggest that lately some in the scholarly community have divested themselves from this norm and have taken to the notion that leadership is actually a *process* that can be taught, shared, distributed, and collectively enacted. These scholars have also begun to popularize the view that leadership can be a shared influence process and that the role of leadership does *not* have to originate solely from a hierarchical leader. Rather, leadership can derive from any member of a group or social system who can offer the skills and talent that are needed by the project or system at the time (Hunt, 2004; Ropo, Eriksson, & Hunt, 1997). Of course, at this point, there exists far less empirical study in this area than in the older, more established leadership theories, but in the past two decades, momentum in the study of shared leadership has grown and taken great strides.

Therefore, in this chapter we will cover five main areas regarding shared leadership. First, we will identify the historical theoretical precursors to the development of shared leadership theory. Then we review studies of shared leadership that have begun to document its antecedents and outcomes. We then discuss some of the techniques that can be used to measure shared leadership, some of which have been used to great effect and some of which we would suggest using, based on the results of some of the more recent empirical study. Our fourth section will focus on the future of shared leadership research and some ideas for theory building and empirical research that can further expand our knowledge about this area of leadership. Finally, we will close with a view toward the future of leadership in organizations.

Sometimes, in order to go forward, we first need to go back. In the case of leadership study, Bass and Avolio (1993) point out that "new" theories related to the field of leadership are often re-pioneered versions of older theories (Yukl, 2002). In order to not fall into the selective memory trap, we will spend just a little time reviewing some of the historical underpinnings of shared leadership and how our current understanding of the shared leadership experience has been influenced by offerings from the fields of organizational behavior, psychology, teamwork, sociology, and leadership.

Historical Bases of Shared Leadership

It generally appears that prior to the Industrial Revolution, very little thought was given to the scientific study of leading others, or leadership. It was during this period, especially toward the 1830s and on, that the impact from the changes that were occurring at an increasingly rapid pace began to be studied in any scientific manner (Nardinelli, 2008). Of course, there were many people, from manufacturers to philosophers, who were writing about the phenomena that were affecting the global stage, but the main focus of their work centered on the transfer and movement of knowledge about technological advances (Stewart, 1998, 2003). However, Stewart (2003) noted that as late as the end of the 18th century, many of those who were considered scientists also began to address the scientific measurement of the social and managerial occurrences of the day. It was at the beginning of the 19th century when economists such as Jean Baptiste Say (1803/1964) wrote that entrepreneurs "must possess the art of superintendence and administration" (p. 330). The main interests of economists prior to his writing this were land and labor, and to some extent, capital. Eventually, the idea that leadership did have a role in business began to be more understood; however, this idea of leading others still focused mainly on the command and control activities that would be generated from the hierarchical leader. It was only later in that century that slight hints of shared leadership can be detected in management writing as another form of leading others (Pearce & Conger, 2003).

One of the earliest management thinkers in the area of systemic organizational and leadership approaches was Daniel C. McCallum. He developed one of the first groupings of principles related to management that could span various industries and were mainly focused on leadership. One of these principles was unity of command, where orders came from the top, and work was carried out by those down subsequent levels of the hierarchy (Wren, 1994). The overwhelming majority of the Industrial Revolution writing on leadership was focused on a top-down, command-and-control perspective (e.g., Montgomery, 1836, 1840; Wren, 1994). This perspective became firmly ensconced by the turn of the 20th century and was captured in what came to be known as "scientific management" (Gantt, 1916; Gilbreth, 1912; Gilbreth & Gilbreth, 1917; Taylor, 1903, 1911).

If we simply rested on the writing of the aforementioned authors and social philosophers, we could easily draw the conclusion that the absolute control of employee behavior by the employers is the only way our forebearers knew. However, if we step outside of these scholars, we notice small leadership nudges in another direction. One of the people who noticed and then wrote about her dissonant observations was a management consultant and community activist named Mary Parker Follett. She wrote about a concept called the *law of the situation* (Follett, 1924). She thought that instead of following the articulated leader in any and all situations, it sometimes made more sense to follow the person in the group who had the most knowledge about the situation in which the group was operating. Clearly, her ideas were a sharp departure from the normally accepted, hierarchical leadership model of the day—yet, they also appear to be quite closely associated with the idea of shared leadership theory.

Although Follett was a popular management consultant and speaker during the 1920s, the majority of the business community of the time discounted many of her ideas and writings. Some of this was a result of the economic reality of the time; things were so uncertain, especially during the 1930s and 1940s that the idea of losing control to anyone was anathema to the organizational leadership of the time (Drucker, 1954). However, Peter Drucker calls her "the brightest star in the management firmament" for that era (Drucker, 1995, p. 2).

Another pivotal pillar to the development of shared leadership in our historical review was the writing done by Hollander (1961) and quickly followed by others, which dealt with the idea that a leader can emerge or be selected by members of a leaderless group (e.g., Bartol & Martin, 1986; Hollander, 1978; Stein & Heller, 1979). It is clear that this type of theory building is integral to our deeper understanding of the psychological underpinnings for the emergence of a leader who has not been "chosen" by the upper management. The difference between shared leadership and emergent leadership is that whereas emergent leadership deals mainly with the choosing of an ultimate leader, the concept of shared leadership deals more with the idea that multiple leaders can and will emerge over time, based on the needs and situation in which the group finds itself (Pearce, 1997; Pearce & Sims, 2002).

An additional component that allows us a foundational look at the development of shared leadership theory is the literature on substitutes for leadership (e.g., Kerr & Jermier, 1978). Those writings suggest that there are possible substitutes for a hierarchical leader that can manifest themselves under certain circumstances. For example, in work that is highly routinized, the need for a leader or supervisor to oversee all facets of each individual's work is unnecessary. Taking this idea a step further, shared leadership can also serve as a substitute for a more formally designated leader.

The concept of self-leadership (Manz, 1986) can also be seen as emergent from the theory of leadership substitutes. Manz and Sims (1980) identified self-management, or self-leadership, as a possible substitute for a more traditionally appointed, vertical leader. They believed that (1) the more individual group members knew and understood about the organization's needs, the more highly skilled they were, and (2) the more motivated they were to engage in activities that were productive, the more likely their ability to lead themselves would mitigate the need for proximal control, direction, and supervision. Taking this idea just a little further, we can draw the conclusion that this could also work well at the group level and lead to the development of shared leadership in a group as each individual displayed his or her abilities, skills, organizational understanding, and motivation to achieve (Pearce & Conger, 2003).

Finally, the theory of empowerment should be briefly explored as a foundational component to shared leadership. This is a topic that has interested many in the field of leadership (e.g., Blau & Alba, 1982; Conger & Kanungo, 1988; Cox, Pearce, & Sims, 2003; Manz, 1986: Manz & Sims, 1989, 1990; Mohrman, Cohen, & Mohrman, 1995; Pearce & Sims, 2000, 2002) and deals mainly with the issue of power (e.g., Conger & Kanungo, 1988). Often, the primary focus in management research is on those at the top of the organization and their activities. Empowerment, however, focuses on the devolvement of power from those central power sources to those who are dealing with circumstances on a daily basis about

which they might have higher levels of decision-making qualifications than those at the top.

Most of the literature and research in empowerment is focused on the individual (e.g., Conger & Kanungo, 1988), although there are some who are researching this phenomenon at the group level (e.g., Mohrman et al., 1995). It must be clearly noted that although empowering leadership or empowerment is definitely the act of sharing leadership, it is also not the equivalent of the shared leadership that can be created by a group. In order for shared leadership to fully exist in a group, members must be actively engaged and participative in the leadership process (Conger & Pearce, 2009). Because of this, it is evident that empowerment is a critical and necessary component for the development of shared leadership in a group.

In this section, we have very briefly discussed some of the most important historical underpinnings to the development of shared leadership theory—from the Industrial Revolution, which began in Great Britain but which quickly spread to the rest of the globe, to the pioneers in the area of "scientific management," to several interesting and valuable streams of research that allow us more clarity when beginning our own exploration of shared leadership theory. In the following section, we will delve further into the literature on shared leadership, exploring both the antecedents and outcomes of this important leadership concept.

Recent Evidence on the Antecedents and Outcomes of Shared Leadership

Recently, shared leadership has been receiving increasing attention in both the practitioner (e.g., Pearce, Manz, & Sims, 2010) and academic literature (e.g., Carson, Tesluk, & Marrone, 2007; Wassenaar & Pearce, 2012). Although the vast majority of the writing on shared leadership has been conceptual in nature, a modicum of empirical advance is worth noting. This empirical work has identified both antecedents and outcomes of shared leadership in a wide variety of contexts—ranging from hospitals, to research and development, to the blue-collar world of manufacturing, to the white-collar world virtual teams of knowledge workers, and even to the c-suite ranks of top management teams. Below, we briefly review the empirical evidence on shared leadership to date. That said, there is still a large amount of work that needs to be done to further understand the role of shared leadership in organizational systems.

Some of the Antecedents of Shared Leadership

One of the most fascinating angles when studying any phenomenon in organizational behavior is to investigate its antecedents, or more simply put, what potential activities or behaviors result in an outcome. Lately, researchers have been focusing their efforts on developing a richer and deeper understanding of the precursors to the evolution of shared leadership in groups and organizations. In this vein, they have discovered three main groups of antecedents to shared leadership, which we will briefly explain in the following paragraphs.

Hierarchical/vertical leaders. Not surprisingly, hierarchical or vertical leaders have been found to have a considerable influence on the development and occurrence of shared leadership. For example, the actions or behaviors of the vertical leader are directly related to the development of group members' satisfaction with their work and activities (George et al., 2002; Shamir & Lapidot, 2003). Additionally, trust in the hierarchical leader is directly correlated to the shared leadership formation in groups (George et al., 2002; Olson-Sanders, 2006), and it serves as a facilitating force for smooth social interactions (Dirks & Ferrin, 2002), which in turn directly affect the group's ability to share leadership effectively. Shamir and Lapidot (2003) were able, in their study of the Israeli Defense Forces, clearly to conclude that leader and follower goal alignment contribute to the development of shared leadership. They also confirmed that group members' trust in, and satisfaction with, their leaders is directly related to the degree to which shared leadership exists in those groups. Similarly, Elloy (2008) discovered that when the vertical leader allows group members latitude in decision making, the incidence of shared leadership increased.

The gender of the vertical leader has been found to be important when considering the development of shared leadership (Konu & Viitanen, 2008). In their study that was conducted in several major Finnish healthcare organizations, Konu and Viitanen (2008) uncovered that teams who have a female vertical leader are more likely to share leadership among group members. Their research also suggests that the reason for this higher incidence of shared leadership in these female-led groups is that these leaders are more likely to be inclined to nurture those around them than are their male counterparts (Paris, Howell, Dorfman, & Hanges, 2009).

Finally, the behavior of the vertical leader has been found to be integrally important to the development of shared leadership in a group (Hooker & Csikszentmihalyi, 2003). In the qualitative work done by Hooker and Csikszentmihalyi (2003), six vertical leader behaviors were found to support the development of shared leadership: (1) valuing excellence, (2) providing clear goals, (3) giving timely feedback, (4) matching challenges and skills, (5) diminishing distractions, and (6) creating freedom. Taken together, these studies identify the important role that vertical leadership has in the display and development of shared leadership.

Support structures. Another important group of antecedents that have been studied in the past few years are those that enhance our understanding of the support structures that are in place or can be developed to aid in a group's development of shared leadership. For example, technology has been, is, and will continue to be a foundational underpinning to the development of shared leadership in groups (Wassenaar et al., 2010). Cordery, Soo, Kirkman, Rosen, and Mathieu (2009) realized that critical components in the development and sustainability of shared leadership in virtual teams are the support structures, both social and technological, that enable group members to communicate more easily, fluidly transporting information across time and geography. These support mechanisms can be constituted of the technical infrastructure that is in place, which supports communication between members of a group or others, and training (employee training, orientations, or other organized learning environments) that augments the skills of the group.

Elloy (2008) discovered that when an organization provided team training, and when it encouraged and facilitated communication between employees within a paper mill that the development of shared leadership was greatly facilitated. Another line of research that has been gaining momentum in both the academic and practitioner literatures is specifically related to executive coaching (Bono, Purvanova, Towler, & Peterson, 2009; Elmhirst, 2008; Leonard & Goff, 2003). The incidence of coaching in organizations has been extolled as essential in leader and team development, yet very little empirical research has, as of yet, been done—particularly as it relates to groups. However, Carson et al. (2007), as well as Cordery et al. (2009), did uncover that coaching was positively related to the demonstration of shared leadership.

Culture and empowerment. Context of leadership has been gaining increasing attention in the literature (e.g., Antonakis, Avolio, & Sivasubramaniam, 2003). Clearly, there must be more ways that cause or lead to an environment in which leadership is shared than just the activities of the vertical leader or how much support a group or its members receive. One of these is culture (Pearce, 2008). For example, Konu and Viitanen (2008) learned that a group's values are an important predictor of shared leadership. Moreover, in the same study in which they explored coaching and its contribution to sharing leadership, Carson et al. (2007) found that internal environment—a concept similar to cultural values—was also a contributor to shared leadership, thus further providing confirmation for our belief that organizational culture or context is a contributing factor in the development of shared leadership.

Wood (2005) also discovered that if a team and its members perceive that they are empowered, they are more likely to behave in a way that shares leadership. He was exploring the question of whether members of top management teams in church organizations could even occur in what is normally considered a highly developed hierarchical organization. It was a revealing outcome, especially when taking into account our previous explorations of the incidence of shared leadership throughout history and how, against our initial expectations or knowledge, it also did occur in many religious denominations, particularly through the Middle Ages (Coss, 1996).

Other antecedents. There are three other interesting and valuable antecedents that have been explored in the research literature as precursors to shared leadership. The first is relationship longevity. Ropo and Sauer (2003) conducted a longitudinal qualitative study of orchestras, uncovering the fact that the length of relationships, also called relationship longevity, between various members, such as orchestra leaders, sponsors, members, or other possible group members is an important foreshadowing to sharing leadership between the various orchestral constituents. Hooker and Csikszentmihalyi (2003), in their study of university research teams, discovered that flow (Csikszentmihalyi, 1990) and the development of a state of flow was a foundational link in the development of shared leadership in the creative group. Our final antecedent is proximity. It was studied by Balthazard, Waldman, Howell, and Atwater (2004), who found that face-to-face teams are more likely to develop shared leadership than virtual teams, which builds on the work of Antonakis and Atwater (2002).

Summary. As we can clearly observe from the varied possible antecedents that we have just examined, there are many precursors, or causes that enable shared leadership to occur in groups. We, as researchers, are merely at the beginning of the exploration of these antecedents, and there is enormous opportunity for further research in this area. Developing a more complete understanding of these causes will only further enable organizations and groups to capitalize on the benefits or outcomes of sharing leadership, which we will explore in some detail in the next section.

Outcomes Associated With Shared Leadership

Broadly speaking, there are three levels of analysis regarding outcomes in organizational behavior and leadership research—individual-, group-, and organization-level outcomes—and outcome variables span from intermediate-type outcomes, such as attitudes, behaviors, and cognitions, to effectiveness or performance outcomes (Luthans, 2010). Below we review the extant literature on the outcomes empirically associated with shared leadership.

Individual-level outcomes. At least six individual-level outcomes have been associated with shared leadership. Individual satisfaction is one of the most widely researched individual-level variables in organizational behavior (e.g., Cranny, Smith, & Stone, 1992), and two of studies have specifically examined the effects of shared leadership on satisfaction. First, Avolio, Jung, Murray, and Sivasubramaniam (1996), in a study of undergraduate project teams, found team member satisfaction to be positively related to shared leadership. Next, Shamir and Lapidot (2003), in a study of Israeli military officer training, found that shared leadership was positively related to satisfaction with, as well as trust in, hierarchical leaders. Thus, shared leadership has been linked to satisfaction with both team members as well as team leaders.

Building on the work of Bandura (1986), George et al. (2002), in a nursing study, found shared leadership to be directly related to follower self-efficacy. Also in the hospital environment, Klein, Zeigert, Knight, and Xiao (2006), found shared leadership to be positively associated with the skill development of junior medical staff. Finally, Hooker and Csikszentmihalyi (2003), in a study of R&D laboratories, found mimetic effects of shared leadership. That is, as followers learned shared leadership from the lead scientist in their original PhD training laboratory, they mimicked those lead scientist behaviors to develop shared leadership in their own laboratories. This is similar to what Bass, Waldman, Avolio, and Bebb (1987) called the "falling dominoes effect," noted for transformational leadership mimetic effects. Accordingly, shared leadership has been empirically associated with multiple individual level outcomes.

Group-/team-level outcomes. At least 15 group-/team-level, intermediate-type outcomes have been associated with shared leadership. Moreover, at

least six studies have identified group effectiveness/performance outcomes of shared leadership.

Group confidence or potency (e.g., Gully, Incalcaterra, Joshi, & Beaubien, 2002) has received considerable attention in recent years. In this vein, Pearce (1997); Hooker and Csikszentmahalyi (2003); and Pearce, Yoo, and Alavi (2004) all found shared leadership to be positively associated with team confidence or potency. Similarly, Solansky (2008), in a laboratory study, found that shared leadership was associated with higher levels of motivation and cognitive advantage, whereas Pearce et al. (2004) found shared leadership predictive of social integration, and Balthazard et al. (2004) found shared leadership to positively predict group cohesion (e.g., Evans & Dion, 1991). It is important to note that Hooker and Csikszentmahalyi (2003) also linked shared leadership with group empowerment (Conger & Pearce, 2009) and sense of flow (Csikszentmahalyi, 1990). Together these studies suggest that shared leadership is a useful predictor of cognitive outcomes in groups.

An important group-level behavioral variable in organizational behavior research is organizational citizenship behavior (OCB; e.g., Organ, 1988), and leadership has been found to be an important predictor of OCB (e.g., Pearce & Herbik, 2004). Moving to the shared leadership level of analysis, Pearce (1997) found shared leadership to be predictive of team citizenship behavior and team networking behavior. Relatedly, Balthazard et al. (2004) found shared leadership was positively predictive of a constructive interaction style and negatively associated with a defensive interaction style. Klein et al. (2006) also found shared leadership to be positively related to swift coordination of activities, as well as reliability. Khourey-Bowers, Dinko, and Hart (2005), in a study of 216 educators in 17 school districts who were part of a change management plan, found that shared leadership facilitated information exchange among teachers. Finally, in a study of 32 United States and Mexico strategic alliances, Rodríguez (2005) found that shared leadership can facilitate the development of intercultural fit. As such, shared leadership appears to be an important predictor of group-level behavioral outcomes.

Six studies have specifically linked shared leadership to group/team effectiveness and performance. For example, Pearce and Sims (2002) found that shared leadership, relative to vertical leadership, was a more useful predictor of team effectiveness in 71 change management teams from the point of view of managers, internal customers, and team members. Similarly, Olson-Sanders (2006) found that shared leadership was positively linked with new product development performance orientation and team effectiveness. In the same vein, Carson et al. (2007) found that shared leadership predicted consulting team performance, and Avolio et al. (1996) found shared leadership to be appreciably related to group members' self-ratings of effectiveness. Moving to the virtual team arena, Carte, Chidambaram, and Becker (2006), in a study of 22 virtual teams, also found shared leadership to be a significant predictor of team performance. Moreover, Pearce et al. (2004) found that, controlling for team size and vertical leadership, shared leadership was positively related to problem-solving quality and an increased perception of task effectiveness. Taken together, these studies clearly suggest a shared leadership to group performance link.

Organization-level outcomes. Although the effects of shared leadership on individuals and groups are important, perhaps most importantly one should consider the effects of shared leadership at the organizational level of analysis. In this regard, four studies help to shed some light. First, O'Toole, Galbraith, and Lawler (2003), in a qualitative study of shared leadership at the top of organizations of 25 firms, concluded that 17 firms experienced positive effects, whereas 8 experienced negative effects. Potentially more significantly, using multiple regression analysis, Ensley, Hmieleski, and Pearce (2006) conducted a two-sample study of shared leadership in entrepreneurial firms. Their first sample of 66 firms was drawn from the Inc. 500, which are the fastest growing, privately held firms in the United States. Their second sample was a random national sample of United States-based firms, drawn from Dun & Bradstreet's market identifiers database. In both samples, they found that, controlling for CEO leader behavior, shared leadership predicted the financial performance of the firms.

Furthermore, Manz, Shipper, and Stewart (2009) conducted a qualitative study of shared leadership at W. L. Gore & Associates. As an organization, Gore has consciously decided not to implement an articulated hierarchical structure but rather to advocate a system called "natural leadership." Here are some examples: Associates move into a leadership role once they have gained enough credibility with their peers to gain influence, or if they have demonstrated their expertise in a given situation, which Gore also calls knowledge-based decision making. By creating this type of environment, Gore has been able to minimize employee turnover to approximately 5%, and in 2007, they received 34,585 applications for only 272 jobs. Just as telling, Gore's team and their work together yielded revenues of more than $2 billion in 2007, which placed them near the top of Forbes annual ranking of privately held companies (Manz et al., 2009). As such, the initial evidence on shared leadership indicates that it can have a potential powerful effect on organizational performance outcomes.

Summary. In sum, shared leadership appears to be an important predictor of several outcome variables that span attitudinal, behavioral, cognitive, and effectiveness outcomes, at the individual, group, and organizational levels of analysis. In the following section, we explore the measurement of shared leadership.

The Measurement of Shared Leadership

To date, there has been little research that examines the various methods by which to measure shared leadership. This is not surprising, especially since this field is still quite new and the complexity in its measurement can be, on the surface, daunting. However, as the field continues to grow, it will become ever more critical for a more clear understanding of the most effective methods that can be used to measure shared leadership as we search for more answers about this theory. Pearce and Conger (2003) noted five methods that can be and are currently the most commonly used to measure shared leadership; of these five, three are quantitative and survey based and two are qualitative and observation based.

In order to study shared leadership at the group level, whether (1) as whole, the individual or "sum of its parts," or even (2) the social network of the group, a revised traditional leadership items list can be used for the three quantitative survey approaches. As an example, when examining the entire team, or the whole group, the approach that uses items where (1) the group is the entity and is the source of influence and (2) the group as a whole is the target of influence has proven to yield valuable insights. When using variables that have been conceived at the group level of analysis, researchers are able to perform analyses comparable to those that are conducted at the individual leader level of data (e.g., regression, SEM; Antonakis, Bendahan, Jacquart, & Lalive, in press; Mundlak, 1978; Yammarino, 1990). There are several examples of this approach in Pearce and Conger (2003), Avolio et al. (1996), Pearce (1997), Ensley et al. (2006), and Pearce and Sims (2002). This method is particularly attractive in that the collection of data is fairly innocuous to the participants in the study, especially as it relates to individual group member anonymity. However, a potential shortcoming of this method is that important variance in contributions by individual members of the group could potentially be smoothed. It is also important to note that there is some debate whether simply measuring constructs at the group level of analysis is sufficient to determine outcomes of group-level variables (James, Demaree, & Wolf, 1984, 1993; Kozlowski & Klein, 2000; Yammarino, 1990; Yammarino & Bass, 1990; Yammarino, Dansereau, & Kennedy, 2001).

The second method, which measures the "group as a sum of its parts," utilizes items that measure individual group members as the basis for influence and the total group as the target of influence. There are three options when using this method that can be used to create group-level variables. One of these options is that the level of shared leadership can be evaluated using the dominant member's results. This means using the highest rated individual's scores. The second option involves doing the opposite of the first and measuring shared leadership by using

the scores of the individual rated lowest on leadership, also known as the "weakest link." The third option assesses shared leadership by using what is called the "behavioral average option." This method is similar to the method mentioned in the previous paragraph, the group as a whole approach.

Some research has been begun by Pearce and colleagues (Pearce & Conger, 2003), but additional data should be collected to further explore these methods before truly meaningful results can be discussed. Ideally, once this has occurred, these group-level variables can then be utilized in research in a similar vein as those variables that are used at the individual leader level. The main strength of this research is that it allows the researcher to explore the influence of single group members on the overall leadership of the group. However, unlike the previous method of research where the effort involved for the respondent in data collection was relatively minimal, a key weakness of this method is that it requires a considerable investment of time from each participant because each respondent must answer the same item multiple times, thus increasing the possibility of respondent fatigue.

The final quantitative method, which studies the group as a social network, focuses on items that measure individual group members as both sources of influence and also the targets of influence. The primary variable that is measured at the group level by using this method is the degree to which leadership behaviors are centralized and/or directed by one or a few or, alternatively, if these same leadership behaviors are dispersed and/or shared by a wider group of team members. A primary component of this line of research, the investigation of social networks, has been eventually to be able to predict who, in a group, will become a central, or controlling member. It seems possible that this method can be used in a similar manner as those that use individual leader data to predict shared leadership, primarily by taking into account the opposite of the centrality score as a predictor of shared leadership. However, another interesting and valuable direction of research is using the compliment of the centrality score to carry out analyses that uncover the density of leadership in groups. For example, a potential avenue for research would be to examine whether or not shared leadership behaviors can be predicted by locating the density.

The positive strengths of this approach are that it allows for the following areas of examination: (1) the extent that each member is involved in group or team leadership; (2) how dispersed the leadership really is on the team; and (3) what patterns of interaction exist between individuals, primarily those who are the sources of influence in the group, and how influence moves within and through the group. However, as with the previous method of analysis, the weaknesses of this method also are both that it is taxing to the participants, primarily with regard to the time required to fill out the instrument, and that the methods ultimately used to analyze the collected data are usually quite complex. Finally, it is important to note that this particular method does not measure influence that emerges from the group as a whole or influence that is aimed at the whole group.

As we mentioned earlier in this section, there are also two qualitative methods that have lately been used to measure shared leadership. They are (1) leadership sociograms (Pearce, 2002) and (2) ethnographic methods (e.g., Manz et al., 2009). A primary focus in the leadership sociogram method is the documentation of individual and group patterns of interactions and the observation of group meetings. There are two primary strengths to this method. The first is that it allows a far more comprehensive understanding of group dynamics to be developed than the questionnaire-based methods. The second is that the data collected can be quantified and used as a source of data for a social network analysis. The main weaknesses of this approach are that it is time intensive, as it requires a researcher to be located in the same place as the group for what can be extended periods of time, and also that even with this co-location, key interactions between group members may be missed, as they might occur outside of the observed meetings.

The fifth method, our second qualitative approach, involves utilizing ethnography as a tool for analysis. This method requires the researcher to invest immersive time in the organization or group, observing the interactions and interplay between members in their natural setting(s). This observation does not focus only on the group that is being studied and their meeting(s), but rather it focuses on the group and its members in the context of their daily activities and interactions. The strength of this approach is that it allows the researcher the most holistic understanding of the group and its dynamics. The weakness is similar to that of the previous qualitative method, leadership sociograms, in that it requires an even more extensive investment of time commitment on the part of the researcher.

Although we have highlighted the basic characteristics, strengths, and weaknesses of five of the most prevalent and promising methodological avenues for the further research of shared leadership theory, by no means does this suggest our list is exhaustive. We also do not believe that each of these methods is perfect or cannot be developed. For example, adding an element of contextual research, especially in situations where qualitative data is collected, can add another valuable facet to our understanding of both the antecedents and the outcomes of shared leadership (Liden & Antonakis, 2009). Further research should be done to compare the efficacy of each of these methods in various contexts. Additionally, we do not suggest that this methodological list is complete, but rather, we look forward to the additional research methods that might be attempted in the future as the research of shared leadership theory evolves.

The Future of Shared Leadership

Although much of this chapter is devoted to exploring the development of shared leadership theory, especially as it relates to the empirical research that has already been conducted to examine the antecedents and outcomes of this phenomenon, the reality is that there is still a tremendous amount of interesting and valuable work that must be done on shared leadership. In order to aid this endeavor, we would like to take time to highlight some of the gaps in our knowledge about shared leadership, in the hope that by doing so we will broaden the field for research rather than restrict it. Thus, the following section will describe some possible directions for research in the area of shared leadership. Several important categories for future research include (1) the relationships that exist between shared and vertical leadership; (2) which dynamics (or fundamental factors) are present when leadership is shared in groups and/or organizational settings? (3) what steps are necessary to implement shared leadership? (4) what outcomes are linked to shared leadership? (5) how should shared leadership be assessed and codified? (6) how does culture—organizational, ethnic, and national—affect or influence shared leadership? and (7) what are the possible limits or liabilities of shared leadership? Below we draw attention to the more specific research questions and ideas that could advance leadership dialogue in the area of shared leadership. The possibilities are seemingly endless. They are exciting, and as we discover more about shared leadership theory, the implications for practice are even more profound.

The Relationship Between Shared and Vertical Leadership

Typically, researchers focus their studies on the behavior or attributes of a single leader, the person who either is the appointed or formal leader or the person who appears to be the most influential in a group. We call the relationship between this person and the group members around them a "vertical" relationship, implying that there exists a hierarchy and followers. We call this relationship "vertical leadership" (Gerstner & Day, 1997). Although some researchers have suggested that shared and vertical leadership are mutually exclusive, there are a number in the academic community who believe that shared and vertical leadership are actually intertwined and interdependent (Pearce & Conger, 2003).

Obviously, just these questions open up the opportunity for extensive research. However, in order to simplify the dialogue, we can summarize three primary areas that should be examined: (a) what are the activities and roles in which vertical leaders should engage that will facilitate or catalyze the evolution of shared leadership in groups or organizations? (b) in what ways can the vertical leader become an obstacle

to the development or display of shared leadership? and (c) how would, or even can, the two forms of leadership work together to elevate the effectiveness of an organization or a group?

Context, or the environment in which the group or organization finds itself, is another important issue when considering the relationship between vertical and shared leadership. We assume that there are some settings that would be more hospitable or conducive to the parallel incidence of these two leadership forms—but what are they? Would there be some situations that simply, by their nature, make the coexistence of vertical and shared leadership impossible? Are there circumstances in which strong direction, in the guise of vertical leadership, is needed? Or conversely, if a group or organization is in need of increased levels of group consent, harmony, or engagement, is shared leadership the more valuable form of organization?

Another cadre of research questions are those that relate to the life cycle of the group. Does vertical leadership occur more often at the inception or creation of a new group? So then, does shared leadership occur more frequently in more established groups or groups that are at the later stages of a project? What about internal or external events, such as crisis? Can these events cause the form of leadership to shift from one to the other? More subtly, will shared leadership shift in form or "strength" based on the life stage of the group? These are all important questions for future research.

The Fundamentals (or Dynamics) of Shared Leadership

One of the main areas relating to shared leadership process that poses considerable interest to researchers are the roles or bases of leadership. Pearce and Conger (2003) found it apparent that most of the authors who contributed their thoughts on shared leadership believed that shared leadership, as a process, was dependent on demonstrable and conclusive bases of leadership ranging on a continuum from vertical to shared. Shifts in leadership forms take place as they are needed and are primarily driven by things like the group's or organization's environment, challenges facing the group or organization, or skills that are ascending or descending in primacy at a certain point in time (Gerstner & Day, 1997). Pearce and Conger (2003) point out that because of this, shared leadership is then a powerful solution to a foundational organizational problem: that not one person in any organization is able to function effectively in all of the possible leadership aspects that are needed in either a group or an organizational context.

One of the areas of interest, in this regard, in the exploration of shared leadership theory is the roles that are most effective or even relevant when sharing leadership in groups. Clearly, not all leadership roles are consistently present or even necessary in shared leadership environments. Rather some of them, in various permutations, can either facilitate or hinder the development and outcomes of shared leadership in groups or organizations. Additionally, some of these leadership roles can become more or less critical at certain times in the life cycle of the team. What has become evident through the initial research in shared leadership theory is that in order to move forward in a thorough way, a comprehensive and clearly defined set of leadership roles would be extremely helpful when exploring and testing our hypotheses about the shared leadership phenomenon.

And what about how influence works in a shared leadership environment? Both Locke (2003) and Seibert, Sparrowe, and Liden (2003) discuss the idea that some influence strategies are more appropriate than others in a situation where shared leadership is present. Pearce and Sims (2002) provide some valuable insights on the subject of influence creation, the five types of leadership, and some outcomes of shared leadership. As an example, aversive leadership is negatively related to team self-ratings of their team's effectiveness. They also discovered that directive leadership was negatively related to both internal customer and manager ratings of the team's effectiveness. Finally, they found that shared empowering, transactional and transformational leadership were positively related to team self-ratings of team effectiveness.

Causes or Antecedents of Shared Leadership

One of the most fundamentally interesting areas for research in shared leadership theory is the investigation into the causes, or antecedents of shared leadership. Pearce (1997) raised the question of whether or not there is a process of "serial emergence." Although this seems a simplistic model for what is a more complex process of leading groups, it does allow the research community to begin to question how this process of sharing leadership starts.

Based on the potential avenues for research into the causes of shared leadership, we can suggest the following four overarching research areas: (a) what are the most standard causes that enable shared leadership? (b) which of these causes are more significant than others? (c) how does the situation assist or detract from some of these causes? and (d) can certain leadership typologies or roles, or which external factors, or the group life cycle help to classify certain causal agents for shared leadership?

Enabling or Facilitating Factors

There are many possible factors that facilitate shared leadership that were proposed through the work of Pearce and Conger (2003), but not many have been explored in any great detail. For example, here are a few factors that appear to be important facilitating factors: (1) the competence of group members; (2) the complexity of the task itself; (3) the mental models and shared knowledge of members in the group; (4) the leadership prototypes of the group; (5) the status, influence, and power of each group member; (6) the diversity of the group; (7) the proximity of the group members; (8) the familiarity or personal attraction for group members to one another; (9) the amount, extent, and timing of group member turnover; (10) the life-cycle of the group or project; and (11) the size of the group.

Is it possible for a group to move from a vertical leadership model to one of shared leadership? Or can a group develop shared leadership from its inception? How best to achieve that goal? What are some of the "best practices" and/or interventions that can best enable the development of sharing leadership in a group or organization? So far, very little research has been done in the area of implementing shared leadership, especially at the organizational level of analysis.

How does organizational design affect shared leadership? What types of rewards, performance measurement, or other processes are important to encourage shared leadership? Do these rewards work best at the individual or the group level, or perhaps a combination of both?

Clearly, this is just a small array of the possible questions that can be asked about the implementation of shared leadership in groups, but even more so, about the study of shared leadership theory in a larger sense. In the following section, we will briefly explore the influence that cross-cultural values might also play in the development of shared leadership.

Culture and Shared Leadership

As mentioned in the previous section, it makes sense, especially due to the wide array of cultures, to wonder how these differences in values and norms affect the possibility of sharing leadership in organizations and groups. There are many factors that form culture, and they shape how cognitions and perceptions occur in groups all over the world. For example, power distance, or the degree to which group members of a specific culture expect that power in the group, organization, or society be distributed unequally (Hofstede, 1980; House et al., 1999; Pearce, 2008; Pearce & Osmond, 1999), can greatly influence the behavior of individuals or groups toward a leader in organizations. Research (Pearce, 2008) has also demonstrated that countries with cultures that are nurturing or aggressive have fascinating implications for how leaders lead and develop those around them. For example, societies that are more nurturing are interested in developing the potential of the people around them, rather than competing. They are concerned with growing the totality of their society and community rather than

simply focusing on their own little piece. Contrast this to societies in which aggressive behavior is the norm. These groups are more likely to be materialistic, aggressive, and competitive. They are far more interested in goal achievement, but this achievement can often occur at the expense of those around them. These societies are particularly at a disadvantage when it comes to sharing leadership. They cause people to jockey for control and power, and once they have it, they are far less likely to relinquish that control to anyone around them, regardless of the other's skills (Pearce, 2008).

Another aspect to study when examining culture and shared leadership is whether the society is collectivist or individualist. People who live in a more collectivist society will be more inclined to work in groups, even those made up of relatives or other groups and organized communities, and will expect that in return for their loyalty to the group, they will be taken care of by the community or group in which they are a member. We can compare this to the individualistic societies where this is completely the opposite. People who are in individualistic societies are far more self-reliant and independent. They do not gravitate toward working in teams and find that they are more interested in personal freedom than working with others (Pearce, 2008).

Our overall knowledge of how organizational culture, politics, and design affect or influence shared leadership is still quite scant. A good example of this is the question of whether shared leadership can occur in an organization where the cultural norm values a vertical or top-down form of leadership. Another example of an organization in which the development of shared leadership might be difficult would be one that does not articulate clear goals or vision or where there is not an emphasis on excellence. Would shared leadership still be able to develop under these circumstances, perhaps under the aegis of an organizational maverick or perhaps in a remote location that is not as affected by the organization's norms and culture? These are many of the other questions that comprise a rich, varied, and valuable dialogue in shared leadership study for many years to come, particularly as our organizations continue to evolve along with the knowledge economy.

The Future of Organizational Leadership

As we forge further into the knowledge era, our models of leadership will continue to evolve to embrace the paradigmatic shift away from leadership as merely a hierarchical role to leadership as an unfolding social process, that is, a shared leadership-type perspective (Wassenaar et al., 2010). This evolutionary process, as with many others, brings to light several questions beginning with the most simple: Can leadership be shared effectively? Yes. Pearce, Manz, and Sims (2009) have uncovered numerous organizations where shared leadership is affecting real outcomes. Examples include how the medical team at a trauma center treats patients more quickly and safely; how sharing leadership in Alcoholics Anonymous helps people who are struggling to heal their addictions more effectively; or how Southwest Airlines attributes their success not to how they structure their costs, but rather to how their corporate culture of feedback from all points of the hierarchy can enable leadership to originate from any level.

Is developing shared leadership challenging? Yes. Having said that, we firmly believe that most people are capable of being both followers *and* leaders and that shared leadership is an organizational imperative for the age of knowledge work (Pearce, 2010). Although there are circumstances where shared leadership approaches might not work, the research evidence demonstrates that shared leadership can positively affect individual, group, and organizational level outcomes, including organizational performance.

Does this mean that shared leadership is a panacea? No. There will nearly always be a need for hierarchical leadership in our modern organizations (Leavitt, 2005). As documented by several studies (e.g., Ensley et al., 2006; Hooker & Csikszentmihalyi, 2003; Pearce & Sims, 2002; Shamir & Lapidot, 2003) shared and hierarchical leadership work in tandem to effect individual, group, and organizational outcomes.

Are there circumstances where we do not advocate shared leadership? Yes. For example, shared leadership is applicable only to tasks where there is interdependency between the individuals involved. To force fit any particular potential organizational process simply does not seem wise. We might further speculate that certain other preconditions are necessary for shared leadership to flourish. For instance, it seems important that the individuals involved should have well-developed knowledge, skills, and abilities—not only for the technical aspects of their tasks but also for how to engage effectively as both followers and leaders if shared leadership is to be effective. These are but a few caveats regarding shared leadership: Shared leadership, and related approaches, require far more research, not only on their outcomes but also on their antecedents and moderators. As research continues to delve deeper into leadership processes, we will yield more insights for the organizations of the future.

Case Studies

The following cases are two examples where leadership is shared. One is a scenario where the employees of United Baggage Claims service are given the ability to make decisions based on each passenger's situation. The other is an example drawn from the famous Napa restaurant The French Laundry and its Chef, Thomas Keller.

Lost Bag on United

You never want United Airlines to lose your bag. In order to get it back, you will have to wade through a convoluted maze of 800 numbers, claim forms, and airline schedules—all while they survey you to find out how well they are servicing your claim. The main number to the people who are supposed to help you takes you to a call center in India where ostensibly helpful people attempt to locate a bag on the other side of the world. They are extremely concerned with getting you to fill out a survey at the end of the call on how they did and how well they helped you. However, after three days with a missing bag and calls from an airport telling me my bag was in one place, when in reality, it had never left the airport where I had asked for it not to be delivered, a United employee honestly said: "We get this all the time. A lot of our call centers are in India. They're in a different country; a different world; a world away. People call and are told all the time that their bag is in one place, but when I check, I find that they are really in a different place. They don't understand, and they don't care." Quote 11:05 p.m., Friday, August 6, 2010, Montreal.

The reason this is happening is that many companies judge their call center employees solely on how long they spend on their service calls, which in essence, turns the concept of service into a disservice. In addition, when they don't understand what you are saying, they just give up, or tell you what they think you want to hear in order to get the call completed. They are obsequious in order to get you to feel as if they have helped, yet no actual help or resolution has actually occurred. The actual ability or desire to help and resolve, although on the surface appears to be genuine, is in reality only a cover in order to increase customer service ratings at the moment of the call, when the customer is hoping that the diffident United call center employee actually did resolve the lost bag. Yet these survey results are what is portrayed to the public as how wonderfully United treats its "valuable" customers.

This is one example of how leadership is ostensibly shared, by giving the call center employees the power to appear to resolve problems through their own initiative and abilities. However, when the capacity for them to actually truly execute their jobs is hampered by systems, bureaucracy, or other rules, they are potentially even more unempowered than if they simply had to pass along the problems to their supervisors for solving.

Sharing the Menu-Thomas Keller and The French Laundry

Typical chefs rule their kitchens. They design the menu and the theme, the style of cuisine. They select the vendors, the ingredients, and how they are presented to the customers in their final preparation. Traditionally, it is the job of the chef de cuisine,

the sous chef, or any of the rest of the kitchen and wait staff to simply repeat the vision of the head chef, but never to interpret or improvise and never, ever to create.

This is not the case in the land of Chef Thomas Keller. In his kitchens, each part of a growing group of restaurants scattered around the United States, he takes a different tack, one of vision and empowerment. He sets the vision: that of extremely high quality ingredients and preparations, based on seasonal and local organic ingredients, served in both traditional and innovative ways in memorable settings. Then he hires people who can execute that vision with little hands-on guidance from him. He states, "Cooking is a simple equation: product and execution. If you have quality product and people who are going to execute it; bringing the two together, a strong team with a common goal and building relationships with suppliers, you've got great food."

He goes on to say, "Chefs have a new responsibility. No longer is there just one restaurant, one menu. This means we have to hand down to our younger chefs the opportunities that we have. That can mean writing a book, or creating a menu, or sourcing a new sort of supply. They have a determination to, every day, evolve their work a little better than the day before." June, 2010.

By managing his kitchen in this way, he is able to immediately accomplish several things. First, he is able to hire some of the most talented, up-and-coming people who want to learn from him yet who are also interested in developing their own flavors in their cooking. Second, these people will understand very clearly how the environment that Chef Keller creates is different. Because they recognize this difference, they are more committed to the overall vision and success of the French Laundry Group because, at the end of the day, they are a foundational part of their overall success.

Favorite meal, roasted chicken.

These two small vignettes are excerpted from the upcoming book *Share the Lead* by Craig L Pearce,

Charles C. Manz, and Henry P. Sims Jr., reproduced with permission from Stanford University Press.

Discussion Questions

1. Where have you experienced shared leadership? What were some of the positive aspects? Why? Were there some things about shared leadership that you felt could work better?

2. Are there some situations in which shared leadership might work better than others?

3. In addition to some of the future areas for research in the area of shared leadership mentioned in the chapter, what other possible directions do you think that research in this area could go?

Supplementary Reading

Pearce, C. L. (2008, July 7). Follow the leaders. *Wall Street Journal*, pp. R8.

References

Antonakis, J., & Atwater, L. (2002). Leader distance: A review and a proposed theory. *The Leadership Quarterly*, 13, 673–704.

Antonakis, J., Avolio, B. J., & Sivasubramaniam, N., (2003). Context and leadership: An examination of the nine-factor full-range leadership theory using the Multifactor Leadership Questionnaire. *The Leadership Quarterly*, 14, 261–295.

Antonakis, J., Bendahan, S., Jacquart, P., & Lalive, R. (2010). On making causal claims: A review and recommendations. *The Leadership Quarterly*, 21, 1086–1120.

Antonakis, J., Cianciolo, A. T., & Sternberg, R. J. (2004). *The nature of leadership*. Thousand Oaks, CA: Sage.

Avolio, B. J., Jung, D., Murray, W., & Sivasubramaniam, N. (1996). Building highly developed teams: Focusing on shared leadership process, efficacy, trust, and performance. In M. M. Beyerlein, D. A. Johnson, & S. T. Beyerlein (Eds.), *Advances in interdisciplinary studies of work teams* (pp. 173–209). Greenwich, CT: JAI.

Balthazard, P., Waldman, D., Howell, J., & Atwater, L. (2004, January). Shared leadership and group interaction styles in problem-solving virtual teams. *Proceedings of the 37th annual Hawaii international conference on system sciences* 43(HICSS, Vol. 1, p. 10043b).

Bandura, A. (1986). *Social foundations of thought and action: A social cognitive theory.* Englewood Cliffs, NJ: Prentice Hall.

Bartol, K. M., & Martin, D. C. (1986). Women and men in task groups. In R. D. Ashmore & F. K. Del Boca (Eds.), *The social psychology of female-male relations.* (pp. 259–310). New York: Academic Press.

Bass, B. M., & Avolio, B. J. (1993). Transformational leadership: A response to critiques. In J. G. Hunt, B. R. Baliga, H. P. Dachler, & C. A. Schriesheim (Eds.), *Emerging leadership vistas* (pp. 29–40). Lexington, MA: D. C. Heath.

Bass, B. M., & Bass, R. (2008). *The Bass handbook of leadership: Theory, research, and managerial applications.* New York: Simon & Schuster.

Bass, B. M., Waldman, D. A., Avolio, B. J., & Bebb, M. (1987). Transformational leadership and the falling dominoes effect. *Group & Organization Studies* [now named *Group & Organization Management*], 12, 73–87.

Blau, J. R., & Alba, R. D. (1982). Empowering nets of participation. *Administrative Science Quarterly*, 27, 363–379.

Bono, J., Purvanova, R., Towler, A., & Peterson, D. (2009). A survey of executive coaching practices. *Personnel Psychology*, 62, 361–404.

Carlyle, T. (1894). *On heroes and hero worship and the heroic in history*. London: Chapman and Hall, Ltd. (Original work published 1841)

Carson, J., Tesluk, P., & Marrone, J. (2007). Shared leadership in teams: An investigation of antecedent conditions and performance. *Academy of Management Journal*, 50, 1217–1234.

Carte, T. A., Chidambaram, L., & Becker, A. (2006). Emergent leadership in self-managed virtual teams: A longitudinal study of concentrated and shared leadership behaviors. *Group Decision and Negotiation*, 15, 323–343.

Conger, J. A., & Kanungo, R. N. (1988). The empowerment process: Integrating theory and practice. *Academy of Management Review*, 13, 639–652.

Conger, J. A., & Pearce, C. L. (2009) Using empowerment to motivate people to engage in effective self- and shared leadership. In E. A. Locke (Ed.), *Principles of organizational behavior* (pp. 201–216). New York: John Wiley.

Cordery, J., Soo, C., Kirkman, B., Rosen, B., & Mathieu, J. (2009). Leading parallel global virtual teams: Lessons from Alcoa. *Organizational Dynamics*, 38, 204–216.

Coss, P. R. (1996). *The knight in medieval England*. Conshohocken, PA: Combined Books.

Cox, J. F., Pearce, C. L., & Sims, H. P., Jr. (2003). Toward a broader agenda for leadership development: Extending the traditional transactional-transformational duality by developing directive, empowering and shared leadership skills. In S. E. Murphy & R. E. Riggio (Eds.). *The future of leadership development* (pp. 161–180). Mahwah, NJ: Lawrence Erlbaum.

Cranny, C. J., Smith, P. C., & Stone, E. F. (1992). *Job satisfaction: How people feel about their jobs and how it affects their performance*. Lexington, MA: Lexington Books.

Csikszentmihalyi, M. (1990). *Flow: The psychology of optimal experience*. New York: Harper & Row.

Day, D. V., Gronn, P., & Salas, E. (2004). Leadership capacity in teams. *The Leadership Quarterly*, 15, 857–880.

Day, D. V., Gronn, P., & Salas, E. (2006). Leadership in team-based organizations: On the threshold of a new era. *The Leadership Quarterly*, 17, 211–216.

Day, D. V., & O'Connor, P. M. G. (2003). Leadership development: Understanding the process. In S. E. Murphy & R. E. Riggio (Eds.). *The future of leadership development* (pp. 11–28). Mahwah, NJ: Lawrence Erlbaum.

Dirks, K. T., & Ferrin, D. L. (2002). Trust in leadership: Meta-analytic findings and implications for research and practice. *Journal of Applied Psychology*, 87, 611–628.

Drucker, P. F. (1954). *The practice of management*. New York: Harper & Row.

Drucker, P. F. (1995). *Management in time of great change*. New York: Penguin Putnam.

Elloy, D. F. (2008). The relationship between self-leadership behaviors and organization variables in a self-managed work team environment. *Management Research News*, 31, 801–810.

Elmhirst, K. (2008). Executive coaching. *Leadership Excellence*, 25(1), 11.

Ensley, M. D., Hmieleski, K. M., & Pearce, C. L. (2006). The importance of vertical and shared leadership within new venture top management teams: Implications for the performance of startups. *The Leadership Quarterly*, 17, 217–231.

Evans, C. R., & Dion, K. L. (1991). Group cohesion and performance: A meta-analysis. *Small Group Research*, 22, 175–186.

Figueira, T. J., Brennan, T. C, & Sternberg, R. H. (2009). *Wisdom from the ancients: Leadership lessons from Alexander the Great to Julius Caesar*. New York: Fall River Press.

Follett, M. P. (1924). *Creative experience*. New York: Longmans Green.

Gantt, H. L. (1916). *Industrial leadership*. New Haven, CT: Yale University Press.

George, V., Burke, L. J., Rodgers, B., Duthie, N., Hoffmann, M. L., Koceja, V., et al. (2002). Developing staff nurse shared leadership behavior in professional nursing practice. *Nursing Administration Quarterly*, 26(3), 44–59.

Gerstner, C. R., & Day, D. V. (1997). Meta-analytic review of leader-member exchange theory: Correlates and construct issues. *Journal of Applied Psychology*, 82, 827–844.

Gilbreth, F. B. (1912). *Primer of scientific management*. New York: Van Nostrand Reinhold.

Gilbreth, F. B., & Gilbreth, L. M. (1917). *Applied motion study*. New York: Sturgis & Walton.

Gully, S. M., Incalcaterra, K. A., Joshi, A., & Beaubien, J. M. (2002). A meta-analysis of team-efficacy, potency, and performance: Interdependence and level of analysis as moderators of observed relationship. *Journal of Applied Psychology*, 87, 819–832.

Hofstede, G. H. (1980). *Culture consequences: International differences in work-related values*. London: Sage.

Hollander, E. P. (1961). Some effects of perceived status on responses to innovative behavior. *Journal of Abnormal and Social Psychology*, 63, 247–250.

Hollander, E. P. (1978). *Leadership dynamics: A practical guide to effective relationships*. New York: Free Press.

Hooker, C., & Csikszentmihalyi, M. (2003). Flow, creativity, and shared leadership: Rethinking the motivation and structuring of knowledge work. In C. L. Pearce & J. A. Conger (Eds.), *Shared leadership: Reframing the hows and whys of leadership* (pp. 217–234). Thousand Oaks, CA: Sage.

House, R. J., Hanges, P. J., Ruiz-Quintanilla, S. A., Dorfman, P. W., Javidan, M., Dickson, M., et al. (1999). Cultural influences on leadership in organizations: Project GLOBE. In W. H. Mobley, M. J. Gessner, & V. Arnold (Eds.), *Advances in global leadership* (Vol. 1, pp. 171–234). Stamford, CT: JAI.

Hunt, J. G. (2004). What is leadership? In J. Antonakis, A. T. Cianciolo, & R. J. Sternberg (Eds.), *The nature of leadership* (pp. 19–47). Thousand Oaks: Sage.

James, L. R., Demaree, R. G., & Wolf, G. (1984). Estimating within-group interrater reliability with and without response bias. *Journal of Applied Psychology*, 69, 85–99.

James, L. R., Demaree, R. G., & Wolf, G. (1993). rwg: An assessment of interrater agreement. *Journal of Applied Psychology*, 78, 306–310.

Kerr, S., & Jermier, J. (1978). Substitutes for leadership: Their meaning and measurement. *Organizational Behavior and Human Performance*, 22, 374–403.

Khourey-Bowers, C., Dinko, R. L., & Hart, R. G. (2005). Influence of a shared leadership model in creating a school culture of inquiry and collegiality. *Journal of Research in Science Teaching*, 42, 3–24.

Klein, K. J., Ziegert, J. C., Knight, A. P., & Xiao, Y. (2006). Dynamic delegation: Shared, hierarchical, and deindividualized leadership in extreme action teams. *Administrative Science Quarterly*, 51, 590–621.

Konu, A., & Viitanen, E. (2008). Shared leadership in Finnish social and health care. *Leadership in Health Services*, 21, 28–40.

Kozlowski, S. W. J., & Klein, K. J. (2000). A multilevel approach to theory and research in organizations: Contextual, temporal, and emergent processes. In K. J. Klein & S. W J. Kozlowski (Eds.), *Multilevel theory, research, and methods in organizations* (pp. 3–90). San Francisco: Jossey-Bass.

Leavitt, H. J. (2005). *Top down: Why hierarchies are here to stay and how to manage them more effectively*. Boston: Harvard Business School Press.

Leonard, H. S., & Goff, M. (2003). Leadership development as an intervention for organizational transformation. *Consulting Psychology Journal*, 55, 58–67.

Liden, R. C., & Antonakis, J. (2009). Considering context in psychological leadership research. *Human Relations*, 62, 1587–1605.

Locke, E. A. (2003). Leadership: Starting at the top. In C. L. Pearce & J. A. Conger (Eds.), *Shared leadership: Reframing the hows and whys of leadership* (pp. 271–284). Thousand Oaks, CA: Sage.

Luthans, F. (2010). *Organizational behavior*. New York: McGraw-Hill.

Manz, C. C. (1986). Self-leadership: Toward an expanded theory of self-influence processes in organizations. *Academy of Management Review*, 11, 585–600.

Manz, C. C., Shipper, F., & Stewart, G. L. (2009). Everyone a team leader: Shared influence at W. L. Gore & Associates. *Organizational Dynamics*, 38, 239–244.

Manz, C. C., & Sims, H. P., Jr. (1980). Self-management as a substitute for leadership: A social learning theory perspective. *Academy of Management Review*, 5, 361–367.

Manz, C. C., & Sims, H. P., Jr. (1989). *Super leadership: Leading others to lead themselves*. New York: Prentice Hall.

Manz, C. C., & Sims, H. P., Jr. (1990). *Super leadership: Leading others to lead themselves*. New York: Berkley Books.

Mohrman, S. A., Cohen, S. G., & Mohrman, A. M. (1995). *Designing team-based organizations: New forms for knowledge work*. San Francisco: Jossey-Bass.

Montgomery, J. (1836). *The theory and practice of cotton spinning; or the carding and spinning master's assistant*. Glasgow, Scotland: John Niven, Trongate.

Montgomery, J. (1840). *The cotton manufacture of the United States of America contrasted and compared with that of Great Britain*. London: John N. Van.

Mundlak, Y. (1978). Pooling of time-series and cross-section data. *Econometrica*, 46(1), 69–85.

Nardinelli, C., (2008). *Industrial revolution and the standard of living*. Library of Economics and Liberty. Available at http://www.econlib.org/library/Enc/IndustrialRevolutionandtheStandardofLiving.html

Olson-Sanders, T. (2006). Collectivity and influence: The nature of shared leadership and its relationship with team learning orientation, vertical leadership and team effectiveness (Doctoral dissertation, George Washington University, 2006). Retrieved from ABI/INFORM Global (Publication No. AAT 3237041).

Organ, D. W. (1988). *Organizational citizenship behavior: The good soldier syndrome*. Lexington, MA: Lexington Books.

O'Toole, J., Galbraith, J., & Lawler, E. E., III. (2003). The promise and pitfalls of shared leadership: When two (or more) heads are better than one. In C. L. Pearce & J. A. Conger (Eds.), *Shared leadership: Reframing the hows and whys of leadership* (pp. 250–268). Thousand Oaks, CA: Sage.

Paris, L., Howell, J., Dorfman, P., & Hanges, P. (2009). Preferred leadership prototypes of male and female leaders in 27 countries. *Journal of International Business Studies*, 40, 1396–1405.

Pearce, C. L. (1997). *The determinants of change management team (CMT) effectiveness: A longitudinal investigation*. Unpublished doctoral dissertation, University of Maryland, College Park.

Pearce, C. L., (2002, August). Quantitative and qualitative approaches to the study of shared leadership. In C. L. Pearce (symposium chair), *Shared leadership: Reframing the hows and whys of leadership.* Presented at the annual conference of the Academy of Management, Denver, CO.

Pearce, C. L. (2008, July 7). Follow the leaders. *The Wall Street Journal*, p. R8.

Pearce, C. L. (2010). Leading knowledge workers: Beyond the era of command and control. In C. L. Pearce, J. A. Maciariello, & H. Yamawaki (Eds.), *The Drucker difference* (pp. 35–46). New York: McGraw-Hill.

Pearce, C. L., & Conger, J. A. (Eds.). (2003). *Shared leadership: Reframing the hows and whys of leadership.* Thousand Oaks, CA: Sage.

Pearce, C. L., Conger, J. A., & Locke, E. (2008). Shared leadership theory. *The Leadership Quarterly*, 19, 622–628.

Pearce, C. L., & Herbick, P. A. (2004). Citizenship behavior at the team level of analysis: The role of team leader behavior, team dynamics, the team's environment, and team demography. *Journal of Social Psychology*, 144, 293–310.

Pearce, C. L., Manz, C. C., & Sims, H. P., Jr. (2009). Where do we go from here? Is shared leadership the key to team success? *Organizational Dynamics*, 38, 234–238.

Pearce, C. L., Manz, C. C., & Sims, H. P., Jr. (in press). *Share the lead.* Palo Alto, CA: Stanford University Press.

Pearce, C. L., & Osmond, C. P., (1999). From workplace attitudes and values to a global pattern of nations: An application of latent class modeling. *Journal of Management*, 25, 759–778.

Pearce, C. L., & Sims, H. P., Jr. (2000). Shared leadership: Toward a multi-level theory of leadership. In M. M. Beyerlein, D. A. Johnson, & S. T. Beyerlein (Eds.), *Advances in interdisciplinary studies of work teams* (pp. 115–139). Greenwich, CT: JAI.

Pearce, C. L., & Sims, H. P., Jr. (2002). Vertical versus shared leadership as predictors of the effectiveness of change management teams: An examination of aversive, directive, transactional, transformational, and empowering leader behaviors. *Group Dynamics, Theory, Research, and Practice*, 6, 172–197.

Pearce, C. L., Yoo, Y., & Alavi, M. (2004). Leadership, social work, and virtual teams: The relative influence of vertical versus shared leadership in the nonprofit sector. In R. E. Riggio & S. Smith Orr (Eds.), *Improving leadership in nonprofit organizations* (pp. 160–203). San Francisco: Jossey-Bass.

Riggio, R. E., Chaleff, I., & Lipman-Blumen, J. (Eds.). (2008). *The art of followership: How great followers create great leaders and organizations.* San Francisco: Jossey-Bass.

Rodriguez, C. (2005). Emergence of a third culture: Shared leadership in international strategic alliances. *International Marketing Review*, 22, 67–95.

Ropo, A., Eriksson, P., & Hunt, J. G. (1997). Reflections on conducting processual research on management and organizations. *Scandinavian Journal of Management*, 13, 331–335.

Ropo, A., & Sauer, E. (2003). Partnerships of orchestras: Towards shared leadership. *International Journal of Arts Management*, 5(2), 44–55.

Say, J. B. (1964). *A treatise on political economy.* New York: Augustus M. Kelley. (Original work published 1803)

Seibert, S. E., Sparrowe, R. T., & Liden, R. C. (2003). A group exchange structure approach to leadership in groups. In C. L. Pearce & J. A. Conger (Eds.), *Shared leadership: Reframing the hows and whys of leadership* (pp. 173–192). Thousand Oaks, CA: Sage.

Shamir, B., & Lapidot, Y. (2003). Shared leadership in the management of group boundaries: A study of expulsions from officers' training courses. In C. L. Pearce & J. A. Conger (Eds.), *Shared leadership: Reframing the hows and whys of leadership* (pp. 235–249). Thousand Oaks, CA: Sage.

Solansky, S. (2008). Leadership style and team processes in self-managed teams. *Journal of Leadership & Organizational Studies*, 14, 332–341.

Stein, R. T., & Heller, T. (1979). An empirical analysis of the correlations between leadership status and participation rates reported in the literature. *Journal of Personality and Social Psychology*, 37, 1993–2002.

Stewart, L. (1998). A meaning for machines: Modernity, utility, and the eighteenth century British public. *Journal of Modern History*, 70, 259–294.

Stewart, L., (2003). Science and the eighteenth-century public: Scientific revolutions and the changing format of scientific investigation. In M. Fitzpatrick, P. Jones, C. Knelworf, & I. McAlmon (Eds.), *The Enlightenment world* (pp. 234–246). London: Routledge.

Taylor, F. W. (1903). *Shop management.* New York: Harper & Row.

Taylor, F. W. (1911). *Principles of scientific management.* New York: Harper & Brothers.

Wassenaar, C. L., & Pearce, C. L. (2012). Shared leadership 2.0: A 2010 glimpse into the state of the field. In M. Uhl-Bien & S. Ospina, (Eds.), *Advancing Relational leadership theory* (pp. 421–432). Charlotte, NC: Information Age.

Wassenaar, C. L., Pearce, C. L., Hoch, J., & Wegge, J. (2010). Shared leadership meets virtual teams: A match made in cyberspace. In P. Yoong (Ed.), *Leadership in the digital enterprise: Issues and challenges* (pp. 15–27). Hersey, PA: IGI Global.

Wood, M. S. (2005). Determinants of shared leadership in management teams. *International Journal of Leadership Studies,* 1(1) 64–85.

Wren, D. A. (1994). *The evolution of management thought* (4th ed.). New York: John Wiley.

Yammarino, F. J. (1990). Individual- and group-directed leader behavior descriptions. *Educational and Psychological Measurement,* 50, 739–759.

Yammarino, F. J., & Bass, B. M. (1990). Transformational leadership and multiple levels of analysis. *Human Relations,* 43, 975–996.

Yammarino, F. J., Dansereau, F., & Kennedy, C. J. (2001). A multiple-level multidimensional approach to leadership: Viewing leadership through an elephant's eye. *Organizational Dynamics,* 29, 149–163.

Yukl, G. A. (2002). *Leadership in organizations* (5th ed.). Englewood Cliffs, NJ: Prentice Hall.

CHAPTER 14

E-leadership

*Re-Examining Transformations
in Leadership Source and Transmission*

Bruce J. Avolio[1]
University of Washington

John J. Sosik
Pennsylvania State University

Surinder S. Kahai
Binghamton University

Bradford Baker
University of Maryland

1. Introduction

Thomas Edison suggested at the turn of the 20th century that human beings have an enormous capacity to build amazing technology but figuring how to best implement it, remains a formidable challenge (see www.edisonfordwinterestates.org). This certainly appears to be true of the advanced information technology (AIT) that has been developed since the mid-1990s and deployed in organizations because there have been amazing transformations in what technology can now do *for* and *to* us. Yet, how such technology is implemented in organizations and its effects on the way people work together has not been fully examined nor understood. Although the potential impact of AIT has been recognized by both leadership scholars and practitioners as important, what we know about the interaction between AIT and leadership still remains at the very nascent stages of development.

The position we take in this updated review regarding the examination of e-leadership is broader than simply focusing on how leaders use AIT when interacting virtually. Specifically, we attempt to "zoom out" in our examination of leadership and AIT, by considering how AIT and leadership—in the broadest sense—affect each other over time, distance, and cultures. We do so, because, information is a fundamental building block for considering how organizations function. Consequently, to the extent that information generation and distribution in organizations is changing as a function of advances in information technology, we suggest that what actually constitutes an organization is also transforming, which then centrally affects how we view leadership in current and future organizations.

We argue that e-leaders are affected by time, distance, and cultural considerations in how they actively shape their followers', customers' and society's views and use of AIT, and potentially the context that embeds them. Work on strategic leadership suggests that there are windows of opportunities defined by market, economic, societal, and political factors that place limits on when technologies can be developed and/or adopted (Finkelstein, Hambrick, & Cannella, 2007), and therefore when leaders are required to communicate these factors to followers or customers. For example, the determination of when and how to best apply technologies to develop and introduce an innovative computer for the higher-education market was essential to the success of NeXT, the company Steve Jobs founded after leaving Apple in 1985. To overcome market-defined time limitations in the fast-paced computer industry, Jobs recognized the importance of eliminating social and physical distance among his top managers and designers. To close the time/space gaps and create a more participative context, he used a mix of intensive company retreats and technology. This approach facilitated discussions among employees about NeXT's vision and culture and how customers could use the new technology his employees were creating (Nathan, 1986). Thus, e-leadership not only considers how AIT mediates leadership influence processes, but also describes how leadership influences the creation, adaption, or adoption of AIT by all constituents within what we call the *total leadership system* (described below), and how technology may aid leaders to better reveal, frame, and communicate truths

hidden within the ambiguities of complex social systems and their contexts (Heidegger, 1977).

In their review of e-leadership, Avolio, Kahai, and Dodge (2001) indicated, "we chose the term e-leadership to incorporate the new emerging context for examining leadership" (p. 617). The authors went further in their discussion to emphasize that they would focus on how AIT was mediating social influence processes that are typically associated with leadership at individual, group, and organization levels. However, in their abstract, they also stated, "organizational structures, including leadership, may themselves be transformed as a result of interactions with Advanced Information Technology" (p. 615) and further into their review, they suggested that "leaders will need to play a more proactive role in creating the social structures that foster the implementation of AIT" (p. 617).

Reflecting on their main focus, we assume that Avolio et al. (2001) used adaptive structuration theory specifically because they were interested in not only how leaders appropriate technology, but also how technology impacts leadership. Consequently, we set out here to examine how leaders lead virtually, as well as how teams interact virtually, but this in our view is only a very small piece of the transformation that is occurring in organizations as a consequence of introducing AIT. Yet, we cannot focus on every aspect of organizations or organizational theory in this updated review, so we direct our attention specifically to examining how AIT and leadership interact with each other to affect individuals, groups, organizations, and larger communities.

Looking back and building on Avolio et al. (2001), our focus here is to examine the changing complex leadership dynamic that is affected by the introduction of new forms of AIT. Dasgupta (2011) perhaps articulated this broader focus best stating, "leadership and technology, therefore enjoy a recursive relationship, each affecting and at the same time being affected by the other; each transforming and being transformed by the other" (p. 2). Similarly, Avolio and Kahai (2003) in their discussion of how technology is affecting leadership, viewed e-leadership as being "a fundamental change in the way leaders and followers related to each other within organizations and between organizations"(p. 15).

With this focus in mind, we examine how the interaction between leadership and AIT will permanently change what we conceive of as representing an organization in which future practitioners lead and future leadership scholars study leadership, as noted by Avolio et al. (2001), when they stated, "the repeated appropriation of information technology generates or transforms social structures, which over time become institutionalized" (p. 621). Fundamentally, we build on the foundational question guiding earlier work on e-leadership to ask, *how does the appropriation of AIT affect the total leadership system in organizations and in turn, how does leadership affect the appropriation of AIT in the sense of their co-evolution?* We assess whether leadership is the source of organizational structures/processes and how leadership affects and is affected by the structures arising from the appropriation of the AIT. Referring to Katz and Kahn's (1978) notion that organizations are interconnected systems whereby a change in one aspect of the system will affect changes in other parts, we emphasize from the outset of this article that we are considering both social and technical systems, as well as their interaction over time.

Our review of the literature indicates that advances in AIT and its appropriation at all levels of organizations and societies have far outpaced the practice and science of leadership. Indeed, it seems fair to say that the field of leadership has largely assumed what we might call an anthropological approach to understanding how AIT affects the leadership dynamics in organizations, communities, and societies. By anthropological, we mean the leadership field has studied the traces left behind after AIT has been appropriated, following what the impact has been, versus predicting what it could be. This includes but is not limited to how AIT has dis-intermediated the relationship between leaders and leaders, leaders and followers, leaders and their organization, community and nation states, global and non-global team members, governments and the citizens they serve, and the business enterprise and its customers.

We begin our discussion by first highlighting critical aspects of the original discussion on e-leadership in terms of some of the fundamental operational definitions and theoretical frameworks used to interpret what constituted e-leadership at that time. Next, we examine how e-leadership has evolved in both science and practice over the past ten plus years, exploring it from a micro to macro perspective. We then examine emerging areas that were not included in the 2001 review (e.g., gamification, explained below) that are changing the way organizational members and consumers interact around the globe. After these discussions, we provide a review and integration of the existing literature, in Table 14.1, and propose a framework to guide future work on e-leadership, in Figure 14.1. Finally, we conclude with recommendations for exploring over the next decade what constitutes e-leadership in all of its many forms and functions.

2. Reflecting Back to Prescribe Forward

Avolio et al. (2001) led their discussion of e-leadership by stating that, "We believe it is perhaps too early to identify any empirically based, systematic, patterned variations or to draw any broad conclusions about e-leadership" (p. 616). Since that statement was first published, our updated review suggests that although there are certain broad conclusions one can derive from the leadership literature, such as how different leadership styles interact with different AIT systems to produce different patterns of interaction and performance, providing more specific recommendations and conclusions still remains elusive. However, we are confident in saying that AIT affects the leadership dynamic, sometimes augmenting it, and sometimes substituting or subtracting from it, but if pushed to offer a specific set of axioms or practical guidelines for exploring this leadership domain, at present such specificity does not seem justified.

Certain points made in the 2001 article did offer appropriate guidance for future work on e-leadership and remain relevant today, including for example, the statement, "In the case of e-leadership, the context not only matters, it is a part of the construct being studied" (p. 616). Avolio (2007) made a clear call for the field of leadership to focus its energies on understanding the context in which leadership was not only embedded, but in the case of e-leadership part and parcel. A call for more theory and research on the context in which leadership is embedded coincided with many other calls in the field of leadership to do the same (Bass, 2008).

As stated in Avolio et al. (2001), "E-leadership is defined as a social influence process mediated by AIT to produce a change in attitudes, feelings, thinking, behavior, and performance with individuals, groups, and/or organizations" (p. 617). Yet, the original definition of e-leadership may have also benefited from placing greater emphasis on the importance of the context in the original definition (cf. Avolio, 2007; Bass, 2008), which might be revised as follows: *E-leadership is defined as a social influence process embedded in both proximal and distal contexts mediated by AIT that can produce a change in attitudes, feelings, thinking, behavior, and performance.* Also in retrospect, there could have been greater emphasis placed on what constitutes the source or *locus* of e-leadership, and how the source of leadership is transmitted when it is mediated through AIT, as we discuss below.

In terms of specific theoretical considerations that were provided in 2001, the suggestion that leadership and technology influence each other reciprocally, as emphasized by Weick (1990) and Orlikowski, Yates, Okamura, and Fujimoto (1995), is clearly in line with emerging leadership theory and research that has appeared over the last decade, such as work on authentic leadership theory (see Avolio & Gardner, 2005). Adaptive Structure Theory (AST; DeSanctis & Poole, 1994), which was the foundational theoretical framework used by Avolio et al. (2001) to examine e-leadership, remains useful in determining how the appropriation of AIT by leaders and their peers or followers can affect how those leaders lead through technology, and how leadership itself affects the use of technology.

Looking back, AST views technology in terms of what it called its *structural features* and *spirit.* Specifically, information technology is not simply used, but rather appropriated in ways that is based on how the technology is interpreted by the user. Hence, users may appropriate technology in ways that were not intended by the designer or *spirit,* that is to say, unfaithfully. Avolio et al. (2001) stated that the, "appropriation of structures and its outcomes can reaffirm existing structures, modify them, or give rise

to new structures" (p. 615). Also, Avolio et al. suggested that leadership should be viewed as a *system* that can serve as the source of structures that can faithfully or unfaithfully guide actions in line with the spirit of both leadership and AIT. For example, we have recently seen the rapid growth of crowd sourcing in all aspects of business and community challenges, which in spirit promotes collective or shared leadership on a very broad and dynamic scale. Creating such a collective leadership system that can encompass thousands of individuals influencing each other towards a specific goal or mission, along with the AIT to support that leadership, is exactly what DeSanctis and Poole (1994) meant when they referred to the faithful appropriation of technology.

The appropriation concept in AST is an area that the field of leadership has only begun to scratch the surface of in terms of examining how AIT is appropriated within and between different levels of analysis. The leadership field's collective understanding of what has been appropriated, and how, seems primarily post hoc. However, how a leadership system operates impacts how technology is appropriated. Leaders can affect appropriation by manipulating institutional structures of signification, legitimization, and domination (Chatterjee, Grewal, & Sambamurthy, 2002). These structures create norms and values regarding how organizational members should engage in structuring actions. Leaders can manipulate structures of signification, which give meaning and serve as cognitive guides, through inspirationally motivating behaviors that offer a vision for the organization and how AIT fits into that vision. Leaders can influence the structures of legitimization, which legitimize behavior, by discussing opportunities and risks with the application of AIT. By believing in AIT, participating in AIT strategy and projects, and using AIT, leaders can be role models and send signals that legitimize their followers' participation in AIT projects and adoption of AIT. Leaders can manipulate structures of domination, which regulate behavior, through mandates and policies regarding AIT adoption and use.

However, technology may not always be appropriated in accord with the structures enabled or created by a leader. Indeed, when authoritarian leadership conflicts with an emergent and complex leadership dynamic, as in what has been referred to as the "Arab Spring," the appropriation of technology such as Twitter and Facebook to launch protests has radically changed who was and who was not in control. Of course, these technologies can also be used to create havoc and chaos among large groups, which presents the possibility for misusing AIT to serve the purposes of radical groups/leaders interested in destabilizing populations.

Nevertheless, we suspect that the founders of both Twitter and Facebook may not have built into the spirit of their respective AIT systems the idea of *regime change,* however that is how those technologies were appropriated. We also are witnessing the same type of transformation happening in many aspects of business, where AIT is changing not only the way customers interact with organizations and what is offered and delivered, but also how organizations configure their leadership and operational systems to add value for their customers. AIT has empowered customers through websites, blogs, and other means of connecting, to provide transparent and oftentimes nearly instant feedback on products on services. At the same time, AIT is now being used to track customer purchasing patterns and preferences, and then aligning ads and offerings that could no doubt manipulate consumers and violate a range of privacy issues.

The importance of relationships in terms of AIT was certainly noted even in the early work that was done connecting groupware systems and leadership (Sosik, Avolio, & Kahai, 1997). Specifically, this line of research examined different styles of leadership and how individuals interacted within a groupware system setting, showing how different leadership styles manipulated experimentally (either in facilitation or in groups) affected how groups interacted and their outcomes. In these experiments, anonymity was consistently shown to be a powerful moderator when examined in the context of leader and followers e-collaborations. Today, this finding may not seem so surprising in that when we provide consumers with the protection of anonymity, we see how this construct has transformed the way products and services are graded (e.g., Amazon.com, Trip Advisor, Angie's

List), and how leaders of Fortune 500 companies are judged (e.g., Glassdoor.com). What was shown in early research regarding the effects of anonymity on the interactions within group support systems (see, Sosik et al., 1997, where anonymity enhanced the effects of transformational over transactional leadership on solution originality, group efficacy, and satisfaction with the task) has largely been shown in online interactions around the globe.

In sum, looking back to 2001, we remain confident the theoretical framework that guided the foundational work on e-leadership remains sound and still generative as a foundation for future research. The inclination that leadership and AIT systems co-evolve, perhaps not always in the most constructive or even beneficial ways, still makes sense. Also, that context matters even in how we define e-leadership, is more apparent today than it might have been in 2001. Yet, we also see that the practice field has far outpaced what we know about how leadership and AIT will affect each other. This is also true in the recommendations and training that organizations have provided to leaders and teams on how best to appropriate AIT whether in one to one, one to many, many to many, or virtual team settings.

We proceed by examining what happened over the last decade and how what has transpired might shape the next decade or two in terms of leadership research, theory, and practice. Yet, we remain grounded in our focus guided by a question that was posed in the future directions section in Avolio et al. (2001) where the authors stated, "How does the organizational context, including the specification of levels of analysis, affect how we conceptualize, define, and measure e-leadership?" (p. 658).

***

6. How AIT Is Transforming the Ways We Work at Meso-Levels

Following from Kahai (2013), we organize the type of general changes occurring at work with the following themes: (1) increasing use of AIT in organizations, (2) greater transparency and openness, (3) the rise of social networks, (4) constant contact, and (5) increase use of tracking devices. In the following sections, we discuss these respective changes and how they are influencing the loci and mechanisms of leadership.

6.1. Increasing Use of AIT in Organizations

As new tools emerge to connect us in social networks and support the development of online distributed communities, the definition of what constitutes a "virtual team" has expanded. The creation of social media, such as blogs and micro-blogs, content communities, social networking sites, virtual worlds are examples of where the boundaries of virtual teaming may be stretched beyond our traditional notions of such teams (Kaplan & Haenlein, 2010).

Avolio et al. (2001) devoted significant attention to virtual teams in their exploration of e-leadership. Yet, a greatly expanded literature has emerged that identifies three key dimensions that are commonly characteristic of virtual teams: (1) relatively limited lifespan, dependent on transient organizational or task needs, (2) team dispersion in terms of geographical, social, or temporal space, and (3) technological enablement (Jarvenpaa & Leidner, 1999; Powell, Piccoli, & Ives, 2004). Indeed, there is a growing body of research on virtual teaming that examines how communication technology use is related to aspects of mediated team collaboration. Powell et al. (2004) summarizing this literature identified research on virtual team inputs (e.g., team design, cultural differences), socio-emotional processes (e.g., trust, cohesion), and outputs (e.g., team performance, satisfaction). Past research suggests that although collaborative technologies can enable virtual teamwork, key aspects of FtF interaction are often attenuated or completely absent-especially visual cues, the immediacy of feedback, and a sense of presence of self, others, and objects (Dennis, Fuller, & Valacich, 2008). These technological limitations can lead to difficulties related to collaboration activities including the sharing of ideas, convergence with solutions or decisions, and the coordination of work (Powell et al., 2004).

Ultimately, collaborative technology can either enable or hinder a sender's ability to exchange data and information (both content and cues), and the capability of that information to change understanding or behavior of other virtual team members. Montoya et al. (2011) reported that higher-performing teams perceived communication in a 3D Collaborative Virtual Environment (CVE) to be easier than the lower performing teams. For members of higher performing teams, results suggested that communication difficulties were mitigated as communication was perceived to be more natural and teammates more responsive. Higher-performing teams perceived they were better able to coordinate their teamwork by developing clear strategies and reaching consensus as compared to lower-performing teams.

Cameron and Webster (2005) found that a common form of communication in virtual teams is instant messaging (IM). In their analysis of how IM was appropriated, Cameron and Webster (2005) reported that IM spirit is characterized by informality and is perceived to be much less rich than FtF communication. Cameron and Webster's (2005) results demonstrated that employees use IM not only as a replacement for other communication channels, but also as an additional method for collaboration. However, one of the potential downsides of appropriating IM is where participants jumped the communication queue in front of waiting others.

Constant access to AIT, pressures to reduce travel expenses, and increased presence of Millennials in the workplace are fueling a shift to greater incidence of electronic communication in organizations either through virtual teams or on a broader community scale (Kahai, 2013). This sort of transformative shift can lead to significant changes in what we consider to be the loci and mechanisms of leadership. For instance, electronic communication was expected to reduce the effects of domination by a few and enable more equal participation in organizations, shifting the locus of leadership to a collective level (Sproull & Kiesler, 1986). However, forces against promoting such collective interactions or shifts in leadership locus remain today across many organizations, communities, and societies. For example, Weisband, Schneider, and Connolly (1995) reported that influence behaviors and their effects did not get evened out by the use of electronic communication channels when deep status differences existed within the group. Early research on the appropriation of AIT suggests that the shift to greater electronic communication may be accompanied by a shift to the collective as the locus of leadership, but this may occur more readily where the members of the collective are of equal status, or when a culture for collaboration is already in place that facilitates that type of appropriation of AIT.

Electronic communication may affect how one's emotions are conveyed (Kahai, 2013). Most electronic media reduce the nonverbal cues (Kahai & Cooper, 1999). The extraction of emotion via less media rich technologies may then contribute to receivers seeing positive messages as less positive and negative messages as more negative (Byron, 2008). As noted by Daft and Lengel (1984), the medium of information (e.g., FtF, telephone) affects the richness of information. Also, while users of electronic media are known to compensate for the challenges they encounter in using AIT (Kock, 2004), they are less likely to compensate for transmitting emotions in that they may not fully appreciate the inability of receivers to perceive the emotions or tone they are trying to convey (Kruger, Epley, Parker, & Ng, 2005). The inability of leaders to convey their emotions accurately or to interpret those displayed by others can make it challenging to connect with followers and energize them when using AIT (Erez, Misangyi, Johnson, LePine, & Halverson, 2008). This may be especially problematic for charismatic or transformational leaders who often use emotions to positively influence or motivate followers (Bass, 2008).

Until recently, the manifestation of emotions in CMC and other technology platforms for e-leadership has been limited to text-based messages and emoticons, while the measurement of emotions has been restricted to self-report instruments (e.g., Manser, Cooper, & Trefusis, 2012) and experience sampling techniques where respondents are periodically paged throughout the day via electronic devices, instant messages, or Twitter and requested to report their affective states (Hektner, Schmidt, & Csikszentmihalyi, 2006). However, promising advances in technology are now making the experience, expression, and recognition of

emotions more realistic and relevant for e-leadership research and practice. We believe this progress will lead to the heightening of leaders' and followers' awareness of the potential for technology to add to, rather than detract from, the emotional experience associated with leadership events. One such technology is called *affective haptics,* which Arafsha, Masudul Alam, and El Saddik (2012) defined as, "computer systems that affect a human's emotional condition by the sense of touch" (p. 350). Building upon earlier technology that can recognize human faces and understand the expression of emotions displayed (Pentland & Choudhury, 2000), this type of AIT involves the exchange of power (e.g., heat, pressure, vibrations) through contact with parts of the human body via tactile sensors or jackets simulating feelings of touching and/or being touched, controlled by a programmed interaction algorithm (MacLean, 2008). Research on the use of touch for recognizing and expressing emotion via computer interfaces is just emerging. Smith and MacLean (2007) demonstrated how emotions could be transmitted between couples and strangers using haptic devices; couples in close personal relationships reported greater liking of experienced and recognized emotions in virtual contexts than did strangers. As such, a history of interactions and sufficient levels of trust between leaders and followers interacting online may be a prerequisite for the use of haptic devices to simulate emotional motivational responses that occur in leader-follower relationships. However, we need to be cautious that individuals or groups do not use this technology to build relationships based on false data, premises, or intentions.

Reviews of the leadership literature (Bass, 2008; Yukl, 2010) suggest that human failings (e.g., distorted perceptions, biases, fatigue, etc.) can produce dysfunctional emotions (e.g., anger, fear, despair) in leaders and followers, thereby potentially yielding suboptimal e-leadership processes and outcomes. This possibility, coupled with the societal trend that personal presence is optional for many activities that can now be performed virtually (e.g., online training and education, working from home, socializing online), raises the interesting possibility that in the future robots may serve in certain leadership and followership roles because they are not influenced by emotions. Samani, Koh, Saadatian, and Polydorou (2012) pointed out that humans make bad decisions because they are not able to fully process the range of emotions they experience throughout the day, but robots can be programmed to express only positive or neutral emotional states. However, these authors failed to recognize that robots might be programmed to express negative emotions, such as anger and rage, reflecting the dark side of leadership. Samani et al. (2012) suggested that, "the robot assigned to handle high-risk trading should not only have character traits which will ensure that it will constantly remain analytical and disciplined, but it should also be instilled with a sense of disappointment and shame towards other robot associates" (p. 162). Other researchers are more skeptical arguing that robots cannot yet think creatively (Goldenberg & Mazursky, 2002), exercise moral judgment, accumulate experiences with each action they perform, or interpret unfolding events (Dreyfus, Dreyfus, & Athanasiou, 2000).

We believe the possibility of robot technology fully controlling e-leadership processes and outcomes is unlikely, yet interesting to consider. Nevertheless, if technology is developed to the point that robots can recognize and express emotions, monitor psychological states and conditions, and suggest actions to humans without the capacity to make moral judgments, placing robots in e-leadership roles as advocated by Samani et al. (2012) would require careful scrutiny. Research on authentic (Luthans & Avolio, 2003), ethical (Brown & Treviño, 2006), and destructive forms of leadership (Eubanks & Mumford, 2010) suggests some potential danger in such initiatives; robots may provide leaders and followers with the impetus to do things that they would have not done in the past—bypass their own emotions, logic, and reason, and blindly follow robotic directives without adequately considering ethical, cultural, and legal considerations.

6.2. Greater Transparency

Rhue and Sundararajan (2013) have shown increased use of AIT systems and the ubiquitous presence of web-based tools and technologies both increases access to information and organizational leaders as well as levels of transparency. What transpires at all organizational levels around the globe is becoming increasingly available to others because of the Internet and greater reliance on information technology to do one's work (Kahai, 2013). By affecting what people know and think about their leaders, this is potentially affecting the leadership cognitions and in turn choices seen as available and subsequent actions taken.

As noted through our references to big data, followers now have unprecedented access to information that influences their sense-making related to how they interpret their leaders' transmissions. Such increased transparency and openness are occurring in a variety of different ways. Today, whistleblowers have easy access to Internet sites like Wikileaks (http://wikile aks.org/) and online media that they use to expose organizations and their leaders. Recently, we saw a number of classified documents and exchanges within the National Security Agency (NSA), especially those related to its surveillance of U.S. citizens, being exposed by a relatively low-level systems administrator working for the NSA (Hill, 2013). In this instance, just one individual with the right point of contact can send an entire organization into chaos trying to respond to the leaked information.

Another example is that of an observer posting President Obama's offhanded reference to Kanye West as a "jackass" after the latter inappropriately interrupted the 2009 MTV Video Music Awards (Gold, 2009). Such episodes sometimes cause major damage to the reputation of the leader and the organization, especially if taken out of context. For example, at a firm called Cerner, an employee forwarded the email of Cerner's CEO, Neal Patterson, to his managers in which he expressed annoyance with declining work ethic (Murphy, 2006). In Cerner's case, the disclosure of the CEO's email led to a 29% drop in its stock price (Murphy, 2006).

Emerging information technology also provides greater transparency into the efforts, interactions, and performance of employees. Technologies such as Google Apps provides companies with real-time data on who has contributed what and when; in situations where the relationship between effort and performance is somewhat ambiguous, such information can influence how leaders and group members perceive others, trust them, and offer consideration (Kahai, 2013). Gaming virtual worlds, like World of Warcraft, provide a different kind of visibility that facilitates leadership for activities that require individual players to team-up with each other (Reeves, Malone, & O'Driscoll, 2008). Specifically, in this game, one can track individual performance and make team member capabilities, performance, and compensation transparent. Game leaders can then link appropriate rewards during or immediately following a performance cycle, therefore creating greater feelings of equity and meritocracy. Additionally, transparency about how the team is performing and team members' capabilities can also help e-leaders choose or modify their strategies in real-time, helping them select and define the roles of those who are most suitable for a particular task.

In this context, leaders are likely to face greater pressures to be authentic and transparent in their interactions with others. The transparency enabled by AIT is also bringing behaviors, traits, and cognitions related to ethical leadership into focus. After seeing numerous cases of ethical misconduct by organizational leaders, we are now facing the prospect of an increase in such cases because AIT may provide organizational leaders with rather tempting situations that could foster either an abuse of power or even ethical misconduct. We also see that leaders don't have to stick to their internal networks to observe what their employees are doing outside of work. Indeed, a whole industry has now emerged to help companies dig up dirt on their adversaries by hacking into their internal networks and emails, while investigating their Internet footprint (Kane, 2013). Leaders try to justify such actions, at least in cases where they are spying within their internal networks, with the argument that whatever is happening on an organization's internal system is no longer private (Barrett, 2013). Such actions may invariably lead to a loss of trust in leaders and the organizations they represent.

Of course the use of AIT can also reinforce that an organization's leadership is transparent and acting in accord with high ethical standards (Brown, Treviño,

& Harrison, 2005). This can occur where leaders make sure their ethical actions are visible and they engage in explicit communication about standards. Also, by using AIT they can more easily follow up with very large and distributed workforces with suitable reinforcement for the messages and principles that they have shared. Certain traits of the leader one identifies with (such as conscientiousness and agreeableness) and beliefs about morality contribute to the leader being seen as ethical and promoting ethical behavior by others can be reinforced by the stories, actions, and behaviors transmitted via AIT (Brown & Treviño, 2006).

6.3. The Rise of Social Networks and Addressing Geographical Distance

Current AIT is making it easy for individuals and organizations to create social networks, which are then harnessed for communication, coordinated action, and learning. In addition to providing open platforms, such as Facebook, Twitter, and LinkedIn, which allow anyone to join, many AIT products and services enable organizations to build social networks within their firewalls, such as Yammer (www.yammer.com/) and Socialtext (www.socialtext.com). The widespread use of these platforms for social networking is facilitated not only by their ease of use but also by the self-selection of individuals into a network (Kahai, 2013). For instance, whenever two or more people use a particular hash tag in Twitter or Facebook, they automatically become part of a network of those interested in what that hash tag represents. One can see the broad impact of social media on not only what constitutes the loci of leadership, but also these new mechanisms of leadership through which they are transmitted.

Today, social media is enabling the conditions for a shift in the locus of leadership to the broader collective/context. According to a social network perspective (Balkundi & Kilduff, 2006), leadership is viewed as an important social influence process for building social capital in networks. Thus, it is only through an accurate understanding of the network and how it fits and our roles within the network that we figure out what coalitions to build in pursuit of organizational goals. When social media are introduced into the leadership dynamic, such AIT mechanisms facilitate this understanding and, thus, help a leader or leaders to build relevant coalitions and social capital in a more timely and robust manner (Kahai, 2013). Social networks in which social capital resides now represents a significant locus of leadership.

The complexity theory of leadership (Uhl-Bien, Marion, & McKelvey, 2007) suggests that social media are enabling a shift in the locus of leadership more to what we have defined above as context. Different forms of social media today are making organizational interactions more rapid and likely complex by enabling the development of social networks that span hierarchical levels and departmental boundaries (Kahai, 2013). These networks then facilitate messy and imperfect information flows and processing that the normal structure would not handle. Specifically, social networks serve to connect individuals and groups with asymmetrical preferences (knowledge, skills, beliefs, values, etc.) on the fly and allow them to debate an issue to generate a new understanding of complex challenges, which can promote greater alignment and trust in organizations.

Uhl-Bien et al. (2007) considers this emergent and dynamic interaction between individuals and ideas as leadership because this complex dynamic is producing adaptive changes. One example of how social media can facilitate leadership was provided by Thompson (2006), who described the following use of a wiki (called as Intellipedia) by previously isolated U.S. Intelligence agencies: "...the usefulness of Intellipedia proved itself just a couple of months ago, when a small two-seater plane crashed into a Manhattan building. An analyst created a page within 20 min, and over the next two hours it was edited 80 times by employees of nine different spy agencies, as news trickled out. They rapidly concluded the crash was not a terrorist act."

Participatory systems are now common in many Web 2.0 applications, such as healthcare (Patientslikeme for sharing experiences on symptoms and treatments), encyclopediae (Wikipedia for general information on most any topic), commerce and marketplaces (M-Turk for farming out simple repetitive

tasks), astronomy (Galaxy Zoo for classifying galaxies), and bioscience (Foldlt for protein folding). These technologies impact leadership transmissions by promoting self-disclosure and the freedom to share details of leader and followers' work and personal lives in real time. Such disclosure, if properly managed, could allow a leader to be more considerate towards particular followers, who might not share with the leader such details FtF. Self-disclosure by the leader can make him/her seem more approachable, potentially reducing the power distance between leader and followers (Napier & Ferris, 1993).

Organizational leaders can also use social media traces to learn what is on the minds of followers (Balkundi & Kilduff, 2006). For example, at SAP, leaders monitor employee activity on social media to gauge if their message is reaching and impacting employees (Starke, 2011). The potential downside of this type of monitoring is that employees may also feel their privacy is compromised, and they may in turn intentionally mask their response to messages provided by their leaders so they appear engaged.

Mechanisms associated with social media can also facilitate the collective cognition involved in leadership by enabling top leaders to share their vision with others and build the network's social capital efficiently and effectively to support that vision. We actually witnessed the effects of such social media during the 2008 and 2012 U.S. Presidential elections when Barack Obama harnessed social media to connect directly with the electorate, to broadly communicate and reinforce his platform, ultimately winning both elections (Green, 2012).

Those opposed to a leader, however, also may use social media. Activists in Egypt used Facebook, Twitter, and email to form a network of protesters against President Hosni Mubarak and his government in early 2011 (Sutter, 2011). These activists used this network to coordinate powerful protests in the streets during an 18-day revolution, which initially forced President Mubarak to dismiss his government, and eventually driving him out of office.

By making others, including their thoughts and actions, transparent, social media creates new demands for ethical, authentic, and transformational leadership and thus (as discussed earlier) highlights the importance of behaviors, traits, and cognitions associated with leadership. For instance, when leaders learn what is on the minds of others by looking at their social media posts, they could take punitive action against those with whose ideas they don't agree. Sophisticated data mining tools available today make it possible for leaders to profile their employees and take action they may consider as preemptive, such as depicted in the motion picture entitled *Minority Report*. In that movie, the police could arrest and prosecute someone simply for intentions they had that constituted a potential criminal act. IBM recently released an online tool that scans employees' emails and social media posts to flag who might be nursing grudges and who are more likely to divulge company secrets (Schectman, 2013). Because such tools are not designed to make perfect predictions, their use by leaders to take action, such as firing someone who is profiled as likely to divulge company secrets, certainly raises ethical concerns.

The rise of social media has potential implications for future leadership development. There is clearly a need for leaders to understand both the opportunities possible in using social media and the ethical concerns that arise. For example, leaders need to learn about the opportunities for sense-making and relationship development enabled by social media discussed above. While social media is no replacement for social interaction enabled by FtF contact, with organizations spreading their operations worldwide and cutting employee travel budgets, the ubiquitous use of social media offers organizations numerous opportunities for social interaction that would be absent otherwise. And since innovation is a top priority for many organizations and social interaction plays a critical role in promoting innovation (Tsai & Ghoshal, 1998), leaders need to be developed in terms of their understanding of how they can take advantage of social media.

6.4. Constant Contact

Leaders are now in constant contact with followers and constituents due to the ubiquity of mobile devices, which oftentimes requires them to multi-task, while being continually interrupted (MacLean, 2008). Such burdensome demands of AIT use have been linked to performance deficits, stress, and superficial relationships lacking social cohesion and mutual understanding experienced by organizational members (Stokols et al., 2009). These detrimental outcomes may lead to dysfunctional forms of leadership (Eubanks & Mumford, 2010) and fundamentally change leader behavior in virtual settings.

The 24/7 availability of leaders and followers is altering leadership behaviors and interactions whereby both leaders and followers reach out to each other, not only during work, but also afterhours. Availability of leaders and followers to each other may improve task performance via just-in-time updates, guidance, and feedback. Moreover, the fast response times in providing guidance and feedback by a leader when needed by a follower can also be seen as individually considerate behavior contributing to a follower's development. Yet, we also know that constant contact has its downsides (Kahai, 2013). Those who work this way will need to figure out the effective temporal rhythms for their communication activities to avoid excessive stress, burnout, productivity loss, poor work and life balance, as well as getting online when tired and perhaps then saying the wrong thing (Stokols et al., 2009). Such temporal rhythms can define the regularity through which the communication takes place, the purposes of communication, and the communication media used (Maznevski & Chudoba, 2000).

6.5. The Rise of Tracking Devices

The use of inexpensive sensors embedded in various forms of AIT is revolutionizing the tracking of behavior and affect for both organizational and personal applications. Companies are embedding sensors in lanyards and office furniture to collect data about worker behavior, including movements, voice levels, whereabouts, whom they meet, and then link that data with productivity, email traffic, and survey data to learn about behavioral patterns contributing to or detracting from performance (Silverman, 2011).

With Global Positioning Systems (GPS) trackers in cellphones and other devices, organizations can go beyond physical boundaries and collect data about worker location and travel. Today's webcams and other sensor-based technologies enable the detection of emotional states of individuals, which opens up a wide range of opportunities for their use in situations where emotional states can be hard to detect (Weintraub, 2012). For example, after announcing a restructuring plan one could track the emotions of employees coming into work to determine how positive or negative those employees are about the proposed changes.

We can certainly speculate how such tracking technologies may affect the locus and mechanisms of leadership. For instance, we foresee the locus of leadership shifting to the technology when it provides task-oriented guidance and motivation normally provided by a leader. When Cubist Pharmaceuticals employed sensors in a study of 30 sales and marketing workers for tracking purposes, it realized that higher individual productivity was correlated with promoting more not less FtF interactions (Silverman, 2011). They also found that social activity dropped during lunch time after workers returned to their cubicles to check their emails. The company combined these two findings and decided to make its cafeteria more inviting to encourage its workers to eat lunch together, longer, while engaging in social interactions.

We foresee how there are ways in which tracking technologies can affect the mechanisms of leadership including their effect on the behaviors, cognitions, and affect associated with leadership. For instance, leaders can use tracking technologies to learn more about the behaviors of followers or peers in the workplace and therefore react to those behaviors in more of a timely manner, providing guidance, recognition, manipulation or even criticism. Tracking technologies can affect cognitions related to leadership. When one's followers are rewarded on the basis of certain behaviors, tracking technology may make the monitoring and tracking of those behaviors easier to reinforce for good and bad purposes. For instance, with handwashing by health care workers falling below 50% at most hospitals, hospitals are now using sensor-based technology to monitor, track, and reward handwashing behavior (Rosenberg, 2011).

Affect involved in an event or episode of leadership can be difficult to detect, such as in remote meetings and online learning situations that rely on CMC. This can make it challenging for a leader with a high emotional quotient to employ affect-based mechanisms to influence others. As indicated earlier, technologies are now available that enable the detection of emotional states of individuals (Weintraub, 2012). Webcams and wearable technologies in the form of wristbands and headbands can assess the type of affect, such as excitement, boredom, anger, sadness, and frustration experienced by someone being observed. Yet, we must consider the downside of greater transparency and tracking, such as privacy issues (Alge, 2001). For example, Bernstein (2012) theorized, tested, and introduced the notion of a transparency paradox—whereby maintaining constant observation of workers may reduce their performance by inducing those observed to conceal activities through codes and other costly means. Despite the fact that recent studies have exposed the cost associated with "cyber loafing" (Wang, Tian, & Shen, 2013), it is possible that cyber loafing acts as a form of positive deviance and increased transparency might actually result in overall decreased productivity.

7. Macro OB and E-leadership

We have introduced some key macro issues in terms of our discussions of the effects of big data, tracking, social networks and social media on how organizations and leaders will function. Yet, there are certainly numerous implications for e-leadership and AIT when examining strategic change and transformations in organizations, leadership, as well as how organizations relate to each other within and between markets that have been raised in the IT, organizational theory, and leadership literatures (Henderson & Venkatraman, 1992). One common theme in the organizational change literature is that change is often caused by or the result of changes in AIT, or that change is undertaken to implement new technologies (see for example, Gilley, Gilley, & McMillan, 2009; Holt, Armenakis, Feild, & Harris, 2007). Much less studied has been the role of e-leadership and AIT in facilitating or inhibiting organizational change and its impact on leadership and organizational transformation.

Henderson and Venkatraman (1992) were among the first authors to discuss the need for strategic alignment between IT implementation and organizational change, what they referred to as *IT-enabled organizational transformation (OT)*. Subsequently, evidence has been accumulating showing that investing in AIT as part of the organizational change process was considered an important asset for leveraging organizational change. As such, a common theme in the macro change literature was that change often was caused by or the result of changes in AIT (see for example, Gilley et al., 2009; Holt et al., 2007). Much less examined was the role of AIT in facilitating organizational change and the interactive effect of organizational change on the appropriation of new AIT systems. Besson and Rowe (2012) conducted a 20-year review of the literature on IT-enabled OT. Examining their findings, we concluded there was relatively little attention being paid to examining the effects of leadership on IT-enabled OT, and how such IT-enabled changes impact the loci and mechanisms of leadership. For example, we don't know how such changes will affect individual, team, or strategic leadership, as these systems become appropriated into use in ways that might be different as a function of implementing new AIT.

In terms of social transformation, Twitter, Facebook, and social media appeared to play a very central and critical role in the Arab Spring. For example, Khondker (2011) argues, "There is no question that the social networking applications played a vital role in organizing and publicizing social protests" (p. 677). During the anti-Mubarak protests, an Egyptian activist put it succinctly in the following tweet: "We use Facebook to schedule the protests, Twitter to coordinate, and YouTube to tell the world" (Global Voice Advocacy, 2010). Howard et al. (2011) analyzed over 3 million tweets, gigabytes of YouTube content, and thousands of blog posts, and reported that social media played a central role in shaping political debates in the Arab Spring. Finally, based on a survey study conducted by the Dubai School of Government, researchers found that nearly 9 in 10 Egyptians and Tunisians surveyed in March 2011 said they were using Facebook to organize and spread awareness of protests; all but one protest called for on Facebook occurred (Dubai School of Government, 2011).

Event cycles associated with the Arab Spring also illustrate aspects of AST, and how individuals both impact and are impacted by AIT. Specifically, on June 6, 2010, Khaled Said, an Egyptian blogger, was dragged out of a cyber cafe and beaten to death by policemen in Alexandria, Egypt. The cafe owner, Hassan Mosbah, provided details of his murder in a filmed interview. On June 14, 2010, Issandr El Amrani posted the details on the blog site Global Voices Advocacy, and a young Google executive, Wael Ghonim, created a Facebook page titled, "We Are All Khaled Said," which grew to 350,000 members in just six months (Giglio, 2011, p. 15).

The lack of attention to leadership in this more macro-focused literature is not surprising because the work on strategic leadership, without necessarily focusing on AIT, still remains in relatively nascent stages. Currently, there is relatively little research that has examined what constitutes strategic leadership (see Finkelstein et al., 2007, for a notable exception), particularly systems level leadership that might be enabled and distributed by the use of new AIT strategic systems. Thus, we still know very little on how e-leadership, AIT, and their interaction affect strategic leadership and organizational transformation.

8. AIT and Gamification

One of the biggest advances in AIT over the last decade is gamification. Since gamification is new, there is still not a universally accepted definition. However, the following definition has the three major components that are often seen when practitioners talk about gamification—the use of game elements and game design techniques in non-game contexts (Deterding, Dixon, Khaled, & Nacke, 2011; Werbach & Hunter, 2012). Additionally, considering the nascent stage that gamification is in, it is important to emphasize that gamification and games are not the same thing—using the metaphor of grammar, if games are the noun, gamification is the verb.

In our search of the major leadership, management, and IT journals, only one published article was identified using the keyword gamification. Despite the lack of academic focus on the effects of gamification on both leadership and organizations, a 2011 Gartner Research Report estimates that by 2015, more than 50% of organizations that manage innovation will gamify those processes. Eric Schmidt, the current Google Chairman, went so far as to say that, "Everything in the future online is going to look like a game." We focus on gamification in this review because we think it will not only affect the way leaders are developed, but how leaders and their followers will engage one another in organizations in the near future.

A practical example of gamification is Nike+, which uses an accelerometer that fits into the sole of a running shoe. The accelerometer tracks every step a person takes so the device knows how far and how fast a person is running. The device then communicates wirelessly with a smartphone or a computer and aggregates the data. Nike then built a set of applications around Nike+ that makes the experience of running seem more game-like. For example, Nike+ shows a person their longest and quickest runs; runners are able to compare themselves to previous runtimes; and can establish goals and earn medals, trophies, and awards. Nike + is not designed to replace running with a running game, but instead to make the experience of running feel more game-like—and thus, theoretically, more engaging and fun, which is central to the notion of gamification. Imagine if such a device was developed to foster the tracking of leadership.

8.1. Games vs. Simulations

Klabbers (2009) suggests that games and simulations can—and often do—overlap depending on purpose. Simulations have a more specific reference model upon which a "simulation" is designed and built to represent; whereas games frequently have a more open system design, and specific reference models are not required. For example, flight simulators are designed to represent key information needed to train pilots by exposing them to different scenarios. Whereas with a flight game, the system is open, focused on entertainment (versus learning), and the players have freedom to act within the space provided. According to Klabbers (2009), all simulations are a type of game, but not all games are simulations. Games can serve many functions, one of which is to simulate.

Gamification is about "gamifying" an experience to make it more game-like and thus more engaging and fun in the real world. Gamification examines the different elements of games and applies those same elements to non-game contexts. For example, Nike + "gamifies" the construct of self-awareness by making a runner aware of their performance using the game elements of badges, leaderboards, etc. A gamified leadership development experience could do the same thing by rewarding players with badges or points for completing leadership assessments or for taking on specific leadership challenges such as forming a team. A gamification system with this goal would get players motivated about taking on the challenge of leadership development in part because of a welcoming and engaging user interface. The game could onboard players to teach them how to navigate and interact with it. The players would then get increasingly difficult challenges as they progressed through the system, and finally—if successful—they would achieve a degree of mastery around a specific leadership goal/challenge that they established at the beginning of the process.

A current limitation to what we know about gamification deals with its relationship with extrinsic rewards, typically used with transactional forms of leadership (Bass, 1985). Gamification tends to be heavily influenced by its use of extrinsic rewards through points, badges, and leaderboards. Many gamified sites and gamification platforms assume that a virtual reward is inherently motivating. However, this can be a poor substitute for what some people want—or, worse, it potentially ignores the powerful effects of intrinsic motivation. Here, as

Werbach and Hunter (2012, p. 62) argue, "The lesson for gamification is simple: Don't mindlessly attach extrinsic motivators to activities that can be motivated using intrinsic regulators."

Deci, Koestner, and Ryan (1999) reported in their meta-analysis that types of rewards matter and that a demotivating effect is more pronounced with certain types of rewards than others. Specifically, tangible rewards tend to produce the largest demotivating effect and reduce intrinsic motivation. Tangible rewards are often thought of as the more rewarding, such as giving a bonus, but have the greatest risk of lowering intrinsic motivation. Unexpected rewards have the least effect of crowding out intrinsic motivation.

In sum, we view gamification and games as some of the most exciting frontiers for exploring leadership and its development with respect to AIT. By designing gamification systems and games that engage players in real challenges that leaders face, we can manipulate and introduce different conditions to systematically examine the impact on leaders, followers, and their interactions in that every move in a game is coded. A virtual game can become a virtual lab for exploring a broad range of leadership topics that have been examined in less interesting, dynamic, and restricted contexts. Imagine a thousand players around the world being engaged in a game to develop a new global organization to address a particular societal challenge. The possibilities of introducing different conditions, examining social network formations, examining how verbal and non-verbal behaviors affect the dynamics of leadership, and how virtual teams form and disband seem endless. Indeed, it seems fair to say, that the use of gamification for studying leadership is indeed no game!

9. AIT and E-leadership Development

Regarding the relationship between leadership development and the recent increases/prevalence of Web 2.0 platforms and social media (Facebook, blogs, Twitter, etc.), according to social cognitive theory (Bandura, 1986), individuals acquire values,

skills, and standards of behavior through basic social learning processes (e.g., vicarious learning, verbal persuasion) involving interactions with significant others (e.g., mentors). Leadership learning and development can occur both formally, but also informally through vicarious learning and social cues, as demonstrated in previous research (DeRue & Wellman, 2009).

Halic, Lee, Paulus, and Spence (2010) suggested that a "technological tool works better when they are coupled with compatible pedagogical conceptions" (p.211), in terms of fostering development. This goes back to a common argument within e-learning platforms—that e-learning is most effective when it is "blended" with technology and FtF facilitation. An example of this blended approach was reported by Gifford (2010), who explored a model for effectively using blogs in a leadership course to enhance critical thinking capacity by providing more effective reflection opportunities. Gifford conducted his experiment over the course of two academic semesters using the Watson (2001) "what?—so what?—now what?" model, which promotes a more thorough reflection process, while encouraging critical thinking based upon an experience. Gifford (2010) demonstrated that students using the Watson (2001) model for a blogging reflection exercise averaged higher grades and more consistently met the objectives of the assignment when compared with students given guiding questions for blogging.

Several types of AIT may be used to accelerate leadership development in organizations. For example, the Internet offers a vast amount of searchable information on business trends, financial forecasts, and personal information about leaders, peers, and followers. With Google Glass, leaders can don headgear that quickly creates three-dimensional imagery and accesses information from the Internet. This information may help judgment and enhance the leader's ability to display appropriate forms of leadership behavior across a range of situations.

Big data on followers' history of interactions and work patterns collected by tracking sensors can provide leaders with information on how to best motivate and monitor followers (Silverman, 2011). For example, leaders can use crowd sourcing technologies to collect opinion data on ideas, products, and services that can be used by them to help solve organizational problems and support innovation (Boudreau & Lakhani, 2013). In addition, we expect that future leader developers will create and use applications that leverage facial/emotional recognition technology to recognize followers' psychological and/or emotional states as well as their own (Pentland & Choudhury, 2000) in fostering leader self-awareness and regulation and emotional intelligence (Mayer, Caruso, & Salovey, 2000). Finally, we can also foresee the use of games as being a new frontier for addressing leadership development.

Some authors are also exploring how massive multi-player games can be used as a means for developing leadership. Reeves et al. (2008) argued that the challenges facing players who serve as game leaders, in large community games, are similar to those faced by leaders in real organizations. Leaders have to recruit, assess, motivate, reward, and retain talented team members. They need to capitalize on a group's competitive advantage and analyze multiple streams of constantly changing data to make quick decisions that have wide-ranging and long-lasting effects. Added to these leadership challenges is the need for leaders to build and retain a volunteer workforce in a fluid, complex, and digitally mediated environment.

Some preliminary research by Ducheneaut and Moore (2005) showed how games can provide opportunities for learning social skills, managing, and leading in small groups, and coordinating and cooperating with people. In 2008, Deloitte Consulting launched the Deloitte Leadership Academy as a web-based portal to enhance leadership development for their employees across the world. Deloitte partnered with BadgeVille, a web-based gamification platform, which gamified the web portal so players were able to earn badges, points, and virtual rewards for completing leadership training.

In the early 2000's, the U.S. Army released a video game called *America's Army* that was used as both a recruiting tool and a means to educate players about the values of U.S. soldiers. Since its debut, the game has become the most successful recruiting tool in the history of the U.S. Army. However, the game is more than just a recruiting tool—it is also designed to teach players about the values of the U.S. Army.

In sum, we expect that with the advances occurring in AIT, there is a broad range of factors that will affect how we interpret the locus and the mechanisms of leadership. Clearly, much of what we have discussed provides a broad and deep agenda for future leadership theory and research to consider, as the context in which leadership is enacted is clearly changing.

In Table 14.1, we provide a high level summary of the literature covered in this review. The purpose of this table is not to offer a comprehensive summary of the literature, but rather to point to trends and gaps where more research is needed. Table 14.1 follows the framework we have used throughout this article in terms of the loci of leadership and its transmission mechanism to highlight some of the typical research we have uncovered in this review.

10. Conclusions and Implications

Throughout this article, we have highlighted some of the important changes occurring in terms of leadership source and transmission due to rapid advances and use of AIT. Also, wherever possible, we have discussed the practical implications and reservations we might have for using AIT in cases like tracking people or prematurely judging intentions. Consequently, in this final section, we briefly highlight some of the main conclusions we have drawn from this updated review of the e-leadership literature, as well as offer a model to guide future work in this area:

- The gap between the practice and implementation of AIT and what we know about its effects has grown over the last decade, when the term e-leadership was first introduced. Today, even more powerful technologies are being appropriated, and generally speaking, we have relatively little understanding of the potential effects of these technologies on the leadership dynamic in or outside organizations, as well as how leadership appropriates AIT faithfully or unfaithfully.

Table 14.1 Current and Emerging Trends in E-leadership Research

Source/locus of e-leadership	Transmission of E-leadership			
	Traits	Cognition	Affect	Behavior
Individual	Gender, self-efficacy, extraversion associated with Internet and computer use (Jackson et al., 2003; Ventatesh & Morris, 2000), suggest that trait profiles (Yukl, 2010) may influence e-leadership. Follower traits influence effectiveness of virtual interactions (Furutani et al., 2007; Hoch & Kozlowski, 2012). Emerging questions: How will follower traits affect the way people choose to engage in virtual simulations and games including such things as choice of avatars, the type of leadership roles assumed or followership, likelihood of engaging in shared leadership, etc.?\n\nCan we use virtual interactions to determine traits of participants without	Follower perceptions about how they are treated by distant leaders are important in online interactions (Antonakis & Atwater, 2002). Social presence of leaders in online communities is important for follower perceptions of leader authenticity (Kramer & Winter, 2008). Understanding follower expectations and distributed cognitions are required to frame coherent vision (Jaffe, 2012). Mobile technologies and social networks facilitate transactive memory required for shared leadership (Small et al., 2009.) Emerging questions:\n\nHow will real time access to information impact the expected level of transparency in leader and follower interactions? How	Positive attitudes toward AIT appropriation are associated with openness to experience, agreeableness, introversion or extraversion (Orr et al., 2009).\n\nAffective Events Theory (Weiss & Cropanzano, 1996) hold promise for understanding how e-leadership events evolve and impact both emotions and the sustainability of groups and organizations.\n\nRobotic leaders may produce more reasonable outcomes because they are not influenced by emotions as are humans (Samani et al., 2012); but robots currently have limitations regarding moral judgment, creativity, and accumulation of experiences (Dreyfus et al., 2000; Goldenberg & Mazursky, 2002). Emerging questions:	Transformational leadership and anonymity promote individuals' flow state and creativity in GDSS (Sosik, Avolio, Kahai, & Jung, 1998). Structure and goal setting are important in early stages of online interactions (Weisband, 2008).\n\nConflict resolution behavior is needed for managing global teams (Nardon & Steers, 2008).\n\nEncouragement and coordination facilitates user effectiveness in virtual worlds (Montoya et al., 2011). Emerging questions:\n\nTo what extent is the type of leader behavior observed through the lens of AIT judged in the same way, as the same behavior exhibited FtF? How might leaders use

(Continued)

Table 14.1 (Continued)

Source/locus of e-leadership	Transmission of E-leadership			
	Traits	Cognition	Affect	Behavior
	using surveys/tests and might this be abused by organizations?	might access to the information change the dynamics of the ways leader sand teams' process information and come to decisions? Might leaders use pseudo-transparent interactions to manipulate followers on a massive scale?	How will access to information via AIT that can detect nonverbal cues and emotions shape the interactions with leaders and followers in real time in groups or potentially below in dyadic interactions? How might this information be used to manipulate followers to onboard with initiatives?	AIT to foster and solidify the perceptions of their style of leadership? With AIT making it easier for leaders to collect information about others, how is a leader's ethical conduct influenced?
Dyad	Negative trait affectivity makes individuals pessimistic and then they perceive life events as more stressful (Watson & Slack, 1993). Individuals with paranoid tendencies (skeptical or argumentative dimension of personality) actively search for and selectively attend to signs of mistreatment in the behaviors of others in relationships. Gaming technology used to simulate challenging leadership situations, when repeated until sufficient skill levels can	Commonalities in how dyad members communicate and evaluate events increase communication effectiveness and mutual liking (House et al., 2004). Followers in effective leader-member exchanges have a cognitive decision-making style compatible with that of the leader (Graen & Uhl-Bien, 1995). Emerging questions: How might AIT such as Google Glass or Big Data access build shared cognitive forms of trust between dyad members in the initial stages	AIT can make it challenging for leaders and followers to convey and interpret emotions accurately and connect with others (Kahai, 2013). Haptic and other emotional recognition and response devices hold promise for understanding emotional bonds between distant leaders and follower relationships (MacLean, 2008; Mignonac & Herrbach, 2004). Emerging questions: Can these new emerging technologies accelerate the development of relationships in teams?	New forms of CWB will emerge as new web-based processes and programs make their way into employees' personal and professional lives (Klotz & Buckley, 2012). Emerging question: How will the shifting terrain of AIT create or buffer followers from DL and how might these same contexts allow for new forms of CWB to emerge as a possible response to DL? Given similar provision of specific leader behaviors and

| Source/locus of e-leadership | Transmission of E-leadership | | | |
	Traits	Cognition	Affect	Behavior
	be attained, may be used to build self-efficacy and resilience associated with positive leader-follower relationships (Luthans & Avolio, 2003). Social support provided by online communities also may serve as a source of hope and optimism for leader-follower dyads facing challenging events (DeAndrea et al., 2011). Emerging Question: Davis (2001) cognitive-behavioral pathological use of the internet (PUI) model offers insights into how unethical leadership may emerge in online communities. How might negative trait characteristics and PUI get exacerbated in dyadic AIT contexts? Could these conditions be mitigating through gaming and gamification?	of their relationship and maintain or destroy it over time? Can virtual worlds, serious gaming, or groupware support learning orientations and processes associated with high-quality leader-member exchanges? At what point in the history of a relationship is it optimum to use AIT to accelerate the development of a more balanced dyadic relationship? Can the use of AIT facilitate the cultural integration among individual dyads working across time, distance and cultural boundaries?	How might this technology also accelerate mishaps and conflicts based on interpreting data inaccurately?	potential negative effects of Facebook, what is the quality of on-line leader-follower relationships compared to FtF relationships? Is a leader who is "friended" on Facebook by a follower provided with the same level of trust, respect, and commitment as a leader influencing followers in FtF contexts? What online behaviors constitute being "friended"? How does self-disclosure by leaders and followers enabled by social media affect leader-follower relationships? What is the level of authenticity associated with such self-disclosure?
Group	Team traits serve as inputs and influence the execution of teamwork processes and task work, which are likely to	Group support systems facilitate interpretation of events and collaboration quality (Smith-Slater &	Online extreme communities may support study of destructive forms of leadership (DeAndrea et al., 2011). 3D Collaborative Virtual	Transformational leadership and anonymity promotes group potency, positive comments, learning, and

(Continued)

Table 14.1 (Continued)

Source/locus of e-leadership	Transmission of E-leadership			
	Traits	Cognition	Affect	Behavior
	alter subsequent emergent states, teamwork, and task work (Marks, Mathieu, & Zaceara, 2001). Emerging questions: How might AIT be used to accelerate the development and disbanding of teams? What are the implications for team development where all interactions are recorded and available for review at any time in the team's developmental trajectory?	Anderson, 1994; Kahai et al., 2003). Greater transparency enabled by AIT is affecting what people know and think about their leaders and others in their group (Kahai, 2013). Emerging questions: How might AIT be used to examine processes that promote and sustain innovation in organizations? Will greater transparency in group interactions fostered by AIT promote more or less task versus relationship conflict?	Environments (CVEs) produce more visual cues to teams (Montoya et al., 2011) and thus have the capacity to increase trust and affective leadership. Emerging questions: What is the potential for creating contagion effects through social networks that could spread viral movements that might be destructive? How might abusive leaders use AIT to solidify control of their agenda and groups?	creativity in GDSS (Kahai et al., 2003; Sosik et al., 1997). Influence behavior evens across group members when status is equal but not otherwise (Weisband et al., 1995). Greater transparency enabled by AIT may control ethical misconduct by leaders who choose to manipulate the message for self-gain. Emerging questions: Can we scale groups larger than what is typically associated with FtF teams using AIT to promote more rapid and integrative interactions? What does shared leadership look like in teams that are interacting via AIT and how does having a permanent record of team interactions impact trust building in the early formation of teams?

Table 14.1 (Continued)

Source/locus of e-leadership	Traits	Cognition	Affect	Behavior
		Transmission of E-leadership		
Organization	Emerging questions: Considering the fact that entire organizations are being judged on their traits through sites like Glassdoor.com, how will this impact the relationships between stakeholders and firms?	IS-enabled organizational transformation plays a major role in the dialectical nature of how organizational change impacts and is impacted by AIT (Besson & Rowe; 2012). Emerging questions: What are the ethical implications of IS-enabled OT, especially considering that managers are implementing changes that allow for more monitoring of employees? What is the effect of AIT on making the ethical actions and standards of a leader visible? How can social media enable leaders to learn what is on the minds of their followers? How can leaders use this information for prosocial and self-serving purposes? What is the potential for a leader to build social capital by sharing her/his vision via social media?	Emerging questions: How might organizations use haptic devices and tracking sensors to promote climates and cultures of shared positive organizational behavior, positive psychological capital, and character strengths and virtues associated with organizational effectiveness? How might leaders use these devices to create "Orwellian Big Brother" cultures where every word and behavior is recorded?	Though crowdsourcing fits into the traditional definition of a virtual team (Powell et al., 2004), as new tools emerge to connect us in social networks and support the development of online distributed communities, crowdsourcing is expanding the definition of what is a "virtual team." (Boudreau & Lakhani, 2013) Emerging Question: What will constitute the definition of an organization in the future, and how might rapid cycle organizations that go from start up to closing off, affect the way leaders and followers interact?

(Continued)

Table 14.1 (Continued)

Source/locus of e-leadership	Traits	Transmission of E-leadership		
		Cognition	Affect	Behavior
Context	Social media and virtual worlds may help satisfy needs and create social identities that can be used by organizations to facilitate cultural integration (Eisenbeiss et al., 2012) or cultural segregation (DeAndrea et al., 2011). Emerging questions: As we consider strategic leadership, what are now the context and boundaries for studying this topic, given how AIT opens up connections to such a broader range of stakeholders? How might organizations use AIT to foster a change in market identity with stakeholders that leaders are attempting to drive?	Associations between contextual elements and followers' attitudes mediated by transformational leadership in remote environments can impact how such leadership is perceived (Kelley & Kelloway, 2012). Emerging questions: How do different types of environments such as ones that are 'strong' or 'weak' contexts impact on the way that leadership is perceived when filtered through AIT? What sort of elements in the context can foster support for more positive leadership development? How does the view enabled by social networking technology of the network a leader belongs to facilitate the building of relevant coalitions and social capital (Kahai, 2013)?	Social media has the power to convey, organize, and focus affect that is so powerful it can lead to global changes (e.g., the Arab Spring; Khondker, 2011). Emerging questions: Considering how quickly information can now spread globally, what are the implications for authenticating information? Could unverified information lead to online witch-hunts? How will the examination of 'big data' affect the way that leaders make decisions in terms of time, quality and impact?	There is a strong correlation between online and offline leadership (Jang & Ryu, 2011); Leadership qualities can be transmitted and developed in MMORPGs (Ducheneaut & Moore, 2005; Reeves et al, 2008). Emerging questions: What are the boundaries of leadership that are developed virtually–are they more or less expansive? Can they withstand situations where there are real world, as opposed to virtual, consequences. How does social media enable the emergent and dynamic interactions that produce adaptive change?

- Although AIT has provided numerous platforms for collaboration and wide participation among various stakeholders, the shift in locus from individual to a shared or collective leadership in most organizations remains a stretch goal as opposed to reality. Clearly, organizations and their leaders are quickly learning how to appropriate many of these AIT applications to gather, interpret, and disseminate information and knowledge. But, as yet, these technologies have not dramatically changed the way organizations are led, nor have they fundamentally changed the way we study leadership, or even theorize about it.

- Opportunities to examine how AIT can completely transform the way leaders are developed hardly is mentioned in the leadership literature at all, more so in the practice literature, but is beginning to appear in terms of applications to support development (e.g., using online learning/development tools). This area, along with gamification, represents one of the most fundamentally transformative means for developing leadership to emerge in the last 100 years. To the extent we are seeing the use of this technology emerge in arenas such as healthcare and examining/fostering well-being, we have no doubt that these AIT systems will infiltrate the assessment and development of leadership.

- As noted throughout this article, there are many ethical considerations that need to be addressed as the appropriation of AIT far exceeds our capacity to determine what we should or should not be using in leadership roles and events. As Heidegger (1977) argued, "What is dangerous is not technology. There is no demonry of technology, but rather there is the mystery of its essence. The essence of technology, as a destining of revealing, is the danger" (p. 14). If the technology is available, it will be used, and therefore creating a forum to discuss what are the ethical considerations associated with the appropriation of AIT for e-leadership seems like critical imperatives for the field of leadership.

- Other than the GDSS research, there has been relatively little reported in the leadership literature focusing on how different styles and orientations of leadership interact with the appropriation of some of the latest AIT. Indeed, in this instance the "black box" of leadership is not only in the traditional mediators or mechanisms, but also includes the leadership styles and outcomes. Since its publication, the original Avolio et al. (2001) article is in the top 5% of articles cited in *The Leadership Quarterly* (since 2001), suggesting there has been a lot of attention given to the topics covered in this original review. Indeed, based on Google Scholar, this article has been cited nearly 300 times as of October 2013.

- Although referenced sporadically throughout the review, there has been relatively little attention paid to the impact of social, cultural, and physical distance that is mediated on e-leadership. We know of no research that has actually examined both social and physical distance together to determine how it affects the appropriation of AIT and in turn the impact it has on the appropriation of virtual leadership tools and processes.

- We need to consider what constitutes the *total leadership system* in organizations, which we define as representing vertical, horizontal, and diagonal forms of leadership, as well as leadership exhibited by individuals and through groups/entities. This entails examining leadership within and across all organizational levels based on the new connections made possible with AIT—including leading peer-to-peer and leading up management levels. Although prior research has examined the cascading and bypass effects of leadership, none of this research has examined what happens when leadership processes are connected via AIT. Indeed, the total leadership system and how it is appropriated and developed are now emerging in organizations, making the individual as leader more background, and the collective and its dynamic connections the focal point.

- How organizations are structured in the future, and how organizations change and transform will no doubt be affected by the appropriation of AIT. It may be time to totally rethink what constitutes an organization and in turn, its leadership.

In Figure 14.1, we provide a framework depicting the interactive effects of AIT and leadership on individual, team, and organizational interactions. On the x-axis we project time going back to the original e-leadership publication, then well into the future. On the y-axis we present the emergence of AIT platforms. We then depict the evolution of the Web over a 20-plus year interval from Web 1.0 to what might be called "beyond the web," portraying at each level, how AIT is interacting with the leadership dynamic from bottom left-as a central organizing link to top right-where all interactions are embedded in a dynamic way with the AIT of the future. At each level, we point to themes that tie together both the practice of e-leadership and the research that has emerged, or we project to emerge overtime, while trying to highlight key issues.

In conclusion, perhaps it suffices to say, that although the term e-leadership was introduced into the literature now more than a decade ago, the sun is still rising and shedding light on the earliest developments in this area, with much more to go before it hits its zenith.

Figure 14.1	The Evolution of E-leadership Through the Emergence of AIT Platforms Over Time

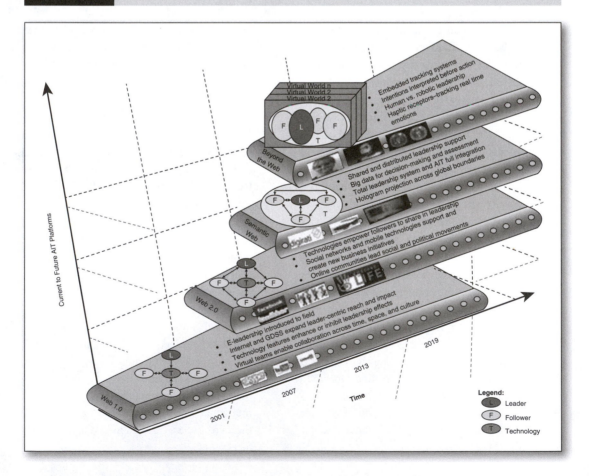

Acknowledgment

The authors wish to thank Natalie A. Fitzgerald and Niko Nakai for their assistance with the literature review for this article.

Note

1. Corresponding author at: Mark Pigott Chair in Business Strategic Leadership, Foster School of Business at the University of Washington. *E-mail address:* bavolio@u .washington.edu (B.J. Avolio).

References

Alderfer, C. P. (1972). *Existence, relatedness, and growth: Human needs in organizational settings.* New York, NY: Free Press.

Alge, B. J. (2001). Effects of computer surveillance on perceptions of privacy and procedural justice. *Journal of Applied Psychology,* 86(4), 797–804.

Amichai-Hamburger, Y. (2005). Personality and the Internet. In Y. Amichai-Hamburger (Ed.), *The social net: Understanding human behavior in cyberspace* (pp. 27–56). New York, NY: Oxford University Press.

Antonakis, J., & Atwater, L. (2002). Leader distance: A review and a proposed theory. *The Leadership Quarterly,* 23(6), 673–704.

Arafsha, F., Masudul Alam, K., & El Saddik, A. (2012). Emojacket: Consumer centric wearable affective jacket to enhance emotional immersion. *Proceedings of the 2012 International Conference on Innovations in Information Technology* (pp. 350–355).

Avolio, B. J. (2007). Promoting more integrative strategies for leadership theory-building. *American Psychologist,* 62(1), 25–33.

Avolio, B. J., & Gardner, W. L. (2005). Authentic leadership development: Getting to the root of positive forms of leadership. *The Leadership Quarterly,* 16(3), 315–338.

Avolio, B. J., & Kahai, S. S. (2003). Adding the "E" to E-leadership. *Organizational Dynamics,* 31, 325–338.

Avolio, B. J., Kahai, S. S., & Dodge, G. E. (2001). E-leadership: Implications for theory, research, and practice. *The Leadership Quarterly,* 11(4), 615–668.

Balkundi, P., & Kilduff, M. (2006). The ties that lead: A social network approach to leadership. *The Leadership Quarterly,* 17(4), 419–439.

Balthazard, P., Waldman, D., & Warren, J. (2009). Predictors of the emergence of transformational leadership in virtual decision teams. *The Leadership Quarterly,* 20(5), 651–663.

Bandura, A. (1986). *Social foundations of thought and action: A social cognitive theory.* Englewood Cliffs, NJ: Prentice-Hall.

Barrett, P. M. (2013, April 3). Harvard digs a deeper hole on cheating, e-mail. *BusinessWeek Online* (Retrieved from http://www.businessweek.com/articles/2013-0 4-03/harvard-digs-a-deeper-hole-on-cheating-e-mail).

Bass, B. M. (1985). *Leadership and performance beyond expectations.* New York, NY: Free Press.

Bass, B. M. (2008). *The Bass handbook of leadership: Theory, research and managerial applications* (4th ed.). New York, NY: Free Press.

Bass, B. M., Waldman, D. A., Avolio, B. J., & Bebb, M. (1987). Transformational leadership and the falling dominoes effect. *Group & Organization Studies,* 12(1), 73–87.

Bernstein, E. (2012). The transparency paradox: A role for privacy in organizational learning and operational control. *Administrative Science Quarterly,* 57(2), 181–216.

Besson, P., & Rowe, F. (2012). Strategizing information systems-enabled organizational transformation: A transdisciplinary review and new directions. *The Journal of Strategic Information Systems,* 22(2), 103–124.

Birnholtz, J., Dixon, G., & Hancock, J. (2012). Distance, ambiguity and appropriation: Structures affording impression management in a collated organization. *Computers in Human Behavior,* 28, 1028–1035.

Boudreau, K. J., & Lakhani, K. R. (2013). Using the crowd as an innovation partner. *Harvard Business Journal,* 91(4), 60–69.

Brown, M. E., & Treviño, L. K. (2006). Ethical leadership: A review and future directions. *The Leadership Quarterly,* 27(6), 595–616.

Brown, M. E., Treviño, L. K., & Harrison, D. A. (2005). Ethical leadership: A social learning perspective for construct development and testing. *Organizational Behavior and Human Decision Processes,* 97(2), 117–134.

Byron, K. (2008). Carrying too heavy a load? The communication and miscommunication of emotion by email. *Academy of Management Review,* 33(2), 309–327.

Cairncross, F. (1997). *The death of distance: How the communication revolution is changing our lives.* Boston, MA: Harvard Business School Press.

Cameron, A., & Webster, J. (2005). Unintended consequences of emerging communication technologies: IM in the workplace. *Computers in Human Behavior,* 22(1), 85–103.

Carsten, M., Uhl-Bein, M., West, B., Patera, J., & McGregor, R. (2010). Exploring social constructions of followership: A qualitative study. *The Leadership Quarterly,* 21(3), 543–562.

Chak, K., & Leung, L. (2004). Shyness and locus of control as predictors of Internet addiction and Internet use. *Cyber Psychology & Behavior,* 7(5), 559–570.

Chatterjee, D., Grewal, R., & Sambamurthy, V. (2002). Shaping up for e-commerce: Institutional enablers of the organizational assimilation of web technologies. *MIS Quarterly,* 26(2), 65–89.

Chun, J. U., Yammarino, F. J., Dionne, S. D., Sosik, J. J., & Moon, H. K. (2009). Leadership across hierarchical levels: Multiple levels of management and multiple levels of analysis. *The Leadership Quarterly,* 20(5), 689–707.

Daft, R., & Lengel, R. (1984). Information richness: A new approach to managerial behavior and organization design. *Research in Organizational Behavior,* 6, 191–233.

DasGupta, P. (2011). Literature review: E-leadership. *Emerging Leadership Journeys,* 4, 1–36.

Davis, R. A. (2001). A cognitive-behavioral model of pathological Internet use. *Computers in Human Behavior,* 17(2), 187–195.

DeAndrea, D. C., Tom Tong, S., & Walther, J. B. (2011). Dark sides of computer-mediated communication. In W. R. Cupach, & B. H. Spitzberg (Eds.), *The dark side of close relationships II* (pp. 95–118). New York, NY: Routledge.

Deci, E. L., Koestner, R., & Ryan, R. M. (1999). A meta-analytic review of experiments examining the effects of extrinsic rewards on intrinsic motivation. *Psychological Bulletin,* 125(6), 627–668.

Deci, E. L., & Ryan, R. M. (2000). The 'what' and 'why' of goal pursuits: Human needs and the self-determination of behavior. *Psychological Inquiry,* 22 (4), 227–268.

Dennis, A. R., Fuller, R. M., & Valacich, J. S. (2008). Media, tasks, and communication processes: A theory of media synchronicity. *MIS Quarterly,* 32(3), 575–600.

DeRue, D. S., & Ashford, S. J. (2010). Who will lead and who will follow? A social process of leadership identity construction in organizations. *Academy of Management Review,* 35(4), 827–847.

DeRue, D. S., & Wellman, N. (2009). Developing leaders via experience: The role of developmental challenge, learning orientation, and feedback. *Journal of Applied Psychology,* 94(4), 859–875.

DeSanctis, G., & Poole, M. S. (1994). Capturing the complexity in advanced technology use: Adaptive Structuration Theory. *Organization Science,* 5(2), 121–147.

Deterding, S., Dixon, D., Khaled, R., & Nacke, L. (2011). From game design elements to gamefulness: defining gamification. *Proceedings of the 15th International Academic Mind Trek Conference: Envisioning Future Media Environments* (pp. 9–15).

Dreyfus, H. L., Dreyfus, S. E., & Athanasiou, T. (2000). *Mind over machine.* New York, NY: Free Press.

Dubai School of Government (2011). Arab social media report. Retrieved on May 22, 2013 from. http://www.dsg.ae/en/ASMR2/ASMRHome2.aspx

Ducheneaut, N., & Moore, R. J. (2005). More than just 'XP': Learning social skills in massively multiplayer online games. *Interactive Technology and Smart Education,* 2(2), 89–100.

Eberly, M. B., Johnson, M., Hernandez, M., & Avolio, B. J. (2013). An integrative process model of leadership: Examining loci, mechanisms, and event cycles. *American Psychologist,* 68(6), 427–443.

Eisenbeiss, M., Blechschmidt, B., Backhaus, K., & Freund, P. A. (2012). "The (real) world is not enough:" Motivational drivers and user behavior in virtual worlds. *Journal of Interactive Marketing,* 26(1), 4–20.

Erez, A., Misangyi, V. F., Johnson, D. E., LePine, M. A., & Halverson, K. C. (2008). Stirring the hearts of followers: Charismatic leadership as the transferal of affect. *Journal of Applied Psychology,* 93(3), 602–616.

Eubanks, D. L., & Mumford, M. D. (2010). Destructive leadership: The role of cognitive processes. In B. Schins, & T. Hansborough (Eds.), *When leadership goes wrong: Destructive leadership, mistakes, and ethical failures* (pp. 23–48). Charlotte, NC: Information Age.

Finkelstein, S., Hambrick, D. C., & Cannella, A. A. (2007). *Strategic leadership: Theory and research on executives, top management teams, and boards.* Oxford, UK: Oxford University Press.

Furutani, K., Kobayashi, T., & Ura, M. (2007). Effects of Internet use on self-efficacy: Perceived network-changing possibility as a mediator. *AI & Society,* 23(2), 251–263.

Gajendran, R. S., & Joshi, A. (2012). Innovation in globally distributed teams: The role of LMX, communication frequency, and member influence on team decisions. *Journal of Applied Psychology,* 97(6), 1252–1261.

Galvin, P. M., Balkundi, P., & Waldman, D. A. (2010). Spreading the word: The role of surrogates in charismatic leadership processes. *Academy of Management Review*, 35(3), 477–494.

Gifford, G. T. (2010). A modern technology in the leadership classroom: Using blogs for critical thinking development. *Journal of Leadership Education*, 9(1), 165–172.

Giglio, M. (2011). The Facebook freedom fighter. *Newsweek*, 157(8), 14.

Gilley, A., Gilley, J., & McMillan, H. (2009). Organizational change: Motivation, communication, and leadership effectiveness. *Performance Improvement Quarterly*, 21(4), 75–94.

Global Voice Advocacy. (2010). Retrieved on May 21, 2013 from, advocacy.globalvoicesonline.org

Gold, M. (2009, Sept 16). Obama, Kanye West and trouble with Twitter. *Los Angeles Times Online* (Retrieved from http://articles.latimes.com/2009/sep/16/entertainment/et-abctwitterl 6).

Goldenberg, J., & Mazursky, D. (2002). *Creativity in product innovation*. Cambridge, UK: Cambridge University Press.

Gomes, T. (2010, February 13). Do smart phones thwart public records laws? NPR.org. Retrieved from. npr.org/templates/story/story.php?storyId=123573568

Graen, G. B., & Uhl-Bien, M. (1995). Relationship-based approach to leadership: Development of leader-member exchange (LMX) theory of leadership over 25 years: Applying a multi-level multi-domain perspective. *The Leadership Quarterly*, 6(2), 219–247.

Green, J. (2012, November 21). Corporations want Obama's winning formula. *BusinessWeek Online* (Retrieved from http://www.businessweek.com/articles/2012-11-21/corporations-want-obamas-winning-formula).

Halic, O., Lee, D., Paulus, T., & Spence, M. (2010). To blog or not to blog: Student perceptions of blog effectiveness for learning in a college-level course. *The Internet and Higher Education*, 13(4), 206–213.

Hammel, G. (2009, March 25). *The Facebook generation vs. the Fortune 500* ([blog] Retrieved from http://blogs.wsj.com/management/2009/03/24/the-facebook-generation-vs-the-fortune-500/).

Hannah, S. T., Schaubroeck, J. M., Kozlowski, S. W. J., Lord, R. G., Trevino, L. K., Avolio, B. J., et al. (2013). Multi-level influences of abusive leaders on follower values, moral conation, and ethical intentions and behaviors. *Journal of Applied Psychology*, 98, 579–592.

Hassanzadeh, V., Gholami, R., Allahyar, N., & Noordin, N. (2012). Motivation and personality traits of TESL postgraduate students towards the use of information and communications technology in second language teaching. *English Language Teaching*, 5(4), 74–86.

Heidegger, M. (1977). *The question concerning technology and other essays*. New York, NY: Harper.

Hektner, J. M., Schmidt, J. A., & Csikszentmihalyi, M. (2006). *Experience sampling method: Measuring the quality of everyday life*. Thousand Oaks, CA: Sage.

Henderson, J. C., & Venkatraman, N. (1992). *Strategic alignment: A model for organizational transformation through information technology*. New York, NY: Oxford University Press.

Hernandez, M., Eberly, M. B., Avolio, B. J., & Johnson, M. D. (2011). The loci and mechanisms of leadership: Exploring a more comprehensive view of leadership theory. *The Leadership Quarterly*, 22(6), 1165–1185.

Hill, K. (2013, June 10). Why NSA IT guy Edward Snowden leaked top secret documents. *Forbes Online* (Retrieved from http://www.forbes.com/sites/kashmirhill/2013/06/10/why-nsa-it-guy-edward-snowden-leaked-top-secret-documents/).

Hoch, J. E., & Kozlowski, S. W. J. (2013). Leading virtual teams: Hierarchical leadership, structural supports, and shared team leadership. *Journal of Applied Psychology*, http://dx.doi.org/10.1037/a0030264 (Advance online publication).

Holt, D., Armenakis, A., Feild, H., & Harris, S. (2007). Readiness for organizational change: The systematic development of a scale. *The Journal of Applied Behavioral Science*, 43(2), 232–255.

House, R. J., Hanges, P. J., Javidan, M., Dorfman, P. W., & Gupta, V. (2004). *Culture, leadership and organizations: The GLOBE study of 62 societies*. Thousand Oaks, CA: Sage.

Howard, P. N., Duffy, A., Freelon, D., Hussain, M., Mari, W., & Mazaid, M. (September 11). Opening closed regimes: What was the role of social media during the Arab Spring? Retrieved from. http://pitpi.org/index.php/2011/09/11/opening-closed-regimes-what-was-the-role-of-social-media-during-the-arab-spring/

Ives, B., & Jungles, I. (2008). APC forum: Business applications of virtual worlds and serious gaming. *MIS Quarterly*, 7(3), 151–156.

Jackson, L. A., von Eye, A., Biocca, F. A., Barbatsis, G., Fitzgerald, H. E., & Zhao, Y. (2003). Personality, cognitive style, demographic characteristics and Internet use-Findings from the HomeNetToo project. *Swiss Journal of Psychology*, 62(2), 79–90.

Jaffe, E. (2012). Rewired: Cognition in the digital *age*. *Association for Psychological Science Observer*, 25(2)

([Online]. Retrieved from www.psychologicalscience .org/index.php/publications/observer/2012/february-12/rewired.html).

Jang, Y. B., & Ryu, S. H. (2011). Exploring game experiences and game leadership in massively multiplayer online role-playing games. *British Journal of Educational Technology,* 42(4), 616–623.

Jarvenpaa, S., Knoll, K., & Leidner, D. (1998). Is anybody out there? Antecedents of trust in virtual teams. *Journal of Management Information Systems,* 14(4), 29–64.

Jarvenpaa, S., & Leidner, D. (1999). Communication and trust in global virtual teams. *Organizational Science,* 10(6), 791–815.

Jiang, L. C., Bazarova, N. N., & Hancock, J. T. (2013). From perception to behavior: Disclosure reciprocity and the intensification of intimacy in computer-mediated communication. *Communication Research,* 40(1), 125–143.

Judge, T. A., & Bono, J. E. (2001). Relationship of core self-evaluation traits, self-esteem, generalized self-efficacy, locus of control, and emotional stability with job satisfaction and job performance: A meta-analysis. *Journal of Applied Psychology,* 86(1), 80–92.

Judge, T. A., Heller, D., & Mount, M. K. (2002). Five-factor model of personality and job satisfaction: A meta-analysis.*Journal of Applied Psychology,* 87(3), 530–541.

Kahai, S. S. (2013). Leading in a digital age: What's different, issues raised, and what we know. In M. C. Bligh, & R. E. Riggio (Eds.), *Exploring distance in leader-follower relationships: When near is far and far is near* (pp. 63–108). New York, NY: Routledge.

Kahai, S. S., & Cooper, R. B. (1999). The effect of computer-mediated communication on agreement and acceptance. *Journal of Management Information Systems,* 16(1), 165–188.

Kahai, S. S., Sosik, J. J., & Avolio, B.J. (2003). Effects of leadership style, anonymity and rewards in an electronic meeting system context. *The Leadership Quarterly,* 14(4), 499–524.

Kahai, S. S., Sosik, J. J., & Avolio, B.J. (2013, August). Effects of transformational leadership and media on collaboration and performance in virtual teams. In N. S. Hill & N. M. Lorinkova (Chairs), *Leadership in virtual groups: Looking back and charting paths forward.* Symposium conducted at the meetings of the *Academy of Management,* Orlando, FL.

Kane, C. (March 22). Want to spy on somebody? It's easier than ever. CNBC.com. Retrieved from. www.cnbc .com/id/100583418.

Kaplan, A., & Haenlein, M. (2010). Users of the world, unite! The challenges and opportunities of social media. *Business Horizons,* 53(1), 59–68.

Katz, D., & Kahn, R. L. (1978). *The social psychology of organizations.* New York, NY: Wiley.

Kelley, E., & Kelloway, E. K. (2012). Context matters: Testing a model of remote leadership. *Journal of Leadership & Organizational Studies,* 19(4), 437–449.

Khondker, H. (2011). Role of the new media in the Arab Spring. *Globalizations,* 8(5), 675–679.

Klabbers, J. (2009). Terminological ambiguity: Game and simulation. *Simulation & Gaming,* 40(4), 446–463.

Klotz, A., & Buckley, M. R. (2012). A historical perspective of counterproductive work behavior targeting the organization. *Journal of Management History,* 79(1), 114–132.

Kock, N. (2004). The psychobiological model: Towards a new theory of computer-mediated communication based on Darwinian evolution. *Organization Science,* 15(3), 327–348.

Kramer, N. C., & Winter, S. (2008). Impression management 2.0: The relationship of self-esteem, extraversion, self-efficacy, and self-presentation within social networking sites. *Journal of Media Psychology,* 20(3), 106–116.

Kross, E., Verduyn, P., Demiralp, E., Park, J., Lee, D. S., Lin, N., et al. (2013). Facebook use predicts declines in subjective well-being in young adults. *PLoS One,* 8(8).

Kruger, J., Epley, N., Parker, J., & Ng, Z. (2005). Egocentrism over e-mail: Can we communicate as well as we think? *Journal of Personality and Social Psychology,* 89(6), 925–936.

Lord, R. G., Foti, R. J., & De Vader, C. L. (1984). A test of leadership categorization theory: Internal structure, information processing, and leadership perceptions. *Organizational Behavior and Human Performance,* 34(3), 343–378.

Luthans, F., & Avolio, B. J. (2003). Authentic leadership development. In K. S. Cameron, J. E. Dutton, & R. E. Quinn (Eds.), *Positive organizational scholarship* (pp. 241–258). San Francisco, CA: Berrett-Koehler.

MacLean, K. E. (2008). Haptic interaction design for everyday interfaces. *Reviews of Human Factors and Ergonomics,* 4(1), 149–193.

Manser, R., Cooper, M., & Trefusis, J. (2012). Beliefs about emotions as a metacognitive construct: Initial development of a self-report questionnaire measure and preliminary investigation in relation to emotion regulation. *Clinical Psychology and Psychotherapy,* 19(3), 235–246.

Marks, M. A., Mathieu, J. E., & Zaccaro, S. J. (2001). A temporally based framework and taxonomy of team processes. *Academy of Management Review,* 26(3), 356–376.

Mayer, D. M., Kuenzi, M., Greenbaum, R., Bardes, M., & Salvador, R. (2009). How low does ethical leadership flow? Test of a trickle-down model. *Organizational Behavior and Human Decision Processes,* 108(1), 1-13.

Mayer, J. D., Caruso, D. R., & Salovey, P. (2000). Selecting a measure of emotional intelligence: The case for ability scales. In R. Bar-On, & J. D. A. Parker (Eds.), *The handbook of emotional intelligence* (pp. 320–342). New York, NY: Jossey-Bass.

Maznevski, M. L., & Chudoba, K. M. (2000). Bridging space over time: Global virtual team dynamics and effectiveness. *Organization Science,* 11(5), 473–492.

McClelland, D. C. (1978). Managing motivation to expand human freedom. *American Psychologist,* 33(3), 201–210.

Merriman, K., Schmidt, S., & Dunlap-Hinkler, D. (2007). Profiling virtual employees: The impact of managing virtually. *Journal of Leadership & Organizational Studies,* 14(1), 6–15.

Mignonac, K., & Herrbach, O. (2004). Linking work events, affective states, and attitudes: An empirical study of managers' emotions. *Journal of Business and Psychology,* 19(2), 221–240.

Montoya, M. M., Massey, A. P., & Lockwood, N. S. (2011). 3D collaborative virtual environments: Exploring the link between collaborative behaviors and team performance. *Decision Sciences,* 42(2), 451–476.

Morgeson, F. P., & Hofmann, D. A. (1999). The structure and function of collective constructs: Implications for multilevel research and theory development. *Academy of Management Review,* 24(2), 249–265.

Mowday, R. T., & Sutton, R. I. (1993). Organizational behavior: Linking individuals and groups to organizational contexts. *Annual Review of Psychology,* 44(1), 195–229.

Murphy, R. M. (2006, April 27). Zero to $1 billion. *CNN* Money.com. Retrieved from. http://money .cnn.com/2006/04/26/smbusiness/zerocover_fsbbil lion_fsb/.

Nacke, L. E., Grimshaw, M. N., & Lindley, C. A. (2010). More than a feeling: Measurement of sonic user experience and psychophysiology in a first-person shooter game. *Interacting with Computers,* 22(5), 336–343.

Napier, B. J., & Ferris, G. R. (1993). Distance in organizations. *Human Resource Management Review,* 9(3), 321–357.

Nardon, L., & Steers, R. M. (2008). The new global manager: Learning cultures on the fly. *Organizational Dynamics,* 37(1), 47–59.

Nathan, J. (Producer) (1986). *Steve Jobs: Keeper of the vision.* [Documentary]. United States: Jonathan Nathan Productions. Available at youtube.com/watch? v=WHsHKzYOV2E.

Orlikowski, W. J., Yates, J., Okamura, K., & Fujimoto, M. (1995). Shaping electronic communication: The meta-structuring of technology in the context in use. *Organization Science,* 6, 423–444.

Orr, E. S., Sissic, M., Ross, C. Simmering, M. G., Arseneault, J. M., & Orr, R. R. (2009). The influence of shyness on the use of Facebook in an undergraduate sample. *Cyber Psychology & Behavior,* 12(3), 337–340.

Pearce, C. L., & Conger, J. A. (2003). *Shared leadership: Reframing the hows and whys of leadership.* Thousand Oaks, CA: Sage.

Pentland, A., & Choudhury, T. (2000). Face recognition in smart environments. *IEEE Computers,* 33(3), 50–55.

Pinheiro, C. A. (2011). *Social network analysis in telecommunications.* New York, NY: Wiley.

Powell, A., Piccoli, G., & Ives, B. (2004). Virtual teams: A review of current literature and directions for future research. *The Database for Advances in Information Systems,* 35(1), 6–36.

Reeves, B., Malone, T. W., & O Driscoll, T. (2008). Leadership's online labs. *Harvard Business Review,* 86(5), 58–66.

Rhue, L., & Sundararajan, A. (2013). Digital access, political networks and the diffusion of democracy. *Social Networks* (Retrieved from http://dx.doi.org/10 .1016/j.socnet.2012.06.007).

Rosenberg, T. (2011, April 25). *Better hand-washing through technology* ([Blog] Retrieved from http://opinionator .blogs.nytimes.com/2011/04/25/better-hand-wash ing-through-technology/?_r=0)

Samani, H. A., Koh, J. T., Saadatian, E., & Polydorou, D. (2012). Towards robotics leadership: An analysis of leadership characteristics and the roles robots will inherit in future human society. Inj. S. Pan, S. M. Chen, & N. T. Nguyen (Eds.), *ACIIDS 2012PartII, LNAI 7197* (pp. 158–165). Berlin, DE: Springer-Verlag.

Schaubroeck, J. M., Hannah, S. T., Avolio, B. J., Kozlowski, S. W., Lord, R. G., Treviño, L. K., et al. (2012). Embedding ethical leadership within and across organization levels. *Academy of Management Journal,* 55(5), 1053–1078.

Schectman, J. (2013, January 29). *IBM security tool can flag "disgruntled employees"* ([Blog] Retrieved from http:// blogs.wsj.com/cio/2013/01/29/ibm-security-tool- can-flag-disgruntled-employees/).

Schepers, J., Wetzels, M., & Ruyter, K. D. (2005). Leadership styles in technology acceptance: Do followers practice what leaders preach? *Managing Service Quality,* 15(6), 496–505.

Sheldon, K. M., Abad, N., & Hinsch, C. (2011). A two-process view of Facebook use and relatedness need-satisfaction: Disconnection drives use, and connection rewards it. *Journal of Personality and Social Psychology,* 100(4), 766–775.

Silverman, R. (2011, October 10). Latest game theory: Mixing work and play. *Wall Street Journal* (Retrieved from http://online.wsj.com/news/articles/SB1000142 405297020429450457661537178379524 8).

Sisask, M., Mark, L., & Varnik, A. (2012). Internet comments elicited by media portrayal of a familicide-suicide case. *Crisis: The Journal of Crisis Intervention and Suicide Prevention,* 33(4), 222–229.

Small, G. W., Moody, T. D., Siddarth, P., & Bookheimer, S. Y. (2009). Your brain on Google: Patterns of cerebral activation during Internet searching. *American Journal of Geriatric Psychiatry,* 17(2), 116–126.

Small, G. W., & Vorgan, G. (2008). Meet your iBrain. *Scientific American Mind,* 19(5), 42–49.

Smith, J., & MacLean, K. (2007). Communicating emotion through a haptic link: Design space and methodology. *International Journal of Human Computer Studies,* 65(4), 376–387.

Smith-Slater, J., & Anderson, E. (1994). Communication convergence in electronically supported discussions: An adaptation of Kincaid's convergence model. *Telematics and Informatics,* 11(2), 111–125.

Sosik, J. J. (1997). Effects of transformational leadership and anonymity on idea generation in computer-mediated groups. *Group & Organization Management,* 22(4), 460–487.

Sosik, J. J., Avolio, B. J., & Kahai, S. S. (1997). The impact of leadership style and anonymity on group potency and effectiveness in a GDSS environment journal *of Applied Psychology,* 82(1), 89–103.

Sosik, J. J., Avolio, B. J., Kahai, S. S., & Jung, D. I. (1998). Computer-supported work group potency and effectiveness: The role of transformational leadership, anonymity, and task interdependence. *Computers in Human Behavior,* 14(3), 491–511.

Sosik, J. J., & Cameron, J. C. (2010). Character and authentic transformational leadership behavior: Expanding the ascetic self toward others. *Consulting Psychology Journal: Practice and Research,* 62(4), 251–269.

Sosik, J. J., Chun, J. U., Blair, A. L., & Fitzgerald, N. A. (2013). Possible selves in the lives of transformational faith community leaders. *Psychology of Religion and Spirituality* (in press) (http://psycnet.apa.org/index .cfm?fa=buy.optionToBuy&id=2013-20577-001).

Sosik, J. J., & Dinger, S. L. (2007). Relationships between leadership style and vision content: The moderating role of need for approval, self-monitoring, and need for social power. *The Leadership Quarterly,* 18(2), 134–153.

Sosik, J. J., Godshalk, V. M., & Yammarino, F. J. (2004). Transformational leadership, learning goal orientation, and expectations for career success in mentor-protege relationships: A multiple levels of analysis perspective. *The Leadership Quarterly,* 15(2), 241–261.

Sosik, J. J., Kahai, S. S., & Avolio, B. J. (1999). Leadership style, anonymity, and creativity in group decision support systems: The mediating role of optimal flow. *The Journal of Creative Behavior,* 33(4), 1–30.

Spreitzer, G. M. (1995). Psychological empowerment in the workplace: Dimensions, measurement and validation. *Academy of Management Journal,* 38(5), 1442–1465.

Sproull, L., & Kiesler, S. (1986). Reducing social context cues: Electronic mail in organizational communication. *Management Science,* 32(11), 1492–1512.

Starke, M. (June 3). CEOs and the social media monster. MarcusStarke.com. Retrieved on May 22, 2013 from. marcusstarke.com/leadership/ceos-and-the-social-media-monster

Stokols, D., Mishra, S., Gould-Runnerstrom, M., & Hipp, J. (2009). Psychology in an age of ecological crisis: From personal angst to collective action. *American Psychologist,* 64(3), 181–193.

Sutanto, J., Tan, C., Battistini, B., & Phang, C. (2011). Emergent leadership in virtual collaboration settings: A social network analysis approach. *Long Range Planning,* 44(5), 421–439.

Sutter, J. (2011, February 21). The faces of Egypt's "Revolution 2.0". *CNN* (Retrieved from http://www .cnn.com/2011/TECH/innovation/02/21/egypt.inter net. revolution/).

Tajfel, H., & Turner, J. C. (1986). The social identity theory of intergroup behavior. In W. G. Austin, & S. Worchel (Eds.), *The social psychology of intergroup relations* (pp. 7–24). Chicago, IL: Nelson-Hall.

Thompson, C. (2006, December 3). Open-source spying. *The New York Times Online* (Retrieved from http:// www.nytimes.com/2006/12/03/magazine/03intelli gence.html?pagewanted=all).

Toma, C. L., & Hancock, J. T. (2012). What lies beneath: The linguistic traces of deception in online dating profiles. *Journal of Communication,* 62(1), 78–97.

Tsai, W., & Ghoshal, S. (1998). Social capital and value creation: The role of intrafirm networks. *Academy of Management Journal,* 41(4), 464–476.

Uhl-Bien, M., Marion, R., & McKelvey, B. (2007). Complexity leadership theory: Shifting leadership from the industrial age to the knowledge era. *The Leadership Quarterly,* 18(4), 298–318.

Ventatesh, V., & Morris, M. G. (2000). Why don't men ever stop to ask for directions? Gender, social influence, and their role in technology acceptance and usage behavior. *MIS Quarterly,* 24(1), 115–139.

Walker, S. K., Dworkin, J., & Connell, J. H. (2011). Variation in parent use of information and communications technology: Does quantity matter? *Family & Consumer Sciences Research Journal,* 40(2), 106–119.

Walther, J. B. (2008). Computer-mediated communication and virtual groups. In E. A. Konijn, S. Utz, M. Tanis, & S. B. Barnes (Eds.), *Mediated interpersonal communication* (pp. 271–290). New York, NY: Taylor and Francis/Routledge.

Wang, J., Tian, J., & Shen, Z. (2013). The effects and moderators of cyber-loafing controls: an empirical study of Chinese public servants. *Information Technology and Management,* http://dx.doi.org/10.1007/sl0799-013-0164-y (Advance online publication).

Watson, S. (2001). Reflection toolkit. Retrieved on May 17, 2013 from. www.nationalserviceresources.org/files/legacy/filemanager/download/615/nwtoolkit.pdf

Watson, D., & Slack, L. A. (1993). General factors of affective temperament and their relation to job satisfaction over time. *Organizational Behaviour and Human Decision Processes,* 54(2), 181–202.

Weick, K. F. (1990). Technology as equivoque: Sense making in new techniques. In P. S. Goodman, & L. S. Sproull (Eds.), *Technology and organizations* (pp. 1–44). San Francisco, CA: Jossey-Bass.

Weintraub, K. (October 15). Affective programming grows in effort to read faces. *The New York Times* ([Online]. Retrieved from www.nytimes.com/2012/10/16/science/affective-programming-grows-in-effort-to-read-faces.html).

Weisband, S. (2008). *Leadership at a distance: Research in technologically-supported work.* New York, NY: Erlbaum.

Weisband, S. P., Schneider, S. K., & Connolly, T. (1995). Computer-mediated communication and social information: Status salience and status differences. *Academy of Management,* 32(4), 1124–1151.

Weiss, H. M., & Cropanzano, R. (1996). Affective events theory: A theoretical discussion of the structure, causes and consequences of affective experiences at work. *Research in Organizational Behaviour,* 19, 1–74A.

Wellman, B., & Gulia, M. (1999). Net surfers don't ride alone: Virtual communities as communities. In M. A. Smith, & P. Kollock (Eds.), *Communities in cyberspace* (pp. 167–194). London, UK: Routledge.

Werbach, K., & Hunter, D. (2012). *For the win: How game thinking can revolutionize your business.* Philadelphia, PA: Wharton Digital Press.

Wofford, J. C., & Goodwin, V. L. (1994). A cognitive interpretation of transactional and transformational leadership theories. *The Leadership Quarterly,* 5(2), 161–186.

Wordsworth, W. (1926). Book third: residence at Cambridge. In E. de Selincourt (Ed.), *The prelude or growth of a poet's mind; An autobiographical poem: Edited from the manuscripts with introduction, textual and critical notes by Ernest de Selincourt.* Oxford, UK: Clarendon Press.

Yammarino, F. J. (1994). Indirect leadership: Transformational leadership at a distance. In B. M. Bass, & B.J. Avolio (Eds.), *Improving organizational effectiveness through transformational leadership* (pp. 26–47). Thousand Oaks, CA: Sage.

Yukl, G. (2010). *Leadership in organizations* (7th ed.) Upper Saddle River, NJ: Prentice Hall.

Zimmer, M. (2010). But the data is already public: On the ethics of research in Facebook. *Ethics and Information Technology,* 72(4), 313–325.

CHAPTER 15

Complexity Leadership Theory

Mary Uhl-Bien

University of Nebraska

Russ Marion

Clemson University

Introduction

The field of leadership is in the midst of a paradigm shift, in which traditional models are giving way to new conceptualizations of leadership and organizing. Predominant theories, such as transformational leadership and leader–member exchange (LMX), are reaching maturity, the stage Hunt and Dodge (2000) refer to as Consolidation/Accommodation in the evolution of concepts—their major contributions have already been made, research is matter-of-fact, and overall research declines (Reichers & Schneider, 1990). More significantly, they are insufficient to explain the complex realities of leadership and management today (Lewin, 1999; Marion & Uhl-Bien, 2001; Pearce & Conger, 2003; Plowman & Duchon, 2008). As described by Hamel (2009), the principles of 'modern' management are over 100 years old. We need to develop new foundations for leadership:

'Scholars and practitioners must rebuild management's underpinnings [which] will require hunting for new principles in fields as diverse as anthropology, biology, design, political science, urban planning, and theology' (Hamel, 2009, p. 93).

Complexity leadership scholars are doing just this—using complexity concepts from the physical sciences to develop new foundations for theorizing about leadership. Similar to biology and physics, where complexity radically transformed views regarding orderliness of the universe (Wheatley, 1992), complexity is helping leadership scholars overcome the limits of bureaucratic logics in thinking about the dynamics of order in organizational life. Complexity is providing a new lexicon for leadership research and practice—one that considers leadership as occurring in both formal *and* informal processes, and as emerging in and interacting with complex interactive dynamics.

Source: The Sage Handbook of Leadership by editors Alan Bryman, David Collinson, Keith Grint, Brad Jackson, and Mary Uhl-Bien, 2011, pp. 468–482. SAGE Publications. Reprinted with permission.

Although the language is new, complexity focuses on concepts of informal organization and leadership emergence that are age old. We have known them since the earliest writings in the study of management and leadership (Barnard, 1938; Follett, 1924; Roethlisberger & Dickson, 1939; Selznick, 1949). Despite this, organizational studies chose to focus on formal structures and systems of organizations, adopting the zeitgeist of the times (Hunt & Dodge, 2000) by assuming predictable states of adaptation to the environment (Burns & Stalker, 1961; Galbraith, 1973; Katz & Kahn, 1978; Lawrence & Lorsch, 1967; Scott, 1987) and static equilibrium models (e.g., contingency theory, punctuated equilibrium, ecology, strategic choice) (Brown & Eisenhardt, 1997; Eisenhardt & Tabrizi, 1995; Stacey, 1995). As management scholars have discovered, these models do not fit today's contexts of dynamic and continual change (Browning, Beyer, & Stetler, 1995; Eisenhardt & Schoonhoven, 1990).

Because of this a new, 'dynamic equilibrium,' paradigm has emerged in organizational studies in the last two decades (Anderson, 1999; Boisot & Child, 1999; Davis, Eisenhardt, & Bingham, 2009; Galunic & Eisenhardt, 2001; Meyer, Gaba, & Colwell, 2005; Osborn & Hunt, 2007; Pettigrew et al., 2003). Complexity leadership theory provides a leadership model to fit with this emerging, dynamic organization paradigm (Uhl-Bien, Marion, & McKelvey, 2007). It describes a model for the 'leadership of emergence' in organizations and social systems (Lichtenstein & Plowman, 2009).

In this chapter we overview the field of complexity leadership and position it in the dynamic organization paradigm in organization studies (Eisenhardt & Tabrizi, 1995; Lewin, 1999). Because complexity leadership is an emerging area in the field and unfamiliar to many leadership scholars, we begin with a chronological review that describes how complexity theory entered into management and leadership discourse. We then provide an overview of the current state of the field. We conclude by discussing methodological issues associated with studying complexity leadership and identifying the most promising areas for future research.

Due to space limitations we do not provide a detailed review of complexity principles—excellent resources are available discussing complexity science as it relates to

organizations (Anderson, 1999; Cilliers, 1998; Marion, 1999; Stacey, Griffin, & Shaw, 2000) and leadership (Hazy, Goldstein, & Lichtenstein, 2007; Uhl-Bien & Marion, 2008; Wheatley, 1998). We refer readers who are interested in learning more about core complexity concepts and principles to those and other sources (e.g., Kauffman, 1995; Mainzer, 1997; Waldrop, 1992).

Chronological Development of Complexity Approaches to Leadership

For many leadership scholars and practitioners, the first exposure to the promise of complexity for the study of organizational leadership was Margaret Wheatley's *Leadership and the New Science* (Wheatley, 1992, 1999). In this book, Wheatley described the possibilities of the 'new science' of complexity for advancing scientific management principles, based in Newtonian mechanics, to 'scientific leadership' principles, based in complexity and complex adaptive systems. According to Wheatley, 'scientific leadership' shifts the perspective from managerial leadership, grounded in hierarchical ordering and control, to a complexity view of leadership as emergent order that arises in the combinations of many individual actions. Leadership from this perspective acknowledges the deep relationship between individual activity and the whole (Wheatley, 1992).

Applying the metaphor of 'living systems' found in complexity to leadership in organizations, Wheatley introduced concepts such as emergence and self-organizing processes. From this view, change results not from top-down, preconceived strategic plans or mandates of any single individual or boss, but from local actions that occur simultaneously around the system linking up with one another to produce powerful emergent phenomena. Wheatley described how, in complexity, management would not be about command-and-control but sharing information and catalyzing 'local' connections to generate emergence and adaptability (Wheatley, 1999). Leadership would not lie in formal structure, but in the interconnected actions of individuals acting out of personal values or vision and engaging with one another through dialogue.

In 1995, Ralph Stacey conveyed a similar theme with his article applying complexity to strategic change (see also Stacey, 1996). Stacey suggested that complex adaptive systems offer a superior alternative to predominant static views. Rather than organizations tending toward *equilibrium* (stability, regularity, and predictability) as described by strategic choice and ecology views, Stacey proposed that strategic change is more accurately described using complexity concepts of *far from equilibrium* states. In equilibrium, change is driven by negative feedback processes toward predictable states of adaptation to the environment. In far from equilibrium (i.e., complexity), creative, innovative, and continually changing behavior is driven by negative *and* positive feedback to 'paradoxical states of stability and instability, predictability and unpredictability' (Stacey, 1995, p. 478). As described by Stacey (1995, p. 478):

> The transformational process is one of internal, spontaneous self-organization amongst the agents of a system, provoked by instabilities, and potentially leading to emergent order. . . . *The dynamics of success then have to do with being kept away from equilibrium adaptation in states of instability, irregularity and unpredictability.* [emphasis added]

In other words, Stacey introduced to leadership the powerful but paradigm-shifting concept that changeable organizations are those in which informal feedback networks are sustained *away from equilibrium* (i.e., edge of chaos). Instead of order and control, these organizations operate on 'disorderly' dynamics of contradiction, conflict, tension, and dialogue (cf. Heifetz & Laurie, 2001). Moreover, these dynamics occur primarily in the informal network system—not the formal stabilizing systems—in the organization.

The role of strategic management, then, is not to reduce the level of uncertainty (i.e., diminishing surprise in the organization) but to accept and even promote uncertainty, surprise, unknowability, and open-endedness. In direct contrast to leadership approaches advocating the critical role of organizational leaders in establishing vision and aligning employees around that vision, Stacey says that in changeable systems it is not possible to specify meaningful pictures of a future state (i.e., a vision): '. . . consensus around some picture of a future state removes the chaos which changeable systems must experience if they are to innovate' (p. 491). Rather than focusing on individual leaders and actions of those at the top, Stacey (1995) suggested strategic management research should focus on leadership in the group dynamics and spontaneously self-organizing political and organizational learning processes through which innovation occurs.

Furthermore, given that managers operate paradoxically—in a formal hierarchy with a focus on efficiency and control while also in informal networks seeking to undermine these hierarchies and controls to allow for creativity and changeability—Stacey (1995) states that research programs exploring the dual processes of formal and informal leadership are of paramount importance for strategic management. He calls for research investigating how leaders affect and are affected by the informal networks of which they are a part, as well as how leaders encourage these networks to engage in promoting conflict and dialogue within boundaries. Consistent with shared leadership perspectives, Stacey describes the need for attention to 'leadership which is located not simply in one person but shifts from person to person according to task needs or emotional states of groups of people operating in informal networks' (p. 492).

In a separate series of studies in high-velocity organizations, Kathleen Eisenhardt provided empirical evidence that, in retrospect, is consistent with Stacey's assertions. Eisenhardt was drawn to complexity when traditional equilibrium-based and contingency views were not able to explain findings regarding organizations operating in rapidly changing industries. Eisenhardt, like Stacey (1995), began to suggest that complexity approaches are better suited for development 'of a more dynamic organizational paradigm' that captures key features of firms that are 'continuously adaptive' (Eisenhardt & Tabrizi, 1995).

For example, Eisenhardt and Schoonhoven (1990) described a 'surprising result' in which effects of the founding team and environment grew—rather than faded—with time, similar to amplifying effects and sensitive dependence on initial conditions in chaos theory (Gleick, 1987). They proposed that chaos dynamics may have been at play and could represent an interesting avenue for future research.

In Eisenhardt and Tabrizi (1995), the authors called into question traditional depictions of organic processes as lacking structure (Burns & Stalker, 1961; Lawrence & Lorsch, 1967). Their findings show that these organizations *do* have structure, just not structures that match descriptions in the literature. These structures combine elements of both adaptation and formal control. For example, continuously changing organizations have fast processes in uncertain situations that are 'improvisational,' in that they combine real-time learning through design iterations and testing (i.e., adaptation), but also have the focus and discipline of milestones (i.e., formal structure). Moreover, they have leaders who, rather than restricting information, suppressing conflict, and centralizing decision-making (i.e., formal structure and control), allow for the essential dynamics of real-time interaction, intuition, and improvisation (i.e., adaptation). These leaders allow for flexibility (i.e., adaptation) while also having high-level reporting relationships that give them final decision-making authority on key issues of budget, team composition, and project timetable (i.e., formal structure). They conclude (p. 108):

> Thus our work joins a small but growing number of studies that challenge the relevance of organic processes to effective organization (Jelinek and Schoonhoven, 1990; Weick, 1993; Brown and Eisenhardt, 1995b) and relate closely to emergent ideas on balancing order and disorder within complex, adaptive systems.

Similarly, Browning et al. (1995) 'found' complexity when they were analyzing data from their qualitative research in the semiconductor industry. Investigating how cooperation can arise and persist in a highly competitive industry, their data did not fit systems theories positing internal processes toward homeostasis. They realized, instead, that their findings were better explained by complexity theory. For example, individual contributions became self-amplifying in that they 'gave birth to a moral community and created structures that in turn created other structures' (p. 145). Moreover these activities occurred in an environment in which the top leader's non-directive leadership style created an egalitarian culture that encouraged innovation and self-organization. In this managerial environment, individuals in the organization could structure situations and activities according to needs. They could 'create structures that fit the moment' (p. 142)—allowing them flexibility and fluidity to modify structures they found useful and keep inventing new ones.

In 1997, Brown and Eisenhardt used complexity theory to explore continuous change in the context of multiple-product innovation. They challenged punctuated equilibrium models assuming radical and intermittent change, suggesting instead that: 'While the punctuated equilibrium model is in the foreground of academic interest, it is in the background of the experiences of many firms' (p. 1). Their findings show that many organizations are more accurately described as continuously changing, and such organizations are 'semistructured' rather than over-structured (mechanistic) or under-structured (organic). Semistructures are sufficiently rigid to allow change to happen, but not so rigid that change cannot occur: while some responsibilities, meetings, and priorities were set, the design process itself was almost completely unfettered.

According to their data, the most adaptive organizations—those that exhibited the most prolific, complex, and continuous change—were poised at the 'edge of chaos that exists between order and disorder' (p. 29). This 'dissipative equilibrium. . .requires constant managerial vigilance to avoid slipping into pure chaos or pure structure' (p. 29). In these systems, unsuccessful managers were those who engaged in too much structuring. These managers used what could be considered traditional leadership approaches—they began with the future, developed a strategy (i.e., planning and visioning), and then worked to execute (i.e., implementation). In so doing, they kept getting bogged down, however, in implementation—in the day-to-day business. They were continually waylaid by problems with current product development and a focus on maintaining current revenues. Managers in successfully changing organizations neither rigidly planned nor chaotically reacted. They began by getting rid of lock-step and bureaucratic process, increasing communication, and adding project-level responsibilities, and then 'choreographed transitions' between past and future projects that were neither haphazard nor rigid. This involved looking out to the future to identify next opportunities, eventually linking current and future projects in seamless transitions (see also Brown & Eisenhardt, 1998).

The findings from Eisenhardt (Brown & Eisenhardt, 1997; Eisenhardt & Schoonhoven, 1990; Eisenhardt & Tabrizi, 1995) and Browning et al. (1995), combined with the writings of Stacey (1995) and Wheatley (1992), began to suggest a new view of management as more fluid, enabling, and adaptive than predominant theorizing at the time. By the end of the 1990s, evidence was beginning to mount for the potential of complexity to offer a new paradigm for management and leadership. This sentiment was crystallized in a special issue of *Organization Science* focusing on the implications of the science of complexity for the field of organizational studies. As stated by Arie Lewin (1999, p. 215):

This rediscovery of the characteristics of open systems begs a reexamination of the underlying management logic that dominates the view of the role of managers. . . . The idea that organizations can naturally evolve effective strategies, structures, and processes and self-adjust to new strategies and environmental changes *implies that managers should facilitate, guide, and set the boundary* conditions in which successful self-organization can take place. [emphasis added]

This new managerial logic would focus on things such as managing the organizational levers of dissipative energy; designing organizational systems that facilitate emergent processes such as improvisation, product champions, and emergent strategies; and openness to bottom-up processes and acceptance of equifinal outcomes (Lewin, 1999).

In an article introducing complexity to leadership research in 2001, Marion and Uhl-Bien made

a similar call for a new leadership logic grounded in complexity. Describing complexity as a science of complexly interacting systems, they argued that complexity changes the dialogue in leadership away from managing and controlling and toward *enabling*. Instead of viewing leadership as interpersonal influence, they described complexity leadership as providing linkages to 'emergent structures' within and among organizations. At the macro leadership level (e.g., leadership *of* the organization; Boal & Hooijberg, 2001), this means that the focus of leadership should be on how to foster and speed up the emergence of distributed intelligence (DI) (McKelvey, 2008). At the micro level (e.g., leadership *in* the organization, Boal & Hooijberg, 2001), this means creating the conditions that enable productive, but largely unspecified, future states:

This recognizes that leaders cannot control the future (e.g., determinism) because in complex systems such as organizations, unpredictable (and sometimes unexplainable) internal dynamics will determine future conditions. Rather, micro-level complex leaders need to influence networks, creating atmospheres for formation of aggregates and meta-aggregates (e.g., the emergent structure concepts of complexity theory to be discussed below) in ways that permit innovation and dissemination of innovations so critical for 'fitness' of the firm. (Marion & Uhl-Bien, 2001, p. 391)

Drawing from Marion's 1999 book *The Edge of Organization*, they explained these dynamics as a combination of microdynamic (e.g., correlation, interaction, and randomness) and macrodynamic forces. Microdynamics represent bottom-up (emergent) behaviors that occur when individuals interact, leading to both coordinated behavior and random behavior (i.e., aggregation). Macro-dynamics represent the emergence of the larger systems from the interactions at the micro-level. Macro-level behaviors are driven by the micro-dynamics and characterized by 'bottom-up' coordination and non-linear behavior to generate emergence and self-organization (rather than leader-designed outcomes).

Applying this to al-Qaeda, Marion and Uhl-Bien (2003) offered an illustration of complexity leadership. Arguing that the nature of Islamic militancy spawned a complexly structured organization led according to complexity leadership principles, they showed how al-Qaeda emerged through a process of aggregation and autocatalysis characteristic of complex adaptive systems. Rather than resulting from strategic plans of a set of leaders, al-Qaeda emerged through a process of bottom-up aggregation (i.e., linking-up of various terrorist cells) enabled by direct and indirect leadership processes (e.g., forging alliances that helped increase the power of the network, capitalizing on opportunities emerging out of network dynamics, serving as tags to catalyze al-Qaeda's structure and activities). Al-Qaeda leaders did not create this movement; they were created by it. Thus, the authors conclude, the case shows that leadership is not necessarily a person or a formal role but a phenomenon created by, and residing in, a complex adaptive system.

As Marion and Uhl-Bien were beginning their complexity work, Ralph Stacey was rapidly advancing the concepts he initiated in the 1990s into a perspective known as complex responsive processes (Stacey, 2000; 2001b; Stacey, Griffin, & Shaw, 2000). Beginning with Mead's responsive processing (1934), Stacey described a social process as one in which each gesture from one animal calls forth a response from another, and together, gesture and response form a social act (Stacey, 2000, 2001b). From this perspective, the social is a responsive process of meaningful signaling in continuous cycles of cooperative and competitive interaction (Stacey, 2000, 2001b). Intellect plays a role in this process, but, contrary to traditional perspectives, Stacey proposes that mind is not an autonomous individual first thinking and then choosing an action; rather, it is individuals in relationship *continuously evoking and provoking responses in one another* (with responses influenced by past history). In this process, Stacey argues, both individual mind and social emerge in relationships between people—i.e., Stacey sees mind and social as occurring in 'the space between' (cf. Bradbury & Lichtenstein, 2005).

Whereas this presents a radical departure from traditional positivist and realist views, it is consistent with complexity notions of emergence (Goldstein,

2007; Marion & Uhl-Bien, 2001). Stacey elaborates Mead's (1934) concept of social by using complexity concepts to explain how interactions between large numbers of agents, each responding to others on the basis of local organizing principles, produce coherent patterns with the potential for novelty. In this way, complexity explains the way in which global coherence can arise in the context of large numbers of local interactions. When richly connected enough (i.e., edge of chaos), this process of self-organizing interaction can produce coherent and novel patterns in itself, and this occurs *without any blueprint or program* (cf. Uhl-Bien, 2006). With this, Stacey returns to his position in the 1995 article regarding the importance of recognizing paradoxical states of stability/instability and predictability/unpredictability at the same time (2001a). His point:

> Interaction itself is sufficient to account for coherent pattern in relating. There is no need to posit causal powers in some system above, beneath, behind or in front of that interaction. (Stacey, 2001a, p. 462)

Applied to leadership, Stacey makes a strong case for moving beyond the dominant voice in management theory that speaks in the language of design, regularity, and control. Instead, he calls for researchers to acknowledge the voices from the fringes of organization theory, complexity sciences, psychology, and sociology that define a participative perspective (Stacey et al., 2000; Streatfield, 2001). From this view, managers are not *outside* the organization system, which is thought of as an objective, pre-given reality that can be modeled, designed, and under their control; instead, they are themselves members of the complex networks they form, and through their inter-subjective voices they interact to co-evolve a jointly constructed reality (cf. Fairhurst & Grant, 2010; Hosking 2007; Hosking, Dachler, & Gergen, 1995). This suggests, then, that managers/ leaders are not 'in control' even though they may be 'in charge' (Stacey et al., 2000; see also Stacey & Griffin, 2008; Streatfield, 2001).

Back in the USA, Marion and Uhl-Bien were hearing strong interest in pursuing the potential of complexity for advancing leadership theory and research. In response they organized two conferences in 2005—the first at the Center for Creative Leadership (Greensboro, NC) with Ellen Van Velsor and Cindy McCauley, and the second at George Washington University (Executive Leadership Program), with Margaret Gorman and Jim Hazy. These conferences were designed to bring together top leadership scholars with complexity scholars to explore the possibilities for advancing a new theory of complexity leadership. The conferences resulted in two books (Hazy et al., 2007; Uhl-Bien & Marion, 2008) and two special issues (*Emergence: Complexity & Organization*, Vol. 8, Issue 4, 2006; *The Leadership Quarterly*, Vol. 18, Issue 4, 2007). They also resulted in collaborations and publications, as conference participants set out to develop and investigate theoretical frameworks for the study of complexity leadership.

Today, complexity leadership research is burgeoning, with writing increasing exponentially since 2005. To describe the current state of the field, in the section below we present the major theoretical framework for the study of complexity leadership and review related research with respect to this framework.

Current State of the Field

From the review above we can see the core concepts that comprise a complexity approach to leadership. Complexity leadership theory is the study of leadership based in complexity science (Hazy et al., 2007; Uhl-Bien & Marion, 2008); it is grounded in a complexity, rather than a bureaucratic (Weber, 1947), paradigm. It assumes that leadership is not generated in authority and control (i.e., the formal managerial structure) but in the interconnected actions of individuals acting out of personal values or vision, and engaging with one another through dialogue (Wheatley, 1992). From this perspective, order is not designed and directed, but emergent from the combinations of many individual actions: Local actions that occur simultaneously around the system link up with one another to produce powerful emergent phenomena (Lichtenstein & Plowman, 2009; Uhl-Bien & Marion, 2009). In this way, complexity suggests very

much a shared, or distributed, view of leadership (Gronn, 2002; Pearce & Conger, 2003).

Complexity leadership theory acknowledges the deep relationship between individual activity and the whole (Wheatley, 1992). It focuses on the rich interplay between local and global. As described by Goldspink and Kay (2004), complexity helps bridge the micro–macro divide in the social sciences by helping explain the relationship between the constitutive elements of the social system (people) and the emergent phenomena resulting from their interactions (e.g., organizations). In this way, levels of analysis are not so much about individual, dyad, group, organization (levels generated from hierarchical, linear, bureaucratic ordering) but about how phenomena emerge from the complex and nonlinear interplay between heterogeneous agents and complexity dynamics.

For many leadership scholars this will be hard to get one's head around. This is because our leadership training is heavily positivist, and we typically don't even know it. We are trained in a scientific method that advocates reductionism (studying individual level variables) and determinism (showing linear causality) (Marion & Uhl-Bien, 2001; Stacey, 1995). But there is a new science, one in which change and constant creation signal new ways of maintaining order and structure (Wheatley, 1992). Complexity leadership advances leadership theory and research into this new science and its new scientific method (Hazy et al., 2007; Uhl-Bien & Marion, 2008). By offering a leadership theory to fit the emerging dynamic organizational paradigm (Eisenhardt & Tabrizi, 1995), it takes leadership out of the Industrial Age and places it into the modern, connectionist Knowledge Era (Uhl-Bien et al., 2007).

Knowledge Era organizations are poised at the 'edge of chaos' that exists between order and disorder, stability and instability—continuously changing, rather than giving in to equilibrium, stability-seeking tendencies (Eisenhardt & Tabrizi, 1995; Pettigrew et al., 2003; Stacey, 1995). In essence, they must attempt to operate as complex adaptive systems (Martin & Eisenhardt, 2010). Yet keeping an organization in an adaptive state (i.e., far from equilibrium, edge of chaos) is counter to everything we have been taught and assumed (Plowman & Duchon, 2008). Moreover, it is no easy task. As shown by Houchin and MacLean (2005), stabilizing forces in organizations are strong—in conditions of anxiety caused by disequilibrium, the pressures on managers to seek equilibrium in the form of comfort and security are often overwhelming. Organizational managers give in to these pressures to reduce anxiety by taking actions that avoid conflict, maintain control and minimize change, thereby creating complex *recursive* rather than complex *adaptive* systems. As Houchin and MacLean (2005) point out, complex recursive systems, because they do not adapt, often experience only short-term survival.

Although complexity approaches describe how organizations maintain an adaptive, rather than recursive, state the findings of Houchin and MacLean (2005) require complexity scholars to acknowledge that organizations are *not* naturally complex adaptive systems. Instead they are bureaucracies (Hales, 2002). As we know, bureaucracy is not designed to be adaptive (Heckscher, 1994). *We argue that this is why complexity leadership is needed: complexity leadership offers managers and leaders a framework for understanding how they can help organizations operate more like complex adaptive systems.* Complexity leadership does this by enabling and interacting with complex adaptive dynamics in organizations (Hazy, 2006; Marion & Uhl-Bien, 2001; Uhl-Bien et al., 2007). The primary role of complexity leadership is to show how, in contexts of larger organizing frameworks (most often bureaucracy), organizational leaders can create conditions suitable to complex adaptive dynamics, and then interact with these dynamics to generate productive outcomes for the firm (Uhl-Bien & Marion, 2009).

To grasp this, we need to understand two key concepts: (1) complexity leadership functions and (2) complexity dynamics and emergence. Therefore, we turn to these next.

Complexity Leadership Functions

One of the challenges in advancing a paradigm of complexity leadership theory is in addressing terminology. As can be seen from the review above, complexity clearly suggests an alternative view of leadership. But what is this view, and how can it be described?

Some scholars do not give it a specific name, instead referring to it simply as a new view of leadership (Stacey et al., 2000; Wheatley, 1992, 1999). These scholars, not without justification, argue that the distributed and interactive view of leadership is the true reality of leadership and therefore we should acknowledge that reality and move ahead.

Other scholars recognize that complexity suggests additional forms of leadership. For example Hazy (2006), drawing from complexity concepts, identified three new forms of leadership associated with complexity: leadership of convergence, leadership of variety, and leadership of unity. Leadership of convergence catalyzes the activities of a system toward a particular attractor. Leadership of variety catalyzes an exploration and experimentation process to increase the variety of possibilities available to the system and also creates the conditions that enable transformation from one attractor to another. Leadership of unity balances tension and catalyzes coherence and a sense of oneness in the system over time. Surie and Hazy (2006) added another kind of leadership: generative leadership. Generative leadership is defined as leadership that fosters innovation, organizational adaptation, and high performance over time. It does this by seeking out, fostering, and sustaining generative relationships that yield new learning relevant for innovation.

Drawing from organization and management theory, Uhl-Bien et al. (2007) offered a slightly different perspective. They identified three functions of leadership: administrative, adaptive, and enabling. Administrative leadership is managerial leadership associated with the bureaucratic elements of organizations. It occurs in formal, managerial roles and reflects traditional management processes and functions aimed at driving business results: strategic direction and alignment, budgeting, resource allocation, regulatory, scheduling, etc. It aligns organizational members with the business needs of the firm (e.g., through efficiency and control). It comprises the *administrative function* of the organization.

Adaptive leadership, similar to Stacey's complex responsive processing (Johannessen & Aasen, 2007), reflects the 'complexity' view of leadership. It describes leadership as emerging in and from the dynamic interaction of heterogeneous agents as they work interdependently in organizations. It occurs in the complex adaptive systems of organizations. Adaptive leadership varies from Stacey's view, however, in its focus on adaptive work (cf. Heifetz, 1994). As defined by Uhl-Bien and Marion (2009), adaptive leadership is an informal leadership process that occurs in intentional interactions of interdependent human agents (individuals or collectives) as they work to generate and advance novel solutions in the face of adaptive needs of the organization (cf. Heifetz & Laurie, 2001; Johannessen & Aasen, 2007). It is productive of new ideas, innovation, adaptability, and change (Uhl-Bien et al., 2007). It comprises the *adaptive* function of the organization.

Hence, the model presented by Uhl-Bien and Marion (Uhl-Bien & Marion, 2009; Uhl-Bien et al., 2007) identifies two primary functions related to leadership in organizations: administrative and adaptive. The administrative function drives toward business results; the adaptive function drives toward innovation (product innovation) and adaptability (process innovation). The administrative function is motivated toward efficiency and control (e.g., exploitation) while the adaptive function is motivated toward creative interaction and innovation (e.g., exploration).

These two functions operate in dynamic tension with one another (Houchin & MacLean, 2005). This tension is reflected in pressures from administrators to bureaucratize organizational processes (e.g., formalization) and pressures from organizational members to operate and adapt more informally and flexibly. For example, Christiansen and Varnes (2007) described how numerous micro-decisions and negotiations that occur in a networked dynamic tend to preempt the decision making of managers, thus relegating manager meetings to the role of approval or non-approval. Eisenhardt and Tabrizi (1995) describe the suppressing effect of the administrative function on adaptive processes: 'The results also show that planning and rewarding for schedule attainment are ineffective ways of accelerating pace' (p. 84). Koch and Leitner (2008) found evidence for purely emergent bottom-up processes, in which employees intrinsically and without explicit orders took initiative to innovate in ways that deliberately bypassed and even ignored formal processes (e.g., financial incentive systems, suggestion schemes, patent rules), often keeping these activities secret until they were mature enough to be presented to management. Osborn and Marion (2009) found that, in alliances, administrative leadership in the form of transformational leadership was useful for returning profit to the mother institution but dysfunctional for innovation within the alliance itself. Similar findings were reported by Martin and Eisenhardt (2010).

To address the dynamic tension between administrative and adaptive functions, complexity leadership theory introduces a third leadership function: enabling leadership (Uhl-Bien & Marion, 2009; Uhl-Bien et al., 2007). Enabling leadership operates in the interface, the dynamic tension, between the administrative and adaptive functions. It recognizes both needs of the organization as legitimate, so it works to 'loosen up the organization—stimulating innovation, creativity and responsiveness and learn[ing] to manage continuous adaptation to change—without losing strategic focus or spinning out of control' (Dess & Picken, 2000, p. 19).

Enabling leadership does this in two ways. First, it enables adaptive climates and conditions conducive to complexity dynamics (Uhl-Bien & Marion, 2009; Uhl-Bien et al., 2007). Adaptive climates create relational dynamics characterized by rich interaction, interconnectivity, and information flow (cf. Anderson, Issel, & McDaniel, 2003; Lichtenstein & Plowman, 2009; Plowman, Solansky, et al., 2007; Regine & Lewin, 2000). For example, adaptive climates are characterized by such things as empowerment, trust, psychological safety, networking, and rewards for collaboration and creativity that allow for members to openly share, disagree, and conflict over ideas and perspectives (cf. Edmondson, 1999; Heifetz & Laurie, 2001). They see conflict not as destructive, but as the 'fuel that drives system growth and enables learning and adaptive behaviors, which make innovation possible' (Andrade, Plowman, & Duchon, 2008, p. 24). Adaptive climates provide resources (time, budget, expertise, heterogeneity) and space (physical layout, location; Barry & Price, 2004; Thomke & Nimgade, 2007) that encourage complexity dynamics (e.g., adaptive tension, conflicting constraints, aggregation). This type of enabling leadership recognizes the value of highly adaptive leaders and enables them by allowing latitude, resources, protection, and sponsorship. Moreover, it protects adaptive dynamics from the stifling and suppressing elements of administrative leadership and bureaucracy.

Secondly, enabling leadership loosens up the administrative structures and systems to help adaptive leadership advance and champion innovative outcomes into the formal system. When adaptive outcomes emerge they need to be incorporated into the system to generate business results. Enabling leadership helps break down barriers that might shut out adaptive initiatives along the way or inhibit them from getting heard by the right audience. They do this by clearing hurdles, providing protection, and opening administrative channels. Enabling leaders also provide cover for adaptive initiatives (e.g., high-level sponsorship), help adaptive leaders get to the right audience, and use their authority to help the initiative gain visibility (e.g., become tags; Boal & Schultz, 2007; Hunt, Osborn, & Boal, 2009; Marion & Uhl-Bien, 2001; Plowman, Solansky, et al., 2007). For example, as found by Plowman, Solansky, et al. (2007) in their study of emergence in Mission Church, when the administrative leaders began to see the breakfasts in a new light, the Sunday morning program took on a new meaning:

> [The leader's] exact words were 'that café needs a kick in the pants' and those were his exact words and so I thought okay and once that whole transition was made from getting two pastors out of preaching to ten people at 9 o'clock and go serve the 200 who were sitting right below you, you know, that was huge. I think that was huge. . . . From that moment on when [the leader] decided to get involved. . . . that's when it really evolved. (p. 352)

Hence, complexity leadership theory (CLT) identifies three leadership functions (Uhl-Bien & Marion, 2009; Uhl-Bien et al., 2007). CLT proposes that adaptability occurs in the adaptive function; the adaptive function generates and advances adaptive outcomes (e.g., product innovation, process innovation, learning) for the firm. These adaptive outcomes are converted into business results by the administrative function. Because these two functions operate in dynamic tension, enabling leadership works in the interface of adaptive and administrative to maintain appropriate entanglement between these functions (Uhl-Bien & Marion, 2009; Uhl-Bien et al., 2007).

Complexity Dynamics and Emergence

A key contribution of complexity to leadership research is the study of interactive dynamics and emergence. Contrary to conventional leadership research, which largely examines individuals, absent context or process (Osborn, Hunt, & Jauch, 2002), the essence of CLT is that leadership is generated in the context of richly networked interactions. *Complexity is at its core a theory of interactive dynamics and emergence.* While complexity leadership certainly acknowledges individuals with respect to leadership *functions* (not styles, e.g., individuals can engage in one or more functions), in CLT leadership functions are considered in terms of how they interact with complexity dynamics. Thus, CLT is a pure contextual theory of leadership (Osborn et al., 2002): it sees leadership as embedded in context.

Although CLT is consistent with social construction views of leadership (Fairhurst & Grant, 2010), it adopts a different focus. Instead of examining socioemotional processes (e.g., meaning-making, trust, power), it seeks to identify social mechanisms (Hedström & Swedberg, 1998) associated with complexity dynamics—CLT examines complexity dynamics as 'social mechanisms' (Hedström & Swedberg, 1998) that arise when humans interact under complexity conditions (Uhl-Bien et al., 2007). In complexity, social mechanisms are not variables; they are not individual-level constructs, but dynamic, nonlinear processes. They are predictable in a *non-linear* sense—in their process but not in their outcomes (Uhl-Bien & Marion, 2009).

Complexity dynamics are the force behind emergence in complexity theory. Emergence occurs when 'system-level order spontaneously arises from the action and repeated interaction of lower level system components without intervention by a central component' (Chiles, Meyer, & Hench, 2004, p. 502; see also Lichtenstein, 2000; Plowman, Baker, et al., 2007). Emergence describes a situation in which order does not result from imposition of an overall plan by a central authority, but from the action of interdependent agents purposefully pursuing individual plans based on local knowledge and continuously adapting to feedback about the actions of others (Chiles et al., 2004; Hayek, 1988; Stacey, 1995; Tsoukas & Chia, 2002).

Emergence dynamics include social mechanisms such as conflicting constraints, correlation, and amplification (Lichtenstein & Plowman, 2009; Marion & Uhl-Bien, 2003; Plowman, Solansky, et al., 2007; Uhl-Bien et al., 2007). Conflicting constraints is an initiating mechanism that helps foster generation of new ideas and initial adaptations. It occurs under conditions of interdependence when interacting agents, brought together by common need, must work through adaptive tension generated by heterogeneous perspectives to produce an adaptive response (e.g., an idea for doing something differently, a change in process, a variation from standard procedure; see also Marion & Uhl-Bien, 2001).

Correlation and amplification are aggregation mechanisms. Correlation occurs when interacting agents compromise a measure (but not all) of their individual need preferences to the needs of others and the emerging alliance (Marion & Uhl-Bien, 2001). Marion and Uhl-Bien (2003) found correlation dynamics occurring in training camps in al-Qaeda, where nationalistic differences were set aside in pursuit of common goals. Plowman, Solansky, et al. (2007) found in their case study of Mission Church that correlation was fostered by church leaders who used common language to foster meaning, collective action, and organizational identity among church members and staff.

Amplification occurs when incipient networks that formed to generate a creative or adaptive endeavor expand to include formal and informal supporters. Formal supporters may include organizational structures that will play roles in advancing the idea, such as marketing, legal, branding departments. Informal support may include groups whose own ideas can benefit from alliance or who can piggyback on the original idea. Lichtenstein and Plowman (2009) argue that leaders foster amplification by allowing experiments, encouraging rich interactions, and supporting collective action (see also Lichtenstein, 2000). Chiles et al. (2004) examined the development of Branson, Missouri, into the musical giant it has become. They found that positive feedback processes enhanced an amplification process that helped account for the rapid development of that town. Plowman et al. (2007) studied radical change in a declining, inner-city church, and found that small changes occurred to amplify the actions of an emergent change. Tsoukas and Chia (2002) observed that recursive feedback tended to amplify small ideas into large ones.

Learning is a by-product outcome of these complexity dynamics. Learning occurs when ideas collide, merge, diverge, elaborate in sets, or are extinguished. It emerges from the interaction of ideas, tasks, information, resources, beliefs, worldviews, visions, and adaptive agents. According to Fonseca (2002), knowledge emerges as individuals and social settings interact to create meaning. Schreiber, Marion, Uhl-Bien, and Carley (2006) simulated the capacity of a system to learn, and found that moderate levels of coupling plus moderately demanding vision produced better learning than did low coupling and vision or high coupling and vision. Allen (2001) argued for what he called the fundamental importance of microdiversity in generating learning within a group.

A different perspective of emergence is offered by Goldstein (2007), who argues that bottom-up self-organization cannot occur without significant enabling and constraining factors (e.g., managerial influence). He describes emergence from the standpoint of *self-transcending constructions*, in which pre-existing order is transformed into emergent order. From this perspective, emergent order does not appear 'out of the blue' (i.e., order is not free, Goldstein, 2007; see also Osborn & Hunt, 2007). It comes from a continuous build-up of structures along with an ongoing shifting and merging of structures with one another to generate new structures. It is not self-organizing in a pure sense, but rather emergent organizing in the contexts of already-existing structures (cf. Uhl-Bien & Marion, 2009). As described by Goldstein (2007), the leader's role in such contexts is to 'recognize, identify, foster, sift, provide, shape and constrain resources of order to be used for emergent modifications' (p. 91).

Goldstein's perspective is consistent with Hunt, Osborn, and Boal's (2009) complexity model of strategic leadership, which emphasizes managers' roles in patterning of attention and network development. These processes are proposed to stimulate social construction to create new information and knowledge from the dialogue and discussion of all participants. They may also influence complexity dynamics of N, K, P, and C: 'new individuals within the system may be included (a change of N), new combinations of interaction may be fostered (a change in K), new schema may emerge (a change in P), and new connections with those traditionally outside the system may be made (a change in C)' (Hunt et al., 2009, p. 514 see also Kauffman, 1995; Marion, 1999; Osborn & Hunt, 2007; Schneider & Somers, 2006).

Support for these dynamics is offered by Osborn and Marion (2009), who found that leaders who engaged in attention-patterning behaviors, consolidated the interactive dynamics of the groups (e.g., Goldstein's K and P), thus enhancing creativity. Moreover, consistent with pattern recognition, Plowman et al. (2007) found that leaders interpret adaptations as they began to accumulate and skillfully used language by giving meaning to emergent changes and drawing attention to the pattern that was forming.

In addition to the perspectives above, Cunha and Cunha (2006) offer a complexity view of strategic management. Similar to Uhl-Bien et al.'s (2007) entangled adaptive and administrative functions, they suggest that a complexity theory of strategy involves a combination of freedom with a clear organizational infrastructure of strategy, design, and process that allows strategic improvisation to flourish. From this perspective, complexity leaders manage to achieve a 'paradoxical state' of ample freedom (of employees) and strong control (provided by clear strategic direction):

> Through improvisation and simple rules, organizational members become empowered to make decisions, and strategy takes the form of strategic decision making at many organizational levels, in the context of an enabling organizational design. (p. 844)

Finally, Goldstein, Hazy, and Lichtenstein (2010) suggest that truly adaptable organizations are those in which leaders (i.e., managers) create 'ecologies of innovation' by encouraging and supporting experiments in novelty and building new organizational pathways that allow these experiments to materialize into novel offerings and improvements. They present a framework for leadership to help spawn emergence that comes about through a recognition, amplification, and dissemination of seeds of innovation that come from micro-level diversity or experiments in novelty. As they describe, a primary objective of generative leadership (cf. Surie & Hazy, 2006) in facilitating emergence is fostering and amplifying novelty generation within an ecology of innovation.

In sum, complexity leadership theory is a process theory of leadership that seeks to understand the complexity dynamics comprising the social mechanisms of emergence in organizations. It assumes that adaptive leadership is embedded in context and generated in 'the space between' (Bradbury & Lichtenstein, 2005): it arises when interacting agents operating under conditions of complexity generate adaptive responses in organizations. These responses emerge when adaptive leadership and complexity dynamics work to generate innovation, adaptability, and learning for the firm. Complexity dynamics are social mechanisms associated with generation of new ideas (e.g., conflicting constraints) and flow of these ideas within the organization (e.g., correlation, amplification). Managers (i.e., enabling leaders) can help foster these dynamics by enabling complexity conditions and dynamics and supporting adaptive leadership processes.

Organizations that operate in accordance with complexity leadership are characterized by rich adaptive functions producing adaptive leadership and complexity dynamics, and flexible administrative functions (administrative leadership) that capitalize on these dynamics to produce strong business results for the firm. In such organizations, strategic leadership is not restricted to actions of those at the top, but emerges from the actions and interactions of individuals as they make adaptations in local contexts throughout the organization (Tsoukas & Chia, 2002).

Conclusions

The field of complexity leadership is still quite young. Borrowing again from Hunt and Dodge (2000), complexity leadership approaches are clearly in the Introduction Elaboration stage of the evolution of concepts (Reichers & Schneider, 1990). In this stage, scholars attempt to legitimize the concept with books and articles to educate people about the topic. They also offer preliminary findings to provide evidence of the concept as a real phenomenon (Hunt & Dodge, 2000). From the books and articles that have appeared in the last decade we can see evidence of both of these—education about the concept (e.g., Hazy et al., 2007; Stacey et al., 2000; Uhl-Bien & Marion, 2008) and preliminary findings to support its legitimacy (e.g., Lichtenstein & Plowman, 2009; Martin & Eisenhardt, 2010; Plowman, Baker, et al., 2007; Plowman, Solansky, et al., 2007).

Complexity leadership scholars now need to engage in programmatic empirical research. Much of this work is already under way, and we expect to see a variety of empirical studies appearing in the literature in the next five years. Given that the ontology of complexity is closer to critical realism (Goldspink & Kay, 2004; Reed, 2009) than the logical positivism of conventional leadership theories (e.g., transformational leadership, LMX implicit leadership theories),

we expect that most of this research will not use traditional survey methodologies but instead more qualitative and agent-based modeling approaches, including grounded theory, rigorous case studies (e.g., Chiles et al., 2004; Plowman, Baker, et al., 2007), dynamic network analysis (Carley, 1992, 1997; Carley & Hill, 2001; Uzzi & Spiro, 2005), simulation and modeling (Davis, Eisenhardt, & Bingham, 2007; Harrison, Lin, Carroll, & Carley, 2007), and network studies (Kilduff, Crossland, & Tsai, 2007).

Moreover, the study of complexity dynamics will adopt more of a process than a variance theory approach (Mohr, 1982) consistent with mechanism-based theorizing (Davis & Marquis, 2005). As described by Chiles et al. (2004, p. 502):

> Unlike traditional variance theory, which uses variation in a small set of well-defined independent variables to explain variance in a dependent variable and to predict specific outcomes of simple phenomena, process theory calls for a high level of abstraction, predicts how general patterns of change will unfold, and develops post hoc explanations of a sequence of events over time by telling a story about how or why a phenomenon evolved from the temporal ordering and interaction of myriad events.

Using process theory and mechanism-based theorizing, complexity leadership scholars can investigate complexity dynamics that comprise mechanisms of emergence—dynamics such as conflicting constraints, correlation, amplification, etc. Complexity leadership scholars should also investigate the conditions under which these dynamics occur. According to complexity theory, these conditions will be generated in dis-equilibrium (e.g., far-from-equilibrium, edge of chaos) (Lichtenstein & Plowman, 2009) and fostered by heterogeneity, interdependence, dynamic interaction, and adaptive tension (Uhl-Bien & Marion, 2009).

Complexity leadership scholars also need to investigate complexity leadership functions. For example, as described by Stacey (1995), research is needed to identify how leaders affect and are affected by the informal networks of which they are a part, as well as how leaders encourage these networks to engage in complexity dynamics. We also need to examine adaptive leadership not as an individual behavior but as a collective leadership process, and enabling leadership as a function distinct from empowerment. Moreover, a complexity theory of strategy suggests that rather than focusing on strategic leadership as the behaviors of those at the top, we must explore strategy as emergent within the organization and identify the enabling organizational designs that foster it (Cunha & Cunha, 2006; Stacey, 1995).

The findings of MacLean and colleagues (Houchin & MacLean, 2005; MacIntosh, MacLean, & Burns, 2007; MacLean & MacIntosh, 2002) suggest important areas for future research. First, the findings reported in MacIntosh et al. (2007) that only two of 25 organizations they studied achieved levels of fluidity, innovation, and performance consistent with edge of chaos states, indicates that maintaining organizations in adaptive states may be one of the greatest challenges faced in organizations today. We believe this indicates all the more reason to generate greater understanding of how organizations can engage in complexity leadership practices that help them overcome pressures to return to equilibrium and instead act in ways that enable adaptive states. However, this recommendation comes with a caution. MacIntosh et al.'s (2007) findings that managers' attempts to generate disequilibrium in organizations used 'unhealthy' organizational practices (e.g., rapid job rotation, high performance demands, circulating organizational fictions such as rumor and counter-rumor) indicate that complexity leadership scholars need to be careful that managerial actions used to generate 'edge of chaos' conditions do not result in deteriorating health outcomes for organizational members.

In conclusion, as demonstrated by this review, complexity leadership theory offers a rich and rigorous theoretical framework that identifies important new directions for leadership research. It is situated in the dynamic organizational paradigm investigating firms that are 'continuously adaptive' (cf. Eisenhardt & Tabrizi, 1995). CLT suggests that adaptive states are those poised at the edge or chaos

between order and disorder. Maintaining these states requires constant managerial vigilance to avoid slipping into pure chaos or pure structure.

A critical implication of CLT is this: complexity leadership theory recognizes that although organizations are bureaucracies, they do not have to be *bureaucratic*. According to complexity leadership, a key role of managers is to facilitate, guide, and set the boundary conditions in which successful emergence (e.g., self-organization) can take place and be effectively entangled with organizational systems. A key role of adaptive leadership is to engage with complexity dynamics to generate and advance adaptive outcomes for the firm.

Although complexity approaches represents a sharp break from orthodox perspectives by adopting ontological assumptions rooted in dynamic tension, emergent novelty, perpetual disequilibrium, and increasing heterogeneity, they do not render past paradigms obsolete—instead, they go a step beyond these paradigms while remaining complementary to them (Chiles et al., 2004). The same is true of complexity leadership theory. By focusing on the entangled nature of administrative and adaptive leadership functions, and their interactions with the dynamics of complexity and emergence in organizations, complexity leadership offers an exciting advancement to leadership theory while adding new pieces to help fill in the complex puzzle of leadership in organizations and social systems.

References

Allen, P. M. (2001). A complex systems approach to learning in adaptive networks. *International Journal of Innovation Management, 5*(2), 149–180.

Anderson, P. (1999). Complexity theory and organization science. *Organization Science, 10*(3), 216–232.

Anderson, R. A., Issel, L., & McDaniel, R. (2003). Nursing homes as complex adaptive systems: relationship between management practice and resident outcomes. *Nursing Research, 52*(1), 12–21.

Andrade, L., Plowman, D., & Duchon, D. (2008). Getting past conflict resolution: a complexity view of conflict. *Emergence: Complexity and Organization (E:CO), 10*(1), 23–28.

Barnard, C. I. (1938). *The functions of the executive.* Cambridge, MA: Harvard University Press.

Barry, H., & Price, I. (2004). Quantifying the complex adaptive workplace. *Facilities, 22*(1), 8–18.

Boal, K., & Hooijberg, R. (2001). Strategic leadership research: moving on. *The Leadership Quarterly, 11*(4), 515–549.

Boal, K., & Schultz, P. (2007). Storytelling, time, and evolution: the role of strategic leadership in complex adaptive systems. *The Leadership Quarterly, 18*(4), 411–428.

Boisot, M., & Child, J. (1999). Organizations as adaptive systems in complex environments: the case of China. *Organization Science, 10*(3), 237–252.

Bradbury, H., & Lichtenstein, B. M. B. (2005). Relationality in organizational research: Exploring the space between. *Organization Science, 11*(5), 551–564.

Brown, S., & Eisenhardt, K. (1995b). Product innovation as core capability: The art of dynamic adaptation. Working paper, Department of Industrial Engineering and Engineering Management, Stanford University.

Brown, S. L., & Eisenhardt, K. M. (1997). The art of continuous change: linking complexity theory and time-paced evolution in relentlessly shifting organizations. *Administration Science Quarterly, 42*(1), 1–34.

Brown, S. L., & Eisenhardt, K. M. (1998). *Competing on the edge: strategy as structured chaos.* Boston: Harvard Business School Press.

Browning, L. D., Beyer, J. M., & Stetler, J. C. (1995). Building cooperation in a competitive industry: Sematech and the semiconductor industry. *Academy of Management Journal, 38*(1), 113–151.

Burns, T., & Stalker, G. M. (1961). *The management of innovation.* New York: Barnes and Noble.

Carley, K. (1992). Organizational learning and personnel turnover. *Organizational Science, 3*, 20–46.

Carley, K. (1997). Organizational adaptation. *Annals of Operations Research, 75*, 25–47.

Carley, K., & Hill, V. (2001). Structural change and learning within organizations. In A. Lomi & E. R. Larsen (eds), *Dynamics of organizational societies.* Cambridge, MA: AAAI/MIT Press, pp. 63–92.

Chiles, T. H., Meyer, A. D., & Hench, T. J. (2004). Organizational emergence: the origin and transformation of Branson, Missouri's musical theaters. *Organization Science, 15*(5), 499–519.

Christiansen, J. K., & Varnes, C. J. (2007). Making decisions on innovation: meetings or networks? *Creativity & Innovation Management, 16*(3), 282–298.

Cilliers, P. (1998). *Complexity and postmodernism: understanding complex systems.* London: Routledge.

Cunha, M. P., & Cunha, J. V. (2006). Towards a complexity theory of strategy. *Management Decision, 44*(7), 839–850.

Davis, G. F., & Marquis, C. (2005). Prospects for organization theory in the early twenty-first century: institutional fields and mechanisms. *Organization Science, 16*(4), 332–343.

Davis, J. P., Eisenhardt, K. M., & Bingham, C. (2007). Developing theory through simulation methods. *Academy of Management Review, 32*(2), 480–499.

Davis, J. P., Eisenhardt, K. M., & Bingham, C. (2009). Optimal structure, market dynamism, and the strategy of simple rules. *Administrative Science Quarterly, 54*, 413–452.

Dess, G., & Picken, J. C. (2000). Changing roles: leadership in the 21st century. *Organizational Dynamics, 28*(3), 18–34.

Edmondson, A. (1999). Psychological safety and learning behavior in work teams. *Administrative Science Quarterly, 44*(2), 350–383.

Eisenhardt, K. M., & Schoonhoven, C. B. (1990). Organizational growth: linking founding team, strategy, environment, and growth among U.S. semiconductor ventures, 1978–1988. *Administrative Science Quarterly, 35*(3), 504–529.

Eisenhardt, K. M., & Tabrizi, B. N. (1995). Accelerating adaptive processes: product innovation in the global computer industry. *Administrative Science Quarterly, 40*(1), 84–110.

Fairhurst, G., & Grant, D. (2010). The social construction of leadership: a sailing guide. *Management Communication Quarterly, 24*(2), 171–210.

Follett, M. P. (1924). *Creative experience.* New York: Longmans Green.

Fonseca, J. (2002). *Complexity and innovation in organizations.* London: Routledge.

Galbraith, J. R. (1973). *Designing complex organizations.* Reading, MA: Addison Wesley.

Galunic, D. C., & Eisenhardt, K. M. (2001). Architectural innovation and modular corporate forms. *Academy of Management Journal, 44*(6), 1229–1249.

Gleick, J. (1987). *Chaos: making a new science.* New York: Viking.

Goldspink, C., & Kay, R. (2004). Bridging the micro–macro divide: a new basis for social science. *Human Relations, 57*(5), 597–618.

Goldstein, J. (2007). A new model of emergence and its leadership implications. In J. Hazy, J. Goldstein, & B. Lichtenstein (eds), *Complex systems leadership theory.* Mansfield, MA: ISCE Publishing.

Goldstein, J., Hazy, J., & Lichtenstein, B. (2010). *Complexity and the nexus of leadership: Leveraging nonlinear science to create ecologies of innovation*. Englewood Cliffs, NJ: Palgrave Macmillan.

Gronn, P. (2002). Distributed leadership as a unit of analysis. *The Leadership Quarterly, 13*(4), 423–451.

Hales, C. (2002). 'Bureaucracy-lite' and continuities in managerial work. *British Journal of Management, 13*, 51–66.

Hamel, G. (2009). Moon shots for management. *Harvard Business Review*, February, 91–98.

Harrison, J. R., Lin, Z., Carroll, G. R., & Carley, K. M. (2007). Simulation modeling in organizational and management research. *Academy of Management Review, 32*(4), 1229– 1245.

Hayek, F. A. (1988). *The fatal conceit*. London: Routledge.

Hazy, J. K. (2006). Measuring leadership effectiveness in complex socio-technical systems. *Emergence: Complexity and Organization (E:CO), 8*(3), 58–77.

Hazy, J., Goldstein, J., & Lichtenstein, B. (2007). *Toward a theory of leadership in complex systems*. Mansfield, MA: ISCE Publishing Company.

Heckscher, C. (1994). Defining the post-bureaucratic type. In C. Heckscher & A. Donnellon (Eds.), *The post-bureaucratic organization: New perspectives on organizational change*. Thousand Oaks, CA: Sage, pp. 14–62.

Hedström, P., & Swedberg, R. (1998). *Social mechanisms: an analytical approach to social theory*. Cambridge: Cambridge University Press.

Heifetz, R. A. (1994). *Leadership without easy answers*. Cambridge, MA: Harvard University Press.

Heifetz, R. A., & Laurie, D. L. (2001). The work of leadership. *Harvard Business Review, 79*(11), 131–141.

Hosking, D. M. (2007). Not leaders, not followers: A post-modern discourse of leadership processes. In B. Shamir, R. Pillai, M. Bligh, & M. Uhl-Bien (eds), *Follower-centered perspectives on leadership: A tribute to the memory of James R. Meindl*. Greenwich, CT: Information Age Publishing, pp. 243–264.

Hosking, D. M., Dachler, H. P., & Gergen, K. J. (eds). (1995). *Management and organization: Relational alternatives to individualism*. Brookfield, USA: Avebury.

Houchin, K., & MacLean, D. (2005). Complexity theory and strategic change: An empirically informed critique. *British Journal of Management, 16*(2), 149–166.

Hunt, J. G., & Dodge, G. (2000). Leadership deja vu all over again. *The Leadership Quarterly, 11*, 435–458.

Hunt, J. G., Osborn, R., & Boal, K. (2009). The architecture of managerial leadership: Stimulation and channeling of organizational emergence. *The Leadership Quarterly, 20*(4), 503–516.

Jelinek, M., & Schoonhoven, M. (1990). *The Innovation Marathon*. London: Basil-Blackwell.

Johannessen, S., & Aasen, T.M.B. (2007). Exploring innovation processes from a complexity perspective. Part I: theoretical and methodological approach. *International Journal of Learning and Change, 2*(4), 420–433.

Katz, D., & Kahn, R. L. (1978). *The social psychology of organizations*, 2nd ed. New York: John Wiley and Sons.

Kauffman, S. (1993). *Origins of order: Self-organization and selection in evolution*. Oxford: Oxford University Press.

Kauffman, S. A. (1993). *The origins of order*. New York: Oxford University Press.

Kauffman, S. A. (1995). *At home in the universe: The search for the laws of self-organization and complexity*. New York: Oxford University Press.

Kilduff, M., Crossland, C., & Tsai, W. (2007). Pathways of opportunity in dynamic organizational networks. In M. Uhl-Bien & R. Marion (Eds.), *Complexity leadership, part 1*, Vol. 5. Charlotte, NC: Information Age Publishing, pp. 83–100.

Koch, R., & Leitner, K. (2008). The dynamics and functions of self-organization in the fuzzy front end: Empirical evidence from the Austrian semiconductor industry. *Creativity and Innovation Management, 17*(3), 216–226.

Lawrence, P. R., & Lorsch, J. W. (1967). *Organization and environment*. Cambridge, MA: Harvard University Press.

Lewin, A. (1999). *Complexity: life at the edge of chaos*, 2nd ed. Chicago: University of Chicago Press.

Lichtenstein, B. (2000). Emergence as a process of self-organizing: New assumptions and insights from the study of nonlinear dynamic systems. *Journal of Organizational Change Management, 13*, 526–544.

Lichtenstein, B., & Plowman, D. (2009). The leadership of emergence: A complex systems leadership theory of emergence at successive organizational levels. *The Leadership Quarterly, 20*(4), 617–630.

MacIntosh, R., MacLean, D., & Burns, H. (2007). Health in organization: Towards a process-based view. *Journal of Management Studies, 44*(2), 206–221.

McKelvey, B. (2008). Emergent strategy via complexity leadership: Using complexity science and adaptive tension to build distributed intelligence. In M. Uhl-Bien &

R. Marion (Eds.), *Complexity leadership, part 1: conceptual foundations* Charlotte, NC: Information Age Publishing, pp. 225–268.

MacLean, D., & MacIntosh, R. (2002). One process, two audiences: On the challenges of management research. *European Management Journal, 20*, 383–92.

Mainzer, K. (1997). *Thinking in complexity,* 3rd edn. New York: Springer-Verlag.

Marion, R. (1999). *The edge of organization: chaos and complexity theories of formal social organizations.* Newbury Park, CA: Sage.

Marion, R., & Uhl-Bien, M. (2001). Leadership in complex organizations. *The Leadership Quarterly, 12,* 389–418.

Marion, R., & Uhl-Bien, M. (2003). Complexity theory and al-Qaeda: examining complex leadership. *Emergence: A Journal of Complexity Issues in Organizations and Management, 5,* 56–78.

Martin, J. A., & Eisenhardt, K. (2010). Rewiring: cross-business-unit collaborations in multibusiness organizations. *Academy of Management Journal, 53*(2), 265–301.

Mead, G. H. (1934). *Mind, self, and society.* Chicago: University of Chicago Press.

Meyer, A., Gaba, V., & Colwell, K. (2005). Organizing far from equilibrium. *Organization Science, 16*(5), 456–473.

Mohr, L. B. (1982). *Explaining organizational behavior.* San Francisco: Jossey-Bass.

Osborn, R., & Hunt, J. G. (2007). Leadership and the choice of order: Complexity and hierarchical perspectives near the edge of chaos. *The Leadership Quarterly, 18*(4), 319–340.

Osborn, R., Hunt, J. G., & Jauch, L. R. (2002). Toward a contextual theory of leadership. *The Leadership Quarterly, 13*(6), 797.

Osborn, R., & Marion, R. (2009). Contextual leadership, transformational leadership and the performance of international innovation seeking alliances. *The Leadership Quarterly, 20*(2), 191–206.

Pearce, C. L., & Conger, J. A. (2003). *Shared leadership: reframing the hows and whys of leadership.* Thousand Oaks, CA: Sage.

Pettigrew, A. M., Whittington, R., Melin, L., Sanchez-Runda, C., van den Bosch, F., Ruigrok, W., & Numagami, T. (2003). *Innovative forms of organizing.* London: Sage.

Plowman, D., & Duchon, D. (2008). Dispelling the myths about leadership: From cybernetics to emergence. In M. Uhl-Bien & R. Marion (eds), *Complexity leadership, part 1: conceptual foundations.* Charlotte, NC: Information Age Publishing, pp. 129–154.

Plowman, D., Solansky, S., Beck, T., Baker, L., Kulkarni, M., & Travis, D. (2007). The role of leadership in emergent, self-organization. *The Leadership Quarterly, 18,* 341–356.

Plowman, D. A., Baker, L. T., Beck, T. E., Kulkarni, M., Solansky, S. T., & Travis, D. V. (2007). Radical change accidentally: The emergence and amplification of small change. *Academy of Management Journal, 50*(3), 515–543.

Reed, M.I. (2009). Critical realism: Philosophy, method or philosophy in search of a method? In A. Bryman and D. Buchanan (Eds.), *The Sage handbook of organizational research methods.* London: Sage, pp. 430–448.

Regine, B., & Lewin, R. (2000). Leading at the edge: how leaders influence complex systems. *Emergence: A Journal of Complexity Issues in Organizations and Management, 2*(2), 5–23.

Reichers, A. E., & Schneider, B. (1990). Climate and culture: an evolution of constructs. In B. Schneider (Ed.), *Organizational climate and culture.* San Francisco: Jossey-Bass, pp. 5–39.

Roethlisberger, F. J., & Dickson, W. J. (1939). *Management and the worker.* Cambridge, MA: Harvard University Press.

Schneider, M., & Somers, M. (2006). Organizations as complex adaptive systems: Implications of complexity theory for leadership research. *The Leadership Quarterly 17*(4), 351–365.

Schreiber, C., Marion, R., Uhl-Bien, M., & Carley, K. (2006). Multi-agent based simulation of a model of complexity leadership. Paper presented at the International Conference on Complex Systems, Boston.

Scott, W. R. (1987). *Organizations: rational, natural, and open systems,* 2nd ed. Englewood Cliffs, NJ: Prentice Hall.

Selznick, P. (1949). *TVA and the grass roots.* Berkeley: University of California Press.

Stacey, R. D. (1995). The science of complexity: An alternative perspective for strategic change processes. *Strategic Management Journal, 16*(6), 477–495.

Stacey, R. D. (1996). *Complexity and creativity in organizations.* San Francisco: Berrett-Koehler.

Stacey, R. D. (2000). The emergence of knowledge in organizations. *Emergence, 2*(4), 23–39.

Stacey, R. D. (2001a). What can it mean to say that the individual is social through and through? *Group Analysis, 34,* 457–471.

Stacey, R. D. (2001b). *Complex responsive processes in organizations: Learning and knowledge creation.* London: Routledge.

Stacey, R. D., & Griffin, R. W. (2008). What contribution can insights from the complexity sciences make to the theory and practice of development management? *Journal of International Development, 20*(6), 804–820.

Stacey, R. D., Griffin, D., & Shaw, P. (2000). *Complexity and management: Fad or radical challenge to systems thinking*. London: Routledge.

Streatfield, P. J. (2001). *The paradox of control in organizations*. London: Routledge.

Surie, G., & Hazy, J. (2006). Generative leadership: Nurturing innovation in complex systems. *Emergence: Complexity and Organization, 8*(4), 13–26.

Thomke, S., & Nimgade, A. (2007). *Ideo product development. Harvard Business School case (9-600-143)*. Boston: Harvard Business School Publishing.

Tsoukas, H., & Chia, R. (2002). On organizational becoming: Rethinking organizational change. *Organization Science, 13*(5), 567–582.

Uhl-Bien, M. (2006). Relational leadership theory: Exploring the social processes of leadership and organizing. *The Leadership Quarterly, 17*, 654–676.

Uhl-Bien, M., & Marion, R. (2008). *Complexity leadership, part 1: Conceptual foundations*. Charlotte, NC: Information Age Publishing.

Uhl-Bien, M., & Marion, R. (2009). Complexity leadership in bureaucratic forms of organizing: A meso model. *The Leadership Quarterly, 20*, 631–650.

Uhl-Bien, M., Marion, R., & McKelvey, B. (2007). Complexity leadership theory: Shifting leadership from the industrial age to the knowledge era. *The Leadership Quarterly, 18*(4), 298–318.

Uzzi, B., & Spiro, J. (2005). Collaboration and creativity: The small world problem. *American Journal of Sociology, 111*(2), 447–504.

Waldrop, M. M. (1992). *Complexity: The emerging science at the edge of order and chaos*. New York: Simon & Schuster.

Weber, M. (1947). *The theory of social and economic organization* (A. H. Henderson & T. Parsons, trans.). Glencoe, IL: Free Press.

Weick, K. E. (1993). The collapse of sensemaking in organizations: The Mann Gulch disaster. *Administrative Science Quarterly, 38*(4), 628–652.

Wheatley, M. J. (1992). *Leadership and the new science: Learning about organization from an orderly universe*. San Francisco: Berrett-Koehler.

Wheatley, M. J. (1999). *Leadership and the new science*, 2nd ed. San Francisco: Berrett-Koehler.

CHAPTER 16

Leading Global Teams[1]

Lena Zander[2]
Uppsala University

Audra I. Mockaitis
Monash University

Christina L. Butler
Kingston University

1. Introduction

As organizations become more diverse and ever new forms of organizing emerge, working in global teams is fast becoming the rule rather than the exception. Multinational teams of all shapes and sizes have been called the 'heart' of globalization (Snow, Snell, Canney Davision, & Hambrick, 1996) and are routinely used to cope with our increasingly competitive, complex and culturally diverse 21st century world (DiStefano & Maznevski, 2000; Raviin, Thomas, & Ilsev, 2000). In the midst of technological advances of the last decade, global virtual teams, defined as nationally, geographically, and culturally diverse groups that communicate almost exclusively through electronic media (Jarvenpaa & Leidner, 1999), rose to the fore of organizational innovations (Townsend, DeMarie, & Hendrickson,

1998). Team members work across temporal and spatial boundaries, most often in the absence of face-to-face interaction, to coordinate their activities toward the attainment of common goals from different locations around the globe. Global virtual teams and collocated teams came to be viewed as end poles on a continuum with most global teams ending up somewhere in between based on their degree of face-to-face interaction (Kirkman, Rosen, Tesluk, & Gibson, 2004). Yet, it seems that these new organizational forms are surfacing more quickly than scholars are able to study them; research on global and virtual team leadership, in particular, is lagging behind (Malhotra, Majchrzak, & Rosen, 2007; Zigurs, 2002). It is our overall objective to increase the knowledge about leading global teams.

Global teams, as defined by Maloney and Zellmer-Bruhn (2006), differ from other teams on the following

---

two characteristics: (1) a globally dispersed work environment, and (2) heterogeneity on multiple dimensions. We have chosen to focus specifically on national cultural heterogeneity, a salient characteristic of global teams, as nationality has been found to override other demographic and tenure-based categorizations in such teams (Butler, 2006; Earley & Mosakowski, 2000) and with respect to leadership (Zander & Romani, 2004). Our knowledge about leading global teams is still limited (Davis & Bryant, 2003; Joshi & Lazarova, 2005), but since teams are multicultural in composition and virtual in action they stand at the crossroads of two literature streams—multicultural team research and virtual team research (Steers, Sanchez-Runde, & Nardon, 2010).

There is growing attention devoted to studying virtual teams, and although progress has been made with respect to comparing collocated and virtual teams, the literature does not to any large extent distinguish between single and multi-country types of virtual teams. Much of the work is still conceptual or purely practitioner oriented. There is a limited number of empirical studies on leading virtual teams in general (Malhotra et al., 2007; Zigurs, 2002), and fewer still that are cross-cultural (Davis & Bryant, 2003; Joshi & Lazarova, 2005). With regard to research on multicultural teams, we find that the accumulation of knowledge on the processes and outcomes of multicultural teams is prolific (Stahl, Maznevski, Voigt, & Jonsen, 2010). The literature about leading multicultural teams is less extensive (Zander & Butler, 2010), but it is expanding as is our knowledge about leading virtual teams. We will demonstrate this when we discuss leadership competences, styles, strategies and modes as well as recent cultural research about the team leader such as biculturalism, global mindsets and cultural intelligence.

In this article, we aim to identify key emerging themes and directions in which global team leadership is heading and provide some suggestions for future research. Our review of the trends will center on the issues that have emerged in recent years. We will first turn to the literature on virtual teams for an understanding of leading in a virtual context, then to the literature on multicultural teams for an insight into multicultural team leadership and finally to recent culture research to add to our knowledge of

global team leaders. In contrast to the more common practice of examining leadership from only the leaders' perspective, it is our ambition to incorporate both team leaders' and members' perspectives for a more holistic and complex picture of global team leadership. Our review results in three themes for global team leadership: global leaders as boundary spanners, bridge makers and blenders; people-oriented leadership in global teams; and leveraging global team diversity. We thus ground our ideas for a future research agenda on leading global teams in emerging cutting-edge work before concluding with some reflections and managerial implications.

2. Leading Virtual Teams

The virtual context has enabled teams to complete tasks more efficiently and quickly than ever before, and access the best resources and people in locations around the globe. Not surprisingly, these positive aspects are coupled with challenges. Given the virtual context that global virtual teams (GVTs) work in, members' different cultural backgrounds, the interface of technology, and the fact that members are often not in synch because of different time zones, the role of leading virtual teams is riddled with complexity. Because GVT members often cannot see their leader, one might get the sense that virtual team leaders need to have special knowledge or qualities or display certain types of behaviors to be effective.

In their recent review, Jonsen, Maznevski, and Canney Davison (2012) highlight some of the leader challenges and virtual team aspects that have received attention in the general GVT literature. These are rather straightforward leader actions, such as maintaining communication, establishing relationships and managing conflict. In fact, much of the literature on GVTs highlights the importance of communication and trust (e.g., Aubert & Kelsey, 2003; Jarvenpaa & Leidner, 1999; Krebs, Hobman, & Bordia, 2006; Zigurs, 2002). But this is not as simple as it sounds, because GVT members often rely on team leaders to provide direction and inspiration from a distance. GVT leaders must possess excellent asynchronous communication skills, and must be especially effective in synchronous and face-to-face communication since there are often limited opportunities for such interaction (Davis & Bryant, 2003). GVT leaders should also be technologically savvy and possess an ability to match the technology to the specific requirements of the team and its tasks (e.g., rich versus lean communication media); they must be engaging, culturally sensitive and approachable, by communicating frequently with all members (Davis & Bryant, 2003; Jonsen et al., 2012; Zigurs, 2002). Although there is much literature about the challenges of working in GVTs there is very little empirical research on actually leading GVTs (Joshi & Lazarova, 2005; Jonsen et al., 2012; Malhotra et al., 2007). In the following sections we highlight some of the literature that has aimed to address this gap with respect to leader competencies and styles seen as important for GVT performance.

2.1. Leader Competencies

In GVTs "distance amplifies dysfunction" (Davis & Bryant, 2003, p. 310). To overcome the added challenges associated with distance and to prevent dysfunction, GVT leaders must possess certain competencies. Joshi and Lazarova (2005) sought answers to the question of what competencies are identified as important for leaders in multinational virtual teams. In their study of multicultural teams in a single corporation from around the globe, they compared the competencies identified by team members and leaders, as well as those considered important by team members who were collocated with and distant from their team leader. The following competencies were identified as important by a large percentage of team leaders and team members: direction and goal setting, communication, facilitating teamwork and motivating and inspiring. However, team leaders and team members differed in their views about other competencies. For example, managing cultural diversity was mentioned as important by 65% of team leaders, but only 5% of members. Empowering was mentioned only by team leaders, and mentoring and coaching and resource acquisition—only by team members.

Boundary spanning was more important for team members than leaders. Slight differences were found across countries. For example, boundary spanning was

mentioned only by Anglo country respondents (from the U.S.A. and UK/Ireland). There were generally few respondents from countries other than the U.S.A., and statistical tests were not conducted to ascertain any meaningful cross-national differences. Davis and Bryant (2003) conducted interviews with 68 global virtual team members and leaders (all managers in MNEs located in Asia and Europe) and identified several competencies that leaders of GVTs must possess including that GVT leaders must engage in boundary spanning activities.

In their study of multicultural GVTs from Europe, Mexico and the U.S.A., Kayworth and Leidner (2001–2002) found that effective GVT leaders act as mentors, are communicative and are able to manage multiple leadership roles. They are also empathetic, and possess both a task-focus and relational skills (Bell & Kozlowski, 2002; Kayworth & Leidner, 2001–2002). And, they must be able to instill a sense of community or personal connection in the team to develop trust. Knowing when to switch between a task and relationship orientation is an important skill in achieving this goal. It thus appears that there are clear ideas about the competencies needed of global virtual team leaders, due to the specific contextual factors that determine these competencies. Yet, interestingly, research has also found differences in the views of GVT members and leaders regarding the qualities that are important for leading teams to success. One quality that stands out is the leader as boundary spanner, a still emergent topic in the literature.

2.2. Leadership Styles

A number of studies have examined the effectiveness of transformational leadership in teams. In a single country study Carte, Chidambaram, and Becker (2006) found no differences between high and low performing teams regarding transformational leadership behaviors. Joshi, Lazarova, and Liao (2009) however found the opposite for multicultural geographically dispersed virtual teams. In highly geographically dispersed teams, a lack of shared context can jeopardize a shared team identity.

Inspirational leaders serve as the bridge between team members and link them with a common goal or vision. In their study, teams that were more geographically dispersed had more positive perceptions about inspirational leadership, commitment to the team and team trust (Joshi et al., 2009). Similarly Davis and Bryant (2003) found that transformational leadership had positive effects on global virtual team outcomes, whereas laissez-faire leadership and team outcomes displayed a negative relationship. As Davis and Bryant put it, the leader must lead with "both the head and the heart" (2003, p. 319).

Bell and Kozlowski (2002) argue that there is little scope for traditional leadership in GVTs, such as development and shaping of team processes, and the monitoring and management of ongoing team performance. They posit that because there is only limited face-to-face interaction in these teams, leaders need to distribute and delegate leadership functions and responsibilities to team members. Kirkman et al. (2004) demonstrate that highly empowered teams are significantly associated with higher levels of team process improvement (and customer satisfaction) than less empowered teams. To accomplish well-functioning empowered GVTs, team leaders need to provide clear directions as well as specific individual goals (Kirkman et al., 2004). Bell and Kozlowski (2002) argue that leaders should be more proactive and structuring, developing mechanisms that can become reinforced by the GVT members themselves. Team leaders can achieve this by establishing routines early in the project (Bell & Kozlowski, 2002).

Davis and Bryant (2003) concluded that self-leadership, or leadership distributed to all members of the team, is linked to GVT success or failure. Teams in which self-leadership was discouraged were less effective than teams that supported self-leadership. Teams in which flexibility meant changing leadership roles depending on the situation were more effective than teams that lacked this competence. However, a key question is whether fully distributed leadership or self-managed leadership is more effective in global virtual teams, when members are in different geographic locations and have different cultural backgrounds, or if a leader needs to act as a linchpin among members. This has not been explored in empirical studies. Muethel and Hoegl (2010) argue on theoretical grounds that

shared leadership should be effective in global virtual teams as it enhances the monitoring and influencing opportunities for members in different locations, the speed of decision-making, accountability of team members toward all others, task coordination and group cohesion. The extent to which individual team members will embrace shared leadership will be influenced and impeded by their respective countries' institutional and cultural characteristics, e.g., cultural values and norms (Muethel & Hoegl, 2010). We think testing these ideas empirically would be a promising avenue for enhancing our knowledge on GVTs.

3. Leading Multicultural Teams

We have found extensive reading on the topic of leading global multicultural teams (MCTs) of interest to practitioners (see, e.g., Brett, Behfar, & Kern, 2006; Maznevski, 2008; Miller, Fields, Kumar, & Ortiz, 2000; Steers et al., 2010). For example, Michael Miller, Ronald Fields, Ashish Kumar, and Rudy Ortiz have all been active managers of multicultural project teams and share their experiences and insights on how to tap the creative potential of multicultural project teams through leadership and creating a strategic vision (Miller et al., 2000). They also list, and vividly illustrate with examples, dos and don'ts regarding intercultural work, and conclude that "although it is impossible for any manager to know everything about all cultures and ethnic groups, it is important to learn as much as possible. The very act of expressing genuine interest in an individual and his background improves morale and understanding. This improvement translates into more effective project performance" (Miller et al., 2000, p. 22). Realizing this thoughtful lesson into practice, however, is easier said than done, as we will discuss in the following.

Brett et al. (2006) draw our attention to four cultural barriers in multicultural teams: conflicting decision-making norms, conflicting attitudes toward hierarchy, direct versus indirect communication, and trouble with language fluency and accents. The former two barriers will be addressed further below in this article. The latter two are related to communication; this is not surprising given that a sizeable portion of the multicultural team research touches on this topic in some way. Even in the smaller subsection of team leadership studies we find work where communication is in focus. For example, in the studies we reviewed, communicating vision, goals, and directions, engaging in feedback and developing routines together, avoiding communication breakdowns and steering the team on the right track stood out as important leader actions (see, e.g., Ayoko, Hartel, & Callan, 2002; Matveev & Nelson, 2004).

Steers et al. (2010, p. 265) single out "mastering intercultural communications by listening for contextual messages behind content messages" as one of the main leadership challenges for leaders of multicultural teams. Team leaders must also facilitate communication among team members, make communication norms explicit, and help build mutual understanding (Steers et al., 2010). These are essential competences for effective bridge makers acting between people within a team (we will address bridge making in more detail later in this article). Not only do team leaders differ in their communication styles, but members with different national backgrounds can also differ in their communication preferences. For example employees' preferred form and frequency of communication with their immediate manager was found to vary across countries and cultural clusters (Zander, 2005). This adds to the complexity of 'hearing' what is not being said, i.e., understanding the contextualized communication. The content may be just as difficult to grasp as when speakers are less than fluent, have unfamiliar accents or dialects. Senior managers from multinational firms interviewed by Schweiger, Atamer, and Calori (2003) were surprised to find that language challenges were much more prevalent and more difficult to overcome than they expected when working in global teams given that English was the *lingua franca* in their respective organizations.

The topic of communication challenges in global teams is far from exhausted, and language in global teams has only started to receive attention. Leaders need to possess certain competences, and possibly leadership styles, to be able to overcome such challenges. We will first focus our review on leader competences before turning to examining recent research on leadership styles in multicultural teams.

3.1. Leader Competencies

In the literature on MCTs, leadership is not often specified as crucial for team performance, although it is frequently concluded that management matters (Zander & Butler, 2010). To cast light on what competencies team leaders need to effectively lead MCTs, Hajro and Pudelko (2010) carried out 70 interviews with MCT leaders and members from five multinational firms. Interestingly they found that leadership was precisely what was perceived as critical to MCT performance. Specifically, knowledge management and transfer were reported as the most important MCT leader competence, with cross-cultural awareness following closely. As is typical of bridge makers in MCTs, team leaders play an important role in facilitating interaction between team members and resolving conflicts (Hajro & Pudelko, 2010). Bridge makers are similar to boundary spanners, although boundary spanners span boundaries between the team and various other organizational units or groups while bridge makers bridge cultural and linguistic boundaries between people within multicultural groups (Liljegren & Zander, 2011).

Not surprisingly Hajro and Pudelko (2010) emphasize that an inability to simultaneously work with people from different backgrounds together with a lack of insight into, sensitivity toward, and accommodation of different cultures are among the major reasons for MCT failure. Cross-cultural competence is essential for team leadership, and team leadership is critical for the functioning of the MCT. Beliefs as to what is the most important element of cross-cultural competence tend to vary across countries and cultures. For example, in a comparison of the perceptions of Russian and American managers, who were members of MCTs, Russians ranked a cross-cultural personality orientation (e.g., cultural empathy and interest in intercultural interaction) as most important, whereas cross-cultural skills (e.g., an understanding and clear communication of team's goals, norms and roles) were the most important to the Americans (Matveev & Milter, 2004). These results beg the immediate question of what the implications are for global team leadership if the leader is perceived as strong on only one of these, when global team members vary in their expectations, as the Russian and American respondents did in the study above.

Additionally, our review of multicultural team leadership identified that leaders are expected to possess a competence of recognizing and bridging divergent member perceptions and acceptance of leadership roles, communication skills, ways of organizing work, etc. We raise the questions of how relevant bridge making skills are in the global context, and how these can be carried out in a virtual setting with globally dispersed team members.

3.2. Leadership Styles

Transformational leadership, like charismatic leadership, has been widely studied in general but not so much in the context of MCTs (Kearney & Gebert, 2009). The positive effects of transformational leadership on outcomes such as employee motivation, satisfaction and performance (see Judge & Piccolo, 2004 for a review) were found by Kearney and Gebert (2009) in a team setting in their study of 62 R&D teams in a multinational company. They established that transformational leadership can unleash the potential in MCTs by tapping the variance and benefits provided by diversity leading to positive performance. Notably no link between transformational leadership and performance could be found in homogenous teams; there was even a detrimental effect on performance for high levels of transformational leadership (Kearney & Gebert, 2009). These are controversial findings in the light of statements that transformational leadership has been found to be the most reliable predictor of team performance (see, e.g., Schaubroeck, Lam, & Peng, 2011). In Schaubroeck et al.'s (2011) study of bank teams in Hong Kong versus in the U.S.A., they found that team members' trust in the leader was critical

for the link between transformational leadership and team performance. Interestingly, Hoffman, Bynum, Piccolo, and Sutton (2011) found that American managers' congruence with organizational values was related to a positive effect of transformational leadership on group effectiveness.

Servant leadership, which has been around since 1970 (Barbuto & Wheeler, 2006) has recently started to attract more attention and has been found to explain variance in team performance (Schaubroeck et al., 2011). Both transformational and servant leadership are people-oriented leadership styles emphasizing the importance of valuing people, listening, mentoring and empowering followers (Stone, Russell, & Patterson, 2004). Stone et al. (2004) argue that the primary difference between the two is that servant leadership focuses on the follower and the understanding of the role of the leader as being of service to the follower (Greenleaf, 1977), whereas transformational leadership focuses on the organization, specifically on building follower commitment toward organizational goals. Given this differentiation, an immediate question is whether the more interpersonal nature of servant leadership can be as successful in virtual multicultural teams as it is in collocated multicultural teams. Additionally, we also query whether trust and person-organization value congruence would have similar mediating effects when transformational leadership is used in global teams, given the culturally based differences in members' leadership preferences.

3.3. Leadership Strategies and Modes

In the face of cultural complexities, which threaten team process and outcomes yet can provide opportunities to benefit from and leverage cultural differences, team leaders opt for different cultural strategies. Based on in-depth case studies, observation, interviews and informal discussions with team leaders and members in multicultural R&D, electrical engineering and product development teams, Chevrier (2003) identified three different leadership strategies and how these were more or less successfully enacted. The first strategy is 'laissez-faire leadership'; where cross-cultural differences are neither managed nor drawn upon, but largely ignored. Instead, the leader relies on the team members' tolerance and self-control when facing culturally ambiguous or conflicting situations. When team members begin to feel frustrated, they need to release tension by talking and it is often done within their own cultural subgroup, with the high risk of cementing the already strong faultlines in their team. The second strategy involves team leaders and members in a 'cultural trial-and-error' process. Attempts to create more personal relationships among those involved are essential for this form of probing and finding ad hoc solutions for cross-cultural differences one by one. However, this pragmatic way of handling and occasionally leveraging cultural differences suffers from temporal limitations, which could reinforce polarization and negative stereotyping, instead of creating a mutually permanent functioning work environment for the team members. The third leadership strategy is based on setting up a 'common team culture', e.g., using professional or corporate cultural values or ways of organizing work as a basis. Although this has the potential to create a stable setting where cultural differences can be handled and thrive within a shared frame of norms and appropriate behaviors, the downside is that the creation often becomes a common-denominator-culture that dampens rather than encourages cultural exchange and falls short of leveraging cultural differences.

One alternative to avoiding a 'common-denominator-culture' has been proposed by Maznevski and Zander (2001), namely, combining team culture creation with individualized leadership. They argue that this combination could also defuse the power paradox, which occurs when, for example, some team members appreciate, respect and trust a leader who practices delegation of authority and empowerment, whereas these same leader behaviors are unacceptable to other team members. Because they prefer more directive or hands-on leadership, these team members can easily lose their belief in and respect for a leader who does not act in the expected way. The power paradox, in this example, embodies the two cultural barriers based on conflicting attitudes; namely with respect to hierarchy and to

decision-making norms (Brett et al., 2006). A team leader who is stuck in such a power paradox will become ineffective unless it can be resolved. Wu, Tsui, and Kinicki (2010) recently demonstrated problems with individualized leadership in single culture teams—they found that it disturbs the creation of common team norms, which are positively related to team effectiveness. It remains an empirical question whether this problem also would occur in globally dispersed virtual teams.

Chevrier (2003) suggests an alternative team leadership strategy to those she identified in her research discussed above. She bases that strategy on two assumptions: first, that multicultural team effectiveness is dependent on a deep understanding of the cultural issues at hand, and second, that such an understanding will not occur simply through team member interaction. She proposes that a cultural mediator helps team members to decipher cultural meaning systems and integrate cognitive understanding of others into action. This is another bridge making activity complementing those we briefly touched upon earlier in this article. Such a role does not necessarily have to be held by the team leader; team members could also act as cultural bridge makers and become influential in the team process, e.g., in decision-making (Liljegren & Zander, 2011).

As we have highlighted, team leadership does not necessarily have to be carried out by a single individual, the team leader, but could be seen as a set of activities that needs to be done by one or several individuals. This reasoning within contemporary leadership research was applied by Zander and Butler (2010) in their work on developing team leadership modes. They add three leadership modes to traditional single leadership. Zander and Butler (2010) use two leadership dimensions, activities (distributed versus focused) and authority (horizontal versus vertical) to characterize the four team leadership modes: single, paired, rotated, and shared leadership. The choice of leadership mode for a given team is based on the team's multicultural composition, which is analyzed in terms of faultlines and status cues (Zander & Butler, 2010). The Zander and Butler model builds on an initial fit argument. It is not proposed to be used in a static or rigid way but flexibly, in line with the dynamics of multicultural processes. The idea is that an informed choice of team leadership mode may give the multicultural team a higher probability of success and a lower probability of destructive conflict in need of later managerial intervention. Zander and Butler (2010) argue that it is possible to align and develop leadership modes in accordance with the needs of the team, as well as the strategic and operational demands of the multinational firm. How organizations do so, and which leadership strategies are most effective in culturally diverse global teams are salient topics. Specifically, examining how organizations select and apply different leadership modes in managing and leveraging diversity in order to ensure high performance of the global team would be a valuable addition to the leadership literature.

4. The Team Leader

As companies become more global and increasingly use multicultural virtual teams, employees who have the cognitive aptitude and experience to think and act 'globally' are increasingly sought after. The challenge for managers is to accurately identify these internationally minded individuals to act as global team leaders.

People are indeed being exposed to more and more cultures (Friedman & Liu, 2009; Tsui, Nifadkar, & Ou, 2007). At least three identifiable streams of research have developed around this external process. The first of these is the many-faceted construct of the 'global mindset' (e.g., Javidan, Dorfman, deLuque, & House, 2006). Global mindset is argued to be crucial for global leaders to be able influence individuals, groups and organizations that are unlike them. These global leaders may be seen to be international (e.g., Anthias, 2001) or cosmopolitan rather than bound by one, two or a few cultures. Other people seem to adapt easily and well in emotional, behavioral and cognitive terms to new cultural contexts and so display what Earley and colleagues (Earley, 2002; Earley & Ang, 2003; Earley, Murnieks, & Mosakowski, 2007) have termed cultural intelligence or CQ. Lastly, an

increasing number of people identify with two (or more) cultural identities and so may demonstrate biculturalism, a process of intrapersonal cultural diversity switching easily between two or more cultures (Bunderson & Sutcliffe, 2002; Hong, Morris, Chiu, & Benet-Martinez, 2000; LaFromboise, Coleman, & Gerton, 1993).

Global mindset is related to biculturalism and cultural intelligence (Earley et al., 2007) in that an individual can also develop and refine at least some elements of it (e.g., the cognitive competences that lead to intercultural empathy). It also differs significantly from biculturalism and cultural intelligence in that it alone includes a strategic element. Biculturalism may lead to cultural intelligence of cultures beyond those internal to the bicultural. Cultural intelligence might be understood as the cultural competence component, albeit a modified one, of global mindset. These three distinct constructs do overlap, and each may contribute in some distinct way to leading global teams.

4.1. Global Mindset and Cultural Intelligence

Global team leaders need to possess cultural competence and awareness as we have discussed earlier, but such competence is clearly not sufficient, if they are to be seen as successful by the organizations which employ them. Other factors, such as global business savvy, clearly contribute to this success as part of the bigger package. Global mindset (Hitt, Javidan, & Steers, 2007; Javidan et al., 2006; Javidan, Steers, & Hitt, 2007; Jeanett, 2000; Levy, Beechler, Taylor, & Boyacigiller, 2007; Murtha, Lenway, & Bagozzi, 1998; Perlmutter, 1969; Redding, 2007) is argued to bring competitive advantage to organizations through its dual focus on cultural competence and strategic organizational impact. Perl-mutter (1969) ground breaking work on ethno-, poly-, and geocentric orientations implicitly build on the idea of a global mindset, or in his terminology geocentricism. Until recently the construct has been ill-defined covering a wide range of factors and levels of analysis (e.g., individual skills, attitudes, and behaviors; organizational strategies, policies, practices and structures) tied to the global agenda. Levy et al. (2007) synthesize the literature to define global mindset as a multidimensional individual level "highly complex cognitive structure characterized by an openness to and articulation of multiple cultural and strategic realities on both global and local levels, and the cognitive ability to mediate and integrate across this multiplicity" (p. 27). It encompasses both cultural and strategic perspectives and draws on underlying constructs of cosmopolitanism and cognitive complexity. It is at one and the same time based in cognition, behavior and a 'way of being'. It is of interest to understand how the cultural and strategic competences encompassed by global mindset play out when leading global teams in a virtual context.

Cultural intelligence consists of meta-cognitive, cognitive, motivational, and behavioral components (Ang & Van Dyne, 2008; Ang et al., 2007; Van Dyne, Ang, & Koh, 2008). It has been shown to be a key predictor of integration in multinational teams (Flaherty, 2008), but also of international assignment effectiveness (Kim, Kirkman, & Chen, 2008), expatriate adjustment and performance (Shaffer & Miller, 2008), and task performance in culturally diverse settings (Ang et al., 2007). These are all relevant for success as a global team leader. Discussions of cultural intelligence in the leadership literature, though, remain largely conceptual (e.g., Alon & Higgins, 2005; Mannor, 2008). In one recent exception, Groves and Feyerherm (2011) tested the moderating effects of cultural diversity on leader and team performance. Data from 99 leaders and 321 of their followers with an average team size of about 4 people including the leader showed that leader cultural intelligence is a function of the leadership context. A leader's cultural intelligence contributes to team member perceptions of the performance of the leader and the team where teams are characterized by high national and ethnic diversity. As this composition is typical for global teams these findings are of interest to examine whether they also are applicable for global teams that act in a virtual context.

4.2. Biculturals and Biculturalism

Born biculturals, individuals who have two cultural backgrounds (e.g., parents from two different national cultures, or are members of an ethnic minority relative to the society's dominant majority), are often assumed to already have the ability to quickly switch frames between the two cultures as required and provide a managerial solution to bicultural work situations including teams (Brannen & Thomas, 2010). Indeed, recent experimental work has shown that Chinese-Western participants who have been primed with pictures of Chinese and Western cultural icons actually do think differently using different parts of their brains to process information depending on the prime (Ng & Han, 2009). Global team leaders do need to think differently to span boundaries and make bridges as we discussed. While it is tempting to assume that a born bicultural has the capability to do so, empirical evidence demonstrates that it is important to distinguish between someone who is 'simply' a born bicultural and someone who actually demonstrates bicultural fluency or biculturalism. Indeed Lücke and Roth (2008) develop a culture-cognitive conceptualization of biculturalism to argue that individuals who are not born biculturals can develop biculturalism also through social experiences in later life.

Friedman and Liu (2009) identify four factors that research has shown to enhance or constrain the cognitive flexibility of biculturals, whether born or learned. These factors are (1) 'need for cognitive closure', (2) assimilation strategies, (3) 'bicultural integration', and (4) lay theory of race. High 'need for cognitive closure' individuals dislike ambiguity and so are more likely than low 'need for cognitive closure' individuals to follow the cultural rules they were brought up with (Chiu, Morris, Hong, & Menon, 2000; Kruglanski, 1990). Further while some individuals may choose a 'positive' integration assimilation strategy, other may choose 'negative' separation or marginalization assimilation strategies as they acculturate (Berry, 1990; see also Bourhis, Moise, Perrault, & Senecal, 1997; Mana, Orr, & Mana 2009; Roccas & Brewer, 2002). In addition high 'bicultural integration' individuals make fewer situational attributions, implying cultural assimilation; individuals low in 'bicultural integration' make greater situational attributions, implying cultural contrast (Benet-Martinez & Haritatos, 2005). Low 'bicultural integration' results in 'mismatching' in performance appraisals (Mok, Cheng, & Morris, 2010) and pay allocation (Friedman, Liw, Chi, Hong, & Sung, 2008, as cited in Friedman & Liu, 2009) that can lead to managerial problems rather than solutions. Lastly some biculturals hold an 'essentialist' view or lay theory of race as stable and enduring. They view their two cultures, minority and majority, as separate entities. In experimental work, biculturals who hold such a view respond to majority culture primes with minority culture responses (No et al., 2008). Depending on biculturals' need for cognitive closure, application of 'positive' or 'negative' assimilation strategies, level of bicultural integration, and the absence or the presence of a 'lay theory of race', the degree of biculturalism, and the associated sought-after competence of cognitive flexibility will vary.

Some born biculturals do indeed possess amazing cognitive flexibility and behavioral adaptability in the workplace. In their journey to bicultural fluency (Bell & Nkomo, 2001) they use a wide range of techniques to achieve success. This immediately accessible cultural competence repertoire is what makes biculturals, whether born or learned, of critical interest for the leadership of global teams. Dickerson (2006) reports on the wide variety of techniques including the tapping of new social networks that Latino and black women leaders in the labor movement use to access and negotiate societal hierarchies. The 'switching techniques' of Navajo women managers (Muller, 1998) and the 'expanding' persuasive influence of American Indian managers (Warner & Grint, 2006) are examples of managers who have developed active biculturalism. These examples of non-White US leaders illustrate the organizational system constraints these individuals face and their ability to liberate themselves from these constraints while becoming and remaining successful players in mainstream organizational systems (Ospina & Foldy, 2009). The ability to liberate oneself to 'switch' and 'expand' influence, for example, will allow a bicultural, whether born or learned, in the position of a global team leader to span boundaries and bridge differences.

Mirroring the 'negative' lens of the diversity literature more generally (Shore et al., 2009), earlier work on biculturalism focused on the often negative immigrant experience in a relatively stable external context and the conclusions that a positive identity is a necessary condition for bicultural life success generally. Although we have not uncovered any empirical work on bicultural leaders of global teams, newer work on biculturalism contrasts positive with negative identities, flexibility and liberation with constraint, salience with categorization, and dynamic with stable environments. This positive focus parallels developments noted above in respect of multicultural teams and elsewhere in the organization literature (e.g., the literature on inclusion of diverse individuals (Bilimoria, Joy, & Liang, 2008; Roberson, 2006)). These contrasts match more closely with the current complex dynamic and global environment, and suggest that bicultural team leaders of global teams might more successfully leverage the positive cognitive contributions of adaptability (e.g., the boundary-spanning and bridge-making roles discussed above) while at the same time more successfully minimize cognitive constraints experienced by team members, a third role that we label 'blender' (Butler, Zander, Mockaitis, & Sutton, 2012). The success of biculturals in this newly identified role together with the two roles noted above is a topic that holds both theoretical and practical relevance worthy of future empirical inquiry.

5. Discussion—Emerging Research Themes and a Future Research Agenda

The literature on global team leadership is far from abundant, but when reviewing recent work on virtual team leadership, multicultural team leadership, and the team leader we could clearly identify three emerging themes that are highly relevant for future research on leading global teams (see Figure 16.1 for a graphical illustration of the literature review and the emerging themes).

These three emerging themes are: (1) global team leaders as boundary spanners, bridge makers, and blenders, (2) people-oriented leadership in global teams, and (3) leveraging global team diversity, which will be discussed in detail below.

5.1. Global Team Leaders as Boundary Spanners, Bridge Makers, and Blenders

As much of the research on global team leadership concentrates on the leader's competencies and challenges in leading the team, it would be valuable to consider the multiple roles of global team leaders. The first theme that surfaced is the expectation and desire for global team leaders to be engaged in *boundary spanning* activities between organizational units, *bridge making* activities across cultural and linguistic differences between people within the team, as well as *blending* subgroups within teams.

Boundary spanning was identified as a leader competence important in virtual teams (Davis & Bryant, 2003; Joshi & Lazarova, 2005) and multicultural teams (Hajro & Pudelko, 2010). Wiesenfeld and Hewlin (2003) argue that boundary spanning is the most important role of managers. To do this effectively, managers must identify with multiple groups and be able to attain synergies between them. However, as Wiesenfeld and Hewlin (2003) argue, managers must have established legitimacy within these groups. This means that the leader must be viewed as

Figure 16.1   Leading Global Teams: Literature Review and Emerging Research Themes

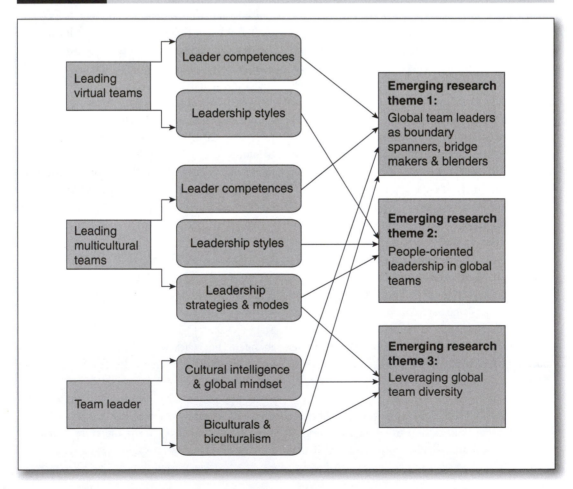

such by the group members. Legitimacy necessitates trust. In global virtual teams this is even more important, as members are dispersed; team members must be confident that their leader will represent their interests to other groups both within and external to the organization. As if the task of leading a global team was not challenging enough, the team leader as boundary spanner must also possess chameleon-like abilities, identifying with the virtual team as a whole and each of its members, as well as with multiple other groups. However, according to Wiesenfeld and Hewlin (2003), in order for boundary spanning to be achieved well, the leader cannot prioritize one identity over another, so as not to jeopardize the trust of the groups that are given lower priority. The leader must demonstrate commitment to all groups among which synergies are to be attained. How do global team leaders balance their multiple roles in different groups as well as their relationships within those groups? What are the qualities of effective boundary spanning by global team leaders? Given the critical importance of identification for connecting global members (Martins & Schilpzand, 2011), how do boundary spanning leaders of global teams identify with the global team and other groups, and what is the relationship between identification and effective leadership?

Bridge makers facilitate intra-team communication, interaction, and resolve conflicts by bridging cultural and linguistic boundaries between team members (Liljegren & Zander, 2011). As we touched on earlier, tuning in to and identifying cultural cues, reading the in-between lines of 'hidden' contextual information (Steers et al., 2010) can enable communication and resolve communication misunderstandings before these become a reality. This makes bridge making an essential part of what team leaders need to do to leverage the full potential of a multicultural team (Maznevski, 2008). Bridge making is also the essence of the leadership strategy proposed by Chevrier (2003), who argues that mere interaction between team members will not release synergy effects from drawing on different cultures. Successful synergetic team outcomes can only be achieved through a deep understanding of each others' cultural backgrounds and world views. This leads us to query whether the team leader's bridge making role changes

character, increases in importance, or possibly becomes redundant in the virtual working environment of global teams. Other questions include whether a team leader can be a bridge maker in cyber space where team members are not in spatial and temporal proximity to each other, and whether bridge making is dependent on acting in real time, or if delayed team leader responses will aggravate rather than alleviate the situation.

We build on Abreu's and Peloquin's (2004) understanding that bridge makers foster understanding, interdependence, cohesion, and recognition across cultural boundaries in a team. If we examine recent research by Jenster and Steiler (2011) on 31 GVTs operating across 22 countries, we find a significant relationship between team leaders' personal support and expression of inclusion, and team members' motivation and team cohesiveness.

This leads Jenster and Steiler (2011) to argue for an increased effort in supporting team members to bridge gaps between team leader and members when working in a global virtual context. Examining the potential effects of team leaders' personal support and inclusive actions, together with a bridge making cultural repertoire on global team outcomes constitutes an exciting new research agenda with both theoretical and practical implications.

Global team leaders also need to act as blenders, uniting the subgroups and splits (see Lau & Murnighan, 1998, 2005, for a discussion of group faultlines) present in the many 'in-between' multinational groups (Butler, 2010) that fall somewhere on the team composition spectrum between 'highly heterogeneous' and 'highly homogeneous'. Research on intergroup leadership (e.g., national political parties) has found that leaders often remain insular reinforcing boundaries between groups rather than encouraging understanding (Kellerman, 2004) creating conflict between groups leading to intergroup rivalry. Those who demonstrate biculturalism as discussed above should be more able than others to employ, for example, switching techniques to 'move' immediately and rapidly between subgroups.

The standard solution offered by the intergroup literature has been for leaders to develop a superordinate goal to create a bridge to reduce intergroup dislike (likely drawn from social norms) Hornsey and Hogg (2000) emphasize that maintaining, not weakening, subgroup identities, while locating them within the context of a binding superordinate identity, is a way to avoid such 'superordinate identity' bridges making things worse rather than better. Other research (e.g., Brewer, 1999; Hinkle & Brown, 1990; Kosterman & Feshbach, 1989; Park & Judd, 2005) has shown that the solution lies in offering up a greater range of strategies, something which should come naturally to those demonstrating biculturalism.

Pittinsky (2010) proposes the creation of a workplace culture where enacting individual acts of liking (likely to be drawn from individual experience) is the accepted way of behaving where national diversity is present. He further emphasizes the need for leaders to develop high-quality individual relationships with followers from all subgroups, not just their own. Biculturals are more likely to be able to blend the team into such a 'liking' culture. Shore et al. (2011) advocate focusing simultaneously on both the satisfaction of belonging and the need for uniqueness which each team member processes (Brewer, 1991) to increase inclusion of all team members and cite strategies to achieve this such as incorporating high group task difficulty coupled with high group autonomy (Man & Lam, 2003) and smaller group size and greater group interdependence (Beal, Cohen, Burke, & McLendon, 2003).

Although these types of blending strategies seem more likely to succeed when undertaken by someone demonstrating biculturalism, are they the strategies that biculturals in the role of global team leader actually use? Further are these strategies, or indeed other strategies, significantly more likely to succeed when undertaken by an individual demonstrating biculturalism than when undertaken by someone high on cultural intelligence, demonstrating a global mindset or, indeed, anyone else leading the so-called 'in-between global teams' in particular and global multicultural teams in general?

Lastly, how are team leader roles such as boundary spanning, bridge making and blending enacted in a global virtual environment? Butler et al. (2012) suggest that fostering of the qualities, skills, and competences required for effective global leadership actually

occurs simultaneously when performing these three unique roles within and across groups. Their significance lies in the ability to manage paradoxical situations occurring when working across national and cultural borders. Will these roles take on a new guise, can these roles satisfy the needs of global team members, or possibly serve other purposes? These are central questions in future research on leading global teams.

5.2. People-Oriented Leadership in Global Teams

At the crossroads of virtual and multicultural team leadership research the focus was clearly on people-oriented leadership styles making it our second emerging theme. Transformational and inspirational leadership together with the less researched servant leadership, all viewed as stimulating, encouraging and supporting types of leadership, were found to have positive effects in both global virtual teams and in multicultural collocated teams.

The people-oriented leadership trends echo a general move away from the more 'traditional' leadership preoccupied with order giving, control and distinct role boundaries between those who lead and those who are led. This is possibly a response to contemporary changes in work values and expectations, where a sense of duty and loyalty to a single employer is being replaced by a need for individual experience to achieve through a variety of employers and a plethora of work arrangements. To retain talent and skills, and not lose knowledgeable human resources, managers become competent in and practice people-oriented aspects of leadership. This people-oriented leadership trend is, however, not solely driven by individual work preferences but also by harsh labor market realities, where competition and financial turbulence have led to restructuring, outsourcing, downsizing, alliance formation, and other organizational changes with far-reaching implications for the people who work in these organizations.

Team members in our review ranked people-oriented leadership styles, such as transformational, inspirational and servant leadership, highly, and empirical studies established a direct link between leadership style and team effectiveness with only a few noted exceptions, such as the mediating need for member trust in the team leader in one study and person-organization value congruence in another, for transformational leadership to be effective. The picture is less clear, however, with respect to the effectiveness of distributed leadership or empowering global teams. On the one hand, the virtual team leadership literature poignantly questions whether there is any other way to successfully lead geographically distributed virtual teams. On the other hand, some have also found that empowering was prioritized by team leaders, not the team members. This is not surprising perhaps, as the cross-cultural leadership literature describes how leadership styles, behaviors and prototypes, and employee preferences for leadership practices vary significantly across countries and cultures (see, e.g., House, Hanges, Javidan, Dormán, & Gupta, 2004; Smith, Peterson, & Schwartz, 2002; Zander, 1997), suggesting that in a global team, members will hold different leadership models. With this follows the risk of a team leader experiencing the afore mentioned power paradox (Maznevksi & Zander, 2001) and becoming ineffective.

In a recent meta-analysis of cultural effects in studies using Hofstede's dimensions from the last three decades, Taras, Kirkman, and Steel (2010) demonstrated that culture significantly explains variance in employee receptivity to certain leadership styles as well as team-related attitudes and perceptions; this underscores the likelihood of facing a power paradox, and the difficulty of selecting the right leadership style when leading multicultural teams. Watson, Johnson, and Zgourides (2002) found that for ethnically diverse teams interpersonal leadership activities were more important than for non-diverse teams, where task leadership was critical. And, as demonstrated by Zander (1997, 2005) and Zander and Romani (2004) employees' interpersonal leadership preferences vary significantly across countries and cultures. A central question for future research on leading global teams is whether a power paradox can surface and take on the same magnitude in virtual teams, when team members often work asynchronically, separated by both time and space

and are not necessarily aware of each other's conflicting leadership preferences, as in collocated teams. If so, then the global team leader will become a less effective leader.

Team members' evaluations of team leader effectiveness are, however, not solely dependent on what leadership style is used. Sauer (2011) demonstrated that perceived leader effectiveness was the result of an interaction between leadership style (empowering versus directive behavior) and how the leader's status is judged (low versus high status as measured by age, number of years of experience and appearance of the incoming leader) by team members. These results are similar to findings in gender-based leadership research aptly denoted female first and leader second (Scott & Brown, 2006). Different leadership styles, such as 'autocratic' versus 'democratic', are interpreted differently depending on whether the leader is a man or a woman (see, e.g., Eagly & Carli, 2003; Scott & Brown, 2006). Recent research findings in collocated teams indicate that incoming team leader status characteristics and other visible demographics matter for team members' perceptions and evaluations about the effectiveness of the leader's style. This leads us to pose the question of whether these results hold when there is a lack of, or limited, face-to-face visibility in the virtual environment facing global teams? Other research questions include how incoming global team leaders assume leadership or become acknowledged as team leaders, how they form and norm a team culture, organize work and lead the team to success. In essence, will team members' perceptions of leadership effectiveness still be related to incoming global team leaders' status characteristics and/or actions when they work in a virtual working environment?

That global team leaders should motivate and inspire, coach and mentor, and take a personal interest in team members, was viewed as essential by team members in the studies we reviewed. These competences are of course of value to any group leader, who wishes to engage in people-oriented leadership styles, but in a virtual and cross-cultural context they need to be coupled with a cross-cultural awareness, highlighted as critical in a number of the studies we reviewed. We need further research regarding how feasible, effective and successful people-oriented leadership practices are in the virtual and multicultural context of a global team, where team leaders and members hold and prefer different leadership models, and whether team outcomes will vary between transformational, inspirational, service-oriented, empowering, distributed, and shared leadership styles and modes.

5.3. Leveraging Global Team Diversity

More work is still needed on the role of the leader in managing and leveraging multicultural diversity in global virtual teams, our third emerging theme. We are still seeking answers to many questions about recognizing cultural differences and their interaction with the virtual team context, and the emergence of subgroups and faultlines based on cultural and other team member characteristics, as well as how to recognize and manage them in virtual teams. All of these questions pose further challenges for global team leaders. However, even the leader, who has cross-cultural competence, will find this task daunting without adequate knowledge about how diversity affects team functioning and outcomes. The literature in this area is not unequivocal.

According to Earley and Mosakowski (2000), effective teams are those that have a strong team culture (a sense of purpose and goals) and shared expectations. In the early stages of the team, cultural diversity is expected to negatively influence team functioning, however, over time, the relationship between diversity and performance becomes curvilinear; this is also a finding by Watson et al. (2002). Others argue that cultural diversity is not as important as other factors. For example, Davis and Bryant (2003, p. 330) suggest that a strong organizational culture trumps any national cultural differences, and global team members leave their "cultural identity at the door," especially in cases where organizational culture is particularly strong.

In the meta-analysis of diversity effects in multicultural teams by Stahl, Maznevski, et al. (2010), diversity was found to lead to process losses with respect to increased conflict and lower social

integration but also increased creativity. Multicultural teams that were collocated experienced more conflict and lower social integration than dispersed (virtual) teams. Although these findings suggest that the virtual context may to some extent diminish the effects of diversity, others have found that cultural differences may be especially strong when they appear to be concealed by the virtual context (Mockaitis, Rose, & Zettinig, 2012). Because global team members cannot readily see one another or easily engage in face-to-face interaction, surface-level diversity becomes less important, and deeper-level diversity, such as values diversity, becomes more salient. Some researchers have argued that cultural diversity will have stronger effects on team outcomes than surface-level diversity in global teams (Martins, Gilson, & Maynard, 2004).

Stahl, Makela, Zander, and Maznevski (2010) argue that perhaps the literature on team diversity has placed too much emphasis on the negative aspects of diversity, and this has limited our understanding about the dynamic nature of diversity in teams. There is a positive side to diversity as well. Diversity can result in deeper interaction and richer communication, enhance learning, increase creativity and satisfaction, and have additional benefits (Stahl, Makela, et al., 2010). However, Stahl, Makela, et al. (2010) explain that the focus on managing diversity in multicultural teams has been on theories that help to understand or mitigate the problems that arise in such teams (e.g., social identity theory, faultlines, similarity-attraction theory, etc.). They do not focus on multicultural virtual teams. Yet, given all of the distance barriers created by the virtual context (physical geographic distance, communication lags, interaction barriers, etc.) that the global team leader must manage, a positive approach to leveraging the benefits of diversity as opposed to managing in order to minimize its negative effects would be a refreshing direction and a novel addition to the literature on global team leadership. Here we can refer back to our team leadership modes discussion, repeat that the global virtual context places extra-ordinary challenges on leadership as team member interaction is not going on in real time (nor in real life) to any larger extent. In which way, if at all can the leadership modes be used to leverage, not just manage, cultural diversity in global virtual teams?

Leaders, who demonstrate biculturalism together with those, who possess cultural intelligence or a global mindset, can move comfortably between different cultures, and demonstrate inter-cultural empathy and personal liking, may be most suited to the task of leading successful global teams. Empirical data is thus far quite thin underlining the need for future research that questions the nature of the relationship between biculturalism, cultural intelligence and global mindset, the relative impact of biculturalism, cultural intelligence and global mindset on global team performance, and strategies for effective bicultural, cultural intelligence and global mindset leadership of global teams. Under such a perspective, research into how leaders can bring out the best qualities of different team members would be rather informative from theoretical and practical perspectives.

6. Concluding Reflections and Managerial Relevance

Our review has shown that, surprisingly, given the rise of global teams, both multicultural team and global virtual leadership remain under-researched areas. The combination of multinational, multilinguistic and multicultural team dimensions, and a geographically dispersed virtual context, lead to teams of a different kind, not just of a different degree, as team complexities and dynamics are not just amplified, but new leadership challenges are also introduced. This places new demands on global team leadership and global team leaders.

Several compelling research trends and questions for future research emerged in our literature review, all firmly grounded in multicultural and virtual team leadership research and recent work on biculturalism, which deliberately pose questions regarding leadership and leaders of global teams. We identified and discussed three emerging research themes in more detail. The first theme is that of global leaders as boundary spanners, bridge makers, and blenders. The second theme concerns people-oriented leadership in

global teams, and the third theme addresses leveraging global team diversity.

We were surprised that the *raison d'être* of a global team leader did not receive any explicit in-depth attention. What will change when a multicultural leader has to work virtually, and correspondingly when a virtual team leader faces a multicultural team? Hajro and Pudelko (2010) found that the multicultural team leaders they studied ranked virtual team leadership at the bottom of the list of team leader competences. Only a little more than half of the global virtual leaders (and only 5% of the team members) viewed managing cultural diversity as important in Joshi's and Lazarova's (2005) study. Is this an example of not understanding the challenges and implications for others' daily work until we experience them ourselves, or is it an indication of something else?

Popular belief has it that younger generations, computer and internet savvy from an early age, do not feel as inhibited when communicating electronically as older generations do. If this is so, then will members of the younger generation be better, more effective and efficient, global team leaders? Are the younger generations also possibly short-circuiting cultural communication misunderstandings using text messaging abbreviations and an emerging internet communication protocol; will the need for team leaders to boundary span, bridge make and blend decrease or possibly diminish in the future? Or will they find that socializing virtually is quite different from leading work virtually? Will the simplified accessibility of electronic media for virtual face-to-face interaction lead to a changed role for the team leader; an increased use of alternative team leadership modes; or possibly diminish the need for a single team leader altogether?

Additionally, electronic advancements may be global in use and outreach, but this does not necessarily mean that they are globally accessible to all, or that internet skills or experience with electronic platforms are uniformly distributed, not even among the younger generations. Cultural values, expectations and preferences may also enhance, or inhibit, contemporary technology-driven communication. At the same time we must remember that leadership preferences may change at a variable or slower rate and differ across countries and cultures, leaving global team leaders with interpersonal challenges and opportunities to be negotiated and leveraged, while adapting to and learning from fast-paced electronic advancements.

Globalization and changes in attitudes also contribute to the rising number of born biculturals, e.g., in 2008 the U.S. Census Bureau projected that by 2050 minorities will become the majority with 54% of the American population being of non-White European origin. Although we cannot predict how many people will demonstrate biculturalism, such changing demographic patterns are a particularly interesting issue to pursue in light of the rapidly accumulating literature on biculturalism. This phenomenon also rekindles the old question of leader traits and characteristics but offers a new prism through which to examine it, by querying whether biculturals possess a specific set of competences which would make them particularly successful as global team leaders.

For practitioners our literature review on leading global teams is of immediate and very hands-on use as it highlights emerging themes important for the future. For global team leaders a specific set of leadership roles (i.e., boundary spanners, bridge makers and blenders) stand out together with a set of people-oriented leadership styles (i.e., transformational, empowering and shared leadership) and a focus on team performance in form of leveraging global team diversity. Knowledge about differences between team members' and team leaders' leadership expectations is helpful for leaders in terms of understanding team members' leadership preferences as well as for the decision-makers who select team leaders for their global teams. Here discussions as to the advantages of choosing those who display cultural intelligence, global mindset or who are biculturals demonstrating biculturalism as global team leaders can be most helpful. Vast cross-national differences regarding expectations about leadership and management practices are not a new phenomenon in contemporary multinational organizations. However, some of our findings may pose challenges for human resource managers, for example that team leaders and team members differ as to

what they list as most important leadership competences and styles. Mentoring and coaching were important for team members, while empowering and managing diversity came highly ranked on the team leaders' agenda. A more nuanced understanding of team leaders' and members' differing expectations, together with a cultural awareness of differences in leadership preferences across countries, will strengthen team leaders' ability to overcome the power paradox described in our review. Our review also highlighted that use of different leadership modes, such as paired, rotated or shared leadership, rather than just resorting to the standard single team leader option, could be applied strategically, not just to manage cultural differences but to actually leverage them. This is certainly invaluable for team leaders and global leaders alike.

With this article we have contributed to the extant literature on leading global teams. The current state of the field is presented and analyzed; we have outlined where contemporary research is heading, and identified some themes that deserve focused attention in the future. We can easily set an even longer research agenda as our thoughts spin around various combinations of virtual and multicultural team leadership challenges. However, we need to get much closer to the heart of the matter to find out whether there is something more to leading global teams than what we know from leading virtual multicultural teams today, as we believe that work in multinational organizations will not only be organized in and around global teams, but that global teams could actually become the new fluid global firms of tomorrow.

Notes

1. The authors wish to thank the JWB Special Issue editors Rick Steers, Carlos Sanchez-Runde, Luciara Nardon for insightful comments, the Editor-in-Chief John Slocum and Jan Olavarri, Assistant to the Editor-in-Chief, for support in what has been a pleasurable writing experience.

2. Corresponding author. *E-mail addresses:* lena.zander@fek.uu.se (L Zander), audra.mockaitis@monash.edu (A.I. Mockaitis), christina.butler@kingston.ac.uk (GL Butler).

References

Abreu, B., & Peloquin, S. (2004). The issue is: Embracing diversity in our profession. *The American Journal of Occupational Therapy, 58:* 353–359.

Alon, I., & Higgins, J. (2005). Global leadership success through emotional and cultural intelligences. *Business Horizons, 48:* 501–512.

Ang, S., & Van Dyne, L. (2008). *Handbook of cultural intelligence: Theory, measurement.* and applications, Armonk, NY: ME Sharpe.

Ang, S., Van Dyne, L. Koh, C. Ng, K., Templer, K. J., Tay, C., et al. (2007). Cultural intelligence: Its measurement and effects on cultural judgment and decisionmaking, cultural adaptation, and task performance. *Management and Organization Review, 3:* 335–371.

Anthias, F. (2001). New hybridites, old concepts: The limits of "culture". *Ethnic & Racial Studies, 24:* 619–649.

Aubert, B. A., & Kelsey, B. L. (2003). Further understanding of trust and performance in virtual teams. *Small Group Research, 34:* 575–618.

Ayoko, O. B., Hartel, C. E. J., & Callan, V. J. (2002). Resolving the puzzle of productive and destructive conflict in culturally heterogenous workgroups: A communication accommodation theory approach. *The International Journal of Conflict Management, 13:* 165–195.

Barbuto, J. E., & Wheeler, D. W. (2006). Scale development and construct clarification of servant leadership. *Group & Organizational Management, 31:* 300–326.

Beal, D. J., Cohen, R., Burke, M. J., & McLendon, C. L. (2003). Cohesion and performance in groups: A meta-analytic clarification of construct relations. *Journal of Applied Psychology, 88:* 989–1004.

Bell, B. S., & Kozlowski, S. W. (2002). A typology of virtual teams: Implications for effective leadership. *Group & Organization Management, 27(1):* 14–49.

Bell, E. L., & Nkomo, S. M. (2001). *Our separate ways: Black and white women and the struggle for professional identity.* Boston: Harvard Business School Press.

Benet-Martinez, V., & Haritatos, J. (2005). Bicultural identity integration (BII): Components and psychological antecedents. *Journal of Personality, 73:* 1015–1050.

Berry, J. W. (1990). Psychology of acculturation. In J. Berman (Ed.), *Cross-cultural perspectives: Nebraska symposium on motivation,* (pp. 201–235). Lincoln: University of Nebraska Press.

Bilimoria, D., Joy, S., & Liang, X. (2008). Breaking barriers and creating inclusiveness: Lessons of organizational transformation to advance women faculty in academic science and engineering. *Human Resource Management, 47:* 423–441.

Bourhis, R., Moise, L., Perrault, S., & Senecal, S. (1997). Towards an interactive acculturation model: A social psychological approach. *International Journal of Psychology, 32:* 369–386.

Brannen, M. Y., & Thomas, D. C. (2010). Bicultural individuals in organizations: Implications and opportunity. *International Journal of Cross-Cultural Management, 10:* 5–16.

Brewer, M. B. (1991). The social self: On being the same and different at the same time. *Personality and Social Psychology Bulletin, 17:* 475–482.

Brewer, M. B. (1999). The psychology of prejudice: Ingroup love or outgroup hate? *Journal of Social Issues, 35:* 429–444.

Bunderson, J. S., & Sutcliffe, K. M. (2002). Comparing alternative conceptualizations of functional diversity in management teams: Process and performance effects. *Academy of Management Journal, 45:* 875–893.

Butler, C. L. (2006). The influence of status cues on collective identity in teams of different national composition. *Academy of management best papers proceedings.*

Butler, C. L. (2010). *The challenge of the 'in-between' multinational team: Is a bicultural leader the answer?* Paper presented at the academy of management annual meeting, Montreal, Canada.

Butler, C. L., Zander, L., Mockaitis, A. I., & Sutton, C. (2012). The global leader as boundary spanner, bridge maker and blender. *Industrial and Organizational Psychology: Perspectives on Science and Practice 5(2)* 240–243.

Brett, J., Behfar, K., & Kern, M. C. (2006). Managing multicultural teams. *Harvard Business Review, 84:* 84–91.

Carte, T. A., Chidambaram, L., & Becker, A. (2006). Emergent leadership in self-managed virtual teams: A longitudinal study of concentrated and shared leadership behaviors. *Group Decision and Negotiation, 15:* 323–343.

Chevrier, S. (2003). Cross-cultural management in multinational project groups. *Journal of World Business, 38:* 141–149.

Chiu, C. Y., Morris, M. W., Hong, Y. Y., & Menon, T. (2000). Motivated cultural cognition: The impact of implicit cultural theories on dispositional attribution varies as a function of need for closure. *Journal of Personality and Social Psychology, 78:* 247–259.

Davis, D. D., & Bryant, J. L. (2003). Influence at a distance: Leadership in global virtual teams. *Advances in Global Leadership, 3:* 303–340.

Dickerson, N. (2006). We are a force to be reckoned with: Black and Latina women's leadership in the contemporary US labor movement. *Working USA, 9(3):* 293–313.

DiStefano, J. J., & Maznevski, M. L. (2000). Creating value with diverse teams in global management. *Organizational Dynamics, 29:* 45–63.

Eagly, A. H., & Carli, L. L. (2003). The female leadership advantage: An evaluation of the evidence. *The Leadership Quarterly, 14:* 807–834.

Earley, P. C. (2002). Redefining interactions across cultures and organizations: Moving forward with cultural intelligence. *Research in Organizational Behavior, 24:* 271–299.

Earley, P. C., & Ang, S. (2003). *Cultural intelligence: Individual interactions across cultures.* Palo Alto, CA: Stanford University Press.

Earley, P. C., Murnieks, C., & Mosakowski, E. (2007). Cultural intelligence and the global mindset. *Advances in International Management 19:* 75–103.

Earley, P. C., & Mosakowski, E. (2000). Creating hybrid team cultures: An empirical test of transnational team functioning. *Academy of Management Journal, 43(1):* 26–49.

Flaherty, J. (2008). The effects of cultural intelligence on team member acceptance and integration in multinational teams. In S. Ang & L. Van Dyne (Eds.), *Handbook of cultural intelligence: Theory, measurement, and applications* (pp. 192–205). Armonk, NY: M.E. Sharpe.

Friedman, R., & Liu, W. (2009). Biculturalism in management: Leveraging the benefits of intrapersonal diversity. In R. Wyer, C. Y. Chiu, & Y. Y. Hong (Eds.), *Understanding culture: Theory, research, and application* (pp. 343–360). Hove, East Sussex: Psychology Press.

Friedman, R., Liw, W., Chi, S., Hong, Y. Y., & Sung, L. K. (2008). *Western exposure: The effects of foreign experience on Taiwanese managers' cognition.* Unpublished manuscript.

Greenleaf, R. K. (1977). *Servant leadership: A journey into the nature of legitimate power and greatness.* New York: Paulist Press.

Groves, K. S., & Feyerherm, A. E. (2011). Leader cultural intelligence in context: Testing the moderating effects of team cultural diversity on leader and team performance. *Group and Organization Management, 36(5):* 535–566.

Hajro, A., & Pudelko, M. (2010). An analysis of core-competences of successful multinational team leaders. *International Journal of Cross Cultural Management, 10(2):* 175–194.

Hinkle, S., & Brown, R. (1990). Intergroup comparisons and social identity: Some links and lacunae. In D. Abrams & M. Hogg (Eds.), *Social identity theory: Construction and critical advance* (pp. 48–70). London: Harvester Wheatsheaf.

Hitt, M. A., Javidan, M., & Steers, R. M. (2007). The global mindset: An introduction. *Advances in International Management, 19:* 1–10.

Hoffman, B. J., Bynum, B. H., Piccolo, R. F., & Sutton, A. W. (2011). Person-organization congruence: How transformational leaders influence work group effectiveness. *Academy of Management Journal, 54:* 779–796.

Hong, Y. Y., Morris, M., Chiu, C Y., & Benet-Martinez, V. (2000). Multicultural minds: A dynamic constructivist approach to culture and cognition. *American Psychologist, 55:* 709–720.

Hornsey, M. J., & Hogg, M. A. (2000). Assimilation and diversity: An integrative model of subgroup relations. *Personality and Social Psychology Review, 4:* 143–156.

House, R. J., Hanges, P. J., Javidan, M., Dorfman, P. W., & Gupta, V. (2004). *Culture, Leadership, and Organizations.* Thousand Oaks, CA: Sage Publications.

Jarvenpaa, S. L., & Leidner, D. E. (1999). Communication and trust in global virtual teams. *Organization Science, 10:* 791–815.

Javidan, M., Dorfman, P. W., De Luque, M. S., & House, R. J. (2006). In the eye of the beholder: Cross cultural lessons in leadership from project GLOBE. *Academy of Management Perspectives, 20:* 67–90.

Javidan, M., Steers, R. M., & Hitt, M. A. (2007). Putting it all together: So what is a global mindset and why is it important? *Advances in International Management, 19:* 215–226.

Jeanett, J. P. (2000). *Managing with a global mindset.* London: Prentice Hall.

Jenster, N. P., & Steiler, D. (2011). Turning up the volume in interpersonal leadership: Motivating and building cohesive global virtual teams during times of economic crisis. *Advances in Global Leadership, 6:* 267–297.

Jonsen, K., Maznevski, M. L., & Canney Davison, S. (2012) Global virtual team dynamics and effectiveness. In G. Stahl, I. Björkman, & S. Morris (Eds.), *Handbook of research in international human resource management* (pp. 363–392). Edward Elgar Publishing: London, in press.

Joshi, A., & Lazarova, M. B. (2005). Do global teams need global leaders? Identifying leadership competences in multinational teams. In D. L. Shapiro (Ed.), *Managing multinational teams: Global perspectives* (pp. 281–301). Amsterdam: Elsevier.

Joshi, A., Lazarova, M. B., & Liao, H. (2009). Getting everyone on board: The role of inspirational leadership in geographically dispersed teams. *Organization Science, 20:* 240–252.

Judge, T. A., & Piccolo, R. F. (2004). Transformational and transactional leadership: A meta-analytic test of their relative validity. *Journal of Applied Psychology, 89:* 755–768.

Kayworth, T. R., & Leidner, D. E. (2001-2002). Leadership effectiveness in global virtual teams. *Journal of Management Information Systems, 18(3):* 7–40.

Kearney, E., & Gebert, D. (2009). Managing diversity and enhancing team outcomes: The promise of transformational leadership. *Journal of Applied Psychology, 94(1):* 77–89.

Kellerman, B. (2004). *Bad leadership: What it is, how it happens, why it matters.* Boston: Harvard Business School Press.

Kim, K., Kirkman, B., & Chen, G. (2008). Cultural intelligence and international assignment effectiveness: A conceptual model and preliminary findings. In S. Ang & L. Van Dyne (Eds.), *Handbook of cultural intelligence: Theory measurement, and applications* (pp. 71–90). Armonk, NY: M.E. Sharpe.

Kirkman, B. L., Rosen, B., Tesluk, P. E., & Gibson, C. B. (2004). The impact of team empowerment on virtual team performance: The moderating role of face-to-face interaction. *Academy of Management Journal, 47:* 175–192.

Kosterman, R., & Feshbach, S. (1989). Towards a measure of patriotic and nationalistic attitudes. *Political Psychology, 10:* 2257–2274.

Krebs, S. A., Hobman, E. V., & Bordia, P. (2006). Virtual teams and group member dissimilarity: Consequences for the development of trust. *Small Group Research, 37:* 721–741.

Kruglanski, A. (1990). Motivations for judging and knowing: Implications for causal attributions. In Higgins, E. T., & Sorrentino, R. M. (Eds.), *The handbook of motivation and cognition: Foundation of social behavior* (vol. 2, pp. 333–368). New York: Guilford Press.

LaFromboise, T., Coleman, H. L. K., & Gerton, J. (1993). Psychological impact of biculturalism: Evidence and theory. *Psychological Bulletin, 114:* 395–412.

Lau, D., & Murnighan, J. K. (1998). Demographic diversity and faultlines: The compositional dynamics of organizational groups. *Academy of Management Review, 23:* 325–340.

Lau, D., & Murnighan, J. K. (2005). Interactions within groups and subgroups: The effects of demographic fault-lines. *Academy of Management Journal, 48:* 645–659.

Levy, O., Beechler, S., Taylor, S., & Boyacigiller, N. A. (2007). What we talk about when we talk about 'global mindset': Managerial cognition in multinational corporations. *Journal of International Business Studies, 38:* 231–258.

Liljegren, S., & Zander, L. (2011). *The importance of being a bridge maker: Power and influence in international and multicultural boards of directors.* Paper presented at the academy of management annual meeting, San Antonio, USA.

Lücke G., & Roth, K. (2008). *An embeddedness view of biculturalism.* South Carolina CIBER Working Paper Series, Working Paper D-08-07.

Malhotra, A., Majchrzak, A., & Rosen, B. (2007). Leading virtual teams. *Academy of Management Perspectives,* February: 60–70.

Maloney, M. M., & Zellmer-Bruhn, M. (2006). Building bridges, windows, and cultures: Mediating mechanisms between team heterogeneity and performance in global teams. *Management International Review, 46:* 697–720.

Man, D. C., & Lam, S. S. K. (2003). The effects of job complexity and autonomy on cohesiveness in collectivistic and individualistic work groups: A cross-cultural analysis. *Journal of Organizational Behavior, 24:* 979–1001.

Mana, A., Orr, E., & Mana, Y. (2009). An integrated acculturation model of immigrants' social identity. *Journal of Social Psychology, 149:* 450–473.

Mannor, M. (2008). Top executives and global leadership: At the intersection of cultural intelligence and strategic leadership theory. In S. Ang & L. Van Dyne (Eds.), *Handbook of cultural intelligence: Theory, measurement, and applications* (pp. 91–106). Armonk, NY: M.E. Sharpe.

Martins, L. L., Gilson, L. L., & Maynard, M. T. (2004). Virtual teams: What do we know and where do we go from here? *Journal of Management, 30:* 805–835.

Martins, L. L., & Schilpzand, M. C. (2011). Global virtual teams: Key developments, research gaps, and future directions. *Research in Personnel and Human Resource Management, 30:* 1–72.

Matveev, A. V., & Milter, R. G. (2004). The value of intercultural competence for performance of multicultural teams. *Team Performance Management, 10(6):* 104–111.

Matveev, A. V., & Nelson, P. E. (2004). Cross cultural communication competence and multicultural team performance: Perceptions of American and Russian managers. *International Journal of Cross Cultural Management, 4(2)*: 253–270.

Maznevski, M. L. (2008). Leading global teams. In M. E. Medenhall, J. S. Osland, A. Bird, G. R. Oddou, & M. L. Maznevski (Eds.), *Global leadership: Research, practice, and development (pp. 94–113)*. Milton Park: Routledge.

Maznevski, M. L., & Zander, L. (2001). Leading global teams: Overcoming the challenge of power paradoxes. In M. Medenhall, T. Kuehlmann, & G. Stahl (Eds.), *Developing global business leaders: Policies, processes, and innovations (pp. 157-174)*. Westport, CT: Quorum Books.

Miller, D. M., Fields, P. E. R., Kumar, P. E. A., & Ortiz, P. E. R. (2000). Leadership and organizational vision in managing a multiethnic and multicultural project team. *Journal of Management in Engineering, 16(6)*: 18–22.

Mockaitis, A. I., Rose, E. L., & Zettinig, P. (2012). The power of individual cultural values in global virtual teams. *International Journal of Cross-Cultural Management 12(2)*: 193–210.

Mok, A., Cheng, C. Y., & Morris, M. W. (2010). Matching versus mismatching cultural norms in performance appraisal: Effects of the cultural setting and bicultural identity integration. *International Journal of Cross Cultural Management, 10(1)*: 17–35.

Muethel, M., & Hoegl, M. (2010). Cultural and societal influences on shared leadership in globally dispersed teams. *Journal of International Management, 16*: 234–246.

Muller, H. J. (1998). American Indian women managers: Living in two worlds. *Journal of Management Inquiry, 7(1)*: 4–28.

Murtha, T. P., Lenway, S. A., & Bagozzi, R. P. (1998). Global mindset and cognitive shifts in a complex multinational corporation. *Strategic Management Journal, 19*: 97–114.

Ng, S., & Han, S. (2009). The bicultural self and the bicultural brain. In R. S. Wyer, C. Y. Chiu, & Y. Y. Hong (Eds.), *Understanding culture: Theory, research, and application* (pp. 329–342). Hove, East Sussex: Psychology Press.

No, S., Hong, Y. Y., Liao, H. Y., Lee, K., Wood, D., & Caho, M. M. (2008). Race and psychological essentialism: Lay theory of race moderators Asian Americans' responses toward American culture. *Journal of Personality and Social Psychology, 95*: 991–1004.

Ospina, S., & Foldy, E. (2009). A critical review of race and ethnicity in the leadership literature: Surfacing context, power and the collective dimensions of leadership. *The Leadership Quarterly, 20(6)*: 876–896.

Park, B., & Judd, C. (2005). Rethinking the link between categorization and prejudice within the social cognition perspective. *Personality and Social Psychology Review, 9*: 108–130.

Perlmutter, H. (1969). The tortuous evolution of the multinational corporation. *Columbia Journal of World Business, 4*: 9–18.

Pittinsky, T. (2010). A two-dimensional model of intergroup leadership. *American Psychologist, 65(3)*: 194–200.

Raviin, E. C., Thomas, D. C., & Ilsev, A. (2000). Beliefs about values, status and legitimacy in multicultural groups: Influences on intragroup conflict. In P. C. Earley & H. Singh (Eds.), *Innovations in international and crosscultural management* (pp. 17–51). Thousand Oaks, CA: Sage.

Redding, G. (2007). The chess master and the 10 simultaneous opponents: But what if the game is poker? Implications for the global mindset. *Advances in International Management, 19*: 49–73.

Roberson, Q. M. (2006). Disentangling the meanings of diversity and inclusion in organizations. *Group and Organization Management, 31*: 212–236.

Roccas, S., & Brewer, M. (2002). Social identity complexity. *Personality & Social Psychology Review, 6*: 88–106.

Sauer, S. J. (2011). Taking the reins: The effects of new leader status and leadership style on team performance. *Journal of Applied Psychology, 96*: 574–587.

Schaubroeck, J., Lam, S. S. K., & Peng, A. C. (2011). Cognition-based and affect-based trust as mediators of leaders behavior influences on team performance. *Journal of Applied Psychology, 96*: 863–887.

Schweiger, D. M., Atamer, T., & Calori, R. (2003). Transnational project teams and networks: Making the multinational organization more effective. *Journal of World Business, 38*: 127–140.

Scott, K. A., & Brown, D. J. (2006). Female first, leader second? Gender bias in the encoding of leadership behavior. *Organizational Behavior and Human Decision Processes, 101(2)*: 230–242.

Shaffer, M., & Miller, G. (2008). Cultural intelligence: A key success factor for expatriates. In S. Ang & L. Van Dyne (Eds.), *Handbook of cultural intelligence: Theory, measurement, and applications* (pp. 107–125). Armonk, NY: M.E. Sharpe.

Shore, L. M., Chung, B., Dean, M. A., Ehrhart, K. H., Jung, D., Randel, A., et al. (2009). Diversity and inclusiveness: Where are we now and where are we going? *Human Resource Management Review, 19:* 117–133.

Shore, L. M., Randel, A. E., Chung, B. G., Dean, M. A., Ehrhart, K. H., & Singh, G. (2011). Inclusion and diversity in work groups: A review and model for future research. *Journal of Management, 37:* 1262–1289.

Smith, P. B., Peterson, M. F., & Schwartz, S. H. (2002). Cultural values, sources of guidance, and their relevance to managerial behavior a 47-nation study. *Journal of Cross-Cultural Psychology, 33(2):* 188–208.

Snow, C. C., Snell, S. A., Canney Davison, S., & Hambrick, D. C. (1996). Use transnational teams to globalize your company. *Organizational Dynamics, 24(4):* 50–67.

Stahl, G. K., Maznevski, M. L., Voigt, A., & Jonsen, K. (2010). Unraveling the effects of cultural diversity in teams: A meta-analysis of research on multicultural work groups. *Journal of International Business Studies, 41:* 690–709.

Stahl, G. K., Makela, K., Zander, L., & Maznevski, M. L. (2010). A look at the bright side of multicultural team diversity. *Scandinavian Journal of Management, 26:* 439–447.

Steers, R. M., Sanchez-Runde, C. J., & Nardon, L. (2010). *Management across cultures: Challenges and strategies.* Cambridge: Cambridge University Press.

Stone, A. G., Russell, R. F., & Patterson, K. (2004). Transformational versus servant leadership: A difference in leader focus. *The Leadership and Organization Development Journal, 25(4):* 349–361.

Taras, V., Kirkman, B. L., & Steel, P. (2010). Examining the impact of cultures' consequences: A three-decade, multilevel, meta-analytic review of Hofstede's cultural value dimensions. *Journal of Applied Psychology, 95:* 405–439.

Townsend, A. M., DeMarie, S. M., & Hendrickson, A. R. (1998). Virtual teams: Technology and the workplace of the future. *The Academy of Management Executive, 12(3):* 17–29.

Tsui, A., Nifadkar, S., & Ou, A. Y. (2007). Cross-national, cross-cultural organizational behavior research: Advances, gaps, and recommendations. *Journal of Management, 33:* 426–478.

Van Dyne, L., Ang, S., & Koh, C. (2008). Development and validation of the CQS: The cultural intelligence scale. In S. Ang & L. Van Dyne (Eds.), *Handbook of cultural intelligence: Theory, measurement, and applications* (pp. 16–38). Armonk, NY: M.E. Sharpe

Warner, L. S., & Grint, K. (2006). American Indian ways of leading and knowing. *Leadership, 21(2):* 225–244.

Watson, W. E., Johnson, L., & Zgourides, G. D. (2002). The influence of ethnic diversity on leadership, group process, and performance: An examination of learning teams. *International Journal of Intercultural Relations, 26:* 1–16.

Wiesenfeld, B. M., & Hewlin, P. F. (2003). Splintered identify and organizational change: The predicament of boundary spanning mangers. *Research on Managing Groups and Teams, 5:* 27–52.

Wu, J. B., Tsui, A. S., & Kinicki, A. J. (2010). Consequences of differentiated leadership in groups. *Academy of Management Journal, 53:* 90–106.

Zander, L. (1997). *The licence to lead—an 18 country study of the relationship between employees' preferences regarding interpersonal leadership and national culture* (published Ph.D. dissertation). Stockholm School of Economics and the Institute of International Business, Stockholm.

Zander, L. (2005). Communication and country clusters: A study of language and leadership preferences. *International Studies of Management and Organisation, 35(1):* 84–104.

Zander, L., & Butler, C. L. (2010). Leadership modes: Success strategies for multicultural teams. *Scandinavian Journal of Management, 26(3):* 258–267.

Zander, L., & Romani, L. (2004). When nationality matters: A study of departmental, hierarchical, professional, gender and age-based employee groupings' leadership preferences across 15 countries. *International Journal of Cross-Cultural Management, 4(3):* 291–315.

Zigurs, I. (2002). Leadership in virtual teams: Oxymoron or opportunity? *Organizational Dynamics, 31(4):* 339–351.

CHAPTER 17

Inspiring Democracy in the Workplace

From Fear-Based to Freedom-Centered Organizations

Traci L. Fenton

WorldBlu

Albert Einstein once wrote, "All that is truly great and inspiring is created by the individual who can labor in freedom." There's just one problem with Einstein's dictum: most people don't labor in freedom each day; they labor in fear. According to a recent Zogby International/Workplace Democracy Association poll, one out of every four Americans today feel like they work in a dictatorship. Contrast that with a whopping 80 percent of American workers who feel that if they had more freedom at work they could do a better job.

As last year's Arab Spring clearly demonstrated, no one wants to live in a dictatorship. So why do so many of us choose to *work* in one each day? Why do we continue to believe that fear and control—rather than work environments that release and free people—will produce the most engaged, innovative, and competitive workplaces? They don't.

We have evolved from the Industrial Age, a manufacturing-centric period in which the command-and-control model of business arguably worked, to a new *Democratic* Age, an age of unprecedented transparency, voice, and the tools of engagement and influence that enable a global power-to-the-people ethos unlike anything we've ever before seen.

This new Democratic Age requires that businesses and their leaders embrace an entirely new operating system, one that is based on freedom—not the outdated model of fear and control.

For the past 14 years, I've been researching this new model of business around the world, as well as growing my own freedom-centered company after leaving a job at a fear-based Fortune 500 company. Along that way, I've discovered a core idea that seems to be the keynote for this new age. The idea is simple, straightforward, and very powerful:

When we consciously choose to design our workplaces based on freedom, rather than fear and control, we unleash human greatness, build world-class organizations, and change the world for the better.

What's So Wrong With Fear?

When I speak around the world on the topic of the advantages of building freedom-centered—rather than fear-based—workplaces, I often get quizzical looks from CEOs and executives. They ask me, "What's so wrong with a little fear in the workplace? It gets people motivated, that's for sure!"

While fear can be a short-term motivator, it doesn't have a lasting positive impact. And it certainly doesn't help promote full engagement—not to mention loyalty—in the workplace. Fear leads directly to a variety of negative organizational outcomes:

- Unwillingness of leaders to share enough financial information about a company and its fiscal health to inform good decision making
- Lack of opportunity for employees to have real influence and decision-making power in their jobs
- Lack of opportunity for employees to directly address challenges or move forward with opportunities
- Lack of emotional safety around trying new ideas and making mistakes
- Lack of clarity around how long employees will have a job
- Feelings of being invisible, unvalued, and voiceless at work

There are many other forms of fear, but they all tend to produce the same effect—to shut us down and make us disengage. And disengagement, mainly due to outdated command-and-control structures, has reached epic proportions. According to a 2011 Gallup Employee Engagement poll, only 30 percent of American workers feel engaged at work, which means that 70 percent are disengaged! The traditional model of business simply isn't as effective as it once was.

HCL Goes Fearless

HCL, a freedom-centered company based just outside Delhi, India, with operations in more than 25 countries worldwide, knows how to choose freedom over fear when it comes to making decisions. In sharp contrast to massive, often fear-based layoffs, HCL, a $5 billion company with nearly 80,000 employees, took a decidedly different approach.

Back in 2005, Vineet Nayar, HCL's new CEO, decided to transform HCL from a traditional command-and-control organization to a freedom-centered, democratic workplace. Things were going along relatively smoothly with the transition until the global recession hit in 2008. The economic downturn provided an unexpected opportunity to see if a mind-set of freedom would prevail even in difficult financial conditions, or if HCL and its leaders would revert to tightening their control over the organization, as so many do when times are challenging.

Like most companies at the time, HCL got hit hard. The challenge? The company's leadership team needed to find a way to reduce the organization's expenses by $100 million, or they would have to lay people off. Instead of hunkering down and lapsing into a mind-set of fear and secrecy, however, the C-suite took the opposite tack. They fearlessly and authentically opened up the organization's operations and became even more transparent. They went to their employees and explained the situation and then asked them what they thought they should do to cut expenses. Appropriate forums were provided for employees to share ideas for how the company could cost costs without cutting jobs.

Hundreds of ideas were submitted, and 76 were implemented. The result? The company saved a total of $260 million by opening up and making decisions based on freedom and possibility rather than myopic fear and control. HCL was able to build on the ideas of its employees to turn the recession into an opportunity—and as a result not one employee was let go.

HCL's transition to a freedom-centered, democratic model has had a significant and positive impact on its bottom line, even throughout the recent global recession. HCL is one among only five companies in the overall global technology sector (alongside Apple,

Google, Lenovo, and Cognizant) to achieve a five-year revenue compound annual growth rate of more than 30 percent.

During the 2008–2009 recession, sustaining a freedom-centered mind-set among top leaders as well as employees allowed HCL to grow its revenues by 21 percent, while most of its competitors saw revenues shrink. When I attended HCL's global conference in the spring of 2010, and later visited its headquarters in India a few months later, I was impressed with how genuinely happy and engaged employees were at every level of the organization. They knew a freedom-centered approach wasn't easy and required a tremendous amount of discipline, but the net effect was worth the effort. Since becoming freedom-centered and democratic, HCL has tripled its revenue and income and doubled its overall market capitalization.

Vineet Nayar explains: "HCL recognizes that its greatest asset is its employees—the 80,000 'HCLites' that deliver value and directly interface with HCL's customers every day. The average age of an 'HCLite' is 27 years old and we believe that employees of the 'Gen Y' generation are not going to adapt to today's corporate structures. Instead, organizations must adapt their corporate structures to create an environment where these employees can thrive. The job of the CEO is to enable, enthuse, and encourage employees, and to transfer the onus of change at HCL from executive management to the employees. Creating a democratic workplace within HCL has enabled us to achieve this goal."

> *Adopt a mind-set based on freedom rather than control.*

The Framework of Freedom

The first step toward successfully building a freedom-centered workplace is to adopt a mind-set based on freedom rather than control. The second thing is to create the right democratic design framework.

The word *democracy* conjures up a lot of different things for people, especially when you apply it to business. A popular misconception about organizational democracy is that there are no leaders, no decisions ever get made, and it takes an eternity to get anything done. This is wrong. You still have leaders in a democratic organization. In fact, you have something even better: distributed leadership, which makes the organization stronger. Decisions are made throughout the organization by those who have the most knowledge or will be most impacted by the decision, not just by those in the C-suite. Voting and consensus are simply ways of making decisions, but they aren't democracy in and of themselves.

And while sometimes the decision-making process may take longer because of a commitment to giving people voice, in my experience organizations make up time in the execution stage because everyone is in alignment.

Organizational democracy is the new model of organizational *design* for a Democratic Age, and out of this new model of design grows a healthy, freedom-centered culture.

The Principles of Organizational Democracy

After I resigned from my very *undemocratic* Fortune 500 job, I spent a decade researching organizational democracy globally. In the process, I discovered 10 democratic design principles that create a democratic ecology within a company.

They are principles such as transparency, accountability, dialogue and listening, decentralization, choice, integrity, and more (see Figure 17.1). For an organization to successfully practice organizational democracy, all 10 principles must be in operation.

I focused on 10 *principles*—not practices— because principles are scalable, adaptable, and universal, whereas practices are not. The value comes when all 10 principles are in operation. It is at the intersection of these 10 principles where the spark of freedom takes place.

Who's Doing It?

Is a freedom-centered culture, achieved through the framework of organizational democracy, simply a utopian ideal, or is it something that is practical and used in more than just a few progressive companies?

| Figure 17.1 | The Worldblu™ 10 Principles of Organizational Democracy |

For an organization to successfully practice organizational democracy, *all* ten principles must be in operation.

Principle	Description
Purpose + **Vision**	When an organization and its individual employees know their reason for existing and have a sense of intentional direction.
Dialogue + **Listening**	When we listen and engage in conversations in a way that brings out new levels of meaning and connection.
Fairness + **Dignity**	When each person is treated justly and regarded impartially.
Transparency	When ideas flow freely and information is openly and responsibly shared.
Accountability	When each person and the organization as a whole is responsible to each other and their community for their actions.
Individual + **Collective**	When individuals understand the unique contribution they make towards achieving collective goals.
Choice	When each person is encouraged to exercise their right to choose between a diversity of possibilities.
Integrity	When each person and the organization as a whole steadfastly adheres to ethical and moral principles.
Decentralization	When power is appropriately shared among people throughout the organization.
Reflection + **Evaluation**	When there is a commitment to continuous feedback and development and a willingness to learn from the past and apply lessons to improve the future.

Well, that's something I wanted to know the answer to myself.

So in 2007 my team and I developed a scorecard tool that measures the level of organizational democracy within a company. Since then, we've certified dozens of companies around the world, ranging from small, five-person operations all the way up to Fortune 500 companies with 85,000+ employees, with revenues from $1 million to $6 billion.

These are companies that distribute airplane parts, brew world-class beer, make cleaning products, deliver online television, provide dialysis services, and bake bread. Many of these organizations are leading their industries. They include Zappos, Hulu, DaVita, HCL Technologies, WD-40, Brainpark, Great Harvest Bread Company, NixonMcInnes, and dozens more from across North America, South America, Europe, and Asia.

They use a democratic operating system because it improves the bottom line by

- Making them more efficient and productive
- Boosting innovation
- Allowing them to attract and retain top talent, especially Gen Y top candidates
- Lowering absenteeism
- Allowing them to provide A+ customer service

Moving to Freedom

One company that successfully made the transition from an undemocratic to a democratic framework is DaVita. The company—headquartered in Denver—provides dialysis services at more than 1,600 clinics across the United States. DaVita is a Fortune 400 company with more than 35,000 employees, and it is now a WorldBlu-certified democratic workplace. But life wasn't always so democratic at DaVita.

Back in 1999 the situation was bleak. Senior executives had bailed out, the company was under investigation by the SEC and teetering on the edge of bankruptcy, and employee morale was at an all-time low. Then DaVita hired a new CEO, Kent Thiry. Soon after Kent arrived and had time to survey the situation, he told his employees, "We need to stop thinking of ourselves as a corporation and need to think of ourselves as a democratic community."

So the company started to implement changes that gave real power to the people:

1. Instead of the secret-society mentality that characterizes many workplaces, DaVita opened up and began holding regular town hall meetings where honest and authentic conversations started to happen. At these meetings, the CEO

TOOLS FOR BUILDING A FREEDOM-CENTERED WORKPLACE

Chaordix

Chaordix works with companies to develop crowdsourcing communities for idea creation, market prediction, testing, and problem-solving. Crowds are invited to submit, discuss, vote on, and identify the insights and answers that will help strengthen an organization and move ideas forward.

www.chaordix.com

The Great Game of Business

The Great Game of Business is an organization that teaches companies how to implement Open-Book Management, enabling employees to use financial information to improve decision-making, engagement, and the overall health of the company.

www.ggob.com

Podio

Podio is an online work platform that gives power to the people to design, manage, and collaborate in a democratic way. Combining hundreds of specialized and flexible work apps with messaging, tasks, reporting, and workflow and contact management, Podio enables companies to build and shape an online workplace customized to their needs.

www.podio.com

Reframeit

Reframeit is a technology-supported process for sustainable decision making that works by engaging the collective intelligence of employees and providing decision makers with a data-driven basis for choices that might otherwise be dominated by anecdotes and impressions.

www.reframeit.com

Rypple

Rypple is a social performance platform built for teams to provide continuous, action-ready feedback, coaching, and recognition to their teams in real time.

www.rypple.com

and the COO would share the mistakes they made in the preceding year and how they planned to improve. This simple change cultivated a learning, rather than blaming, atmosphere within DaVita.

2. Employees throughout the organization were empowered to make decisions with real impact on DaVita, voting on things ranging from a company name change to its strategic direction.

3. Instead of power being centralized at the top of a pyramid, power was decentralized from corporate headquarters out to the 1,600 clinics, where local employees were empowered to run things in the way they felt would best serve their community.

4. And rather than calling himself the CEO, Kent Thiry now refers to himself as "the Mayor," focusing on serving his village and teammates (rather than his company and employees).

The bottom-line result of this democratic transition? DaVita went from near-bankruptcy to $6 billion in revenue and more than $400 million in profit, and it enjoys steady growth, low turnover, and high morale. DaVita is now the undisputed leader in its industry.

The Role of a Leader in a Freedom-Centered Company

If the role of a leader or a CEO in a traditional company is to be a dictator, or at best a *benevolent* dictator,

what is the role of a leader in a freedom-centered, democratic workplace?

The role of a leader in this new workplace is to be a visionary, coach, guide, and facilitator of people, ideas, and talent. But above all, the job is to be an *environmentalist*. Freedom-centered leaders must themselves cultivate a mind-set of freedom and make sure that their organization's overall environment stays freedom-centered as well. They must be vigilant about daily finding ways to eliminate fear and uncertainty, as best they can, so that employees will feel they can work in freedom, with an expansive sense of possibility, which will ultimately impact the company at the bottom line.

> *Being a visionary, coach, guide, and facilitator of people, ideas, and talent.*

Freedom-centered workplace design and leadership are intelligent, economically viable, and spiritually advanced, and expect and require the best of people.

To that end, when we consciously choose to design our workplace environments based on freedom rather than fear and control, we will join dozens of companies worldwide that are unleashing human greatness, building world-class organizations, and changing the world for the better—one employee at a time. And we can help bring about Albert Einstein's vision of a workplace where individuals can labor in freedom, creating all that is truly great and inspiring in the process.

PART IV

Culture and Inclusion

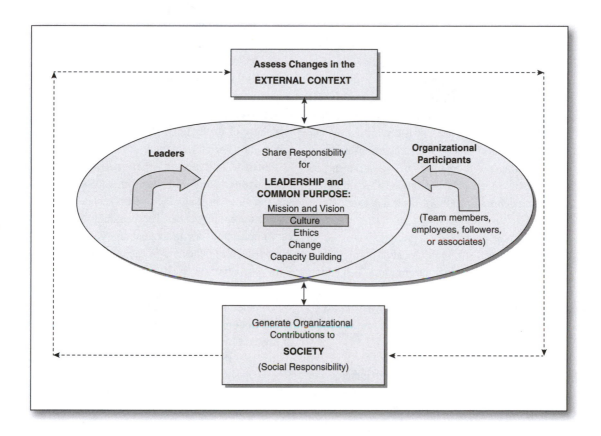

Overview

Culture is the life force of an organization—its DNA. It is where the real values and underlying beliefs, practices and behavioral norms, symbols, ceremonies, and customs exist. This section explores the meaning and influence of organizational culture and the inclusion of global and national cultures with other forms of diversity in the organization.

In recent years, the term *inclusion* has been added to the dialogue on diversity. Inclusion and diversity are distinct yet related concepts. "Diversity focuses on organizational demography [that is, workforce composition, including race, sex, disability, ethnicity, and so on], whereas inclusion focuses on the removal of obstacles to the full participation and contribution of employees in organizations."[1] Real inclusion entails bringing people with varied backgrounds and unique perspectives into the organization and creating a climate in which they can thrive, learn, and contribute their capabilities to the organization's processes and outcomes. An underlying assumption of inclusion is that the human community—in this case, an organizational community—has a greater chance of understanding key issues, engaging in creative or innovative work, and creating effective, sustainable change by involving heterogeneous stakeholders in a mutual problem-solving arena.[2] As a result, inclusion enriches the organization's culture and builds its capacity.

Culture and Climate

This section begins with a discussion of organizational culture. Edgar Schein's (Chapter 18) conception of organizational culture provides a perspective for examining other chapters in this section. He explains that culture is a powerful force in the organization and often operates invisibly outside of our awareness. Culture is a product of a group's accumulated learning and is passed to new group members or generations through socialization or acculturation.

Schein defines the culture of a group as

a pattern of shared basic assumptions learned by a group as it solved its problems of external adaptation and internal integration, which has worked well enough to be considered valid and, therefore, to be taught to new members as the correct way to perceive, think, and feel in relation to those problems.

Culture should be observable and increase our understanding of a set of events if the concept is to be useful. Accordingly, models and studies of culture need to incorporate several observable events and underlying forces—observed behavioral regularities when people interact; group norms; espoused values, formal philosophy; rules of the game; climate; embedded skills; habits of thinking, mental models, and/or linguistic paradigms; shared meanings; root metaphors or integrating symbols; and formal rituals and celebrations. Once these forces and events are perceptible, leaders and members can more readily understand how culture influences their organization and what aspects need to be adapted or changed. This understanding is especially useful for examining the role of culture in bringing about or inhibiting genuine inclusion of diverse groups in the organization.

The internal culture of today's global workplace consists of individuals and groups from different national cultures. Michàlle Mor Barak (Chapter 19) emphasizes that leaders and members in this global context need to understand cultural differences and similarities among national groups, and develop proficiency in cross-cultural communication. The author details two major studies by Geert Hofstede and Robert House et al. that provide perspective on various cultural dimensions. Building on an earlier framework developed by Inkeles and Levinson, Hofstede surveyed IBM employees in 40 different countries to measure differences along four value dimensions: power distance, individualism versus collectivism, masculinity versus femininity, and avoidance of uncertainty. He later added long-term versus short-term orientation.

Hofstede discovered that national culture accounted for more differences in work-related values and attitudes than other factors such as position, profession, age, or gender. These findings had significant implications for individual and group expectations related to behaviors in the workplace. As Mor Barak explains,

Whether employees expect their supervisor, for example, to be authoritative and give clear instructions that they will closely follow or whether they expect to operate independently and have egalitarian relationships with their supervisors depends to a large extent on the cultural perception of power distance in their society.

Hofstede's study provided considerable advances in the study of national cultures in the workplace, but it was also critiqued for its inherent Western bias, limited conceptualization of culture, and less than rigorous methodology.

The Global Leadership and Organizational Behavior Effectiveness (GLOBE) study conducted by Robert House et al. examined the relationship among societal culture, organizational culture, and organizational leadership effectiveness. The study team consisted of 170 social scientists and management scholars from 61 countries who collected data from

17,000 middle managers in three different industries. It differed from Hofstede's study in several ways: it was a cross-cultural study conceptualized by multicultural researchers; the industry selection and instrument design were completed with the full participation of multinational researchers; and data were collected in each country by investigators who were natives of the culture or had extensive knowledge and experience in the country.

Robert House et al. studied nine cultural attributes: performance orientation, assertiveness, future orientation, human orientation, institutional collectivism, in-group collectivism, gender egalitarianism, power distance, and uncertainty avoidance. They found six universally shared dimensions of leadership, including charismatic/value based, team oriented, self-protective, participative, humane oriented, and autonomous.

According to Mor Barak, effective interaction in cross-national settings depends to a great extent on the ability of leaders and members to convey a clear message that people in different cultures can comprehend the way the communicator intended them to understand it. She defines communication as the use of symbols (including words, tone of voice, gestures, or use of objects or artifacts) to convey meaning. Miscommunication is more likely to occur between participants from different cultures, and it occurs when the original intent of the person transmitting the message is different from the meaning that is received by the other person. As a result, leaders and members need to understand cultural differences and become competent in cross-cultural communication to succeed in a diverse, cross-national workplace.

Donna Chrobot-Mason and Nicholas Aramovich (Chapter 20) examine the effect of organizational climate on inclusion and retention of diverse members. They cite the work of Schneider, Gunnarson, and Niles-Jolly, who define climate as "the atmosphere that employees perceive as created in their organizations by practices, procedures and rewards." Chrobot-Mason and Aramovich researched the relationship between employee perceptions of an affirming climate for diversity and the employee's intent to stay with or leave the organization (turnover). They

also hypothesized that four psychological outcomes mediate the relationship between employees' perceptions of diversity climate and their intentions to turnover: employees' identification with the organization, climate for innovation, psychological empowerment, and identity freedom.

They found employees are less likely to report intentions to leave the organization when they feel they work in a climate where they have equal access to opportunities and are treated fairly. Their findings support claims in the diversity literature that when organizations develop a diversity affirming climate, they accrue the positive benefits of diversity, including greater creativity, innovation, and an improved bottom line. Identity freedom, employees' perception that they can be themselves at work and express their unique perspectives, allows employees to feel empowered to make decisions affecting their work, feel encouraged to develop innovative solutions, and identify with the organization. Additionally, the study found that a diversity affirming climate supported these positive outcomes across employee gender and race. In other words, majority members benefitted equally from this organizational climate.

Inclusion

The next three chapters focus on organizational inclusion of three specific forms of diversity: lesbian, gay, bisexual, and transgender members (LGBT); women; and generational differences. Steven Schmidt, Rod Githens, Tonette Rocco, and Martin Kormanik (Chapter 21) review the small core of research on lesbian, gay, bisexual, and transgender individuals in U.S. workplaces. In practice, LGBT inclusion policies and practices in corporations have exceeded empirical research on the topic. The Human Rights Campaign Foundation measures employers' commitment to equal treatment and inclusion of LGBT employees, consumers, and investors using a Corporate Equality Index with criteria in four categories: nondiscrimination polices; equal benefits; organizational competency in LGBT inclusion; and public commitment. Their 2014 report shows that

304 businesses from the Fortune 500 list received a rating of 100% on the index.[3] These companies

- implement nondiscrimination policies covering sexual orientation and gender identity;
- update benefits packages for both-partner benefits, including retirement benefits and transgender-inclusive benefits; and
- demonstrate competency in LGBT inclusion through actions such as diversity training and educational programs, optional self-identification by employees to measure recruitment and retention, senior leaders' accountability for diversity and inclusion goals, gender transition guidelines, LGBT/Allies employee groups and diversity councils, and public engagement of the LGBT community (pp. 20, 24, 28, 30–33, 36).

In contrast to business practices, Schmidt, Githens, Rocco, and Kormanik examine research on LGBT workplace issues to determine what articles have been published, what topics were covered, what research methodologies were used, and what research needs to be addressed in the future. Their review discovered research on several workplace and organizational issues, including organizational change to promote inclusion of LGBT members in the workplace, LGBT-focused diversity initiatives such as eliminating discrimination and preventing harassment, human resource policies such as benefits for same-sex partners, career development, and workplace education content and training concerning LGBT diversity in the workplace and curriculum development. The authors argue there are significant gaps in this area of research, and the field is ripe for studies to fill these voids.

A considerable body of research has been conducted on the topic of women and leadership. Crystal Hoyt (Chapter 22) affirms the research focus on women and leadership has shifted from asking, "Can women lead?" (which is now a moot point) to "Are there leadership style and effectiveness differences between women and men?" and "Why are women underrepresented in elite leadership roles?" Studies on leadership style and effectiveness differences between women and men found the only robust

gender difference was that women lead in a more democratic or participative style than men. This difference, however, appears to be adaptive in that the use of these styles by women resulted in more favorable evaluations. Women's styles were also found to be more transformational than men's since women engage in more contingent reward and blend individualized consideration with inspirational motivation components of transformational leadership.

While women hold 51% of management and professional positions, Hoyt asserts that research on underrepresentation of women in elite roles demonstrates that many women must successfully navigate what Eagly and Carli call the *leadership labyrinth*. Women have to circumvent barriers all along the road to reaching top executive positions. More women are reaching these executive positions, but there are still less than 3% women who are Fortune 500 CEOs, 15.7% with seats on Fortune 500 boards, and 16.8 % in the U.S. Congress. To reach top levels, women can work to balance communal and agentic leadership qualities, and their organizations can implement policies and practices to support their rise to the executive suite such as providing line management positions with appropriately demanding assignments or changing the norm for excessively long work hours.

John Becton, Harvell Walker, and Allison Jones-Farmer (Chapter 23) emphasize that organizations in the United States currently have three generations of employees working together—Baby Boomers (born between 1945 and 1964), Generation X (born between 1965 and 1979), and Millennials or Generation Y (born in 1980 or later). Common stereotypes have been attributed to each of these groups—for instance, Baby Boomers are considered achievement oriented, independent, in control of their own destinies, respectful of authority, loyal, attached to organizations, and diligent on the job. There is some empirical evidence for many of the stereotypical values associated with each group, but does this mean organizations need to find different ways to manage and work with each generational group? Publicity in the general press has managers and human resources specialists wondering how they should respond.

The researchers wanted to determine if the three generations differ in workplace behavior as is often predicted by common generational stereotypes. They examined job mobility behaviors (rather than attitudes and values) in three areas: job mobility behaviors, compliance with work rules and policies, and willingness to work overtime. They found generational differences in the three workplace behaviors were relatively small, though there were some differences in workplace behavior. The researchers conclude that the cost of tailoring organizational practices to fit each generation outweighs the potential benefits of designing flexibility into human resource practices and strategies that address the needs of all employees.

Notes

1. Roberson, Q. M. (2006). Disentangling the meanings of diversity and inclusion in organizations. *Group & Organization Management, 31*(2), 217.

2. See Hickman, G. R. (2010). *Leading change in multiple contexts: Concepts and practices in organizational, community, political, social, and global change settings* (p. 246). Thousand Oaks, CA: Sage.

3. Human Rights Campaign Foundation. (2014). *Corporate equality index 2014: Rating American workplaces on lesbian, gay, bisexual and transgender equality* (p.16). Washington, DC: Author.

Part IV — Chapters

18. The Concept of Organizational Culture: Why Bother?

    Edgar H. Schein

19. Culture and Communication in the Global Workplace

    Michàlle E. Mor Barak

20. The Psychological Benefits of Creating an Affirming Climate for Workplace Diversity

    Donna Chrobot-Mason and Nicholas P. Aramovich

21. Lesbians, Gays, Bisexuals, and Transgendered People and Human Resource Development: An Examination of the Literature in Adult Education and Human Resource Development

    Steven W. Schmidt, Rod P. Githens, Tonette S. Rocco, and Martin B. Kormanik

22. Women and Leadership

    Crystal L. Hoyt

23. Generational Differences in Workplace Behavior

    John Bret Becton, Harvell Jack Walker, and Allison Jones-Farmer

CHAPTER 18

The Concept of Organizational Culture

Why Bother?

Edgar H. Schein
Massachusetts Institute of Technology

Culture is an abstraction, yet the forces that are created in social and organizational situations deriving from culture are powerful. If we don't understand the operation of these forces, we become victim to them. Cultural forces are powerful because they operate outside of our awareness. We need to understand them not only because of their power but also because they help to explain many of our puzzling and frustrating experiences in social and organizational life. Most importantly, understanding cultural forces enables us to understand ourselves better.

What Needs to Be Explained?

Most of us in our roles as students, employees, managers, researchers, or consultants work in and have to deal with groups and organizations of all kinds. Yet we continue to find it amazingly difficult to understand and justify much of what we observe and experience in our organizational life. Too much seems to be "bureaucratic," "political," or just plain "irrational." People in positions of authority, especially our immediate bosses, often frustrate us or act incomprehensibly, and those we consider the "leaders" of our organizations often disappoint us.

When we get into arguments or negotiations with others, we often cannot understand how our opponents could take such "ridiculous" positions. When we observe other organizations, we often find it incomprehensible that "smart people could do such dumb things." We recognize cultural differences at the ethnic or national level but find them puzzling at the group, organizational, or occupational level. Gladwell (2008) in his popular book *Outliers* provides some vivid examples of how both ethnic and organizational cultures explain such anomalies as airline crashes and the success of some law firms.

As managers, when we try to change the behavior of subordinates, we often encounter "resistance to change" at a level that seems beyond reason. We observe departments in our organization that seem to be more interested in fighting with each other than getting the job done. We see communication problems and misunderstandings between group members that should not be occurring between "reasonable" people. We explain in detail why something different must be done, yet people continue to act as if they had not heard us.

As leaders who are trying to get our organizations to become more effective in the face of severe environmental pressures, we are sometimes amazed at the degree to which individuals and groups in the organization will continue to behave in obviously ineffective ways, often threatening the very survival of the organization. As we try to get things done that involve other groups, we often discover that they do not communicate with each other and that the level of conflict between groups in organizations and in the community is often astonishingly high.

As teachers, we encounter the sometimes-mysterious phenomenon that different classes behave completely differently from each other even though our material and teaching style remains the same. If we are employees considering a new job, we realize that companies differ greatly in their approach, even in the same industry and geographic locale. We feel these differences even as we walk in the door of different organizations such as restaurants, banks, stores, or airlines.

As members of different occupations, we are aware that being a doctor, lawyer, engineer, accountant, or manager involves not only learning technical skills but also adopting certain values and norms that define our occupation. If we violate some of these norms, we can be thrown out of the occupation. But where do these come from and how do we reconcile the fact that each occupation considers its norms and values to be the correct ones? How is it possible that in a hospital, the doctors, nurses, and administrators are often fighting with each other rather than collaborating to improve patient care? How is it possible that employees in organizations report unsafe conditions, yet the organization continues to operate until a major accident happens?

The concept of culture helps to explain all of these phenomena and to "normalize" them. If we understand the dynamics of culture, we will be less likely to be puzzled, irritated, and anxious when we encounter the unfamiliar and seemingly irrational behavior of people in organizations, and we will have a deeper understanding not only of why various groups of people or organizations can be so different but also why it is so hard to change them.

Even more important, if we understand culture better, we will understand ourselves better and recognize some of the forces acting within us that define who we are. We will then understand that our personality and character reflect the groups that socialized us and the groups with which we identify and to which we want to belong. Culture is not only all around us but within us as well.

FIVE PERSONAL EXAMPLES

To illustrate how culture helps to illuminate organizational situations, I will begin by describing several situations I encountered in my experiences as a consultant.

DEC

In the first case, Digital Equipment Corporation (DEC), I was called in to help a management group improve its communication, interpersonal relationships, and decision making (Schein, 2003). DEC was founded in the middle 1950s and was one of the first companies to successfully introduce interactive computing, something that today we take completely for granted. The company was highly

(Continued)

(Continued)

successful for twenty-five years but then developed a variety of difficulties, which led to its sale to the Compaq Corporation in 1996. I will be referring to the DEC story many times in this book.

After sitting in on a number of meetings of the top management, I observed, among other things: (1) High levels of interrupting, confrontation, and debate, (2) excessive emotionality about proposed courses of action, (3) great frustration over the difficulty of getting a point of view across, (4) a sense that every member of the group wanted to win all the time, and (5) shared frustration that it took forever to make a decision that would stick.

Over a period of several months, I made many suggestions about better listening, less interrupting, more orderly processing of the agenda, the potential negative effects of high emotionality and conflict, and the need to reduce the frustration level. The group members said that the suggestions were helpful, and they modified certain aspects of their procedure, such as lengthening some of their meetings. However, the basic pattern did not change. No matter what kind of Intervention I attempted, the basic style of the group remained the same. How to explain this?

Ciba-Geigy

In the second case, I was asked, as part of a broader consultation project, to help create a climate for innovation in an organization that felt a need to become more flexible to respond to its increasingly dynamic business environment. This Swiss Chemical Company consisted of many different business units, geographical units, and functional group. It was eventually merged with the Sandoz Company and is today part of Novartis.

As I got to know more about Ciba-Geigy's many units and problems, I observed that some very innovative things were going on in many places in the company. I wrote several memos describing these innovations, added other ideas from my own experience, and gave the memos to my contact person in to the company with the request that he distribute them to the various business unit and geographical managers who needed to be made aware of these ideas.

After some months, I discovered that those managers to whom I had personally given the memo thought it was helpful and on target, but rarely, if ever, did they pass it on, and none were ever distributed by my contact person. I also suggested meetings of managers from different units to stimulate lateral communication but found no support at all for such meeting. No matter what I did, I could not seem to get information flowing laterally across divisional functional, or geographical boundaries. Yet everyone agreed in principle the innovation would be stimulated by more lateral communication and encouraged me to keep on "helping." Why did my helpful memos not circulate?

Cambridge-at-Home

This third example is quite different. Two years ago I was involved in the creation of an organization devoted to allowing people to stay in their homes as they aged. The founding group of ten older residents of Cambridge asked me to chair the meetings to design this new organization.

To build strong consensus and commitment, I wanted to be sure that everyone' s voice would be heard even if that slowed down the meetings. I resisted Robert's *Rules of Order* in favor of a consensus building style, which was much slower but honored everyone's point of view. I discovered that this consensus approach polarized the group into those who were comfortable with the more open style and those who thought I was running the "worst meetings ever." What was going on here?

Amoco

In the fourth example, Amoco, a large oil company that was eventually acquired by British Petroleum, decided to centralize all of its engineering functions into a single service unit. Whereas engineers had previously been regular full-time members of projects, they were now supposed to "sell their services" to clients who would be charged for these service, The engineers would now be "internal consultants" who would be "hired" by the various projects. The engineers resisted this new arrangement violently, and many of them threatened to leave the organization. Why were they so resistant to the new organizational arrangements?

Alpha Power

In the fifth example, Alpha Power, an electric and gas utility that services a major urban, area was faced with becoming more environmentally responsible after being brought up on criminal charges for allegedly failing to report the presence of asbestos in one of its local units that suffered an accident. Electrical workers, whose "heroic" self-image of keeping the power on no matter what, also held the strong norm that one did not report spills and other environmental and safety problems if such reports would embarrass the group. I was involved in a multi-year project to change this self-image to one where the "heroic" model was to report all safety and environmental hazards even if that meant reporting on peers and even bosses. A new concept of personal responsibility, teamwork, and openness of communication was to be adopted. Reporting on and dealing with environmental events became routine, but no matter how clear the new mandate was, some safety problems continued if peer group relations were involved. Why? What could be more important than employee and public safety?

How Does the Concept of Culture Help?

I did not really understand the forces operating in any of these cases until I began to examine my own assumptions about how things should work in these organizations and began to test whether my assumptions fitted those operating in my client systems. This step of examining the *shared* assumptions in an organization or group and comparing them to your own takes us into "cultural" analysis and will be the focus from here on.

It turned out that in DEC, senior managers and most of the other members of the organization shared the assumption that you cannot determine whether or not something is "true" or "valid" unless you subject the idea or proposal to intensive debate. Only ideas that survive such debate are worth acting on, and only ideas that survive such scrutiny will be implemented. The group members assumed that what they were doing was discovering truth, and, in this context, being polite to each other was relatively unimportant. I become more helpful to the group when I realized this and went to the flip chart and just started to write down the various ideas they were processing. If someone was interrupted, I could ask him or her to restate his or her point instead of punishing the interrupter. The group began to focus on the items on the chart and found that this really did help their communication and decision process. I had finally understood and accepted an essential element of their culture instead of imposing my own.

By this intervention of going to the flip chart, I had changed the *microculture* of their group to enable them to accomplish what their organizational culture dictated.

In Ciba-Geigy, I eventually discovered that there was a strong shared assumption that each manager's job was his or her private "turf" not to be infringed on. The strong image was communicated that "a person's job is like his or her home, and if someone gives unsolicited information, it is like walking into someone's home uninvited." Sending memos to people implies that they do not already know what is in the memo, which is seen to be potentially insulting. In this organization, managers prided themselves on knowing whatever they needed to know to do their job. Had I understood this aspect of their culture, I would have asked for a list of the names of the managers and sent the memo directly to them. They would have accepted it from me because I was the paid consultant and expert.

In my Cambridge meetings, different members had different prior experiences in meetings. Those who had grown up with a formal Robert's *Rules of Order* system on various other nonprofit boards were adamant that this was the only way to run a meeting. Others who had no history on other boards were more tolerant of my informal style. The members had come from different subcultures that did not mesh. In my human relations training culture, I had learned the value of involving people to get better implementation of decisions and was trying to build that kind of microculture in this group. Only when I adapted my style to theirs was I able to begin to shape the group more toward my preferred style.

In Amoco, I began to understand the resistance of the engineers when I learned that their assumptions were "good work should speak for itself," and "engineers should not have to go out and sell themselves." They were used to having people come to them for services and did not have a good role model for how to sell themselves.

In Alpha, I learned that in the safety area, all work units had strong norms and values of self-protection that often over-rode the new requirements imposed on the company by the courts. The groups had their own experience base for what was safe and what was not safe and were willing to trust that. On the other hand, identifying environmental hazards and cleaning them up involved new skills that workers were willing to learn and collaborate on. The union had its own cultural assumption that under no conditions would one "rat out" a fellow union member, and this applied especially in the safety area.

In each of these cases, I initially did not understand what was going on because my own basic assumptions about truth, turf, and group relations differed from the shared assumptions of the members of the organization or group. And my assumptions reflected my "occupation" as a social psychologist and organization consultant, while the group's assumptions reflected in part their occupations and experiences as electrical engineers, chemists, nonprofit organization board members, and electrical workers.

To make sense of such situations requires taking a "cultural perspective," learning to see the world through "cultural lenses," becoming competent in "cultural analysis" by which I mean being able to perceive and decipher the cultural forces that operate in groups, organizations, and occupations. When we learn to see the world through cultural lenses, all kinds of things begin to make sense that initially were mysterious, frustrating, or seemingly stupid.

Culture: An Empirically Based Abstraction

Culture as a concept has had a long and checkered history. Laymen have used it as a word to indicate sophistication, as when we say that someone is very "cultured." Anthropologists have used it to refer to the customs and rituals that societies develop over the course of their history. In the past several decades, some organizational researchers and managers have used it to describe the norms and practices that organizations develop around their handling of people or as the espoused values and credo of an organization. This sometimes confuses the concept of culture with the concept of climate, and confuses culture as what *is* with culture as *what ought to be*.

Thus managers speak of developing the "right kind of culture," a "culture of quality," or a "culture of customer service," suggesting that culture has to do with certain values that managers are trying to inculcate in their organizations. Also implied in this usage is the assumption that there are better or worse cultures, stronger or weaker cultures, and that the "right" kind of culture would influence how effective organizations are. In the managerial literature, there is often the implication that having a culture is necessary for effective performance, and that the stronger the culture, the more effective the organization.

Researchers have supported some of these views by reporting findings that certain cultural dimensions do correlate with economic performance, but this research is hard to evaluate because of the many definitions of culture and the variety of indexes of performance that are used (Wilderom Glunk, and Maslowski, 2000). Consultants and researchers have touted "culture surveys" and have claimed that they can improve organizational performance by helping organizations create certain kinds of cultures, but these claims are often based on a very different definition of culture than the one I will be arguing for here (Denison, 1990; Sackman and Bertelsman, 2006). As we will see, whether or not a culture is "good" or "bad," "functionally effective," or not, depends not on the culture alone but on the relationship of the culture to the environment in which it exists.

Perhaps the most intriguing aspect of culture as a concept is that it points us to phenomena that are below the surface, that are powerful in their impact but invisible and to a considerable degree unconscious. Culture creates within us mindsets and frames of reference that Marshak (2006) identified as one of a number of important *covert* processes. In another sense, culture is to a group what personality or character is to an individual. We can see the behavior that results, but we often cannot see the forces underneath that cause certain kinds of behavior. Yet, just as our personality and character guide and constrain our behavior, so does culture guide and constrain the behavior of members of a group through the shared norms that are held in that group.

Culture as a concept is thus an abstraction. If an abstract concept is to be useful to our thinking, it should be observable yet increase our understanding of a set of events that are otherwise mysterious or not

well understood. From this point of view, I will argue that we must avoid the superficial models of culture and build on the deeper, more complex anthropological models. Those models refer to a wide range of observable events and underlying forces, as shown in the following list.

- **Observed behavioral regularities when people interact:** The language they use, the customs and traditions that evolve, and the rituals they employ in a wide variety of situations (for example, Goffman, 1959, 1967; Jones and others, 1988; Trice and Beyer, 1993; Van Maanen, 1979b).

- **Group norms:** The implicit standards and values that evolve in working groups, such as the particular norm of "a fair day's work for a fair day's pay," that evolved among workers in the Bank Wiring Room in the Hawthorne studies (for example, Hotnans, 1950; Kilmann and Saxton, 1983).

- **Espoused values:** The articulated publicly announced principles and values that the group claims to be trying to achieve, such as "product quality" or "price leadership" (for example, Deal and Kennedy, 1982, 1999).

- **Formal philosophy:** The broad policies and ideological principles that guide a group's actions toward stockholders, employees, customers, and other stakeholders such as the highly publicized "HP Way" of the Hewlett-Packard Co. (for example, Ouchi, 1981; Pascale and Athos, 1981; Packard, 1995).

- **Rules of the game:** The implicit, unwritten rules for getting along in the organization, "the ropes" that a newcomer must learn to become an accepted member, "the way we do things around here" (for example, Schein, 1968, 1978; Van Maanen, 1976, 1979b; Ritti and Funkhouser, 1987).

- **Climate:** The feeling that is conveyed in a group by the physical layout and the way in which members of the organization interact with each other, with customers, or with other outsiders (for example, Ashkanasy, and others 2000; Schneider, 1990; Tagiuri and Litwin, 1968).

- **Embedded skills:** The special competencies displayed by group members in accomplishing certain tasks, the ability to make certain things that get passed on from generation to generation without necessarily being articulated in writing (for example, Argyris and Schon, 1978; Cook and Yanow, 1993; Henderson and Clark, 1990; Peters and Waterman, 1982; Ang and Van Dyne, 2008).
- **Habits of thinking, mental models, and/or linguistic paradigms:** The shared cognitive frames that guide the perceptions, thought, and language used by the members of a group and are taught to new members in the early socialization process (for example, Douglas, 1986; Hofstede, 1991, 2001; Van Maanen, 1979b; Senge, Roberts, Ross, Smith, and Kleiner, 1994).
- **Shared meanings:** The emergent understandings that are created by group members as they interact with each other (for example, Geertz, 1973; Smircich, 1983; Van Maanen and Barley, 1984; Weick, 1995, Weick and Sutcliffe, 2001; Hatch and Schultz, 2004).
- **"Root metaphors" or integrating symbols:** The ways that groups evolve to characterize themselves, which may or may not be appreciated consciously, but that get embodied in buildings, office layouts, and other material artifacts of the group. This level of the culture reflects the emotional and aesthetic response of members as contrasted with the cognitive or evaluative response (for example, Gagliardi, 1990; Hatch, 1990; Pondy, Frost, Morgan, and Dandridge, 1983; Schultz, 1995).
- **Formal rituals and celebrations:** The ways in which a group celebrates key events that reflect important values or important "passages" by members such as promotion, completion of important projects, and milestones (Trice and Beyer, 1993, Deal and Kennedy, 1982, 1999).

All of these concepts and phenomena relate to culture and/or reflect culture in that they deal with things that group members share or hold in common, but none of them can usefully be thought of as *the* culture of a country, organization, occupation, or group. You might wonder why we need the word *culture* at all when we have so many other concepts such as norms, values, behavior patterns, rituals, traditions, and so on. However, the word *culture* adds several other critical elements to the concept of sharing. The concept of culture implies structural stability, depth, breadth, and patterning or integration.

Structural Stability

Culture implies some level of structural stability in the group. When we say that something is "cultural" we imply that it is not only shared but also stable because it defines the group. After we achieve a sense of group identity, which is a key component of culture, it is our major stabilizing force and will not be given up easily. Culture is something that survives even when some members of the organization depart. Culture is hard to change because group members value stability in that it provides meaning and predictability.

Depth

Culture is the deepest, often unconscious part of a group and is therefore less tangible and less visible. From this point of view, most of the categories used to describe culture listed earlier can be thought of as *manifestations* of culture, but they are not the "essence" of what we mean by culture. Note that when something is more deeply embedded that also lends stability.

Breadth

A third characteristic of culture is that after it has developed, it covers *all* of a group's functioning. Culture is pervasive and influences all aspects of how an organization deals with its primary task, its various environments, and its internal operations. Not all groups have cultures in this sense, but the concept connotes that if we refer to "the culture" of a group, we are referring to all of its operations.

Patterning or Integration

The fourth characteristic that is implied by the concept of culture and that further lends stability is patterning or integration of the elements into a larger paradigm or "Gestalt" that ties together the various elements and resides at a deeper level. Culture implies that rituals, climate, values, and behaviors tie together into a coherent whole, and this pattern or integration is the essence of what we mean by "culture." Such patterning or integration ultimately derives from the human need to make our environment as sensible and orderly as we can (Weick, 1995). Disorder or senselessness makes us anxious, so we will work hard to reduce that anxiety by developing a more consistent and predictable view of how things are and how they should be. Thus: "Organizational cultures, like other cultures, develop as groups of people struggle to make sense of and cope with their worlds" (Trice and Beyer, 1993, p. 4).

How then should we think about this "essence" of culture, and how should we formally define it? The most useful way to arrive at a definition of something as abstract as culture is to think in dynamic evolutionary terms. If we can understand where culture comes from, how it evolves, then we can grasp something that is abstract, that exists in a group's unconscious, yet that has powerful influences on a group's behavior.

Any social unit that has some kind of shared history will have evolved a culture. The strength of that culture depends on the length of time, the stability of membership of the group, and the emotional intensity of the actual historical experiences they have shared. We all have a common-sense notion of this phenomenon, yet it is difficult to define it abstractly. The formal definition that I propose and will work with builds on this evolutionary perspective and argues that the most fundamental characteristic of culture is that it is a product of social *learning*.

Culture Formally Defined

The culture of a group can now be defined as a pattern of shared basic assumptions learned by a group as it solved its problems of external adaptation and internal integration, which has worked well enough to be considered valid and, therefore, to be taught to new members as the correct way to perceive, think, and feel in relation to those problems.

Culture by this definition tends toward patterning and integration. But a given group may not have the kind of learning experiences that allow it to evolve a culture in this sense. There may be major turnover leaders or members, the mission or primary task may change, the underlying technology on which the group is built may evolve, or the group may split into subgroups that develop their own subcultures leading to what Joanne Martin and her colleagues define as *differentiated* cultures and/or *fragmented* cultures (Martin, 2002).

We all know of groups, organizations, and societies where there are beliefs and values that work at cross purposes with other beliefs and values leading to situations full of conflict and ambiguity. But if the concept of culture is to have any utility, it should draw our attention to those things that are the product of our human need for stability, consistency, and meaning. Culture formation, therefore, is always, by definition, a striving toward patterning and integration, even though in many groups, their actual history of experiences prevents them from ever achieving a clear-cut unambiguous paradigm.

Culture Content

If a group's culture is that group's accumulated learning, how do we describe and catalogue the content of that learning? Group and organizational theories distinguish two major sets of problems that all groups, no matter what their size, must deal with: (1) Survival, growth, and adaptation in their environment; and (2) Internal integration that permits daily functioning and the ability to adapt and learn. Both of these areas of group functioning will reflect the macrocultural context in which the group exists and from which are derived broader and deeper basic assumptions about the nature of reality, time, space, human nature, and human relationships. Each of these areas will be explained in detail in later chapters.

The Process of Socialization or Acculturation

After a group has a culture, it will pass elements of this culture on to new generations of group members (Louis, 1980; Schein, 1968; Van Maanen, 1976; Van Maanen and Schein, 1979). Studying what new members of groups are taught is, in fact, a good way to discover some of the elements of a culture, but we only learn about surface aspects of the culture by this means. This is especially so because much of what is at the heart of a culture will not be revealed in the rules of behavior taught to newcomers. It will only be revealed to members as they gain permanent status and are allowed into the inner circles of the group where group secrets then are shared.

On the other hand, *how* people learn and the socialization processes to which they are subjected may indeed reveal deeper assumptions. To get at those deeper levels, we must try to understand the perceptions and feelings that arise in critical situations, and we must observe and interview regular members or "old timers" to get an accurate sense of the deeper-level assumptions that are shared.

Can culture be learned through anticipatory socialization or self-socialization? Can new members discover for themselves what the basic assumptions are? Yes and no. We certainly know that one of the major activities of any new member when she or he enters a new group is to decipher the operating norms and assumptions. But this deciphering can only be successful through the rewards and punishments that are meted out by old members to new members as they experiment with different kinds of behavior. In this sense, there is always a teaching process going on, even though it may be quite implicit and unsystematic.

If the group does not have shared assumptions, as will sometimes be the case, the new members' interaction with old members will be a more creative process of building a culture. But once shared assumptions exist, the culture survives through teaching them to newcomers. In this regard, culture is a mechanism of social control and can be the basis of explicitly manipulating members into perceiving, thinking, and feeling in certain ways (Van Maanen and Kunda, 1989; Kunda, 1992). Whether or not we approve of this as a mechanism of social control is a separate question that will be addressed later.

Can Culture Be Inferred From Only Behavior?

Note that the definition of culture that I have given does not include overt behavior patterns, though some such behavior, especially formal rituals, would reflect cultural assumptions. Instead, this definition emphasizes that the shared assumptions deal with how we perceive, think about, and feel about things. We cannot rely on overt behavior alone because it is always determined both by the cultural predisposition (the perceptions, thoughts, and feelings that are patterned) and by the situational contingencies that arise from the immediate external environment.

Behavioral regularities can occur for reasons other than culture. For example, if we observe that all members of a group cower in the presence of a large and loud leader, this could be based on biological reflex reactions to sound and size, individual learning, or shared learning. Such a behavioral regularity should not, therefore, be the basis for defining culture, though we might later discover that, in a given group's experience, cowering is indeed a result of shared learning and therefore a manifestation of deeper shared assumptions. Or, to put it another way, when we observe behavioral regularities, we do not know whether or not we are dealing with a cultural manifestation. Only after we have discovered the deeper layers that I am defining as the essence of culture can we specify what is and what is not an "artifact" that reflects the culture.

Do Occupations Have Cultures?

The definition provided previously does not specify the size or location of the social unit to which it can legitimately be applied. We know that nations, ethnic groups, religions, and other kinds of social units have cultures in this sense. I called these *macrocultures*. Our experience with large organizations also tells us that even globally dispersed corporations such as IBM or Unilever have corporate cultures in spite of the obvious presence of many diverse subcultures within the larger organization.

But it is not clear whether it makes sense to say that medicine or law or accounting or engineering have cultures. If culture is a product of joint learning leading to shared assumptions about how to perform and relate internally, then we can see clearly that many occupations do evolve cultures. If there is strong socialization during the education and training period and if the beliefs and values learned during this time remain stable as taken-for-granted assumptions even though the person may not be in a group of occupational peers, then clearly those occupations have cultures. For most of the occupations that will concern us, these cultures are global to the extent that members are trained in the same way to the same skill set and values. However, we will find that macrocultures also influence how occupations are defined, that is, how engineering or medicine is practiced in a particular country. These variations make it that much more difficult to decipher in a hospital, for example, what is national, ethnic, occupational, or organizational.

Summary and Conclusions

In this chapter, I have introduced the concept of culture and have argued that it helps to explain some of the more seemingly incomprehensible and irrational aspects of what goes on in groups, occupations, organizations, and other kinds of social units that have common histories. I reviewed the variety of elements that people perceive to be "culture," leading to a formal definition that puts the emphasis on shared learning experiences that lead to shared, taken-for-granted basic assumptions held by the members of the group or organization.

In this sense, any group with a stable membership and a history of shared learning will have developed some level of culture, but a group that either has had a great deal of turnover of members and leaders or a history lacking in any kind of challenging events may well lack any shared assumptions. Not every collection of people develops a culture, and, in fact, we tend to use the terms "group," "team," or "community" rather than "crowd" or "collection of people" only when there has been enough of a shared history so that some degree of culture formation has taken place.

After a set of shared assumptions has come to be taken for granted it determines much of the group's behavior, and the rules and norms that are taught to newcomers in a socialization process that is a reflection of culture. We noted that to define culture, we must go below the behavioral level because behavioral regularities can be caused by forces other than culture. We noted that even large organizations can have a common culture if there has been enough of a history of shared experience.

We also noted that culture and leadership are two sides of the same coin in that leaders first start the process of culture creation when they create groups and organizations. After cultures exist, they determine the criteria for leadership and thus determine who will or will not be a leader. But if elements of a culture become dysfunctional, it is the unique function of leadership to perceive the functional and dysfunctional elements of the existing culture and to manage cultural evolution and change in such a way that the group can survive in a changing environment. The bottom line for leaders is that if they do not become conscious of the cultures in which they are embedded, those cultures will manage them. Cultural understanding is desirable for all of us, but it is essential to leaders if they are to lead.

References

Ang, S., & Van Dyne, L. (Eds.). (2008). *Handbook of cultural intelligence.* Armohk, NY: M. E. Sharpe.

Argyris, C., & Schon, D. A. (1978). *Organizational Learning.* Reading, MA: Addison-Wesley.

Ashkanasy, N. M., Wilderom, C. P. M., & Peterson, M. F (Eds.). (2000). *Handbook of organizational culture and climate.* Thousand Oaks, CA: Sage.

Cook, S. D. N., & Yanow, D. (1993). Culture and organizational learning. *Journal of Management Inquiry*, 2(4), 373–390.

Deal, T. E., & Kennedy, A. A. (1982). *Corporate cultures*. Reading, MA: Addison-Wesley.

Deal, T. E., & Kennedy, A. A. (1999). *The new corporate cultures*. New York: Perseus.

Denison, D. R., Haaland. S., & Goelzer, P. (2003). *Corporate culture and organizational effectiveness: Is there a similar pattern around the world?* (pp. 205–227) Greenwich: Jai Press.

Douglas, M. (1986). *How institutions think*. Syracuse, NY: Syracuse University Press.

Gagliardi, P. (Ed.) (1990). *Symbols and artifacts: Views of the corporate landscape*. New York: Walter de Gruyter.

Geertz, C. (1973). *The interpretation of cultures*. New York: Basic Books.

Gladwell, M. (2008). *Outliers*. New York: Little Brown.

Goffman, E. (1959). *The presentation of self in every day life*. New York: Doubleday.

Goffman, E. (1967). *Interaction ritual* Hawthorne, NY: Aldine.

Hatch, M. J. (1990). The symbolics of office design. In P. Gagliardi (Ed.), *Symbols and Artifacts*. New York: Walter de Gruyter.

Hatch, M. J., & Schultz, M. (Eds.). (2004). *Organizational identity: A reader*. Oxford, UK: Oxford University Press.

Henderson, R. M., & Clark, K. B. (1990). Architectural innovation: The reconfiguration of existing product technologies and the failure of established firms. *Administrative Science Quarterly*, 35, 9–30.

Hofstede, G. (1991). Cultures *and organizations*. London: McGraw-Hill.

Homans, G. (1950). *The human group*. New York: Harcourt Brace Jovanovich.

Jones, M. O., Moore, M. D., & Snyder, R. C. (Eds.). (1988). *Inside organizations*. Newbury Park, CA: Sage.

Kilmann, R. H., & Saxton, M. J. (1983). *The Kilmann-Saxton culture gap survey*. Pittsburgh, PA: Organizational Design Consultants.

Kunda, G. (1992). *Engineering culture*. Philadelphia: Temple University Press.

Louis, M. R. (1980). Surprise and sense making. Administrative *Science Quarterly*, 25, 226–251.

Marshak, R. J. (2006). *Covert processes at work*. San Francisco: Berrett-Koehler.

Martin, J. (2002*). Organisational culture: Mapping the terrain*. Newbury Park, CA:

Ouchi, W. G. (1981). *Theory Z*. Reading, MA: Addison-Wesley.

Packard, D. (1995). *The HP way*. New York: Harper Collins.

Pascale, R. T., & Athos, A. G. (1981). *The art of Japanese management*. New York: Simon & Schuster.

Peters, T. J., & Waterman, R. H., Jr. (1982). *In search of excellence*. New York:. Harper & Row.

Pondy, L. R., Frost, P. J., Morgan, G., & Dandridge, T. (Eds.). (1983). *Organizational symbolism*. Greenwich, CT: JAI Press.

Ritti, R. R., & Funkhouser, G. R. (1987). *The ropes to skip and the ropes to know* (3rd ed.). Columbus, OH: Grid.

Sackmann, S. A. & Stiftung, B. (2006). *Success factor: Corporate culture*. Guetersloh, Germany: Bertelsman Stiftung.

Schein, E. H. (1968). Organizational socialization and the profession of management. *Industrial Management Review*, 9, 1–15.

Schneider, B. (Ed.). (1990). *Organizational climate and culture*. San Francisco: Jossey-Bass.

Schultz, M. (1995). *On studying organizational cultures*. New York: De Gruyter.

Senge, P., Roberts, C., Ross, R. B., Smith, B. J., & Kleiner, A. (1994). *The fifth discipline field book*. New York: Doubleday Currency.

Smircich, L. (1983). Concepts of culture and organizational analysis. *Administrative Science Quarterly*, 28, 339–358.

Tagiuri, R., & Litwin, G. H. (Eds.). (1968). *Organizational climate: Exploration of a concept*. Boston: Division of Research, Harvard Graduate School of Business.

Trice, H. M., & Beyer, J. M. (1993). The *cultures of work organizations*. Englewood Cliffs, NJ: Prentice-Hall.

Van Maanen, J. (1976). Breaking in: Socialization at work, in R. Dubin (Ed.), *Handbook of work organization and society*. Skokie, IL: Rand McNally.

Van Maanen, J. (1979b). The self, the situation, and the rules of interpersonal relations. In W. Bennis, J. Van Maanen, E. J. Schein, & F. I. Steele (Eds.), *Essays in interpersonal dynamics* (pp. 43–101). Homewood, IL: Dorsey Press.

Van Maanen, J., & Schein, E. H. (1979). Toward a theory of organizational socialization. In B. M. Staw, & L. L. Cummings (Eds.), *Research in organizational behavior* (Vol. 1). Greenwich, CT: JAI Press.

Van Maanen, J., & Barley, S. R. (1984). Occupational communities: Culture and control in organizations. In B. M. Staw & L. L. Cummings (Eds.), *Research in organizational behavior* (Vol. 6). Greenwich, CT: JAI Press.

Van Maanen, J., & Kunda, G. (1989). Real feelings: Emotional expression and organizational culture. In B. Staw (Ed.), Research *in organizational behavior* (Vol. 11). Greenwich, CT: JAI Press.

Weick, K. (1995). *Sensemaking in organizations.* Thousand Oaks, CA: Sage.

Weick, K., & Sutcliffe, K. M. (2001). *Managing the unexpected.* San Francisco: Jossey-Bass.

Wilderom, C. P. M., Glunk, U., & Maslowski, R. (2000). Organizational culture as a predictor of organizational performance. In N. M. Ashkanasy, G. P. M. Wilderom, & M. F. Peterson (Eds.), *Handbook of organizational culture and climate* (pp. 193–209). Thousand Oaks, CA: Sage.

CHAPTER 19

Culture and Communication in the Global Workplace

Michàlle E. Mor Barak

University of Southern California

The Jack Welch of the future cannot be me. I spent my entire career in the United States. The next head of General Electric will be somebody who spent time in Bombay, in Hong Kong, in Buenos Aires. We have to send our best and brightest overseas and make sure they have the training that will allow them to be global leaders who will make GE flourish in the future.

—Jack Welch, CEO of U.S.-based General Electric in a speech to GE employees[1]

To succeed in managing a workforce that is increasingly diverse and multinational, managers need knowledge about cultural differences and similarities among nations. They also need to be sensitive to these differences, which can contribute to their effectiveness in cross-cultural communication. Human behavior and interpersonal interactions are reflective of the values and norms of specific societies. These cultural values and behavioral norms differ between societies, but until recently, they have been considered quite stable within societies. In recent decades, however, this perception has been changing as scholars became more aware of the impact of the global trends of immigration and worker migration on national cultures (see Chapters 4 and 5). In today's global business world, a manager has to understand cultural differences among societies and their meaning in business relations. In addition, she or he needs to be sensitive to cultural nuances within societies that are associated with the diversity of that society. In this chapter, we examine the cultural context in the global workplace and

---

Source: Culture and Communication in the Global Workplace by Michàlle E. Mor Barak, pp. 175–195. In *Managing Diversity: Toward a Globally Inclusive Workplace,* 3rd ed. by Michàlle E. Mor Barak (2014). Copyright © SAGE Publications, Inc. Reprinted with permission.

analyze communication patterns that facilitate or block effective cross-cultural communication.

The Cultural Context for the Global Workplace

What is *culture?* The Latin origin of the word refers to the tilling of the soil, although the common everyday use of the word refers to refinement, particularly through education, literature, and the arts. In this book, we refer to the broader meaning of the word *culture* as used by social scientists. There are many definitions of culture in the social psychological and anthropological literature,[2] but the most widely accepted definition is the one proposed in the mid-20th century by Kroeber and Kluckhohn (1952) after analyzing 160 definitions of the concept of *culture* and synthesizing the following definition:

> Culture consists of patterns, explicit or implicit, of and for behavior acquired and transmitted by symbols, constituting the distinctive achievements of human groups, including their embodiments in artifacts; the essential core of culture consists of traditional (historically derived and selected) ideas and especially their attached values; culture systems may, on the one hand, be considered as products of action, on the other as conditioning elements of further action. (p. 181)

Using the analogy of computer programming, Hofstede, Hofstede, and Minkov (2010) call culture "software of the mind," noting that the patterns of thinking, feeling, and acting embedded in a culture are like "mental programs." They define *culture* as "the collective programming of the mind which distinguishes the members of one group or category of people from another" (p. 6). Although culture does not determine the exact behavior for human beings the way programs dictate how computers function, it does delineate the expectations, actual or anticipated, and behaviors within a specific social context. Others define *culture* as a "set of beliefs and values about what is desirable

and undesirable in a community of people, and a set of formal or informal practices to support the values" (Javidan & House, 2001, p. 292). Understanding societal culture can be complex because it includes two sets of elements at once: The first are the ongoing cultural practices that inform us about the current perceptions of specific cultures, and the second are the strongly held values that inform us about aspirations and direction that cultures wish to develop (Dorfman, Javidan, Hanges, Dastmalchian, & House, 2012; Javidan, Stahl, Brodbeck, & Wilderom, 2005).

If culture is the sum of the learned and shared patterns of thought and behaviors that are characteristic of a given people, how are national cultures around the world different from one another? To answer this question, Geert Hofstede, a Dutch social scientist, embarked on a multinational study examining national cultures (Hofstede, 1980, 1997, 2001; Hofstede & Hofstede, 2004; Hofstede et al., 2010). In his initial book, *Culture's Consequences,* Hofstede (1980) presented a statistical analysis of about 117,000 questionnaires collected in 1967 and 1973 from employees working in IBM subsidiaries in 40 different countries. Studying individuals who worked for the same organization was assumed to provide the researchers with a good environment for studying national cultures because all the employees were thought to share the same organizational culture and environment. This allowed the researchers to focus on the differences in the participants' responses as indicative of national cultural differences. In other words, the researchers assumed that being employed by the same organization (IBM) has created a common organizational culture and, therefore, whatever differences in values and norms would be evident between employees who worked in different countries would be the result of national cultural differences. The most important result of this analysis was a theoretical formulation of four value dimensions for representing differences among national cultures: power distance, uncertainty avoidance, individualism-collectivism, and masculinity/femininity. A fifth dimension—long- versus short-term orientation—was added a decade later (Hofstede, 1997).

It is important to note from the outset that Hofstede's research (e.g., 1980, 1997, 2001) was widely lauded for its breakthrough contribution to the study of culture (e.g., Kirkman, Lowe, & Gibson, 2006; Søndergaard, 1994), yet it was criticized for its lack of scientific rigor and even outright cultural bias (e.g., Ailon, 2008; McSweeney, 2002). Because of its enduring and widespread influence, we devote the following sections to discussing the strengths of the work as well as its limitations.

Cultural Value Dimensions

Social anthropologists have long agreed that all societies face the same basic problems—they differ only in the way they answer these problems.[3] Hofstede (1980), based on an earlier framework developed by Inkeles and Levinson (1969), examined culture in the different countries along four axes: (a) *power distance*—the relationship with authority and social inequality; (b) *individualism vs. collectivism*—the relationship between the individual and the group; (c) *masculinity vs. femininity*—the tendency toward assertiveness in contrast to modesty; and (d) *avoidance of uncertainty*—the control of aggression and expressions of emotions. Interestingly, Hofstede (1980) found that national culture, as measured along these axes, explained more of the differences in work-related values and attitudes than did position within the organization, profession, age, or gender. Following the discovery and write-up of the four original cultural dimensions that were previously stated, Hofstede (2001) decided to add a fifth dimension to his model. This dimension was based on the answers of student samples from 23 countries to the Chinese Value Survey (CVS). The study's instrument was developed by Michael Harris Bond in Hong Kong based on values suggested by Chinese scholars and seemed was to reflect Confucian teachings in both of its poles. The fifth dimension was *long- versus short-term orientation*—the tendency for thrift and perseverance and respect for tradition and fulfilling social obligations. Table 19.1 provides the definitions for each dimension with some country-specific examples.

These five dimensions have clear implications for individual and group expectations related to acceptable behaviors in the workplace. Whether employees expect their supervisor, for example, to be authoritative and give clear instructions that they will closely follow or whether they expect to operate independently and have egalitarian relationships with their supervisors depends to a large extent on the cultural perception of power distance in their society. Next is a description of the cultural differences in expected and acceptable behaviors in the workplace, according to Hofstede's five axes.

Power Distance

In large power distance societies, such as Latin countries (Latin American and Latin European, like France and Spain), as well as Asian and African countries, the hierarchical system in society is considered existential. Applying this principle to the workplace, supervisors and subordinates consider themselves as existentially unequal. There are many supervisors and many layers of management with large salary differentials between people at the top and at the bottom, as well as in between. Subordinates expect to be told what to do, and superiors are entitled to special privileges. Hofstede and colleagues (2010) note that, in high power distance societies, "The ideal boss, in the subordinates' eyes, is one they feel most comfortable with and who they respect most, is a benevolent autocrat or 'good father'" (p. 73). In contrast, in small power distance societies, such as the United States, Canada, Great Britain, and Denmark, subordinates and supervisors consider themselves as existentially equal. The hierarchical strata in the organizations are considered permeable, providing the possibility for both subordinates and supervisors to move up or down the ladder, and supervisors are expected to be accessible to subordinates. The ideal boss is "a resourceful (and therefore respected) democrat" (Hofstede et al., 2010, p. 74). There is evidence that congruence between managers' societal values of power distance and the culture of the organization in which the manager works can reduce job-related stress. For example, Joiner (2001)

Table 19.1	**Dimensions of Cultural Difference**

Dimension	*Definition*[1]	*Country-Specific Examples*[2]
Power distance	*Power distance* refers to the extent to which the less powerful members of institutions and organizations within a country expect and accept that power is distributed unequally.	Large power distance: Malaysia, Guatemala, Panama, Philippines, Mexico Small power distance: Austria, Israel, Denmark, New Zealand, Ireland
Individualism vs. collectivism	*Individualism* pertains to societies in which the ties between individuals are loose. *Collectivism* pertains to societies in which people are integrated into strong cohesive in-groups, which throughout a lifetime continue to protect them in exchange for unquestioning loyalty.	High individualism: United States, Australia, Great Britain, Canada, the Netherlands High collectivism: Guatemala, Ecuador, Panama, Venezuela, Colombia
Masculinity vs. femininity	*Masculinity* pertains to societies in which gender roles are clearly distinct. *Femininity* pertains to societies in which social gender roles overlap (both men and women are supposed to be modest, tender, and concerned with quality of life).	High masculinity: Japan, Austria, Venezuela, Italy, Switzerland High femininity: Sweden, Norway, the Netherlands, Denmark, Costa Rica
Avoidance of uncertainty	*Avoidance of uncertainty* refers to the extent to which the members of a culture feel threatened by uncertain or unknown situations—the extent to which they need predictability in the form of written and unwritten rules.	Weak uncertainty avoidance: Greece, Portugal, Guatemala, Uruguay, Belgium Strong uncertainty avoidance: Singapore, Jamaica, Denmark, Sweden, Hong Kong
Long-term vs. short-term orientation	Long-term orientation refers to the fostering of virtues oriented toward future rewards, in particular, perseverance and thrift. Short-term orientation refers to the fostering of virtues related to the past and present, in particular, respect for tradition, preservation of "face," and fulfilling social obligations.	Long-term orientation: China, Hong Kong, Taiwan, Japan, Korea Short-term orientation: Zimbabwe, Canada, Philippines, Nigeria, Pakistan

Source: Adapted from Hofstede (1980, 1997, 2001).

Notes:

1. Definitions for the four cultural dimensions are drawn from Hofstede (1997, pp. 28, 51, 113), and the fifth cultural dimension is drawn from Hofstede (2001, pp. 356, 359). These definitions are also cited in Hofstede's more recent work with colleagues (e.g., Hofstede et al., 2010).

2. Country-specific identifications in this table and throughout the chapter are based on Hofstede's study among IBM employees worldwide and Michael Bond's CVS study among students. Scores and rankings for the more than 60 countries included in the original study on each of the four cultural dimensions can be found in Hofstede (1980, 1997; Hofstede et al., 2010), and those for 23 countries included in the CVS study on the fifth dimension can be found in Hofstede (2001; Hofstede et al., 2010).

found that managers in Greece, a country characterized by a large power distance, were comfortable with the so-called Eiffel Tower organizational culture, characterized by centralization and formalizations, and that the congruence between this type of organizational culture and the Greek culture contributed to reduced levels of stress among the managers.

Individualism Versus Collectivism

The individualism/collectivism dimension refers to the extent to which people see themselves as an integral part of a social group with primary alliance to the group or as separate individuals with primary responsibility for themselves and their very immediate family only. In collectivist societies, such as many Latin American countries as well as Arab-speaking countries, people are born into extended families or other in-groups, which continue to protect them in exchange for loyalty. This reality is evident in the workplace where the relationship between the employer and the employees in the organization is seen as a family relationship. There are mutual obligations with strong loyalty on the part of the employee connected to an employer's commitment for protection and security in return. In a strong collectivist-oriented context, there is a clear preference for group-oriented human resource (HR) management practices (Aycan, Al-Hamadi, Davis, & Budhwar, 2007). Employee loyalty in this context refers to an unwritten contract that requires employees to be faithful to their duties, to their managers and coworkers, and to their organization. Loyalty often serves as a mediator between the perception of a familiar (collectivistic) organizational climate and job performance and often means that employees are more likely to follow orders, behave according to expectations, and do the best job they know how to do (Jen, Chou, Lin, & Tsai, 2012; Umiker, 1995). Hiring preference is given to relatives, first to relatives of high-ranking members of the organization and then to others. The assumption underlying this practice is that hiring relatives of employees reduces the company's business risk (due to familiarity with the new hires) and increases employee loyalty. Even

when employees do not perform to expectation, they can still expect to hold onto their jobs because of the family loyalty value. A strong collectivist orientation, such as in many countries in the Middle East, often translates into commitment to the work organization (Fischer & Mansell, 2009; Robertson, Al-Khatib, & Al-Habib, 2002). A study of 365 employees from Saudi Arabia, Kuwait, and Oman provides support for the proposition that a collectivist orientation is associated with a strong group commitment and belief in participatory work ethics (Robertson et al., 2002) and two sets of meta-analyses of employee commitment across cultures indicate that greater collectivism was associated with higher organizational commitment and lower intention to leave (Fischer & Mansell, 2009).

In individualist societies, such as the United States, Australia, Great Britain, and Canada, people are expected to act on their own interests. For example, employees in these individualist societies would most likely view their supervisor as rewarding individual efforts, unlike employees in collectivistic societies, who are more likely to perceive supervisory actions as rewarding team or work group collaboration. The relationship between employees and employers is based, therefore, not on group loyalty but on complementing self-interests. Employers' decisions related to hiring and promotions are expected to be based on skills, achievements, and merit; favoritism and nepotism are strongly discouraged. In approaching work assignments, employees in a collectivist society would emphasize working together and will view the relationships as more important than the task, whereas the reverse will be true in the individualist society where the task will prevail over the relationship. A study comparing social support of employees in a U.S.-based company with that of employees in its former subsidiary in Israel found significant differences that are rooted in the collectivist-individualist leanings, respectively, of these two societies (Mor Barak, Findler, & Wind, 2003). Using the statistical method of factor analysis, which allowed the researchers to identify clusters of relationships between variables, the researchers examined the sources of social support for employees in the two societies. They found that employees in the United States clearly delineated between three types of support providers: (a) their supervisor; (b) their coworkers; and (c) support providers from outside the work environment—their spouses/partners, family members, and friends. The Israeli employees did not make such distinctions. For the Israeli employees, living in a collectivist society, the lines between supervisors, coworkers, and family/friends networks were blurred because a coworker, or supervisor for that matter, could also have been a friend or a family member.

Masculinity Versus Femininity

The masculinity/femininity dimension refers to the extent to which dominant values in the society emphasize assertiveness, competition, and material achievements, attributes associated with masculine qualities, as compared with feminine qualities such as relationships among people, care for others, and care for quality of life in general. Hofstede (1980, 1997, 2005) justifies anchoring these qualities in the gender-related terminology of the ancient, universal, gender-role differences between men as hunters, fighters, and providers and women as caretakers and nurturers of the family. In masculine societies, such as Japan, Italy, Mexico, and the United States, assertiveness, ambition, and competitiveness are expected and rewarded in the work context. In contrast, employees who show modesty, solidarity, and care for others are valued more in feminine societies such as Sweden, Norway, the Netherlands, and Denmark. In feminine societies, there is a preference for solving work-related conflicts by compromise and negotiation whereas in masculine societies, power struggles and direct confrontation may be more common in conflict resolution. Managers in feminine societies take into consideration their employees' needs and strive for consensus whereas managers in masculine societies are expected to be assertive and decisive. The balance between work and family is also very different in both types of societies. In the Scandinavian countries (identified as feminine societies), fathers often take time out from work to take care of a young or sick child. In a review of paternity leave statistics in the European Union (EU), almost all fathers in Sweden and the majority of fathers in Norway and in Finland take paternity leave (Dermott, 2001; O'Brien, 2009). In contrast, in masculine societies, the mother typically takes care of the children, and the father is expected to continue with his work as usual. In some countries, such as Japan and South Korea, the traditional cultural expectation was that women retire completely from the workforce once they had their first child and devote full time to raising their children. When Britain's prime minister Tony Blair limited his schedule but continued to work when his fourth child, Leo, was born in May 2000, a public debate ensued about the justification of such an action with some criticizing his action as irresponsible and others hailing it as an example for paternal responsibility. Britain is, of course, near the masculine end of the scale.

Avoidance of Uncertainty

Avoidance of uncertainty is a dimension that refers to the extent to which people in a society feel anxious about ambiguous situations and the steps that they are willing to take to create stability through formalization of rules and regulations. In high uncertainty avoidance societies, such as Belgium, Japan, and France, there are many rules that govern the behavior of employees as well as the work process. In contrast, in low uncertainly avoidance societies such as Great Britain, Jamaica, and South Africa, there are fewer regulations and a general belief that there should not be more rules than are strictly necessary. High job mobility is prevalent and expected in societies with low uncertainty avoidance and job stability and lifetime employment are more common and cherished in societies with high uncertainty avoidance. Hofstede and colleagues (2010) note the importance of the anxiety component of uncertainty avoidance and its impact on time orientation in the work context:

In strong uncertainty avoidance societies people like to work hard, or at least to be always busy. Life is hurried, and time is money. In weak uncertainty avoidance societies people are quite able to work hard if there is a need for it, but they are not driven by an inner urge towards constant activity. They like to relax. Time is a framework to orient oneself in, but not something one is constantly watching. (p. 210)

Long- Versus Short-Term Orientation

The long- versus short-term orientation is the fifth dimension that was added after the introduction of the original four dimensions to address differences in East-West cultural orientations. Designed by Chinese scholars and reflecting Confucian principles, the CVS provided the initial evidence for this dimension among students in 23 different countries (Hofstede, 2007; Hofstede & Bond, 1988). Long-term orientation refers to the fostering of virtues oriented toward future rewards: in particular, perseverance and thrift. Short-term orientation refers to the fostering of virtues related to the past and present, in particular, respect for tradition, preservation of "face," and fulfilling social obligations.

In long-term-oriented cultures, a person's responsibility for family and for work are not separate and not viewed as in competition. In fact, the two seem to support each other and therefore family enterprises are very common. The long-term pole on the continuum is associated with persistence, perseverance, and tenacity in pursuit of goals and this value orientation is seen as supporting entrepreneurial initiatives. These values are paired with the values of thrift and a sense of comfort with hierarchy, all leading to the availability of capital and to a stable work relationship within a family or close-knit work enterprise. At the other end of the continuum, the short-term orientation places great emphasis on personal steadiness and stability, which could suppress risk-seeking behaviors that are required to support entrepreneurial activities.

On the continuum of long- versus short-term orientation, Asian countries scored toward the long-term pole while the rest of the countries scored at the medium- or short-term pole. The top long-term scorers were China, Hong Kong, Taiwan, Japan, and Korea (Hofstede, 2007). No Western countries scored more

than medium term; the United States, Britain, and Canada scored in the short-term orientation range, as did countries of Africa. High scores on the long-term dimension were strongly correlated with the countries' economic success in the last quarter of the 20th century (Hofstede & Hofstede, 2004, p. 223). The authors noted that long-term orientation is identified as a major explanation for the explosive growth of the East Asian economies during that period.

Summary and Critique of Hofstede's Framework

Hofstede's original work received wide acclaim for its pioneer nature and has since been cited and used in a vast number of research projects around the world, but it was also criticized for its less than rigorous theoretical framework and less than perfect research methods (e.g., Ailon, 2008; McSweeney, 2002). The strengths of the work included an ambitious effort to measure and quantify the values that distinguish one culture from another along five unified dimensions and a demonstration of the significance of national cultures to management theory and practice. As a result, the books promoted sensitivity to cultural diversity in the workplace at the very time that global businesses were expanding. It also undermined the assumption that management knowledge that originated in the United States could be universally applied and emphasized the need to learn different cultures and adapt management practices to local values and norms. The typology that Hofstede put forth in his work has been widely applied and has become exceptionally influential (e.g., Baskerville, 2003; Bhagat, 2002; Bing, 2004; Chandy & Williams, 1994; Cronje, 2011; Hart, 1999; Kirkman et al., 2006; Søndergaard, 1994; Triandis, 2004; Yoo, Donthu, & Lenartowicz, 2011).

In a retrospective piece, Michale Minkov and Geert Hofstede (2011) summarize what they call "the Hofstede doctrine," noting that Hofstede's body of work has a distinct identity with five major contributions to cross-cultural research: (a) generating a paradigm shift in the study of culture, from treating it as a single (though, admittedly complex) variable to unpackaging culture into independent measurable dimensions; (b) creating cultural dimensions that are meaningful on a national level, underpinned by variables that correlated across nations, not across individuals or organizations; (c) the five dimensions address basic universal problems that all societies have to deal with; (d) the cultural dimensions are thought to reflect stable national differences that, though evolving, remain quite the same, or move in a similar direction as to render them quite consistent over time; (e) the work was based on a very large data set demonstrating the importance and relevance of national culture to organizational behavior, management practices, and to society at large.

Hofstede's work has been criticized on several levels, including its limited conceptualization of culture, its less than rigorous methodology, and its inherent Western cultural bias (e.g., Ailon, 2008; Baskerville, 2003; Eckhardt, 2002; Harrison & McKinnon, 1999; Kitayama, 2002; McSweeney, 2002; Robinson, 1983; Singh, 1990). The work was criticized because it seemed to identify culture with nations and because it has operated under the assumption that within each nation there was a uniformed and relatively static culture. This notion of a unified national culture is particularly problematic in light of the increased diversity within nations. One glaring example from Hofstede's (1980) initial study was the use of an all-White sample (because of the apartheid regime of the time) to represent the totality of the South African national culture. Another stream of criticism related to the validity and reliability of the study's measures as well as the limited research methodology. For example, even though the total number of questionnaires was very large—117,000—this number includes both waves of the questionnaire that were administered in 1968 and 1969 and again from 1971 to 1973. The large number in and of itself does not ensure representativeness. In fact, in some of the countries the samples were very small (e.g., 58 in Singapore and 37 in Pakistan). Hofstede's (2001) claim that the sample sizes were sufficient because to the homogeneity of values within national samples is highly questionable because the basic premise of homogeneous national cultures cannot be substantiated (McSweeney, 2002). Finally, an interesting analysis by Ailon (2008) uses a mirroring technique to deconstruct Hofstede's book *Culture's Consequences* (1980) using the book's own assumptions and logic. The author demonstrates that, despite his explicit efforts to remain "culturally neutral," the book's specific Western cultural lens is evident throughout the chapters. For example, with respect to the uncertainty avoidance dimension, Ailon (2008) notes, "Hofstede strongly disagrees with the claim that company rules should not be broken, thus expressing low uncertainty avoidance value" (p. 423), yet the book itself manifests what appears to be a very high intolerance for the unpredictable ambiguous, or uncertain. In other words, it manifests very high uncertainty avoidance (p. 893). Ailon found several inconsistencies in both theory and methodology and cautions against an uncritical reading of Hofstede's cultural dimensions.

A central concern among all of Hofstede's critics is the author's central premise that *national cultures are uniform* and therefore could be represented by relatively small samples (1980, p. 65) and could be measured, quantified, compared, and graphed quite precisely on the continuum of each of the five dimensions. McSweeney (2002) notes that "if the aim is understanding then we need to know more about the richness and diversity of national practices and institutions—rather than merely assuming their 'uniformity' and that they have an already known national cultural cause" (p. 112). Ailon (2008) sums up her criticism with a positive note, highlighting Hofstede's pioneering work on the backdrop of the period of his initial research: "Hofstede, it should be remembered, worked within the discursive limits of the 1970's, and he did so impressively, at least in so far as the popularity of *Culture's Consequences* indicated" (p. 901).

It is important to remember that the cultural dimensions offered by Hofstede's work were in many respects the first attempt to scientifically characterize the very broad concept of culture in a multinational context. Judging by the numerous researchers who found this conceptual framework useful, the author's contribution has been enormous. Yet, as national cultures become more diverse with an influx of immigrants, migrant workers, and the migration of businesses (painstakingly demonstrated in the first part of this book), it is important to pay attention to diversity within national cultures and to the change in the culture of those nations as a result of infusion of other cultures over time. Any manager who attempts to shortcut her or his learning process by looking for broad brush characterizations of "uniform" and "constant" national cultures may be doing a disservice to herself or himself. It has been the premise of this book all along that in today's increasingly diverse workforce, a more nuanced understanding of, sensitivity for, and proficiency in the cultural differences not only *between* but *within* national cultures is essential.

The GLOBE Study

A different attempt to identify cultural dimensions in an international context is the Global Leadership and Organizational Behavior Effectiveness (GLOBE) research program. GLOBE is a multiyear program of cross-cultural research designed to examine the relationship between societal culture, organizational culture, and organizational leadership effectiveness (Dorfman et al., 2012; House, Hangers, Javidan, Dorfman, & Gupta, 2004; Javidan, House, Dorfman, Hanges, & Sully de Luque, 2006). The project was conceived in 1991 by Robert J. House from the Wharton School at the University of Pennsylvania who assembled a team of approximately 170 social scientists and management scholars from 61 countries representing major geographic regions throughout the world to collaborate on the study. The researchers collected data from over 17,000 middle managers in three industries: financial services, food processing, and telecommunications, as well as archival measures of country economic prosperity and the physical and psychological well-being of the cultures studied.

GLOBE has several distinguishing features. First, it is truly a cross-cultural research program. The constructs were defined, conceptualized, and operationalized by the multicultural team of researchers. Second, the industries were selected through a polling of the country investigators, and the instruments were designed with the full participation of the researchers representing the different cultures. Finally, the data in each country were collected by

investigators who were either natives of the cultures studied or had extensive knowledge and experience in that culture.

The authors derived nine cultural dimensions from the literature and measured them both as practices (the way things are) and values (the way things ought to be) (Dorfman et al., 2012; Javidan, Dorfman, Sully de Luque, & House, 2006). The nine cultural attributes that were described in the study were:

- *Performance orientation*: The degree to which a collective encourages and rewards group members for performance improvement and excellence
- *Assertiveness*: The degree to which individuals are assertive, confrontational, and aggressive in their relationships with others
- *Future orientation*: The extent to which individuals engage in future-oriented behaviors such as delaying gratification, planning, and investing in the future
- *Human orientation*: The degree to which a collective encourages and rewards individuals for being fair, altruistic, generous, caring, and kind to others
- *Institutional collectivism*: The degree to which organizational and societal institutional practices encourage and reward collective distribution of resources and collective action
- *In-group collectivism*: The degree to which individuals express pride, loyalty, and cohesiveness in their organizations or families
- *Gender egalitarianism*: The degree to which a collective minimizes gender inequality
- Power distance: The degree to which members of a collective expect power to be distributed equally
- *Uncertainty avoidance*: The extent to which a society, organization, or group relies on social norms, rules, and procedures to alleviate unpredictability of future events.

The study authors focused on leadership, which they defined through a process of cross-cultural discussions as "the ability of an individual to influence, motivate, and enable others to contribute toward the effectiveness and success of the organizations of which they are members" (House et al., 2004, p. 15). The principal outcome of the study was the development of six universally shared dimensions of leadership: charismatic/value based, team oriented, self-protective, participative, humane oriented, and autonomous.

Cross-Cultural Communication

Effective interactions in today's global business world depend to a great extent on the ability to convey a clear message that people in different cultures can comprehend in the way the communicator intended them to understand it. Business communication can be interpreted very differently depending on the cultural orientation of a particular country. For example, in masculine societies, an effective manager is one who communicates directly, assertively, and even aggressively. Those from feminine-leaning societies may interpret such behavior as unfriendly, arrogant, and even rude. A Swedish manager reading a help-wanted advertisement for a salesperson in the United States might be taken aback by the requirement that the qualified candidate be "aggressive." On the other hand, British managers may interpret a Chinese manager's modesty and humility in stating his qualifications as a weakness. Although the cross-fertilization of ideas generated from a diverse workforce can be beneficial to organizations, some research indicates that congruence between organizational cultural and the culture of the wider society could produce beneficial outcomes. For example, a study of Mexican workers indicates that such congruence, along the axes noted by Hofstede and his colleagues, contribute to job satisfaction and organizational commitment (Madlock, 2012).

An incident in the city of Najaf during the 2003 war in Iraq (see Box 19.1), demonstrates one leader's bold and effective use of nonverbal, cross-cultural communication that probably saved many lives that day. Unable to speak Arabic and with no interpreter on site, the commander of the U.S. Army's 101st Airborne Division was unable to use language to communicate his nonaggressive intentions to the Arabic-speaking crowd. In a spur-of-the-moment decision, he instructed his soldiers to kneel on one knee, smile, and point their weapons to the ground. This vulnerable yet friendly posture was clearly understood by the crowd that responded likewise by smiling and sitting on the ground. Luckily, in the Najaf incident, the nonverbal body language was sufficiently universal to convey the peaceful intentions of the soldiers and to prevent what could have been a deadly incident.

BOX 19.1: LEADERSHIP THROUGH EFFECTIVE CROSS-CULTURAL COMMUNICATION SAVES THE DAY IN NAJAF

Early in June 2003 during the U.S. war in Iraq, the U.S. Army's 101st Airborne Division on a mission to secure the area entered the city of Najaf. It was an uneventful patrol. The search turned up nothing. The Shia Muslim population, which traditionally has not supported Saddam's rule, seemed curious and friendly, but didn't get too close. The local population had cautiously welcomed the U.S. troops. Word came from the Grand Ayatollah Sistani that he was willing to meet with the American commander, but he asked first that the U.S. soldiers secure his compound.

As the troops started down the road toward the Ayatollah's compound, the crowd that assembled there to watch the American soldiers mistook their intentions to mean that they were progressing toward the Imam Ali shrine located in Najaf. The Imam Ali shrine is the burial site of the prophet Muhammad's son-in-law and considered one of the holiest sites in the world for Shia Muslims.

(Continued)

(Continued)

The once-friendly crowd became alarmed and chaos ensued. Earlier warm greetings were replaced with angry shouts and gestures as hundreds of people attempted to block the soldiers' way. Clerics appeared with a message from the Grand Ayatollah that the soldiers were progressing at his invitation, but their message was drowned out.

Realizing the explosive situation at hand and unable to verbally convey his peaceful intentions, the colonel told his men to stay calm. He instructed the soldiers to smile, get down on one knee, and point their weapons to the ground. The puzzled soldiers reluctantly complied. A hush fell on the crowd. Then slowly the crowd responded in kind—relaxing, smiling, and sitting on the ground. The tension was diffused, but the colonel realized that the situation was still potentially volatile. "Turn around," he ordered his men, "just turn around and go." The soldiers complied, and as they were leaving, the colonel turned around and bowed apologetically to the crowd as if saying, "Sorry for the misunderstanding." A potentially deadly confrontation was prevented.

Source: Chilcote (2003).

Although in the business world the stakes do not often involve human lives, they do involve people's livelihood. Cross-cultural miscommunication can result in lost opportunities—such as losing a job or a business deal—that could be detrimental to the financial and economic well-being of individuals and organizations. Conversely, effective cross-cultural communication can open up employment and business opportunities that may not be otherwise available to the participants.

Effective Cross-Cultural Communication

Communication, in its most basic form, is the use of symbols to convey meaning. Symbols can include words, tone of voice, gestures, or use of objects (artifacts). It refers to "the process through which people, acting together, create, sustain, and manage meaning through the use of verbal and nonverbal signs and symbols from a particular context" (Conrad & Poole, 2012, p. 5). Broadly defined, communication is multidimensional (Neuliep, 2008) and relates to three types of goals: (a) instrumental goals (e.g., performing tasks), (b) relational goals (e.g., negotiating conflicts), and (c) identity management (e.g., conveying a desired self-image) (Bernstein, 1975; Clark & Delia, 1979; Halliday, 1978).

Cross-cultural communication is particularly challenging and involves several potential barriers to communication that are related to the use of verbal and nonverbal methods to convey meanings that may or may not be the same in the cultures of origin of the participants (see Figure 19.1 for illustration).

When people use symbols that elicit meaning in another person, whatever the original intent was, or even without conscious intent, they are still communicating. Often the message that is received may be different from the one that was intended because of cultural barriers on the part of receivers and transmitters. Take, for example, gender differences in perceptions of sexual meanings. A man may perceive a woman's behavior as flirtatious when her original intent was simply courteous and entirely nonsexual, leading to severe misunderstandings. Add to that the cultural layer when, for example, it is entirely acceptable and chivalrous for a French businessman to compliment a woman colleague on her dress in the French cultural context. An American businesswoman might perceive the exact same behavior as inappropriate and may even

Figure 19.1	Barriers to Effective Cross-Cultural Communication

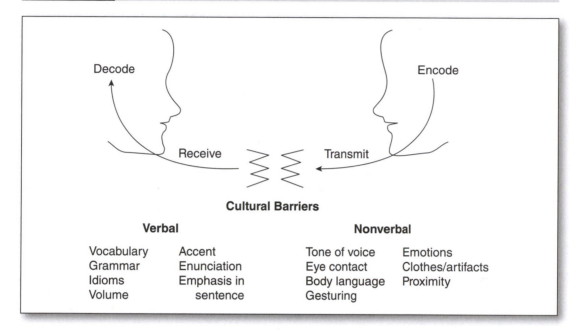

interpret it as sexual harassment. Miscommunication occurs when the original intent of the person transmitting the message is different from the meaning that is received by the other person, and it is more likely to occur between participants who belong to different cultures.

Verbal Communication

The use of different languages often creates a barrier to communication because one or both sides are not as articulate as they could be in their native tongues. For example, a Dutch person who speaks Flemish but is also fluent in French may not be as familiar with the vocabulary, grammar, and idioms of the language as would be a native French speaker. Articulating her thoughts (encoding) would be more difficult for her, and the end message may not be exactly what she intended to convey. In addition, her accent, enunciation, and emphasis in sentence intonation (the "music" of the language) may make it difficult for the listener to clearly comprehend what she was saying and to be distracted from the message.

When conducting international business, the choice of which language to use (e.g., one's own or the host country's language) is more than a practical matter. It is a choice of whether to signify national pride on the one hand or to demonstrate respect for the host country's culture on the other. Foreign leaders often speak their own language and communicate through an interpreter, even when they are fluent in the host country's language, to show a sense of national pride. For example, when the supersonic plane the *Concorde* was designed, there was a bitter argument between the French and the British who collaborated on the project, perhaps reflecting the age-old rivalry and animosity between the two countries.[4] At one point, work was halted after the French insisted that the plane should have a Gallic final letter *e* in its name, whereas the British stolidly referred to it as "Concord." Eventually the French spelling was adopted (Arnold, 2003). On the other hand, saying a few words, such as "hello" or "good evening," in the host country's language can go a long way. When John F. Kennedy gave his famous speech in front of the Berlin town hall and said, "All free men, wherever they may live, are citizens of Berlin, and, therefore, as a free man, I take pride in the words, '*Ich bin ein Berliner*'" (I am a Berliner), more than a million West Berliners responded with a roar of approval.[5] Similarly, when Bill Clinton spoke at the funeral of Yitzhak Rabin, the prime minister of Israel who was assassinated because of his work toward peace in the Middle East, he began his English speech by saying two words in Hebrew, "*Shalom Chaver*"—"Goodbye (also doubles as Peace) My Friend." The people of Israel were so touched by this gesture that these words later appeared in poems, in everyday phrases, and on bumper stickers. Willy Brandt, the former German chancellor, once commented, "If I'm selling to you, I speak your language. If I am buying, *dann müssen Sie Deutsch sprechen*" (then you must speak German) (Nurden, 1997, p. 39).

Linguistic diversity is an important aspect of global diversity. Managing a workforce that does not share a common language can present a major challenge to both employees and management. Although most of the discussion related to the use of foreign languages in business refers to international organizations with business partners or subsidiaries in different countries, verbal communication may also present a challenge within countries. In Guinea, for example, a large segment of the population barely speak French, the official language of Guinea (Auclair, 1992); India has two main languages (Hindi and English), 14 official languages, and thousands more languages and dialects (The World Factbook, 2012); and in South Africa's metropolitan area of Alexandra, nine major Bantu languages are claimed as home language, and many residents also speak some English, Afrikaans, or Portuguese (McCall, Ngeva, & Mbebe, 1997). Linguistic diversity is strongly related to people's and nations' history, heritage, and sense of identity and can influence economic and political development both positively and negatively. As Ginsburgh and Weber (2011) point out, on the one hand suppression and elimination of linguistic diversity was part of the ugly heritage of colonialism and should be condemned. On the other hand, a plethora of languages within a nation (e.g., 527 language in Nigeria, 217 in the Democratic Republic of Congo, thousands in India) could cause difficulties such as miscommunication, institutional

wastefulness, inefficiencies, and—when tied to strong ethnic, national, or religious identity—even war (Ginsburgh & Weber, 2011).

Often, misunderstandings occur when one person is not familiar with all aspects of the other's language. A classic example of such mistaken translation resulted in a horned Moses holding the Ten Commandments in the famous Michelangelo statue (circa 1513). The original biblical Hebrew text describes Moses coming down Mount Sinai after meeting God "with his face radiating" or literally with rays of light coming out of his face (Exodus 34:29). However, the Hebrew word for *ray* is the same as the word for *horn—keren*. Michelangelo, relying on Jerome's vulgate translation of the Old Testament, which apparently confused the two meanings, sculpted the famous statue of Moses with two horns protruding from his head. On the other hand, sometimes the use of a foreign language can add a different dimension to the discussion because people who are not native speakers can pick up errors that native speakers will not see. Adler and Gundersen (2008, p. 74) describe an example of a business using this perceptual characteristic to its advantage: The Canadian National Railway gives reports written in English to bilingual francophone employees to proofread and reports written in French to bilingual anglophones for proofreading.

Language Fluency and Cultural Fluency

When dealing with foreign languages and different cultures, language fluency and cultural fluency are not the same—although they are related. Language fluency refers to the possession of linguistic skills that allow one to function much like a native speaker of the language. Cultural fluency refers to the ability to identify, understand, and apply the communicative behaviors of members of the other group; it is the ability to go back and forth between two or more cultures, to send and receive messages in a way that assures that the meanings of the messages of both the sender and receiver regularly match (Glazier, 2003; Molinsky, 2005; Staub, 2009). Children of immigrants who grow up speaking the language of their parents at home, but without connection to their broader cultural heritage, are facing great difficulties when returning to their homeland, although they may speak the language fluently. For example, according to U.S. laws, legal aliens who committed a crime may be deported to their home country. After the 9/11 terrorist attack in 2001, the United States began enforcing its immigration laws more vigorously and more immigrants who committed crimes were deported. Among the deportees was a large group of Cambodian nationals who grew up in the United States and were highly acculturated to the American culture. Although their parents spoke Khmer at home, they did not teach them about their cultural heritage because they wanted to forget the horrors of the Khmer Rouge and the Pol Pot regime. As a result, although they were fluent in Khmer, these deportees experienced great difficulties adjusting to the Cambodian way of life and culture.[6]

Nonverbal Communication

Nonverbal barriers to cross-cultural communication include body language—movements, gestures, and postures—as well as the use of artifacts such as personal adornments and the physical setting. Trust and respect are often conveyed through nonverbal rather than verbal communication. A case in point is controversy in the U.S. media ignited by President Obama's bow to the Japanese emperor during his Asian tour in November of 2009. Some interpreted the bow as a culturally sensitive sign of respect, but others noted that this is an indication of subservience that is unbefitting a U.S. president (MSNBC News, 2009; National Public Radio, 2009). Obama's defenders attributed the bow to his multicultural background and worldly awareness, while his critics thought it was a sign of his naiveté and a behavior unbefitting the presidency citing a tradition that the U.S. president bows to no one. The supporters also noted that the bow, a typical Asian form of greeting, was also accompanied by a very Western firm handshake, while the critics noted that the very low bow, practically a 90-degree angle, was a gesture of extreme deference and subordination. Either way, it is clear that this one nonverbal gesture spoke volumes and was discussed more than any of the speeches the president and his hosts gave during the tour. In addition to body gestures, artifacts can also be used to transfer important information and those, too, need to be understood and interpreted in their specific cultural and national context (see Box 19.2 for an example of the use of the physical setting to convey respect in different cultures).

BOX 19.2: HOW CAN THE IMPORTANT GUEST SIT AT THE HEAD OF A ROUND TABLE? THE USE OF THE PHYSICAL SETTING TO CONVEY RESPECT IN BUSINESS COMMUNICATION

To convey respect to a high-ranking visitor, Europeans and North Americans have the person sit at the head of a rectangular table. A round table is typically reserved for occasions when the participants are presumed to be equals. A prime example is the famous legend of King Arthur of Camelot and his Knights of the Round Table. King Arthur conveyed the equality among his chosen knights through the use of a round table. Similarly, in modern times, the representatives to the UN Security Council all sit at a round table. The assumption of these Western cultures is that there is no way to identify a more- or less-respected seat at a round table and therefore no way to indicate the relative ranking of the participants.

(Continued)

(Continued)

In the Chinese culture, on the other hand, the ranking of the participants can be clearly identified by the way they sit at a round table: The highest ranking participant in a meeting will be seated directly facing the main entrance to the room, and the rest of the participants, in descending order of rank, will be seated to his or her left and right sides until the lowest-ranking person will have his or her back to the entrance. This follows a similar logic of circular-ranked importance expressed in the Chinese perception of geography. The Chinese tradition indicates that the imperial palace is the most important place in the world, and from there, in circles of decreased importance, are the other areas of Beijing, the rest of China, and the rest of the world.

Clothing has long been used to communicate rank (e.g., the cardinal robes and the queen's crown), mood (e.g., mourning clothes), occasion (e.g., wedding outfits in different cultures), and even seasons (e.g., the geisha's seasonal kimono colors or light and dark business attire in the West, depending on the time of year). Clothes are an extension of the body and closely relate to the person's gender, age, socioeconomic status, and national origin. When doing business in a foreign country, one often faces the question of whether to wear the business attire that is common in one's own culture or in the host country. Although in modern times the Western business suit goes a long way for men, it is not the same for women. Western clothes may be perceived as inappropriately revealing by many cultures, and wearing them might be interpreted as disrespectful to the host culture and be perceived as offensive. On the other hand, wearing a traditional outfit, such as the Muslim attire of *abaya, burqah,* or *hijab,*[7] may be seen as confining or even degrading by Western women. The U.S. Army's policy of "strongly encouraging" army servicewomen to conform to Saudi rules and wear *abayas* while serving in Saudi Arabia has long been controversial.[8] When Madeleine Albright, the U.S. secretary of state during the Clinton presidency, visited Egypt and Saudi Arabia in 1999, she found a middle-ground solution. Although she did not wear the traditional Muslim attire that is expected from women in that country, she wore dresses and skirts that were longer than the ones she wore in Washington. She also donned a wide-brimmed hat, thus walking the fine line between conveying respect for her hosts' culture and her own.

In contrast, Mahatma Gandhi, the father of modern India and the leader of its liberation movement from Great Britain, wore just a loincloth during his visit to England in 1931, shocking the conservative British society. The British media interpreted his attire as primitive and disrespectful, but Gandhi was sending a clear message of independence and defiance as well as respect for Indian culture and traditions: "It was a rejection not only of the material products of Europe, but also of the European value system with its criteria of decency" (Tarlo, 1996, p. 75).

Over the years, more work organizations and international bodies relaxed strict clothing requirements to accommodate the traditional or religious attire. For example, Disney allowed a Muslim employee at its Orange County park to wear a specially designed head-scarf after initially objecting to her religious head covering. Initially, Noor Abdallah who worked at a ticket booth in the Disneyland park, was told that she could not wear the hijab and was offered another job away from the public. After she refused, the park worked with her to design a covering—a blue scarf topped with a beret—to match her costume and meet her religious demands ("Disney, Muslim Worker," 2010). In preparation for the 2012 Olympic competitions in London, FIFA (Fédération Internationale de Football Association) overturned its ban on women playing football with their heads covered, opening the doors to women athletes from traditional Muslim countries to compete in the Olympics. Other international sports bodies have also relaxed clothing rules in a way that allowed more Muslim women to compete in the game such as judo player Wodjan Ali Seraj Abdulrahim, Saudi Arabian runner Sarah Attar, and U.S. fencer Ibtihaj Muhammad (Khaleeli, 2012).

Cross-Cultural Communication Styles

A question that is very relevant for any business transaction is whether and to what extent members of a particular cultural group will alter their preferred communication style when interacting with members from another cultural group. Utilizing the theoretical perspective presented earlier, will members of collectivist cultures become more direct and task oriented in their communication with members of individualist cultures? Will members of individualist cultures become more concerned with the needs of others and in preserving harmony in the transaction? Or will one or both groups become more entrenched in their own communication style?

It is plausible to assume that adapting to the other's communication style will generate a perception of similarity and familiarity that will contribute to creating a positive atmosphere in cross-cultural encounters (e.g., Byrne's 1971 similarity attraction paradigm; Foley, Linnehan, Greenhaus, & Weer, 2006; Lee & Gudykunst, 2001). Intergroup contact theory and research, originally proposed as a "contact hypothesis" by Allport (1954), suggests that intergroup contact typically reduces prejudice (Brown & Hewstone, 2005; Harrington & Miller, 1992; Pettigrew, Tropp, Wagner, & Christ, 2011). Allport's original conditions for optimal contact, such as equal status and common goals, facilitate the effect but are not necessary conditions and there are other positive outcomes for intergroup contact such as greater trust. Research findings apply to many types of groups including different ages, gender, nations, ethnicities, race, sexual orientation, and different abilities and the major mediators between intergroup contact and such positive outcomes are affective—reduced anxiety and empathy (Pettigrew et al., 2011). On the other hand, because cross-cultural encounters create uncertainly and provoke anxiety, participants may resort to the familiarity of their own cultural norms and even more strongly exhibit their normative communication styles, especially when the contact is nonvoluntary or threatening (Lau, Lam, & Deutsch Salamon, 2008; Laurent, 1984; Pettigrew et al., 2011; Tse, Francis, & Walls, 1994). A study conducted in New Zealand supports the latter (see Box 19.3).

BOX 19.3: ARE MEMBERS OF A CULTURAL GROUP INTERACTING WITH A MEMBER OF ANOTHER GROUP MORE LIKELY TO CHANGE THEIR ORIGINAL COMMUNICATION STYLE OR REINFORCE IT?

Pekerti and Thomas (2003) examined intercultural and intracultural communication styles between two groups in New Zealand: Anglo-Europeans, representing a low-context individualist culture, and East Asians, representing high-context collectivist culture. Participants in the experiment were 96 students at a large New Zealand university, one half of whom were Anglo-European New Zealanders (Pakeha) and one half of whom were students from Asia (primarily from China) who were first generation with less than 10 years in New Zealand (to control for acculturation). Students were randomly assigned to one of two conditions—interaction with members of their own cultural group or interaction with members of the other cultural group.[9] The assignment was ranking of 15 crimes by their severity, and participants were given no more than 15 minutes to rank the crimes by consensus. The interactions were videotaped and coded by independent observers for the occurrence and intensity of each cultural communication behavior. The results showed

(Continued)

(Continued)

that interacting with members of a different culture increased the tendency to use the cultural communication style of their own culture. Specifically, in interactions with Anglo-Europeans, the Asian students were more likely than they were with members of their own culture to accommodate and change their opinions in order to preserve harmony. A similar trend was apparent with the Anglo-Europeans students who were more likely than they were with members of their own cultural group to be direct and task oriented in their interaction with Asian students. The authors attribute this behavior to the uncertainly involved in cross-cultural interactions, which increases people's tendency to rely on their own cultural norms. The authors conclude that in cross-cultural communication, the dominant tendency is exaggeration of one's own cultural behaviors rather than adaptation.

The tendency to resort to the familiarity of one's own cultural norms may be even stronger when facing a conflict. Sometimes due to misunderstanding, cultural ignorance, or fear of losing face, this behavior could have a toll both in human relationships and in financial outcomes. Mangaliso (2001) describes an incident in a South African mining company that mushroomed into a labor dispute and a prolonged strike that cost the company greatly—all because management was unable to appropriately communicate with its workers. In the beginning of the labor dispute, the workers invited top management to address them on the issue in a public forum. Management denied their request, however, and responded instead by sending messages through envoys and written statements posted on bulletin boards. In the high-context collectivist culture of the South African workers, management's impersonal and task-oriented communication was entirely inappropriate. It failed to take into consideration the South African concept of *ubuntu,* meaning humaneness, consideration for compassion and community—similar to the Chinese concept of *quanxi,* the Korean *chaeboel,* and the Spanish *simpatia* (mentioned in Chapter 9) all indicating a cultural emphasis on relationships (Sanchez-Burks & Lee, 2007; Triandis, Marin, Lisansky, & Betancourt, 1984). Frustrated and humiliated, the workers began a strike that lasted for more than 2 weeks and resulted in several hundreds of employees being fired and several million dollars of company losses. One of the employee representatives was reported to have said, "The only thing that employees wanted was for top management to come and address us. Just to speak to us" (Mangaliso, 2001, p. 23). In retrospect, the strike and its costly consequences could have been avoided if management understood the cultural context of its workers and was able to communicate with them in an appropriate manner.

Summary and Conclusion

To succeed in managing a workforce that is increasingly diverse and multinational, managers need to understand cultural differences and to become competent in cross-cultural communication. This chapter examines the cultural context of the global workplace and analyzes communication patterns that facilitate or block effective cross-cultural communication.

Research on cultural dimensions and the wealth of research inspired by Geert Hofstede's pioneering work provide an important context for understanding cross-cultural interactions in the workplace. His four axes of *power distance* (authority and social inequality), *individualism vs. collectivism* (cohesion and loyalty to the group), *masculinity vs. femininity* (competition in contrast to care for others), and *avoidance of uncertainty* (tolerance for ambiguity) have clear implications for individual and group expectations related to acceptable behaviors in the workplace.

Whether employees expect to be rewarded, for example, for individual excellence or for a team effort depends to a large extent on the cultural perception of individualism versus collectivism in their society. The GLOBE project, led by Robert J. House, examined nine cultural dimensions of leadership worldwide through a longitudinal study in 62 world cultures. The principal outcome of the study was the development of six universally shared dimensions of leadership: (a) charismatic/value based, (b) team oriented, (c) self-protective, (d) participative, (e) humane oriented, and (f) autonomous.

Defined as *the use of symbols to convey meaning,* communication in today's global environment has become largely cross-cultural. Cross-cultural communication involves several potential barriers that are related to the use of verbal and nonverbal methods to convey meanings that may or may not be the same in the cultures of origin of the participants. Miscommunication occurs when the original intent of the person transmitting the message is different from the meaning that is received by the other person, and it is more likely to occur between participants who belong to different cultures. Often, misunderstandings occur when one person is not familiar with all aspects of the other's language, is not fluent or articulate in the language used for the business transaction, or miscommunicates or misreads nonverbal communication such as movement or gestures.

Effective communication with employees, customers, shareholders, regulators, and other business partners presents a serious challenge, even when conducted within the same cultural framework. The challenge is compounded when communication involves two or more diverse cultural contexts. When one partner to a business communication misreads the cultural clues encoded in the other person's message, the transaction can result in a misunderstanding, hurt emotions, conflicts, and lost business opportunities. On the other hand, making the effort to understand other cultures and to communicate effectively within them can go a long way in fostering trust, conveying respect, and eventually securing mutually beneficial business deals.

Notes

1. See Javidan and House (2001, p. 289).

2. For a summary table of key definitions of culture, see Erez and Earley (1993).

3. See, for example, Margaret Mead (1935/2001) and Ruth Benedict (1934/1989).

4. The interesting historical/political context to the inception of the *Concorde* project was the project was designed in response to the space race between the United States and the Soviet Union in the 1960s. Its goal was to demonstrate the technological abilities of Western Europe as a center of world power, independent from the United States and the Soviet Union. This was the impetus for France and England to put aside their historical animosity and work collaboratively on this project ("History of the Supersonic Airliner," 2001; "The World," 2003).

5. See "Text: Kennedy's Berlin Speech" (2003).

6. See "The World" (2003).

7. *Abaya* is a head-to-toe, traditional Muslim dress made from black, lightweight fabric that has two layers; *burqah* similarly provides cover from head to toe and, in addition, covers the face so that only the eyes are exposed, sometimes behind a netlike fabric; and *hijab* is a traditional Muslim head scarf.

8. Lieutenant Colonel Martha McSally has led a long struggle to end this policy by the Pentagon. McSally, who was the first woman U.S. service member to fly in combat, was stationed in Saudi Arabia where she was forced to wear the *abaya* and travel in the rear seats of vehicles in accordance with local custom. Congressman Langevin joined McSally's fight and called the army's requirement "gender discrimination," saying that "women make first-class soldiers and should not be treated like second-class citizens" ("Langevin Seeks," 2002).

9. The study used a 2 × 2 (culture x condition) design, and in assignment to the two experimental conditions, the researchers used blocks by gender, age, and culture to control for possible effects of these variables on the outcome variable of communication style.

References

Adler, N. J., & Gundersen, A. (2008). *International dimensions of organizational behavior* (5th ed.). Mason, OH: Thomson South-Western.

Ailon, G. (2008). Mirror, mirror on the wall: Culture's consequences in a value test of its own design. Academy of Management Review, 33(4), 885–904.

Allport, G. W. (1954). *The nature of prejudice.* New York: Doubleday, Anchor.

Arnold, J. (2003, October 10). Why economists don't fly Concorde. *BBC News.* Retrieved September 12, 2004, from http://news.bbc.co.uk/2/hi/business/2935337.stm

Auclair, M. (1992). Out in Africa: Going where no communicator has gone before. *Communication World, 9*(3), 43–45.

Aycan, Z., Al-Hamadi, A. B., Davis, A., & Budhwar, P. (2007). Cultural orientations and preferences for HRM policies and practices: The case of Oman. *The International Journal of Human Resource Management, 18*(2), 11.

Baskerville, R. F. (2003). Hofstede never studied culture. *Accounting, Organizations and Society, 28,* 1–14.

Benedict, R. (1989). *Patterns of cultures.* Boston: Mariners Books. (Original work published 1934).

Bernstein, B. (1975). *Class, codes, and control: Theoretical studies toward a sociology of language.* New York: Schoken.

Bhagat, R. S. (2002). Book review of Culture's consequences: Comparing values, behaviors, institutions, and organizations across nations (2nd ed.). *Academy of Management Review, 27,* 460–462.

Bing, J. W. (2004). Hofstede's consequences: The impact of his work on consulting and business practices. *Academy of Management Executive, 18*(1), 80–87.

Brown, R., & Hewstone, M. (2005). An integrative theory of intergroup contact. In M. P. Zanna (Ed.), *Advances in experimental psychology* (Vol. 37, pp. 256–284). Elsevier Academic Press.

Byrne D. (1971). *The attraction paradigm.* New York: Academic.

Chandy, P. R., & Williams, T. G. E. (1994). The impact of journals and authors on international business. *Journal of International Business Studies, 25,* 715–728.

Chilcote, R. (2003, June 4). *Cooler heads prevail in Najaf.* Retrieved May 25, 2004, from www.cnn.com/2003/WORLD/meast/04/03/otsc.irq.chilcote.najaf/

Clark, R. A., & Delia, J. G. (1979). Topoi and rhetorical competence. *Quarterly Journal of Speech, 65,* 165–206.

Conrad, C., & Poole, M. S. (2012). *Strategic organizational communication in a global economy* (7th ed.). New York: Wiley-Blackwell.

Cronje, J. C. (2011). Using Hofstede's cultural dimensions to interpret cross-cultural blended teaching and learning. *Computers & Education, 56*(3), 596–603.

Dermott, E. M. (2001). New fatherhood in practice? Parental leave in the U.K. *The International Journal of Sociology and Social Policy, 21*(4–6), 145.

Disney, Muslim worker agree on hijab substitute. (2010, September 29). *USA Today.* Retrieved from www.usatoday.com/news/religion/2010-09-29-disney-muslim_N.htm

Dorfman, P., Javidan, M., Hanges, P., Dastmalchian, A., & House, R. (2012). GLOBE: A twenty year journey into the intriguing world of culture and leadership [Special issue]. *Journal of World Business, 47*(4), 504–518.

Eckhardt, G. (2002). Book review of *Culture's Consequences: Comparing values, behaviors, institutions, and organizations across nations* (2nd ed.). *Australian Journal of Management, 27,* 89–94.

Erez, M., & Earley, P. C. (1993). *Culture, self-identity and work.* Oxford: Oxford University Press.

Fischer, R., & Mansell, A. (2009). Commitment across cultures: A meta-analytical approach. Journal of International Business Studies, 40, 1339–1358.

Foley, S., Linnehan, F., Greenhaus, G. H., & Weer, C. H. (2006). The impact of gender similarity, racial similarity, and work culture on family-supportive supervision. *Group & Organization Management, 31*(4), 420–441.

Ginsburgh, V., & Weber, S. (2011). *How many languages do we need? The economics of linguistic diversity.* Princeton, NJ: Princeton University Press.

Glazier, J. A. (2003). Developing cultural fluency: Arab and Jewish students engaging in one another's company. *Harvard Educational Review, 73*(2), 141–163.

Halliday, M. A. K. (1978). *Language as social semiotic.* Baltimore, MD: University Park Press.

Harrington, H. J., & Miller, N. (1992). Research and theory in intergroup relations: Issues of consensus and controversy. In J. Lynch, C. Modgil, & S. Modgil (Eds.), *Cultural diversity and the schools* (Vol. 2, pp. 159–178). London: Falmer.

Harrison, G. L., & McKinnon, J. L. (1999). Cross-cultural research in management control systems design: A review of the current state. *Accounting, Organizations and Society, 24,* 483–506.

Hart, W. B. (1999). Interdisciplinary influences in the study of intercultural relations: A citation analysis of the *International Journal of Intercultural Relations. International Journal of Intercultural Relations, 23,* 575–589.

Hofstede, G. (1980). Culture's consequences: International differences in work related values. Beverly Hills, CA: Sage.

Hofstede G. (1997). *Cultures and organizations: Software of the mind.* New York: McGraw-Hill.

Hofstede, G. (2001). *Culture's consequences: Comparing values, behaviors, institutions, and organizations across nations* (2nd ed.). Thousand Oaks, CA: Sage.

Hofstede, G. (2007). Asian management in the 21st century. *Asia Pacific Journal of Management, 24,* 411–420.

Hofstede, G., & Bond, M. H. (1988). The Confucius connection: From cultural roots to economic growth. *Organizational Dynamics, 16*(4), 4–21.

Hofstede, G., & Hofstede, G. J. (2004). *Cultures and organizations: Software of the mind* (2nd ed.). New York: McGraw-Hill.

Hofstede, G., Hofstede, G. J., & Minkov, M. (2010). *Cultures and organizations: Software of the mind* (3rd ed.). New York: McGraw-Hill.

House, R. J., Hangers, P. J., Javidan, M., Dorfman, P. W., & Gupta, V. (2004). *Culture, leadership, and organizations: The GLOBE Study of 62 societies.* Thousand Oaks, CA: Sage.

Inkeles, A., & Levinson, D. J. (1969). National character: The study of modal personality and sociocultural systems. In G. Lindzey & E. Aronson (Eds.), *The handbook of social psychology* (2nd ed., pp. 418–506). Reading, MA: Addison-Wesley.

Javidan, M., & House, R. (2001). Cultural acumen for the global manager: Lessons from Project GLOBE. *Organizational Dynamics, 29*(4), 289–305.

Javidan, M., House, R., Dorfman, P. W., Hanges, P. J., & Sully de Luque, M. (2006). Conceptualizing and measuring cultures and their consequences: A comparative review of GLOBE's and Hofstede's approaches. *Journal of International Business Studies, 37,* 897–914.

Javidan, M., Stahl, G. K., Brodbeck, F., & Wilderom, C. P. M. (2005). Cross-border transfer of knowledge: Cultural lessons from project GLOBE. *Academy of Management Executive 19*(2), 59–76.

Jen, C., Chou, L., Lin, C., & Tsai, M. (2012). The influence of the perception of a familial climate on job performance: Mediation of loyalty to supervisors and moderation of filial behavior. *International Journal of Psychology, 47*(3), 169–178.

Joiner, T. A. (2001). The influence of national culture and organizational culture alignment on job stress and performance: Evidence from Greece. *Journal of Managerial Psychology, 16*(3), 229.

Khaleeli, H. (2012, July 23). Sports hijabs help Muslim women to Olympic success. *The Guardian.*

Kirkman, B. L., Lowe, K. B., & Gibson, C. B. (2006). A quarter century of Culture's consequences: A review of empirical research incorporating Hofstede's cultural values framework. Journal of International Business Studies, 37, 285–320.

Kitayama, S. (2002). Culture and basic psychological processes—Toward a system view of culture: Comment on Oyserman et al. *Psychological Bulletin, 128,* 89–96.

Kroeber, A. L., & Kluckhohn, C. (1952). *Culture: A critical review of concepts and definitions.* Cambridge, MA: Harvard University Press.

Langevin seeks to author legislation to ban forced wearing of the abaya by American servicewomen in Saudi Arabia. (2002, May 8). Congressman Langevin [Press release]. Retrieved from www.house.gov/apps/list/press/ri02_langevin/050802abayaamend.htm

Lau, D. C., Lam, L. W., & Deutsch Salamon, S. (2008). The impact of relational demographics on perceived managerial trustworthiness: Similarity or norms? *The Journal of Social Psychology, 148*(2), 187–209.

Laurent, A. (1984). The cultural diversity of Western conceptions of management. *International Studies of Management and Organizations, 13,* 75–96.

Lee, C. M., & Gudykunst, W. B. (2001). Attraction to interethnic interactions. *International Journal of Intercultural Relations, 25,* 373–387.

Madlock, P. E. (2012). The influence of cultural congruency, communication, and work alienation on employee satisfaction and commitment in Mexican organizations. *Western Journal of Communication, 76*(4), 380–396.

Mangaliso, M. P. (2001). Building competitive advantage from Ubuntu: Management lessons from South Africa. *Academy of Management Executive, 15*(3), 23–33.

McCall, G. J., Ngeva, J., & Mbebe, M. (1997). Mapping conflict cultures: Interpersonal disputing in a South African black township. *Human Organization, 56*(1), 71–78.

McSweeney, B. (2002). Hofstede's model of national cultural differences and their consequences: A triumph of faith—a failure of analysis. *Human Relations, 55*(1), 89–118.

Mead, M. (2001). *Sex and temperament in three primitive societies.* New York: HarperCollins. (Original work published 1935).

Minkov, M., & Hofstede, G. (2011). The evolution of Hofstede's doctrine. *Cross Cultural Management: An International Journal, 18*(1), 10–20.

Molinsky, A. L. (2005). Language fluency and the evaluation of cultural faux pas: Russians interviewing for jobs in the United States. *Social Psychology Quarterly, 68*(2), 103–120.

Mor Barak, M. E., Findler, L., & Wind, L. (2003). Cross-cultural aspects of diversity and well-being in the workplace: An international perspective. *Journal of Social Work Research and Evaluation, 4*(2), 49–73.

MSNBC News. (2009, November 26). *Obama's bow in Japan sparks some criticism. Conservative commentators accuse president of groveling to foreign leader.* Retrieved November 30, 2009, from www.msnbc .msn.com/id/33978533/ns/ politics-white_house/

National Public Radio. (2009, November 16). *The presidential bow.* Retrieved November 30, 2009, from http:// minnesota.publicradio.org/collections/special/ columns/news_cut/ archive/2009/11/the_presiden tial_bow.shtml?refid=0

Neuliep, J. W. (2008). *Intercultural communication: A contextual approach* (4th ed.). Thousand Oaks, CA: Sage.

Nurden, R. (1997, October 30). Teaching tailored for business people's every demand. *The European,* p. 9.

O'Brien, M. (2009). Fathers, parental leave policies, and infant quality of life: International perspectives and policy impact. *The ANNALS of the American Academy of Political and Social Science, 624*(1), 190–213.

Pekerti, A. A., & Thomas, D. C. (2003). Communication in intercultural interaction: An empirical investigation of indicentric and sociocentric communication styles. *Journal of Cross-Cultural Psychology, 34*(2), 139–154.

Pettigrew, T. F., Tropp, L. R., Wagner, U., & Christ, O. (2011). Recent advances in intergroup contact theory. *International Journal of Intercultural Relations, 35*(3), 271–280.

Robertson, C. J., Al-Khatib, J. A., & Al-Habib, M. (2002). The relationship between Arab values and work beliefs: An exploratory examination. *Thunderbird International Business Review, 44*(5), 583.

Robinson, R. V. (1983). Book review of *Culture's Consequences:* International differences in work-related values. *Work and Occupations, 10,* 110–115.

Sanchez-Burks, J., & Lee, F. (2007). Culture and workways. In S. Kitayama & D. Cohen (Eds.), *Handbook of cultural psychology* (Vol. 1, pp. 346–369). New York: Guilford.

Singh, J. P. (1990). Managerial culture and work-related values in India. *Organization Studies, 11,* 75–101.

Søndergaard, M. (1994). Research note: Hofstede's consequences: A study of reviews, citations and replications. *Organization Studies, 15,* 447–456.

Staub, K. J. (2009). Facilitating supervisee cultural fluency for a multicultural society. *Perspectives on Administration and Supervision, 19,* 45–50.

Tarlo, E. (1996). *Clothing matters: Dress and identity in India.* Chicago: University of Chicago Press.

Text: Kennedy's Berlin speech. (2003, June 26). BBC News, UK edition. Retrieved May 23, 2004, from http:// news.bbc.co.uk/2/hi/europe/3022166.stm

The World. (2003, October 23). National Public Radio [Radio broadcast].

The World Factbook. (2012). *Languages, Central Intelligence Agency.* Retrieved from www.cia.gov/library/publica tions/the-world-factbook/fields/2098.html

Triandis, H. C. (2004). The many dimensions of culture. *Academy of Management Executive, 18*(1), 88–93.

Triandis, H. C., Marin, G., Lisansky, J., & Betancourt, H. (1984). Simpatia as a cultural script of Hispanics. *Journal of Personality and Social Psychology, 47,* 1363–1375.

Tse, D. K., Francis, J., & Walls, J. F. (1994). Cultural differences in conducting intra- and inter-cultural negotiations: A Sino-Canadian comparison. *Journal of International Business Studies, 25,* 537–555.

Umiker, W. (1995). Workplace loyalty in the 1990s. *The Health Care Supervisor, 13*(3), 30–35.

Yoo, B., Donthu, N., & Lenartowicz, T. (2011). Measuring Hofstede's five dimensions of cultural values at the individual level: Development and validation of CVSCALE. *Journal of International Consumer Marketing, 23*(3–4), 193–210.

CHAPTER 20

The Psychological Benefits of Creating an Affirming Climate for Workplace Diversity

Donna Chrobot-Mason[1]
University of Cincinnati

Nicholas P. Aramovich
University of Illinois at Chicago

Ever since dramatic shifts in the demographics of the workforce were predicted more than two decades ago, diversity researchers and authors have been writing about the need for organizations to create a work environment that supports and values diverse employees (e.g., Cox, 1994; Konrad, Prasad, & Pringle, 2006; Shore et al., 2011). They have argued that diversity is a double-edged sword; it has the potential for positive and negative outcomes. Moreover, the difference between these two dramatically different scenarios often depends on the work environment and the extent to which diversity is managed or mismanaged.

The argument goes as follows. When diversity is managed effectively and the work environment supports and values a diverse workforce, employees from all demographic backgrounds feel included within their organization and believe that their ideas, opinions, and suggestions are welcome. The eventual outcome is the espoused potential benefits of a diverse workforce that comprise the business case for diversity (Konrad, 2003; Kulik & Roberson, 2008), namely, that employees will realize their full potential at work and greater creativity and innovation will result from the variety of perspectives, experiences, backgrounds, and work styles that a diverse workforce may bring (Milliken & Martins, 1996; Page, 2007; Williams & O'Reilly, 1998), positively impacting the bottom-line.

This proposition, known as the cognitive resource perspective or, more recently, the resource-based view of diversity, is a theoretical approach used to

Source: Article by Donna Chrobot-Mason and Nicholas P. Aramovich in *Group & Organization Management,* 2013 38(6), pp. 659–689. SAGE Publications. Reprinted with permission.

explain the positive effects of diversity on workplace outcomes. Richard and Miller (2013) define the resource-based knowledge view as a set of conditions in which diversity becomes a competitive advantage. "The coordination and combination of employees' knowledge, skills, and abilities become the firms' human resources and capital, and a source of competitive advantage to the extent the resources are valuable, rare, hard to imitate, and strategically difficult to substitute" (Richard & Miller, 2013, p. 241). This perspective suggests that demographic diversity is accompanied by diversity on underlying attributes such as values, beliefs, attitudes, and personality (McGrath, Berdahl, & Arrow, 1995; Webber & Donahue, 2001). As demographic diversity increases, so does the group's cognitive resources and ability to engage in more complex problem solving and thinking (Hambrick & Mason, 1984; Page, 2007; Roberge & van Dick, 2010).

The flip side of the argument, however, is that when the work environment fails to support diverse employees, negative outcomes may result, such as an increase in harassment and discrimination (Schneider, Hitlan, & Radhakrishnan, 2000), intergroup conflict (Jehn, Bezrukova, & Thatcher, 2008), and turnover (McKay et al., 2007). Research examining the faultline theory of diversity and conflict support this argument. Faultline theory suggests that demographic differences resulting in subgroups or coalitions increase the salience of in-group/out-group differences, resulting in further polarization and competition and conflict (Lau & Murnighan, 2005). When diversity climate perceptions are characterized by a belief that the organization is unfair or when personnel practices favor certain groups over others, demographic differences become more salient and faultlines crack open, exposing the organization to negative work outcomes (Jehn & Bezrukova, 2010).

Overall, research examining the effects of diversity on workplace outcomes has been characterized as limited and inconsistent (Curtis & Dreachslin, 2008; van Knippenberg & Schippers, 2007; Webber & Donahue, 2001). This inconsistency is likely because the relationship is more complex than was originally thought (Harrison & Klein, 2007; Kochan et al., 2003). One explanation for these mixed results is the

organizational climate created for a diverse workforce; some organizations effectively manage diversity while others mismanage the potentially valuable resources found within a diverse workforce (Jayne & Dipboye, 2004).

Although the resource-based view of diversity is commonly cited as support for the competitive advantage of diversity, few studies have empirically examined the veracity of its claims. Most research in this area has focused on the link between diverse representation within an organization (e.g., the proportion of various racial and gender demographic groups represented in the organization) and objective business performance measures indicating financial performance (Dwyer, Richard, & Chadwick, 2003; Kochan et al., 2003; Richard, Murthi, & Ismail, 2007). In a recent review of the literature on diversity as a source of competitive advantage, Richard and Miller (2013) summarize the empirical work on the diversity-performance relationship as quite scarce. In fact, the studies reviewed found no support for a main effect of diversity on firm business performance, but rather support for a moderated relationship in which business strategy, organizational culture and design, and human resource management practices all played a significant role in determining the extent to which diversity positively impacted firm performance.

Though many scholars have argued that diverse groups result in creative ideas, innovative solutions, and improved decision making by raising divergent ideas and opinions about how best to improve organizational effectiveness (De Dreu & West, 2001; Phillips, Northcraft, & Neale, 2006), there still exists a need to explore the conditions under which diversity leads to positive workplace outcomes. Gonzalez and DeNisi (2009), for example, call for additional research in this area. They challenge scholars to explore the association between diversity climate and organizational diversity, including how climates are perceived and managed. Thus, there remains a significant gap in the literature that the present study seeks to fill. To do so, we focus on three goals. First, we examine the link between diversity climate perceptions and turnover intentions. Second, we explore four psychological variables as mediators of this relationship to more fully understand how and why diversity climate perceptions influence employee retention. And finally, we assess whether such relationships hold consistently across racial and gender subgroups.

Conceptualizing an Affirming Climate for Diversity

Scholars have long argued that organizational climate is an important construct, because it impacts employee performance and satisfaction (L. R. James, James, & Ashe, 1990), and touches nearly every aspect of organizational life (Kuenzi & Schminke, 2009). Schneider, Gunnarson, and Niles-Jolly (1994) write that climate is "the atmosphere that employees perceive is created in their organizations by practices, procedures, and rewards" (p. 18). They go on to say that "Employees observe what happens to them (and around them) and then draw conclusions about their organization's priorities" (p. 18). Thus, employees form an overall perception of what is valued and deemed a high priority within their organization based largely on what management does, not what it says (Schneider et al., 1994). For example, organizations that create a climate for innovation experience a more innovative and creative workforce (Schneider et al., 1994) and organizations that create a strong service climate positively impact customers' perceptions of service quality (Schneider, White, & Paul, 1998).

Although practical guidelines for creating a positive diversity climate can be found abundantly in the popular press (e.g., Chavez & Weisinger, 2008), only a handful of empirical studies exist focusing on diversity climate. Early research demonstrated that a *diversity climate* exists and employees do indeed develop an overall impression of the extent to which the organization values diversity based on its practices, policies, procedures, and rewards (Kossek & Zonia, 1993; Mor Barak, Cherin, & Berkman, 1998).

The conceptualization of diversity climate has evolved over time. Early research was highly pragmatic and each study conceptualized diversity climate differently, depending on the specific organization involved. Recent work has attempted to take a more theoretically based approach to the study of diversity

climate and conceptualize the construct as multidimensional. Although to date there is no single widely used measure of diversity climate, there is overlap and convergence in how diversity climate is conceptualized. Diversity climate has often been defined as consisting of two core diversity practices: fair treatment and integration (McKay, Avery, & Morris, 2008; Mor Barak et al., 1998; Roberson, 2006). For example, McKay et al. (2008) define diversity climate as "employees' shared perceptions that an employer utilizes fair personnel practices and socially integrates underrepresented employees into the work environment" (p. 350). Gelfand, Nishii, Raver, and Schneider (2005) define diversity climate as "employees' shared perceptions of the policies, practices, and procedures that implicitly and explicitly communicate the extent to which fostering and maintaining diversity and eliminating discrimination is a priority in the organization" (p. 104). Likewise, we define diversity climate, at least in part, as consisting of perceptions of a set of diversity practices aimed at providing fair and equal opportunities to all employees.

Beyond what may be referred to as fair diversity practices, many scholars have theorized that diversity climate also consists of the interpretation of such practices. That is, an important element of diversity climate includes employee perceptions of the extent to which they feel valued and the degree to which diversity is viewed as a competitive advantage. For example, Cox (1991, 1994) defined three types of organizations: monolithic, plural, and multicultural. Cox distinguished a multicultural organization from one that is monolithic (demographically and culturally homogeneous) and one that is plural (diverse representation at lower levels only), by defining a multicultural organization as one in which members of all sociocultural backgrounds can contribute and achieve their full potential. Unlike a plural organization, in which differences are simply tolerated, in a multicultural organization, organizational members view diversity as a valuable resource and competitive advantage.

Thus, a review of the literature suggests that diversity climate is complex and multifaceted (Herdman & McMillan-Capehart, 2010). An affirming climate for diversity consists of management practices to create a work environment defined as providing equal access and fair treatment to all. The creation of an affirming climate for diversity also depends on employee perceptions that diversity is valued and the extent to which diverse employees are encouraged to contribute fully to the organization (Joshi & Roh, 2013).

To define an affirming climate for diversity for purposes of the present study, we drew heavily on Cox's (1991, 1994) conceptualization of a multicultural organization. Cox identified and described six dimensions of a multicultural organization. *Full structural integration* is achieved when all demographic groups are adequately represented within various organizational levels, functions, and work groups. *Integration in informal networks* occurs when all organizational members have equal access to and are included in social and informal networking activities. *Low cultural bias* is evident in organizations where steps are taken to identify and eliminate discrimination and prejudice in the workplace. *Intergroup cohesion* is observed when the organization achieves an optimal level of conflict involving work tasks, while minimizing conflict due to social identity group differences, such as race and gender. *Acculturation* refers to the method by which cultural differences are resolved in organizations. Cox argues that acculturation should involve a two-way process in which minority and majority group members have some influence on organizational norms and values and minority group members are not expected to assimilate or shed their identity when coming to work. Finally, Cox suggests that a multicultural organization may be characterized by the extent to which *organizational identification* occurs for all employees.

Turnover: A Key Outcome of an Affirming Climate for Diversity

As mentioned earlier, previous research has focused primarily on the link between diverse representation within an organization and objective business performance. Research examining the relationship between diversity climate and outcomes is limited to a handful of studies. McKay et al. (2008) found that diversity

climate plays an important role in predicting sales performance. Findler, Wind, and Mor Barak (2007) examined social work managers in Israel and found a significant direct relationship between climate variables (i.e., fairness, inclusion, stress, and social support) and general health and well-being, job satisfaction, and organizational commitment.

While a variety of consequences of diversity climate have been explored in the literature (van Knippenberg, Homan, & van Ginkel, 2013), employee satisfaction and its opposite, turnover, are often mentioned as a key outcome and reason to invest in fostering a positive diversity climate. This is likely due to the fact that the cost of turnover in organizations is well documented and considered significant enough that organizations are advised to take steps to reduce turnover (Kacmar, Andrews, Van Rooy, Steilberg, & Cerrone, 2006).

Creating an affirming climate to support a diverse workforce is one strategy to improve employee satisfaction and commitment and, thereby, reduce turnover (Hicks-Clarke & Iles, 2000). When employees of color see similar others succeeding in the workplace, they perceive that they, too, will be permitted to succeed in the organization (Thomas, 2005) and, thus, will be less likely to turn over. Several studies report a significant negative relationship between an affirming diversity climate and turnover intentions (Kaplan, Wiley, & Maertz, 2011; McKay et al., 2007; Stewart, Volpone, Avery, & McKay, 2011). Using a multiorganizational sample, Kaplan et al. (2011) found that positive perceptions of diversity climate were related to decreased turnover intentions. McKay et al. (2007) found that people from underrepresented groups had higher rates of turnover than White men, a finding consistent with previous research on turnover. In addition, however, they found that high turnover among underrepresented groups is especially high if such group members perceive that the organization is not committed to supporting diversity. Thus, our first hypothesis attempts to replicate previous findings by predicting that diversity climate will be negatively related to turnover intentions.

Hypothesis 1: An affirming climate for diversity has a negative effect on turnover intentions.

Psychological Outcomes of Diversity Climate Perceptions

After reviewing the extant literature examining the relationship between diversity climate and outcomes, it quickly becomes apparent that work remains to be done in this area and additional outcome variables and/or mediators should be examined. The resource-based view of diversity suggests that demographic diversity leads to a competitive business advantage because it is accompanied by diversity in values, beliefs, attitudes, and personality, resulting in additional cognitive resources that enable employees to engage in more complex problem-solving and higher-order thinking (Hambrick & Mason, 1984; Webber & Donahue, 2001). Although this theory remains largely untested, Ely and Thomas (2001) found that firms that adopt an integration and learning perspective have a high value for diversity and view it as a resource for learning, change, and renewal throughout the entire organization. When firms value diversity and embrace the opportunity to learn from a diverse workforce, their employees have the chance to experience constructive intergroup conflict and explore diverse viewpoints, which facilitates opportunities for cross-cultural learning and enhances performance. Likewise, Cox (1994) suggests that the goal of managing diversity is to maximize the ability of all employees to contribute to organizational goals and achieve their full potential.

To create a work climate that is affirming for diverse employees such that the benefits of diverse perspectives are realized, a better understanding of the complex relationship between diversity climate and work outcomes is necessary (Curtis & Dreachslin, 2008). To advance the field and illuminate the proverbial black box one must ask: How, why, and under what conditions do diversity practices have a positive impact on employees' perceptions that their differences contribute to and enhance their work?

According to Cox's (1994) Interactional Model of Cultural Diversity (IMCD) model, the relationship between diversity climate and organizational effectiveness outcome variables is mediated by the extent to which employees experience positive affect and achievement within the organization.

The IMCD is consistent with previous research that finds organizational commitment mediates the effect of diversity climate perceptions on turnover intentions (McKay et al., 2007). Kaplan et al. (2011) also examined a mediator of turnover intentions. They found that calculative attachment (defined as a rational calculation of the probability of attaining important goals in the future through continued membership) fully mediated the relationship between diversity climate perceptions and turnover intention. Although only a handful of empirical studies have examined mediators of diversity climate and turnover, theoretical work in this area suggests that diversity climate has a positive impact on organizational outcomes like employee retention, *because* employees experience positive psychological outcomes in a work environment characterized by fair and supportive procedures, practices, and policies.

Therefore, one of the goals of the present study was to empirically examine the role of a variety of mediators to clarify the relationship between diversity climate perceptions and turnover intentions. We predict that when employees perceive their demographic group is tolerated, but not valued as a result of perceived unfair or unequal management practices, they will experience marginalization. Furthermore, when employees feel marginalized, they are less likely to contribute their unique perspectives and will disengage from their work or even disengage from the organization itself and ultimately find employment elsewhere. Conversely, when employees work in an organization characterized as engaging in a set of fair and inclusive management practices, employees will perceive that they are an important part of the organization and that their group identity is valued, which, in turn, affects their perception that diverse perspectives and backgrounds contribute to the work. In the present study, we have identified four psychological outcomes that we predict will mediate the relationship between diversity climate perceptions and turnover intentions.

Recently, the extent to which organizational members identify with or are committed to their organization has been examined as a key mediator or moderator of the relationship between diversity climate and workplace outcomes. For example, McKay et al. (2007) demonstrated that organizational commitment mediates the relationship between positive perceptions of workplace diversity climate and turnover intentions. Gonzalez and DeNisi (2009) found partial support for diversity climate as a moderator of the relationship between organizational identification, organizational commitment, and intentions to quit. Therefore, in the present study, we examine *organizational identification* as a potential psychological outcome of diversity climate perceptions that mediates the relationship between diversity climate and turnover intentions. We define organizational identification as the extent to which employees identify with, are involved in, and enjoy a sense of belonging and membership in an organization (Allen & Meyer, 1990). This is consistent with Cox (1991, 1994) who argues that within a multicultural organization, organizational identification occurs for all employees.

In a recent review of the literature supporting diversity as a competitive advantage, Richard and Miller (2013) suggest research supports the notion that diverse groups are more likely to come up with creative ideas and innovative solutions by raising divergent ideas and options about how best to improve organizational effectiveness. Yet, the literature also seems to be clear that an affirming climate for diversity is necessary to achieve such positive outcomes (van Knippenberg et al., 2013). Research has found that the introduction of minority viewpoints leads to more divergent thinking, consideration of alternative perspectives, and greater information processing (Nemeth, 1986; Tomasetto, Mucchi-Faina, Alparone, & Pagliaro, 2009). In support of this, Yang and Konrad (2011) found a three-way interaction among employee involvement, variation in involvement, and racioethnic diversity on innovation. They conclude that ensuring high levels of involvement among members of historically marginalized racioethnic groups enhances innovation.

Furthermore, there is evidence to support that a climate for innovation is related to employee well-being (King, de Chermont, West, Dawson, & Hebl, 2007). Based on this research as well as literature citing the business case for diversity, which argues that creativity and innovation resulting from diversity can be a competitive advantage (Konrad, 2003; Kulik &

Roberson, 2008), we predict perceived *climate for innovation* will mediate the relationship between diversity climate perceptions and turnover intentions. When employees perceive an affirming climate for diversity, they are more likely to also perceive a climate in which innovative and creative ideas are valued and encouraged. This perception eventually relates to lower turnover.

The resource-based view of diversity also predicts that a positive outcome of diversity is an organization's enhanced ability to engage in complex problem solving. Again, the notion that minority viewpoints lead to more divergent thinking and consideration of alternative perspectives (Nemeth, 1986; Tomasetto et al., 2009) suggests that heterogeneous employee groups may be better equipped than homogeneous groups to solve organizational problems and improve organizational performance. Yet, this potential benefit of diversity will only be realized if employees perceive an affirming climate for diversity and this perception is then associated with the belief that they are empowered to make decisions and encouraged to engage in problem solving. There is evidence to suggest that when employees perceive they are empowered, this perceived empowerment is related to positive outcomes, such as increased job satisfaction and work productivity/effectiveness as well as lower job-related strain and propensity to leave the organization (Koberg, Boss, Seniem, & Goodman, 1999; Spreitzer, Kizilos, & Nason, 1997). Therefore, we predict that perceptions of *psychological empowerment* will mediate the relationship between diversity climate perceptions and intentions to turnover.

Finally, we consider Cox's (1994) IMCD model to identify an additional possible mediator, as well as a recent review highlighting the importance of *identity work* in navigating the self in diverse work contexts (Roberts & Creary, 2013). Cox argues that identity is central to how diversity impacts behavior in organizations. He illustrates the important relationship of identity to the career experience of minority group members and suggests that there is a cost to the individual and the organization when members attempt to repress expression of group identity (Cox, 1991). Such individuals may feel pressure to act in ways that may be unnatural for them and a strong desire to fit in with the dominant group may lead to additional stress that likely has a negative impact on work performance. Cox (1991) asserts that "people are at their best when they can be themselves" (p. 59). Roberts and Creary (2013) likewise argue that navigating the self is critical to working in a diverse workplace and involves identity construction and negotiation processes that unfold as people interpret and act on their differences. Roberts and Creary go on to say that as employees act on these differences in constructive ways, they open possibilities for differences to become sources of creativity and resilience (p. 73). In this paper, we define *identity freedom* as the extent to which employees feel free to express their identity at work. We predict that identity freedom will mediate the relationship between diversity climate perceptions and intentions to turn over. When employees perceive an affirming climate for diversity, they are more likely to experience freedom to express their identity as well as different perspectives and opinions, which, in turn, lead to positive work outcomes, such as lower intention to turnover.

> **Hypothesis 2:** The overall effects of an affirming climate for diversity on turnover intentions will be mediated by four psychological outcome variables: organizational identification, climate for innovation, psychological empowerment, and identity freedom.

Subgroup Differences

In addition to examining turnover as a key outcome of diversity climate and various mediators of this relationship, a final goal of this study was to examine whether the four psychological outcomes mediated the relationship between diversity climate perceptions and turnover intentions regardless of racial and gender subgroup differences. Although decades of research on racial and gender differences have yielded important findings that suggest that Whites and men experience a dramatically different workplace from people of color and women (Cox, Welch, & Nkomo, 2001; Powell, 1999), there is research to support the assertion that an affirming climate for diversity has positive work outcomes for all organizational members.

For example, Phillips, Duguid, Thomas-Hunt, and Uparna (2013) report that the information-processing benefits of diversity do not come solely from the contributions of social minorities, but also come from dominant group members such as Whites. Other research suggests that diversity climate perceptions are significantly related to turnover intentions for Whites as well as racial minority groups (Kaplan et al., 2011; McKay et al., 2007). For example, McKay et al. (2007) found that diversity climate perceptions mediated by organizational commitment were positively related to turnover intentions for White men and women as well as non-White groups. Dobbin, Sutton, Meyer, and Scott (1993) suggest that all demographic groups benefit from equal opportunity and affirmative action initiatives, because such processes demand that organizations examine and rationalize their staffing procedures, resulting in more objective decision making and increased perceptions of fairness. Thus, creating a work environment characterized by fair treatment, for example, may be beneficial for all employees regardless of racial or gender group differences. Therefore, we hypothesize that the psychological outcome variables will mediate the relationship between diversity and turnover regardless of gender or racial group membership.

> **Hypothesis 3:** Four psychological outcome variables (organizational identification, identity freedom, psychological empowerment, and climate for innovation) mediate the relationship between diversity climate and turnover intentions across subgroups.

Method

Sample

Participants were 1,731 public employees from a large municipality in the United States. The largest group of employees ($n = 866$; 50%) comprised police officers. Approximately 15% of the sample consisted of firefighters ($n = 254$) and the remaining 35% were represented by other departments such as city planning, parks and recreation, and internal support services ($n = 611$). Of the 1,731 survey respondents, approximately 70% ($n = 1,192$) were men and 30%

($n = 515$) were women (24 people failed to indicate their gender). Approximately 81% ($n = 1,400$) of the participants were Caucasian/White and 19% ($n = 331$) were non-Caucasian. Approximately 10% ($n = 179$) were Hispanic/Latino, 5% ($n = 86$) were African American, 2% ($n = 32$) were Asian, and 2% ($n = 34$) were Native American. The majority of respondents were between 36 and 45 years of age (36%; $n = 624$). Most employees were tenured between 6 and 10 years in the organization.

Procedure

The diversity climate survey used in the present study was developed to guide diversity training initiatives within the municipal organization and provide a baseline measure of employee perceptions and attitudes. We worked closely with the Diversity Coordinator to develop and revise the survey. A volunteer task force was created including representatives from all departments and levels to administer the surveys. Prior to administering the surveys, task force members participated in a training session in which they were provided with materials intended to inform them of the goals of the survey, when and how respondents would receive feedback, and steps taken to ensure respondent confidentiality. A task force member or representative then facilitated each survey administration session. Employees completed the surveys in meetings of their work groups during work time. The entire organization (approximately 2,300 employees) was invited to participate in the survey during a 3.5-week period. Facilitators collected the completed surveys at these meetings, placed them in envelopes immediately, and mailed them to an outside vendor for data keying to ensure respondent confidentiality. The overall response rate was 81%.

Measures

Affirming climate for diversity. We developed a measure of diversity climate that included four subscales (Structural Integration, Informal Integration, Low Cultural Bias, and Intergroup Cohesion). In developing our measure, we drew heavily on Cox's (1991, 1994) conceptualization of a multicultural organization. *Low Cultural Bias* was measured using 7 of the 15 items from the Workplace Prejudice/Discrimination Inventory (K. James, Lovato, & Cropanzano, 1994). These 7 items were selected because they assessed employee perceptions of the existence of bias, prejudice, and discrimination in the workplace. The 8 items not taken from the original survey were eliminated due to redundancy with other items or because they measured more informal types of discrimination, such as social isolation. Items indicating the existence of bias and discrimination in the workplace were reverse scored so that high scores indicated a lack of bias in the workplace.

Items comprising the other three subscales in the diversity climate measure (*Informal Integration, Intergroup Cohesion,* and *Structural Integration*) were developed based on Cox's definition of these dimensions (see Cox, 1991). Although other diversity climate measures were consulted during development of these subscale items, no existing measures seemed to adequately capture the multicultural dimensions defined by Cox. Thus, new items were developed by the first author and revised with input from the diversity director of the organization in which the survey was administered as well as other diversity scholars. Examples include the following: "I feel excluded from casual conversations with members of other demographic groups" (Informal Integration–Reverse), "Minority input is effectively considered at all levels in the organization" (Structural Integration), and "There are tensions between members of different groups in this organization" (Intergroup Conflict–Reverse). For all items, responses ranged from *strongly disagree* (1) to strongly *agree* (7).

Psychological Outcome Variables

Organizational identification was measured using five items from the affective subscale of the organizational commitment measure developed by Allen and Meyer (1990). *Psychological empowerment* was measured using the three-item Self-Determination subscale from Spreitzer's (1995) Psychological

Empowerment scale. Four new items for *perceived climate for innovation* were developed. To develop these items, the authors consulted literature on the business case for diversity as well as research on innovation (cited previously). Based on this literature, the authors generated a list of behaviors that might be expected if employees worked in an environment in which they were expected and rewarded for contributing to innovative and creative ideas. Four items were developed to assess employees' perceptions that creative solutions and new ideas are supported and encouraged at work (e.g., "In my work unit, we are encouraged to come up with new and creative ideas"). *Identity freedom* was developed based on Cox's (1991, 1994) dimension of acculturation as well as work by Shore et al. (2011) on inclusion. Cox and Shore describe a positive diverse work environment as one in which employees can express their true identity at work rather than attempt to suppress differences. We developed a five-item scale to assess the extent to which employees feel they can "fit in" and contribute fully at work without having to assimilate. A sample item is, "I feel that I can fit in at work without having to change who I am."

Turnover

Turnover intentions were measured using a three-item subscale of the Michigan Organizational Assessment Questionnaire (MOAQ; Seashore, Lawler, Mirvis, & Cammann, 1982). These items assessed the extent to which employees actively thought about leaving the organization (e.g., "It is likely that I will actively look for a new job (outside the organization) in the next year").

Control Variables

Because of their conceptual and empirical links with turnover and organizational identification, *organizational tenure* and *job level* were used as control variables when testing hypotheses (Griffeth, Hom, & Gaertner, 2000; Mathieu & Zajac, 1990). Tenure was measured using a 5-point scale (1 = *less than 1 year*, 2 = *1–5 years*, 3 = *6–10 years*, 4 = *11–15 years*, 5 = *more than 15 years*). Job level was also measured with a 5-point scale

(1 = *clerical/paraprofessional*, 2 = *professional*, 3 = *supervisor*, 4 = *manager*, 5 = *senior manager*).

Results

Analysis Plan

Our analysis involved three stages. In the first stage, we sought to establish the number of dimensions necessary to represent employees' perceptions of diversity climate. Our diversity climate survey consisted of items measuring four distinct climate dimensions (Structural Integration, Informal Integration, Lack of Cultural Bias, and Intergroup Cohesion). However, prior theory has conceptualized diversity climate as comprised of two dimensions, fair treatment and integration. Therefore, using a randomly selected half of our sample, we conducted exploratory factor analysis (EFA) to determine the number of diversity climate dimensions. In the second stage, we used confirmatory factor analysis (CFA) on the second half of the data set to replicate the results of our EFA and establish a measurement model. At this stage, we tested for method bias and assessed whether the measurement model was invariant across three subgroups of employees: White males, White females, and non-Whites. In the final data analysis stage, we created a structural equation model (SEM) to test our hypotheses regarding the relationships between diversity climate perceptions and turnover, and to test whether this relationship was mediated by four psychological variables. In addition, we assessed whether these relationships were generally consistent across various subgroups of employees.

Stage 1: *EFA*

Prior to analyses, all survey items were assessed for missing values, outliers, and univariate skewness and kurtosis. Missing data were replaced via mean substitution and 25 cases classified as multivariate outliers were deleted. To determine the underlying factor structure of the survey items, we conducted a

Table 20.1	Results of Exploratory Factor Analysis

Original item	Equal treatment	Equal access	Empowerment	Climate for innovation	Organizational identification	Turnover intentions	Identity freedom
IC3	**0.75**	0.00	0.12	−0.15	0.06	0.03	−0.06
LOCB5	**0.72**	0.12	0.00	0.06	0.02	−0.04	−0.12
LOCB2	**0.69**	−0.14	−0.07	0.09	0.00	0.00	0.09
LOCB6	**0.69**	−0.22	−0.09	0.15	−0.04	0.05	0.00
IIN1	**0.67**	0.15	0.04	−0.06	−0.15	0.02	−0.06
IC2	**0.66**	0.05	0.07	−0.08	0.09	−0.07	−0.13
LOCB3	**0.59**	0.24	−0.14	0.06	0.02	0.01	−0.08
IIN3	**0.56**	−0.06	0.05	−0.01	0.02	−0.01	0.17
LOCB1	**0.45**	0.05	−0.03	−0.01	−0.04	0.06	0.11
LOCB4	0.42	0.06	0.02	−0.03	−0.14	0.02	0.32
IIN2	0.38	0.27	−0.03	−0.01	0.15	0.03	−0.03
IIN5	0.07	**0.73**	−0.03	0.00	−0.08	0.06	0.01
SI1	0.08	**0.71**	0.08	−0.08	0.02	−0.08	0.01
SI4	−0.04	**0.65**	−0.03	0.09	0.06	0.01	−0.02
SI2	0.04	**0.51**	−0.07	0.10	−0.09	0.03	0.00
IIN4	0.22	**0.47**	0.02	−0.03	−0.05	0.02	0.03
SI5	0.20	0.42	−0.16	0.13	−0.04	0.11	−0.09
IC4	0.29	0.40	0.09	−0.14	0.12	−0.04	0.00
LOCB7	0.24	0.31	0.04	0.03	0.00	−0.06	0.10
IC5	0.10	0.29	0.08	0.08	0.07	−0.04	0.18
EMP3	0.01	−0.02	**0.86**	−0.03	0.02	0.04	−0.02
EMP2	−0.01	−0.06	**0.77**	0.11	−0.10	0.02	−0.01
EMP1	−0.01	−0.01	**0.73**	0.03	0.01	0.00	−0.03
CI1	−0.01	0.06	−0.06	**0.77**	0.02	−0.02	−0.05
CI3	0.07	0.04	0.10	**0.72**	−0.03	0.00	−0.02
CI4	−0.14	0.10	0.09	**0.70**	−0.01	0.02	0.02
CI2	0.10	−0.04	0.06	**0.66**	0.05	−0.01	−0.09
OID2	0.05	−0.07	−0.05	−0.02	**0.84**	−0.09	−0.06
OID3	−0.16	0.14	−0.01	0.00	**0.74**	0.08	−0.01

Original item	Equal treatment	Equal access	Empowerment	Climate for innovation	Organizational identification	Turnover intentions	Identity freedom
OID4	0.03	−0.08	−0.02	0.11	**0.68**	0.00	0.13
OID5	0.07	−0.06	0.02	−0.02	0.43	0.21	−0.08
TRN3	−0.04	0.02	−0.02	0.01	0.02	**−0.93**	0.03
TRN1	0.03	−0.09	−0.02	0.02	0.03	**−0.87**	−0.01
TRN2	−0.02	0.05	−0.04	−0.02	−0.24	**−0.53**	−0.11
IF2	0.04	0.00	−0.05	−0.08	−0.07	0.06	**0.93**
IF1	−0.05	0.00	−0.03	−0.07	0.01	0.00	**0.92**
IF5	0.01	0.04	0.10	0.13	0.05	−0.05	**0.52**
IF4	0.28	−0.10	0.02	0.10	0.06	−0.04	0.40
IF3	0.14	0.23	0.04	0.12	0.04	−0.05	0.34

Note: Factor loadings ≥.45 are in boldface and used in subsequent CFA. CI = climate for innovation; EMP = psychological empowerment; IC = intergroup cohesion; IF = identity freedom; IIN = informal integration; LOCB = lack of cultural bias; OID = organizational identification; SI = structural integration; TRN = intentions to turnover; CFA = confirmatory factor analysis.

series of EFAs with principal axis factoring as the extraction method and Promax rotation. To remain in the analysis, an item's communality estimate after extraction must have been greater than .25, and only items with loadings greater than .45 on the factors were interpreted (Tabachnick & Fidell, 2001). Based on these criteria, 12 items were not included in the subsequent CFA.

Results indicated that the most interpretable factor solution consisted of seven factors (please see Table 20.1). All factors had initial eigenvalues greater than 1.0 and collectively accounted for 59% of the variance in the measured items. Two of the seven factors emerged as diversity climate dimensions, consisting exclusively of items from the Lack of Cultural Bias, Informal Integration, Intergroup Cohesion, and Structural Integration scales. The first of these factors (α =.87) consisted of nine items; five items from the Lack of Cultural Bias scale, two items from the Intergroup Cohesion scale, and two items from the Informal Integration scale. Generally, these items dealt with issues of treatment in the workplace, and we therefore chose to call this factor, *Equal Treatment*.

The second of these factors (α =.80) consisted of five items; two items from the Informal Integration scale and three items from the Structural Integration scale. Because all of these items reflect employees' perceptions of equal accessibility to organizational level, resources, and informal networks, we chose to call this five-item factor *Equal Access*. Together, these two dimensions measure perceptions of diversity practices involving equal access and treatment to foster an affirming climate for diversity.

All other items generally loaded on their respective scales. However, in cases in which factor loadings were below .45, those items were dropped from subsequent analyses. This resulted in removal of one item from the Organizational Identification scale and two items from the Identity Freedom scale. Even after removal of such items, these scales demonstrated strong internal consistency. Cronbach's alpha was as follows: Organizational Identification (.80), Identity Freedom (.82), Psychological Empowerment (.83), Climate for Innovation (.83), and Turnover Intentions (.87). Means, standard deviations, correlations, and reliabilities of the final scales are provided in Table 20.2.

| Table 20.2 | | | | | | Descriptive Statistics for Diversity Climate Scales and Psychological Outcome Variables | | | | | | |

		Sample 1			Sample 2								
	α	M	SD	α	M	SD	1	2	3	4	5	6	7
1. Equal treatment	.87	4.80	1.25	.87	4.72	1.28	—	.67	.41	.55	.46	.33	−.33
2. Equal access	.80	5.01	1.21	.77	4.92	1.21	.69	—	.44	.50	.52	.38	−.35
3. Organizational identification	.80	5.04	1.48	.76	4.93	1.47	.39	.40	—	.47	.48	.36	−.51
4. Identity freedom	.82	5.33	1.33	.80	5.25	1.33	.60	.55	.44	—	.52	.49	−.38
5. Climate for innovation	.83	5.34	1.20	.85	5.27	1.25	.48	.52	.49	.55	—	.59	−.42
6. Psychological empowerment	.83	5.41	1.23	.83	5.36	1.28	.33	.34	.25	.50	.51	—	−.35
7. Turnover intentions	.87	2.54	1.71	.86	2.70	1.77	−.36	−.35	−.52	−.41	−.40	−.25	—

Note: Results below the diagonal are for Sample 1 (N = 853) and results above the diagonal are for Sample 2 (N = 853). All correlations are significant at *p* <.01.

Stage 2: CFA

After finding evidence to support a two-dimensional conceptualization of diversity climate involving equal access and equal treatment, we moved to the second stage of the analysis in which we replicated the EFA results using CFA. We conducted the CFA with M*plus* 4.0 (Muthén & Muthén, 2006), using the second half of our sample. Our analysis also evaluated whether method bias was of concern and the measurement invariance across three different employee subgroups. Model fit was assessed using model chisquare (χ^2), the comparative fit index (CFI), the Tucker–Lewis index (TLI), the root mean squared error of approximation (RMSEA) and standardized root mean squared residual (SRMR). Values close to or above.95 for the CFI and TLI, close to.06 or less for the RMSEA, and.09 or less for the SRMR indicate good model fit (Hu & Bentler, 1999).

Our measurement model consisted of seven latent factors representing the constructs of Equal Treatment, Equal Access, Identity Freedom, Organizational Identification, Psychological Empowerment, Climate for Innovation, and Turnover Intentions. All items were specified to load only on their respective factors, which were allowed to correlate with one another. Inspection of the modification indices after the first model fitting suggested that correlating the uniquenesses between Items 1 and 3 of the turnover scale would significantly improve model fit. Because both items contained the words "looking for a new job," it seemed reasonable that they shared common variance and, therefore, we retained this correlation in all subsequent models.

Results indicated that the measurement model fit the data well, $\chi^2(383) = 861.26$, CFI =.96, TLI =.95, RMSEA =.04, SRMR =.04, and all items loaded significantly on their respective factors. In addition, this seven-factor model fit significantly better than several alternative measurement models, including a six-factor model in which the items representing Equal Treatment and Equal Access factors were forced to load on a single diversity climate factor, $\Delta\chi^2(6) = 291.02$, *p* <.001, and a one-factor model in which all survey items were forced to load on a single global factor, $\Delta\chi^2(21) = 3{,}035.44$, $p < .001$. Therefore, these results confirmed the seven-factor structure of the previous EFA.

We next determined the extent to which method bias was present in the data using the measured response style technique (Podsakoff, MacKenzie, & Podsakoff, 2012). Briefly, this technique involves assessing the extent to which four common participant response styles (acquiescence, disacquiescence, extreme responding, and midpoint responding) inflate the correlations among survey items. Following procedures described in Weijters, Schillewaert, and Geuens (2008), we assessed whether factor loadings in our measurement model were reduced when accounting for these response style biases. Results of this analysis revealed that factor loadings did not change in a model that accounted for these response styles, indicating that correlations among survey items were not upwardly inflated by method factors.

Finally, we determined whether the seven-factor measurement model was invariant across three subgroups of employees: White men ($n = 478$), White women ($n = 211$), and non-Whites ($n = 156$). At a minimum, measurement equivalence across groups is established by demonstrating that: (a) the same number of factors holds across groups and (b) groups have equal factor loadings on the factors (Raju, Lafitte, & Byrne, 2002). To test measurement equivalence, we first fit the seven-factor measurement model across all three groups, allowing each group to have unique factor loadings. Results indicated this model fit well, suggesting an invariant seven-factor structure across groups, $\chi^2(1{,}149) = 1{,}758.11$, CFI $=.95$, TLI $=.94$, RMSEA $=.04$, SRMR $=.05$. Next, the factor loadings for each group were constrained to be equivalent to one another. Results indicated that this model also fit the data well, $\chi^2(1{,}195) = 1{,}816.32$, CFI $=.95$, TLI $=.94$, RMSEA $=.04$, SRMR $=.05$, and did not differ from the fit of the first model that allowed factor loadings to vary freely, $\Delta\chi^2(46) = 58.21$, ns. These results established measurement equivalence, indicating that the subgroups conceptualized all seven factors comparably.

Stage 3: Structural Equation Modeling

To test Hypotheses 1 and 2, we first created a SEM in which Equal Treatment and Equal Access directly predicted all other variables, and the four psychological outcomes (Identify Freedom, Psychological Empowerment, Climate for Innovation, and Organizational Identification) predicted Turnover Intentions. The two control variables, Organizational Tenure and Job Level predicted Organizational Identification and Turnover Intentions. Results revealed that this model fit the data well, $\chi^2(435) = 974.01$, CFI $=.96$, TLI $= .95$, RMSEA $=.04$, SRMR $=.04$, but also revealed several nonsignificant direct effects from diversity climate perceptions to the other variables, and significant positive correlations between the four psychological outcome variables. This suggested that the model could be improved by eliminating nonsignificant paths and specifying direct relationships from one psychological outcome variable to another.

Therefore, a revised model was created in which Equal Treatment and Equal Access predicted all other variables, and direct relationships between the psychological outcome variables were specified. In addition, nonsignificant paths were eliminated using a model-trimming procedure recommended by Kline (2005). In this procedure, nonsignificant paths are eliminated one at a time based on theoretical and empirical grounds. After removing each path, overall model fit is evaluated by a significant change in model chi-square. If this change is significant, the path is retained, and if nonsignificant, the path is removed. The only exception we made to this process was that the paths involving control variables were retained, even though they were nonsignificant. Results of this process revealed that the final "trimmed" model fit the data well, $\chi^2(442) = 984.08$, CFI $=.95$, TLI $=.95$, RMSEA $=.04$, $SRMR =$, and just as well as the original structural model, $\Delta\chi^2(7) = 10.07$, ns, indicating that trimming the nonsignificant paths resulted in a more parsimonious model that still fit the data well. The final structural model and parameter estimates appear in Figure 20.1.

Figure 20.1	Results of structural model

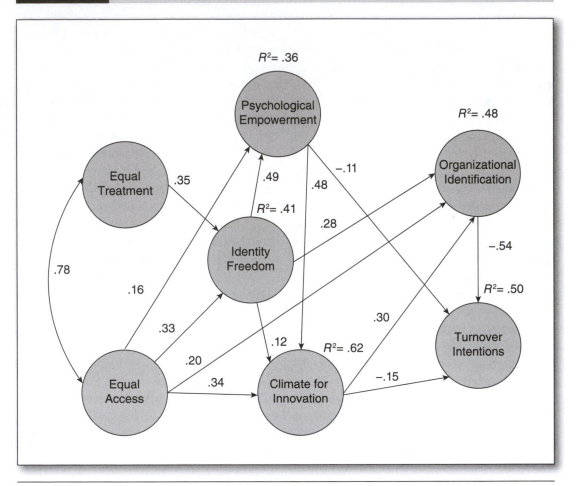

Note: Structural path coefficients are standardized. All coefficients in the model larger in magnitude than ±.11 are significant at $p <.05$. Although not shown in the model, Turnover Intentions and Organizational Identification were regressed on two control variables, employees' organizational tenure and job level. None of these paths were statistically significant.

To test Hypotheses 1 and 2, the total effects of diversity climate perceptions on Turnover Intentions, as well as the other study variables from the final structural model presented in Figure 20.1, were calculated. These results appear in Table 20.3.

In support of Hypothesis 1, Equal Treatment and Equal Access had a negative total effect on Intentions to Turnover. In support of Hypothesis 2, the overall effect of both diversity climate perception variables on turnover was entirely mediated through the four psychological outcome variables. Specifically, as can been seen in Table 20.3, there were no direct effects of

diversity climate perceptions on Turnover Intentions. The total effects of these variables were equal to their total indirect effects, indicating complete mediation. In addition, the diversity climate perception variables had a significant overall effect on all four psychological outcome variables. Specifically, Equal Treatment had a significant direct effect on Identify Freedom and significant total effects on Psychological Empowerment, Climate for Innovation, and Organizational Identification, as mediated through Identify Freedom. Equal Access had significant direct and indirect effects on four psychological outcome variables.

To test Hypothesis 3 and determine whether the four psychological outcome variables mediated the effect of diversity climate perceptions on turnover intentions across various subgroups, we fit the revised structural model described above (first including all paths) to the data for each employee subgroup. Then, following a similar model-trimming process, nonsignificant paths were eliminated with the goal of creating a more parsimonious model for each subgroup that still fit the data well. Goodness of fit statistics and total, direct, and indirect effects of the diversity climate dimensions on Turnover Intentions and psychological outcome variables for the models that resulted from this process for each group are presented in Table 2.4.

Results indicated that these models generally fit the data well, with goodness of fit criteria at or close to conventional cutoffs for each subgroup. In support of Hypothesis 3, the effects of Equal Treatment and Equal Access on Turnover Intentions were mediated by the four psychological outcomes across all three employee subgroups, as evidenced by significant total

indirect effects (see Table 20.3). In addition, the pattern of total, direct, and indirect effects of the diversity climate dimensions on the psychological outcomes was consistent across subgroups.

Discussion

The results of this study support the argument articulated in the diversity literature, which is that when organizations manage diversity well and engage in management practices perceived as fair to a diverse workforce, they reap important benefits. Our results suggest that when employees feel they work in an environment in which they have equal access to opportunities and are treated fairly, they are less likely to report intentions to leave the organization. In addition, four psychological outcomes (identify freedom, psychological empowerment, climate for innovation, and organizational identification) fully mediate the relationship between diversity climate perceptions and turnover intentions.

Table 20.3	**Total, Direct, and Indirect Effects of Diversity Climate Perceptions on Study Variables**				
Diversity climate dimension	*Identity freedom*	*Empowerment*	*Climate for innovation*	*Organizational identification*	*Turnover intentions*
Equal treatment					
Total effect	.35***	.17***	.12***	.14***	−.13***
Direct effect	.35***	—	—	—	—
Total of all indirect effects	—	.17***	.12***	.14***	−.13***
Equal access					
Total effect	.33***	.32***	.53***	.45***	−.36***
Direct effect	.33***	.16***	.34***	.20***	—
Total of all indirect effects	—	.16***	.19***	.25***	−.36***

Note: Total effects are equal to the sum of direct effects plus total indirect effects.

*p <.05. **p <.01. ***p <.001.

| Table 20.4 | Total, Direct, and Indirect Effects of Diversity Climate Perceptions on Study Variables Across Employee Subgroups |

Group	Model fit	Diversity climate dimension	Identity freedom	Empowerment	Climate for innovation	Organizational identification	Turnover intentions
White men (*n* = 478)	$\chi^2(444) =$	Equal treatment					
	759.31	Total effect	.27**	.13*	.11*	.05*	−.07*
	CFI =.95	Direct effect	.27**	—	—	—	—
	TLI =.95	Total indirect effects	—	.13*	.11*	.05*	−.07*
	RMSEA =.04	Equal access					
	SRMR =.04	Total effect	.43***	.42***	.57***	.55***	−.42***
		Direct effect	.43***	.21***	.29***	.23***	—
		Total indirect effects	—	.21***	.28***	.27***	−.42***
White Women (*n* = 211)	$\chi^2(445) =$	Equal treatment					
	621.66	Total effect	.33***	.18*	.12***	.14*	−.26***
	CFI =.94	Direct effect	.33***	—	—	—	−.18*
	TLI =.94	Total indirect effects	—	.18*	.12***	.14*	−.08*
	RMSEA =.04	Equal access					
	SRMR =.06	Total effect	.28**	.15*	.52***	.28***	−.25***
		Direct effect	.28**	—	.45***	—	—
		Total indirect effects	—	.15*	.07*	.28***	−.25***

Group	Model fit	Diversity climate dimension	Identity freedom	Empowerment	Climate for innovation	Organizational identification	Turnover intentions
Non-Whites (n = 156)	$\chi^2(445) =$	Equal treatment					
	651.61	Total effect	.43***	.25**	.14**	.22**	−.21**
	CFI =.90	Direct effect	.43***	—	—	—	—
	TLI =.90	Total indirect effects	—	.25**	.14**	.22**	−.21**
	RMSEA =.06	Equal access					
	SRMR =.07	Total effect	.34**	.20*	.48***	.61***	−.42***
		Direct effect	.34**	—	.37***	.43***	—
		Total indirect effects	—	.20*	.11*	.18*	−.42***

Note: CFI = comparative fit index; TLI = Tucker–Lewis index; RMSEA = root mean squared error of approximation; SRMR = standardized root mean squared residual.

*p <.05. **p <.01. ***p <.001.

Of these four psychological variables, it appears that identity freedom plays a key role in mediating the relationship between diversity climate perceptions and turnover intentions. Specifically, equal treatment and equal access predicted identity freedom, which, in turn, predicted psychological empowerment, climate for innovation, and organizational identification. Thus, it may be that diversity climate perceptions significantly affect the extent to which employees feel that they can be themselves at work. Moreover, when employees feel free to be themselves and to express their unique perspective, they feel empowered to make decisions affecting their work, feel encouraged to develop innovative solutions, and are more likely to identify with the organization.

In addition, the present research found that these relationships were generally consistent across employee gender and race. The findings suggest that it is important for organizations to take steps to create an affirming climate for diversity for all employees, regardless of demographic differences, and that efforts to do so should encourage employees to tap into and take advantage of their differences in a way that contributes to greater innovation and problem-solving capability (Joshi & Roh, 2013; Konrad, 2003).

The results of the present research also support previous work showing that diversity climate is multidimensional (Herdman & McMillan-Capehart, 2010). Specifically, we found support for two dimensions of diversity climate related to Cox's (1991, 1994) theoretical work on multicultural organizations. The first dimension, equal access, involves employee perceptions that all employees have access to resources and power, and have the opportunity to take advantage of developmental opportunities within the organization. The second dimension, equal treatment, involves the perception that employees from all demographic groups are treated in the same way, and that discrimination, conflict, and exclusion along demographic lines is minimal. In addition, we found support for four psychological variables that may be considered outcomes of diversity climate perceptions yet are still an important part of creating an affirming climate for diversity. Furthermore, the results of the measurement equivalence/invariance analyses in the present study suggest that all employees (regardless of race or gender) conceptualize diversity climate similarly.

Finally, our findings add to the present diversity literature by providing a better understanding of how diversity climate impacts turnover intentions. Specifically, when employees perceive that organizational practices are fair and believe that they are valued and have equal opportunities to fully participate in and excel within the organization, they will feel a strong sense of identification with the organization, which reduces the likelihood of turnover.

Implications

This research suggests that organizations must realize the importance of going beyond the recruitment and hiring of a diverse workforce. To truly benefit from diversity, organizations must also allocate the resources to create an environment that supports a diverse workforce. These resources will be well-spent, as diversity climate seems to have a significant impact on all employees, including White males, White females, and non-Whites.

This research has also helped clarify the construct of diversity climate, which we hope will advance the field and suggest additional implications for practitioners. Organizations can better focus their resources by taking steps to positively impact employee perceptions of equal access and equal treatment. Employee attitude surveys should contain survey items that focus on diversity climate perceptions as well as the extent to which employees feel that they can be themselves at work and fully contribute their unique perspectives to their work group. Organizations can then track these results and trends over time and also assess any demographic differences in employee perceptions. These data can be used to make organizational changes to improve the climate for diversity.

These findings may also prove to be useful in developing diversity training content and framing diversity in such a way that resistance is minimized (Thomas, 2008). A study conducted by the Society for Human Resource Management (SHRM) found that 76% of organizations provide some type of diversity training (Fegley, 2006). In addition, diversity training is estimated to be a nearly $8 billion industry (Anand & Winters, 2008). Although this information suggests that the overwhelming majority of organizations conduct diversity training, scholars have criticized these programs for many reasons, among them the fact that many programs involve divisive or emotionally damaging exercises, are not developed based on clear training objectives or goals, are unconnected to procedures and programs that will lead to change, and lack follow-up (Chrobot-Mason, Hays-Thomas, & Wishik, 2008). As a result, many diversity training initiatives may actually cause more harm than good and resistance to such programs is often high. The results of this study may help facilitate the development of more constructive and effective diversity training programs. Organizations may find it useful to develop diversity training content that focuses on behaviors that foster an environment in which members have equal access, are treated equally, and experience identity freedom within the organization.

Limitations and Future Research

There are several limitations of this study that are important to consider when conducting future research in this area. Perhaps the biggest limitation is the correlational nature of the data, which necessarily limits conclusions about causal relationships. Even though our final structural model specifies causal relations that are consistent with previous theoretical and empirical work, caution should be exercised in making definitive conclusions about cause and effect relations.

Another limitation involves not having a large enough sample size to examine racial subgroups (e.g., African Americans, Hispanics, Asians, and Native Americans) and, therefore, collapsing these groups into the single category of non-Whites. Because Anderson and Gerbing (1988) recommend a minimum sample size of 150 to obtain meaningful SEM parameter estimates, it was necessary to place all non-White employees into a single category. Thus, future research is needed to examine various racial subgroups to determine if diversity climate is conceptualized differently or leads to different outcomes among various demographic groups. Furthermore, additional outcomes of diversity climate should be examined to expand the scope of the business justification for diversity management. For example, an affirming climate for diversity may impact other employee attitudinal or behavioral outcomes such as organizational citizenship behaviors (OCB) and it may also have an impact on more external outcomes, such as customer retention or corporate image.

Conclusion

Diversity in the workplace has the potential to be an organizational benefit, but also an organizational liability. Research in this area seems to suggest that the key contributing factor in determining such an outcome is the extent to which the organization engages in a set of diversity practices that lead to positive psychological outcomes such that employees feel valued and encouraged to fully contribute to the workplace. Although it may be a difficult decision to invest in resources to measure diversity climate and implement initiatives to improve employee perceptions of climate, our results suggest that organizations that do so will ultimately be making a wise decision.

Declaration of Conflicting Interests

The author(s) declared no potential conflicts of interest with respect to the research, authorship, and/or publication of this article.

Funding

The author(s) received no financial support for the research, authorship, and/or publication of this article.

Note

1. Corresponding Author: Donna Chrobot-Mason, University of Cincinnati, Edwards 1 Room 5120-F, Cincinnati, OH 45221-0094, USA. Email: Donna.Chrobot-Mason@UC.edu

References

Allen, N. J., & Meyer, J. P. (1990). The measurement and antecedents of affective, continuance, and normative commitment to the organization. *Journal of Occupational Psychology, 63,* 1–18.

Anand, R., & Winters, M. (2008). A retrospective view of corporate diversity training from 1964 to the present. *Academy of Management Learning & Education, 7,* 356–372.

Anderson, J. C., & Gerbing, D. W. (1988). Structural equation modeling in practice: A review and recommended two-step approach. *Psychological Bulletin, 103,* 411–423.

Chavez, C., & Weisinger, J. Y. (2008). Beyond diversity training: A social infusion for cultural inclusion. *Human Resource Management, 47,* 331–350.

Chrobot-Mason, D., Hays-Thomas, R., & Wishik, H. R. (2008). Understanding and defusing resistance to diversity training and learning. In K. Thomas (Ed.), *Diversity resistance in organizations* (pp. 23–54). Mahwah, NJ: Lawrence Erlbaum.

Cox, T., Jr. (1991). The multicultural organization. *Academy of Management Executive, 5,* 34–47.

Cox, T., Jr. (1994). *Cultural diversity in organizations.* San Francisco, CA: Berrett-Koehler.

Cox, T., Jr., Welch, J., & Nkomo, S. M. (2001). Research on race and ethnicity: An update and analysis. In R. T. Golembiewski (Ed.), *Handbook of organizational behavior* (pp. 255–286). New York, NY: Marcel Dekker.

Curtis, E. F., & Dreachslin, J. L. (2008). Diversity management interventions and organizational performance: A synthesis of current literature. *Human Resource Development Review, 7,* 107–134.

De Dreu, C. K. W., & West, M. A. (2001). Minority dissent and team innovation: The importance of participation in decision making. *Journal of Applied Psychology, 86,* 1191–1201.

Dobbin, F., Sutton, J. R., Meyer, J. W., & Scott, W. R. (1993). Equal employment opportunity law and the construction of internal labor markets. *American Journal of Sociology, 99*, 396–427.

Dwyer, S., Richard, O. C., & Chadwick, K. (2003). Gender diversity in management and firm performance: The influence of growth orientation and organizational culture. *Journal of Business Research, 56*, 1009–1019.

Ely, R. J., & Thomas, D. A. (2001). Cultural diversity at work: The effects of diversity perspectives on work group processes and outcomes. *Administrative Science Quarterly, 46*, 229–273.

Fegley, S. (2006). *Workplace diversity and changes to the EEO-1 process survey report*. Alexandria, VA: Society for Human Resource Management.

Findler, L., Wind, L. H., & Mor Barak, M. E. (2007). The challenge of workforce management in a global society: Modeling the relationship between diversity, inclusion, organizational culture, and employee well-being, job satisfaction and organizational commitment. *Administration in Social Work, 31*, 63–94.

Gelfand, M. J., Nishii, L. H., Raver, J. L., & Schneider, B. (2005). Discrimination in organizations: An organizational-level systems perspective. In R. L. Dipboye & A. Colella (Eds.), *Discrimination at work: The psychological and organizational bases* (pp. 89–116). Mahwah, NJ: Lawrence Erlbaum.

Gonzalez, J. A., & DeNisi, A. S. (2009). Cross-level effects of demography and diversity climate on organizational attachment and firm effectiveness. *Journal of Organizational Behavior, 30*, 21–40.

Griffeth, R. W., Hom, P. W., & Gaertner, S. (2000). A meta-analysis of antecedents and correlates of employee turnover: Update, moderator tests, and research implications for the next millennium. *Journal of Management, 26*, 463–488.

Hambrick, D. C., & Mason, P. A. (1984). Upper echelons: The organization as a reflection of top managers. *Academy of Management Review, 9*, 193–206.

Harrison, D. A., & Klein, K. J. (2007). What's the difference? Diversity constructs as separation, variety, or disparity in organizations. *Academy of Management Review, 32*, 1199–1228.

Herdman, A. O., & McMillan-Capehart, A. (2010). Establishing a diversity program is not enough: Exploring the determinants of diversity climate. *Journal of Business and Psychology, 25*, 39–53.

Hicks-Clarke, D., & Iles, P. (2000). Climate for diversity and its effects on career and organizational attitudes and perceptions. *Personnel Review, 29*, 324–345.

Hu, L., & Bentler, P. M. (1999). Cutoff criteria for fit indexes in covariance structure analysis: Conventional criteria versus new alternatives. *Structural Equation Modeling, 6*, 1–55.

James, K., Lovato, C., & Cropanzano, R. (1994). Correlational and known-group comparison validation of a Workplace Prejudice/Discrimination Inventory. *Journal of Applied Social Psychology, 24*, 1573–1592.

James, L. R., James, L. A., & Ashe, D. K. (1990). The meaning of organizations: The role of cognition and values. In B. Schneider (Ed.), *Organizational climate and culture* (pp. 40–84). San Francisco, CA: Jossey-Bass.

Jayne, M. E., & Dipboye, R. L. (2004). Leveraging diversity to improve business performance: Research findings and recommendations for organizations. *Human Resource Management, 43*, 409–424.

Jehn, K. A., & Bezrukova, K. (2010). The faultline activation process and the effects of activated faultlines on coalition formation, conflict, and group outcomes. *Organizational Behavior and Human Decision Processes, 112*, 24–42.

Jehn, K. A., Bezrukova, K., & Thatcher, S. (2008). Conflict, diversity, and faultlines in workgroups. In C. K. W. De Dreu & M. J. Gelfand (Eds.), *The psychology of conflict and conflict management in organizations* (pp. 179–210). New York, NY: Taylor & Francis.

Joshi, A., & Roh, H. (2013). Understanding how context shapes team diversity outcomes. In Q. M. Roberson (Ed.), *The Oxford handbook of diversity and work* (pp. 209–219). New York, NY: Oxford University Press.

Kacmar, K. M., Andrews, M. C., Van Rooy, D. L., Steilberg, R. C., & Cerrone, S. (2006). Sure everyone can be replaced . . . but at what cost? Turnover as a predictor of unit-level performance. *Academy of Management Journal, 49*, 133–144.

Kaplan, D. M., Wiley, J. W., & Maertz, C. P. (2011). The role of calculative attachment in the relationship between diversity climate and retention. *Human Resource Management, 50*, 271–287.

King, E. B., de Chermont, K., West, M., Dawson, J. F., & Hebl, M. R. (2007). How innovation can alleviate negative consequences of demanding work contexts: The influence of climate for innovation on organizational outcomes. *Journal of Occupational and Organizational Psychology, 80*, 631–645.

Kline, R. B. (2005). *Principles and practice of structural equation modeling* (2nd ed.). New York, NY: Guilford.

Koberg, C. S., Boss, R. W., Seniem, J. C., & Goodman, E. A. (1999). Antecedents and outcomes of empowerment:

Empirical evidence from the health care industry. *Group & Organization Management, 24*, 71–91.

Kochan, T., Bezrukova, K., Ely, R., Jackson, S., Joshi, A., Jehn, K., . . . Thomas, D. (2003). The effects of diversity on business performance: Report of the diversity research network. *Human Resource Management, 42*, 3–21.

Konrad, A. M. (2003). Defining the domain of workplace diversity scholarship. *Group & Organization Management, 28*, 4–17.

Konrad, A. M., Prasad, P., & Pringle, J. K. (2006). *Handbook of workplace diversity*. Thousand Oaks, CA: Sage.

Kossek, E. E., & Zonia, S. S. (1993). Assessing diversity climate: A field study of reactions to employer efforts to promote diversity. *Journal of Organizational Behavior, 14*, 61–81.

Kuenzi, M., & Schminke, M. (2009). Assembling fragments into a lens: A review, critique, and proposed research agenda for the organizational work climate literature. *Journal of Management, 35*, 634–717.

Kulik, C. T., & Roberson, L. (2008). Diversity initiative effectiveness: What organizations can (and cannot) expect from diversity recruitment, diversity training, and formal mentoring programs. In A. P. Brief (Ed.), *Diversity at work* (pp. 265–317). Cambridge, UK: Cambridge University Press.

Lau, D. C., & Murnighan, J. K. (2005). Interactions within groups and subgroups: The effects of demographic faultlines. *Academy of Management Journal, 48*, 645–659.

Mathieu, J. E., & Zajac, D. M. (1990). A review and meta-analysis of the antecedents, correlates, and consequences of organizational commitment. *Psychological Bulletin, 108*, 171–194.

McGrath, J. E., Berdahl, J. L., & Arrow, H. (1995). Traits, expectations, culture and clout: The dynamics of diversity in work groups. In S. E. Jackson & M. N. Ruderman (Eds.), *Diversity in work teams: Research paradigms for a changing workplace* (pp. 17–46). Washington, DC: American Psychological Association.

McKay, P. F., Avery, D. R., & Morris, M. A. (2008). Mean racial-ethnic differences in employee sales performance: The moderating role of diversity climate. *Personnel Psychology, 61*, 349–374.

McKay, P. F., Avery, D. R., Tonidandel, S., Morris, M. A., Hernandez, M., & Hebl, M. R. (2007). Racial differences in employee retention: Are diversity climate perceptions the key? *Personnel Psychology, 60*, 35–62.

Milliken, F. J., & Martins, L. L. (1996). Searching for common threads: Understanding the multiple effects of diversity in organizational groups. *Academy of Management Review, 21*, 402–433.

Mor Barak, M. E., Cherin, D. A., & Berkman, S. (1998). Organizational and personal dimensions of diversity climate. *Journal of Applied Behavioral Science, 34*, 82–104.

Muthén, L. K., & Muthén, B. O. (2006). M*plus* 4.0 [Computer software]. Los Angeles, CA: Muthén & Muthén.

Nemeth, C. J. (1986). Differential contributions of majority and minority influence processes. *Psychological Review, 93*, 10–20.

Page, S. E. (2007). Making the difference: Applying a logic of diversity. *Academy of Management Perspectives, 21*, 6–20.

Phillips, K. W., Duguid, M., Thomas-Hunt, M., & Uparna, J. (2013). Diversity as knowledge exchange: The roles of information processing, expertise, and status. In Q. M. Roberson (Ed.), *The Oxford handbook of diversity and work* (pp. 1571–78). New York, NY: Oxford University Press.

Phillips, K. W., Northcraft, G. B., & Neale, M. A. (2006). Surface-level diversity and decision-making in groups: When does deep-level similarity help? *Group Processes and Intergroup Relations, 9*, 467–482.

Podsakoff, P. M., MacKenzie, S. B., & Podsakoff, N. P. (2012). Sources of method bias in social science research and recommendations on how to control it. *Annual Review of Psychology, 63*, 539–569.

Powell, G. (1999). *Handbook of gender and work*. Thousand Oaks, CA: Sage.

Raju, N. S., Lafitte, L. J., & Byrne, B. M. (2002). Measurement equivalence: A comparison of methods based on confirmatory factor analysis and item response theory. *Journal of Applied Psychology, 87*, 517–529.

Richard, O. C., & Miller, C. D. (2013). Considering diversity as a source of competitive advantage in organizations. In Q. M. Roberson (Ed.), *The Oxford handbook of diversity and work* (pp. 239–250). New York, NY: Oxford University Press.

Richard, O. C., Murthi, B. P. S., & Ismail, K. (2007). The impact of racial diversity on intermediate and long-term performance: The moderating role of environmental context. *Strategic Management Journal, 28*, 1213–1233.

Roberge, M. E., & van Dick, R. (2010). Recognizing the benefits of diversity: When and how does diversity increase group performance? *Human Resource Management Review, 20*, 295–308.

Roberson, Q. A. (2006). Disentangling the meanings of diversity and inclusion in organizations. *Group & Organization Management, 31*, 212–236.

Roberts, L. M., & Creary, S. J. (2013). Navigating the self in diverse work contexts. In Q. M. Roberson (Ed.), *The Oxford handbook of diversity and work* (pp. 73–97). New York, NY: Oxford University Press.

Schneider, B., Gunnarson, S. K., & Niles-Jolly, K. (1994). Creating the climate and culture of success. *Organizational Dynamics, 23*, 17–29.

Schneider, B., White, S. S., & Paul, M. C. (1998). Linking service climate and customer perceptions of service quality: Test of a causal model. *Journal of Applied Psychology, 83*, 150–163.

Schneider, K. T., Hitlan, R. T., & Radhakrishnan, P. (2000). An examination of the nature and correlates of ethnic harassment experiences in multiple contexts. *Journal of Applied Psychology, 85*, 3–12.

Seashore, S. E., Lawler, E. E., Mirvis, P., & Cammann, C. (Eds.). (1982). *Observing and measuring organizational change: A guide to field practice.* New York, NY: Wiley.

Shore, L. M., Randel, A. E., Chung, B. G., Dean, M. A., Ehrhart, K. H., & Singh, G. (2011). Inclusion and diversity in work groups: A review and model for future research. *Journal of Management, 37*, 1262–1289.

Spreitzer, G. M. (1995). Psychological empowerment in the workplace: Dimensions, measurement, and validation. *Academy of Management Journal, 38*, 1442–1465.

Spreitzer, G. M., Kizilos, M. A., & Nason, S. W. (1997). A dimensional analysis of the relationship between psychological empowerment and effectiveness, satisfaction, and strain. *Journal of Management, 23*, 679–704.

Stewart, R., Volpone, S. D., Avery, D. R., & McKay, P. (2011). You support diversity, but are you ethical? Examining the interactive effects of diversity and ethical climate perceptions on turnover intentions. *Journal of Business Ethics, 100*, 581–593.

Tabachnick, B. G., & Fidell, L. S. (2001). *Using multivariate statistics* (4th ed.). Boston, MA: Allyn & Bacon.

Thomas, K. M. (2005). *Diversity dynamics in the workplace.* Belmont, CA: Thomson-Wadsworth.

Thomas, K. M. (2008). *Diversity resistance in organizations.* New York, NY: Lawrence Erlbaum.

Tomasetto, C., Mucchi-Faina, A., Alparone, F., & Pagliaro, S. (2009). Differential effects of majority and minority influence on argumentation strategies. *Social Influence, 4*, 33–45.

van Knippenberg, D., Homan, A. C., & van Ginkel, W. P. (2013). Diversity cognition and climates. In Q. M. Roberson (Ed.), *The Oxford handbook of diversity and work* (pp. 220–238). New York, NY: Oxford University Press.

van Knippenberg, D., & Schippers, M. C. (2007). Work group diversity. *Annual Review of Psychology, 58*, 515–541.

Webber, S. S., & Donahue, L. M. (2001). Impact of highly and less job-related diversity on work group cohesion and performance: A meta-analysis. *Journal of Management, 27*, 141–162.

Weijters, B., Schillewaert, N., & Geuens, M. (2008). Assessing response styles across modes of data collection. *Journal of the Academy of Marketing Science, 36*, 409–422.

Williams, K. Y., & O'Reilly, C. A. (1998). Demography and diversity in organizations. *Research in Organizational Behavior, 20*, 77–140.

Yang, Y., & Konrad, A. M. (2011). Diversity and organizational innovation: The role of employee involvement. *Journal of Organizational Behavior, 32*, 1062–1083.

CHAPTER 21

Lesbians, Gays, Bisexuals, and Transgendered People and Human Resource Development

An Examination of the Literature in Adult Education and Human Resource Development

Steven W. Schmidt[1]
East Carolina University

Rod P. Githens
University of Louisville

Tonette S. Rocco
Florida International University

Martin B. Kormanik
O.D. Systems

I ssues related to lesbian, gay, bisexual, and transgender (LGBT) individuals in U.S. workplaces have captured the attention of organizations recently, causing favorable changes in relatively short time periods. The Human Rights Campaign Corporate Equality Index measures an employer's "commitment to equal treatment of employees, consumers, and investors, irrespective of [an employee's] sexual orientation or gender identity and expression" (Corporate Equality Index, 2007, p. 12) using a scale of 0% to 100%. The

Source: Article by Steven W. Schmidt, Rod P. Githens, Tonette S. Rocco, and Martin B. Kormanik in *Human Resource Development Review,* 2012, 11(3), pp. 326–348. SAGE Publications. Reprinted with permission.

2010 report noted that 305 businesses received a perfect 100% rating. That number was a 45% increase over the previous year, and those 305 businesses represent over 9.3 million full-time employees (Corporate Equality Index, 2010). Even in these challenging economic times, "the Corporate Equality Index once again demonstrates that businesses recognize the importance of working with and providing for lesbian, gay, bisexual, and transgender workers and consumers" (Corporate Equality Index, 2010, p. 1).

From a research standpoint, however, LGBT workplace issues have not received a great deal of attention. Ragins (2004) notes that they "constitute one of the largest, but least studied, minority groups in the workforce" (p. 35). An examination of LGBT workplace issues is appropriate for HRD researchers. LGBT individuals constitute a sexual minority (Kameny, 1971; Leonard, 2003) that could benefit from conceptual, empirical, and theoretical work connecting the issue of sexual minorities as a distinct group to diversity and other concerns of HRD.

Is the lack of research-related attention on this topic related to lack of interest on the part of, or lack of acceptance by, the academic community? In 2008, Githens, Schmidt, Rocco, and Gedro hosted the first preconference on LGBT issues in HRD at the Academy of Human Resource Development (AHRD) International Conference. AHRD proved to be slower in its acceptance of the topic. Schmidt and Githens (2010) reported that some reviewers for their preconference felt the topic was extremely important, however, one reviewer wondered whether it was a topic the organization wanted to promote and others questioned the importance of the topic in general. The session went on to become the highest-attended preconference held that year. Feedback from participants of the 2008 LGBT preconference demonstrated a demand for guidelines on evidence-based practice on LGBT issues in HRD.

The purpose of this chapter is to examine the literature in human resource development and adult education to determine what work has been done related to HRD, identify the topics which were covered, types of articles published, and research methods used and use this information to create a research agenda to address the intersection of LGBT issues and HRD. To do this, we searched the literature asking these questions: What types of articles are published

(e.g., conceptual, literature reviews, empirical studies) and what methods are used? To what extent does the literature address the concerns of LGBT people? Do the articles published provide an adequate foundation for future research? What topics, trends, issues should form future research agendas?

This review includes research from the fields of adult education and human resource development because of the close-knit and overlapping relationship between the two disciplines. Three of the four authors of this chapter are in both fields, some graduate programs house programs of study in both fields, and some HRD programs grew from adult education programs. The search of the adult education literature begins in 1994 just before the first article by Hill (1995) was published on LGBT issues. Work on this topic in adult education spawned the work in HRD where the first article was published by Gedro, Cervero, and Johnson-Bailey (2002). The search of HRD literature begins in 2001 just before that first article appeared in *Human Resource Development International*.

This review is organized as follows: A conceptual framework for diversity and LGBT inclusion will be presented followed by article analysis by content and by research approaches employed. Summary tables regarding article content and research approaches are then presented. Content-related and research approach-related themes will be discussed, followed by a discussion of gaps in current research and recommendations for future research.

Diversity and LGBT Inclusion: A Conceptual Framework

Given the substantial demographic changes of recent years in the U.S. workforce, workforce diversity has become a compelling force for organizational change (Robinson & Dechant, 1997). Although race, ethnicity, gender and culture have traditionally been the dimensions of diversity that have received the most attention in the workplace (Ross-Gordon & Brooks, 2004), the concept of diversity has been expanded to include a broader spectrum of factors. Diversity refers to:

the multitude and full range of human differences. We each bring our diversity—our different perspectives, experiences, and identity—to all we do in life. As we tap into those differences . . . we bring innovation, new perspectives, fresh viewpoints to bear on the bottom line, creating competitive advantage that only a wide range of talents and ideas can offer. (Jamison & Miller, 2006, p. 1)

Diversity encompasses visible and non-visible aspects of identities by which individuals categorize themselves and others (Ely & Thomas, 2001). These specific identities are also known as dimensions of diversity, and they cover a range of individual characteristics. Diversity is composed of "variations in race, gender, ethnicity, nationality, sexual orientation, physical abilities, social class, age, and other such socially meaningful categorizations, together with the additional differences caused by or signified by these markers" (Ferdman, 1995, p. 37). Additional dimensions were traditionally viewed as less salient, but can be as powerful, include educational background, geographic location, income, marital status, military experience, parental status, religious beliefs, and work experience (Loden & Rosener, 1991).

Diversity, according to Cox (1993), includes representation of people from different groups within a social system. Decisions are made about who to include and who to exclude when discussing diversity. What factors create social systems? Who is included and who is excluded? Arguably, social dominance and social identity play a role (Sidanius & Pratto, 1999). While LGBT individuals and allies might respond in one way to this question, there are others whose definitions would exclude those populations. Indeed, Cox (1993) posits that "most individuals have relatively high awareness of the identity that most distinguishes them from the majority group in a particular setting and considerably less awareness of other identities" (p. 50). Diversity and the knowledge surrounding it therefore is continually evolving. Harris (2007) summarizes this evolution as follows: "For decades, the focus (of diversity initiatives) had been on recruitment efforts and talent management programs related to African Americans, Hispanics, and other people of color. Even though corporations focused on race, those

issues helped open the door for discussions on gender, age, and, most recently, sexual orientation and gender identity" (p. 64).

In the development of a business case for diversity, organizations have identified numerous benefits. Cultures in which diversity is valued have been associated with increases in the quality of group performance, creativity of ideas, cooperation, and the number of perspectives and alternatives considered (Brickson, 2000). Inclusion of different demographic groups brings different styles, insights, and perspectives into an organization, fostering mutual contact and a decrease in stereotyping (Ely & Thomas, 2001). A high level of acceptance of diversity increases mutual learning and employees' readiness for organizational change (Iles & Hayers, 1997). Acceptance ensures that individual differences in values, opinions, and beliefs are encouraged and accepted (McMillan-Capehart, 2006). Some organizations see a strategic imperative for managing diversity, realizing that having a proactive HR policy on diversity enhances competitive advantage (Jayne & Dipboye, 2004). Conversely and specifically related to LGBT individuals, Liddle, Luzzo, Hauenstein, and Schuck (2004) note that fear of harassment and discrimination in the workplace can result in a variety of negative consequences. These include feelings of isolation, anxiety, reduced creative energy, and decreased levels of collaboration. They also note that "hostile workplaces may force LGBT employees to stay closeted (that is, to hide their LGBT identities)" (p. 35), which may adversely affect the employee's physical health (Liddle et al., 2004). These findings are similar to those of Cox (1993), who posits that the negative work outcomes associated with a poor diversity climate include increased absenteeism, lower productivity, and higher turnover.

While organizations may attend to workforce diversity for many reasons, Yang (2005) notes that institutional influence may be due to coercive pressure from statute and mandate, normative pressure exerted by community and professional associations, and mimetic pressure to adopt competitors' practices. Legislation is not enough to facilitate positive diversity outcomes (Gilbert & Ivancevich, 2000). Instead, organizations can create more positive effects by simultaneous pressures than by any force working alone (Yang, 2005). The literature consistently shows that any organizational efforts to encourage employment of a diverse workforce will be wasted if that effort is not matched by an effort to ensure that the organization's structures (e.g., policies, procedures) and culture are inclusive and supportive of differences (Jamison & Miller, 2006; Kwak, 2003; Thomas, 1990; Thomas & Ely, 1996). Some organizations make the mistake of emphasizing certain minority groups in their diversity initiatives at the expense of other groups. Focusing on some and ignoring others can send confusing messages to employees and can result in opposition to diversity efforts (Loden, 1996). The way all employees are treated with respect to their individualities is critical to employee satisfaction and drives performance.

Much of the inequity in organizations occurs because employees are treated the same and differences are ignored (Wilson, 1997). Effectively managing diversity means acknowledging differences, including "acknowledging individual employee needs and then accommodating these needs" (p. 18). Told to treat every employee the same to comply with laws on workplace equity, managers are confused when told to treat employees differently because of individuals' diverse characteristics, values, backgrounds, and experiences. Sense making about workforce diversity is difficult (Roberson & Stevens, 2006), especially since, as noted earlier, lifestyle and societal attitude changes around aspects of diversity are occurring at such a rapid pace and with such complexity that they are sometimes difficult to manage.

Although there has been increased interest in learning about the management of LGBT issues in HRD, extensive research is still needed (Ward, 2003; Ward & Winstanley, 2005). In terms of research, sexuality can be as significant of a defining social category as race, class, gender, disability, and occupation (Kormanik, 2009, Kudlick, 2003; Ragins & Cornwell, 2001; U.K. Government, 2003), yielding important implications for workforce learning and performance. Organizations differ in their perspectives of including sexual minorities in their diversity initiatives, on a spectrum from hostility to advocacy (Rocco, Landorf, & Delgado, 2009). "While most

companies understand that this is a core dimension of peoples' diversity, they are less inclined to defend the rights of LGB employees when they are threatened" (Loden, 1996, p. 85). Loden noted organizations may come under attack by community and religious groups opposed to LGBT rights and fear the loss of some customers. Such perspectives have implications for organizational culture, productivity, and commitment of LGBT employees and others who value respect for their LGBT colleagues.

In some instances, discussion of the disenfranchisement of a group may be trivialized because the prevalence of that population is not large enough (Gonsiorek, Sell, & Weinrich, 1995). To help place sexuality in context with other workforce populations of interest to HRD research and practice we provide demographic figures for comparative groups. For example, the U.S. civilian labor force is 13% Hispanic, 12% African American, 5% Asian, and 2% multirace (U.S. Census Bureau, 2008). Approximately 4% of the U.S. workforce has some form of disabling condition (U.S. Census Bureau, 2006). Organizations spend time, money, and other resources on HRD programs to identify and address the needs of these discrete populations. In comparison, approximately 7% of the population identifies as lesbian, gay, or bisexual (Witeck & Combs, 2006), with some reporting numbers as high as 17% (Gonsiorek et al., 1995). When considering these statistics, it is important to remember that the definition of sexuality is laden with social, psychological, and political meanings. Given the perceived risk involved in self-disclosure of identity and concerns with anonymity, these figures are generally accepted as a "floor measure" or absolute minimum.

Research Design

Both adult education and human resource development journals and conference proceedings were searched. In adult education we searched the proceedings from the annual Adult Education Research Conference, *Adult Education Quarterly*, and *New Directions in Adult and Continuing Education*. In human resource development we searched the proceedings from the annual Academy of Human Resource Development Conference, *Advances in Developing Human Resources (ADHR)*; *Human Resource Development International (HRDI)*, *Human Resource Development Quarterly (HRDQ)* and *Human Resource Development Review (HRDR)*.

The search terms listed here were used to search the adult education and human resource development literature. Search terms used in both fields were sexual orientation, gay and lesbian, gender identity, sexual minority, queer, bisexual, transex*, transgen*. Articles with these terms as keywords, in the titles, or in the abstracts were then read for relevance to HRD. Articles and papers were included if they were related to HRD. Any publication that was not on a topic related to HRD was excluded.

Identifying Literature in Adult Education

A search (using the terms listed above) of the table of contents of the Adult Education Research Conference proceedings from 1994 to 2009 uncovered 26 papers on LGBT issues in adult education. Topics covered in these 26 papers included sexual identity development; rights, citizenship, and policy issues; queer knowledge and pedagogy; straight allies; podcasting; HIV; reparative therapy; and male development. The authors determined that to qualify for inclusion in this review, papers had to focus on both LGBT issues and a workplace-related topic. Additionally, that intersection of topics (LGBT issues and the workplace) had to be the major, rather than a peripheral focus, of the paper. Out of the 26 papers, three papers directly addressed HRD issues: learning and participation at an LGBT employee conference (Gedro, 2007a), employee resource groups (Githens & Aragon, 2007), and approaches to diversity for LGBT change agents (Githens, 2009b).

The search of *Adult Education Quarterly* and *New Directions in Adult and Continuing Education* produced 13 articles. Two articles appeared in *Adult Education Quarterly* between 1994 and 2009. Neither article was relevant to HRD and was not included in this review based on criteria noted earlier.

New Directions in Adult and Continuing Education (NDACE), the monograph series in the field, published nine chapters in Hill's special issue dedicated to sexual minorities, included seven chapters related to HRD (2006a). These chapters covered straight privilege and career development (Rocco & Gallagher, 2006), lesbians' experiences in organizations (Gedro, 2006), organizational issues (Hill, 2006c; Muñoz & Thomas, 2006), workplace policies (Hornsby, 2006), sexual identity development in the workplace (King & Biro, 2006), and the experience of being queer in an organization (Hill, 2006b).

Identifying Literature in Human Resource Development

Our search (using the terms listed above) revealed that 28 papers that mentioned LGBT issues were published in the proceedings of the annual AHRD conference from 2000–2009. Only 10 AHRD proceedings papers from 2000–2009 dealt with LGBT issues in HRD as the main focus for the paper. The other 18 articles noted LGBT issues in peripheral ways (as a dimension of diversity, for example).

Twelve articles were published in three of the four HRD-related publications. In 2004, "How Lesbians Learn to Negotiate the Heterosexism of Corporate America" was published in *HRDI*, making it the first article on LGBT issues published in the four AHRD journals. *HRDQ* published an editorial by Gedro (2007b) entitled "Conducting Research on LGBT Issues: Leading the Field All over Again." The February 2009 edition of *ADHR*, edited by Rocco, Gedro, and Kormanik (2009), focused on LGBT issues in HRD. The 10 articles addressed topics such as workplace diversity initiatives, LGBT career development, work-life balance and same-sex couples, transgender issues in the workplace, LGBT employee groups, and workplace allies.

Analysis of Articles

After identifying and reading the abstracts of the papers related to LGBT issues, the authors held discussions by phone and e-mail to create an inductively developed categorization scheme. The categories developed included the following: Identity development, pedagogy/classroom issues, research approaches and needs, social change and policy, and workplace and organizational issues (see Table 21.1). Three of those categories, identity development,

pedagogy/classroom issues, and social change and policy, were then omitted from this work because those papers focused on adult education in ways not relevant to HRD. The broad category of workplace and organizational issues included all papers that we concluded were related to HRD. Workplace and organizational issues was inductively subdivided as

Table 21.1 Categorization of Papers

Category	Number of publications	Publications by type
Identity development	8	ADHR, 1
		AERC Conf, 7
Pedagogy/classroom issues	9	ADHR, 1
		AEQ, 1
		AERC Conf, 4
		AHRD Conf, 1
		NDACE, 2
Social change and policy	8	AERC Conf, 8
Research approaches and needs	6	AEQ, 1
		AERC Conf, 3
		AHRD Conf, 1
		HRDQ, 1
Workplace and organizational issues	30	ADHR, 8
		AERC Conf, 4
		AHRD Conf, 10
		HRDI, 1
		NDACE, 7
Total	61	ADHR, 10
		AEQ, 2
		AERC Conf, 26
		AHRD Conf, 12
		HRDI, 1
		HRDQ, 1
		NDACE, 9

Note: A list of specific papers in each category is available on request.

follows: Organizational change, LGBT-focused diversity initiatives, HR policy, career development, and workplace education.

Research approaches used in the articles will be discussed first, followed by a topical summary of the findings from the articles addressing workplace and organizational issues.

Research Approaches Used

Overall, the literature on LGBT issues in HRD and adult education is heavier on conceptual papers than empirical studies and literature reviews. See Table 21.2 for a summary of types of paper (empirical/non empirical) in each thematic categorization scheme.

All of the chapters in the *NDACE* issue were conceptual pieces. One of the two articles published in *AEQ* was empirical while the other article was a literature review. Nine of the 26 papers presented at AERC presented findings from qualitative empirical studies. Of the 12 AHRD conference papers dealing with LGBT issues in HRD, only three were empirical

studies. Three of the 12 conference presentations were innovative, or discussion-type sessions, and one was a preconference on LGBT issues and HRD. The remaining five presentations were conceptual pieces, including reviews of literature.

Nine of the 12 articles presented in the four HRD-related journals were conceptual pieces or literature reviews. One was qualitative, one was mixed methods, and the other was an editorial. There is a complete lack of articles reporting quantitative empirical findings.

Workplace and Organizational Issues

The subcategories that emerged from the workplace and organizational issues category are organizational change, LGBT-focused diversity initiatives, HR policy, career development, and workplace education. We present an overview of the papers we found that fit each category. Some papers are related to more than one category.

Table 21.2 Research Methods Used in LGBT-Related Papers

	Conceptual	Lit. review	Position papers	Qualitative empirical	Quantitative empirical	Mixed method empirical
Identity development	3	0	0	5	0	0
Pedagogy/ classroom issues	6	0	0	2	0	0
Social change and policy	3	0	1	5	0	0
Research approaches and needs	0	2	3	1	0	0
Workplace and organizational issues	19	0	2	7	0	2
Total	31	2	6	20	0	2

Organizational Change

Organizations have approached civil rights legislation and social pressure to diversify workforces from different perspectives ranging from hostile, compliant, inquiry, inclusion, and advocacy (Rocco, Landorf, et al., 2009). Hostility is the most negative and advocacy the most positive perspective toward inclusion of LGBT workers. These perspectives are held by individuals and the organization and may not be the same for both. Organizational change initiatives under each perspective differ as do their diversity initiatives.

Valuing diversity "was originally conceived without reference to sexual identity, gender identity, or gender expression" (Hill, 2006b, p. 9). Hill explains that most organizations have failed to consider the relationship between sexuality, technologies, culture, and society within the workplace. This intersection is key in discussions on LGBT issues and organizational change. Human sexuality includes opposite sex and same sex sexual orientations, gender identity, and gender expression (Hill, 2006b; Kormanik, 2009). Organizations are blind to the materials that straight employees bring to the workplace that proclaim their sexuality and orientation such as pictures of partners, sharing memories with colleagues about personal moments, and even appearance and style (Rocco & Gallagher, 2006). Yet when LGBT workers bring in similar materials these items can be construed as offensive by some. Organizations that sell consumer goods capitalize on sexuality in their marketing campaigns yet "policy statements and training programs [focused] on sex discrimination and sexual harassment [are written] ignoring sexual orientation and gender identity (Kormanik, 2009, p. 25)." Hornsby (2006) suggests that organizational policy changes that include sexual minorities through inclusive language and particular attention to sexual minority issues can drive organizational change. To drive organizational change, harassment policies must be enforced, domestic partner benefits established, preparations made to address resistance, and commitment from leaders must be visible (Munoz & Thomas, 2006).

LGBT employees and allies have sought changes through workplace advocacy efforts because of the need for organizational changes in policies, practices, and individual attitudes. These efforts occur through the informal efforts of individuals and groups, employer-sponsored groups for LGBT people and allies (sometimes known as employee resource groups, affinity groups, or employee networks), outside workplace groups affiliated with unions or other workplace-oriented organizations (sometimes known as LGBT Caucuses), and more subversive groups that exist outside of traditional organizational structures (Githens & Aragon, 2009). Advocacy for LGBT employees exists in all sectors of the economy. However, those in the corporate sector have achieved changes more quickly than those working in the public sector, due to social and political factors (i.e., governmental employers are less risk adverse due to political constituencies) and economic factors (i.e., capitalism results in an increased drive to retain talented employees within corporate settings) (Githens, 2009a).

As an example of corporate activism on the individual level, Gedro, Cervero, and Johnson-Bailey (2004) examined how lesbian managers/executives navigated heterosexism. They found that the women felt a personal responsibility to advocate for change by educating others about the heterosexism they and other LGBT people faced. MacDonnell's (2009) work illustrates how such activism can result in both small-scale local changes and larger policy changes. Her study described the policy and practice positions developed by the provincial nursing association as a result of insights from Canadian nurses who advocate for lesbian health issues. In this example, individual advocacy, scholarly research, and professional policy development converged to result in changes that benefit both patients and nurses.

Advocates for LGBT workplace changes often seek change for personal, professional, and political reasons (Humphrey, 1999). Gedro (2007a) examined the learning of attendees at a national LGBT workplace conference using transformative learning theory (Mezirow, 1997) and Friere's emancipatory theory of transformation (Friere, 1970). In Gedro's study, HR departments were often identified by participants as ineffective in addressing LGBT issues; the conference emboldened these participants to make changes in their organizations that HR did not (Gedro, 2007a). The conference provided participants with ideas for strategizing and making the case for more inclusive workplaces, despite the structural and personal obstacles they might encounter.

The role of allies has been a salient theme in studies examining advocacy within workplaces. Brooks and Edwards (2009) found that LGBT employees want allies who foster emotionally inclusive environments for LGBT colleagues, who provide uncompromising support for the safety of LGBT colleagues by combating homophobia, and who advocate to others for equity and inclusion in policies and practices. In considering what motivates allies to do this work, both Gedro (2007a) and Brooks and Edwards found that allies had a transformational experience that illuminated the importance of advocating for LGBT issues. In Gedro's study, the LGBT workplace conference provided transformational experiences for the allies. These allies' perspectives were transformed both in revealing their own personal heterosexism and their responsibility to seek workplace changes rather than being complacent in letting others seek change. In a case study of a long-term change effort within one organization, Githens (2009b) found that while initial enthusiasm from allies could help in moving a workplace advocacy effort forward at critical points, the LGBT employees' perseverance brought changes to fruition. Brooks and Edwards' study found that allies range from (a) those who are personally supportive on an individual level to LGBT colleagues to (b) those who quietly advocate in their own immediate circles of influence to (c) one ally-activist who started a national movement of allies working for LGBT equity.

LGBT-Focused Diversity Initiatives

Workforce diversity initiatives differ in their inclusiveness of sexual minority issues, in their perceived value by non-minority employees, and in the operationalization of their implementation. Rocco, Landorf, et al. (2009) proposed a framework for examining organizations' approaches to addressing sexual minority issues within diversity initiatives, including hostility, compliance, inquiry, inclusion, and advocacy. Workforce diversity programs most often focus on four areas: increasing workplace representation of traditionally underrepresented groups, eliminating discrimination, preventing harassment, and promoting inclusion. In each of these goal areas, the focus has been primarily race and gender (Maxwell, 2005). When gender has been cited as a workforce diversity factor, the espoused focus has been on the differences in workplace issues, challenges, and needs of women and men. Most organizations have policy statements and training programs on sex discrimination and sexual harassment. The need for compliance has resulted in organizations' gender diversity programs focusing primarily on sex discrimination and sexual harassment (Kormanik, 2009). Gender diversity programming has minimally covered the broader spectrum of sexuality. Only recently have organizations put sexual orientation into their non-discrimination policies, with an even smaller number adding gender identity (see Heller, 2006; Human Rights Campaign Foundation [HRCF], 2006). Without a need for compliance, discussion of sexual orientation and gender identity is omitted from diversity initiatives.

Githens (2009b) explored the ways LGBT individuals use education to seek equitable policies and improve campus climates. The qualitative study examined the approaches to diversity education by activists seeking domestic partner benefits. The results showed the importance of building coalitions focused on action. Initiatives geared toward identity-oriented policy changes required LGBT individuals to call others into action and keep them motivated to seek culture and climate changes that support the initiative. Kormanik's (2009) mixed methods study was undertaken in concert with a diversity initiative. The research examined employees' awareness development around five facets of sexuality—sex discrimination, sexual harassment, sexual attraction, sexual orientation, and transgender issues. The results showed differences in awareness, suggesting that each facet of sexuality should be treated as a discrete diversity factor. The results also showed that awareness development around sexual orientation and gender identity was less developed than for sex discrimination, sexual harassment, and sexual attraction, confirming the need to raise awareness is greater for the facets of sexual orientation and gender identity.

Rocco, Gallagher, Gedro, Hornsby, and van Loo's (2006) conference panel explored the social construction of heterosexist identity in terms of diversity training, career development and succession planning for LGBT workers, the effects of heterosexism on LGBT career development, and strategies to overcome heterosexism in the workplace. Githens and colleagues' (2008) preconference symposium focused on developing HRD practices that are inclusive of sexual minority employees. Hill (2006b) reflected on the resistance encountered when organizations acknowledge the worth of sexual minorities as part of workforce diversity. The resistance was in the form of backlashes to diversity change, e.g., straight employees demanding equal time or attention. Evidence-based practices exist that may help HRD professionals avoid resistance that can result from attempts to create fully inclusive workplaces. Examples of evidenced-based practices are couching the message that the organization is gay-friendly in the concept of equal opportunity for all workers and allowing workers to "select themselves out of positions" (Hill, 2006b, p. 13) when they feel their moral or religious sentiments are compromised.

HR Policy

Issues related to HR policy persist as some of the most tangible measures of an organization's level of support for LGBT people. Research related to these issues addresses ways in which organizations address policies and practices related to wages, insurance, leaves of absences, and work/life balance.

Much of the effort to bring LGBT-friendly organizational changes over the last 10 years has focused on persuading employers to adopt benefits for same-sex partners of employees (Githens, 2008; Githens, 2009a; Muñoz & Thomas, 2006). Benefits have likely been at the center of attention due to the clear inequities that have presented themselves between LGBT and heterosexual employees. Hornsby and Munn (2009) explain that 29% to 33% of employees' earnings come from their benefits packages. LGBT employees not receiving inclusive benefits lose a substantial portion of their income, when compared to the total compensation of heterosexual colleagues. Companies offer domestic partner health benefits in an effort to remain competitive, in response to public pressure, and/or to not engage in unfair practices (HRCF, 2010).

The simple adoption of these benefits is not without problems. Some employers require extra documentation for employees to prove a domestic partnership, such as a declaration of permanent relationship, joint ownership of assets, or joint residence for a specified period (Hornsby, 2006). Despite these specific requirements, most employers do not require any such documentation for heterosexual employees, not even a marriage certificate when adding a new spouse to employer-provided benefits. Another example of an inequity is requiring same-sex domestic partners to annually recertify their partnerships to maintain benefits eligibility (Hornsby & Munn, 2009). Employers rarely ask married heterosexual couples to certify annually that they continue to be married and rarely require more than checking a box to indicate marital status. Some employers that have inclusive policies have failed to update their documents and forms with inclusive language (e.g., using "spouse" but not including "partner") (Hornsby & Munn, 2009). This causes problems for LGBT employees who are not aware of the inclusive policies and the benefits being offered.

An additional concern originates in federal tax policy. Both the employer-paid portion and the employee-paid portion of domestic partner health benefits are taxed as employee income by the federal government, while not being taxed for married couples. Hornsby and Munn (2009) recommend that employers provide compensation to cover those additional costs. Van Loo and Rocco (2008) examined approaches to measuring earnings differences between heterosexuals, bisexuals, gays, and lesbians. Although there are some problems with all such research due to issues of how to identify LGBT individuals in large scale studies (van Loo & Rocco, 2008), past research in the U.S. has found consistently lower wages for gay men than heterosexual men. Research on lesbians' earnings has been less conclusive (van Loo & Rocco, 2008).

Work-life benefits consider employees' needs outside of the workplace. Benefits receiving the most attention include provisions that allow for caring for children through on-site daycare, parental leave for mothers and fathers, and flextime arrangements. Munn, Gedro, Hornsby, and Rocco (2009) contend that these policies and the research about these benefits primarily address the needs of women (and sometimes men) in heterosexual marriages. Munn and her colleagues contend that LGBT individuals are required to educate their heterosexual superiors, colleagues, and subordinates about their specific needs, which may vary from the work-life benefits currently offered by many employers. Additionally, the needs of transgender employees differ from the needs of LGB and heterosexual employees and should be carefully considered (Davis, 2009). For example, employers can ensure that hormone therapy and sex reassignment surgery are available through employer-provided benefits for those individuals who need access to those health services.

Career Development

Due to the historical career risks for LGBT workers, it is not surprising that one scholar has written four conceptual papers (Gedro, 2006, 2007c, 2009) and conducted one empirical study on lesbian executives' career development strategies (Gedro et al., 2004). For LGBT employees, career development is challenging due to the dilemma of whether to hide or disclose their identity in a multitude of work-related interactions. These dilemmas around identity and openness are an aspect of identity management (Gedro, 2009a). Identity has to be managed for LGBT people at the same time individuals are developing their identities as LGBT. Furthermore, "challenges associated with disclosure are not simply faced once and overcome; instead, they may be engaged on an ongoing or periodic basis throughout life" (Hill, 2009, p. 350). Since individuals'

career pathways emerge when they are adolescents, this false heterosexual identity combined with fear of harassment, can limit career choices. Gedro (2009a) explains that heterosexual individuals do not consider the safety or appropriateness of a career choice in terms of sexual orientation. Lesbians do not have to consider "accommodating men or conforming to traditional gender roles" (Gedro, 2009a, p. 59) when making career choices, nor is their non-adherence to traditional gender roles judged negatively as it is in the case of gay men. Men advance in their careers often through relationship building and bonding with other men. Masculinity and heterosexuality play prominent roles in these relationships putting gay men at a disadvantage.

Heterosexism costs organizations in decreased productivity and increased turnover of LGBT individuals (Rocco & Gallagher, 2006). Fearing harassment, editing every word one says in order to conceal one's true identity, and not being able to be an authentic individual require effort. The effort required to manage identity at work is not available to increase productivity. Organizations which maintain hostile environments toward minorities lose those same minorities, the investments made to develop them, and incur replacement costs. Lesbian corporate executives learned to manage their identities and negotiate heterosexism in corporations by developing skills in prescreening other employees to determine their receptivity to lesbians, disclosing strategically, and using their position to educate others on the challenges faced by lesbians (Gedro et al., 2004).

Workplace Education

Workplace education is the systematic development of the knowledge, skills, and attitudes required by a person in order to effectively perform a given task or job (Patrick, 2000). While at one point, the terms "training" and "education" may have been distinctly different, Schmidt (2006) notes that "the line between training and education is blurred to the point that the terms may be interchangeable" (p. 9). They will be used interchangeably in this chapter. Different than learning in the workplace, which can be informal and incidental, training is planned and purposeful. It is important to note that in this chapter, workplace education initiatives are examined separate from *general* diversity initiatives and *general* diversity training. The distinction is related to course content. In diversity related training and initiatives, LGBT issues are one of many dimensions of diversity pulled together and studied as parts of the whole concept. Workplace education issues look at the relationship between LGBT employees and different aspects of educational processes in the workplace.

There is a small body of research on LGBT issues in workplace education. Research on LGBT issues in workplace training has addressed education for HIV/AIDS prevention among sex workers and healthcare workers (Hill, 2005). Much discussion revolves around the development of curriculum to support LGBT inclusion in the workplace, including the degree to which training materials and workplace trainers acknowledge LGBT employees and issues in training programs. This concept, also known as queering the curriculum (Chapman & Gedro, 2007) has been researched in multiple educational settings, including the workplace. Chapman and Gedro (2007) concluded that queering the curriculum is an effective way to promote exploration of GLBT issues, as well as diversity and inclusion, in the workplace.

Gaps in HRD Research and Recommendations for Future Research

The authors of this chapter have concluded that a small group of scholars, many of whom are either LGBT or dedicated allies, are conducting research and writing about LGBT issues in HRD. Research should be conducted from multiple perspectives and not remain the purview of the minority group. Heterocentric bias may be present when studies repeatedly ignore the concerns of a whole category of people (van Loo & Rocco, 2008).

Gaps in the diversity research are related to basic education on LGBT issues in the workplace and on initiatives designed to raise awareness among all employees. However, sexual orientation is not regularly included as a variable considered in diversity studies, organizational development/culture, or any studies where race and gender are seen as important variables (van Loo & Rocco, 2008). Sometimes scholars simply do not consider LGBT employees as a variable because it may be invisible. Other times scholars choose not to include survey items about sexual minority status and concerns for fear of offending other survey respondents (Munn, Rocco, Bowman, & van Loo, 2011). Future research should investigate whether adding survey items about sexual minority status and concerns are offensive to participants. If found to be the case, research should also focus on what HRD practitioners can do in terms of diversity initiatives and organizational development to change these attitudes. Dismissing LGBT concerns and over issues of sensitivity can prevent the pursuing of legitimate research.

Research could examine which types of advocacy efforts are most effective in various types of organizations. For example, more aggressive approaches may lead to changes in one type of organization, while more passive or subtle approaches may be more effective in other types of organizations. The organizational perspectives from hostility to advocacy could benefit from research at the organizational, management and individual levels (Rocco, Landorf, et al., 2009). Questions that could be asked are: What is the relationship between the organizational perspective and the individual worker's perspective toward sexual minority inclusion? How do organizations identify with these perspectives? How does an organization move from being hostile to being an advocate for inclusion? A repeated theme in the literature has been the reaction of HR to LGBT concerns, as opposed to leading changes on these issues. As the HR profession seeks to be more proactive overall, research could examine how HR professionals successfully execute leadership on making changes to foster climates, policies, and practices that are friendlier to LGBT employees.

Kormanik's (2009) facets of sexual orientation and gender identity research should be conducted in other parts of the country with government and private sector workers and with a mix of organizations that foster the different perspectives toward sexual minority inclusion (Rocco, Landorf, et al., 2009). The facets of sexual orientation and gender identity can be examined also using qualitative and quantitative measures as in a survey sent to workers in specific industries. As progress on LGBT issues continues at a fast pace, issues related to workplace climate for LGBT issues are fluid and dynamic. For example, areas ripe for research are the effect of an employee coming out during the selection process, an employee coming out after starting a new position, the effect on productivity when LGBT employees are open about their sexuality, and the effect on collegiality when employees are open about sexuality. Specifically, these issues need to be considered in male-dominated fields, with quickly changing cultures and policies. For example, the U.S. military no longer condones discrimination in its policies. Surveys of military personnel showed the majority of military personnel were either neutral or positive about changing the "Don't Ask Don't Tell" policy, with those having knowingly served with LGBT personnel having more positive feelings on the topic (Westat, 2010). In sectors and industries such as this, opinions and practices are changing quickly, leading to the need for continual investigation to understand how leaders can best foster inclusive environments.

Another area to investigate is to examine the factors that predict long-term motivation and persistence by allies. Brooks and Edwards (2009) and Gedro et al. (2004) provide insights into some steps that activists take to improve climate and culture. However, a systematic study examining the role of both activists and HR in improving organizational climate and culture for LGBT workers could prove helpful for practice. Additionally, research should focus on coalition building as a way to improve workplace culture and climate.

The research on compensation disparities for gay men points to a need for additional research to understand the reasons for the disparities and to understand how HRD professionals can help prevent them. Other promising areas for research relate to the implementation of work-life benefits that allow for leaves of absence and flextime. Lastly, although domestic partner benefits have seen widespread adoption among large, publicly traded companies, we know that adoption has been slower in governmental agencies (Githens, 2008) and among small employers

(HRCF, 2009). Changes in these policies in governmental agencies tie back to complicated public policy debates. However, research among small employers could be fruitful in helping HR professionals and activists understand the antecedents present in small organizations that offer benefits.

Gaps in research on career development and LGBT employees are many, and include research on LGBT employees' career development and mobility in different types of occupations and careers. Research that specifically focuses on the experiences of gay men, lesbians, bisexuals and transgender employees in the workplace is also needed.

As noted earlier, research on LGBT issues in workplace training has focused on education for HIV/AIDS prevention among sex workers and healthcare workers. These two different types of employees demonstrate the fact that the concepts of workers and the workplace are broad; as is the concept of workplace training. Research has yet to take off in this area, and opportunities abound for future research on workplace education and LGBT issues such as cultural competence on LGBT issues for workplace trainers, and the development of curriculum that supports LGBT inclusion in the workplace.

Concluding Thoughts

Creating an inclusive and diverse workforce is relevant to the HRD profession in a sometimes-hostile political climate where the rhetoric can be centered on the purported immorality of LGBT people as a justification for the denial of civil rights. In this climate, HRD scholars and scholar-practitioners charged with increasing diversity because of legal mandates or moral correctness are searching for guidance. It is important to note that sexual orientation has been, and continues to be, mentioned in presentations and publications related to general diversity training, issues of gender in HRD, and women's career development.

We intend to stimulate thinking and challenge traditionally held views that have dismissed LGBT issues as a pathological condition of interest primarily to healthcare professionals—an organizational undiscussable—rather than a legitimate issue for HRD. In line with the precepts of critical human resource development (HRD) we share a purpose which "works towards reform aligned with purposes of justice, equity, and participation;" knowledge which "is understood to be contested;" inquiry which focuses "on power issues seeking to understand how socio-political processes" shape how we understand cognition, identity, and meaning; and, methods which "are practices that expose and challenge prevailing economic ideologies and power relations constituting organizational structures of inequity" (Fenwick, 2005, p. 228-229). Sexuality, as an invisible social identity in the workplace, has implications for both research and practice (Clair, Beatty, & MacLean, 2005; Ward & Winstanley, 2005). Additionally, in an environment where organizations need the productivity and full participation of all types of talent, this issue is a bottom-line business concern as well.

This chapter provides a summary of the small core of research from which to build and provides several fruitful areas for future research. The overarching theme from this body of work is that while many HR professionals are sincere and want to address these issues, they have often reacted or failed to act rather than provide proactive leadership on LGBT issues.

Declaration of Conflicting Interests

The author(s) declared no potential conflicts of interest with respect to the research, authorship, and/or publication of this chapter.

Funding

The author(s) received no financial support for the research, authorship, and/or publication of this chapter.

Note

1. **Corresponding Author:** Steven W. Schmidt, East Carolina University, 221B Ragsdale Hall, Greenville, NC 27858, USA Email: SCHMIDTST@ecu.edu

References

Brickson, S. (2000). Exploring identity: Where are we now. *Academy of Management Review, 25*, 1, 147–148.

Brooks, A. K., & Edwards, K. (2009). Allies in the workplace: Including LGBT in HRD. *Advances in Developing Human Resources, 11*(1), 136–149.

Chapman, D. D., & Gedro, J. (2007). Queering the HRD curriculum. In F. M. Nafukho (Ed.), *Academy of Human Resource Development Conference Proceedings* (pp. 579–586). Bowling Green, OH: AHRD.

Clair, J. A., Beatty, J. E., & MacLean, T. L. (2005). Out of sight but not out of mind: Managing invisible social identities. *Academy of Management Review, 30*(1), 78.

Corporate Equality Index. (2007). Washington, DC: Human Rights Campaign.

Corporate Equality Index. (2010). Washington, DC: Human Rights Campaign.

Cox, T. (1993). *Cultural diversity in organizations: Theory, research and practice.* San Francisco, CA: Berrett-Koehler.

Davis, D. (2009). Transgender issues in the workplace: HRD's newest challenge/opportunity. *Advances in Developing Human Resources, 11*(1), 109–120.

Ely J., & Thomas, D. A. (2001). Cultural diversity at work: The effects of diversity perspectives on work group processes and outcomes. *Administrative Science Quarterly, 46*, 229–273.

Fenwick, T. J. (2005). Conceptions of critical HRD: Dilemmas for theory and practice. *Human Resource Development International, 8*, 225–238.

Ferdman, B. (1995). Cultural identity and diversity in organizations: Bridging the gap between group differences and individual uniqueness. In M. Chemers, S. Oskamp, & M. Costanzo (Eds.), *Diversity in organizations: New perspectives for a changing workplace* (pp. 37–61). Thousand Oaks, CA: Sage.

Friere, P. (1970). *Pedagogy of the oppressed.* New York, NY: Seabury.

Gedro, J. (2006). Lesbians: Identifying, facing, and navigating the double bind of sexual orientation and gender in organizational settings. In R. J. Hill (Ed.), *New Directions for Adult and Continuing Education,* (pp. 41–50). San Francisco, CA: Jossey-Bass.

Gedro, J. (2007a). Antecedents and consequences of participation in a national lesbian, gay, bisexual, and transgender (LGBT) workplace conference. In L. Servage & T. Fenwick (Eds.) *Adult Education Resource Conference Proceedings,* (pp. 211–216). Edmonton, Alberta, Canada: University of Alberta.

Gedro, J. (2007b). Conducting research on LGBT issues: Leading the field all over again! *Human Resource Development Quarterly, 18*, 153–158.

Gedro, J. (2007c). LGBT Career Development. In F. Nafuko, T. Chermack & C. Graham (Eds.), *Academy of Human Resource Development Conference Proceedings* (pp. 691–699). Indianapolis, IN: Academy of Human Resource Development.

Gedro, J. (2009). Lipstick or golf clubs? Lesbian presentations and representations of leadership, and the implications for HRD. In T. J. Chermack (Ed.), *Proceedings AHRD 2009 International Research Conference* (pp. 2995–3017). Bowling Green, OH: Academy of Human Resource Development.

Gedro, J., Cervero, R., & Johnson-Bailey, J. (2002). How lesbians have learned to negotiate the heterosexism of corporate America. In Egan, T., & Lynham, S. (Eds.), *Academy of Human Resource Development Conference Proceedings* (pp. 373–380). Bowling Green, OH: AHRD.

Gedro, J., Cervero, R., & Johnson-Bailey, J. (2004). How lesbians learn to negotiate the heterosexism of corporate America. *Human Resource Development International, 7*, 181–195.

Gilbert, J. A., & Ivancevich, J. M. (2000). Valuing diversity: A tale of two organizations. *Academy of Management Executive, 14*(1), 93–105.

Githens, R. P. (2008). Capitalism, identity politics, and queerness converge: LGBT employee resource groups. In T. J. Chermack (Ed.), *Proceedings AHRD 2008 International Research Conference* (pp. 209–216). Bowling Green, OH: Academy of Human Resource Development.

Githens, R. P. (2009a). Capitalism, identity politics, and queerness converge: LGBT employee resource groups. *New Horizons in Adult Education and Human Resource Development, 23*(3), 18–31.

Githens, R. P. (2009b). Diversity and ressentiment in educating for LGBTQ-friendly changes in a university. In R. L. Lawrence (Ed.), *Proceedings of the 50th Annual Adult Education Research Conference* (pp. 125–130). Chicago, IL: National-Louis University.

Githens, R. P., & Aragon, S. R. (2007). LGBTQ employee groups: Who are they good for? How are they organized? In L. Servage & T. Fenwick (Eds.), *Adult Education Research Conference Proceedings* (pp. 223–228). Edmonton, Alberta, Canada: University of Alberta.

Githens, R. P., & Aragon, S. R. (2009). LGBT employee groups: Goals and organizational structures. *Advances in Developing Human Resources, 11*(1), 121–135.

Githens, R. P., Schmidt, S. W., Rocco, T. S., & Gedro, J. (2008). Workforce diversity: developing inclusive HRD practices for sexual minorities/LGBT employees. In T. J. Chermack (Ed.), *Proceedings AHRD 2008 International Research Conference* (pp. 35–37). Bowling Green, OH: Academy of Human Resource Development.

Gonsiorek, J. C., Sell, R. L., & Weinrich, J. D. (1995). Definition and measurement of sexual orientation. *Suicide and Life-Threatening Behavior, 25*, 40.

Harris, W. (2007). Finding your place in the world. *Black Enterprise, 38*(4), 64–65.

Heller, M. (2006). More employers broadening nondiscrimination policies to include transgender workers. *Workforce Management, 85*(12), 62–63.

Hill, N. L. (2009). Affirmative practice and alternative sexual orientations: Helping clients navigate the coming out process. *Clinical Social Work Journal, 37*, 346–356.

Hill, R. J. (1995). Gay discourse in adult education: A critical review. *Adult Education Quarterly, 45*, 142–158.

Hill, R. J. (2005). Poz-itively transformational: Sex workers and HIV/AIDS education. In J. P. Egan (Ed.), *New directions for adult and continuing education,* (pp. 75–84). San Francisco, CA: Jossey-Bass.

Hill, R. J. (2006a). *New directions for adult and continuing education.* San Francisco, CA: Jossey-Bass.

Hill, R. J. (2006b). What's it like to be queer here? In R. J. Hill (Ed.), *New Directions for Adult and Continuing Education* (pp. 7–16). San Francisco, CA: Jossey-Bass.

Hill, R. J. (2006c). Queer challenges in organizational settings: Complexity, paradox, and contradiction. In R. J. Hill (Ed.), *New Directions for Adult and Continuing Education* (pp. 97–102). San Francisco, CA: Jossey-Bass.

Hornsby, E. E. (2006). Using policy to drive organizational change. In R. J. Hill (Ed.), *New directions for adult and continuing education* (pp. 73–83). San Francisco, CA: Jossey-Bass.

Hornsby, E. E., & Munn, S. L. (2009). University work-life benefits and same-sex couples. *Advances in Developing Human Resources, 11*(1), 67–81.

Human Rights Campaign Foundation. (2006). *Workplace gender transition guidelines.* Retrieved from http://www.hrc.org/issues/workplace/equal opportunity/4863.htm

Human Rights Campaign Foundation. (2009). *Domestic partner benefits: Prevalence among private employees.* Retrieved from http://www.hrc.org/issues/workplace/benefits/11612.htm

Human Rights Campaign Foundation (2010). *Workplace database*. Retrieved from http://www.hrc.org/employersearch/

Humphrey, J. C. (1999). Organizing sexualities, organized inequalities: Lesbians and gay men in public service occupations. *Gender, Work and Organization, 6,* 134–151.

Iles, P., & Hayers, P. K. (1997). Managing diversity in transnational project teams: A tentative model and case study. *Journal of Managerial Psychology, 12*(2), 95–117.

Jamison, C. L., & Miller, F. A. (2006, May). Diversity is dead. *ASTD Links, 5*(4). Retrieved from http://www.astd.org/astd/Publications/ASTD_Links/2006/April/Home

Jayne, M. A., & Dipboye, R. L. (2004). Leveraging diversity to improve business performance: Research findings and recommendations for organizations. *Human Resource Management, 43,* 409–424.

Kameny, F. E. (1971). Homosexuals as a minority group. In E. Sagarin (Ed.), *The other minorities: Nonethnic collectives classified as minority groups* (pp. 50–65). Waltham, MA: Xerox College.

King, K. P., & Biro, S. C. (2006). A transformative learning perspective of continuing sexual identity development in the workplace. In R. J. Hill (Ed.), *New directions for adult and continuing education* (pp. 17–27). San Francisco, CA: Jossey-Bass.

Kormanik, M. B. (2009). Sexuality as a diversity factor: An examination of awareness. *Advances in Developing Human Resources, 11*(1), 24–36.

Kudlick, C. J. (2003). Disability history: Why we need another "other." *American Historical Review, 108,* 763.

Kwak, M. (2003). The paradoxical effects of diversity. *Sloan Management Review, 44*(3), 7.

Leonard, A. S. (2003). The gay rights workplace revolution. *Human Rights, 30*(3), 14–16.

Liddle, B. J., Luzzo, D. A., Hauenstein, A. L., & Schuck, K (2004). Construction and validation of the Lesbian, Gay, Bisexual and Transgender climate inventory. *Journal of Career Assessment, 12*(1), 33–50.

Loden, M. (1996). *Implementing Diversity*, Chicago. Irwin.

Loden, M., & Rosener, J. B. (1991). *Workforce America: Managing employee diversity as a vital resource.* Homewood, IL. Irwin.

MacDonnell, J. A. (2009). Gender, sexuality, and the organizational context: Nurses who advocate for lesbian health. In T. J. Chermack (Ed.), *Proceedings AHRD 2009 International Research Conference* (pp. 3541–3544). Bowling Green, OH: Academy of Human Resource Development.

Maxwell, M. (2005). It's not just Black and White: How diverse is your workforce? *Nursing Economics, 23,* 139–140.

McMillan-Capehart, A. (2006). Heterogeneity or homogeneity: Socialization makes the difference when diversity is at stake. *Performance Improvement Quarterly, 19*(1), 83–99.

Mezirow, J. (1997). Transformative learning: Theory to practice. *New Directions for Adult and Continuing Education, 74,* 5–12.

Munn, S. L., Gedro, J., Hornsby, E. E., & Rocco, T. S. (2009). Lesbians, gays, and work-life balance. In T. J. Chermack (Ed.), *Proceedings AHRD 2009 International Research Conference* (pp. 3711–3715). Bowling Green, OH: Academy of Human Resource Development.

Munn, S. L., Rocco, T. S., Bowman, L., & van Loo, J. (2011). *Work-life research and the representation of sexual minorities.* Naples, Italy: Critical Management Studies Conference. Available at http://www.organizzazione.unina.it/cms7/proceedings/proceedings_stream_37/Munn_et_alii.pdf

Munoz, C. S., & Thomas, K. M. (2006). LGBTQ issues in organizational settings: What HRD professionals need to know and do. *New Directions for Adult and Continuing Education 2006*(112), 85–95.

Patrick, J. (2000). Training. In N. Chmiel (Ed.), *Introduction to work and organizational psychology* (pp. 100–125). Oxford, UK: Blackwell.

Ragins, B. R. (2004) Sexual orientation in the workplace: The unique work and career experiences of gay, lesbian and bisexual workers. *Research in Personnel and Human Resources Management, 23,* 35–120

Ragins, B. R., & Cornwell, J. M. (2001). Pink triangles: Antecedents and consequences of perceived workplace discrimination against gay and lesbian employees. *Journal of Applied Psychology, 86,* 1244.

Roberson, Q. M., & Stevens, C. K. (2006). Making sense of diversity in the workplace: organizational justice and language abstraction in employees' accounts of diversity-related incidents. *Journal of Applied Psychology, 91*(2), 379.

Robinson, G. & Dechant, K. (1997). Building a business case for diversity. *The Academy of Management Executive, 13*(3), 21.

Rocco, T. S., & Gallagher, S. J. (2006). Deconstructing heterosexual privilege with new science metaphors. In M. Hagen & E. Goff (Eds.), *Proceedings of the 47th Adult Education Research Conference* (pp. 312–317). Minneapolis-St. Paul, MN: University of Minnesota.

Rocco, T. S., Gallagher, S., Gedro, J., Hornsby, E. E., & van Loo, J. (2006). Sexual orientation, diversity, and issues of workplace equity. In F. M. Nafukho (Ed.), *Academy of Human Resource Development Conference Proceedings* (pp. 1040–1045). Bowling Green, OH: AHRD.

Rocco, T. S., Gedro, J., & Kormanik, M. B. (Eds.). (2009). Sexual minority issues in HRD. *Advances in Developing Human Resources. 11*(1).

Rocco, T. S., Landorf, H., & Delgado, A. (2009). Framing the issue/framing the question: A proposed framework for organizational perspectives on sexual minorities. *Advances in Developing Human Resources, 11*(1), 7–23.

Ross-Gordon, J. M., & Brooks, A. K. (2004). Diversity in human resource development and continuing professional education: What does it mean for the workforce, clients, and professionals? *Advances in Developing Human Resources, 6*(1), 69–85.

Schmidt, S. W. (2006). *The relationship between job training satisfaction and overall job satisfaction* (Unpublished doctoral dissertation). University of Wisconsin–Milwaukee, WI.

Schmidt, S. W., & Githens, R. P. (2010). A place at the table? The organization of a pre-conference symposium on LGBT issues in HRD. *New Horizons in Adult Education and Human Resource Development, 24*(1), 59–62.

Sidanius, J., & Pratto, F. (1999). *Social dominance: An intergroup theory of social hierarchy and oppression.* Cambridge, UK: Cambridge University Press.

Thomas, D., & Ely, R. (1996). Making differences matter: A new paradigm for managing diversity. *Harvard Business Review, 74*(5), 79–90.

Thomas, R., Jr. (1990). From affirmative action to affirming diversity. *Harvard Business Review, 68* (2), 107–117.

U.K. Government: Minister urges councils to promote diversity. (2003, July 7). *M2 Presswire*, p. 1.

U.S. Census Bureau. (2006). *United States disability status.* Retrieved from: http://factfinder.census.gov/servlet/DTTable?_bm=y&-geo_id=01000US&-ds_name=ACS_2006_EST_G00_&-_lang=en&-_caller=geoselect&-state=dt&-format=&-mt_name=ACS_2006_EST_G2000_C18020

U.S. Census Bureau. (2008). *United States employment status.* Retrieved from http://factfinder.census.gov/servlet/STTable?_bm=y&-geo_id=01000US&-qr_name=ACS_2008_3YR_G00_S2301&-ds_name=ACS_2008_3YR_G00_

van Loo, J. B., & Rocco, T. S. (2008). Conceptualizing an inclusive economic approach to GLBT labor issues: Current research and future directions. In T. J. Chermack (Ed.), *Proceedings AHRD 2008 International Research Conference* (pp. 194–200). Bowling Green, OH: Academy of Human Resource Development.

Ward, J. H. (2003). Setting the diversity agenda straight. *Business & Professional Ethics Journal, 22*(3), 73.

Ward, J., & Winstanley, D. (2005). Coming out at work: Performativity and the recognition and renegotiation of identity. *Sociological Review, 53*, 447.

Westat. (2010). *Support to the DoD comprehensive review working group analyzing the impact of repealing "Don't Ask, Don't Tell."* (Vol. 1: findings from the surveys). Rockville, MD: Author.

Wilson, T. (1997). *Diversity at work: The business case for equity.* Toronto, Ontario, Canada: Wiley.

Witeck, B., & Combs, W. (2006, February). Getting a clearer picture. In *Quirk's Marketing Research Review.* Washington, DC: Author.

Yang, Y. (2005). Developing cultural diversity advantage: The impact of diversity management structures. In K. M. Weaver (Ed.), *Academy of Management 2005 Annual Meeting Proceedings.* Briarcliff Manor, NY: Academy of Management.

CHAPTER 22

Women and Leadership

Crystal L. Hoyt

University of Richmond

When you meet a human being, the first distinction you make is "male or female?" and you are accustomed to make the distinction with unhesitating certainty.

—Sigmund Freud

Description

Writers in the popular press have shown an enduring interest in the topic of gender and leadership, reporting stark and meaningful differences between women and men (Book, 2000; Bowman, Worthy, & Greyser, 1965). These differences turned from a view of women as inferior to men (e.g., some posited that women lacked skills and traits necessary for managerial success; Hennig & Jardin, 1977) to the more modern popular view that extols the superiority of women in leadership positions (Book, 2000; Helgesen, 1990). However, for a variety of reasons, including methodological hindrances, a predominance of male researchers largely uninterested in the topic, and an academic assumption of gender equality in leadership, academic researchers ignored issues related to gender and leadership until the 1970s (Chemers, 1997). The increasing numbers of women in leadership positions

and women in academia, brought about by dramatic changes in American society, have fueled the now robust scholarly interest in the study of female leaders.

Scholars started out asking, "Can women lead?" but that is now a moot point. In addition to the increasing presence of women in corporate and political leadership roles, we can point to highly effective female leaders including former prime ministers such as Benazir Bhutto (Pakistan), Margaret Thatcher (UK), Gro Marlem Brundtland (Norway), and Indira Gandhi (India), and current world leaders such as Chancellor Angela Merkel of Germany and President Dilma Rousseff of Brazil. Beyond politics we can point to a number of highly effective female leaders including PepsiCo's CEO Indra Nooyi, Avon's CEO Andrea Jung, Four-Star General Ann E. Dunwoody, and the founder of Teach for America, Wendy Kopp. The primary research question now is "Are there leadership style and effectiveness differences between women and men?"

which is often subsumed under a larger question: "Why are women underrepresented in elite leadership roles?" This chapter explores empirical evidence related to these issues of gender and leadership by first examining style and effectiveness differences between men and women, then discussing the gender gap in leadership and prominent explanations for it, and, finally, addressing approaches to promoting women in leadership.

Gender, Leadership Styles, and Leadership Effectiveness

As more women are occupying positions of leadership, questions as to whether they lead in a different manner from men and whether women or men are more effective as leaders have garnered greater attention. Increasingly, writers in the mainstream press are asserting that there are indeed gender differences in leadership styles, and that women's leadership is more effective in contemporary society (Book, 2000; Helgesen, 1990; Rosener, 1995). However, academic researchers have a greater diversity in their views; indeed, many argue that gender has little or no relationship to leadership style and effectiveness (Dobbins & Platz, 1986; van Engen, Leeden, & Willemsen, 2001; Powell, 1990).

Early research examining style differences between women and men compared either interpersonally oriented and task-oriented styles or democratic and autocratic styles. In a meta-analysis, Eagly and Johnson (1990) found that, contrary to stereotypic expectations, women were not found to lead in a more interpersonally oriented and less task-oriented manner than men in organizational studies. These differences were found only in settings where behavior was more regulated by social roles, such as experimental settings. The only robust gender difference found across settings was that women led in a more democratic, or participative, manner than men. Another meta-analysis examining research between 1987 and 2000 found similar results (van Engen & Willemsen, 2004).

It is important to consider these results in conjunction with findings from a large-scale meta-analysis of the literature on evaluations of female and male leaders who were equated on all characteristics and leadership behaviors (Eagly, Makhijani, & Klonsky, 1992). These studies revealed that women were devalued compared with men when they led in a masculine manner (autocratic or directive; e.g., Bartol & Butterfield, 1976), when they occupied a typically masculine leadership role (e.g., athletic coaches or managers in manufacturing plants; see Knight & Saal, 1984), and when the evaluators were men. These findings indicate that women's greater use of democratic style appears to be adaptive in that they are using the style that produces the most favorable evaluations.

More recent research has examined gender differences in transformational leadership (Bass, 1985; Burns, 1978; see Chapter 9). A meta-analysis by Eagly, Johannesen-Schmidt, and van Engen (2003) found small but robust differences between female and male leaders on these styles such that women's styles tend to be more transformational than men's, and women tend to engage in more contingent reward behaviors than men. Although these styles predict effectiveness, recent findings suggest that the devaluation of female leaders by male subordinates has been shown to extend to female transformational leaders (Ayman, Korabik, & Morris, 2009).

In addition to leadership style, the relative effectiveness of male and female leaders has been assessed in a number of studies (Jacobson & Effertz, 1974; Tsui & Gutek, 1984). In a meta-analysis comparing the effectiveness of female and male leaders, men and women were equally effective leaders, overall, but there were gender differences such that women and men were more effective in leadership roles that were congruent with their gender (Eagly, Karau, & Makhijani, 1995). Thus, women were less effective to the extent that the leader role was masculinized. For example, women were less effective than men were in military positions, but they were somewhat more effective than men were in education, government, and social service organizations, and substantially more effective than men were in middle management positions, where communal interpersonal skills are highly valued. In addition, women were less effective than men were when they supervised a higher proportion of male subordinates or when a greater proportion of male raters assessed the leaders' performance.

In sum, empirical research supports small differences in leadership style and effectiveness between men and women. Women experience slight effectiveness disadvantages in masculine leader roles, whereas roles that are more feminine offer them some advantages. Additionally, women exceed men in the use of democratic or participatory styles, and they are more likely to use transformational leadership behaviors and contingent reward, styles that are associated with contemporary notions of effective leadership.

The Glass Ceiling Turned Labyrinth

We still think of a powerful man as a born leader and a powerful woman as an anomaly.

—Margaret Atwood

Evidence of the Leadership Labyrinth

Although the predicament of female leaders has improved significantly in recent decades, there is still a long way to go. Women earn 57% of the bachelor's degrees, 60% of the master's degrees, more than half of the doctorate degrees, and nearly half of the first professional degrees awarded in the United States (Catalyst, 2011b), and they make up nearly half of the U.S. labor force (47.2%; U.S. Bureau of Labor Statistics, 2010a). However, women are still underrepresented in the upper echelons of America's corporations and political system. Women are among the leadership ranks in American organizations occupying more than half of all management and professional positions (51.5%; Catalyst, 2011c) and a quarter of all chief executive officer (CEO) positions (25.5%; U.S. Bureau of Labor Statistics, 2010b). However, more elite leadership positions show a different story. For example, women represent less than 3% of Fortune 500 CEOs, and hold only 15.7% of the Fortune 500 board seats and a mere 14.4% of the Fortune 500 executive officer positions (Catalyst, 2011a, 2011c).

On the political front, women currently hold only 90 of the 535 seats in the U.S. Congress (16.8%; 17% in the Senate and 16.8% in the House of Representatives); women of color occupy just 24 seats (Center for American Women and Politics, 2011). Indeed, as of August 2011, the world average of women's representation in national legislatures or parliaments is 19.3%, with the United States ranked 70th out of 187 countries (Inter-Parliamentary Union, 2011). Moreover, women represent just 6.1% of military officers at the level of brigadier general and rear admiral or higher (U.S. Department of Defense, 2008).

The invisible barrier preventing women from ascending into elite leadership positions was initially dubbed the glass ceiling, a term introduced into the American vernacular by two Wall Street Journal reporters in 1986 (Hymowitz & Schellhardt, 1986). Even in female-dominated occupations, women face the glass ceiling, whereas White men appear to ride a glass escalator to the top leadership positions (Maume, 1999; Williams, 1992, 1995). Eagly and Carli (2007) recently identified limitations with the glass ceiling metaphor, including that it implies that everyone has equal access to lower positions until all women hit this single, invisible, and impassable barrier. They put forward an alternative image of a leadership labyrinth conveying the impression of a journey riddled with challenges all along the way, not just near the top, that can and has been successfully navigated by women (Figure 22.1).

Understanding the Labyrinth

The leadership gap is a global phenomenon whereby women are disproportionately concentrated in lower-level and lower-authority leadership positions than men (Powell & Graves, 2003). Discussions of women's underrepresentation in high-level leadership positions generally revolve around three types of explanations (Figure 22.2). The first set of

Figure 22.1	The Leadership Gap

Educational and Work Attainment	
Women	Men
In Managerial/Professional Positions	
50.8%	49.2%
In U.S. Labor Force	
46.7%	53.3%
Earning Bachelor's Degrees	
57.5%	42.5%
The Leadership Gap	
Women	Men
CEOs in Fortune 500 Companies	
3%	97%
Holding Board Seats in Fortune 500 Companies	
15.2%	84.8%
Members of U.S. Congress	
16.8%	83.2%

explanations highlights differences in women's and men's investments in human capital. The next category of explanations considers gender differences between women and men. The final type of explanation focuses on prejudice and discrimination against female leaders.

Human Capital Differences

One prominent set of explanations for the labyrinth is that women have less human capital investment in education, training, and work experience than men (Eagly & Carli, 2004, 2007). This supposed lack of human capital is said to result in a dearth of qualified women, sometimes called a "pipeline problem." However, a closer look at the numbers reveals that women are indeed in the pipeline but that the pipeline is leaking. As already discussed, women are obtaining undergraduate degrees at a far higher rate than men, and women are earning professional and doctorate degrees at a rate greater or nearly equal to that of men, but they are still vastly underrepresented in top leadership positions. In the domain of law,

although women earn 45.9% of all law degrees and make up 45.4% of associates, they make up only 19.4% of partners (American Bar Association, 2011). And even though women represent only about one third of those graduating with MBAs from the top 10 business schools (Catalyst, 2011d), their representation in the upper echelons of American business pales in comparison. Finally, there is clear evidence that the lack of women reaching the top is not due to the fact that not enough time has passed for natural career progression to occur (Heilman, 1997).

Women do have somewhat less work experience and employment continuity than men, driven largely by the disproportionate responsibility women assume for child rearing and domestic duties (Bowles & McGinn, 2005; Eagly & Carli, 2007). Although a common explanation for the gender disparity in experience is that women are more likely than men to quit their jobs, there is no consistent research evidence to that effect (Eagly & Carli, 2004). However, there is evidence that women experience greater losses than men do after quitting because women are more likely to quit for family-related reasons (Keith &

McWilliams, 1999). Domestic and child-rearing expectations impose an added burden on women climbing the leadership ladder, especially on those women who cannot afford to pay for domestic help. Although men's participation in domestic labor has increased significantly in recent years (Galinsky, Aumann, & Bond, 2008), women continue to do the majority of the child care responsibilities and household chores (Belkin, 2008; Craig, 2006; Pailhe & Solaz, 2006). Women respond to these work–home conflicts in a variety of ways (Bowles & McGinn, 2005). Some women choose not to marry or have children, others choose to become "superwomen" and attempt to excel in every role, and others take leaves of absence, take sick days, or choose part-time employment to juggle these work–home conflicts (Hewlett, 2002; Nieva & Gutek, 1981). Antiquated workplace norms make it difficult for women to rise in the leadership ranks: Those who take advantage of workplace leave and flexibility programs are often marginalized, and those who take time off from their careers often find reentry difficult and often enter at a lower level than the level they left (Williams, 2010). A related explanation for the leadership gap is that this culturally prescribed division of labor leads women to self-select themselves out of leadership tracks by choosing "mommy track" positions that do not funnel into leadership positions (Belkin, 2003); however, research does not support this argument (Eagly & Carli, 2004; Williams, 2010).

Although women occupy more than half of all management and professional positions (Catalyst, 2011c), they have fewer developmental opportunities at work than do men. Many of these gender differences in developmental opportunities may be driven in part by the prejudice women experience in the domain of leadership. In addition to having fewer responsibilities in the same jobs as men, women are less likely to receive encouragement, be included in key networks, and receive formal job training than their male counterparts (Knoke & Ishio, 1998; Morrison & Von Glinow, 1990; Ohlott, Ruderman, &

Figure 22.2   Understanding the Leadership Labyrinth

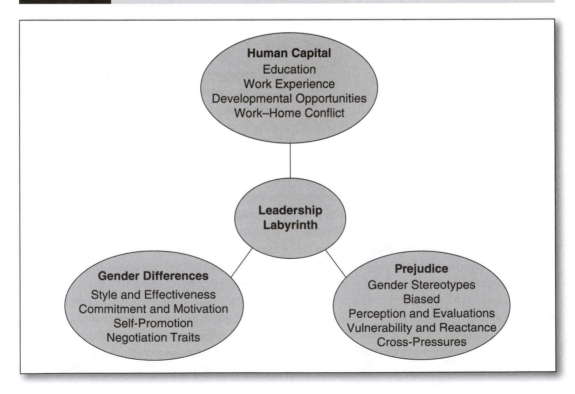

McCauley, 1994; Powell & Graves, 2003). One important developmental experience that affects career success is effective mentor relationships (Ensher & Murphy, 2005), and women confront greater barriers to establishing informal mentor relationships than men do (Powell & Graves, 2003). Additionally, women are disproportionately represented in business positions that are less visible, have less responsibility, and do not lead to top leadership positions. For example, women are clustered in the fields of accounting, education, and the velvet ghetto of human resource management (Bowles & McGinn, 2005). Relatedly, when women are promoted to leadership positions they are more likely than men are to be placed on a "glass cliff": They are more likely to be appointed to precarious leadership situations associated with greater risk and criticism (Ryan, Haslam, Hersby, & Bongiorno, 2011).

In sum, there is scant support for the notions that women receive less education than men, that they quit their jobs more often than men do, or that they opt out of the leadership track for the mommy track. There is support for the notion that women have less work experience and more career interruptions than men, largely because women assume significantly more domestic responsibility. Finally, women receive less formal training and have fewer developmental opportunities at work than men, both of which likely are related to prejudice against female leaders.

Gender Differences

Other arguments attempting to explain the leadership gap revolve around the notion that women are just different from men. One argument in this vein is that women's underrepresentation in elite leadership positions is a result of differences in leadership style and effectiveness. As discussed earlier in this chapter, any substantial leadership style differences between women and men should not disadvantage women and can even offer a female advantage (Eagly & Carli, 2007; Vecchio, 2002). Another oft-cited barrier to women's advancement is the presumed gender difference in commitment to employment and motivation to lead. However, research indicates that women show the same level of identification with and

commitment to paid employment roles as men do, and both women and men view their roles as workers to be secondary to their roles as parents and partners (Bielby & Bielby, 1988; Thoits, 1992). Empirical research does indicate that women are less likely than men are to promote themselves for leadership positions (Bowles & McGinn, 2005). For example, women are more likely to take on informal, as opposed to official, leadership roles, and use terms such as facilitator or organizer instead of leader (Andrews, 1992; Fletcher, 2001). A meta-analytic review of the research literature on leader emergence revealed that although women were less likely than men were to emerge as group leaders, they were more likely to serve as social facilitators than men were (Eagly & Karau, 1991). This research must be interpreted in light of the social costs, or backlash, women experience when they promote themselves or are competent in positions of authority (Rudman & Glick, 2001). Women face significant gender biases and social disincentives when they self-promote. Unlike men, for example, self-promoting women are seen as less socially attractive and less hirable (Rudman, 1998). Thus, women who want to pursue leadership positions may choose not to do so because they have internalized these expectations or are simply aware of the social costs of ambition (Bowles & McGinn, 2005; Powell & Graves, 2003).

Another claim is that men are more likely than women to have the traits necessary for effective leadership. Effective leadership, however, is marked by an androgynous mixture of traits including intelligence, social skills, initiative, and the ability to persuade (Eagly & Carli, 2007). Social science research has shown some small sex differences in traits related to effective leadership, such as integrity, assertiveness, gregariousness, and risk taking; however, these differences favor women as much as they do men (Eagly & Carli, 2007; Feingold, 1994; Franke, Crown, & Spake, 1997). One gender difference that advantages men in leadership is that men are more likely than women to ask for what they want (Babcock & Laschever, 2003). Reaching elite leadership positions is not done in a vacuum: People must negotiate with others to access the right positions, experiences, opportunities, resources, and assistance in both the professional and domestic spheres. Not only are women less likely to negotiate than men are (Small, Gelfand, Babcock, & Gettman, 2007), the negotiations needed to ascend the leadership hierarchy often are unstructured, ambiguous, and rife with gender triggers—exactly the type of situation that particularly disadvantages women (Bowles & McGinn, 2005). Moreover, women face greater social costs for initiating negotiation than men do, so their lower levels of negotiation may represent an adaptive response to social disincentives (Bowles, Babcock, & Lai, 2007).

In sum, women are no less effective at leadership, committed to their jobs, or motivated for leadership roles than men. However, women are less likely to self-promote and negotiate than men. Furthermore, research shows a few small sex differences in traits associated with effective leadership, although these differences equally advantage women and men.

Prejudice

One prominent explanation for the leadership gap revolves around gender biases stemming from stereotyped expectations that women take care and men take charge (Hoyt & Chemers, 2008). Stereotypes are cognitive shortcuts that influence the way people process information regarding groups and group members. People assign characteristics to groups, or individual members of groups, regardless of the actual variation in characteristics between the members (Hamilton, Stroessner, & Driscoll, 1994). Gender stereotypes are pervasive, well documented, and highly resistant to change (Dodge, Gilroy, & Fenzel, 1995; Heilman, 2001). Gender stereotypes both describe stereotypic beliefs about the attributes of women and men, and prescribe how men and women ought to be (Burgess & Borgida, 1999; Glick & Fiske, 1999). Men are stereotyped with agentic characteristics such as confidence, assertiveness, independence, rationality, and decisiveness, whereas women are stereotyped with communal characteristics such as concern for others, sensitivity, warmth, helpfulness, and nurturance (Deaux & Kite, 1993; Heilman, 2001).

Gender stereotypes are easily and automatically activated, and they often lead to biased judgments

(Fiske, 1998; Kunda & Spencer, 2003). In addition to facing gender-based prejudice, women of color often also confront racial or ethnic prejudice (Bell & Nkomo, 2001). A vivid illustration of gender-based prejudice can be seen in the evaluation of men and women auditioning for symphony orchestras. In the 1970s and 1980s, male-dominated symphony orchestras made one simple change: All applicants were asked to audition while hidden behind a screen. This small change greatly increased the proportion of women in symphony orchestras (Goldin & Rouse, 2000). Merely seeing the applicant's sex evoked stereotype-based expectations in the judges' minds that resulted in a significant bias toward selecting men.

In leadership roles, gender stereotypes are particularly damaging for women because agentic, as opposed to communal, tendencies often are indispensable (Chemers & Murphy, 1995). According to role congruity theory, the agentic qualities thought necessary in the leadership role are incompatible with the predominantly communal qualities stereotypically associated with women, thus resulting in prejudice against female leaders (Eagly & Karau, 2002). Although the masculine construal of leadership has decreased somewhat over time, it remains pervasive and robust (Koenig, Eagly, Mitchell, & Ristikari, 2011). Thus, in the leadership role, women are confronted with cross-pressures: As leaders, they should be masculine and tough, but as women, they should not be "too manly." These opposing expectations for women often result in the perception that women are less qualified for elite leadership positions than men, and in harsh evaluations of effective female leaders for not being "female enough."

This prejudice against female leaders helps explain the numerous findings indicating less favorable attitudes toward female than male leaders, greater difficulty for women to attain top leadership roles, and greater difficulty for women to be viewed as effective in these roles (Eagly & Karau, 2002). The penalties for violating one's gender stereotypes are clearly illustrated in the classic 1989 Supreme Court case Price Waterhouse v. Ann Hopkins. Price Waterhouse told Hopkins that she would not make partner because she was too masculine, going as far as advising her to go to charm school, wear jewelry and makeup, and be less aggressive. In the end, the Court ruled that Price Waterhouse was discriminating based on gender stereotypes (Fiske, Bersoff, Borgida, Deaux, & Heilman, 1991). Gender bias was also evident in the media coverage of the 2008 U.S. presidential primaries involving Hillary Clinton. As Katie Couric noted after Clinton bowed out of contention, "One of the great lessons of that campaign is the continued and accepted role of sexism in American life, particularly the media . . . if Senator Obama had to confront the racist equivalent of an 'Iron My Shirt' poster at campaign rallies or a Hillary nutcracker sold at airports . . . the outrage would not be a footnote, it would be front page news" (Couric & Co., 2008).

Gender biases can be particularly detrimental in the decision-making processes for selecting elite leaders, given that the generally unstructured nature of those decisions allows biased decisions without accountability (Powell & Graves, 2003). Not only are the decision makers influenced by the stereotypes that disadvantage women in the leadership role, but also they may succumb to homosocial reproduction, a tendency for a group to reproduce itself in its own image (Kanter, 1977). People prefer similar others and report the most positive decisions about and evaluations of people who are most similar to them, biases that can clearly disadvantage women when male leaders are looking for replacements.

These stereotypic expectations not only affect others' perceptions and evaluations of female leaders, but also can directly affect the women themselves. Women who make up a very small minority of a male-dominated group are seen as tokens representing all women; they experience significant pressure as their highly visible performance is scrutinized and they are perceived through gender-stereotyped lenses (Kanter, 1977). Women often are very aware of their gender and the accompanying stereotypes (Sekaquaptewa & Thompson, 2003). Research shows that women respond in one of two ways to the gender-based leadership stereotype: Either they demonstrate vulnerability by assimilating to the stereotype, or they react against it by engaging in stereotype-countering behaviors (Hoyt, 2010). Whether the threat of the gender-leader stereotype is met with

vulnerability or reactance responses depends on factors such as the leader's self-efficacy, the explicitness of the stereotype, the type of task, the group sex-composition, and the power that the leader holds (Bergeron, Block, & Echtenkamp, 2006; Davies, Spencer, & Steele, 2005; Hoyt & Blascovich, 2007, 2010; Kray, Reb, Galinsky, & Thompson, 2004; Kray, Thompson, & Galinsky, 2001). Furthermore, although female leaders may demonstrate reactance to certain solitary gender stereotype threats, when such threats are combined women are likely to demonstrate deleterious vulnerability responses (Hoyt, Johnson, Murphy, & Skinnell, 2010). In sum, substantial empirical evidence reveals that gender stereotypes can significantly alter the perception and evaluation of female leaders and directly affect women in or aspiring to leadership roles.

Navigating the Labyrinth

The number of women who successfully navigate the labyrinth is on the rise (Eagly & Carli, 2007). A confluence of factors contributes to this increase in effective female leaders (Figure 22.3). Changes in organizations are beginning to make it easier for women to reach top positions. The culture of many organizations is changing; gendered work assumptions such as the male model of work, the notion of uninterrupted full-time careers, and the separation of work and family are being challenged (Cooper & Lewis, 1999; Williams, 2010). Moreover, many organizations are valuing flexible workers and diversity in their top echelons. These organizations can augment women's career development by involving them in career development programs and formal networks, and offering work–life support. In addition, assigning more women to high-visibility positions and developing effective and supportive mentoring relationships for women are key strategies for reducing the leadership gap (Bell & Nkomo, 2001; Ensher & Murphy, 2005; Ragins, Townsend, & Mattis, 1998).

Although the gendered division of labor contributes to the leadership gap, there is recent evidence of increasing parity in the involvement of women and men in child care and housework (Eagly & Carli, 2007).

| **Figure 22.3** | Leadership Effectiveness |

In balancing work and home life, an appealing approach for women is structural role redefinition (Hall, 1972). This approach involves negotiating with both family and colleagues to renegotiate role expectations both at work and at home. For example, at home women can negotiate workload between spouses, team up with friends and family members, and, if able, hire help when necessary (Bowles & McGinn, 2005). At work, women can work for family-friendly reforms such as job-protected maternity leaves. Beyond work–home issues, negotiations for valued positions, experiences, and resources are important social interactions on the road to top leadership positions. Thus, another approach to reducing the leadership gap is to enhance women's negotiation power and restructure negotiations to their advantage (Bowles & McGinn, 2005). For example, research has shown that the term negotiation is laden with gendered connotations, so one approach would be to reframe negotiation situations in nongendered terms such as "asking" situations.

Women who are aware of the labyrinth may circumvent barriers by starting their own ventures (Wirth, 2001). Women-owned businesses account for 40% of all privately owned businesses, employ more than 13 million people, and generate $1.9 trillion in sales; businesses owned by women of color grew faster than all privately held businesses between 2002 and 2008 (Center for Women's Business Research, 2008). Women's successful foray into entrepreneurship is working to change the face of business, and by extension leadership, as we know it.

Many of the impediments women face in the leadership domain stem from the incongruity between the female gender role and the leadership role. Women face a double standard in the leadership role: They must come across as extremely competent but also as appropriately "feminine," a set of standards men are not held to (Eagly & Carli, 2003). One way women can increase their perceived warmth and their influence is by combining communal qualities such as warmth and friendliness with agentic qualities such as exceptional competence and assertiveness (Carli, 2001; Rudman & Glick, 2001). Additionally, the transformational leadership style is particularly beneficial for women because it is not a markedly masculine style. This style encompasses traditionally feminine behaviors such as being considerate and supportive, and is strongly associated with leadership effectiveness (see Chapter 9). Recent research suggests that blending individualized consideration with inspirational motivation is prudent for women seeking leadership advancement (Vinkenburg, van Engen, Eagly, & Johannesen-Schmidt, 2011). The incongruity between the leadership role and the female gender role does appear to be decreasing (Eagly & Carli, 2007). Recent research indicates that women have become significantly more masculine—for example, becoming more assertive and valuing leadership and power more as job attributes, without losing their femininity (Konrad, Ritchie, Lieb, & Corrigall, 2000; Twenge, 2001). In addition, evidence suggests that the leadership role is starting to be seen as less masculine and more androgynous (Koenig et al., 2011; Schein, 2001).

Motives for Removing the Barriers

While the barriers discussed in the previous sections are generally conceived to be against women, the labyrinth can be generalized to encompass other nondominant groups such as ethnic, racial, and sexual minorities as well. There are a number of important motivations for removing these barriers into the upper echelons of leadership.

First, doing so will fulfill the promise of equal opportunity by allowing everyone the possibility of taking on leadership roles, from the boardroom to the Senate floor. This larger and more demographically diverse pool of candidates not only makes it easier to find talented people, but it also facilitates greater levels of organizational success.

Second, promoting a richly diverse group of women into leadership roles will not only help make societal institutions, businesses, and governments more representative, but it can also contribute to more ethical, productive, innovative, and financially successful organizations that demonstrate higher levels of collective intelligence and are less rife with conflict (Bernardi, Bosco, & Columb, 2009; Catalyst, 2004; Forsyth, 2010; Miller & Del Carmen Triana, 2009; Nielsen & Huse, 2010; Woolley, Chabris, Pentland, Hashmi, & Malone, 2010).

Despite these barriers, women are showing a greater presence in top leadership positions. With changes in workplace norms and developmental opportunities for women; greater gender equity in domestic responsibilities; greater negotiation power of women, especially regarding the work–home balance; the effectiveness and predominance of women-owned businesses; and changes in the incongruity between women and leadership, we likely will see more women in elite leadership roles.

Strengths

A consideration of the effects of gender on leadership has important implications for a comprehensive understanding of leadership. Contemporary approaches to gender and leadership involve questions that directly affect leadership success, such as style and effectiveness differences between men and women, and the varied barriers confronting women. Gender is integral to contemporary notions of effective leadership styles that have morphed from a traditional masculine, autocratic style to the more feminine or androgynous styles of democratic and transformational leadership. Developing a more androgynous conception of leadership will enhance leadership effectiveness by giving people the opportunity to engage in the best leadership practices, and not by restricting people to those behaviors that are most appropriate for their gender.

Research on gender and leadership is productive in both dispelling myths about the gender gap and shining a light on aspects of the gender barriers that are difficult to see and therefore are often overlooked. For example, gender biases generally are no longer overt but more often take the form of subtle and implicit preconceptions and discrimination, making them particularly potent and pernicious. These biases have a detrimental impact on the perception and evaluation of women, and they limit the range of leadership behavior deemed appropriate for women. In addition, awareness of these biases can threaten women in the leadership role. The changes needed to overcome these problems within organizations and society can occur only when we are aware of these often subtle and disguised prejudices.

Understanding the many components of the labyrinth will give us the tools necessary to combat this inequality from many perspectives, including individual, interpersonal, organizational, and societal approaches. In addition, this research addresses larger, more significant considerations about gender and social systems. For example, it acknowledges the profound power division between men and women, and it opens up dialogue on structural questions such as the gendered division of work in society. By not ignoring issues of gender and leadership but rather avidly attempting to understand them, we can help ensure that women have equal opportunity in attaining influential leadership positions, that organizations and constituents have access to the greatest talent pool when selecting leaders, and that there is greater gender diversity in the ranks of leadership, which has been linked to organizational success.

Criticisms

Issues of gender and leadership can be subsumed under a more general topic of leadership and diversity. This perspective involves an understanding of the impact of various demographic characteristics on leadership, including—but not limited to—gender, race, ethnicity, and sexual orientation (Chemers & Murphy, 1995; Hoyt & Chemers, 2008). However, unlike the research examining gender and leadership, research into minority leaders is scant (Hoyt & Chemers, 2008). Although some of the issues surrounding minorities in leadership may bear similarities to those surrounding women (e.g., minorities also face negative stereotypes and resulting difficulties ascending the leadership hierarchy), the underlying dynamics and mechanisms are no doubt distinct (Gurin, 1985; Stangor, Lynch, Duan, & Glass, 1992). Leadership researchers should put a greater emphasis on understanding the role of race, ethnicity, sexual orientation and other types of diversity, as well as important interactive effects between, for example, race and gender (Smith & Stewart, 1983), in leadership processes.

Much of the research examining gender in leadership has taken place in Western contexts; research on gender and leadership in other contexts is sparse. Because most of the findings regarding female leaders stem from the culturally defined role of women in society, many of the findings discussed in this chapter will not generalize well across cultures in which the roles of women and men differ. Therefore, we must realize the limited generalizability of the extant literature on gender and leadership, and researchers should expand their purview to address gender and leadership from a cross-cultural perspective. A final criticism concerns the dearth of essential, complementary research agendas on the domestic sphere. Research on gender and leadership focuses on decreasing the gender gap in leadership positions, thereby lessening gender segregation at work; however, the leadership gap will not be closed without a concurrent focus on closing the gender gap at home.

Application

Although the gender gap in influential leadership positions remains clearly visible, there is evidence that it is starting to close. Understanding the obstacles that make up the labyrinth and tactics to eradicate the inequality will make it easier for women to reach top positions. The labyrinth has many barriers, and the necessary changes occur at many levels, ranging from individual and interpersonal levels to organizational and societal levels. Prejudice plays an important role in the interpersonal and individual levels; the first step in dealing with these biases is to become aware of them in others and in ourselves. Women are faced with the problem of needing to bolster their leadership competence with appropriate "femaleness": Adopting behaviors such as individualized consideration and inspirational motivation is a promising approach to overcome these biased expectations. In addition, women's use of effective negotiation techniques can aid them in procuring the resources they need at work and at home to augment their leadership advancement.

Changes are also taking place at more macro-organizational and societal levels that will contribute to greater gender equality in leadership. For example, changes in organizational culture, women's career development, mentoring opportunities for women, and increased numbers of women in strategic positions will increase the presence of women in prominent leadership roles. At the societal level, structural changes regarding a more equitable distribution of child rearing and domestic duties are also contributing to the influx of women into elite positions.

References

American Bar Association. (2011). *Commission on women in the profession: A current glance at women in the law 2011*. Retrieved September 23, 2011, from http://www.americanbar.org/content/dam/aba/uncategorized/2011/cwp_current_glance_statistics_2011.authcheckdam.pdf

Andrews, P. H. (1992). Sex and gender differences in group communication: Impact on the facilitation process. *Small Group Research, 23*(1), 74–94.

Ayman, R., Korabik, K., & Morris, S. (2009). Is transformational leadership always perceived as effective? Male subordinates' devaluation of female transformational leaders. *Journal of Applied Social Psychology, 39,* 852–879.

Babcock, L., & Laschever, S. (2003). *Women don't ask: Negotiation and the gender divide.* Princeton, NJ: Princeton University Press.

Bartol, K. M., & Butterfield, D. A. (1976). Sex effects in evaluating leaders. *Journal of Applied Psychology, 61,* 446–454.

Bass, B. M. (1985). Leadership: Good, better, best. *Organizational Dynamics, 13,* 26–40.

Belkin, L. (2003, October 26). The opt-out revolution. *The New York Times,* p. 42.

Belkin, L. (2008, June 15). When mom and dad share it all. *The New York Times.* Retrieved June 15, 2008, from http://www.nytimes.com/2008/06/15/magazine/15parenting-t.html?ref=jobs&pagewanted=all

Bell, E., & Nkomo, S. (2001). *Our separate ways: Black and white women and the struggle for professional identity.* Boston: Harvard Business School Press.

Bergeron, D. M., Block, C. J., & Echtenkamp, B. A. (2006). Disabling the able: Stereotype threat and women's work performance. *Human Performance, 19*(2), 133–158.

Bernardi, R. A., Bosco, S. M., & Columb, V. L. (2009). Does female representation on boards of directors associate with the "Most Ethical Companies" list? *Corporate Reputation Review, 12,* 270–280.

Bielby, D. D., & Bielby, W. T. (1988). She works hard for the money: Household responsibilities and the allocation of work effort. *American Journal of Sociology, 93,* 1031–1059.

Blank, R., & Slipp, S. (1994). *Voices of diversity.* New York: AMACOM.

Book, E. W. (2000). *Why the best man for the job is a woman.* New York: HarperCollins.

Bowles, H. R., Babcock, L., & Lai, L. (2007). Social incentives for gender differences in the propensity to initiate negotiations: Sometimes it does hurt to ask. *Organizational Behavior and Human Decision Processes, 103,* 84–103.

Bowles, H. R., & McGinn, K. L. (2005). Claiming authority: Negotiating challenges for women leaders. In D. M. Messick & R. M. Kramer (Eds.), *The psychology of leadership: New perspectives and research* (pp. 191–208). Mahwah, NJ: Lawrence Erlbaum.

Bowman, G., Worthy, N., & Greyser, S. (1965). Are women executives people? *Harvard Business Review, 43*(4), 14–28, 164–178.

Burgess, D., & Borgida, E. (1999). Who women are, who women should be: Descriptive and prescriptive gender stereotyping in sex discrimination. *Psychology, Public Policy, & Law, 5,* 665–692.

Burns, J. M. (1978). *Leadership.* New York: Plenum.

Carli, L. L. (2001). Gender and social influence. *Journal of Social Issues, 57,* 725–741.

Catalyst. (2004). *The bottom line: Connecting corporate performance and gender diversity.* New York: Author.

Catalyst. (2011a). *Statistical overview of women in the workplace.* Retrieved September 30, 2011, from http://www.catalyst.org/publication/219/statistical-overview-of-women-in-the-workplace

Catalyst. (2011b). *U.S. labor force, population, and education.* Retrieved October 2, 2011, from http://www.catalyst.org/publication/202/us-labor-force-population-and-education

Catalyst. (2011c). *U.S. women in business.* Retrieved September 21, 2011, from http://www.catalyst.org/publication/132/us-women-in-business

Catalyst. (2011d). *Women MBAs.* Retrieved November 15, 2011, from http://www.catalyst.org/publication/250/women-mbas

Center for American Women and Politics. (2011). *Women in elective office 2011*. Retrieved September 21, 2011, from http://www.cawp.rutgers.edu/fast_facts/levels_of_office/documents/elective.pdf

Center for Women's Business Research. (2008). *Key facts about women owned businesses 2008*. Retrieved May 28, 2009, from http://www.nfwbo.org/facts/index.php

Chemers, M. M. (1997). *An integrative theory of leadership*. Mahwah, NJ: Lawrence Erlbaum.

Chemers, M. M., & Murphy, S. E. (1995). Leadership and diversity in groups and organizations. In M. M. Chemers, S. Oskamp, & M. A. Constanzo (Eds.), *Diversity in organizations: New perspectives for a changing workplace* (pp. 157–190). Thousand Oaks, CA: Sage.

Cooper, C. L., & Lewis, S. (1999). Gender and the changing nature of work. In G. N. Powell (Ed.), *Handbook of gender and work* (pp. 37–46). Thousand Oaks, CA: Sage.

Couric & Co. (2008). *Katie Couric's notebook: Sexism and politics*. Retrieved May 29, 2009, from http://www.cbsnews.com/blogs/2008/06/11/couricandco/entry4174429.shtml

Craig, L. (2006). Does father care mean fathers share? A comparison of how mothers and fathers in intact families spend time with children. *Gender and Society, 20*, 259–281.

Dasgupta, N., & Asgari, S. (2004). Seeing is believing: Exposure to counterstereotypic women leaders and its effect on automatic gender stereotyping. *Journal of Experimental Social Psychology, 40*, 642–658.

Davies, P. G., Spencer, S. J., & Steele, C. M. (2005). Clearing the air: Identity safety moderates the effects of stereotype threat on women's leadership aspirations. *Journal of Personality and Social Psychology, 88*, 276–287.

Deaux, K., & Kite, M. (1993). Gender stereotypes. In F. L. Denmark & M. Paludi (Eds.), *Psychology of women: A handbook of theory and issues* (pp. 107–139). Westport, CT: Greenwood.

Dobbins, G. H., & Platz, S. J. (1986). Sex differences in leadership: How real are they? *Academy of Management Review, 11*, 118–127.

Dodge, K. A., Gilroy, F. D., & Fenzel, L. M. (1995). Requisite management characteristics revisited: Two decades later. *Journal of Social Behavior and Personality, 10*, 253–264.

Eagly, A. H., & Carli, L. L. (2003). The female leadership advantage: An evaluation of the evidence. *Leadership Quarterly, 14*, 807–834.

Eagly, A. H., & Carli, L. L. (2004). Women and men as leaders. In J. Antonakis, R. J. Sternberg, & A. T. Cianciolo (Eds.), *The nature of leadership* (pp. 279–301). Thousand Oaks, CA: Sage.

Eagly, A. H., & Carli, L. L. (2007). *Through the labyrinth: The truth about how women become leaders*. Boston: Harvard Business School Press.

Eagly, A. H., Johannesen-Schmidt, M. C., & van Engen, M. (2003). Transformational, transactional, and laissez-faire leadership styles: A meta-analysis comparing women and men. *Psychological Bulletin, 129*, 569–591.

Eagly, A. H., & Johnson, B. T. (1990). Gender and leadership style: A meta-analysis. *Psychological Bulletin, 108*(2), 233–256.

Eagly, A. H., & Karau, S. J. (1991). Gender and the emergence of leaders: A meta-analysis. *Journal of Personality and Social Psychology, 60*, 685–710.

Eagly, A. H., & Karau, S. J. (2002). Role congruity theory of prejudice toward female leaders. *Psychological Review, 109*, 573–598.

Eagly, A. H., Karau, S. J., & Makhijani, M. G. (1995). Gender and the effectiveness of leaders: A meta-analysis. *Psychological Bulletin, 117*, 125–145.

Eagly, A. H., Makhijani, M., & Klonsky, B. (1992). Gender and the evaluation of leaders: A meta-analysis. *Psychological Bulletin, 111*, 3–22.

Ensher, E. A., & Murphy, S. E. (2005). *Power mentoring: How successful mentors and protégés get the most out of their relationships*. San Francisco: Jossey-Bass.

Feingold, A. (1994). Gender differences in personality: A meta-analysis. *Psychological Bulletin, 116*, 429–456.

Fiske, S. (1998). Stereotyping, prejudice, and discrimination. In D. T. Gilbert, S. T. Fiske, & G. Lindzey (Eds.), *The handbook of social psychology* (4th ed., Vol. 2, pp. 982–1026). Boston: McGraw-Hill.

Fiske, S., Bersoff, D. N., Borgida, E., Deaux, K., & Heilman, M. E. (1991). Social science research on trial: Use of sex stereotyping research in *Price Waterhouse v. Hopkins*. *American Psychologist, 46*(10), 1049–1060.

Fletcher, J. K. (2001). *Disappearing acts: Gender, power, and relational practice at work*. Boston: MIT Press.

Forsyth, D. R. (2010). *Group dynamics* (5th ed.). Belmont, CA: Wadsworth.

Franke, G. R., Crown, D. F., & Spake, D. F. (1997). Gender differences in ethical perceptions of business practices: A social role theory perspective. *Journal of Applied Psychology, 82*, 920–934.

Freud, S. (1965). *New introductory lectures on psychoanalysis: Femininity*. New York: W. W. Norton.

Galinsky, E., Aumann, K., & Bond, J. (2008). *Times are changing: Gender and generation at work and at home.* Retrieved November 14, 2011, from http://familiesandwork.org/site/research/reports/Times_Are_Changing.pdf

Glick, P., & Fiske, S. T. (1999). Sexism and other "isms": Independence, status, and the ambivalent content of stereotypes. In W. B. Swann, Jr., & J. H. Langlois (Eds.), *Sexism and stereotypes in modern society: The gender science of Janet Taylor Spence* (pp. 193–221). Washington, DC: American Psychological Association.

Goldin, C., & Rouse, C. (2000). Orchestrating impartiality: The impact of "blind" auditions on female musicians. *American Economic Review, 90*(4), 715–741.

Greenwald, A. G., McGhee, D. E., & Schwartz, J. L. K. (1998). Measuring individual differences in implicit cognition: The implicit association test. *Journal of Personality and Social Psychology, 74,* 1464–1480.

Gurin, P. (1985). Women's gender consciousness. *Public Opinion Quarterly, 49,* 143–163.

Hall, D. T. (1972). A model of coping with role conflict: The role behavior of college-educated women. *Administrative Science Quarterly, 17*(4), 471–486.

Hamilton, D. L., Stroessner, S. J., & Driscoll, D. M. (1994). Social cognition and the study of stereotyping. In P. G. Devine, D. L. Hamilton, & T. M. Ostrom (Eds.), *Social cognition: Impact on social psychology* (pp. 291–321). New York: Academic Press.

Heilman, M. E. (1997). Sex discrimination and the affirmative action remedy: The role of sex stereotypes. *Journal of Business Ethics, 16,* 877–889.

Heilman, M. E. (2001). Description and prescription: How gender stereotypes prevent women's ascent up the organizational ladder. *Journal of Social Issues, 57,* 657–674.

Helgesen, S. (1990). *The female advantage: Women's ways of leadership.* New York: Doubleday.

Hennig, M., & Jardin, A. (1977). *The managerial woman.* Garden City, NY: Anchor.

Hewlett, S. A. (2002). *Creating a life: Professional women and the quest for children.* New York: Talk Miramax.

Hoyt, C. L. (2010). Women, men, and leadership: Exploring the gender gap at the top. *Social and Personality Psychology Compass, 4,* 484–498.

Hoyt, C., & Blascovich, J. (2007). Leadership efficacy and women leaders' responses to stereotype activation. *Group Processes and Intergroup Relations, 10,* 595–616.

Hoyt, C., & Blascovich, J. (2010). The role of self-efficacy and stereotype activation on cardiovascular, behavioral and self-report responses in the leadership domain. *Leadership Quarterly, 21,* 89–103.

Hoyt, C. L., & Chemers, M. M. (2008). Social stigma and leadership: A long climb up a slippery ladder. In C. L. Hoyt, G. R. Goethals, & D. R. Forsyth (Eds.), *Leadership at the crossroads: Leadership and psychology* (Vol. 1, pp. 165–180). Westport, CT: Praeger.

Hoyt, C., Johnson, S., Murphy, S., & Skinnell, K. (2010). The impact of blatant stereotype activation and group sex-composition on female leaders. *Leadership Quarterly, 21,* 716–732.

Hymowitz, C., & Schellhardt, T. D. (1986, March 24). The glass ceiling: Why women can't seem to break the invisible barrier that blocks them from the top jobs. *The Wall Street Journal,* pp. D1, D4–D5.

Inter-Parliamentary Union. (2011). *Women in national parliaments.* Retrieved September 21, 2011, from http://www.ipu.org/wmn-e/classif.htm

Jacobson, M. B., & Effertz, J. (1974). Sex roles and leadership perceptions of the leaders and the led. *Organizational Behavior and Human Performance, 12,* 383–396.

Kanter, R. (1977). *Men and women of the corporation.* New York: Basic Books.

Keith, K., & McWilliams, A. (1999). The returns to mobility and job search by gender: Additional evidence from the NLSY. *Industrial & Labor Relations Review, 52*(3), 460–477.

Knight, P. A., & Saal, F. E. (1984). Effects of gender differences and selection agent expertise on leader influence and performance evaluations. *Organizational Behavior and Human Performance, 34,* 225–243.

Knoke, D., & Ishio, Y. (1998). The gender gap in company job training. *Work and Occupations, 25*(2), 141–167.

Koenig, A. M., Eagly, A. H., Mitchell, A. A., & Ristikari, T. (2011). Are leader stereotypes masculine? A meta-analysis of three research paradigms. *Psychological Bulletin, 137,* 616–642.

Konrad, A. M., Ritchie, J. E., Jr., Lieb, P., & Corrigall, E. (2000). Sex differences and similarities in job attribute preferences: A meta-analysis. *Psychological Bulletin, 126,* 593–641.

Kray, L., Reb, J., Galinsky, A., & Thompson, L. (2004). Stereotype reactance at the bargaining table: The effect of stereotype activation and power on claiming and creating value. *Personality and Social Psychology Bulletin, 30,* 399–411.

Kray, L. J., Thompson, L., & Galinsky, A. (2001). Battle of the sexes: Gender stereotype confirmation and reactance in negotiations. *Journal of Personality & Social Psychology, 80,* 942–958.

Kunda, Z., & Spencer, S. J. (2003). When do stereotypes come to mind and when do they color judgment? A goal-based theory of stereotype activation and application. *Psychological Bulletin, 129,* 522–544.

Maume, D. J., Jr. (1999). Glass ceilings and glass escalators. *Work & Occupations, 26*(4), 483.

Miller, T., & Del Carmen Triana, M. (2009). Demographic diversity in the boardroom: Mediators of the board diversity-firm performance relationship. *Journal of Management Studies, 46,* 755–786.

Morrison, A., & Von Glinow, M. A. (1990). Women and minorities in management. *American Psychologist, 45,* 200–208.

National Center for Education Statistics (NCES). (2008). *The condition of education 2008.* Retrieved November 15, 2011, from http://nces.ed.gov/pubs2008/2008031 .pdf

Nielsen, S., & Huse, M. (2010). The contribution of women on boards of directors: Going beyond the surface. *Corporate Governance—An International Review, 18,* 136–148.

Nieva, V. E., & Gutek, B. A. (1981). *Women and work: A psychological perspective.* New York: Praeger.

Ohlott, P. J., Ruderman, M. N., & McCauley, C. D. (1994). Gender differences in managers' developmental job experiences. *Academy of Management Journal, 37,* 46–67.

Pailhe, A., & Solaz, A. (2006). Time with children: Do fathers and mothers replace each other when one parent is unemployed? *European Journal of Population, 24,* 211–236. doi: 10.1007/s10680–007–9143–5

Powell, G. N. (1990). One more time: Do female and male managers differ? *Academy of Management Executive, 4,* 68–75.

Powell, G. N., & Graves, L. M. (2003). *Women and men in management* (3rd ed.). Thousand Oaks, CA: Sage.

Ragins, B. R., Townsend, B., & Mattis, M. (1998). Gender gap in the executive suite: CEOs and female executives report on breaking the glass ceiling. *Academy of Management Executive, 12,* 28–42.

Rosener, J. (1995). *America's competitive secret: Utilizing women as a management strategy.* New York: Oxford University Press.

Rudman, L. A. (1998). Self-promotion as a risk factor for women: The costs and benefits of counter-stereotypical impression management. *Journal of Personality and Social Psychology, 74,* 629–645.

Rudman, L. A., & Glick, P. (2001). Prescriptive gender stereotypes and backlash toward agentic women. *Journal of Social Issues, 57,* 743–762.

Ryan, M. K., Haslam, S. A., Hersby, M. D., & Bongiorno, R. (2011). Think crisis–think female: The glass cliff and contextual variation in the think manager–think male stereotype. *Journal of Applied Psychology, 96,* 470–484.

Schein, V. E. (2001). A global look at psychological barriers to women's progress in management. *Journal of Social Issues, 57,* 675–688.

Sekaquaptewa, D., & Thompson, M. (2003). Solo status, stereotype threat, and performance expectancies: Their effects on women's performance. *Journal of Experimental Social Psychology, 39,* 68–74.

Small, D. A., Gelfand, M., Babcock, L., & Gettman, H. (2007). Who goes to the bargaining table? The influence of gender and framing on the initiation of negotiation. *Journal of Personality and Social Psychology, 93,* 600–613.

Smith, A., & Stewart, A. J. (1983). Approaches to studying racism and sexism in black women's lives. *Journal of Social Issues, 39,* 1–15.

Stangor, C., Lynch, L., Duan, C., & Glass, B. (1992). Categorization of individuals on the basis of multiple social features. *Journal of Personality and Social Psychology, 62,* 207–218.

Thoits, P. A. (1992). Identity structures and psychological well-being: Gender and marital status comparisons. *Social Psychology Quarterly, 55,* 236–256.

Tsui, A. S., & Gutek, B. A. (1984). A role set analysis of gender differences in performance, affective relationship, and career success of industrial middle managers. *Academy of Management Journal, 27,* 619–635.

Twenge, J. M. (2001). Change in women's assertiveness in response to status and roles: A cross-temporal meta-analysis, 1931–1993. *Journal of Personality and Social Psychology, 81,* 133–145.

U.S. Bureau of Labor Statistics. (2010a). *Current population survey, annual averages: Household data.* (Characteristics of the employed, Table 9: Employed persons by occupation, sex, and age). Retrieved September 21, 2011, from http://www.bls.gov/cps/cpsaat9.pdf

U.S. Bureau of Labor Statistics. (2010b). *Current population survey, annual averages: Household data.* (Table 11: Employed persons by detailed occupation, sex, race, and Hispanic or Latino ethnicity). Retrieved September 21, 2011, from http://www.bls.gov/cps/cpsaat11.pdf

U.S. Department of Defense. (2008). *Active duty military personnel by service by rank/grade* (for September 30, 2008). Retrieved April 30, 2009, from http://siadapp .dmdc.osd.mil/personnel/MILITARY/rg0809f.pdf and http://siadapp.dmdc.osd.mil/personnel/MILI-TARY/rg0809.pdf

van Engen, M. L., Leeden, R. van der, & Willemsen, T. M. (2001). Gender, context and leadership styles: A field study. *Journal of Occupational and Organizational Psychology, 74,* 581–598.

van Engen, M. L., & Willemsen, T. M. (2004). Sex and leadership styles: A meta-analysis of research published in the 1990s. *Psychological Reports, 94,* 3–18.

Vecchio, R. P. (2002). Leadership and gender advantage. *Leadership Quarterly, 13,* 643–671.

Vinkenburg, C. J., van Engen, M. L., Eagly, A. H., & Johannesen-Schmidt, M. C. (2011). An exploration of stereotypical beliefs about leadership styles: Is transformational leadership a route to women's promotion? *The Leadership Quarterly, 22,* 10–21.

Williams, C. L. (1992). The glass escalator: Hidden advantages for men in the "female" professions. *Social Problems, 39,* 253–267.

Williams, C. L. (1995). *Still a man's world: Men who do "women's work."* Berkeley: University of California Press.

Williams, J. (2010). *Reshaping the work-family debate: Why men and class matter.* Cambridge, MA: Harvard University Press.

Wirth, L. (2001). *Breaking through the glass ceiling: Women in management.* Geneva: International Labour Office.

Woolley, A. W., Chabris, C. F., Pentland, A., Hashmi, N., & Malone, T. M. (2010). Evidence for a collective intelligence factor in the performance of human groups. *Science, 330,* 686–688.

CHAPTER 23

Generational Differences in Workplace Behavior

John Bret Becton[1]
University of Southern Mississippi

Harvell Jack Walker
Auburn University

Allison Jones-Farmer
Auburn University

Generational Differences in Workplace Behavior

As the average age of the U.S. workforce continues to increase, much attention has focused on the fact that the workforce is largely comprised of three generations (i.e., Baby Boomers, Generation X, and Millennials; Eisner, 2005). The popular press frequently stresses the need for organizations to recruit, reward, and manage these employees differently because of generational differences in attitudes, values, and desires (Jurkiewicz & Brown, 1998; Kupperschmidt, 2000; Macky, Gardner, & Forsyth, 2008). Many have suggested that failure to recognize these differences can lead to negative organizational outcomes such as intergenerational workplace conflict, misunderstanding and miscommunication, poor working relationships, reduced employee productivity, poor employee well-being, lower innovation, and fewer organizational citizenship behaviors (Adams, 2000; Bradford, 1993; Dittman, 2005; Fyock, 1990; Jurkiewicz, 2000; Kupperschmidt, 2000; Smola & Sutton, 2002; Westerman & Yamamura, 2007; Yu & Miller, 2003). As a result, human resource (HR) management specialists, managers, and researchers have expressed interest in identifying ways to manage and work with people from different generations (Cennamo & Gardner, 2008).

Considering the extent to which generational stereotypes are commonly accepted, it is surprising that empirical evidence of generational differences is relatively sparse (Twenge, Campbell,

Hoffman, & Lance, 2010), and the research that exists is somewhat contradictory. One stream of research supports the general stereotypes concerning generational differences in work values (Cennamo & Gardner, 2008; Smola & Sutton, 2002), personal values (Egri & Ralston, 2004; Lyons, Duxbury, & Higgins, 2007), leadership behaviors (Sessa, Kabacoff, Deal, & Brown, 2007), psychological/personality traits (Twenge & Campbell, 2008), turnover intentions, and organizational commitment (D'Amato & Herzfeldt, 2008; for a complete review of evidence for generational differences, see Twenge, 2010). Another stream of research has found few, if any, generational differences in a variety of employee characteristics such as personality and motivation (cf. Hart, Schembri, Bell, & Armstrong, 2003; Jurkiewicz, 2000; Levy, Carroll, Francoeur, & Logue, 2005; Wong, Gardiner, Lang, & Coulon, 2008). More recently, Trzesniewski and Donnellan (2010) found little evidence of generational differences in a variety of traits, attitudes, and behaviors including egotism, self-enhancement, individualism, self-esteem, locus of control, hopelessness, happiness, life satisfaction, loneliness, antisocial behavior, time spent working or watching television, political activity, the importance of religion, and the importance of social status.

Considering these inconsistent findings, there exists a great deal of controversy about whether or not generational differences exist at all (cf. Arnett, 2010; Roberts, Edmonds, & Grijalva, 2010; Terracciano, 2010), with some suggesting that perceived generational differences are a product of popular culture versus social science (Giancola, 2006). Scholars have also noted that observed generational differences may be explained, at least in part, by age, life stage, or career stage effects instead of generation (Arnett, 2010; Carlson & Gjerde, 2009; Foster, Campbell, & Twenge, 2003; Kohut, 1971; Parry & Urwin, 2011). According to this view, human development is punctuated by different life stages that involve unique cognitive, emotional, and behavioral experiences (cf. Levinson, 1980), and differences in attitudes or values that are often attributed to generations may

be explained by the nature of jobs held by older workers or their current life cycle. Studies that examine and test generational differences are valuable because generational studies have important applied and theoretical implications (Trzesniewski & Donnellan, 2010). Accordingly, accepting common generational stereotypes without empirical support can have potentially adverse effects on both research and practice. As a result, more generational research is needed.

In this study, we provide further insight into generational effects in the workplace and make a contribution by investigating possible generational differences in workplace behaviors versus values, attitudes, or personality. Specifically, we draw from generational cohort theory (Mannheim, 1952) and common generational stereotypes regarding attitudes and values to examine if generational membership explains differences in several important workplace behaviors (i.e., job mobility, disciplinary action, and willingness to work overtime). The mixed support for generational differences in values, beliefs, etc. reviewed above suggests efforts intended to promote effective management of workers from different generations may not be necessary. However, we argue that it is important to examine possible generational differences in workplace behaviors before arriving at such a conclusion.

We also make a contribution in our analytic approach. One critical issue in most generational differences studies is the age–generation confound. In an attempt to address this issue, some researchers have suggested segmenting generations into "cusp" and "core" cohort groups (Egri & Ralston, 2004) whereby individuals born within the last 5 years of a generation are considered part of the "cusp" group while those born within the remainder of the generation's birth years are considered part of the "core" group. While this approach provides important insight because it allows researchers to determine if there are any significant differences in the values/behaviors of the "cusp" and "core" groups of each generation, it also has several limitations. For example, there is no theoretical rationale for choosing 5 years to identify the cusp/core group. Additionally, this approach fails to consider that those born in the

cusp/core gen group

earlier years of a generation might also be different from those in the middle or the end of a generation. To address these limitations, we include a measure of individuals' "relative age" (i.e., the difference in each individual's age from the mean age of his/her generation) in each of our analyses. This allows different weighting to be given to those who are far away from the core as defined by the mean of each generation. In other words, someone with a large, positive relative age or large, negative relative age is at the cusp of two generations. While we are unable to completely rule out age, life stage, or career stage effects with this approach, it does provide unique insight into the effects of age increases within each generation.

Generational Cohort Theory

The concept of generations and their effects have long been discussed by researchers in anthropology, sociology, and social psychology (Hung, Gu, & Yim, 2007). A generation, often called a cohort, consists of people of similar age in a similar location who experienced similar social, historical, and life events (Kupperschmidt, 2000; Mannheim, 1972). These shared experiences (e.g., industrialization, fundamental changes, cataclysmic events, and tragedies) differentiate one generation from another (Jurkiewicz & Brown, 1998) because they have a profound effect on the attitudes, values, beliefs, and expectations of generational groups (Abramson & Inglehart, 1995; Inglehart, 1977, 1990; Inglehart & Norris, 2003). Rogler (2002) proposed that the formation of a generation's collective identity occurs in the following ways. First, significant events such as disasters, wars, or revolutions challenge the existing social order and lay the foundation for the emergence of a new generation. Second, these events have a stronger effect on the "coming-of-age" group than on other age groups coexisting during the same period of time because people tend to form value systems during the preadult years whereas the values of older generations are already solidified (McCrae et al., 2002). Third, this shared set of values and goals is supported by peers in the same generation and persists throughout adulthood (Kupperschmidt, 2000; Macky et al., 2008). In summary, commonly experienced life events have a stronger, more enduring effect on the "coming-of-age" cohort group than on other cohort groups who also experienced the same events.

Current Generations in the Workplace

Researchers generally agree that three generations currently dominate the workforce (i.e., Baby Boomers, Generation X, and Millennials), although the labels and periods of years those labels encompass vary (Lyons et al., 2007; Sessa et al., 2007). Because no exact age range for each cohort exists, comparing results of empirical studies of generational differences is difficult. In the passages that follow, we summarize the popular stereotypes related to values and beliefs often associated with Baby Boomers (born between 1945 and 1964), Generation X (born between 1965 and 1979), and Millennials (born in 1980 or later). However, before doing so, we make several notes regarding our summary. First, empirical support for the associated values and beliefs for each generation is lacking and we present them primarily as stereotypes. Second, we note that there is little to no evidence that links important events experienced by generational cohort groups and their stereotypical values/characteristics. Third, the presented stereotypes are associated with Western culture generations. As argued by Parry and Urwin (2011) and discussed in more detail in the future research section of this manuscript, national culture is likely to have a significant influence on generational values, attitudes, and behaviors.

Baby Boomers

Baby Boomers were born between the early 1940s and mid-1960s (Sessa et al., 2007). Boomers, as they are often called, were the result of the persistently high birth rates in America between 1945 and the 1960s and, as a result, this generation is densely populated (Lyons et al., 2007). Because this generation comprises such a large segment of society, Boomers have had a strong generational presence (i.e., significant influence on society). Events that shaped the Boomers generation include the Vietnam War, the Watergate scandal

(Lancaster & Stillman, 2002), Woodstock (Adams, 2000), the civil rights movement, the Kennedy and King assassinations, and the sexual revolution (Bradford, 1993). Boomers are stereotypically described as achievement oriented (O'Bannon, 2001), independent, in control of their own destinies (Mitchell, 1998), respectful of authority (Allen, 2004), loyal and attached to organizations (Hart, 2006; Loomis, 2000), and diligent on the job (Yu & Miller, 2003). Boomers are also often viewed as competitive, and they tend to measure success materially (Eisner, 2005). Some empirical evidence supports many of the stereotypical values associated with Boomers. For example, Egri and Ralston (2004) found that Boomers were higher than both older generations and GenXers in self-enhancement values (e.g., achievement, hedonism, power). Additionally, Boomers were found to be higher in self-reliance, hard work, and work centrality than younger generations (Meriac, Woehr, & Banister, 2010).

Generation X

Generation X, or Gen X (Coupland, 1991), was born between 1965 and 1979 and is defined by life experiences such as the age of economic uncertainty, recessions, high unemployment, inflation, downsizing, and high divorce rates among their parents (Kupperschmidt, 2000; Lyons et al., 2007). It is also worth noting that many GenXers are the children of compulsive workers which is posited to have had a dramatic impact on the attitudes and values of this generation (Eisner, 2005). The popular press has also noted that many GenXers were school-age children who spent part of their day unsupervised at home while their parents worked. Therefore, they are believed to be individualistic, distrustful of corporations, lacking in loyalty, focused on balancing their work and personal lives (Eisner, 2005), financially self-reliant, and entrepreneurial risk takers (de Meuse, Bergmann, & Lester, 2001; Tulgan, 1995). Commonly accepted stereotypes suggest that GenXers are also more likely to leave an employer for more challenging work, a higher salary, or better benefits because they grew up in an era where organizational loyalty and commitment were not regularly rewarded with job security (Hays, 1999; Loomis, 2000). Research appears

to support this assertion as Smola and Sutton (2002) found GenXers to be less loyal, more "me" oriented, expectant of promotion sooner than older generations, and less likely to view work as an important part of one's life. Other perceived characteristics of this generation include being outcome focused, skeptical (Francis-Smith, 2004), and desiring of specific and constructive feedback (Allen, 2004). Empirical support for these stereotypical values is limited, but Egri and Ralston (2004) found that GenXers attributed significantly higher importance to openness to change values (e.g., self-direction, stimulation) but lower importance to self-enhancement values (e.g., achievement, hedonism, power) than Boomers. Additionally, Meriac et al. (2010) found that GenXers were lower in centrality of work than Boomers.

Millennials

There is little agreement regarding the label for the most recent cohort to enter the workforce. Referred to as Millennials, Nexters (Howe, Strauss, & Matson, 2000), the Net Generation (Tapscott, 1998), and Generation Y (Neuborne & Kerwin, 1999), this generation typically begins with birth years between 1980 and 1983 but has no agreed-upon "cutoff" date for inclusion (Sessa et al., 2007). Millennials are the first "high-tech" generation, having never known life before cell phones, personal computers, and ATMs were commonplace (Mitchell, 1998; Ryan, 2000). Additionally, the globalization of society and the marketplace is thought to have had a tremendous impact on their values (Howe et al., 2000). Millennials are the most racially and ethnically diverse of the four generations (Mitchell, 1998) and, as a result, they are thought to value diversity and change (Patterson, 2005). Common stereotypes for this generation include being distrustful of organizations, having a strong desire for meaningful work (Ryan, 2000), holding lifelong learning as a high priority, and viewing family as the key to happiness (Mitchell, 1998). Similar to Boomers, Millennials are thought to feel a strong desire to succeed and measure their own success by the meaningfulness of work (Eisner, 2005). Research findings supporting these contentions are somewhat sparse although

Millennials have been found to value leisure more than other generations and work harder than Generation X (Meriac et al., 2010).

Hypotheses

As discussed in the previous passages, there is a growing body of literature that suggests generations are distinctive from one another because social, historical, and life experiences (i.e., life history patterns) affect individuals' dominant attitudes and values (cf. Beutell & Wittig-Berman, 2008; Cennamo & Gardner, 2008; D'Amato & Herzfeldt, 2008; Egri & Ralston, 2004; Lyons et al., 2007; Sessa et al., 2007; Smola & Sutton, 2002; Twenge & Campbell, 2008). Because life history patterns are, in part, a function of one's generation (i.e., social and cultural events of one's formative years), many have assumed that generational cohort groups differ in several workplace behaviors because they differ in their formative experiences and resulting values. Our objective is to examine if the three generational cohort groups in Western culture detailed above differ in workplace behavior as predicted by common generational stereotypes.

Job Mobility Behaviors

Job mobility refers to patterns of intra- and interorganizational transitions over the history of a person's career (Hall, 1996; Sullivan, 1999), or a person's history of changing jobs. Previous research has found that the number of times individuals leave jobs is related to future turnover (Ghiselli, 1974; Judge & Watanabe, 1995; Munasinghe & Sigman, 2004). Recognizing this tendency, some organizations prefer to "screen out" applicants who have changed jobs frequently in the past in order to have a stable workforce (Griffeth & Hom, 2001).

Commonly held stereotypes suggest several reasons why generations may differ in terms of job mobility behaviors. In Western cultures, many older generation employees (e.g., Boomers) entered the workforce when the predominant career management strategy was to enter a firm, work hard, be loyal

to the organization, and be rewarded with job security (Hall, 1996). During this era, one's career path often entailed a sequence of jobs within a single organization (Levinson, 1978; Whyte, 1956), and employees were described as not only working for organizations but belonging to them (Whyte, 1956). However, more recent generations (e.g., Gen X and Millennials) entered the workforce in an era where downsizing, layoffs, and offshoring were more commonplace. As a result, employee loyalty and commitment were often not consistently reciprocated with job security (de Meuse et al., 2001; Smola & Sutton, 2002; Tulgan, 1995; Twenge & Campbell, 2008), and the career paths of these younger generations are more likely to involve multiple jobs across multiple organizations (Arthur & Rousseau, 1996).

Because of these generational life experiences, many researchers have posited that generations differ in regard to personal values that are related to employer loyalty and decisions to terminate employment. Boomers are thought to be more likely to remain loyal and attached to an organization (Hart, 2006; Loomis, 2000; Patterson, 2005) because they believe in lifetime employment, company loyalty, and paying one's dues to get ahead (Elsdon & Lyer, 1999). On the other hand, GenXers and Millennials are often perceived as willing to leave a job when better opportunities arise or to look for other opportunities when their current employers are not meeting their needs (Crainer & Dearlove, 1999). GenXers are also thought to be less likely to display loyalty to a particular organization because they are more independent, self-reliant (Hart, 2006), and entrepreneurial (O'Bannon, 2001) than previous generations. In fact, Generation X is said to have pioneered the "free agent" workforce, focusing on keeping skills current to improve their security (Eisner, 2005). Similarly, Millennials are thought to be comfortable with change and less likely to view job security as an important factor in their careers (Hart, 2006). These reported generational stereotypes suggest Boomers will differ from GenXers and Millennials regarding their job mobility behaviors. Therefore, we hypothesize the following:

Hypothesis 1. Boomers will exhibit fewer job mobility behaviors than GenXers and Millennials.

Compliance With Work Rules and Policies

In most organizations, control mechanisms such as work rules, policies, and procedures exist to guide employees in the performance of their jobs. Failure to comply with these rules and policies can be detrimental to organizational success (e.g., litigation, inefficiencies, substandard quality of products or services, etc.), and managers must deal with problem behaviors in the workplace to minimize negative organizational consequences (Orey, 2007; Vardi & Weitz, 2004). Managing such misbehavior often involves taking disciplinary action against employees such as suspension, demotion, and, ultimately, termination. Since models of organizational misbehavior include individual values as antecedents of such behavior (Vardi & Weitz, 2004), it is important to investigate possible generational differences in incidences of rules violations and terminations.

Boomers are often described as having a strong work ethic, highly involved in their jobs (Kupperschmidt, 2000), and diligent on the job (Yu & Miller, 2003). Others suggest that most Boomers respect authority (Allen, 2004) and traditional values in the workplace (O'Bannon, 2001). In contrast, younger generations tend to be viewed as fiercely independent (Lancaster & Stillman, 2002; Tapscott, 1998; Zemke, Raines, & Filipczak, 2000), placing little value on tradition and conformity (Lyons et al., 2007). Empirical studies suggest that younger generations are higher in individualistic traits such as self-esteem, assertiveness, and narcissism (Twenge, 2001; Twenge & Campbell, 2001, 2009; Twenge & Foster, 2010; Twenge, Konrath, Foster, Campbell, & Bushman, 2008). There is also some empirical evidence that indicates younger generations are not as concerned with the impression they make on others, are less formal, and are less likely to conform (Cohen, 2007; Twenge & Campbell, 2008). Coupled with the notion that Generation X and Millennials are less loyal to their employers (Hart, 2006), these tendencies may also result in greater disregard for work rules, policies, and procedures. Consequently, the popular stereotypes suggest that older generations are more respectful of work rules than younger generations. By extension, we hypothesize that older generations will be more compliant, resulting in more instances of rules compliance and fewer terminations.

Hypothesis 2. Boomers will exhibit more instances of compliance and experience fewer instances of termination than GenXers and Millennials.

Willingness to Work Overtime

As discussed earlier, scholars suggest that Generation X is much more concerned with work–life balance (Chao, 2005; Eisner, 2005) than any other generation, and the personal values and goals of GenXers are likely more important than work-related goals (Howe et al., 2000). On the other hand, Boomers and Millennials value material and financial success (Eisner, 2005; Yu & Miller, 2003). Boomers are often described as wanting it all and seeking to get it by working long hours (Eisner, 2005). Researchers suggest that Millennials, raised mostly by Boomers, have experienced powerful pressure from parents to explore financially rewarding vocational paths (Twenge, 2010). As a result, Millennials are said to be driven by personal achievement and success (Pew Research Center, 2007). Some have made the observation that GenXers "work to live" whereas Boomers "live to work" (Chao, 2005). Empirical evidence also suggests that Generation X values work–life balance. For example, Burke (1994) found that Generation X rated a balanced lifestyle as one of the most important job factors while company perks and community status were the least important. Other studies have drawn similar conclusions and found that family and personal relationships are more important to Generation X's personal happiness than their work (Arnett, 2000; Eskilson & Wiley, 1999; Smola & Sutton, 2002). Additionally, the Families and Work Institute (2006) reports that GenXers are more family centric than both Boomers and Millennials.

While work–life balance is related to numerous work behaviors, we argue that willingness to work overtime is one way a greater need for work–life balance is manifested. Since the very nature of overtime involves working more hours than the normal workload, working overtime is likely in direct competition with time devoted to family obligations, hobbies, and activities outside of work (Mayo Foundation for Medical Education and Research, 2008). To test the popular stereotypes suggesting that GenXers differ considerably from other generations concerning the value they attach to work–life balance, we hypothesize that GenXers will exhibit less willingness to work overtime in comparison with Boomers or Millennials.

Hypothesis 3. GenXers will report less willingness to work overtime than Boomers or Millennials.

Method

Sample and Procedure

Study participants were job applicants for a variety of positions in two different hospitals located in the southeastern United States. As part of the application process, job seekers completed a biodata questionnaire (to be described in more detail in the Measures section) and an online application that included birth date. A total of 8,128 applicants were available for analysis. The sample consisted of 1,641 (20.2%) Baby Boomers, 4,972 (61.2%) GenXers, and 1,515 (18.6%) Millennials. The mean age of Baby Boomers was 48.5 years old ($SD = 4.79$), the mean age of GenXers was 30.8 years old ($SD = 5.05$), and the mean age of Millennials was 21.5 years old ($SD = 1.38$). The sample consisted of 301 (3.7%) Native Americans, 116 (1.4%) Asian/Pacific Islanders, 237 (2.9%) Hispanics, 3,955 (48.7) African Americans, and 3,211 (39.5%) Caucasians. A total of 308 (3.8%) did not disclose their race. The sample was comprised of 6,828 (83.2%) females and 1,300 (15.8%) males while 83 (1%) failed to provide their gender.

Measures

To measure differences in workplace behaviors among individuals from different generations, we drew from applicant responses to a biodata measure on an employment application. The instrument used in the present study was developed and validated for use as a selection device in the health care industry (Becton, Matthews, Hartley, & Whitaker, 2009). The biodata instrument presented 40 multiple-choice questions and scenarios that asked applicants about previous life experiences related to high school, college, and work assignments. A sample of items from this instrument was selected for the present study, matching the content of the items to the behaviors of interest.

Job Mobility Behaviors

Job mobility behaviors were measured via two biodata items. The first item asked applicants to indicate the longest time ever spent in one job and response options included 1 (*less than three months*), 2 (*three to six months*), 3 (*six months to one year*), 4 (*one to two years*), 5 (*two to five years*), and 6 (*more than five years*). To aid in the interpretation of our results, the data were re-coded to reflect a more quantitative measure by calculating the midpoint of each category in months (i.e., 1 = 1.5 months, 2 = 4.5 months, etc.). The second item asked applicants the number of jobs held in the last five years and response options included 1 = one, 2 = two, 3 = three, 4 = four, and 5 = five or more. A summary of mean responses to job mobility behavior items by generation is given in Table 23.1.

Compliance With Work Rules

Compliance behaviors were measured using two biodata items. The first item asked applicants to report how their most recent supervisor would rate their attendance. Response options included 1 (*bottom 5%*), 2 (*lower than most*), 3 (*typical of most people*), 4 (*higher than most*), and 5 (*top 5% of all employees*).

The second item asked applicants how their most recent supervisor would rate their appearance as it related to adherence to dress code. Response options included 1 (*never appropriate*), 2 (*sometimes appropriate*), 3 (*usually appropriate*), and 4 (*always appropriate*). A summary of compliance behaviors by generation is given in Table 23.2.

Terminations

Terminations were assessed using a biodata item asking the number of times an applicant had been fired in the past. Response options for this question included 1 (*never*), 2 (*I left a job to avoid being fired*), 3 (*I have been fired once*), and 4 (*I have been fired at least twice*). A summary of terminations by generation is given in Table 23.3.

Willingness to Work Overtime

Willingness to work overtime was measured with one biodata item. This item asked applicants how

| **Table 23.1** | Job Mobility and Control Variables. Sample Means With Standard Deviations Given in Parentheses |

	Job mobility		
Generation	Longest number of months spent in single job	Number of jobs held in the last 5 years	Age
Boomers	72.9 (20.2)	2.0 (1.0)	48.5 (4.8)
Gen X	48.5 (24.7)	2.5 (1.1)	30.8 (5.0)
Millennials	22.6 (16.6)	2.6 (1.1)	21.5 (1.4)
Total	48.6 (27.4)	2.4 (1.1)	32.6 (9.8)

| **Table 23.2** | Compliance With Work Rules |

	Attendance rating				
Generation	Bottom 5% (%)	Lower than most (%)	Typical of most (%)	Higher than most (%)	Top 5% (%)
Boomers	0.18	0.31	13.73	34.05	51.74
Gen X	0.22	0.60	20.90	33.66	44.62
Millennials	0.00	0.40	17.36	34.92	47.26
Total	0.17	0.50	18.79	33.97	46.55
	Appearance rating				
Generation	Never appropriate (%)	Sometimes appropriate (%)	Usually appropriate (%)	Always appropriate (%)	
Boomers	0.06	0.18	5.24	94.52	
Gen X	0.08	0.20	4.89	94.83	
Millennials	0.14	0.48	6.77	92.62	
Total	0.09	0.25	5.30	94.36	

Table values represent the sample percent of a given generation who selected the corresponding column category response.

Table 23.3	Terminations

Generation	Employment history			
	Never been fired (%)	*Quit since likely to be fired (%)*	*Fired once (%)*	*Fired at least twice (%)*
Boomers	78.86	1.91	15.37	3.87
Gen X	80.03	1.79	16.08	2.10
Millennials	87.85	2.06	8.85	1.24
Total	81.22	1.86	14.62	2.30

Table values represent the sample percent of a given generation who selected the corresponding column category response.

Table 23.4	Willingness to Work Overtime

Generation	Willingness to work overtime				
	Never when asked (%)	*Rarely when asked (%)*	*Occasionally when asked (%)*	*Most times when asked (%)*	*Every time when asked (%)*
Boomers	0.24	0.92	11.72	43.28	43.83
Gen X	0.22	0.87	13.31	47.49	38.11
Millennials	0.69	1.31	10.27	47.21	40.52
Total	0.31	0.96	12.44	46.58	39.71

Table values represent the sample percent of a given generation who selected the corresponding column category response.

often their most recent supervisor would say they were willing to work overtime. Response options included 1 (*never when asked*), 2 (*rarely when asked*), 3 (*occasionally when asked*), 4 (*most times when asked*), and 5 (*every time when asked*). A summary of willingness to work overtime by generation is given in Table 23.4.

Control Variables

Scholars have argued that it is difficult to separate the effects of age and generation (Macky et al., 2008; Twenge & Campbell, 2008), and this is a challenge for all generational research (Parry & Urwin, 2011). For example, including age as a covariate is inappropriate because it has a naturally high correlation with generational cohort (Egri & Ralston, 2004). Further, due to the partial nature of coefficients in statistical models, it is not possible to interpret the effect of generation while holding age constant. Thus, in an attempt to explore a potential age confound, we included a control variable labeled "relative age." Relative age was calculated for each applicant by subtracting the mean age for their generation from their own age, and thus measures the distance from their age to the average of their generation (see Table 23.1 for a summary of mean age by generation). The "relative age" is computed by subtracting an individual's age from the mean age of his/her generation. Thus, someone with a "relative age" of 5 is 5 years older than the average for his/her generation. Including this measure as a control variable allowed us to examine the effects of age increases within each generation and provides insight into the potential age confound. In addition to controlling for relative age in our analyses, we also included (when significant) an interaction term between "relative age" and generation. This allows for possible differences in the slope of the relationship between age and the response variables by generation.

Gender was also included as a control variable because research suggests that males and females differ considerably with respect to job mobility (Booth, Franscesconi, & Garcia-Serrano, 1999; Keith & McWilliams, 1997) and willingness to work overtime (Becker & Moen, 1999; Keene & Reynolds, 2005).

Data and Analysis

Due to the different response formats associated with our items (i.e., interval, ordinal, etc.), we used a variety of analyses to test our hypotheses. Additionally, several of the response options were selected by a small percentage of participants and we combined these categories with the next response option. We do not believe this adjustment influenced our results considering the model parameters in an ordinal logistic regression are invariant to collapsing adjacent categories (Greenland, 1994; Murad, Fleischman, Sadetzki, Geyer, & Freedman, 2003), and doing so when some categories are very sparse can improve the asymptotic fit of the maximum likelihood analysis.

The response options for the items relating to job mobility in Hypothesis 1 were measured on an interval scale, thus hierarchical multiple regression analysis was used to test Hypothesis 1. Hypothesis 2 concerns compliance with work rules and terminations. The response options for each of these questions were ordinal. For the item relating to attendance, we combined the first two response options (1 = *bottom 5%*; 2 = *lower than most*) with the third response

option (3 = *typical of most*) because these two options were selected by less than 1% of the sample for each category. This recoding resulted in three categories for attendance rating (3 = *typical of most or lower*; 4 = *higher than most*; 5 = *top 5%*) and ordinal logistic regression was used to test for generational differences. Similarly, the response options for appearance ratings were ordinal, and the two lowest categories (1 = *appearance is never appropriate*; 2 = *appearance is sometimes appropriate*) were combined with the third response option (3 = *appearance is usually appropriate*). This adjustment created a binary coding of the appearance variable (3 = *appearance is not always appropriate*; 4 = *appearance is always appropriate*) and binary logistic regression was used to test Hypothesis 2 with respect to appearance rating. The response options for terminations were ordinal (e.g., 1 = *never*; 2 = *I left a job to avoid being fired*; 3 = *I have been fired once*; 4 = *I have been fired at least twice*) and did not require any adjustment; thus, ordinal logistic regression was used to test Hypothesis 2 with respect to terminations. Finally, we combined the lowest two response options for willingness to work overtime (1 = *never work when asked*; 2 = *rarely work when asked*) with the third category (3 = *occasionally work when asked*) and used ordinal logistic regression to test Hypothesis 3.

Results

Intercorrelations among the study variables are presented in Table 23.5. The correlations among age, longest number of months spent in a single job, and number of jobs held in the last 5 years were computed using Pearson's product moment correlation. All correlations involving attendance rating, appearance rating, and employment history were computed using Spearman's rank correlation. Hypothesis 1 posited that Boomers would exhibit fewer job mobility behaviors than GenXers and Millennials. Table 23.6 presents the hierarchical regression analysis used to test this hypothesis. Step 1 included only the control variables (i.e., gender and relative age). Step 2 included the controls and main effects for generation (R^2 = .34, p < .001). Step 3 included the controls, main effects for generation, and the interaction between relative age and generation ($R^2 = .014$, $p < .001$). We contend that the relative age × generation interactions provided additional insight by investigating the effects of age increases on the variable of interest within each generation. As predicted, the main effect for generation indicated that Boomers reported longer time in one job than GenXers and Millennials. Specifically, when comparing individuals of the same gender and relative age, GenXers spent, on average, 24.16 fewer months on the job (95% CI −25.32, −23.00) than Boomers, while Millennials spent, on average, 50.21 fewer months on the job (95% CI −51.66, −48.76) than Boomers.

The significant relative age × generation interactions imply that the association between relative age and the time spent on the job differs due to generation. For Boomers, each additional year of relative age translates into an average job tenure of .69 months longer (95% CI .48 .89). For Gen X, an additional year of relative age translates into 2.11 additional months of job tenure (difference between Boomers and Gen X is 1.42 months, 95% CI 1.18, 1.66). For Millennials, relative age seems even more important to job tenure, and an additional year of age is associated with 3.63 months longer on the job (difference between Boomers and Millennials is 2.94, 95% CI 2.15, 3.74). These results indicate that there are significant job tenure mean differences between Boomers and Gen X and between Boomers and Millennials when controlling for relative age and the interaction between relative age and generation.

A similar analysis was performed to test for generational differences in the number of jobs held in the last 5 years (see Table 23.6). The second step of the hierarchical regression that included the main effects showed a significant change in unexplained variability ($R^2 = .03$, $p < .001$), as did the third step that included the interaction term between generation and relative age ($R^2 = .02$, $p < .001$). Results revealed that Boomers had fewer jobs in the past 5 years than either GenXers or Millennials. More specifically, GenXers of the same relative age and gender had an average of .45 more jobs (95% CI .39, .50) than Boomers, while Millennials averaged .55 more jobs (95% CI .48, .63) than Boomers. The significant relative age main effect indicated that an additional year of relative age is related to a .02 decrease in the average number of jobs held in the last 5 years (95% CI −.03, −.01) for Boomers. Additionally, the significant

Table 23.5   Correlation Coefficients Among Study Variables

	Age	Longest number of months spent in single job	Number of jobs held in the last 5 years	Attendance rating	Appearance rating
Longest number of months spent in single job	0.565**				
Number of jobs held in the last 5 years	−0.220**	−0.272**			
Attendance rating	0.026*	0.090**	−0.056**		
Appearance rating	0.029**	0.056**	−0.014	0.133**	
Employment history	−0.191**	−0.160**	−0.087**	0.000	0.017

**Correlation is significant at the .01 level. *Correlation is significant at the .05 level.

Table 23.6 Regression Analysis of Job Mobility Behaviors

Variable	Longest time in one job					Number of jobs in the past 5 years				
	b	95% CI	β	R^2	ΔR^2	b	95% CI	β	R^2	ΔR^2
Step 1				.09					.02	
Constant	52.59	(51.17, 54.01)				2.45	(2.40, 2.51)			
Sex (1 = female)	-4.75***	(-6.30, -3.20)	-.06			-.05	(-.11, .02)	-.02		
Relative age	1.81***	(1.69, 1.94)	.30			-.03***	(-.04, -.03)	-.14		
Step 2				.42	.33***				.05	.03***
Constant	76.35	(74.92, 77.84)				2.09	(2.02, 2.16)			
Sex (1 = female)	-4.30***	(-5.53, -3.05)	-.06			-.07*	(-.13, -.00)	-.02		
Relative age	1.81***	(1.71, 1.91)	.30			-.03***	(-.04, -.03)	-.14		
Gen X	-24.16***	(-21.33, 23.00)	-.43			.45***	(.39, .50)	.20		
Millennial	-50.20***	(-51.66, -48.74)	-.71			.57***	(.49, .64)	.20		
Step 3				.43	.01***				.07	.02***
Constant	76.45	(75.03, 77.87)				2.10	(2.03, 2.17)			
Sex (1 = female)	-4.41***	(-5.64, -3.18)	-.06			-.07*	(-.14, -.01)	-.03		
Relative age	.69***	(.48, .89)	.12			-.02***	(-.03, -.01)	-.09		
Gen X	-24.16***	(-25.32, -23.00)	-.43			.45***	(.39, .50)	.20		
Millennial	-50.21***	(-51.66, -48.76)	-.71			.55***	(.48, .63)	.20		
Gen X × age	1.42***	(1.18, 1.66)	.21			-.02***	(-.04, -.01)	-.09		
Millennial × age	2.94***	(2.15, 3.74)	.03			.20***	(.16, .25)	.13		

Note: For this analysis, the generation variables were coded as Gen X = 1, 0 otherwise; and Millennial = 1, 0 otherwise.

*p <.05. **p <.01. ***p <.001.

Table 23.7	Ordinal Multinomial Regression Analysis of Attendance				
Variable	β	SE b	Wald's X^2	e^β (odds ratio)	95% CI e^β
Lower than most people	−5.42	.15	1,301.07***	.004	(.003,.006)
Typical of most people	−1.84	.07	688.65***	.16	(.14,.18)
Higher than most	−.28	.07	16.86***	.76	(.67,.87)
Millennial	−.19	.07	8.02**	.83	(.73,.94)
Gen X	−.34	.05	39.36***	.71	(.64,.79)
Sex (1 = female)	−.21	.06	12.755***	.81	(.73,.91)
Relative age	.003	.005	.489	1.00	(.99, 1.01)

Note: The last response category, "In the top 5%," was the reference category. The Boomers category was used as the reference category for generation, and male was used as the reference category for sex.

*$p < .05$. **$p < .01$. ***$p < .001$.

relative age × Gen X interaction suggests that an additional year of relative age resulted in a .04 decrease in the average number of jobs held in the last 5 years when compared to Boomers (difference between Boomers and GenXers is −.02, 95% CI −.04, −.01). Conversely, an additional year of age for Millennials results in an average *increase* of .18 jobs in the last 5 years as compared to Boomers (difference between Millennials and Boomers is .20, 95% CI .16, .25). Thus, comparable Millennials who are older in their generation tend to have held more jobs in the past 5 years, while comparable Boomers and GenXers who are older in the generation tend to have held fewer jobs, on average, in the past 5 years. These results suggest that there are still significant mean differences in the number of jobs held in the past 5 years between Boomers and Gen X and between Boomers and Millennials when controlling for relative age and the interaction between relative age and generation. Taken collectively, results of both hierarchical regression analyses for the longest time spent in one job and for the number of jobs held in the past 5 years lend support for Hypothesis 1.

Hypothesis 2 predicted that Boomers would exhibit more instances of compliance with work rules

and fewer terminations than GenXers and Millennials. Tables 23.7–23.9 contain results of the regression analyses used to test the hypothesized generational effects on appearance, attendance, and terminations.

Concerning attendance, results indicated that there was overall significance associated with the fitted model containing relative age, gender, and generation as predictors of attendance behaviors (log likelihood = −8,670.33, $\chi^2 = 56.19$, $df = 4$, $p < .001$). However, the interaction between relative age and generation was not significant, thus not included in the fitted model. The reported proportional odds ordinal logistic regression model (see Table 23.7) compares the odds of a respondent selecting the next higher category over the combined adjacent and lower categories. Because of the categorical nature of the generational variable and gender control variable, the odds for each of these variables are compared relative to a specific reference category. For all logistic regression models in this paper, we selected male as the referent category for gender and Boomer as the referent category for generation. Thus, for example, the Gen X coefficient ($e^\beta = .71$, 95% CI .64, .79) is interpreted as the odds of a Gen X member selecting the next higher attendance category as compared to a

Table 23.8 Binary Logistic Regression Analysis of Appropriate Appearance

Variable	β	SE b	Wald's X^2	e^β (odds ratio)	95% CI e^β
Usually appropriate	−2.27	.13	291.28***	.10	(.08,.13)
Millennial	.34	.15	5.13*	1.40	(1.04,1.87)
Gen X	−.03	.13	.05	.97	(.78,1.25)
Sex (1 = female)	−.77	.11	49.03***	.46	(.38,.58)
Relative age	−.01	.01	1.44	.99	(.97,1.01)

Note: The last response category "always appropriate" was used as the reference category. The Boomers category was used as the reference category for generation, and male was used as the reference category for sex.

*p <.05. **p <.01. ***p <.001.

Table 23.9 Ordinal Multinomial Regression Analysis of Termination

Variable	β	SE b	Wald's X^2	e^β (odds ratio)	95% CI e^β
Never been fired	.956	.08	132.7***	2.60	(2.21,3.06)
Left because likely to be fired	1.09	.08	169.5***	3.00	(2.51,3.48)
Fired once	3.26	.11	923.2***	25.90	(21.00,31.95)
Millennial	−.68	.10	46.0***	.51	(.42,.62)
Gen X	−.07	.07	1.1	.93	(.81,1.07)
Sex (1 = female)	−.44	.07	36.2***	.65	(.56,.75)
Relative age	.02	.01	12.6***	1.0	(1.01,1.03)

Note: The last response category "fired twice or more" was used as the reference category. The Boomers category was used as the reference category for generation, and male was used as the reference category for sex.

*p <.05. **p <.01. ***p <.001.

Boomer of the same relative age and gender. Because this odds ratio is less than 1, it implies a 29% reduction in the odds of GenXers selecting a higher attendance category compared to Boomers. Similarly, the odds of comparable Millennials responding in the next higher attendance category is .83 that of Boomers (95% CI .73, .94). This implies a 17% reduction in the odds of comparable Millennials rating their attendance in the higher category than Boomers.

Table 23.8 presents the binary logistic regression results used to test generational differences for the appearance dimension of Hypothesis 2. Again, the relative age × generation interactions were not significant and thus excluded from our final model. The final model indicated a significant association between generation and appropriate appearance (log likelihood = −1,719.02, χ^2 = 55.23, df = 4, p <.001). The results indicate that when controlling for relative age and gender, Millennials' odds of responding in the category of "usually appropriate" is 1.4 times higher than that of a Boomer (95% CI 1.05, −1.87). However, the odds of GenXers responding in the "usually appropriate" category was not significantly different from that of Boomers (e^β=.99, 95% CI .97, 1.01).

Results of the ordinal logistic regression analyses for generational effects on terminations (see Table 23.9) indicated that there was an association between generation and disciplinary action (log likelihood = −4,829.8, χ^2= 107.5, df= 4, p <.001). Again, this final model did not include the relative age × generation interactions because they were not significant in the original model. Our findings revealed that the odds of Millennials selecting the next higher response category over that of the combined lower categories was .51 times less than Boomers (95% CI .42, .62). However, the odds of GenXers responding in a higher disciplinary category was not significantly different than Boomers (95% CI .81, 1.1).

Taken collectively, results of the three analyses regarding attendance, appearance, and terminations provide partial support for Hypothesis 2. It is important to note that the relative age × generation interactions were not significant in all three analyses, indicating that increases in age within each generation have similar effects on the workplace behavior associated with Hypothesis 2.

Hypothesis 3 predicted that GenXers would be less willing to work overtime than other generations. Table 23.10 presents the ordinal logistic regression analysis used to test this prediction. The interaction between generation and relative age was originally included in our model but found to be not significant, and thus excluded from the final model. Our final model indicated an association between generation and willingness to work overtime (log likelihood = −7,963.13, χ^2=43.71, df=4, p <.001). Further, results suggested that the odds of selecting the next higher response category over that of the combined lower categories differed significantly between GenXers and Boomers.

More specifically, the odds of GenXers responding in a higher willingness to work overtime category is .82 times lower (95% CI .73, −.94), on average, than Boomers. As expected, there was no significant difference between comparable Millennials and Boomers in terms of the odds of willingness to work

Table 23.10 Ordinal Multinomial Regression Analysis of Willingness to Work Overtime

Variable	β	SE b	Wald's X^2	e^β (odds ratio)	95% CI e^β
Never or occasionally when asked	−2.24	.07	946.86***	.11	(.09,.12)
Most times when asked	.03	.07	.15	1.03	(.90,1.17)
Millennial	−.09	.07	1.65	.92	(.80,1.05)
Gen X	−.20	.05	13.68***	.82	(.73,.91)
Female	−.30	.06	26.59***	.74	(.66,.83)
Relative age	−.00	.00	.07	1	(.99,1.01)

Note: The last response category "every time when asked" was used as the reference category. The Boomers category was used as the reference category for generation, and male was used as the reference category for sex.

* p <.05. ** p <.01. *** p <.001.

overtime. These results provide support for Hypothesis 3 and indicate that GenXers are less likely to work overtime as compared to Boomers and Millennials.

Discussion

The results of the present study suggest that while generational differences exist in some workplace behaviors, the popular generational stereotypes are not always consistent with workplace behaviors. As mentioned earlier, these findings deviate from the majority of existing generational differences research in that our study focused on job behaviors versus attitudes or values. We believe our results can be instructive and have important implications for management and HR practices.

Overall, our results suggest that organizations should be cautious in taking the advice of some scholars to implement HR strategies that recognize the unique values and characteristics of each generation versus general strategies applied to all generations of employees (D'Amato & Herzfeldt, 2008). Although we did find evidence of some generational differences in workplace behavior, the effects sizes were quite small as evidenced by the small, but statistically significant changes in R^2 in the hierarchical regression analysis, and the odds ratios near 1.0 in the ordinal logistic regression analyses. As such, we tend to agree with others who have argued that the cost of tailoring HR practices to each generation may outweigh the potential benefits (Kowske, Rasch, & Wiley, 2010). Moreover, we caution practitioners to avoid treating employees simply as members of generations, ignoring the fact that other individual differences likely play a more prominent role in workplace behaviors than generational differences (cf. Twenge, 2010). Rather than developing HR strategies that target specific generations, organizations may be better served by designing greater flexibility into HR practices and strategies in order to address the needs and values of all employees regardless of generational cohort group.

The inclusion of relative age in our analyses also has important implications. This approach allowed us to compare increases in age within each generation on the investigated workplace behaviors. In terms of our specific findings, the significant relative age × generation interaction effects for job mobility behaviors indicated that increases in age within younger generations (i.e., GenXers and Millennials) had a greater effect on these behaviors than increases in age within the Boomer generation. These results suggest that we should interpret our findings regarding generational differences in job mobility behaviors with caution. More specifically, generational differences in job mobility behaviors may be attributed to age or life stage effects versus a pure generational effect. For example, some scholars argue that human development is characterized by different life stages that are unique in terms of cognitive, emotional, and behavioral experiences (cf. Levinson, 1980). As such, the nature of jobs held by older workers or their current life cycle may explain the lower job mobility behaviors for Boomers. However, the relative age × generation interactions were not significant for the other workplace behaviors, providing more evidence of generational effects on workplace behaviors. Additionally, inspecting the results of the study seems to suggest that at least some of the differences cannot be explained simply by age. For example, we found that participants from older generations generally reported being fired fewer times than younger generations. If age alone influenced results, we would expect the opposite because older generations have been in the workforce longer and have had more opportunities to be fired.

Limitations and Future Research

While our study reveals some interesting results, we should note several potential limitations. Due to the cross-sectional nature of our data, we were unable to explicitly test for age, life stage, or career stage effects. While the relative age measure used in our analyses provides unique insight into these issues, we encourage future researchers to further investigate generational differences using other data collection methods such as longitudinal designs. As suggested by an anonymous reviewer, another possibility is for future researchers to use additional individual variables (e.g., number of children, applying for full-time or part-time jobs) as proxies for family or life stage effects. Unfortunately, the field data collection design prevented us from collecting this type of data because participants were applying for actual jobs, and it would be illegal for us to ask specific questions about number of children, marital status, etc. Similarly, we echo Parry and Urwin's (2011) call for future research to explicitly consider other within-generation individual characteristics such as ethnicity or national culture.

The nature of the data used for analyses presents another possible limitation. We collected data from participants' self-reported biodata items on an employment application and the accuracy of self-report data is often debated. However, research has shown that the accuracy of biodata can be maximized by using several strategies. First, the more objective (i.e., verifiable) the biodata items, the greater the accuracy (Becker & Colquitt, 1992; Schrader & Osburn, 1977; Shaffer, Saunders, & Owens, 1986). All items used in the current study were objective and verifiable. Second, informing applicants their responses are subject to independent verification reduces the likelihood of faking or giving socially desirable answers (Kluger & Colella, 1993). All participants in this study signed an acknowledgment that their responses may be verified and dishonest answers would result in disqualification from the hiring process. Although the authors feel that adequate measures were taken to ameliorate the effects of faking or giving socially desirable responses, we cannot completely rule out such concerns. Future research would benefit from assessing generational differences in workplace behavior using sources such as official employment records of disciplinary action, rules violations, terminations, etc.

A final limitation concerns statistical significance and sample size. While our study did find significant differences between generational cohort groups on several work-related behaviors, our sample size was very large. With large samples, even small effects can be found to be highly significant. Thus, results should be interpreted in light of effect sizes, which were small.

Conclusion

The current study extended previous research on the effects of generational differences in the workplace by investigating actual employee behaviors. While results indicated some generational differences in workplace behavior exist, the effect sizes for these relationships were small. As such, we caution organizations from exerting much effort to redesign practices and policies in an attempt to more effectively manage workers from different generations.

Note

1. Correspondence concerning this article should be addressed to John Bret Becton, University of Southern Mississippi, Department of Management and International Business, 118 College Dr. #5077, Hattiesburg, MS 39406, USA. E-mail: bret.becton@usm.edu doi: 10.1111/jasp.12208

References

Abramson, P. R., & Inglehart, R. (1995). *Value change in global perspective*. Ann Arbor, MI: University of Michigan Press.

Adams, S. J. (2000). Generation X: How understanding this population leads to better safety programs. *Professional Safety, 45,* 26–29.

Allen, P. (2004). Welcoming Y. *Benefits Canada, 28,* 51–53.

Arnett, J. J. (2000). High hopes in a grim world. *Youth & Society, 31,* 267–286.

Arnett, J. J. (2010). Oh, grow up! Generational grumbling and the new life stage of emerging adulthood—Commentary on Trzesniewski & Donnellan (2010). *Perspectives on Psychological Science, 5,* 89–92.

Arthur, M. B., & Rousseau, D. M. (1996). *The boundaryless career: A new employment principle for a new organizational era*. New York: Oxford University Press.

Becker, P. E., & Moen, P. (1999). Scaling back: Dual-career couples' work-family strategies. *Journal of Marriage and the Family, 61,* 995–1007.

Becker, T., & Colquitt, A. (1992). Potential versus actual faking of a biodata form: An analysis along several dimensions of item type. *Personnel Psychology, 45,* 389–406.

Becton, J. B., Matthews, M. C., Hartley, D. L., & Whitaker, D. H. (2009). Biodata as a predictor of turnover, organizational commitment, & job performance in the healthcare industry. *International Journal of Selection and Assessment, 17,* 189–202.

Beutell, N. J., & Wittig-Berman, U. (2008). Work-family conflict and work-family synergy for generation X, baby boomers, and satisfaction outcomes. *Journal of Managerial Psychology, 23,* 507–523.

Booth, A. I., Franscesconi, M., & Garcia-Serrano, C. (1999). Job tenure and job mobility in Britain. *Industrial and Labor Relations Review, 53,* 43–70.

Bradford, F. W. (1993). Understanding Gen X. *Marketing Research, 5,* 54.

Burke, R. J. (1994). Generation X: Measures, sex and age differences. *Psychological Reports, 74,* 555–562.

Carlson, K. S., & Gjerde, P. F. (2009). Preschool personality antecedents of narcissism in adolescence and emerging adulthood: A 20-year longitudinal study. *Journal of Research in Personality, 43,* 570–578.

Cennamo, L., & Gardner, D. (2008). Generational differences in work values, outcomes and person-organisation values fit. *Journal of Managerial Psychology, 23,* 891–906.

Chao, L. (2005). For Gen Xers, it's work to live: Allowing employees to strike balance between job and life can lead to better retention rates. *Wall Street Journal,* Eastern edition, November 29, B6.

Cohen, J. S. (2007). Dressed for success? Or unfairly singled out? *Chicago Tribune,* September 2.

Coupland, D. (1991). *Generation X: Tales for an accelerated culture.* New York: St. Martin's Griffin.

Crainer, S., & Dearlove, D. (1999). Death of executive talent. *Management Review,* July–August, 17–23.

D'Amato, A., & Herzfeldt, R. (2008). Learning orientation, organizational commitment, and talent retention across generations. *Journal of Managerial Psychology, 23,* 929–953.

de Meuse, K. P., Bergmann, T. J., & Lester, S. (2001). An investigation of the relational component of the psychological contract across time, generation, and employment status. *Journal of Managerial Issues, 13,* 102–118.

Dittman, M. (2005). Generational differences at work. *Monitor on Psychology, 36,* 54–55.

Egri, C. P., & Ralston, D. A. (2004). Generation cohorts and personal values: A comparison of China and the United States. *Organization Science, 15,* 210–220.

Eisner, S. P. (2005). Managing generation Y. *SAM Advanced Management Journal, 70,* 4–15.

Elsdon, R., & Lyer, S. (1999). Creating value and enhancing retention through employee development: The Sun Microsystems experience. *Human Resource Planning, 22,* 39–48.

Eskilson, A., & Wiley, M. G. (1999). Solving for X: Aspirations and expectations of college students. *Journal of Youth & Adolescence, 28,* 51–70.

Families and Work Institute. (2006). Generation and gender in the workplace. American Business Collaboration. Retrieved April 23, 2009, from http://familiesandwork.org/site/research/reports/mai.html.

Foster, J. D., Campbell, W. K., & Twenge, J. M. (2003). Individual differences in narcissism: Inflated self-views across the lifespan and around the world. *Journal of Research in Personality, 37,* 469–486.

Francis-Smith, J. (August 26, 2004). Surviving and thriving in the multigenerational workplace. *Journal Record, 1.*

Fyock, C. D. (1990). *America's work force is coming of age.* Toronto: Lexington Books.

Ghiselli, E. E. (1974). Some perspectives for industrial psychology. *American Psychologist, 29,* 80–87.

Giancola, F. (2006). The generation gap: More myth than reality? *Human Resource Planning, 29,* 32–37.

Greenland, S. (1994). Alternative models for ordinal logistic regression. *Statistics in Medicine, 13,* 1665–1677.

Griffeth, R. W., & Hom, P. W. (2001). *Retaining valued employees.* Thousand Oaks, CA: Sage.

Hall, D. T. (1996). Protean careers of the 21st century. *Academy of Management Executive, 10,* 8–16.

Hart, K. A. (2006). *Generations in the workplace: Finding common ground.* Retrieved April 14, 2007, from www.mloonline.com

Hart, P. M., Schembri, C., Bell, C. A., & Armstrong, K. (2003). *Leadership, climate, work attitudes and commitment: Is Generation X really that different?* Paper presented at Academy of Management Meeting, Seattle, Washington.

Hays, S. (1999). Gen X and the art of the reward. *Workforce, 78,* 44–47.

Howe, H., Strauss, W., & Matson, R. J. (2000). *Millennials rising: The next great generation.* New York: Vintage.

Hung, K. H., Gu, F. F., & Yim, C. K. (2007). A social institutional approach to identifying generational cohorts in China with a comparison with American consumers. *Journal of International Business Studies, 38,* 836–853.

Inglehart, R. (1977). *The silent revolution: Changing values and political styles among Western publics.* Princeton, NJ: Princeton University Press.

Inglehart, R. (1990). *Culture shift in advanced industrial society.* Princeton, NJ: Princeton University Press.

Inglehart, R., & Norris, P. (2003). *Rising ride: Gender equality and cultural change around the world.* Cambridge: Cambridge University Press.

Judge, T., & Watanabe, S. (1995). Is the past prologue: A test of Ghiselli's hobo syndrome. *Journal of Management, 21*, 211–229.

Jurkiewicz, C. L. (2000). Generation X and the public employee. *Public Personnel Management, 29*, 55–74.

Jurkiewicz, C. L., & Brown, R. G. (1998). GenXers vs Boomers vs Matures: Generational comparisons of public employee motivation. *Review of Public Personnel Administration, 18*, 18–37.

Keene, J., & Reynolds, J. (2005). The job costs of family demands: Gender differences in negative family-to-work spillover. *Journal of Family Issues, 26*, 275–299.

Keith, K., & McWilliams, A. (1997). Job mobility and gender-based wage growth differentials. *Economic Inquiry, 35*, 320–333. Retrieved from Academic Search Premier database.

Kluger, A., & Colella, A. (1993). Beyond the mean bias: The effect of warning against faking on biodata item variances. *Personnel Psychology, 46*, 763–780.

Kohut, H. (1971). *The analysis of self.* New York: International Universities Press.

Kowske, B. J., Rasch, R., & Wiley, J. (2010). Millennials' (lack of) attitude problem: An empirical examination of generational effects on work attitudes. *Journal of Business Psychology, 25*, 265–279.

Kupperschmidt, B. R. (2000). Multigeneration employees: Strategies for effective management. *The Health Care Manager, 19*, 65–76.

Lancaster, L. C., & Stillman, D. (2002). *When generations collide: Who they are, why they clash, how to solve the generational puzzle at work.* New York: Harper Collins.

Levinson, D. (1978). *The seasons of a man's life.* New York: Knopf.

Levinson, D. J. (1980). Toward a conception of the adult life course. In N. J. Smelser & E. H. Erikson (Eds.), *Themes of work and love in adulthood* (pp. 265–289). Cambridge, MA: Harvard University Press.

Levy, L., Carroll, B., Francoeur, J., & Logue, M. (2005). *The generational mirage? A pilot study into perceptions of leadership of Generations X and Y.* Hudson Global Resources, Sydney.

Loomis, J. E. (2000). *Gen X.* Indianapolis, IN: Rough Notes Co.

Lyons, S. T., Duxbury, L., & Higgins, C. (2007). An empirical assessment of generational differences in basic human values. *Psychological Reports, 101*, 339–352.

Macky, K., Gardner, D., & Forsyth, S. (2008). Generational differences at work: Introduction and overview. *Journal of Managerial Psychology, 23*, 857–861.

Mannheim, K. (1952). The sociological problem of generations. In K. Mannheim (Ed.), *Essays on the sociology of knowledge* (p. 306). London: RKP (first published 1923).

Mannheim, K. (1972). The problem of generations. In P. G. Altbach & R. S. Laufer (Eds.), *The new pilgrims: Youth protest in transition* (pp. 101–138). New York: David McKay.

Mayo Foundation for Medical Education and Research. (2008). Work-life balance: Ways to restore harmony and reduce stress. Retrieved April 22, 2009, from http://www.mayoclinic.com/health/work-life-balance/WL00056

McCrae, R. R., Costa Jr, P. T., Terracciano, A., Parker, W. E., Mills, C. J., De Fruyt, F., et al. (2002). Personality trait development from age 12 to age 18: Longitudinal, cross-sectional, and cross-cultural analyses. *Journal of Personality and Social Psychology, 83*, 1456–1468.

Meriac, J. P., Woehr, D. J., & Banister, C. (2010). Generational differences in work ethic: An examination of measurement equivalent across three cohorts. *Journal of Business Psychology, 25*, 315–324.

Mitchell, S. (1998). *American generations: Who they are. How they live. What they think.* Ithaca, NY: New Strategist.

Munasinghe, L., & Sigman, K. (2004). A hobo syndrome? Mobility, wages and job turnover. *Labour Economics, 11*, 191–218.

Murad, H., Fleischman, A., Sadetzki, S., Geyer, O., & Freedman, L. (2003). Small samples and ordered logistic regression. *The American Statistician, 57*, 155–160.

Neuborne, E., & Kerwin, K. (February 15, 1999). Generation Y. *Business Week*, Online. Retrieved April 3, 2009, from http://www.businessweek.com/1999/ 99_07/ b3616001.htm

O'Bannon, G. (2001). Managing our future: The Generation X factor. *Public Personnel Management, 30*, 95–109.

Orey, M. (2007). Fear of firing. *Business Week*, April 23, 52.

Parry, E., & Urwin, P. (2011). Generational differences in work values: A review of theory and evidence. *International Journal of Management Reviews, 13*, 79–96.

Patterson, C. (January 2005). *Generational diversity: Implications for consultation and teamwork.* Paper presented at the meeting of the Council of Directors of School Psychology Programs on Generational Differences, Deerfield Beach, FL.

Pew Research Center. (2007). *How young people view their lives, futures, and politics: A portrait of "Generation*

Next." Retrieved April 23, 2009, from http://people-press.org/report/3000/a-portrait-of-generation-next

Roberts, B. W., Edmonds, G., & Grijalva, E. (2010). Is it Developmental Me, not Generation Me: Developmental changes are more important than generational changes in narcissism—Commentary on Trzesniewski & Donnellan (2010). *Perspectives on Psychological Sciences, 5*, 97–102.

Rogler, L. H. (2002). Historical generations and psychology: The case of the Great Depression and World War II. *The American Psychologist, 57*, 1013–1023.

Ryan, M. (September 10, 2000). Gerald Celente: He reveals what lies ahead. *Parade Magazine*, pp. 22–23.

Schrader, A., & Osburn, H. (1977). Biodata faking: Effects of induced subtlety and position specificity. *Personnel Psychology, 30*, 395–404.

Sessa, V. I., Kabacoff, R. I., Deal, J., & Brown, H. (2007). Generational differences in leader values and leadership behaviors. *The Psychologist-Manager Journal, 10*, 47–74.

Shaffer, G. A., Saunders, V., & Owens, W. A. (1986). Additional evidence for the accuracy of biographical data: Long-term retest and observer ratings. *Personnel Psychology, 39*, 791–809.

Sherman, R. O. (2008). One size doesn't fit all: Motivating a multigenerational staff. *Nursing Management, 39*, 8–10.

Smola, K., & Sutton, C. (2002). Generational differences: Revisiting generational work values for the new millennium. *Journal of Organizational Behavior, 23*, 363–382.

Sullivan, S. E. (1999). The changing nature of careers: A review and research agenda. *Journal of Management, 25*, 457–484.

Tapscott, D. (1998). *Growing up digital: The rise of the net generation.* New York: McGraw-Hill.

Terracciano, A. (2010). Secular trends and personality: Perspectives from longitudinal and cross-cultural studies—Commentary on Trzesniewski & Donnellan (2010). *Perspectives on Psychological Science, 5*, 93–96.

Trzesniewski, K. H., & Donnellan, M. B. (2010). Rethinking "Generation Me" a study of cohort effects from 1976–2006. *Perspectives on Psychological Science, 5*, 58–75.

Tulgan, B. (1995). *Managing Generation X: How to bring out the best in young talent.* New York: Nolo Press.

Twenge, J. M. (2001). Changes in women's assertiveness in response to status and roles: A cross-temporal meta-analysis, 1931–1993. *Journal of Personality and Social Psychology, 81*, 133–145.

Twenge, J. M. (2010). A review of the empirical evidence on generational differences in work attitudes. *Journal of Business and Psychology, 25*, 201–210.

Twenge, J. M., & Campbell, S. M. (2008). Generational differences in psychological traits and their impact on the workplace. *Journal of Managerial Psychology, 23*, 862–877.

Twenge, J. M., & Campbell, S. M. (2009). *The narcissism epidemic: Living in the age of entitlement.* New York: Free Press.

Twenge, J. M., Campbell, S. M., Hoffman, B. J., & Lance, C. E. (2010). Generational differences in work values: Leisure and extrinsic values increasing, social and intrinsic values decreasing. *Journal of Management, 36*, 1117–1142.

Twenge, J. M., & Campbell, W. K. (2001). Age and birth cohort differences in selfesteem: A cross-temporal meta-analysis. *Personality and Social Psychology Review, 5*, 321–344.

Twenge, J. M., & Foster, J. D. (2010). Birth cohort increases in narcissistic personality traits among American college students 1982–2009. *Social Psychological and Personality Science, 1*, 99–106.

Twenge, J. M., Konrath, S., Foster, J. D., Campbell, W. K., & Bushman, B. J. (2008). Egos inflating over time: A crosstemporal meta-analysis of the Narcissistic Personality Inventory. *Journal of Personality, 76*, 875–901.

Vardi, Y., & Weitz, E. (2004). *Misbehavior in organizations.* Mahwah, NJ: Lawrence - Erlbaum.

Westerman, J. W., & Yamamura, J. H. (2007). Generational preferences for work environment fit: Effects on employee outcomes. *Career Development International, 12*, 150–161.

Whyte, W. H. (1956). *The organization man.* Garden City, NY: Anchor Books.

Wong, M., Gardiner, E., Lang, W., & Coulon, L. (2008). Generational differences in personality and motivation: Do they exist and what are the implications for the workplace? *Journal of Managerial Psychology, 23*, 878–890.

Yu, H. C., & Miller, P. (2003). The generation gap and cultural influence—A Taiwan empirical investigation. *Cross Cultural Management, 10*, 23–41.

Zemke, R., Raines, C., & Filipczak, B. (2000). *Generations at work: Managing the clash of veterans, boomers, Xers and Nexters in your workplace.* New York: AMA Publications.

PART V

Ethics

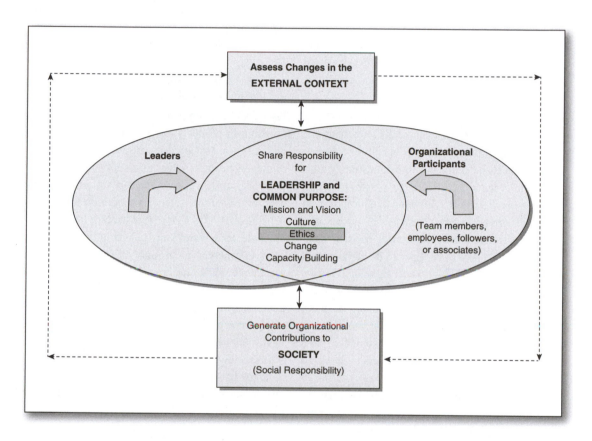

Overview

Ethics in organizations, as in other areas of life, compel leaders and participants to take into account the impact of their actions in relation to others. Ethics should guide every aspect of organizational life beginning with developing and implementing ethical leadership policies, procedures, and practices for leaders and members; creating and carrying out the organization's common purpose; care and treatment of all stakeholders; decision making and strategy; and social responsibility, among other elements.

Despite the expectation for organization leaders and members to act ethically, Mark Schwartz (Chapter 25) asks, "Why do most people, including employees and government regulators, remain so skeptical of corporate executives' ethical leadership capabilities?" One main contributor to this distrust is the inclination of individuals in leader roles to openly promote ethical values and concurrently base organizational reward systems primarily on financial performance. Ethical actions or decisions on behalf of the organization often do not count as a part of the reward system. Schwartz identifies three key elements drawn from existing literature for building an ethical corporate culture:

1. A set of core ethical values infused throughout the organization in its policies, processes, and practices

2. A formal ethics program, including a code of ethics, ethics training, an ethics hotline, and an ethics officer

3. The continuous presence of ethical leadership (i.e., an appropriate tone at the top as reflected by the board of directors, senior executives, and managers)

These three elements are mutually reinforcing and work in concert to create an ethical culture. Schwartz argues ethical leadership entails demonstrating morally appropriate conduct through personal actions, interpersonal relations, promotion of ethical conduct to organization members through two-way communication, reinforcement, and ethical decision making. He suggests two dimensions to the development of a moral reputation by leaders: the moral person, who acts with integrity, honesty, and trustworthiness in his or her personal life; and the moral manager, who visibly role models ethical conduct and applies reward systems that hold everyone accountable. Both dimensions must be present for leaders to develop a moral reputation.

Joanne Ciulla (Chapter 24) extends the discourse on ethical leadership by examining the role of leadership in shaping organizational values. Values are what people believe are important or morally worthy. All leaders hold values, whether they are stated or unstated, but how they act on these values in the organization is what matters most.

She argues that how we assess the impact of a leader's values depends on one's leadership theory. For example, transforming and servant leadership emphasize the moral relationship of leaders and followers to each other, and the importance of values in the process. Burns' theory focuses on modal values (modes of behavior or conduct such as honesty, fairness, or courage) and end values (goals or standards such as liberty, equality, or justice), while Greenleaf

emphasizes the requirement of organizational leaders and followers to carry out the value of serving organizational members and caring for the least privileged in society.

Ciulla presents several examples of leadership values in action with illustrations from companies such as Malden Mills and Merck. The CEO of Malden Mills acted on the values of his faith when he provided full salaries to his employees after his textile factory burned down. Merck's leaders decided to give away a vaccine to treat river blindness to victims in 35 developing countries based on the values in their mission statement: "We are in the business of preserving and improving human life." Merck's actions inspired other company leaders to follow suit by investing in products for poor and disenfranchised people. These leaders demonstrated the significance of shaping business values through their actions.

Leader authenticity is the focus of an emerging area of research. Arran Caza and Brad Jackson (Chapter 26) offer a review of nascent literature on authentic leadership. This leadership concept developed a coherent focus only in 2003, but it has attracted considerable attention among scholars and practitioners. The authors speculate the appeal of authentic leadership stems from widespread disillusionment with the performance of leaders in business, politics, and religion, and people's desire for selfless, enlightened leadership.

Drawing on concepts of authenticity by both Harter and Kernis, Caza and Jackson propose a four part definition

"authentic leaders" are defined as leaders who exhibit four behavioural tendencies: self-awareness, which is accurate knowledge of one's strengths, weaknesses, and idiosyncratic qualities; relational transparency, which involves genuine representation of the self to others; balanced processing, which is the collection and use of relevant, objective information, particularly that which challenges one's prior beliefs; and an internalized moral perspective, which refers to self-regulation and self-determination, rather than acting in accordance with situational demands.

They emphasize that all four components of the definition must be true for leadership to be considered authentic.

Studies of authentic leadership thus far cluster in three areas: antecedents of authentic leadership such as a positive organizational context; consequences of authentic leadership, including improved well-being and greater leadership effectiveness; and mechanisms of authentic leadership such as attitudinal changes and changes in the relationships that followers have with leaders. Caza and Jackson stress the need for further development of authentic leadership theory and substantially more empirical research.

Some forms of leadership are dysfunctional and harmful to the organization and its participants. In these cases, leaders have a responsibility to engage in truthful self-reflection and self-correction. Participants have a responsibility to themselves and their organizations not to become victims of poor, unethical, or abusive behavior. We look to organizational leaders to model ethical behavior, but, regrettably, there are examples of leaders not rising to the occasion. With the increase in shared leadership in new era organizations comes shared responsibility by leaders and members to uphold ethical behavior in the organization.

Melissa Carsten and Mary Uhl-Bein (Chapter 27) studied followers' responses to unethical requests by leaders. Followers must make a decision to stand up to an unethical request—by challenging the request, refusing it, or responding with an ethical alternative—or they can go along with the leader's request and essentially become complicit with the unethical behavior.

Followers' responses to an unethical request are associated with their belief about the follower role. If followers see their role as co-producers of leadership (the premise of shared leadership), then they are likely to stand up to the leader's request. If they see their role as passive and obedient ("I'm just following orders"), then they are likely to comply with the unethical request. Passive followers displace their responsibility for unethical behavior or crimes of obedience by blaming the leader, while followers who believe in coproduction of leadership take responsibility for their actions. Another moderator of followers' behavior is their belief about the romance of leadership. Followers who romanticize leaders have an inflated view of leaders' importance and a tendency to attribute success or failure to the knowledge and effectiveness of leaders.

Carsten and Uhl-Bein's study found followers with weaker co-production beliefs are more likely to comply with a leader's unethical request while followers with stronger co-production beliefs are less likely to comply. Individuals with stronger co-production beliefs, who do not romanticize leaders, are least likely to obey leaders' unethical request and displace responsibility for their actions. The researchers warn that effects of co-production beliefs can be diminished by followers' belief in the romance of leadership and other factors such as a strong bureaucracy that may make it more difficult for even active followers to take initiative.

Birgit Schyns and Jan Schilling (Chapter 28) conducted a meta-analysis to examine the effects and outcomes of destructive leadership. Destructive leadership focuses on the dark side of leadership where leaders behave in ways that are detrimental to followers. Literature on this phenomenon use various terms to describe it, including *destructive leadership*, *abusive supervision*, *toxic leadership*, *petty tyranny*, and others.

The authors define destructive leadership as "a process in which over a longer period of time the activities, experiences and/or relationships of an individual or the members of a group are repeatedly influenced by their supervisor in a way that is perceived as hostile and/or obstructive." They group the research into four categories: leader-related concepts such as follower resistance toward the leader; job-related concepts involving job satisfaction concerns; organization-related concepts such as turnover; and individual follower–related concepts including stress and well-being.

As the authors hypothesized, their research found followers of destructive leaders are likely to have negative attitudes toward their leaders, show resistance toward them, have more negative attitudes toward their jobs and the organization as a whole, and experience a negative effect on their personal lives. These consequences are costly to the organization in terms of turnover, diminished performance, and harm to followers. Leaders and members need to make every effort to eliminate destructive leadership in the organization and avoid its occurrence from the outset.

Debra Comer and Susan Baker (Chapter 29) offer the viable option of "courageous coalitions" for active followers who face unethical behavior such as destructive leadership in organizations. They argue that it takes considerable moral courage to stand alone and advocate for change, but people can often tackle problems by working together as a coalition. Forming a coalition allows members to exert more influence toward raising the organization's ethical bar.

The authors contend that even morally courageous coalitions need leadership. They provide specific steps for leaders or initiators to consider before asking others to join them in concerted action. These four steps require contemplation to identify issues, ideas, values, and motivation for the proposed change; observation to assess the organization's ethical culture and identify likely consequences; preparation by identifying available recourses and resources such as a compassionate supervisor or manager; and enlisting the support of others to build a coalition.

Part V — Chapters

CHAPTER 24

Developing and Sustaining an Ethical Corporate Culture

The Core Elements

Mark S. Schwartz

York University

1. Unethical Corporate Activity

It can be argued that of all the issues faced by boards of directors, executives, and managers, unethical corporate activity is one of the most significant in terms of its potential negative impact and one of the most difficult to properly address. The range of illegal and unethical activity taking place is extensive and includes corruption, bribery, receiving and giving gifts and entertainment, kickbacks, extortion, nepotism, favoritism, money laundering, improper use of insider information, use of intermediaries, conflicts of interest, fraud, aggressive accounting, discrimination, sexual harassment, workplace safety, consumer product safety, and environmental pollution (U.S. Sentencing Commission, 2010). Unfortunately, one does not have to look very far to see significant examples of crime and unethical activity within or on behalf

of business organizations and the serious negative impacts such scandals have had on investors, employees, customers, competitors, the natural environment, and society (e.g., Enron, WorldCom, Tyco, Parmalat, Siemens, Madoff Investments, BP). This list does not include the more basic legal yet unethical practices by firms and their agents, including acts of dishonesty, disloyalty, disrespect, or promise breaking, all of which can also result in unnecessary harm to stakeholders. However, beyond the major scandals that are often the focus of media scrutiny, lawsuits or government prosecutions are the more difficult and challenging ethical dilemmas managers face. For example, consider the following firm-level ethical dilemmas with which many managers must wrestle:

- Should production be moved overseas, leading to worker layoffs?

- Should affirmative action policies be adhered to, leading to other qualified candidates being bypassed?
- Should consumer products be sold in third world countries with less stringent consumer protection laws when their sale would not be legally permitted in the firm's home country?

Or consider the following individual-level ethical dilemmas managers might face:

- Should I break confidentiality and indicate to a work colleague who is also a good friend that he/ she is about to be laid off?
- Should I accept an expensive bottle of wine during the holiday season from a current supplier if the firm does not forbid this?
- Should I join my work colleagues when a potential client is being taken to an adult entertainment club?
- Should I report my supervisor who is acting in an abusive manner toward other employees and thereby risk losing my own job?

How can firms prevent significant unethical behavior while simultaneously providing proper guidance to managers and employees in how to address more challenging day-to-day ethical dilemmas? While a vast array of potential solutions have been presented, many theorists (e.g., Brass, Butterfield, & Skaggs, 1998) argue that the presence of an ethical corporate culture is a necessary, although insufficient, condition if the extent to which illegal or unethical activity is taking place is to be minimized. An ethical corporate culture not only helps avoid major illegal or unethical corporate scandals but also leads to more appropriate ethical behavior at all firm levels. This theoretical position is at least initially supported by empirical evidence. For example, the 2009 National Business Ethics Survey of 2,852 U.S. employees conducted by the Ethics Resource Center (2010) found that in stronger ethical cultures, far fewer employees feel pressure to commit misconduct (4% versus 15%), the rates of observed misconduct are much lower (39% versus 76%), employees who observe misconduct are more likely to report it (43% versus 28%), and those who report misconduct are less likely to experience retaliation

(4% versus 24%). In reviewing the academic literature, Mcdonald (2009, p. 357) suggests: "The results highlight the important role that organisational culture plays in ethical decision making."

However, there are several difficulties with an approach focusing on developing an ethical corporate culture to help combat illegal or unethical activity. The initial challenge lies in understanding what exactly defines an ethical corporate culture. Before this can be done, however, one must start with defining the broader corporate culture concept found in the organizational theory literature. While several definitions exist, for the purposes of this article, corporate culture is simply considered a representation of the organization's shared assumptions, values, and beliefs. Building on this general definition, Treviño and Nelson (2011, p. 153) suggest that an ethical corporate culture represents a slice or subset of the organization's broader culture and is "maintained through a complex interplay [and alignment] of formal [i.e., policies, leadership, authority structures, reward systems, training programs] and informal organizational systems [i.e., peer behavior and ethical norms]." In terms of how an ethical corporate culture can lead to expected ethical behavior, employees can act in accordance with the firm's ethical norms either through a socialization process (i.e., employees feel they are expected to behave accordingly) or an internalization process (i.e., employees adopt the ethical norms as their own). The goal, then, is for firms to ensure that within their broader corporate culture of shared values and beliefs, a strong ethical corporate culture also exists rather than a weak culture. Only when this takes place will employees be more likely to conform to desired ethical norms.

A second difficulty lies in asking whether its existence—however defined—will actually make a difference with respect to all employees and managers. For the purposes of this article, this position is rejected as being clearly unrealistic as illegal and unethical activity will always continue, despite the existence of even an ideal ethical corporate culture. For example, there are many individuals in the fraud-prevention field who accept a 20–60–20 rule. Namely, 20% of a given workforce will always do the right thing; that is, act legally or ethically regardless of one's circumstances or work environment. Another 20% will always engage in illegal or unethical behavior when the opportunity exists, the rewards are sufficient, and there is a perceived low likelihood of getting caught. The remaining 60% of the workforce, while basically honest, will decide to engage in illegal or unethical behavior depending on the environment in which they work and factors like managerial pressure, peer pressure, or reward systems or the belief that they are acting in the firm's best interests. Such employees can be referred to as 'fence sitters'. Turning this fact into a potential opportunity, it is this 60% that can arguably be most influenced to do the right thing when they work within an ethical corporate culture. Consequently, these fence sitters are the target group of this article. The goal is to identify measures that can help mitigate or minimize—as opposed to completely eliminate—the extent to which illegal or unethical activity takes place within or on behalf of businesses.

However, even among fence sitters, an additional preliminary hurdle remains. Are employees who can be socialized to act in an ethically appropriate manner even able to initially recognize that they are in the midst of an ethical dilemma? For example, one study found that when asked to describe a moral dilemma they had experienced, two-thirds of 18- to 23-year-olds were "unable to answer the question or described problems that are not moral at all, like whether they could afford to rent a certain apartment or whether they had enough quarters to feed the meter at a parking spot" (Brooks, 2011). When this additional ethical awareness hurdle is added, those who would normally act ethically or those who can be socialized to act ethically may not do so because they may not recognize they are facing an ethical dilemma. The actual distribution of those employees who would always act ethically, might act ethically, or never act ethically when lack of ethical awareness is also taken into account, would actually approximate something closer to 10–50–40 rather than 20–60–20.

Regardless of the actual distribution, it becomes extremely important for board members, executives, and managers to understand how to best develop and sustain an ethical corporate culture with respect to employees who can be sensitized to become aware they are facing ethical dilemmas or employees who can be influenced by their work environments. While recognizing there is no one-size-fits-all solution for all business organizations, one can certainly postulate

that certain core elements should be in place to have the greatest chance of developing and maintaining an ethical corporate culture.

A key question then arises: What critical elements are necessary to develop and sustain an ethical corporate culture? Based on a review of the extant literature, this article argues that three key elements must necessarily exist if crime, corruption, and other illegal or unethical activity within and on behalf of businesses are to be minimized through building an ethical corporate culture:

1. A set of *core ethical values* infused throughout the organization in its policies, processes, and practices;

2. A *formal ethics program,* including a code of ethics, ethics training, an ethics hotline, and an ethics officer; and

3. The continuous presence of *ethical leadership* (i.e., an appropriate tone at the top as reflected by the board of directors, senior executives, and managers).

While these three elements are distinct, they also overlap, relate to, and reinforce each other. As part of an effort to consolidate the extensive theoretical and empirical business ethics research that has been conducted to date, each of the three key elements necessary to develop and maintain an ethical corporate culture will now be discussed.

2. First Pillar: Core Ethical Values

A set of core ethical values appears to be critical in establishing an ethical corporate culture. As articulated by Hunt, Wood, and Chonko (1989, p. 79), "corporate values have long been referred to as the central dimension of an organization's culture." An ethical corporate culture has, in turn, been recognized as important to ethical decision making. Indeed, O'Fallon and Butterfield (2005, p. 397) state that "research generally supports the notion that ethical climates and cultures have a positive influence on ethical decision making." Despite the recognized importance of core ethical

Hypernorms

universal ethical values

values, however, research likewise suggests that many employees perceive their firms to be lacking ethical values. For example, of 23,000 U.S. employees surveyed, only 15% felt they worked in a high-trust environment, only 13% had highly cooperative working relationships with other groups or departments, and only 10% felt their organization holds people accountable for results (Covey, 2004).

Although there are a number of potential ethical values from which a firm may choose, it could be argued that one needs to attempt to identify those ethical values that can be considered universal in nature. To the greatest extent possible, the selected moral values should retain their significance despite differences in culture, religion, time, and circumstance. A large number of diverse individuals and social groups should view the values as being fundamentally important in guiding or evaluating behavior, actions, or policies. Along these lines, universal moral values are considered to be similar to *hypernorms*,

which Donaldson and Dunfee (1999) describe as "deep moral values" (p. 27) representing "a convergence of religious, political, and philosophical thought" (p. 44). Hypernorms are considered "so fundamental that, by definition, they serve to evaluate lower-order norms [while]. . . reaching to the root of what is ethical for humanity" (p. 44). One list that has been proposed suggests the following set of universal core ethical values for all business firms (Schwartz, 2005):

- *Trustworthiness*, including honesty, promise keeping, integrity, transparency, reliability, and loyalty;
- *Respect*, including respect for human rights;
- *Responsibility*, including accountability, accepting fault, and not blaming others;
- *Fairness*, including notions of process, impartiality, and equity;
- *Caring*, including sensitivity toward others and avoiding unnecessary harm; and

Table 24.1	Ethical Dilemmas and Potential Application of Ethical Values
Ethical Dilemma	*Application of Ethical Values*
Should I break confidentiality and indicate to a friend that he/she is about to be laid off?	While values like loyalty to one's friend or caring (i.e., trying to avoid unnecessary harm) suggest breaching confidentiality and disclosing the information to one's friend, other aspects of *trustworthiness* (e.g., *loyalty* to the firm, *honesty*, and *promise keeping*) suggest maintaining confidentiality despite pressure to do otherwise.
Do I accept an expensive bottle of wine during the holiday season from a current supplier if the firm does not forbid this?	While one might argue that accepting gifts is the norm and there is no current apparent conflict of interest, the ethical values of *fairness* (e.g., perceived conflict of interest) and *loyalty* to the firm and its owners suggest otherwise. At a minimum, if refusing the bottle of wine would be problematic, then the gift should become the property of the firm rather than the property of the individual receiving the gift.
Do I fully disclose a mistake made to a client or customer when they will not notice and the mistake is significant?	This issue can place potential negative financial considerations of losing the client into conflict with ethical values. The core values of *trustworthiness* (i.e., *loyalty, honesty, promise keeping, integrity*) clearly suggest that disclosure must take place. *Respect* for the client suggests that disclosure should take place. *Responsibility* also suggests that accountability for the mistake should be taken, and *fairness* would require compensation to be provided if the mistake caused any loss to the client/customer.

- *Citizenship,* including obeying laws, assisting the community, and protecting the environment.

Can the application of such core ethical values actually assist managers and employees in determining the appropriate course of ethical conduct? To help illustrate their potential, Table 24.1 provides a brief analysis of how several of the aforementioned core ethical values can be applied to resolve typical ethical dilemmas faced in the workplace.

If applied to business practices, core ethical values can sometimes constrain the firm's self-interest; however, in other cases, consistently applying such values helps ensure the long-term financial prosperity of the firm. Regardless of whether applying ethical values always leads to profit maximization, it can be argued that all business firms should attempt to infuse core ethical values throughout their organizations as the basic starting point for establishing an ethical corporate culture. This infusion should take place within the firm's (1) policies, (2) processes, and (3) practices.

2.1. Policies

First, whenever possible, core ethical values must be made explicit in the firm's policy documents. The most important document in which values should be present is the firm's code of ethics, and they should be stated up-front. Values should also be included in the firm's annual report, public accountability statement, or social report, and they should be indicated as clearly as possible on the homepage of the firm's website. Although being explicit about ethical values might expose a firm to additional critique from academics, the media, non-governmental organizations (NGOs), customers, and even employees, this should be considered a necessary step toward establishing an ethical corporate culture. Of course, even firms like Enron—despite being quite explicit in its office banners and training videos about the company's core ethical values, including integrity, honesty, and respect—failed to live up to them. This makes it clear that values must be incorporated into other processes and practices, too.

2.2. Processes

Values only become alive and lead to a more ethical corporate culture when they are infused and observed throughout the firm's processes. The first process involves hiring; namely, the right people need to be recruited. There are various methods that can be used to build ethical values (e.g., honesty, integrity) into the hiring process, such as testing and interviews. Certain questions (e.g., "Have you ever faced an ethical dilemma before? If so, how did you handle it?") have the potential to reveal an applicant's general awareness of ethical issues and his/her perspective on ethical decision making. Certain answers (e.g., "I don't think I've ever faced an ethical dilemma") suggest a lack of awareness and might represent a red flag during the hiring process. Hiring ethical leaders at the more senior levels can be critical if an ethical tone at the top is to be established.

While concerns have been raised over the use and effectiveness of integrity testing, this tool also remains an important measure for employers to screen out 'executive psychopaths,' who—despite their polish, charm, and cool decisiveness—are "cunning, manipulative, untrustworthy, unethical, parasitic, and utterly remorseless," thus making them dangerous to their companies (Morse, 2004, p. 20). Ethical values should be considered the filter or gate through which potential new employees or managers must pass before financial performance factors may even be considered when hiring. Firms might ponder utilizing a group decision-making approach when hiring at the senior levels (as opposed to one-on-one hiring interviews only) as this process better facilitates raising ethical red flags regarding candidates.

Ethical values should also be part of any orientation process, such as ethics training. Performance appraisals should also consider employees' behavior with respect to ethical values: "An effective performance management system is a key component of the ethical culture. The system plays an essential role in alignment or misalignment of the ethical culture because people pay attention to what is measured, rewarded, and disciplined" (Treviño St Nelson, 2011, p. 172). While it is sometimes more difficult in a performance appraisal to measure behavior that conforms to ethical values, it is easier to identify actions that fail to reflect such values. Promotion decisions should also be based on the ethical values. When employees are promoted only on the basis of their financial performance when they have not lived up to values only reinforces the perception for other employees that the firm does not consider ethical values to be important. This can have a potentially severe impact on the firm's ethical corporate culture. Disciplinary or even dismissal decisions should also be based on whether individuals live up to values. Most important is that, to the greatest extent possible, the firm aligns its reward system—including compensation—with its ethical values.

2.3. Practices

If the firm has a set of core ethical values, it needs to be perceived to live up to them; that is, it must 'walk the talk.' Without this general perception, ethical values quickly become meaningless. To prevent this from occurring, there are a variety of practices that should explicitly incorporate the firm's values. All decision making and behavior at every level and function should be based on the firm's ethical values, whenever possible. This includes not only at the executive, manager, and employee levels, but also at the board of directors level. Surveys of employees and customers should attempt to include feedback on performance of the firm and its agents with respect to ethical values. All meetings, additional training efforts, and speeches—especially by senior managers—should make explicit reference to core ethical values. The aforementioned actions reinforce core ethical values, helping to sustain an ethical corporate culture.

Another method entails building ethical values into stories about the actions/decisions of employees, managers, or senior executives, which gives greater meaning to the organization's culture. This storytelling should include positive tales in which an employee, manager, or even the chief executive officer (CEO) acted consistently with the firm's core ethical values, despite financial pressure to do otherwise. However, it should also include negative stories whereby the firm failed to live up to its values, as well

as discussions about why the mistakes were made and how to avoid such mistakes in the future.

3. Second Pillar: Formal Ethics Program

Most commentators agree that a formal, comprehensive ethics program is necessary to help establish and ensure an ethical corporate culture, particularly for larger organizations. In fact, changing regulations have virtually made it a requirement for large firms and public firms to ensure they have such programs in place. For example, the U.S. Federal Sentencing Guidelines for Organizations (FSGOs), which were enacted by the U.S. Sentencing Commission (1991), are referred to when judges sentence organizations for violating U.S. federal law. The FSGOs permit firms to have their fines reduced if they are able to establish that they possessed an effective compliance and ethics program prior to the offense. Revised in 2004 and again in 2010, the FSGOs now suggest that an ethical organizational culture is necessary before a firm can be considered to have an effective compliance and ethics program designed to prevent illegal and unethical behavior. The FSGOs (Section 8B2.1) state: "To have an effective compliance and ethics program, an organization shall promote *an organizational culture that encourages ethical conduct* and a commitment to compliance with the law" [emphasis added]. The FSGOs go on to identify the minimum requirements for a firm to be considered as possessing an effective program, including a code of ethics, ethics training, an individual responsible for the ethics program, and a reporting system for improper behavior. In a similar fashion, the U.S. Sarbanes-Oxley Act (SOX) requires firms to ensure the presence of certain ethics program elements. Not only are public firms essentially required to possess a code of conduct or ethics, but SOX also suggests certain minimum content for the code while requiring that firms have appropriate whistle-blowing channels.

Numerous commentators now also provide more specific recommendations regarding each element of an effective ethics program (see Schwartz, 2004). For example, codes of ethics should be easy to understand

and non-legalistic, include relevant examples, avoid a negative tone, and include expected behaviors and sanctions. The code-development process should involve employees, apply to everyone in the organization, and include a sign-off process whereby employees indicate they have read, understand, and will comply with the code. Ethics training with relevant examples should be conducted by managers whenever possible. The code should be reinforced regularly at meetings and through emails, newsletters, and high-level speeches. Often referred to as an *ethics* or *compliance officer,* an administrator who has direct access to the board of directors and who cannot be fired by the CEO should be appointed to oversee the ethics program. To the greatest extent possible, a reporting mechanism should also be established to provide for anonymity and confidentiality with no fear of reprisals; any code enforcement must be fair and consistent. Finally, regular monitoring and auditing of the ethics program's effectiveness should take place, as well as periodic revisions.

All these measures are part of developing a comprehensive and effective ethics program. Ultimately, the program should be based on the previously discussed core ethical values. However, a firm that possesses core ethical values infused throughout its policies, processes, and practices—even when supported by a comprehensive ethics program—is not sufficient. The presence of ethical leadership is also necessary, as will now be discussed.

4. Third Pillar: Ethical Leadership

Beyond infusing ethical values throughout the organization and developing a comprehensive ethics program, to achieve an ethical corporate culture, there must also be an ethical tone at the top. In fact, many suggest that an ethical corporate culture is contingent upon ethical leadership: "The moral tone of an organization is set best by top management. . .workers generally get their ethical cues by observing what their bosses do" (James, 2000, p. 54). According to Brown, Treviño, and Harrison (2005, p. 117), "Leaders should be the key source of ethical guidance for employees." They define ethical leadership as "The demonstration of normative-ly appropriate conduct through personal actions and interpersonal relationships, and the promotion of such conduct to followers through two-way communication, reinforcement, and ethical decision-making" (p. 120). Others have even suggested that a relationship exists between ethical leaders and the presence of values within an organization: "Ethics is central to leadership because of the. . .impact leaders have on establishing the organization's values" (Northouse, 2001, p. 255). Of course, ethical leadership must be demonstrated not just by the CEO and other senior executives in the C-suite, but at every level, including first-line supervisors and retail store managers.

The relationship between ethical leadership and ethical behavior has also been observed. According to Hitt (1990, p. 3), "results of research studies demonstrate that the ethical conduct of individuals in organizations is influenced greatly by their leaders." Perceptions among employees that their managers possess a set of core ethical values and act upon them has been shown to significantly impact the firm's ethical corporate culture. Based on a survey of more than 10,000 U.S. employees, a study by Treviño, Weaver, Gibson, and Toffler (1999, p. 142) supports this point:

> When employees perceived that supervisors and executives regularly pay attention to ethics, take ethics seriously, and care about ethics and values as much as the bottom line, all of the outcomes [i.e., employees less likely to engage in unethical/illegal behavior, have greater awareness of ethical/legal issues, more likely to look for advice within the firm, willing to deliver bad news to management, willing to report ethical violations, and more committed to the organization] were significantly more positive.

Despite the recognized importance of ethical leadership within business, there appears to be a perception that such leadership is lacking. For example, a 2010 Gallup survey of more than 1,000 U.S. adults found that only 15% perceived business executives as having 'very high' or 'high' honesty and ethical standards, even lower than auto mechanics at 28% and TV reporters at 23% (Gallup, 2010). In a 2009 survey of 1,024 of its readers from around the world, *Harvard Business Review* found that 76% of respondents had less trust in U.S. senior management than they had the previous year, and 51% had less trust in senior management at non-U.S. companies (Polodny, 2009). This suggests that there is significant room for improvement in society's perception of business leaders' ethical values.

Why do most people, including employees and government regulators, remain so skeptical of corporate executives' ethical leadership capabilities? One reason is the inherent conflict between executives' desire to act in a manner that fulfills their fiduciary obligations to shareholders (i.e., maximize the bottom line) versus engaging in what the public considers to be ethical behavior (i.e., putting people before profits). For the general public, which does not possess a fiduciary obligation to stockholders, this perceived conflict of interest and corresponding perceptions of excessive corporate and executive greed is arguably the underlying basis for the anti-Wall Street movement. For governments, such perceptions appear to drive continuous calls for enhanced corporate governance regulations to restrain errant conduct. Thus, how exactly can managers and executives exemplify ethical leadership and reverse current negative perceptions?

Creating perceptions of ethical leadership is no easy task. Because most employees will not have direct contact with their senior managers, the firm's leaders must attempt to develop a reputation for ethical leadership. Various studies have examined how an ethical reputation is developed. Treviño, Brown, and Pincus-Hartman (2003) suggest there are two dimensions to ethical leadership: a 'moral person' dimension and a 'moral manager' dimension. The *moral person* dimension requires the manager to act with integrity, honesty, and trustworthiness. It is based on the manager treating people with respect and dignity, and living a moral life at the personal level. The *moral manager* dimension is affected not only by visibly role-modeling ethical conduct but also by applying a reward system to hold everyone accountable, and by regularly

and openly communicating with all employees about the importance of ethical values. If one is perceived as being a strong moral manager but a weak moral person, he/ she would be seen as a hypocrite; that is, he/ she talks about the importance of ethics but does not act accordingly. To be an ethical leader, a manager must be perceived as both a strong moral manager and a strong moral person.

Probably the most significant means of demonstrating ethical leadership is to ensure that all decision making is in accordance with the aforementioned ethical values. This becomes increasingly apparent when executives are seen to make such decisions even at great financial cost to the firm. Ethical values must be seen to take priority over other interests, or they quickly become irrelevant. In one famous example, as the founder of his accounting firm, the then-28-year-old Arthur Andersen refused to yield to the questionable demands of an important railway client during an audit. He lost the client as a result, but when the client later went bankrupt, Arthur Andersen developed a reputation as someone who could be trusted to act with integrity. This decision set an ethical tone for the firm for many years, leading to Arthur Andersen later acting as a watchdog over the entire accounting industry. Unfortunately, such ethical behavior did not continue in the long term at Arthur Andersen, and its culture—especially in relation to its client, Enron—began to focus more on generating revenue than on the ethical values originally underlying its auditing business.

In another high-profile case, former Johnson St. Johnson CEO James Burke relied on his firm's credo to withstand the 1982 Tylenol crisis and derive a long-term competitive advantage from the event. Under Burke's leadership, the company placed customer safety ahead of financial considerations: it recalled Tylenol nationwide, despite the massive cost. Similarly, former Alcoa CEO, Paul O'Neil, developed a reputation for caring about the safety of his employees. He did this by visiting plants and indicating to personnel that there would be no budget limits for safety matters; they should spend as much as necessary to fix all safety hazards, regardless of the cost. O'Neil distributed his home phone number such that safety problems could be reported, and he flew to speak in person with employees who had been injured on the job. As another example, following a series of scandals at the Canadian bank CIBC related to its dealings with Enron and a $2.4 billion settlement with investors, the new CEO, Gerald McCaughey, decided to voluntarily accept a compensation package that delayed the vesting of his share options extensively and also included a provision that his compensation could be taken away retroactively if a scandal was later discovered to have occurred during his term as CEO of the bank. Such actions could be seen to demonstrate a commitment to ethical values, including integrity, caring, and responsibility, leading to a perception of the CEO as an ethical leader.

Unfortunately, however, a multitude of companies have failed to establish such an ethical tone at the top, leading to significant scandals that sometimes caused their downfall. For example, U.S. firms and their former CEOs, such as WorldCom (Bernie Ebbers), Tyco International (Dennis Kozlowski), and Adelphia (John Rigas); Canadian firms, such as Hollinger (Conrad Black) and Livent (Garth Drabinsky); and the Italian firm Parmalat (Calisto Tanzi) appear to have lacked an appropriate tone at the top. These examples represent firms with unethical leadership, leading to behavior that cost them "billions of dollars a year due to increased absenteeism, health care costs, lost productivity, and expended costs associated with defending actionable claims" (Brown & Mitchell, 2010, p. 588).

In other cases, highly successful CEOs, such as Harry Stonecipher of Boeing and Mark Hurd of HP, were forced to resign following the discovery of inappropriate relationships. Even Enron—despite possessing a comprehensive compliance and ethics program—collapsed at least in part due to an unsuitable tone at the top led by former CEO Jeffrey Skilling, who emphasized bottom-line results over ethical values. Kenneth Lay, also former CEO and chairman of Enron, demonstrated a lack of ethical leadership when he requested that Enron's managers use his sister's travel agency for all of their overseas flights. Similarly, the U.S. government bailout of American International Group (AIG), the collapse of Lehman Brothers, and the sale of Merrill Lynch appear to demonstrate how the self-interested pursuits of these firms' senior leaders led to severe financial repercussions for their investors, clients, employees, and other stakeholders. All of these examples seem to support the claim that "Leadership which lacks ethical conduct can be dangerous, destructive, and even toxic" (Toor & Ofori, 2009, p. 533).

To summarize, an ethical leader is trustworthy, honest, transparent, responsible, caring, respectful, and fair; acts with integrity; and puts the interests of the firm and other stakeholders before his/her own personal interests. All of this must be demonstrated through the leader's actions, not just through words. In fact, only greater cynicism among employees will occur if the leader talks about the importance of ethical behavior but does not act accordingly. Regardless of the financial implications, senior executives' failure to act ethically must lead to disciplinary action by their firm's board of directors, in order to ensure a sense of accountability. Without ethical leadership across the organization, including at the board of directors level, there is little chance of establishing and sustaining an ethical corporate culture.

5. Discussion and Conclusion

Figure 24.1 summarizes the interaction of all three elements necessary to develop and sustain an ethical corporate culture within a firm. Once an ethical

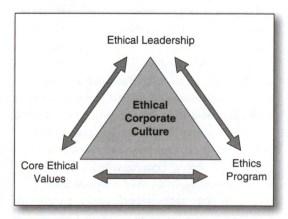

| **Figure 24.1** | Key Elements of an Ethical Corporate Culture |

corporate culture is developed and hopefully sustained, the assumption is that the extent of crime, corruption, and unethical activity within organizations or on their behalf will be minimized. Of course, developing an ethical corporate culture is only the first step, as multiple challenges must continually be overcome. For example, developing and sustaining an ethical corporate culture becomes exceptionally difficult for large multinational organizations with tens if not hundreds of thousands of employees around the world, each with his/her own distinct ethical perspective and culture. As such, a general or overarching corporate culture does not exist or would at least be extremely difficult to identify in any large multinational organization. Constant acquisitions or mergers between firms that possess very distinct ethical corporate cultures make it even more difficult to establish and maintain consistent ethical norms across an entire organization. A single change in top management can also have a significant negative impact on ethical corporate cultures, as demonstrated with respect to CEO Jeffrey Skilling at Enron. While difficult economic conditions or intense competition that might lead to financial ruin can actually strengthen ethical corporate culture due to increased scrutiny, such conditions might also intensify the pressure on firms to reject their ethical norms in favor of the bottom line.

Unfortunately, it is often difficult to measure the success of an ethical corporate culture in terms of outcomes, as one cannot always identify scandals that were avoided as a result of ethical work environments. In any event, while firms must undertake significant and sustained efforts to ensure high ethical standards, such efforts must take place along with the decisions and actions of other stakeholders, including governments (e.g., through regulation, enforcement, incentives), employees (e.g., where to work), customers (e.g., which companies' products to buy or services to use), suppliers (e.g., which companies to work with), creditors (e.g., where to lend), shareholders (e.g., where to invest, shareholders resolutions), NGOs (e.g., through the development of ethical codes and pressure tactics), academics (e.g., through normative research), and the media (e.g., through investigative reporting). As a multi-pronged approach, all of these stakeholders can collectively place additional pressure or create incentives to encourage firms and their agents to engage in legal and ethical behavior.

With respect to firms' own efforts, there are three fundamental elements that form the basis of an ethical corporate culture: (1) the existence of a set of *core ethical values,* (2) the establishment of a *formal ethics program,* and (3) the continuous presence of *ethical leadership.* As a summary, Table 24.2 highlights the key recommendations and provides better-known corporate examples of the good and bad for each of the three pillars of an ethical corporate culture.

With significant corporate scandals taking place in 2010—such as Toyota's recall troubles, leading to approximately $50 million in fines and billions of dollars in related expenses; Goldman Sachs betting against a sub-prime mortgage product while simultaneously recommending the product to its own clients, leading to a $550 million settlement; and BP's massive oil spill in the Gulf of Mexico, spurring establishment of a $20 billion compensation fund-one might question whether these firms had *all* three elements clearly present.

Without all three of these elements firmly in place, each of these firms arguably developed corporate cultures that emphasized financial considerations over the health, safety, or general wellbeing of other stakeholders. For example, some suggest that Toyota has a secretive corporate culture in Japan that disagrees with disclosing safety defects (Linebaugh, Searcey, & Shirouzu, 2010), and Goldman Sachs' corporate culture focus on revenue generation, egos, and bonuses is viewed as contributing to its clients being misled (Morgenson St. Story, 2010). Similarly, a U.S. government commission referred to BP as possessing a culture of complacency, with profits taking priority over safety, which partially led to the Gulf oil spill (Crooks, 2010). Future research might examine the extent to which firms like these that suffer ethical scandals are deficient in terms of infusing ethical values throughout the organization, possessing a weak ethics program, and/or lacking ethical leadership. Research might also examine whether such firms succeed in developing and sustaining ethical corporate cultures following such incidents based on the presence of the three core elements or if any changes in ethical culture tend to be merely short term in nature.

While all three elements are distinct, they also reinforce and support each other. For example,

Table 24.2	Three Pillars of an Ethical Corporate Culture: Recommendations and Examples

	Recommendations	*Examples*
(1)(a) Core ethical values: Policy	Establish a set of core ethical values for the firm, including trustworthiness, responsibility, caring, citizenship, fairness, and respect. Emphasize that when in conflict, the ethical values must take priority over the bottom line. The ethical values should be posted prominently in the firm's code of ethics and on the home page of the firm's website.	*Good:* Johnson & Johnson's credo establishes stakeholder priorities by stating that its first responsibility is to the users of its products and services while its final responsibility is to its stockholders. *Bad:* Toyota's actions leading to the brake pedal recall appeared to equate the value of 'safety' with 'quality' rather than making safety a priority in and of itself.
(1)(b) Core ethical values: Process	An ethical values filter should be applied to decision making, including hiring, performance appraisals, and firing. Whether one acts in accordance with the ethical values should be directly tied to the firm's compensation/ reward system.	*Good:* The firm Veritas (Latin for *truth*) fired its chief financial officer when it was discovered that he had lied on his resume years before about having a master of business administration. *Bad:* Enron's performance appraisal system (i.e., the 'rank and yank' process of dismissing the bottom 10% of performers) appears to have contributed to pressures to cut ethical corners.
(1)(c) Core ethical values: Practice	All firm-level and managerial-level decision making should be based on and explicitly refer to the core ethical values whenever possible.	*Good:* BankBoston's application of the ethical value of respect during layoffs in the 1990s led to the provision of job retraining, educational grants, and support of non-profit employment for employees who were laid off. *Bad:* Enron's complete disregard for its explicit values as indicated in its code of ethics, including respect and integrity (i.e., honesty)
(2)(a) Formal ethics program: Code	Ensure employee involvement in code creation or revision to help achieve buy-in and ensure realism. Code should apply to all firm's agents, including contractors and suppliers.	*Good:* Wal-Mart's 'Statement of Ethics' applies to all relevant stakeholders, including the firm's suppliers, consultants, law firms, public relations firms, contractors, and other service providers. *Bad:* WorldCom lacked a code of ethics based on CEO Bernie Ebber's view that having such a code was a "colossal waste of time."

(Continued)

Table 24.2   (Continued)

	Recommendations	Examples
(2)(b) Formal ethics program: Implementation	Annual sign-off of the code should take place. Relevant examples should be used during training. Manager should conduct training whenever possible.	*Good:* Johnson & Johnson periodically surveys its employees to evaluate how well the company lives up to its credo responsibilities. The firm ensures that the credo remains at the heart of the corporate culture by training its managers in the credo-based Johnson & Johnson 'Standards of Leadership.' *Bad:* Enron's training video 'Vision and Values' includes CEO Jeffrey Skilling's statement: "Out there... there's a desire to cut corners, but we can't have that at Enron."
(2)(c) Formal ethics program: Administration	A well-communicated whistleblowing channel should be established with protections provided against retaliation. Refer to the whistleblowing channel as a 'helpline' rather than a 'hotline.' Annual audit of the ethics program's effectiveness should take place with modifications made if necessary.	*Good:* Following its bribery scandal, Siemens created an ethics and risk compliance department with 600 employees, developed a training program, and changed the reporting system at the highest levels to try to prevent future misconduct. *Bad:* BP's alleged failure to protect its employees who raised safety complaints, in part leading to the Gulf oil spill.
(3) Ethical leadership	All actions and decisions at all levels throughout the organization should exemplify ethical leadership up to and including the board of directors. Managers should ensure that their personal behavior does not conflict with their ethical reputation at work.	*Good:* Johnson & Johnson's CEO James Burke's decision to recall Tylenol nationwide based on the company's redo and despite the financial cost. *Bad:* HP CEO Mark Hurd's concealed relationship with a marketing consultant and his submission of inaccurate expense reports.

ethical values become the basis for ethics programs, which can in turn enhance ethical leadership. As discussed, ethical leadership is critical for the successful infusion of ethical values throughout the organization and the potential effectiveness of ethics programs. When all three elements of an ethical corporate culture are in place, employees are not only sensitized to recognize the ethical dilemmas they or their firms face, but will also hopefully have the motivation, ability, and confidence to respond in an ethically appropriate manner with such ethical behavior being supported and rewarded by all managerial levels of the organization. Such ethical sensitivity will hopefully not only take place for macro-level ethical issues, such as whether to open up operations in a country run by a repressive regime, but also for micro-level issues, such as whether to hire a friend who is highly qualified for a job position. Nevertheless, due to human nature, crime, corruption, and other factors, illegal or unethical activity will never be completely eliminated for a certain percentage of the workforce regardless of whatever efforts are undertaken. However, business firms have an ethical obligation to make reasonable attempts to minimize the presence of crime and unethical activity for the good of all society.

References

Brass, D. J., Butterfield, K. D., & Skaggs, B. C. (1998). Relationships and unethical behavior: A social network perspective. *Academy of Management Review,* 23(1), 14–31.

Brooks, D. (2011, September 12). If it feels right. . . *New York Times.* Retrieved September 13, 2011, from http://www.nytimes.com/2011/09/13/opinion/if-it-feels-right.html?_r=1

Brown, M. E., & Mitchell, M. S. (2010). Ethical and unethical leadership: Exploring new avenues for future leadership. *Business Ethics Quarterly,* 20(4), 583–616.

Brown, M. E., Treviño, L. K., & Harrison, D. A. (2005). Ethical leadership: A social learning perspective for construct development and testing. *Organizational Behavior and Human Decision Processes,* 97(2), 117–134.

Covey, S. (2004). *The 8th habit.* New York: Free Press.

Crooks, E. (2010, November9). 'Bad calls' preceded Gulf of Mexico blast. *Financial Times.* Retrieved September 12, 2011, from http://www.ft.eom/intl/cms/s/0/a51cfcbc-ec0c-11df-b50f-00144feab49a.html#axzz23 Qc6jZB

Donaldson, T., & Dunfee, T. W. (1999). *Ties that bind: A social contracts approach to business ethics.* Boston: Harvard Business School Press.

Ethics Resource Center. (2010). *The importance of ethical culture: Increasing trust and driving down risks.* Retrieved September 12, 2011, from http://www.ethics.org/files/u5/ CultureSup4.pdf

Gallup (2010). *Honesty/ethics in professions.* Retrieved September 12, 2011, from http://www.gallup.com/poll/1654/honesty-ethics-professions.aspx

Hitt, W. D. (1990). *Ethics and leadership: Putting theory into practice.* Columbus, OH: Battelle Press.

Hunt, S. D., Wood, V. R., & Chonko, L. B. (1989). Corporate ethical values and organizational commitment in marketing. *Journal of Marketing,* 53(3), 79–90.

James, H. S., Jr. (2000). Reinforcing ethical decision making through organizational structure. *Journal of Business Ethics,* 28(1), 43–58.

Linebaugh, K., Searcey, D., & Shirouzu, N. (2010, February 8). Secretive culture led Toyota astray. *Wall Street Journal.* Retrieved from http://online.wsj.com/article/SB100 01424052748704820904575057505573309631238.html

Mcdonald, G. (2009). An anthology of codes of ethics. *European Business Review,* 21(4), 344–372.

Morgenson, G., & Story, L. (2010, May 18). Clients worried about Goldman's dueling goals. *New York Times.* Retrieved September 12, 2011, from http://www.nytimes.com/2010/05/19/business/19client.html?_r=1&dbk

Morse, G. (2004). Executive psychopaths. *Harvard Business Review,* 82(10), 20–22.

Northouse, P. G. (2001). *Leadership theory and practice* (2nd ed.). London: Sage Publications.

O'Fallon, M. J., & Butterfield, K. D. (2005). A review of the empirical ethical decision-making literature: 1996–2003. *Journal of Business Ethics,* 59(4), 375–413.

Podolny, J. M. (2009). The buck stops (and starts) at business school. *Harvard Business Review,* 87(6), 62–67.

Schwartz, M. S. (2004). Effective corporate codes of ethics: Perceptions of code users. *Journal of Business Ethics,* 55(4), 321–341.

Schwartz, M. S. (2005). Universal moral values for corporate codes of ethics. *Journal of Business Ethics,* 59(1), 27–44.

Toor, S. R., & Ofori, G. (2009). Ethical leadership: Examining the relationships with full range leadership model, employee outcomes, and organizational culture. *Journal of Business Ethics,* 90(4), 533–547.

Treviño, L. K., Brown, M., & Pincus-Hartman, L. (2003). A quantitative investigation of perceived executive ethical leadership: Perceptions from inside and outside the executive suite. *Human Relations,* 56(1), 5–37.

Treviño, L. K., & Nelson, K. A. (2011). *Managing business ethics* (5th ed.). New York: John Wiley.

Treviño, L. K., Weaver, G. R., Gibson, D. G., & Toffler, B. L. (1999). Managing ethics and legal compliance: What works and what hurts. *California Management Review,* 41(2), 131–151.

U.S. Sentencing Commission. (1991). *U.S. Federal Sentencing Guidelines for Organizations.* Retrieved September 12, 2011, from http://www.ussc.gov/Guidelines/Organizational_Guidelines/guidelines_chapter_8.htm

U.S. Sentencing Commission. (2010). Organizations receiving fines or restitution. *Sourcebook for Federal Sentencing Statistics.* Retrieved September 12, 2011, from http://www.ussc.gov/Data_and_Statistics/Annual_Reports_and_Sourcebooks/2010/Table51.pdf

CHAPTER 25

The Importance of Leadership in Shaping Business Values

Joanne B. Ciulla

University of Richmond

Few doubt that leaders play a role, either as founders or promoters of values in organizations. So the more important question is not 'Whose values?' but 'What values?' Just because a leader has values doesn't mean that they are good ones. Furthermore, the question is not so much about what a leader values, but what a leader actually does to demonstrate his or her values. This chapter is about how leaders translate values into action and actions into enduring organizational values. I first examine how we have come to think about the values of business leaders and success. I also reflect on what theories of leadership say about how leaders influence followers. Then I argue that the language of *having values* is often inadequate for understanding individual and organizational ethics. Lastly, I look at the leadership of P. Roy Vagelos of Merck & Company to illustrate the how the values of founders and current leaders shape the values of their own organizations, and can shape the values of the industries in which they operate.

Old Assumptions About the Values and Virtues of Business Leaders

Some of our attitudes towards the values of business leaders can be traced to the Protestant work ethic, which included the belief that accumulation of wealth was a sign that one was among God's chosen. One of the Calvinists' favorite Biblical passages was "Seest thou a man diligent in his business? He shall stand before kings" (Proverbs xxii 29). This equation of business success and salvation seemed to stick even in the secular world. In the 18th century, Benjamin Franklin tempered the Protestant work ethic with enlightenment ideals. He believed that business

Source: "The Importance of Leadership in Shaping Business Values," by Joanne B. Ciulla in *Long Range Planning,* Vol. 32, No. 2, pp. 166–172. Copyright © 1999 Elsevier Science Ltd. All rights reserved. Reprinted with permission.

leaders should strive for wealth so that they can use it in a humane way to help society. Franklin thought good character was necessary for success. In his autobiography he listed eleven virtues needed for success in business and in life: temperance, silence, order, resolution, sincerity, justice, moderation, cleanliness, tranquillity, chastity, and humility. Virtues tell us what we should be like and what we have to do to be that way. Values are what we believe to be important or morally worthy. We usually assume that values motivate us to act, but this isn't always the case. Some are satisfied to have a value and not act on it. This is not possible with a virtue. A person may value courage, but never do anything brave or heroic. Whereas one cannot possess the virtue of courage unless he or she has done something courageous.

America is somewhat distinct in its history of celebrating the values and character of business leaders. For example, in the 19th century, William Makepeace Thayer specialized in biographies of chief executive officers. His books focused on how the values leaders formed early in life contributed to their success. Thayer summed up the moral path to success this way: "Man deviseth his own way, but the Lord directeth his steps".[1] As the number of business journalists grew in America, some dedicated themselves to lionizing business leaders. The Scottish immigrant Bertie Charles (B.C.) Forbes elevated the moral adulation of business leaders into an enduring art form, imitated by business publications throughout the world. When he started Forbes magazine in 1916, Forbes described it as "a publication that would strive to inject more humanity, more joy, and more satisfaction into business and into life in general".[2] His goal was to convey Franklin's message that work, virtue, and wealth lead to happiness and social benefit.

The 18th and 19th century advocates of the work ethic preached that strong moral character was the key to wealth. By early 20th century the emphasis on moral character shifted to an emphasis on personality. In Dale Carnegie's 1936 classic *How to Win Friends and Influence People,* psychology, not morality, was the key to success in business. This was true in leadership theory as well. Scholars were more interested in studying the personality traits of leaders than their values. This is in part because through

most of the 20th century many prominent leadership scholars were psychologists.

The mythologies of business leaders remain popular, even though many of them are not great philanthropists or particularly morally virtuous or advocates of enlightened self-interest.[3] Today business leaders are more likely to be celebrated in the first person than in the third. Consider, for example, the popularity of autobiographies by Al Dunlap, Donald Trump, and Bill Gates, all of whom enjoy touting their own virtues and values to the public.

Recent books such as *Business as a Calling,* by Michael Novak, draw the traditional Protestant connection between success in business and God's favor.[4] Novak, who is a Catholic, argues that successful business people are more religious than other professionals. He cites two studies to back up his view. The first looked at church attendance by elites from the news media, business, politics, labor unions, the military, and religion. It found that groups with the highest proportion of weekly church attendance after religious professionals, were the military at 49% and then business at 35%. The second study, a Conference Board survey of senior executives at Fortune 500 companies, reported that 65% of the respondents said they worshipped at churches or synagogues regularly.[5] Novak infers that church going affects business values. However, we need more evidence than church attendance to connect religious values with the values a leader brings to work. After all, for some going to church is nothing more than *going to church.*

Leadership Theories and Values

The legacy of the Protestant work ethic and its attitudes toward business present a paradox. Are business leaders successful because of their virtues? or Are they virtuous because they are successful? In the literature of leadership studies both seem to be true, depending on how one defines leadership.

Leadership scholars have spent way too much time worrying about the definition of leadership. Some believe that if they could agree on a common definition of leadership, they would be better able to understand it. Joseph Rost gathered together 221 definitions of leadership. After reviewing all of his definitions, one discovers that the definition problem was not really about definitions *per se*. All 221 definitions say basically the same thing—leadership is about one person getting other people to do something. Where the definitions differ was in how leaders got other followers to act and how leaders came up with the something that was to be done. For example, one definition from the 1920s said, "[Leadership is] the ability to impress the will of the leader on those led and induce obedience, respect, loyalty, and cooperation".[6] Another definition from the 1990s said, "Leadership is an influence relationship between leaders and followers who intend real changes that reflect their mutual purposes".[7] We all can think of leaders who fit both of these descriptions. Some use their power to force people to do what they want, others work with their followers to do what everyone agrees is best for them. The difference between the definitions rests on a normative question: "How should leaders treat followers?"

The scholars who worry about constructing the ultimate definition of leadership are asking the wrong question, but inadvertently trying to answer the right one. The ultimate question about leadership is not "What is the definition of leadership?" The whole point of studying leadership is, "What is good leadership?" The use of word *good* here has two senses, morally good and technically good or effective. If a good leader means *good* in both senses, then the two should form a logical conjunction. In other words, in order for the statement "She is a good leader" to be true, it must be true that she is effective *and* she is ethical.

The question, "What constitutes a good leader?" lies at the heart of many public debates about leadership today. We want our leaders to be good in both ways. Nonetheless, we are often more likely to say leaders are good if they are effective, but not moral, than if they are moral, but not effective. Leaders face a paradox. They have to stay in business or get reelected in order to be leaders. If they are not minimally effective at doing these things, their morality as leaders is usually irrelevant, because they are no longer leaders. In leadership, effectiveness sometimes must take priority over ethics. What we hope for are leaders who know when ethics should and when

ethics shouldn't take a back seat to effectiveness. History tends to dismiss as irrelevant the morally good leaders who are unsuccessful. President Jimmy Carter was a man of great personal integrity, but during his presidency, he was ineffective and generally considered a poor leader. The conflict between ethics and effectiveness and the definition problem are apparent in what I have called, "the Hitler problem".[8] The answer to the question "Was Hitler a good leader?" is yes, if a leader is defined as someone who is effective or gets the job they set out to do done. The answer is no, if the leader gets the job done, but the job itself is immoral, and it is done in an immoral way. In other words leadership is about more than being effective at getting followers to do things. The quality of leadership also depends on the means and the ends of a leader's actions. The same is true for Robin Hood. While in myth some admire him, he still steals from the rich to give to the poor. His purpose is morally worthy, but the way that he does it is not. Most of us would prefer leaders who do the right thing, the right way for the right reasons.

The way that we assess the impact of a leader's values on an organization also depends on one's theory of leadership. Many still carry with them the "Great Man" theory—leaders are born and not made. Personality traits, not values catapult leaders to greatness. This theory has been articulated in different ways. Thomas Carlyle wrote about the traits of heroes such as Napoleon. Niccolo Machiavelli described the strategic cunning of his 'Prince'. Friedrich Nietzsche extolled the will to power of his 'superman'. While the innate qualities of leaders are primary factors in these theories, it is not always clear what makes people want to follow great men.

Charismatic leadership is a close relative to the Great Man Theory. Charismatic leaders have powerful personalities. However the distinguishing feature of charismatic leadership is the emotional relationship that charismatic leaders establish with followers. Charismatic leaders range from a John F. Kennedy, who inspired a generation to try and make the world better, to the cult leader Jim Jones, who lead his followers into suicide. The values of charismatic leaders shape the organization, but in some cases these values do not live on when the charismatic leader is gone.

Other theories of leadership focus on the situation or context of leadership. They emphasize the nature of the task that needs to be done, the external environment, which includes historical, economic, and cultural factors, and the characteristics of followers. Lee Iacocca was the right leader for Chrysler when it went bankrupt, but we don't know if he would be the right leader at some other phase of the firm's history. Ross Perot was a good business man, but many doubted his ability to be effective as a political leader. Situational theories don't explicitly say anything about values, but one might surmise that in some situations a person with particularly strong moral values must emerge as a leader. For example, Nelson Mandela and Vaclav Havel seemed to have been the right men at the right time. They both offered the powerful kind of moral leadership required for peaceful revolutions in South Africa and the Czech Republic.

A third group of scholars combine trait theories with situational models and focus on the interaction between leaders and followers. The leader's role is to guide the organization along paths that are rewarding to everyone involved. Here values are sure to play an important role, but again it matters what the values are and what they mean to others in the organization. The Ohio studies and the Michigan studies both measured leadership effectiveness in terms of how leaders treated subordinates and how they got the job done. The Ohio Studies looked at leadership effectiveness in terms of 'consideration' or the degree to which leaders act in friendly and supportive manner, and 'initiating structure' or the way that leaders structure their own role and the role of subordinates in order to obtain group goals.[9] The Michigan Studies measured leaders on the basis of task orientation and relationship orientation.[10] Implicit in these theories and studies is an ethical question. Are leaders more effective when they are kind to people, or are leaders more effective when they use certain techniques for structuring and ordering tasks? Is leadership about moral relationships or techniques?—probably both.[11]

Transforming Leadership and Servant Leadership are normative theories of leadership. Both emphasize the relationship of leaders and followers to each other and the importance values in the process of leadership. James MacGregor Burns' theory of transforming leadership rests on a set of moral assumptions about the relationship between leaders and followers.[12] Burns argues that leaders have to operate at higher need and value levels than those of followers. Charismatic leaders can be transforming leaders, however, unlike many charismatic leaders, the transforming leader engages followers in a dialogue about the tension and conflict within their own value systems. Transforming leaders have very strong values, but they do not force them on others.[13] Ultimately, the transforming leader develops followers so that they can lead themselves.

Burns' theory addresses two pressing moral questions. The morality of means (and this also includes the moral use of power) and the morality of ends. Burns' distinction between transforming and transactional leadership, and modal and end-values offers a way to think about the question "What is a good leader?" both in terms of the relationship of leaders to followers and the means and ends of actions. Transactional leadership rests on the values found in the means of an act. These are called modal values which are things like, responsibility, fairness, honesty and promise-keeping. Transactional leadership helps leaders and followers reach their own goals by supplying lower level wants and needs so that they can move up to higher needs. Transforming leadership is concerned with end-values, such as liberty, justice, and equality.

Servant leadership has not gotten as much attention as transformational leadership in the literature, but in recent years interest in it by the business community has grown. Servant leaders lead because they want to serve others. In *Servant Leadership,* Robert K. Greenleaf says people follow servant leaders freely because they trust them. Like the transforming leader, the servant leader also tries to morally elevate followers. Greenleaf says servant leadership must pass this test: "Do those served grow as persons? Do they *while being served* become healthier, wiser, freer, more autonomous, more likely themselves to become servants?" He goes on and adds a Rawlsian proviso, "*And,* what is the effect on the least privileged in society?"[14] In both transforming leadership and servant leadership, leaders not only have values, but they help followers develop their own values, which will hopefully overlap or be compatible with those of the organization.

The Problem of Only *Having* Values

Social scientists like to talk about values because they are descriptors. When a poll asks voters if they prefer better schools or lower taxes, we assume that if the majority pick better schools, it means most respondents value education. Ask people about their values and they will tell you what they think is important. Different types of moral statements and concepts *do* different things. For example the statement 'you ought not to kill' prescribes, 'Do not kill' commands, 'Killing is wrong' evaluates, and 'Killing is wrong because I value life' explains, and 'Killing is against my values, which include the value of human life' describes. Values are static concepts. You have to make a lot of assumptions to make a value *do* something. You have to assume that because people value something they act accordingly, but we know this isn't the case. While values change all the time, having a value does not mean that one has or will do something about it.

Since values themselves do not have agency, the main way that a leader influences the organization is through his or her words and actions. One way to understand a leader's values is through their vision. The CEO who says his or her vision is to double market share by the year 2000 has a goal, not a vision. All businesses want to make profits. Visions must have an implicit or explicit moral component to them.[15] Often the moral component has to do with improving the quality of life, particularly in the case of making a product safer, environmentally friendly, or more affordable to those who need it. A leader's vision should tell us where we want to go, why it's good to go there, and the right way for us to get there.

The only way to understand if a business leader's values have an impact is to look at how his or her values connect with actions. Hypocrisy is the most extreme form of values not meeting up with actions. Hypocrites express strong moral values that they do not hold and then act against them. For example, a company that advertises its commitment to green products while continuing to sell products that don't meet it's own espoused green standards is hypocritical.[16] What is most odd about some hypocrites is that

they are not always complete liars. Some know they should live up to the values they talk about, but simply do not or will not.

Another problem with values and actions is what Frederick B. Bird calls 'moral silence'. Moral silence is the opposite of hypocrisy. Morally silent leaders act and speak as if they do not hold certain moral values, when they actually do. The company president who cuts 1000 jobs from the payroll may publicly state that he cut jobs to fill what he considers his most important obligation to protect shareholder value. When in fact he is guilt ridden because he really believes that his greatest moral obligation is to his employees. Leaders sometimes lack the ability or the moral courage to act on their values. Similarly, there are some who have values, but are either too busy, distracted, or lazy to act on those values. Consider the case of a female corporate executive who has strong convictions about giving women opportunities for career advancement, but does not go out of her way or take advantage of opportunities to ensure that women in her company have these opportunities.

Often leaders don't realize that the values they hold are in practice contradictory or inconsistent. Once a colleague and I conducted an ethics seminar for the presidents of a large conglomerate. The CEO of the corporation was an enthusiastic participant. During the seminar he expressed his feelings about the importance of honesty and integrity in business. However, as the participants discussed our case studies, it became clear that there were a number of situations in which protecting the company's integrity meant losing business or money. The CEO actively agreed with these conclusions. However, the others in the seminar pointed out to him that quarterly sales determined the compensation for each business unit. The CEO set profit targets for each business unit and used a formula to determine compensation. When it came to performance, he valued the numbers more than anything else. What the CEO failed to realize was that he was espousing the value of integrity, but in effect saying that employees would be punished if they did not act with integrity (with firing) *and* punished if they did act with integrity (with reduced compensation). Some thought that if the CEO really valued integrity, he should make some adjustment to the incentive system to take into account business lost for ethical reasons. One brave man wondered out loud if the CEO didn't really value profits over integrity.

Often companies write codes of ethics or mission statements but don't to think through what the values in the statement mean in terms of how they manage their businesses. In 1983 the Harvard Business School wrote a glowing case study of how CEO Jim Beré developed the Borg-Warner code of ethics.[17] Borg-Warner is a conglomerate of automotive, financial services, and security service businesses. Its code began with the statement, "We believe in the dignity of the individual", and "We believe in the common-wealth of Borg Warner and its people". An elegant framed copy of the code was hung offices and factories of Borg-Warner's various businesses. Their ethics code also said, "we must heed the voice of our natural concern for others" and "grant others the same respect, cooperation, and decency we seek for ourselves".[18]

Warner Gear, a division of Borg Warner, manu-factured gears for cars and boats. In 1984 it made a text book turn around in labor relations and produc-tivity. After years of losing money and engaging in endless labor disputes, the union and management finally agreed to cooperate. They formed effective quality circles that saved the company millions of dollars in waste and inefficiency. Company profits soared in 1985.[19] However, in July of that year, with no warning to the managers or employees who implemented the turnaround, Borg Warner announced it was shipping part of Warner Gear to Kenfig, Wales to save on labor costs. This meant that the factory would lose 300 jobs. While the business decision may have been warranted, the way that it was implemented did not show decency and respect for those who had worked so hard to make the firm successful. All the energy, good will, and commit-ment of the employees didn't matter, and neither did the grand values that hung on the wall.

Lastly, there are cases where a business leader acts on values that he has never made any concerted effort to express in words to employees. On 11 December 1995 Malden Mills, a textile factory in Massachusetts, burnt down. The owner, Aaron Feuerstein, immedi-ately decided to give out Christmas bonuses and pay his employees full salaries until the factory was repaired. In the midst of massive corporate downsiz-ings this story of kindness captured the public imagi-nation. Feuerstein was a quiet man running a family business. The business itself was known for treating workers fairly, but Feuerstein had never been one to publicly articulate his own values. Given the publicity of his actions after the fire, he was asked by the press to talk about his values. He then explained that his business values came from his Jewish faith and the teachings of the Talmud. Yet for most employees, *where* he got his values didn't matter as much as *what* he did with them.

The point of these examples is to show that a leader's values do indeed shape the values of the firm when they are paired with policies and actions that breathe life into them. The way in which founders influence the values of the company is by setting out their mission, what they want to do, and how they want to do it. But most importantly, their actions write the story of the organization's values. The story can be a morally good one or an evil one. Either way, the role of leaders who come after the founder is to tell and add to the story of the company and its val-ues. This includes ethical lessons learned from its mistakes as well as its moral triumphs.

Howard Garner believes that great leaders are also great story tellers. He says leadership is a process in the minds of individuals who live in a culture. Some stories tend to become more predominant in this process, such as stories that provide an adequate and timely sense of identity for individuals.[20] The story of the fire at Malden Mills will become part of the com-pany's mythology. It not only conveys a message of moral commitment to employees, but it sets a moral standard for those who will take Feuerstein's place.

Leaders' values matter when they are repeatedly reflected in their actions. However, a leader's values and his or her will to act on them are also shaped by the history and the culture of the organization itself. As I pointed out earlier, we sometimes mythologize business leaders because they are successful or imag-ine that their lone values are responsible for doing some heroic action. But as we saw earlier, there can be a gap between having values and acting on them. This gap is often narrowed or widened by the values already present in the story of the organization.

One of the more dramatic illustrations of business leadership and values is the case of P. Roy Vagelos, CEO of Merck & Co., Inc.[21] Prior to becoming CEO, Vagelos was director of Merck Sharp & Dohme's research laboratories. In 1979 a researcher named William Campbell had a hunch that an antiparasite drug he was working on called Ivermectin might work on the parasite that caused river blindness, a disease that threatens the eyesight and lives of 85 million people in 35 developing countries. He asked Vagelos if he could have the resources to pursue his research. Despite the fact that the market for this drug was essentially the poorest people in the world, Vagelos gave Campbell the go ahead. While the decision was Vagelos', it was also reinforced by the Merck's axiom 'health precedes wealth'.

Campbell's hunch about Ivermectin proved to be right and he developed a drug called 'Mectizan', which was approved for use by the government in 1987. By this time Vagelos had become the CEO of Merck. Now that the drug was approved he sought public underwriting to produce Mectizan. Vagelos hired Henry Kissinger to help open doors for Merck. They approached several sources including the US Agency for International Development and the World Health Organization, but couldn't raise money for the drug. Merck was left with a drug that was only useful to people who couldn't buy it. Vagelos recalled, "We faced the possibility that we had a miraculous drug that would sit on a shelf".[22] After reviewing the company's options, Vagelos and his directors announced that they would give Mectizan away for free, forever, on 21 October 1987. A decade later the drug giveaway cost Merck over $200 million. By 1996 Mectizan had reached 19 million people. In Nigeria alone it saved 6 million people from blindness.

Few business leaders ever have the opportunity to do what Vagelos did. His values guided his decisions in this case, but so did the values of the founder. George C. Merck, son of the company's American founder said that from the very beginning Merck's founders asserted that medicine was for people not profits. However, he quickly added that they also believed that if medicine is for people, profits will follow.[23]

Like many corporate mission statements Merck's says its mission "is to provide society with superior products and services". The statement goes on to assert, "We are in the business of preserving and improving human life". "All of our actions must be measured by our success at achieving this goal". It concludes that "We expect profits from work that satisfies customer needs and that benefits humanity".[24] The values in Merck's mission statement are as grand as the ones in Borg Warner's. However, the corporate leaders prior to Vagelos acted on and hence reinforced these values long before Vagelos donated Mectizan. After WWII tuberculosis thrived in Japan. Most Japanese couldn't afford to buy Merck's powerful drug, Streptomycin, to fight it. Merck gave away a large supply of the drug to the Japanese public. The Japanese did not forget. In 1983 the Japanese government allowed Merck to purchase 50.02% of Banyu Pharmaceutical. At the time this was the largest foreign investment in a Japanese company. Merck is currently the largest American pharmaceutical company in Japan. The story makes Merck's mission statement come alive. It is the kind of story that employees learn and internalize when they come to work there.

Vagelos' moral leadership in this case extended beyond his organization into the industry. As Michael Useem points out, Merck has become the benchmark by which the moral behavior of other pharmaceutical companies are judged. Sometimes the moral actions of one CEO or company set the bar higher for others. Useem observes that the message hit home at Glaxo. In comparing Glaxo to Merck, a business writer once called Glaxo "a hollow enterprise lacking purpose and lacking soul".[25] Merck's values seemed to inspire Glaxo's new CEO Richard Sykes. In 1993 Glaxo invested in developing a drug to combat a form of tuberculosis connected to Aids and found mostly among the poor. In 1996 Glaxo donated a potent new product for malaria. Similarly, Dupont is now giving away nylon to filter guinea worms out of drinking water in poor countries and American Cyanamid is donating a larvacide to control them.

A cynic might regard Merck's donation of Streptomycin and Mectizan as nothing more than public relations stunts. But what is most interesting about the actions of Merck's leaders is that while they believed that "by doing good they would do well", at the time that they acted it was unclear exactly when and how the company would benefit. Neither the Japanese after the war nor the poor people of the world who are threatened by river blindness looked likely to return the favor in the near future. While this wasn't an altruistic act, it was not a purely self-interested one either. Since it was unclear if, when, and how Merck would benefit, it is reasonable to assume that Merck's leaders and the values upon which they acted were authentic. They intentionally acted on their values. Any future benefits required a leap of faith on their part.

Business leaders' values matter to the organization only if they act on them. In business ethics and in life we always hope that doing the right thing, while costly and sometimes painful in the short run, will pay off in the long run.

Notes

1. R. M. Huber, *The American Idea of Success*, p. 53, McGraw-Hill, New York (1971).

2. B. C. Forbes, Fact and comment, *Forbes* 60(1 October), 10 (1947).

3. See 'The challenge for America's rich" and "Philanthropy in America", *The Economist* 30 May, 17, 23-25 (1998).

4. M. Novak, *Business as a Calling*, The Free Press, New York (1996).

5. "God Gets Down to Business", Across the board, *The Conference Board* 14(5), 11-12 (1988).

6. B. V. Moore, The May Conference on leadership, *Personnel Journal 6*, 124 (1927).

7. J. Rost, *Leadership for the Twenty-First Century*, p. 102, Praeger, New York (1991).

8. J. B. Ciulla, Leadership ethics: Mapping the territory, *Business Ethics Quarterly* January (1995).

9. E. A. Fleishman, The description of supervisory behavior, *Personnel Psychology* 37, 1-6 (1953).

10. Results from the earlier and later Michigan Studies are discussed in R. Leikert, *New Patterns of Management*, McGraw-Hill, New York (1961), and *The Human Organization: Its Management and Value*, McGraw-Hill, New York (1967).

11. G. Yukl, *Leadership in Organizations*, 2nd ed, Prentice-Hall, Englewood Cliffs, NJ (1989), p. 96.

12. Burns uses the terms *transforming* and *transformational* in his book. However, he prefers to refer to his theory as *transforming* leadership.

13. J. MacGregor Burns, *Leadership*, pp. 42-43, Harper & Row, New York (1978).

14. R. Greenleaf, *Servant Leadership*, p. 23, Paulist Press, New York (1977).

15. B. Nanus, *Visionary Leadership*, Jossey-Bass, San Francisco (1992).

16. F. B. Bird, *The Muted Conscience*, p. 4, Quorum Books, Westport, CT (1996).

17. K. E. Goodpaster, The beliefs of Borg-Warner, Harvard Business School case 9-383-091, The President and Fellows of Harvard College (1983).

18. P. E. Murphy, *80 Exemplary Ethics Statements*, p. 27, University of Notre Dame Press, Notre Dame, IN (1998).

19. J. B. Ciulla, and K. E. Goodpaster, Building trust at Warner Gear, Harvard Business School Case Services 0-386-0011, p. 11, The President and Fellows of Harvard College (1985).

20. H. Gardner, *Leading Minds*, p. 22, Basic Books, New York (1995).

21. The information about this case is from M. Useem, *The Leadership Moment*, Chap. 1, Times Business Books, New York (1998).

22. *Ibid.*, p. 23.

23. *Ibid.*, p. 29.

24. p. 29.

25. p. 31.

CHAPTER 26

Authentic Leadership

Arran Caza
Wake Forest University

Brad Jackson
University of Auckland

Introduction

Recent corporate and political scandals have prompted media portrayals of a 'global leadership crisis', which in turn has led to discussion of the nature of leadership, with both its advantages and disadvantages (Kets De Vries & Balazs, Chapter 28). In these discussions, authentic leadership has assumed an important position among strength-based approaches, having been advanced as a potential solution to the challenges of modern leadership. While authentic leadership research only developed a coherent focus in 2003, it has since attracted considerable theoretical attention and continues to figure prominently in practitioners' treatment of leadership. Ladkin and Taylor (2010) note that it has provided the focus for three special issues of academic journals: *The Leadership Quarterly* (2005/1), the *Journal of Management Studies* (2005/5), and the *European Management Journal* (2007/2).

Authentic leadership has also provided the inspiration for numerous popular books and articles (e.g. George, 2003; Goffee & Jones, 2005; Irvine & Reger, 2006). These are supported by a strong and growing interest in authentic leadership among practitioners in many industries and professions (e.g. Gayvert, 1999; George, Sims, McLean, & Mayer, 2007; Kouzes & Posner, 2008; Nadeau, 2002; O'Connor, 2007; Pembroke, 2002; Shelton, 2008). In one striking example, the American Association of Critical Care Nurses declared authentic leadership to be one of their six necessities for a healthy working environment (American Association of Critical Care Nurses, 2005).

As a nascent endeavour, authentic leadership research is still in the process of defining itself, and so this review is primarily formative rather than summative in nature. We describe the history and content of authentic leadership theory, overview its theoretical tenets, and review the empirical evidence that has been provid ed to date. We conclude by highlighting some prominent opportunities and challenges that appear to lie ahead for authentic leadership theory.

Source: The Sage Handbook of Leadership by editors Alan Bryman, David Collinson, Keith Grint, Brad Jackson and Mary Uhl-Bien, 2011, pp. 352–364. SAGE Publications. Reprinted with permission.

Motivations and Origins of Authentic Leadership Theory

Luthans and Avolio's (2003) chapter on authentic leadership development is generally credited with being the starting point of the research programme on authentic leadership (e.g. Avolio, Walumbwa, & Weber, 2009; Gardner, Avolio, & Walumbwa, 2005; Walumbwa, Avolio, Gardner, Wernsing, & Peterson, 2008). This programme is usually described as the union of Avolio's interest in fullrange leadership (e.g. Avolio, 1999) with Luthans' work on positive organizational behaviour (Luthans, 2002). Nonetheless, these and other authors recognize that there had been some prior work concerning authenticity and leadership (Avolio, Gardner, & Walumbwa, 2005), particularly in the field of education (e.g. Henderson & Hoy, 1983; Hoy & Henderson, 1983), as well as Luthans' consideration of positive leadership (Luthans, Luthans, Hodgetts, & Luthans, 2001). Related issues had also figured in studies that had not explicitly focused on authenticity. For example, leaders who engaged in self-monitoring, which is a behavioural tendency to intentionally adjust one's behaviour to fit the current context (Snyder, 1974), had been shown to be perceived as less sincere and more manipulative, and to therefore receive poorer group performance from followers (Sosik, Avolio, & Jung, 2002).

Nonetheless, Luthans and Avolio (2003) noted that most of the previous work had examined the negative consequences of a lack of authenticity, rather trying to understand authenticity per se. Their chapter was a call to focus primarily on authentic leadership itself. In this sense, authentic leadership theory can be seen as a part of the growing popularity of positive perspectives throughout the social sciences, including psychology (Seligman & Csikszentmihalyi, 2000), organizational studies (Cameron, Dutton, & Quinn, 2003) and organization behaviour (Luthans, 2002). Consistent with this, authentic leadership scholars have explicitly recognized their intellectual debt to the humanistic values of psychologists such as Rogers (1963) and Maslow (1968) as important influences upon the development of this new positive perspective on leadership (Avolio & Gardner, 2005).

However, the most important influence on the development of authentic leadership theory most likely emerged from the post-charismatic critiques of transformational leadership (Michie & Gooty, 2005). As described by Díaz-Sáenz (Chapter 22), the construct of transformational leadership was developed in the 1970s as a way to understand highly influential political leaders (Burns, 1978), and was subsequently applied to business and organizational contexts throughout the 1980s (e.g. Bass, 1985). Transformational leadership involves a number of specific behaviours and effects, but these are generally united by the leader's ability to craft and convey a compelling vision that leads followers to adopt the leader's mission as their own (Bass & Avolio, 1997). For example, transformational leaders were described as exhibiting 'idealized influence,' in that followers came to judge them as embodying desirable beliefs and therefore being worthy of emulation (Jung & Avolio, 2000).

Several commentators noted potential danger in the influence and adulation generated by transformational leaders (e.g. Conger & Kanungo, 1998). For example, it was suggested that the extreme personal identification of followers with a transformational leader could create follower dependence on the leader (see Trevino & Brown, 2007), and this fear was supported by empirical evidence (e.g. Kark, Shamir, & Chen, 2003). Moreover, the ethical basis for transformation was also questioned, since the leader's intentional alteration of followers' values seemed to risk—perhaps even require—manipulation (Beyer, 1999; Price, 2003). In fact, Bass described both Ghandi and Hitler as transformational leaders (Bass, 1985). Empirical evidence also showed that transformational leadership did not necessarily have to be ethical (Howell & Avolio, 1992).

The response to these concerns by the leading theorists of transformational leadership was to draw a distinction between 'authentic' transformational leaders and 'pseudo' transformational leaders (Bass & Steidlmeier, 1999). They noted that 'to be truly transformational, leadership must be grounded in moral foundations' (1999, p. 181). In this reformulation, leaders who are not morally and ethically sound may exhibit influence and charisma, but they are only pseudo-transformational. Authentically transformational leaders are distinguished by their personal moral character, the admirable values that comprise their agenda, and the ethical means they use when interacting with others. Consistent with this, as discussed below, authentic leadership theory stressed the moral component of leadership from the outset.

Defining Authentic Leadership

Authentic leadership theory makes distinctions between three types or levels of authenticity: an individual's personal authenticity; a leader's authenticity as a leader; and authentic leadership as a phenomenon in itself (Shamir & Eilam, 2005; Yammarino, Dionne, Schriesheim, & Dansereau, 2008). These three types of authenticity are argued to be hierarchically inclusive, such that one cannot be an authentic leader without being individually authentic and authentic leadership is not possible without the intervention of an authentic leader (Gardner, Avolio, Luthans, May, & Walumbwa, 2005).

In this context, 'authenticity' is defined based on psychological research, particularly that of Harter (2002) and Kernis (2003). Harter (2002) emphasied the origins of the term in ancient Greek philosophy and described two components of authenticity: knowing one's true self and acting in accord with that true self. In consequence, 'authenticity is thus an entirely subjective, reflexive process that, by definition, is experienced only by the individual him- or herself' (Erickson, 1994, p. 35). If an individual believes she is being authentic, then by definition, she is (Avolio & Gardner, 2005; Harter, 2002). However, this phenomenological emphasis contrasts with some other approaches, which require empirical validation (e.g. Terry, 1993). In this vein, Kernis (2003) defined authenticity as consisting of four components: full awareness and acceptance of self; unbiased processing of self-relevant information; action consistent with true self; and a relational orientation that values openness and truth in close personal relationships. Combining these two views, authentic

leadership scholars define authenticity as having clear and certain knowledge about oneself in all regards (e.g., beliefs, preferences, strengths, weaknesses) and behaving consistently with that self-knowledge (Gardner, Avolio, Luthans, et al., 2005; Ilies, Margeson, & Nahrgang, 2005).

Building on this definition, and particularly the four components in Kernis (2003), 'authentic leaders' are defined as leaders who exhibit four behavioural tendencies: self-awareness, which is accurate knowledge of one's strengths, weaknesses, and idiosyncratic qualities; relational transparency, which involves genuine representation of the self to others; balanced processing, which is the collection and use of relevant, objective information, particularly that which challenges one's prior beliefs; and an internalized moral perspective, which refers to self-regulation and self-determination, rather than acting in accordance with situational demands (Gardner, Avolio, Luthans, et al., 2005; Walumbwa et al., 2008). It should be noted that the definition explicitly requires all four components be true of both the leader's thoughts and actions (Gardner, Avolio, Luthans, et al., 2005; Ilies et al., 2005). In contrast, some observers have noted that individuals may be authentically self-aware yet choose to behave in a self-inconsistent or inauthentic fashion (Harter, 2002; Kernis, 2003). Others have argued against the inclusion of a moral component, questioning whether there is any inherent difference between an authentic person who leads and an authentic leader (Shamir & Eilam, 2005; Sparrowe, 2005). Nonetheless, most authentic leadership theory has been based on the tenet that anyone lacking even one of the four behaviours cannot be an authentic leader, suggesting that some consensus has developed in support of the four-part definition (Avolio et al., 2009; Walumbwa et al., 2008).

Given the four behaviours required of authentic leaders, 'authentic leadership' is then defined in terms of the consequences of those behaviours:

A pattern of leader behavior that draws upon and promotes both positive psychological capacities and a positive ethical climate, to foster greater self awareness, an internalized moral perspective, balanced processing of information, and relational transparency on the part of leaders working with followers, fostering positive self-development (Walumbwa et al., 2008, p. 94).

We should note that in the opening of this chapter, we referred to authentic leadership theory as a new focus for research; however, many of the central participants might object to our characterization. When definitions of authentic leadership are stated, they are typically accompanied by claims that this is not a new type of leadership or a new label for an existing phenomenon, but rather a concern with what is fundamental in leadership (e.g., Avolio & Gardner, 2005; Avolio et al., 2009; Chan, Hannah, & Gardner, 2005; May, Chan, Hodges, & Avolio, 2003). It has been claimed that authentic leadership, as here defined, is the 'root construct of all positive, effective forms of leadership' (Avolio et al., 2005, p. xxii).

Theoretical Claims

In the seven years since its formal introduction, authentic leadership has been the focus of significant theoretical attention. A number of authors have discussed its antecedents and consequences, at all levels and in all areas of organizational life. It is beyond the scope of this chapter to restate the full arguments developing these claims. Instead, we provide a brief summary of the claims that have been made, so that interested readers may pursue the original source material for those matters with which they are most concerned.

Antecedents of Authentic Leadership

Numerous potential sources of authentic leadership have been proposed, which can be broadly grouped into environmental factors and individual differences. The environmental antecedents include facilitative support, particularly through established norms of authenticity (Chan et al., 2005) and a positive organizational context (Avolio, Gardner, Walumbwa, Luthans, & May, 2004; Gardner, Avolio, Luthans, et al., 2005; Luthans & Avolio, 2003). Such facilitative factors are predicted to assist the ongoing development of authentic leadership. Other, more

active, environmental factors have also been proposed, including role models (Gardner, Avolio, Luthans, et al., 2005) and direct intervention through training (Avolio & Luthans, 2006; Luthans & Avolio, 2003). These more active environmental considerations are predicted to initiate or accelerate the development of authentic leadership.

Among the individual differences that have been singled out in creating authentic leadership, personal history is particularly important (Gardner, Avolio, Luthans, et al., 2005; Luthans & Avolio, 2003). Authentic leaders' interpretations of the events in their past are predicted to create a personal meaning system (Goldman & Kernis, 2002) based on specific leadership moments or 'triggers' that shape their approach to leadership (Avolio & Luthans, 2006; George & Sims, 2007). In addition to these developmental experiences, authentic leadership is said to be enhanced by a highly developed personal morality (Hannah, Lester, & Vogelgesang, 2005), higher levels of psychological capital (Avolio & Luthans, 2006; Luthans & Avolio, 2003), and a tendency towards concern for others in the form of self-transcendent values and other-directed emotions (Hannah, et al., 2005; Michie & Gooty, 2005). Ilies and colleagues (2005) also offered a series of propositions about distinct antecedents for each of the four behavioural components of authentic leadership; these included positive self-concept, emotional intelligence, integrity, an incremental theory of ability, and low self-monitoring.

Consequences of Authentic Leadership

The hypothesized effects of authentic leadership are extensive and varied, offering potential benefit to leaders, their organizations as wholes, and to individual followers. For themselves, authentic leaders are predicted to experience more positive emotions (Chan et al., 2005; Gardner, Avolio, Luthans, et al., 2005), improved well-being (Chan et al., 2005; Gardner, Avolio, Luthans, et al., 2005; Ilies et al., 2005), and greater leadership effectiveness (Eigel & Kuhnert, 2005). For groups and organizations, the most discussed benefit is fostering a more positive culture or climate (Gardner, Avolio, Luthans, et al., 2005; Mazutis & Slawinski, 2008; Shirey, 2006a; Woolley, Caza, Levy,

& Jackson, 2007), although authentic leadership has also been linked to organizational learning (Mazutis & Slawinski, 2008) and entrepreneurial success (Jensen & Luthans, 2006b; Shirey, 2006b).

However, the most dramatic benefits proposed to arise from authentic leadership are those for individual followers; gains in some of the most important outcomes of practical and theoretical concern have been proposed to result from authentic leadership. Behaviourally, followers of authentic leaders are predicted to exert greater effort, engage in more organizational citizenship behaviour, and enjoy better work performance (Avolio et al., 2004; Chan et al., 2005; Gardner, Avolio, Luthans, et al., 2005; Walumbwa et al., 2008), as well as having higher levels of creativity (Ilies et al., 2005). Followers are also predicted to experience a variety of improved attitudes and mindsets. The most frequently mentioned change is an increased trust in leadership (Avolio et al., 2004; Chan et al., 2005; Dasborough & Ashkanasy, 2005; Gardner, Avolio, Luthans, et al., 2005; Hannah et al., 2005), but many other benefits have been proposed, including positive emotions (Avolio et al., 2004; Chan et al., 2005; Dasborough & Ashkanasy, 2005; Jensen & Luthans, 2006a), task engagement (Avolio et al., 2004; Gardner, Avolio, Luthans, et al., 2005), higher motivation (Ilies et al., 2005), greater commitment (Avolio, et al., 2004; Jensen & Luthans, 2006a; Walumbwa et al., 2008), and more satisfaction (Avolio et al., 2004; Ilies et al., 2005; Jensen & Luthans, 2006a; Walumbwa et al., 2008). In addition, since follower development is fundamental to authentic leadership, predictions have been made about the developmental benefits experienced by followers, including greater empowerment (Avolio et al., 2004; Ilies et al., 2005), moral development (Hannah et al., 2005; Ilies et al., 2005), improved well-being (Gardner, Avolio, Luthans, et al., 2005; Ilies et al., 2005), and increases in psychological capital (Avolio et al., 2004; Avolio & Luthans, 2006; Gardner & Schermerhorn, 2004; Ilies et al., 2005; Woolley et al., 2007).

Mechanisms of Authentic Leadership

To explain the many benefits expected to arise from authentic leadership, authors have suggested a number of mechanisms. These are generally of two sorts. The first is attitudinal change, such that some of the beneficial attitude changes are used to explain behavioural and developmental changes (e.g., authentic leadership increases task engagement, which contributes to improved performance; Gardner, Avolio, Luthans, et al., 2005). The other mechanisms involve changes in the relationships that followers have with their leaders and their organizations. These include greater identification with the leader and the organization (Avolio et al., 2004; Ilies et al., 2005), improved communication between parties (Mazutis & Slawinski, 2008), imitation of positive role models (Gardner, Avolio, Luthans, et al., 2005; Ilies et al., 2005), and greater social exchange (Chan et al., 2005; Ilies et al., 2005), all of which have been suggested as ways to explain the dramatic benefits promised to arise from authentic leadership.

In reviewing the lists of antecedents, consequences, and mechanisms, one may be struck by the overlap in some areas. For example, psychological capital has been proposed as both an antecedent and a consequence of authentic leadership. Similarly, a more positive organizational climate is predicted to contribute to authentic leadership, be a benefit resulting from authentic leadership, and be a constituent part of the authentic leadership phenomenon itself. The complexities and potential confusions of such multifunctional relationships have been recognized by authentic leadership scholars, and comprise an area that has been suggested as needing greater attention (e.g., Gardner, Avolio, Luthans, et al., 2005; Luthans & Avolio, 2009). This and other future directions for the development of authentic leadership are discussed below, after a review of the empirical evidence concerning the predictions described here.

Empirical Findings

Despite the many important theoretical predictions associated with authentic leadership, and the topic's apparently considerable popularity among academics and practitioners, surprisingly little empirical research has been conducted to date. As a part of their theory-building efforts, Yammarino and colleagues (2008) searched and found only four research reports. Our more recent search found little more. In February 2009, we conducted a keyword search of the ABI-Inform and EBSCO databases, using 'lead*' and 'authen*' as word stems. We then conducted ISI forward citation searches on the authentic leadership pieces we found, as well as searching the bibliographies of all identified pieces. We found only seven empirical reports: the three book chapters and one journal article previously identified by Yammarino and colleagues (2008), as well as two other journal pieces and one refereed conference paper. Each of these is summarized in Table 26.1.

Looking across these studies reveals at least two important patterns. The first is their relative success in finding support for theoretical predictions. Allowing for the limitations imposed by their designs, the studies suggest that leader authenticity is in fact a relevant and potentially important issue for followers. Organization members care about how authentic their leaders are, and they appear to respond favourably to those they perceive as authentic. Follower attributions of leader authenticity have been linked to positive emotion (Dasborough & Ashkanasy, 2005; Jensen & Luthans, 2006a), organizational commitment (Jensen & Luthans, 2006a; Walumbwa et al., 2008), psychological capital

Table 26.1 Summary of Empirical Research in Authentic Leadership

Source	Design	Participants	Authentic leadership operationalization	Key findings
Dasborough & Ashkanasy (2005) Study 1	Three focus groups	Sample of 24 employees from three randomly selected Australian organizations	None	Followers describing negative emotional interactions with supervisors attributed their negative emotion to: 1. Supervisor's inconsistency with previous behaviour 2. Supervisor's failure to keep them informed 3. Supervisor's lack of technical skill 4. Supervisor's lack of concern for anything but income/performance
Dasborough & Ashkanasy (2005) Study 2	Experimental: video of charismatic leader requesting effort on behalf of	One hundred and thirty-seven undergraduate students in Australia	Manipulated trough (in)consistency between 'we' or 'I' phrasing in video and email	Leader inconsistency led to follower attributions of manipulation (vs sincerity), causing

(Continued)

Table 26.1   (Continued)

Source	Design	Participants	Authentic leadership operationalization	Key findings
	organization, for collective goals. Follow-up email from leader uses either 'we' phrasing (authentic condition) or 'I' phrasing (inauthentic condition)			negative emotion and reducing positive emotion. Follower positive emotion predicted trust in leader and ratings of transformational leadership. Negative emotion, trust, and transformational leadership influenced follower intention to comply with request
Eigel & Kuhnert (2005)	Semi-structured clinical interviews	Twenty-one board-elected executives of large public corporations in diverse industries	None. Describe five 'Leadership Development Levels' (LDL) and link the highest, level 5, to authentic leadership	LDL 5 is associated with leadership effectiveness in all environments, assessed by subject matter experts
Pittinsky & Tyson (2005)	Six structured focus group discussions	Snowball sample of 28 African Americans born between 1965 and 1980, stratified for low, middle, and high SES	Structured question format about 'what makes an African American leader authentic' (p. 262)	Found seven 'authenticity makers': 1. Experience of racism—recognize its importance 2. Policy positions—equality, affirmative action, community development, etc. 3. Party affiliation—liberal 4. Speech patterns and mannerisms 5. Experience of struggle—easy life is 'not real'

Source	Design	Participants	*Authentic leadership operationalization*	*Key findings*
				6. Black Church participation 7. Connection to other African Americans—embrace historical events, reach out socially, etc.
Jensen & Luthans (2006a)	Survey	Convenience sample of 179 employees in 62 Midwestern firms that had been in operation for less than 10 years	'Authentic entrepreneurial leadership' as summed scale composed of selected items from MLQ (Bass & Avolio, 1997), future orientation (Knight, 1997), and ethical climate (Victor & Cullen, 1988)	Followers who perceived their managers as more authentic reported greater job satisfaction, organizational commitment, and work happiness
Jensen & Luthans (2006b)	Survey	Convenience sample of 76 owner-founders of small Midwestern businesses that had been in operation for less than 10 years	Authentic entrepreneurial leadership, as in Jensen & Luthans (2006a)	Managers' self-reported psychological capital predicted self-reported levels of authentic entrepreneurial leadership
Woolley & colleagues (2007)	Survey	Stratified random sample of 863 working adults in New Zealand	Authentic Leadership Questionnaire (ALQ) using a second-order construct composed of self-awareness, relational transparency, internal moral perspective, and balanced processing (see Walumbwa et al., 2008)	Followers who perceived their supervisors as more authentic reported greater psychological capital. This relationship was predominantly mediated by followers' assessment of their supervisor's positive impact on the work environment Second-order factor structure of ALQ supported.

(Continued)

Table 26.1 (Continued)

Source	Design	Participants	Authentic leadership operationalization	Key findings
Walumbwa & colleagues (2008) Study 1	Survey	Two hundred and twenty-four full-time employees of US manufacturer; 212 full-time employees of state-owned firm in Beijing	ALQ (Walumbwa et al., 2008)	American and Chinese samples showed measurement equivalence
Walumbwa & colleagues (2008) Study 2	In-class survey	One hundred and seventy-eight American adult students and 236 evening students working full time in the USA	ALQ (Walumbwa et al., 2008)	Authentic leadership measured by ALQ shown to be a related to, but distinct from, ethical leadership and transformational leadership. Followers who perceived their supervisors as more authentic reported greater OCB, organizational commitment, and satisfaction with supervisor
Walumbwa & colleagues (2008) Study 3	Two-stage survey (six weeks apart)	Four hundred and seventy-eight employees of 11 US MNCs in Kenya, and their supervisors (N= 104)	ALQ (Walumbwa et al., 2008)	Followers who perceived their supervisors as more authentic reported greater job satisfaction and had higher supervisor-rated job performance

(Woolley et al., 2007), and performance (Eigel & Kuhnert, 2005; Walumbwa et al., 2008).

The second pattern, which has already been noted earlier by others (Yammarino et al., 2008), is that the empirical data are almost entirely at the individual level. To the extent that conclusions from focus groups can be considered collective or aggregate phenomena, there may be some preliminary evidence at a collective level (Dasborough & Ashkanasy, 2005; Pittinsky & Tyson, 2005), but this is tenuous. Similarly, while one study examined organizational climate as a potential mechanism for authentic leadership's effect on followers (Woolley et al., 2007), the measurement remained at the individual level. Despite the theoretical emphasis upon the collective and relational effects associated with authentic leadership, nothing beyond individual perception and behaviour has yet been tested.

In summary, the empirical evidence concerning authentic leadership is limited. There are only seven published research reports, and only four of these were subject to peer review. Authentic leadership has only been measured at the individual level, and has almost exclusively concerned followers' attributions of leader authenticity. As such, we may tentatively conclude that the construct of authenticity is meaningful to followers, and that individual followers' attributions of leader authenticity are associated with beneficial attitudes and behaviours. However, the strongest conclusion to be drawn is that much more empirical research is needed.

Opportunities, Questions, and Concerns

Definition of Authenticity

The two foundational sources on which this literature bases its definition of authenticity (i.e., Harter, 2002; Kernis, 2003) may not be compatible concerning the phenomenological status of authenticity, which in turn creates some conflict in the definition of authentic leadership. More importantly, current operationalizations are inconsistent with the definition of authenticity as a personal experience. With only one exception (Jensen & Luthans, 2006b), the empirical measurement of authentic leadership involves observer attributions of authenticity, taking no account of the leader's experience. Whereas follower responses to a leader's authenticity are clearly determined by their attributions of that leader's authenticity, these attributions are not necessarily accurate (e.g. Douglas, Ferris, & Perrewe, 2005; Ferris et al., 2007). In recognition of this, the awkward distinction between 'genuine' authentic leaders and 'pseudo' authentic leaders has already been raised (Chan et al., 2005). Moreover, even when third-party judgements are accurate, they still do not reflect the phenomenological nature of a leader's authenticity

(Harter, 2002; Harter, Waters, Whitesell, & Kastelic, 1998). This conflict can be seen in current writing, where authenticity is defined as purely phenomenological (Avolio & Gardner, 2005; Avolio et al., 2004; Chan et al., 2005; Erickson, 1994), but also as depending on follower responses: 'followers authenticate the leader' (Gardner, Avolio, Luthans, et al., 2005, p. 348; see also Goffee & Jones, 2005).

Ontological Status of Authenticity

Even more fundamental than clearly defining a construct is the need to answer the question of the extent to which authenticity is even possible. The assumption underlying authentic leadership theory derives from the modernist psychological belief that each individual has a 'true' self, one that is independent of context and behavioural presentations; in other words, there is something constant to be authentic about (Goffman, 1959; James, 1890). Doubts have been raised about the appropriateness of this belief (Erickson, 1994). Conceptually, it has been argued that one's self is an ongoing project, rather than an essential constant (Ricoeur, 1992; Sparrowe, 2005), and this may be particularly relevant now, given that modern society and technology have made life so fluid and complex as to make a single constant self either impossible or impractical (Gergen, 1991). Moreover, others have argued that even if there is a relatively 'true' self, it is necessarily defined in relation to others, and thus cannot be constant in the sense required for authenticity (Peterson, 2005; Sandelands, 1998). In either case, authenticity, as the sort of behavioural goal implied by authentic leadership theory, becomes a paradox: the simple act of intentionally 'being authentic' undercuts any possibility of achieving it (Guthey & Jackson, 2005; Hochschild, 1983).

Clarity of Nomological Status and Level of Analysis

In part owing to potential confusion in the definition of authentic leadership, it is sometimes unclear where authentic leadership begins and ends. For example, as noted above, authors variously treat a positive organizational climate as a source of authentic leadership, a part of authentic leadership, and a consequence of authentic leadership. Such issues need to be clarified, not only for purposes of defining the nature of the construct but also its appropriate level of analysis. For example, Kernis' (2003) definition of authenticity is restricted to the individual level by including only a personal orientation towards truthful relationships; in contrast, the definition of authentic leadership includes reference to the actual leader–follower relationship, which is necessarily not at the individual level of analysis. Although different elements of the authentic leadership phenomenon may operate at different levels, these need to be made distinct (see Yammarino et al., 2008 for a proposal to address this issue).

Contextualizing Authentic Leadership

Although the authentic leadership questionnaire has been shown to function well and have predicted relationships with outcomes in four different cultures and a variety of settings (Walumbwa et al., 2008; Woolley et al., 2007), there is also evidence that the meaning and effect of authentic leadership can vary by context (Chan, 2005). Pittinsky and Tyson (2005) showed that what counts as authentic depends on the particular leader and follower in question, and others show that the effects of authenticity may vary by gender and/or personal values (Harter et al., 1998; Woolley et al., 2007). It has also been suggested that other differences may be important, including ethnicity, class, and education (Eagly, 2005). Similarly, interpersonal congruence and cultural values may also be moderators of the effect of authentic leadership (Chan, 2005; Chan et al., 2005; Ilies et al., 2005; Woolley & Jackson, 2010).

Authentic Leadership Versus Authentic Leadership Development

The motivation to develop practical interventions has been an explicit part of authentic leadership theory from the beginning, and has arguably been the one thing that all writers in this area share (Cooper,

Scandura, & Schriesheim, 2005; Eagly, 2005; Eigel & Kuhnert, 2005; Ilies et al., 2005; Luthans & Avolio, 2003; Shamir & Eilam, 2005; Sparrowe, 2005). However, there appears to be an increasing emphasis on the issues of development and intervention. The initial work tended to emphasize the nature and effect of authentic leadership, and this early emphasis was arguably crystallized by the scale development paper (Walumbwa et al., 2008), which specifically defined and measured how much authentic leadership a given leader exhibited. In contrast to this early emphasis on understanding authentic leaders, more recent discussions suggest a subtle shift towards emphasizing development over authenticity per se (e.g., Avolio, 2007, p. 29ff; see also Faber, Johanson, Thomas, & Vogelzang, 2007). That is, the discussion of authentic leadership development now seems more concerned with whether a given leadership intervention authentically (i.e. genuinely) develops leadership ability (e.g., Avolio, Walumbwa, & Weber, 2009, p. 423). Interestingly, it seems that the focus may be moving from developing *authentic leadership* to *authentically developing* leadership (Luthans & Avolio, 2009, pp. 303–304). Given some reports that current leadership interventions offer little benefit (Reichard & Avolio, 2005), this may be an appropriate move, and it is not inconsistent with the previous work; however, it is nonetheless an important change in focus. Developing authentic leadership is much more specific than authentically developing effective leadership of any sort. Whereas either focus, or both, may be fruitfully pursued in the future, it will be important for authors to clearly specify which matter they are concerned with to avoid the sort of fundamental confusion that had plagued other research programmes: for example, organizational citizenship behaviour (OCB) and the nature of 'extra-role' Organ (1997).

Role of Emotion

Emotions have had a central role in the development of authentic leadership theory. They figure prominently as antecedents and consequences of authenticity (Dasborough & Ashkanasy, 2005; Gardner, Avolio, Luthans et al., 2005; Hannah et al.,

2005; Ilies et al., 2005; Michie & Gooty, 2005). In addition, the most common definition given for authenticity is taken from Harter (2002) and refers to being true to one's inner thoughts and feelings. However, the role of feelings in authenticity has received little attention (see Zhang, Wang, & Caza, 2008). Far more attention has been paid to authenticity with regard to values and morality than to emotion. This is surprising, given the prevalence of emotion management in most organizational contexts (Glaso & Einarsen, 2008; Goffman, 1973), and the strong intuitive link that practitioners make between authenticity and emotion (Turner & Mavin, 2008). For an extended discussion of the link between leadership and emotion, see Ashkanasy and Humphrey (Chapter 27).

Embodied Authentic Leadership

Notions of embodiment and how the body functions within the field of organizational studies have received increasing attention, but are still relatively rare in leadership studies (see Sinclair, Chapter 37). Nonetheless, the issue of embodiment is a potentially important one for authentic leadership theory. For example, Ladkin and Taylor (2010) note that the widely publicized incident involving Hillary Clinton breaking down in tears during the Democratic primary election shows that authenticity has an embodied, aesthetic dimension (see also Hansen & Bathurst, Chapter 19). Ladkin and Taylor (2010) argue that the way in which the leader's 'self' is embodied is a critical determinant of the experience of authentic leadership, noting that,

> Although it may be obvious, for the purposes of our argument, it is important to point out that it is the leaders' body, and the way in which he or she uses it to express their 'true self', which is the seemingly invisible mechanism through which authenticity is conveyed. (Ladkin & Taylor, 2010, p. 65)

They highlight how the system of method acting developed by Constantin Stanislavski uses the somatic sense of self (i.e., the body) to contribute to the feelings of authenticity, and how through engaging with somatic clues, leadership can be performed in a way which is experienced as authentic, both to the leaders and their followers. They close by inviting researchers to empirically investigate how leaders who are widely considered to be 'authentic' actually experience themselves at a somatic level of awareness. In concert with this, there is a need to better understand how followers make aesthetically based assessments of their experiences with leaders (e.g., Rule & Ambady, 2008, 2009; Nana, Burch, & Jackson, 2010).

Disadvantages of Authenticity

One element that all of the authentic leadership theory reviewed here shares is the implicit belief that authenticity is wholly desirable, that it produces only positive outcomes. However, it seems unlikely that authenticity is in all ways and at all time unremittingly beneficial. For example, Harter (2002) shows that inauthenticity may be important for some kinds of positive change (see also Ibarra, 1999; Kernis, 2003). It also may be possible to be too authentic, such that authenticity not only limits possibilities but also actually produces negative results (Harter, 2002; Woolley et al., 2007). Although the potential drawbacks of authenticity have yet to be examined, it seems unlikely that one could understand the phenomenon of authentic leadership without addressing them. It is to this task that we turn to in the concluding section of this chapter.

Conclusions

In the past decade, authentic leadership has seized the popular imagination in a way that few leadership ideas have. This is evident in the business media and through our interactions with managers in the MBA and executive development classes that we teach. Many people seem taken with the idea of authenticity and are keen to learn more about it. In part, we suspect that authenticity's appeal derives from its face validity and commonsense value. After all, who would advocate for inauthentic leaders? However, we believe that the source of the appeal goes deeper still. Authentic leadership resonates with widespread disillusionment about the performance of business, political, and religious leaders. Authentic leadership seems to provide a ready answer to concerns about the intentions and morality of these leaders. This combines with managers' fears and concerns about their own leadership ability to make the notion of authenticity particularly appealing. As the wellworn clichée runs, authentic leadership is an idea whose 'time has come.' It is a powerful response to the entrenched scepticism and suspicion towards established leaders and it accords with a general desire for selfless, enlightened leadership.

Given this general appeal, it is not surprising that leadership scholars have been attracted to the concept of authenticity. As we have shown in this review, in a relatively short period of time significant strides have been made in defining the concept and its antecedents, mechanisms, and consequences. Unfortunately, however, most of this work has been confined to the theoretical realm; there are very few empirical studies. This imbalance is unhealthy and will need to be rectified if the concept is to have a sustainable future within the larger field of leadership studies. In terms of direction, we used the previous section to highlight the issues that seem most pressing and most promising. We also believe that more variety in methods and data are essential, including mixed sources of data and multiple levels of analysis.

These empirical developments are important to sustain the momentum of authentic leadership and to respond to its critics. In fact, somewhat ironically, the most encouraging sign for the future of authentic leadership theory may be in the intensity of the critical response it has provoked (e.g., Caza & Carroll, in press; Collinson, Chapter 13). The idea of authenticity clearly has great power to provoke and attract attention. We do not believe that the critics' concerns are insurmountable, but it is important to the further development of authentic leadership theory that they be addressed. As described in this chapter, this will likely require new directions, additional techniques, and a broader constituency than has previously been engaged in the theory's development.

References

American Association of Critical Care Nurses. (2005). *AACN standards for establishing and sustaining healthy work environments.* Aliso Viejo, CA: American Association of Critical Care Nurses.

Avolio, B. J. (1999). *Full leadership development: building vital forces in organizations.* Newbury Park, CA: Sage.

Avolio, B. J. (2007). Promoting more integrative strategies for leadership theory-building. *American Psychologist,* 62(1), 25–33.

Avolio, B. J., & Gardner, W. L. (2005). Authentic leadership development: getting to the root of positive forms of leadership. *The Leadership Quarterly,* 16(3), 315–338.

Avolio, B. J., Gardner, W. L., & Walumbwa, F. O. (2005). Preface. In W. L. Gardner, B. J. Avolio, & F. O. Walumbwa (eds), *Authentic leadership theory and practice: origins, effects, and development,* Vol. 3. New York: Elsevier, pp. xxi–xxix.

Avolio, B. J., Gardner, W. L., Walumbwa, F. O., Luthans, F., & May, D. R. (2004). Unlocking the mask: a look at the process by which authentic leaders impact follower attitudes and behaviors. *The Leadership Quarterly,* 15(6), 801–823.

Avolio, B. J., & Luthans, F. (2006). *The high impact leader: moments matter in accelerating authentic leadership development.* New York: McGraw-Hill.

Avolio, B. J., Walumbwa, F. O., & Weber, T. J. (2009). Leadership: current theories, research, and future directions. *Annual Review of Psychology,* 60, 421–449.

Bass, B. M. (1985). *Leadership and performance beyond expectations.* New York: Free Press.

Bass, B. M., & Avolio, B. J. (1997). *Full-range of leadership development: manual for the Multifactor Leadership Questionnaire.* Palo Alto, CA: Mind Garden.

Bass, B. M., & Steidlmeier, P. (1999). Ethics, character, and authentic transformational leadership behavior. *The Leadership Quarterly,* 10(2), 181–217.

Beyer, J. M. (1999). Taming and promoting charisma to change organizations. *The Leadership Quarterly,* 10, 307–331.

Burns, J. M. (1978). *Leadership.* New York: Harper & Row.

Cameron, K. S., Dutton, J. E., & Quinn, R. E. (2003). *Positive organizational scholarship: foundations of a new discipline.* San Francisco, CA: Berrett-Koehler Publishers.

Caza, A., & Carroll, B. (In press). Critical theory and POS. In K. S. Cameron & G. M. Spreitzer (eds), *Handbook of positive organizational scholarship.* Oxford: Oxford University Press.

Chan, A. (2005). Authentic leadership measurement and development: Challenges and suggestions. In W. L. Gardner, B. J. Avolio, & F. O. Walumbwa (eds), *Authentic leadership theory and practice: origins, effects, and development*, Vol. 3. New York: Elsevier, pp. 227–250.

Chan, A., Hannah, S. T., & Gardner, W. L. (2005). Veritable authentic leadership: Emergence, functioning, and impacts. In W. L. Gardner, B. J. Avolio, & F. O. Walumbwa (eds), *Authentic leadership theory and practice: Origins, effects, and development*, Vol. 3. New York: Elsevier, pp. 3–41.

Conger, J. A., & Kanungo, R. N. (1998). *Charismatic leadership in organizations*. Thousand Oaks, CA: Sage.

Cooper, C. D., Scandura, T. A., & Schriesheim, C. A. (2005). Looking forward but learning from our past: Potential challenges to developing authentic leadership theory and authentic leaders. *The Leadership Quarterly*, 16(3), 475–493.

Dasborough, M. T., & Ashkanasy, N. M. (2005). Follower emotional reactions to authentic and inauthentic leadership influence. In W. L. Gardner, B. J. Avolio, & F. O. Walumbwa (eds), *Authentic leadership theory and practice: Origins, effects, and development*, Vol. 3. New York: Elsevier, pp. 281–300.

Douglas, C., Ferris, G. R., & Perrewe, P. L. (2005). Leader political skill and authentic leadership. In W. L. Gardner, B. J. Avolio, & F. O. Walumbwa (eds), *Authentic leadership theory and practice: Origins, effects, and development*, Vol. 3. New York: Elsevier, pp. 139–154.

Eagly, A. H. (2005). Achieving relational authenticity in leadership: Does gender matter? *The Leadership Quarterly*, 16(3), 459–474.

Eigel, K. M., & Kuhnert, K. W. (2005). Authentic development: leadership development level and executive effectiveness. In W. L. Gardner, B. J. Avolio, & F. O. Walumbwa (eds), *Authentic leadership theory and practice: Origins, effects, and development*, Vol. 3. New York: Elsevier, pp. 357–385.

Erickson, R. J. (1994). Our society, our selves: becoming authentic in an inauthentic world. *Advanced Development Journal*, 6(1), 27–39.

Faber, M., Johanson, R., Thomas, A., & Vogelzang, M. (2007). Charge it up: Developing authentic leaders. *Critical Care Nurse*, 27(2), 98–98.

Ferris, G. R., Treadway, D. C., Perrewe, P. L., Brouer, R. L., Douglas, C., & Lux, S. (2007). Political skill in organizations. *Journal of Management*, 33(3), 290–320.

Gardner, W. L., Avolio, B. J., Luthans, F., May, D. R., & Walumbwa, F. (2005). 'Can you see the real me?' A self based model of authentic leader and follower development. *The Leadership Quarterly*, 16(3), 343–372.

Gardner, W. L., Avolio, B. J., & Walumbwa, F. O. (2005). *Authentic leadership theory and practice: Origins, effects, and development*. New York: Elsevier.

Gardner, W. L., & Schermerhorn, J. R. (2004). Unleashing individual potential: Performance gains through positive organizational behavior and authentic leadership. *Organizational Dynamics*, 33(3), 270–281.

Gayvert, D. R. (1999). Leadership and doctrinal reform. *Military Review*, 79(3), 18–22.

George, B. (2003). *Authentic leadership: Rediscovering the secrets of creating lasting value*. San Francisco, CA: Jossey Bass.

George, B., & Sims, P. (2007). *True North: Discover your authentic leadership*. San Francisco, CA: Jossey-Bass.

George, B., Sims, P., McLean, A. N., & Mayer, D. (2007). Discovering your authentic leadership. *Harvard Business Review*, 85(2), 129–138.

Gergen, K. J. (1991). *The saturated self: Dilemmas of identity in contemporary life*. New York: Basic Books.

Glaso, L., & Einarsen, S. (2008). Emotion regulation in leader–follower relationships. *European Journal of Work and Organizational Psychology*, 17(4), 482–500.

Goffee, R., & Jones, G. (2005). Managing authenticity: the paradox of great leadership. *Harvard Business Review*, December, 87–94.

Goffman, E. (1959). *The presentation of self in everyday life*. Garden City, NY: Doubleday Anchor.

Goffman, E. (1973). On face-work. In W. G. Bennis, E. H. Berlow, E. H. Schein, & F. I. Steele (Eds.), *Interpersonal dynamics: Essays and readings on human interaction*, 3rd edn. Homewood, IL: Dorsey, pp. 175–189.

Goldman, B. M., & Kernis, M. H. (2002). The role of authenticity in healthy psychological functioning and subjective well-being. *Annals of the American Psychotherapy Association*, 5(Nov/Dec), 18–20.

Guthey, E., & Jackson, B. (2005). CEO portraits and the authenticity paradox. *Journal of Management Studies*, 42(5), 1057–1082.

Hannah, S. T., Lester, P. B., & Vogelgesang, G. R. (2005). Moral leadership: Explicating the moral component of authentic leadership. In W. L. Gardner, B. J. Avolio, & F. O. Walumbwa (eds), *Authentic leadership theory and practice: Origins, effects, and development*, Vol. 3. New York: Elsevier, pp. 43–81.

Harter, S. (2002). Authenticity. In C. R. Snyder & S. J. Lopez (eds), *Handbook of positive psychology*, New York: Oxford University Press, pp. 382–394.

Harter, S., Waters, P. L., Whitesell, N. R., & Kastelic, D. (1998). Level of voice among female and male high school students: Relational context, support, and gender orientation. *Developmental Psychology,* 34(5), 892–901.

Henderson, J. E., & Hoy, W. K. (1983). Leader authenticity: The development and test of an operational measure. *Educational and Psychological Research,* 3(2), 63–75.

Hochschild, A. R. (1983). *The managed heart.* Berkeley, CA: University of California Press.

Howell, J. M., & Avolio, B. J. (1992). The ethics of charismatic leadership: Submission or liberation? *Academy of Management Executive,* 6(2), 43–54.

Hoy, W. K., & Henderson, J. E. (1983). Principal authenticity, school climate and pupil-control orientation. *Alberta Journal of Educational Research,* 29(2), 123–130.

Ibarra, H. (1999). Provisional selves: Experimenting with image and identity in professional adaptation. *Administrative Science Quarterly,* 44(4), 764–791.

Ilies, R., Morgeson, F. P., & Nahrgang, J. D. (2005). Authentic leadership and eudaemonic well-being: Understanding leader–follower outcomes. *The Leadership Quarterly,* 16(3), 373–394.

Irvine, D., & Reger, J. (2006). *The authentic leader.* Sanford, FL: DC Press.

James, W. (1890). *The principles of psychology.* New York: Dover.

Jensen, S. M., & Luthans, F. (2006a). Entrepreneurs as authentic leaders: Impact on employees' attitudes. *Leadership and Organization Development Journal,* 27(8), 646–666.

Jensen, S. M., & Luthans, F. (2006b). Relationship between entrepreneurs' psychological capital and their authentic leadership. *Journal of Managerial Issues,* 18(2), 254–275.

Jung, D. I., & Avolio, B. J. (2000). Opening the black box: An experimental investigation of the mediating effects of trust and value congruence on transformational and transactional leadership. *Journal of Organizational Behavior,* 17(8), 949–964.

Kark, R., Shamir, B., & Chen, G. (2003). The two faces of transformational leadership: Empowerment and dependency. *Journal of Applied Psychology,* 88, 246–255.

Kernis, M. H. (2003). Toward a conceptualization of optimal self-esteem. *Psychological Inquiry,* 14(1), 1–26.

Knight, G. A. (1997). Cross-cultural reliability and validity of a scale to measure firm entrepreneurial orientation. *Journal of Business Venturing,* 12, 213–225.

Kouzes, J. M., & Posner, B. Z. (2008). *The leadership challenge,* San Francisco, CA: Jossey-Bass.

Ladkin, D., & Taylor, S. V. (2010). Enacting the 'true self': Towards a theory of embodied authentic leadership, *The Leadership Quarterly,* 21, 64–74.

Luthans, F. (2002). The need for and meaning of positive organizational behavior. *Journal of Organizational Behavior,* 23(6), 695–706.

Luthans, F., & Avolio, B. J. (2003). Authentic leadership development. In K. S. Cameron, J. E. Dutton, & R. E. Quinn (eds), *Positive organizational scholarship: Foundations of a new discipline.* San Francisco, CA: Berrett-Koehler Publishers, pp. 241–258.

Luthans, F., & Avolio, B. J. (2009). The 'point' of positive organizational behavior. *Journal of Organizational Behavior,* 30(2), 291–307.

Luthans, F., Luthans, K. W., Hodgetts, R. M., & Luthans, B. C. (2001). Positive approach to leadership (PAL): implications for today's organizations. *Journal of Leadership Studies,* 8(2), 3–20.

Maslow, A. (1968). *Towards a psychology of being.* New York: Van Nostrand.

May, D. R., Chan, A. Y. L., Hodges, T. D., & Avolio, B. J. (2003). Developing the moral component of authentic leadership. *Organizational Dynamics,* 32(3), 247–260.

Mazutis, D., & Slawinski, N. (2008). Leading organizational learning through authentic dialogue. *Management Learning,* 39(4), 437–456.

Michie, S., & Gooty, J. (2005). Values, emotions, and authenticity: Will the real leader please stand up? *The Leadership Quarterly,* 16(3), 441–457.

Nadeau, K. (2002). Peasant resistance and religious protests in early Philippine society: Turning friars against the grain. *Journal for the Scientific Study of Religion,* 41(1), 75–86.

Nana, E., Burch, G., & Jackson, B. (2010). Attributing leadership personality and effectiveness from leaders' faces: An exploratory study. *Leadership and Organizational Development Journal,* 31(8), 223–246.

O'Connor, S. J. (2007). Capacity, morality and authenticity in the quest for cancer nursing leadership. *European Journal of Oncology Nursing,* 11(3), 209–211.

Organ, D. W. (1997). Organizational citizenship behavior: It's construct clean-up time. *Human Performance,* 10(2), 85–97.

Pembroke, N. (2002). Rising leaders need authentic leadership. *Clergy Journal,* 78(8), 17–19.

Peterson, R. A. (2005). In search of authenticity. *Journal of Management Studies,* 42(5), 1083–1098.

Pittinsky, T. L., & Tyson, C. J. (2005). Leader authenticity markers: Findings from a study of perceptions of African American political leaders. In W. L. Gardner, B. J. Avolio, & F. O. Walumbwa (eds), *Authentic leadership theory and practice: Origins, effects, and development,* Vol. 3. New York: Elsevier, pp. 253–279.

Price, T. L. (2003). The ethics of authentic transformational leadership. *The Leadership Quarterly,* 14(1), 67–81.

Reichard, R. J., & Avolio, B. J. (2005). The status of leadership intervention research: A meta-analytic summary. In W. L. Gardner, B. J. Avolio, & F. O. Walumbwa (eds), *Authentic leadership theory and practice: origins, effects, and development.* New York: Elsevier, pp. 203–226.

Ricoeur, P. (1992). *Oneself as another.* Chicago, IL: University of Chicago Press.

Rogers, C. R. (1963). The actualizing tendency in relation to 'motives' and to consciousness. In *Nebraska symposium on motivation,* Vol. 11. Lincoln, NE: University of Nebraska Press, pp. 1–24.

Rule, N., & Ambady, N. (2008). The face of success: inferences from chief executive officers' appearance predict company profits. *Psychological Science,* 19, 109–111.

Rule, N. O., & Ambady, N. (2009). She's got the look: inferences from female chief executive officers' faces predict their success. *Sex Roles,* 61, 644–652.

Sandelands, L. E. (1998). *Feeling and form in social life.* Lanham, MD: Rowan & Littlefield Publishers.

Seligman, M. E. P., & Csikszentmihalyi, M. (2000). Positive psychology: An introduction. *American Psychologist,* 55, 5–14.

Shamir, B., & Eilam, G. (2005). 'What's your story?' A life-stories approach to authentic leadership development. *The Leadership Quarterly,* 16(3), 395–417.

Shelton, K. (2008). Authentic leaders add value. *Leadership Excellence,* 25(2), 22.

Shirey, M. R. (2006a). Authentic leaders creating healthy work environments for nursing practice. *American Journal of Critical Care,* 15(3), 256–267.

Shirey, M. R. (2006b). Building authentic leadership and enhancing entrepreneurial performance. *Clinical Nurse Specialist,* 20(6), 280–282.

Snyder, M. (1974). The self-monitoring of expressive behavior. *Journal of Personality and Social Psychology,* 30, 526–537.

Sosik, J. J., Avolio, B. J., & Jung, D. I. (2002). Beneath the mask: examining the relationship of self-presentation attributes and impression management to charismatic leadership. *The Leadership Quarterly,* 13(3), 217–242.

Sparrowe, R. T. (2005). Authentic leadership and the narrative self. *The Leadership Quarterly,* 16(3), 419–439.

Terry, R. W. (1993). *Authentic leadership: Courage in action.* San Francisco, CA: Jossey-Bass.

Trevino, L. K., & Brown, M. E. (2007). Ethical leadership: a developing construct. In D. Nelson & C. L. Cooper (eds), *Positive organizational behavior: Accentuating the positive at work.* Thousand Oaks, CA: Sage, pp. 101–116.

Turner, J., & Mavin, S. (2008). What can we learn from senior leader narratives? The strutting and fretting of becoming a leader. *Leadership & Organization Development Journal,* 29(4), 376–391.

Victor, B., & Cullen, J. B. (1988). The organizational bases of ethical work climates. *Administrative Science Quarterly,* 33(1), 101–125.

Walumbwa, F. O., Avolio, B. J., Gardner, W. L., Wernsing, T. S., & Peterson, S. J. (2008). Authentic leadership: development and validation of a theory-based measure. *Journal of Management,* 34(1), 89–126.

Woolley, L., Caza, A., Levy, L., & Jackson, B. (2007). Three steps forward and one step back: Exploring relationships between authentic leadership, psychological capital, and leadership impact. *Proceedings of the Australia and New Zealand Academy of Management.*

Woolley, L., & Jackson, B. (2010). The importance of 'mucking-in' for authentic leadership: An exploratory mixed methods study. Paper presented at the Academy of Management Meeting in Montreal, August.

Yammarino, F. J., Dionne, S. D., Schriesheim, C. A., & Dansereau, F. (2008). Authentic leadership and positive organizational behavior: A meso, multi-level perspective. *The Leadership Quarterly,* 19(6), 693–707.

Zhang, G., Wang, L., & Caza, A. (2008). Effects of leaders' emotional authenticity on leadership effectiveness and followers' trust. *Proceedings of the Australia and New Zealand Academy of Management.*

CHAPTER 27

Ethical Followership

An Examination of Followership Beliefs and Crimes of Obedience

Melissa K. Carsten[1]
Winthrop University

Mary Uhl-Bien
University of Nebraska

Most discussions about organizational ethics emphasize the role that leaders play in modeling, promoting, and reinforcing ethical behavior in the workplace (Brown & Trevñino, 2006; Kohlberg, 1969; Treviño, 1986; Treviño, Brown, & Hartman, 2003). The basic assumption in the literature and in practice is that leader behaviors (Walumbwa & Schaubroeck, 2009) and their effects on climate (Trevino, Butterfield, & McCabe, 1998; Trevino, Weaver, Gibson, & Toffler, 1999) are the most critical antecedents to ethical behavior in organizations. However, the ethical lapses during the past decade (e.g., WorldCom) show that it is often the *leaders* who act unethically and/or demand unethical actions from followers (Whittington & Pany, 2009). Indeed, the 2011 National Business Ethics Survey conducted by the Ethics Resource Center (2012) found that 34% of employees "had a negative view of their supervisor's ethics." These findings clearly indicate that relying on leader ethical behavior is not enough. We need to also focus on the role of followers in maintaining ethical behavior in organizations (Hollander, 1995; Perreault, 1997).

An area that has been identified as important regarding the role of followers in organizational ethics is followers' responses to unethical requests by a leader (Uhl-Bien & Carsten, 2007). Followers face ethical dilemmas when leaders approach them with inappropriate requests, such as asking them to engage in behaviors that are clearly unethical. In such situations, followers must make a decision: They can choose to stand up to the unethical request (e.g., by challenging the leader's directive, refusing to engage in unethical behavior, or proposing alternative courses of action) or they can go along with the leader's request,

---

Source: Article by Melissa K. Carsten and Mary Uhl-Bien in *Journal of Leadership & Organizational Studies,* 2013, 20(1), pp. 49–61. SAGE Publications. Reprinted with permission.

in essence becoming complicit with the unethical behavior. This choice will likely be associated with their beliefs about the follower role and how followers should interact with leaders. For followers to be able to stand up to a leader's unethical request, they must not view their followership role as passive and obedient. Instead, they must feel a responsibility as an active participant in the leadership process (Baker, 2007; Carsten, Uhl-Bien, West, Patera, & McGregor, 2010; Chaleff, 2009; Hirschhorn, 1990; Kelley, 1992; Uhl-Bien & Carsten, 2007; Uhl-Bien & Pillai, 2007).

Burgeoning research on followership suggests that individuals hold a variety of beliefs about the role followers should play in the leadership process (Carsten et al., 2010; Sy, 2010). For example, Carsten et al. (2010) found that some followers construct their roles along traditional definitions of followers being deferent and blindly obedient, whereas others construct their roles around partnership and contribution and focus on engaging in more leader-like (e.g., influencing, voicing, decision making) than follower-like behaviors (Carsten et al., 2010). According to Shamir (2007), this more active and engaging dimension comprises the "coproduction" of leadership, which involves leaders and followers working together to effect important organizational outcomes.

Building from these initial findings, Carsten and Uhl–Bien (2009) developed and validated a measure of follower beliefs in the coproduction of leadership—the extent to which people believe their role as a follower is to partner with leaders in an effort to coproduce positive leadership outcomes. Their findings show that follower belief in the coproduction of leadership is significantly and positively related to behaviors such as voice and upward influence behavior and negatively related to beliefs in power distance and legitimacy of authority. These results suggest that individuals with a stronger belief in the coproduction of leadership are more likely to voice ideas and concerns, influence leaders to gain support and resources, and are less likely to see their role as ineffectual or insignificant. Taken together, these results suggest that followers' beliefs about coproduction are related to how individuals enact the follower role in organizations.

Coproduction beliefs may increase understanding of the choices followers make when faced with an unethical request by a leader. For example, followers with weaker coproduction beliefs likely act more traditionally as followers, seeing that it is their responsibility to defer to a leader by obeying and following the leader's unethical request. Followers with stronger coproduction beliefs are likely to believe it is their duty to object to a leader's unethical request for the good of the organization (Carsten et al., 2010). Such followers are likely to work to find an ethical solution in the face of an unethical request by a leader and less likely to see themselves as powerless to a leader's directive. Thus, it is likely that followers with stronger coproduction beliefs demonstrate "ethical followership" by responding to a leader's unethical request in ways that help maintain ethical behavior in the workplace, whereas followers with weaker coproduction beliefs may demonstrate "unethical followership" by being complicit in the unethical behavior.

The purpose of this study was to conduct an initial investigation into the concept of ethical/unethical followership. Specifically, we examined whether follower beliefs in the coproduction of leadership predict their intentions to stand up to, or comply with, unethical requests by a leader. Followers who comply with unethical requests, meaning they engage in unethical behavior under leaders' directives, can be described as engaging in "crimes of obedience" (Kelman & Hamilton, 1989). They likely are able to act in this way because they displace responsibility for the unethical act from themselves to their leader (Bandura, 1991; Milgram, 1965, 1974; Rost, 1979).

We begin by reviewing research on obedience to authority and discuss displacement of responsibility as a necessary precursor to obedient responses. In addition, we also address disobedient responses that followers may have to an unethical request by a leader. Given that fewer studies have looked at the relationship between personal characteristics and disobedience (Perreault, 1997), we examined both the obedient and disobedient (e.g., constructive resistance) responses that followers may have to unethical demands of superiors. Following this, we discuss research on coproduction beliefs (Carsten & Uhl-Bien, 2009) and romance of leadership (Meindl, Ehrlich, & Dukerich, 1985) to understand whether these beliefs play a role in predicting both

| **Figure 27.1** | Theoretical Model With Hypotheses |

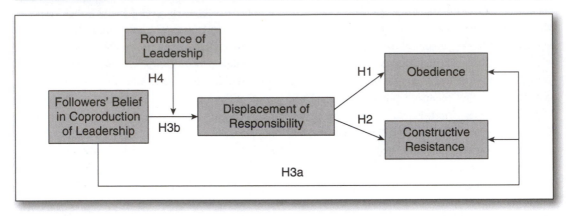

displacement of responsibility and a follower's ulti- mate decision to obey or disobey a leader's unethical request. The theoretical model that was tested in this study, and explained more thoroughly in the sections below, is shown in Figure 27.1.

Followers Reactions to Unethical Requests By a Leader

Crimes of Obedience

Kelman and Hamilton (1989, p. 46) define crimes of obedience as "acts performed in response to orders from authority that are considered illegal or immoral by the larger community." Throughout history, crimes of obedience have occurred in the My Lai massacre, Nazi concentration camps, and more recently in the destructive corporate business practices of compa- nies such as Enron, WorldCom, and Arthur Anderson (Zahra, Priem, & Rasheed, 2007). In the business setting, crimes of obedience occur when subordi- nates willingly follow an unethical or illegal directive of a superior. For example, evidence suggests that the ethical violations that occurred at Enron were, in some cases, ordered by top management to inflate corporate revenue (Carsten & Uhl-Bien, 2007).

According to Hollander (1995), ethical lapses such as this occur because leaders are perceived to have "power over" followers, and followers believe they are too weak to counter the unethical demands of their leaders (Biggart & Hamilton, 1984). For crimes of

obedience to occur, Kelman and Hamilton (1989) suggested that followers must see the leader's power and authority as legitimate. The perception of legiti- macy leaves followers feeling powerless, as if they have no choice but to obey their leader's commands (Tyler, 1997). In essence, followers feel they must take a "one-down" position in the presence of their lead- ers, obeying a leader's directive because their lower status role requires them to do so (Baker, 2007; Ravlin & Thomas, 2005).

Research on obedience confirms these status effects. In addition, it shows that individuals who obey unethical directives also displace responsibility onto the authority figure, perceiving they were not at fault because they were in a subordinate position (Milgram, 1974). This displacement of responsibility is a key ele- ment of moral disengagement—a social–cognitive mechanism that allows individuals to engage in unethical acts by disconnecting the moral ramifica- tions of an action from their own involvement in that action (Bandura, 1991). According to Bandura, Underwood, and Fromson (1975), individuals may displace responsibility for unethical or immoral actions onto a leader because they perceive the leader to have greater agency than they do. This helps them escape the negativity of their immoral behavior by attributing responsibility for that behavior onto some- one other than themselves (Bandura, 1999).

Bandura (1991) stated that one's propensity to displace responsibility is a trait-like characteristic. Similarly, Blass (2009) suggested that those who par- ticipate in it are more likely to engage in obedience than those who feel responsibility for the unethical dilemma. Rost (1979) argued that actors who displace responsibility are likely to believe they can avoid punishment because it is the authority figure who is responsible for the unethical act. Milgram's studies (1965) found that actors who continued to inflict harm on participants who were clearly demonstrating pain and discomfort stated they were simply "following orders." These participants further stated that it was the *experimenter* who was responsible for the pain that was inflicted on the learner because the experimenter was the "expert."

Hence, a large body of research supports the strong link between an individual's propensity to displace responsibility and their subsequent obedience to authority figures (see Blass, 2009, for a review; see also Burger 2009; Milgram, 1965, 1974; Wood & Bandura, 1989). Therefore, we believe displacement of responsibility will be a key mechanism in the relationship between followership beliefs and crimes of obedience. Specifically, we hypothesize that followers who demonstrate intent to engage in crimes of obedience by complying with a leader's unethical request are likely to do so because they have displaced responsibility on to the leader.

Hypothesis 1: Displacement of responsibility is positively associated with intent to obey a leader's unethical request.

Constructive Resistance

Whereas displacement of responsibility has been linked to obedience in unethical situations, few studies have investigated the reactions of individuals who fail to displace responsibility (i.e., those who assume personal responsibility) or the various ways in which individuals may choose to *disobey* (Modigliani & Rochat, 1995). Thus, we examine antecedents to resistance, given that so few studies have explored resistance to unethical requests by a leader.

Obedience studies conducted by Milgram (1965, 1974) and others (see Blass, 2009, for a review) suggest that approximately 35% of individuals resist the unethical demands of a leader. In a replication of Milgram's experiment, Modigliani and Rochat

(1995) found that participants who protested the leader's instructions early in the experiment showed greater felt responsibility and a greater likelihood of disobeying the experimenter at the end of the experiment when the electric shock became unbearable for the participant. Milgram (1974) concluded that the difference between those who obeyed and those who protested was likely due to complex differences in personal characteristics. However, his early experiments did not reveal such differences. As a result, subsequent research has largely focused on the situational characteristics that predict whether someone obeys or disobeys (Milgram, 1965; also see Miller, Collins, & Brief, 1995, for a review), and only a handful of studies have looked at the personal characteristics that predict *disobedient responses* (Blass, 1991; Kelman & Hamilton, 1989).

According to a review by Blass (1991), several personality and social belief variables may predict obedience/disobedience to unethical requests. For example, personality variables such as authoritarianism (Elms & Milgram, 1966) and trust in superiors (Blass, 1991) have been associated with higher levels of obedience. Blass (1991) also suggests that an individual's belief in power and status differentials may explain why one obeys or disobeys unethical demands. In addition to these followership-oriented characteristics, other individual-level variables have also been associated with obedience in unethical situations. For example, a review by Treviño (1986) showed that individual difference variables such as locus of control, field dependence, and ego strength influence decisions to act ethically.

Related to the discussion of moral disengagement, the decision to resist may be associated with a propensity to displace responsibility elsewhere—in this case, onto the leader (Hinrichs, 2007). Whereas followers who displace responsibility are likely to engage in unethical conduct, followers who believe that the decision to act ethically falls on them rather than the leader likely show resistance to a leader's unethical request (Bandura, 1999; Rost, 1979). Indeed, there is evidence that the decision to disobey is associated with felt responsibility (Wood & Bandura, 1989) and that the rate of disobedience increases when individual responsibility is made salient by an experimenter or bystanders (Milgram, 1974).

One form of disobedience may involve followers' constructively challenging their leader's request. Tepper, Duffy, and Shaw (2001) argued that constructive resistance occurs when followers directly object to a leader's request by making suggestions for alternative actions or presenting reasons for noncompliance. In these situations, followers may use such resistance strategies to open a line of dialogue with their leader when they perceive that a leader's request is imprudent or illogical (Tepper et al., 2006). Followers who respond to a leader's request with constructive resistance score high on conscientiousness and receive high performance ratings from managers (Tepper et al., 2006). In the face of an unethical request proposed by a leader, constructive resistance has the potential to provide the most positive outcomes with regard to upholding ethical codes.

Given the risk associated with resisting a leader's request (see Milliken, Morrison, & Hewlin, 2003), we hypothesized that followers who engage in constructive resistance do so only if they feel a high degree of responsibility for the ethical dilemma (i.e., they score low on displacement of responsibility). Specifically, followers who maintain a sense of personal responsibility likely do not see themselves as safeguarded against the negative ramifications of unethical conduct. Thus, they are likely to be concerned about remorse and regret associated with obeying unethical demands of a leader (Rost, 1979). Indeed, followers who fail to displace responsibility are likely to feel it is their duty to speak up, present reasons for noncompliance, and recommend alternative courses of action that better serve their department or organization.

Hypothesis 2: Displacement of responsibility is negatively associated with followers' intention to constructively challenge their leader's unethical request.

Followers' Belief in the Coproduction of Leadership

Consistent with the discussion of status effects and obedience to authority, emerging work on followership is examining the beliefs individuals have about the role that followers play in the leadership process (Carsten et al., 2010; De Cremer & Van Dijk, 2005; De Vries & Van Gelder, 2005; Gerber, 1988). For example, Carsten and colleagues (Carsten et al., 2010; Carsten & Uhl-Bien, 2009) developed a construct that measures followers' belief in the coproduction of leadership. Belief in the coproduction of leadership is defined as the extent to which an individual believes that followers should partner with leaders to influence and enhance the leadership process. These beliefs about the follower role, and the extent to which followers should partner with leaders, develop over time as individuals began to interact with others in positions of authority (Kuhn & Laird, 2011; Louis, 1980; Ravlin & Thomas, 2005). When acting as a follower, individuals rely on their beliefs to direct their behavior. The theory of reasoned action states that beliefs form the foundation for attitudes, which in turn affect behavioral intentions (see Ajzen & Fishbein, 1977, for a review; see also Ajzen, 1991; Conner & Armitage, 1998; Fishbein & Ajzen, 1975). Indeed, Conner and Armitage (1998) suggest that beliefs may be a stronger predictor of behavioral intentions than attitudes alone, as demonstrated by research suggesting that the best way to change behavior is to change the person's underlying beliefs.

Carsten et al. (2010) have argued that individuals with weaker coproduction beliefs endorse a role definition of followership involving obedience and deference because they perceive that leaders have more expertise and agency, and they trust that the leader knows the best course of action for the group. Individuals with stronger coproduction beliefs endorse a role definition that involves partnering with leaders to improve the overall functioning of the work unit; they believe followers play an integral role in the leadership process. Indeed, early validation work by Carsten and Uhl-Bien (2009) shows that followers with stronger coproduction beliefs engage in voice and upward influence behavior and are undeterred by status and power differentials.

These findings have implications for ethical behavior in organizations. In particular, they suggest that followers who maintain weaker coproduction of leadership beliefs are likely to engage in crimes of obedience because they believe the follower role is best served by following a leader's directives without question. On the other hand, followers who have stronger coproduction beliefs may constructively challenge their leaders when faced with an unethical directive. Such individuals see followers as active participants in the leadership process and are more likely to challenge requests they perceive as potentially damaging to the organization.

We also expect that followers' coproduction beliefs are indirectly related to these outcomes through displacement of responsibility. For example, because followers with weaker coproduction beliefs strongly endorse the legitimacy of authority (Carsten & Uhl-Bien, 2009), we hypothesize they are likely to displace responsibility onto their leaders for unethical conduct, and subsequently place themselves in a "one-down position" (Kelman & Hamilton, 1989; Ravlin & Thomas, 2005). These followers may disengage and subsequently obey the unethical request because they believe they are less knowledgeable and less agentic than their leaders (Bandura, 1999). For those with stronger coproduction beliefs, who reject blind obedience (opting instead for a more collaborative role in the leadership process), we hypothesize they will engage in less displacement of responsibility and show a propensity to directly object to their leader's unethical request through constructive resistance.

Hypothesis 3a: Belief in the coproduction of leadership is negatively associated with intention to obey and positively associated with intention to constructively resist a leader's unethical request.

Hypothesis 3b: The relationship between belief in the coproduction of leadership and intentions to obey or constructively resist a leader's unethical request is mediated by displacement of responsibility.

Romance of Leadership

In addition to beliefs about followership, we expect that followers' beliefs about the romance of leadership will predict their intention to obey or constructively resist a leader's unethical request. Meindl et al. (1985) showed that followers maintain beliefs about the importance of leadership relative to other contextual

factors in predicting the ultimate success or failure of an organization. Followers who romanticize leaders have an inflated view of a leader's importance in affecting organizational outcomes (Meindl & Ehrlich, 1987), are more likely to perceive leaders as transformational and charismatic (Awamleh & Gardner, 1999), and have a tendency to attribute success or failure to a leader's level of knowledge and effectiveness (Konst, Vonk, & Van Der Vlist, 1999; Weber, Rottenstreich, Camerer, & Kenz, 2001) rather than other factors involved in producing an organizational outcome. Those who romanticize leaders often downplay contextual factors, such as the effort or expertise of subordinates, in explaining why organizations succeed or fail (see Bligh & Schyns, 2007, for a review).

Although research has not directly linked the romance of leadership to crimes of obedience, Hinrichs (2007) developed a theoretical model wherein he proposed that individuals who romanticize leaders are likely to obey unethical directives. Hinrichs (2007) argued that followers who romanticize leaders perceive the leader as all-powerful and therefore defer judgment to their leader. They believe the organization is better served by following a leader's request rather than relying on their own judgment.

In the present study, we expect that the romance of leadership will interact with coproduction beliefs to predict displacement of responsibility. Specifically, we hypothesize that individuals with weaker coproduction beliefs are likely to displace responsibility regardless of whether followers romanticize their leaders, whereas individuals with a stronger coproduction belief who romanticize leaders are likely to show greater levels of displacement of responsibility than those who do not romanticize leaders. This prediction is in line with research showing that individuals with a romanticized view of leadership see leaders as having greater importance, accountability, and responsibility for organizational processes and procedures (Meindl et al., 1985). Under situations where the leader has asked the follower to engage in unethical conduct, we expect those who romanticize leaders to show a propensity to displace responsibility, because they believe it is the leader who is ultimately responsible for organizational outcomes. Thus, we hypothesize that less displacement of responsibility occurs among followers with stronger coproduction beliefs who do not romanticize leadership.

> *Hypothesis 4*: Romance of leadership moderates the relationship between coproduction of leadership beliefs and displacement of responsibility such that followers with stronger coproduction beliefs who do not romanticize leaders are less likely to displace responsibility than any other group.

Method

Pilot Study

Prior to testing the hypothesized model, a pilot study was conducted with undergraduate business students at a university in the Southeastern United States. The purpose of the pilot study was to ensure that the scenario used to convey the unethical situation was believable and understandable (see Alexander & Becker, 1978). Additionally, we wanted to assess whether enough variance was generated on the outcome measures to test the full hypothesized model. Participants in the pilot study included 149 students enrolled in an introductory management course. Respondents were 54% female with an average age of 22 years. Approximately 54% of these students indicated they were working, and 20% were working full time.

Data were collected from students over two separate time periods. At Time 1, a research assistant visited each class and asked students for assistance in completing a personality and beliefs survey for a class project. Measures collected at Time 1 included coproduction of leadership beliefs, romance of leadership, and demographics. At Time 2, approximately 5 weeks later, the principal investigator visited the same classes and asked students to participate in a study on leadership and ethics. The Time 2 survey included a scenario detailing the unethical situation and a series of questions asking whether the participant intended to obey or disobey the manager's request.

The scenario, originally published by Weber (1991), depicted a situation where an employee at an automotive company was asked to investigate an operating problem on one of the company's new luxury automobiles. Soon after beginning the investigation, the employee's manager approached and asked the employee to fabricate the data and change the findings of the study.

Table 27.1	Means, Standard Deviations, Alpha Reliabilities, and Intercorrelations for Pilot Study								

Variables	Mean	SD	1	2	3	4	5	6	7
1. Gender	1.54	.49	—						
2. Age	21.59	3.7	−.09	—					
3. Employed	1.36	.48	−.02	−.01	—				
4. Coproduction of Leadership	4.07	.57	.01	−.01	−.07	.76			
5. RLS	3.88	.59	−.06	.01	.18*	.23*	.79		
6. Obedience	2.13	.99	−.09	−.09	.10	−.25*	.04	—	
7. Constructive Resistance	4.12	.57	.01	.06	.01	.25**	.05	−.43**	.84

Note: N = 149. RLS = Romance of Leadership Scale. Cronbach's alpha reliability presented on the diagonal. Gender coded 1 = Male and 2 = Female. Employed coded 1 = Yes and 2 = No.

*p <.05. **p <.01.

Table 27.2 Regression Analysis for Pilot Study

	Beta	R^2	ΔR^2	F
Model Predicting Obedience				
Step 1		.02	.02	.90
Age	.04			
Gender	−.12			
Employed	−.08			
Step 2		.08	.06	3.17*
Coproduction beliefs	−.21*			
RLS	.13			
Model Predicting Constructive Resistance				
Step 1		.01	.01	.17
Age	.09			
Gender	.01			
Employed	.01			
Step 2		.08	.07	3.87*
Coproduction beliefs	.23*			
RLS	−.07			

Note. N = 149. RLS = Romance of Leadership Scale. Betas reported from final model. Codes: 1 = Male and 2 = Female, 1 = Employed and 2 = Unemployed.

*$p < .05$. **$p < .01$.*

Weber's original scenario was modified slightly for this study. First, the name of the employee was changed to a gender neutral name and the scenario was revised to ensure that the manager's request to fabricate data was clear to participants. Students were asked to put themselves in the position of the employee and indicate their intention to obey or disobey the manager's request. Students were then asked a single question regarding their intent to obey the manager's request, as well as a series of questions regarding whether they would directly challenge their manager using constructive resistance strategies (see scale information below).

Results from the pilot study indicated the scenario was believable. More than 94% of the respondents indicated they believed a situation such as this happens in the workplace. In addition, data from the pilot study showed variance in both the single obedience item as well as the measures of constructive resistance (see means, standard deviations, alpha reliabilities, and intercorrelations in Table 27.1). The results of the pilot study also provided evidence that students' coproduction of leadership beliefs, as measured at Time 1, predicted their intention to obey or resist the unethical requests of a leader at Time 2 (see Table 27.2). Specifically, students with stronger coproduction beliefs were less likely to obey, ($\Delta R^2 = .06$, $F = 3.17$, $p < .05$) and more likely to constructively resist the unethical requests of a leader ($\Delta R^2 = .07$, $F = 3.87$, $p < .05$). Having found that the scenario was believable, and produced sufficient variance in the outcome measures, the full theoretical model was tested with a sample of working adults throughout the United States.

Participants and Procedure

Data were collected from working adults who had voluntarily enrolled in Zoomerang's online research panel. Zoomerang compiles a panel of adults who are interested in participating in social science and marketing research. The surveys were conducted online, and all participants were guaranteed anonymity. Two-hundred and twenty-five working adults were asked to complete the first of two surveys designed to test the theoretical model shown in Figure 27.1. The Time 1 survey assessed employees' belief in the coproduction of leadership, their belief in the romance of leadership, their propensity to displace responsibility, and their demographic characteristics. The Time 2 survey, collected approximately 4 weeks later, included the scenario, as well as questions gauging whether participants intended to obey or constructively resist the leader's unethical request. Of those contacted, 161 participants responded to both surveys and were included in the final data set (response rate = 72%). The sample was primarily male (48% female, 52% male), with an average age of 39 years ($SD = 8.3$) and an average tenure in their current organization of 11 years ($SD = 12$). The majority of the respondents (72%) identified themselves as entry-level/front-line employees, 6% said they were first-line supervisors, and 17% identified themselves as middle managers.

Measures

Follower Belief in the Coproduction of Leadership was measured with Carsten and Uhl-Bien's (2009) 5-item measure ($\alpha = .74$). This measure asks participants to think about their beliefs regarding the role of followers in relation to leaders in organizations and respond to each item using a 6-point strongly disagree–strongly agree response scale. The 5-point scale is commonly used in belief research (Anderson, 1995; Dweck, 1996), because beliefs are assumed to be robust and stable, thus eliminating the need for a "neutral" scale midpoint. A sample item is, "As part of their role, followers must be willing to challenge superiors' assumptions." In previous studies, this

scale has shown good reliability (ranging from .73 to .84) as well as construct and predictive validity (Carsten & Uhl-Bien, 2009).

Romance of Leadership was measured with Meindl's (1998) 6-item Romance of Leadership Scale (RLS; $\alpha = .77$). A sample item from this scale is, "When it comes right down to it, the quality of leadership is the single most important influence on the functioning of an organization." With the exception of the coproduction of leadership scale described above, all other measures, including the RLS, were collected using a 5-point response scale ranging from strongly disagree to strongly agree.

Displacement of Responsibility was measured with Bandura, Barbaranelli, Caprara, and Pastorelli's (1996) 4-item measure, which is part of the moral disengagement scale ($\alpha = .81$). The scale asks about general propensity to displace responsibility and is not situation specific. A sample item from this scale is, "If people are not disciplined then they cannot be blamed for misbehaving." Previous research has found the scale to have good reliability and validity.

Intention to Obey the Leader's Unethical Request was measured with one item written specifically for this study. Participants were asked whether they agreed or disagreed with the following statement: "I would obey my manager's request." Research on single-item measures compared with measures of the same construct using multiple items shows that, depending on the issue being addressed, a single-item can provide equally valid ratings (Gardner, Cummings, Dunham, & Pierce, 1998; Loo, 2002; Wanous, Reichers, & Hudy, 1997). Specifically, "If the construct being measured is sufficiently narrow or is unambiguous to the respondent, a single item may suffice" (Sackett & Larson, 1990, p. 247). In this case, the construct meets those criteria in that it is a straightforward assessment of whether an individual would obey the manager's request.

Constructive Resistance was assessed with Tepper et al.'s (2001) 4-item measure of resistance to downward influence attempts ($\alpha = .72$). Participants were asked whether they would engage in each of the behaviors if they were in the actor's position. A sample item from this scale is, "I would present a logical reason for taking a different approach to the problem."

Social Desirability was measured with Paulhus's (1991) 18-item scale. According to Randall and Fernandes (1991), studies that ask participants to place themselves in ethical dilemmas should include some measure of impression management. Paulhus's (1991) measure assesses the tendency to manage impressions by asking participants a series of statements about their own behavior. A sample item from this is scale is, "I have said something bad about a friend behind his or her back."

Results

Means, standard deviations, reliabilities, and correlations for all study variables are shown in Table 27.3. To test the model depicted in Figure 27.1, separate regression analyses were conducted for each hypothesis, controlling for social desirability and demographic variables thought to influence an individual's

intention to engage in unethical behavior. For example, research has shown that gender (Arlow, 1991) and rank in the organization (Barnett & Karson, 1989) are both associated with intent to engage in unethical behavior.

Hypotheses 1 and 2 predicted that an individual's propensity to displace responsibility at Time 1 would be associated with their intention to obey (Hypothesis 1) or constructively resist (Hypothesis 2) a manager's unethical request at Time 2. The results supported Hypotheses 1 and 2 (see Table 27.4). Specifically, after controlling for social desirability, gender, and rank in the organization, those who displaced responsibility were more likely to obey ($\Delta R^2 = .11$, $F = 23.07$, $p < .01$) and less likely to constructively resist ($\Delta R^2 = .04$, $F = 4.31$, $p < .05$) a leader's unethical request.

Hypothesis 3a predicted a direct relationship between belief in the coproduction of leadership and intent to obey or constructively resist a leader's unethical request; Hypothesis 3b predicted that

Table 27.3	Means, Standard Deviations, Alpha Reliabilities, and Intercorrelations (Field Study)

Variables	Mean	SD	1	2	3	4	5	6	7	8
1. Gender	1.48	.50	—							
2. Age	39.5	8.3	.05	—						
3. Social desirability	2.66	.68	−.02	.18*	.70					
4. Coproduction belief	4.18	.69	−.01	.12	.05	.74				
5. RLS	3.81	.56	.04	.03	.12	.16*	.77			
6. Displacement of Responsibility	2.23	.77	−.16*	−.12	.03	−.45†	−.03	.81		
7. Obedience	2.30	1.04	−.07	−.23†	.13	−.35†	−.13	.47†	—	
8. Constructive Resistance	3.89	.59	.08	.04	.12	.33†	.26†	−.21†	−.38†	.72

Note: N =161. RLS = Romance of Leadership Scale. Cronbach's alpha reliability presented on the diagonal. Gender coded 1 = Male and 2 = Female.

*p <.05. †p <.01.

Table 27.4	Regression Analyses for Displacement of Responsibility Predicting Obedience and Constructive Resistance (Field Study)

	Beta	R^2	ΔR^2	ΔF
Hypothesis 1: Model Predicting Obedience to Authority				
Step 1		.13	.13	4.74**
Gender	.01			
Rank				
Entry level	.43**			
Supervisor	.32**			
Middle manager	.32**			
Social desirability	.17			
Step 2		.24	.11	23.07**
Displacement of responsibility	.35**			
Hypothesis 2: Model Predicting Constructive Resistance				
Step 1		.04	.04	1.27
Gender	.07			
Rank				
Entry level	−.23*			
Supervisor	−.12			
Middle manager	−.07			
Social desirability	.10			
Step 2		.08	.04	4.31*
Displacement of responsibility	−.17*			

Note: N = 161. Betas reported from final model. Gender coded 1 = Male and 2 = Female. Comparison group for dummy variables = director/ executive.

*p <.05. **p <.01.

displacement of responsibility mediates these relationships. The findings showed a direct effect between coproduction of leadership beliefs and both obedience (ΔR^2 = .10, F = 19.06, p <.01) and constructive resistance (ΔR^2 = .19, F = 14.89, p <.01), indicating support for Hypothesis 3a (see Table 27.5).

For Hypothesis 3b, mediation was assessed using Preacher and Hayes (2004) application of the Sobel (1982) test with bootstrapping. Preacher and Hayes (2004) showed that the Baron and Kenny (1986) method does not allow for testing the significance of the indirect effect in mediation models. As an alternative to hand calculating the

Table 27.5	Regression Analyses for Coproduction of Leadership Predicting Obedience and Constructive Resistance (Field Study)

	Beta	R^2	ΔR^2	ΔF
Hypothesis 3a: Model Predicting Obedience to Authority				
Step 1		.13	.13	4.74**
Gender	−.06			
Rank				
Entry level	.27*			
Supervisor	.26*			
Middle manager	.27*			
Social desirability	.18			
Step 2		.23	.10	19.06**
Coproduction beliefs	−.33**			
Hypothesis 3a: Model Predicting Constructive Resistance				
Step 1		.04	.04	1.27
Gender	.09			
Rank				
Entry level	−.11			
Supervisor	−.06			
Middle manager	−.01			
Social desirability	.10			
Step 2		.13	.09	14.89**
Coproduction beliefs	.30**			

Note: N = 161. Betas reported from final model. Gender coded 1 = Male and 2 = Female. Comparison group for dummy variables = director/executive.

p < .05. **p* < .01.

Sobel test, they provided instructions and SPSS macros to test for mediation using the steps outlined by Baron and Kenny, and in addition they provided a direct test of the null hypothesis that the difference between "c" and "c" is zero. This method also offers bootstrapping results, which are important to report when testing mediation hypotheses on small samples that may violate the assumption of normality for total and specific indirect effects (Shrout & Bolger, 2002).

The results of this analysis showed that displacement of responsibility mediated the relationship between beliefs in the coproduction of leadership and intention to obey a leader's unethical request

($Z = -3.84$, $p < .01$). However, no support was found for an indirect effect of coproduction beliefs on intentions to use constructive resistance. Thus, the results suggest that Hypothesis 3b was supported for obedience, but not for constructive resistance (see Table 27.6).

The final hypothesis predicted that the relationship between belief in the coproduction of leadership and displacement of responsibility is moderated by an individual's belief in the romance of leadership (see Table 27.7). The results support the hypothesis. Individuals with stronger coproduction beliefs, who romanticize leaders, are more likely to displace responsibility than individuals with stronger coproduction beliefs who do not romanticize leaders ($\Delta R^2 = .02$, $F = 3.99$, $p < .05$). Indeed, the results from a simple slopes analysis indicate that the relation between coproduction beliefs and displacement of responsibility was significant for followers scoring high, $t(161) = 1.98$, $p < .05$, and low, $t(161) = -2.77$, $p < .01$, on the romance of leadership. The relationship between coproduction beliefs the romance of leadership, whereas individuals with weaker coproduction beliefs were found to engage in displacement

Table 27.6	Indirect Effects of Coproduction Beliefs on Reactions to Unethical Requests Through Displacement of Responsibility (Field Study)

				Bootstrapping, Percentile 95% CI	
Dependent Variable	Effect	SE	z	Lower	Upper
Obedience	−.29	.07	−3.84**	−.46	−.13
Constructive Resistance	.01	.04	.34	−.06	.12

Note: CI = confidence interval. N = 161. 1,000 bootstrap samples.

**p < .01.

Table 27.7	Moderation Analysis With Coproduction of Leadership Beliefs and RLS Predicting Displacement of Responsibility (Field Study)

Variables Entered at Each Step	Beta	R^2	ΔR^2	F
Step 1		.01	.01	.09
Social desirability	.07			
Step 2		.13	.13	11.95*
Coproduction of leadership	−.34**			
RLS	.12			
Step 3		.15	.02	3.99*
Coproduction × RLS	.16*			

Note: N = 161. RLS = Romance of Leadership Scale. Betas reported from final model.

*p < .05. **p < .01.

Figure 27.2

Interaction Plot of
Coproduction Beliefs and
RLS on Displacement of
Responsibility

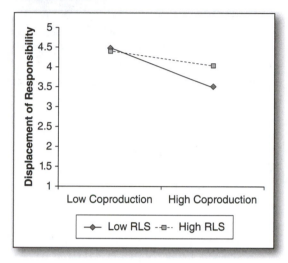

of responsibility regardless of their belief in the romance of leadership (see Figure 27.2). Thus, support was found for Hypothesis 4.

Discussion

The purpose of this study was to investigate issues of "ethical followership" by examining the antecedents of disobedience in an unethical situation. Specifically, personal characteristics such as followers' belief in the coproduction of leadership and the romance of leadership were examined to predict whether followers choose to obey or resist a leader's unethical request.

The results of this study show that followers with weaker coproduction beliefs are more likely to engage in crimes of obedience by complying with a leader's unethical directive, whereas followers with stronger coproduction beliefs are less likely to do so. Furthermore, the relationship between coproduction beliefs and obedience appears to manifest through displacement of responsibility. This mediating effect suggests that individuals with weaker coproduction beliefs are likely to obey a leader's unethical directive because they displace responsibility onto the leader. Followers with stronger coproduction beliefs, on the

other hand, were only found to displace responsibility when they had a stronger belief in romance of leadership. That is, romance of leadership moderated the relationship between coproduction of leadership and displacement of responsibility. Thus, it appears that individuals with stronger coproduction beliefs, who fail to romanticize leaders, show the lowest levels of displacement of responsibility and are least likely to obey a leader's unethical request.

The findings regarding constructive resistance are a bit more nuanced. The regression results show main effects between coproduction beliefs and constructive resistance, as well as displacement of responsibility and constructive resistance. But, contrary to the hypothesis, displacement of responsibility did not mediate the relationship between coproduction beliefs and constructive resistance. This indicates that displacement of responsibility does not explain the association between coproduction beliefs and constructive resistance and suggests there may be another mechanism through which coproduction beliefs are related to a follower's decision to resist a leader's request.

According to the theory of reasoned action (Ajzen, 1991), an individual's beliefs and attitudes interact with context to influence behavior. Indeed, the followers interviewed by Carsten et al. (2010) spoke candidly about the effects of leadership styles and organizational climates (e.g., authoritarian or empowering) on their ability to act on their beliefs: Strong bureaucracy diminished followers' ability to take initiative and move things forward. Applied to this study, strong bureaucracy may make it hard to constructively resist, even though followers do not displace responsibility. In other words, maintaining a sense of personal responsibility may not be sufficient to allow followers to constructively resist—they may also need to believe the context will allow them to act on their beliefs and their feelings of responsibility.

A fruitful area for future research is examination of the contextual factors associated with a follower's belief that he/ she can successfully resist an unethical request from a leader. These factors will likely be associated with a follower's sense of power to act. For example, rather than displacement of responsibility, future research may consider mediators such as relationship quality with the leader (e.g., leader–member exchange), association power (e.g., relationships with powerful others who can provide backup to the follower), and sense of dependency on the organization (e.g., ability to find another job). Research could also consider ethical climates from the standpoint of followership, specifically, whether the follower perceives the organization values an ethical climate to the extent that it will support an individual's efforts to constructively resist a leader's unethical request. Another issue to examine involves the "followership climate" in terms of the number of followers (and leaders) holding stronger or weaker coproduction beliefs. Climates associated with stronger coproduction beliefs (among followers and leaders) are more likely to be associated with ethical followership than climates associated with weaker coproduction beliefs.

Our findings also have important theoretical implications. The results shown here are interesting in that they are in line with emerging research on followership showing that individuals with stronger coproduction beliefs are more likely to speak up with ideas or solutions to problems (Carsten & Uhl-Bien, 2012) and that individuals with weaker coproduction beliefs show a stronger belief in legitimacy of authority (Carsten et al., 2010; Carsten & Uhl-Bien, 2009). The results also support and extend previous research on the relationship between legitimacy of authority and obedience (Blass, 2009; Milgram, 1974) by showing that followers' beliefs about their role (as opposed to the leader's role) can predict their response to unethical situations and that displacement of responsibility is a necessary precursor for obedience (Rost, 1979; Wood & Bandura, 1989).

Moreover, the results are consistent with findings regarding the romance of leadership. For example, individuals who score high on the romance of leadership perceive that leaders are extremely important in determining organizational outcomes (Meindl, 1990; Meindl & Ehrlich, 1987; Meindl et al., 1985). This heightened perception of a leader's importance may affect the decision that followers make about who is ultimately responsible for the ethical conduct of an organization. Indeed, our findings show that even though individuals may see followers as equal partners in the leadership process (i.e., they have stronger beliefs in the coproduction of leadership), they may still overly attribute a leader's importance in determining ethical conduct, largely believing that the

leader, rather than followers, is responsible for setting and maintaining the ethical tone.

Limitations

The results of this study should be interpreted with caution until they have been replicated in a variety of settings and with multiple methodologies. For example, our research is nonexperimental, which limits our ability to draw conclusions about causation. Furthermore, our research can only draw conclusions about one's behavioral intentions rather than their actual behavior in unethical situations. Future research may want to examine how followers actually react to the unethical demands of a superior either in a lab study or by asking participants to describe unethical situations and how they responded.

In addition, future research may want to create a more balanced look at ethical followership by collecting perceptions of both leaders and followers. For example, it may be that followers see themselves as contributing to the ethical conduct of an organization, but leaders see these followers as detracting from the organizational mission or goals. Finally, because this study was conducted using a North American sample, these findings may not generalize across cultures. For example, differences in how followers perceive power distance or uncertainty avoidance across cultures may also influence their willingness to constructively challenge leaders in the face of an unethical request.

Conclusion

This study reveals the important, and often overlooked, role that followers play in the maintenance of ethical conduct in organizations. By establishing the important relationships between follower beliefs, displacement of responsibility, and obedience, we begin to understand the follower side of ethical leadership and appreciate the role that followers play in challenging their leaders to uphold ethical codes. Although this study is only the first step toward understanding the differences between ethical and unethical followership, it lays a foundation for future research to begin a more balanced appreciation of how both leaders and followers can work together to coproduce ethical outcomes in organizations.

Declaration of Conflicting Interests

The authors declared no potential conflicts of interest with respect to the research, authorship, and/or publication of this article.

Funding

The authors received no financial support for the research, authorship, and/or publication of this article.

Note

1. Corresponding Author: Melissa K. Carsten, Winthrop University, College of Business Administration, 518 Thurmond Building, Rock Hill, SC 29733, USA Email: carstenm@winthrop.edu

References

Ajzen, I. (1991). The theory of planned behavior. *Organizational Behavior and Human Decision Processes, 50,* 179–211.

Ajzen, I., & Fishbein, M. (1977). Attitude-behavior relations: A theoretical analysis and review of empirical research. *Psychological Bulletin, 84,* 888–918.

Alexander, C. S., & Becker, H. J. (1978). The use of vignettes in survey research. *Public Opinion Quarterly, 42,* 93–104.

Anderson, C. A. (1995). Implicit theories in broad perspective. *Psychological Inquiry, 6,* 286–321.

Arlow, P. (1991). Personal characteristics in college students' evaluations of business ethics and corporate social responsibility. *Journal of Business Ethics, 10,* 63–69.

Awamleh, R., & Gardner, W. L. (1999). Perceptions of leader charisma and effectiveness: The effects of vision content, delivery, and organizational performance. *Leadership Quarterly, 10,* 345–373.

Baker, S. D. (2007). Followership: Theoretical foundation of a contemporary construct. *Journal of Leadership & Organizational Studies, 14,* 50–60.

Bandura, A. (1991). Social cognitive theory of moral thought and action. In W. M. Kurtines & J. L. Gewirtz (Eds.), *Handbook of moral behavior and development* (Vol. 1, pp. 45–103). Hillsdale, NJ: Erlbaum.

Bandura, A. (1999). Moral disengagement in the perpetration of inhumanities. *Personality and Social Psychology Review, 3,* 193–209.

Bandura, A., Barbaranelli, C., Caprara, G., & Pastorelli, C. (1996). Mechanisms of moral disengagement in the exercise of moral agency. *Journal of Personality and Social Psychology, 71,* 364–374.

Bandura, A., Underwood, B., & Fromson, M. E. (1975). Disinhibition of aggression through diffusion of responsibility and dehumanization of victims. *Journal of Research in Personality, 9,* 253–269.

Barnett, J. H., & Karson, M. J. (1989). Managers, values, and executive decisions: An exploration of the role of gender, career stage, organizational level, function, and the importance of ethics, relationships and results in managerial decisionmaking. *Journal of Business Ethics, 8,* 747–771.

Baron, R. M., & Kenny, D. A. (1986). The moderator-mediator variable distinction in social psychological research: Conceptual, strategic and statistical considerations. *Journal of Personality and Social Psychology, 51,* 1173–1182.

Blass, T. (1991). Understanding behavior in the Milgram obedience experiment: The role of personality, situations, and their interactions. *Journal of Personality and Social Psychology, 60,* 398-413.

Blass, T. (2009). From New Haven to Santa Clara: A historical perspective on the Milgram obedience experiments. *American Psychologist, 64,* 37–45.

Bligh, M. C., & Schyns, B. (2007). The romance lives on: Contemporary issues surrounding the romance of leadership. *Leadership, 3,* 343–360.

Biggart, N. W., & Hamilton, G. G. (1984). The power of obedience. *Administrative Science Quarterly, 29,* 540–549.

Brown, M. E., & Treviño, L. K. (2006). Ethical leadership: A review and future directions. *Leadership Quarterly, 17,* 595–616.

Burger, J. M. (2009). Replicating Milgram: Would people still obey today? *American Psychologist, 64,* 1–11.

Carsten, M. K., & Uhl-Bien, M. (2009). *Implicit followership theories (IFT): Developing and validating an IFT Scale for the study of followership.* Paper presented at the 2009 Annual Meeting of the Southern Management Association, Ashville, NC.

Carsten, M. K., & Uhl-Bien, M. (2012). Follower beliefs in the co-production of leadership: examining upward communication and the moderating role of context. *Journal of Psychology, 220,* 210–220.

Carsten, M. K., Uhl-Bien, M., West, B. J., Patera, J., & McGregor, R. (2010). Exploring social constructions of followership: A qualitative study. *Leadership Quarterly, 21,* 543–562.

Chaleff, I. (2009). *The courageous follower: Standing up to and for our leaders* (3rd ed.). San Francisco, CA: Berrett-Koehler.

Conner, M., & Armitage, C. J. (1998). Extending the theory of planned behavior: A review and avenues for further research. *Journal of Applied Social Psychology, 28,* 1429–1464.

De Cremer, D., & Van Dijk, E. (2005). When and why leaders put themselves first: Leader behavior in resource allocations as a function of feeling entitled. *European Journal of Social Psychology, 35,* 553–563.

De Vries, R. E., & Van Gelder, J. (2005). Leadership and the need for leadership: Testing an implicit followership theory. In B. Schyns & J. R. Meindl (Eds.), *Implicit leadership theories: Essays and explorations* (pp. 277–304). Greenwich, CN: IAP.

Dweck, C. S. (1996). Implicit theories as organizers of goals and behavior. In P. M. Gollwitzer & J. A. Bargh (Eds.), *The psychology of action: Linking cognition and motivation to behavior* (pp. 69–90). New York, NY: Guilford Press.

Elms, A. C., & Milgram, S. (1966). Personality characteristics associated with obedience and disobedience towards authoritative command. *Journal of Experimental Research into Personality, 1,* 282–289.

Ethics Resource Center. (2012). *2011 National Business Ethics Survey: Workplace ethics in transition.* Retrieved from http://www.ethics.org/nbes/files/FinalNBES-web.pdf

Fishbein, M., & Ajzen, I. (1975). *Belief, attitude, intention, and behavior: An introduction to theory and research.* Reading, MA: Addison-Wesley.

Gardner, D. G., Cummings, L. L., Dunham, R. B., & Pierce, J. L. (1998). Single-item versus multiple-item measurement scales: An empirical comparison. *Educational and Psychological Measurement, 58,* 898–915.

Gerber, G. W. (1988). Leadership roles and the gender stereotype traits. *Sex Roles, 18,* 649–668.

Hinrichs, K. T. (2007). Follower propensity to commit crimes of obedience: The role of leadership beliefs. *Journal of Leadership & Organizational Studies, 14,* 69–76.

Hirschhorn, L. (1990). Leaders and followers in a postindustrial age: A psychodynamic view. *Journal of Applied Behavioral Science, 26,* 529–542.

Hollander, E. P. (1995). Ethical challenges in leader-follower relationships. *Business Ethics Quarterly, 5,* 55–65.

Kelley, R. E. (1992). *The power of followership: How to create leaders people want to follow and followers who lead themselves.* New York, NY: Doubleday.

Kelman, H. C., & Hamilton, V. L. (1989). *Crimes of obedience: Toward a social psychology of authority and responsibility.* New Haven, CT: Yale University Press.

Kohlberg, L. (1969). *Stages in the development of moral thought and action.* New York, NY: Holt, Rinehart & Winston.

Konst, D., Vonk, R., & Van Der Vlist, R. (1999). Inferences about causes and consequences of behavior of leaders and subordinates. *Journal of Organizational Behavior, 20,* 261–271.

Kuhn, E. S., & Laird, R. D. (2011). Individual differences in early adolescents' beliefs in the legitimacy of parental authority. *Developmental Psychology, 47,* 1353–1365.

Loo, R. (2002). A caveat on using single-item versus multi-pleitem scales. *Journal of Managerial Psychology, 17,* 68–75.

Louis, M. R. (1980). Surprise and sensemaking: What newcomers experience entering unfamiliar organizational settings. *Administrative Science Quarterly, 25,* 226–251.

Meindl, J. R. (1998). The romance of leadership as a followercentric theory: A social construction approach. In F. Dansereau & F. J. Yammarino (Eds.), *Leadership: The multiple-level approaches* (pp. 285–298). Stamford, CT: JAI Press.

Meindl, J. R. (1990). On leadership: An alternative to the conventional wisdom. In B. M. Staw & L. L. Cummings (Eds.), *Research in organizational behavior* (pp. 159–203). Greenwich, CT: JAI Press.

Meindl, J. R., & Ehrlich, S. B. (1987). The romance of leadership and the evaluation of organizational performance. *Academy of Management Journal, 30,* 91–109.

Meindl, J. R., Ehrlich, S. B., & Dukerich, J. M. (1985). The romance of leadership. *Administrative Science Quarterly, 30,* 78–102.

Milgram, S. (1965). Some conditions of obedience and disobedience to authority. *Human Relations, 18,* 57–76.

Milgram, S. (1974). *Obedience to authority: An experimental view.* New York, NY: Harper & Row.

Miller, A. G., Collins, B. E., & Brief, D. E. (1995). Perspectives on obedience to authority: The legacy of the Milgram experiments. *Journal of Social Issues, 51,* 1–19.

Milliken, F. J., Morrison, E. W., & Hewlin, P. F. (2003). An exploratory study of employee silence: Issues that employees don't communicate upward and why. *Journal of Management Studies, 40,* 1453–1476.

Modigliani, A., & Rochat, F. (1995). The role of interaction sequences and the timing of resistance in shaping obedience and defiance to authority. *Journal of Social Issues, 51,* 107–123.

Paulhus, D. L. (1991). Measurement and control of response bias. In J. P. Robinson & P. R. Shaver (Eds.), *Measures of personality and social psychological attitudes* (pp. 17–59). San Diego, CA: Academic Press.

Perreault, G. (1997). Ethical followers: A link to ethical leadership. *Journal of Leadership Studies, 4,* 78–89.

Preacher, K. J., & Hayes, J. F. (2004). SPSS and SAS procedures for estimating indirect effects in simple mediation models. *Behavior Research Methods, Instruments, & Computers, 36,* 717–731.

Randall, D. M., & Fernandes, M. F. (1991). The social desirability response bias in ethics research. *Journal of Business Ethics, 10,* 805–817.

Ravlin, E. C., & Thomas, D. C. (2005). Status and stratification in organizational life. *Journal of Management, 31,* 966–987.

Rost, J. C. (1995). Leadership: A discussion about ethics. *Business Ethics Quarterly, 5,* 129–142.

Sackett, P. R., & Larson, J. R., Jr. (1990). Research strategies and tactics in industrial and organizational psychology. In M. D. Dunnette & L. M. Hough (Eds.), *Handbook of industrial and organizational psychology* (2nd ed., Vol. 1, pp. 419–489). Palo Alto, CA: Consulting Psychologists Press.

Shamir, B. (2007). From passive recipients to active coproducers: Followers' roles in the leadership process. In B. Shamir, R. Pillai, M. C. Bligh, & M. Uhl-Bien (Eds.), *Followercentered perspectives on leadership: A tribute to the memory of James R. Meindl* (pp. ix–xxxix). Greenwich, CT: Information Age Publishing.

Shrout, P. E., & Bolger, N. (2002). Mediation in experimental and nonexperimental studies: New procedures and recommendations. *Psychological Methods, 7,* 422–445.

Sobel, M. E. (1982). Asymptotic confidence intervals for indirect effects in structural equation models. In S. Leinhardt (Ed.), *Sociological methodology 1982* (pp. 290–312). Washington, DC: American Sociological Association.

Sy, T. (2010). What do you think of followers? Examining the content, structure, and consequences of implicit followership theories. *Organizational Behavior & Human Decision Processes, 113,* 73–84.

Tepper, B. J., Duffy, M. K., & Shaw, J. D. (2001). Personality moderators of the relationship between abusive supervision and subordinates' resistance. *Journal of Applied Psychology, 86,* 974–983.

Tepper, B. J., Uhl-Bien, M., Kohut, G. F., Rogleberg, S. G., Lockhart, D. E., & Ensley, M. D. (2006). Subordinates' resistance and managers' evaluations of subordinates' performance. *Journal of Management, 32,* 185–209.

Treviño, L. K. (1986). Ethical decision making in organizations: A person-situation interactionalist model. *Academy of Management Review, 11,* 601–617.

Treviño, L. K., Brown, M., & Hartman, L. P. (2003). A qualitative investigation of perceived executive ethical leadership: Perceptions from inside and outside the executive suite. *Human Relations, 56,* 5–37.

Treviño, L. K., Butterfield, K., & McCabe, D. (1998). The ethical context in organizations: Influences on employee attitudes and behaviors. *Business Ethics Quarterly, 8,* 447–476.

Treviño, L. K., Weaver, G. R., Gibson, D. G., & Toffler, B. L. (1999). Managing ethics and legal compliance: What works and what hurts. *California Management Review, 41,* 131–151.

Tyler, T. R. (1997). The psychology of legitimacy: A relational perspective on voluntary deference to authorities. *Personality and Social Psychology Review, 1,* 323–345.

Uhl-Bien, M., & Carsten, M. K. (2007). Being ethical when the boss is not. *Organizational Dynamics, 36,* 187–201.

Uhl-Bien, M., & Pillai, R. (2007). The romance of leadership and the social construction of followership. In B. Shamir, R. Pillai, M. C. Bligh, & M. Uhl-Bien (Eds.), *Follower-centered perspectives on leadership: A tribute to the memory of James R. Meindl* (pp. 187–209). Greenwich, CT: Information Age Publishing.

Walumbwa, F., & Schaubroeck, J. (2009). Leader personality traits and employee voice behavior: Mediating roles of ethical leadership and work group psychological safety. *Journal of Applied Psychology, 94,* 1275–1286.

Wanous, J. P., Reichers, A. E., & Hudy, M. J. (1997). Overall job satisfaction: How good are single-item measures? *Journal of Applied Psychology, 82,* 247–252.

Weber, J. (1991). Adapting Kohlberg to enhance the assessment of managers' moral reasoning. *Business Ethics Quarterly, 1,* 293–318.

Weber, R. A., Rottenstreich, Y. S., Camerer, C. F., & Knez, M. (2001). The illusion of leadership: Misattribution of cause in coordination games. *Organization Science, 12,* 582–598.

Whittington, O. R., & Pany, K. (2009). *Principles of auditing and other assurance services* (17th ed.). Columbus, OH: McGraw-Hill.

Wood, R., & Bandura, A. (1989). Social cognitive theory of organizational management. *Academy of Management Journal, 14,* 361–384.

Zahra, S. A., Priem, R. L., & Rasheed, A. A. (2007). Understanding the causes and effects of top-management fraud. *Organizational Dynamics, 36,* 122–139.

CHAPTER 28

How Bad Are the Effects of Bad Leaders?

A Meta-Analysis of Destructive Leadership and Its Outcomes

Birgit Schyns[1]
Durham University, UK

Jan Schilling
University of Applied Administrative Sciences, Hanover, Germany

1. Introduction

Traditionally, research into leadership has often been guided by the quest to find the most effective person or method to lead. Popular concepts such as transformational leadership (e.g., Bass, 1985) but even more recent developments such as ethical (e.g., Brown, Trevino, & Harrison, 2005) or authentic leadership (e.g., Walumbwa, Avolio, Gardner, Wernsing, & Peterson, 2008) focus on positive leader behavior and its effects. Sometimes the term 'leadership' is even limited to an exercise of personal influence resulting in enthusiastic commitment of followers: "proponents of this view argue that a person who uses authority and control over rewards, punishments, and information to manipulate or coerce followers is not really 'leading' them" (Yukl & van Fleet, 1992, p. 148). However, a recent stream of research (often under the label of 'supervision' or 'supervisory behavior') acknowledges that there is also a dark side to leadership (Conger, 1990): Regardless of what researchers and practitioners may consider ideal, some leaders behave in ways that are detrimental to their followers and often the organization as a whole.

There are two main reasons for the growing interest in the dark side of leadership: First, there is the question of the prevalence of and costs as a result of destructive leaders. While Aryee, Sun, Chen, and

Debrah (2008) consider abusive supervision, as the one concept that has dominated empirical research in this area, as a "low base rate phenomenon" (p. 394), other studies report a strong prevalence of destructive leader behaviors in organizations. For example in the Netherlands, Hubert and van Veldhoven (2001) report a prevalence rate of about 11%. Even higher prevalence rates have been found in a Norwegian study (Aasland, Skogstad, Notelaers, Nielsen, & Einarsen, 2010) where about a third of employees report to have been subject to some type of destructive leadership behavior "often" within the six months prior to the questioning. In the US, abusive supervision affects an estimated 13.6% of U.S. workers (Tepper, 2007) at a cost of $ 23.8 billion annually for US-companies (e.g., due to employee absenteeism, employee turnover, and lowered effectiveness; Tepper, Duffy, Henle, & Lambert, 2006). These numbers underline the high practical importance of this area of research.

The second reason for the interest in destructive leader behaviors stems from the findings that their effects on individual followers are quite severe. A large variety of outcomes have been studied in relation to destructive leadership behaviors. Examples include effects on job tension and emotional exhaustion (e.g., Harvey, Stoner, Hochwarter, & Kacmar, 2007), resistance behavior (e.g., Bamberger & Bacharach, 2006), deviant work behavior (e.g., Duffy, Ganster, & Pagon, 2002), reduced family well-being (e.g., Hoobler & Brass, 2006), and intention to quit and job satisfaction (e.g., Tepper, 2000). Both prevalence rates and potential serious effects of destructive leader behaviors make it a concept worthwhile of deeper investigation.

While for some time, a lot of literature focusing on detrimental aspects of leadership was narrative in nature (e.g., Lipman-Blumen, 2004; Sutton, 2007), making quantitative research syntheses next to impossible, research in this area has now also attracted substantial interest from quantitative researchers. Tepper (2007) stated in his qualitative literature review that most of the studies on abusive supervision have been conducted during just the last few years. Thus, the time seems ripe for a meta-analysis, quantifying the effect sizes that we can expect when leaders show destructive behaviors.

While meta-analyses already exist in the area of constructive leadership (i.e., Judge & Piccolo, 2004; Judge, Piccolo, & Ilies, 2004; Wang, Oh, Courtright, & Colbert, 2011) as well as in the field of general workplace harassment/aggression (i.e., Bowling & Beehr, 2006), a comprehensive quantitative review of destructive leadership is still absent. To our knowledge, only Hershcovis (2011) has undertaken such an endeavor. However, her intention was to meta-analytically compare supervisor-initiated aggression to other constructs of workplace aggression. Hence, she does not give a full overview of the consequences of destructive leadership but rather focuses on some outcome variables selected based on their usefulness for this comparison. Other meta-analyses have only focused on specific aspects of destructive leadership (i.e., supervisor aggression, Hershcovis & Barling, 2010; non-contingent punishment, Podsakoff, Bommer, Podsakoff, & MacKenzie, 2006).

In summary, while there is increasing evidence that destructive leaders cause serious problems for followers, organizations, and society, research in this area is lacking both an integration of the diverse concepts and a comprehensive, quantitative review of the consequences of destructive leadership. Such a review will not only provide a state-of-the-art overview of our knowledge in this area but also prospects for future theoretical and empirical developments. In fields of research like destructive leadership that are in a relatively early stage, a major problem concerns the inconsistency of the terminology (cp. Tepper, 2007). Hence, we will start by limiting the focus of our review by discussing the boundaries of destructive leadership and distinguishing it from the broader concept of destructive leader behavior. We will then discuss the different constructs of destructive leadership used in previous research to develop a definition and conclude which concepts we will include in our meta-analysis and why. Subsequently, we will briefly review prior research in this area and derive assumptions regarding the relationship between destructive leadership and different outcomes, before explaining how we conducted this meta-analysis and what the results were. We end with a discussion regarding what we know about destructive leadership so far and directions for future research.

2. Distinguishing Destructive Leader Behavior and Destructive Leadership?

It is not an easy task to define destructive leadership for two main reasons. First, as already mentioned, some researchers claim that leadership can by definition only be positive (see Yukl & van Fleet, 1992). They reject the concept of destructive leadership as being an oxymoron and advocate for different terms to capture the negative side of leader behavior (e.g., supervision, management, or headship). Second, and perhaps as a consequence of this view, we see a rather scattered landscape of different terms, concepts, and studies all interested in the dark side of leader behavior but with some important differences. Leadership researchers only recently adopted the topic from other areas such as bullying and counterproductive work behavior (Tepper, 2007; Thoroughgood, Tate, Sawyer, & Jacobs, 2012). It therefore seems necessary to answer two main questions: Why should we speak of *leadership* with respect to the dark side of leader behavior? What exactly encompasses the term 'destructive leadership'? To answer these questions, we first need to establish a border between destructive *leadership* and the more general term of destructive *leader behavior*.

Thoroughgood and colleagues (2012) define destructive leader behavior as voluntary acts (committed by a person in a leadership, supervisory, or managerial position) which most people would perceive as harmful and deviant towards followers and/or the organization and which can either be physical or verbal, active or passive, direct or indirect. While others have made similar distinctions (e.g. Einarsen, Aasland, & Skogstad, 2007), it seems important to us to note that Thoroughgood and colleagues do <u>not</u> speak of destructive leadership but destructive leader behavior (unlike Einarsen et al., 2007). From our point of view, it is important to acknowledge that while it is self-evident that not everything a leader does is leadership, the comprehensiveness of the term 'destructive leadership' is still debatable due to the difficulty of the term leadership itself. Yukl (2006) summarizes the wide range of different definitions of leadership by stating that defining leadership is always to some degree arbitrary and subjective. However, most definitions share the assumption that leadership involves "a process whereby intentional influence is exerted by one person over other people to guide, structure, and facilitate activities and relationships in a group and organization" (Yukl, 2006, p. 3). Hence, while destructive leader behavior can encompass a wider variety of harmful behavior which is not related to the leadership task (e.g., taking drugs at work, stealing from the organization; cp. Thoroughgood et al., 2012), the term of destructive leadership should be limited to those aspects which include follower-targeted influence (which is a key aspect in defining leadership). In summary, we argue here that destructive leadership is not the same as destructive leader or supervisor behavior as the latter refers to any type of negative behavior committed by a person in a leadership position, including counterproductive work behavior. In this meta-analysis, we focus on leader behaviors that are targeted towards the followers (and thus represent leadership) rather than the organization.

3. Different Conceptualizations and a Definition: What Is Destructive Leadership?

Even though concepts such as the negative side of charismatic leadership (often called personalized charisma, Howell, 1998) or narratives about political leaders such as Hitler or Stalin (e.g., Burns, 2003; Kellerman, 2004) have been part of the leadership discussion for a long time, the quantitative study of destructive leadership is a relatively recent one. Different conceptualizations of similar ideas have emerged almost at the same time. Examples of such conceptualizations include abusive supervision (e.g., Tepper, 2000), destructive leadership (Einarsen et al., 2007), toxic leadership (Lipman-Blumen, 2004), and petty tyranny (Ashforth, 1994). Table 28.1 gives an overview of the different types of destructive leadership found in the literature. There are a few key aspects in which the definitions of these concepts differ which we will outline below.

(1) *Perception versus actual behavior:* As is the case with constructive leadership, destructive leadership tends to be assessed from the follower's point of view. However, some definitions of the concepts included here explicitly refer to follower's perception of the leader's behavior (e.g., abusive supervision: Tepper, 2000) whereas others only refer to the leader's behavior (e.g., social undermining: Duffy et al., 2002). We argue that leader behavior can only have an effect when it is perceived by followers and in that sense, probably all the different concepts of destructive leadership include an element of perception.

(2) *Intent:* Another question is whether or not the behavior shown by the leader is intentionally or unintentionally destructive. Some definitions of destructive leadership include the notion of intent (e.g., despotic leadership: De Hoogh & Den Hartog, 2008), other do not (e.g., petty tyranny: Ashforth, 1997) or do not do so explicitly (e.g., supervisor aggression: Inness, Barling, & Turner, 2005). While it is quite difficult to empirically differentiate these different notions (see the discussion between Hershcovis, 2011, and Tepper & Henle, 2011), some authors stress that the intent does not have to be real but that the perception of intent is the key element here (e.g., social undermining: Duffy et al., 2002). We can assume that leader behavior that is perceived to be intentionally destructive is more harmful than behavior that is unintentionally destructive but both can be considered destructive.

(3) *Physical, verbal, and non-verbal behavior:* Destructive leadership can encompass a wide variety of behaviors, including verbal and non-verbal behavior or even physical violence. While some definitions rule out physical behavior (e.g., Tepper, 2000), others include it in their definition (e.g., destructive leadership: Einarsen, Skogstad, Leseth, & Aasland, 2002). Even though physical violence may be a rather unlikely form of destructive leadership, it seems advisable to not completely exclude it from the definition in order not to limit the scope of destructive leadership too much in this early stage of research.

(4) *Inclusion of outcomes:* Some definitions of destructive leadership explicitly refer to outcomes (e.g., Einarsen et al., 2002), others define the concept in more neutral terms (e.g., petty tyranny: Ashforth, 1997). An interesting discussion can be undertaken regarding the question as to whether or not the conceptualization of destructive leadership should refrain from including references to outcomes. On the one hand, a more neutral approach to assessing leaders' destructive behavior would be useful as, otherwise, testing correlations between the construct and its potential outcomes can be redundant. On the other hand, practically it can be difficult to differentiate destructive behavior from the destructiveness regarding its outcomes. We follow the arguments of Thoroughgood and colleagues (2012) in that we focus on the perceived nature of the target behavior rather than on its specific consequences as this may lead to the incorrect inclusion or exclusion of certain behaviors.

Following this summary and consistent with the definition of leadership by Yukl (2006), we will define destructive leadership as *"a process in which over a longer period of time the activities, experiences and/or relationships of an individual or the members of a group are repeatedly influenced by their supervisor in a way that is perceived as hostile and/or obstructive".* Some aspects of this definition deserve further explanation.

(1) *Influence:* Exerting influence on followers is at the heart of most of the definitions of leadership (Yukl, 2006), which makes it also a key feature of destructive leadership. This means that a leader uses destructive leadership to achieve a certain aim and at least unintentionally (see discussion above) influences the activities and relationships within the group.

(2) *Supervisor:* While many definitions of leadership in general do not define who exerts the influence, a definition on destructive leadership

Table 28.1 Types of Destructive Leadership Used in the Studies Included in the Meta-analysis and Articles That Introduced the Concept

Type of destructive leadership	Articles that introduced the concept	Perception	(Perceived) Intent	Duration/frequency	Physical, verbal, and non-verbal behavior	Target	Inclusion of outcomes
Petty tyranny	Ashforth (1997)	N	N		V/NV	F	N
Abusive supervision	Tepper (2000)	Y	N	Y	V/NV	F	N
Coercive power	Elangovan and Xie (2000)	N					Y
Abusive supervisory behaviors	Yagil (2005)	Y		Y	V/NV	F	N
Social undermining	Duffy et al. (2002)	N	Y	Y	V/NV	F/C[a]	Y
Supervisory abuse[b]	Bamberger and Bacharach (2006)	Y	N	Y	V/NV	F	N
Supervisor verbal abuse	Grandey et al. (2007)			Y	V	F	N
Unsupportive managerial behaviors	Rooney and Gottlieb (2007)			Y	V/NV	F	N
Aversive leadership	Bligh et al. (2007)	Y			V/NV	F	N
Destructive leadership	Einarsen et al. (2002)	N	N	Y	V/NV/P	F/O[c]	Y
Tyrannical leadership[d]	Hauge et al. (2007)	N	N	Y	V/NV/P	F/O[e]	Y
Despotic leadership	De Hoogh and Den Hartog (2008)	N	Y		V/NV/P	F/O	N

Note: N = No; Y = Yes; V = Verbal; NV = Nonverbal; P = Physical; F = Follower; O = Organization; C = Colleagues.

[a] In our meta-analysis, only supervisor behavior towards followers is included.

[b] Definition based on Tepper but different instrument used. We assume the same characteristics as valid for Tepper.

[c] Only follower related behavior is included in our meta-analysis.

[d] This is part of the destructive leadership model by Einarsen et al. (2002) and therefore follows the same definition.

[e] Only follower related behavior is included in our meta-analysis.

needs to be clear about this aspect and focus on hierarchical mistreatment (cp. Tepper, 2007). While not impossible, it seems rather unlikely that a person without formal authority can emerge and stay in a position of an informal leader in an organizational context by behaving destructively (at least in the long run). Many conceptions of destructive leader behavior include the abuse of formal power as an important means to intimidate and punish reluctant followers.

(3) *Repetition over a longer period of time:* To qualify as destructive leadership, it seems also important that the negative influence on the group members is exerted not just once or twice but repeatedly over a longer period of time. This aspect roots deeply in the literature on workplace bullying (e.g. Einarsen, Hoel, Zapf, & Cooper, 2003) as it is important to distinguish destructive leadership from short-term conflicts or single destructive acts. It has to be stressed that a boss who has a bad day and takes it out on his or her followers should not be considered as a destructive leader (Tepper, 2007).

(4) *Perceived hostility and/or obstructiveness:* As stated before, destructive leadership should be defined by the nature of the target behavior rather than its consequences (Thoroughgood et al., 2012). Hence, the core of destructive leadership lies in the hostile and hindering nature of the leader's behavior. While constructive leadership is defined as reaching common agreements about work and facilitating individual and collective efforts to achieve shared goals (cp. Yukl, 2006), destructive leadership on the contrary involves hostile behavior (like public ridiculing, taking credit for subordinates' successes, and scapegoating subordinates; Keashly, Trott, & MacLean, 1994) as well as impeding cooperative work in the team (like giving someone the silent treatment and prohibiting interaction with coworkers; Tepper, 2000). As stated above, it is important to note

that hostility and obstructiveness can only be subjective evaluations "subordinates make on the basis of their observations of their supervisors' behavior" (Tepper, 2007, p. 4).

(5) *Individual or group:* There is an ongoing discussion about the level of analysis in leadership research (see, e.g., Yammarino, Dionne, Chun, & Dansereau, 2005). Some conceptualizations of leadership explicitly refer to the individual level relationships (e.g., Leader-Member Exchange; Graen & Uhl-Bien, 1995) whereas others imply group level relationships (i.e., the leader behaves the same towards all members of his/her group, e.g., transformational leadership: Bass, 1985). We assume that destructive leadership can refer to both levels, in the sense that leaders might target only one or few members of their group, and/or only one or few members of their group perceive destructive leadership, or they are generally destructive towards all of their followers.

4. Sharpening the Focus: What Is Not Destructive Leadership?

An important issue raised by this definition of destructive leadership is the question as to whether or not laissez-faire leadership (non-leadership) can be included as a type of destructive leadership. Skogstad, Einarsen, Torsheim, Aasland, and Hetland (2007) argue in this direction and state that destructive leadership can take both active, manifest as well as passive, indirect forms. Skogstad and colleagues (2007) underline that not only the direct forms of supervisor hostility but also a lack of initiative and support can have negative effects on subordinates' satisfaction and performance. This argument is supported by their own empirical results (i.e., laissez-faire leadership is related to higher levels of role conflict, role ambiguity, and conflict with co-workers; Skogstad et al., 2007) as well as those of others (e.g., Judge & Piccolo, 2004).

However, as a concept should not be defined by its consequences (see above), the question remains if the term 'destructive' is really appropriate when talking about laissez-faire leadership. Padilla, Hogan, and Kaiser (2007) note that destructive leadership results in harmful, long-term ramifications. The very broad conception by Skogstad and others (2007) may blur important differences within the field of the dark side of leadership. While it is certainly true that laissez-faire is an ineffective leadership style (i.e., inappropriate to achieve follower satisfaction and effective performance), we see a clear qualitative difference between non-leadership and active supervisor hostility as described by the concepts such as abusive supervision (Tepper, 2000) or petty tyranny (Ashforth, 1994). The latter can be expected to have much more severe and potentially even qualitatively different detrimental consequences (for a similar argument see Ashforth, 1994).

An even more difficult aspect of the dark side of leadership is the so-called supportive-disloyal leadership (Einarsen et al., 2007) which is described as showing (too much) consideration for the welfare of followers while violating organizational goal attainment. Such leaders may steal resources from the organization, protect their followers from work, and grant their employees more benefits than they are obliged to (Einarsen et al., 2007). The difficulty with this concept is that this kind of leadership is normally not regarded as hostile by the followers as they may benefit from it (at least in the short run). While there can be no doubt that it is a destructive leader behavior with regard to the organization, supportive-disloyal can be expected to produce quite different reactions on part of the followers than other forms of destructive leadership such as abusive supervision or tyrannical leadership (see Einarsen et al., 2002).

Therefore, it should be treated as a separate area of destructive leader behavior in order not to blur the important differences between these concepts.

In summary, it now seems necessary to distinguish between *destructive* and *negative leadership* (cp. Schilling, 2009). In contrast to our definition of destructive leadership, negative leadership is used as an overarching term including commonly disliked and denounced behaviors ranging from ineffective (such as laissez-faire leadership) and anti-organizational behavior (such as supportive-disloyal leadership) to

destructive aspects in the sense of our definition (cp. Kellerman, 2004).

In conclusion, in our definition of destructive leadership, we are inclusive in the sense that we include as many concepts as possible without blurring the concept. Other than excluding 'non-leadership' ('laissez-faire') and supportive-disloyal leadership for the reasons indicated above, we therefore decided to include a broad range of behaviors in our definition. Thus, we include verbal, non-verbal, and physical behavior as part of destructive leadership. With respect to the target of the behavior, we decided to focus on the follower as a target. The reason, as indicated above, is related to the question of leadership versus general destructive leader behavior. In our meta-analysis, we were not so much interested in leaders' general 'misbehavior' (which could also include, e.g., counterproductive work behavior) than in leadership behavior directed towards the followers.

5. Destructive Leadership and Outcomes: Theoretical Framework

Conducting a meta-analysis means that in terms of the constructs examined, we have to rely on research that has been conducted so far in the area for the selection of outcome variables. In reviewing the relevant literature in the field, we found that most of the outcomes of destructive leadership are assessed from a follower's point of view. Theoretically, and in line with our definition of destructive leadership, focusing on follower-related outcomes makes sense, as part of our definition is that destructive leadership is focused on influencing followers. As we outlined above, this is different from general destructive leader behavior as defined by Thoroughgood and colleagues (2012). The latter also refers to destructive behavior against the company, meaning that a different set of outcomes might be more relevant.

Outcomes under study in the area of destructive leadership can broadly be differentiated into leader-related concepts, job-related concepts, organization-related concepts, and individual follower-related concepts (see Fig. 28.1). While there are certainly outcomes that can be classified under several of these categories, we broadly used the following guidelines of categorization: Probably the easiest category to define is leader-related concepts. Here, we subsumed concepts that related directly to the leader such as follower resistance towards the leader (e.g., Bligh, Kohles, Pearce, Justin, & Stovall, 2007) and leader identification (Ashforth, 1997). These are dyadic concepts, in the sense that they are attitudes or behaviors shown by individual followers to individual leaders. One of the main concepts categorized as job-related is job satisfaction (e.g., Tepper, 2000). While different conceptualizations can comprise different aspects of job satisfaction (e.g., the supervisor or the organization), we argue that job satisfaction a) is often assessed with one question (Wanous, Reichers, & Hudy, 2000) relating directly to the job or b) assesses different facets that make up a job. Where specific aspects were differentiated (e.g., the supervisor), these were summarized under the respective other category (in this example, attitudes towards the leader).

Organization-related concepts comprise concepts that directly affect the organization such as organizational commitment or turnover. While one could argue that these concepts are influenced by a myriad of antecedents and also do not only affect the organization (e.g., people who leave the organization also leave their supervisor and their team), it seemed most appropriate to summarize them under

organization-related concepts as they convey an attitude towards the organization as a whole.

We summarized stress, well-being, and performance under individual follower-related concepts as they are consequences that relate to the individual follower. Arguably, performance is broader and relates to the job as well as the organization, however, we categorized this variable as individual follower-related concept in order for it not to be confused with performance of the organization as a whole.

In the following, we will outline the expected relationships between destructive leadership and those outcomes as well as how we think the relationships will differ from each other with respect to their strength. We will also discuss differences in the effect sizes between destructive and constructive leadership.

5.1. Leader-Related Concepts

Several studies have looked into leader-related concepts, mainly follower resistance towards the leader (e.g., Bligh et al., 2007) and attitudes towards the leader (e.g., leader identification; Ashforth, 1997). The assumption is that followers show resistance towards destructive leaders. Tepper, Duffy, and Shaw (2001) argue that resistance such as ignoring request can be a way of frustrating leaders in a way that "is somewhat ambiguous from the target's perspective in terms of intent" (p. 975) and thus a good way to

Figure 28.1 Outcomes of Destructive Leadership

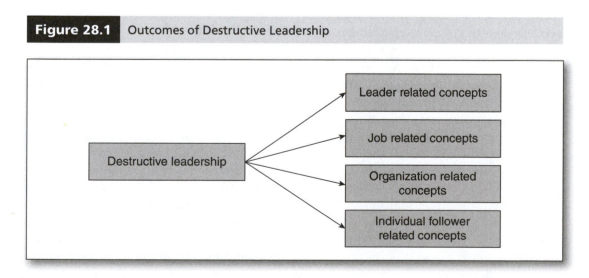

retaliate to leaders. Their results confirm that abusive supervision is positively related to resistance. With respect to attitudes towards leaders, an example is Duffy and Ferrier's (2003) study examining trust in the supervisor. They argue that abusive supervision should lower trust in the supervisor and indeed found empirical support for this hypothesis. On a more general level, it is likely that followers change their attitudes and behaviors towards the source of destructive behavior, that is, their leader. Based on the available theory and results, we assume:

H1. Destructive leadership will have negative relationships with positive leader-related concepts (such as trust) and positive relationships with negative leader-related concepts (such as resistance).

5.2. Job-Related Concepts

In the context of destructive leadership, the concept most examined is job satisfaction. Many studies argued and found that destructive leadership is negatively related to job satisfaction (e.g., Tepper, 2000; Tepper, Duffy, Hoobler, & Ensley, 2004) as supervisors form a significant part of one's job and, thus contribute to making a job a pleasant or unpleasant experience. Part of destructive leadership is putting forwards unreasonable demands or ridiculing followers, which are behaviors that make the daily experience of going to work displeasing. Other job-related attitudes under investigation were job dedication (Aryee et al., 2008) and work motivation (Elangovan & Xie, 2000). Being dedicated to a job that involves destructive leader behavior is likely to be difficult, even if the follower is dedicated to his/her profession in general. The same is true for motivation: Keeping up motivation in the light of abuse is unlikely in the longer run. Again, the assumption that destructive leadership is negatively related to these concepts was generally supported. Given prior theory and results we assume:

H2. Destructive leadership will have negative relationships with positive job-related concepts and positive relationships with negative job-related concepts.

5.3. Organization-Related Concepts

Organization-related concepts that have been examined in prior research include turnover intention (Ashforth, 1997), counterproductive work behavior (Mitchell & Ambrose, 2007), justice (Zellars, Tepper, & Duffy, 2002), and commitment (Burris, Detert, & Chiaburu, 2008). Regarding turnover intention, Ashforth (1997) found that petty tyranny is positively related to turnover intention. He argues that this is due to the unpredictability of petty tyrants which creates work alienation. Mitchell and Ambrose (2007) argue that in addition to direct retaliation to the supervisor, followers of abusive leaders will also show what they call 'displaced' deviance towards the organization. Their results support this assumption. With respect to justice, Tepper (2000) argues that followers of abusive supervisors will perceive his/her behavior as unjust and thus evaluated procedural justice as low. This notion was supported in his study. Arguably, commitment to an organization that 'allows' destructive leadership should be low as followers might think that the organization fails to protect them. This notion was empirically supported (e.g., Burris et al., 2008).

H3. Destructive leadership will have negative relationships with positive organization-related concepts and positive relationships with negative organization-related concepts.

5.4. Individual Follower-Related Concepts

Outcomes of destructive leadership on individual followers examined in prior research include affectivity, stress, well-being, and performance. In the context of abusive supervision and outcomes, affectivity is often used as a control variable (e.g., Breaux, Perrewe, Hall, Frink, & Hochwarter, 2008). Destructive leadership is often found to be positively related to negative affectivity (e.g., Tepper et al., 2004) and negatively related to positive affectivity (e.g., Wu & Hu, 2009). Technically, affectivity could also be an antecedent of destructive leadership, as people might differ in how they evaluate a leader's behavior based on their general affectivity. Stress and well-being are probably the most examined outcomes of destructive leadership, as it almost seems a matter of course that destructive leadership is positively related to stress and negatively related to well-being. Long-term and frequent exposition to destructive behavior from a person that is in charge is likely to cause stress and lead to lower well-being. Sample studies examining stress are Chen and Kao (2009) and Tepper (2000) and for well-being Hobman, Restubog, Bordia, and Tang (2009) and Burris and colleagues (2008). Results for the relationship between destructive leadership and individual performance tend to support the notion that destructive leadership is negatively related to performance (e.g., Aryee, Chen, Sun, and Debrah (2007)). Theoretically, there are different reasons to assume that destructive leadership is likely to have an impact on individual performance: First, followers may lower their efforts in the face of a destructive leader. Second, negative relationships between destructive leadership and motivation or well-being could explain why the performance of followers of destructive leaders is low.

H4. Destructive leadership will have negative relationships with positive individual follower-related concepts and positive relationships with negative individual follower-related concepts.

5.5. Strength of Relationships

Looking at the different relationships outlined above, we can assume that not all of them will be of the same strength. In terms of the size of effects, we can assume that attitudes and behaviors that are directed towards the 'destructive' leader would be more strongly related to destructive leadership than relationships to job- or organization-related attitudes and behaviors. Attitudes towards the source of the negative experiences and direct 'retaliation' are likely to be influenced solely by the leader whereas other attitudes and behaviors are influenced by other sources as well.

H5. The effect sizes found for the relationships between destructive leadership and leader-related attitudes and behaviors will be higher than those for job- or organization-related attitudes and behaviors.

5.6. Destructive and Constructive Leadership

Based on Baumeister, Bratslavsky, Finkenauer, and Vohs (2001), Einarsen and colleagues (2007) assume that destructive leadership has stronger effects than positive leadership. While it is beyond the scope of this meta-analysis to directly compare effects of destructive and constructive leadership, we will examine the *size of the effects* of destructive leadership on various outcome variables and compare our results to prior meta-analyses on constructive leadership. In line with Baumeister and colleagues (2001) and Einarsen and colleagues (2007), we argue that negative behavior should have stronger effects than positive behavior. Thus:

H6. The effect sizes found for the relationships between destructive leadership and follower attitudes and behaviors will higher be than those for constructive leadership and follower attitudes and behaviors.

6. Method

6.1. Search Strategy and Inclusion/Exclusion Criteria

In order to identify articles to be included in the meta-analysis, we used three approaches (following procedures of other meta-analyses; cp. Judge & Piccolo, 2004; Judge, Colbert, & Ilies, 2004; Hershcovis & Barling, 2010). First, we reviewed the reference list of Tepper's (2007) overview article. Second, we conducted a literature research in PsycINFO, Google Scholar, and Web of Science to identify further studies. As there is at this stage not a unitary term in use for destructive leadership, we used a variety of search terms, such as abusive supervision, abusive leadership, destructive supervision, and destructive leadership. We restricted our search to keywords, title, and abstract. The cut-off date for this search was end of September 2010. Table 28.2 depicts the search terms used and the number of articles found for each of those terms. Third, we also contacted colleagues working and publishing in this field on an individual basis to uncover some unpublished research.

Using all search strategies outlined above, we found 260 articles. The PsycINFO search yielded 104 studies. All other searches combined yielded another 156 articles.

We used several strategies to identify studies relevant for our meta-analysis. First, we reviewed the abstracts of the articles found. Based on the criteria outlined below, we discarded 44 articles after reading the abstracts. In the second stage, we reviewed the remaining 216 articles. Of those articles, 61 were deemed relevant, 152 were not relevant, and 3 were not available. Reasons for non-inclusion in our meta-analysis were: The articles reported no quantitative data (e.g., review or theoretical articles as well as qualitative papers were excluded), the study did not refer to hierarchical relationships (e.g., some studies referred to peer, rather than leadership behavior), the study did not use behavior as a unit of measurement (e.g., some studies focused on traits), the study did not take place in a formal work context (e.g., some studies comprised samples in mentoring relationships), the

Table 28.2   Search Terms and Number of Articles Found in PsycINFO

Search term	Number of articles found
Abusive supervision	46
Supervisor abuse	1
Abusive leadership	1
Bossing	9
Despotic leadership	2
Despotic supervision	0
Destructive leadership	11
Destructive supervision	0
Narcissistic leadership	4
Narcissistic supervision	0
Negative leadership	13
Negative supervision	7
Petty tyranny	2
Psychopathic leadership	1
Psychopathic supervision	0
Toxic leadership	4
Toxic supervision	0
Tyrannical leadership	2
Tyrannical supervision	1
Total N of articles found in PsycINFO	104

article was not written in English, the study did not include a form of destructive leadership (see above, we excluded studies that used laissez-faire leadership as a form of destructive leadership), or the study did not refer to personal leadership (e.g., some studies comprised structural or HRM type of leadership). We also excluded studies that did not differentiate the perpetrator of the negative behavior (e.g., some studies focus on workplace aggression in general independent of who shows the aggression, e.g., some studies reported in Hershcovis, 2011). Finally, some articles did not contain enough information to be included in our meta-analysis. We also excluded articles that reported on the same data set for a second time.

6.2. Coding Procedure

For all studies relevant to our meta-analysis, we identified the measurement of destructive leadership used. Table 28.1 gives an overview of the concepts used in the studies included in the meta-analysis and the article that introduced the concept. We did not further exclude studies here but rather included all studies satisfying our criteria outlined above. While this led to the inclusion of a variety of different assessments of destructive leadership, they all share a common core reflecting our definition of destructive leadership. From the different kinds of measurement, the abusive supervision scale (Tepper, 2000) was by far the most often used instrument. While the majority of studies (Brown et al., 2005) used the full 15-item version, some studies (Baumeister et al., 2001) used shorter versions ranging from 3 to 13 items taken from Tepper (2000) (see Appendix A). Three studies combined some of Tepper's items with those of other scales to measure abusive supervision.

Next, we identified all other variables included in each of the studies. Due to the focus of our study, we only included outcome variables (i.e., variables that may actually be affected by destructive leadership). Hence, demographic variables and follower personality were not incorporated into our analyses.

We then examined in how far studies used the same correlates of destructive leadership so that a meaningful meta-analysis of the respective relationships could be undertaken. Wherever possible, based on the number of studies using the same construct, we analyzed studies using the same construct (e.g., job satisfaction). However, as the outcomes were quite varied, we categorized them so that more studies could be included in each meta-analytic calculation of relationships. To achieve this, qualitative content analysis was chosen as an approach that combines the strengths of the grounded theory approach in the discovery of 'natural' categories with strategies from traditional content analysis (cp. Schilling, 2006). This included the basic processes of comparing the outcome variables and their constituting (sample) items found in the studies to develop categories. The first step was to find simple categories based on the constructs found in the different studies. Most outcome variables could be coded on the basis of their name as they were used in enough studies (e.g., positive affectivity, affective commitment, and job satisfaction). As a rule of thumb we created an outcome category if a variable was used in at least six different studies (cp. Locke, 2002). The second step was to analyze the rest of the variables to find commonalities in order to combine small categories (subsuming old or formulating new categories; Conger, 1998). For example, we defined a category 'follower resistance towards leader' which included variables such as leader-directed deviance, aggression, and retaliation; that is, variables which shared the idea of negative behavior towards the (destructive) leader. The two categories 'well-being' and 'organizational performance' were kept as first-order categories of outcome variables even though they comprised less than six studies as they could not meaningfully be combined with other outcome variables. Finally, we structured the thus established category system by subsuming the categories to four higher-level groupings based on their focus (leader, job, organization, and individual follower). This categorization was conducted in line with our theoretical considerations outlined under "Destructive leadership and outcomes: theoretical framework". Table 28.3 depicts all categories used and gives examples of the concepts that were summarized under each category.

For 2/3 of the articles, two raters conducted the categorization of the outcome criteria jointly. The codes were discussed and a coding scheme developed and applied. For the remaining 1/3 of the articles, two raters independently coded the variables with regard to the category system outlined above. A computation of the inter-rater-reliability for the categorized outcome variables used in these studies yielded a value of .90 (Cohen's kappa), which signifies high inter-rater agreement.

For all relevant studies, the correlations between destructive leadership and outcomes were extracted. Appendix A1 indicates the studies that were used for each of the correlations. The numbers vary considerably as some outcomes were studied more commonly than others. Overall, 57 articles (some reporting

more than one study) reported relevant results and all necessary information to be included in our meta-analyses.

6.3. Analyses

We used the program Comprehensive Meta-Analysis (Borenstein, Hedges, Higgins, & Rothstein, 2005) to conduct our meta-analyses. For each category of outcomes, we conducted a separate analysis. Where several correlations between the same constructs/ outcome categories were reported in one

Table 28.3　Categories Used in the Meta-analysis.

Category	Sample concepts
Leader-related concepts	
Follower resistance towards leader	Aggression, supervisor-directed deviance
Attitudes towards leader	Trust, liking
Job-related concepts	
Job satisfaction	Job satisfaction
Job-related attitudes	Dedication, involvement, motivation
Organization-related concepts	
Turnover intention	Intention to turnover, intention to quit
Counterproductive work behavior	Organizational deviance, counter-productive behavior at work
Justice	Distributive justice, pay fairness, procedural justice
Organizational performance	
Commitment	Affective commitment, organizational commitment
Individual follower-related concepts	
Affectivity	Positive affectivity, negative affectivity
Positive self-evaluation	Self-esteem, core self-evaluation, self-efficacy
Follower stress	Exhaustion, depression
Follower well-being	Life-satisfaction, physical well-being
Individual performance	OCB, performance, work effort

study, we used several approaches to including them in our meta-analysis: First, if the correlations were independent (e.g., the same relationships were reported for different samples), we treated them as independent, including all relevant correlations in our analyses. Second, where dependent correlations were reported, for example, between several types of destructive leadership and the same outcome, or between destructive leadership and outcomes that were coded into the same category, we averaged the correlations. While there are different methods to correct these average correlations, most of them tend to lead to higher estimates of correlations (Hunter & Schmidt, 2004). Using the average therefore constitutes a conservative estimate of the overall correlation. Given that we assumed we would find relatively large effects and given also the possible practical implications of over-estimating effect sizes, we decided to use a conservative estimate.

We conducted all analyses twice, once with the raw correlations and a second time with the corrected correlations (corrected for unreliability where this information was available in the primary studies). We will, however, interpret only the meta-analytic results of the raw correlations as the corrected correlations constitute the upper limit of the estimation of the population correlation and, given we expect large effects, we decided to follow a conservative estimation in order not to exaggerate the effects of destructive leadership.

7. Results

Table 28.4 depicts the results of our meta-analyses. The results are very much in line with our expectations, showing that destructive leadership is negatively related to positive leader-related concepts and positively related to negative leader-related concepts, thus supporting H1. As we only found studies examining positive job-related attitudes to include in our meta-analyses, we can only in part support H2 in so far as destructive leadership is negatively related to positive job-related concepts. We assumed in H3 that destructive leadership will have negative relationships with positive organization-related concepts and

positive relationships with negative organization-related concepts. Our results support this hypothesis. We also found support for H4 (Destructive leadership will have negative relationships with positive individual follower-related concepts and positive relationships with negative individual follower-related concepts), although the relationship between destructive leadership and positive affectivity was rather low. For all results it has to be noted, however, that the variance within the studies (Q_{within}) is often large, indicating heterogeneity of results.

As expected in Hypothesis 5, the strongest effects we found were for attitude towards the leader, indicating that destructive leader behavior is directly related to how followers feel about their leader. However, the relationship between destructive leadership and follower resistance (towards the leader), while still a strong effect and in the expected direction, is weaker than some of the other relationships, indicating that attitudes maybe more strongly affected by destructive leadership than behavior, at least where the leader is directly concerned.

The second strongest effect (though much smaller than the one for leader-related attitudes) emerged for counterproductive work behavior. This shows the wider effects of destructive leadership, in the sense that more general job-related behaviors are affected by destructive leadership behavior. While direct resistance towards the leader contains a greater risk of punishment by the leader, general counterproductive work behavior may be a safer (i.e., more clandestine) way to retaliate upon one's leader for his destructive leadership.

Job-related concepts such as job satisfaction and organization-related concepts such as turnover intention and the experience of justice also showed medium-sized correlations to destructive leadership although interestingly not as high as counterproductive work behavior.

As expected well-being, negative affectivity, and stress were found to be related to destructive leadership, indicating that this type of leader behavior has effects that are wider than just work-related. The relationship with occupational stress is not as strong as those for the two other variables. This may be a hint that an impairment of one's personal well-being

Table 28.4	Outcomes of Meta-analysis—Correlations Between Destructive Leadership and Outcomes

Concept	Q_b	k	N	r	*CI* Lower limit	*CI* Upper limit	Q_w
Leader-related concepts							
Follower resistance (overall)	7.770**	8	2176	.295	.256	.333	
Abusive		6	1637	.263	.217	.308	131.773***
Other		2	539	.387	.313	.457	10.050**
Attitude towards leader (overall)	14.306***	7[a]	1582	−.571	−.604	−.537	
Abusive		2	192	−.521	−.618	−.408	7.106***
Other		4	720	−.511	−.563	−.454	27.611***
Job-related concepts							
Job satisfaction (overall)	37.620***	21[a]	8707	−.336	−.355	−.317	
Abusive		10	2724	−.272	−.307	−.237	45.372***
Other		10	5313	−.347	−.370	−.323	9.521
Job-related attitudes (overall)	2.189	6	2784	−.319	−.352	−.285	
Abusive		2	501	−.263	−.343	−.180	1.684
Other		4	2283	−.330	−.366	−.293	33.536***
Organization-related concepts							
Turnover intention (overall)	59.872***	11[a]	6034	.313	.290	.335	
Abusive		5	2440	.222	.184	.260	13.594***
Other		5	2924	.339	.306	.371	32.213***
Counterproductive work behavior (overall)	23.352***	19[a]	7610	.377	.358	.397	
Abusive		13	5219	.395	.372	.418	127.898***
Other		5	1721	.292	.248	.334	20.158***
Justice (overall)	18.068***	12	4625	−.321	−.346	−.294	
Abusive		11	2965	−.278	−.311	−.244	57.352***
Other		1	1660	−.393	−.433	−.352	0.000

Concept	Q_b	k	N	r	CI Lower limit	CI Upper limit	Q_w
Organizational Performance		2	333	.039	−.069	.146	
Commitment (overall)	5.540**	14	3821	−.212	−.242	−.182	
Abusive		10	3033	−.194	−.228	−.159	31.018***
Other		4	788	−.283	−.346	−.217	14.916***
Individual follower-related concepts							
Affectivity							
-Positive affectivity (overall)	0.068	8	2514	−.094	−.133	−.055	
Abusive		5	1839	−.097	−.142	−.051	2.324
Other		3	675	−.085	−.160	.009	24.486***
-Negative affectivity (overall)	13.564**	15	6860	.339	.318	.360	
Abusive		10	4881	.364	.339	.388	97.350***
Other		5	1979	.276	.234	.316	6.373
Positive self-evaluation (overall)	4.982**	13	2856	−.172	−.208	−.136	
Abusive		7	1504	−.211	−.259	−.161	51.430***
Other		6	1352	−.129	−.181	−.076	22.861***
Stress (overall)	32.089***	24	12,093	.243	.226	.259	
Abusive		12	3836	.314	.285	.343	55.980***
Other		12	8258	.210	.189	.230	91.769***
Well-being (overall)	28.188***	4	1057	−.346	−.398	−.291	
Abusive		3	990	−.366	−.419	−.311	28.188***
Other		1	67	−.010	−.250	−.231	0.000
Individual performance (overall)	2.011	12	4657	−.204	−.231	−.176	
Abusive		7	1946	−.180	−.223	−.136	11.012
Other		5	2711	−.221	−.256	−.184	17.095

"other" refers to studies that used instruments other than abusive supervision.

** $p < .05$.

*** $p < .001$.

[a] Where a study used both abusive supervision and another instrument, the correlations reported in this study were averaged and included in the overall calculation but deleted from the moderator analysis.

and the experience negative emotions are more strongly affected by destructive leadership while occupational stress is influenced by other factors (e.g., the availability of coping resources). The experience that colleagues are exposed to the same kind of destructive leader behavior may work as a moderator in this relationship resulting in lower levels of stress (i.e., 'a problem shared is a problem halved'). We also found smaller but significant effects for organizational commitment, follower positive self-evaluation, and individual performance. These concepts are clearly influenced by a wider range of factors outside the leader's control but it is still striking that destructive leadership has an effect even on those aspects of their followers' lives.

As abusive supervision was the most often used concept in the studies we found, we compared the correlations between studies using the instrument assessing abusive supervision introduced by Tepper (2000) and outcomes, on the one hand, and studies using a different instrument to assess destructive leadership (e.g., petty tyranny) and outcomes, on the other hand. The results are depicted in Table 28.4. At first glance the pattern of results of the moderator analysis does not seem to be very clear. However, looking a bit more closely, it seems that abusive supervision yields higher correlations than other instruments for more personal concepts such as affectivity and well-being. It is also more strongly related to attitudes and behavior directed towards the leader and CWB. In studies using instruments other than Tepper's questionnaire, we found higher correlations with outcomes such as resistance, turnover intention, justice, and performance. These seem to be more directly related to the job than the outcomes abusive supervision is more highly related to. Although this is speculation, we can assume that the reason for these differences is due to item contents: Reviewing the items of the abusive supervision instrument by Tepper in comparison to those of the other instruments, abusive supervision may have a stronger personal connotation as some of the behaviors listed seem less work-relevant than behaviors subsumed under other concepts. That means that the differences in correlations could be due to specificity matching (Brunswick, 1956).

We also compared our results to meta-analyses of constructive leadership. We assumed (Hypothesis 6) that the effect sizes found for the relationship between destructive leadership and follower attitudes and behaviors will be higher than those for constructive leadership and follower attitudes and behaviors. We selected the meta-analyses to compare our results to on the basis that (a) they report meta-analytic results of a constructive leadership concept (e.g., transformational leadership, LMX), (b) they include one or more outcomes that were included in our meta-analysis, and (c) they were not integrated in newer meta-analyses (e.g., Judge & Piccolo, 2004, integrated the 'older' meta-analyses of Lowe, Kroeck, & Sivasubramaniam, 1996; Fuller, Patterson, Hester, &Stringer, 1996). We found these meta-analyses using PsycINFO and the search terms "meta-analysis" and "leadership".

As shown in Table 28.5, the pattern of results for destructive versus constructive leadership is slightly mixed. Most of the correlations are higher for constructive rather than destructive leadership with the exception of commitment and well-being. Interestingly, the pattern of results is different for different constructive leadership concepts: For the constructive leadership concepts LMX and transformational leadership all correlations are higher than those for destructive leadership. Thus, our sixth hypothesis was not supported.

8. Discussion

The aim of this meta-analysis was to summarize quantitatively the relationships that destructive leadership has with leader-related, job-related, organization-related, and more general person-related outcomes. One of the most interesting results of our meta-analysis is the fact that the pattern of results is not only as expected but also how narrow the confidence intervals are. This means that we can be rather confident in drawing conclusions about the expected strength and direction of the relationships between destructive leadership and outcomes. As expected, the results were strong for the outcomes related to the supervisor him/herself. Followers of destructive leaders are likely to have negative attitudes towards the leader and show resistance towards her/him. Indeed, the relationship between destructive leadership and attitudes towards the leader was the strongest effect we found. This is in line with, for example, Tepper and colleagues' (2001) argument regarding direct retaliation towards the leader. The relationship between destructive leadership and attitudes towards the leader was stronger than the relationship between destructive leadership and the more behavioral resistance variable. We can only speculate as to why this is the case, but followers might shy away from direct resistance to avoid further

destructive leadership behavior and a spiral of abuse, whereas attitudes are hidden from the leader.

Although, due to the correlative nature of the data, we cannot draw conclusions about causal relationships, we can assume that a destructive leader will find it difficult to convince the follower to 'follow', which will ultimately challenge his/her own position. Of course, for a while, destructive leadership might work in terms of achieving goals. Indeed, Bardes and Piccolo (2010) argue that goal setting can contribute to the emergence of destructive leader behaviors. Thus, these behaviors might be used to

Table 28.5 Outcomes of Destructive and Constructive Leadership

Outcome	Destructive leadership	Constructive leadership	Concept	Source for constructive leadership
Attitude tow./ satisfaction with leader	−.57	.68	Consideration	Judge et al. (2004)
		.27	Initiating structure	Judge et al. (2004)
		.62	LMX	Gerstner and Day (1997)
		.71	Transformational leadership	Judge and Piccolo (2004)
		.55	Contingent reward	Judge and Piccolo (2004)
Job satisfaction	−.34	.40	Consideration	Judge et al. (2004)
		.19	Initiating structure	Judge et al. (2004)
		.46	LMX	Gerstner and Day (1997)
		.23	Democratic leadership	Gastil (1994)
		.58	Transformational leadership	Judge and Piccolo (2004)
		.64	Contingent reward	Judge and Piccolo (2004)
Turnover intention	.31	−.28	LMX	Gerstner and Day (1997)
Commitment	−.21	.35	LMX	Gerstner and Day (1997)
Well-being	−.35	.26	Different constructive styles	Kuoppala, Lamminpaa, Liira, and Vainio (2008)
Individual performance	−.20	.22	Transformational leadership	Wang et al. (2011)

achieve goals. However, the relationship between destructive leadership and follower resistance implies that followers will in the long run not comply with the leader (at least if they do not have to fear severe punishment for this behavior). Of course, we cannot rule out that follower resistance is the cause of destructive leadership behavior rather than the other way round. More longitudinal research is needed to clarify causal effects.

Destructive leadership is also negatively related to positive attitudes towards the job. Supervisors constitute a large part of one's job and also have the power to shape the jobs of their followers. Some of this 'shaping' may be part of the destructive leadership (e.g., non-contingent punishment, Ashforth, 1994) and, therefore, it is not surprising that followers also lower their attitudes towards their job. Again, of course, we cannot rule out that negative job attitudes cause or contribute to destructive leadership. That would mean that supervisors' destructive behaviors are reactive. While this could be the case, it seems that not all supervisors react to negative attitudes or behaviors in a destructive way and that as a reaction this will likely aggravate rather than solve the problem, making it unlikely that destructive leadership is (solely) a reaction towards negative attitudes. In addition, prior longitudinal research into the relationship between bullying in the workplace and job satisfaction indicated that bullying causes lower job satisfaction rather than job satisfaction causing bullying (Rodriguez-Munoz, Baillien, De Witte, Moreno-Jimenez, & Pastor, 2009).

We also found that followers of destructive leaders have more negative attitudes towards their organization as a whole. Burris and colleagues (2008) argue for an overspill of negative feelings towards the supervisor to negative feelings towards the organization. This could be not only due to the leader being perceived as representative of the organization but also due to the perception that the organization does not intervene to protect their employees. Regardless of the reasons for the negative attitudes, destructive leadership seems to have a broader impact in the organization, in so far as employees regard the organization as a whole more negatively. This likely leads to costs for the organization as followers' turnover intention increases (e.g., Van Dick et al., 2004) and, probably, their performance decreases (e.g., Meyer, Stanley, Herscovitch, & Topolnytsky, 2002). The very strong correlation between destructive leadership and counterproductive work behavior should be particularly worrisome in this respect.

The high correlation we found could be due to three reasons: First, we assume that counterproductive work behavior in this context serves as an act of retaliation towards the leader which may prove safer than direct resistance towards the leader (displaced deviance, Mitchell & Ambrose, 2007). Second, destructive leaders may be seen as role models for their followers, conveying the message that negative behavior is appropriate in this organization. This explanation is closely related to the idea of Brown and colleagues (2005) concerning the process of social learning in the area of ethical leadership. Finally, destructive leadership and counterproductive work behavior could be a sign of a more general negative organizational culture that is permissive of these types of negative behavior. Kusy and Holloway (2009) point out two aspects of organizational culture that help or hinder toxic leader behavior: (a) system dynamics and (b) values. System dynamics are antecedents as they refer to the extent to which an organization encourages or discourages these leader behaviors. Values refer to principles and standards of dealing with toxic leaders. In any case, organizations should have a high degree of self-interest to deal with destructive leaders.

It seems that the effects of destructive leadership are even wider, touching the personal life of employees. Though to a lesser extent than leader-related, job-related, and organizational effects, we found that destructive leadership is also closely related to negative affectivity and to the experience of occupational stress (and negatively to personal well-being, respectively). Of course, we cannot rule out that the relationship is in the opposite direction, so that, for example, stress leads to a higher perception of destructive leadership. However, Ferris, Zinko, Brouer, Buckley, and Harvey (2007) argue that, for example, strategic bullying leads to control loss in followers and thereby increases stress.

Ultimately, the consequence of these relationships could be societal costs if employees become unable to work for a prolonged period of time.

While a meta-analytic comparison of destructive and constructive leadership behavior was beyond the scope of our meta-analysis, we compared our results to meta-analyses of constructive leadership behaviors, such as transformational leadership. In line with Baumeister and colleagues (2001) and Einarsen and colleagues (2007), we expected destructive leadership to have stronger effects than constructive forms of leadership. However, a comparison of results did not confirm this notion. One interesting point to note here is that not all outcomes of destructive leadership have also been studied under constructive conditions and notably many negative outcomes have (to our knowledge) not been subject to meta-analyses yet. Here, future research is needed to clarify if destructive leadership has stronger effects on negative outcomes then constructive leadership.

9. Limitations of the Study

Some limitations or our study are based in the data available from primary research. Probably the biggest drawback of our meta-analysis is that all our analyses are based on correlations. Most available research into destructive leadership is cross-sectional in nature (with the notable exception of some of Tepper's studies, e.g., Tepper et al., 2009). We, therefore, cannot draw conclusions about causal effects. In addition, studies on destructive leadership and its outcomes tend to use self-report data only. This means that there is a potential for a method bias. However, the correlation differences we found between the different outcome variables will likely be similar but might differ in strength when method bias is avoided. While using self-report data only is a clear limitation, the issue lies in the nature of the research: A lot of the constructs summarized under destructive leadership explicitly refer to the perception of leader hostility as a defining attribute of destructive leadership. In addition, some of the outcomes are highly subjective.

Given that the field is relatively new, there were limits as to the possibility of analyzing moderators. We found large within studies heterogeneity which points to moderating influence. However, given the limited amount of moderators included in primary research, we were not able to include moderators here other than one on the measurement of destructive leadership.

Relatedly, we summarized different outcomes into categories to achieve a larger number of studies included in our individual analyses. However, that means that we cannot say much about differentiated effects. For example, under the heading of counterproductive work behavior different behaviors such as organizational and interpersonal deviance (i.e., negative behavior towards coworkers), active as well as passive counterproductive behavior are summarized. This limits in how far differentiated relationships between destructive leadership and outcomes could be examined.

We found only two studies which examined the relationship between destructive leadership and performance: De Hoogh and Den Hartog (2008) assessed perceived top management team effectiveness. Detert, Trevino, Burris, and Andiappan (2007) used different measures on the organizational level such as operating profit and actual turnover. De Hoogh and Den Hartog found no relationship between despotic leadership and organizational performance. Detert and colleagues only found one significant relationship out of the five they tested and that was with product loss (in this case, food loss). From these two studies, we cannot derive a clear conclusion regarding the relationship between destructive leadership and organizational performance. It seems that most of the results point to a zero or rather low relationship which is probably due to the fact that there are a myriad of influences on organizational performance and (bad) leadership is only one of them. In addition, based on our definition, we focused narrowly on destructive leadership rather than more general destructive leader behavior. Destructive leader behavior might be more strongly related to organizational performance as it would have a more direct effect on organizational performance (e.g., in the sense of stealing or fraud) than destructive leadership. At the same time, destructive leadership might have a long-term effect via low follower motivation or high turnover rates, where destructive leader behaviors might have more immediate effects.

Finally, all meta-analyses may be subject to the file drawer problem (Rosenthal, 1979). This refers to the tendency that negative or inconclusive results often remain unpublished by their authors (Sackett, 1979). With regard to our study, this bias may cause an overestimation of effects concerning the consequences of destructive leadership. While to our knowledge there still is no 'silver bullet' to solve this problem, we tried to minimize it by directly contacting colleagues working in this field asking for unpublished studies.

10. Methodological Suggestions for Future Research

Most of the studies we found are cross-sectional and mono-method. Future research should, therefore, try to collect longitudinal data to determine the direction of the relationship. It is not inconceivable that destructive leadership is a reaction of a leader towards an adverse situation in the workplace (e.g., low follower commitment, high counter-productive work behavior). Ideally, leaders would be assessed from a point in time when they first lead a team in order to examine if their (perceived) behavior changes with their followers' attitudes and behaviors.

With respect to counterproductive work behavior but also other types of behavior, it would be interesting to examine in a more differentiated way which behaviors are most strongly affected by destructive leadership and if there is a difference in the effects depending on how long a follower is working for a destructive leader. One could assume that the types of counterproductive work behavior shown by followers get more severe the longer they serve under a destructive leader. For example, counterproductive work behavior may start with some withdrawal behaviors such as longer breaks and ultimately continue to aggression against co-workers and customers.

In addition to subjective data, future research should consider assessing data using diary studies,

for example, asking participants to note incidents of destructive leadership and measuring their stress objectively. A further methodological suggestion is to collect peer ratings of destructive leadership, such as asking colleagues in how far a person is subjected to destructive leadership rather than indicating in how far they themselves perceive destructive leadership towards themselves. In addition, multi-level analysis could be used to assess the level of consensus among followers regarding the destructive leadership of their leader.

Interestingly, there are very few studies focusing on team-related consequences of destructive leadership (for exceptions see: Duffy et al., 2002; Duffy, Ganster, Shaw, Johnson, & Pagon, 2006; Fox & Stallworth, 2010; Hobman et al., 2009). It would be interesting to investigate if destructive leadership necessarily impairs coworker support and fosters conflicts in a team or may even lead to higher team cohesiveness (i.e., by having a 'common enemy').

As very few studies included organizational performance data, this is another area where research into destructive leadership can be enhanced by using objective data. More research is needed to examine in how far destructive leadership is related not only to 'soft' criteria but also to 'hard' performance data. Likely, the relationship between destructive leadership and organizational performance will be mediated by follower-related attitudes such as job satisfaction and well-being which will likely lead to a lower follower productivity.

11. Future Research and Theoretical Developments

The limitations of our study not only stress the importance of advancing empirical research on destructive leadership in different ways but also underline the necessity of developing a comprehensive theoretical model. While this endeavor is beyond the scope of our paper, the results of our study lead to several suggestions for future research in the area of destructive leadership and point to necessary "ingredients" of a theoretical model. The starting point for the development of a comprehensive model of destructive leadership is to look for theories that can inform such a model.

11.1. Theoretical Foundations for a Comprehensive Model

To get a more complete picture, a theoretical model of destructive leadership has to develop ideas regarding the mechanisms which underlie the empirical relationships between destructive leadership and its antecedents and consequences. First, social learning—as also described for ethical leadership by Brown et al. (2005)—could be major basis for a better understanding of destructive leadership. According to social learning, followers imitate the destructive behavior of their supervisor in the form of resistance, counterproductive work behavior, or workplace bullying. This can explain the link between destructive leadership and follower outcomes.

The trickle-down model of abusive supervision (Mayer, Bardes, Hoobler, Wayne, & Marinova, submitted for publication) which is also based on social learning theory may serve to identify antecedents. They argue that leadership behaviors of higher-level leaders are adopted on lower levels. Therefore, higher-level destructive leadership can 'trickle down' to all levels in the organization. Psychological hardiness (Maddi, 2006) may have a buffering effect on the relationship between the perception of destructive leadership on part of higher-level leaders and its imitation of a lower-level leader.

Social learning and trickle down models may have a greater impact when there is high power distance between leader and follower. This may not only increase the emergence of destructive leadership but also aggravate the effects of destructive leadership as the follower might feel he/she cannot react to the behavior (cp. Tepper, 2007) and therefore might develop symptoms of learned helplessness (Seligman, 1975).

Second, the perception of (interactional) injustice and follower reactions to it may be an important explanation for the impact of destructive leadership (Bies & Tripp, 2005; Colquitt, Conlon, Wesson, Porter, & Ng, 2001). For example, followers may try to 'restore justice' by changing their perception of the relationship with their leader or by taking action against the leader ('getting even'). Perceived injustice (e.g., in the form of higher-level destructive leadership) and psychological contract breach can also be important sources for the emergence of destructive leadership. But as Tepper (2007) argues, not all leaders who believe that they have been mistreated abuse their followers. This relationship is likely to be moderated by characteristics of the leader and his/her followers. Followers who appear to be weak and vulnerable (e.g., high in neuroticism; Costa & McCrae, 1992) or provocative and difficult (e.g., low in agreeableness; Costa & McCrae, 1992) can be expected to be more likely targets of destructive leadership than their more emotionally stable and/or agreeable coworkers (Aquino & Byron, 2002; Tepper, 2007).

Agreeableness and neuroticism (Costa & McCrae, 1992) as personality traits of the leader should be influential moderators in the relationship between perceived injustice and the execution of destructive leadership. As Tepper (2007) already outlined, supervisors low in agreeableness and/or high in neuroticism should be more likely to show destructive leadership as they are less concerned about the effects of their behavior and experience greater anger and frustration (and react to it more impulsively), respectively.

Third, destructive leadership can be perceived as an extreme social stressor which may lead us to understand how negative emotions and counterproductive work behavior arise as a consequence of destructive leadership (e.g., the stressor-emotion model; Spector & Fox, 2005). This may also prove helpful to explain the use of functional (e.g., seeking social support) and especially dysfunctional forms of coping (e.g., problem drinking; Bamberger & Bacharach, 2006) as reactions to destructive leadership. While this list of possible mechanisms is certainly not exhaustive, they may serve as starting points to explain the impact of destructive leadership. A high degree of neuroticism may aggravate the relationship between destructive leadership and negative affect and stress (Costa & McCrae, 1992).

As stated before, some conceptualizations of destructive leadership explicitly or implicitly include the notion of (perceived) intent (e.g., De Hoogh & Den Hartog, 2008). It seems likely that if followers perceive intent, the effects on their attitudes and behaviors are stronger than when they do not perceive intent (e.g., when they perceive the leader as reacting towards circumstances or simply as incompetent). Future research could examine this idea by either comparing different forms of destructive leadership directly or simply asking followers whether or not they think the leader uses destructive behavior with a specific aim. At the same time, irrespective of their followers' perception of their intention, some leaders may use destructive leadership intentionally to achieve particular results, for example, higher productivity or attempting to bully an employee into leaving, while others might not be aware of the effects of their behavior. It would be interesting to examine in future research in how far actual intent is related to leaders' attributes (e.g., narcissism or psychopathy; cp. Paulhus & Williams, 2002) and how it affects followers. However, actual intent might be very difficult to assess as it requires the respective leader to state intent.

Fourth, Padilla and colleagues (2007) introduced what they call the toxic triangle, referring to the characteristics of leaders and followers as well as the environmental context. They argue that destructive leadership is a result of all those characteristics. We have concentrated on *leaders' behaviors* in our meta-analysis as it is the most widely examined aspect in this research area. That means that we looked at destructive leader behavior in isolation and did not take into account the environment in which destructive leadership happens (see e.g., Kusy & Holloway, 2009, for a discussion around organizational environment). Nevertheless, integrating leader, follower, and organizational characteristics (e.g., as potential moderators) is necessary to get a more complete picture of the dynamics of destructive leadership. For example, destructive leadership could be just shown by one or a few individual leaders or it could be part of an organizational culture. Such a culture would be characterized by social norms which legitimate destructive leadership as a means of exercising authority (Tepper, 2007). We can expect that destructive leadership emerges much easier and also has different effects (at least in terms of the strength of effects) if it is part of a culture (rather than an isolated phenomenon). In case of the former, followers might be able to transfer to a different department to escape the destructive leadership. They may also feel more encouraged to raise the issue with other people in the organization if the destructiveness is not widespread. Likewise, high power distance (Hofstede, 2001) as part of an industry and/or national culture may also influence the emergence of destructive leadership (Mulvey & Padilla, 2010) as this kind of negative leader behavior may be conceived as an acceptable expression of unequal power distributions in social organizations (Tepper, 2007). Further possible influences of the organizational and societal environment like checks and balances (e.g., media power, and legislation), organizational complexity, instability and dynamism, and perceived threat are outlined by Mulvey and Padilla (2010).

12. Conclusion

In conclusion, our meta-analysis shows the expected negative effects of destructive leadership and thereby confirms the urgency for organizations to deal with prevalent destructive leadership and avoid the occurrence of destructive leadership in the first place. Some of the effect sizes we found are rather substantial, underlining the importance of leaders and leadership in organizations. In terms of the future of destructive leadership research, this meta-analysis has shown many gaps in our knowledge and thereby serves as a call for more conceptual work as well as empirical studies in this important area of organizational behavior.

Note

1. Corresponding author at: Durham Business School, Durham University, Mill Hill Lane Durham DH1 3LB, UK. Tel.: +44 191 334 5173; fax: +44 191 3345201. E-mail address: birgit.schyns@durham.ac.uk (B. Schyns).

Appendix A	Articles Included in the Meta-analysis That Use a Measurement of Abusive Supervision

Abusive supervision articles	N of items
Aryee, Chen, Sun, and Debrah (2004)	10
Aryee, Chen, Sun, and Debrah (2007)	10
Aryee, Sun, Chen, and Debrah (2008)	10
Biron (2010)	15
Breaux, Perrewe, Hall, Frink, and Hochwarter (2008)	15
Brown, Trevino, and Harrison (2005)	No info
Burris, Detert, and Chiaburu (2008)	4 (adapted)
Detert, Trevino, Burris, and Andiappan (2007)	3 (adapted)
Duffy and Ferrier (2003)	5 (adapted)
Dupre, Inness, Connelly, Barling, and Hoption (2006)	15
Harris, Kacmar, and Zivnuska (2007)	11
Harvey and Keashly (2006)	15
Harvey, Stoner, Hochwarter, and Kacmar (2007)	15
Hobman, Restubog, Bordia, and Tang (2009)	13
Hoobler and Brass (2006)	15
Inness, Barling, and Turner (2005)	15
Kiazad, Restubog, Zagenczyk, Kiewitz, and Tang (2010)	15
Mayer, Bardes, Hoobler, Wayne, and Marinova (submitted for publication)	15
Mitchell and Ambrose (2007)	5
Rafferty, Restubog, and Jimmieson (2010)	15
Tate and Jacobs (2010)	15
Tepper (2000)	15
Tepper, Carr, Breaux, Geider, Hu, and Hua (2009)	5 (Study 1)
	15 (Study 2)
Tepper, Duffy, Hoobler, and Ensley (2004)	15
Tepper, Duffy, and Shaw (2001)	15
Tepper, Henle, Lambert, Giacalone, and Duffy (2008)	15
Tepper, Moss, Lockhart, and Carr (2007)	15
Thau, Bennett, Mitchell, and Marrs (2009)	Combined measurement (Study 1)
	5 (Study 2)
Thau and Mitchell (2010)	5
Wu and Hu (2009)	15
Yagil (2005)	15 (Study 2)
Yagil (2006)	15
Zellars, Tepper, and Duffy (2002)	Combined measurement

Appendix A1 | Studies Included in the Meta-analysis

Concept	Name of study
Leader-related concepts	
Follower resistance (9 samples)	Bligh et al. (2007)
	Dupre et al. (2006)
	Hershcovis and Barling (2010)
	Hoobler and Brass (2006)
	Kim and Shapiro (2008)
	Tepper et al. (2001)
	Tepper et al. (2007)
	Thau and Mitchell (2010)
Attitude towards leader (7 samples)	Ashforth (1997)
	Brown et al. (2005)
	Duffy and Ferrier (2003)
	Duffy et al. (2006)
	Rooney and Gottlieb (2007)
	Tate and Jacobs (2010)
	Elangovan and Xie (2000)
Job-related concepts	Bligh et al. (2007)
Job satisfaction (21 samples)	Breaux et al. (2008)
	Duffy et al. (2006)
	Einarsen et al. (2002)
	Elangovan and Xie (2000)
	Fox and Stallworth (2010)
	Harris et al. (2007)
	Harvey and Keashly (2006)
	Hauge, Skogstad, and Einarsen (2007)
	Hershcovis and Barling (2010)
	Hobman et al. (2009)
	Lim and Teo (2009)
	Reeds and Bullis (2009)
	Rooney and Gottlieb (2007)
	Tate and Jacobs (2010)
	Tepper et al. (2004)
	Tepper (2000)

Concept	Name of study
	Tepper et al. (2009)
Job-related attitudes (6 samples)	Aryee et al. (2004)
	Aryee et al. (2008)
	Ashforth (1997)
	Duffy et al. (2006)
	Elangovan and Xie (2000)
	Gould-Williams (2007)
Organization-related concepts	
Turnover intention (13 samples)	Ashforth (1997)
	Burris et al. (2008)
	Duffy et al. (2006)
	Fox and Stallworth (2010)
	Gould-Williams (2007)
	Harvey et al. (2007)
	Harvey and Keashly (2006)
	Hershcovis and Barling (2010)
	Lim and Teo (2009)
	Rooney and Gottlieb (2007)
	Tate and Jacobs (2010)
	Tepper et al. (2009)
Counter productive work behavior (21 samples)	Biron (2010)
	Duffy et al. (2002)
	Duffy et al. (2006)
	Hershcovis and Barling (2010)
	Inness et al. (2005)
	Kim and Shapiro (2008)
	Lim and Teo (2009)
	Mayer et al. (submitted for publication)
	Mitchell and Ambrose (2007)
	Tate and Jacobs (2010)
	Tepper et al. (2008)
	Tepper et al. (2009)
	Thau et al. (2009)

(Continued)

Appendix A1 (Continued)

Concept	Name of study
	Thau and Mitchell (2010)
	Yagil (2005)
Justice (12 samples)	Aryee et al. (2007)
	Burris et al. (2008)
	Detert et al. (2007)
	Duffy and Ferrier (2003)
	Gould-Williams (2007)
	Hoobler and Brass (2006)
	Tepper (2000)
	Tepper et al. (2007)
	Thau and Mitchell (2010)
	Zellars et al. (2002)
Organizational Performance (2 samples)	Detert et al. (2007)
	De Hoogh and Den Hartog (2008)
Commitment (15 sample)	Aryee et al. (2007)
	Ashforth (1997)
	Burris et al. (2008)
	Duffy and Ferrier (2003)
	Duffy et al. (2002)
	Elangovan and Xie (2000)
	Harvey and Keashly (2006)
	Hershcovis and Barling (2010)
	Lim and Teo (2009)
	Tepper et al. (2004)
	Tepper (2000)
	Tepper et al. (2008)
	Tepper et al. (2009)
Individual follower-related concepts	
Affectivity (positive) (8 samples)	Bowling, Beehr, Bennett, and Watson (2010)
	Breaux et al. (2008)
	Duffy et al. (2002)
	Harvey et al. (2007)
	Tepper et al. (2004)

Concept	Name of study
	Wu and Hu (2009)
	Zellars et al. (2002)
Affectivity (negative) (15 samples)	Aryee et al. (2004)
	Aryee et al. (2008)
	Biron (2010)
	Bowling et al. (2010)
	Breaux et al. (2008)
	Duffy et al. (2002)
	Duffy et al. (2006)
	Kim and Shapiro (2008)
	Tepper et al. (2009)
	Tepper et al. (2006)
	Thau et al. (2009)
	Wu and Hu (2009)
	Zellars et al. (2002)
Positive self-evaluation (13 samples)	Ashforth (1997)
	Bligh et al. (2007)
	Bowling et al. (2010)
	Duffy et al. (2002)
	Hobman et al. (2009)
	Inness et al. (2005)
	Kiazad, Restubog, Zagenczyk, Kiewitz, and Tang (2010)
	Rafferty et al. (2010)
	Rooney, Gottlieb, and Newby-Clark (2009)
	Tepper et al. (2009)
	Wu and Hu (2009)
	Yagil (2006)
Stress	Aryee et al. (2004)
	Aryee et al. (2008)
	Ashforth (1997)
	Bamberger and Bacharach (2006)
	Breaux et al. (2008)

(Continued)

Appendix A1　(Continued)

Concept	Name of study
	Burris et al. (2008)
	Chen and Kao (2009)
	Duffy et al. (2002)
Stress	Einarsen et al. (2002)
	Elangovan and Xie (2000)
	Fox and Stallworth (2010)
	Gould-Williams (2007)
	Grandey, Kern, and Frone (2007)
	Harvey et al. (2007)
	Hershcovis and Barling (2010)
	Hobman et al. (2009)
	Nyberg, Westerlund, Magnusson Hanson, and Theorell (2008)
	Rafferty et al. (2010)
	Rooney and Gottlieb (2007)
	Rooney et al. (2009)[1]
	Tepper (2000)
	Tepper et al. (2007)
	Thau and Mitchell (2010)
	Wu and Hu (2009)
	Yagil (2006)
Well-being	Burris et al. (2008)
	De Hoogh and Den Hartog (2008)
	Hershcovis and Barling (2010)
	Hobman et al. (2009)
	Tepper (2000)
Individual performance	Aryee et al. (2007)
	Aryee et al. (2004)
	Aryee et al. (2008)
	Ashforth (1997)
	Bligh et al. (2007)
	Burris et al. (2008)
	Elangovan and Xie (2000)
	Gould-Williams (2007)

Concept	Name of study
	Harris et al. (2007)
	Hershcovis and Barling (2010)
	Hoobler and Brass (2006)
	Thau, Aquino, and Bommer (2008)
	Zellars et al. (2002)

This study reports the same sample as Rooney and Gottlieb and therefore was not included in our meta-analysis.

References*

* References included in the meta-analysis.

Aasland, M. S., Skogstad, A., Notelaers, G., Nielsen, M. B., & Einarsen, S. (2010). The prevalence of destructive leadership behaviour. *British Journal of Management, 21,* 438—152.

Aquino, K., & Byron, K. (2002). Dominating interpersonal behavior and perceived victimization in groups: Evidence for a curvilinear relationship. *Journal of Management, 28,* 69–87.

*Aryee, S., Chen, Z. X., Sun, L. Y., & Debrah, Y. A. (2004). Examining the mediating and moderating influences on the relationships between abusive supervision and contextual performance in a Chinese context. *Paper presented at the 4th Asia Academy Management Conference, December 16–18, Shanghai, China.*

*Aryee, S., Chen, Z. X., Sun, L. Y., & Debrah, Y. A. (2007). Antecedents and outcomes of abusive supervision: Test of a trickle-down model. *Journal of Applied Psychology, 92,* 191–201.

*Aryee, S., Sun, L. Y., Chen, Z. X. G., & Debrah, Y. A. (2008). Abusive supervision and contextual performance: The mediating role of emotional exhaustion and the moderating role of work unit structure. *Management and Organization Review, 4,* 393–411.

Ashforth, B. E. (1994). Petty tyranny in organizations. *Human Relations, 47,* 755–778.

*Ashforth, B. E. (1997). Petty tyranny in organizations: A preliminary examination of antecedents and consequences. *Canadian Journal of Administrative Sciences, 14,*126–140.

*Bamberger, P. A., & Bacharach, S. B. (2006). Abusive supervision and subordinate problem drinking: Taking resistance, stress and subordinate personality into account. *Human Relations, 59,* 723–752.

Bardes, M., & Piccolo, R. F. (2010). Aspects of goals and reward systems as antecedents of destructive leadership.

In B. Schyns, & T. Hansbrough (Eds.), *When leadership goes wrong: Destructive leadership, mistakes, and ethical failures.* Charlotte, NC: Information Age Publishing.

Bass, B. M. (1985). *Leadership and performance beyond expectations.* New York: Free Press.

Baumeister, R. F., Bratslavsky, E., Finkenauer, C., & Vohs, K. D. (2001). Bad is stronger than good. *Review of General Psychology, 5,* 323–370.

Bies, R. J., & Tripp, T. M. (2005). The study of revenge in the workplace: Conceptual, ideological, and empirical issues. In S. Fox, & P. E. Spector (Eds.), *Counterproductive work behavior: investigations of actors and targets* (pp. 65–81). Washington, DC: American Psychological Association.

*Biron, M. (2010). Negative reciprocity and the association between perceived organizational ethical values and organizational deviance. *Human Relations, 63,* 875–897.

*Bligh, M., Kohles, J. C., Pearce, C. L., Justin, J. E., & Stovall, J. F. (2007). When the romance is over: Follower perspectives of aversive leadership. *Applied Psychology: An International Review, 56,* 528–557.

Borenstein, M., Hedges, L., Higgins, J., & Rothstein, H. (2005). *Comprehensive meta-analysis version 2.* Englewood, NJ: Biostat.

Bowling, N. A., & Beehr, T. A. (2006). Workplace harassment from the victim's perspective: A theoretical model and meta-analysis. *Journal of Applied Psychology, 91,* 998–1012.

*Bowling, N. A., Beehr, T. A., Bennett, M. M., & Watson, C. P. (2010). Target personality and workplace victimization: A prospective analysis. *Work and Stress, 24,* 140–158.

*Breaux, D., Perrewe, P., Hall, A., Frink, D., & Hochwarter, W. (2008). Time to try a little tenderness? The detrimental effects of accountability when coupled with abusive supervision. *Journal of Leadership and Organizational Studies, 11,* 111–122.

*Brown, M. E., Trevino, L. K., & Harrison, D. A. (2005). Ethical leadership: A social learning perspective for construct development and testing. *Organizational Behavior and Human Decision Processes, 97,* 117–134.

Brunswick, E. (1956). *Perception and the representative design of psychological experiments* (2nd ed.). Berkeley: University of California Press.

Burns, J. (2003). *Transformational leadership.* New York: Atlantic Monthly Press.

*Burris, E. R., Detert, J. R., & Chiaburu, D. S. (2008). Quitting before leaving: The mediating effects of psychological attachment and detachment on voice. *Journal of Applied Psychology, 93,* 912–9222.

*Chen, H. C., & Kao, H. S. R. (2009). Chinese paternalistic leadership and non-Chinese subordinates' psychological health. *International Journal of Human Resource Management, 20,* 2533–2546.

Colquitt, J. A., Conlon, D. E., Wesson, M. J., Porter, C. O. L. H., & Ng, K. Y. (2001). Justice at the millennium: A meta-analytic review of 25 years of organizational justice research. *Journal of Applied Psychology, 86,* 425–445.

Conger, J. A. (1990). The dark side of leadership. *Organizational Dynamics, 19,* 44–55.

Conger, J. A. (1998). Qualitative research as the cornerstone methodology for understanding leadership. *The Leadership Quarterly, 9,*107–121.

Costa, P. T., Jr., & McCrae, R. R. (1992). *Revised NEO Personality Inventory (NEO-PI-R) and NEO Five-Factor (NEO-FFI) Inventory Professional Manual.* Odessa, FL: PAR.

*De Hoogh, A. H. B., & Den Hartog, D. N. (2008). Ethical and despotic leadership, relationships with leader's social responsibility, top management team effectiveness and subordinates' optimism: A multi-method study. *The Leadership Quarterly, 19,* 297–311.

*Detert, J. R., Trevino, L. K., Burris, E. R., & Andiappan, M. (2007). Managerial modes of influence and counter-productivity in organizations: A longitudinal business-unit-level investigation. *Journal of Applied Psychology, 92,* 993–1005.

*Duffy, M. K., & Ferrier, W. J. (2003). Birds of a feather? How supervisor-subordinate dissimilarity moderates the influence of supervisor behaviors on workplace attitudes. *Group Organization Management, 28,* 217–248.

*Duffy, M. K., Ganster, D. C., & Pagon, M. (2002). Social undermining in the workplace. *Academy of Management Journal, 45,* 331–351.

*Duffy, M. K., Ganster, D. C., Shaw, J. D., Johnson, J. L., & Pagon, M. (2006). The social context of undermining behavior at work. *Organizational Behavior and Human Decision Processes, 101,* 105–126.

*Dupre, K. E., Inness, M., Connelly, C. E., Barling, J., & Hoption, C. (2006). Workplace aggression in teenage part-time employees. *Journal of Applied Psychology, 91,* 987–997.

Einarsen, S., Aasland, M. S., & Skogstad, A. (2007). Destructive leadership behaviour: A definition and conceptual model. *The Leadership Quarterly, 18,* 207–216.

Einarsen, S., Hoel, H., Zapf, D., & Cooper, C. L. (2003). The concept of bullying at work: The European tradition. In S. Einarsen, H. Hoel, D. Zapf, & C. L. Cooper (Eds.), *Bullying and emotional abuse in the workplace: International perspectives in research and practice* (pp. 3–30). London: Taylor & Francis.

*Einarsen, S., Skogstad, A., Leseth, A. M. S. B., & Aasland, M. S. (2002). Destructive leadership: A behavioural model. *Forskningved Institutt for samfunnspsykologi, 2002,* 55–59.

*Elangovan, A. R., & Xie, J. L. (2000). Effects of perceived power of supervisor on subordinate work attitudes. *Leadership and Organization Development Journal, 21,*319–328.

Ferris, G. R., Zinko, R., Brouer, R. L., Buckley, M. R., & Harvey, M. G. (2007). Strategic bullying as a supplementary, balanced perspective on destructive leadership. *The Leadership Quarterly, 18,* 195–206.

*Fox, S., & Stallworth, L. E. (2010). The battered apple: An application of stressor-emotion-control/support theory to teachers' experience of violence and bullying. *Human Relations, 63,* 927–954.

Fuller, J. B., Patterson, C. E. P., Hester, K., & Stringer, D. Y. (1996). A quantitative review of research on charismatic leadership. *Psychological Reports, 78,* 271–287.

Gastil, J. (1994). A meta-analytic review of the productivity and satisfaction of democratic and autocratic leadership. *Small Group Research, 25,* 384–410.

Gerstner, C. R., & Day, D. V. (1997). Meta-analytic review of leader-member exchange theory: Correlates and construct issues. *Journal of Applied Psychology, 82,* 827–844.

*Gould-Williams, J. (2007). HR practices, organizational climate and employee outcomes: Evaluating social exchange relationships in local government. *International Journal of Human Resource Management, 18,* 1627–1647.

Graen, G. B., & Uhl-Bien, M. (1995). Development of leader-member exchange (LMX) theory of leadership over 25 years: Applying a multi-level multi-domain perspective. *The Leadership Quarterly, 6,* 219–247.

*Grandey, A. A., Kern, J. H., & Frone, M. R. (2007). Verbal abuse from outsiders versus insiders: Comparing frequent, impact on emotional exhaustion, and the role of emotional labor. *Journal of Occupational Health Psychology, 12,* 63–79.

*Harris, K. J., Kacmar, K. M., & Zivnuska, S. (2007). An investigation of abusive supervision as a predictor of performance and the meaning of work as a moderator of the relationship. *The Leadership Quarterly, 18,* 252–263.

*Harvey, S., & Keashly, L. (2006). Lowered trust in management as a mediating state between abusive supervision, work attitudes and intention to leave. *ASBBSE E-Journal,* 2(1) (Retrieved from: http://www.asbbs .org/files/2006/ASBBS%20E-Journal%202006%20 HTM%20Files/lowered%20trust%20asbbs%20e-jour nal%202006.pdf)

*Harvey, P., Stoner, J., Hochwarter, W., & Kacmar, C. (2007). Coping with abusive supervision: The neutralizing effects of ingratiation and positive affect on negative employee outcomes. *The Leadership Quarterly, 18,* 264–280.

*Hauge, L. J., Skogstad, A., & Einarsen, S. (2007). Relationships between stressful work environments and bullying: Results of a large representative study. *Work and Stress, 21,* 220–242.

Hershcovis, M. S. (2011). Incivility, social undermining, bullying...Oh My! A call to reconcile constructs within workplace aggression research. *Journal of Organizational Behavior, 32,* 499–519.

Hershcovis, M. S., & Barling, J. (2010). Towards a multi-foci approach to workplace aggression: A meta-analytic review of outcomes from different perpetrators. *Journal of Organizational Behavior, 31,* 24–44.

*Hobman, E. V., Restubog, S. L. D., Bordia, P., & Tang, R. L. (2009). Abusive supervision in advising relationships: Investigating the role of social support. *Applied Psychology: An International Review, 58,* 233–256.

Hofstede, G. (2001). *Culture's consequences: Comparing values, behaviors, institutions, and organizations across nations.* Thousand Oaks, CA: Sage.

*Hoobler, J. M., & Brass, D. J. (2006). Abusive supervision and family undermining as displaced aggression. *Journal of Applied Psychology, 91,* 1125–1133.

Howell, J. M. (1998). Two faces of charisma: Socialized and personalized leadership in organizations. In J. A. Conger, & R. N. Kanungo (Eds.), *Charismatic leadership: The elusive factor in organizational effectiveness* (pp. 213–236). San Francisco, CA: Jossey-Bass.

Hubert, A. B., & van Veldhoven, M. J. P. M. (2001). Risk sectors for undesirable behaviour and mobbing. *European Journal of Work and Organizational Psychology, 10,* 415–424.

Hunter, J. E., & Schmidt, F. L. (2004). *Methods of meta-analysis—Correcting error and bias in research findings.* Thousand Oaks, CA: Sage.

Inness, M., Barling, J., & Turner, N. (2005). Understanding supervisor-targeted aggression: A within-person, between-jobs design. *Journal of Applied Psychology, 90,* 731–739.

Judge, T. A., & Piccolo, R. (2004). Transformational and transactional leadership: A meta-analytic test of their relative validity. *Journal of Applied Psychology, 89,* 755–768.

Judge, T. A., Colbert, A. E., & Ilies, R. (2004). Intelligence and leadership: A quantitative review and test of theoretical propositions. *Journal of Applied Psychology, 89,* 542–552.

Judge, T. A., Piccolo, R. F., & Ilies, R. (2004). The forgotten ones? A re-examination of consideration, initiating structure, and leadership effectiveness. *Journal of Applied Psychology, 89,* 36–51.

Keashly, L., Trott, V., & MacLean, L. M. (1994). Abusive behavior in the workplace: A preliminary investigation. *Violence and Victims, 9,* 341–357.

Kellerman, B. (2004). *Bad leadership: What it is, how it happens, why it matters.* Boston, MA: Harvard Business School Press.

*Kiazad, K., Restubog, S. L. D., Zagenczyk, T. J., Kiewitz, C., &Tang, R. L. (2010). In pursuit of power: The role of authoritarian leadership in the relationship between supervisors' Machiavellianism and subordinates' perceptions of abusive supervisory power. *Journal of Research in Personality, 44,* 512–519.

*Kim, T. Y., & Shapiro, D. L. (2008). Retaliation against supervisory mistreatment: Negative emotion, group membership, and cross-cultural difference. *International Journal of Conflict Management, 19,* 339–358.

Kuoppala, J., Lamminpaa, A., Liira, J., & Vainio, H. (2008). Leadership, job well-being, and health effects—A systematic review and a meta-analysis. *Journal of Occupational and Environmental Medicine, 50,* 904–915.

Kusy, M., & Holloway, E. (2009). *Toxic workplacel: Managing toxic personalities and their systems of power.* San Francisco, CA: John Wiley.

*Lim, V. K. G., & Teo, T. S. H. (2009). Mind your E-manners: Impact of cyber incivility on employees' work attitude and behavior. *Information Management, 46,* 419–425.

Lipman-Blumen, J. (2004). *The allure of toxic leaders: Why we follow destructive bosses and corrupt politicians-and how we can survive them.* New York: Oxford University Press.

Locke, K. (2002). The grounded theory approach to qualitative research. In F. Drasgow, & N. Schmitt (Eds.), *Measuring and analyzing behavior in organizations—Advances in measurement and data analysis* (pp. 17–43). San Francisco: Jossey-Bass.

Lowe, K. B., Kroeck, K. G., & Sivasubramaniam, N. (1996). Effectiveness correlates of transformational and transactional leadership: A meta-analytic review of the MLQ literature. *The Leadership Quarterly, 7*, 385–425.

Maddi, S. R. (2006). Hardiness: The courage to grow from stresses. *The Journal of Positive Psychology, 1*, 160–168.

*Mayer, D. M., Bardes, M., Hoobler, J. M., Wayne, S. J., & Marinova, S. V. (submitted for publication). *The (bad) apple doesn't fall far from the tree: A trickle-down model of abusive supervision*. Manuscript (Personnel Psychology).

Meyer, J. P., Stanley, D. J., Herscovitch, L., & Topolnytsky, L. (2002). Affective, continuance, and normative commitment to the organization: A meta-analysis of antecedents, correlates, and consequences. *Journal of Vocational Behavior, 61*, 20–52.

*Mitchell, M. S., & Ambrose, M. L. (2007). Abusive supervision and workplace deviance and the moderating effects of negative reciprocity beliefs. *Journal of Applied Psychology, 92*, 1159–1168.

Mulvey, P. W., & Padilla, A. (2010). The environment of destructive leadership. In B. Schyns, & T. Hansbrough (Eds.), *When leadership goes wrong: Destructive leadership, mistakes and ethical failures*. Charlotte, NC: Information Age Publishing.

*Nyberg, A., Westerlund, H., Magnusson Hanson, L. L., & Theorell, T. (2008). Managerial leadership is associated with self-reported sickness absence and sickness presenteeism among Swedish men and women. *Scandinavian Journal of Public Health, 36*, 803–811.

Padilla, A., Hogan, R., & Kaiser, R. B. (2007). The toxic triangle: Destructive leaders, susceptible followers, and conducive environments. *The Leadership Quarterly, 18*, 176–194.

Paulhus, D. L., & Williams, K. M. (2002). The dark triad of personality: Narcissism, Machiavellism, and psychopathy. *Journal of Research in Personality, 36*, 556–563.

Podsakoff, P. M., Bommer, W. H., Podsakoff, N. P., & MacKenzie, S. B. (2006). Relationships between leader reward and punishment behavior and subordinate attitudes, perceptions, and behaviors: A meta-analytic review of existing and new research. *Organizational Behavior and Human Decision Processes, 99*, 113–142.

*Rafferty, A. E., Restubog, S. L. D., & Jimmieson, N. L. (2010). Losing sleep: Examining the cascading effects of supervisors' experience of injustice on subordinates' psychological health. *Work and Stress, 24*, 36–55.

*Reed, G. E., & Bullis, R C. (2009). The impact of destructive leadership on senior military officers and civilian employees. *Armed Forces & Society, 36*, 5–18.

Rodriguez-Munoz, A., Baillien, E., De Witte, H., Moreno-Jimenez, B., & Pastor, J. C. (2009). Cross-lagged relationships between workplace bullying, job satisfaction and engagement: Two longitudinal studies. *Work and Stress, 23*, 225–243.

*Rooney, J. A., & Gottlieb, B. H. (2007). Development and initial validation of a measure of supportive and unsupportive managerial behaviors. *Journal of Vocational Behavior, 71*, 186–203.

*Rooney, J. A., Gottlieb, B. H., & Newby-Clark, I. R. (2009). How support-related managerial behaviors influence employees: An integrated model. *Journal of Managerial Psychology, 24*, 410–427.

Rosenthal, R. (1979). The file drawer problem and tolerance for null results. *Psychological Bulletin, 86*, 638–641.

Sackett, D. L. (1979). Bias in analytic research. *Journal of Chronic Diseases, 32*, 51–63.

Schilling, J. (2006). On the pragmatics of qualitative assessment: Designing the process for content analysis. *European Journal of Psychological /Assessment, 22*, 28–37.

Schilling, J. (2009). From ineffectiveness to destruction: A qualitative study on the meaning of negative leadership. *Leadership, 5*, 102–128.

Seligman, M. E. P. (1975). *Helplessness: On depression, development and death*. San Francisco: Freeman.

Skogstad, A., Einarsen, S., Torsheim, T., Aasland, M., & Hetland, H. (2007). The destructiveness of Laissez-faire leadership behaviour. *Journal of Occupational Health Psychology, 12*(1), 80–92.

Spector, P. E., & Fox, S. (2005). The stressor-emotion model of counterproductive work behavior. In S. Fox, & P. E. Spector (Eds.), *Counterproductive work behavior: Investigations of actors and targets* (pp. 151–174). Washington, DC: American Psychological Association.

Sutton, R. I. (2007). *The no asshole rule: Building a civilized workplace and surviving one that isn't*. New York: Warner Business Books.

Tate, B. W., & Jacobs, R. R. (2010). Progressing by stepping back: An assessment of negative leader behavior. *Poster presented at the 2010 SIOP conference in Chicago*.

*Tepper, B. J. (2000). Consequences of abusive supervision. *Academy of Management Journal, 43*, 178–190.

Tepper, B. J. (2007). *Abusive supervision* in work organizations: Review synthesis, and research agenda. *Journal of Management, 33*, 261–289.

*Tepper, B. J., Carr, J. C., Breaux, D. M., Geider, S., Hu, C., & Hua, W. (2009). Abusive supervision, intentions to quit, and employees' workplace deviance: A power/

dependence analysis. *Organizational Behavior and Human Decision Processes, 109,* 156–167.

*Tepper, B. J., Duffy, M. K., Henle, C. A., & Lambert, L. S. (2006). Procedural injustice, victim precipitation, and abusive supervision. *Personnel Psychology, 59,* 101–123.

*Tepper, B. J., Duffy, M. K., Hoobler, J., & Ensley, M. D. (2004). Moderators of the relationships between coworkers' organizational citizenship behavior and fellow employees' attitudes. *Journal of Applied Psychology, 89,* 455–465.

*Tepper, B. J., Duffy, M. K., & Shaw, J. D. (2001). Personality moderators of the relationship between abusive supervision and subordinates' resistance. *Journal of Applied Psychology, 86,* 974–983.

Tepper, B. J., & Henle, C. A. (2011). A case for recognizing distinctions among constructs that capture interpersonal mistreatment in work organizations. *Journal of Organizational Behavior, 32,* 487–498.

*Tepper, B. J., Henle, C. A., Lambert, L. S., Giacalone, R. A., & Duffy, M. K. (2008). Abusive supervision and subordinates' organization deviance. *Journal of Applied Psychology, 93,* 721–732.

*Tepper, B. J., Moss, S. E., Lockhart, D. E., & Carr, J. C. (2007). Abusive supervision, upward maintenance communication, and subordinates' psychological distress. *Academy of Management Journal, 50,* 1169–1180.

*Thau, S., Aquino, K., & Bommer, W. H. (2008). How employee race moderates the relationship between non-contingent punishment and organizational citizenship behaviors: A test of the Negative Adaptation Hypothesis. *Social Justice Research, 21,* 297–312.

*Thau, S., Bennett, R. J., Mitchell, M. S., & Marrs, M. B. (2009). How management style moderates the relationship between abusive supervision and workplace deviance: An uncertainty management theory perspective. *Organizational Behavior and Human Decision Processes, 108,* 79–92.

*Thau, S., & Mitchell, M. S. (2010). Self-gain or self-regulation impairment? Tests of competing explanations of the supervisor abuse and employee deviance relationship through perceptions of distributive justice perceptions. *Journal of Applied Psychology, 95,* 1009–1031.

Thoroughgood, C. N., Tate, B. W., Sawyer, K. B., & Jacobs, R (2012). Bad to the bone: Empirically defining and measuring destructive leader behavior. *Journal of Leadership and Organizational Studies, 19,* 230–255.

Van Dick, R., Christ, O., Stellmacher, J., Wagner, U., Ahlswede, O., Grubba, C., et al. (2004). Should I stay or should I go? Explaining turnover intentions with organizational identification and job satisfaction. *British Journal of Management, 15,* 351–360.

Walumbwa, F. O., Avolio, B. J., Gardner, W. L., Wernsing, T. S., & Peterson, S. J. (2008). Authentic leadership: Development and validation of a theory-based measure. *Journal of Management, 34,* 89–126.

Wang, G., Oh, I.-S., Courtright, S. H., & Colbert, A. E. (2011). Transformational leadership and performance across criteria and levels: A meta-analytic review of 25 years of research. *Group and Organization Management, 36,* 223–270.

Wanous, J. P., Reichers, R. E., & Hudy, J. T. (2000). Overall job satisfaction: How good are single-item measures? *Journal of Applied Psychology, 82,* 247–252.

*Wu, T. Y., & Hu, C. (2009). Abusive supervision and employee emotional exhaustion: Dispositional antecedents and boundaries. *Group and Organization Management, 34,* 143–169.

*Yagil, D. (2005). Employees' attribution of abusive supervisory behaviors. *International Journal of Organizational Analysis, 13,* 307–326.

*Yagil, D. (2006). The relationship of abusive and supportive workplace supervision to employee burnout and upward influence tactics. *Journal of Emotional Abuse, 6,* 49–65.

Yammarino, F. J., Dionne, S. D., Chun, J. U., & Dansereau, F. (2005). Leadership and levels of analysis: A state-of-the-science review. *The Leadership Quarterly, 16,* 879–919.

Yukl, G. (2006). *Leadership in organizations* (6th ed.). Upper Saddle River, NJ: Pearson-Prentice. Hall.

Yukl, G., & van Fleet, D. D. (1992). Theory and research on leadership in organizations. In M. D. Dunette, & L. M. Hough (Eds.), *Handbook of industrial and organizational psychology* (pp. 147–199). Palo Alto: Consulting Psychologists Press.

*Zellars, K. L., Tepper, B. J., & Duffy, M. K. (2002). Abusive supervision and subordinates' organizational citizenship behavior. *Journal of Applied Psychology, 87,* 1068–1076.

CHAPTER 29

I Defy With a Little Help From My Friends

Raising an Organization's Ethical Bar
Through a Morally Courageous Coalition

Debra R. Comer
Hofstra University

Susan D. Baker
Morgan State University

> Never doubt that a small group of thoughtful, committed citizens can change the world. Indeed, it is the only thing that ever has.
>
> —Margaret Mead[1]

> If engineers agree that they will not submit to pressure to write dishonest reports and then stick with that agreement, employers will not be able to increase the pressure by saying, in effect, "If you don't, I'll get somebody who will." Hence honest engineers will not be penalized If no such agreement is in force, even an honest engineer may well consider it futile to resist the pressure and therefore not do so.
>
> —Edwin M. Hartman[2]

Many people lament that an organization without ethical leadership cannot be an ethical place and that any attempt to change the status quo would be pointless. Yet, the pair of quotes above suggests that collective action can promote ethical behavior in an organization. "Moral courage is often lonely courage,"[3] but there is strength in numbers, and people can tackle ethical problems in their

Source: "I Defy with a Little Help from My Friends: Raising an Organization's Ethical Bar Through a Morally Courageous Coalition," by Debra R. Comer and Susan D. Baker in Moral Courage in *Organizations: Doing the Right Thing at Work*, editors Debra R. Comer and Gina Vega. Copyright © 2011. Reprinted with permission from M.E. Sharp, Inc.

organizations by working together. When they recognize that they are not alone, they see the possibility of change and refuse to tolerate morally problematic conduct. In this chapter we explore how a group of right-minded individuals can collaborate to raise their company's ethical bar. We begin by answering this question: How can a few people who would like to do the right thing persuade others in their organization to join them in a morally courageous coalition? After considering how employees often respond to wrongdoing in their organizations, we glean lessons from organizational culture change, social movements, and ethical leaders and role models to offer practical advice for those seeking to effect bottom-up change to make their organization more ethical.

The Response to Wrongdoing in the Workplace

Barbara, a new cashier in a retail store, noticed her supervisor's habit of making bigoted comments about customers from certain demographic groups and treating them rudely. Barbara cringed every time she had to listen to her supervisor, but she could not bring herself to do anything about his remarks.

At shift change in a convenience store, the clerk closing for the evening shift was counting money. As Janelle restocked shelves, she noticed that the clerk was placing only some of the money in the store's safe—and pocketing the rest. Not wanting to believe what she was seeing, Janelle moved to another work area to distance herself from the theft. The next day, when the store manager was upset about the $100 missing from the safe's daily receipts, Janelle reluctantly came forward to describe what she had witnessed.

An electronics retailer employed teenagers after school and during the summers. Whenever monthly sales goals were met, the division manager threw congratulatory parties at which alcohol was served to all employees, even those younger than legal drinking age. Jamal expressed concern to his senior managers, who laughed dismissively and told him, "Loosen up! Everyone gets to celebrate."

Dan, a student working the late shift at a fast-food restaurant, felt uncomfortable because the shift manager, ignoring the sexual harassment policy in the company's handbook, frequently commented on female employees' appearance. Dan's coworkers, Rita and Jasmine, confided in him that they disliked the suggestive remarks, planned on quitting, and were telling their friends not to apply for vacant positions there. After graduation, Dan landed a job at a respected design firm. He noticed that this company's handbook had no sexual harassment policy and worried what would happen should harassment occur, but decided that there was nothing he could do.

All of these situations involve employees who observed unethical behavior at their workplace. At times, as in the example involving Barbara, the new cashier, a person spots wrongdoing but does not report it to anyone. Or, in the case of Janelle, the convenience store employee, a person may report wrongdoing only after someone else is already aware of it. Sometimes, as in the scenario about underage drinking at Jamal's company or the one about sexual harassment at the fast-food restaurant where Dan worked, those in authority see wrongdoing and condone it or are the ones committing the act, leaving a concerned employee wondering what to do. And at other times, as in the case of the design firm that had not drafted a sexual harassment policy, a well-intentioned employee, Dan, wants to protect his company from ethical pitfalls, but ends up doing nothing. Indeed, even though organizations in the private, public, and nonprofit sectors have poured resources into compliance programs and ethics training for employees, alarming numbers of employees still do not report the ethical violations they witness.[4] Why? The two main reasons that employees remain silent about the unethical behavior they observe in the workplace are (1) they do not believe reporting misconduct to their managers would make a difference, and (2) they fear retaliation by management.[5]

Making the Workplace More Ethical Requires Organizational Change

The Challenge of Organizational Change

Can an unethical organization become more ethical? Many employees see no point in reporting or trying by other means to eliminate the unethical behavior entrenched in their organizations. Organizational change requires effort, persistence, follow-through, and follow-up. Inertia, fear, and laziness are common obstacles, as even those in favor of change may resign themselves to living with suboptimal circumstances because of the anticipated difficulty and unknown outcome of doing something new. Even greater resistance comes from those who stand to lose advantages that current conditions confer.[6] Real change requires that people leave their comfort zone and put collective interests before self-interests.[7]

Warren Buffet's leadership at Salomon Brothers in the early 1990s provides a compelling and encouraging account of the possibility of truly transforming an organization's culture to a more ethical one and assures us that "an unethical culture need not be permauent."[8] Buffet cooperated fully with the authorities in the wake of the bond trading scandal involving Salomon's former CEO and chair. In his capacity as new CEO and chair, he restored the company's tarnished reputation by overhauling its leadership, policies, structures, behavior, and beliefs. He behaved ethically himself, focused his employees' attention on the ethical implications of their behavior, rewarded ethical deeds, and fired miscreants. The events that transpired at Salomon Brothers show how the discovery of an organization's transgression can serve as a catalyst for change.[9] When crisis underscores the need to abandon past practices, employees and other stakeholders clamor for rehabilitation. They look for "changes in management, in reward structures, and in codes of conduct. . . [as signs that] the organization is determined to purge negative influences and focus its energy on renewal."[10]

But instead of waiting until their organization crashes, shouldn't employees promote change that would prevent such disgrace? And must these would-be agents of change inhabit the executive suite? What happens when individuals seek to make their organization more ethical by opposing the immoral behavior of their superiors? The mantra of organizational change guru John Kotter is that change will not happen unless the highest echelon of management leads or, at the very least, deeply supports it.[11] Indeed, those seeking to initiate bottom-up change to make their organization more ethical receive sobering advice: they are warned to become marketable—in case they lose their jobs.[12]

Why is organizational change, and bottom-up change in particular, so arduous? Systems and practices persist in organizations not necessarily because they are functional but because they are ingrained.[13] Organizational transformation therefore "requires changing structures, understandings, and beliefs that have long been taken for granted as normal, neutral, and legitimate."[14] Furthermore, those most likely to perceive a need for change are not those most advantaged by existing arrangements.[15] The former need to contend with the latter, who will want to preserve their comfortable position.[16] Ideas and examples from social movements can shed light on how bottom-up change can happen.

Collective Action in Organizations

More than thirty years ago, scholars recognized that the lessons of social movements could inform change within organizations.[17] But there was—and continues to be—a lack of attention to the potential of intra-organizational coalitions. A coalition is a group formed apart from the formal structure of its members' organization in order to achieve a common goal through shared action; "coalitions form because they allow their members to exert more influence than they could as independent individuals."[18] There is strength in unity, and collective action can be an effective path to ethical organizational transformation.[19] Consider the example of the engineers mentioned at the beginning of this chapter: if all the engineers stand together, none of them will have to behave dishonestly; nobody will be penalized; and principled behavior will prevail. If just one or two good apples can envision a more ethical organization and inspire like-minded colleagues to collaborate with them in the quest to achieve that vision, they can change their organization.

Morally Courageous Coalitions

Many people do nothing when they observe misbehavior in their workplaces. They believe that speaking up and taking action would, at best, be useless and, could, at worst, result in retaliation against them. But others *do* step up to try to make a change. Upward dissent in organizations is "one mechanism by which employees can offer corrective feedback about troubling or flawed organizational policies and practices."[20] The "principled organizational dissenter" calls for the organization in which he or she works to put an end to moral improprieties.[21] Typically, this person works alone and does not participate in designing or implementing the desired changes.[22] In contrast, we focus here on principled dissenters who work collectively and aspire not only to draw to attention to, but also to fix, the problems they identify in their organizations. These dissenters unite with others in a morally courageous coalition to strive to change situations. Rather than merely grabbing the bullhorn to report problems, coalition members take the bull by the horns to help solve problems.[23]

Leadership of Morally Courageous Coalitions

How do like-minded dissenters come together in a morally courageous coalition to achieve their common goal? They join forces behind a leader, someone who envisions a better future—and then articulates that vision in a way that arouses others to help implement it.[24] Even in a collective, there is usually one person who forms the group or emerges later as a leader. Key leadership behaviors include "providing motivation, building. . . commitment. . . , and articulating a vision that draws an emotional and enthusiastic response; and. . . plotting a movement strategy and assembling the resources and assigning responsibilities to see that strategy carried out."[25] Because the coalition is attempting to undo inveterate patterns, it must have enough members to accomplish the task.[26] But because quality of membership matters as well as quantity, leaders need to tap into their networks to find members who can provide information, knowledge, and influence to facilitate goal accomplishment.[27] A leader attracts followers by stirring emotions "that may stimulate them to acts of courage."[28] Leaders of coalitions must "establish their credibility to potential followers" in order to convince them that their coalition is worth joining.[29]

- During World War II, German soldiers killed tens of thousands of Jews in western Belorussia and confined others to ghettos. A Jewish resistance group that came to be known as the Bielski partisans chose to reclaim their dignity by refusing either to live in the ghetto or to perish in the death camps; instead, they escaped to the Belorussian forests and encouraged others to join them. Between 1942 and 1944, the entrepreneurial and politically savvy Tuvia Bielski led his brothers and trusted entourage to create a community within the forest that ultimately saved more than 1,200 Jewish lives. Whereas other partisan groups accepted only those who could fight and pull their weight, Bielski welcomed all Jews—including the elderly, young children, and those with no particular survival skills.[30]

- Another charismatic leader was Harvey Milk, the first openly gay man to hold public office in the United States. Famous for opening his speeches with "My name is Harvey Milk, and I'm here to recruit you,"[31] this businessman-turned-grassroots-activist organized the members of the gay community in San Francisco in the mid-1970s by inspiring them to join the fight for their civil rights. In the words of Milk's campaign manager, "What set Harvey apart from you or me was that he was a visionary. He imagined a righteous world inside his head and then he set about to create it for real, for all of us."[32] According to his successor on the San Francisco Board of Supervisors, Harvey Milk gave others the hope "to envision new possibilities. . . and create a different future."[33]

- A third change agent who reshaped her world by building a morally courageous coalition is Liberian Leymah Gbowee. As a parent and a social worker, Gbowee saw the harsh effects of the Liberian civil war on her own children and on the traumatized former boy soldiers exploited by both dictator Charles Taylor and the civilian warlords who fought him for control of Liberia.[34] In 2001, she asked the women at her church to join her in expressing moral outrage through prayer vigils, sit-ins, and peace marches.[35] Within two years, her Christian coalition had enlisted the support of Muslim women in opposition to the war. Her nonviolent coalition attracted international attention and forced Taylor and the warlords to enter into peace negotiations. The coalition's persistence eventually awoke the consciences of many Liberians and drove Taylor into exile in 2003.[36]

Although Bielski, Milk, and Gbowee operated in different times and places, all of them led coalitions by articulating inspirational visions that gained the support and commitment of followers.

Morally Courageous Coalitions in Organizations

Bielski, Milk, and Gbowee led groups that operated outside the powerful systems they opposed. Those seeking to effect change as organizational insiders have unique challenges as they seek to dismantle current policies and practices. To raise their organization's ethical bar, members of a morally courageous coalition must be mindful of the political feasibility of their proposed actions and be sure to secure support for their ideas.[37] Those at the top are likely to resist if "their immediate interests [are] well served by existing power relations and patterns of resource allocation."[38] It is therefore important for coalition members to have an ally who strongly identifies with their goal of change and has a position sufficiently high in the hierarchy. Such an individual is well situated to appeal to the moral values of organizational decision makers whose cooperation is needed to fix the problem.[39]

As we have mentioned, any modification of the status quo that threatens the privileged place of the elite can be a hard sell. Consequently, it is essential to tie the desired change to a goal that appears nonradical—and therefore minimally threatening—to those who would otherwise object.[40] Even if senior managers cannot appreciate the intrinsic value of making their organization more ethical, it may still be possible to convince them of the instrumental benefits by portraying movement toward a more principled organization as a means to help the organization's bottom line.[41] If an organization considers itself progressive or dedicated to continuous improvement, change-seekers can tie their proposal to such avowed commitment. For example, employees who want their company to "go green" to protect the planet may demonstrate that Earth-friendly processes would facilitate the company's achievement of strategic goals.[42] By the same token, a coalition may persuade budget-conscious managers to raise workers' low wages by explaining that fair compensation would reduce the costs of employee theft.[43] Members of a morally courageous coalition can also legitimize their goals to senior management by pointing out that successful industry rivals have already implemented these goals or that achieving the goals would comply with standards set by professional organizations or funding agencies. After Starbucks became a pioneer by offering health insurance to part-time employees, other retailers followed suit.[44] Likewise, an initiative to promote gender equity at the University of Michigan succeeded in large part because it was sponsored and funded by the respected National Science Foundation (NSF), which had spearheaded a similar nationwide program.[45]

Building a Coalition to Implement Ethical Change

There is widespread agreement that leaders in top management positions set the ethical tone for their organization and play a major role in shaping their organization's ethical culture and standards.[46] In contrast, less is known about individuals at lower levels who initiate action to raise their organizations' ethical bar. Yet, employees are more likely to find ethical role models in their immediate supervisors and peers than in their CEOs and top managers.[47] After all, they interact more regularly with supervisors and peers, who influence them informally "below the organizational radar."[48] Lower-level employees whose exemplary behavior earns the respect of their colleagues can orchestrate bottom-up change in their organizations by persuading others to follow their lead. But before those who seek ethical change branch out to connect with like-minded coworkers, they need to do some groundwork by themselves. Then, after careful contemplation, observation, and preparation, they can proceed to recruit others to join them. We now offer you specific steps for building a morally courageous coalition in your organization.[49]

Contemplation, Observation, and Preparation: Getting Your Act Together Before Asking Others to Act With You

Contemplation

First, identify the issue you are facing: Have you observed unethical behavior (your supervisor bullies or harasses others) or practices (salespeople accept expensive gifts or bribes from vendors, customers, or contractors) that you want to eliminate? Is there an unfair policy in your organization that you seek to change (domestic partners are denied health benefits)? Or do you have an idea for a new practice or policy that could enhance your organization's ethical health (the organization could emphasize ethics role-playing in its already existing mentoring program for new employees)?

Next, carefully examine your own feelings about what to do. What possible actions might you take? What would be the ideal outcome? Reviewing the values you learned as a child from your parents, other close family members, guardians, or teachers is a good starting point. But that alone is insufficient because your early-childhood role models may not have modeled workplace behaviors.[50] Consider, then, ethical individuals you have admired in your work environment: what would they advise you to do? As you reflect on this question, you may also want to think about the consequences of *not* acting. If you had to explain to your closest relatives, friends, or colleagues why you had not acted in this situation, could you do so proudly? Would you want others to act as you did in the same circumstances?

Observation

After your initial self-exploration, your next step is an assessment of the likely consequences of your possible actions. To develop a realistic appraisal of your organization's response to your ideal outcome and the challenges you may encounter, pay attention to top managers and supervisors. By observing how they act themselves and how they reward or discipline your coworkers for their ethical or unethical acts, you will learn what is acceptable and unacceptable in your organization.[51]

Preparation

After identifying the issue and desired outcomes, exploring your own ethical feelings and possible actions, and then assessing your organization's ethical culture, your next step is to identify available recourses and resources. Before you can bring others on board, you will have to convince them that your goal is attainable and that you are prepared and not naïvely optimistic. Be sure to check your organization's written code of conduct, the employee handbook, and your industry's professional ethical code. Any or all of these may contain a relevant policy statement or guideline that could validate the change you propose by linking it to sanctioned behavior.[52] But because decision making in organizations depends as much on politics as on logic,[53] it is also important to secure the help of key individuals, such as a sympathetic supervisor in another area of your organization or a senior manager who supports your viewpoint. As noted earlier, it is invaluable to secure the endorsement of like-minded allies whose status within the organizational hierarchy establishes their credibility and gives them access to those with the formal power to change your organization's culture.[54] Other important allies can be external stakeholders whose opinions command the attention of your senior management. In 1994, for example, Exxon Mobil responded to activists' concerns about the social and political risks of its Chad-Cameroon project by asking the World Bank to assess the project's impact on indigenous communities. The World Bank's solutions satisfied Exxon and activists.[55]

After identifying the resources you have, determine what you still need. For example, is there a potential senior ally whom you do not know personally? Make it a priority to recruit a new coalition member who knows this potential ally. Perhaps you have a friend or acquaintance in the organization, someone for whom you have done a favor in the past, who could connect you to this person. Alternatively, recognize that someone in your coalition will have to enlist this senior ally. Then, as a last preparatory step, outline and rehearse your thoughts and practice what you want to say to others you would like to recruit for your coalition. It is not necessary to work out every detail before consulting others; in fact, soliciting the viewpoints of other coalition members as to what to do and how to do it can yield better solutions and increase members' commitment to the coalition and the shared goal.[56]

Enlisting the Support of Others to Build a Coalition

What can you say to persuade coworkers to join you in working toward a more ethical organization? Remember, first, that you are trying to recruit those you know—or suspect may—have concerns similar to your own. Still, in order to spur them to take action, you must frame the issue in a way that pulls them away from the sidelines and into your coalition.[57] You need to direct their attention to a specific problem, guide them to come up with concrete steps for fixing the problem, and motivate them to take part in fixing it. An individual will participate in collective action to the extent that he or she perceives a moral problem, wants to express moral dissatisfaction, and believes that collective action will be effective.[58] Therefore, the content of your discussion needs to be an appeal to prospective members' emotions and values, as well as their sense of reason.[59] Describe the current situation in terms that emphasize the injustice of the status quo and the benefits they would personally reap from changing it. Tell prospective members how they could contribute to the coalition. Assure them that collective effort can succeed to solve the problem by making the proposed change seem less radical and thus more doable,[60] breaking down the proposed change into manageable goals and tasks, and demonstrating your awareness of the organization's political constraints and opportunities.

Strive to anticipate the perspective of each potential coalition member so that you can shape your message to fit that person. Imagine how to align his or her ambitions with your goal. When you approach someone, be sure that you have a private distraction-free setting and block of time. Begin with a quick attention-grabber that focuses the person on what you want to say:[61] a concise statement of what you want to accomplish (along the lines of "I'm Harvey Milk, and I'm here to recruit you !"); an alarming statistic ("Our department's accident rate has increased 25 percent in the past six months!"); a question that requires your colleague to recognize an issue whose seriousness he or she has not yet considered ("How would you feel if the company denied health benefits for your dependents?"); or a picture of the desired results ("Can you imagine how great it would be not to have to worry that someone might find out that our boss is taking kickbacks—and then jump to the conclusion that you and I are doing the same thing?").

Remind your colleague of the long-term benefits that you seek (that is, a more ethical organization) and of any short-term benefits that may accrue,[62] such as the pride of doing the right thing, the personal satisfaction of working with colleagues to achieve a goal, and the political advantage of expanding one's network. Illustrate your ideas with vivid personal experiences or stories. Heed the adage "A picture is worth a thousand words" by developing one striking, easily visualized image that expresses your goal.[63] This shared image creates a common bond and unity of purpose for coalition members— and a shortcut to understanding the end results you all seek.

Build rapport, reinforce your verbal message, and convey hope. Keep your colleague engaged in the discussion by providing your undivided attention, asking for his or her opinions, and listening actively to what he or she would like to accomplish. Check that you understand what your colleague has said by paraphrasing his or her comments.[64] As you try to recruit others into your coalition, be careful not to seem self-righteous. Do not cause others to feel as though you are putting them down for not stepping up to the plate as soon as you have.[65] Instead, welcome them by emphasizing that they, too, can take the higher ground and make a difference. End your conversation by asking for your colleagues' support and agreement to take specific actions, such as identifying and meeting with like-minded colleagues within a week's time or inviting, them to a larger discussion.

You have spoken with others about your moral concerns and given them an assessment of your organization's ethical culture and the resources available to help you address these concerns. You have thereby encouraged those who share your feelings, but were reluctant to act on them, to join your coalition and shoulder some of the work. As your coalition grows and you are no longer alone, you can point to the progress you have already made to keep coalition members motivated and maintain the momentum to focus on and achieve long-term goals.

At this point all of the coalition members should collectively fine-tune the plan to address the issue. Tasks should be assigned according to competencies—and you may or may not want to continue your role as leader. Remember that it is essential to arrange to connect with a senior-level person in your organization who supports your goal and to have this person schedule a meeting with organizational decision makers. Because employees who have solid relationships with their superiors feel freer to express risky information,[66] it makes sense for coalition members who are well connected to ("tight with") key members of senior management to be the group's spokespersons. Use the collective strengths of your coalition members to achieve your common goal.

Conclusion

Unethical behavior persists in organizations when employees believe there is nothing they can do about it. Although the endeavors of one individual acting alone may not be enough to undo entrenched workplace misconduct, the collective efforts of the members of a morally courageous coalition can change their organization. In this chapter, we have recommended that coalitions gain political support and legitimacy for their ideas and position their proposed changes in a way that is least threatening to top management. We have also provided concrete suggestions for building a morally courageous coalition. We hope these ideas will inspire and equip you to join with right-minded colleagues to make your organization more ethical.

Notes

1. This quote has been attributed to Margaret Mead.
2. Hartman, 1996, 76.
3. Miller, 2000, 255.
4. Of the well over half of private-sector, nonprofit, and government employees who asserted that they had witnessed misconduct at their workplace within the past year, an average of 30–40 percent did not report the wrongdoing that they observed (private- and nonprofit-sector respondents had 42 and 38 percent nonreport rates, respectively, while government-sector respondents had 30 percent nonreport rates); Ethics Resource Center, 2008a, 2008b, and 2008c.
5. Ethics Resource Center, 2008a and 2008b; see also Kohn, Chapter 5.
6. Campbell, 2005.
7. Quinn, 2004.
8. Sims, 2000, 75.
9. Sims, 2009, also describes how ethical scandals can prompt corporate leaders to focus on creating a values-driven culture.
10. Pfarrer et al., 2008, 739.
11. Kotter, 1996; Kotter and Rathgeber, 2002.
12. Uhl-Bien and Carsten, 2007.
13. DiMaggio and Powell, 1983; Meyer and Rowan, 1977.
14. Meyerson and Tompkins, 2007, 306.
15. Meyerson and Tompkins, 2007.
16. Misangyi, Weaver, and Elms, 2008.
17. Zald and Berger, 1978. Davis et al., 2005, explored subsequent research on the intersection between social movements and organizations.
18. Stevenson, Pearce, and Porter, 1985, 262. Bruxelles and Kerbrat-Orecchioni, 2004, likewise define a coalition as a temporary group of allies united against another party to achieve their common objective.

19. As Meyerson and Tompkins, 2007, comment: "The possibility of group as institutional change agent suggests intriguing possibilities for the design of change and points to an important topic for future research to address in greater depth" (322). It is telling that the term "change agent," used to denote the person in an organization most responsible for championing and implementing change, appears nearly exclusively as a singular noun. We do not hear or read about "change agents" at an organization. Even though a collective may have a leader, this single individual cannot do everything alone; the power of the group lies in the mutual association of like-minded change-seekers.

20. Kassing, 2009, 434.

21. Graham, 1986; see also Matt and Shahinpoor. Chapter 12.

22. Graham, 1986.

23. Garner, 2009, reported that some organizational dissenters find allies and propose possible solutions to the problems they have identified. Our morally courageous coalitions both initiate and contribute to the implementation of change, as do the institutional entrepreneurs described by Battilana, Leca, and Boxenbaum, 2009.

24. Bass, 1990; Battilana, Leca, and Boxenbaum, 2009; Kouzes and Posner, 2002.

25. Aminzade, Goldstone, and Perry, 2001; also see Campbell, 2005.

26. Having a critical mass ensures that the coalition's collective output will be sufficient, and thus boosts morale by giving members hope that they can succeed. Nelson, 2009, documented the activities of the Red Orchestra *(Rote Kapelle)*, a resistance network that tried to thwart Hitler's fascist regime. Tragically, the group was too small, and many members ultimately lost their lives.

27. Gabbay and Leenders, 2001 ; Knoke, 2009.

28. Jablin, 2006, 107; also see Burns, 1978.

29. Einwohner, 2007, 1310.

30. Tec, 1993.

31. Shilts, 1982.

32. Kronenberg, 2002, 37.

33. Britt, 2002, 80.

34. Tate, 2004, documented the extensive use of child soldiers in the Liberian civil war.

35. Moyers, 2009.

36. Conley, 2008; Moyers, 2009. Also see the documentary, *Pray the Devil Back to Hell.*

37. Campbell, 2005; Misangyi, Weaver, and Elms, 2008.

38. Agócs, 1997, 925.

39. Meyerson and Tompkins, 2007.

40. Scully and Creed, 2005.

41. Thomas, 1991, recognized that few companies would embrace demographic diversity as a moral good, but that many would learn to accept diversity for economic reasons.

42. For a counterpoint on undertaking green management for strategic versus moral reasons, see, respectively, Siegel, 2009, and Marcus and Fremetti, 2009.

43. Alstete, 2006; Niehoff and Paul, 2000.

44. Michelli, 2007; DiMaggio and Powell, 1983, discussed intra-organizational mimicry.

45. Meyerson and Tompkins, 2007.

46. Andreoli and Lefkowitz, 2009; Brown and Treviño, 2006; Schminke, Ambrose, and Neubaum, 2005; Sims and Brinkmann, 2002; Treviño, Brown, and Hartman, 2003.

47. Weaver, Treviño, and Agle, 2005.

48. Ibid., 328.

49. These suggestions draw on current theory and research about organizational culture change, social movements, and ethical leaders and role models, as well as organizational communication.

50. Brown and Treviño, 2006.

51. Brown and Treviño, 2006; Sims and Brinkmann, 2002.

52. Likewise, in Chapter 2, Callahan tells Comer that employees can use professional codes and standards to justify their ethical decisions.

53. Bolman and Deal, 2008.

54. Strang and Jung, 2005, note that change-seekers who cannot obtain institutional support become frustrated and spent.

55. Battilana, Leca, and Boxenbaum, 2009.

56. Maier, 1967; Watson, Michaelsen, and Sharp, 1991.

57. Campbell, 2005.

58. Klandermans, 2003; Misangyi, Weaver, and Elms, 2008. Whereas Gandhi and King encouraged people to do the right thing regardless of the outcome, for the very reason that it is the right thing, few members of organizations are willing to struggle without decent odds of succeeding.

59. Campbell, 2005; Hornsey et al., 2006; Misangyi, Weaver, and Elms, 2008.

60. Battilana, Leca, and Boxenbaum, 2009.

61. Munter, 2006.

62. Veech, 2002.

63. Ibid.

64. Ober, 2001.

65. Those who display unusually virtuous behavior may incur the resentment of others; see Monin, Sawyer, and Marquez, 2008; and Treviño and Victor, 1992.

66. Botero and Van Dyne, 2009.

References

Agócs, C. 1997. Institutionalized resistance to organizational change: Denial, inaction and repression. *Journal of Business Ethics* 16(9), 917–931.

Alstete, J. 2006. Inside advice on educating managers for preventing employee theft. *International Journal of Retail and Distribution Management* 34(11), 833–844.

Aminzade, R. R., Goldstone, J. A., and Perry, E. J. 2001. Leadership dynamics and dynamics of contention. In *Silence and voice in the study of contentious politics,* ed. R. R. Aminzade, J. A. Goldstone, D. McAdam, E. J. Perry, W. H. Sewell, S. Tarrow, and C. Tilley, 126–154. Cambridge: Cambridge University Press.

Andreoli, N., and Lefkowitz, J. 2009. Individual and organizational antecedents of misconduct in organizations. *Journal of Business Ethics* 85(3), 309–332.

Bass, B.M. 1990. From transactional to transformational leadership: Learning to share the vision. *Organizational Dynamics* 18(3), 19–36.

Battilana, J., Leca, B., and Boxenbaum, E. 2009. How actors change institutions: Towards a theory of institutional entrepreneurship. *Academy of Management Annals* 3(1), 65–107.

Bolman, L. G., and Deal, T.E. 2008. *Reframing organizations: Artistry, choice, and leadership.* New York: John Wiley & Sons.

Botero, I. C., and Van Dyne, L. 2009. Employee voice behavior: Interactive effects of LMX and power distance in the United States and Colombia. *Management Communication Quarterly* 23(1), 84–104.

Britt, H. 2002. Harvey Milk as I knew him. In *Out in the Castro: Desire, promise, activism,* ed. W. Leyland, 78–81. San Francisco, CA: Leyland Publications.

Brown, M. E., and Treviño, L. K. 2006. Ethical leadership: A review and future directions. *Leadership Quarterly* 17(6), 595–616.

Bruxelles, S., and Kerbrat-Orecchioni, C. 2004. Coalitions in polylogues. *Journal of Pragmatics* 36(1), 75–113.

Burns, J. M. 1978. *Leadership.* New York: Harper and Row.

Callahan, D., and Comer, D. R. 2011. "But everybody's doing it": Implications of the cheating culture for moral courage in organizations. In *Moral courage in organizations:*

Doing the right thing at work, ed. D. R. Comer and G. Vega, 13–24. Armonk, NY: M.E. Sharpe.

Campbell, J.L. 2005. Where do we stand? Common mechanisms in organizations and social movements research. In *Social movements and organization theory,* ed. G. F. Davis, D. McAdam, W.R. Scott, and M. N. Zald, 41–68. New York: Cambridge University Press.

Conley, K. 2008. The rahble rousers. *O, The Oprah Magazine,* November 18. www.oprah.com/article/omagazine/200812_omag_liberia (accessed Aug 12, 2009).

Davis, G. F., McAdam, D., Scott, W. R., and Zald, M. N., eds. 2005. *Social movements and organization theory.* New York: Cambridge University Press.

DiMaggio, P. J., and Powell, W. W. 1983. The iron cage revisited: Institutional isomorphism and collective rationality in organizational fields. *American Sociological Review* 48(2), 147–160.

Einwohner, R. L. 2007. Leadership, authority, and collective action. *American Behavioral Scientist* 50(10), 1306–1326.

Ethics Resource Center. 2008a. National Business Ethics Survey®: An inside view of private sector ethics. Arlington, VA: Ethics Resource Center.

———. 2008b. National Government Ethics Survey®: An inside view of public sector ethics. Arlington, VA: Ethics Resource Center.

———. 2008c. National Nonprofit Ethics Survey ®: An inside view of nonprofit sector ethics. Arlington, VA: Ethics Resource Center.

Gabbay, S. M., and Leenders, R. T. A. J. 2001. Social capital of organizations: From social structure to the management of corporate social capital. *Research in the Sociology of Organizations* 18, 1–20.

Garner, J. T. 2009. When things go wrong at work: An exploration of organizational dissent messages. *Communication Studies* 60(2), 197–218.

Graham, J. W. 1986. Principled organizational dissent: A theoretical essay. *Research in Organizational Behavior* 8, 1–52.

Hartman, E. 1996. *Organizational ethics and the good life.* New York: Oxford.

Hornsey, M. J., Mavor, K., Morton, T., O'Brien, A., Paasonen, K-E., Smith, J. and White, K. M. 2006. Why do people engage in collective action? Revisiting the role of perceived effectiveness. *Journal of Applied Social Psychology* 36(7) 1701–1722.

Jablin, F. M. 2006. Courage and courageous communication among leaders and followers in groups, organizations, and communities. *Management Communication Quarterly* 20(1), 94–110.

Kassing, J. W. 2009. "In case you didn't hear me the first time": An examination of repetitious upward dissent. *Management Communication Quarterly* 22(3), 416–136.

Klandermans, B. 2003. Collective political action. In *Oxford handbook of political psychology,* ed. D. O. Sears, L. Huddy, and R. Jervis, 670–709. New York: Oxford University Press.

Knoke, D. 2009. Playing well together: Creating corporate social capital in strategic alliance networks. *American Behavioral Scientist* 52(12), 1690–1708.

Kohn, S. M. 2011. For the greater good: The moral courage of whistleblowers. In *Moral courage in organizations: Doing the right thing at work,* ed. D. R. Comer and G. Vega, 60–74. Armonk, NY: M. E. Sharpe.

Kotter, J. P. 1996. *Leading change.* Boston: Harvard Business School Press.

Kotter, J. P. and Rathgeber, H. 2002. *Our iceberg is melting: Changing and succeeding under any conditions.* New York: St. Martin's Press.

Kouzes, J. M., and Posner, B. Z. 2002. *The leadership challenge* (3d ed.). San Francisco: Jossey-Bass.

Kronenberg, A. 2002. Everybody needed milk. In *Out in the Castro: Desire, promise, activism,* ed. W. Leyland, 37–13. San Francisco: Leyland Publications.

Maier, N. R. F. 1967. Assets and liabilities in group problem solving: The need for an integrative function. *Psychological Review* 74(4), 239–249.

Marcus, A. A., and Fremeth, A. R. 2009. Green management matters regardless. *Academy of Management Perspectives* 23(3), 17–26.

Matt, B. F., and Shahinpoor, N. 2011. Speaking truth to power: The courageous organizational dissenter. In *Moral courage in organizations: Doing the right thing at work,* ed. D.R. Comer and G. Vega, 157–170. Armonk, NY: M.E. Sharpe.

Meyer, J. W., and Rowan, B. 1977. Institutionalized organizations: Formalized structure as myth and ceremony. *American Journal of Sociology* 83(2), 340–363.

Meyerson, D., and Tompkins, M. 2007. Tempered radicals as institutional change agents: The case of advancing gender equity at the University of Michigan. *Harvard Journal of Law and Gender* 30, 303–322.

Michelli, J. A. 2007. *The Starbucks experience: 5 principles f or turning ordinary into extraordinary.* New York: McGraw-Hill.

Miller, W. L. 2000. *The mystery of courage.* Cambridge, MA: Harvard University Press.

Misangyi, V. F., Weaver, G. R., and Elms, H. 2008. Ending corruption: The interplay among institutional logics, resources, and institutional entrepreneurs. *Academy of Management Review* 33(3), 750–770.

Monin, B., Sawyer, P.J., and Marquez, M. J. 2008. The rejection of moral rebels: Resenting those who do the right thing. *Journal of Personality and Social Psychology* 95(1), 76–93.

Moyers, B. 2009. Transcript. *Bill Moyers Journal,* June 19. www.pbs.org/moyers/journal/06192009/transcriptl. html (accessed August 12, 2009).

Munter, R. 2006. *Guide to managerial communication: Effective business writing and speaking* (7th ed.). Upper Saddle River, NJ: Pearson Prentice Hall.

Nelson, A. 2009. *Red orchestra: The story of the Berlin underground and the circle of friends who resisted Hitler.* New York: Random House.

Niehoff, B. P., and Paul, R. J. 2000. Causes of employee theft and strategies HR managers can use for prevention. *Human Resource Management* 39(1), 51–64.

Ober, S. 2001. *Contemporary business communication.* Boston: Houghton Mifflin.

Pfarrer, M. D., Decelles, K. A., Smith, K. G., and Taylor, M. S. 2008. After the fall: Reintegrating the corrupt organization. *Academy of Management Review* 33(1), 730–749.

Pray the devil back to hell. 2008. Directed by G. Reticker. Fork Films.

Quinn, R.E. 2004. *Building the bridge as you walk on it: A guide for leading change.* San Francisco: Jossey-Bass.

Schminke, M., Ambrose, M. L., and Neubaum, D. O. 2005. The effect of leader moral development on ethical climate and employee attitudes. *Organizational Behavior and Human Decision Processes* 97(2), 135–151.

Scully, M. A., and Creed, W. E. D. 2005. In *Social movements and Organization theory,* ed. G. F. Davis, D. McAdam, W.R. Scott, and M.N. Zald, 310–332. New York: Cambridge University Press.

Shilts, R. 1982. *The mayor of Castro Street: The life and times of Harvey Milk.* New York: St. Martin's Press.

Siegel, D. S. 2009. Green management matters only if it yields more green: An economic/strategic perspective. *Academy of Management Perspectives* 23(3), 5–16.

Sims, R. 2009. Toward a better understanding of organizational efforts to rebuild reputation following an ethical scandal. *Journal of Business Ethics* 90(4), 453–172.

Sims, R. R. 2000. Changing an organization's culture under new leadership. *Journal of Business Ethics* 25(1), 65–78.

Sims, R. R., and Brinkmann, J. 2002. Leaders as moral role models: The case of John Gutfreund at Salomon Brothers. *Journal of Business Ethics* 35(4), 327–339.

Stevenson, W. B., Pearce, J. L., and Porter, L. W. 1985. The concept of "coalition" in organization theory and research. *Academy of Management Review* 10(2), 256–268.

Strang, D., and Jung, D.-I. 2005. Organizational change as orchestrated social movement: Recruitment to a corporate quality initiative. In *Social movements and organization theory,* ed. G. F. Davis, D. McAdam, W. R. Scott, and M. N. Zald, 280–309. New York: Cambridge University Press.

Tate, T. 2004. How to fight, how to kill: Child soldiers in Liberia. *Human Rights Watch* 16(2) (February), www .hrw.org/reports/2004/liberia0204/liberia0204.pdf (accessed August 29. 2009).

Tec, N. 1993. *Defiance.* New York: Oxford.

Thomas, R. R., Jr. 1991. *Beyond race and gender: Unleashing the power of your total workforce by managing diversity.* New York: AMACOM.

Treviño, L. K., Brown, M., and Hartman, L. 2003. A qualitative investigation of perceived executive ethical leadership: Perceptions from inside and outside the executive suite. *Human Relations* 56(1), 5–37.

Treviño, L. K., and Victor, B. 1992. Peer reporting of nnethical behavior: A social context perspective. *Academy of Management Journal* 35(3), 38–64.

Uhl-Bien, M., and Carsten, M. K. 2007. Being ethical when the boss is not. *Organizational Dynamics* 36(2), 187–201.

Veech, A. 2002. *Managerial communication strategies: An applied casebook.* Upper Saddle River, NJ: Pearson Prentice Hall.

Watson, W., Michaelsen, L. K., and Sharp, W. 1991. Member competence, group interaction, and group decision making: A longitudinal study. *Journal of Applied Psychology* 76(7), 803–809.

Weaver, G. R., Treviño, L. K., and Agle, B. 2005. "Somebody I look up to": Ethical role models in organizations. *Organizational Dynamics* 34(4), 313–330.

Zald, M. N., and Berger, M. A. 1978. Social movements in organizations: Coup d'etat, insurgency, and mass movements. *American Journal of Sociology* 83(4), 823–861.

PART VI

Organizational Change

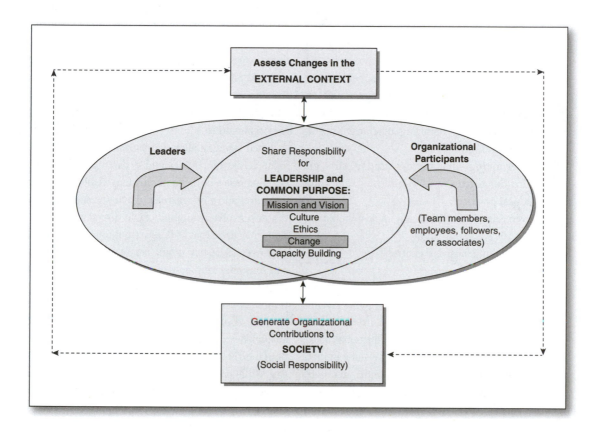

Assess Changes in the **EXTERNAL CONTEXT**

Leaders

Share Responsibility for **LEADERSHIP and COMMON PURPOSE:**
Mission and Vision
Culture
Ethics
Change
Capacity Building

Organizational Participants

(Team members, employees, followers, or associates)

Generate Organizational Contributions to **SOCIETY** (Social Responsibility)

Overview

The dynamic external context (described in Part I) is a major driver of change in new era organizations. Organizations can thrive in this context if leaders and participants identify emerging patterns and seize opportunities presented by external changes. The chapters in this section focus on the organization's strategic leadership and change processes that position it to respond to a rapidly changing environment.

Strategic Leadership

Robert Hoskisson, Michael Hitt, R. Duane Ireland, and Jeffrey Harrison (Chapter 30) detail the role of strategic leadership in setting direction and generating change related to the organization's external context. They define strategic leadership as "the ability to anticipate events, envision possibilities, maintain flexibility, and empower others to create strategic change as necessary." In many contemporary organizations, this function is typically developed by the chief executive officer (CEO) and her or his top management team.

Strategic direction is reflected in the organization's mission, vision, purpose, long-term goals, and values. These elements serve as the organization's true north and guide overall leadership, decision making, and functioning. Key responsibilities and actions for strategic leadership entail

- ensuring that the organization is well positioned economically;
- acquiring, developing, and managing key resources including human capital and an effective organization culture;
- developing and managing relationships with external stakeholders;
- determining and communicating strategic direction together with establishing values and ethical practices;
- overseeing formulation and implementation of specific strategies; and
- establishing balanced controls.

When implementing strategic leadership, the authors assert a more collaborative style that encompasses top-level team members with heterogeneous backgrounds (different experience, functional backgrounds, and education) generally results in better decisions than the traditional commander style. A heterogeneous team provides more information, knowledge, and skills and is positively associated with innovation, strategic change, and a propensity to take stronger competitive actions.

Kurt Matzler, Johann Füller, Britta Koch, Julia Hautz, and Katja Hutter (Chapter 31) offer an option for strategy development that differs from current strategic leadership processes. They argue that Web 2.0 technologies (also called *social software*) have the potential to change the way organizations formulate strategy. These approaches—referred to as *democratizing strategy*, *open strategy*, *open-source strategy*, or *strategy as a practice of thousands*—allow entities to engage large numbers of people in generating, discussing, and evaluating strategy ideas. The technology lets the organization tap into the collective intelligence of the organization from members at all levels with little effort and at low cost.

The researchers explored this open strategy process in four case studies: an Austrian medium-sized automation supplier, a leading German car manufacturer, a major European bank, and a German multinational engineering and electronics company. They explored the organizations' strategy objectives, means, kind of openness, and results. In all four cases, participation levels were high but contributions were not evenly distributed. A small, dense core of active participants dominated the process, and there was a large passive periphery. Executives were surprised by the number, diversity, and quality of contributions from the far reaches of the organization.

Open strategy allows organizations to start dialogue across hierarchies and departments; however, skipping levels of the hierarchy may challenge power structures and strategic roles of managers. Discussion can also evolve in unpredictable directions. Discussions may arise that leaders are not prepared for, and controversial issues might create endless dialogues and tensions. Members of the organization must be prepared for tough critiques and direct or blunt responses. Increased involvement in strategy leads to stronger visions, increased rationality, and enhanced adaptiveness; it can also lead to more politics, cultural inertia, and more constraints imposed on strategy. While open strategy can have positive effects on employee motivation, it can also create frustration among employees if there is inadequate response to their ideas.

The authors emphasize an important prerequisite for open strategy is an open culture that emphasizes transparency and open dialogue—not all organizational cultures are right for this approach. This approach to strategy "changes the role of organization members from implementers of strategy to active shapers of strategy." There are many questions to be answered about open strategy. Not all problems are suited for crowdsourcing, and more research is needed to understand which problems are appropriate for open strategy. The potential in this area of inquiry provide enormous possibilities for new research and practices.

As senior leaders open the strategy process to more participants using Web 2.0 technologies, the "big data" movement is revolutionizing decision making in today's agile companies. Andrew McAfee and Erik Brynjolfsson (Chapter 32) explain how "the big data movement, like analytics before it, seeks to glean intelligence from data and translate that into business advantage." These data sets are larger, are collected faster, and are drawn from a wider variety of sources than ever before in history.

McAfee and Brynjolfsson argue that data-driven decisions are better decisions—and they set out to prove it. They hypothesized that data-driven companies would be better performers than other organizations. They interviewed of 330 executives of public companies in North America about their organizational and technology management practices, and they examined performance data from annual reports and independent sources. Their study found the more data-driven companies performed better on objective financial measures and operational results. Companies in the top third of their industry in the use of data-driven decision making were, on average, 5% more productive and 6% more profitable than their competitors. They use big data to make a wide variety of business decisions from creating new businesses to increasing sales.

Big data is creating a new culture of decision making that changes how decisions are made and who makes them, according to the authors. Companies that want to maintain a competitive edge can no longer rely on making decisions based on the highest-paid person's opinion (HiPPO), they must first ask, "What do the data say?" To manage the change to big data organizations must meet five management challenges: leadership—develop leadership teams that set clear goals, define what success looks like, and ask the right questions; talent management—bring in the right talent such as data scientists and other professionals skilled at working with large quantities of information; technology—acquire the tools to handle the volume, velocity, and variety of big data; decision making—put information and the relevant decision rights in the same location (i.e., situate the data with the people who have the problem-solving techniques to exploit the data); and company culture—create a culture where people use data first (by asking, "What do we know?") rather than relying on hunches.

Change

These major changes in strategy and decision processes will require agility and constant change in the organization. Gill Hickman (Chapter 33) identifies several categories of organization change practices including collective or collaborative approaches, strategic planning, stages of praxis, scenario building, appreciative inquiry, e-practices, and ethical practices. Collective or collaborative change involves leadership and change practices that are embedded (or institutionalized) in the organization's essential systems. These change practices require organizational learning and shared power where leadership, authority, responsibility, and decision-making power are delegated or distributed to individuals and teams throughout the organization.

Strategic planning typically involves creating or updating the organization's vision and mission, conducting an environmental scan, setting strategic direction using goals and strategies, and implementing and updating the plan. While strategic planning processes often originate at the top, new open strategy processes, discussed earlier, allow leaders to start dialogue across levels of the hierarchy and receive ideas from anywhere in the organization.

Regarding stages of praxis, Hickman compares Kurt Lewin's classic three-stage model of change with John Kotter's eight-stage model. Both models begin with establishing a sense of urgency, which initiates the change process, and move through to the final stage of anchoring new change in the culture. Scenario building is an eight-factor process that helps leaders and members use factual information and indicators of early trends to project alternative futures for the organization. Appreciative inquiry is a change process that uses successful processes and practices in the organization to build momentum and construct new realities for the future.

Leading change in virtual teams requires e-practices that combine select components of face-to-face leadership with technology, structured processes, clearly designated roles, frequent communication, and other factors. Finally, effective change processes require ethical practices consisting of authenticity, trust, and reciprocal care to sustain a healthy moral environment.

Steve Kempster, Malcolm Higgs, and Tobias Wuerz (Chapter 34) explore the concept of piloting a change project in successive parts of the organization to enhance the effectiveness and success of change. Pilots have been used in fields such as engineering to test products and services and in psychological research to test experiments, but not in organizational change. The authors point to high failure rates of current change programs and propose that piloting may offer advantages due to its emphasis on experimenting, learning, lowering resistance, and sharing ownership of the change.

They propose a model comprising four interconnected triangles that combine the pilot model with the best features of three traditional change models: rational top-down, emergent/bottom-up, and politically governed. The pilot project is facilitated through distributed leadership (shared leadership), a relational process that incorporates many individuals into leadership rather than a single leader. Distributed leadership provides the organizing activity for a wide process of social influence in the change process.

The concept and process of piloting change will need more examination to explore its potential for generating change in new era organizations. Kempster, Higgs, and Wuerz suggest two propositions for future research: "1) distributed change leadership enables planned, emergent and political change to be executed in a complementary manner; and 2) implementing change through the use of pilots creates the context to enable the effective emergence of distributed leadership."

Organizational change requires the creation of designs or structures that meet the demands of changing environments, organization or business models, technology, and human capacity. Raymond E. Miles, Charles C. Snow, Øystein D. Fjeldstad, Grant Miles, and Christopher Lettl (Chapter 35) explain four traditional and contemporary organization models and their accompanying forms or structures

that emerged from the middle 19th century to the late 20th century. These models include the U-form (unitary) or bureaucratic organization model—developed for large, single-business firms or government organizations to achieve economies of scale through specialization and top-down coordination and control; the M-form (multi-divisional) model—created for firms with multiple divisions where managers operate under delegated authority to meet the goals and objectives of their unit in alignment with the larger organization; the matrix organization—developed to allow flexible integration and application of technologies using multi-functional project teams of members from across and up and down the hierarchy; and the multi-firm network—designed to allow firms to focus their activities on skills or operations where they have the most expertise and outsource non-core activities to specialist providers.

The authors identify a new organization form called *collaborative communities* that is designed to meet the opportunities and challenges of the 21st century. These communities operate in a global context where rapidly expanding and diverse science-based knowledge exists across industry, country, and continental lines. They remove innovative barriers and create new ways to leverage knowledge.

Raymond Miles et al. "expect the most innovative firms to participate with other firms in forming communities of firms capable of collaboratively creating large-scale complex solution as well as sharing knowledge to produce innovations across a set of expandable markets." One example, Syndicom, is a community of practice among medical professionals and innovators of medical devices. Their first collaborative activity was the creation of a community of practice among spine surgeons (SpineConnect) for the purpose of sharing diagnostic and treatment expertise. Their community evolved rapidly and now includes 1,300 spine surgeons and 100 trauma surgeons across the United States, Europe, and Asia.

The authors suggest that collaborative communities can be used to tackle global problems where there is a *global commons*—jointly held resources that benefit the entire community such as grazing land, oceans, and the atmosphere. These communities will need actors who have collaborative capabilities and values, protocols and infrastructure that facilitate collaboration, and shared access to commons.

Part VI — Chapters

CHAPTER 30

Strategic Leadership

Robert E. Hoskisson
Rice University

Michael A. Hitt
Texas A&M University

R. Duane Ireland
Texas A&M Uniiversity

Jeffrey S. Harrison
University of Richmond

S trategic leaders can profoundly influence firm performance.[1] Legendary business chief executive officers (CEOs) such as Jack Welch at General Electric, Sam Walton at Walmart, and Akio Morita at Sony led their organizations to greater success than any of their many formidable competitors, yet they were very different in their approaches. Jack Welch was notorious for creating difficult targets for his subordinates and penalizing them when they did not perform. He drove managers to high levels of success or facilitated their departure from the firm, figuring that he was doing them a favor by helping them find some other situation in which they could excel.[2] Sam Walton took a positive and caring approach to the retailing business, treating customers as royalty and

calling employees "associates." He also took an unconventional approach to the market by placing huge stores in rural areas and stocking them from warehouses that were centrally located near groups of stores. Although we now consider these features business-as-usual, they were anything but normal in the early days of Walmart.[3] Akio Morita pushed hard on innovation and adopted a forward-looking, global perspective. He is heralded as a diplomat whose broad vision of Japan's role in the world economy helped Sony and other Japanese companies achieve high levels of success in international markets.[4]

Despite these different approaches, all of these leaders were visionaries, or transformational leaders: they established a clear view of what they wanted to accomplish. They were also agents of change, leading others to make their vision a reality. Effective strategic leadership is a requirement for successful strategic management. **Strategic leadership** is the ability to anticipate, envision, maintain flexibility, and empower others to create strategic change as necessary. Multifunctional in nature, strategic leadership involves managing through others, managing an entire enterprise rather than a functional subunit, and coping with change. Because of the complex and often global orientation of the job, strategic leaders must learn how to effectively influence human behavior in an uncertain environment. By word and/or by personal example, and through their ability to envision the future, effective strategic leaders meaningfully influence the behaviors, thoughts, and feelings of those with whom they work.[5] Transformational leadership entails motivating followers to do more than is expected, to continuously enrich their capabilities, and to place the organization's interests above their own.[6]

This chapter begins by focusing on individual strategic leaders as a key resource for the firm—the personal characteristics that make them effective and the influences on their abilities to make effective strategic decisions. Then we examine top management teams and their influence on organizations, as well as factors associated with executive succession. The rest of the chapter discusses six key components of effective strategic leadership: ensuring that the firm is well-positioned economically, managing key resources, developing and maintaining effective relationships with key stakeholders, determining a strategic direction, overseeing the formulation and implementation of specific strategies, and establishing balanced organizational control systems. These activities influence the amount of value a firm creates and its economic performance.

Strategic Leaders as a Key Resource Through Their Influences on Strategic Decisions

Not all managers have the capacity to become effective strategic leaders. Furthermore, it may be that strategic

leadership skills can be analyzed as a hierarchy in which managers must master lower-level skills before they fine-tune higher-level skills, as illustrated in the following levels from the book *Good to Great* by Jim Collins.[7]

- *Level 1: Highly Capable Individual.* The most basic skills for becoming a capable individual are developing skills and a strong work ethic.
- *Level 2: Contributing Team Member.* Next, a person must be able to work effectively in teams and make useful contributions to the achievement of team goals.
- *Level 3: Competent Manager.* Once the two lower-level skills are mastered, competent management comes from the ability to organize people and resources so as to achieve organizational objectives.
- *Level 4: Effective Leader.* Not all competent managers are effective leaders. Leadership entails the ability to articulate a clear strategic intent and motivate followers to high levels of performance.
- *Level 5: Level 5 Executive.* These are people with unwavering resolve to lead their companies to greatness. Frequently they are humble, attributing success to the team they have assembled rather than focusing on their own personal achievements. A Level 5 leader might also be called a transformational leader.

Although the book *Good to Great* has been criticized, the concept of a skills hierarchy is a useful idea and to a degree has been verified by academic research.[8] People will not be able to contribute well to a team until they have attained a certain level of personal competence. Also, the skills at Levels 1 and 2 (more basic skills) seem essential to becoming an excellent manager or leader. Furthermore, since competent management is defined as an ability to organize people and resources to achieve objectives, it seems reasonable that effective leaders also need these skills. The book suggests that many have lower level skills, whereas very few have higher-level skills (Level 5), suggesting that those with appropriate skills are a key resource for an organization. Steve Jobs, deceased CEO of Apple, is one who exemplified a transformational leader and was definitely a key source of Apple's tremendous success by ushering in an era focused on personal technology through iTunes, iPods, iPhones and iPads. He did this by "his ability to inspire loyalty in customers, his controlling leadership style, and his devotion to simple and elegant product design."[9]

However, besides general skills that any organization might be able to utilize, one must also understand the strategic situation of a particular company in order to make appropriate strategic decisions. Although the ability to establish a strategic vision and create passion and energy among a firm's employees to realize the vision and achieve outstanding performance are essential, research has shown that human and social capital are necessary for understanding the business and are also indicators of future success.[10]

Strategic Leadership Style

Strategic leaders direct the strategic management process in different ways. The CEO sets the tone for the amount of management participation in strategic decisions and the way the decisions are implemented.[11] Some CEOs apply a very traditional "commander" approach, using meetings with top management team members to collect information but then individually deciding on strategies and directing subordinates to carry them out. A more collaborative style entails jointly arriving at strategies and implementation plans with members of the top management team. In other organizations, the CEO may delegate most strategy-making responsibilities to subordinates, allocating resources to them and giving them responsibility for effective utilization.[12] The appropriateness of various decision-making styles tends to vary depending on the competitive situation. In situations in which rapid decisions are required, such as emergencies or unexpected shifts in the business environment, a more directive approach may be more appropriate. However, in general, a more participative style will lead to better decisions because managers share and consider a greater amount of relevant information.[13] Also, implementation may be easier and more successful because managers feel that they are a part of the decisions they are working to implement.[14]

The cultural and functional backgrounds of top managers may also influence the way strategic decisions are made.[15] An ongoing debate exists regarding whether it is appropriate to try to match the backgrounds of managers with the competitive situation in which they will lead. For instance, it may be appropriate for managers with production-operations backgrounds to run businesses that try to achieve low cost positions because of the internal focus on efficiency and engineering.[16] Alternatively, businesses that are seeking to differentiate their products may need someone with training in marketing or research and development (R&D) because of the need for innovation and market awareness. Growth strategies, in general, may call for a person with a strong marketing background, a willingness to take risks, and a high tolerance for ambiguity.[17] Nevertheless, these same characteristics may be inappropriate in turnaround situations. Some evidence also exists that strategic change and innovation are more likely when a manager is younger and has less time in the organization but is well-educated.[18] There is no absolute formula for matching a strategic leader to a competitive situation. The point to understand is that the effectiveness of strategic leadership may depend, in part, on how well the background and skills of a particular leader fit with the challenges the firm is facing.

Managerial Discretion and Decision Biases

Managerial discretion and decision biases can also influence the effectiveness of strategic decisions. Because strategic decisions are intended to help a firm develop one or more competitive advantages, how managers exercise discretion (latitude for action) is critical to the firm's success.[19] Managers often use their discretion when making strategic decisions, including those associated with implementation of strategies.[20] Top executives must be action oriented; thus, the decisions that they make should spur the company to action. However, they are constrained by a number of factors that influence the level of discretion they have when making decisions. Some of these factors are associated with the external environment, such as the industry structure, the rate of market growth in the firm's primary industry, and the degree to which products can be differentiated. Consider, for example, that managers in a firm that produces a basic commodity are fairly limited in determining how they might alter their product to make it more appealing to the market. Characteristics of the organization, including its size, age, resources, and culture, can also influence discretion. For instance, strong organizational cultures can have a significant effect on the decisions that are made. Finally, discretion is influenced by individual characteristics of the manager, including commitment to the firm and its strategic outcomes, tolerance for ambiguity, skills in working with different people, and aspiration levels (see Figure 30.1).

In addition to managerial discretion, decision-making biases can have a significant effect on strategic decisions.[21] Strategic managers tend to rely on a limited set of heuristics, or "rules of thumb," when they make strategic decisions.[22] These heuristics help managers simplify what might otherwise be an overwhelmingly complicated and uncertain decision environment. However, heuristics also can lead to suboptimal decisions.[23] Although dozens of potential decision-making biases have been described in the research literature,[24] five seem to have the most potential for influencing strategic decisions:[25]

- *Reliance on Previously Formed Beliefs.* Executives bring a number of preconceived ideas into any decision process. Some of them are a

Figure 30.1	Factors Affecting Managerial Discretion

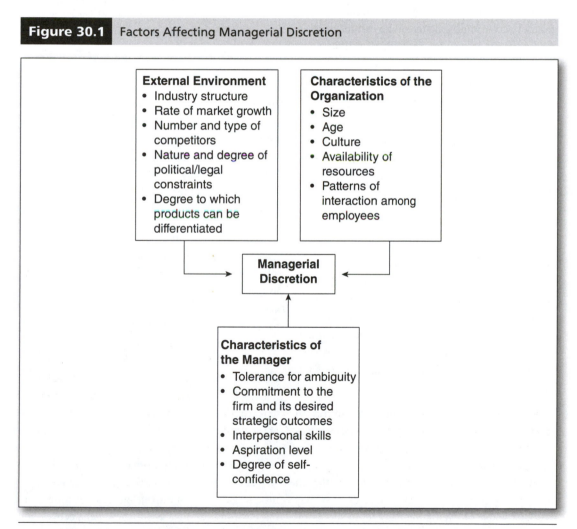

Source: Adapted from S. Finkelstein & D. C Hambrick, 1996. *Strategic leadership: Top executives and their effects on organizations,* St. Paul, MN; West Publishing Company.

function of the executives' past experiences, whereas others are based on things they may have read or heard about, regardless of whether they have any actual empirical validity. Especially important to strategic decisions are beliefs about causality—that is, how the salient decision variables fit together. For instance, executives may believe that particular strategic actions will bring particular firm results. Clearly, experience is a valuable executive resource; however, preconceived ideas may cause decision makers to overlook information that could lead to different conclusions.[26] Stereotypes also fit into this category—that is, when executives hold preconceived notions about the abilities or potential behavior of individuals based on variables such as gender, nationality, religion, or race. Holding a stereotype can result in an executive ignoring the individual skills, background, and performance of a person who is being considered for a strategic position and thereby potentially choosing an individual who will not lead as effectively.

- *Focus on Limited Objectives.* Executives also tend to focus on a limited number of firm targets instead of thinking broadly about other worthwhile objectives.[27] For instance, a primary focus on budgetary controls may lead managers to focus on selected critical performance targets.[28] Too much focus on financial objectives, such as shareholder returns or return-on-equity, can lead to short-sighted decisions, where the firm takes actions with immediate financial benefits while damaging its longer-term performance.[29] It can also lead to neglect of and less favorable relationships with stakeholders that are important to firm competitiveness, such as customers, suppliers, the communities in which firms operate, or even employees.[30]

- *Exposure to Limited Decision Alternatives.* In an effort to simplify decision processes, executives tend to limit the number of alternatives for achieving a particular goal.[31] Instead, they rely on intuition to supplement rationality.[32] The problem is that in an effort to speed up decision processes, they may overlook viable or even potentially more successful alternatives.

- *Insensitivity to Outcome Probabilities.* Frequently, decision makers do not understand, trust, or use outcome probabilities to guide decision processes; that is, they tend to be more influenced by the magnitude of potential decision outcomes rather than the probability that they will occur.[33] They may also consider decision situations as unique and therefore discount information that might otherwise help them assess the probability of success.[34] The obvious danger associated with this bias is that, on the basis of the high potential returns that might accrue, strategic leaders will guide their firms into situations that are unlikely to be successful.

- *Illusion of Control.* As decision makers approach a particular decision situation, they may believe that they have more control over the outcomes from that decision than they actually have.[35] This bias manifests itself in executives assessing lower probabilities of failure, which is related to the previous bias. However, it also results in a feeling among decision makers that they can use their professional skills to fix problems that occur as a decision is implemented.[36] This problem is linked to overconfidence or overoptimism.[37] Consequently, this bias can lead to poor decisions at the outset and inadequate planning for implementation of those decisions.

Hubris, which can be defined as excessive pride, leading to a feeling of invincibility, can magnify the effects of each of these potential biases.[38] CEOs tend to garner media attention, and they may win awards and gain other types of public recognition.[39] Research has shown that when CEOs begin to believe the glowing press accounts and to feel that they are unlikely to make errors, they are more likely to make poor strategic decisions.[40] Top executives need to have self-confidence, but they must also guard against allowing it to reach the point of hubris. Perhaps that is why some of the greatest business leaders of our day exhibit an unusual degree of humility.[41]

Awareness of decision-making biases can help strategic leaders at least partially overcome them. For instance, leaders can provide an open decision-making environment that invites new perspectives and challenges existing assumptions and strategies. Also, problems associated with the neglect of prior probabilities can be addressed through real options analysis (see Chapter 13). In addition, strategic leaders can address problems associated with decision biases by surrounding themselves with a top management team composed of individuals who have divergent views and varying backgrounds. It is important also to evaluate the decision processes used. "A recent McKinsey study of more than 1,000 business investments, for instance, showed that when companies worked to reduce the effects of bias, they raised their returns on investment by seven percentage points."[42]

Top Management Teams

In most firms, complex organizational challenges and the need for substantial information, knowledge, and skills to address these challenges result in a need for teams of executives to provide strategic leadership. The quality of strategic thinking and subsequent strategic decisions made by a top management team affect the firm's ability to innovate and engage in effective strategic change.[43] Top-level managers are an important resource for firms seeking to successfully use the strategic management process.[44]

A top management team is composed of the CEO and other key managers who are responsible for setting the direction of the firm and formulating and implementing its strategies. For instance, a team may include a chief operating officer (COO) and an assortment of other high-ranking officials typically representing the major businesses and/or functional areas of the firm, as well as members of the board of directors. The decisions resulting from strategic thinking that top-level managers engage in influence how the firm is designed, the nature of its strategies, and whether it will achieve its goals. Thus, a critical element of organizational success is having a top management team with superior managerial and decision-making skills.[45]

Several factors influence the ability of top management teams to exercise effective strategic leadership, including team heterogeneity, team power, and executive succession processes.

Top Management Team Heterogeneity

The job of top-level executives is complex and requires a broad knowledge of the firm's operations, as well as the three key parts of the firm's external environment—the general, industry, and competitor environments. (Chapter 3 explores these environments in depth.) The overwhelming complexity and strength of environmental forces, as well as the need to manage a wide variety of stakeholder relationships, require formation of a fairly diverse top management team with a wide variety of strengths, capabilities, and knowledge.[46] This normally requires a heterogeneous top management team composed of individuals with different functional backgrounds, experience, and education. The more heterogeneous a top management team is--the more varied the expertise and knowledge within the team—the more capacity it has to provide effective strategic leadership in formulating strategy.[47]

Steve Ballmer has been Microsoft's chief executive officer since 2000, but Bill Gates only recently (2008) retired from day-to-day operating decisions as chairman of the board. Since that time, Ballmer has replaced almost every major division head at Microsoft and has overseen "a dramatic shift away from the company's PC-first heritage."[48] The Windows Vista operating system was a distinct setback for Microsoft; it was poorly implemented and Windows 7 was mostly a fix of Windows Vista. The upcoming launch of Windows 8, under the leadership of Steven Sinofsky, portends to be much more successful and is based on lessons learned from Vista's failure. Ballmer also hired Qi Lu from Yahoo! to revamp Microsoft search business. This has paid off in Bing (Microsoft's search offering) improving its market share. Microsoft's acquisition of Skype also brought in a new player, Tony Bates, whom he has put in charge to help move this acquisition to the next level of excellence. Ballmer has focused on improving the vision for new products, a function he took over from Gates' former leadership. One former board member, James I. Cash, indicated, "He's learned to manage through people and made a commitment to interdisciplinary work. I think he will come off looking like a real unique and special leader."[49] Although his success with these changes remains to be seen, he has to deal with a large and diverse top management team.

Members of a heterogeneous top management team benefit from discussing the different perspectives that team members advance. In many cases, these discussions increase the quality of the team's decisions, especially when a synthesis emerges from the diverse perspectives that are superior to any one individual's perspective.[50] Having members with substantive expertise in the firm's core functions and businesses is also important to a top management team's effectiveness. In a high-technology industry, it may be critical for a firm's top management team to have R&D expertise, particularly when growth strategies are being implemented.[51] Heterogeneous top management teams have sometimes demonstrated a propensity to take stronger competitive actions and reactions than more homogeneous teams.[52]

More heterogeneity in top management teams is also positively associated with innovation and strategic change.[53] Team heterogeneity may encourage members to "think outside the box" and thus be more creative in making decisions. In essence, thinking outside the box means "thinking beyond the common mental models that shape the way people see the world."[54] Therefore, firms that need to change their strategies are more likely to do so if they have top management teams with diverse backgrounds and expertise. A team with various areas of expertise is more likely to identify environmental changes (opportunities and threats) or changes within the firms that require a different strategic direction.[55] Research also shows that more heterogeneity among top management team members promotes debate, which often leads to better strategic decisions. In turn, better strategic decisions produce higher firm performance.[56]

Once a decision is made, the next challenge is to create a level of cohesion among team members that will facilitate effective implementation of the change. One of the great challenges facing strategic leaders is integrating the diverse opinions and behavior of a heterogeneous team into a common way of thinking and behaving.[57] In general, the more heterogeneous and larger the top management team is, the more

difficult it is for the team to effectively implement strategies.[58] Comprehensive and long-term strategic plans can be inhibited by communication difficulties among top executives who have different backgrounds and different cognitive skills.[59] As a result, a group of top executives with diverse backgrounds may inhibit the process of decision making if it is not effectively managed. In these cases, top management teams may fail to comprehensively examine threats and opportunities, leading to suboptimal strategic decisions.

Virginia Rometty was promoted to CEO of IBM in late 2011. IBM, a top technology firm, is continually changing and has a global strategy. Rometty has played a key part in recent moves, including the acquisition of a consulting arm of PricewaterhouseCoopers as well as helping to establish delivery centers for IT services in China and India. She helped both manage the integration process of the PricewaterhouseCoopers acquisition and formulate the IT service strategies in these large, emerging economies.[60] She obviously has to meet the challenges managing a diverse team among IBM's various businesses, both across services and products as well as across a diverse set of geographic markets. One IBM customer echoed her abilities to facilitate this diversity. Under her direction, IBM staffers engaged in "collaborative problem solving, which I think the future of IT is all about." It will be interesting to see how IBM thrives under Rometty's leadership as she continues to work with Samuel Palmisano, the former CEO, who will remain as chairman of IBM's board.[61]

The CEO and Top Management Team Power

Chapter 11 discusses the board of directors as a governance mechanism for monitoring a firm's strategic direction and for representing stakeholders' interests, especially those of shareholders. Here, we focus on the characteristics that give the CEO and top management team power relative to the board and the influence these characteristics can have on the amount of strategic leadership the board provides.[62] An underlying premise is that higher performance normally is achieved when the board of directors is more directly involved in shaping a firm's strategic direction.[63] However, directors may find it difficult to direct the strategic actions of powerful CEOs and top management teams.[64] Their relative power is at least partially a function of social or business ties with directors and their tenure as members of the team.

It is not uncommon for a powerful CEO to appoint a number of sympathetic outside board members such as friends, family members, or principals in companies with which the firm conducts business. CEOs may also appoint board members who are on the top management team and report directly to the CEO.[65] In either case, the CEO may have significant control over the board's actions. Westphal and Zajac have asked the "central question" of "whether boards are an effective management control mechanism . . . or whether they are a 'management tool', . . . a rubber stamp for management initiatives... and often surrender to management their major domain of decision-making authority, which includes the right to hire, fire, and compensate top management."[66]

Pfizer is an example of a giant pharmaceutical firm which stumbled, at least in part, because of an ineffective board. Jeffrey Kindler, CEO of Pfizer, the world's largest pharmaceutical company, stepped down in December 2010. Pfizer had built an extraordinarily successful company, realizing $68 billion annual sales on blockbuster drugs such as Lipitor and Viagra. However, under Kindler, its stock price had sagged from a high of $49 down to $17 as its pipeline of drugs dried up. Kindler evidently had difficulties trusting his colleagues and, at times, appeared to undermine many of his potential successors. He sought outside ideas from those who may not have had the necessary knowledge. He was also known for micro-managing his executive teams' endeavors. *Fortune Magazine* summed it up this way: "The story of Jeff Kindler's tenure at Pfizer is a saga of ambition, intrigue, back-stabbing, and betrayal-all exacerbated by a board that allowed the problems to fester for years."[67] This suggests that if a board stays too distant from the strategic decision-making processes, political problems can get in the way of the rational process of making decisions, which can confuse the decisions

necessary to create a stable financial future. Ian Read has been appointed as the new Pfizer CEO and Chairman of the board; Read has been a longtime inside manager of the major drug producer.

Despite the highly visible examples of poor governance in low-performing firms, close ties between board members and CEOs do not always lead to less board member involvement in strategic decisions. In fact, research shows that social ties between the CEO and board members may actually increase board members' involvement in strategic decisions. Thus, strong relationships between the CEO and the board of directors may result in positive or negative outcomes for firms, depending on how those relationships are managed.[68] The important point is to recognize and safeguard against the risks.

Another way for a CEO to achieve power relative to the board is to serve as chair of the board.[69] This practice, called CEO duality, has become more common in the United States. Although it varies across industries, duality occurs most often in the largest firms, as exemplified in Ian Read's appointment to both positions in the previously mentioned Pfizer illustration. Increased shareholder activism, however, has brought CEO duality under scrutiny and attack in both U.S. and European firms. Duality has been criticized for causing poor performance and slow response to change in a number of firms, although the research does not provide clear direction.[70]

Historically, an **independent board leadership structure**, in which different people held the positions of CEO and board chair, was believed to enhance a board's ability to monitor top-level managers' decisions and actions, particularly in terms of the firm's financial performance (see Chapter 11).[71] Consistent with this view, the two jobs are always separate in Britain. However, the British model can also lead to problems, particularly to power struggles and confusion regarding firm leadership.[72] Also, **stewardship theory** suggests that top managers want to do the right thing for the firm's shareholders and that reducing the amount of interference with their actions will increase the profit potential of the firm.[73] From this perspective, CEO duality would be expected to facilitate effective decisions and actions. In these instances, the increased effectiveness gained through CEO duality accrues from the individual who wants to perform effectively and be the best possible steward of the firm's assets[74] Because of this person's positive orientation and actions, extra governance and the coordination costs resulting from an independent board leadership structure would be unnecessary. These arguments demonstrate that there is no clear answer regarding the influence of CEO duality on strategic decision making.

An additional influence on the power of the CEO and other top management team members is their tenure in the organization. CEOs with long tenure—on the team and in the organization—have a greater influence on board decisions.[75] And it follows that CEOs with greater influence may take actions in their own best interests, the outcomes of which increase their compensation from the company[76] Long tenure is known to restrict the breadth of an executive's knowledge base. With the limited perspectives associated with a restricted knowledge base, long-tenured top executives typically develop fewer alternatives to evaluate in making strategic decisions.[77] However, long-tenured managers also may be able to exercise more effective strategic control, thereby obviating the need for board members' involvement because effective strategic control generally produces higher performance.[78]

To strengthen the firm, boards of directors should develop an effective relationship with the firm's top management team that makes sense in a particular competitive situation.[79] Specifically, the relative degree of power held by the board and top management team members should be examined in light of the situation. The abundance of resources in a firm's external environment and the volatility of that environment may affect the ideal balance of power between boards and top management teams.[80] For instance, a volatile and uncertain environment may create a situation in which a powerful CEO is needed to move quickly, and a diverse top management team could create less cohesion among team members and prevent or stall a necessary strategic move.[81] By developing effective working relationships, boards, CEOs, and other top management team members are able to serve the best interests of the firm's stakeholders.[82]

Executive Succession Processes

The choice of top executives, especially CEOs, is a critical organizational decision with important implications for the firm's performance.[83] Many companies use leadership screening systems to identify individuals with managerial and strategic leadership potential. The most effective of these systems assess people within the firm and gain valuable information about the capabilities of other companies' managers, particularly their strategic leaders.[84] Based on the results of these assessments, training and development programs are provided for current managers in an attempt to preselect and shape the skills of people who may become tomorrow's leaders. The "ten-step talent" management development program at General Electric, for example, is considered one of the most effective in the world.[85]

Organizations select strategic leaders from two types of managerial labor markets: internal and external.[86] An *internal managerial labor market* consists of the opportunities for managerial positions within a firm, and an *external managerial labor market* consists of career opportunities for managers in organizations other than the one for which they work currently.

In the past, companies have strongly preferred that insiders fill top management positions because of a desire for continuity and a continuing commitment to the firm's current vision, mission, and chosen strategies.[87] Research shows that insider CEOs are more effective and provide more successful change programs after three years.[88] Several benefits are thought to accrue to firms when insiders are selected as new CEOs. Because of their experience with the firm and the industry environment in which they compete, insiders are familiar with company products, markets, technologies, and operating procedures. Also, internal hiring produces lower turnover among existing personnel, many of whom possess valuable firm-specific knowledge such as unique routines, processes, documentation, or trade secrets.

Thus, when the firm is performing well, internal succession is favored because it is assumed that hiring from inside keeps within the firm the important knowledge necessary to sustain the high performance. For an inside move to the top to occur successfully, however, firms must develop and implement effective succession management programs, which help develop managers so that one will eventually be prepared to ascend to the top.[89]

Given the impressive success of General Electric over the past 20-plus years and its highly effective management development program, an insider, Jeffrey Immelt, was chosen to succeed Jack Welch.[90] Similarly, at IBM, Virginia Rometty, also an insider, was selected to replace Samuel Palmisano. However, because of changing competitive landscapes and varying levels of performance, an increasing number of boards of directors have been turning to outsiders to succeed CEOs.[91] Firms often hire an executive recruitment firm, or "headhunter," to help identify and recruit strong candidates. Although valid reasons often exist for selecting an outsider, often this is done because boards have not established well-developed, internal succession places. However, if strategic change is needed often an outsider is selected. For example, research suggests that executives who have spent their entire careers with a particular firm may become "stale in the saddle."[92] Long tenure with a firm seems to reduce the number of innovative ideas top executives are able to develop to cope with conditions their firms face. Given the importance of innovation for a firm's success in today's competitive landscape, an inability to innovate or to create conditions that stimulate innovation throughout a firm is a liability in a strategic leader. The diverse knowledge base and social networks they have developed while working for other organizations is another reason to hire from the external managerial labor market.[93] Unique combinations of diverse knowledge sets might create synergy as the foundation for developing new competitive advantages.

Figure 30.2 shows how the composition of the top management team and CEO succession (managerial labor market) may interact to affect strategy. For example, when the top management team is homogeneous (its members have similar functional experiences and educational backgrounds) and a new CEO is selected from inside the firm, the firm's current strategy is unlikely to change. On the other hand, when a new CEO is selected from outside the firm and the top management team is heterogeneous, there is a high probability that strategy will change. When the new CEO is from inside the firm and a heterogeneous top management team is in place, the strategy may not change, but innovation is likely to continue. An external CEO succession with a homogeneous team creates a more ambiguous situation.

Figure 30.2 Effect of CEO Succession and Top Management Team Composition on Strategy

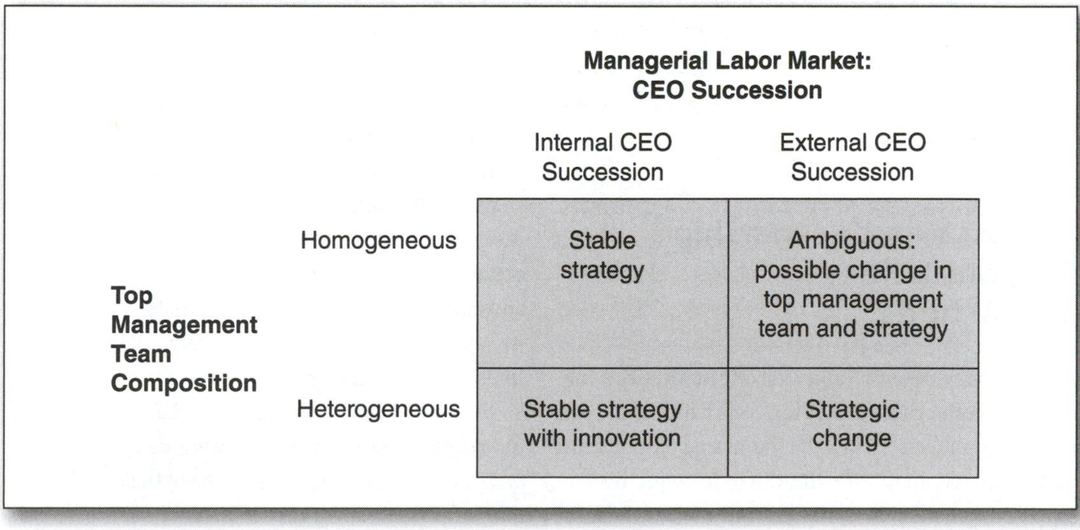

		Managerial Labor Market: CEO Succession	
		Internal CEO Succession	External CEO Succession
Top Management Team Composition	Homogeneous	Stable strategy	Ambiguous: possible change in top management team and strategy
	Heterogeneous	Stable strategy with innovation	Strategic change

© Cengage Learning

Given the need for diverse managerial perspectives in an increasingly competitive marketplace, it is unfortunate that some firms are still reluctant to fill their top jobs with individuals who might bring a different view to the table.[94] In particular, minority groups and especially women are underrepresented in the top positions of major for-profit organizations.[95] From a resource-based perspective, this is unfortunate because it signals that some firms are not taking full advantage of the resources they possess.[96] The stakeholder view also would suggest that a firm that creates a "glass ceiling" for some of its members with regard to their promotion potential is missing opportunities to foster relationships with diverse segments of society.

Nevertheless, women are making slow but steady progress in receiving more appointments in upper-level positions in for-profit firms, particularly in certain industries.[97] For example, Xerox CEO Ursala Burns (took over the helm from Anne Mulcahy and was the first female to female successor CEO among Fortune 500 firms), IBM CEO Virginia Rometty, and Hewlett Packard CEO Meg Whitman (also former CEO of eBay) are examples of women who have broken through the gender barrier. Additionally, organizations are beginning, to utilize women's potential managerial talents through memberships on corporate boards of directors. In the top 100 firms in New York, 17 percent of board members are women.[98] These additional appointments suggest that women's ability to represent stakeholders' and especially shareholders' best interests in for-profit companies at the level of the board of directors is being more broadly recognized.

Key Strategic Leadership Responsibilities and Actions

The primary responsibility for strategic thinking, and the effective strategic leadership that can result from it, rests with the top management team and, in particular, with the CEO. Strategic leadership is an extremely complex, but critical, form of leadership. Strategies cannot be formulated and implemented to achieve above-average returns unless strategic leaders successfully fulfill several important responsibilities.

As described in Chapter 1, the I/O economic, resource-based, and stakeholder perspectives envision the strategic management process from different points of view. The three perspectives also provide different views regarding the primary responsibilities of strategic leaders. From an economic perspective, top managers have the primary responsibility for ensuring that firm strategies will lead to above-average economic performance by monitoring the external environment and positioning the firm optimally in terms of its strategic direction, strategies, and implementation plans.[99] According to the resource-based view, top managers are primarily responsible for making sure their organizations acquire, develop, and utilize resources that lead to achieving competitive advantage.[100] Finally, the stakeholder perspective gives top managers primary responsibility for managing relationships with important constituencies to facilitate the creation of value.[101]

These three perspectives reflect the varied responsibilities and tasks associated with strategic leadership. They emphasize different aspects of a strategic leader's job, but in reality top managers have all of the responsibilities outlined by each of the perspectives, although they may give them a different priority. As illustrated in Figure 30.3, the responsibilities of strategic leaders are translated into specific tasks associated with the strategic management process. These tasks include determining and communicating strategic direction, facilitating and overseeing the formulation and implementation of specific strategies, and establishing balanced controls to ensure that the firm is accomplishing what it should to move in the desired direction. When executed properly, these actions result in the establishment of competitive advantage, creation of greater value for the firm and its stakeholders, and, ultimately, above-average financial performance.

Strategic leaders have substantial decision-making responsibilities that cannot be delegated.[102] The rest of this chapter discusses some of the most important of these, using the responsibilities and tasks found in Figure 30.3 as an outline.

Figure 30.3	Strategic Management Models and Effective Strategic Leadership

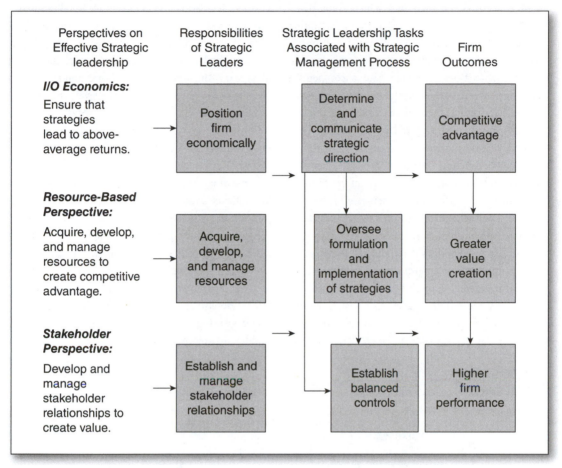

© Cengage Learning.

Ensure That the Firm Is Well Positioned Economically

The I/O economic model is based on the idea that economic performance is determined by a firm's general, industry, and competitor environments and by how well the firm implements the strategy dictated by those environments (see Chapter 1). Consequently, strategic leadership involves selecting industries and industry segments in which to compete and responding to changes that occur in those environments. Effective strategic leaders engage in strategic thinking that leads to the firm and its environment being continuously aligned. Individual judgment plays an important part in learning about and analyzing the firm's external conditions. As Dan DiMicco, CEO of the steel giant Nucor, put it, "What I get paid for is not looking at yesterday, but looking at the future."[103]

Another way to envision the positioning responsibility of strategic leaders is to say that they should clearly define a firm's strategy, which is a manifestation of strategic intent. Strategic intent was defined in the first chapter as the way a firm leverages its resources, capabilities, and core competencies to accomplish its goals in the competitive environment.[104] Unfortunately, the term "strategy" has taken on so many meanings that it can be used to mean almost anything. For instance, some firms may define their strategy in terms of how they treat people, whereas others may talk about particular markets or products. Hambrick and Fredrickson suggest that strategy is "the central, integrated, externally oriented concept of how we will achieve our objectives."[105] Their view is consistent with our definition in Chapter 1 that strategy is an integrated and coordinated set of commitments and actions designed to exploit core competencies and gain a competitive advantage. A firm's fundamental purposes, reflected in its mission and goals, are treated separately from a firm's strategy. Instead, the strategy becomes a vehicle to achieve the firm's purposes. Organizational arrangements such as structures, processes, rewards systems, and functional policies also support but do not define strategy. Strategic leaders use the tools of strategic analysis, including analysis of industries, markets, competitors, and internal strengths and weaknesses, to help them determine firm strategy.[106]

Five important elements that identify a firm's strategy are arenas, growth vehicles, differentiators, staging, and the economic logic that ties all the elements together (see Figure 30.4). *Arenas* involve a firm's scope, which is the breadth of a firm's activities across products, markets, geographic regions, core technologies, and value creation stages. Defining the business is a critical starting point for all strategic planning and management.[107] Firms like Siemens AG, Sony, and General Electric have broad scope because of their involvement in a wide range of industries throughout the world. On the other hand, Frontier Airlines focuses its efforts exclusively on airline transportation in the western United States. McDonald's has wide geographic scope, but most of its revenues come from a particular technology—fast food preparation and delivery.

Growth vehicles also are important to understanding a firm's strategy. Some of the commonly used vehicles are internal development, joint ventures, licensing, franchising, and acquisitions. General Electric has historically engaged in frequent acquisitions to increase the scope of its businesses, as well as many joint ventures to enter new markets (such as China). Choice Hotels used franchising to become one of the fastest growing hotel operators in the country using middle market brands such as the Comfort Inn,

Figure 30.4	The Five Major Elements of Strategy

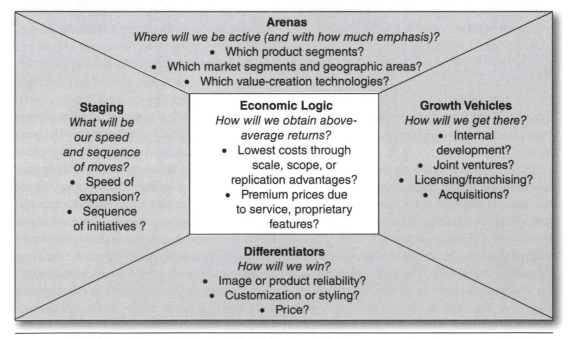

Source: Based on D. C. Hambrick & I. W. Fredrickson. 2005, Are you sure you have a strategy? *Academy of Management Executive.* 19(4): 54, reprinted from 15(4).

Comfort Suites, Cambria Suites, Sleep Inn, Mainstay Suites, Quality Inn, Clarion, EconoLodge, Rodeway Inn, and Suburban Extended Stay throughout the United States and more than 40 countries and territories.[108] On the other hand, hotel and restaurant chains such as Marriott and Starbucks, respectively, have grown rapidly primarily through internal development rather than franchising.

Differentiators help a firm determine how it is expected to win customers in the marketplace. Southwest Airlines attracts customers through rock-bottom prices and by staying on schedule. McDonald's draws people in by offering them dependable quality and convenient locations. A company like General Electric has a more difficult problem in defining a consistent differentiator for its multitude of businesses. In fact, in diversified firms it is probably a better idea to allow the top management team of each distinct business to determine how it will win customers. However, even firms as highly diversified as General Electric may try to establish core competencies that differentiate several businesses in similar ways. For instance, General Electric stresses finding innovative ways to satisfy customer needs. According to CEO Jeffrey Immelt: "For GE, imagination at work is more than a slogan or tagline. It is a reason for being."[109]

Staging has to do with the timing of strategy and the sequence of moves the firm will take to carry it out. It is especially important because of the speed with which the competitive environment is changing.[110] For instance, Microsoft has been criticized because it is sometimes slow to respond to changes in its markets such as the move to mobile computing.[111] However, being fast to market is not a guarantee of success either. Consider that Yahoo! Inc. was an early entrant in the search market, but through a series of missteps, the company now struggles to survive in this market.[112] Strategic leaders must make sure that everything is in place as they execute a strategy. As an example, Boeing had to work out problems with its unions before building its 787 Dreamliner, which required major changes to the firm's manufacturing processes.[113]

The *economic logic* of a strategy pulls together the other four elements. From an economic perspective, a strategy is unsuccessful unless its elements lead to above-average returns. When everything comes together, the results can be outstanding. The Boeing case, however, also illustrates one of the major themes of this book—the need for constant reassessment of strategy in an ever-changing external environment. For example, as consumers demanded cutting-edge products and better service, Dell lost its number one slot to rival Hewlett-Packard, but as the move to mobile and cloud computing illustrates, Apple has become the leader through the iPad tablet and other mobile devices.[114]

Acquire, Develop, and Manage Key Resources

The resource-based perspective focuses attention on the value of organizational resources in achieving competitive advantage. Strategic leaders are primarily responsible for ensuring that their firms acquire and develop the resources they need to achieve competitive success. Briefly mentioned in Chapter 1, *core competencies* are resources and capabilities that serve as a source of competitive advantage for a firm over its rivals. Firms develop and exploit core competencies in many different functional areas. Strategic leaders must verify that the firm's competencies are emphasized in strategy implementation efforts.

Much of Chapter 4 deals with organizational resources and their potential as sources of competitive advantage. However, two resources—human capital and organizational culture—are so closely related to strategic leadership that we discuss them briefly here.

Manage human capital. The ability to manage human capital, or the knowledge and skills of a firm's entire workforce, may be the most critical of the strategic leader's skills.[115] Intellectual capital, including the ability to manage knowledge and create and commercialize innovation, affects a strategic leader's success.[116] Competent strategic leaders also establish the context through which stakeholders (such as employees, customers, and suppliers) can perform at peak efficiency.[117] The crux of strategic leadership is the ability to manage the firm's operations and employees effectively in order to sustain high performance over time.

From the perspective of human capital, employees are viewed as a capital resource that requires investment.[118] These investments are productive, in that much of the development of U.S. industry can be attributed to the effectiveness of its human capital, leading to the conviction in many business firms today that "as the dynamics of competition accelerate, people are perhaps the only truly sustainable source of competitive advantage."[119] Human capital's increasing importance suggests a significant role for the firm's human resource management activities.[120] As a support activity (see Chapter 4), human resource management practices facilitate people's efforts to successfully select and especially to use the firm's strategies.[121]

Finding the human capital necessary to run an organization effectively is a challenge that many firms attempt to solve by using temporary employees. Other firms try to improve their recruiting and selection techniques. Solving the problem, however, requires more than hiring temporary employees; it requires building effective commitments to organizational goals as well. Hiring star players is also insufficient; rather, a strategic leader needs to build an effective organizational team committed to achieving the company's strategic intent.[122]

Increasingly, international experience has become essential to the development necessary for strategic leaders.[123] Because nearly every industry is targeting fast-growing foreign markets, more companies are requiring "global competency" among their top managers. Thus, companies trying to learn how to compete successfully in the global economy should find opportunities for their future strategic leaders to work in locations outside of their home nation. When multinational corporations invest in emerging economies, they are also wise to invest in human capital in foreign subsidiaries.[124] Furthermore, because international management capabilities are becoming important, managing "inpatriation" (the process of transferring host-country or third-country national managers into the domestic market of multinational firms) has become an important means of building global core competencies.[125]

Effective training and development programs increase the probability that a manager will be a successful strategic leader. These programs have grown progressively important as knowledge has become more integral to gaining and sustaining a competitive advantage.[126] Additionally, such programs build knowledge and skills, inculcate a common set of core values, and offer a systematic view of the organization, thus promoting the firm's strategic vision and organizational cohesion. The programs also contribute to the development of core competencies. Furthermore, they help strategic leaders improve skills that are critical to completing other tasks associated with effective strategic leadership, such as determining the firm's strategic direction, exploiting and maintaining the firm's core competencies, and developing an organizational culture that supports ethical practices. Thus, building human capital is vital to the effective execution of strategic leadership.

Strategic leaders must acquire the skills necessary to help develop human capital in their areas of responsibility. This challenge is important, given that most strategic leaders need to enhance their human resource management and collaborative abilities.[127] For example, firms that value human resources and have effective reward plans for employees have obtained higher returns on their initial public offerings.[128] When human capital investments are successful, the result is a workforce capable of learning continuously. Continuous learning and leveraging the firm's expanding knowledge base are linked with strategic success.[129]

Programs that achieve outstanding results in the training of future strategic leaders become a competitive advantage for a firm. General Electric's system of training and development of future strategic leaders is comprehensive and thought to be among the best.[130] Accordingly, it may be a source of competitive advantage for the firm.

Ensure an effective organizational culture. An organizational culture consists of a complex set of ideologies, symbols, and core values that is shared throughout the firm and influences the way business is conducted. Evidence suggests that a firm can develop core competencies in terms of both the capabilities it possesses and the way the capabilities are used to produce strategic actions. In other words, because the organizational culture influences how the firm conducts its business and helps regulate and control employees' behavior, it can be a source of competitive advantage.[131] Thus, shaping the context within which the firm formulates and implements its strategies—that is, shaping the organizational culture—is a central task of strategic leaders.[132]

An organizational culture often encourages (or discourages) the pursuit of entrepreneurial opportunities, especially in large firms.[133] Entrepreneurial opportunities are an important source of growth and innovation; therefore, a key role of strategic leaders is to encourage and promote innovation by pursuing entrepreneurial opportunities.[134] One way to do this is to invest in opportunities as real options—that is, opportunities that provide options to make additional worthwhile investments in the future, if the situation calls for it. For example, a firm may purchase property now because it wants the option to build on it in the future. Chapter 12 describes how large firms use strategic entrepreneurship to pursue entrepreneurial opportunities and to gain first-mover advantages. Chapter 13 covers the real options approach. Medium and small firms also rely on strategic entrepreneurship when trying to develop innovations as the foundation for earning above-average returns. In firms of all sizes, strategic entrepreneurship is more likely to be successful when employees have an entrepreneurial orientation. Five dimensions characterize a firm's entrepreneurial orientation: autonomy, innovativeness, risk taking, proactiveness, and competitive aggressiveness.[135] In combination, these dimensions influence the actions a firm takes in efforts to be innovative and launch new ventures.

Autonomy allows employees to take actions that are free of organizational constraints and permits individuals and groups to be self-directed. *Innovativeness* "reflects a firm's tendency to engage in and support new ideas, novelty, experimentation, and creative processes that may result in new products, services, or technological processes."[136] Cultures with a tendency toward innovativeness encourage employees to think beyond existing knowledge, technologies, and parameters in efforts to find creative ways to add value. *Risk taking* reflects a willingness by employees and their firm to accept risks when pursuing entrepreneurial opportunities. These risks can

include assuming significant levels of debt and allocating substantial other resources (e.g., people) to projects that may not be completed. *Proactiveness* describes a firm's ability to be a market leader rather than a follower. Proactive organizational cultures constantly use processes to anticipate future market needs and to satisfy them before competitors learn how to do so. Finally, *competitive aggressiveness* is a firm's propensity to take actions that allow it to consistently and substantially outperform its rivals.[137]

Changing a firm's organizational culture is more difficult than maintaining it, but effective strategic leaders recognize when change is needed. Incremental changes to the firm's culture typically are used to implement strategies. More significant and sometimes even radical changes to organizational culture are used to support the selection of strategies that differ from those the firm has implemented historically. Regardless of the reasons for change, shaping and reinforcing a new culture require effective communication and problem solving, along with the selection of the right people (those who have the values desired for the organization), effective performance appraisals (establishing goals and measuring individual performance toward goals that fit in with the new core values), and appropriate reward systems (rewarding the desired behaviors that reflect the new core values).[138]

Evidence suggests that cultural changes succeed only when the firm's CEO, other key top management team members, and middle-level managers actively support them.[139] Ronald Johnson was recently hired by J.C. Penney to become its CEO. Johnson was formerly the marketing director for Apple Computer Stores. Johnson's new vision suggests that it will be a "seismic shift cutting across all aspects of the company's pricing, promotion, presentation and products."[140] Such a dramatic change will require all employees, and especially the middle-level and top executives, to implement this new strategy. However, J.C. Penney might experience some customer and supplier pushback regarding its new schemes as they seek to adjust to the "new J.C. Penney." In the store, the floor will convert from the current open seas of racks to 100 individual shop concepts for private and national brands, including Izod, Arizona, and Liz

Claiborne. Each month, J.C. Penney's will stage sales and promotions tied to holidays and special events such as Valentine's Day or the Super Bowl.[141] In this example we see the importance of successfully changing an organization's culture linked to efforts to develop human capital and manage stakeholders to develop competitive advantage.

Develop and Manage Relationships With External Stakeholders

Many of the benefits associated with effective stakeholder management (as outlined in Chapter 1) depend on the actions and attitudes of the top management team, and especially the CEO. A CEO who fosters excellent relationships with key stakeholders can help the organization acquire timely and more accurate information about the external environment, which can enhance planning and decision making.[142] Furthermore, firms that have better reputations because of excellent stakeholder relationships may have the advantage of attracting customers and business partners, giving them more and better strategic options from which to select.[143] Also, a relationship of trust between top managers and external stakeholders can help to facilitate acquisition of valuable resources and reduce transaction costs associated with elaborate contractual safeguards and contingencies that might otherwise be necessary.[144] As the business world continues to increase in complexity and businesses become more interdependent, the leadership role of managing external stakeholders takes on even more strategic importance.[145]

This section emphasizes the responsibilities of top managers in creating and managing relationships with external stakeholders. The last section, derived from the resource-based view, emphasizes the strategic role top managers play in acquiring, developing, and managing internal resources, especially human capital and organizational culture. Although discussed separately, these two perspectives overlap, as do the roles strategic leaders play. For instance, from a resource-based perspective, stakeholder relationships *are* strategic resources that can help a firm acquire additional resources and thereby maintain competitive advantage.[146] Also, the stakeholder perspective includes management of both external *and* internal stakeholders.

Economic positioning also is conceptually linked to the other two perspectives. For instance, external stakeholder management is closely associated with the monitoring that occurs as strategic leaders position their firms in their industries. Also, possession of particular resources and skills positions a firm relative to its competitors. Responsibilities associated with all three of the perspectives result in strategic direction and formulation and implementation of specific strategies (see Figure 30.3).

Determine and Communicate Strategic Direction

The strategic direction of a firm defines its image and character over time, framed within the context of the conditions in which it operates. Like a firm's strategy, it grows out of strategic intent and is a function of the resources and capabilities a firm possesses or wishes to possess, as well as what the firm wants to do for its stakeholders. The CEO is the chief architect of strategic direction, although most top executives obtain input from many people inside and outside the organization.[147] Research has shown that having an effective strategic direction and properly reinforcing it can positively affect performance as measured by growth in sales, profits, employment, and net worth.[148]

Strategic direction is reflected in the firm's mission, vision, purpose, long-term goals, and values, which tend to be interconnected. In fact, sometimes a mission statement includes many of these things, such as Novartis' mission statement found in Table 30.1. Novartis has five divisions representing pharmaceuticals, Alcon (eye care products), Sandoz (generic drugs), vaccines and diagnostics, and consumer health.

A carefully constructed strategic mission should help the firm define the scope of its operations as well as its unique purposes.[149] With regard to scope, Novartis has defined its businesses in terms of customer functions. Specifically, the company's products

Table 30.1	Mission of Novartis

Purpose
We want to discover, develop and successfully market innovative products to prevent and cure diseases, to ease suffering, and to enhance the quality of life. We also want to provide a shareholder return that reflects outstanding performance and to adequately reward those who invest ideas and work in our company.
People
We strive to provide our associates with the safest possible workplace and to promote their health and well-being. We are an integral part of the communities that host our operations. We pay living wages worldwide, contributing to the stability and prosperity of these communities. With more than 120,000 associates in 140 countries worldwide, Novartis associates share a vision of **a better today and tomorrow for patients**—a vision that drives our growth and success. The greatest job satisfaction for our associates is the knowledge that they improve the quality of life for patients with increasing precision and efficiency through breakthrough science and innovation. Our performance-oriented culture and responsible approach attract top experts in all areas—research and development, marketing and sales, finance and administration. Our talented associates have made us a global leader in healthcare. Novartis is committed to rewarding the people who invest ideas and work in our company.

Source: Adapted from the following Website http://www.novartis.com/about-novartis/our-mission/index .shtml, visited on February 21, 2012.

and services prevent and cure diseases, ease suffering, and enhance the quality of life. Typically, purposes are defined in terms of what a firm intends to do for particular stakeholders. For instance, a firm may want to achieve high returns for shareholders or provide a motivating environment for employees. In the Novartis example, in addition to what the company intends to do for its customers, it aspires to help employees realize professional ambitions and to contribute to society and the environment. The company values of openness, innovation, and financial success are also found in the mission statement.

Some firms also include the concept of sustainability in their mission statement. **Sustainable development**, the concept that a firm can and should operate without adversely influencing its environment, has been gaining strategic importance in recent years.[150] The ideal long-term vision has two parts: a core ideology and an envisioned future. The core ideology motivates employees through the company's heritage, and the envisioned future encourages employees to stretch beyond their comfort zones.[151]

"Stretch goals" promote higher levels of personal and organizational performance.[152] The vision of Novartis is reflected by a desire to be recognized for having a positive effect on the fives of customers, employees, the environment, and society. This vision is built on a long history of success in the health sciences. Novartis also wants to remain in the top quartile of its industry based on growth in earnings. Achieving this goal over the long term will require a very high level of motivation among managers and employees. The company will have to continue to innovate and change in order to remain competitive in its volatile and highly competitive industry.

Although the Novartis example is particularly comprehensive, it is not unusual to find many of the components of strategic direction in a strategic mission statement. On the other hand, sometimes strategic direction is not found in a written statement, or it is divided into an assortment of statements with different names and purposes. Also, labels are used in a variety of different ways. What is most important is that the firm has a well-defined strategic direction and that it communicates the direction to internal and, to some extent, external stakeholders. Annual reports, speeches, press releases, training sessions, meetings, interpersonal communication, and comments from executives are all vehicles for communicating strategic direction.[153]

Internal stakeholders, including executives, managers, and employees, need to know the strategic direction so that it can guide them in their decision making. The firm can also communicate certain elements of its strategic direction to external stakeholders to help them know what to expect from the organization. Obviously, investors use such information to help them predict the firm's future performance. However, customers, communities, suppliers, venture partners, special interest groups, and regulators can benefit from understanding what the firm values and how it conducts business. In the wake of recent corporate scandals, this element of strategic direction has been receiving significantly more attention.

Establish values and ethical practices. Mission statements often refer to values associated with ethical practices. In addition, codes of ethics frequently are created to reinforce those values. For instance, United Technologies has a twenty page code of ethics based on the values of trust, respect, and integrity.[154] Nevertheless, values statements and codes of ethics are not a guarantee that managers and employees will act ethically.[155] The infamous sixty-four-page "Code of Ethics" allegedly published by Enron Corporation begins with a statement from CEO Kenneth Lay: "As officers and employees of Enron Corp., its subsidiaries, and its affiliated companies, we are responsible for conducting the business affairs of the companies in accordance with all applicable laws and in a moral and honest manner."[156] Managerial opportunism may explain the behavior and decisions of key executives at Enron, where stockholders lost almost all the value in their Enron stock during the firm's bankruptcy proceeding. The bankruptcy was precipitated by off-balance-sheet partnerships formed by Enron managers.[157] The reputation of Arthur Andersen, Enron's auditor, was also damaged beyond repair, resulting ultimately in the company surrendering its license to practice as certified public accountants.[158]

There were a number of recent departures of CEOs based on ethical lapses and associated corporate scandals. Jon Corzine, former CEO of MF Global, left the organization because it defaulted on its loans and lost control of investors' funds and was forced into bankruptcy. Interestingly, Corzine was a former U.S. senator, former Democratic governor of New Jersey, and ex-CEO of Goldman Sachs, a famous investment bank. In addition, CEO Michael Woodford was forced to resign from Japanese camera maker Olympus after he questioned billions of dollars in takeover costs that had been put in its books by former executives of the company. Although the company used the excuse that Woodford's style was "too independent and not respectful enough of Japanese culture," company representatives have since admitted that it had falsified the books in regard to the costs questioned by Woodford.[159]

Ethical companies encourage and enable people at all organizational levels to act ethically when doing what is necessary to implement the firm's strategies. In turn, ethical practices and the judgment on which they are based create "social capital" in the organization in that "goodwill available to individuals and groups" in the organization increases.[160] Thus, leadership is essential in providing examples upon which to model the ethics values, and the approach that leaders provide influences the values that employees adopt in the interaction with stakeholders.[161] Alternately, when unethical practices evolve in an organization, they become like a contagious disease.[162] Firms that have been reported to have poor ethical behavior, such as practicing fraud or having to restate financial results, see their overall corporate value in the stock market drop precipitously.[163]

News Corp. chairman Rupert Murdoch supervises a global media empire that covers newspapers, cable news companies, as well as newspaper organizations. The *News of the World* tabloid owned by Murdoch but amounting to only 3 percent of the News Corp. assets, participated in phone hacking that caused a scandal that called into question the integrity of the whole media empire. The scandal caused News Corp. stock to drop by $5 billion worth of equity. In the process, those politicians who associated with the CEO of *News of the World,* Rebekah Brooks, a former newspaper executive at News Corp., had their credibility questioned. Andrew Coulson, one of the former executives at News Corp., was indicted and had to be fired by the British Prime Minister, David Cameron, because he had hired Coulson as his press secretary. Much of the scandal could have been avoided had Murdoch and his executives apologized and performed an open investigation into the dealings of *News of the World.* Instead, News Corp. uses this ethic of responding: "If you are attacked from the outside, you defend." They never admitted wrongdoing or sought to get to the bottom of the issue, and created instead a lax focus on ethics. Apparently the newspaper ethic at the *News of the World* tabloid focused on "scoop-obsessed . . . cut throat competition in which the ends—a good story—always justifies the frequently unedifying means."[164] This is an example where the informal ethics of the company leaders caused havoc not only to the individual tabloid (the tabloid was shut down), but also cast doubt on all the media outlets of the News Corp. empire and even impacted the political credibility of the U.K. Prime Minister, David Cameron.[165]

To properly influence employees' judgment and behavior, ethical practices must shape the firm's decision-making process and be an integral part of an organization's culture. In fact, research has found that a value-based culture is the most effective means of ensuring that employees comply with the firm's ethical requirements.[166] Evidence also suggests that managers' values are critical in shaping a firm's cultural values.[167] Consequently, firms should employ ethical strategic leaders—leaders who include ethical practices as part of their long-term vision for the firm, who desire to do the right thing, and for whom honesty, trust, and integrity are important. Strategic leaders who consistently display these qualities inspire employees as they work with others to develop and support an organizational culture in which ethical practices are the expected behavioral norms. In addition to being good examples, top managers may also institute formal programs to manage ethics. Operating much like control systems, these programs help inculcate values throughout the organization.[168]

Additional actions strategic leaders can take to develop an ethical organizational culture include (1) establishing and communicating specific goals to describe the firm's ethical standards (e.g., developing and disseminating a code of conduct); (2) continuously revising and updating the code of conduct on the basis of input from people throughout the firm and from other stakeholders (e.g., customers and suppliers); (3) disseminating the code of conduct to all stakeholders to inform them of the firm's ethical standards and practices; (4) developing and implementing methods and procedures to use in achieving the firm's ethical standards (e.g., using internal auditing practices that are consistent with the standards); (5) creating and using explicit reward systems that recognize acts of courage (e.g., rewarding those who use proper channels and procedures to report observed wrongdoing); and (6) creating a work environment in which all people are treated with dignity.[169] The effectiveness of these actions increases when they are taken simultaneously, thereby making them mutually supportive.

Oversee Formulation and Implementation of Specific Strategies

Strategic leaders are responsible for ensuring that appropriate strategies are both formulated and successfully implemented. Earlier in this chapter we outlined the responsibilities of strategic leaders from three perspectives. Each of these perspectives results in a slightly different but interrelated view of strategy formulation and implementation. I/O economics suggests that strategy is based on evaluation of the external environment and positioning the firm optimally in that environment. Implementation involves developing structures, systems, and programs to reinforce the position.[170] The resource-based view focuses on the acquisition and development of uniquely valuable resources and capabilities that are hard for competitors to imitate, thus leading to competitive advantage. Implementation plans involve making optimal use of and supporting those resources and capabilities.[171] The stakeholder perspective leads to strategies that attempt to make optimal use of relationships with stakeholders to create value. Implementation involves activities such as collecting information from stakeholders, assessing their needs and desires, integrating this knowledge into strategic decisions, effectively managing internal stakeholders, and forming interorganizational relationships with external stakeholders.[172] Chapters 5 through 10 discuss the specific nature of these strategies and how they are implemented.

Strategic direction also influences a firm's specific strategies. For instance, a firm's mission defines its basic approach to corporate-level strategy and may contain clues regarding the resources and skills that form the base for its business-level strategies. In addition, strategic direction serves as a guide to many aspects of a firm's strategy implementation process, including motivation, leadership, employee empowerment, and organizational design. In the case of Novartis, the company is supporting its mission by transforming its headquarters in Basel, Switzerland, into an ultramodern, high-performance workplace that facilitates research and fosters communication and collaboration.[173]

Once strategic leaders have guided the establishment of the firm's strategic direction, strategies, and implementation plans, their final responsibility is to establish organizational control systems to ensure that the plans are actually executed and to measure their success and provide feedback.

Establish Balanced Controls

Organizational controls have long been viewed as an important part of strategy implementation processes. Controls are necessary to help ensure that firms achieve their desired outcomes.[174] Defined as the "formal, information-based . . . procedures used by managers to maintain or alter patterns in organizational activities," controls help strategic leaders build credibility, demonstrate the value of strategies to the firm's stakeholders, and promote and support strategic change.[175] Most critically, controls provide the parameters within which strategies are to be implemented, as well as corrective actions to be taken when implementation-related adjustments are required.

We examine control structures associated with each strategy type (Business-level in Chapter 5, Cooperative Strategy in Chapter 7, Corporate-level in Chapter 8, and International Strategy in Chapter 10). Chapter 11 on corporate governance discusses top executive controls in greater detail, but here we look briefly at financial and strategic controls because strategic leaders are responsible for their development and effective use. Financial control focuses on short-term financial outcomes. In contrast, *strategic control* focuses on the content of strategic actions, rather than their outcomes. Some strategic actions can be correct, but poor financial outcomes may still result because of external conditions, such as a recession in the economy, unexpected domestic or foreign government actions, or natural disasters.[176] Therefore, an emphasis on financial control often produces more short-term and risk-averse managerial decisions because financial outcomes may be caused by events beyond managers' direct control. Alternatively, strategic control encourages lower-level managers to make decisions that incorporate moderate and acceptable levels of risk because outcomes are shared between the business-level executives making strategic proposals and the corporate-level executives evaluating them.

The balanced scorecard. The balanced scorecard is a framework that strategic leaders can use to verify that they have established both financial controls and strategic controls to assess their firm's performance.[177] This technique is most appropriate when dealing with business-level strategies but can also apply to corporate-level strategies.

The underlying premise of the balanced scorecard is that firms jeopardize their future performance possibilities when financial controls are emphasized at the expense of strategic controls,[178] in that financial controls provide feedback about outcomes achieved from past actions but do not communicate the drivers of the firm's future performance.[179] Thus, an overemphasis on financial controls could promote organizational behavior that has a net effect of sacrificing the firm's long-term, value-creating potential for short-term performance gains.[180] An appropriate balance of financial controls and strategic controls, rather than an overemphasis on either, allows firms to effectively monitor their performance.

Figure 30.5	Strategic Controls and Financial Controls In a Balanced Scorecard Framework

Perspectives	Criteria
Financial	• Cash flow • Return on equity • Return on assets
Customer	• Assessment of ability to anticipate customer's needs • Effectiveness of customer service practices • Percentage of repeat businesss • Quality of communications with customers
Internal Business Procesess	• Asset utilization improvements • Improvements in employee morale • Changes in turnover rates
Learning and Growth	• Improvements in innovation ability • Number of new products compared to competitors' • Increases in employees' skills

© Cengage Learning.

Four perspectives are integrated to form the balanced scorecard framework (see Figure 30.5): *financial* (concerned with growth, profitability, and risk from the shareholders' perspective), *customer* (concerned with the amount of value that customers perceive was created by the firm's products), *internal business processes* (with a focus on the priorities for various business processes that create customer and shareholder satisfaction), and *learning and growth* (concerned with the firm's effort to create a climate that supports change, innovation, and growth). Thus, using the balanced scorecard's framework allows the firm to understand how it looks to shareholders (financial perspective), how customers view it (customer perspective), the processes it must emphasize to successfully use its competitive advantage (internal perspective), and what it can do to improve its performance in order to grow (learning and growth perspective). Porsche used a balanced-scorecard approach to promote learning and continuous improvement while maintaining a market-leading position among sports car manufacturers.[181]

Firms use different criteria to measure their standing relative to the scorecard's four perspectives (see Figure 30.5). These criteria should be established on the basis of what the firm is trying to accomplish and its strategic direction. The firm should select the number of criteria that will allow it to have both a strategic understanding and a financial understanding of its performance without becoming immersed in too many details.[182] Several performance criteria, such as those associated with financial and customer as well as purely internal perspectives, will be discussed in Chapter 4. Of course, the criteria frequently are interrelated.

Strategic leaders play an important role in determining a proper balance between strategic controls and financial controls for their firm. This is true in single-business firms as well as in diversified corporations. In fact, most corporate restructuring is designed to refocus the firm on its core businesses, thereby allowing top executives to reestablish strategic control of their separate business units.[183] Thus, both strategic controls and financial controls support effective use of the firm's corporate-level strategy.

Summary

- Effective strategic leadership is a prerequisite to successful use of the strategic management process. Strategic leadership entails the ability to anticipate events, envision possibilities, maintain flexibility, and empower others to create strategic change.

- Strategic leadership skills fall into a hierarchy, where managers must master lower-level skills before they fine-tune higher-level skills. Level 5 Executives have mastered all the skills.

- Strategic leaders differ in the way they direct the strategic management process. A traditional "commander" approach limits manager participation in strategic decisions, whereas a more collaborative style entails jointly arriving at strategies and implementation plans with members of the top management team. The appropriate style depends on the nature of the competitive situation.

- Top managers are constrained by a number of factors that influence the level of discretion they have when making decisions. Some of these factors are associated with the external environment, such as the industry structure, the rate of market growth in the firm's primary industry, and the degree to which products can be differentiated.

- Strategic managers sometimes rely on heuristics, or "rules of thumb," when they make strategic decisions. These heuristics help managers simplify what might otherwise be an overwhelmingly complicated and uncertain decision environment, but they also can lead to suboptimal decisions. Awareness of decision-making biases, use of real options analysis, and formation of a heterogeneous top management team can help strategic decision makers reduce the ill effects of decision biases.

- A top management team is composed of the chief executive officer and other key managers who are responsible for setting the direction of the firm and formulating and implementing its strategies. The quality of strategic thinking and subsequent strategic decisions made by a top management team affect the firm's ability to innovate and engage in effective strategic change.

- The overwhelming complexity and strength of environmental forces, as well as the need to manage a wide variety of stakeholder relationships, require formation of a heterogeneous top management team composed of individuals with different functional backgrounds, experience, and education. The more heterogeneous a top management team is, with varied expertise and knowledge, the more capacity it has to provide effective strategic leadership in formulating strategy.

- Higher firm performance normally is achieved when the board of directors is more directly involved in shaping a firm's strategic direction. However, directors may find it difficult to direct the strategic actions of powerful CEOs and top management teams. The relative power of top managers is at least partially a function of social or business ties with directors, their tenure as members of the top management team, and whether the CEO also serves as chair of the board.

- Organizations select strategic leaders from two types of managerial labor markets—internal and external. Use of the internal or external market depends, in part, on the need for change in the organization.

- Six key components of effective strategic leadership include ensuring that the firm is well-positioned economically, managing key resources, developing and maintaining effective relationships with key stakeholders, determining a strategic direction (which includes establishing values and ethical practices), overseeing the formulation and implementation of specific strategies, and establishing balanced organizational control systems.

- Strategic direction is reflected *in* the firm's mission, vision, purpose, long-term goals, and values, which tend to be interconnected. There are several vehicles, such as annual reports, speeches, and press releases, for communicating strategic direction.

- An effective balance between strategic and financial controls allows for the flexible use of core competencies, but within the parameters indicated by the firm's financial position. The balanced scorecard is a tool that strategic leaders use to develop an appropriate balance between the firm's strategic and financial controls.

Ethics Questions

1. What are the ethical issues influencing managerial discretion? Has the current business environment changed the influence of ethics on managerial discretion? If so, how?

2. How have ethical lapses influenced regulatory changes and how has the current stakeholders' view changed the expectations for strategic leaders in formulating and implementing contemporary strategies?

3. What should a newly appointed CEO from the external managerial labor market do to understand a firm's ethical climate? How important are the CEO's efforts to understand this climate?

4. Are ethical strategic leaders more effective than unethical strategic leaders? If so, why? If not, why not?

5. Assume that you are working in an organization that you believe has an unethical culture. What actions could you take to change that culture to make it more ethical?

6. Is corporate downsizing ethical? If not, why not? If corporate downsizing is ethical, what can strategic leaders do to mitigate the negative effects associated with reducing the size of their firm's labor force?

Notes

1. A. G.Lafley & N. M. Tichy, 2011, The art and science of finding the right CEO, *Harvard Business Review,* 89(10): 66–74.

2. 2006, Leadership styles at GE and Canon, *Strategic Direction,* 22(1): 15–20; R. Barnes, 2004, Executives who didn't survive Jack Welch's GE are now running 3M, Home Depot, *Knight Ridder Tribune Business News,* April 24, 1.

3. B. Moreton, 2009, To *Serve God and Wal-Mart: The Making of Christian Free Enterprise,* Cambridge, MA: Harvard University Press; C. H. Tong & L. I. Tong, 2006, Exploring the cornerstones of Wal-Mart's success and competitiveness, *Competitiveness Review,* 16(2): 143–149.

4. J. Greco, 1999, Akio Morita: A founder of Japan, Inc., *The Journal of Business Strategy,* 20(5): 38–39.

5. A. J. Kinicki, K. J. L. Jacobson, B. M. Galvin, & G, E. Prussia, 2011, A multilevel systems model of leadership, *Journal of Leadership & Organization Studies,* 18(2): 133–149.

6. Z. Zhen & S. J, Peterson, 2011, Advice networks in teams: The role of transformational leadership and members[1] core self-evaluations, *Journal of Applied Psychology,* 96(5): 1004–1017.

7. J. Collins, 2001, *Good to Great: Why Some Companies Make the Leap . . . and Others Don,* New York: Harper Business.

8. R. W. Evans & F. C. Butler, 2011, An upper echelons view of 'Good to Great': Principles for behavioral integration in the top management team, *Journal of Leadership Studies.* 5(2): 89–97.

9. 2011, The magician, *Economist,* October 8, 15.

10. J. Tian, J. Haieblian, & N. Rajagopalan, 2011, The effects of board human and social capital on investor reactions to new CEO selection, *Strategic Management Journal,* 32(7): 731–747.

11. E. Ng & G. Sears, 2012, CEO leadership styles and the implementation of organizational diversity practices: Moderating effects of social values and age, *Journal of Business Ethics,* 105(1): 41–52.

12. M. Carpenter & J. Fredrickson, 2001, Top management teams, global strategic posture, and the moderating role of uncertainty, *Academy of Management Journal,* 44: 533–545; S. F. Slater, 1989, The influence of style on business unit performance, *Journal of Management,* 15: 441–455,

13. L. Markóczy, 2001, Consensus formation during strategic change, *Strategic Management Journal,* 22: 1013–1031; D. Knight, C. L. Pearce, K. G. Smith, J. D. Olian, H. P. Sims, K. A. Smith, & P. Flood, 1999, Top management team diversity, group process, and strategic consensus, *Strategic Management Journal,* 20: 446–465.

14. H. Wang, A. S. Tsui, & K. R. Xin, 2011, CEO leadership behaviors, organizational performance, and employees' attitudes, *Leadership Quarterly,* 22(1): 92–105; M. de Luque, N. T. Washburn, D. A. Waldman, & R. J. House, 2008, Unrequited profit: How stakeholder and economic values relate to subordinates' perceptions of leadership and firm performance, *Administrative Science Quarterly,* 53(4): 626–654.

15. G. Sadri, T. J. Weber, & W. A. Gentry, 2011, Empathetic emotion and leadership performance: An empirical analysis across 38 countries, *Leadership Quarterly, 22(5):* 818–830; M. A. Hitt, M. T. Dacin, B. B. Tyler, & D. Park, 1997, Understanding the differences in Korean and U.S. executives' strategic orientations, *Strategic Management Journal,* 18: 159–167; Slater, The influence of style on business unit

performance; A. S. Thomas, R. J. Litschert, & K. Ramaswamy, 1991, The performance impact of strategy-manager co-alignment: An empirical examination, *Strategic Management Journal*, 12: 509–522.

16. V. Govindarajan, 1989, implementing competitive strategies at the business unit level: Implications of matching managers to strategies, *Strategic Management Journal*, 10:251–269.

17. A. K. Gupta & V. Govindarajan, 1984, Business unit strategy, managerial characteristics, and business unit effectiveness at strategy implementation, *Academy of Management Journal, 27:* 25–41.

18. M. F. Wiersema & K. A. Bantel, 1992, Top management team demography and corporate strategic change, *Academy of Management Journal*, 35: 91–121; K. A. Bantel & S. E. Jackson, 1989, Top management and innovations in banking: Does the composition of the top team make a difference? *Strategic Management journal*, 10: 107–124.

19. C. Crassland & D. C. Hambrick, 2011, Differences in managerial discretion across countries: How nation-level institutions affect the degree to which CEOs matter, *Strategic Management Journal*, 32(8): 797–819; D. C. Hambrick & E. Abrahamson, 1995, Assessing managerial discretion across industries: A multi-method approach, *Academy of Management journal*, 38: 1427–1441; D. C. Hambrick & S. Finkelstein, 1987, Managerial discretion: A bridge between polar views of organizational outcomes, in B. Staw & L. L. Cummings (Eds.), *Research in Organizational Behavior,* Greenwich, CT: JAI Press, 369–406.

20. D. G Sirmon, M. A. Hitt, R. D. Ireland, & B, Gilbert, 2011, Resource orchestration to create competitive advantage: Breadth, depth, and life cycle effects, *Journal of Management*, 37(5): 1390–1412; R. Whittington, 2003, The work of strategizing and organizing: For a practice perspective, *Strategic Organization*, 1: 117–125.

21. M. Workman, 2012, Bias in strategic initiative continuance decisions: Framing interactions and HRD practices, *Management Decision*, 50(1): 21–42; T. K, Das & B. S. Teng, 1999, Cognitive biases and strategic decision processes: An integrative perspective, *Journal of Management Studies*, 36: 757–778; C R. Schwenk, 1995, Strategic decision making, *Journal of Management*, 21: 471–493.

22. D. Kahneman, P. Slovic, & A. Tversky (eds.), 1982, *Judgment under Uncertainty: Heuristics and Biases,* New York: Cambridge University Press; A. Tversky & D. Kahneman, 1974, Judgment under uncertainty: Heuristics and biases, *Science*, 185: 1124–1131.

23. M. S. Gary & R. E. Wood, 2011, Mental models, decision rules and performance heterogeneity, *Strategic Management Journal*, 32: 569–594; Kahneman, Slovic, & Tversky, *Judgment under Uncertainty,*

24. M. H. Bazerman, 1994, *Judgment m Managerial Decision Making*, 3rd ed., New York: Wiley; R. M. Hogarth, 1980, *Judgment and Choice: The Psychology of Decision*, Chichester, UK: Wiley.

25. Das & Teng, Cognitive biases and strategic decision processes; J. G. March & Z. Shapira, 1987, Managerial perspectives on risk and risk taking, *Management Science,* 33: 1404–1418.

26. C. R. Schwenk, 1984, Cognitive simplification processes in strategic decision-making, *Strategic Management Journal*, 5: 111–128.

27. March & Shapira, Managerial perspectives.

28. R. E. Hoskisson, M. A. Hitt, & C W. L. Hill, 1991, Managerial risk taking in diversified firms: An evolutionary perspective, *Organization Science*, 2: 296–314.

29. J. Devan, K. Millan, & P. Shirke, 2005, Balancing short- and long-term performance, *McKinsey Quarterly,* 1: 31–33.

30. J. P. Walsh & W. R. Nord, 2005, Taking stock of stakeholder management. *Academy of Management Review,* 30: 426–438; J. E Post, L. E. Preston, & S. Sauter-Sachs, 2002, *Redefining the Corporation: Stakeholder Management and Organizational Wealth,* Stanford, CA: Stanford University Press.

31. March & Shapira, Managerial perspectives; J. W. Fredrickson, 1984, The comprehensiveness of strategic decision processes: Extension, observations, future directions, *Academy of Management Journal*, 27: 445–466.

32. J. W. Fredrickson, 1986, An exploratory approach to measuring perceptions of strategic decision constructs, *Strategic Management Journal*, 7: 473–483.

33. Z. Shapira, 1995, *Risk Taking: A Managerial Perspective*, New York: Russell Sage Foundation.

34. D. Kahneman & D. Lovallo, 1993, Timid choices and bold forecasts: A cognitive perspective on risk taking, *Management Science*, 39: 17–31.

35. R. Durand, 2003, Predicting a firm's forecasting ability: The roles of organizational illusion of control and organizational attention, *Strategic Management Journal*, 9: 821–838; E. J. Langer, 1975, Illusion of control, *Journal of Personality and Social Psychology*, 32: 311–328.

36. Shapira, *Risk Taking;* C. Vlek & P. J. Stallen, 1980, Rational and personal aspects of risk, *Acta Psycho-logica*, 45: 273–300.

37. D. Garcia, F. Sangiorgi, & B. Urošević, 2007, Overconfidence and market efficiency with heterogeneous assets,

Economic Theory, 30:313–336; R. A. Lowe & A. Arvids, 2006, Overoptimism and the performance of entrepreneurial firms, *Management Science,* 52: 173–186.

38. N. J. Fast, N. Sivanathan, N. D. Mayer, & A. D. Galinsky, 2012, Power and overconfident decision-making, *Organizational Behavior & Human Decision Processes,* 117(2): 249–260; N. J. Hiller & D. C. Hambrick, 2005, Conceptualizing executive hubris: The role of (hyper) core self-evaluations in strategic decision making, *Strategic Management Journal,* 26: 297–319.

39. J. B. Wade, J. F. Porac, T. G. Pollock, & S. D. Graff in, 2006, The burden of celebrity: The impact of CEO certification contests on CEO pay and performance, *Academy of Management Journal,* 49: 643–660.

40. S. Park, J. D. Westphal, & I. Stern, 2011, Set up for a fall: The insidious effects of flattery and opinion conformity toward corporate leaders, *Administrative Science Quarterly,* 56(2): 257–302; M. L. A. Hayward, V. P. Rindova, & T. G. Pollock, 2004, Believing one's own press: The causes and consequences of CEO celebrity, *Strategic Management Journal,* 25: 637–653.

41. Collins, *Good to Great.*

42. D. Kahneman, D. Lovallo, & O. Sibony, 2011, Before you make that big decision, *Harvard Business Review,* 89(6): 50–60.

43. A. Carmenli, A. Tishler, & A. C. Edmondson, 2012, CEO relational leadership and strategic decision quality in top management teams: The role of team trust and learning from failure, *Strategic Organization,* 10(1): 31–54; A. L. Iaquito & J. W. Fredrickson, 1997, Top management team agreement about the strategic decision process: A test of some of its determinants and consequences, *Strategic Management Journal,* 18: 63–75.

44. J. P. Gander, 2010, The managerial limit to the growth of firms revisited, *Managerial & Decision Economics,* 31(8): 549–555; R. Castanias & C. Helfat, 2001, The managerial rents model: Theory and empirical analysis, *Journal of Management,* 27: 661–678.

45. B. Frisch, 2011, Who really makes the big decisions in your company? *Harvard Business Review,* 89(12): 104–111; M. Beer & R. Eisenstat, 2000, The silent killers of strategy implementation and learning, *Sloan Management Review,* 41(4): 29–40; C. M. Christensen, 1997, Making strategy: Learning by doing, *Harvard Business Review,* 75(6): 141–156.

46. K. Talke, S. Salomo, & A. Kock, 2011, Top management team diversity and strategic innovation orientation: The relationship and consequences for innovativeness and performance. *Journal of Product innovation Management,*

28(6): 819–832; C. Pegels, Y. Song, & B. Yang, 2000, Management heterogeneity, competitive interaction groups, and firm performance, *Strategic Management Journal,* 21: 911–923.

47. S. T. Bell, A. J. Villado, M. A. Lukasik, L. Belau, & A. L. Briggs, 2011, Getting specific about demographic diversity variable and team performance relationships: A meta-analysis, *Journal of Management,* 37(3): 709–743.

48. A. Vance, 2012, c:\\Ballmer [Reboots], *Bloomberg Business Week,* January 16, 46–52.

49. Ibid., 49.

50. K. Talke, S. Salomo, & K. Rost, 2010, How top management team diversity affects innovativeness and performance via the strategic choice to focus on innovation fields, *Research Policy,* 39(7): 907–918; D. Knight, C. L. Pearce, K. G. Smith, J. D. Olian, H. P. Sims, K. A. Smith, & P. Flood, 1999, Top management team diversity, group process, and strategic consensus, *Strategic Management Journal,* 20: 446–465.

51. A. S. Alexiev, J. P. Jansen, F. J. Van den Bosch, & H. W. Volberda, 2010, Top management team advice seeking and exploratory innovation: The moderating role of TMT heterogeneity, *Journal of Management Studies,* 47(7): 1343–1364; J. Bunderson, 2003, Team member functional background and involvement in management teams: Direct effects and the moderating role of power and centralization, *Academy of Management Journal,* 46: 458–474.

52. K. Bongjin, M. L. Burns, & J. E. Prescott, 2009, The strategic role of the board: The impact of board structure on top management team strategic action capability, *Corporate Governance: An International Review,* 17(6): 728–743; D. C. Hambrick, T. S. Cho, & M. J. Chen, 1996, The influence of top management team heterogeneity on firms' competitive moves, *Administrative Science Quarterly,* 41: 659–684.

53. W. Yong, W. Zelong, & L. Qiaozhuan, 2011, Top management team diversity and strategic change: The moderating effects of pay imparity and organization slack, *Journal of Organizational Change Management,* 24(3): 267–281; S. Wally & M. Becerra, 2001, Top management team characteristics and strategic changes in international diversification: The case of U.S. multinationals in the European community, *Group & Organization Management,* 26: 165–188; W. Boeker, 1997, Strategic change: The influence of managerial characteristics and organizational growth, *Academy of Management Journal,* 40: 152–170.

54. J. Magretta, 2002, The behavior behind the buzzwords, *MIT Sloan Management Review,* 43(4): 90.

55. Wiersema & Bante, Top management team demography and corporate strategic change; Bantel & Jackson, Top management and innovations in banking.

56. J. J. Distefano & M. L. Maznevski, 2000, Creating value with diverse teams in global management, *Organizational Dynamics*, 29(1): 45–63; T. Simons, L. H. Pelled, & K. A. Smith, 1999, Making use of difference, diversity, debate, and decision comprehensiveness in top management teams, *Academy of Management Journal*, 42: 662–673.

57. A. Carmeli, J. Schaubroeck, & A. Tishler, 2011, How CEO empowering leadership shapes top management team processes: Implications for firm performance, *Leadership Quarterly*, 22(2): 399–411; Z. Simsek, J. F. Veiga, M. H. Lubatkin, & R. H. Dino, 2005, Modeling the multilevel determinants of top management team behavioral integration, *Academy of Management Journal*, 48: 69–84.

58. E. M. Wong, M. E. Ormiston, & P. E. Tetlock, 2011, The effects of top management team integrative complexity and decentralized decision making on corporate social performance, *Academy of Management Journal*, 54(6): 1207–1228; S. Finkelstein & D. C. Hambrick, 1996, *Strategic Leadership: Top Executives and Their Effects on Organizations*, New York: West Publishing, 148.

59. L. Xin, H. Ndofor, R. L. Priem, & J. C. Picken, 2010, Top management team communication networks, environmental uncertainty, and organizational performance: A contingency view, *Journal of Managerial Issues*, 22(4): 436–455; C. C. Miller, L. M. Burke, & W. H. Glick, 1998, Cognitive diversity among upper-echelon executives: Implications for strategic decision processes, *Strategic Management Journal*, 19: 39–58.

60. 2011, Steady as she goes, *Economist*, October 29, 79.

61. S. E. Ante & J. S. Lublin, 2011, IBM picks sales chief as next CEO, *Wall Street Journal*, October 26, B1.

62. T. Buyl, C. Boone, W. Hendricks & P. Matthyssens, 2011, Top management team functional diversity and firm performance: The moderating role of CEO characteristics, *Journal of Management Studies*, 48: 151–177.

63. S. Machold, M. Huse, A. Minichilli, & M. Nordqvist, 2011, Board leadership and strategy involvement in small firms: A team production approach, *Corporate Governance: An International Review*, 19(4): 368–383; L. Tihanyi, R. A. Johnson, R. E. Hosktsson, & M. A. Hirr, 2003, Institutional ownership and international diversification: The effects of boards of directors and technological opportunity, *Academy of Management Journal*, 46: 195–211; W. Q. Judge, Jr. & C. P. Zeithaml, 1992, Institutional and strategic choice perspectives on board involvement in the strategic decision process, *Academy of Management Journal*, 35: 766–794.

64. C. Fracassi & G. Tate, 2012, External networking and internal firm governance, *Journal of Finance*, 67(1): 153–194; G. Kassinis & N. Vafeas, 2002, Corporate boards and outside stakeholders as determinants of environmental litigation, *Strategic Management Journal*, 23: 399–415; B. R. Golden & E. J. Zajac, 2001, When will boards influence strategy? Inclination rimes power equals strategic change, *Strategic Management Journal*, 22: 1087–1111.

65. M. Carpenter & J. Westphal, 2001, Strategic context of external network ties: Examining the impact of director appointments on board involvement in strategic decision making, *Academy of Management Journal*, 44:639–660.

66. J. D. Westphal & È. J. Zajac, 1995, Who shall govern? CEO/board power, demographic similarity, and new director selection, *Administrative Science Quarterly*, 40: 60.

67. P. Elkind, J. Reingold, & D. Burke, 2011, Inside Pfizer's palace coup, *Fortune*, August 15, 76–91.

68. M. A. Abebe, A. Angriawan, & Y. Lui, 2011, CEO power and organizational turnaround in declining firms: Does environment play a role? *Journal of Leadership and Organizational Studies*, 18: 260–273; J. D. Westphal, 1999, Collaboration in the boardroom: Behavioral and performance consequences of CEO-board social ties, *Academy of Management Journal*, 42: 7–24.

69. A. Dey, E. Engel, & X. Liu, 2011, CEO and board chair roles: To split or not to split? *Journal of Corporate Finance*, 17(5): 1595–1618; J. Roberts & P. Stiles, 1999, The relationship between chairmen and chief executives: Competitive or complementary roles? *Long Range Planning*, 32(1): 36–48.

70. Y. Deutsch, T. Keil, & T. Laamanen, 2011, A dual agency view of board compensation: The joint effects of outside director and CEO stock options on firm risk, *Strategic Management Journal*, 32: 212–227; I. Filatotchev & M. Wright, 2011, Agency perspectives on corporate governance of multinational enterprises, *Journal of Management Studies*, 48(2): 471–486; J. Coles J. W. Hescerly, 2000, Independence of the chairman and board composition: Firm choices and shareholder value, *Journal of Management*, 26: 195–214; B. K. Boyd, 1995, CEO duality and firm performance: A contingency model, *Strategic Management Journal*, 16: 301.

71. J. Tang, M. Crossan, & W. G. Rowe, 2011, Dominant CEO, deviant strategy, and extreme performance: The moderating role of a powerful board, *Journal of Management Studies*, 48(7): 1479–1503; C. M. Daily & D. R. Dalton, 1995,

CEO and director turnover in failing firms: An illusion of change? *Strategic Management Journal,* 16: 393–400.

72. Dey, Engel, & Liu, CEO and board chair roles: To split or not to split; J. W. Lorsch & A. Zelleke, 2005, Should the CEO be the chairman? *Sloan Management Reviews,* 46(2): 71–81.

73. R. Albanese, M. T. Dacin, & I. C. Harris, 1997, Agents as stewards, *Academy of Management Review,* 22: 609–611; J. H. Davis, F. D. Schoorman, & L. Donaldson, 1997, Toward a stewardship theory of management, *Academy of Management Review,* 22: 20–47.

74. C. S. Tuggie, D. G. Sirmon, G. R. Reutzel, & L. Bierman, 2010, Commanding board of director attention: Investigating how organizational performance and CEO duality affect board members, attention to monitoring, *Strategic Management Journal,* 31(9): 946–968.

75. M. A. Carpenter, 2002, The implications of strategy and social context for the relationship between top management team heterogeneity and firm performance, *Strategic Management Journal,* 23: 275–284; J. D. Westphal & E. J. Zajac, 1997, Defections from the inner circle: Social exchange, reciprocity and diffusion of board independence in U.S. corporations, *Administrative Science Quarterly,* 42(1): 161–183.

76. J. G. Combs & M. S. Skill, 2003, Managerialist and human capital explanations for key executive pay premiums: A contingency perspective, *Academy of Management Journal,* 46: 63–73.

77. D. Souder, Z. Simsek, & S. G. Johnson, 2012, The differing effects of agent and founder CEOs on the firm's market expansion, *Strategic Management Journal,* 33(1): 23–41.

78. R. A. Johnson, R. E. Hoskisson, & M. A. Hitt, 1993, Board involvement in restructuring: The effect of board versus managerial controls and characteristics, *Strategic Management Journal,* 14 (summer special issue): 33–50.

79. E. E. Lawler III, D. Finegold, G. Benson, & J. Conger, 2002, Adding value in the boardroom, *MIT Sloan Management Review,* 43(2): 92–93.

80. Boyd, CEO duality and firm performance.

81. M. Carpenter & J. Fredrickson, 2001, Top management teams, global strategic posture, and the moderating role of uncertainty, *Academy of Management Journal,* 44: 533–545.

82. A. P. Kakabadse, N. K. Kakabadse, & R. Knyght, 2010, The chemistry factor in the Chairman/CEO relationship, *European Management Journal,* 28(4): 285–296; M. Schneider, 2002, A stakeholder model of organizational leadership, *Organization Science,* 13: 209–220.

83. Lafley & Tichy, The art and science of finding the right CEO; M. Sorcher & J. Brant, 2002, Are you picking the right leaders? *Harvard Business Review,* 80(2): 78–55; D. A. Waldman, G. G. Ramirez, R. J. House, & P. Puranam, 2001, Does leadership matter? CEO leadership attributes and profitability under conditions of perceived environmental uncertainty, *Academy of Management Journal,* 44: 134–143.

84. J. M. Citrin, 2012, When naming a CEO, ignore the market reaction, *Harvard Business Review,* 90(1/2): 30; A. Kakabadse & N. Kakabadse, 2001, Dynamics of executive succession, *Corporate Governance,* 1(3): 9–14.

85. B. Kowitt, 2011, The man powering up GE, *Fortune,* December 26, *58–65;* R. Charan, 2000, GE's ten-step talent plan, *Fortune,* April 17, 232.

86. R. E. Hoskisson, D. Yiu, & H. Kim, 2010, Capital and labor market congruence and corporate governance: Effects on corporate innovation and global competitiveness, in D. B. Audretsch, G. B. Dagnini, R. Faraci, & R. E. Hoskisson (Eds.), *New Frontiers in Entrepreneurship: Recognizing, Seizing, and Executing Opportunities,* New York: Springer, 67–93.

87. W. Shen & A. A. Cannella, 2003, Will succession planning increase shareholder wealth? Evidence from investor reactions to relay CEO successions, *Strategic Management Journal,* 24: 191–198.

88. Y. Zhang & N. Rajagopalan, 2010, Once an outsider, always an outsider? CEO origin, strategic change, *and* firm performance, *Strategic Management Journal,* 31 (3): 334–346.

89. Y. Zhang & N. Rajagopalan, 2010, CEO succession planning: Finally at the center stage of the boardroom, *Business Horizons,* 53(5): 455–462; D. C. Carey & D. Ogden, 2000, CEO *Succession: A Window on How Boards Can Get It Right When Choosing a New Chief Executive,* New York: Oxford University Press.

90. S. B. Shepard, 2002, A Talk with Jeff Immelt: Jack Welch's successor charts a course for GE in the 21st century, *Business Week,* January 28, 102–104.

91. L. Greiner, T. Cummings, & A. Bhambri, 2002, When new CEOs succeed and fail: 4-D theory of strategic transformation. *Organizational Dynamics,* 32: 1–16.

92. D. Miller, 1991, Stale in the saddle: CEO tenure and the match between organization and environment, *Management Science,* 37: 34–52.

93. V. Anand, W. H. Glide, & C. C. Manz, 2002, Thriving on the knowledge of outsiders: Tapping organizational social capital, *Academy of Management Executive,* 16(1): 87–101.

94. J. M. Barron, D. V. Chulkov, & G. R. Waddell, 2011, Top management team turnover, CEO succession type, and strategic change, *Journal of Business Research,* 64(8): 904–910; N. A. Ashkanasy, C. E. J. Härtel, & C. S. Daus, 2002, Diversity and emotion: The new frontiers in organizational behavior research, *Journal of Management,* 28: 307–338.

95. G. N. Powell, D. A. Butterfield, & J. D. Parent, 2002, Gender and managerial stereotypes: Have the times changed? *Journal of Management,* 28: 177–193.

96. B. Srinidhi, F. A. Gui, & J. Tsui, 2011, Female directors and earnings quality, *Contemporary Accounting Research,* 28(5): 1610–1644; K. Campbell & A. M. Vera, 2010, Female board appointments and firm valuation: Short and long-term effects, *Journal of Management & Governance,* 14(1): 37–59.

97. 2011, Growth of women on boards, in C-suites a 'truot', *Financial Executive,* 27(10): 10; C. E. Helfat, D. Harris, & P. J. Wolfson, 2006, The pipeline to the top: Women and men in the top executive ranks of U.S. corporations, *Academy of Management Perspectives,* 20(4): 42–64.

98. Growth of women on boards, in C-suites a 'trot'.

99. O. Chatain, 2011, Value creation, competition, and performance in buyer-supplier relationships, *Strategic Management Journal,* 32: 76–102; R. D. Ireland & M. A. Hitt, 2005, Achieving and maintaining strategic competitiveness in the 21st century: The role of strategic leadership, *Academy of Management Executive,* 19(4): 63–77, originally published in 12(1): 43–57; A. Cannella, Jr., A. Pettigrew, & D. Hambrick, 2001, Upper echelons: Donald Hambrick on executives and strategy, *Academy of Management Executive,* 15(3): 36–52; D. Lei, M. A. Hitt, & R. Bettis, 1996, Dyriamic core competencies through meta-learning and strategic context, *Journal of Management,* 22: 547–567.

100. D. G. Sirmon, M. A. Hitt, R. D. Ireland, & B. Gilbert, 2011, Resource orchestration to create competitive advantage: Breadth, depth, and life cycle effects, *Journal of Management,* 37(5): 1390–1412.

101. J. S. Harrison, D. A. Bosse, & R. A. Phillips, 2010, Managing for stakeholders, stakeholder utility functions and competitive advantage, *Strategic Management Journal,* 31: 58–74; J. S. Harrison, 2003, *Strategic Management of Resources and Relationships,* New York: Wiley; R. E. Freeman, 1984, *Strategic Management: A Stakeholder Approach,* Boston: Pitman.

102. Finkelstein & Hambrick, *Strategic Leadership,* 2.

103. S. Berfield, 2006, Most inspiring steel boss, *Business Week,* December 18, 61.

104. G. Hamel & C. K. Prahalad, 1989, Strategic intent, *Harvard Business Review,* 67(3): 63–76.

105. D. C. Hambrick & J. W. Fredrickson, 2005, Are you sure you have a strategy? *Academy of Management Executive,* 19(4): 51–62, reprinted from 15(4).

106. H. A. Ndofor, D. G. Sirmon, & X. He, 2011, Firm resources, competitive actions and performance: Investigating a mediated model with evidence from the in-vitro diagnostics industry, *Strategic Management Journal,* 32: 640–657.

107. D. F. Abell, 1980, *Defining the Business: The Starting Point of Strategic Planning,* Englewood Cliffs, NJ: Prentice Hall.

108. 2012, Choice Hotels International, http://www.wikinvest.com, February 20.

109. 2012, General Electric, http://www.ge.com/company/advertising, February 20.

110. S. Mohammed & S. Nadkarni. 2011, Temporal diversity and team performance: The moderating role of team temporal leadership, *Academy of Management Journal,* 54(3): 489–508; K. M. Eisenhardt & S. L. Brown, 1998, Time pacing: Compering in markets that won't stand still, *Harvard Business Review,* March-April: 59–69.

111. A. Vance, 2012, c:\\Ballmer [Reboots], *Bloomberg Business Week,* January 16, 49.

112. A. Efrati, A. Das, V. Monga, & J. S. Lublin, 2012, Yahoo CEO faces big new problems, *Wall Street Journal,* February 15, B3.

113. D. Kesmodel, O. C. D. Michaels, 2011, For Boeing, it's been a long, strange trip—after three-year delay, plane maker readies 787 Dreamliner production, *Wall Street Journal,* September 21, B1.

114. 2012, IT leaders continue to juggle multiple priorities in 2012, *CIO,* January 19, 2.

115. R. E. Ployharr, C. H. Van ldderkinge, & W. J. MacKenzie, 2011, Acquiring and developing human capital in service contexts: The interconnectedness of human capital resources, *Academy of Management Journal,* 54: 353–368; J. A. Oxman, 2002, The hidden leverage of human capital, *MIT Sloan Management Review,* 43(4): 79–83.

116. N. Argyres, 2011, Using organizational economics to study organizational capability development and strategy, *Organization Science,* 22: 1138–1143; D. J. Teece, 2000, *Managing Intellectual Capital: Organizational, Strategic and Policy Dimensions,* Oxford, UK: Oxford University Press.

117. C. Fernandez–Araoz, B. Groysberg, & N. Nohria, 2011, How to hang on to your high potentials, *Harvard Business Review,* 89(10): 76–83.

118. J. Pfeffer, 2010, Building sustainable organizations; The human factor, *Academy of Management Perspectives*, 24(1): 34–45; C. A. Lengnick-Hall & J. A. Wolff, 1999, Similarities and contradictions in the core logic of three strategy research streams, *Strategic Management Journal*, 20: 1109–1132.

119. S. A. Snell & M. A. Youndt, 1995, Human resource management and firm performance: Testing a contingency model of executive controls, *Journal of Management*, 21: 711–737.

120. F. DiBmraardino, 2011, The missing link: Measuring and managing financial performance of the human capital investment, *People & Strategy*, 34(2): 44–49; W. Watson, W. H. Stewart, & A. Barnir, 2003, The effects of human capital, organizational demography, and interpersonal processes on venture partner perceptions of firm profit and growth, *Journal of Business Venturing*, 18: 145–164; D. Ulrich, 1998, A new mandate for human resources, *Harvard Business Review*, 76(1): 124–134.

121. P. M. Wright & G. C. McMahan, 2011, Exploring human capital: Purring 'human' back into strategic human resource management, *Human Resource Management Journal*, 21: 93–104; J. Pfeffer, 1994, *Competitive Advantage through People*, Boston: Harvard Business School Press, 4.

122. Carmeli, Tishler, fie Edmondson, CEO relational leadership and strategic decision quality in top management teams; L. Graton, 2001, *Living Strategy: Putting People at the Heart of Corporate Purpose*, London: Financial Times/Prentice Hall.

123. J. S. Sidhu & K. W. Volberda, 2011, Coordination of globally distributed teams: A co–evolution perspective on offshoring. *International Business Review*, 20: 278–290; A. Yan, G. Zhu, & D. T. Hall, 2002, International assignments for career building: A model of agency relationships and psychological contracts, *Academy of Management Review*, 27: 373–391.

124. C. Keen & Y. Wu, 2011, An ambidextrous learning model for the internationalization of firms from emerging economies, *Journal of International Entrepreneurship*, 9(4): 316–339,

125. M. Harvey, T. Kiessling, & M. Moeller, 2011, Globalization and the inward flow of immigrants: Issues associated with the inpatriation of global managers. *Human Resource Development Quarterly*, 22(2): 177–194; M. G. Harvey & M. R. Buckley, 1997, Managing inpatriates: Building a global core competency, *Journal of World Business*, 32(1): 35–52.

126. C. Gaimon, G. F. Ozkan, & K. Napoleon, 2011, Dynamic resource capabilities: Managing workforce knowledge with a technology upgrade, *Organization Science*, 22(6): 1560–1578; C. A. Bardett & S. Ghoshal, 2002, Building competitive advantage through people, *MIT Sloan Management Review*, 43(2): 34–41; D. M. De Carolls & D. L. Deeds, 1999, The impact of stocks and flows of organizational knowledge on firm performance: An empirical investigation of the biotechnology industry, *Strategic Management Journal*, 20: 953–968.

127. J. Abele, 2011, Bringing minds together, *Harvard Business Review*, 89(7/8): 86–93; R. Cross & L. Prusak, 2002, The people who make organizations go—or stop, *Harvard Business Review*, 80(6): 105–112.

128. S. B. Bach, W. Q. Judge, & T. J. Dean, 2008, A knowledge-based view of IPO success: Superior knowledge, isolating mechanisms, and the creation of market value, *Journal of Managerial Issues*, 20(4): 507–525; T. M. Welbourne & L. A. Cyr, 1999, The human resource executive effect in initial public offering firms, *Academy of Management Journal*, 42: 616–629.

129. Gaimon, Ozkan, & Napoleon, Dynamic resource capabilities: Managing workforce knowledge with a technology upgrade; Bartlett & Ghoshal, Building competitive advantage through people.

130. H. Collingwood & D. L. Coutu, 2002, Jack on Jack, *Harvard Business Review*, 80(2): 88–94.

131. A. Klein, 2011, Corporate culture: Its value as a resource for competitive advantage, *Journal of Business Strategy*, 32(2): 21–28; A. K. Gupta & V. Govindarajan, 2000, Knowledge management's social dimension: Lessons from Nucor steel, *Sloan Management Review*, 42(1): 71–80; C. M. Fiol, 1991, Managing culture as a competitive resource: An identity-based view of sustainable competitive advantage, *Journal of Management*, 17: 191–211; J. B. Barney, 1986, Organizational culture: Can it be a source of sustained competitive advantage? *Academy of Management Review*, 11: 656–465.

132. A. J. Bock, T. Opsahl, G. George, & D. M. Gann, 2012, The effects of culture and structure on strategic flexibility during business model innovation, *Journal of Management Studies*, 49: 279–305; J. Kotier, 2011, Corporate culture: Whose job is it? *Forbes*, http://blog.forbes.com/johnkotter, February 17.

133. H. Lin & E. F. McDonough III, 2011, Investigating the role of leadership and organizational culture in fostering innovation ambidexterity, *IEEE Transactions on Engineering Management*, 58(3): 497–509.

134. M. A. Hitt, R. D. Ireland, D. G. Sirmon, & C. A. Trahms, 2011. Strategic entrepreneurship: Creating value for individuals, organizations and society, *Academy*

of Management Perspectives, 25(2): 57–75; D. S. Elenkov, W. Judge, & P. Wright, 2005, Strategic leadership and executive innovation influence; An international multi-cluster comparative study, *Strategic Management Journal,* 26: 665–682.

135. B. A. George, 2011, Entrepreneurial orientation: A theoretical and empirical examination of the consequences of differing construct representations, *Journal of Management Studies,* 48(6): 1291–1313; G. T. Lumpkin & G. G. Dess, 1996, Clarifying the entrepreneurial orientation construct and linking it to performance, *Academy of Management Review,* 21: 135–172.

136. Lumpkin & Dess, Clarifying die entrepreneurial orientation construct and linking it to performance, 142.

137. Ibid, 137.

138. D. Park, R. Chinta, M. Lee, J. Turner, & L. Kilbourne, 2011. Macro-fit versus micro-fit of the organization with its environment: Implications for strategic leadership. *International Journal of Management,* 28(2): 488–492; R. A. Burgelman & Y. L. Doz, 2001, The power of strategic integration, *Sloan Management Review,* 42(3): 28–38; P. H. Fuchs, K. E. Mifflin, D. Miller, & J. O. Whitney, 2000, Strategic integration: Competing in the age of capabilities, *California Management Review,* 42(3): 118–147.

139. A. M. L. Raes, M. G. Heijltks, U. Glunk, & R. A. Roe, 2011, The interface of the top management team and middle managers: A process model, *Academy of Management Review,* 36: 102–126; H. N. Nguyen & S. Mohamed, 2011, Leadership behaviors, organizational culture and knowledge management practices: An empirical investigation, *Journal of Management Development,* 30(2): 206–221; J. E. Dutton, S. J. Ashford, R. M. O'Neill, E. Hayes, & E. E. Wierba, 1997, Reading the wind: How middle managers assess the context for selling issues to top managers, *Strategic Management Journal,* 18: 407–425.

140. N. Zmuda, 2012, JCP reinvention is bold bet, but hardly fail-safe, *Advertising Age,* January 30, 1–22,

141. K. Talley, 2012, Penney CEO says profit won't suffer, *Wall Street Journal,* January 27, B6.

142. J. Peloza & J. Shang, 2011, How can corporate social responsibility activities create value for stakeholders? A systematic review, *Journal of the Academy of Marketing Science,* 39: 117–135; R. E. Freeman & W. M. Evan, 1990, Corporate governance: A stakeholder interpretation, *journal of Behavioral Economics,* 19: 337–359.

143. S. Helm, 2011, Employees' awareness of their impact on corporate reputation, *Journal of Business Research,* 64(7): 657–663; C J. Fombrun, 2001, Corporate reputations as economic assets, in M. A. Hitt, R. E. Freeman,

& J. S. Harrison, *Handbook of Strategic Management,* Oxford, UK: Blackwell Publishers, 289–312.

144. M. Pirson & D. Malhorra, 2011, Foundations of organizational trust: What matters to different stakeholders? *Organization Science,* 22(4): 1087–1104.

145. M. A. Hitt, K. T. Haynes, & R. Serpa, 2010, Strategic leadership for the 21st century, *Business Horizons,* 53: 437–444.

146. B. Neville, S. Bell, & G. Whitwell, 2011, Stakeholder salience revisited: Refining, redefining, and refueling an underdeveloped conceptual tool, *Journal of Business Ethics,* 102(3): 357–378; D. Lavie, 2006, The competitive advantage of interconnected firms: An extension of the resource-based view, *Academy of Management Review,* 31: 638–658.

147. J. E. Rogers, 2011, The CEO of Duke Energy on learning to work with green activists, *Harvard Business Review,* 89(5): 51–54; R. C Ford, 2002, Darden restaurants CEO Joe Lee on the importance of core values: Integrity and fairness, *Academy of Management Executive,* 16(1): 31–36; P. W. Beamish, 1999, Sony's Yoshihide Nakamura on structure and decision making, *Academy of Management Executive,* 13(4): 12–16.

148. J. R. Baum, E. A. Locke, & S. A. Kirkpatrick, 1998, A longitudinal study of the relation of vision and vision communication to venture growth in entrepreneurial firms, *Journal of Applied Psychology,* 83: 43–54.

149. M. Wasden, 2011, Why you need an identity crisis, *Finweek,* December 15, 38; R. D. Ireland & M. A. Hitt, 1992, Mission statements: Importance, challenge, and recommendations for development, *Business Horizons,* 35(3): 34–42.

150. D. Kiron, N. Kraschwitz, K. Haanaes, & L. von Streng Velken, 2012, Sustainability nears a tipping point, MIT *Shan Management Review,* 53(2): 69–74; G. Kassinis & N. Vafeas, 2006, Stakeholder pressures and environmental performance, *Academy of Management Journal,* 49: 145–159,

151. L. M. Levin, 2000, Vision revisited, *Journal of Applied Behavioral Science,* 36: 91–107; J. C. Collins & J. I. Porras, 1996, Building your company's vision, *Harvard Business Review,* 74(5): 65–77.

152. S. B. Sitkin, K. E. See, C. Miller, M. W. Lawless, & A. M. Carton, 2011, The paradox of stretch goals: Organizations in pursuit of the seemingly impossible, *Academy of Management Review,* 36(3): 544–566; S. Kerr & S. Landauer, 2004, Using stretch goals to promote organizational effectiveness and personal growth, *Academy of Management Executive,* 18(4): 134–138; K. R. Thompson, W. A. Hochwarter, & N. J. Mathys, 1997, Stretch targets: What makes them effective? *Academy of Management Executive,* 11(3): 48–59.

153. R. Goffee & G. Jones, 2006, Getting personal on the topic of leadership: Authentic self-expression works for those at the top, *Human Resource Management international Digest*, 14(4): 32–40.

154. 2012, *Code of Ethics*, Hartford, CT; United Technologies, http://utc.com/Governance/Ethics/Code+of+Eihics, accessed on February 21.

155. K. M. Gilley, C. J. Robertson, & T. C. Mazur, 2010, The bottom-line benefits of ethics code commitment, *Business Horizons*, 53(1): 31–37; J. M. Stevens, H. K. Steensma, D. A. Harrison, & P. L. Cochran, 2005, Symbolic or substantive document? Influence of ethics codes on financial executives' decisions, *Strategic Management Journal*, 26: 181–195.

156. 2006, *Enron Code of Ethics July 2000*, The Smoking Gun, http://www.thesmokinggun.com/graphics/packageart/enron/enron.pdf, December 15.

157. S. Forest, W. Zellner & H. Timmons, 2001, The Enron debacle, *Business Week*, November 12, 106–110.

158. E. Feldman, 2006, A basic quantification of the competitive implications of the demise of Arthur Andersen, *Review of Industrial Organization*, 29: 193–212.

159. S. Adams, 2011, Steve jobs, Jon Corzine among 201l's biggest CEO departures, *Forbes*, December 8, 30.

160. R. Rumelt, 2011, *Good strategy/bad strategy*, New York: Crowne Business; P. S. Adler & S.-W. Kwon, 2002, Social capital: Prospects for a new concept, *Academy of Management Review*, 27: 17–40.

161. E. Wallace, L. Chernatony, & L. Buil, 2011, How leadership and commitment influence bank employees' adoption of their bank's values, *Journal of Business Ethics*, 101(3): 397–414; T. A. Stewart, 2001, Right now the only capital that matters is social capital, *Business* 2.0, December, 128–130.

162. V. Anand, B. E. Ashforth, & M. Joshi, 2005, Business as usual: The acceptance and perpetuation of corruption in organizations, *Academy of Management Executive*, 19(4): 9–23; D. J. Brass, K. D. Butterfield, & B. C. Skaggs, 1998, Relationships and unethical behavior: A social network perspective, *Academy of Management Review*, 23: 14–31.

163. W. Wallace, 2000, The value relevance of accounting: The rest of the story, *European Management Journal*, 18(6): 675–82.

164. L. Grove, M. Giglio, D. Ephron, & W. Underhill, 2011, Rupert's red menace, *Newsweek*, July 25, 40–44.

165. P. M. Barrett, F. Gillette, R. Farzad, J. Browning, L. Fortado, & T. Penny, 2011, Ink-stained wretchedness, *Bloomberg Businessweek*, July 18, 4–6; S. Forbes, 2011, Why Rupert Murdoch will survive and thrive again, 2011, *Forbes*, July 18, 30.

166. C. C. Maurer, P. Bansal, & M. M. Crossan, 2011, Creating economic value through social venues: introducing a culturally informed resource–based view, *Organization Science*, 22: 432–448; L. K. Trevino, G. R. Weaver, D. G. Toffler, & B. Ley, 1999, Managing ethics and legal compliance: What works and what hurts, *California Management Review*, 41(2): 131–151.

167. T. Yaffe & R. Kark, 2011, Leading by example; The case of leader OCB, *Journal of Applied Psychology*, 96(4): 806–826; J. A. Petrick & J. F. Quinn, 2001, The challenge of leadership accountability for integrity capacity as a strategic asset, *Journal of Business Ethics*, 34: 331–343; R. C. Mayer, J. H. Davis, & F. D. Schoorman, *1995, An* integrative model of organizational trust, *Academy of Management Review*, 20: 709–734.

168. J. R. Cohen, L. W. Pant, & D. J. Sharp, 2001, An examination of differences in ethical decisionmaking between Canadian business students and accounting professionals, *Journal of Business Ethics*, 30: 319–336; G. R. Weaver, L K. Trevino, & P. L. Cochran, 1999, Corporate ethics programs as control systems: Influences of executive commitment and environmental factors, *Academy of Management Journal*, 42: 41–57.

169. R. T. Mowday, 2011, Elevating the dialogue on professional ethics to the next level: Reflections on the experience of the Academy of Management, *Management & Organization Review*, 7(3): 505–509; N. N. Leila Trapp, 2011, Staff attitudes to talking openly about ethical dilemmas: The role of business ethics conceptions and trust, *Journal of Business Ethics*, 103(4): 543–552; P. E. Murphy, 1995, Corporate ethics statements: Current status and future prospects, *Journal of Business Ethics*, 14: 727–740.

170. P. Fuck & R. Badhara, 2011, Fire, snowball, mask, movie: How leaders spark and sustain change, *Harvard Business Review*, 89(11): 145–148; L. G. Hrebiniak & W. F. Joyce, 2001, Implementing strategy: An appraisal and agenda for future research, in M. A. Hitt, R. E. Freeman, & J. S. Harrison (eds.), *Handbook of Strategic Management*, Oxford, UK: Blackwell Publishers, 433–463.

171. J. A. Martin, 2011, Dynamic managerial capabilities and the multibusiness team: The role of episodic teams in executive leadership groups, *Organization Science*, 22(1): 118–140; J. B. Barney, 1995, Looking inside for competitive advantage, *Academy of Management Executive*, November, 49–61.

172. R. Kanter, 2011, How great companies think differently, *Harvard Business Review*, 89(11): 66–78; B. R. Barringer, & J. S. Harrison, 2000, Walking a tightrope: Creating value through interorganizational relationships, *Journal of Management*, 26: 367–404.

173. 2012, Basel Headquarters, Novarás, http://www.novartis.com/abom-novams/iocarions/fcasel-headquarters.shtml, accessed on February 23.

174. M. Z. Elbashir, P. A. Collier, & S. G. Sutton, 2011, The role of organizational absorptive capacity in strategic use of business intelligence to support integrated management control systems, *Accounting Review*, 86(1): 155–184; J. H. Gittell, 2000, Paradox of coordination and control, *California Management Review*, 42(3): 101–117; L. J. Kirsch, 1996, The management of complex tasks in organizations: Controlling the systems development process, *Organization Science*, 7: 1–21.

175. M. D. Shields, K. J. Deng, & Y. Kato, 2000, The design and effects of control systems: Tests of direct-and indirect-effects models, *Accounting, Organizations and Society*, 25: 185–202; R. Simons, 1994, How new top managers use control systems as levers of strategic renewal, *Strategic Management Journal*, 15: 170–171.

176. R. E. White, R. E, Hoskisson, D. W. Yin, & G. D. Bruton, 2008, Employment and market innovation in Chinese business group affiliated firms: The role of group control systems, *Management & Organization Review*, 4(2): 225–256; K. J. Laverty, 1996, Economic "short-termism": The debate, the unresolved issues, and the implications for management practice and research, *Academy of Management Review*, 21: 825–860.

177. E. E. Tapinos, R. G. Dyson, & M. M. Meadows, 2011, Does the balanced scorecard make a difference to the strategy development process? *Journal of the Operational Research Society*, 62(5): 888–899; R. S. Kaplan & D. P. Norton, 2000, *The Strategy-Focused Organization: How Balanced Scorecard Companies Thrive in the New Business Environment*, Boston: Harvard Business School Press.

178. N. Jarrar & M. Smith, 2011, Product diversification: The need for innovation and the role of a balanced scorecard, *journal of Applied Management Accounting Research*, 9(2): 43–60; B. E. Becker, M. A. Huselid, & D. Ulrich, 2001, *The HR Scorecard: Linking People, Strategy, and Performance*, Boston: Harvard Business School Press, 21.

179. Kaplan & Norton, *The Strategy-Focused Organization*.

180. L. Yuan, L. Xiyao, L. Yi, & R. R. Barnes, 2011, Knowledge communication, exploitation and endogenous innovation; The moderating effects of internal controls in SMEs, *R&D Management*, 41(2): 156–172; R. S. Kaplan & D. P. Norton, 2001, Transforming the balanced scorecard from performance measurement to strategic management: Part I, *Accounting Horizons*, 15(1): 87–104.

181. J. D. Gunkel & G. Probst, 2003, Implementation of the balanced scorecard as a means of corporate learning: The Porsche case, Cratifield, UK: European Case Clearing House.

182. R. S. Kaplan & D. P. Norton, 2008, Mastering the management system, *Harvard Business Review*, 86(1): 62–77; M. A. Mische, 2001, *Strategic Renewal: Becoming a High-Performance Organization*, Upper Saddle River, NJ: Prentice Hall, 181.

183. K. P. Coyne, S. Coyne, & S. T. Coyne, 2010, When you've got to cut costs now, *Harvard Business Review*, 88(5): 74–82; R. E. Hoskisson, R. A. Johnson, L. Tihanyi, & R. E White, 2005, Diversified business groups and corporate refocusing in emerging economies, *Journal of Management*, 31: 941–965; R. E. Hoskisson & M. A, Hitt, 1994, *Downscoping: How to Tame the Diversified Firm*, New York: Oxford University Press.

CHAPTER 31

Open Strategy

Towards a Research Agenda

Kurt Matzler
University of Innsbruck, Austria

Johann Füller
University of Innsbruck, Austria

Katja Hutter
University of Innsbruck, Austria

Julia Hautz
University of Innsbruck, Austria

Daniel Stieger
University of Innsbruck, Austria

Introduction

Information systems and strategizing practices have become inseparable (Whittington, 2014). As organizations are increasingly adopting Web 2.0 technologies, new opportunities for internal collaboration emerge. Web 2.0, also labeled social software, or—in the context of organizations—Enterprise 2.0, supports group interaction, the establishment of communities, and the creation and the exchange of content (von Krogh, 2012). As with knowledge management, which underwent a fundamental transformation through social software (von Krogh, 2012), there is reason to believe that social software radically changes the way companies formulate and implement strategies, allowing more open and participatory modes of strategizing. These new approaches—variously labeled as "democratizing strategy" (Stieger, Matzler, Chatterjee, & Ladstätter-Fussenegger, 2012), "open strategy" (Whittington, Cailluet, & Yakis-Douglas, 2011), "open-source strategy" (Newstead & Lanzerotti, 2010), or "strategy as a practice of thousands" (Dobusch & Müller-Seitz,

2012)—involve a large number of people in generating, discussing, and evaluating strategy ideas. Social software is fundamentally disrupting the way employees cooperate and deal with knowledge (Bebensee, Helms, & Spruit, 2011; von Krogh, 2012), enabling peer production and unbounded collaboration. These systems are built on easy to use and intuitive applications like blogs, wikis, social bookmarking, editing platforms, etc., and infrastructure and open platforms that reap considerable economies of scale.

The idea of democratizing strategy is not new. Almost two decades ago, C. K. Prahalad said in an interview: "Strategy is not only created by people at the top of a company or its planning department. Strategy needs the wealth of information and knowledge possessed by people at the 'coalface' to make it happen, by people who are continually dealing with customers, competitors, technologies, and suppliers. Democratizing strategy creates a new way of thinking about a process for pooling collective knowledge and commitment in an organization and channeling it" (Prahalad, 1995). In a similar vein, Gary Hamel wrote: "Strategy making must be democratic. . . The capacity to think creatively about strategy is distributed widely in an enterprise" (Hamel, 1996). Interestingly, these revolutionary thoughts on strategizing remained unheard—in theory as well as in practice. Strategy is still believed to be formulated deliberately at the top and implemented below (Mintzberg, 2009). Strategy development has traditionally been exclusive (i.e., the job of the top management team) and secretive to protect competitive advantages (Whittington et al., 2011). However, strategy work is changing dramatically. The ideas of open innovation (Chesbrough, 2003), crowdsourcing (Howe, 2006), and collective intelligence (Page, 2007; Surowiecki, 2004) have had a profound impact on how organizations create value, how they externally and internally collaborate, and how they make decisions. Chesbrough and Appleyard (2007) introduced the idea of open innovation to strategy. They argue that the notion of intellectual commons, peer production, and collective innovation requires a rethinking of how companies formulate and implement their strategies. Crowdsourcing requires the collaboration of a large number of people to tap into the collective intelligence of an organization. Until recently, this has been costly and difficult. However, social software offers new

opportunities for collaboration and allows the involvement of a larger crowd—with little effort and at low cost. Information systems are enablers and shapers of crowdsourcing (Majchrzak & Malhotra, 2013). Social software tools increase outreach and information richness, they enable remote and asynchronous collaboration, they allow for cognitive diversity, independence, and additive aggregation (which are requirements for the wisdom of the crowd, see Surowiecki, 2004). Social software enables companies to tap into the power of collective intelligence, bringing employee involvement in strategy processes to the next level (Stieger et al., 2012).

Strategy work is being revolutionized. It seems that a number of forces (societal, cultural, organizational and technological) push companies to open their strategy processes. Open strategy might become a major new phenomenon in strategy research and practice, raising many questions to be answered (Whittington et al., 2011). The open strategy approach seems to have two major benefits. First, it allows companies to gather knowledge and expertise from all parts of the organization, and to tap into the wisdom of the crowd (Surowiecki, 2004). Under certain parameters (i.e., diversity, independence, decentralization, and correct aggregation of information), large groups of people can be better at problem solving, fostering innovation, coming to wise decisions, and predicting the future than an elite few (Surowiecki, 2004)—diversity trumps ability (Page, 2007). This observation should be particularly relevant for strategy processes. Indeed, it has been acknowledged recently that the paradigm of collective intelligence and crowdsourcing (which usually is used for external sourcing, e.g., open innovation) can be applied inside a company as well (Bonabeau, 2009; Bonabeau & Meyer, 2001). To understand whether and how Web 2.0-based open strategy initiatives improve strategies is an important question for research.

Second, strategy rarely is a product of an individual strategist or a homogenous strategy team. Rather it is a process of social interaction, based on the beliefs and shared understandings of an organization's members (Mintzberg, Allstrand, & Lampel, 2009). It is also known that if the "implementers do not own the strategy," strategy implementation is likely to fail (Giles, 1991). Insufficient buy-in or insufficient understanding of the strategy among those who implement it is a common reason for poor implementation. Hence, involvement of a larger number of employees in the strategy process has long been recognized as a means to create a shared understanding, stronger commitment, and effective implementation (Sterling, 2003). Opening up the strategy process to broadly involve employees might be an important means to increase implementation commitment and improve execution. Web 2.0 technologies allow removing communication barriers and promoting inclusion, enabling an organization-wide dialogue. Employees can participate in open discussions, contribute their ideas, and comment on their peers' opinions and thus collectively develop and contribute to strategies.

Building on four case studies (an Austrian medium-sized automation supplier, a leading German car manufacturer, a major European bank, and a German multinational engineering and electronics company), we explore the phenomenon of open strategy. Whereas first experiences show that web-based social technology features (e.g., transparency, inclusion, independence, peer review, etc.) positively influence the quality of strategy ideas and identification and implementation commitment, there are a number of potential risks (e.g., discussions can evolve in unpredictable ways, management might have to decide against the "crowd", critical knowledge or secrets are difficult to protect, etc.). Also, it needs to be investigated for which topics and under which conditions open strategy is a suitable approach, as well as how the process needs to be designed, how individuals can be motivated to contribute, what the role of management is, how corporate culture affects and is affected by opening strategy, how strategies emerge in such initiatives, etc.

In this chapter, based on the qualitative analysis of four cases, the following research questions for the emerging new paradigm of open strategy are identified and discussed: 1) What are the effects of inclusion-exclusion in open strategizing? 2) What is the social structure of the organization in strategizing, where are the nodes in the social network, where are the talents? 3) How do roles and power structures change? 4) Open strategy and consensus/dissensus: why and how do they emerge, what are the effects? 5) What is opening strategy's impact on politization? What is the influence of e.g., transparency, anonymity, etc.? 6) How does open strategy influence

motivation? How can managers effectively react to overwhelming numbers of contributions? What is their role?, and 7) What is the role of organizational culture? In the following section, we present the cases and discuss the implications of our findings.

Case Studies

Our first case is an Austrian medium-sized automation supplier as described in one of our previous papers (Stieger et al., 2012). An Intranet platform was installed and all employees were invited to discuss four strategy topics (success factors/strengths, future customer solutions, process improvement, new technologies). Out of 370 employees, 216 registered at the Intranet platform. Roughly half of them actively contributed to the strategy dialogue. Online software was developed and specially tailored to the demands of an intra-company crowdsourcing platform. The platform exposed the central topics the crowd should discuss. These central topics were the major questions the employees should work on. They were anchored in the menu structure, so that they could be easily found when navigating. Participants could start threads and assign them to one of those topics. A thread was a new direction of discussion which was not addressed before. It was a specific dialogue between participants focusing on one central idea. Participants could state their opinion and take part in the dialogue by adding posts to such a thread. Participants could directly comment on a post with another post. By implementing a feature for anonymous publishing, fear of evaluation was minimized. Asynchronous communication was supported by storing the threads. Each participant could view the contributions of others and respond them. During the first day the platform was online, 22 threads and 203 comments on those threads were posted. After two weeks, 135 threads had grown to a total of 1,374 comments.

The second case is based on an ongoing corporate-wide innovation platform called 'Business Innovation Community' (BI Community) initiated by Daimler, a leading German car manufacturer (Füller, Hutter, Hautz, & Matzler, 2014; Matzler, Füller, Koch, Hautz, & Hutter, 2013). The wiki-based software application allows employees to interactively and collaboratively develop ideas on new business concepts.

Thereby new areas of growth and future business models, independent of existing products but linked to the company's core business, should be identified. Every employee in the company, regardless of business unit affiliation, hierarchy level or profession, is invited to join and to submit ideas as well as to provide feedback. Moreover, user profiles are publicly accessible on the community platform in order to be able to link virtual identities with the real-life person, i.e., the employee. The corporate innovation platform enabling this bottom-up approach was launched on 1st August 2008 and attracted about 30,000 employees who submitted more than 2,000 ideas. Just like in an open-source setting, submitted ideas can be modified as well as extended by other participants. To date, over 35 new business models have emerged from the platform and are currently being tested and further developed. 'Car2go' (www.car2go.com/)—a car-sharing model in urban transportation—emerged from the BI community. The flexible mobility concept with the minute-to-minute pay option has so far attracted more than 100,000 registered customers and more than two million rentals. It offers over 600 electronically driven vehicles (Füller et al., 2014).

In our third case, the German Bank Hypo Vereinsbank placed great importance on engaging their employees in an open strategy project with the title "If I was my customer . . ." (in German: "Wenn ich mein Kunde wär' . . ."). The project started with the "Excellent customer experience" initiative (in German: "Exzellente Kundenerlebnisse"), run in cooperation with two external partners, the innovation agency HYVE AG and the creative agency Berger Baader Hermes (BBH). Due to an internal restructuring program in 2010, the bank wanted to become the "best customer bank". The open strategy initiative allowed 8,000 employees and managers—responsible for private customers and small and medium sized enterprises (SMEs)—the opportunity to develop and define future service and consulting standards which could later be implemented in their daily work routine. Over six weeks employees were invited to describe an excellent customer experience based on a concrete practical example, thereby focusing on the employees' behaviors rather than processes, products or systems of the bank. 2,592 employees participated and contributed 900 new standards and 1,500 comments.

The initial "If I was my customer . . ." project soon turned into an industry-wide best practice example. A follow-up project, "You are the bank." (In German: "Du bist die Bank."), was launched with the goal of implementing the predefined service and consulting guidelines through all branches in the country.

The fourth case concerns a company-wide idea contest set up by a German multinational engineering and electronics company. The contest platform was intended to generate ideas and gather validation for a strategy concept within a particular organizational sector. This strategy would have the scope to impact 25,000 employees, and the organization wanted to engage the employees in the development process in order to gain as much buy-in as possible. The contest targeted the entire work force from one sector to submit strategies for creating and validating new business opportunities. The contest launched on April 11, 2011 and ran for two months. In total, 466 employees submitted 138 ideas. Further employees provided 628 evaluations and 355 detailed suggestions for improvements related to submitted concepts and ideas. At the end of the contest period five sector experts within the organization picked the top 50 ideas, which were presented to the board, who further selected three winners. The three winning ideas were further developed and business plans prepared.

Table 31.1 summarizes the four cases with their strategy objectives, means, kind of openness, and the results. In the following section of the paper we discuss our observations, the results of our qualitative interviews, and our theoretical reflections. Overall, 29 qualitative, semi-structured interviews were conducted. The objective was to explore experiences and identify benefits, critical issues and risks of open strategy projects. Interviewees included employees and managers from different hierarchical levels of the organizations.

Results

Participation

The objective of an open strategy project is to involve a large number of employees in strategy projects. As highlighted by one interviewee ". . . we don't want to simply let the employees know which direction

| **Table 31.1** | **Open Strategy Cases** | | | |

	BM (anonymized Austrian automation supplier)	Daimler	Hypo Vereinsbank (HVB)	EEC (anonymized Engineering and electronics company)
Strategy issue	Understand success factors and identify new technological solutions. Create a dialogue with employees.	Develop new business models: "Contribute to the achievement of Daimler's profitable growth targets by generating, evaluating and implementing growth options above and beyond the current business."	Implement "Excellent Customer Experience" strategy and derive service standards that can be implemented.	Submit strategies for creating and validating business opportunities with growth potential in sector X.
Means	Intranet-based corporate-wide platform with social software functionalities	Intranet-based corporate wide platform called 'Business Innovation Community' with social software functionalities	Intranet platform with social software functionalities: 2 phases: 1) define service standards ("If I was my customer. . ."), 2) then implementing them in a second phase ("You are the bank").	Intranet-based corporate contest platform
Openness	The intranet platform was accessible for two weeks to discuss four questions: 1. Success factors/strengths? 2. Future customer solutions? 3. Process improvement? 4. New technologies? During that time-span, participants were free to start new threads, assign them to one of the four topics, and comment on other people's posts.	Open to all employees, regardless of business unit affiliation, hierarchy level, or profession. When submitting ideas, users are asked to describe the idea and evaluate their proposals regarding market potential, volume of sales, potential risk, 'time-to-market'. Employees interactively and collaboratively generate, develop, and discuss ideas on new BM.	Open non-stop, giving 6,000 employees and managers the chance to post ideas, discuss and modify them and exchange experiences with colleagues, and describe everyday customer experiences in order to derive concrete service standards that can now be implemented.	Open for eight weeks to all employees from one business sector. Participants can submit ideas, evaluate ideas, or actively engage in discussions about submitted idea proposals, or chat with other participants by leaving messages on other members' profiles.

(Continued)

Table 31.1	(Continued)			
	BM (anonymized Austrian automation supplier)	Daimler	Hypo Vereinsbank (HVB)	EEC (anonymized Engineering and electronics company)
Results	• Of the 370 employees, 216 registered • 135 threads; 1,374 comments • 2 new, so far unknown technological issues were brought up	• Launch in August, 2008 • 30,000 employees registered • More than 2,000 ideas • 35 new business models, currently being tested for their market potential (e.g., car2go)	• 2,592 employees took part • In six weeks, the service standards were defined and summarized in six major categories. • Currently, the company is in the middle of implementing using the "You are the bank!" platform (employees discuss standards and contribute to implementation)	• 466 participants • 138 ideas were submitted • 355 suggestions for improvements • Several ideas have been tested, patents examined, project strategies developed, and business plans drawn up

we are heading. We would like to encourage them to follow us and even contribute to the strategy with their ideas and comments."

In all four cases, participation rates were high (BM=260 of 370; Daimler=30,000 of 270,000; HVB=2,400 of 6,000; and EEC=466 of 25,000 addressed employees). However, as has also been observed in open source and online innovation communities before (for a review see Füller et al., 2014), participation levels are not evenly distributed. Typically a small, dense, active core of participants dominates open strategy initiatives and there is a large, passive "periphery". In the first case, the medium-sized automation supplier, an "impact factor" was used as a measure of active participation and impact. Based on citations of posts, participants were rewarded with points for their contribution (Stieger et al., 2012). The top three participants had an impact-factor of 1,700, 1,480 and 1,120 respectively. They received a high impact factor by starting two

discussion topics with high numbers of comments posted by others. 51 participants (i.e., 20% of the participants) generated an impact factor higher than 100 and one third of all registered participants generated an impact higher than 30 points. 130 participants (i.e., half of the participants) did not receive any points at all; they did not write any comments and/ or no other person commented on their posts. In the Daimler case, approximately 50% of all ideas on the platform were provided by the 22 most active idea submitters, and 50% of all comments were submitted by the 10 most active commenting participants (Füller et al., 2014). Of those 1,049 participants that answered a survey about participation, 153 submitted at least one idea and 213 commented on ideas of others. There are various reasons for non-participation: no access (e.g., production plants), fear of exposure, no interest/ time, etc. Hauptmann and Steger (2013) argue that social networks within organizations create a kind of "parallel world." This "parallel world" might exclude many organizational members (e.g., digital natives versus elder cohorts), and individuals who are active in these networks do not necessarily represent the whole organization but rather an exclusive section of organization members. Hence, while on the one side social software- based open strategy initiatives enable the inclusion of more employees in strategy processes, there still remains the inclusion-exclusion problem (Hauptmann & Steger, 2013). Some employees might feel excluded because they do not have sufficient access (e.g., in production plants), or because they lack the skills, have a fear of exposure or not enough time (Füller et al., 2014). There are many positive effects of increasing the scope of involvement in strategy processes, such as "improved strategy execution, higher quality decisions, better understanding of deliberate strategy, enhanced organizational learning, stronger organizational commitment, higher job satisfaction, more adaptive core competencies, the development of competitive advantage and improved organizational performance." (Collier, Fishwick, & Floyd, 2004). However, studies also show that when (middle) managers are excluded from strategy-related conversations, this leads to alienation, lack of motivation to implement strategies, and intra-organizational conflict (Wooldridge, Schmid, & Floyd, 2008). Hence, the inclusion-exclusion problem in open strategy projects might be a serious issue and needs strong attention in research and in practice.

The fact that only a small, dense, active core contributes most to open strategy projects raises the question of how employees can be incentivized to participate and to contribute. Companies can use incentives (monetary and non-monetary) to foster enough crowd activity on the open strategy platform. These can be given to the most active contributors that generate the most influential contributions or to the best contributions that are selected and implemented. Open strategy platforms are built to draw on the collective intelligence of the community, facilitating interaction, information exchange, topic-related discussion, and community building and thus cooperation. However, a certain degree of competition among the participants will always occur. This competition can be spurred by incentives or by employees' desire for recognition, career prospects, and

reputation gains. Higher levels of competition can be expected when companies use both financial and non-financial rewards. In that case, open strategy projects are characterized by cooperation and competition, a phenomenon that has been labeled "communition" (Hutter, Hautz, Füller, Mueller, & Matzler, 2011) in the context of innovation communities. Diverse fields of literature such as economics (Greenhalgh & Rogers, 2006), game theory (Brandenburger & Nalebuff, 1996), knowledge sharing (Tsai, 2002), team performance (Beersma et al., 2003), innovation (Quintana-García & Benavides-Velasco, 2004), and problem solving (Qin, Johnson, & Johnson, 1995), studied the question of whether competition or cooperation is more beneficial. Social interdependence theory (Deutsch, 1949; Johnson & Johnson, 2005) argues that the structure of interdependencies among individuals determines cooperative and competitive behavior among them. Positive levels of interdependence lead to cooperative interactions via higher expectations of assistance and support, harmony, and trusting and friendly relationships, whereas negative interdependencies result in competitive interactions such as pursuing individual goals and win-lose rewards, increasing mistrust, and restricting information and resource exchange (Ghobadi & D'ambra, 2011). Studies in innovation communities found ambiguous results regarding hybrid structures (for a review see Bullinger, Neyer, Rass, & Moeslein Kathrin, 2010), and it remains to be studied how cooperation and competition among employees in social software-based open strategy projects influences the quality of contributions and acceptance of strategies.

Contributions to Strategy

In all four cases, executives were positively surprised by the number and quality of contributions. Many ideas came from the "far reaches" of the organizations, and executives were surprised how widely the ability to think creatively about strategy was distributed in the company. Daimler's car sharing business model was an outcome of the open strategy project; in the case of the automation supplier, two new technologies were brought to the surface by employees, and in the HVB project, a senior manager attributed an increase in the customer satisfaction score directly to employee involvement. Several interviews confirmed the benefits of including a large number of employees: "Due to the new tool the blue collar worker also has a chance to make his idea visible. Traditional communication ways are crossed over" stated one executive, and another one said: "The diversity of ideas is remarkable . . . it was a great reality check . . . of what our organization already knew and developed. The contest generated feedback from geographical regions and functional roles that would have never been involved using our traditional processes; we would have never engaged 450 employees to take such a strategy project seriously, think about it and contribute ideas and feedback."

These outcomes confirm Gary Hamel's view on strategy as a revolution: "Strategy making must be democratic . . . The capacity to think creatively about strategy is distributed widely in an enterprise. It is impossible to predict exactly where a revolutionary idea is forming" (Hamel, 1996). The use of social software, where individuals can contribute, comment, criticize and evaluate ideas, allows more cognitive diversity, which improves the ability of a group to process information as it increases variety in knowledge and perspectives (Kellermanns, Walter, Floyd, Lechner, & Shaw, 2011). The focus of the four cases analyzed was on different phases of strategy formulation. The first case (automation supplier) and the fourth case (EEC) focused on strategic analysis identification of ideas (e.g., success factors, strengths and weaknesses, future solutions), the second case (Daimler) focused on the more complex issues of developing business models (describe the idea and evaluate the proposal regarding market potential, volume of sales, potential risk, and 'time-to-market'), the third case focused on strategy implementation (i.e., involving employees to develop ideas to operationalize the strategy and contribute ideas for implementation). Although in all four cases valuable contributions were made by the employees, the question arises for which strategy topics social software-based open strategy is most suitable. Not all problems are suited for crowdsourcing (Boudreau & Lakhani, 2013). Some authors argue that the tasks given to a crowd should be of a modular, self-contained, closed

solution type (Afuah & Tucci, 2012; Majchrzak & Malhotra, 2013). This has led some researchers to suggest that crowdsourcing tasks should be split into phases, e.g., invite contributors to suggest ideas, let these ideas be evaluated by the crowd or by a jury, then re-invite the crowd to discuss specific questions and develop ideas further (Hutter et al., 2011). Such staged approaches could work well in strategy projects. However, much research is needed to understand which problems are suited for open strategy and how the process can be structured and managed.

Another interesting research avenue is enabled by social software. When log file data is available, social network supported open strategy initiatives allow the use of social network analysis that can contribute to answering important research questions. Identifying strategically relevant and influential professionals is difficult and problematic, and understanding why some are more influential and involved is still an important issue in strategy research (Pappas & Wooldridge, 2007; Wooldridge et al., 2008). Hence, social software-based open strategy projects should give rise to social network analysis to investigate the network structure, positions, influential people, and their behavior in strategizing.

Dialogues Across Hierarchies and Departments

Stieger et al. (2012) argue that social technologies and collaboration software allow companies to tap into the crowd of their employees on a greater scale than ever before and to integrate the organization's members in a strategy dialogue. This allows companies to start dialogues across hierarchies and departments, as evidenced by these statements: "It's a good tool to get people talking and to get an impression about the atmosphere in the company" (executive), "I've got great concepts, and I'd like to share my idea without filtering to improve my reputation" (employee), "Within the . . . community you can communicate with like-minded peers across hierarchical levels and geographical regions" (employee), "For the first time, we can "jump" hierarchies, I have direct contact to employees in the lowest ranks" (executive), and "Usually the communication of strategy runs down the hierarchy and the communication channel. With the contest platform we had a different angle to communicate, a completely new way of receiving the input and feedback from the employees and to get them engaged and directly contributing to the strategic direction" (executive). Hence, these more open forms of strategy-making that lead to more transparency and more inclusion of different actors (Whittington et al., 2011) might change traditional roles of managers in strategy processes. "Jumping" hierarchies might challenge power structures and strategic roles of managers. Especially middle managers have been viewed as very critical for strategies, as they synthesize, facilitate, champion, ratify and implement (Burgelman, 1991; Floyd & Lane, 2000). In traditional strategy processes middle managers are uniquely positioned in the evaluation of information as they have more knowledge of the strategic situation of the organization than operating managers and are more familiar with operational matters than top managers (Floyd & Lane, 2000). The fact that social software based open strategy allows communication across hierarchies and departments raises the important question of how roles and power structures in such forms of strategizing change.

Research in online innovation communities has shown that interaction and collaboration establishes social relationships and creates a sense of community (Abfalter, Zaglia, & Mueller, 2012; Gebauer, Füller, & Pezzei, 2013). It has been shown that such communities develop a shared language, a joint history, and over time, possibly common values and beliefs (Lakhani & Hippel, 2003). The formation of a sense of community across hierarchies, departments, and organizational units might have a number of positive effects but might also lead to dysfunctional behavior, e.g. when there is disagreement between the community and management decisions. Da Cunha and Orlikowski (2008) have shown that, in the context of a long-time change project in a major company, employees in online forums developed three practices through which they vented their negative emotions and tensions: constructing counter-narratives, sharing protest stories, and expressing solidarity. How social software-based open strategy projects foster a sense of community among employees and what the positive and negative effects are should be a promising and important research question.

Unpredictability

Companies that open their strategy processes must be aware that in such projects discussions can evolve in unpredictable directions. The "crowd" might reveal topics that are slumbering under the surface or come up with strategies or solutions management is not prepared for (Stieger et al., 2012). Statements like "How can an 'outsider' start criticizing my project idea and trying to get approval from other participants. Apparently, he wants to take over my idea!" or "Some employees like to discuss ideas over and over and miss the chance to implement" demonstrate that extensive critique might not be well received by participants. Controversial issues that emerge might create endless discussions and tensions. Literature on strategic consensus assumes that shared strategic thinking improves coordination and integration of collective efforts, smoothes implementation of strategy and ultimately enhances organizational performance (Bourgeois, 1980; Kellermanns et al., 2011). Sam Palmisano, former CEO of IBM, described his experience with IBM's Innovation Jam to include all employees in the formulation of corporate values this way: "They [the employees] were thoughtful and passionate about the company they want to be a part of. They were also brutally honest. Some of what they wrote was painful to read, because they pointed out all the bureaucratic and dysfunctional things that get in the way of serving clients, working as a team or implementing new ideas. But we were resolute in keeping the dialogue free-flowing and candid. And I don't think what resulted-broad, enthusiastic, grassroots consensus-could have been obtained in any other way"[1]. Management has to be prepared for harsh critique, and for employees to directly and bluntly address issues they consider important. In an open strategy process, where "employees would feel free to share their thoughts and opinion, however politically charged they might be" and where "the internal debate about strategy, direction, and policy would be open, vigorous, and uncensored" (Hamel, 2007) unpredictable issues might emerge, and employees might take sides in debates and identify with and commit to controversial issues. There is a high risk that, when debates and disputes persist for a longer time, community members will become divided and polarized into different and incompatible groups (Smith, 1999), whereby members become disengaged and alienated (Mortensen & Hinds, 2001). In the context of an online discussion forum-based change management project, Da Cunha and Orlikowski (2008) found that employee engagement in online forums can have the paradoxical effect of resisting and facilitating implementation at the same time. The online forum facilitated expression of resentment, frustration, and solidarity and thus provided an outlet for the employee's emotions, while this at the same time defused negative emotions and frustrations and dampened interest to openly resist the change program.

In open strategy projects, dissensus among employees and between employees and management might emerge and it remains to be studied how such dissensus be solved or how such dissensus across hierarchies and departments influences strategy projects and their success.

Misuses. Social media platforms can blur the line between private life and work life (Hauptmann & Steger, 2013) and this may mislead employees to misapply social media for private conversations and congest open strategy platforms with irrelevant content, as evidenced with this statement: "Other participants did have fun posting topics like canteen food". While there is a lot of evidence that increased involvement in strategy leads to stronger visions, increased rationality, and enhanced adaptiveness, there is also evidence that increased involvement may lead to more politics, cultural inertia and more constraints imposed on strategy (Collier et al., 2004). Statements like "Are you under-worked? The participation is not stated in your job description so concentrate on our core-business' was the reaction of my colleague when I started checking out the platform", "Mobbing, jealousy, time concern, lack of understanding, lack of feedback and resonance are major reasons why colleagues might avoid participation" or "I submitted an idea, but it somehow disappeared in the system…I have no idea about the current status of my submission…" demonstrate that misuses and politization might be problematic issues. Denyer et al. (2011), in their study on the use of social software

within organizations, come to a very disillusioning conclusion: "The use of the technology to serve political ends by those within the organization, may include power, suppression, hiding behind the technology or other forms of abuse" (Denyer et al., 2011). Research on middle management (Guth & Macmillan, 1986) has shown that there are several specific ways in which middle management hindered strategy implementation, including foot-dragging and sabotage. Also, middle manager perceptions of the strategy process can be colored by individual and unit self-interest. As open strategy widens the scope of involvement, the question arises how employees (middle managers, and employees in the lower ranks) might misuse such open strategy platforms, form coalitions, politicize, pursue self-interest, etc. Hence, questions like "What is opening strategy's impact on politization?" and "What is the influence of e.g., transparency, anonymity, etc.?" need utmost attention in future research.

Motivation and Responsiveness

Studies on employee involvement in strategy process have shown a long list of positive effects such as: "improved strategy execution, higher quality decisions, better understanding of deliberate strategy, enhanced organizational learning, stronger organizational commitment, higher job satisfaction, more adaptive core competencies, the development of competitive advantage and improved organizational performance" (Collier et al., 2004). Open strategy has a positive effect on employee's motivation; they "feel that they are taken seriously, so this open strategy project increases acceptance of the strategy and fosters implementation" (executive). This results in a high engagement and can lead to an overwhelming number of ideas: "They [the employees] come with a long list of things they would change—many managers are just overwhelmed with the aggregation of the sheer number of ideas/suggestions" (executive) or "In a sense we got the whole organization involved, and purely the amount of feedback we received by far exceeded anything that we received for other strategy projects, which had a larger magnitude financially" (executive).

As has been shown by Stieger et al. (2012), this can create a serious problem for managers, especially if their role is not clearly specified. From the employee's perspective not adequately responding to ideas can lead to frustration and bewilderment, as evidenced by the following statements: "Resignation, who is responsible for further development—no feedback, no comments, what happened with my idea—I was left alone with my submission." "What happened with my submission? I received pretty good community feedback and now? What's the next step? Did I pass the gate? I would love to read more about the activity on the community on our company blog or the intranet. Make it more transparent. Keep employees engaged" (employee), and "Experts equipped with power inside the organization should take up the ideas as a mentor and provide valuable feedback and discuss next steps towards implementation. Otherwise ideas will be buried in oblivion and their submitters loose interest due to missing resonance" (employee). Hence, appropriately reacting to ideas, recognition, clarifying roles of managers, etc. are important issues that have to be addressed in open strategy projects.

Culture

Stieger et al. (2012) argue that the critical challenge for social software-based open strategy is not related to "the technological infrastructure, but in creating a suitable process to encourage and guide employees in their participation". One senior manager described open strategy as "a vehicle to implement a new form of collaboration within the company" and another one said that wide participation of employees in such open strategy projects "is not simply a trend. It is an in inevitable change approaching us." The executive vice president of Strategy and Marketing at Red Hat, a company that introduced an open strategy process, said: "A traditional strategic planning model would not work at Red Hat. Red Hat had a deeply entrenched and open source-inspired culture that prized transparency and collaboration"[2]. Besides technological, societal, and organization issues, Whittington et al. (2011), also see cultural change as a driver of open strategy.

Postmodern-skepticism and the belief that knowledge is no longer organized hierarchically in organizations or in society is a cultural force that drives companies to open their strategy processes. Hence, it can also be argued that an open culture that emphasizes transparency and open dialogues, where employees have no fear of exposure, seems to be an important prerequisite for open strategy. Obviously culture matters, and it is to be researched which cultural environment best fits an open strategy approach, what topics are suitable for open strategy projects, and how opening strategy changes the culture in an organization.

Conclusion

Open strategy seems to radically change the strategist's work (Whittington et al., 2011). More open, inclusive, and transparent ways of strategizing offer new opportunities to tap into the knowledge of employees, regardless of their position, and to create more identification with and more commitment to a strategy. However, open strategy also creates some challenges for organizations. In this paper we described four cases of open strategy and identified seven critical issues based on our observations and on our qualitative interviews. These issues raise important research questions and have wide implications for managerial practice. It remains to be studied how opening strategy influences the outcome of strategy work (i.e., quality of strategy and quality of execution). As knowledge is increasingly democratized, strategies that are built on the "wisdom of the crowd" (i.e., knowledge of all organizational members) may be more realistic and executable. Strategy formation is a process of social interaction, based on the beliefs and shared understandings of an organization's members (Mintzberg et al., 2009). Involving all employees in strategy making might increase identification and commitment and, as a consequence, improve execution and performance.

In open strategy projects, the role of top management is changing from authors of strategy to editors of strategy (Skarzynski & Gibson, 2008). The more transparent and inclusive approach to strategy also changes the role of employees from implementers of strategy to active shapers of strategy. Managers might not have to "sell" their strategy anymore to employees, who, have being part of its formulation, "own" the strategy. Middle managers' role in strategy has been described as synthesizing, facilitating, championing, and implementing (Burgelman, 1991; Floyd & Lane, 2000). A major question to study is how roles of managers and employees on all levels change, when strategy dialogues across hierarchies, departments, and organizational units are made possible. How do social software-based open strategy projects foster a sense of community among employees, and what are the positive and negative effects?

A third major research question relates to predictability. A big advantage of an exclusive and secretive strategy process is that is easier to manage and to control. In this regard, opening strategy entails major risks. How can and should managers react to unforeseen and uncomfortable ideas and discussions? What is their role? How should they intervene? How can dissensus among employees, departments, etc., be solved when individuals and groups commit themselves to opposing ideas? How does such dissensus influence the quality of a strategy and its implementation?

Social software-based open strategy also poses some significant threats to organizations. Users of social software might organize within online communities and "develop a life of their own" (Wiertz & de Ruyter, 2007). This may also be the case in open strategy projects and politization, bulling, or misusing the open strategy platform for private and irrelevant topics are potential consequences. Management is challenged with understanding which interventions are beneficial or obstructive in building vibrant and effective platforms and communities (Haefliger, Moneiro, Foray, & Von Krogh, 2011).

While it seems that involving employees in strategy projects on a large scale increases their motivation and their commitment, management has to be aware that it cannot appropriately react to all suggestions and ideas. As employees publicly expose themselves with their contributions, neglecting or rejecting suggestions, ideas, or contributions might have contrary effects. As has been observed in the cases, managers had to deal with an overwhelming number of contributions. Hence, it has to be studied how employees can be kept motivated and engaged during and after an open strategy project. This especially involves the role of managers in reacting to contributions, selecting ideas, recognizing contributions, and dealing with them. Opening strategy does not imply that decisions are democratized: "Openness refers to the sharing of views, information and knowledge, not a democracy of actual decision making" (Whittington et al., 2011). Hence, decision making power remains with top-management. Whether and how top management can decide against the opinion of a "crowd" involved in the process and how involved employees react to such decisions is to be studied. Studies in the context of involving users via open innovation communities in co-creation projects show how strong reactions can be when participants, who during the initiative develop a sense of community, perceive the sponsoring company's decision as unfair (Gebauer et al., 2013).

In this paper we explored forms of open strategy within firms. However, open strategy may also involve external stakeholders, e.g., customers, suppliers, partners, etc. Whittington et al. distinguish between internal and external openness of strategy (Whittington et al., 2011), where in the latter case external actors are included (Dobusch & Kapeller, 2013). Opening strategy to externals adds much complexity to the process and likely leads to new questions and concerns, e.g., the issue of knowledge leakage (Hustad & Teigland, 2008) or the management of community boundaries, for which current strategy literature offers little guidance (Haefliger et al., 2011). In this context, von Krogh (2012) points at two important issues: 1) how can critical knowledge be protected from spilling over with social software and 2) how can the value of knowledge, and in turn the value of a knowledge-intensive company, be ensured when this value rests on "the quality, distinctiveness, and ownership of data, information, and knowledge" (p. 158)?

Finally, opening strategy requires an open culture. Not every company and not every problem might be suitable for such an initiative. Cultural antecedents and consequences for open strategy seem to be another major theme for research in this context.

We close this chapter with a final consideration. Open strategy might have the potential to disrupt the consultancy industry. Consulting firms are hired for their specialized knowledge and for their capabilities, however "as access to knowledge is democratized, opacity fades and clients no longer have to pay the fees of big consulting firms." (Christensen, Wang, & van Bever, 2013). Social-media supported platforms might be the enabling technology. Companies might start with small and simple open strategy projects (e.g., SWOT-Analysis, idea generation) and learn the benefits of the approach, improve processes, extend the scope and step-by-step realize that fewer and fewer strategy problems require consultants. A McKinsey study from 2011 (Bughin, Hung Byers, & Chui, 2011) found that of those companies that use social technologies (e.g., social networking, blogs, Wikis), they do so to scan the external environment (73%), find new ideas (73%), manage projects (55%), and develop strategic plans (43%). In these companies open strategy has already gotten a foothold.

Notes

1. "Our Values at Work on Being an IBMer" www.ibm.at, cited in: Skarzynski, P., & Gibson, R. 2008. *Innovation to the Core*. Boston: Harvard Business Press.
2. http://www.managementexchange.com/story/democratizing-corporate-strategy-process-red-hat

References

Abfalter, D., Zaglia, M. E., & Mueller, J. 2012. Sense of virtual community: A follow up on its measurement. *Computers in Human Behavior*, 28(2): 400–404.

Afuah, A., & Tucci, C. L. 2012. Crowdsourcing As a Solution to Distant Search. *Academy of Management Review*, 37(3): 355–375.

Bebensee, T., Helms, R., & Spruit, M. 2011. Exploring Web 2.0 applications as a means of bolstering up knowledge management. *Electronic Journal of Knowledge Management*, 9: 1–9.

Beersma, B., Hollenbeck, J. R., Humphrey, S. E., Moon, H., Conlon, D. E., & Ilgen, D. R. 2003. Cooperation, Competition, and Team Performance: Toward a Contingency Approach. *Academy of Management Journal*, 46(5): 572–590.

Bonabeau, E. 2009. Decisions 2.0: The power of collective intelligence. *Sloan Management Review*(Winter): 45–52.

Bonabeau, E., & Meyer, C. 2001. Swarm Intelligence: A Whole new Way to Think about Business. *Harvard Business Review*(May): 107–114.

Boudreau, K. J., & Lakhani, K. 2013. Using the crowd as an innovation partner. *Harvard Business Review*(April): 61–69.

Bourgeois, L. J. 1980. Performance and consensus. *Strategic Management Journal*, 1(3): 227–248.

Brandenburger, A., & Nalebuff, B. 1996. *Co-opetition*. New York: Doubleday/Currency.

Bughin, J., Hung Byers, A., & Chui, M. 2011. How social technologies are extending the organization. *McKinsey Quarterly*(November): 1–10.

Bullinger, A., C., Neyer, A.-K., Rass, M., & Moeslein Kathrin, M. 2010. Community-Based Innovation Contests: Where Competition Meets Cooperation. *Creativity and Innovation Management*, 19(3): 290–303.

Burgelman, R. 1991. Intraorganizational ecology of strategy-making and organizational adaptation: Theory and field research. *Organization Science*, 2: 239–262.

Chesbrough, H. 2003. *Open innovation: The new imperative for creating and profiting from technology* (1st ed.). Boston: Harvard Business School Press.

Chesbrough, H., & Appleyard, M. M. 2007. Open innovation and strategy. *California Management Review*, 50(1): 57–76.

Christensen, C. M., Wang, D., & van Bever, D. 2013. Consulting on the cuspt of disruption. *Harvard Business Review*(October): 107–114.

Collier, N., Fishwick, F., & Floyd, S. W. 2004. Managerial Involvement and Perceptions of Strategy Process. *Long Range Planning*, 37(1): 67–83.

da Cunha, J. V., & Orlikowski, W. J. 2008. Performing catharsis: The use of online discussion forums in organizational change. *Information and Organization*, 18(2): 132–156.

Denyer, D., Parry, E., & Flowers, P. 2011. "Social", "Open" and "Participative"? Exploring Personal Experiences and Organisational Effects of Enterprise 2.0 Use. *Long Range Planning*, 44(5–6): 375–396.

Deutsch, M. 1949. A theory of cooperation and competition. *Human Relations*, 2(2): 129–152.

Dobusch, L., & Kapeller, J. 2013. Open strategy between crowd and community: Lessons from Wikimedia and Creative Commons, *Academy of Management Meeting*. Orlando, FL.

Dobusch, L., & Müller-Seitz, G. 2012. Strategy as a practice of thousands? *Academy of Management Best Paper Proceedings.*

Floyd, S. W., & Lane, P. J. 2000. Strategizing Throughout the Organization: Managing Role Conflict in Strategic Renewal. *Academy of Management Review,* 25(1): 154–177.

Füller, J., Hutter, K., Hautz, J., & Matzler, K. 2014. Internal innovation communities: The influence of motives and barriers on employees' participation intensity. *Journal of Product Innovation Management,* (forthcoming).

Gebauer, J., Füller, J., & Pezzei, R. 2013. The dark and the bright side of co-creation: Triggers of member behavior in online innovation communities. *Journal of Business Research,* 66(9): 1516–1527.

Ghobadi, S., & D'ambra, J. 2011. Coopetitive knowledge sharing: An analytical review of literature. *The Electronic Journal of Knowledge Management,* 9(4): 307–317.

Giles, W. G. 1991. Making strategy work. *Long Range Planning,* 24(5): 75–91.

Greenhalgh, C., & Rogers, M. 2006. The value of innovation: The interaction of competition, R&D and IP. *Research Policy,* 35(4): 562–580.

Guth, W. D., & Macmillan, I. C. 1986. Strategy implementation versus middle management self-interest. *Strategic Management Journal,* 7(4): 313–327.

Haefliger, S., Moneiro, E., Foray, D., & Von Krogh, G. 2011. Social software and strategy. *Long Range Planning,* 44: 297–316.

Hamel, G. 1996. Strategy as revolution. *Harvard Business Review* (July-August): 69–82.

Hamel, G. 2007. *The future of management.* Boston: Harvard Business Press.

Hauptmann, S., & Steger, T. 2013. "A brave new (digital) world"? Effects of In-house Social Media on HRM. *Zeitschrift für Personalsforschung,* 27(1): 26–46.

Howe, J. 2006. The Rise of Crowdsourcing. *Wired Magazine* (14.06): 5.

Hustad, E., & Teigland, R. 2008. *Implementing social networking media and Web 2.0 in multinationals: Implications for knowledge management.* Paper presented at the Proceedings of the 9th European Conference on Knowledge Management.

Hutter, K., Hautz, J., Füller, J., Mueller, J., & Matzler, K. 2011. Communitition: The Tension between Competition and Collaboration in Community-Based Design Contests. *Creativity & Innovation Management,* 20(1): 3–21.

Johnson, D. W., & Johnson, R. T. 2005. New Developments in Social Interdependence Theory. *Genetic, Social, and General Psychology Monographs,* 131(4): 285–358.

Kellermanns, F. W., Walter, J., Floyd, S. W., Lechner, C., & Shaw, J. C. 2011. To agree or not to agree? A meta-analytical review of strategic consensus and organizational performance. *Journal of Business Research,* 64(2): 126–133.

Lakhani, K., & Hippel, E. V. 2003. How Open Source Software Works: "Free" User-to-User Assistance. *Research Policy,* 32(6): 923–942.

Majchrzak, A., & Malhotra, A. 2013. Towards an information systems perspective and research agenda on crowdsourcing for innovation. *The Journal of Strategic Information Systems,* 22(4): 257–268.

Matzler, K., Füller, J., Koch, B., Hautz, J., & Hutter, K. 2013. Open Strategy-a new strategy paradigm? In K. Matzler, H. Pechlaner, & B. Renzl (Eds.), *Strategie und Leadership:* 37–58. Wiesbaden: Gabler.

Mintzberg, H. 2009. Rebuilding companies as communities. *Harvard Business Review*(July- August): 1–4.

Mintzberg, H., Allstrand, B., & Lampel, J. 2009. *Strategy Safari.* Harlow et al.: Prentice Hall.

Mortensen, M., & Hinds, P. J. 2001. Conflict and shared identity in geographically distributed teams. *International journal of conflict management,* 12(3): 212–238.

Newstead, B., & Lanzerotti, L. 2010. Can you open-source your strategy? *Harvard Business Review*(October): 32.

Page, S. E. 2007. *The Difference - How the Power of Diversity Creates Better Groups, Firms, Schools and Societies.* Princeton, NJ: Princeton University Press.

Pappas, J. M., & Wooldridge, B. 2007. Middle Managers' Divergent Strategic Activity: An Investigation of Multiple Measures of Network Centrality. *Journal of Management Studies,* 44(3): 323–341.

Prahalad, C. K. 1995. New view of strategy: An interview with C. K. Prahalad. *European Journal of Management,* 13(2): 131–138.

Qin, Z., Johnson, D. W., & Johnson, R. T. 1995. Cooperative Versus Competitive Efforts and Problem Solving. *Review of Educational Research,* 65(2): 129–143.

Quintana-García, C., & Benavides-Velasco, C. A. 2004. Cooperation, competition, and innovative capability: a panel data of European dedicated biotechnology firms. *Technovation,* 24(12): 927–938.

Skarzynski, P., & Gibson, R. 2008. *Innovation to the core.* Boston: Harvard Business Press.

Smith, A. D. 1999. Problems of conflict management in virtual communities. In M. A. Smith, & P. Kollock

(Eds.), *communities in cyberspace*: 134–163. New York: Routledge.

Sterling, J. 2003. Translating strategy into effective implementation: Dispelling the myths and highlighting what works. *Strategy & Leadership*, 31(3): 27-34.

Stieger, D., Matzler, K., Chatterjee, S., & Ladstätter-Fussenegger, F. 2012. Democratizing Strategy: How crowdsourcing can be used for strategy dialogues. *California Management Review*, 54(4): 1–26.

Surowiecki, J. 2004. *The wisdom of crowds: Why the many are smarter than the few and how collective wisdom shapes business, economies, societies and nations*. London: Abacus.

Tsai, W. 2002. Social Structure of "Coopetition" Within a Multiunit Organization: Coordination, Competition, and Intraorganizational Knowledge Sharing. *Organization Science*, 13(2): 179–190.

von Krogh, G. 2012. How does social software change knowledge management? Toward a strategic research agenda. *The Journal of Strategic Information Systems*, 21(2): 154–164.

Whittington, R. 2014. Information systems strategy and Strategy-as-Practice: a Joint Agenda. *The Journal of Strategic Information Systems*, (forthcoming).

Whittington, R., Cailluet, L., & Yakis-Douglas, B. 2011. Opening Strategy: Evolution of a Precarious Profession. *British Journal of Management*, 22(3): 531–544.

Wiertz, C., & de Ruyter, K. 2007. Beyond the Call of Duty: Why Customers Contribute to Firm Hosted Commercial Online Communities. *Organization Studies*, 28(03): 347–376.

Wooldridge, B., Schmid, T., & Floyd, S. W. 2008. The Middle Management Perspective on Strategy Process: Contributions, Synthesis, and Future Research. *Journal of Management*, 34(6): 1190–1221.

CHAPTER 32

Big Data

The Management Revolution

Andrew McAfee
Massachusetts Institute of Technology

Erik Brynjolfsson
Massachusetts Institute of Technology

"You can't manage what you don't measure."

There's much wisdom in that saying, which has been attributed to both W. Edwards Deming and Peter Drucker, and it explains why the recent explosion of digital data is so important. Simply put, because of big data, managers can measure, and hence know, radically more about their businesses, and directly translate that knowledge into improved decision making and performance.

Consider retailing. Booksellers in physical stores could always track which books sold and which did not. If they had a loyalty program, they could tie some of those purchases to individual customers. And that was about it. Once shopping moved online, though, the understanding of customers increased dramatically. Online retailers could track not only what customers bought, but also what else they looked at;

how they navigated through the site; how much they were influenced by promotions, reviews, and page layouts; and similarities across individuals and groups. Before long, they developed algorithms to predict what books individual customers would like to read next—algorithms that performed better every time the customer responded to or ignored a recommendation. Traditional retailers simply couldn't access this kind of information, let alone act on it in a timely manner. It's no wonder that Amazon has put so many brick-and-mortar bookstores out of business.

The familiarity of the Amazon story almost masks its power. We expect companies that were born digital to accomplish things that business executives could only dream of a generation ago. But in fact the use of big data has the potential to transform traditional businesses as well. It may offer them even greater opportunities for competitive advantage (online businesses have always known that they were competing on how well they understood their data). As we'll discuss in more detail, the big data of this revolution is far more powerful than sure and therefore manage more precisely than ever before. We can make better predictions and smarter decisions. We can target more-effective interventions, and can do so in areas that so far have been dominated by gut and intuition rather than by data and rigor.

As the tools and philosophies of big data spread, they will change long-standing ideas about the value of experience, the nature of expertise, and the practice of management. Smart leaders across industries will see using big data for what it is: a management revolution. But as with any other major change in business, the challenges of becoming a big data–enabled organization can be enormous and require hands-on—or in some cases hands-off—leadership. Nevertheless, it's a transition that executives need to engage with today.

What's New Here?

Business executives sometimes ask us, "Isn't 'big data' just another way of saying 'analytics'?" It's true that they're related: The big data movement, like analytics before it, seeks to glean intelligence from data and translate that into business advantage. However, there are three key differences:

Volume

As of 2012, about 2.5 exabytes of data are created each day, and that number is doubling every 40 months or so. More data cross the internet than were stored in the entire internet just 20 years ago. This gives companies an opportunity to work with many petabyes of data in a single data set—and not just from the internet. For instance, it is estimated that Walmart collects more than 2.5 petabytes of data every hour from its customer transactions. A petabyte is one quadrillion bytes, or the equivalent of about 20 million filing cabinets' worth of text. An exabyte is 1,000 times that amount, or one billion gigabytes.

Velocity

For many applications, the speed of data creation is even more important than the volume. Real-time or nearly real-time information makes it possible for a company to be much more agile than its competitors.

IDEA IN BRIEF

Data-driven decisions are better decisions—it's as simple as that. Using big data enables managers to decide on the basis of evidence rather than intuition. For that reason it has the potential to revolutionize management.

Companies that were born digital, such as Google and Amazon, are already masters of big data. But the potential to gain competitive advantage from it may be even greater for other companies.

The managerial challenges, however, are very real. Senior decision makers have to embrace evidence-based decision making. Their companies need to hire scientists who can find patterns in data and translate them into useful business information. And whole organizations need to redefine their understanding of "judgment."

For instance, our colleague Alex "Sandy" Pentland and his group at the MIT Media Lab used location data from mobile phones to infer how many people were in Macy's parking lots on Black Friday—the start of the Christmas shopping season in the United States. This made it possible to estimate the retailer's sales on that critical day even before Macy's itself had recorded those sales. Rapid insights like that can provide an obvious competitive advantage to Wall Street analysts and Main Street managers.

Variety

Big data takes the form of messages, updates, and images posted to social networks; readings from sensors; GPS signals from cell phones, and more. Many of the most important sources of big data are relatively new. The huge amounts of information from social networks, for example, are only as old as the networks themselves; Facebook was launched in 2004, Twitter in 2006. The same holds for smartphones and the other mobile devices that now provide enormous streams of data tied to people, activities, and locations. Because these devices are ubiquitous, it's easy to forget that the iPhone was unveiled only five years ago, and the iPad in 2010. Thus the structured databases that stored most corporate information until recently are ill suited to storing and processing big data. At the same time, the steadily declining costs of all the elements of computing—storage, memory, processing, bandwidth, and so on—mean that previously expensive data-intensive approaches are quickly becoming economical.

As more and more business activity is digitized, new sources of information and ever-cheaper equipment combine to bring us into a new era: one in which large amounts of digital information exist on virtually any topic of interest to a business. Mobile phones, online shopping, social networks, electronic communication, GPS, and instrumented machinery all produce torrents of data as a by-product of their ordinary operations. Each of us is now a walking data generator. The data available are often unstructured—not organized in a database—and unwieldy, but there's a huge amount of signal in the noise, simply waiting to be released. Analytics brought rigorous techniques to decision making; big data is at once simpler and more powerful. As Google's director of research, Peter Norvig, puts it: "We don't have better algorithms. We just have more data."

How Data-Driven Companies Perform

The second question skeptics might pose is this: "Where's the evidence that using big data intelligently will improve business performance?" The business press is rife with anecdotes and case studies that supposedly demonstrate the value of being data-driven. But the truth, we realized recently, is that nobody was tackling that question rigorously. To address this embarrassing gap, we led a team at the MIT Center for Digital Business, working in partnership with McKinsey's business technology office and with our colleague Lorin Hitt at Wharton and the MIT doctoral student Heekyung Kim. We set out to test the hypothesis that data-driven companies would be better performers. We conducted structured interviews with executives at 330 public North American companies about their organizational and technology management practices, and gathered performance data from their annual reports and independent sources.

Not everyone was embracing data-driven decision making. In fact, we found a broad spectrum of attitudes and approaches in every industry. But across all the analyses we conducted, one relationship stood out: The more companies characterized themselves as data-driven, the better they performed on objective measures of financial and operational results. In particular, companies in the top third of their industry in the use of data-driven decision making were, on average, 5% more productive and 6% more profitable than their competitors. This performance difference remained robust after accounting for the contributions of labor, capital, purchased services, and traditional IT investment. It was statistically significant and economically important and was reflected in measurable increases in stock market valuations.

EXPERTISE FROM SURPRISING SOURCES

Often someone coming from outside an industry can spot a better way to use big data than an insider, just because so many new, unexpected sources of data are available. One of us, Erik, demonstrated this in research he conducted with Lynn Wu, now an assistant professor at Wharton. They used publicly available web search data to predict housing-price changes in metropolitan areas across the United States. They had no special knowledge of the housing market when they began their study, but they reasoned that virtually real-time search data would enable good near-term forecasts about the housing market—and they were right. In fact, their prediction proved more accurate than the official one from the National Association of Realtors, which had developed a far more complex model but relied on relatively slow-changing historical data.

This is hardly the only case in which simple models and big data trump more-elaborate analytics approaches. Researchers at the Johns Hopkins School of Medicine, for example, found that they could use data from Google Flu Trends (a free, publicly available aggregator of relevant search terms) to predict surges in flu-related emergency room visits a week before warnings came from the Centers for Disease Control. Similarly, Twitter updates were as accurate as official reports at tracking the spread of cholera in Haiti after the January 2010 earthquake; they were also two weeks earlier.

So how are managers using big data? Let's look in detail at two companies that are far from Silicon Valley upstarts. One uses big data to create new businesses, the other to drive more sales.

Improved Airline ETAs

Minutes matter in airports. So does accurate information about flight arrival times: If a plane lands before the ground staff is ready for it, the passengers and crew are effectively trapped, and if it shows up later than expected, the staff sits idle, driving up costs. So when a major U.S. airline learned from an internal study that about 10% of the flights into its major hub had at least a 10-minute gap between the estimated time of arrival and the actual arrival time—and 30% had a gap of at least five minutes—it decided to take action.

At the time, the airline was relying on the aviation industry's long-standing practice of using the ETAs provided by pilots. The pilots made these estimates during their final approach to the airport, when they had many other demands on their time and attention. In search of a better solution, the airline turned to PASSUR Aerospace, a provider of decision-support technologies for the aviation industry. In 2001 PASSUR began offering its own arrival estimates as a service called RightETA. It calculated these times by combining publicly available data about weather, flight schedules, and other factors with proprietary data the company itself collected, including feeds from a network of passive radar stations it had installed near airports to gather data about every plane in the local sky.

PASSUR started with just a few of these installations, but by 2012 it had more than 155. Every 4.6 seconds it collects a wide range of information about every plane that it "sees." This yields a huge and constant flood of digital data. What's more, the company keeps all the data it has gathered over time, so it has an immense body of multidimensional information spanning more than a decade. This allows sophisticated analysis and pattern matching. RightETA essentially works by asking itself "What happened all the previous times a plane approached this airport under these conditions? When did it actually land?"

After switching to RightETA, the airline virtually eliminated gaps between estimated and actual arrival times. PASSUR believes that enabling an airline to know when its planes are going to land and plan accordingly is worth several million dollars a year at each airport. It's a simple formula: Using big data leads to better predictions, and better predictions yield better decisions.

Speedier, More Personalized Promotions

A couple of years ago, Sears Holdings came to the conclusion that it needed to generate greater value from the huge amounts of customer, product, and promotion data it collected from its Sears, Craftsman, and Lands' End brands. Obviously, it would be valuable to combine and make use of all these data to tailor promotions and other offerings to customers, and to personalize the offers to take advantage of local conditions. Valuable, but difficult: Sears required about eight weeks to generate personalized promotions, at which point many of them were no longer optimal for the company. It took so long mainly because the data required for these large-scale analyses were both voluminous and highly fragmented—housed in many databases and "data warehouses" maintained by the various brands.

In search of a faster, cheaper way to do its analytic work, Sears Holdings turned to the technologies and practices of big data. As one of its first steps, it set up a Hadoop cluster. This is simply a group of inexpensive commodity servers whose activities are coordinated by an emerging software framework called Hadoop (named after a toy elephant in the household of Doug Cutting, one of its developers).

Sears started using the cluster to store incoming data from all its brands and to hold data from existing data warehouses. It then conducted analyses on the cluster directly, avoiding the time-consuming complexities of pulling data from various sources and combining them so that they can be analyzed. This change allowed the company to be much faster and more precise with its promotions. According to the company's CTO, Phil Shelley, the time needed to generate a comprehensive set of promotions dropped from eight weeks to one, and is still dropping. And these promotions are of higher quality, because they're more timely, more granular, and more personalized. Sears's Hadoop cluster stores and processes several petabytes of data at a fraction of the cost of a comparable standard data warehouse.

Shelley says he's surprised at how easy it has been to transition from old to new approaches to data management and high-performance analytics. Because skills and knowledge related to new data technologies were so rare in 2010, when Sears started the transition, it contracted some of the work to a company called Cloudera. But over time its old guard of IT and analytics professionals have become comfortable with the new tools and approaches.

The PASSUR and Sears Holding examples illustrate the power of big data, which allows more accurate predictions, better decisions, and precise interventions, and can enable these things at seemingly limitless scale. We've seen big data used in supply chain management to understand why a carmaker's defect rates in the field suddenly increased, in customer service to continually scan and intervene in the health care practices of millions of people, in planning and forecasting to better anticipate online sales on the basis of a data set of product characteristics, and so on. We've seen similar payoffs in many other industries and functions, from finance to marketing to hotels and gaming, and from human resource management to machine repair.

Our statistical analysis tells us that what we're seeing is not just a few flashy examples but a more fundamental transformation of the economy. We've become convinced that almost no sphere of business activity will remain untouched by this movement.

A New Culture of Decision Making

The technical challenges of using big data are very real. But the managerial challenges are even greater—starting with the role of the senior executive team.

> *Big data's power does not erase the need for vision or human insight.*

Muting the HiPPOs

One of the most critical aspects of big data is its impact on how decisions are made and who gets to make them. When data are scarce, expensive to obtain, or not available in digital form, it makes sense to let well-placed people make decisions, which they do on the basis of experience they've built up and patterns and relationships they've observed and internalized. "Intuition" is the label given to this style of inference and decision making. People state their opinions about what the future holds—what's going to happen, how well something will work, and so on—and then plan accordingly. (See "The True Measures of Success," by Michael J. Mauboussin, in this issue.)

For particularly important decisions, these people are typically high up in the organization, or they're expensive outsiders brought in because of their expertise and track records. Many in the big data community maintain that companies often make most of their important decisions by relying on "HiPPO"—the highest-paid person's opinion.

To be sure, a number of senior executives are genuinely data-driven and willing to override their own intuition when the data don't agree with it. But we believe that throughout the business world today, people rely too much on experience and intuition and not enough on data. For our research we constructed a 5-point composite scale that captured the overall extent to which a company was data-driven. Fully 32% of our respondents rated their companies at or below 3 on this scale.

New Roles

Executives interested in leading a big data transition can start with two simple techniques. First, they can get in the habit of asking "What do the data say?" when faced with an important decision and following up with more-specific questions such as "Where did the data come from?," "What kinds of analyses were conducted?," and "How confident are we in the results?" (People will get the message quickly if executives develop this discipline.) Second, they can allow themselves to be overruled by the data; few things are more powerful for changing a decision-making culture than seeing a senior executive concede when data have disproved a hunch.

When it comes to knowing which problems to tackle, of course, domain expertise remains critical. Traditional domain experts—those deeply familiar with an area—are the ones who know where the biggest opportunities and challenges lie. PASSUR, for one, is trying to hire as many people as possible who have extensive knowledge of operations at America's major airports. They will be invaluable in helping the company figure out what offerings and markets it should go after next.

As the big data movement advances, the role of domain experts will shift. They'll be valued not for their HiPPO-style answers but because they know what questions to ask. Pablo Picasso might have been thinking of domain experts when he said, "Computers are useless. They can only give you answers."

Five Management Challenges

Companies won't reap the full benefits of a transition to using big data unless they're able to manage change effectively. Five areas are particularly important in that process.

Leadership

Companies succeed in the big data era not simply because they have more or better data, but because they have leadership teams that set clear goals, define what success looks like, and ask the right questions. Big data's power does not erase the need for vision or human insight. On the contrary, we still must have business leaders who can spot a great opportunity, understand how a market is developing, think creatively and propose truly novel offerings, articulate a compelling vision, persuade people to embrace it and work hard to realize it, and deal effectively with customers, employees, stockholders, and other stakeholders. The successful companies of the next decade will be the ones whose leaders can do all that while changing the way their organizations make many decisions.

GETTING STARTED

You don't need to make enormous up-front investments in IT to use big data (unlike earlier generations of IT-enabled change).

Here's one approach to building a capability from the ground up.

1. Pick a business unit to be the testing ground. It should have a quant-friendly leader backed up by a team of data scientists.

2. Challenge each key function to identify five business opportunities based on big data, each of which could be prototyped within five weeks by a team of no more than five people.

3. Implement a process for innovation that includes four steps: experimentation, measurement, sharing, and replication.

4. Keep in mind Joy's Law: "Most of the smartest people work for someone else." Open up some of your data sets and analytic challenges to interested parties across the internet and around the world.

Talent Management

As data become cheaper, the complements to data become more valuable. Some of the most crucial of these are data scientists and other professionals skilled at working with large quantities of information. Statistics are important, but many of the key techniques for using big data are rarely taught in traditional statistics courses. Perhaps even more important are skills in cleaning and organizing large data sets; the new kinds of data rarely come in structured formats. Visualization tools and techniques are also increasing in value. Along with the data scientists, a new generation of computer scientists are bringing to bear techniques for working with very large data sets. Expertise in the design of experiments can help cross the gap between correlation and causation. The best data scientists are also comfortable speaking the language of business and helping leaders reformulate their challenges in ways that big data can tackle. Not surprisingly, people with these skills are hard to find and in great demand. (See "Data Scientist: The Sexiest Job of the 21st Century," by Thomas H. Davenport and D.J. Patil, in this issue.)

Technology

The tools available to handle the volume, velocity, and variety of big data have improved greatly in recent years. In general, these technologies are not prohibitively expensive, and much of the software is open source. Hadoop, the most commonly used framework, combines commodity hardware with open-source software. It takes incoming streams of data and distributes them onto cheap disks; it also provides tools for analyzing the data. However, these technologies do require a skill set that is new to most IT departments, which will need to work hard to integrate all the relevant internal and external sources of data. Although attention to technology isn't sufficient, it is always a necessary component of a big data strategy.

Decision Making

An effective organization puts information and the relevant decision rights in the same location. In the big data era, information is created and transferred, and expertise is often not where it used to be. The artful leader will create an organization flexible enough to minimize the "not invented here" syndrome and maximize crossfunctional cooperation. People who understand the problems need to be brought together with the right data, but also with the people who have problem-solving techniques that can effectively exploit them.

Company Culture

The first question a data-driven organization asks itself is not "What do we think?" but "What do we know?" This requires a move away from acting solely on hunches and instinct. It also requires breaking a bad habit we've noticed in many organizations: pretending to be more data-driven than they actually are. Too often, we saw executives who spiced up their reports with lots of data that supported decisions they had already made using the traditional HiPPO approach. Only afterward were underlings dispatched to find the numbers that would justify the decision.

Without question, many barriers to success remain. There are too few data scientists to go around. The technologies are new and in some cases exotic. It's too easy to mistake correlation for causation and to find misleading patterns in the data. The cultural challenges are enormous, and, of course, privacy concerns are only going to become more significant. But the underlying trends, both in the technology and in the business payoff, are unmistakable.

The evidence is clear: Data-driven decisions tend to be better decisions. Leaders will either embrace this fact or be replaced by others who do. In sector after sector, companies that figure out how to combine domain expertise with data science will pull away from their rivals. We can't say that all the winners will be harnessing big data to transform decision making. But the data tell us that's the surest bet.

CHAPTER 33

Organizational Change Practices

Gill Robinson Hickman

University of Richmond

Which Practices Do We Employ to Implement Change?

The focus of considerable scholarship on leading change stems from studies of change practices in organizations. Researchers strive to determine which practices generate the most effective processes and outcomes. This section highlights several categories of practice—collective or collaborative approaches, strategic planning and goal setting, stages of praxis, and ethical practices—and links them to concepts of organizational change and leadership. Additionally, several practices including environmental scanning (periodic or continuous), scenario planning, and scenario building help to address several questions raised earlier in the chapter about the environment. Which primary factors or indicators in the environment are important to organizational well-being and survival? What are the indicators? How do organizational leaders and members proceed in this environment?

Collective/Collaborative Approaches

The literature on organizational leadership and change includes a small and diffuse body of research on collective or collaborative change approaches. Included in this category are institutionalized-leadership and change practices, organizational learning, and empowerment or shared power. These practices are interrelated and mutually reinforcing, as indicated in Figure 33.1. They function to support teleological, dialectical, and chaos/complexity change in conjunction with collective concepts of leadership.

Institutionalized-Leadership and Change Practices

O'Toole (2001) and his colleagues surveyed more than 3,000 leaders at various organizational levels in 10 large companies in Asia, Europe, and North America. They also interviewed 20–40 of the individuals who completed the survey from each company. O'Toole

| **Figure 33.1** | Collective/Collaborative Practices |

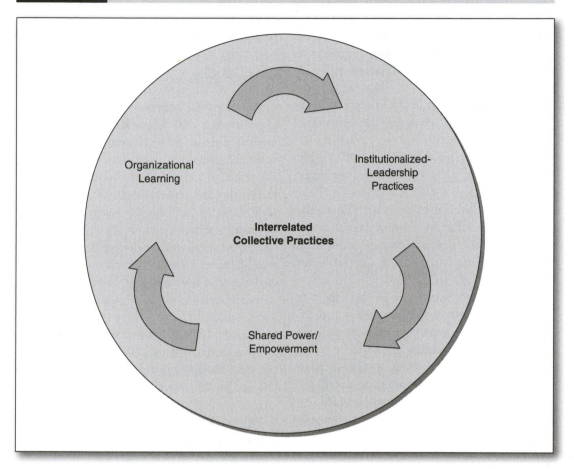

discovered that companies with the highest collective leadership capacity used systems that used institutionalized-leadership and change practices throughout their organizations. "We found that there is something palpably different about a company that emphasizes building enabling systems versus one that depends on a single personality at the top" (O'Toole, 2001, p. 168). Similar to Kelley's (1988) description of effective or exemplary followers, O'Toole (2001) made the following discovery:

> [People throughout these companies] act more like owners and entrepreneurs than employees.... Take the initiative to solve problems.... Willingly accept accountability for meeting commitments and [living organizational values]... Share a

common philosophy and language of leadership.... [and] create, maintain, and adhere to systems and procedures designed to measure and reward ... distributed leadership behaviors. (pp. 160–161)

Two major institutional practices when used together contributed to long-term success: coherence and agility. Coherence encompasses the common behaviors that are found throughout an organization and that are directed toward achieving the organization's goals, and agility represents the organization's institutionalized ability to detect and cope with changes in the external environment, especially when the changes are hard to predict (O'Toole, 2001,

p. 167). O'Toole found that the successful companies focused on building human capacity collectively rather than relying on a small number of individuals to lead and change the organization.

O'Toole (2001) measured each organization's effectiveness using 12 leadership systems:

- *Vision and strategy:* Extent to which corporate strategy is reflected in goals and behaviors at all levels.
- *Goal setting and planning:* Extent to which challenging goals are used to drive performance.
- *Capital allocation:* Extent to which capital allocation decisions are objective and systematic.
- *Group measurement:* Extent to which actual performance is measured against established goals.
- *Risk management:* Extent to which the company measures and mitigates risk.
- *Recruiting:* Extent to which the company taps the best talent available.
- *Professional development:* Extent to which employees are challenged and developed.
- *Performance appraisal:* Extent to which individual appraisals are used to improve performance.
- *Compensation:* Extent to which financial incentives are used to drive desired behaviors.
- *Organizational structure:* Extent to which decision-making authority is delegated to lower levels.
- *Communications:* Extent to which management communicates the big picture.
- *Knowledge transfer:* Extent to which necessary information is gathered, organized, and disseminated. (p. 165)

The highest-performing companies intentionally selected specific systems to emphasize and did not attempt to focus on all of the systems. To develop collective capacity throughout the organization, leaders and members had to ensure that their professional development, performance appraisal, and compensation systems foster coherent practices. These practices ensure alignment among systems so that a compensation system for project teams, for example, includes rewards for collaborative teamwork and does not unintentionally perpetuate competitive individual performance.

Organizational Learning

Organizational learning is a process that adapts the organization and its members to change in the external environment by encouraging experimentation and innovation, continually renewing structures and practices, and using performance data to assess and further develop the organization (London & Maurer, 2004, p. 244). The Technology Solutions case in Chapter 2 shows the company's emphasis on learning and continuous self-development in its employees through sharing ideas to spark new thoughts, seeking guidance from any member of the organization, and providing access to the newest and most innovative ideas possible.

Donald Schön (1971) was one of the early scholars to recognize the need for organizational learning as a process to foster change collectively. He made the following contention:

[Organizational participants] must become able not only to transform our institutions, in response to changing situations and requirements; we must invent and develop institutions which are "learning systems," that is to say, systems capable of bringing about their own continuous transformations. (p. 30)

Since Schön's initial work, organizational-learning systems have become an integral component of the change literature. Senge (1990) popularized organizational learning as a generative process that enhances the capacity of organizational participants to create. He stated that five essential elements must develop as an ensemble to create a fundamental learning organization:

- Personal mastery—continually clarifying and deepening personal vision, focusing energies, developing patience, and seeing reality objectively;

- Mental models—changing ingrained assumptions, generalizations, pictures and images of how the world works;
- Shared vision—unearthing shared "pictures of the future" that foster genuine commitment;
- Team learning—aligning and developing the capacity of a team to create the results its members truly desire; and
- Systems thinking—integrating all the elements by fusing them into a coherent body of theory and practice. (pp. 6–10)

Several theories and concepts of leadership incorporate learning as a part of organizational development and change. Transformational, adaptive, and task relations-and-change leadership encourage organizational learning by similar means, including challenging people to question assumptions; take risks; be innovative and creative; reframe problems and cultivate new approaches; analyze information about events, trends, and changes in the external environment; and then pursue new opportunities, meet unknown conditions or threats, and solve problems.

According to Berson, Nemanich, Waldman, Galvin, and Keller (2006), the literature on organizational learning implies that leadership can influence learning among organizational members and foster a learning culture. Individuals in leadership roles need to develop three essential organizational characteristics to facilitate a learning culture: participation—involvement of organizational members in processes such as decision making, learning, inquiry, challenge, and the creation of greater autonomy; openness—receptiveness to diverse ideas, tolerance, and free flow of information; and psychological safety—freedom to take risks, trust, and support (pp. 580–581).

Shared Power or Empowerment

Movement toward shared power or empowerment is a logical course of action as organizations place greater reliance on the collective or collaborative capabilities of their members to innovate and respond in turbulent or dynamic environments. Shared power or empowerment entails two components: delegating or distributing leadership, authority, responsibility, and decision-making power, formally vested in senior executives, to individuals and teams throughout the organization, and equipping organization members with the resources, knowledge, and skills necessary to make good decisions (Hughes, Ginnett, & Curphy, 2006, p. 537).

Like the example of empowerment at Johnsonville Sausage Company, discussed in Chapter 3, senior executives must examine themselves to determine whether they are willing and ready to share power with employees as coleaders or partners in the process of leading change. Inauthentic attempts at empowerment can be more detrimental to organizational members than maintaining the status quo. Hughes et al. (2006) indicated that "empowered employees have latitude to make decisions, are comfortable making these decisions, believe what they do is important, and are seen as influential members of their team" (p. 539). The authors further described the following best practices for empowerment:

- having leaders in the organization decide whether the organization really wants or needs empowerment;
- creating a clear vision, goals, and accountabilities;
- developing others (through coaching, forging a partnership, developing knowledge and skills, promoting persistence, and transferring skills);
- delegating decision making to followers;
- leading by example; and
- making empowerment systemic—a strategic business practice that is reinforced in selection, performance appraisal, rewards, training, organizational structure, and so on. (pp. 539–542)

Strategic Planning

Executive leaders initiate strategic planning as a part of their overall design to adapt, change, and position the organization to thrive in a highly competitive and turbulent environment. Strategic planning generally originates from the top and involves members at various levels of the organization in certain components of the process. In business settings, companies use strategic planning to establish and sustain competitive advantage in their industry. Nonprofit and government agencies also use strategic planning to provide intentional direction to their organizations and adapt to external changes that affect their services and stakeholders.

Primary components of strategic planning include creating or updating the vision and mission, conducting an environmental scan, setting strategic direction using goals and strategies, and implementing and updating the plan. A vision, much like a compass, points an organization toward its desired end goal, or "true north." It is a realistic, credible, and appealing future for the organization that sets a clear direction; defines a more successful and desirable future; fits the organization's history, culture, and values; and reflects the aspirations and expectations of major stakeholders (Miller & Dess, 1996; Nanus, 1992; Yukl, 2006). A good vision links the present to the future, energizes people and garners commitment, gives meaning to work, and establishes a standard of excellence (Daft & Lane, 2005, p. 516). A mission is the tangible form of the vision that identifies the organization's purpose or reason for existing and identifies its uniqueness or distinctiveness (Miller & Dess, 1996, p. 9).

The vision and mission serve as a base or foundation for planning the organization's future (teleological change), whereas the strategic component involves specific positioning of the organization for competitive advantage or effective service delivery on the basis of factors outside the organization. Relying on multiple sources and multiple disciplines or inputs, leaders and members use environmental scanning to gather information about trends in the external environment:

- Stakeholder analysis—an assessment of the expectations, wants, and needs of all parties that have an interest or stake in the organization, including leaders, team members, managers, employees, customers/clients, recipients of services, and investors/shareholders, among others;
- Competitors' activities—knowledge of competitors' products, services, and methodologies through benchmarking and other information-gathering approaches;
- Demographic changes—changes in the age, ethnic composition, growth, or decline of the population;

- Social and lifestyle changes—women in the workforce, health and fitness awareness, erosion of educational standards, spread of addictive drugs, concern for the environment;
- Technological changes—advances in and use of all forms of technology;
- Economic changes—stock market indices, budget deficits, consumer-spending patterns, inflation rates, interest rates, trade deficits, unemployment rates;
- Legislative/regulatory and political changes—changes in crime laws, environmental protection laws, deregulation, antitrust enforcement, laws protecting human rights and employment; and
- Global changes—economic alliances, changes in consumer tastes and preferences, economic development, international markets, and poverty and disease rates. (Dess, Lumpkin, & Eisner, 2008, pp. 19, 44–50, 380)

The executive leadership team uses information from the environmental scan to determine the organization's opportunities and threats along with its strengths and weaknesses. On the basis of this analysis, the team identifies core competencies (capabilities that combine expertise and application skills) in the organization, evaluates whether there is a need for a major change in strategy, and identifies promising strategies along with possible outcomes of each strategy (Yukl, 2006, pp. 378–380). Frequently, a broad cadre of managers and members are invited to participate in the strategy formulation process. Strategies represent desired states of affairs that the organization wants to reach or end points toward which organizational efforts are directed (Daft & Lane, 2005, p. 526). They are the indicators of the organization's progress toward its vision, mission, and strategic direction.

Clearly, strategic leadership uses strategic-planning processes to bring about strategic change in organizations. Strategic planning is also compatible with teleological and dialectical change. As stated earlier, teleological change is constructed internally by leaders and members of the organization, yet this form of change cannot be fully effective without considering the kind of information that the environmental scanning component of strategic planning highlights. Dialectical change can also benefit from the environmental-scanning component of strategic planning, even though strategic positioning may or may not be feasible in dialectical change.

Strategic planning is often a lengthy process in many organizations. With the increasing pace and unique patterns of change in society, organizations will need continuous scanning and highly participative processes with a broader base of members (beyond executive levels) to determine appropriate action in the short term while planning for the long term. The strategic-planning process may assume a different structure or different characteristics in a less-predictable and less controlled environment of continuous change, experimentation, and learning. Some communication scholars and practitioners suggest that planning strategically may mean engaging in scenario planning—exploring possible outcomes of what could happen in the future and planning for those possibilities (Ströh & Jaatinen, 2001, p. 162). Scenario planning, similar to Peter Schwartz's (see Chapter 1) concept of scenario building, uses information from continuous-scanning processes to develop and plan for probable scenarios, while keeping plans flexible and adjustable.

Stages of Praxis

Kurt Lewin (1951) provided some of the earliest research on stages of praxis in organizational change. His force-field model identified three fundamental stages of change: unfreezing—the stage where organizational participants recognize that their old methods are no longer useful, often due to crises, threats, or new opportunities; changing—the phase where people seek new ways of doing things and choose new approaches; and refreezing—the stage in which leaders and participants implement the new approaches and establish them in the organizational culture (Yukl, 2006, p. 286). Lewin's earlier work provided a foundation for subsequent models (Kanter, 1983b; Kanter, Stein, & Jick, 1992; Kotter, 1996; Nadler, Shaw, & Walton, 1995) that expanded the stages, methods, and practices of organizational change. Figure 33.2 compares Lewin's three-stage model to a much later eight-stage model developed by John Kotter (1996). Kotter's model provides a fitting structure for examining praxis shared by other familiar models.

The Unfreezing Stage

The purpose of unfreezing old ways of doing things (Lewin, 1951), establishing a sense of urgency (Kanter et al., 1992; Kotter, 1996), or initiating a galvanizing event (an action or situation that requires a change response) (Kanter, 1983a, p. 22) is to draw attention to the critical need for organizational change. This sense of urgency or galvanizing event may stem from a current or impending crisis. Yet it is just as likely to come from the organization's inability to adapt—that is, the ability of its members to see and take action to address the gap between the current organization and its need to modify or change its culture, structure, behaviors, and responsibilities. According to Kotter (1996), this stage involves identifying and discussing crises, potential crises, or major opportunities that may galvanize or inspire change (p. 21). Crises include economic threats, like the situation at Technology Solutions; competitive threats; changing markets; shifting demographics; or other changes in the external or internal environment. A galvanizing event may present a crisis or entail a new opportunity, such as launching new products; developing new markets, innovations, or services; and interacting with stakeholders in new ways, such as engaging in community volunteering or environmental sustainability programs.

Both crises and opportunities can create fresh or revitalized momentum in an organization, especially when these crises or opportunities are acknowledged as authentic by members of the organization. Many people fear change and resist change efforts even in situations where a crisis or beneficial innovation is justified. There are multiple reasons why members of organizations resist change:

1. Lack of trust—distrust of the people who propose the change;

2. Belief that change is unnecessary—satisfaction with the status quo and no clear evidence of serious problems with the current way of doing things;

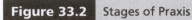

Figure 33.2   Stages of Praxis

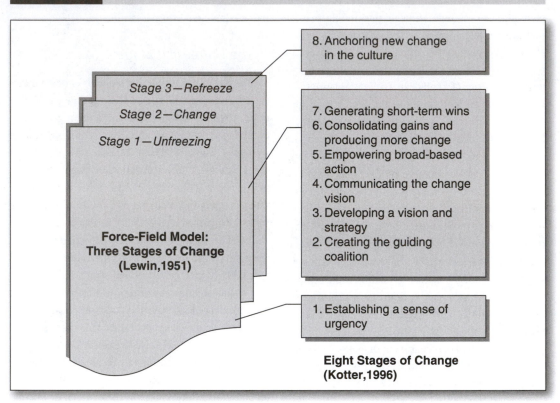

3. Belief that the change is not feasible—a view that the change is unlikely to succeed, too difficult, or likely to fail like some previous efforts;

4. Economic threats—fear that the change may benefit the organization but result in personal loss of income, benefits, or job security;

5. Relative high costs—concern that the cost of change may be higher than the benefits due to loss of resources already invested in the current approach or loss of performance as employees learn the new procedures and debug the new system;

6. Fear of personal failure—organizational members' reluctance to abandon known skills or expertise and their insecurity about mastering new ways of doing things;

7. Loss of status and power—fear of shifts in power for individuals or subunits that may result in loss of status in the organization;

8. Threat to values and ideals—resistance to change that appears incompatible with personal values or strongly held values embedded in the organization's culture; and

9. Resentment of interference—opposition of individuals to perceived control, manipulation, or forced change by others in situations where they have no choice or voice in the change. (Yukl, 2006, pp. 285–286)

Despite these fears, various organizations have implemented successful change processes by using the stages approach with effective forms of leadership and change.

The Changing Phase

Lewin (1951) referred to the next stage simply as the changing phase; later scholars (Kanter et al., 1992; Kotter, 1996; Nadler et al., 1995) defined several additional stages in the changing phase. Specifically, Kotter delineated six stages—creating the guiding coalition, developing a vision and strategy, communicating the change vision, empowering broad-based action, generating short-term wins, and consolidating gains and producing more change (p. 21).

Creating the guiding coalition involves putting together a group with enough power to lead the change and getting the group to work together as a team. This group could comprise the tags, described earlier as members of the organization who lead with or without authority, often in a temporary capacity, to influence people and the processes of meaning making, cooperation, and action taking. They have the kind of influence that moves others to action through their facilitation of cooperation, interaction, and resonance among individuals involved in change or adaptive processes.

Developing a vision and strategy relates to the processes described in strategic planning or creating an image of a realistic, credible, and appealing future for the organization that energizes people, inspires commitment, gives meaning to work, and establishes a standard of excellence. The guiding coalition then develops a strategy to achieve the vision.

Communicating change[1] requires that change leaders use every vehicle possible to communicate constantly the new vision and strategies to organizational members and model the behavior expected of employees. In four case studies of planned change, the researcher concluded that "creating [and communicating] vision, maintaining buy-in to mission, sense-making and feedback, establishing legitimacy, and communicating goal achievement" are essential elements for maintaining commitment to organizational change (Lewis, 2000, p. 151).

Ströh and Jaatinen (2001) suggested that single incidents of change, such as a crisis, require different approaches to communication than do continuous changes (p. 159). They caution that technical communication channels, such as newsletters, electronic and face-to-face updates, or annual reports, are good but not sufficient in organizations where continuous change is a way of life. Effective communication channels need to be consciously embedded and facilitated in the continuous change process

through dialogue, relationship building, diversity of ideas, and participative decision making for change (p. 159).

The use of dialogue, discourse, or conversation is a prominent theme in the literature on communicating change (Ford & Ford, 1995; Heracleous & Barrett, 2001; Jabri, 2004; Kellett, 1999). Kellett (1999) pointed out that creating collaborative learning through dialogue is one approach to generating continuous and intentional change in organizations (p. 211). Creating dialogic conversations is an intentional process with fundamental characteristics and guidelines:

- Dialogue provides a "container" for collective thinking with dedicated time to allow the process to emerge;
- The purpose of dialogue is to create thoughtful exchange, generate mutual understanding, make assumptions explicit, and take action with regard to the issues people care about and need to discuss;
- The spirit of inquiry is essential to dialogue and involves focusing on connections, embracing diverse perspectives, and allowing shared understanding to transform us;
- The process of reflective questioning relies on our ability to listen, value others, and address deep issues; and
- A dialogue is a practical approach for developing a meaningful vision or mission statement, understanding what needs to change and how the change aligns with other factors in the organization, and understanding and negotiating conflicts expressed in the dialogue process. (Kellett, 1999, p. 212)

Another key communication role in continuous change involves building relationships within and across the organization and building trans organizational relationships to develop networks and achieve creativity, innovation, mutual problem solving, and shared meaning. Given this emphasis on relationships between entities, one researcher remarked, "Relationships are all there is to reality and nothing exists independent of its relationships with the environment" (McDaniel, 1997, p. 24).

Dialogue that encourages diversity of ideas is critical for continuous change in organizations. Yet diversity brings both conflict and cooperation, "marked by the struggle of multiple voices to be heard" (Kellett, 1999, p. 213). Dialectic communication is a process through which change occurs:

> In a change process, if there is an effective negotiation or resolution of core dialectics between the stakeholders, it is likely to be a collaborative change that is marked by a respect for difference. If, as Baxter and Montgomery say, "Relational well-being is marked by the capacity to achieve 'both/and' status" (p. 6), then "healthy" organizational change will be marked by talking through dialectics, or at least the respect for differences as they figure into change decisions. (p. 213)

Communication in continuous change environments is highly participatory by necessity. Organizations must facilitate dialogue within and across groups to generate and sustain a free flow of information, diversity of ideas, high levels of cooperation, and substantive involvement in decision making.

Empowering broad-based action requires getting rid of obstacles, changing systems or structures that undermine the change vision, and encouraging risk taking and nontraditional ideas, activities, and actions (Kotter, 1996, p. 21). Earlier in the chapter, empowerment was described as delegating or distributing leadership, authority, responsibility, and decision-making power and equipping organizational members with the resources, knowledge, and skills necessary to make good decisions. Empowerment can facilitate broad-based action in the change process when leaders and members fully endorse and incorporate it in their organizational values, culture, and practices. Organizational systems can be configured to reinforce empowerment in selection, performance appraisal, rewards, and training processes along with communication and work structures.

Generating short-term wins involves making change visible by recognizing, rewarding, and celebrating achievements along the way. This includes setting and achieving short-term goals that support the change initiative; recognizing and rewarding people who made the wins possible; demonstrating or showcasing completed projects and new products or services; publicizing new ventures, partnerships, or collaborative work arrangements; and recognizing monthly, quarterly, or annual accomplishments. Kotter (1996) identified three characteristics of a good short-term win—it's visible and large numbers of people can see it for themselves, it's unambiguous, and it's clearly related to the change effort (pp. 121–122). He pointed out that one possible drawback to acknowledging and celebrating short term wins is the tendency of some people to lose momentum and motivation for completing the larger change. As a result, recognition of intermediate successes needs to be balanced with a realistic perspective that much more remains to be done. Clear or visible gauges of the work ahead are as important as indicators of successes to date.

Consolidating gains and producing more change occur when the guiding coalition, tags, and participants in change throughout the organization learn from and use the gains at each juncture to develop expertise and experience for producing more change. Because complex organizations function through interdependencies—people work in cross-functional and project teams across the organization and between organizations—change in one part of the system produces a kaleidoscope effect by changing all or most parts of the system. In other words, change in interconnected systems produces more change. This is a good outcome for the achievement and sustainability of the larger change, but it can be frustrating in the short run.

> According to Kotter (1996), cumulative gains along the way provide increased credibility to change all systems, structures, and policies that no longer fit the transformation vision. Actions in this stage include hiring, promoting, and developing people who can implement the change vision and reinvigorating the process with new projects, themes, and change agents (pp. 21, 143).

Refreezing or Anchoring New Approaches in the Culture

This phase represents the last stage of change, as defined by Lewin or Kotter, respectively. Both Lewin and Kotter recognized this stage as the fitting time and place to establish or anchor new approaches and behaviors in the organizational culture (shared assumptions, beliefs, values, language, etc.). Many scholars (Deal & Kennedy, 2000; Kotter, 1996; Schein, 1992) acknowledge that culture is the most difficult element to change in an organization, and it is much more challenging to alter culture in mature organizations. Schein (1992) offered several primary and secondary ways to influence cultural change. Each of these factors reinforces the connection between new behaviors and organizational success:

Primary ways to influence culture

- *Attention*—the amount of attention leaders focus on certain issues or factors in the organization;
- *Reactions to crises*—the values and assumptions expressed by leaders during crises;
- *Role modeling*—the messages about values and expectations leaders communicate through their actions or through deliberate modeling such as coaching and teaching;
- *Allocation of rewards*—the criteria used in the organization to allocate rewards; and
- *Criteria for selection and dismissal*—values expressed through criteria for recruiting, selecting, promoting, and dismissing members of the organization.

Secondary ways to influence culture

- *Design of systems and procedures*—placing an emphasis on the new approaches or change in budgets, planning processes, reports, training programs, performance reviews, and so on;
- *Design of organizational structure*—designing an organizational structure that facilitates the philosophy, working relationships or interdependencies, and flexibility needed to implement change and adapt to the environment;

- *Rites and rituals of the organization*—the ritualization of certain types of behaviors can serve as a powerful reinforcer of leaders' assumptions;
- *Design of facilities*—designing facilities that reflect the change in approach or philosophy such as open layouts; open access to conference rooms, dining facilities, and workout spaces; or similar offices for all members of the organization;
- *Stories, legends, and myths*—transmitting stories about actual events, people, or actions that exemplify the philosophy, values, and approaches that are important for change in the culture; and
- *Formal statements*—conveying the new or modified philosophy, values, and approaches in organizational publications and other appropriate venues. (Schein, 1992, pp. 230–252; Yukl, 2006, pp. 290–293)

A final factor in refreezing or anchoring new change in the culture is developing a means to ensure ongoing leadership development. If change is dependent only on individuals currently serving in formal (chief executive officer) and informal (tags) leadership roles, then change processes will likely end when these individuals leave. This statement may seem obvious; however, lack of adequate leadership development has been the downfall of many promising attempts to generate organizational change. Individual and team leadership development along with O'Toole's (2001) concept of institutionalizing leadership in the people and systems of organizations provide the greatest potential for initiating, developing, and benefiting from change.

The practices identified in the stages-of-praxis category most often apply to teleological (intentional and constructed change) and strategic change. These stages can also facilitate evolutionary change when organizations need to adopt new structures, organizational types, or traits. They can apply to the maturity and revitalization phases of life-cycle change, especially as organizations face inertia or potential demise. Organizations in the maturity phase of life-cycle change have the hardest time embracing new opportunities or structures due to their entrenched organizational culture and history of success. Communicating a change strategy or vision among organizational members can foster dialectical change.

Different phases can require different forms of leadership. For example, charismatic leadership frequently succeeds in generating a sense of urgency by inspiring a motivating vision or purpose in the hearts and minds of organizational members. In the case of invisible leadership, however, the purpose itself may be the motivating factor (charisma of purpose) that drives organizational members to work toward a goal. Strategic leadership can help organizational participants shape the vision and strategies that will focus the change effort, and transactional and task relations-and-change leadership may empower broad-based action to implement changes in behavior, work structures, or processes and generate short-term wins. Transformational leadership can operate during most stages of praxis; it may be particularly effective during the stage of consolidating gains and producing more change during the last phase involving anchoring new approaches in the culture. Co leadership or exemplary followership functions throughout the stages of praxis in a team effort to accomplish the common purpose of the change.

Scenario Building

Schwartz (1996) advocated an eight-step process of scenario building (also discussed in Chapter 1) that helps leaders and members take a long view in a world of uncertainty (p. 3). He contended that scenarios are not predictions but mechanisms to help people learn. Scenario building involves more than guessing. It requires a process that uses factual information and indicators of early trends to project alternative futures. The eighth factor, which corresponds with Willis Harman's (1998) concept of "acting with feedback" (pp. 193–194), fosters ongoing learning and flexibility as leaders and participants move toward a desired common goal. Although scenario building is a method used most often in business or organizational settings, it provides a useful means for

developing informed action in other settings, including nonprofit and government agencies.

Scenario building is especially useful for teleological change and strategic leadership due to its planned, constructed approach. However, it may also be relevant to dialectical change, including chaos and complexity theory and collective or collaborative forms of leadership, because it helps organizations prepare for multiple possibilities and identify early indicators in uncertain environments. In virtual or multichannel organizations, scenario building is highly compatible with e-leadership, which uses technology such as groupware to brainstorm and generate multiple responses simultaneously.

Appreciative Inquiry

Appreciative inquiry (AI) is an organizational change practice developed by Cooperrider and Srivastva (1987). It focuses on aspects of the organizations that are working well—the positive history and stories, best organization members, and the relationships that contribute to advancement—rather than on negatives, such as distrust, resistance, and barriers to positive possibilities. AI begins with and retains the "positive principle"—hope, excitement, caring, esprit de corps, urgent purpose, joy in creating something meaningful together—to sustain momentum throughout the process (Fitzgerald, Murrell, & Miller, 2003, p. 6). The process has five essential phases:

1. Choose the positive as the focus for inquiry.

2. Inquire into stories of life-giving forces.

3. Locate themes that appear in the stories and select topics for further inquiry.

4. Create shared images for a preferred future.

5. Find innovative ways to create that future. (Seo, Putnam, & Bartunek, 2004, p. 95)

AI uses a social constructionist approach to organizational change, a teleological model that focuses on the human ability to construct new realities for the organization through an intended process of change. Cooperrider and Srivastva's (1987) AI model departs from previous change approaches because it fully supports the idea that "organizational members have the capacity to create their own future," it rejects interventionist approaches that focus on problem-solving with a heavy emphasis on positivist methods, and it employs less linear methods, such as "stories, narratives, dreams, and visions that stimulate human imagination and meaning systems" (Seo et al., 2004, p. 96).

AI has received positive attention and considerable use by practitioners. Yet there has been little academic research conducted on this method. Future researchers need to raise and examine several methodological and organizational questions regarding AI: Do the methodologies and philosophy used in AI omit significant factors from the change process? For example, does the "positive only" approach of appreciative inquiry resolve underlying problems, conflicts, and mistakes in the organization or does it inadvertently mask or ignore them? Can positivist methodologies (survey research, experiments, etc.) in combination with AI methodologies (dialogues, interviewing, imagining) add or reveal vital information for organizational change that would not be apparent or available using AI methodologies alone? How does AI compare to other theories of change and organizational development? What are the comparative outcomes of AI in relation to other organizational change approaches over time?

E-Practices

Leading change in virtual teams requires some of the same practices as those used by face-to-face (FTF) teams, as well as some different practices. In a study of effective practices in virtual teams, Lurey and Raisinghani (2001) found that these teams, like their FTF counterparts, must have a shared purpose, their members must rely on each other to perform the work, and team leaders must facilitate positive group processes, generate team-based reward systems, and select the most appropriate team members for projects or change initiatives (p. 532). Virtual teams need additional factors to be effective:

- added connectivity among team members through more structured or formal processes including clearly developed and designated roles for team members and very explicit team goals; and

- more attention to communication issues that enhance personal contact and connection among team members such as facilitating face-to-face interaction when possible and identifying and using the most appropriate technology for the people and project. (p. 532)

Respondents in Lurey and Raisinghani's (2001) study used daily e-mail, personal telephone calls, and voice mail most frequently. Other means of communication, including group-telephone and online-computer conferencing, FTF interaction, groupware, shared databases, and videoconferencing, received less frequent use. The researchers suggested that the availability and use of videoconferencing may be effective in bringing together geographically dispersed team members.

To enhance successful e-practices, Zigurs (2003) made the following recommendations for virtual team leaders:

- provide training on participation in virtual teams;
- use team-building exercises in face-to-face processes, when possible;
- provide for both task and relational roles;
- establish standards for communication of contextual cues with each message;
- use process-structuring tools but build in adaptability for individual needs;
- use frequent communication and feedback to nurture emergent leadership and self-leadership that moves the team forward;
- put special and continuous emphasis on relational development; and
- anticipate unintended consequences and debrief the team's responses and approaches to these events. (p. 348)

Virtual organizations and multichannel corporations need the capacity to innovate, change, and respond quickly to meet the needs of customers or service recipients in a round-the-clock Internet environment. Change in virtual organizations and virtual divisions of multichannel organizations entails practices that are information rich and highly collaborative. Stace, Holtham, and Courtney (2001) suggested that these organizations base their design on principles of self-management, collaborative behavioral protocols, shared strategic intent, and equitable sharing of returns (p. 417). They advised that organizations base their e-practices on time spent in productive interchange, trust developed between people, and territory, defined as psychological space and a stake in outcomes (p. 417).

On the basis of current information, e-practices seem to apply to teleological (planned, constructed) and dialectical change, including chaos and complexity theory, in multichannel and virtual organizations. They align with virtual leadership, or e-leadership, and may be fitting for other collective forms of leadership, such as adaptive, team, and invisible. Research on effective virtual or e-practices is still developing. E-change may ultimately constitute a new form of change with its own characteristics and processes.

Ethical Practices

Ethics require leaders and followers in organizations to take into account the impact of their actions in relation to others. Ethics are principles of right conduct or a system of moral values. The guiding question for ethical decisions and practices in leading change is, what ought to be done in regard to coworkers and customers (Gini, 2004, p. 28)? Gini (2004) pointed out that "ethics is primarily a communal, collective enterprise" (p. 28), which makes ethical practices especially relevant in this era of collective and collaborative approaches to leading organizational change, including adaptive, ubuntu, Tao, invisible, team, and virtual leadership.

Critical issues for ethical practices in leading change consist of authenticity, trust, and reciprocal care, among others. Authenticity entails honesty—with one's self and others, between and among organizational leaders and members, and between organizational members and other partners, collaborators, and stakeholders. Authenticity is critically important in the practice of empowerment or shared power, which is a fundamental component of collective or collaborative leadership and change. Ciulla (2004) maintained that "the obvious difference between authentic and bogus empowerment rests on the honesty of the relationship between leaders and followers" (p. 76). She warned that it is not adequate for members of an organization to "feel" empowered; they must "be" empowered to make decisions, take action, and be accountable for their efforts on behalf of the organization (p. 76).

Leaders in positions of authority have a choice to share power with members of the organization or not, but bogus empowerment is both inauthentic and ineffective in the long run. Leaders must weigh the risk in each direction. If organizational leaders choose empowerment or shared power, they need to develop the training, resources, systems, and practices that support it. Most of all, senior leaders must have enough self-knowledge and introspection to know whether they are truly capable of sharing power or whether they fear that most organizational members are unable to handle shared power appropriately, and, therefore, members' mistakes will reflect negatively on leaders. If leaders decide not to empower members, they need to develop substantial capacity within the senior executive team to lead change in a dynamic environment. They must assess the potential impact on their competitive position or service delivery in relation to similar organizations with and without shared power among their members.

Authenticity is a significant factor in developing a sense of urgency or establishing a galvanizing event in the stages-of-praxis approach. Organizational members will likely become indifferent and highly suspect of any change effort when executive leaders attempt to revitalize an organization by "creating" a scare tactic to generate a sense of urgency. Instead, organizational leaders and members must build an honest, compelling case for revitalization on the basis of information, involvement, and commitment.

Openness, or transparency, is included here under the rubric of authenticity. Openness reinforces authenticity and trust by making processes, decisions, and information open and available to members of the organization. In the Technology Solutions case, members indicated that the company's transparency practices—a "no secrets" policy, free sharing of ideas, the open-door policy among all company members, and the discussions during company meetings—contribute to an open and innovative environment. Team members at Johnsonville Sausage performed budgeting and finance, hiring and firing, scheduling, and quality control. Processes, decisions, and information in the organization were transparent, enabling members to take appropriate actions. Members were fully aware of the company's financial status and competitive position in the market, and they knew whether cost cutting, layoffs, or downsizing were necessary for the company to thrive.

Earlier in this book, I cited Tapscott and Williams (2006), who discussed the idea that openness, or the new-era transparency, goes beyond disclosure of information to internal members of the organization. It includes a vast array of external collaborators. As a result, senior leaders need to decide whether they can honestly practice openness in the organization. If they decide to implement openness in the organization's innovations, processes, decisions, and information, then they need to develop systems and practices that support transparency along with procedures that protect some (but not all) confidential and proprietary information. If leaders decide not to practice full transparency, they still need to develop an organizational culture of trust where members experience authenticity and integrity in leader-member relationships. They also will need to evaluate the potential impact on their competitive position or service delivery of maintaining a highly proprietary and confidential organization.

Trust is the foundation of a relationship between and among leaders and members of an organization. Robert Solomon (2004) contended, "*Trust* characterizes an entire network of emotions and emotional attitudes, both between individuals and within groups and by way of a psychodynamic profile of entire societies" (p. 95). He characterized trust as a social role, a reciprocal relationship, a dynamic decision that makes leadership possible, something to be given that transforms a relationship at its most basic

level (pp. 95–99). Honesty builds trust so that members have confidence in a leader's word that the need for change is authentic, that power is indeed shared, and that the member has true agency to effect change in the organization, while leaders have confidence that members can lead themselves, build competence, use their shared power to advance the change initiative, and sustain commitment to the organization's purpose.

Reciprocal care develops from a relationship of trust where "every person matters and each person's welfare and dignity is the concern of us all" (Allen et al., 1998, p. 57). Leading change in a collective or collaborative context creates greater interdependence and mutual responsibility between organizational leaders and members. The leader-follower relationship shifts from a traditional dynamic, where leaders assume responsibility for members, to a shared dynamic, where leaders and members assume responsibility for each other. This relationship involves reciprocal care for the rights, treatment, diversity, and well-being of leaders and members.

Leaders and members in organizations with ethical practices establish a "healthy moral environment," where ethical behavior and expectations are explicitly stated and conscientiously practiced and where ethical practices are not inadvertently undermined by contradictory messages in the organizations' environments (Ciulla, 1995, p. 494). The ethical practices of authenticity, trust, transparency, and reciprocal care apply to leadership and change concepts in this chapter and are necessary for collective or collaborative approaches. They provide the essential underpinning for the communal, collective enterprise of ethics in the process of leading change.

Conclusion

Although there is no one approach or formula to choosing the most appropriate practices for leading change, leaders and members of companies, nonprofit organizations, and government agencies can use the guiding questions in each of the chapters on organizational change to assess and select their options. Organizational members can inspire and generate change that allows their organizations to flourish in the midst of a turbulent environment when they consider and select mutually reinforcing forms of leadership, change, and practice. Table 33.1 in the introduction provides examples of connecting components of organizational change—concepts of change, concepts of leadership, and change practices. Intentional consideration of all three components of change is more than an analytical tool, though it definitely serves that purpose. It is a means of preparing people and their organizations for new ventures into the unknown, fueled by human innovation and advanced technologies.

Note

1. I am deeply indebted to my late colleague Fredric M. Jablin for his help in identifying articles and sources for the discussion on communication in this section.

References

Allen, K. E., Bordas, J., Hickman, G. R., Matusak, L. R., Sorenson, G. J., & Whitmire, K. J. (1998). Leadership in the 21st century. In B. Kellerman (Ed.), *Rethinking leadership: Kellogg leadership studies project 1994–1997* (pp. 41–62). College Park, MD: James MacGregor Burns Academy of Leadership.

Berson, Y., Nemanich, L. A., Waldman, D. A., Galvin, B. M., & Keller, R. T. (2006). Leadership and organizational learning: A multiple levels perspective. *Leadership Quarterly, 17*, 577–594.

Ciulla, J. B. (1995). Messages from the environment: The influence of policies and practices on employee responsibility. In J. T. Wren (Ed.), *The leader's companion: Insights on leadership through the ages* (pp. 492–499). New York: Free Press.

Ciulla, J. B. (2004). *Ethics, the heart of leadership* (2nd ed.). Westport, CT: Praeger.

Cooperrider, D. L., & Srivastva, S. (1987). Appreciative inquiry in organizational life. In R. W. Woodman & W. A. Pasmore (Eds.), *Research in organizational change and development* (Vol. 1, pp. 129–169). Greenwich, CT: JAI Press.

Daft, R. L., & Lane, P. G. (2005). *The leadership experience* (3rd ed.). Mason, OH: Thomson/ South-Western.

Deal, T. E., & Kennedy, A. A. (2000). *Corporate cultures: The rites and rituals of corporate life*. Cambridge, MA: Perseus Books.

Dess, G. G., Lumpkin, G. T., & Eisner, A. B. (2008). *Strategic management: Creating competitive advantages* (4th ed.). New York: McGraw-Hill/Irwin.

Fitzgerald, S. P., Murrell, K. L., & Miller, M. G. (2003). Appreciative inquiry: Accentuating the positive. *Business Strategy Review, 14*(1), 5–7.

Ford, J. D., & Ford, L. W. (1995). The role of conversations in producing intentional change in organizations. *Academy of Management Review, 20*(3), 541–570.

Gini, A. (2004). Moral leadership and business ethics. In J. B. Ciulla (Ed.), *Ethics, the heart of leadership* (2nd., pp. 25–43). Westport, CT: Praeger.

Harman, W. W. (1998). *Global mind change: The promise of the 21st century*. San Francisco: Berrett-Koehler.

Heracleous, L., & Barrett, M. (2001). Organizational change as discourse: Communicative actions and deep structures in the context of information technology implementation. *Academy of Management Journal, 44*, 755–778.

Hughes, R. L., Ginnett, R. C., & Curphy, G. J. (2006). *Leadership: Enhancing the lessons of experience* (5th ed.). Boston: McGraw-Hill.

Jabri, M. (2004). Team feedback based on dialogue: Implications for change management. *Journal of Management Development, 23*(2), 141–151.

Kanter, R. M. (1983a). *The change masters: Innovations for productivity in the American corporation*. New York: Simon & Schuster.

Kanter, R. M. (1983b). Change masters and the intricate architecture of corporate culture change. *Management Review, 72*(10), 18–28.

Kanter, R. M. S., Stein, B. A., & Jick, T. (1992). *The challenge of organizational change: How*

Kellett, P. M. (1999). Dialogue and dialectics in managing organizational change: The case of a mission-based transformation. *Southern Communication Journal, 64*(3), 211–213.

Kelley, R. E. (1988). In praise of followers. *Harvard Business Review, 66*(6), 142–148.

Kotter, J. P. (1996). *Leading change*. Boston: Harvard Business School Press.

Lewin, K. (1951). *Field theory in social science: Selected theoretical papers*. New York: Harper.

Lewis, L. K. (2000). Communicating change: Four cases of quality programs. *Journal of Business Communication, 37*(2), 128–155.

London, M., & Maurer, T. J. (2004). Leadership development: A diagnostic model for continuous learning in dynamic organizations. In J. Antonakis, A. T. Cianciolo, & R. J. Sternberg (Eds.), *The nature of leadership* (pp. 222–245). Thousand Oaks, CA: Sage.

Lurey, J. S., & Raisinghani, M. S. (2001). An empirical study of best practices in virtual teams *Information and Management, 38*, 523–544.

McDaniel, R. R. J. (1997). Strategic leadership: A view from quantum and chaos theories. *Health Care Management Review, 22*(1), 21–37.

Miller, A., & Dess, G. G. (1996). *Strategic management* (2nd ed.). New York: McGraw-Hill.

Nadler, D., Shaw, R. B., & Walton, A. E. (1995). *Discontinuous change: Leading organizational transformation.* San Francisco: Jossey-Bass.

Nanus, B. (1992). *Visionary leadership: Creating a compelling sense of direction for your organization.* San Francisco: Jossey-Bass.

O'Toole, J. (2001). When leadership is an organizational trait. In W. Bennis, G. M. Spreitzer, & T. G. Cummings (Eds.), *The future of leadership: Today's top leadership thinkers speak to tomorrow's leaders* (pp. 158–174). San Francisco: Jossey-Bass.

Schein, E. (1992). *Organizational culture and leadership* (2nd ed.). San Francisco: Jossey-Bass.

Schön, D. A. (1971). *Beyond the stable state.* New York: Random House.

Schwartz, P. (1996). *The art of the long view: Paths to strategic insight for yourself and your company.* New York: Currency Doubleday.

Senge, P. M. (1990). *The fifth discipline: The art and practice of the learning organization.* New York: Doubleday/Currency.

Seo, M., Putnam, L., & Bartunek, J. (2004). Dualities and tensions of planned organizational change. In M. S. Poole & A. H. Van de Ven (Eds.), *Handbook of organizational change and innovation* (pp. 73–107). New York: Oxford University Press.

Solomon, R. (2004). Ethical leadership, emotions, and trust: Beyond "charisma." In J. B. Ciulla (Ed.), *Ethics, the heart of leadership* (2nd ed., pp. 83–102). Westport, CT: Praeger.

Stace, D., Holtham, C., & Courtney, N. (2001). E-change: Charting a path towards sustainable e-strategies. *Strategic Change, 10*, 403–418.

Ströh, U., & Jaatinen, M. (2001). New approaches to communication management for transformation and change in organisations. *Journal of Communication Management, 6*(2), 148–165.

Tapscott, D., & Williams, A. D. (2006). *Wikinomics: How mass collaboration changes everything.* New York: Portfolio.

Yukl, G. A. (2006). *Leadership in organizations* (6th ed.). Upper Saddle River, NJ: Prentice-Hall.

Zigurs, I. (2003). Leadership in virtual teams: Oxymoron or opportunity? *Organizational Dynamics, 31*, 339–359.

Applications and Reflections

The applications and reflections section provides an opportunity to relate the concepts and practices of leading change in Chapters 2–4 to several real-life situations. These situations illustrate the challenges of leading change in various types of organizations, including business, religious, government, education, and nonprofit/ nongovernmental organizations.

Application 1 Business

The New Rules

by Betsy Morris

Even now, nearly five years after his retirement from General Electric, Jack Welch commands the spotlight. He is still power-lunching, still making the gossip columns, still the charismatic embodiment of the star CEO. His books are automatic bestsellers. More than any other single figure, he stands as a model not just for the can-do American executive but for a way of doing business that revived the U.S. corporation in the 1980s and dominated the world's economic landscape for a quarter-century. Just try to find an executive who hasn't been influenced by his teachings. What came to be known as Jack's Rules are by now the business equivalent of holy writ, bedrock wisdom that has been open to interpretation, perhaps, but not dispute.

But the time has come: Corporate America needs a new playbook. The challenge facing U.S. business leaders is greater than ever before, yet they have less control than ever—and less job security. The volatility of the markets is so unpredictable, the pressure from hedge funds and private-equity investors so relentless, the competition from China and India so intense, that the edicts of the past are starting to feel out of date. In executive suites across the country, a dramatic rethinking is underway about fundamental assumptions that defined Welch and his era. Is an emphasis on market share really the prime directive? Is a company's near-term stock price—and the quarterly earnings per share that drive it—really the best measure of a CEO's success? In what ways is managing a company to measure of a CEO's success? In what ways is managing a company to please Wall Street bad for competitiveness in the long run?

Jack Welch, needless to say, is having none of it. When Fortune caught up with him recently, he was as confident and outspoken as ever. "I'm perfectly prepared to change," says Welch (who co-writes a column in Business Week with his wife, Suzy). "Change is great." But, he asserts, he sees no reason to back away from the principles by which he and other star CEOs like Roberto Goizueta of Coca-Cola managed. If applied correctly, Welch contends, his rules can work forever.

Sorry, Jack, but we don't buy it. The practices that brought Welch, Goizueta, and others such success were developed to battle problems specific to a time and place in history. And they worked. No one questions today that bloated bureaucracy can kill a business. No one forgets the shareholder—far from it. Yet those threats have receded. And they have been replaced by new ones. The risk we now face is applying old solutions to new problems.

Early on, Welch argued that lagging businesses—those not No. 1 or No. 2 in their markets—should be fixed, sold, or closed. In a 1981 speech titled "Growing Fast in a Slow-Growth Economy," he announced that GE would no longer tolerate low-margin and low growth units. GE, he told analysts at the Pierre Hotel in New York, "will be the locomotive pulling the GNP, not the caboose following it." As much as any other single event, Welch's words marked the dawn of the shareholder-value movement. And GE eventually became its star. No question who was Welch's boss. His report card: the stock price. His goal: consistent earnings growth.

As his ruthlessly efficient strategy wrenched GE into high performance, the company's stock took off. Soon virtually everything Welch said became gospel—often to the extreme. When Welch embraced Six Sigma, the program began to proliferate all over corporate America.

He talked about being the leanest and meanest and lowest-cost, and corporate America got out its ax. Welch advocated ranking your players and weeding out your weakest, and HR departments turned Darwinian. As time went on, the mantra of shareholder value took on a life of its own. Cheered on by academics, consulting firms and investors, more and more companies tried to defy history (and their own reality) to sustain growth and dazzle Wall Street as Welch was doing. Accounting tricks, acquisition mania, outright thievery—executives went overboard. "It became all about 'real men make their numbers,'" says one CEO. "What were we thinking?"

This, says Harvard Business School's Rakesh Khurana, is the legacy of the Old Rules. Managing to create shareholder value became managed earnings became managing quarter to quarter to please the Street. "That meant a disinvestment in the future," says Khurana, author of Searching for a Corporate Savior. "It was a dramatic reversal of everything that made capitalism strong and the envy of the rest of the world: the willingness of a CEO to forgo dividends and make an investment that wouldn't be realized until one or two CEOs down the road." Now, he believes, "we're at a hinge point of American capitalism."

There is another model. In breathtakingly short order, the rock star of business is no longer the guy atop the Fortune 500 (today Rex Tillerson at ExxonMobil), but the very guy those Fortune 500 types used to love to ridicule: Steve Jobs at Apple. The biggest feat of the decade is not making the elephant dance, as Lou Gerstner famously did at IBM, but inventing the iPod and transforming an industry. Dell spectacularly upended Compaq and Hewlett-Packard, yet few big companies paid close enough attention to see that new technologies and business models were negating the power of economies of scale in myriad ways. Nobody has proved that more than Google.

Yet in the corridors of corporate power, the old rules continue to cast an outsized shadow. Many CEOs are following a playbook that has, at best, been distorted by time. "How do you think about building shareholder value when a lot of people are really just going to hold the share for the moment?" says Jim Collins, a former Stanford Business School professor and the author of Good to Great and Built to Last.

"The idea of maximizing shareholder value is a strange idea when [many shareholders] are really share flippers. That's a real change. That does make the notion of building a great company more difficult."

That doesn't mean everything about Welch's era is wrong. Indeed, we named him "manager of the century" in 1999. Were he at GE today, he might well be in the forefront of the current wave of rethinking, as his successor, Jeffrey Immelt, surely is. Still, in the way of all good analogies, we must begin by tearing down the old so that we can really open ourselves to something different. In that spirit, then, here are seven old rules whose shortcomings have become apparent and seven replacements that point toward a new model for success. Some of the old rules are inspired directly by Welch's teachings; others are not. You may not agree with all of our conclusions (Welch certainly didn't—see "Welch Fires Back"). We welcome the debate. What's most important is to get the discussion started.

Old rule: Big dogs own the street.

New rule: Agile is best; being big can bite you.

Until the very end of the last century, big meant good in the business world. B-schools taught the benefits of economies of scale. The greater your revenue, the more you could spread fixed costs across units sold. With size came dominance—of airwaves, store shelves, supply chains, distribution channels. Until the mid-1990s, a company's market value usually tracked its revenue.

Then strange things started to happen. Microsoft's market cap passed IBM's in 1993, even though Bill Gates' $3 billion in revenue was one-twenty-second that of IBM. Scale didn't insulate GM from near-catastrophic decline. The big dogs seemed to hit a wall. (The median Fortune 500 company is now three times the size it was in 1980, in real terms, and thus much harder to manage.) Citigroup, built through acquisitions by Sandy Weill to deliver consistent earnings, suddenly found the market focused on whatever bad news emerged in Citi's far flung units instead of on the smoothness of its overall performance. Big Pharma used to be prized for its unmatched R&D spending; now it is the smaller biotech firms that generate the cutting-edge drugs—and drug makers Merck, Bristol-Myers, and Eli Lilly all have smaller market caps than biotech Genentech, despite significantly higher revenue and profits.

Technological advances and changing business models have diminished the importance of scale, as outsourcing, partnering, and other alliances with specialty firms (with their own economies of scale) have made it possible to convert fixed costs into variable ones. Dell, it turned out, was not an anomaly, it was just the beginning—a pioneer at all this, keeping its costs down by outsourcing disk drives, memory chips, monitors, and more, freeing itself to focus on (and clean up in) direct selling and just-in-time assembly.

Old rule: Be no. 1 or no. 2 in your market.

New rule: Find a niche, create something new.

Nobody wants to be a laggard, of course, and there is much to be said for being the market leader. Nike, Wal-Mart and Exxon certainly don't wish they were anything else. But more and more, market domination is no safety net. Disney's stranglehold on animated films meant nothing once Pixar's digital innovation hit the scene. AOL's established user base couldn't slow down Google.

Look at Coca-Cola, whose still-strong No. 1 position in cola turned out to be not an insurance policy but proof of what consulting firm McKinsey calls the "incumbent's curse." Coke's arch rivalry with Pepsi was always about market share—capturing it or defending it by tenths of a percentage point in grocery stores, restaurants, and faraway lands. Coke executives defined their industry as "share of stomach"—that is, the total ounces of liquid an average person consumes in a day and what percentage of it can be filled with Coke. CEO Roberto Goizueta told Jack Welch in a conversation in Fortune a decade ago that the soft drink industry wouldn't run out of growth until "that faucet in your kitchen sink is used for what God intended"—dispensing Coke from the tap.

But eventually Coke's monomaniacal focus backfired. When bottled waters like Evian and Poland Spring began to gain traction, Coke didn't pay sufficient attention. Its board vetoed management's proposal to buy Gatorade in 2000 (sending the sports drink into the arms of Pepsi). Such niche products were viewed as low-volume distractions. Yet last year, in a turnabout that would have been inconceivable a decade ago, soda sales fell, and water, sports drinks, and energy drinks all soared. The jaw dropper: Energy drinks—which boast a profit margin of 85%, according to Bernstein Research—are now expected to out earn every other category of soft drink within three years.

Not everyone missed the opportunity. Out in Corona, California, tiny Hansen Natural Corp. didn't care about being No. 1 or No. 2. CEO Rodney Sacks was instead noticing how consumers were migrating from carbonated soft drinks to juices, iced teas, and "functional drinks." So in the 1990s he began moving Hansen beyond its base as a maker of natural sodas (Mandarin Lime, Orange Mango) toward vitamin and energy drinks. Never mind that the energy-drink market was tiny then. "We look for niches and see how they grow," he says. Since launching an energy drink called Monster four years ago (deftly packaged in a dramatic-looking 16-ounce can adorned with a claw mark), Hansen's sales have quadrupled to $348 million, vaulting its shares to $79 from a split-adjusted $2.

Coke has gotten religion. CEO Neville Isdell's team is pushing an array of new drinks, including a half dozen of its own energy entries that have earned the company a significant stake in the U.S. market. "We believe there is value in those niches," Isdell told Fortune this spring. "It will not drive the volume number, but volume is something we've often chased to the detriment of the long-term business."

Starbucks, on the other hand, is a drink-seller that has avoided the incumbent's trap. "We've never said we wanted to be No. 1 or No. 2," says CEO Jim Donald. Starbucks isn't a brand per se; it's more an identity that's morphed from a product (a latte) to a place to get wireless, to a place with music to meet friends. "If we said we wanted to be the No. 1 coffee company, that's what would be on our mind," Donald says. Instead, the company has kept moving, evolving, trying new things. "It doesn't matter where you end up," says Donald. "It matters that you're the company of choice."

Old rule: Shareholders rule.

New rule: The customer is king.

Whenever you ask a CEO about the importance of customers, you hear the requisite platitudes. But in fact, customers have often lost out in the relentless push to maximize shareholder value (as represented by the stock price) and to maximize it immediately. One Bain & Co. study found a huge gap between the perceptions of executives—80% of whom think they are doing an excellent job of serving customers—and the perceptions of customers themselves: Only 8% of them agree. Every four years, according to Bain, the average company loses more than half its customers. Aggressive pricing (on hotel phone bills, rental-car gas charges, and credit card fees, to name a few examples) has increased as the profit pressure on companies has mounted, says Bain's Fred Reichheld. Abusing customers this way, says Reichheld, "destroys the future of a business." He believes that such behavior—and not scandals like Enron and Tyco—is why fewer than half of all Americans have a favorable opinion of business today.

This is shareholder-value theory taken to the extreme: the tail wagging the dog. One CEO, who asked not to be named, describes the pressures this way: Businesses became disconnected from their fundamentals, producing "perceived value" instead of real value, because that's what the stock market rewards. When investor-driven capitalism took over from managerial-driven capitalism, as Harvard's Khurana puts it, CEOs began managing the company by earnings per share instead of focusing on details like new products, service calls, customer-satisfaction scores—all those things that are supposed to produce the earnings per share.

Yet some renegades thumbed their noses at Wall Street and truly kept the consumer experience front and center. Think Apple, which has from inception been predicated on dreaming up what customers want before they know it. Or look at Genentech, whose employees are greeted each day by billboards of the cancer patients who take its drugs, to remind everyone of the importance of their work. At GE, CEO Immelt has instigated what he calls "dreaming sessions" to brainstorm with key customers. He also requires all businesses to be judged using a metric called Net Promoter Score, developed by Reichheld and his colleagues at Bain, that measures how likely a customer is to have you back. "When everything is focused on delivering for customers, that makes employees proud," Reichheld says. "They become the powerful engine."

Old rule: Be lean and mean.

New rule: Look out, not in.

In 1995 Jack Welch "went nuts," as he later put it, over Six Sigma, a set of methods for improving quality—plus a powerful way to reduce costs—that had been developed by Motorola in the 1980s. At GE's annual managers' meeting in Boca Raton the following January, he told his troops that embracing Six Sigma would be the company's most ambitious undertaking ever. GE's "best and the brightest" were redeployed to put the methods into action. And it worked. Welch would later write that Six Sigma helped drive operating margins to 18.9% in 2000 from 14.8% four years earlier.

No wonder that after Welch adopted Six Sigma (to which he devotes a chapter of his book *Winning*), more than a quarter of the Fortune 200 followed suit. Yet not all firms were able to find the same magic. In fact, of 58 large companies that have announced Six Sigma programs, 91% have trailed the S&P 500 since, according to an analysis by Charles Holland of consulting firm Qualpro (which espouses a competing quality-improvement process).

One of the chief problems of Six Sigma, say Holland and other critics, is that it is narrowly designed to fix an existing process, allowing little room for new ideas or an entirely different approach. All that talent—all those best and brightest—were devoted to, say, driving defects down to 3.4 per million and not on coming up with new products or disruptive technologies. Innovation is "a meta-stable entity," says Vishva Dixit, vice president for research of Genentech, who oversees 800 scientists at a company that has created some of the most revolutionary anticancer drugs on the market. "Nothing will kill it faster than trying to manage it, predict it, and put it on a timeline."

An inward-looking culture can leave firms vulnerable in a business world that is changing at a breakneck pace—whether it's Craigslist stealing classified ads from local newspapers or VoIP threatening to make phone calls virtually free. "The availability of information and the opening of key markets is exploding," says Clay Christensen, a Harvard Business School professor and the author of The Innovator's Dilemma, "and now you put a few million Chinese and Indian engineers to the test of disrupting us too." No business can afford to focus its energies on its own navel in that environment. "Getting outside is everything," says GE's Immelt (who still deploys Six Sigma). From the day he took over as CEO, he says, he knew the company would need to be "much more forward-facing in the future than we ever were in the past." He explains: "It's not about change. It's about sudden and abrupt and uncontrollable change. If you're not externally focused in this world, you can really lose your edge."

Old rule: Rank your players; go with the A's.

New rule: Hire passionate people.

At GE under Welch, employees were ranked as A, B, or C players, and the bottom group was relentlessly culled. "We're an A-plus company," Welch told his executives in 1997, according to Robert Slater's book, *Jack Welch and the GE Way*. "We want only A players. Don't spend time trying to get C's to be B's. Move them out early."

Pretty soon places as diverse as Charles Schwab and Ford began ranking employees. But as with Six Sigma, the practice became overdone. Welch's "vitality curve," in the hands of less deft managers, became the "dead man's curve," or "rank and yank." Everybody, it seemed, was expendable. There was a price to pay. According to a Rutgers and University of Connecticut poll in 2002, 58% of workers believed most top executives put their own self-interest ahead of the company's, while only 33% trusted that their bosses have the firm's best interests at heart. "All of a sudden, when big companies had to change and respond to the marketplace and move quickly, they found out they couldn't, because they didn't have people engaged and aligned around the corporate mission," says Xerox CEO Anne Mulcahy. "Then being big is a disadvantage. If you're not nimble, there's no advantage to size. It's like a rock."

While studying companies trying to transform themselves, Christopher Bartlett of Harvard Business

School and a colleague found the major obstacle was inefficient use of increasingly disenfranchised employees. "People don't come to work to be No. 1 or No. 2 or to get a 20% net return on assets," Bartlett says. "They want a sense of purpose. They come to work to get meaning from their lives."

Steve Jobs has emphasized that Apple hires only people who are passionate about what they do (something that, to be fair, Welch also talked about). At Genentech, CEO Art Levinson says he actually screens out job applicants who ask too many questions about titles and options, because he wants only people who are driven to make drugs that help patients fight cancer. GE still ranks employees, but Immelt has also added a new system of rating—red, yellow, or green—on five leadership traits (including creativity and external focus).

Employees are rated against themselves, not one another. Immelt doesn't talk about jettisoning the bottom 10%. He talks about building a team. "When you're 18 years old, you say, 'The iPod is neat,'" Immelt explains, "but people don't dream about making a gas turbine. If we can recruit the best 22-year-olds, we can double and triple in size. If not, then we're already way too big. You've got to be pragmatic about what turns people on."

Old rule: Hire a charismatic CEO.

New rule: Hire a courageous CEO.

As big shareholders began to throw their weight around in the 1980s, boards sacked their CEOs and named dazzling replacements. And the celebrity CEO was born. The stars of that era were a varied crew: Jacques Nasser, Lou Gerstner, George Fisher, Michael Armstrong, Jack Welch, Ken Lay, Al Dunlap, Sandy Weill, Carly Fiorina. Some got more credit than they deserved, others more blame. A voracious business press helped burnish (or break) reputations. The bull market fueled the myth that a truly superior CEO could hit earnings targets quarter after quarter and propel the stock price unrelentingly higher.

But the tactics used by this generation of leaders— squeezing costs, deftly managing financial and accounting decisions, using acquisitions to grow—did not always provide long-term solutions. (A McKinsey study of 157 companies that bulked up through acquisition in the 1990s found that only 12% grew significantly faster than their peers, and only seven firms generated returns that were above industry-average.) Today many of those methods have fallen out of favor. Tellingly, one top management tool du jour is the stock buyback, which can buoy share prices and pacify investors—but also indicates that the CEO has no better ideas for deploying capital.

If the celebrity CEO needed a spotlight, then today's leaders need internal fortitude. Of 940 executives surveyed by Boston Consulting Group last year, 90% said organic growth was "essential" to their success. But less than half were happy with the return on their R&D spending. And therein lies the rub: Organic growth is not a quick fix.

Real growth requires placing big bets that probably won't pay off until far into the future—and today's impatient culture offers little incentive. What practically killed Xerox was its leaders' resistance to making the technological leap from analog copying to digital, which was almost guaranteed (as most such changes are) to cut margins. By the time they were finally forced to, their business was in free fall. The company was eventually charged with improperly accelerating revenues and overstating earnings. (It settled without admitting wrongdoing and paid a $10 million fine.)

"You have to change when you're at the top of your game in terms of profit," says Mulcahy, who cleaned up the mess, made the changes to digital and color, and is now trying to jump-start revenue. "It's hard to do. Your business looks its best. Your margins are at their best. All that makes your job easier. Then you're like, 'Oh, shit, here we go again.' You've got to jump into that risk pool, and once again you're in this mode of 'You know, this could fail.'"

Never before has a CEO more needed to take risks, but rarely has Wall Street been less receptive. A recent Booz Allen study found that a CEO is vulnerable to ouster if his stock price has lagged behind the S&P 500 by an average of 2% since he took the top job. Cisco Systems CEO John Chambers says he knows a number of colleagues who are planning to step down because of the difficulty of balancing the short-term pressures of the Street with what's in the long-term best interest of the company.

But standing tall is precisely what all those corner-office pros get paid the big bucks for, isn't it? "You have to have the courage of your convictions," says Chambers. Immelt agrees that you must be willing to spend time "in the wilderness with no love." And directors need some courage too: to resist pressure to judge a CEO by the company's stock price today and get back to harder measures like return on invested capital. Hark back again to that seminal Jack Welch speech in 1981. It hardly took the world by storm—in fact, Welch has talked about how little it seemed to impress analysts that day, barely moving the stock. But leadership is not about following the rules of the past. It is about standing up for what you believe is best, regardless of the consequences.

Old rule: Admire my might.

New rule: Admire my soul.

Today bravado is dangerous. Soft-drink companies became bad guys when they were slow to leave the school lunchroom. Nike got smacked by sweatshop allegations. Try surfing wakeupwalmart.com to see how powerful a critical community of Internet activists can be. That old notion that has served Goldman Sachs so well is creeping back into vogue: It's okay to be greedy as long as it's "long-term greedy." Says Isdell at Coke: "I do not [agree with] Milton Friedman—that the role of the corporation is solely to make money. Our legitimization in society is a very important part of what we do."

Having a "soul" as a corporation is more than contributing to causes or being transparent about executive compensation or adhering to environmental regulation (though it is certainly all of those things). It is defining a company's vision in a sustainable, long-term way—and to hell with what the hedge funds or other pay-me-now investors say. CEOs must get better at courting long-term investors—explaining their strategies, saying exactly what they intend to do, avoiding the temptation to sugarcoat. "There is so much pressure to hit your numbers," says Genentech's Levinson. "I've been very clear with Wall Street since 1995 that if we see an opportunity to make better drugs and more money down the road at a short-term cost, we will do that every time. And you need to know that's the kind of company we are."

That's easier to do, of course, when you're a glamorous, fast-growing little biotech. So it raises the question: Does the rest of corporate America have the moral fiber to defy the present, when needed, and focus on the future? And do shareholders have patience enough to support them? In other words, are they willing to be long-term greedy—or are they just greedy?

Welch Fires Back

Neutron Jack Defends His Turf

by Betsy Morris

Jack Welch was about to head to a television studio for what he calls "the best job I've ever had"—on-air analyst for the Boston Red Sox pre-game cable show—when we caught up with him. As usual, he had no shortage of opinions.

- On the power of size. It's great to be big. Being big doesn't mean you have to be slow. It doesn't mean you have to have tons of layers. It doesn't mean you can't have highly entrepreneurial people. . . . You can get fat. Monopolies are often guilty of not moving. If GE had stayed pat and we didn't grow in financial services and we stayed No. 1 in light bulbs, we'd have been in deep yogurt. But that doesn't mean you don't want to be big and strong.

- On leadership. You want to be No. 1. There's nothing wrong with that. You don't want to be a loser. Nos. 3, 4, and 5 don't have the same flexibility. You don't have the same level of resources. You can't do R&D at the same level. I agree being No. 1 in a static environment is not by itself sufficient. No. 4 might have smarter management that uses money more wisely. What you do with the resources that come from being a leader—that's what determines your future.

- On keeping lean. I was all for de-layering and flattening organizations. Today I'd flatten them even more. Some companies are still too hierarchical. Some are right out of Bethlehem Steel.

- On exploiting niches. It's not inconsistent at all with wanting to be No. 1, No. 2. In a big company you'd better be out exploring new niches. Today's niches, tomorrow's big things. Those aren't inconsistent.
- On customers. When has there ever been a divergence between shareholders and customers? No one is out saying, "Let's screw this customer today, and if we do, our share price might go up 20 cents." They're just not doing it.
- On looking outward. GE in the 1990s was all about looking outward. We traveled to other companies constantly to bring back best practices. It is one of the great ways to multiply the intellect in your organization.
- On ranking employees. That was very controversial. Weed out the weakest. The Red Sox and the Mets are playing tonight. Guess what? They're not putting on the field guys in the minors. It's all about fielding the best team. It's been portrayed as a cruel system. It isn't. The cruel system is the one that doesn't tell anybody where they stand.

Reflection

- Which leadership and change concepts best fit each of the new rules?
- What concepts and practices can businesses use to counter an "inward-looking culture"?
- Christopher Bartlett and Steve Jobs emphasize purpose and passion in employees' work. What can companies do to inspire authentic purpose and passion?
- Considering concepts and practices of leading change in this chapter, what argument would CEOs use to convince their board of directors and stockholders of the importance of "balancing the short-term pressures of [Wall Street] with what's in the long-term interest of the company"?

Application 2 Religious Organization

Wanted: Excited Christians: Declining Congregations Are Either Being Pruned for Growth, or Burned for Their Failure to Grow

by Carol Ann Keys

I know all the things you do, and that you have a reputation for being alive—but you are dead. Wake up! Strengthen what little remains, for even what is left is almost dead. I find that your actions do not meet the requirements of my God. Go back to what you heard and believed at first; hold to it firmly. Repent and turn to me again. If you don't wake up, I will come to you suddenly, as unexpected as a thief.

—Revelation 3:1–3

Once upon a time, in a land not so far away, there was a little church of The Presbyterian Church in Canada. This church had a long and proud history in its land, and the people of this church believed that God would bless them for their faithfulness forever. Every Sunday the little congregation gathered to worship its Lord in a dignified and orderly manner. But the years went by and slowly the congregation began to fall asleep, and attendance at the little church started to fall quietly away.

First the younger people left and later the Sunday school shut down. The younger generation was bored and disinterested in what the little church had to offer. The message of the good news of Jesus Christ was not being presented to them in a manner which ignited their interest or held their attention. The culture in the land was changing at a pace unprecedented in its history, but the little congregation insisted that the Lord must be worshipped in the same way. The young people said "Okay," and they registered their kids in Sunday morning hockey or went Sunday shopping or slept in.

The people told themselves, "Young people aren't interested in religion, there is nothing we can do." And so one by one the people of the little church grew older and began to die, and soon even the mighty Presbyterian Church Women folded. "What are we to do?" said the session members to each other. "There aren't enough people here to pay our expenses. How will we be able to continue to worship the Lord?"

Two of the elders of the little church joined with their minister to form a committee of session, which grew to include three more people from the congregation. They were charged with finding a solution to this problem. Faithful servants of the Lord, they worked tirelessly to find the clues they needed, and after many months of searching they reported back. "We have sought a vision from God," they said, "and this is what He told us: We need to open the doors of our little church to everyone in the land. We need to meet the people at the level of their culture and at their point of greatest need, and then we need to deliver the good news of Jesus Christ to them in a way they will enjoy and understand. We need to reach out to everyone in this land, young and old, rich and poor, and be the example of Jesus Christ in word and deed. We need to show our land that this little church has a purpose, and a mission, and that we are ready, able and willing to act on it. We need to explain to everyone in the land who we are, and why we are here, and tell them and show them who their neighbor is—because they no longer know. The people of this land have forgotten about the Lord."

The session was uneasy. They liked their little church the way it was. They liked the people they had. Most of all they liked the way they worshipped. The committee tried to show the people of the church they had nothing to fear. The minister gave them scriptural assurance that change has been the call of God to his people throughout all time. The committee told stories of other Presbyterian churches that had successfully made the transition from old to new worship styles resulting in phenomenal growth. They asked the people of the little church to read a contemporary translation of the Bible in order to add value and insight to their understanding of the Lord's purposes for his church. They challenged the little church to better discipleship.

Hopefully, they rationalized, this would help the congregation at the little church understand that "reformed and reforming" has been the cry of the Presbyterian Church since its Reformation inception. Most of all, however, the committee longed to show the little church how wonderful the new music of the Christian church could be. They had seen for themselves how younger people in growing Presbyterian churches had positively responded to changes in worship music and worship style—music which did not include the use of an organ. "What," they asked their people, "would you be willing to give up to bring Jesus Christ back to the people of this land?"

The people of the little church listened to the committee but they didn't like what they heard. It was a John 1:5 kind of thing; the people saw the light, but they preferred the darkness. The committee knew that unless the little church could grasp and truly understand its biblical reason for existence (and then embrace what it has been commanded to do) then there was little reason for them to continue as a congregation in the church of Jesus Christ. The little church did not have new people coming to it because new people were never truly wanted or even invited. There wasn't any sincere thought put into the fact that younger people, who were so desperately needed in this little church, did not understand or enjoy the traditional worship practices. Especially the organ. What were they willing to give up? Nothing. The people of the little church just didn't see it as their issue. As far as they were concerned, the little church was open for business and everyone was welcome to join them in a service of traditional worship on any Sunday morning at 10:30—just like the sign on the front lawn said.

The committee of session was disbanded and the minister sent on her way. The two elders and their families left the little church because God had given them a glorious opportunity to see the possibilities available to any church. An exciting church, they had learned, does not need be an oxymoron. To be an exciting church you simply need to have excited Christians. The little church had been far from either.

Today the congregation at the sleepy little church continues to worship in a land not so far away. Their finances are faltering and they are without a minister.

There appears to be no particular anxiety about death at this little church. It is accepted, and so far as God allows these things to be seen, there will not be a fairy tale ending. Their light is very dim, and they will sleep away their existence until they breathe no longer.

Carol Ann Keys has lived this story.

SOURCE: From "Wanted: Excited Christians," by C. A. Keys, 2007, *Presbyterian Record*, 26 (2), pp. 26–27. This article was first published in the *Presbyterian Record*, March 2007. Reprinted with permission.

REFLECTION

Many congregations, regardless of denomination, face these circumstances. According to the life-cycle theory, this church is facing imminent decline or death. Yet most congregations in similar situations do not want to see their churches close.

- What concepts and practices of leading change can congregations use to revitalize or recover and prevent the continuing decline described by Carol Keys?
- Use the guiding questions throughout the chapter (and summarized in the conclusion) to develop a change proposal for churches in this situation.

Application 3 Government

Virtual Networks: An Opportunity for Government

by Frank DiGiammarino and Lena Trudeau

Meeting the Changing Needs of Citizens

The interactive web is forcing some of government's time-worn institutions to rethink their relationship with their most important client: the public. A good illustration of this kind of reckoning can be found in our municipal library systems, which—in the age of Amazon.com and Barnes and Noble megastores—are under increasing pressure to stay relevant and engaged with the communities they serve.

"The younger generation today is wired differently than people in my generation," said sixty-nine-year-old Harry Courtright, explaining to the New York Times last summer why the fifteen-branch library system he oversees in Arizona's Maricopa County jettisoned the once sacred Dewey decimal system of classifying books in favor of one designed for the majority of users, who come to browse without a particular title in mind.

Courtright and his colleagues are facing fundamental questions of identity. What is a library in the twenty-first century? How does the role of librarian change in light of customer reviews and other peer-to-peer networking opportunities that online bookstores routinely provide? Will the one-third of Americans who count themselves among Generation Y ultimately expect public libraries to work more like Netflix? Will we eventually be a society of on-demand books?

The implications for government, which delivers a wide range of services to an ever more sophisticated public, are immense. Libraries provide just one example of the opportunity virtual networks offer public-sector leaders—faced with expanding mandates, increasingly constrained budgets, and unwieldy organizational structures—to rethink their service delivery model.

Emergence of the Virtual Network

The paradigms that define our current understanding of organizations can be traced back to the 1930s and early public administration scholars like Luther Gulick, who claimed that organizations should departmentalize work by purpose, process, clientele, or place and should not combine dissimilar activities in single agencies. Gulick argued that although most work contains all four elements, systems must organize around only one of these core principles, to the exclusion of the other three. Today's government institutions reflect this thinking, with agencies that provide services and information often managed in vertical silos.

Virtual networks, in contrast, place a premium on breaking down these silos and connecting various audiences across (and within) them for better delivery to the citizen. The "wiki" platform for virtual collaboration takes its name from the Hawaiian word for "fast" and features built-in functionality that allows quick content analysis—users can see the labels that have been applied to content, how content has been edited and reviewed, and the relationships that have formed between various pieces of data. This allows for nearly limitless access and searchability that is shifting the structure of thought from the hierarchical and vertical to the diffuse and horizontal. Particularly in light of Generation Y's increasing role in the federal workforce, government leaders have the responsibility to understand the nature of this evolution and embrace virtual networks as a way to be more efficient while remaining relevant.

"While the government is still buying Rolodexes, the younger generations have 600 friends on Facebook and 250 professional colleagues on LinkedIn," said Steve Ressler, 27, a cofounder of Young Government Leaders, a professional organization of more than 1,000 younger federal employees from more than thirty departments and agencies. "It's very important for us to see Web 2.0 technologies in the workplace. We are used to working horizontal, are not afraid of authority, and want our ideas heard."

Technology and Leadership

The cause of deploying Web 2.0 in government continues to gain committed champions, and the mounting success stories can be attributed more to leadership than technology. In April 2006, the Office of the Director of National Intelligence (ODNI) created the classified "Intellipedia" wiki site to allow 16 intelligence agencies to quickly and collaboratively share classified information. Without compromising security, the goal was to transcend traditional silos and gain the agility required to combat loosely connected networks of terrorists and similarly diffuse but urgent threats. The site allows frontline agents to post information on any aspect of intelligence along with other agencies in the intelligence community.

This powerful collaborative tool has been put to practical use on several occasions, including the 2006 crash of a small plane into a New York City high-rise. Within two hours, Intellipedia garnered more than eighty updates, enough to determine with confidence that the crash was not a terrorist act. Intellipedia has also been useful in providing up-to-date, peer-driven intelligence on North Korean missile tests, bomb-making by Iraqi insurgents, and instability in Nigeria. In testimony presented to Congress on September 10, 2007—6 years after the terrorist attacks of September 11—Director of National Intelligence Admiral Michael McConnell lauded Intellipedia for enabling "experts from different disciplines to pool their knowledge, form virtual teams, and quickly make complete intelligence assessments.... The solution does not require special networks or equipment but has dramatically changed our capability to share information in a timely manner."

"It's not complicated technology; it's not expensive," says Assistant Secretary of Homeland Security for the Transportation Security Administration (TSA) Kip Hawley. "The biggest challenge, the biggest learning, is that somebody has to make the decision to just go ahead and do it." In addition to TSA's classified involvement with Intellipedia, Hawley has overseen the launch of a new blog for the traveling public and an internal IdeaFactory, where TSA's 43,000 frontline transportation security officers can confer collectively on job-related issues and ideas. The site empowers employees to share ideas on how to improve the organization across multiple lines; these ideas are available for every employee to see and evaluate. Employees vote for the ideas they like and offer constructive criticism. Within a week of its launch, TSA employees had submitted more than 150 ideas, offered more than 650 comments, and voted on ideas more than 800 times.

The Collaboration Project

Hawley recently discussed these initiatives at the first meeting of The Collaboration Project, the

National Academy of Public Administration's newly launched leadership forum that uses research, best practices, and other resources to help apply the benefits of Web 2.0 and collaborative technology in government.

The Collaboration Project

The National Academy is taking the lead on Web 2.0 in government by launching The Collaboration Project—an independent leadership forum to jump-start the cause of collaborative technology to drive innovation and change in government. Designed for leaders looking to overcome the technical, organizational, and cultural barriers involved, the project convenes members in person and through a virtual collaboration space to share best practices, case studies, white papers, and leadership tools for implementation.

"This is a big idea that's being introduced to a somewhat alien culture," said National Academy president and chief executive officer Jenna L. Dorn, "but we are convinced that collaborative technology has the potential to transform government in America, to tap into the expertise of people outside the hierarchy of any single agency or department, to make government more transparent, and to open the door to a broader array of experts focused on solving a particular problem or to citizens who want to contribute to making government work better."

The Collaboration Project kicked off operations with its first in-person meeting in February, drawing a diverse group of key decision makers, including congressional staff, chief information officers (CIOs), chief technology officers, chief financial officers, and other senior leaders from more than a dozen federal agencies, including the Environmental Protection Agency (EPA), Coast Guard, Government Accountability Office, Small Business Administration, and Departments of Homeland Security, Transportation, and Defense.

TSAs Kip Hawley inspired meeting participants with his presentation on the successful Web 2.0 advances at his agency. "It's self-policing," Hawley told the audience, explaining how the various parties collaborate in responsible and inventive ways without the need for excessive oversight by forum monitors. "We've found that the lighter the touch on editing, the better the quality of ideas and the quality of the discussion."

SOURCE: From "Virtual Networks: An Opportunity for Government," by F. DiGiammarino and L. Trudeau, 2008, *Public Manager,* 37(1), pp. 5–11. Reprinted with permission.

Reflection

- What factors in today's environment challenge Luther Gulick's ideas about how government should function?
- Which concepts and practices of leading change contributed to the changes in public agencies described by DiGiammarino and Trudeau?
- What other change or opportunities could virtual networks offer internal and external stakeholders?

Application 4 Education

Revolution From the Faculty Lounge: The Emergence of Teacher-Led Schools and Cooperatives

by Joe Williams

Progressivism in Wisconsin

In Wisconsin, the home of legendary progressive crusader "Fighting Bob" LaFollette, the concept of teacher cooperatives has been taking a slightly different turn. In Milwaukee, a city where charter schooling and even private school vouchers have been part of the landscape of education for several years, teachers have also begun taking to the idea of running small schools that they feel will better meet the needs of their students.

Unlike the teachers who work for the EdVisions cooperative, teachers at Milwaukee's teacher cooperative schools remain employees of the Milwaukee Public Schools and dues paying members of the Milwaukee Teachers' Education Association (MTEA), but they provide their services to district-sponsored charter schools as an autonomous team. (All the cooperative schools are district-sponsored charters, rather than independent charters, because this arrangement allows the teachers to continue to participate in the state's teacher retirement system.) They don't own their practice in an economic sense, but they are allowed by both the district and their union to own what happens within their autonomous school communities. The teachers select their colleagues, decide on the work assignments, determine the expenditures, and—most importantly, they say—shape the learning program.

"The teachers in these cooperatives literally 'own' what happens in their schools, which creates a climate where accountability and flexibility go hand-in-hand," observes Milwaukee Superintendent William Andrekopoulos. Unionized teachers in Milwaukee have already formed 11 professional partnerships that run charter schools under the state's laws that allow for worker cooperatives. Wisconsin's cooperatives are organized under Chapter 185 of the state's statutes and are tax exempt nonprofit organizations. All full-time teachers at the school site are automatically considered members of the cooperative, and all have the same rights and privileges.

The I.D.E.A.L. Charter School opened in the fall of 2001 as the first teacher cooperative in Milwaukee. The partners collectively hold the charter, although, because of a quirk in the state's charter school law, only one teacher signs it. The teachers continue as district employees and are paid the contract rate, but they can decide how many teachers of what type the school needs, and so they can reallocate expenditures. There is a memorandum of understanding with the MTEA, the bargaining agent for the district's teachers, that waives certain provisions of the master contract. The union has been cooperative, the board of education is happy, and the teachers are protected but still have full control of "professional issues."

Any teacher in the district may apply for a vacant teaching position at any cooperative, but the existing team has the right to interview all the candidates and to select the teachers that the district will then assign to the school. The current agreement allows these interviews up until an established deadline, after which teachers must fill the vacancies using traditional seniority rights—a practice that some members of the cooperatives hope to eliminate in the future since teacher selection is crucial to the team building that allows cooperatives to thrive.

What Happens in These Co-ops?

While the hallways and classrooms of cooperative schools don't always look entirely different from what you would find in a typical school, it is the regular partner meetings that stand out as unconventional. Unlike the often-inflexible, compliance-based cultures that exist in traditional schools—where the principal implements district-wide edicts and there is little room to make meaningful adjustments based on the particular needs of individual schools—partner meetings under the professional partnership model demonstrate what is possible when teachers have a say over what happens in schools.

"All the teachers are at the table," says Avalon's Whalen, who now works as a consultant for EdVisions, helping other teams of teachers around the nation to form cooperatives. At Avalon, about 12 weeks before the doors first opened to students, the teachers got together and simply divided up the lengthy list of tasks that needed to be completed. The concept of "professionalism," Whalen says, ends up meaning something different when you have complete ownership of the work experience. It often means that teachers willingly participate in cafeteria duty, bathroom duty, and hallway duty, for example, because a professional team has determined that resources would be better spent on instruction than on school aides. It isn't that the aides wouldn't be nice to have, Whalen notes, but such costs can be converted into hiring additional teachers, which keeps class sizes lower and keeps the focus on student instruction.

Sometimes the decisions confronting the teacher/owners of a school aren't particularly interesting to much of the outside world, but they illustrate the kinds of everyday issues that can't be easily solved by large, bureaucratic school systems. Signs are also beginning to emerge that teachers will use this new level of flexibility to better understand and respond to the academic needs of their students.

At the Milwaukee Learning Laboratory and Institute, for example, which opened in the fall of 2005, the partnership's teachers determined in the first few months that their students needed to hone their organization, research, and study skills. The students were so weak in these areas that it limited their learning in other subject areas, such as science. For some students, an inability to work on their own was making their lessons irrelevant.

The teachers decided to alter the student schedules midstream to provide an ad hoc course in study skills. They created the time for this unplanned instruction by dropping science class for one marking period. Once the students at the small school were brought up to speed on their research and study skills, the partnership changed the schedules again, so that all students doubled up on science for the final marking period. Thus the students made up for the lost classes and, because they had a better grip on handling homework and research, made better use of their science time than they would have otherwise. "We could never have done that in a large high school that wasn't run by the teachers," said David Coyle, the lead teacher under the partnership arrangement.

Teachers who are members of these cooperatives spend a great deal of time honing the decision-making process, since that is the professional cornerstone on which the school culture is built. "We've had to struggle at times with the question of whether or not we make decisions by consensus or by majority rule," Avalon's Whalen says. "The vast majority of decisions end up being made by consensus, but the tough ones end up being by majority rule."

Conceptually, since the EdVisions and Milwaukee teacher co-op schools are public "schools of choice," there is a connection between the decisions the teachers make about their offerings and the desires of students in the marketplace. If students don't want to attend these schools, they cease to exist.

There are also some built-in levers that ensure the quality of the team members. Teachers who don't cut it in the partnerships, based on evaluations by a cooperative peer-review system, are allowed to return to the traditional employment pool of the district with their seniority intact. The same applies to teachers who decide on their own that the partnership model just isn't a good fit.

One of the Milwaukee teacher cooperatives, Advanced Language and Academic Studies (ALAS), was started by a group of teachers who had grown frustrated working in the perennially troubled South Division High School, a school serving primarily Latinos on Milwaukee's South Side. "We were frustrated with the fact that no one would take responsibility for what was happening," said Linda Peters, the lead teacher at ALAS. In some ways, it was remarkable that the rebellious South Division teachers found one another at all. But, in addition to a burning desire actually to do something to help their students, they had one thing in common: they all avoided the large high school's teachers lounge like the plague. "It was like a den of negativity," one South Division refugee remarked.

At ALAS, there is no room for negativity, teachers say. As soon as a problem is identified, it becomes the professional team's collective responsibility to solve it. There is no need to establish study commissions or run decisions through myriad layers of district-level bureaucracy. Identify a problem, decide collectively on a solution, and implement it. The model is about streamlined school operations. The hours are long, and the hats the teacher/owners wear are many. The partners meet regularly to tackle problems as they arise, and, because there is no principal, they can't leave until someone has taken charge of whatever situation the staff collectively deems worthy of an intervention.

Teachers say the most important change they sought from their teacher union contract was the ability to choose like-minded colleagues who share their vision of education. If anything, teachers say they would like even more flexibility on this issue for the sake of preserving school culture. "We're really hard on ourselves. The pressure comes from within," says Kevin Kuschel, who was driven to join the co-op, in part, by his belief that bilingual students were more capable of taking Advanced Placement courses in subjects like history than South Division seemed to believe. "This is our baby, and we want the baby to be successful," Kuschel continues.

Even students see the difference in terms of staff cohesion when teacher partners work as a team. "The students understand the staff is a unit. There is no playing one teacher off against another," Roxanne Mayeur, a teacher at Milwaukee's Community High School, told the Milwaukee Journal Sentinel. "We don't think administrators are useless or a negative thing, [but] it is important that this movement be about teachers having more of a voice."[1]

Mark Van Ryzin, a doctoral candidate at the University of Minnesota who has studied the teacher partnerships in both Milwaukee and Minnesota, says that virtually anything is possible. "With these professional partnerships, teachers can not only make more of the day-to-day decisions but can also undertake whole-school reform and redesign" if they believe that's what's necessary to contribute to student learning. "If the teachers, as a group, are more comfortable in a traditional classroom-based school, that is what they create. If the teachers are reformers at heart, they can incorporate any sort of pedagogical or technological innovation and create a very different kind of school," Van Ryzin points out. "The ultimate authority lies with them."

Lead Teachers, Not Principals

Generally, there are no principals at these teacher-led schools, so that the teacher voice will drive every decision regarding the education to be delivered. Instead of a principal, most professional partnerships of teachers operate with a single teacher who is designated as the "lead teacher." These individuals are responsible for running partner meetings and other events and for dealing with the state or district bureaucracies when that's necessary.

Yet, even when the school community is sensitive to the need to share responsibilities, many foundations and government agencies that work with the schools rely upon traditional norms and require the signature of the school principal on forms. Teachers said this can be a tricky hurdle,

organizationally, because it means one person ends up getting a lot of additional responsibility dumped into his or her lap. In Wisconsin, for example, the wording of the state's charter school law contributes to the piling-on for lead teachers because it states that charters may be granted only to sole individuals, not teams of teachers, so one teacher's name automatically ends up on the charter contract. Several lead teachers interviewed in Milwaukee expressed hints of frustration that they end up doing the work of principals without the pay bump that serving as a principal usually provides.

Teachers in partnership schools also point out that some forms of decision making are more fun—professionally speaking—than others. Everyone "wants to make a decision about the budget, but no one wants to call a snow day," says Avalon's Whalen. She suggests that there are some tasks—usually far removed from instruction—that teachers still want someone else to deal with.

Many outsiders are quick to point out that ultimately someone must be in charge of handling the day-to-day administrative duties. But supporters of the partnerships say the fact that the "partnership" is responsible for the school doesn't mean that there's "nobody in charge." Rather, it means that the partnership—rather than a district central office—decides who's in charge and in charge of what. Some partnerships, for example, might opt to hire an administrator to support the work of the teachers; others may decide to contract out for administrative services, either because they prefer to have more time with students or because they prefer not to have administrative work.

One thing that becomes clear at all of these teacher-run schools is that the workload for teachers is considerably heavier than under traditional arrangements. Some observers worry that this will work against bringing these teacher-run schools to scale. Simply put, they say, these types of school ownership arrangements aren't for everyone, and teachers must decide for themselves whether the professional satisfaction they gain is worth the cost in additional time and responsibility. "One of the things I worry about is whether or not we can get enough people to keep buying into this approach," Whalen says. "You can't hire the teacher who thinks that teaching is a nine-month job. It really is a full-time commitment."

Note

1. Sarah Carr, "Where Teachers Rule: A School with No Principal?" Milwaukee Journal Sentinel, July 18, 2005.

Source: From "Revolution From the Faculty Lounge: The Emergence of Teacher-Led Schools and Cooperatives," by Joe Williams, 2007, *Phi Delta Kappan,* 89(3), pp. 210–216. Reprinted with permission.

Reflection

- What forms of collective leadership do teacher-led schools illustrate?
- What strengths and weaknesses do these forms of leadership present for public schools?
- How can teacher cooperatives align their concepts of change and leadership with change practices to take advantage of their strengths and decrease weaknesses?
- Who are the stakeholders in teacher-led schools? How do these schools benefit or create problems for each group of stakeholders?

Application 5 Nonprofit

Adult Literacy Center

The mission of the Adult Literacy Center (ALC) is to help adults develop basic reading and communication skills through one-on-one tutoring so that they can fulfill their goals and their roles as citizens, workers, and family members. For adults with limited literacy skills, voting, reading a newspaper, or even ordering food at a restaurant is a difficult task. Illiteracy is commonly correlated with higher school dropout, unemployment, and crime rates and increased poverty. Even more problematic, illiteracy has intergenerational consequences—children of adults with limited literacy are more likely to have limited literacy skills.

The need for adult literacy education in Montclair Township was first identified by the Edgemont Group of Montclair Township with the founding of the Adult Literacy Center's predecessor, Reading to Succeed Project (RSP) in 1987. The RSP was formed in response to the ever increasing problem of adult literacy found throughout the township. It is estimated that 52%, or 94 million, Americans read below the sixth-grade level, a number growing at a rate of 2 million per year. The Literacy at Work study estimated the economic impact and business losses attributable to basic skill deficiencies run into the hundreds of millions of dollars. The Adult Literacy Center's role as a nonprofit literacy program in reversing this trend is accomplished through the dedicated work of a small, full-time staff that helps integrate and connect tutors and students in one-on-one relationships to improve basic reading skills.

The Adult Literacy Center served 320 students in 2007, a sizable number given the current levels of staffing, funding, and space, but this number is only a fraction of the township's 100,000 adults in need. The staff consists of four full-time employees, including the executive director, office manager, education resource coordinator, and trainer/volunteer coordinator; the seven part-time employees, who work between 4 and 20 hours per week; and the volunteer tutors, whose number totals approximately 100.

Jane Atwater, the executive director, has been at ALC for 3 years; however, she has become increasingly frustrated in her position, and rumors are circulating among staff members that she plans to leave. A large part of her frustration stems from the board of directors. Turnover on the board has been very high, and only one fourth of the members are continuing in their position. The continuing members provide little stability because they are consumed with arguing about which of them will become president. Board and subcommittee meetings are sporadic and lack substance. Board members do not fully understand their roles and have not played a vital role in fundraising, friend raising, or policy setting policy and direction for the executive director. Their attempt to develop a strategic plan resulted in a document without a clear vision or strategic direction and with only a few goals.

Jane spends most of her time developing and submitting grant applications to keep the center running. Even though the ALC filmed a moving documentary with testimony from graduates about the success of the program, the center lost its grant funding from the township due to inadequate documentation and assessment of student progress. They had little or no data (such as pre- and posttests) to support their case for continued funding.

Students speak in glowing terms about the program and their supportive tutors. However, among the full-time staff, many personnel problems are brewing—in-fighting, claims of favoritism, and employee turnover. Allegations of favoritism stem from board member interference in hiring decisions—that is, board members using their influence to hire certain part-time staff or volunteers into full-time positions. As a result, there is ongoing resentment and limited teamwork among the staff.

The executive director is at her wits' end. She has solicited the help of a nonprofit institute at a nearby university to help turn this situation around.

Source: This application is based on the research of members of the Leading Change class: Sean Baran, Sam Beese, Marlene Bennett, Kristen Berlacher, Lauren Bifulco, Rachel Brushett, Drake Bushnell, Liz Friend, Whitney McComis, Meagan Powell, Luke Purcell, Lindsey Reid, David Roberts, Killian Tormey, and Will Vanthunen.

Reflection

- How should Jane Atwater and the nonprofit institute begin the change process in this situation?
- Considering the various stakeholders, what concepts and practices of leading change should they consider?

CHAPTER 34

Pilots for Change

Exploring Organisational Change Through Distributed Leadership

Steve Kempster[1]
Lancaster University, Lancaster, UK

Malcolm Higgs
Southampton University, Southampton, UK

Tobias Wuerz
Horvath and Partners, Düsseldorf, Germany and Lancaster University, Lancaster, UK

Introduction

The implementation of pilot processes is not common in organisational change management. As a corollary little is known about how and why pilots could be useful to enhanced efficacy of organisational change. Similarly little attention has been given to processes of distributed leadership in organisational change. The purpose of this chapter is to develop a theoretical argument relating to how the key "dynamics of change management" can be integrated for enhanced efficacy by distributed change leadership through the mechanism of pilots.

There is considerable discussion suggesting that organisations are responding to the challenges of change more and more frequently. A longitudinal study of 50 British firms has shown that the pace at which organisations are changing is accelerating (Whittington and Mayer, 2002). Although organisations seek to address both the external challenges and the development of internal capabilities (Barney, 2001) through internal changes, the success rate of the change programmes launched within organisations is poor, varying in failure between 70 and 90 per cent (Balogun and Hope Hailey, 2008; Higgs and Rowland, 2005).

In engineering, pilots are widely used to detect failures of new developments and to increase the success rate of the launch of a new product or service. In psychological research the use of pilots for controlled experiments has been thoroughly developed over many years (Orne, 1962). However, little work has transferred to understanding the role of pilots within organisational change. This is a much overlooked phenomenon. It arguably should be capable of being applied within organisations to reduce the failure rate of change programmes. We explore how pilots could be applied with particular attention to the notion of distributed leadership. Distributed leadership places emphasis on a relational process that draws on many being involved with leadership rather than the sole individual leader; more than the formal property of the individual leader, but rather embracing informal and emergent aspects alongside formal roles (Senior and Fleming, 2006, p. 268). Johnson-Cramer et al. (2003) have highlighted the importance of drawing together the "change dynamics" of political change, emergent change, planned change and learning and innovation if effectiveness of change initiatives are to be enhanced. Two related questions address this issue and are central to this chapter: How can the "change dynamics" of rational planning, politics and emergence be drawn together effectively? What is the appropriate leadership approach to draw these dynamics together? We will argue that the concept of distributed leadership through piloting change may constitute a significant method to do this and as a consequence increase the success rate of organisational change programmes.

The extant literature on organisational change management has recognised the potential of pilots as a tool for change management (Balogun and Hope Hailey, 2008; Kanter et al., 1992; Higgs and Rowland, 2005). Yet discussions on the use of pilots in change management are limited. Searching "pilots and change management" in Google Scholar generated links to themes regarding environmental sustainability and understandably research on cockpit design and pilots! Searching "pilot sites and change management" through up discussions on lean management and sustainability: in essence a dearth of exploration and discussion of pilots in the field of change management.

Prominent change management texts are also limited in discussion. For example, Senior and Fleming (2006), Burnes (2009) and Kotter (1995, 1996) do not mention pilots, Carnall (2007) refers to the use of pilots twice (pp. 48, 156) as "techniques" linked with "breakthrough teams" (p. 48), or mentioned as "part of the process" in the context of discussing leadership. No other comments are developed and this limited discussion is most prevalent in other texts. Hayes (2002) refers to pilots in terms of the work of Balogun and Hope Hailey (2008) but only cite their work. Balogun and Hope Hailey (2008) explicitly develop the importance of pilots under the notion of "start points" (p. 33) but the discussion is not extensive. Although not referring to pilots explicitly, Higgs and Rowland (2005) identify the importance of emergent experimental network-based action that appeared to provide successful change management when guided by planned frameworks (p. 145). They showed strong evidence through interviews with managers of the importance of experimentation. As discussed earlier, peer reviewed articles are very light on the ground in terms of examining the usefulness of pilots to change management. The few (and this is very few) examinations of pilots in change management are limited to non-refereed editorials (see e.g., Polaniecki, 2006; Wolfberg and Stumborg, 2007).

Thus the concept of pilots as a mechanism for organisational change appears to be largely limited to anecdotal comments. Is the dearth of examination in both practitioner and academic journals a consequence of the limited value of pilots? Or simply that attention has not been brought to the concept? Or does the concept of pilots as a mechanism for organisational change lack an underpinning supportive theoretical structure to encourage debate and exploration? This chapter addresses these three questions through our central purpose to provide a theoretical foundation for the use of pilots within change connected with notions of distributed leadership.

We first identify the key areas affecting change management—what we call the "dynamics of change management". Such dynamics reflect planned change, emergent change, political dynamics within change, along with addressing resistance, participation and commitment as well as learning.

The difficulty of potentially integrating such concepts is arguably a dominant cause for limited success in change interventions. Johnson-Cramer et al. (2003) argue that for effective change management to occur change management needs to be able to draw upon each in a complementary manner. We then outline the notion of distributed leadership as having significant potential to enable this elusive complementarity. We review debates on the manifestation of this form of leadership in organisational contexts. A synthesis suggests a hybrid or blended version of distributed leadership as most suitable to embrace the preceding discussion on integrating the dynamics of change management.

Subsequently we propose a theoretical processual model for distributed change leadership through pilots. We illustrate how this model integrates the dynamics of change management. Finally we outline research opportunities and organizational change implications in terms of improving success rate of change management interventions and explore the potential implications of implementing distributed change leadership through pilots.

Prior to examining the dynamics of change management we define what we mean by a pilot. In this chapter, we define a change management pilot as a mechanism to facilitate sociological and psychological processes of change through the act of designing, experimenting and implementing localised structural or operational changes. The definition of distributed leadership will be outlined shortly.

The Dynamics of Change Management

Change management as an academic discipline is arguably highly fragmented and offers a multitude of partly competing, partly complementary theories and models (By, 2005; Whelan-Berry and Somerville, 2010). We suggest that debates in change management can be summarised into the following three perspectives: rationally planned change management (Kotter, 1995; Beer and Nohria, 2000; Higgs and Rowland, 2005); politically governed change management (Buchanan and Badham, 1999) and emergent, bottom-up based change management

(Stace and Dunphy, 1998; Higgs and Rowland, 2005)—the last embraces notions of individual and team-based learning that emerges within continuous change. We provide a brief review of each perspective to illustrate the theoretical tension of competing dynamics of change. We emphasise that these are not mutually exclusive. Rather we suggest that an additional dynamic is required to become mutually complementary: namely distributed change leadership through pilots.

Perspective No. 1: Rational Planning of Change Management

Rational planning is perceived to be built around a temporal, three tiered understanding of organisational change: first, an understanding of the organisational current state; second, identifying where the organisation wants to be (the future state); and third, design the transition state (Beckhard and Harris, 1987). The transition is understood as a discontinuous step change (Balogun and Hope Hailey, 2008) that moves the organization from one state of quasi-stable equilibrium to another (Lewin, 1964). The change can be and needs to be planned and the process of planning is assumed as being rational (Balogun and Hope Hailey, 2008; Kotter, 1995). That does not mean that power and diverging interests are overlooked, but rather seen as contingencies to be incorporated into planning in order to achieve the identified future state.

The variety of differing approaches within the planned perspective can be distinguished by their degree of context-sensitivity regarding the design of the transition towards the future state of the firm. Through seven in-depth longitudinal case studies Pettigrew and Whipp (1991) identified that "one-fits-all" approaches are not applicable to all situations. The context sensitivity was recognised by Lewin (1967, p. 215) where unfreezing, moving and refreezing "may involve quite different problems in different cases" (see Burnes, 2004, for a review of Lewin's work and the applicability of this to both planned and emergent change). Paradoxically Lewin's recognition of complexity is captured in Weick's (1995) reversal of Lewin's model where the three phases are: "freeze—study the complex system at a point in time; adjust—encourage and stimulate adjustments to achieve necessary changes; and unfreeze—allow the system to continue functioning having made the necessary adjustments" (Higgs and Rowland, 2005, p. 125). This is a significant point that will be encapsulated in the discussion to follow on political and emergent change and the role of pilots in change.

A general criticism of the effectiveness of planned theories is that organisations continuously change and rarely reflect a state of quasi-stable equilibrium (see e.g., Burnes, 2009; Senior and Fleming, 2006). Further, there are severe limitations on the capability of "change agents" to process the information needed for a rational decision (for bounded rationality see Buchanan and Huczynski, 2004; and also Quinn, 1980). Finally, there is no obvious reason why the decision and design process of a change programme should be made exempt from the influences of power, politics and self-interests (Dawson, 2003).

For example, Johnson-Cramer et al. (2003) outline an argument for purposive change management. They suggest that "organizations can enhance the likelihood of purposive change by creating more aligned and coherent changes and by shaping the context into which these design elements are introduced" (p. 1868).

Sitting within the planned perspective Balogun and Hope Hailey (2008, pp. 33-35) are among the few that explicitly mention "pilots" as a tactical choice for change management. These authors do not examine how pilots can mitigate some of the concerns associated with the planned perspective. Pilots can embrace the planned and organised sense of top-down and formally strategically driven change orientation. Rather this sense of institutional need and legitimatisation of the need for change is most helpful when addressing divergent interests and conflicts. A pilot can be the structure through which the plans become realised. Importantly though a pilot mechanism can embrace the inevitable divergent views of political processes.

Perspective No. 2: Politically Governed Change Management

As an alternative to the "*n*-step" (Dawson, 2003, p. 82) approaches of Kanter et al. (1992) and Kotter (1995), organisational change management is anchored

to a focus on the interests, conflicts and the power of the individuals within the organisation (Dawson, 1994, 2003; Pettigrew and Whipp, 1991; Wilson, 1992). While the planned perspective community propose a rational analysis of the environment as a solution in order to be able to develop an effective change design (see e.g., Balogun and Hope Hailey, 2008), Pettigrew and Whipp (1991) are sceptical about the viability of this recommended rational design and decision process.

For the proponents of the political approach, the decision-making process of individuals and of organisations is far from being linear, objectively rational or aligned with the needs of the organisation (Pettigrew and Whipp, 1991). On the individual level, experiences and routines often quickly replace information gathering and a conscious decision process. While a new manager or change agent for instance may try to understand her/his environment in order to derive a considered solution, an experienced manager often derives a solution to a given problem on the basis of his former politically orientated experience (Beer and Nohria, 2000; Buchanan and Badham, 1999; Miller, 1993). This, together with the impact of personal interests and conflicts (Morgan, 1998) leads to different perceptions of the change context and accordingly to different beliefs about a suitable change design (Buchanan and Badham, 1999). The diversity of individual decisions further increases when the organisation is facing an "out-of-ordinary" situation (Wilson et al., 1986). In essence, the political perspective perceives a messy, untidy change process in which all people involved try to push their view forward by blocking other ideas and compromising with third parties (see e.g., Ford, 2006). It follows that the change design is a subject of negotiation and politics instead of being a result of a pure rational analysis of contingency factors (see Buchanan and Badham, 1999; Saka, 2003).

Criticism of this political approach to change management is first levelled at its relative slowness in the context of organisational needs and would be not able to realise emergent opportunities or to cope with emergent problems (Butcher and Atkinson, 2000). A second point of criticism deals with the implicitly accepted imbalance between politically more skilled and less skilled professions or departments in an organisation thereby distorting change towards the most powerful (Townley, 1993).

A pilot approach may be able to blend rational planning analysis with political diversity. Quinn (1980, p. 10) briefly mentions pilots in terms of "pockets of commitment" in the political process. Balogun and Hope Hailey (2008, pp. 29-31) place the use of pilots as a design choice that appears to implicitly allow for the blending of interests through the political process evolving around planned approaches. If a change is perceived to inevitably create "winners and losers" in terms of conflicts or interests and such are resolved through power (Morgan, 1998), the political process is an ever present inevitable dynamic that a pilot can respond to. Pilots, by their very nature as a testing ground, seek to respond to the flux of events and enable the pulse and complexity of organisational reality to be inculcated in a way that a strictly planned top-down and rational approach can simply not deliver (Buchanan and Badham, 1999; Littler et al., 2003; Quinn, 1980; Saka, 2003). The embracing of divergent views as part of the pilot mechanism can be interpreted within notions of distributed leadership—a collective process of sense making. Not always harmonious and often manifest with conflict. Yet blending planned with political provides a sense of cohesion and direction to the sense-making process. We suggest that the institutionally recognised and legitimised pilot guides collective sense making that enables change to become grounded in the political complexity of the organisational context. Further such distributed sense making provides the opportunity for emergence and learning.

Perspective No. 3: Emergent and Bottom-Up Oriented Change Management

As response to the poor success rate of planned change programmes (Butcher and Atkinson, 2000) state a failure rate of above 70 percent; similar with Higgs and Rowland (2005) a "new" approach for "effective corporate renewal" (Beer and Nohria, 2000, p. 158) was proposed: namely the notion of emergence and "bottom-up". The proponents of this approach build on criticism of the rational, planned approach and anticipate that senior management is

not able to know the challenges and appropriate answers for the detailed contextualised issues within each part of the organisation (Beer and Nohria, 2000; Page et al., 2008). They also see an incremental, politically influenced but centrally steered change management approach as insufficient to realise effective change. Butcher and Atkinson (2000) argue that each kind of centrally steered decision process restricts the capacity to respond to a fast changing environment. Higgs and Rowland (2005) place emphasis to the systemic nature in which change occurs. Building on the work of Stacey (1996), Shaw (1997) and Wheatley (2006), they suggest that top-down programmatic change is limited to the extent that it cannot embrace systemic contextualised differences. Rather, stories of change by informants described a reality of "somewhat unstructured and messy activities and interventions" (Higgs and Rowland, 2005, p. 145); responding systemically and politically to the situation as it occurred.

The change management approach suggested by Beer and Nohria (2000) views the starting point for effective organisational change at the outer edges of the firm with front-line employees being empowered to change or eliminate what is hindering them and to create ways to enhance the organisation (Beer and Nohria, 2000). Since the resulting small, pragmatic changes are directly rooted in the day-to-day operational processes, an effective implementation is argued to be more likely than in organisation wide top-down programmes (Butcher and Atkinson, 2000; similarly argued in Beer and Nohria, 2000). Furthermore Higgs and Rowland (2005) argue that, due to the complexity and interrelatedness of organisational systems, such effective changes can spread rapidly throughout the organisation.

If an organisation is structured to enable emergent, bottom-up change, Beer et al. argue that the leadership task of the senior management is to facilitate the emerging changes: making successful "pockets" visible to the whole organisation and providing resources for local change agents (Beer and Nohria, 2000; similarly argued in Saka, 2003).

Heifetz and Laurie (1997) suggest senior managers need to regulate the pressure on the organisation to change. In this way the critical task of senior leadership is to periodically align the corporate structure and direction to the newly emerged practices (Beer and Nohria, 2000). The debate on emergence and localness speaks to the change task being dispersed throughout the organisation. As such it poses questions on the nature of the form of leadership relevant to enable this local and contextualised participative activity to occur. This different form of leadership has its accent on localised learning—understanding, designing and experimenting (Rowland and Higgs, 2008).

Embracing emergent change realities within an organised structure resonates with the design of a pilot process if there is an acceptance that the top-down plan will inevitably be modified to suit local realities. We suggest that such local realities cannot be designed into the pilot from the beginning. This is too complex and arguably unknown. However, the importance of strategic alignment and legitimisation of the change strategy to embrace the political change dynamic gives weight to the need for a planned approach to the objectives and purpose of the initial pilot. Yet the unfolding movement of the pilot to local contexts seeks to incorporate a learning dynamic alongside the collective engagement.

The learning from experiments lies at the heart of the practice of pilots. Pilots have been utilised in a variety of disciplines such as science, engineering, project management and IT. Common to all of the above is the necessity to learn about the technical capability of the planned concept in practice. The experimental nature of the pilot places emphasis on learning. The process of learning may not only improve the practical and local applicability of the change intervention towards desired goals and plans, but it has the potential to catalyse commitment through involvement (Higgs and Rowland, 2005; Stacey, 1996). The importance of commitment and involvement has been argued as a cornerstone to change management as exulted, for example, by Kanter (1984), Kotter (1996) and Pendelbury et al. (1998). Should such commitment and shared ownership occur alongside the learning from re-designing the pilot to the local context then the issues of resistance, so commonly debated within prescribed *n*-step remedies, may be greatly mitigated.

In Search of a Synthesis of the Three Perspectives

The three different perspectives on organisational change management are often presented as mutually exclusive. The rational planning group recommends certain "recipes" and a rigorous examination of the environment in order to effectively bring the organisation from one state to another: discontinuous steps leading from one quasi-stable period to another. The proponents of the political perspective argue against linearity and understand organisational change as an incremental process that inevitably twists and turns influenced by ever changing interests, conflicts and power. Through the perspective of emergent change the flux of events and ideas occur from the roots of the organisation. Such change cannot be effectively planned from the top of the organisation.

Each approach to change management has its specific limitations and its strengths. Using practices from only one perspective limits the potential contribution the other perspectives can offer (Johnson-Cramer et al., 2003). The benefits of planning, with strong clear top-down leadership, responsive to political interests that drawing on broad constituencies of support throughout the organisation, alongside the engagement of local participation in design, testing and implementation, is arguably the change management panacea. After all Kotter's (1995, 1996) important contribution with the prescribed "8 steps" has strong resonance with this. Yet the comparison to Kotter's work captures the essence of our argument. It is a prescription for leadership. A prescription that draws on underpinning conceptualisation of change dynamics, but draws on essentialist notions of leadership: a focus on the leader to drive forward the anticipated change—a mythical sacred model (Grint, 2010). We wish to suggest connecting the change dynamics to new emerging debates in leadership studies: namely leadership as a process within the leader-follower relationship (Uhl-Bien, 2006). Within this conceptualisation of leadership we situate distributed leadership. It offers a very different orientation to change management, particularly if enabled through the mechanism of a pilot.

Distributed Leadership

Assuming an ontology of leadership as focusing on "leader-follower" relations suggests a broader "examination [than] individual attributes alone" (Uhl-Bien, 2006, p. 671). Within the context of distributed leadership the relational focus needs to embrace a model of leadership that is an "emergent property of a group or network of interacting individuals working with an openness of boundaries [y] [and] the varieties of expertise are distributed across the many, not the few" (Bennet et al., 2003, p. 7).

Fundamental to the notion of distributed leadership is a systemic perspective—viewing individual leader agency within relational networked activity (Ross et al., 2005). In this way Gronn's (2002) argument for a recognition of the limitations of relying on one person as an expert on all matters consequently necessitates a shift in leadership conceptualisation towards what Thorpe et al. (2008) suggest as "collaborative and reciprocal relationships" (p. 38). The important context that both Gronn and Thorpe et al. address is the socially imbued notion of the heroic leader. The work of the late James Meindl (1995) has done much to bring critical attention to the social historicism of leadership. Captured in the notion of the "romance of leadership" Meindl (1995) sought to "loosen the traditional assumptions about the significance of leaders to leadership" (p. 330). Such loosening is difficult to achieve because of its questioning of deeply rooted implicit theories of leadership that draw on taken-for-granted assumptions. Grint (2010) captures the essence of these assumptions with his notion of the sacredness of leadership. Followers look to leaders who "offer certainty, identity, and absolution from guilt and anxiety" (Grint, 2010, p. 100). The sacred relates to existential desires by followers for individualistic, heroic leader identities. It is this reified sacredness that Kotter (1996), for example, assumes as a foundation to his thesis of change leadership.

These socially constructed notions of the romantic and heroic leader role are prevalent in writings on change management. An axiom that has resonated in our teaching and consulting practice in change management relates to the need of followers for strong leadership in a crisis or more broadly ambiguous and uncertain situations which typically characterise change. Thus to assume a distributed approach that is disconnected to deeply imbued follower (and leader) expectations is likely to remain merely a theoretical proposition.

This proposition has been explored in the empirical work of Collinson and Collinson (2009). Examining leadership practices within the further education sector they showed that despite considerable attention and advocacy for a distributed approach to leadership—an approach that at face value resonated with espoused values within the educational context—there was a desire for what Collinson and Collinson (2009) described as blended leadership: followers sought both certainty of unambiguous top-down direction and vision linked with participative, collaborative and networked local activity. This empirical finding also connects with Gronn's (2009) reflections on distributed leadership. His advice was to suggest a hybrid form of distributed leadership: "not the case of either or but that both leadership understandings, individual and collective count" (p. 383). Work by Rowland and Higgs (2008), in a study of change leaders in 33 organisations, provides further support for this in a change context. Furthermore, they identified that the reliance on "heroic" views of leadership impacted adversely on the success of a change.

This emerging pragmatic conceptualisation of distributed leadership is central to our argument in terms of both top-down and bottom-up leadership. A synthesis is encapsulated by Parry and Bryman (2006) as "an emergent property of a social system, in which 'leaders' and 'followers' share in the process of enacting leadership [y] [and] effective leadership depends upon multiple leaders for decision-making and action-taking" (p. 455). The key aspects we wish to give emphasis to are: an emergent and systemic relationship; multiple leaders—implicit in this is our assumption at all levels; decision making and action taking—our assumption here is increasing localisation. Drawn together Cope et al. (2011) suggest distributed leadership can be seen "in terms of an 'organizing' activity anchored in a wide process of social influence that is not the exclusive function of a designated leader" (p. 275).

Distributed Change Leadership Through Pilots: Connecting the Change Management Dynamics

Building from the above we suggest that distributed leadership may be significant for the success of organisational change management. We have outlined a theoretical framework that captures a systemic interconnected model of distributed change leadership. This is shown in Figure 34.1.

Figure 34.1 draws on the three dynamics of change management. We connect these to enable an emergent whole, rather than see them as competing perspectives. On each of the three connecting lines between the three dynamics we have situated the important aspects that become enabled through the use of pilots. What we seek to show then is an emergent whole that

is composed of four interconnected sub-triangles (or four interconnected subsystems):

1. The central triangle (system) is the pilot mechanism. This enables the other three triangles (systems) to occur.

2. Rational top-down planning triangle (system).

3. Emergent/bottom-up triangle (system)—this incorporates learning.

4. Politically governed triangle (system).

Returning to the central triangle, the first and subsequent pilots require careful consideration to enable integration of the whole system. It is through the pilot catalyst that we suggest distributed change leadership would become manifest drawing on the change dynamics.

We place emphasis to the notion of a sequencing of pilots. The dynamic of a sequential process enables testing, learning and involvement. Testing in terms of

---

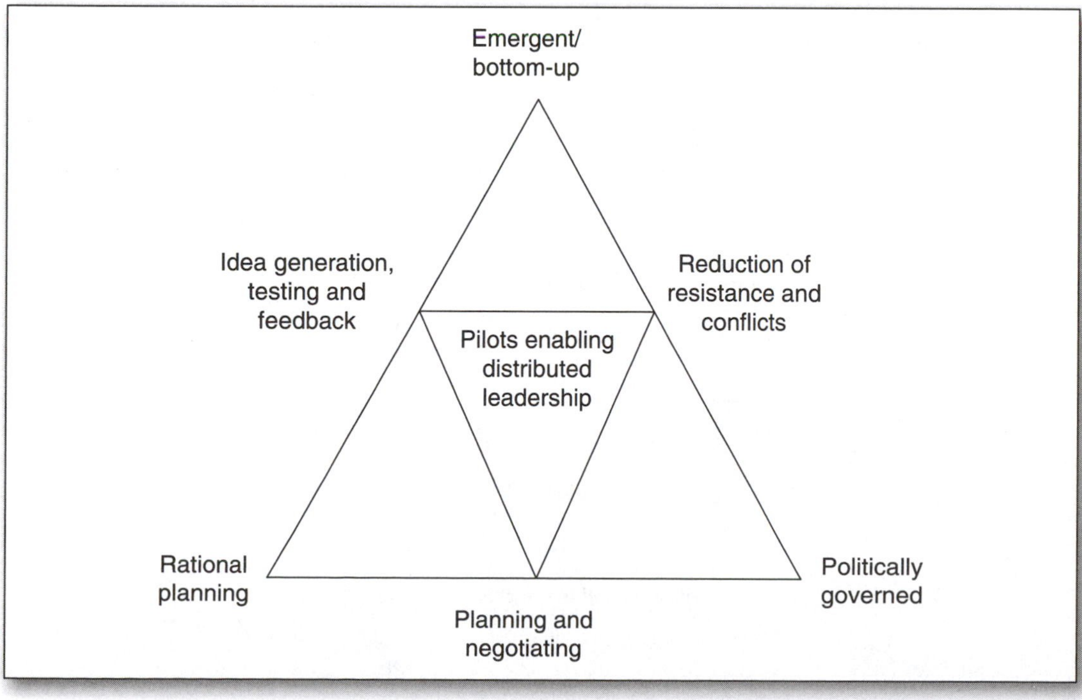

Figure 34.1   Dimensions of Distributed Change Leadership Through Pilots

local adaptation of the change design to allow for local nuance; learning in terms of both transferring previous learning and to capture and incorporate ideas emerging from different contexts; and involvement in terms of engaging people in participating in the process—lowering resistance through shared ownership of the change design relevant to the locality. In this way sequencing pilots rather than a one-off singular pilot supports an effective adaptation of the top-down change programme to different local needs through bottom-up engagement while the overall

strategy of the change is maintained. Thus the notion of successive pilots provides for continual application of the three dynamics of change management. We reflect this pilot sequencing linked to the three change dynamics in Figure 34.2.

The trigger for a pilot arguably comes from the rational and/or the political approach to change management; a sense of political and powerful voices as a consensus of the need for change. Through planning and negotiation the circumstances of the pilot are decided. The test results, namely the arguments for

---

Figure 34.2 Pilots Creating Complementary Change Dynamics

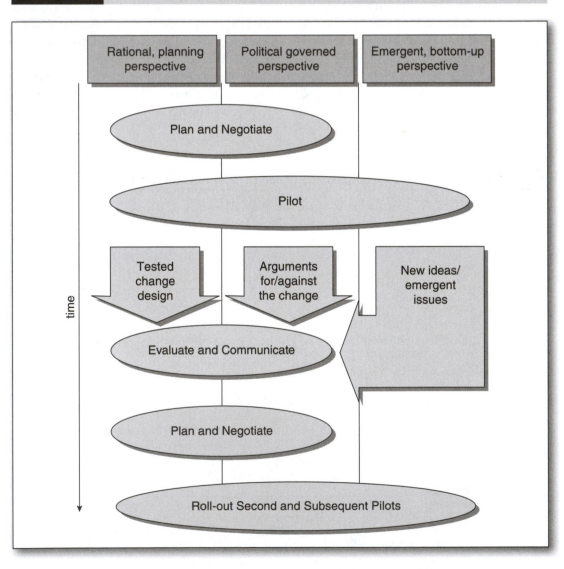

and against the change and emergent ideas, are evaluated and the success or failure of the pilot is communicated. It is at this stage where the different perspectives are connected. The iterative piloting on different organisational levels increases the degree of acceptance of the change gained through pilots. Buchanan et al. (2005) have shown that managers at all levels in an organisation wish to explicitly see decisions and actions legitimised by alignment with a top-down change programme. This is an important dynamic to enable rather than frustrate the distribution of idea generation, decisions and action at the local level. The notion of localised and simplified echoes the work of Nutt (2004). Nutt argues that organisational change design should seek to embrace simplification and devolution—developing the notion of de-development. The mechanism of pilots appears to be a useful vehicle for realisation of such devolution set within a structure and responds to Nutt's (2004) call for implementation processes (p. 1,100). The process shown in Figure 34.2 allows for the development of trust (identified as important to change management (Coleman, 1990). This is engendered through greater distributed engagement and ownership.

Interrelated with learning and support is the incorporation of emergent ideas. A purely top-down planned change can be argued to face difficulties of implementation as a consequence of being unable to appreciate or embrace the complexity of the context in which the change is to occur (Bloodgood and Morrow, 2003). Tyrrall and Parker (2005) illustrate through their study of change in British Rail the difficulty of communications and control from top-down structures (p. 518). We argue that the absorption of new ideas through distributed supportive and legitimised participation of a pilot approach at a local level can stimulate a learning culture and associated commitment towards the change. This strongly reflects the findings of Jones et al. (2005) that showed that readiness to change and success of change initiatives was greatly enhanced in contexts of strong human relations. We suggest that such contexts are engendered by distributed change leadership through pilots.

Our purpose in this chapter has been to explore how to enable complementarity of the change dynamics. We have argued that distributed leadership alongside the mechanism of pilots to be an important catalyst in change management. There is both limited extant understanding of change through pilots and certainly, to our knowledge, there has been no discussion on linking notions of distributed leadership with organisational change management. Similarly no discussions have drawn together distributed leadership with change through the mechanism of pilots. Our frameworks in Figures 34.1 and 34.2 provide such integration and conceptualisation of the notion of distributed change leadership through pilots.

Conclusion

At the outset of this chapter we drew attention to the statement by Johnson-Cramer et al. (2003) who argue that effective change management needs to be able to draw upon each of the three perspectives of rational change, politically shaped change and emergent change. Our contribution has been to reframe these three perspectives; away from a sense of competing interpretations and towards a sense of complementarity. In this way we have addressed the question that frames this chapter: how can the change dynamics of rational planning, politics and emergence be drawn together effectively? We have achieved this through our suggested theoretical framework of distributed change leadership through pilots captured in Figures 34.1 and 34.2. An aspect we seek to make salient is that a pilot creates the opportunity for distributed leadership and distributed leadership enables pilots to create successful change: in a sense two sides of the same coin.

In light of our theoretical argument we suggest a number of areas for future research linked to the following two propositions:

P1. Distributed change leadership enables planned, emergent and political change to be executed in a complementary manner.

P2. Implementing change through the use of pilots creates the context to enable the effective emergence of distributed leadership.

Research is required to explore the manifestation of distributed leadership within particular contexts.

A number of questions relate to this research agenda. For example, are there a variety of forms of distributed change leadership? How does context enable or disable the emergence of distributed leadership? Can distributed change leadership occur without the mechanism of pilots? In essence our proposition requires testing in a variety of ways. Such methods might reflect designing an intervention in line with our process outlined in Figure 34.2 and examining the journey of the implementation. For example, exploring how, within the organisational context, top-down planned leadership connects with political interactions? How are pilot mechanisms designed in light of these interactions? How do local settings become involved in the pilot in terms of design, testing and learning? How does local leadership become enabled and what does this leadership look like? How does this leadership within the pilot address issues of resistance? How does the emergent ideas and learning from the pilot become transferred? To address these exploratory questions organisationally based case studies seem a most appropriate method to provide insights into the processes and interactions that form the basis for distributed change leadership.

Alternative to testing the above questions a series of cases could seek to examine current practices of using pilots within organisational change as an explanatory approach. Focusing on a grounded theory approach (Kempster and Parry, 2011) each case could be explored to explain what has occurred in particular contexts. Such grounded theories can be compared to our suggested theoretical framework from which a revised (abductive) theory or new (retroductive) theory can be developed. We have no doubts that aspects of planned top-down change alongside politics, emergence and learning dynamics will be present. However, the nature of how they inter-relate and the form of effective leadership in this change context is more equivocal. The recent work of Harris (2012) is illuminating in this respect. Addressing the context of school principal leadership Harris (2012) outlines evidence that schools who are successful have redesigned and restructured so that leadership can be more widely shared and spread. The redesign "connects to motivation and learning resulting, potentially, in improved organisational outcomes" (p. 13). It is not clear in this research what the mechanisms for enabling distributed leadership were within the change initiative. However, the process described of "redesign" appears to have enabled the manifestation of distributed leadership. It may be that rather than formal pilots an informal or even metaphoric pilot process occurred. Researching the nature of pilots—formal and informal—may reveal that much change management practice activity does occur through pilots and researchers have not been attuned to this and made visible this practice.

The practical implications described above of improved organisational outcomes in the educational context explicitly illustrate considerable potential of applying our argument for distributed change leadership through pilots. First, we would suggest enhanced motivation and reduced resistance could be anticipated. Second, the focus of the change can be enhanced and refined for applicability in a variety of local contexts through learning and innovation. Third, a sense of strategic alignment to organisational needs through integrated cohesion that is guided by a legitimate top-down process. Harris (2012) has shown, in the school context that distributed leadership appears to lead to organisational success. So a distributed change leadership approach through pilots would seem most useful. However, in practical terms many issues arise. For example, is the organisational culture and leadership practice sympathetic to such an orientation? If power is needed to be distributed away from central control is this acceptable? More questions are likely to be raised about the change purpose and design requiring greater depth of understanding of the change.

There is likely to be a slower pace of change to enable successive pilots to occur and for learning to be adapted into the change process. So in practical terms there may be many issues that the application of distributed change leadership through pilots throws up that needs careful and thoughtful consideration.

The need for enhancing the effectiveness of change interventions is unequivocal. We suggest that it is the lack of attention into how to address the competitive relationship between the change dynamics that has had significant impact on intervention effectiveness. We have suggested the notion of distributed change leadership as having, in theory, potential to give insight into how the change dynamics can be complementary (shown in Figure 34.1). We have outlined a processual view of how distributed change leadership through pilots can occur (shown in Figure 34.2). The need for empirical testing is essential and we have outlined ideas for future research in this regard.

There is a dearth of discussion on the value and application of pilots in processes of organisational change management. Similarly there is very limited discussion on the notion of distributed leadership in organisational change. We hope this chapter may stimulate attention to both of these areas in order to help advance leadership of change and enhance the design and implementation of change interventions for greater success.

Note

1. Corresponding author Dr. Steve Kempster can be contacted at: s.kempster@lancaster.ac.uk.

References

Balogun, J. and Hope Hailey, V. (2008), *Exploring Strategic Change*, 3rd ed., Pearson Education Ltd, Harlow.

Barney, J. (2001), "Is the resource-based 'view' a useful perspective for strategic management research? Yes", *Academy of Management Review*, Vol. 26 No. 1, pp. 41–56.

Beckhard, R. and Harris, R.T. (1987), *Organizational Transitions: Managing Complex Change*, 2nd ed., Addison-Wesley, Reading, MA.

Beer, M. and Nohria, N. (2000), "Cracking the code of change", *Harvard Business Review*, June-July, pp. 133–141.

Bennet, N., Wise, C., Woods, P. and Harvey, J.A. (2003), *Distributed Leadership: A Review of Literature*, National College of School Leadership, Nottingham.

Bloodgood, J.M. and Morrow, J.L. Jr (2003), "Strategic organizational change: exploring the roles of environmental structure, internal conscious awareness and knowledge", *Journal of Management Studies*, Vol. 40 No. 7, pp. 1761–1782.

Buchanan, D. and Badham, R. (1999), "Politics and organizational change: the lived experience", *Human Relations*, Vol. 52 No. 5, pp. 609–629.

Buchanan, D. and Huczynski, A. (2004), *Organizational Behaviour*, 5th ed., Pearson Education, Essex.

Buchanan, D. Fitzgerald, L., Ketley, D., Gollop, R., Jones, J.L., Saint Lamont, S., Neath, A. and Whitby, E. (2005), "No going back: a review of the literature on sustaining organizational change", *International Journal of Management Reviews*, Vol. 7, pp. 189–205.

Burnes, B. (2004), "Kurt Lewin and the planned approach to change: a re-appraisal", *Journal of Management Studies*, Vol. 41 No. 6, pp. 977–1002.

Burnes, B. (2009), *Managing Change: A Strategic Approach to Organisational Dynamics*, 5th ed., FT Prentice Hall, London.

Butcher, D. and Atkinson, S. (2000), "The bottom-up principle", *Management Review*, Vol. 89 No. 1, pp. 48–53.

By, R.T. (2005), "Organisational change management: a critical review", *Journal of Change Management*, Vol. 5 No. 4, pp. 369–380.

Carnall, C. (2007), *Managing Change in Organizations*, 5th ed., FT Prentice Hall, London.

Coleman, J.S. (1990), *Foundations of Social Theory*, Harvard University Press, Cambridge, MA.

Collinson, D. and Collinson, M. (2009), "Blended leadership': employee perspectives on effective leadership in the UK further education sector", *Leadership*, Vol. 5 No. 3, pp. 365-380.

Cope, J., Kempster, S. and Parry, K. (2011), "Exploring distributed leadership in the small business context", *International Journal of Management Reviews*, Vol. 13 No. 3, pp. 270–285.

Dawson, P. (1994), *Organizational Change. A Processual Approach*, Paul Chapman Publishing, Liverpool.

Dawson, P. (2003), *Understanding Organizational Change: The Contemporary Experience of People at Work*, Sage, London.

Ford, R. (2006), "Open-processional change: three principles of reciprocal-relational power", *Journal of Change Management*, Vol. 6 No. 2, pp. 193–216.

Grint, K. (2010), "The sacred in leadership: separation sacrifice and silence", *Organizations Studies*, Vol. 31 No. 1, pp. 89–107.

Gronn, P. (2002), "Distributed leadership as a unit of analysis", *Leadership Quarterly*, Vol. 13 No. 4, pp. 423–451.

Gronn, P. (2009), "Leadership configurations", *Leadership*, Vol. 5 No. 3, pp. 381–394.

Harris, A. (2012), "Distributed leadership: implications for the role of the principal", *Journal of Management Development*, Vol. 3 No. 1, pp. 7–17.

Hayes J. (2002), *The Theory and Practice of Change Management*, Palgrave, New York, NY.

Heifetz, R.A. and Laurie, D.L. (1997), "The work of leadership", *Harvard Business Review*, Vol. 75 No. 1, pp. 124–134.

Higgs, M. and Rowland, D. (2005), "All changes great and small: exploring approaches to changes and its leadership", *Journal of Change Management*, Vol. 5 No. 2, pp. 121–151.

Johnson-Cramer, M.E., Cross, R.L. and Yan, A. (2003), "Sources of fidelity in purposive organizational change: lessons from a re-engineering case", *Journal of Management Studies*, Vol. 40 No. 7, pp. 1837–1870.

Jones, R.A., Jimmieson, N.L. and Griffiths, A. (2005), "The impact of organizational culture and reshaping capabilities on change implementation success: the mediating role of readiness for change", *Journal of Management Studies*, Vol. 42 No. 2, pp. 361–386.

Kanter, R.M. (1984), *The Change Masters*, Routledge, London.

Kanter, R.M., Stein, B.A. and Jick, T.D. (1992), *The Challenge of Organizational Change*, The Free Press, New York, NY.

Kempster, S. and Parry, K. (2011), "Grounded theory and leadership research: a critical realist perspective", *Leadership Quarterly*, Vol. 22 No. 1, pp. 106–120.

Kotter, J.P. (1995), "Leading change: why transformation efforts fail", *Harvard Business Review*, Vol. 73 No. 2, pp. 59–67.

Kotter, J.P. (1996), *Leading Change*, Harvard Business School Press, Boston, MA.

Lewin, K. (1964), *Field Theory in Social Science*, Harper and Row, New York, NY.

Lewin, K. (1967), *Resolving Social Conflicts*, Harper and Row, New York, NY.

Littler, C.R., Wiesner, R. and Dunford, R. (2003), "The dynamics of delayering: changing management structures in three countries", *Journal of Management Studies*, Vol. 40 No. 2, pp. 225–256.

Meindl, J.R. (1995), "The romance of leadership as a follower centric theory: a social constructionist approach", *The Leadership Quarterly*, Vol. 6 No. 3, pp. 329–341.

Miller, D. (1993), "The architecture of simplicity", *Academy of Management Review*, Vol. 18 No. 1, pp. 116–138.

Morgan, G. (1998), *Images of Organizations: The Executive Edition*, Berett-Koehler Publishers, Sage, San Francisco, CA.

Nutt, P. (2004), "Organizational de-development", *Journal of Management Studies*, Vol. 41 No. 7, pp. 1083–1103.

Orne, M.T. (1962), "On the social psychology of the psychological experiment: with particular reference to demand characteristics and their implications", *American Psychologist*, Vol. 17 No. 13, pp. 776–783.

Page, M., Wallace, M., McFarlane, W. and Lawd, J. (2008), "Emergent change and its implications for professional autonomy and managerial control: a case study from Midwifery", *Journal of Change Management*, Vol. 8 No. 3, pp. 249–263.

Parry, K.W. and Bryman, A. (2006), "Leadership in organizations", in Clegg, S., Hardy, C., Lawrence, T. and Nord, W. (Eds), *The Sage Handbook of Organization Studies*, 2nd ed., Sage, London, pp. 447–468.

Pendelbury, J., Grouard, B. and Meston, F. (1998), *The Ten Keys to Successful Change Management*, John Wiley, Chichester.

Pettigrew, A. and Whipp, R. (1991), *Managing Change for Competitive Success*, Blackwell, Oxford.

Polaniecki, P. (2006), "Teaching through TV: transformative encounters with constructed reality", in Duncum P. (Ed.), *Visual Culture in the Art Class: Case Studies*, National Art Education Association, Reston, VA, pp. 39–46.

Quinn, J.B. (1980), "Managing strategic change", *Sloan Management Review*, Vol. 21 No. 4, pp. 3–20.

Ross, L., Rix, M. and Gold, J. (2005), "Learning distributed leadership: part 1", *Industrial and Commercial Training*, Vol. 37 No. 3, pp. 130–137.

Rowland, D. and Higgs, M.J. (2008), *Sustaining Change: Leadership that Works*, Jossey-Bass, London.

Saka, A. (2003), "Internal change agents' view of the management of change problems", *Journal of Organizational Change Management*, Vol. 16 No. 5, pp. 480–496.

Shaw, P. (1997), "Intervening in the shadow systems of organizations: consulting from a complexity perspective", *Journal of Organizational Change*, Vol. 10 No. 3, pp. 235–250.

Senior, B. and Fleming, S. (2006), *Organizational Change*, 3rd ed., Pearson Education, Harlow.

Stace, D. and Dunphy, D. (1998), *Beyond the Boundaries Leading and Recreating the Successful Enterprise*, McGraw-Hill, Sydney.

Stacey, R.D. (1996), *Complexity and Creativity in Organizations*, Berrett-Koehler Publishers, San Francisco, CA.

Thorpe, R., Gold, J., Anderson, L., Burgoyne, J., Wilkinson, D. and Malby, B. (2008), *Towards 'Leaderful' Communities in the North of England: Stories from the Northern Leadership Academy*, Oak Tree Press, Cork.

Townley, B. (1993), "Foucault, power/knowledge, and its relevance for human resource management", *Academy of Management Review*, Vol. 18 No. 3, pp. 518–545.

Tyrrall, D. and Parker, D. (2005), "The fragmentation of a railway: a study of organizational change", *Journal of Management Studies*, Vol. 42 No. 3, pp. 507–537.

Uhl-Bien, M. (2006), "Relational leadership theory: exploring the social processes of leadership and organizing", *The Leadership Quarterly*, Vol. 17 No. 1, pp. 654–676.

Weick, K.E. (1995), *Sense-Making in Organizations*, Sage, Thousand Oaks, CA.

Wheatley, M. (2006), *Leadership and the New Science: Discovering Order in a Chaotic World*, Berrett-Hoehler Publishers, Sage, San Francisco, CA.

Whelan-Berry, K.S. and Somerville, K.A. (2010), "Linking change drivers and the organizational change process: a review and synthesis", *Journal of Change Management*, Vol. 10 No. 2, pp. 175–193.

Whittington, R. and Mayer, M. (2002), *Organizing for Success in the Twenty-First Century: A Starting Point for Change*, Chartered Institute of Personnel and Development, London.

Wilson, D.C. (1992), *A Strategy of Change: Concepts and Controversies in the Management of Change*, Routledge, London.

Wilson, D.C., Butler, R.J., Cray, D., Hickson, D.J. and Mallory, G.R. (1986), "Breaking the bounds of organization in strategic decision making", *Human Relations*, Vol. 39 No. 4, pp. 309–332.

Wolfberg, A. and Stumborg, M. (2007), "Achieving clarity in a constantly changing environment", *Reflections*, Vol. 8 No. 3, pp. 11–22.

Further Reading

Atkinson, D.J. and Day, M. (2004), "Large-scale transitional procurement change in the aerospace industry", *Journal of Purchasing and Supply Management*, Vol. 10 No. 6, pp. 257–268.

Bolden, R., Petrov, G. and Gosling, J. (2007), *Developing Collective Leadership in Higher Education: Final Report*, LFHE, London.

Brown, S.L. and Eisenhardt, K.M. (1997), "The art of continuous change: linking complexity theory and time-paced evolution in relentlessly shifting organisations", *Administrative Science Quarterly*, Vol. 42 No. 1, pp. 1–34.

Buchanan, D. and Dawson, P. (2007), "Discourse and audience: organizational change as multi-story process", *Journal of Management Studies*, Vol. 44 No. 5, pp. 669–686.

Collins, D. (1998), *Organizational Change: Sociological Perspectives*, Routledge, London.

Cummings, T. and Huse, E. (1989), *Organization Development and Change*, West Publishing Company, New York, NY.

Davis, S.A. (1967), "An organic problem-solving method of organizational change", *Journal of Applied Behavioural Science*, Vol. 3 No. 1, pp. 3–21.

Dunford, R.W. (1990), "A reply to Dunphy and Stace", *Organization Studies*, Vol. 11 No. 1, pp. 131–134.

Dunphy, D. and Stace, D. (1988), "Transformational and coercive strategies for planned organizational change: beyond the OD model", *Organizational Studies*, Vol. 9 No. 3, pp. 339–355.

Hemelin, B.E. (1998), "Toward an economic theory of leadership: leading by example", *The American Economic Review*, Vol. 88 No. 5, pp. 1188–1206.

Lipitt, R., Watson, J. and Westley, B. (1958), *The Dynamics of Planned Change: A Comparative Study of Principles and Techniques*, Harcourt, Brace and World, New York, NY.

March, J.G. and Simon, H.A. (1993), *Organizations*, Cambridge Press, Blackwell, Oxford.

Pettigrew, A. (1985), "Examining change in the long-term context of culture and politics", in Srivastra, S. *et al.* (Eds), *Executive Power*, Jossey-Bass, London, pp. 649-670.

Schein, E. (1996), "Kurt Lewin's change theory in the field and in the classroom: notes toward a model of managed learning", *Systems Practice*, Vol. 9 No. 1, pp. 27–47.

CHAPTER 35

Designing Organizations to Meet 21st-Century Opportunities and Challenges

Raymond E. Miles
University of California, Berkeley

Charles C. Snow
Pennsylvania State University

Øystein D. Fjeldstad
Norwegian School of Management, Oslo, Norway

Grant Miles
University of North Texas

Christopher Lettl
Vienna University of Economics and Business, Vienna, Austria

Τhe 21st-century promises to offer abundant opportunities if the firms and nations of the world can design organizational mechanisms to fully utilize the knowledge generated by modern science while finding solutions for the problems that economic progress has created–including global warming and the starkly visible income inequalities that exist across various segments of the global economy. Fortunately, in both the public and private sectors, our understanding of how the global economy works has increased, as evidenced by the emergence of widely effective business and management approaches that are spreading around the world. Indeed, it is our belief that recent experiments

Source: "Designing Organizations to Meet 21st-Century Opportunities and Challenges," by Raymond E. Miles, Charles C. Snow, Øystein D. Fjeldstad, Grant Miles and Christopher Lettl in *Organizational Dynamics*, Vol. 39, No. 2, pp. 93–103. Copyright © 2010 Elsevier Inc. All rights reserved. Reprinted with permission.

involving new organizational approaches will prove to be valuable in addressing not only the exciting economic opportunities of this century but also the pressing challenges that currently plague global society. In order to explore current organizational developments, we present a dynamic theory of organization design and show how it explains the four major designs that have appeared in the U.S. since the latter half of the 1800s: U-form, M-form, matrix, and multi-firm network. We describe how the components of each of these traditional designs reflect the economic and sociopolitical conditions of their birth period. We then use our theory to predict the shape of a new organizational design—*a collaborative community*—as well as its uses and benefits. Overall, we observe that recent decades have brought an increased awareness that global resources are *commons* in the keeping of all nations and societies. Such shared interests require the use of *community values* and *collaborative capabilities* in emerging organizational designs if their full benefits are to be obtained and shared. We describe two types of situations in which large-scale multiparty collaboration is required in order to successfully pursue global opportunities or to resolve global problems: (1) situations in which a large number of actors depend on and contribute to a commons and (2) situations in which a large number of actors share a common goal and each actor provides its complementary contribution to the larger system in a coordinated manner.

A Theory of Organization Design

A theory of organization design provides a conceptual map of the factors and processes involved in the creation and shaping of new business and organizational models. A theory of organization design must explain both the elements of organizational designs and the forces that motivate the search for new configurations of those elements. Within the field of architecture, it is well established that a good design must encompass both function and form, and especially the fit between them. A firm's *business model* articulates its function—how the firm *creates and*

captures value. It includes the firm's resources and activities, as well as the relationships within which resources and activities are embedded. An *organizational form* is the *structure* and *processes* that the firm uses to arrange and focus tangible resources such as money and equipment and intangible resources such as knowledge. Thus, in our theory, the core elements of organization design are a firm's business model and a supporting organizational form that enables the firm to pursue it. While the core elements of organization design are easy enough to identify and describe, the remaining properties of the theory require more insight into the dynamics of organizational behavior. First, the theory must help explain why new organizational forms appear—what drives managers and firms to experiment with new approaches. And, second, it must also specify the capabilities that are required by new business models and their supporting organizational structures and processes, as well as indicate the changes in managerial values and beliefs that are needed in order to facilitate the development and application of those capabilities. Examining organizational evolution over the past 150 years, it appears to us that pioneering firms and managers begin to experiment with new designs when growing scientific and technical knowledge offer new opportunities to create and appropriate wealth. In the middle of the 19th century, advances in steam power were joined by advances in communications and metallurgy; that convergence required new business and organizational models to create and bring new products and services to growing markets. Similarly, in the early part of the 20th century, advances in internal combustion technologies and, decades later, in jet propulsion technologies intersected with advances in electronics and chemistry to create the possibility of bringing a wide range of products and services to a set of growing markets, and thereby help push the invention and adoption of new organizational forms. Clearly, a complex pattern of knowledge-driven dynamics are at work today prompting experiments with new business and organizational models in an effort to capitalize on the opportunities presented by a constantly expanding global marketplace. Two other important patterns in organizational evolution are also worth noting. First, each new organizational design builds on the most useful features of previous designs. Experiments with a new design are undertaken because of the problems and limitations of existing designs. The solutions that are developed help to preserve and extend the strengths of existing designs while bypassing their limitations. Second, each new design adds a new set of capabilities without displacing the usefulness of older skills. Organizations, guided by the human beings who design and operate them, are able to learn and improve, and their ever-increasing capability gives them the flexibility they need to adapt to their changing environments.

In summary, our theory of organization design states that business models and organizational forms evolve as pioneering firms and managers experiment with new approaches in order to broaden their use of knowledge and extend their market reach. Market opportunities arise because the invention and development of technologies enable firms to create and commercialize products and services based on those technologies. As pioneering firms learn how to build and operate new types of organizations, the essential capabilities and management processes of the new forms become widely apparent. And, finally, when a new organizational design becomes fully articulated, and numerous real-life examples accumulate, all firms can consider the new design for adoption, with adoptive success highly dependent on the successful development of supporting capabilities and values. In the following sections, we discuss how our theory of organization design helps to explain the emergence over time of the four major designs that are visible today as well as the changes in managerial capabilities and values each new design has required.

The Specialized, Vertically Integrated U-Form Organization

As noted above, the middle and latter decades of the 19th century brought new technological advances that offered the promise of greatly expanded business models in industries such as transportation, communications, and the production of iron and steel. However, the typical firms in the early decades of the century were small, owner-managed enterprises that bought supplies and materials from, and sold products and services to, local markets. Synergies among steel and telegraphy technologies facilitated—indeed pushed—plans for enlarged railroad services, as steel mills produced the rails and equipment needed along routes assisted by improved telegraph services. Entrepreneurs began to envision new business models in each of these industries, and they argued for broader legal rights and experimented with new organizational structures and processes capable of integrating various related technologies. Such large-scale enterprises facilitated expansion westward and helped the economy become a newly recognized force in international trade. However, the early decades of large, single-business firms, referred to as U-form (unitary) organizations, brought not only economic success, but also a growing recognition of both the deficiencies of that design and the capabilities needed for its efficient operation. It was not until the 1920s that the more successful U-form firms were utilizing a full complement of efficient coordinating and control mechanisms and reliably managing workforces kept stable by wages, working conditions, and supervisory methods that reflected the contributions of scholars in Scientific Management and Human Relations. (See Table 35.1 for a summary of the main features of traditional organizational designs.)

The value transformation that contributed to changes toward more effective leadership and management in private, vertically integrated U-form firms had parallels in the public sector. German sociologist Max Weber, writing in the late 19th and early 20th centuries, argued that the bureaucratic form of organization in government agencies was essential to the operation and maintenance of democratic forms of government, both because it was the most efficient method of structuring work and because the authority vested in the hierarchy of offices was legitimate (based on the credentialed merits of the office holders and supported by clear and rational policies). Improved stability and performance in the public sector was crucial to the stream of reforms made in that sector, including the enhancement of the rights of women, minorities, and immigrants. Similar social progress resulted in greater employee rights and improved treatment and opportunities in the private sector, along with steadily improving firm performance. Thus, beginning with the

Table 35.1	Traditional Organizational Designs	
Organizational Design	*Purpose*	*Coordination and Control Mechanisms*
U-Form	Achieve economies of scale through specialization	Lower-level units coordinated and controlled by higher-level units
M-Form	Respond to differentiated customer demand and achieve economies of scope	Division level oversees functions
Matrix	Combine responsiveness to differentiated customer demand with varied technological expertise	Dual hierarchy (products and functions)
Multi-Firm Network	Flexible, rapid assembly of multiple specialized capabilities to achieve economies of scale and experience	Hierarchy of the lead firm over the total network and hierarchy within network member firms

earliest organizational designs and extending to the present, knowledge about organizational design and management has flowed back and forth between the private and public sectors.

The Multi-Divisional (M-Form) Organization

While Henry Ford's automobile plants, supplied by parts from company-owned steel plants and other dedicated suppliers, produced a constantly growing stream of one-model, one-color vehicles that made the company an early U-form icon, it was another automobile company that pioneered the most popular organizational design of the 20th century. In the 1920s, as the automobile industry grew rapidly, executives at General Motors Corp., led by Alfred P. Sloan, developed an organizational structure to manage a group of automobile firms that had been acquired by entrepreneur William C. Durant. This structure became the M-form (for multi-divisional) in which each division (a former independent firm) focused on meeting the needs and preferences of an existing and/or emerging segment of the automobile industry, while sharing market and technological information across the set of divisions through corporate staff departments. Sloan and his colleagues worked their way through the challenges of balancing the operational freedom delegated to division managers with the need for financially

sound performance and coordinated technological advances across the firm. By the end of World War II, the M-form organization was widely used by U.S. firms and was copied, with appropriate modifications and improvements, by large European and Japanese firms during the 1950s and 1960s. The M-form organization challenged managers to learn the new skill of delegation, a challenge insight-fully discussed by management scholar and consultant Peter Drucker in the 1940s and 1950s, which he christened Management by Objectives (MBO). MBO is a process in which managers share information and reach agreement on goals up and down the hierarchy, rather than relying on the top-down coordination and control approaches prevalent in the U-form. Of course, in many firms managers found it difficult to delegate because their managerial values and beliefs came mostly from experiences in U-form organizations. As had occurred with centralized firm structures, experiments in decentralization paralleling those in the private sector emerged in some government agencies during the Great Depression (especially in rural electrification), and the ability to plan, coordinate, and delegate was an important contributor to the success of U.S. military forces in World War II. Similarly, the core organizational concept of integrating policies and actions while maintaining the benefits of diversity and innovation at local and regional levels was exactly that addressed by the U.S. federal-state governance model, with similar versions found in the U.K. and other European countries. Such part-whole organizational and managerial challenges remain visible today as, for example, in the European Union, which is trying to maintain the unique traditions and values of sovereign nations while obtaining the benefits of collective action.

The capabilities required to support divisionally structured firms and other organizations, such as delegation and joint goal setting across hierarchical levels, reflect particular managerial philosophies. Upper-level M-form managers must respect the talents and decisions of division leaders, respect that when freely and fully demonstrated is usually reciprocated. The question of whether human nature will accommodate the beliefs and behaviors essential to increased self-governance has been debated over the centuries, dating to Aristotle and the early Greek experiments with democratic governance. Aristotle concluded that human nature, in its mature form, could accommodate the simultaneous pursuit of individual well being and a concern for the welfare of others. Similarly, Thomas Jefferson and other early designers of the American political system believed it was possible to accommodate both the differentiated preferences of state leaders and the integrated needs of the larger federation, a philosophy shared by Sloan and other successful M-form pioneers. Further, as new organizational designs evolved beyond the M-form, managerial values had to evolve as well.

The Matrix Organization

In the post-World War II era, while large firms in established industries were moving increasingly toward the M-form design, firms in industries based on the rapid utilization of new technologies in electronics and chemistry found the M-form too restrictive. Technology-intensive firms such as Texas Instruments Inc. and TRW Inc. searched for ways to create new products and markets around the innovations flowing out of the research stimulated by the war effort. The result was an organizational design called the matrix that would allow the flexible integration and application of technologies from a variety of sources to the development of new products and markets. In the matrix design, downstream operating units draw on various upstream capabilities in the operation of existing businesses and in developing and delivering new products and services for new customers. It is a hybrid structure with two distinct hierarchies, established around customers and functions, respectively. A core component of this organizational design is the multi-functional project team that pulls together resources representing the various research and development (R&D) and operating units of the firm as well as personnel from suppliers and even customers. The matrix assembles skills and resources across as well as up and down the hierarchy. The dual hierarchies are typically supplemented with various horizontal processes of coordination and control. Overall, the matrix design seeks to capture both the efficiency and specialization of the U-form and the customer focus and flexibility of the M-form. The price that is paid for simultaneous efficiency and flexibility is a great deal of organizational complexity. Similar experiments in the start-up firms that collectively came to be called Silicon Valley exploited technologies in the fields of electronics, scientific measuring instruments, and computers. The pace of technological development tended to favor younger, smaller firms that could move quickly in new directions, and the flow of managers and scientists from university laboratories to firms brought values that supported free information exchange and collaboration across different types of teams and firms.

The Multi-Firm Network

Managers in the 1970s and beyond began to recognize the costs of maintaining the large, vertically integrated firms that had become common in mature industries. As younger, smaller firms began to move far more quickly in a variety of technical areas, larger firms could not keep pace, and far-sighted managers of the older firms began to sell off or close plants and to cut back on sales and other staff by contracting with smaller independent suppliers and distributors. What emerged from downsizing and subcontracting moves in the late 1970s and throughout the 1980s was the multi-firm network organization, in which firms restricted their activities to those areas along the value chain where they had the most skills—and thus the larger competitive advantage—while outsourcing their non-core activities to specialist providers. While most relationships among firms in early networks were managed by contracts, some firms began to realize that both upstream suppliers and downstream distributors were repositories of technical and market knowledge that could be of value to the producing firms. Firms that established cross-firm relationships that allowed such knowledge to be used to the common advantage of all supply chain members began to out-compete the more rigidly structured network firms in their industries. Also, as had occurred in the past, some managers were unable to recognize the possible gains from inter-firm cooperation and innovation because they believed that cooperation would lead to others benefiting from their proprietary knowledge—a belief system most suited to earlier organizational forms. Moreover, as in previous periods, one can see the overlap of managerial values and beliefs in the private and public sectors. The wide diffusion of market-oriented network organizations in the 1980s coincided with the rapid increase in beliefs among national politicians and policymakers of the value of free-market enterprise. Indeed, the moral glorification of the successes of capitalism and its free-market mechanisms was an important element in the ideological disputes between the allied U.S. and U.K. leaders and the leaders of the Soviet Union. The ultimate dismantling of the Soviet Union's centralized economic system and the movement towards a market-based economy by Russia and its former Eastern Bloc satellites was hailed as a triumph for neoclassical economic and ideological beliefs. Now that the global community is beginning to recognize not only the benefits but also the costs and dangers of unfettered capitalism, such as the global financial crisis, climate change, and social inequity, the time appears to be ripe for further experimentation with organizational designs and governance processes.

The Newest Organizational Designs

Our theory of organization design predicts that emerging designs will enable firms in rapidly developing sectors to more fully utilize growing scientific

and technical knowledge in the creation of an ever-broadening range of product and service innovations. The new designs, the theory suggests, will be a response to the reality that leading economic sectors such as computers, biotechnology, nanotechnology, electronic medical equipment, telecommunications, and energy are not only awash in growing knowledge within firms but also that those firms operate in a global marketplace in which rapidly expanding and diverse science-based knowledge exists across industry, country, and continental lines. In response to this complex reality, individual firms will find it less advantageous to attempt to compete solely by innovating on their own and will increasingly seek opportunities to participate in knowledge communities driving innovations across segments of the global marketplace. Thus, we expect the most innovative firms to participate with other firms in forming communities of firms capable of collaboratively creating large-scale complex solutions as well as sharing knowledge to produce innovations across a set of expandable markets.

Focusing specifically on the variables in our theory, we expect emerging organizational designs to be built, first, on *business models* that identify ways of creating and appropriating economic wealth by combining widely distributed knowledge and, increasingly, knowledge contained in communities of individuals and/or firms focused on a particular technology or subject. Next, the corresponding *organizational forms* will require ways to structure knowledge resources and manage them in order to more effectively benefit from the development of new products and services for a range of complementary markets. Such efforts will retain the useful features of existing firms and their organizational structures and processes while adding new capabilities designed to remove innovation barriers and offer new ways to leverage accumulating knowledge. Lastly, the process of developing new capabilities will direct attention to the management philosophies that are essential in order to complete the development of new designs and support their new approach to knowledge utilization and innovation.

We believe that a viable new organizational type is presently available, as pioneering managers and firms have succeeded in bringing together the capabilities, structures, and processes to create *collaborative communities* of independent firms capable of producing virtually continuous product and market innovations. While our international research team has observed various forms of multi-firm collaboration in several industry settings and countries, the model we describe here is based largely on three designed innovation communities that we have been monitoring for a number of years: Technical and Computing Graphics (TCG Group), Syndicom, and Blade.org. TCG Group was formed in the mid-1970s in Sydney, Australia and remains today a group of small innovative firms that collaborate with one another and with outside firms on technological and product innovations in the information technology (IT) sector. Syndicom is a U.S. startup firm that over the past five years has facilitated the design and development of communities of practice among medical professionals, as well as several innovation communities in the medical devices industry. Blade.org, a collaborative community of more than 250 firms in the computer server marketplace, was established in 2006 by IBM Corp. and several other founding firms. Blade.org is focused on the development and adoption of open blade server platforms, the fastest-growing segment of the computer server market.

Combining Business and Organizational Models at the Firm and Community Levels

In each of our three research cases, firm and community business models have co-evolved over time. Consisting at the time of 13 small firms, TCG Group's business model was based on each firm having its own professional contacts across the growing and dynamic computer and telecommunications industries in Southeast Asia, including contacts with larger local and international firms in various segments of these industries. A typical TCG innovation project explored an opportunity for a TCG firm to create a customized product for a large corporate customer. Within TCG, there was the expectation that each project be an opportunity for the creation of a "triangulation" network that

included (a) the principal customer (e.g., Telstra), (b) the lead TCG firm (and other invited TCG partner firms), and (c) an external technology-development company (e.g., Hitachi). The triangulation network scheme assured the assembly of all the business components from financing through design to delivery of the product, plus the accumulation of knowledge within and across the TCG firms that was essential to further collaborative innovation. Given its collaboration-driven business model, TCG considered both its linkages among internal firms and its relationships with principal customers and technology partners to be learning opportunities sustained by trusting, mutually beneficial interactions.

Both Syndicom and Blade.org are "designed" communities, in the sense that both had commercial purposes from the outset that would enable their members to compete more effectively by participating in a community-based organizational form. The first collaborative activity undertaken by Syndicom was the creation of a community of practice among spine surgeons for the purpose of sharing diagnostic and treatment expertise. Beginning with a small set of leading surgeons invited by the founding group, Syndicom created a secure Internet-based software system called SpineConnect that permitted the posting of patients' digitalized X-rays and the sharing of surgeon knowledge and recommendations. This system provides an infrastructure for collaboration among the community members. Recognizing that many surgeons might be reluctant to ask for or offer knowledge, the founding surgeons group took the lead in posting unusual cases and providing timely and thorough consultative comments. Other spine surgeons soon joined the initial group, and this community of 25–30 members became the prototype as well as strong advocates of the value of collaborative communities. SpineConnect evolved rapidly, and today communities using SpineConnect exist across the United States, Europe, and Asia, totaling more than 1300 spine surgeons and 100 trauma surgeons, the vast majority of whom believe that their collaborative efforts have substantially improved patient diagnosis and care. Syndicom has also created collaborative communities among other surgeon groups who are involved in the early application of new medical devices. In addition to the innovative SpineConnect communities, Syndicom has engaged in even more entrepreneurial collaboration within the medical community. Surgeons in certain specialties often have ideas for improved designs of medical devices and equipment. Some surgeons work directly with medical equipment manufacturers on device designs, usually for a one-time fee. This means that any financial returns derived from successful products go almost entirely to the device manufacturers. With encouragement from the surgeons involved in SpineConnect, Syndicom has assisted in the creation of several medical device design communities, each involving surgeons, patent attorneys, medical engineers, and device manufacturing firms. The first of these communities, CollabCom1, was created in 2006, and it quickly generated a device patent. All members of CollabCom1 work on innovation projects with only an equity share and no upfront or flat-fee payments. To date, Syndicom, an equity shareholder in each community, has helped to create five such communities that in turn have generated device designs, patents in process, and designs licensed to device manufacturers. Syndicom's expertise in the design, formation, and development of collaborative innovation communities demonstrates that trust-based knowledge sharing and utilization among a community of professionals and related firms—a process that typically occurs spontaneously and sporadically—can be deliberately designed and activated quickly and efficiently.

Blade.org is a collaborative community of firms focused on the development and adoption of open blade server platforms, the fastest-growing segment of the computer server market. "Blades" are small dart-shaped devices which, when plugged into a rectangular enclosure, perform as powerful computer servers. A blade server "solution" consists of combinations of hardware, software, and service components. The main benefits to a company that buys a customized blade server solution are lower fixed costs due to the smaller physical space required to house the equipment, lower energy costs to operate the equipment, and ease of maintenance and data management tasks. Blade.org was established in 2006 by IBM, Intel Corp., and six other founding firms to increase the number of

blade platform solutions available for customers and to accelerate the process of bringing them to market. From the original eight founding companies, Blade.org has rapidly grown to a community of more than 250 member firms, including leading blade hardware and software providers, developers, distribution partners, and end users from several countries (though most of Blade.org's member firms are in the United States). In less than two years after the founding of Blade.org, its member firms had developed 60 solutions, an indication of the overall success of the community in creating new products on a nearly continuous basis. Eschewing the current business model of contracting with a select group of suppliers and distributors to form an "ecosystem" around IBM's new blade technology, the founding firms stated that their goal was to build a developer community of firms that would focus on expanding the number of solutions that could be made available through their collaborative efforts. Building on its earlier experiences in open source software development, IBM did not attempt to drive all innovation on blade applications itself. Instead, it opened the specifications to its BladeCenter server chassis and invited the community's member firms to play the leading role in developing blade-based solutions. Blade.org is a largely self-governing community, but it has a principal office that provides infrastructure services and strategic initiatives that benefit the community as a whole. The member firms develop solutions through a variety of processes including Web site postings of previous solutions, the work of volunteer technical committees, and participation in quarterly all-member meetings and other community-wide events. Multi-firm collaboration occurs both within and outside Blade.org, in the sense that member firms collaborate with their customers (end users) in the development of customized solutions, and collaborate with one another in small temporary networks to produce solutions for existing or new customers. On any given innovation project, collaboration can occur in one or more of four ways: (1) bilateral collaboration (a Blade.org member firm collaborates with its customer on a new solution, perhaps using consulting advice from IBM as the inventor of the blade technology); (2) direct collaboration (two or more member firms work together on the development of a new solution); (3) pooled collaboration

(Blade.org member firms contribute ideas, information, and experiences to a central database called Bladeuser.org that is accessible by other member firms to pursue innovation projects); and (4) external collaboration (a Blade.org member firm works with a non-Blade.org firm on a one-off innovation project). In summary, the Blade.org case example shows that a complete market exploration business model can be efficiently and effectively pursued by organizing a collaborative community of complementary firms. IBM and the other founders provide community leadership. The community is self-governed, supported by a common infrastructure for collaboration, and guided by collaborative protocols stated in its bylaws and membership agreement.

Lessons Learned About Large-Scale Multi-Firm Collaboration

Several principles of community-based collaboration stand out from our observations of TCG Group, Syndicom, and Blade.org. First, the process of multi-firm collaboration tends to fuel itself. Across each of these communities, member firms have reported that knowledge sharing has grown almost constantly as firms work with one another, develop innovative products and services, and jointly share in the rewards of their success. In psychological terms, collaboration is intrinsically motivating–the process itself is enjoyable as well as productive. Thus, overall, it seems clear that when new business models are linked to collaborative structural and managerial mechanisms, the opportunities to apply knowledge to new arenas of wealth creation and appropriation continue to expand. As each of these communities has developed its collaborative expertise, the attitudes and values of members have evolved in a supportive manner. For example, at Syndicom the initial surgeon cluster in the SpineConnect community succeeded quickly after two widely respected spine surgeons took the initiative to post their most challenging cases and offer their own comments on other surgeons' cases. In the next few community clusters, top surgeons played a similar leadership role, and the demonstrated collaborative skills quickly spread

across each new cluster. Such role-modeling behavior demonstrates that trust-based communities of practice, which normally evolve informally over lengthy periods of time, can be designed and brought quickly to effective knowledge-sharing levels. Moreover, such behavior can be sustained in a commercially oriented community. Maximally effective collaboration occurs among caring participants who value the contributions of their fellow members (individuals and firms) and are concerned with their equitable treatment. Finally, the effective governance of a collaborative community requires the use of a facilitative management philosophy rather than a hierarchical command-and-control philosophy. The Blade.org community, for example, is designed and operated as a platform upon which the member firms can build collaborative relationships that they use to develop innovative solutions. Member firms in a community governed by a facilitative philosophy and infrastructure can focus on forming the temporary collaborative networks they need to generate product and market innovations. In this sense, community members are self-managing.

Using Collaborative Community Designs to Tackle 21st-Century Global Challenges

Over the last century and a half, as our discussion has indicated, the evolution of organizational designs—business models and organizational forms—has benefited from the interplay of management practices and experiences across the public and private sectors. Thus, leadership approaches and hierarchical coordination mechanisms gained legitimacy in public agencies and private U-form firms, as managers were increasingly assigned on the basis of their credentials and issued their directives in accordance with rationally developed policies. Similarly, the opportunities and challenges of shared corporate and divisional governance in M-form firms had parallels in the interaction of federal and state government policies and procedures. Further, recognition of the benefits of team-based problem solving has grown across military and civilian government organizations as well as in the innovation efforts of matrix-structured private firms. Last, the challenges and benefits of relationships among upstream and downstream firms in global supply chains are, in many instances, not merely a reflection but an actual component of the global economy–in that a sizeable number of multinational firms are themselves large enough to be placed among the 100 largest national economies. At this point, it seems appropriate to consider how currently developing community-based organizational forms suggest design principles and properties that might benefit the long-term health of firms, national economies, and the global community, including the ability of each to generate, use, and distribute wealth and resources. Specifically, we believe there are two major types of situations where the principles and processes of collaborative communities can be usefully applied at the national and international levels. First, both research and practical attention needs to be directed at the critical feature of communities called *commons*, jointly held resources that benefit the entire community. Many such commons exist throughout the global economy, and many more could be created that would benefit the entire world. One type of jointly held resource is tangible–such as grazing land, oceans, and the atmosphere. According to the "tragedy of the commons," some individuals, firms, and countries may exploit and pollute resources to the detriment of fellow community members. Recent experience and research, however, suggest that commons can be managed collaboratively to conserve—even creatively use—common resources. For example, in the city of Kalundborg, Denmark, a set of voluntary exchanges between public and private organizations has produced significant benefits in the form of cost reductions and resource conservation. These exchanges initially involved waste outputs from some organizations becoming useful inputs to other organizations, simultaneously creating both an economic and social benefit. In the future, such exchanges may have broader uses, but it is important to point out that these synergistic ideas and experiments are not likely to be recognized or put into place by existing sociopolitical processes and regional or global institutions. They require collaboration among actors who perceive themselves to be members of a community and are committed to acting in the community's behalf. Another, more recent type of commons is much

less tangible, such as a body of knowledge that can be accessed by community members to be used for their own purposes. Such commons may actually grow and improve with use rather than be depleted, and collaboration among community members both utilizes and replenishes the commons. Thus, firms and countries that view themselves as members of the global community are motivated to form commons that they can contribute to and use to progress both individually and jointly. Second, we need to understand better all of the situations in which a *shared goal*, such as an economy based on clean energy or the equitable development of a worldwide market for a particular product category, can only be accomplished by a set of actors (people, firms, and governments) who each provide their complementary contribution to the larger system in a coordinated manner. For example, IBM is making collaboration with global partners an essential part of its R&D strategy. The company has set up what it calls "collaboratories" that match up its researchers with experts from governments, universities, and firms. Having already established six such collaboratories in Saudi Arabia, Switzerland, China, Ireland, Taiwan, and India, IBM is trying to convince countries and companies that it can help them improve their ability to innovate at an important time for the global economy. This example suggests a firm that produces and distributes products and services globally should make efforts to utilize the full range of knowledge and capabilities of the global community. Of course, doing so brings that firm into contact with diverse government regulations on patents, production processes, taxes, environmental protection, and so on. Global sourcing of products and ideas also requires the firm to understand business practices and cultures in a variety of environments. Adapting appropriately to such conditions requires that the firm think of itself as part of the global community—with all of the opportunities and responsibilities that community membership entails. From a design perspective, the challenges faced in such situations include (a) ensuring enough commitment to the common goal so that all of the necessary investments are made, (b) coordinating the efforts of the various contributors, and (c) ensuring that their solutions are compatible and therefore fit together in the larger system.

Effective large-scale multi-party collaboration requires rethinking organization design concepts, capabilities, and values. The process of large-scale collaboration places heavy strains on existing forms of organizing, which typically are based on hierarchy as the primary means of coordination and control. Hierarchy, however, is not well suited to managing the collaborative process, particularly collaboration that extends beyond the boundaries of the firm. Therefore, pioneering firms in knowledge-intensive, rapidly evolving environments are experimenting with organizational designs that are less reliant on hierarchy. We are still in the early phases of those experiments, but the examples described above of TCG Group, Syndicom, and Blade.org share some properties that aid in identifying the architectural elements of the emerging collaborative community-based organizational designs. Those elements are actors (individuals, firms, governments) who have collaborative capabilities and values, protocols and infrastructure that facilitate collaboration, and shared access to commons. Capable actors who have knowledge, information, tools, and values required to set goals and assess the consequences of potential actions for the achievement of those goals do not need managers. Instead, protocols guide their collaborative activities, and the shared infrastructure provides them with the ability to connect with each other, as well as access the same information. The commons is a repository of both knowledge and other resources available to all of the actors, and it can expand and improve with use. Together, these core organizational mechanisms enable large groups of actors to collaborate in the pursuit of opportunities, or the solution to problems, with minimal use of hierarchical mechanisms. In summary, we observe a number of collaborative community designs emerging across a variety of sectors.

Situations involving commons and shared goals are particularly conducive to such designs. Organizing for large-scale collaboration requires revisiting established approaches to leadership, resource allocation and decisional behaviors, and organization structure. A summary of the main features of the collaborative community design is provided in Table 35.2.

Conclusions

Over the last century and a half, firms using traditional organizational designs have made myriad accomplishments, including the building of industrial empires in railroads, steel, automobiles, electronics, and pharmaceuticals and in the management

Table 35.2   Properties of Collaborative Community Designs

Property	Description
Shared interest	Resource commons or common goals
Collaborative values	Willingness to share knowledge, contribute to the success of fellow community members, and seek fairness in community contributions and the distribution of rewards
Community-oriented leadership	A focus on facilitating community growth and sustainability, member collaboration, and promotion of collaborative values and practices
Protocols and infrastructure that support member collaboration	Systems, processes, and norms that support both direct and pooled collaborative relationships among members
Expandable commons	Knowledge and other resource pools that all members can contribute to and draw from

of global supply chains. Traditional organizational designs, however, will not be able to respond effectively to the opportunities and challenges faced by 21st-century firms and nations. New organizational designs that can mobilize large sets of actors who have the ability to self-organize and collaborate are needed. The core ingredients of such designs include collaborative capabilities and values, facilitating infrastructures, and resource commons. The development of effective collaborative community designs is critically important to the global economy, because increasingly our future depends on successfully pursuing shared goals and sustainably developing our global commons.

Selected Bibliography

For interested readers, there is a wealth of information on opportunities and problems in the global economy. For an overview of global opportunities, see Jacques Attali, *A Brief History of the Future: A Brave and Controversial Look at the Twenty-First Century* (New York, NY: Arcade Publishing, 2008) and Mark Tovey (ed.), *Collective Intelligence: Creating a Prosperous World at Peace* (Earth Intelligence Network, 2008). For an optimistic discussion of major global problems and how to solve them, see Jeffrey Sachs, *Common Wealth: Economics for a Crowded Planet* (New York, NY: The Penguin Press, 2008). A framework for developing global governance mechanisms is discussed in Jose Antonio Ocampo, "Rethinking Global Economic and Social Governance," *Journal of Globalization and Development*, 2010, 1(1), 1–27. Theoretical discussions and illustrative examples of the design of common and communities can be found in Elinor Ostrom, "A General Framework for Analyzing Sustainability of Social-Ecological Systems," *Science*, 2009, 325, 419–422; Yochai Benkler, *The Wealth of Networks: How Social Production Transforms Markets and Freedom* (Copyright by Yochai Benkler, 2006); and Raymond E. Miles, Grant Miles, and Charles C. Snow, *Collaborative Entrepreneurship: How Communities of Networked Firms Use Continuous Innovation to Create Economic Wealth* (Stanford, CA: Stanford University Press, 2005). The human factors and motivation on which collaborative community designs depend, such as autonomy, mastery, and purpose, are discussed in Daniel H. Pink, *Drive: The Surprising Truth About What Motivates Us* (New York, NY: Riverhead Books, 2009).

PART VII

Capacity Building

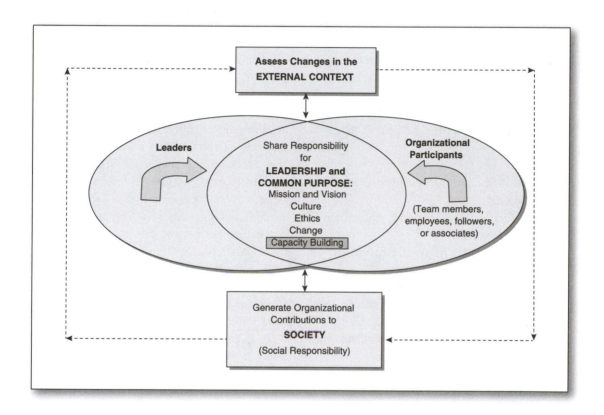

Overview

The organization's ability to meet new and complex challenges from the external context greatly depends on its facility to build capacity among its members. The chapters in this section examine how organizations endeavor to prepare their members for leadership locally, globally, and collectively; and how they facilitate learning and working in Web 2.0 and distributed team settings.

Leader and Leadership Development

David V. Day, John W. Fleenor, Leanne E. Atwater, Rachel E. Sturm, and Rob A. McKee (Chapter 36) review 25 years of research and theory on leader and leadership development. Leader development focuses on the internal development of the individual leader while leadership development focuses on the process of development that involves interactions with multiple individuals such as peers in self-managed teams or leaders and followers. Researchers in this field are less concerned with leadership theory and more concerned with developmental processes (developmental science). In other words, researchers focus on what factors play a role in developing leadership skills and potential, how the development emerges in organizations, and what practices facilitate effective leadership.

Day et al. provide a synopsis of numerous studies and summarize the findings as follows: "[T]hrough the examination of an array of factors including experience, skills, personality, self-development, social mechanisms, 360-degree feedback, self-other agreement, and self-narratives, leadership development represents a dynamic process involving multiple interactions that persist overtime." Overall, the development process

- begins early and is partly influenced by parental modeling;
- involves development and application of multiple skills;
- is shaped by personality and relationships with others;
- can be formed by different theories such as constructive-developmental theory and authentic leadership;
- is measured in different ways including multi-source ratings; and
- should be tailored to current needs of the individual leader.

Most studies to date focus on individual leadership development overtime, but the complex requirements of new era organizations call for members throughout the organization to participate in leadership. One of the authors' recommendations for future study is especially useful for the focus of this text. Greater attention needs to be given to research on the collective aspects of leadership development such as shared leadership. Organizations must develop their members for this new role.

Joyce S. Osland, Allan Bird, and Mark Mendenhall (Chapter 37) examine the research on a specific form of leadership development: global mindset and global leadership capacity. How do organizations prepare their members to lead in a global context? Several studies contend that leaders need a global mindset as a prerequisite and a competitive advantage for leading in transnational organizations. The research in this field is divided on a definition of global mindset. One definition focuses on the necessity of moving beyond ethnocentrism and applying appropriate criteria in different countries and cultures, another emphasizes sense making, and still another highlights a multidimensional approach that joins cultural and strategic considerations.

Osland, Bird, and Mendenhall identify three models of global mindset. The first model is composed of two constructs: cosmopolitanism, an openness and orientation toward the outside world; and cognitive complexity, the ability to generate several competing interpretations of events and their interactive events. The second model identifies global intellectual capital, psychological capital, and social capital as necessary components of global mindset. The third model encompasses the industry-specific, organization-specific, and person-specific antecedents of global mindset within a cultural context.

One research team concluded that global mindset was a necessary but not sufficient condition for global leadership. Osland Bird, and Mendenhall define global leadership as "a process of influencing the thinking, attitudes and behaviours of a global community to work together synergistically toward a common vision and common goals." Research in this area focuses on the capabilities needed by global leaders to be effective and the means to develop global leadership characteristics. Many of the studies identified various competencies that individuals need to become global leaders, but these competencies were not consistent from one study to the next, or the list was too extensive to be useful. Additionally, the competency research focused on the content but did not explain the process that global leaders use.

Reviews of the literature reveal that organizations use varying methods to develop global leadership among their members. The authors recommend a multi-method approach to global leadership development, with each method designed to be high in experiential rigor and time. These programs incorporate such methods as international assignments, short-term developmental assignments, international teams, action learning groups/projects/task forces, international training and development programs, and international meetings and forums, among other components.

Kristin L. Cullen, Charles J. Palus, Donna Chrobot-Mason, and Craig Appaneal (Chapter 38) provide examples from the realm of practice concerning the development of collectivist leadership across the boundaries of an organization and between different organizations. Over the years, the Center for Creative Leadership (CCL) was known for its expertise in individual leadership development using tools such as the 360-degree evaluation mentioned earlier by Day et al. The center has now shifted its focus to fostering the accomplishment of collectives (team, organization, community, and nation) rather than individual leaders.

They begin development sessions with the perspective that leadership is a social process that produces collective outcomes encompassing: direction—agreement on what the collective is trying to achieve; alignment—activities that are coordinated and integrated in service of the shared direction; and commitment—when individuals make the success of the collective a priority. This approach moves the goal of development beyond individual outcomes to collective outcomes.

Kristen Cullen et al. describe their leadership development work with groups that facilitate interaction across boundaries (boundary spanning) to help groups move from a perspective of "us" to "we" (collective leadership). Their boundary spanning leadership model (BSL) uses three strategies. First, groups such as the Defense Department and the State Department (military and diplomats) work separately to clarify and define differences that designate an intergroup boundary. They identify their unique strengths and weaknesses and identify their desired outcomes; then each group shares this information with the other. The second strategy involves forging common ground by developing a shared vision, roles, and responsibilities to learn how they can best collaborate. The third strategy, discovering new frontiers, entails crafting a strategy for working interdependently. Collective leadership development occurs over the long term after groups leave the

center and continue their work toward their shared vision across boundaries.

Members of CCL have begun to use network analysis and new tools to help groups recognize identity-based boundaries, help collectives strategically span these divides, and track changes in cross-boundary activities. The authors implore others to engage in this research to advance the knowledge in collective leadership development.

Learning and Organizational Support

Capacity building among organization members occurs through other forms of learning, in addition to leadership development. Manuel London (Chapter 39) examines generative team learning in the context of Web 2.0 environments. Web 2.0 technologies such as social media, blogs, interactive webinars, and telepresence provide new opportunities for virtual teams to work, learn, problem solve, and innovate together. Loudon cites one researcher who describes team learning as "the acquisition of knowledge, skills, and performance capabilities of an interdependent set of individuals through interaction and experience." Team-learning processes include sharing ideas and information, co-construction of shared models, discussions about team process, experiential learning (doing the work), crossing team boundaries, and storage and retrieval of team capabilities and information.

The author's research focuses on generative learning, which stems from members' openness to new ideas and processes, member self-initiated exploration and experimentation, and new work structures, methods, and processes that produce novel outcomes. He examines team generative learning processes in Web 2.0 environments using a framework of four modes of experiential learning: concrete experience, reflective observation, abstract conceptualization, and active explorations. Using this framework, he analyzes five cases where teams work across boundaries within one organization or across different organizations to generate new solutions to complex challenges. Generative team learning in these cases produced interpersonal insights, communities of practice, and innovations facilitated by Web 2.0 functionality.

Distributed teams are increasingly prevalent in new era organizations. How can organizations provide strong support to these teams to enhance their overall effectiveness? Nathalie Drouin and Mario Bourgault (Chapter 40) sought to identify the dimensions of organizational support that make the strongest impact on the quality of decision making and effective teamwork in distributed project teams. *Perceived organizational support* (POS) refers to idea that "employees are committed to their organizations insofar as they believe that the organization values and cares for them." The authors contend members of distributed project teams must perceive organizational support as beneficial to produce more effective teamwork and improved decision making.

Drouin and Bourgault identified four dimensions of organizational support for distributed project teams based on organizational support theory and research. These dimensions entail strategic staffing—to ensure that teams have members with the knowledge, skills, and competency to perform effectively; training and tools—to provide job training such as long-distance management or time management, and tools including laptops and appropriate hardware and software that team members need for quality decision making and team effectiveness; team autonomy—allowing team self-reliance based on trust that employees will make wise decisions about how to do their jobs; and top management monitoring—organizational control through formal feedback systems used by top management to monitor the progress of a project against a baseline or anticipated outcome.

The researchers used qualitative interviews, case studies, and a custom web questionnaire to test their hypotheses concerning organizational support dimensions and distributed team decision making and effectiveness. They found that strategic staffing is significantly associated with the quality of decision making and team effectiveness. Training and tools positively impact both team effectiveness and the quality of decision making. Team autonomy is a critical dimension that may be even more salient and influential on the quality of decision making in highly culturally diverse teams. Top management monitoring was not found to be useful for projects that were highly distributed; in fact, the reverse appeared to be true. The study offers valuable insight into the type of support organizations need to provide distributed project teams and identifies new possibilities for future research.

Part VII — Chapters

CHAPTER 36

Advances in Leader and Leadership Development

A Review of 25 Years of Research and Theory

David V. Day[1]
University of Western Australia, Australia

John W. Fleenor
Center for Creative Leadership, United States

Leanne E. Atwater
University of Houston, United States

Rachel E. Sturm
University of Houston, United States

Rob A. McKee
University of Houston, United States

1. Introduction and Overview

Leadership development has emerged as an active field of theory building and research, providing a more scientific and evidence-based foundation to augment the long-standing practitioner interest in the topic. This emergence has transpired primarily over the last 10 to 15 years and *The Leadership Quarterly* has played a major role as an important outlet for this work. The purpose of this article is to review those advances, highlight their respective contributions, and identify areas in need of future research.

The purpose of this review is to identify advances in scholarly approaches to leader development (intrapersonal, focused on individual leaders), leadership development (interpersonal, focused on enhancing leadership capacity), and related topics that have been featured in this journal over the previous 25 years. The good news is that much has changed. There have been significant contributions to understanding leadership development (broadly defined to also include leader development) as well as multi-source or 360-degree feedback processes. The latter represent important process tools for enhancing leadership development. Although a lot of new knowledge has been generated in the previous 25 years, there is much more that needs to be learned. For that reason we will review the articles and special issues in *The Leadership Quarterly* since its beginning that have contributed to these scholarly advances. We will also highlight areas where additional focus is needed in terms of building a stronger evidence-based foundation for leadership development and feedback processes.

We begin by elaborating on how and why leadership development is different from the broader field of leadership theory and research. In doing so, we wish to demonstrate that more fully understanding leadership development goes far beyond merely choosing a particular leadership theory and training people in behaviors related to that theory. Leadership development is a complex topic that is deserving of scholarly attention with regard to theory and research independent of what has been studied more generally in the field of leadership.

The structure of this review is as follows. First, the content or the "what" of leadership development will be examined to summarize the phenomena that develop and what factors play a role in developing successful leadership skills and potential. This section will include intrapersonal factors (mainly relevant to leader development) as well as interpersonal factors (relating more to leadership development). Second, we consider process issues or the "how" in leadership development. The goal of this section is to describe the ways in which leadership development emerges in organizations and the practices that can be implemented to facilitate effective leadership. Third, we review a series of recent pieces that address aspects of longitudinal studies of leadership development. These

are theoretical and empirical contributions that provide valuable insights into the longitudinal nature of leadership development. Fourth, we investigate how leadership development has been assessed or evaluated in the literature, thus promoting a scholarly understanding of evaluation methods in leadership development research. We conclude with an agenda for future research on the topic of leadership development. Whereas many of the pieces we review overlap multiple categories, our hope is that this structural framework provides a clear yet comprehensive understanding of the relevant theory and research pertaining to leadership development.

2. Leader and Leadership Development: Research and Theory

There is a relatively long history of leadership theory and research spanning more than a century (Avolio, Reichard, Hannah, Walumbwa, & Chan, 2009); however, in comparison, there is a fairly short history of rigorous scholarly theory and research on the topics of leader and leadership development. As noted by Day (2000), the distinction between developing leaders and developing leadership is potentially an important one. Leader development focuses on developing individual leaders whereas leadership development focuses on a process of development that inherently involves multiple individuals (e.g., leaders and followers or among peers in a self-managed work team). But given the keen attention paid to leadership theory historically, there appears to be a widespread misperception that if the field could just identify and agree on the "correct" leadership theory then the development piece would inevitably follow. It turns out that this is not so simple. Developing individual leaders and developing effective leadership processes involve more than simply deciding which leadership theory is to be used to motivate effective development. This is so because human development involves a complex set of processes that need to be understood. Given that individual leader development occurs in the context of ongoing adult development (Day, Harrison, & Halpin, 2009), we need to focus on development as much as leadership to shed light on how this process unfolds.

One of the reasons leadership theory and research have contributed little to leadership development is a long-standing focus linking personality with leadership. If personality is conceptualized in terms of traits that summarize relatively enduring dispositional tendencies (House, Shane, & Herold, 1996), then its relevance for studying development (i.e., change) is questionable. Another popular approach in leadership research that is likewise limited in its developmental usefulness is the behavioral approach. Although behaviors can be learned, the primary intervention focus associated with leadership behaviors tends to be based on training rather than on longer-term development initiatives. Training typically involves providing proven approaches to solve known problems but the challenges facing contemporary leaders tend to be too complex and ill-defined to be addressed successfully through such relatively short-term training interventions. As a result of these challenges, the nascent fields of leader and leadership development tend to focus less on leadership theory and more on developmental science. In other words, there has been a change in focus associated with studies of leadership development broadly defined, away from leadership research and toward understanding and enhancing developmental processes.

Another important difference is that the nature of leadership development is inherently multilevel and longitudinal (Day, 2011). Specifically, studying development involves mapping and understanding within- and between-person change patterns—as well as those involving groups, teams, and larger collectives—over time. To contribute to greater understanding of how leaders and leadership processes develop and change, relevant theory and research should reflect both the multilevel and the longitudinal nature of development. This longitudinal, multilevel focus means that intrapersonal and interpersonal processes are central to leadership development over time.

3. Intrapersonal Content Issues in Development

In terms of intrapersonal content (see Table 36.1 for a summary), a relevant question is what develops as a function of leader development? Additionally, are there individual differences that affect these interventions?

Researchers such as Lord and Hall (2005) have noted the importance of individual identity in developing leadership skills and expertise as part of the leader development process. Other researchers have examined issues of cognitive and metacognitive skills at the core of leadership potential (Marshall-Mies et al., 2000), as well as various approaches to understanding the underlying patterns of leadership skills (Mumford, Campion, & Morgeson, 2007; Mumford, Marks, Connelly, Zaccaro, & Reiter-Palmon, 2000; Mumford et al., 2000). Moreover, the role of personality has also been examined as a predictor of leadership styles (deVries, 2012) as well as leader performance (Strang & Kuhnert, 2009). All of these issues involving skills, experience, learning, and personality are central to the notion of developing the expert leader (Day et al., 2009; Lord & Hall, 2005). Research and theory on leader self-development also contribute to our conceptual understanding of intrapersonal content issues.

3.1. Experience and Learning in Development

Although there is a long-held assumption on the part of both practitioners and researchers that experience plays an important role in developing effective leadership, research suggests that the empirical evidence for this assumption is far from definitive (Day, 2010). Leadership involves a complex interaction between people and their social and organizational environments (Day, 2000). Therefore, simply correlating a leader's performance with the number of months he or she has been in a job or organization is inadequate (i.e., contaminated and deficient) in capturing the full effects of something as nuanced as experience.

Bettin and Kennedy (1990) addressed these conceptualization and measurement concerns by examining several different ways that experience can be measured in organizations. They argued that a limitation in the research on experience and leader development is the use of tenure or length of time in a job or organization as a proxy for experience. They studied biographies of 84 U.S. Army Captains who all had very similar years of experience. Experience was assessed by experts who rated the biographies according to the knowledge, skills, or practice that

Table 36.1   Intrapersonal and Interpersonal Content Issues in Leadership Development

Topics	Summary	Source
Intrapersonal Experience and leaning	Leaders' previous work history as well as the leadership relevance of previous positions held (as opposed to tenure) should be considered in decisions about the kinds of experiences that enhance leader development.	Bettin and Kennedy (1990)
	Leadership development occurring in adolescence can be shaped, in part, by parental modeling.	Zacharatos et al. (2000)
	A leader's level of experience plays a role in determining how much he or she will learn, but at the same time, not all leaders learn at the same rate or in the same way.	Hirst et al. (2004)
Skills	Although certain kinds of experience may encourage skill development at one point in time in a leader's career, others might be more advantageous at a different time.	Mumford, Marks et al. (2000)
	Whereas individuals with specific skill types are more inclined to hold senior level leadership positions (such as those who scored high on achievement), there is still a fair amount of diversity in terms of ability, personality, and motivational characteristics across leaders at the same level.	Mumford, Zaccaro et al. (2000)
	Six skills relevant for creative problem solving of high-level leaders include general problem solving, planning and implementation, solution construction, solution evaluation, social judgment, and metacognitive processing (i.e., knowledge of one's cognitive processes).	Marshall-Mies et al. (2000)
	As leaders assume more senior positions in an organizational, the acquisition of strategic and business skills will be more important for effective performance than the acquisition of interpersonal and cognitive skills.	Mumford et al. (2007)
	Effective leadership entails developing and integrating wisdom, intelligence, and creativity.	Sternberg (2008)
	Identity, metacognitive, and self-regulation processes are crucial to the refinement of knowledge structures and information processing capabilities associated with leadership expertise.	Lord and Hall (2005)
Personality	Conscientiousness can be a significant predictor of leader performance.	Strang and Kuhnert (2009)
	Different patterns of personality tend to be more equally representative at junior level leadership positions compared to more senior level positions.	Mumford, Zaccaro et al. (2000)
Self-development	Work orientation, mastery orientation, and career-growth orientation facilitate leader self-development activities.	Boyce et al. (2010)

Topics	Summary	Source
	Specific organizational-level (i.e., human resources practices) and group-level (i.e., supervisor style) constructs can promote leader self-development.	Reichard and Johnson (2011)
Interpersonal Social mechanisms	The creation of positive learning environments in which education about other groups occurs, innovation is supported, and cultural communication competence is encouraged, facilitates high quality relationships in diverse leader-member dyads.	Scandura and Lankau (1996)
	Leadership development practices can shape social capital development stages (such as networking, mentoring, leadership training, and job assignments) in a variety of ways.	Galli and Müller-Stewens (2012)
Authentic leadership	Authentic leadership development involves "ongoing processes whereby leaders and followers gain self-awareness and establish open, transparent, trusting and genuine relationships, which in part may be shaped and impacted by planned interventions such as training" (p. 322).	Avolio and Gardner (2005)
	The positive outcomes of authentic leader-follower relationships include heightened levels of follower trust in the leader, engagement, workplace well-being, and sustainable performance.	Gardner et al. (2005)
	Authentic leaders develop authentic followers through positive modeling.	Ilies et al. (2005)
	Positive other-directed emotions (e.g., gratitude, appreciation) will motivate authentic leaders to behave in ways that reflect self-transcendent values (e.g., honesty, loyalty, and equality).	Michie and Gooty (2005)
	The attainment of relational authenticity, wherein followers afford leaders the legitimacy to promote a set of values on their behalf, is challenging for many women in positions of authority, and thus, the development of women leaders should focus on the relational aspects of achieving authenticity as a leader.	Eagly (2005)
	There is a need for empirical evidence evaluating the underlying principles of authentic leadership theory.	Cooper et al. (2005)

the Captains gained from their current position and the leadership relevance of previous positions. When measured in this manner, experience was found to be a significant predictor of leadership performance; however, time in service and number of previous positions were unrelated to leadership performance.

The results of the Bettin and Kennedy (1990) study suggested that whereas time and experience are not mutually exclusive—it does take time to gain experience—it is important for scholars to be mindful that using time as a proxy for experience is limited. Moreover, the authors offered leadership scholars an appropriate conceptualization of experience as the relevant skills, knowledge, and practice acquired while holding various jobs that may be relevant to research on the role of experience in leader development. These findings also have practical implications in terms of taking into account individuals' previous work history as well as the leadership relevance of the previous positions held in making decisions about the kinds of experiences that enhance leader development.

Zacharatos, Barling, and Kelloway (2000) extended this focus on individual experience and leader development by studying adolescents' observations of transformational leadership behaviors exhibited by their respective parents and how this experience was associated with their leadership effectiveness within a team context. Transformational leadership (Bass & Riggio, 2006) is conceptualized around four interrelated components: (a) idealized influence, (b) inspirational motivation, (c) intellectual stimulation, and (d) individualized consideration, and is one of the most frequently studied leadership approaches in the leadership literature (Day & Antonakis, 2012). To better understand how transformational leadership behaviors develop in youths, Zacharatos et al. (2000) invoked social learning theory to explain the influence that parental modeling can have on the development of adolescents' leadership. The research focused on a sample of 112 Canadian high school students who were members of different sports teams. Adolescents' perceptions that their parents demonstrated transformational leadership behaviors were associated with a greater likelihood that these adolescents exhibited similar leadership behaviors. Also, those adolescents who displayed transformational behaviors were rated as more satisfying, effective, and effort-evoking leaders by their peers and coaches in their particular team context. In terms of leadership development, this study suggests that development of leadership (particularly transformational leadership) can start in adolescents and is likely shaped, in part, by parental modeling.

In a year-long empirical study of R&D teams, Hirst, Mann, Bain, Pirola-Merlo, and Richter (2004) examined the role of learning and individual differences in the development of facilitative leadership behaviors. Facilitative leadership endorses respect and positive relationships among team members, constructive conflict resolution, and candid expression of thoughts and attitudes. The authors grounded their hypotheses in action learning theory, proposing that leaders "learn from challenging work, from solving complex problems, and from leading a team, and that they use this knowledge to foster team communication and enhance team performance" (p. 321). But not all leaders learn at the same rate or in the same way. The authors supported their contention that leaders who are better able to learn from their experiences tended to engage in greater levels of facilitative leadership. This learning of facilitative leadership behaviors was, in turn, associated with higher levels of team reflexivity and performance.

Hirst et al. (2004) also found support for their hypotheses that a leader's level of experience will determine how much he or she will learn and, further, experience will moderate the relationship between leadership learning and facilitative leadership. Less experienced leaders simply have more to learn and are more likely to encounter novel situations than their more veteran counterparts. The schemas and implicit leadership theories of inexperienced leaders are likely to be less complex or crystallized, and thus are more amenable to change. This is not meant to suggest that experienced leaders are incapable of learning or translating that learning into their leadership behaviors, but rather that they must work harder to integrate new knowledge into their established cognitive frameworks. Another important finding from this research involved the time lag (ranging from 4 to 8 months) between leadership learning and facilitative leadership behavior enactment. The authors surmised that this "may reflect the interval between gaining new insight and grasping an understanding of how best to translate this knowledge into leadership behavior" (p. 322). In other words, it takes time for leaders to progress from a conceptual understanding of their facilitative role to the procedural expression of their leadership competence through specific facilitative behaviors.

3.2. Skills and Development

At the turn of the 21st century, leadership scholars began focusing attention on the particular leadership skills that can be acquired through development processes. For instance, Mumford, Marks et al. (2000) and Mumford, Zaccaro et al. (2000) used U.S. military samples to examine the skills acquired over the course of a leader's career and how these skills are acquired. The researchers examined complex problem-solving skills, creative thinking skills, social judgment skills, solution construction skills, and leader knowledge or expertise. In order to describe changes in these skills from lower to higher level leadership positions, Mumford, Marks et al. (2000) illustrated that scores on assessments of these skills increased from junior-level positions (e.g., second lieutenant, first lieutenants, and junior captains) to mid-level positions (e.g., senior captains and majors) and from mid-level to upper-level positions (e.g., lieutenant colonels and colonels). They also found that certain skills were more important at certain phases of a leader's career. In particular, technical training was found to be more strongly related to skill increases moving from junior to mid-level positions whereas more advanced professional training was more strongly related to increases in requisite complex problem-solving skills as leaders moved from mid-level to more senior positions.

The findings of Mumford, Marks et al.'s (2000) study of differences in leadership skills across six grade levels of officers in the U.S. Army offer useful theoretical and practical implications for those interested in leadership development. Specifically, their findings supported their proposed organization-based model of leader skill development, which suggests that skill development depends on learning as people interact with their environment. It also explains that skill development can occur over a long period of time and that this process is progressive, moving from simple aspects of development to more complex, integrated components. These findings also suggest that whereas certain kinds of experience may encourage skill development at one point in time in a leader's career, others might be more beneficial at a different time. Thus, they recommended that training assignments should be carefully tailored to current developmental needs, which, of course, is easier said than done.

In a related study, Mumford, Zaccaro et al. (2000) were interested in identifying types or subgroups of individuals entering into the U.S. Army according to ability, personality, and motivational characteristics, as well as determining which of these types were found in more senior positions. They identified seven different types of individual profiles: *Concrete Achievers* were those high on achievement and planning; *Motivated Communicators* were extraverted, dominant, responsible, and high in achievement needs; *Limited Defensives* were introverted, and scored high in areas of sensing, thinking, and judging; *Disengaged Introverts* were also introverted but scored high on intuition, perception, and planning; *Social Adaptors* were extraverted, and scored high in feeling, perception, and openness; *Thoughtful Innovators* were introverted, intuitive, achievement-oriented, and open; and *Struggling Misfits* were those who did not score high on any of the measures.

Results suggested that all seven of these groups were well represented in junior officers, with at least 10% to at most 20% of the officers being found in each subgroup. Whereas group representation was more uniform at the junior officer level, a different pattern of group membership emerged at the more senior level. Specifically, members of three of the subgroups—Motivated Communicators, Thoughtful Innovators, and Social Adaptors—were represented with greater or equal frequency at the senior officer level compared to the junior officer level, with Motivated Communicators and Thoughtful Innovators being especially pronounced with 40% and 26% of the sample, respectively. These findings suggest that whereas individuals with specific skills types are more apt to hold upper level leadership positions there is still a good deal of diversity in terms of ability, personality, and motivational characteristics among leadership incumbents at the same level. The authors encouraged practitioners and scholars to recognize that the development process is holistic in nature and that different types of people will be needed to fill different types of organizational leadership roles.

In an effort to identify and appropriately measure specific skills related to effective senior-level leaders, Marshall-Mies et al. (2000) created and tested an online computer-based cognitive and metacognitive (i.e., knowledge of one's cognitive processes) skill assessment battery called the Military Leadership Exercises. In doing so, they first identified complex cognitive and metacognitive skills relevant for creative problem solving in high-level leaders. The cognitive skills included general problem solving, planning and implementation, solution construction, solution evaluation, and social judgment. Metacognitive processing was measured as individuals' awareness of prior understandings as evidenced by their ability to reevaluate these understandings over time in light of new information. The skills were assessed using complex and domain-specific (i.e., geared towards the military) situational leadership scenarios, which were used to predict performance outcomes. This study contributes to our understanding of leader development by describing skills that are important to senior-level leaders as well as by providing a way in which these skills can be measured.

Other researchers have since investigated different patterns of skills that are important to leaders and leadership development. In particular, Mumford et al. (2007) presented four leadership skill requirements (cognitive, interpersonal, business, and strategic) as a *strataplex,* conceptualized as layered (strata) across the organization and segmented (plex) into a specified number of parts. Findings from their study on approximately 1000 junior, midlevel, and senior managers supported the proposed strataplex approach and demonstrated that specific skill requirements vary by organizational level. In addition, they proposed that as managers are promoted to more senior roles, the acquisition of strategic and business skills will be more important for effective performance than the acquisition of interpersonal and cognitive skills.

Sternberg (2008) provided a WICS approach to leadership, which refers to Wisdom, Intelligence, and Creativity Synthesized. This approach is grounded in the notion that effective leadership entails developing and integrating these three types of skills (wisdom, intelligence, and creativity) that all play an important role in decision making. Accordingly, leadership is a process that involves generating ideas (creativity), then analyzing whether the ideas are good or not (intelligence), and then, ideally, acting on the ideas in a way to achieve a common good (wisdom). Sternberg recommends that one way that leadership potential can be developed is through identifying and encouraging this kind of synthesis.

Lord and Hall (2005) proposed that leadership development is predicated on progressive skills development. Their approach is based on a general theory of learning and expertise, which suggests that changes in information processing and underlying knowledge structures occur as skills are gradually refined. Thus, through the process of skill development a leader advances through novice, intermediate, and expert skill levels. Each level requires increasingly sophisticated knowledge structures and information processing capabilities within broadly defined task, emotional, social, and self-relevant realms. Compared to Hirst et al. (2004), who examined less experienced leaders against more experienced leaders, Lord and Hall focused on the underlying processes involved in moving from a novice (i.e., inexperienced) to an expert (i.e., highly experienced) leader.

The development of leadership skills also requires self-motivation. In that regard, identity, metacognitive, and self-regulation processes are thought to be crucial to the refinement of knowledge structures and information processing capabilities associated with leadership expertise. Through the course of development, identity progresses from the individual level, in which the self is defined in terms of uniqueness from others, to the relational level, in which the self is defined in terms of roles and relationships, to the collective level, in which the self is defined in terms of group or organizational affiliations (Lord & Hall, 2005). Concomitant development of metacognitive skills enables better knowledge access, goal formation, action, and social reactions, which frees up cognitive resources that can be directed toward effective self-regulation. Self-regulation involves the control and communication of emotions to others. As a leader's skills progress into the expert domain over time, the identity and behaviors of a leader are increasingly guided by understanding the situation and collaborating with others.

3.3. Personality and Development

Research has found certain personality traits to be predictive of effective leadership. For example, Strang and Kuhnert (2009) found that the Big Five personality factor of conscientiousness significantly predicted leader performance as measured by the average rating of three sources (subordinate, peer, and supervisor). Moreover, Mumford, Zaccaro et al. (2000) suggested that *patterns* of personality can have an impact on leader skill development and performance. Nonetheless, if personality changes relatively little compared with other personal characteristics in adulthood, then it makes sense to evaluate their predictive value in terms of leadership performance. Other approaches will be discussed that examine more malleable constructs that are thought to change as part of leader development processes (e.g., self-efficacy).

3.4. Self-development

In terms of understanding leader self-development, Boyce, Zaccaro, and Wisecarver (2010) addressed the relative lack of research on the personal characteristics of individuals who engage in leadership self-development activities. Through an empirical examination of junior military leaders, the authors supported a conceptual model in which dispositional characteristics differentially predict leader development activities. The individual characteristics found to be associated with leader development activities were *work orientation* (e.g., job involvement and organizational commitment); *mastery orientation* (greater self-efficacy, conscientiousness, openness to experience, and intellectual maturity); and *career-growth orientation* (greater career exploration and feedback seeking behaviors). Depending on the strength of their mastery and work orientations, individuals were more or less motivated to engage in self-development activities. Those individuals with a stronger career growth orientation were found to be more skilled at performing self-development activities. Overall, the results indicated that work orientation, mastery orientation, and career-growth orientation play key roles in leader self-development.

Further addressing the scarcity of research in the area of self-development of leadership skills, Reichard and Johnson (2011) proposed a multi-level model of leader self-development that describes how leaders are "transformed into continuous self-developers" (p. 34). In this model organizational-level constructs such as human resources practices and resources are linked with group-level phenomena such as norms, supervisor style, and social networks to promote leaders' motivation to develop their leadership and to engage in continuous self-development behavior. Specifically, HR processes (selection, training, and performance appraisal) create group norms (learning, responsibility, and openness), and support the development of individual leader skills and abilities. These individual-level leader characteristics are moderated by supportive group norms to engender an individual's motivation to develop leadership and to engage in continuous self-development. The authors assert that "leader self-development is a cost-effective way for organizations to develop leaders resulting [potentially] in a competitive edge" (p. 33).

4. Interpersonal Content Issues in Development

Given that leadership development is a dynamic process involving multiple individuals spanning various levels of analyses, the content aspects of this process include a variety of interpersonal factors (see Table 36.1). One such approach to understanding the content of leadership development includes a focus on the development of leader-member exchange (LMX) quality. Another relevant approach examines how leadership development practices shape the development of social capital in organizations. Relatedly, a special issue on authentic leadership emphasized the interactive leader-follower quality of authentic leadership and provided developmental strategies related to this leadership approach.

4.1. Social Mechanisms and Development

Leadership development emphasizes the enactment of leadership built on a foundation of mutual trust and respect (Day, 2000). As a result, it is important to understand the development of social interactions that occur within the leadership process. For instance, Boyd and Taylor (1998) conceptually evaluated how the presence of friendship contributes to either effective or ineffective working relationships in the LMX process. Scandura and Lankau (1996) further extended research on LMX by including the potential role that gender and race relations may play in the process of forging effective exchange qualities. More specifically, these authors described how certain social psychological processes (e.g., self-knowledge, interpersonal skills, communication competence, and cultural competence) and contextual influences (e.g., organizational climate/culture, group/organizational composition, economic environment, and organizational support for diversity) moderate the development of high quality relationships in diverse leader-member dyads. They highlighted the importance of leaders creating positive learning environments in which learning about other groups occurs, innovation is supported, and cultural communication competence is encouraged. From this, individuals create more integrated self-concepts that include both intrapersonal and interpersonal dimensions.

More recently, Galli and Müller-Stewens (2012) demonstrated how leadership development practices shape the development of social capital in organizations. In contrast to human capital, which focuses primarily on individual leader attributes (i.e., knowledge, skills, and abilities), social capital considers connections and interactions among individuals within a social context. In an effort to understand how leadership development potentially impacts organizational performance, the authors adopted a case study approach to examine the development of social capital at more strategic levels of the firm. They found that social capital differs regarding its intensity and progresses through stages characterized by contact (e.g., networks, off-sites, mentoring), assimilation (e.g., leadership training, 360-degree feedback), and identification (e.g., job assignments, action learning). Also, their results suggest that leadership development practices vary in their potential impact on social capital development stages; thus, they should be designed accordingly.

4.2. Authentic Leadership Development

In a special issue of *The Leadership Quarterly* on the topic of authentic leadership, Avolio and Gardner (2005) noted that authentic leadership development involves "ongoing processes whereby leaders and followers gain self-awareness and establish open, transparent, trusting and genuine relationships, which in part may be shaped and impacted by planned interventions such as training" (p. 322). Thus, the development of authentic leadership is conceptualized as a more complex process than just the development of authentic leaders. The former involves the development of an authentic relationship (i.e., social capital focus) between leaders and their followers; in contrast, the development of authentic leaders is more intrapersonal in nature (i.e., human capital focus).

Avolio and Gardner (2005) highlighted the environmental and organizational forces that have generated interest in the study of authentic leadership and its development. They described the similarities and defining features of authentic leadership theory in comparison to other perspectives of leadership (e.g., transformational, charismatic, servant, and spiritual leadership). In this vein, a model of the relationships between authentic leadership, follower development, and follower performance was presented (Gardner, Avolio, Luthans, May, & Walumbwa, 2005). The proposed model highlighted the developmental processes of leader and follower self-awareness and self-regulation, as well as the influence of the leaders' and followers' personal histories on authentic leadership and followership. The model also considered the reciprocal effects of an inclusive, ethical, and compassionate organizational climate. Positive modeling was viewed as the primary mechanism through which leaders developed authentic followers and the outcomes of authentic leader-follower relationships included heightened levels of follower trust in the leader, enhanced engagement and workplace well-being, as well as more sustainable performance. Although this approach is commendable for including both leaders and followers in the development process, it is unclear what it offers beyond the well-established effects of leader-member exchange

(LMX) theory. Future tests of authentic leadership development will need to control for LMX in demonstrating a unique contribution to the establishment of authentic relationships.

Ilies, Morgeson, and Nahrgang (2005) presented a somewhat different model of authentic leader development that focused on the elements of authenticity and the processes through which authentic leadership contributes to the well-being of both leaders and followers. Authentic leaders are expected to consider multiple sides and multiple perspectives of an issue, and gather related information in a relatively balanced manner. Similar to what was proposed by Gardner et al. (2005), the focus is on positive modeling as the primary means used by authentic leaders to influence followers and to generate well-being as a positive outcome of authenticity.

Researchers have also stressed the importance of values and behaviors to the understanding and development of authentic leadership. In an investigation of the effects of emotions and values on leader authenticity, Michie and Gooty (2005) posited that emotions and values play a fundamental role in the emergence and development of authentic leadership. The authors' central thesis was that positive other-directed emotions (e.g., gratitude, appreciation) motivate authentic leaders to behave in ways that reflect self-transcendent values (e.g., honesty, loyalty, equality). By stressing the importance of emotions in understanding leadership and followership, this approach represented a somewhat different and novel perspective on the development of authentic leadership.

To further explore the boundary conditions of authentic leadership theory, Eagly (2005) presented a relational view of authenticity in arguing that much more is required of leaders than transparently conveying and acting on their values. Achieving relational authenticity is thought to require that followers afford leaders the legitimacy to promote a set of values on their behalf. Leaders are able to elicit the personal and social identification of followers only when these conditions exist. Eagly suggested that eliciting identification is more difficult for female than male leaders, as it is more generally for members of outsider groups (e.g., minorities, non-natives) who have not traditionally had access to leadership roles.

Because of the interactive effects of gender role and leader role requirements, achieving relational authenticity is challenging for many women in positions of authority. The development of women leaders should therefore focus on the relational aspects of achieving authenticity as a leader. Trends toward participative decision making and transformational leadership may also increase the probability that women and other outsiders will achieve success as leaders.

In a critique of authentic leadership approaches, Cooper, Scandura, and Schriesheim (2005) advised researchers in this area to learn from the mistakes made in other areas of leadership research. They suggested that the core propositions of this theory must first be tested by studying the developmental processes that encompass authentic leadership. Authentic leadership theory, therefore, must be examined through experimental investigations of the hypothesized relationships between its core development processes and essential theoretical constructs. Until the theory has been properly tested (including controlling for the effects of LMX), the authors warned against a rush to push authentic leadership development in practice.

5. Process Issues in Leadership Development

Researchers have also addressed the role of *process* in leader and leadership development (see Table 36.2 for a summary of this literature). Specifically, process factors are those that shape the rate or pattern of development over time. In general, these factors can emerge through organizational practices such as mentoring and coaching, 360-degree feedback, leadership training, job assignments, and action learning among others. In particular, research and theory appearing in *The Leadership Quarterly* has contributed significantly to shaping our scholarly understanding of feedback processes, especially 360-degree feedback. Other process factors related to leadership development that have received attention in this journal include self-other agreement (Fleenor, Smither, Atwater, Braddy, & Sturm, 2010) and the use of narratives and life stories (Ligon, Hunter, & Mumford, 2008; Shamir & Eilam, 2005).

5.1. Feedback as a Process of Development

Corresponding with the emergence of leadership development as a scholarly field of interest, the use of 360-degree feedback as a developmental process to foster self-awareness and competency development has become a major area of research. 360-degree feedback has become almost ubiquitous in organizations of every type (e.g., corporate, government, nonprofit, military, education) and is a prominent process for facilitating development. If used as intended, 360-degree feedback can help people understand systematically the impact of their behavior on others. In general, the approach gathers and reports on ratings of leader behavior and/or effectiveness from multiple sources such as subordinates, peers, bosses, and possibly even external stakeholders such as customers, in addition to self-ratings. These ratings are usually aggregated and therefore remain anonymous, with the exception of ratings provided by the supervisor. A major part of the feedback process is in understanding where the perceptions across different sources converge—as well as diverge—in their perceptions of a focal manager (Hoffman, Lance, Bynum, & Gentry, 2010). Attention is also given to how others' ratings correspond with a leader's self-ratings. The intended focus is typically on leader development but may also include an evaluative component in some organizations. As 360-degree feedback has evolved as an evidence-based process, much of its developmental focus is on identifying leadership skills and competencies that are perceived by various sources to be effective or ineffective.

Table 36.2   Process Issues in Leadership Development

Topics	Summary	Source
360-degree feedback	It is important to consider the pattern of strategic, organizational, and HR-related factors that must be integrated in order to link feedback results to organizational performance. Merely assuming that giving a leader feedback will result in a behavioral change, and ultimately organizational performance improvement, is overly simplistic.	Atwater and Waldman (1998)
	Leaders' reactions to 360-degree feedback vary as a function of the feedback content as well as other factors about the raters and the organizational climate, including whether or not recipients felt the organization was supportive of their developmental efforts.	Facteau et al. (1998)
	Leaders who are high self-monitors do not receive higher 360-degree feedback ratings, suggesting that the impression management styles of high self-monitors do not significantly influence360-degree ratings.	Warech et al. (1998)
	The administration of two feedback interventions has the ability to improve leader effectiveness more so than a single administration of a feedback intervention.	Seifert and Yukl (2010)
	In terms of how political leaders respond to criticism, others' supportive reactions are positively related to collaboration and persuasion strategies as a response to criticism, whereas diverting attention and persuasion are related to unsuccessful resolution of the issue.	Eubanks et al. (2010)

Topics	Summary	Source
	While most leadership development programs have improved leader effectiveness as an ultimate goal, the main roles associated with effective leadership differ according to who is being asked (e.g., focal manager, peers, subordinates, or bosses); hence, effectiveness may be in the eye of the beholder (or evaluator).	Hooijberg and Choi (2000)
Self-other agreement	Leaders who rate themselves similarly to how others rate them are likely to be more effective leaders.	Atwater and Yammarino (1992)
	Self-other agreement does not appear to be related to leadership effectiveness.	Fleenor et al. (1996)
	There is a link between rating agreement and leader effectiveness.	Atwater et al. (1998)
	Whereas self-other agreement appears to be related to leader effectiveness, its relationship to leadership outcomes is complex. Also, self-other agreement can be an important factor in increasing the self-perception accuracy or self-awareness of individuals participating in leadership development programs using multi-source assessments.	Fleenor et al. (2010)
Self-narrative	Authentic leaders can gain self-knowledge, self-concept clarity, and person-role merger, by constructing, developing, and revising the personal narratives they construct about themselves (i.e., life stories).	Shamir and Eilam (2005)
	Continuously revising and updating self-narratives as experiences accrue through written journals or other similar techniques can help enhance the effectiveness of programs and interventions that seek to increase self-awareness.	Sparrowe (2005)
	Various leader performance dimensions can be linked to certain types of experiences.	Ligon et al. (2008)
	For example, experiences that create optimistic views of others and empathy for their suffering are strongly related to outstanding leader performance.	

Because of the interconnected nature of leadership development with 360-degree feedback, these topics will be reviewed together. But to clarify their relationship, leadership development is inherently longitudinal in terms of studying individual and collective change over time; it is multilevel in focusing on intrapersonal and interpersonal changes; and 360-degree feedback is a process used to facilitate this development. It should also be made clear that 360-degree feedback is not a tool such as a personality assessment or other type of psychological inventory. Instead, it is a process of collecting multisource ratings, summarizing these data into an accessible format, and presenting these summaries as a way of fostering self-awareness and the development of individual leaders. This feedback process might be used with larger collectives such as teams and organizations, but its primary use is with individual leaders.

Although many of the articles pertaining to 360-degree feedback and leader development have been published in more practitioner-oriented journals, *The Leadership Quarterly* has published a variety of empirically-based articles on the subject of feedback and its relevance to leadership development. One of the fundamental components of effective leadership is self-awareness or self-understanding. Ashford (1989) wrote eloquently on the topic of feedback-seeking behavior and on the importance of recognizing how one is perceived by others in order to develop a more accurate self-view. This self-view subsequently shapes an understanding of one's own strengths and weaknesses, ultimately influencing decision-making and subsequent behavior. The importance of accurate self-assessment (i.e., enhanced self-awareness) has been extended recently to meta-perceptions, which concern not only how an individual views himself or herself and how others view that individual, but also how the individual thinks others view him or her (Taylor & Hood, 2011).

In the 1990s, interest in the process and outcomes of 360-degree feedback gathered momentum. The use of 360-degree feedback as a development tool was being implemented with varying degrees of success around the world and a number of research questions about what influenced its success were being asked. In an attempt to summarize and highlight what was known about 360-degree feedback from a scholarly perspective, Atwater and Waldman (1998) edited a special issue on 360-degree feedback and leadership development for *The Leadership Quarterly*. Unfortunately, implementation of 360-degree feedback was apparently ahead of research on its effectiveness in that only two studies were published on the topic in that special issue. But notably, this special issue was one of the first publications to highlight areas in which more research was needed on the use of 360-degree feedback for leadership development. Additionally, the issue was noteworthy for its focus on the potential impact of organizational culture on the implementation of 360-degree feedback processes.

In their introduction to the special issue, Atwater and Waldman (1998) recommended that researchers adopt configural approaches to 360-degree feedback by considering the pattern of strategic, organizational, and human resources-related factors that must be integrated in order to link feedback results to organizational performance. Merely assuming that giving a leader feedback will result in a behavioral change, and ultimately organizational performance improvement, is overly simplistic. Atwater and Waldman also suggested that researchers closely examine the link between 360-degree feedback and organizational culture. For example, 360-degree feedback initiatives may be effective only in organizations that have a culture of innovation, behaviorally-based appraisal practices, and developmental strategies. In an attempt to change their culture, some organizations may adopt 360-degree feedback in hopes that these practices will result in employees becoming more open, participative, and trusting. Nonetheless, it is an empirical question whether 360-degree feedback can have positive effects on organizational culture. It might be that a 360-degree feedback process would not be successful until the organization has an open, participative, and trusting culture. This was one of the areas in which the guest editors cited the need for more research on 360-degree feedback.

Another area in need of research was related to the determinants and consequences of developmental goal setting that arise as a result of receiving 360-degree feedback. In an attempt to partially address this need, Facteau, Facteau, Schoel, Russell, and Poteet (1998) examined factors related to leaders' reactions to 360-degree feedback. Positive reactions to feedback are an important element in the success of 360-degree feedback in that such reactions likely result in leaders seeking additional feedback and setting developmental goals, both of which are critical to fostering development. Lacking favorable reactions to the feedback, positive behavior change is unlikely to occur.

Facteau et al. (1998) hypothesized that higher overall other ratings, organizational support, and perceived rater ability would be positively related to the reactions of feedback recipients (acceptance and perceived usefulness of peer and subordinate feedback). Their findings were somewhat mixed. Although they found that overall ratings were positively related to the acceptance of feedback, these ratings were not consistently related to perceived feedback usefulness. For example, the recipient may be very accepting of positive ratings but not find them terribly useful. Whether the feedback was perceived as useful had more to do with the degree to which the recipients felt the organization was supportive of their developmental efforts. Overall, this study provided early evidence that leaders' reactions to 360-degree feedback vary as a function of the feedback itself as well as other factors about the raters and the organizational climate. Differences in the reactions of the participants to the feedback, therefore, were not simply attributable to the overall ratings provided to these leaders. The study concluded that organizations that wish to implement successful 360-degree feedback systems will need to consider all of the various factors that may contribute to the leaders' reactions to feedback.

Reporting on the positive effects of 360-degree feedback for leadership development, Warech, Smither, Reilly, Millsap, and Reilly (1998) studied the relationship between leader self-monitoring, personality, and 360-degree feedback ratings from peers and subordinates. This was an important question to address because it would be disconcerting if a leader's degree of self-monitoring (i.e., the desire and ability to fashion a positive image for a particular situation) explained a large amount of variance in 360-degree ratings. That is, if self-monitoring and 360-degree ratings were highly related it might be concluded that such ratings were manipulated to some extent by the impression management styles of high self-monitors. Encouragingly, the authors found that leaders who were high self-monitors did not receive higher overall ratings, thus providing some assurances that 360-degree feedback ratings reflected mainly perceptions of leadership behaviors rather than the result of active impression management.

Atwater and Waldman (1998) recognized that these studies made significant contributions to our understanding of 360-degree feedback and leadership development but stressed that much more work remained to be done in this area. In particular, it was suggested that future research should focus more squarely on the outcomes of 360-degree feedback. Examples of such outcomes included: (a) the extent to which 360-degree feedback initiatives can affect organizational performance; (b) how often 360-degree feedback should be administered to maintain participant interest and continue the developmental process; and (c) the points in leaders' careers at which

360-degree feedback will have the most impact. For the most part, these still remain important but largely unexamined research questions.

Seifert and Yukl (2010) did address one of the questions posed above in terms of repetition of the feedback process. They conducted a longitudinal field experiment of middle managers in which half of the managers received one developmental workshop including 360-degree feedback and the other half participated in a follow-up workshop where they received feedback a second time. In each workshop they were provided with a feedback report of their self and other ratings of their influence tactics, as well as a discussion to help them understand the results of the feedback and ways to use it to more effectively influence others in the future. The managers' overall effectiveness was measured pre-feedback as well as post-feedback. The pre-feedback effectiveness ratings did not differ in the two groups; however, at the second measurement period those who participated in two feedback processes were rated as significantly more effective following feedback than those who received feedback only once. This suggests that additional resources allocated to the feedback process (e.g., doubling the number of feedback sessions) has the potential to improve leader effectiveness. A question that deserves future research attention concerns whether there is compelling economic or financial utility associated with increasing the number of feedback sessions provided to a leader.

Eubanks et al. (2010) took a different approach to looking at feedback in examining how political leaders respond to criticism. They used a historiometric approach to study biographies of 120 world leaders and how the response strategies to the criticism used by the leader related to success in terms of follower reactions and resolution of an issue. Their results demonstrated that others' supportive reactions were positively related to collaboration and persuasion strategies as a response to criticism, whereas diverting attention and persuasion were related to unsuccessful resolution of the issue. Regarding the ultimate conclusion of the event, both collaboration and confrontation were positively related to the outcome although confrontation was also negatively related to unsupportive reactions by others. It is interesting to speculate about strategies that have differing results for popular opinion versus effective resolution. One could speculate that strategies such as persuasion might be used to influence attitudes while ineffectively resolving the issue. The authors suggested that future research might examine events in which leaders receive praise, the types of behaviors that are praised, as well as follower reactions to the praise. In the political arena—especially in democratic countries—criticism and praise will likely elicit very different reactions depending on whether or not members are from one's own political party or an adversarial party.

Most leadership development programs target, as an ultimate goal, improved leader effectiveness. But the question arises: effectiveness according to whom? Hooijberg and Choi (2000) discovered that the main roles associated with effective leadership differ according to who is being asked (e.g., focal manager, peers, subordinates, or bosses). For example, when considering a monitoring role, focal managers and their subordinates found this to be an important leadership role whereas peers and superiors did not. As another example, the role of facilitator was seen as a component of effectiveness from the perspective of subordinates and peers but not from the perspective of bosses or the managers themselves. These findings provide potentially important implications to the leadership development process because they reinforce the idea that effectiveness may be in the eye of the beholder (or evaluator). Are we developing leaders to align with what superiors or subordinates find to be most important? Is it possible to develop a leader who can succeed in all roles? Hooijberg and Choi suggested that 360-degree feedback is a good starting place for managers in understanding the differing expectations of various constituency groups.

5.2. Self-other Agreement as a Process of Development

A debate emerged in the mid-1990s on the topic of self-other agreement (SOA) in ratings and its role in contributing to leader effectiveness. Atwater and Yammarino's (1992) conclusion that leaders who rated themselves similarly to how others rated them were likely be more effective leaders was questioned (Fleenor, McCauley, & Brutus, 1996). According to Atwater and Yammarino, so-called over-estimators who rate themselves higher than do others may inaccurately over-estimate their strengths and underestimate their weaknesses, which could adversely affect their leadership effectiveness. Using a categorization scheme that included level of performance (i.e., good versus poor), Fleenor et al. reported that self-other agreement was unrelated to leadership effectiveness. Unfortunately, the categorization approach that was used suffered from methodological shortcomings (e.g., dichotomizing or otherwise truncating continuous data). Using more sophisticated analyses such as polynomial regression, Atwater, Ostroff, Yammarino, and Fleenor (1998) found relationships between rating agreement and leader effectiveness; however, the relationship was more complex than originally believed.

In a review of the literature on self-other rating agreement, Fleenor et al. (2010) addressed some of these complexities including issues influencing SOA, as well as optimal measurement and analytic techniques for studying this phenomenon. An important conclusion of this review was that whereas self-other agreement was generally related to leader effectiveness, its relationship to various leadership outcomes was not as straightforward. For example, although self-raters who are in agreement with others' ratings are generally most effective, in some contexts over- and under-estimators can be effective. Another conclusion was that self-other agreement can be an important factor in increasing the self-perception accuracy or self-awareness of individuals participating in leadership development programs that use 360-degree feedback or other types of multisource assessments.

Fleenor et al. (2010) also addressed the implications of using sophisticated analytic tools (e.g., polynomial regression) to study self-other agreement. Although psychometrically the most precise of the available techniques for testing hypotheses about SOA, techniques such as polynomial regression are not very useful for providing feedback on self-other agreement to participants in leader development programs. Instead, simpler and more straightforward approaches are recommended. For example, using comparisons of self-ratings to mean ratings across other rater groups (e.g., subordinates or peers) is useful; however, inter-rater agreement should be assessed prior to using mean ratings. An additional suggestion for optimizing the value of 360-degree feedback to leaders was to provide rater training and incentives to raters to guide them in providing quality feedback. Moreover, the anonymity of raters, especially subordinates, is critical in reducing fears of retribution. As mentioned earlier, the role of the rater and his or her definition of effectiveness should also be considered in interpreting 360-degree feedback ratings.

5.3. Self-narrative as a Process of Development

In addition to investigating how the 360-degree feedback and SOA processes can contribute to leadership development, Shamir and Eilam (2005) advanced a self-narrative approach in which leaders' self-stories contribute to their ongoing development. Leaders wrote personal narratives about themselves (i.e., life stories) to help provide insight into the self-relevant meanings they attach to their life experiences. The authors focused on authentic leadership and suggested that by constructing, developing, and revising their life stories, leaders gain self-knowledge, self-concept clarity, and person-role merger, which are necessary elements in their development as authentic leaders. As noted by the authors, "leaders gain authenticity when they act and justify their actions on the basis of the meaning system provided by their life-stories" (p. 396).

Complementing this life-story approach, Sparrowe (2005) offered an explanation of the narrative process through which a leader's authentic self emerges. This perspective is grounded in hermeneutic philosophy (the theory and study of interpretation), proposing that individuals are able to construct their identities from their interpretations of self-narratives created based on their life experiences. An important aspect of these self-narratives is to continuously revise and update them as experiences accrue. Doing so through written journals or other similar techniques can help enhance the effectiveness of programs and interventions that seek to increase self-awareness.

Ligon et al. (2008) also considered the role of hermeneutic philosophy in leadership development. Rather than relying on leaders to interpret their own narratives, these researchers analyzed and coded the developmental events from the early lives of outstanding leaders as chronicled in their biographies. The results supported the proposition that outstanding leaders rely on past experience to assist their sense-making efforts. Although this may seem unsurprising, it suggests that leaders may be engaged in assimilating recent experiences with past experiences in building a coherent personal narrative or life story. Also, patterns of early experiences emerged that distinguished leaders based upon their leadership orientation (socialized or personalized) or style (charismatic, ideological, or pragmatic). For instance, socialized leaders had relatively more experiences that helped to anchor their core values, whereas personalized leadership resulted more from "a life riddled with instability and uncertainty" (p. 329). Ligon et al.'s findings regarding leadership style also suggested that ideological leaders tended to make decisions based on the beliefs and values they formed through early anchoring events, rather than engaging in more proactive fact-finding and analysis activities. Conversely, pragmatic leaders tended to make decisions based on facts and analysis, due in part to "originating" events at the beginning of their careers that helped define their long-term goals and plans for action. Moreover, charismatic leaders were found to have experienced more turning-point or life-redirecting events during their formative years. Finally, and perhaps most interestingly, the study demonstrated that various dimensions of leader performance were related to certain types of experiences. For instance, having had experiences that create optimistic views of others and empathy for their suffering is strongly related to outstanding performance. Consistent with the implications noted by others (e.g., Shamir & Eilam, 2005; Sparrowe, 2005), Ligon and colleagues underscored the importance of the life narrative and its theoretical and practical implications for leadership development research and practice.

6. Longitudinal Perspectives on Leadership Development

As noted previously in this review, the nature of leadership development is inherently multilevel and longitudinal (Day, 2011). Thus, it is important for scholars to map and understand intra- and inter-personal change patterns of leaders over time (see Table 36.3 for a summary and overview). In an attempt to demonstrate the significance of longitudinal research in studying leadership development, Day, Gronn, and Salas (2004) provided a theoretical model outlining how individual leader and follower skills and attributes could contribute to building team leadership capacity. From this model, it was shown how the development of leadership capacity over time can provide for significant leadership resources at subsequent performance episodes. As such, the importance of longitudinal studies was highlighted. This model also was one of the first to attempt to link individual human capital inputs to the development of teamwork, social capital, and shared leadership capacity, among other things. In further elaborating on the longitudinal nature of leader and leadership development, we next focus on conceptual articles related to the longitudinal nature of leadership development as well as the empirical studies described in a special issue of *The Leadership Quarterly* dedicated to longitudinal research.

Table 36.3	Longitudinal Research in Leadership Development	
Topics	*Summary*	*Source*
Developmental theories	Transactional and transformational leader development involves episodic skill acquisition combined with adult constructive development. Feedback enables the evolution of individuals' intellectual capacities, values, and beliefs.	Russell and Kuhnert (1992)
	Team leadership capacity is an outcome of team processes such as teamwork and team learning, which in turn contribute to team member resources such as knowledge, skills, and abilities, helping to shape subsequent performance.	Day et al. (2004)
	Mixed support was found that a leader's order of development influences his or her leadership effectiveness and performance.	McCauley et al. (2006)
	A leader's stage of development is a significant predictor of performance ratings.	Strang and Kuhnert (2009)
	Future developmental experiences and leadership effectiveness are associated with early learning and leadership experiences, as well as developmental factors including temperament, gender, parenting styles, and attachment styles.	Murphy and Johnson (2011)
Longitudinal studies	True longitudinal studies involve the measurement of the same indicators of leadership at multiple points in time; quasi-longitudinal studies measure predictors early in time and assess their impact on leadership outcomes at a later time.	Day (2011)
	Adolescent extraversion is a significant predictor of adult leader emergence and self-ratings of transformational leadership.	Reichard et al. (2011)
	Academic intrinsic motivation during childhood and adolescence is a significant predictor of intrinsic motivation to lead during adulthood.	Gottfried et al. (2011)

Topics	Summary	Source
	Adolescent extraversion, especially when coupled with social skills, is associated with greater leadership potential.	Guerin et al. (2011)
	Subclinical traits are important moderators of the rate of leader development.	Harms et al. (2011)
	While some subclinical traits (i.e., skeptical and imaginative) have a negative relationship with leader development in a military setting others (i.e., cautious, bold, and dutiful) had a positive relationship.	
	Intelligence is a poor predictor of leadership outcomes. Self-esteem is a strong predictor of leadership role occupancy.	Li et al. (2011)
	Enhanced self-esteem mediates the relationship between positive parenting and leadership potential.	Oliver et al. (2011)
	A strong leader identity acts as a time-varying covariate of leadership effectiveness.	Day and Sin (2011)
	An individual's learning goal orientation may also serve as a moderator of developmental trajectories. Evidence from this study suggests two different classes of developmental trajectories.	

6.1. Developmental Theories Applied to Leader Development

In an early conceptual article that considered issues of development over time, Russell and Kuhnert (1992) created a model of leader development based on the integration of three different approaches. Specifically, they combined Kanfer and Ackerman's (1989) episodic model of skill acquisition with Kegan's (1982) approach to adult development based on constructive-developmental theory (McCauley, Drath, Palus, O'Connor, & Baker, 2006), while also incorporating the development of transactional and transformational leadership into the model. Feedback mechanisms were next added to the model to explain changes in leaders' intellectual capacities, values, and beliefs over time. An important contribution of this approach was the crafting of a longitudinal theoretical perspective on leader development through the integration of literatures on skill acquisition, adult development, and leadership.

Russell and Kuhnert's (1992) framework provided a summary of what was known at that time about the processes underlying developmental change related to how leaders understand and act on their environment. With this framework, the authors went beyond the contributions made in individual disciplines (e.g., learning theory, individual differences, performance models) to encompass diverse research from the skill acquisition, human development, and personnel selection literatures. The article provided a framework for future research on how transactional and transformational leaders develop, which led to more systematic investigations of the experiences that contribute to the development of leaders.

McCauley et al. (2006) reviewed the literature on constructive-developmental theory and its relevance for understanding and predicting leader effectiveness. Constructive-developmental theory is a suite of different theories portraying stage theories of adult development. These approaches are mainly concerned with how a person's understanding of self and the world becomes more elaborated and complex over time. There are two main features of development considered from this theoretical perspective. The first concerns so-called *orders of development* (also referred to as levels of psychosocial development), which are organizing principles that guide how individuals gain understanding of themselves and the external world. Successive orders of development build on and transcend the previous orders such that development is from simpler to more complex and interconnected ways of sense-making. The second feature concerns *developmental movement* involving the change from one order of development to another, usually a higher one, driven by new environmental challenges that demand more complex sense-making abilities.

Constructive-developmental theory has been used sporadically in research in the area of leadership development, usually assuming that a leader's order of development influences his or her leadership effectiveness or managerial performance. Constructive-developmental theory delineates six discrete stages of human development based on the notion that individual differences are a product of how individuals construct or arrange experiences relating to themselves and their social environments (McCauley et al., 2006). One such study examined the psychosocial development of a sample of West Point cadets over a four-year time period. They found evidence of positive constructive development changes in approximately half of the cadets in the sample and that higher levels of development were positively related to various peer, subordinate, and superior measures of cadet performance as leaders in their junior and senior years (Bartone, Snook, Forsythe, Lewis, & Bullis, 2007). Despite the generally supportive findings of the Bartone et al.'s (2007) study, in general the proposition about higher levels of development being associated with better leadership effectiveness has found at best mixed support in the empirical literature. McCauley et al. (2006) called for more research integrating constructive-developmental theory with other relevant streams, moving beyond the focus on developmental order to include dynamics of developmental movement, and examining how the theory might relate to teams and organizations.

In an attempt to answer this call for more integrative research utilizing constructive-developmental theory, Strang and Kuhnert (2009) investigated the application of this theory along with individual personality to examine their effects on leader performance as measured by 360-degree (i.e., multisource) ratings. In a study of 67 management executives who participated in an executive development program, the authors examined constructive-developmental stage (conceptualized as Leadership Developmental Level; LDL) as a predictor of multisource leader performance ratings. They found that LDL was a significant predictor of performance ratings from all rater sources (subordinates, peers, and supervisors). More importantly though, they also tested the incremental predictive ability of LDL compared to the Big Five personality factors. Their results indicated that LDL accounted for unique variance in leader performance beyond that accounted for by personality (when using the leader performance ratings from subordinates and peers); however, they cautioned that this relationship was relatively weak. Nonetheless, constructive-developmental theory provides a unique contribution to our current understanding of leadership and represents a fruitful avenue for future leadership development research.

Taking a different perspective based on childhood antecedents of leader development, Murphy and Johnson (2011) examined the so-called seeds of leader development that germinate and root at various stages before adulthood. They suggested that relevant developmental experiences may occur more readily during sensitive periods of childhood and adolescence, which influence development during adulthood. The authors advanced a framework that considers the influence of early developmental factors on leader identity and self-regulation, which have a relationship to future developmental experiences and leadership effectiveness. In this framework, early developmental factors including genetics, temperament, gender, parenting styles, attachment styles, and early learning and as well as early learning leadership experiences such as those associated with education and sports were important to the leader development process. This framework is immersed in contextual factors such as the individual's developmental stage, societal expectations, and the historical setting. The authors ultimately argued for additional longitudinal examinations of leadership development over the lifespan as a means to help advance current leader development practices.

6.2. Longitudinal Studies of Leadership Development

A 2011 special issue of *The Leadership Quarterly* devoted to longitudinal studies of leadership development represented an important milestone in establishing further evidence for leader development processes and the individual difference factors that shape them. The articles in the issue supported the assertion that leaders are products of their life experiences beginning at an early age; however, multiple forces affect leaders' development during their respective life spans. For example, personality characteristics can play an important role in the early development of leaders whereas experience plays a more important role in adulthood. This special issue emphasized the importance of early leader development and the need for more long-term, longitudinal studies of leadership development. Taken together, the research presented in the special issue addressed several key questions related to how leadership develops, including: (a) how do the dispositional characteristics of individuals (e.g., intelligence, temperament, and personality) influence development as leaders, (b) what role do life experiences play in the development of leaders, (c) do early leader development efforts help to develop future leaders in organizations and communities, and (d) what are some individual difference factors that shape the trajectories of leader development?

Three major longitudinal databases were used in several of the articles in this issue. The Fullerton Longitudinal Study (FLS) started in 1979 with 130 one-year-olds and their families. For the first four years, these children were assessed semi-annually and then annually until they reached the age of 17. Data collection in this program is ongoing. Longitudinal data from United States Military Academy at West Point was collected that focused on the leader development of military cadets over the course of their time at the Academy. The U.S. Department of Labor's National Longitudinal Survey of Youth 1979 (NLSY79) tracked young people born between 1957 and 1964, and first interviewed in 1979.

Three of the special issue articles focused on the effects of personality on leadership development. Using the Fullerton database, Reichard et al. (2011)

investigated how the five-factor model of personality (neuroticism, extraversion, openness, conscientiousness, and agreeableness) and intelligence were related to leader emergence and transformational leadership. They found that personality traits predicted leader emergence in early adults. Of the five personality factors, extraversion was the best predictor of leader emergence and self-ratings of transformational leadership. Surprisingly, intelligence was only related to non-work leader emergence. The authors stressed the need for exposure to leadership opportunities for both extraverted and introverted youth to help them develop more fully as leaders in adulthood.

Continuing with the Fullerton data, Gottfried et al. (2011) looked at academic intrinsic motivation (motivation for and enjoyment of school learning without external rewards) during childhood and adolescence as a predictor of three aspects of motivation to lead during adulthood. The three aspects of motivation to lead included two intrinsic motives (affective identity motivation and non-calculative motivation) and one extrinsic motivation (social normative motivation). *Affective identity motivation* to lead concerns the enjoyment of leading, *non-calculative motivation* concerns leading for its own sake and not for the purpose of receiving external advantages, and *social normative motivation* concerns leading to fulfill one's duty. The first two of these motives to lead are intrinsic in nature, whereas the third is guided by external forces. The study revealed that academic intrinsic motivation was highly related to the affective identity and non-calculative components of motivation to lead, supporting the authors' contention that intrinsic motivation is a state that exhibits continuity over the lifetime. Children and adolescents who exhibit academic intrinsic motivation are more likely to become adults who are intrinsically motivated to become leaders. Accordingly, academic intrinsic motivation was unrelated to social normative motivation. In a recurring theme, leader intelligence was of no consequence in predicting motivation to lead.

In a related article, Guerin et al. (2011) focused on the roles of extraversion and intelligence in predicting leadership outcomes. This study explored the early antecedents of extraversion by investigating behavior and temperament in childhood. Extraverted adolescents—especially those who possessed good social skills—showed greater leadership potential, whereas intelligence did not appear to be predictive of leadership potential.

Also using data from FLS, Oliver and associates (2011) examined the role of supportive parenting in adolescence and transformational leadership in young adults. They found that the relationship between positive parenting and leadership potential was mediated by enhanced self-esteem. Quality parenting and self-esteem were measured during adolescence and self-reported transformational leadership was assessed at age 29 while controlling for the effects of socioeconomic status. This study represented one of the first attempts to investigate these relationships across time. Results supported the hypothesis that a stimulating and supportive environment provided by an adolescent's family created a more positive self-concept, which in turn positively influenced the subsequent emergence of transformational leader qualities. Thus, the content of familial support during adolescence was related to self-rated leadership outcomes as an adult.

Taking a different approach to examining personality in leadership development research, Harms, Spain, and Hannah's (2011) study went beyond typical personality assessments (e.g., Big Five) in exploring the role of subclinical personality traits on leadership development over time. The authors argued that there is a need for empirical research using large samples of developing leaders over time to examine the potential influence of personality traits in general, and what they see as character flaws in particular, and their respective influences on leader development. Specifically, Harms et al. were interested in idiosyncratic (i.e., subclinical) traits that do not greatly inhibit daily functioning (as would clinical traits or those used to diagnose psychological pathologies) yet have the potential to lead to negative consequences in certain contexts. Examples include subclinical traits of excitable, skeptical, leisurely (e.g., indifferent to requests of others), colorful (e.g., expressive, dramatic, wants to be noticed), and imaginative (e.g., acting or thinking in unusual ways).

Using the West Point database, Harms et al. (2011) studied a leader development program that had demonstrated an overall positive effect on participants over a span of three years. The authors found subclinical traits to be important moderators of the rate of leader development (i.e., developmental trajectories) during the program, accounting for 11–17% of the variance in the changes in leader development. Whereas the authors found that some of the subclinical traits (i.e., skeptical and imaginative) had negative relationships with leader development, they also found that others (i.e., cautious, bold, colorful, and dutiful) had positive relationships. This provides somewhat of a mixed message with regard to subclinical traits, indicating that they may not always have negative influences on leader development. (It should be noted that these relationships were found in a student military sample where traits such as imaginative may not be highly regarded while dutiful would be.) The results of this study also demonstrated that leader development persists over numerous years and that the effects of personality on this process endure over time. From these results, Harms and colleagues proposed that leader development is a dynamic process in which personality factors moderate developmental processes through enhancing or inhibiting personal change over time. They suggested that with additional research, leadership interventions and executive training programs might be tailored to the specific needs or characteristics of the leader.

Consistent with the individual difference focus of other articles in this issue, Li, Arvey, and Song (2011) investigated the effect of general mental ability, self-esteem, and familial socioeconomic status on leadership role occupancy (whether an individual occupies a leadership role) and leader advancement (an increase in supervisory scope assessed by the number of assigned subordinates). Additionally, gender was examined as a moderating variable. Using the NLSY79 database, Li et al. found that developmental outcomes were not strongly related to general mental ability (a consistent theme across several studies in the special issue). Specifically, they found self-esteem to be strongly predictive of leadership role occupancy across both genders as well as predictive of the rate of leadership advancement for females. An unusual and unexpected finding was that familial socioeconomic status was negatively related to leader advancement for women. It is unclear why this would be the case (i.e., women from higher socioeconomic families having lower levels of development) and replication of this finding is needed before any strong conclusions can be drawn.

Day and Sin (2011) offered yet another perspective on leader development, focusing on developmental trajectories of emerging leaders over a 13-week time span. Within this paradigm, individuals were hypothesized to vary in terms of initial leadership effectiveness levels and follow different developmental trajectories based on different situational and experiential demands, as well as their willingness and ability to learn. The authors found support for the contention that because of its hypothesized impact on individual thinking and behavior assuming a strong leader identity would function as a within-person, time-varying covariate of leadership effectiveness. This echoes the focus on self-identity proposed by authors such as Lord and Hall (2005). Results partially supported an additional hypothesis that an individual's learning goal orientation (an orientation that focuses on one's development rather than demonstrations of competence) would serve as a between-person, cross-level moderator of developmental trajectories, suggesting that how individuals construct and manage goals can affect their development as leaders.

In an integrative review of the articles addressed in this special issue, Day (2011) discussed the difference between true longitudinal investigations of leadership development and what he termed to be quasi-longitudinal studies (following the distinction made between experimental and quasi-experimental designs). True longitudinal studies involve the measurement of the same indicators of leadership at a minimum of three points in time, whereas quasi-longitudinal studies measure predictors early in time and assess their impact on leadership outcomes at a later time. As noted by Day, both methods have value because they each take a long-lens approach to understanding leadership development and the process of developing leaders over time. Guest Editors

Riggio and Mumford (2011) concluded by stating their wishes that this special issue would: (a) encourage more longitudinal research on leader development; (b) draw attention to existing longitudinal databases that are useful for studying the lifelong development of leadership; and (c) encourage more evaluation of leadership development efforts through the use of true longitudinal designs.

7. Evaluation Methods in Leadership Development

A significant obstacle to advancing scholarly interest in leader and leadership development over the years can be traced to methodological and analytical issues. In the 1970s, prominent psychologists and psychometricians (e.g., Cronbach & Furby, 1970) questioned whether we could, or even should, attempt to measure change. Since that time the field has advanced rapidly in understanding ways to measure and model change appropriately. We now know much more about longitudinal methods as well as multilevel modeling than we did even a decade ago. And given the multilevel and longitudinal nature of leadership development (Day, 2011), these are critically important contributions further motivating the advancement of scholarly interest in the topic (see Table 36.4 for a summary).

But it is also important to bring rigorous evaluation methods to understanding content, process, and outcome issues in development. As such, the *evaluation* of developmental interventions is another area that has received theoretical and empirical attention in this journal. In evaluating the effects of leadership development interventions, it should be noted that focusing on job performance and performance change over time is not the most appropriate approach to understanding the development of leaders or leadership. Job performance is affected by many things other than leadership skills. In other words, it is a contaminated as well as deficient criterion if the focus is purportedly on leadership development. Changes in job performance may also have different time lags associated with change compared to those for development. Thus, the appropriate criterion for evaluation efforts is development and its markers rather than performance per se. The field needs to focus on identifying and tracking appropriate markers or proxies of development that go beyond a fixation on rated job performance.

A special issue of *The Leadership Quarterly,* on the evaluation of leadership development interventions was co-edited by Hannum and Craig (2010). Because of the conceptual and measurement challenges inherent in this type of research, evaluating leadership development is often a complex undertaking. Evaluations of leadership development efforts are made more difficult by the contexts in which they occur. For example, participants in leader development programs may represent different organizations, different functional positions, and position levels, which create difficulties in identifying appropriate control groups and conducting rigorous evaluation studies. Additionally, there may be long time periods between interventions and outcome measurements.

Although evaluation methods exist that can meet these challenges, few published studies have focused on the application of these techniques in estimating the behavioral, psychological, or financial effects associated with leadership development initiatives. The aim of this special issue was to present research that demonstrated such methods. Described below are a number of articles from this issue that were particularly innovative.

Three articles offered specific techniques for evaluating leadership development interventions. Following Day's (2000) thinking about the role of social capital in leadership effectiveness, Hoppe and Reinelt (2010) described how Social Network Analysis (SNA) can identify the structure of relationships among people, goals, interests, and other entities within an organization. SNA, for example, can be used to determine if a leadership development intervention resulted in changes in connectivity in an organization. Additionally, the authors presented a typology for classifying different kinds of leadership networks, along with outcomes typically associated with each type of network.

The use of Q-methodology as a data collection tool for evaluating an initiative to develop collective

Table 36.4   Evaluation Methods in Leadership Development

Topics	Summary	Source
Social network analysis	Social Network Analysis (SNA) can identify the structure of relationships among people, goals, interests, and other entities within an organization.	Hoppe and Reinelt (2010)
Q-methodology	Q-methodology can be an effective method for soliciting participants' perceptions of outcomes. This method can reduce the individual viewpoints of the participants down to a few factors depicting shared ways of thinking about outcomes.	Militello and Benham (2010)
Formative and summative evaluation	Mixed methods including both summative evaluation and formative evaluation can be used to evaluate leader self-development.	Orvis and Ratwani (2010)
Hierarchical linear modeling	Hierarchical linear modeling (HLM) can be used to assess multilevel change over time in a leadership development context.	Gentry and Martineau (2010)
Return on leadership development investment	A method for estimating the return on leadership development investment (RODI) was proposed, along with implications for measuring organizational effectiveness.	Avolio et al. (2010)

leadership was described by Militello and Benham (2010). According to the authors, Q-methodology can be an effective method for soliciting participants' perceptions of outcomes. One purpose of this method is to reduce the individual viewpoints of the participants down to a few factors depicting shared ways of thinking about outcomes. It began with the development of a set of statements (the Q-sample) that would be sorted into categories by the participants. To develop the Q-sample, researchers reviewed documents detailing the mission and goals of the initiative being evaluated. They selected statements that were outcome oriented and descriptive of the initiative, which resulted in a Q-sample consisting of 33 statements. Participants then sorted these statements into outcome categories for the purpose of evaluating leader development. This methodology provided a valuable leadership development tool for participants and an evaluation tool for researchers.

Relatedly, Orvis and Ratwani (2010) highlighted the application and integration of formative and summative evaluation approaches for leader self-development. Because of the highly individualized nature of self-development, evaluators often face unique challenges when evaluating these initiatives. They recommended using a mixed-methods approach that applies effectiveness attribute taxonomy for a self-development activity. The authors demonstrated a methodology for applying this taxonomy to evaluate the effectiveness of self-development activities and discussed the practical implications of adopting the taxonomy for evaluation purposes.

Two articles in this issue described statistically based approaches to leadership development evaluation. Gentry and Martineau (2010) presented an application of hierarchical linear modeling (HLM) for assessing multilevel change over time in a leadership development context. One of the difficulties in evaluating leadership development is measuring whether and how participants change during the initiative. Even when change is an integral part of the design and evaluation of the initiative, uncontrolled events (e.g., missing data) may affect the ability of the evaluators to accurately measure change over time. Using data from a longitudinal school team leadership development initiative, the researchers used HLM procedures to examine changes that occurred across participating teams. The results demonstrated how to detect whether teams were significantly different on an initial assessment and predicted progress using an intercept-as-outcomes analysis. It also demonstrated how to detect whether growth rates were different across teams and how these changes could be predicted using a slopes-as-outcomes analysis. An advantage of this type of evaluation approach is that it allows researchers to examine and test whether successful teams improved at faster rates than other teams, rather than merely performing better at the start of the initiative.

In another statistical approach to evaluation, a method for estimating the return on leadership development investment (RODI) was proposed (Avolio, Avey, & Quisenberry, 2010), along with its implications for measuring organizational effectiveness. The authors suggested that the decision-making process involved in deciding to invest in leadership development should be similar to the decision-making process used by organizations whenever there is a decision to incur costs for an anticipated future benefit. The authors described how to estimate the return on leadership development using different assumptions, scenarios, length of the intervention, and level of participants engaged in the development program. They found that the expected return on investment from leadership development interventions ranged from a low negative RODI to over 200% depending on a number of factors.

Taken together, the articles published in this special issue on the evaluation of leadership development initiatives provided state-of-the-science perspectives on the design, analysis, and interpretation of evaluation research. It is invariably stated that any leadership development initiative must include an evaluation component. Unfortunately, this admonition is often ignored in practice. This special issue provided a "way forward" for helping researchers and practitioners involved with leadership development by providing sound advice to more fully integrate evaluation in their interventions and why doing so is critical.

8. Summary and Future Directions

The purpose of this review was to identify scholarly advances and contributions to the field of leadership development published mainly in *The Leadership Quarterly* over its 25-year history. We reviewed both conceptual and empirical articles that collectively examined definitional, content, process, longitudinal, and evaluation issues concerning leader and leadership development. In terms of operationalizing leadership development, Day (2000) posits that leadership is a complex interaction between people and environments that emerges through social systems. He recommends that scholars and practitioners approach leadership development as a process that transcends but does not replace individual leader development. Building upon earlier reviews of the field, the present review provides an in-depth look at how the leadership development field (including that of leader development) has evolved.

The major insights from the review can be summarized as follows: through the examination of an array of factors including experience, skills, personality, self-development, social mechanisms, 360-degree feedback, self-other agreement, and self-narratives, leadership development represents a dynamic process involving multiple interactions that persist over time. The leadership development process tends to start at a young age and is partly influenced by parental modeling. It involves the development and application of a variety of skills (e.g., wisdom, intelligence, and creativity; Sternberg, 2008) and is shaped by factors such as personality and relationships with others. The overall developmental process can be informed by different theories, such as constructive-developmental theory (McCauley et al., 2006) and authentic leadership (Gardner et al., 2005), and can be measured in a variety of ways including multi-source ratings. Wherever possible, developmental practices should be carefully tailored to current developmental needs of the leader.

Leadership is something that all organizations care about. But what most interests them is not which leadership theory or model is "right" (which may never be settled definitively), but how to develop

leaders and leadership as effectively and efficiently as possible. As such, this is an important area of scholarly research and application with myriad unanswered (and even undiscovered) questions to pursue. We next outline some promising avenues for future research.

8.1. Process-oriented Research

Because leadership development is a field that is inherently longitudinal in nature, researchers need to focus on conceptualizing process theories related to the development of leaders and leadership over time and testing these models using relevant methodologies. Leadership as a field has perhaps been preoccupied with proposing and testing static models, even those that hypothesize mediation (i.e., causal) effects. Simply put, cross-sectional methods are incomplete and probably inappropriate for testing hypotheses and research questions related to leadership development. This puts a burden on researchers given the difficulties associated with conducting longitudinal research. But if leadership is a process and not a position, and leadership development is a longitudinal process involving possibly the entire lifespan, then we need to put forward comprehensive process models and test them appropriately.

8.2. Choosing Relevant Outcome Variables

Researchers need to give serious thought to what is hypothesized to develop as a function of leader or leadership development in a given context. This may involve human capital kinds of variables related to individual knowledge, skills, and abilities, or it maybe things that are even more difficult to assess such as the psychosocial stage of adult development (i.e., orders of development) as proposed in constructive-developmental theory (McCauley et al., 2006). Adopting good outcomes (in place of job performance) to study models of leader and leadership development is also important. Of course, there should be a link between development and performance in a job or role but that is likely neither immediate nor straightforward. Related to the use of job performance, another outcome of questionable relevance to studies of leader development is the organizational position or role one holds (i.e., leadership role occupancy). As noted, leadership is conceptualized as a process rather than a position, so using position as an outcome in leader development research has limited meaning (Day, 2011). Although it may be convenient to use such outcomes, it is unclear how to compare positions across different organizations or sectors (e.g., corporate, military, government, or nonprofit). Researchers should always clarify what it is they think will develop over the period that they plan to study leader development processes. In this way, linking process models with relevant outcomes is a pressing research need.

8.3. Focus on Personal Trajectories of Development

It has been noted that "one central challenge facing scientific psychology is the development of comprehensive accounts of why humans progress along different life trajectories" (Smith, 2009, p. 419). A related challenge in the leader development field is crafting comprehensive accounts of why individuals progress along different developmental trajectories as leaders. The good news is that we now have the methods and analytical techniques to appropriately chart and understand these kinds of developmental trajectories. However, we need more in the way of theories and process models to guide our research. Examining different trajectories of development is a related and important concern. There is likely little argument that people start at different places in their developmental journeys as leaders and develop at different rates and in different ways over time. For these reasons, we need to more fully examine individual differences in developmental trajectories and whether a typology of trajectories can be devised to help us understand and more accurately predict how people change over time. In practical terms this would provide guidance for enabling us to better learn from

those who develop more quickly and effectively and to apply the knowledge to help those who struggle to develop as leaders. Admittedly, this is not easy research to conduct because it requires large samples, a longitudinal focus, and appropriate measurement intervals. Despite these challenges, research on charting and understanding developmental trajectories is an area that deserves future research attention.

8.4. Broadening the Developmental Focus

Researchers have tended to examine how individual leaders develop over time. We need to give greater attention to more collective aspects of leadership, whether they are dyadic leader and follower development or even more collective forms such as shared leadership. We know that development tends to occur in an interpersonal context, so incorporating that context into our research designs, methods, and analyses seems like a logical step in advancing the field of leadership development. For that reason, something like social network analysis (e.g., Hoppe & Reinelt, 2010) may be especially appropriate to consider in future studies of leadership development. There is an emerging interest in what some have called network churn or changes in network structure and individual positions within networks over time (e.g., Sasovova, Mehra, Borgatti, & Schippers, 2010). This seems like a logical stream of research to consider in broadening the focus of leadership development. But as we broaden this focus to include collectives, it should be noted that the line between these forms of leadership development and what has historically been considered organization development (OD) becomes blurred. Nonetheless, that should not stop researchers from taking steps to broaden the focus on development and in doing so perhaps will also advance the field of OD.

8.5. Practicing Leadership

We know from the extensive literature on expertise and expert performance that it generally takes 10 years or 10,000 hours of dedicated practice to become an expert in a given field (Ericcson & Charness, 1994). For this reason, it is highly unlikely that anyone would be able to develop fully as a leader merely through participation in a series of programs, workshops, or seminars. The actual development takes place in the so-called white space between such leader development events. However, we lack a clear idea of the ongoing ways in which people practice to become more expert leaders. Such practice may not be intentional or mindful, which may make it more difficult to study. But this notion of ongoing practice through day-to-day leadership activities is where the crux of development really resides. Rather than focusing on implementing better instructional design or putting together what we hope are more impactful developmental interventions, it might be more productive to take a step back and focus on what happens in the everyday lives of leaders as they practice and develop.

8.6. Self-awareness and 360-degree Feedback

Another area for future research is related to the use of 360-degree feedback instruments as measures of self-awareness. It is often assumed that individuals with ratings that mirror those provided by their followers (high self-other agreement) are more self-aware. Indeed, self-other agreement is often used as a proxy for self-awareness in leadership research. For instance, Fleenor et al. (2010) suggested that low rating agreement is an indication of low self-awareness, especially for over-estimators. In much of the research in this area, however, self-awareness is measured with the same instrument used to determine rating agreement (i.e., the instrument also contains a scale that measures self-awareness). In order to test the relationship between self-awareness and leader effectiveness, there is a need to develop valid and independent measures of self-awareness. With better measures, it may be possible to more thoroughly investigate the relationships among self-awareness, rating agreement, and effectiveness for leader development purposes.

9. Limitations

Although we have attempted to provide a comprehensive review of the scholarly literature on leader and leadership development published over the previous 25 years in this journal, there are areas with potential developmental implications that we have chosen not to review. The predominant reason for this decision is that the focal literature is not sufficiently developed or the implications for leadership development are unclear. Alternatively, it might be argued that there are potential developmental implications associated with just about every published leadership article. That is not very helpful in attempting to summarize and synthesize the most highly relevant literature.

In making choices about what to review, we did not address areas such as the genetic bases of leadership (De Neve, Mikhaylov, Dawes, Christakis, & Fowler, 2013), in which leadership role occupancy was used as the criterion (see criticisms of this outcome discussed previously) and for which it is difficult to argue that leadership can be developed if it is genetically determined; cross-cultural leadership (Sadri, Weber, & Gentry, 2011), whereby there are differing perspectives on what are the most important behaviors or competencies that should be developed; political perspectives on leadership (Ammeter, Douglas, Hochwarter, Ferris, & Gardner, 2004) that take a somewhat unique position in terms of how effective leader behavior is defined; and a recent special issue on leader integrity (Simons, Palanski, & Trevino, 2013), of which we have little empirical evidence as to how it might be developed. Although there are emerging literatures in these areas, as noted, we have confined this review to research that pertains most directly to the development of leaders and leadership.

10. Conclusion

As noted by the eminent leadership scholar John Gardner (1990), "In the mid-21st century, people will look back on our present [leadership development] practices as primitive" (p. xix). This statement is consistent with our contention that despite the significant advances in understanding leadership development made over the past 25 years, many of which have been published in the pages of *The Leadership Quarterly*, the field is still relatively immature. This also means the field is replete with opportunities for researchers and theorists. Looking ahead to the ensuing 25 years, it seems certain that if scholars answer the call, the field will continue to progress to a less primitive state. This will stimulate better leadership and, consequently, foster better organizations, communities, and societies.

Notes

1. Corresponding author at: University of Western Australia Business School (M261), 35 Stirling Highway, Crawley, WA, Australia. Tel.: +61 08 6488 3516. E-mail address: david.day@uwa.edu.au (D.V. Day).

References

Ammeter, A. P., Douglas, C., Hochwarter, W. A., Ferris, G. R., & Gardner, W. L. (2004). Introduction to: The Leadership Quarterly special issue on political perspectives in leadership. *The Leadership Quarterly*, 15(4), 433–435.

Ashford, S. J. (1989). Self-assessments in organizations: A literature review and integrative model. In L. L. Cummings, & B. M. Staw (Eds.), *Research in organizational behavior*, Vol. 11. (pp. 133–174) Greenwich, CT: JAI Press.

Atwater, L. E., Ostroff, C., Yammarino, F. J., & Fleenor, J. W. (1998). Self-other agreement: Does it really matter? *Personnel Psychology*, 51(3), 577–598.

Atwater, L., & Waldman, D. (1998). 360 degree feedback and leadership development. *The Leadership Quarterly*, 9(4), 423–426.

Atwater, L. E., & Yammarino, F. J. (1992). Does self-other agreement on leadership perceptions moderate the validity of leadership and performance predictions? *Personnel Psychology*, 45(1), 141–164.

Avolio, B. J., Avey, J. B., & Quisenberry, D. (2010). Estimating return on leadership development investment. *The Leadership Quarterly*, 21(4), 633–644.

Avolio, B. J., & Gardner, W. L. (2005). Authentic leadership development: Getting to the root of positive forms of leadership. *The Leadership Quarterly*, 16(3), 315–338.

Avolio, B. J., Reichard, R. J., Hannah, S. T., Walumbwa, F. O., & Chan, A. (2009). A meta-analytic review of leadership impact research: Experimental and quasi-experimental studies. *The Leadership Quarterly*, 20(5), 764–784.

Bartone, P. T., Snook, S. A., Forsythe, G. B., Lewis, P., & Bullis, R. C. (2007). Psychosocial development and leader performance of military officer cadets. *The Leadership Quarterly*, 18(5), 490–504.

Bass, B. M., & Riggio, R. E. (2006). *Transformational leadership*. Mahwah, NJ: Erlbaum.

Bettin, P. J., & Kennedy, J. K. (1990). Leadership experience and leader performance: Some empirical support at last. *The Leadership Quarterly*, 1(4), 219–228.

Boyce, L. A., Zaccaro, S. J., & Wisecarver, M. Z. (2010). Propensity for self-development of leadership attributes: Understanding, predicting, and supporting performance of leader self-development. *The Leadership Quarterly*, 21(1), 159–178.

Boyd, N. G., & Taylor, R. R. (1998). A developmental approach to the examination of friendship in leader-follower relationships. *The Leadership Quarterly*, 9(1), 1–25.

Cooper, C. D., Scandura, T. A., & Schriesheim, C. A. (2005). Looking forward but learning from our past: Potential challenges to developing authentic leadership theory and authentic leaders. *The Leadership Quarterly*, 16(3), 475–493.

Cronbach, L. J., & Furby, L. (1970). How we should measure "change": Or should we? *Psychological Bulletin*, 74(1), 68–80.

Day, D. V. (2000). Leadership development: A review in context. *The Leadership Quarterly*, 11(4), 581–613.

Day, D. V. (2010). The difficulties of learning from experience and the need for deliberate practice. *Industrial and Organizational Psychology: Perspectives on Science and Practice*, 3(1), 41–44.

Day, D. V. (2011). Integrative perspectives on longitudinal investigations of leader development: From childhood through adulthood. *The Leadership Quarterly*, 22(3), 561–571.

Day, D. V., & Antonakis, J. (2012). Leadership: Past, present, and future. In D. V. Day, & J. Antonakis (Eds.), *The nature of leadership* (pp. 3–25) (2nd ed.). Los Angeles, CA: Sage.

Day, D. V., Gronn, P., & Salas, E. (2004). Leadership capacity in teams. *The Leadership Quarterly*, 15(6), 857–880.

Day, D. V., Harrison, M. M., & Halpin, S. M. (2009). *An integrative theory of leadership development: Connecting adult development, identity, and expertise*. New York: Psychology Press.

Day, D. V., & Sin, H. P. (2011). Longitudinal tests of an integrative model of leader development: Charting and understanding developmental trajectories. *The Leadership Quarterly, 22*(3), 545–560.

De Neve, J. E., Mikhaylov, S., Dawes, C. T., Christakis, N. A., & Fowler, J. H. (2013). Born to lead? A twin design and genetic association study of leadership role occupancy. *The Leadership Quarterly, 24*(1), 45–60.

deVries, R. E. (2012). Personality predictors of leadership styles and the self-other agreement problem. *The Leadership Quarterly, 23*(5), 809–821.

Eagly, A. H. (2005). Achieving relational authenticity in leadership: Does gender matter? *The Leadership Quarterly, 16*(3), 459–474.

Ericcson, K., & Charness, N. (1994). Expert performance: Its structure and acquisition. *American Psychologist, 49*(8), 725–747.

Eubanks, D. L., Antes, A. L., Friedrich, T. L., Caughron, J. J., Blackwell, L. V., Bedell-Avers, K. E., et al. (2010). Criticism and outstanding leadership: An evaluation of leader reactions and critical outcomes. *The Leadership Quarterly, 21*(3), 365–388.

Facteau, C. L., Facteau, J. D., Schoel, L. C., Russell, J. E. A., & Poteet, M. L. (1998). Reactions of leaders to 360-degree feedback from subordinates and peers. *The Leadership Quarterly, 9*(4), 427–448.

Fleenor, J. W., McCauley, C. D., & Brutus, S. (1996). Self-other rating agreement and leader effectiveness. *The Leadership Quarterly, 7*(4), 487–506.

Fleenor, J. W., Smither, J. W., Atwater, L. E., Braddy, P. W., & Sturm, R. E. (2010). Self-other rating agreement in leadership: A review. *The Leadership Quarterly, 21*(6), 1005–1034.

Galli, E. B., & Müller-Stewens, G. (2012). How to build social capital with leadership development: Lessons from an explorative case study of a multibusiness firm. *The Leadership Quarterly, 23*(1), 176–201.

Gardner, J. W. (1990). *On leadership.* New York: The Free Press.

Gardner, W. L., Avolio, B. J., Luthans, F., May, D. R., & Walumbwa, F. (2005). "Can you see the real me?" A self-based model of authentic leader and follower development. *The Leadership Quarterly, 16*(3), 343–372.

Gentry, W. A., & Martineau, J. W. (2010). Hierarchical linear modeling as an example for measuring change over time in a leadership development evaluation context. *The Leadership Quarterly, 21*(4), 645–656.

Gottfried, A. E., Gottfried, A. W., Reichard, R. J., Guerin, D. W., Oliver, P. H., & Riggio, R. E. (2011). Motivational roots of leadership: A longitudinal study from childhood through adulthood. *The Leadership Quarterly, 22*(3), 510–519.

Guerin, D. W., Oliver, P. H., Gottfried, A. W., Gottfried, A. E., Reichard, R. J., & Riggio, R. E. (2011). Childhood and adolescent antecedents of social skills and leadership potential in adulthood: Temperamental approach/withdrawal and extraversion. *The Leadership Quarterly, 22*(3), 482–494.

Hannum, K. M., & Craig, S. B. (2010). Introduction to special issue on leadership development evaluation. *The Leadership Quarterly, 21*(4), 581–582.

Harms, P. D., Spain, S. M., & Hannah, S. T. (2011). Leader development and the dark side of personality. *The Leadership Quarterly, 22*(3), 495–509.

Hirst, G., Mann, L., Bain, P., Pirola-Merlo, A., & Richter, A. (2004). Learning to lead: The development and testing of a model of leadership learning. *The Leadership Quarterly, 15*(3), 311–327.

Hoffman, B. J., Lance, C. E., Bynum, B. H., & Gentry, W. A. (2010). Rater source effects are alive and well after all. *Personnel Psychology, 63*(1), 119–151.

Hooijberg, R., & Choi, J. (2000). Which leadership roles matter to whom? An examination of rater effects on perceptions of effectiveness. *The Leadership Quarterly, 11*(3), 341–364.

Hoppe, B., & Reinelt, C. (2010). Social network analysis and the evaluation of leadership networks. *The Leadership Quarterly, 21*(4), 600–619.

House, R. J., Shane, S. A., & Herold, D. M. (1996). Rumors of the death of dispositional research are vastly exaggerated. *Academy of Management Review, 21*(1), 203–224.

Ilies, R., Morgeson, F. P., & Nahrgang, J. D. (2005). Authentic leadership and eudaemonic well-being: Understanding leader-follower outcomes. *The Leadership Quarterly, 16*(3), 373–394.

Kanfer, R., & Ackerman, P. L. (1989). Motivation and cognitive abilities: An integrative/aptitude-treatment interaction approach to skill acquisition. *Journal of Applied Psychology, 74*(4), 657–690.

Kegan, R. (1982). *The evolving self: Problem and process in human development.* Cambridge, MA: Harvard University Press.

Li, W. D., Arvey, R. D., & Song, Z. (2011). The influence of general mental ability, self-esteem and family socio-economic status on leadership role occupancy and leader advancement: The moderating role of gender. *The Leadership Quarterly, 22*(3), 520–534.

Ligon, G. S., Hunter, S. T., & Mumford, M. D. (2008). Development of outstanding leadership: A life narrative approach. *The Leadership Quarterly, 19*(3), 312–334.

Lord, R. G., & Hall, R. J. (2005). Identity, deep structure and the development of leadership skill. *The Leadership Quarterly, 16*(4), 591–615.

Marshall-Mies, J. C., Fleishman, E. A., Martin, J. A., Zaccaro, S. J., Baughman, W. A., & McGee, M. L. (2000). Development and evaluation of cognitive and metacognitive measures for predicting leadership potential. *The Leadership Quarterly,* 11(1), 135–153.

McCauley, C. D., Drath, W. H., Palus, C. J., O'Connor, P. M., & Baker, B. A. (2006). The use of constructive-developmental theory to advance the understanding of leadership. *The Leadership Quarterly,* 17(6), 634–653.

Michie, S., & Gooty, J. (2005). Values, emotions, and authenticity: Will the real leader please stand up? *The Leadership Quarterly,* 16(3), 441–457.

Militello, M., & Benham, M. K. (2010). "Sorting out" collective leadership: How Q-methodology can be used to evaluate leadership development. *The Leadership Quarterly,* 21(4), 620–632.

Mumford, T. V., Campion, M. A., & Morgeson, F. P. (2007). The leadership skills strataplex: Leadership skill requirements across organizational levels. *The Leadership Quarterly,* 18(2), 154–166.

Mumford, M., Marks, M. A., Connelly, M. S., Zaccaro, S. J., & Reiter-Palmon, R. (2000a). Development of leadership skills: Experience and timing. *The Leadership Quarterly,* 11(1), 87–114.

Mumford, M., Zaccaro, S. J., Johnson, J. F., Diana, M., Gilbert, J. A., & Threlfall, K. (2000b). Patterns of leader characteristics: Implications for performance and development. *The Leadership Quarterly,* 11(1), 115–133.

Murphy, S. E., & Johnson, S. K. (2011). The benefits of a long-lens approach to leader development: Understanding the seeds of leadership. *The Leadership Quarterly,* 22(3), 459–470.

Oliver, P. H., Gottfried, A. W., Guerin, D. W., Gottfried, A. E., Reichard, R. J., & Riggio, R. E. (2011). Adolescent family environmental antecedents to transformational leadership potential: A longitudinal mediational analysis. *The Leadership Quarterly,* 22(3), 535–544.

Orvis, K. A., & Ratwani, K. L. (2010). Leader self-development: A contemporary context for leader development evaluation. *The Leadership Quarterly,* 21(4), 657–674.

Reichard, R. J., & Johnson, S. K. (2011). Leader self-development as organizational strategy. *The Leadership Quarterly,* 22(1), 33–42.

Reichard, R. J., Riggio, R. E., Guerin, D. W., Oliver, P. H., Gottfried, A. W., & Gottfried, A. E. (2011). A longitudinal analysis of relationships between adolescent personality and intelligence with adult leader emergence and transformational leadership. *The Leadership Quarterly,* 22(3), 471–481.

Riggio, R. E., & Mumford, M. D. (2011). Introduction to the special issue: Longitudinal studies of leadership development. *The Leadership Quarterly,* 22(3), 453–456.

Russell, C. J., & Kuhnert, K. W. (1992). New frontiers in management selection systems: Where measurement technologies and theory collide. *The Leadership Quarterly,* 3(2), 109–135.

Sadri, G., Weber, T. J., & Gentry, W. A. (2011). Empathic emotion and leadership performance: An empirical analysis across 38 countries. *The Leadership Quarterly,* 22(5), 818–830.

Sasovova, Z., Mehra, A., Borgatti, S. P., & Schippers, M. C. (2010). Network churn: The effects of self-monitoring personality on brokerage dynamics. *Administrative Science Quarterly,* 55(4), 639–670.

Scandura, T. A., & Lankau, M. J. (1996). Developing diverse leaders: A leader-member exchange approach. *The Leadership Quarterly,* 7(2), 243–263.

Seifert, C. F., & Yukl, G. (2010). Effects of repeated multisource feedback on the influence behavior and effectiveness of managers: A field experiment. *The Leadership Quarterly,* 21(5), 856–866.

Shamir, B., & Eilam, G. (2005). "What's your story?" A life-stories approach to authentic leadership development. *The Leadership Quarterly,* 16(3), 395–417.

Simons, T., Palanski, M., & Trevino, L. (2013). Toward a broader—but still rigorous—definition of leader integrity: Commentary. *The Leadership Quarterly,* 24(3), 391–394.

Smith, G. T. (2009). Why do different individuals progress along different life trajectories? *Perspectives on Psychological Science,* 4(4), 415–421.

Sparrowe, R. T. (2005). Authentic leadership and the narrative self. *The Leadership Quarterly,* 16(3), 419–439.

Sternberg, R. J. (2008). The WICS approach to leadership: Stories of leadership and the structures and processes that support them. *The Leadership Quarterly,* 19(3), 360–371.

Strang, S. E., & Kuhnert, K. W. (2009). Personality and leadership developmental levels as predictors of leader performance. *The Leadership Quarterly,* 20(3), 421–433.

Taylor, S. N., & Hood, J. N. (2011). It may not be what you think: Gender differences in predicting emotional and social competence. *Human Relations,* 64(5), 627–652.

Warech, M. A., Smither, J. W., Reilly, R. R., Millsap, R. E., & Reilly, S. P. (1998). Self-monitoring and 360-degree ratings. *The Leadership Quarterly,* 9(4), 449–473.

Zacharatos, A., Barling, J., & Kelloway, E. K. (2000). Development and effects of transformational leadership in adolescents. *The Leadership Quarterly,* 11(2), 211–226.

CHAPTER 37

Developing Global Mindset and Global Leadership Capabilities

Joyce S. Osland

San Jose State University

Allan Bird

Northeastern University

Mark Mendenhall

University of Tennessee, Chattanooga

The context of leading globally is complex and fraught with disorienting challenges. The term 'global' encompasses more than simple *geographic reach* in terms of business operations. It also includes the notion of *cultural reach* in terms of people and *intellectual reach* in the development of a global mindset. According to a 2010 IBM study of CEOs (IBM, 2010), complexity is the most challenging aspect of their jobs. Complexity results from these aspects of the global context that combine to create significant challenges for global leaders (Lane, Maznevski, Mendenhall & McNett, 2004: 197):

- *Multiplicity* across a range of dimensions.

- *Interdependence* among a host of stakeholders' sociocultural, political, economic and environmental systems.
- *Ambiguity* in terms of understanding causal relationships, interpreting cues and signals, identifying appropriate actions, and pursuing plausible goals.
- *Flux* in terms of quickly transitioning systems, shifting values and emergent patterns of organizational structure and behaviour.

The complexity of the global context can be addressed through paying attention to managing the following four processes (Lane et al., 2004).

- *Collaborating:* working with others in relationships characterized by community, flexibility, respect, trust and mutual accountability.
- *Discovering:* transformational processes leading to new ways of seeing and acting which, in turn, will lead to the creation of new knowledge, actions and things.
- *Architecting:* the mindful design of processes that will align, balance, and synchronize organizational behaviour.
- *Systems thinking:* seeing and/or discovering the interrelationship among components and levels in a complex system and anticipating the consequences of changes in and to the system.

Developing global leaders and global mindset is a high priority and acknowledged requirement for firms (IBM, 2010). The scarcity of business leaders prepared to deal with the global context has been well documented (Gregersen, Morrison & Black, 1998).

Management scholars have responded to this need with both theoretical and empirical research, primarily to determine what we mean by a global mindset and global leadership and, to a much lesser degree, how these competencies can be developed. We review the empirical literature, identify research dilemmas and holes, and raise questions and suggestions to guide future research on global mindset and leadership as well as on how these can be developed. We propose a non-linear framework to describe the process of global leadership development. The chapter ends with the implications for future research on developmental activities for both individuals and firms.

Literature Review of Global Mindset

The importance of a global mindset has grown in recognition by firms and scholars; one indication has been the increasing number of articles on global mindset in practitioner journals (e.g., Cohen, 2007; Javidan, Teagarden & Bowen, 2010; Levy, Beechler, Taylor & Boyacigiller, 2010). It is still difficult, however, to report how widespread the focus is on this competence in today's businesses. Although the

relationship has not been tested empirically, global mindset has long been viewed as a prerequisite and competitive advantage for effectively managing transnational corporations and competing globally (Bartlett & Ghoshal, 1992; Kedia & Mukherji, 1999; Doz & Prahalad, 1991; Ohmae, 1989). Based on their research on large corporations, Bartlett and Ghoshal (1989) concluded that mindset was more important than sophisticated organizational structures and procedures. Gupta and Govindarajan (2002) also stated that the success of individuals, as well as firms, depends on their ability to observe and interpret the complex environment. The complexity and challenges of the global environment call for adaptations in the cognitive processes of global leaders, workers, and firms. In accordance with Ashby's (1956) law of requisite variety, the degree of complexity in the environment should be matched by an equal degree of internal complexity in the form of a 'managerial mindset' or global mindset (Boyacigiller, Beechler, Taylor & Levy, 2004). Thus, the mindset of the chief executive is critical to a company's strategy (Paul, 2000).

The amount of empirical research on global mindset is still fairly limited; questions remain over how to define, measure, and develop it. The varying levels of analysis (organizational, group, individual) in the literature as well as the overlap with other concepts such as global leadership, cultural intelligence, and cross-cultural competence are ongoing sources of confusion (Vanhoegaerden, 2010). Global mindset has become a catch-all phrase 'for everything that is supposedly global or transnational, from individual attitudes, skills, competencies and behaviors to organizational orientations, structures and strategies, to policies and practices' (Levy et al., 2007: 4). The result has been conceptual ambiguity and contradictory empirical findings. The following representative definitions illustrate the conceptual ambiguity surrounding this concept.

Maznevski and Lane (2004: 172) draw attention to the contextual application of cognition and the necessity of moving beyond ethnocentrism in their definition of global mindset as:

> the ability to develop and interpret criteria for personal and business performance that are independent from the assumptions of a single

country, culture, or context; and to implement those criteria appropriately in different countries, cultures, and contexts.

Clapp-Smith, Luthans and Aviolo (2007: 106) adapted a definition crafted by a group of scholars at a Thunderbird School of Global Management forum to include an emphasis on sense-making:

> the cognitive ability that helps individuals figure out how to best understand and influence individuals, groups, and organizations from diverse social/cultural systems.

Levy et al.'s definition (2007: 27) employs a multidimensional approach that joins together both cultural and strategic considerations:

> A highly complex individual-level cognitive structure characterized by an openness to and articulation of multiple cultural and strategic realities on both global and local levels, and the cognitive ability to mediate and integrate across this multiplicity.

The concept of global mindset first appeared in Perlmutter's (1969) taxonomy of the mindsets found in senior MNC executives: ethnocentric (home country mindset), polycentric (host country mindset) and geocentric (world mindset). Bartlett and Ghoshal (1989) expanded geocentrism, calling it the 'transnational' mindset. Subsequent articles on global mindset were based either on consultants' experiences or on academics' conceptualizations (c.f., Adler & Bartholomew, 1992; Begley & Boyd, 2003; Jeannet, 2000; Kefalas, 1998; Paul, 2000; Srinivas, 1995).

The empirical research (see Table 37.1) provides some evidence for these assumptions, but definitive answers are hampered by the lack of definitional and operational consensus on global mindset. Global mindset has been operationalized in a variety of ways: cognitive complexity (Wills & Barham, 1994); cognitive maps of CEOs (Calori, Johnson & Sarnin, 1994); the international experience of top managers (Sambharya, 1996); judgments about international HR policies (Kobrin, 1994); attitudes toward internationalization in managers (Harveston, Kedia & Davis, 2000); thinking 'glocally' in HR executives (Begley & Boyd, 2003); global orientation in managers (Nummela, Saarenketo & Puumalainen, 2004); top management team global orientation (Beechler, Levy, Taylor & Boyacigiller, 2004); conceptualization and contextualization (Arora, Jaju, Kefalas & Perenich, 2004); cosmopolitanism and cognitive complexity of top management teams (Levy, 2005); top management team (TMT) behaviour (Bouquet, 2005); and intellectual capital, social capital and psychological capital (Bowen & Inkpen, 2009).

Table 37.1 A Chronological List of Empirical Research on Global Mindset

Authors	Operationalization of Global Mindset	Method	Findings
Wills & Barham (1994)	Cognitive complexity	Interviews with 60 successful international managers in global organizations	Successful international managers were characterized by cognitive complexity, emotional energy and psychological maturity, in addition to learned behaviours and skills
Calof & Beamish (1994)	Global mindset defined as geocentric	Surveys of 38 Canadian firms	Firms that characterized themselves as geocentric, rather than ethnocentric or polycentric, reported greater international sales and export intensity

Authors	Operationalization of Global Mindset	Method	Findings
Kobrin (1994)	International HR policies as indicators of geocentrism	Survey with geo-centrism index on international HR policies administered to 68 US manufacturing firms	Geocentric mindset is related to geographic scope of firm, but not to global strategy
Calori, Johnson & Sarnin (1994)	Cognitive complexity of CEOs defined as number of constructs and density of links between constructs	Sample of 26 French and British firms in four industries	CEOs of international firms have more complex maps of their industry than other CEOs. Cognitive complexity of the CEOs correlates with the geographic scope of the firm and interorganizational links, generally supporting 'requisite variety'
Sambharya (1996)	Cognitive state of the top management team as measured by their inter-national work experience	Sample of 54 US manufacturing firms	International experience of top management team correlates with international diversification
Murtha, Lenway & Bagozzi (1998)	'Cognitive processes that balance competing country, business functional concerns' in managers	Longitudinal survey administered to 370 managers in 13 country and affiliates and US head office of an MNC	The change to a global strategy resulted in a cognitive shift toward increased global mindset across all managers.
Harveston, Kedia & Davis (2000)	Attitude toward internationalization	Comparison of 224 managers from 60 born global and146 gradually globalized firms	Managers in born global firms have a different and more global mindset, more international experience, higher risk tolerance than managers in gradually globalized firms.
Begley & Boyd (2003)	"Glocal mentality": 1) Thinking globally, 2) thinking locally, 3) thinking globally and locally simultaneously and balance competing demands	Interviews with 39 HR executives in 32 U.S.-based high-tech MNCs	Corporate global mindset emerges from supportive policy development and practices. Although these are desired, their implementation lags behind firms' global expansion.

(Continued)

Table 37.1 (Continued)

Authors	Operationalization of Global Mindset	Method	Findings
Arora, Jaju, Kefalas & Pereuich (2004)	Thinking globally (conceptualization) and acting locally (contextualization)	Questionnaires sent to 65 U.S. textile managers in Georgia and North Carolina	Managers were better at thinking globally than acting locally. Younger age, higher education, foreign family member, international management training, and living and working abroad correlated with higher global mindset.
Beechler, Levy, Taylor & Boyacigiller (2004)	Global orientation of top management team	Surveys of 521 employees working in five countries for two Japanese MNCs	Employee perceptions of top management team's global orientation positively affected employee commitment and excitement about jobs.
Nummela, Saarenketo & Puumalainen (2004)	Global orientation attitude and international entrepreneurial behaviours	Web-based survey of 72 small Finnish information & communications technology companies	Managers' international work experience correlates with global mindset, as does the globalness of their market. Global mindset correlates with international financial performance.
Bouquet (2005)	Top management team behaviours: global scanning, CEO foreign travel, communication with overseas managers and discussions of globalization decisions	Questionnaires sent to 136 CEOs or presidents of MNCs	Global mindset best explained by micro-level attention structures that mediate the relationship between TMT global mindset and firm characteristics. Too little or too much attention to global issues decreases firm performance.
Levy (2005)	Cosmopolitanism and cognitive diversity in top management teams	Content analysis of letters to shareholders of 69 U.S.-based tech firms	Attention to global/external environment and attention breadth was positively inked to a global strategic posture while attention to internal environment was negatively related.
Taylor, Levy, Boyacigiller & Beechler (2008)	Global orientation of top managers and geocentric	Surveys of 1,644 employees at 10 MNCs headquartered in Australia, Israel, Japan, Mexico and United States	Organizational cultures high in adaptability and HRM positively affect employee commitment. TMT orientation mediates HRM system effect.

The dependent variables are measures of global strategy or performance, such as internationalization or international sales. Several studies prove that global mindset correlates with greater international scope (Calof & Beamish, 1994; Kobrin, 1994; Sambharya, 1996; Nummela et al., 2004), global strategic posture (Levy, 2001), and international financial performance (Nummela et al., 2004). In contrast, one study discovered that too much top management team attention being given to global issues (the authors' operationalization of global mindset) was just as harmful to performance as paying too little attention (Bouquet et al., 2003). Global mindset, operationalized as cognitive complexity and cosmopolitanism, also correlated with two internal measures: higher employee commitment and excitement about their job (Beechler et al., 2004). Owing to the nature of their design, most of these studies cannot settle the question of causality. A longitudinal study found that global mindset increased during the implementation of a new global strategy (Murtha, Lenway & Bagozzi, 1998). Some findings suggest, however, that global mindset may follow strategy rather than the general assumption that strategy follows mindset (Levy et al., 1999). More research is needed to specify the contingencies that influence causality. Arora and colleagues (2004) identified a younger age, a higher education, having a foreign family member, having undergone international management training, and living and working abroad as the demographic antecedents of global mindset.

Models of Global Mindset

This section presents three models of global mindset. The first model (Levy et al., 2004, 2007) represents a significant contribution to identifying the construct domain of global mindset. After an extensive review of the literature and a large empirical study (Taylor, Levy, Boyacigiller & Beechler, 2007), they concluded that global mindset has two underlying constructs: cognitive complexity and cosmopolitanism. Cosmopolitanism, an openness and orientation towards the outside world, also includes the personal ability to make one's way into other cultures, through listening, looking, intuiting, and reflecting. Cognitive complexity is the ability to generate several competing interpretations of events and their interactive effects; it refers to the number of constructs or dimensions a person uses to describe a domain (differentiation) and the number of links among the differentiated constructs (integration). Further, Levy et al. (2007) argue that cognitive complexity and cosmopolitanism influence the three stages in the information processing model in the form of paying *attention* to multiple cultural and strategic dynamics, which will lead to a nonjudgmental integrated *interpretation* of cultural and strategic dynamics, and finally, individual *action*. It is worth noting the similarity between these stages and the more performance oriented effectiveness cycle (Bird & Osland, 2004), which consists of perceiving and decoding, identifying effective managerial action, and possessing the behavioural flexibility and discipline to act appropriately.

According to Beechler and Javidan's (2007) Global Mindset Framework, individuals who have a global mindset possess: *global intellectual capital* (knowledge of the global industry, knowledge of global value networks, knowledge of the global organization, cognitive complexity, and cultural acumen); *psychological capital* (positive psychological profile, cosmopolitanism, and a passion for cross-cultural and cross-national encounters); and *social capital* (structural, relational, and cognitive social capital). To describe a global leader's response to the environment, they incorporated Bird and Osland's (2004) effectiveness cycle as the second component in their model. This component describes how individuals interact with the environment. The outcome is their third component—'global leaders who are effective in influencing others in situations of cross-cultural complexity', which is also their definition of global mindset. Bowen and Inkpen (2009) applied this model to a case study of a Brazilian global change leader. According to Javidan et al. (2010), global mindset is the key reason why global managers succeed, and more effective global managers will have a greater degree of global mindset.

A third model, an integrative framework by Bhagat, Triandis, Ram Baliga, Billing & Davis (2007), is a multilevel, meso approach portraying the evolution of a global mindset based on a review of the literature. The model portrays the industry-specific, organization-specific and person-specific antecedents of global mindset within a cultural context. Industry-specific antecedents are: the rapid pace of globalization, a fast product life cycle, economic trade blocks, uniform practices in global marketing and product standardization, and effective government interventions. Organization-specific antecedents include administrative heritage, strategic leadership, the effective monitoring of clients, horizontal coordination mechanisms, knowledge creation and diffusion, and effective knowledge management systems. Person-specific antecedents include cosmopolitanism, cognitive complexity, cultural intelligence, nonjudgmental and universalistic thinking, and a supportive network of family and friends.

Problems with the global mindset research literature fall into one of three deficiencies. First, there is no generally accepted definition, and it has been operationalized in numerous ways. Second, some studies will use international work experience as a surrogate measure, but not all international assignments will have a positive result: some expatriates will buffer themselves and come home relatively unchanged. Third, research has focused on various levels of analysis: individual managers and CEOs, top management teams, and firms as a whole. Is global mindset in individuals the same construct as it is for firms? Are there different types of global mindsets in firms with different strategies or in different industries depending on varying levels of the required global/cultural knowledge and involvement?

Significant further effort is called for in addressing the following aspects of global mindset research.

- Construct a definition for global mindset, and establish construct and content validity.
- Identify different types of global mindset at different levels of analysis.
- Validate a comprehensive global mindset assessment instrument incorporating cognitive complexity.
- Measure the impact of global mindset on performance outcomes.
- Identify and validate GM antecedents at all levels of analysis.

- Identify the characteristics that can be used in selection decisions.
- Identify the cognitive processes related to global mindset.
- Identify the contingencies that influence global mindset.
- Explore the different forms of global mindset and their relationship to global strategies, industries, and particular companies.
- Develop process models of global mindset.
- Establish the antecedents of global mindset effectiveness.
- Explore the outcomes of global mindset.

There is widespread agreement that global mindset relates to global leadership, but the exact relationship has yet to be empirically determined. Some scholars perceive global mindset as the key component of global leadership; others view it as a cognitive and attitudinal component upon which other global leadership competencies are built (Bird & Osland, 2004). Global mindset is a necessary but not sufficient condition for global leadership, according to Kedia and Mukherji (1999). Levy and her colleagues (2007) also question whether it is possible to develop global leadership skills and behaviours without concurrently developing global mindset.

Literature Review of Global Leadership

The construct of global leadership was born out of the needs of corporations in the 1990s to adopt global strategies, expand internationally and compete in the global marketplace (Mendenhall & Osland, 2002; Von Glinow, 2001). Corporations realized that these capabilities were required to develop and implement their new strategic initiatives that called for the creation of company-specific models development efforts (Mendenhall & Osland, 2002). Because this is a young field of study, many of these models and training programmes, including those offered by universities and consulting companies, are not based on an extensive body of empirical research.

In this chapter, global leadership is defined as a process of influencing the thinking, attitudes and behaviours of a global community to work together synergistically toward a common vision and common goals (Adler, 2001; Festing, 2001). Most scholars have approached the global leadership construct by asking two questions: 'What capabilities do global leaders need in order to be effective?' and 'How can these characteristics be developed?' The earliest publications on global leaders were either extrapolations from the domestic leadership literature, interviews and focus groups, or observations from the authors' consulting experiences (c.f., Kets de Vries & Mead, 1992; Rhinesmith, 1993; Brake, 1997). Two sources of current thinking, findings and implications for future research are the *Advances in Global Leadership* volumes (e.g., Mobley, Wang & Li, 2009) and the 2008 volume by Mendenhall, Osland, Bird, Oddou & Maznevski.

Empirical studies on global leadership are described in Table 37.2. Empirical studies of global managers (for example, Dalton, Ernst, Deal & Leslie, 2002) and empirical work on comparative international leadership (for example, the GLOBE project) exist in the field as well (House, Hanges, Javidan, Dorfman & Gupta, 2004). From the extensive study of the impact of culture on leadership in 62 nations, the GLOBE project identified 21 universally accepted leader attributes and the transformational leadership style as generally advisable. Their subjects, however, were not global leaders, but middle managers and executives working in their own countries. These universal attributes may prove to be linked to effective global leadership; however, further research that tests for the presence of these attributes among successful global leaders is needed. As Adler noted, 'A fundamental distinction is that global leadership is neither domestic nor multi-domestic; it focuses on cross-cultural interaction rather than on either single culture description or multi-country comparison' (2001: 77). We have included only those studies with a specified focus on *global* leadership.

As shown in Table 37.2, the methodology utilized to study global leadership has been varied. Kets de Vries and Florent-Treacy's (1999) early effort relied on case studies. Ernst (2000) went beyond interview

or self-reported data to include 360-degree feedback from bosses and subordinates on behaviours, but his findings did not distinguish between domestic and global leadership. Using semi-structured interviews, Kets de Vries and his colleagues (2004) developed an instrument to measure various psycho-dynamic properties associated with global leadership behaviour. Black et al. (1999) and Goldsmith et al. (2003) also developed instruments to measure global leadership. Perhaps because of their recent development, as yet none of these instruments has been validated using commonly accepted standards for development of psychological assessment and testing instruments (Anastasi & Urbina, 1997; Nunnally & Bernstein, 1994). Several studies employed exploratory designs, which are appropriate in a nascent field of study. Although cognitive complexity is frequently mentioned as a global leadership competency, only one study has directly addressed the cognitive processes of expert global leaders (Osland & Bird, 2006; 2007).

While all of the global leader research in Table 37.2 makes a contribution to our understanding, and advances the field, the findings are not definitive. For example, the published research to date has contributed little in the way of construct definition. No rigorous or collectively accepted definition of global leadership has emerged. As a result, there is conceptual confusion accompanied by enduring questions about whether there is a significant difference between global managers and global leaders, or between global and domestic leaders. In both the sample selection and writing, the terms 'global leader' and 'global manager' are frequently used interchangeably, which is puzzling given the significant distinctions between managers and leaders in the leadership literature (Kotter, 1990).

Several studies asked global managers for their opinion about global leader capability without ensuring or clarifying whether they were in fact global leaders. Yeung and Ready (1995) used a global sample of 1200 managers who chose among survey items to elicit their description of global leaders. Adler (2001) did content analysis using archival research and some interviews with 43 political and 38 women global leaders to describe their backgrounds, ascension, and use of power. Black and colleagues (1999)

Table 37.2 A Chronological List of Empirical Research on Global Leadership

Authors	Description	Method	Global Leadership Findings	Global Leadership Development Findings
Wills & Barham (1994)		Interviews with 60 successful international managers in global organizations.	Capabilities: sense of humility, emotional self-awareness and resilience, psychological maturity, curiosity to learn, and personal morality	
Yeung & Ready (1995)	Identifies leadership capabilities in a cross-national study	Surveys of 1,200 managers from 10 major global corporations and 8 countries	Capabilities: articulate vision, values, strategy; catalyst for strategic and cultural change; empower others; results and customer orientation	
Adler (1997)	Describes women global leaders in politics and business	Archival data and interviews with women global leaders from 60 countries	Their number is increasing and they come from diverse backgrounds; are *not* selected by women-friendly countries or companies; use broad-based power rather than hierarchical power; are lateral transfers; symbolize change and unity; and leverage their increased visibility	
Black, Morrison & Gregersen (1999)	Identifies capabilities of effective global leaders and how to develop them	Interviews of 130 senior line and HR executives in 50 companies in Europe, North America and Asia and nominated global leaders	Capabilities: inquisitive, character, duality, savvy	Development occurs via training, transfer, travel, and multicultural teams
Kets de Vries & Florent-Treacy (1999)	Describes excellent global leadership	Case studies involving interviews with 3 global leaders (CEOs)	Identified best practices in leadership, structure, strategy, corporate culture	

Authors	Description	Method	Global Leadership Findings	Global Leadership Development Findings
Rosen, Digh, Singer & Philips (2000)	Identifies leadership universals	Interviews with 75 CEOs from 28 countries; 1058 surveys with CEOs, presidents, managing directors or chairmen; studies of national culture	Leadership Universals: Personal, social, business, and cultural literacies, many of which are paradoxical in nature	Leadership skills attributed to work experience, natural ability, role models, formal training, age and religion
McCall & Hollen Beck (2002)	To identify how to select and develop global executives and understand how they derail	Interviews with 101 executives from 36 countries and 16 global firms nominated as successful global executives	Competencies: open-minded & flexible; culture interest & sensitivity; able to deal with complexity; resilient, resourceful, optimistic, energetic; honesty & integrity; stable personal life; value-added technical or business skills	Strategy drives development. Learning about culture and adaptability is more difficult than business lessons. While they learn like domestic execs, cultural experiences are more complex and may have different lessons and significant others play a greater role. GLD is not an exact science. Global leaders and global jobs are not all alike. Global careers are hazardous. GLD is difficult but not impossible, and they take more responsibility for their own development.
Goldsmith, Greenberg, Robertson & Hu-Chan (2003)	To identify global leadership dimensions needed in the future	Thought leader panels; focus groups with 28 CEOs, focus/ dialogue groups with at least 207 current or future leaders; interviews with 202 high potential next generation leaders; 73 surveys from forum group members	Fifteen dimensions: integrity, personal mastery, constructive dialogue, shared vision, empowerment, developing people, building partnerships, sharing leadership, thinking globally, appreciating diversity, technologically savvy, customer satisfaction, anticipating opportunities, leading change, and maintaining competitive advantage	

(Continued)

Table 37.2 (Continued)

Authors	Description	Method	Global Leadership Findings	Global Leadership Development Findings
Bikson, Treverton, Moini & Lindstrom (2003)	Examines impact of globalization on HR needs, global leadership competencies, and policies and practices needed to produce sufficient global leaders	Structured interviews with 135 U.S. HR and senior managers in public, for-profit, and non-profit sectors. Unstructured interviews with 24 experts on development policies	Insufficient future global leader who have the required integrated skill repertoire; substantive depth in organization's primary business; managerial ability (especially teamwork and interpersonal skills); strategic international understanding; and cross-cultural experience	
Kets de Vries, Vrignaud & Florent-Treacy (2004)	Describes the development of 360-degree feedback instrument, GlobeInvent	Based on semi-structured interviews with a number of senior executives	Twelve dimensions/psychodynamic properties: envisioning, empowering, energizing, designing, rewarding, team-building, outside orientation, global mindset, tenacity, emotional intelligence, life balance, resilience to stress	
Kets de Vries, Vrignaud & Florent-Treacy (2002)				The basic foundation of GLD is: 1) family background that includes culturally diverse parents, early international experience, and bilingualism; 2) early education in international schools, summer camps and international travel; 3)

Authors	Description	Method	Global Leadership Findings	Global Leadership Development Findings
				later education involving exchange programs, foreign language and international MBA programs; 4) spouses and children who are supportive, adventurous, adaptable and mobile.
Caligiuri & Di Santo (2001)				Flexibility, lack of ethnocentrism and openness did not increase after global assignments.
Caligiuri (2004)			Highly effective global leaders had higher scores in conscientiousness and lower neuroticism scores than less effective leaders	Highly effective global leaders lived abroad as a child, had long-term international assignments, and were mentored by people from another culture.
Furuya, Stevens, Bird, Oddou & Mendenhall (2009)	Japanese repatriates, focusing intercultural competencies, competency acquisition transfer	Longitudinal study of 305 Japanese repatriate managers; assessing pre, during and post international assignment	Higher global leader-related predispositional competencies were associated with behavioural competency acquisition and higher levels of job performance on assignment and post repatriation	Managers with higher levels of predispositional competencies developed to a greater degree than those with lower levels.

asked 130 senior line and HR executives, as well as an unspecified number of nominated global leaders, for their opinion on global leadership capabilities and the methods of developing them. Rosen et al. (2000) interviewed 75 CEOs and surveyed 1058 CEOs, presidents, managing directors or chairmen about global leadership capabilities. Goldsmith and his colleagues (2003): (1) asked the opinion of 18 well-known domestic leadership experts and futurists; (2) held focus groups with 28 CEOs, an unspecified number of global managers and 2002 high potential leaders of the 'next' generation; and (3) surveyed 75 forum members from various countries. In the only study to select subjects solely on effectiveness, as judged by others, McCall and Hollenbeck (2002) interviewed 101 executives from varied companies and countries. Although they refer to their sample as global executives, their sampling methods are similar to other global leader studies.

Kets de Vries and Florent-Treacy (1999) began their empirical work with case studies, utilizing a clinical orientation, of three global leaders who were acknowledged as highly successful global CEOs. As the basis of their subsequent research using an assessment instrument that measured global leader dimensions, they relied primarily on participants who attended INSEAD's senior executive seminar on Emotional Intelligence and Leadership and the MBA programme. This convenience sample may well have been composed of global leaders, but their selection criteria, as well as most of the research reviewed here, assumed that global managers were indistinguishable from global leaders. But not all CEOs and global managers are global leaders. Given the limited amount of research in this field, more could be learned from exploratory research on global leaders who are effective. Both of these contentions argue for more careful selection criteria in global leadership research.

Mendenhall and Osland's (2002) review of the empirical and non empirical literature yielded 56 global leadership competencies, a list too large to be useful. The authors concluded that global leadership was a multidimensional construct with at least six core dimensions of competencies: cross-cultural relationship skills, traits and values, cognitive orientation, global business expertise, global organizing expertise, and visioning. This categorization seems applicable for the competencies identified in the empirical studies reviewed here.

Recently Bird, Mendenhall, Stevens and Oddou (2010) conducted a review of the global leadership and expatriate literature to develop a comprehensive delineation of the content domain of intercultural competence required for effective global leadership. They concluded that the intercultural competencies necessary for effective global leadership conceptually reside in three dimensions: *perception management, relationship management* and *self-management*. Each dimension contains competencies that are a prerequisite to strong global leadership. They delineated a total of 16 competencies to focus upon in order to enhance selection and competency-strength levels for leaders engaged in global work. While further research is needed to gain a more sophisticated understanding of the dynamics of intercultural competencies across various cultural and industry contexts, the content domain of key competencies has been defined, and research studies in the field need to move forward and focus on investigating how the known competencies actually operate.

One striking characteristic of the global leadership competency research is that it has usually taken a *content* approach. While useful, this fails to explicate the process that global leaders utilize or to identify the contingencies that influence their behaviour in specific contexts. Are these competencies crucial at all times or important only in certain situations? Leadership requirements can vary by level, culture and situation, as well as by functions and operating units, so competency lists might not apply across the board (Conger & Ready, 2004: 45).

The competency approach also fails to address the conundrum of exemplary global leaders who succeed despite glaring weaknesses. Few leaders live up to the idealized view of leadership that competency lists portray (Conger & Ready, 2004). McCall and Hollenbeck (2002) note that complex, high-level executive jobs are accomplished in various ways by executives with multiple forms of talent. Therefore we would expect that global leaders can be effective without acquiring all competencies. Our research needs to distinguish between global leaders and global leadership and between episodic and long-term global leadership behaviour.

In summary, global leadership is an emerging field. Researchers have yet to focus on global leadership capability at a level of analysis above the individual. Future research is needed on the following global leadership topics.

- Construct a definition for global leadership.
- Distinguish between global managers and global leaders.
- Differentiate global leaders from domestic leaders.
- Determine the competencies that should be used as selection criteria for development programmes, assignments or promotions.
- Develop and/or validate GL assessment instruments.
- Identify global leader cognition and behaviour.
- Identify the contingencies that influence global leader behaviour.
- Investigate the relationship between global strategy and specific types of global leader skills.
- Develop process models of global leadership.
- Establish the antecedents of global leader effectiveness.
- Discover the outcomes of global leadership development training methodologies.

Developing Global Mindset and Global Leadership

Greater recognition of the important role played by global mindset and leadership does not immediately translate into greater competence and practice. A greater focus on development by scholars and practitioners is crucial. One can develop attitudes, abilities and knowledge through international assignments and global projects, but personality characteristics such as openness, flexibility and the reduction of ethnocentrism are, by definition, less amenable to change (Caligiuri & Di Santo, 2001). Therefore, selecting and promoting those who already have the desired personality characteristics

is a critical aspect in developing both global mindset and global leadership. For this reason, more attention is being paid to assessment instruments that measure predispositions to developing global mindset, global leadership, and intercultural competence (for reviews, see Bird, 2008; Stuart, 2009).

Global Mindset Development

To date, published empirical work on global mindset development is still nonexistent, with the exception of Clapp-Smith's (2009) dissertation. Her study on factors that contribute to global mindset development found a strong fit between the outcome, culturally appropriate behaviour, and cultural self-awareness, cognitive complexity and cultural intelligence.

Clapp-Smith, Luthans and Avólio (2007) developed an individual-level process model of global mindset development, based on social cognitive theory, that could be causal, reciprocal or iterative. Global/cultural trigger events lead individuals to enact varying levels of cognitive complexity. The psychological resources or capacities that help an individual translate the cognitive processing into appropriate behavior (i.e., greater cultural intelligence) are hope, optimism, resiliency, and efficacy. In addition, the influence of psychological capacities on cultural intelligence is strengthened by individual characteristics in the form of promotion focus (a self-regulating system concerned with achieving 'the ideal self') and developmental readiness.

The competencies required to develop global mindset are: 1) a foundation for knowledge, 2) cultural competency skills and 3) an understanding of different styles and preferences to facilitate nonjudgmental adaptation (Gupta, 2004). Based on research from cognitive psychology and knowledge development, Gupta and Govindarajan (2002: 120) assert that the individual and organizational development of a global mindset is likely fostered by (a) curiosity about the world and a commitment to becoming better informed about how the world works, (b) an explicit and self-conscious articulation of current mindsets, (c) exposure to diversity and novelty, and (d) a disciplined attempt to develop an integrated perspective that weaves together diverse strands of knowledge about cultures and markets.

The authors hypothesized that global mindset can be developed by (a) hiring diverse employees and managers, (b) providing opportunities such as cross-border teams and projects, short immersion experiences, and expatriate assignments, (c) holding meetings and business unit headquarters in foreign locations, (d) fostering social networks across cultures, and (e) taking formal education courses. It has also been hypothesized that global mindset can be developed with a focus on global issues with structural positions (global jobs, champions, teams), meeting topics and speakers, and incentives and accountability for global performance (Bouquet et al., 2003).

Global Leadership Development

Few models describe the global leadership development process. (For reviews of the literature on global leader development, see Mendenhall et. al., 2008; SHRM, 2010; Suutari, 2002;). The major challenges firms face in establishing global leadership development programmes are (a) establishing valid selection criteria on the global leadership competencies to develop and measure, (b) designing effective training programmes, and (c) retaining their highly sought-after 'graduates'.

Careful selection practices are essential and must be based upon empirical research identifying competencies important for global leadership success. In general, selection practices must also avoid ethnocentrism and be inclusive (Mendenhall, 2001; Osland & Taylor, 2001; Ruben, 1989).

Caligiuri (2004) found that highly effective global leaders in one firm had significantly higher conscientiousness scores and significantly lower neuroticism than less effective ones. (They also had lived abroad with their families, had long-term international assignments, and were mentored by people from a different culture.) According to Kets de Vries and Florent-Treacy (2002), the basic foundation of global leadership development consists of: a family background that includes culturally diverse parents, early international experiences, and bilingualism; an early education in international schools, summer camps, and international travel; a later education involving exchange programmes, foreign language and international MBA programmes; and spouses and children who are supportive, adventurous, adaptable, and mobile.

The Society for Human Resource Management (2010: 5) reported that common development strategies used by firms for their global leaders included temporary assignments; mentoring/coaching; stretch assignments; experiential or action learning assignments; international cross-functional teams; expatriate assignments of both short and long duration; language training; cross-cultural training; 360-degree feedback; and short business trips. Mendenhall and Oddou (2008) argue that the efficacy of global leadership development programmes is directly related to the experiential rigor and amount of time budgeted for development process in trainees. The list above does not reflect inherent experiential rigor or the amount of time devoted to each development strategy. For example, it is possible for a temporary assignment to be either experientially rigorous or weak, and if it is a 'one-off' experience it is unlikely to produce any developments in global leadership competencies (Brownell, 2006).

International assignments have been viewed as the most powerful development tool in facilitating global leadership competencies (Gregersen et al., 1998; Hall, Zhu & Yan, 2001; Mendenhall et al., 2001; SHRM, 2010), since they constitute a transformational experience that develops business savvy, continuous learning, cognitive complexity, behavioural flexibility, cross-cultural skills, and the ability to manage uncertainty (Osland, 2001; SHRM, 2010). However, simply residing overseas is not a guarantee that global leadership competencies will be developed. Caligiuri and Di Santo (2001) found that certain personality characteristics which are desirable in global leaders (flexibility, ethnocentrism, openness) did not increase as a result of global assignments. This type of finding, which was not surprising to scholars who studied expatriation, points to mediating variables that must be accounted for when considering the developmental potential of an expatriate assignment.

A multi-method approach (with each method designed to be high in experiential rigor and time components) is recommended to firms in developing global leadership development programmes: one that utilizes international assignments, short-term developmental assignments, international teams, action learning groups/projects/task forces, international training and development programmes, international meetings and forums, international travel (Ng, Van Dyne & Ang, 2009; Oddou, Mendenhall & Ritchie, 2000; Osland & Taylor, 2001; Roberts, Kossek & Ozeki, 1998; SHRM, 2010), 360-degree evaluations that include input from foreign organizational members (SHRM, 2010), and assessment centres (Stahl, 2001). Of course, as stated above, all methods have to be used mindfully by tying them to company strategy and ensuring that the necessary experiential rigor is in-built so that developmental leadership learning occurs. These programmes should ideally take place across long time periods and not in a single 1–3 day training programme; each method should be utilized within a long-term development strategy (SHRM, 2010).

A stick in the spokes of the above conclusions, however, is the variable of context and learning biases. For example, do managers from different nationalities develop global leadership skills through differing preferential processes or cultural lenses? Preliminary research by Wilson and Yip (2010) found that learning leadership competencies via 'hardships' or 'crucible experiences' was a more common learning vehicle for North American managers than managers from India and Singapore. They also found that Indian executives preferred learning leadership competencies via familial relationships (parents, uncles, cousins) compared to managers from the other countries in their sample, and that superiors or 'bosses' were viewed far less frequently as being vehicles for leadership development by Chinese managers compared to managers from other countries. Wilson and Yip (2010) raise intriguing questions that remain to be empirically answered by the field: 'Are leaders from some countries less likely to learn unique global leadership competencies via crucible experiences?'

'Our current models of leader development draw primarily on the experiences of senior executives from United States and Western European corporations. Does the use of individualism as a tacit frame of reference for current research truncate a more complete understanding of leader development?' (p. 53) They conclude that 'the bid to utilize research findings to prepare managers for future leadership responsibility must take into account the varieties of contexts within which leader development occurs' and that 'those responsible for leader development need a working knowledge of possible variations concerning what leadership learning will be most useful in a particular content' (pp. 53 & 54).

McCall and Hollenbeck's (2002) research makes a major contribution to clarifying the development process of global executives from both an individual and an organizational perspective. Their model consists of five components that lead to 'the right stuff' in global managers (what they need to implement business strategy): talent, mechanisms, experience in a global context and catalysts, with the latter moderated by business strategy. They acknowledge several difficulties in assessing talent: identifying a common standard across cultures, country differences in assessing, promoting and developing managers, wide variability in global executive jobs, and the organization's openness to promoting executives from other nationalities. The mechanism variable in their model consists of selection, succession, development, discovery and recovery, which are all elaborated on below.

Selection and succession refers in part to the organization's need to identify people who are ready to assume global positions when unexpected staffing needs arise; in other words, replacement planning for critical jobs. Development occurs by placing people in jobs that will expand their cultural or business skills, which is often done with people from a culturally diverse background who have a clear interest in international work. Discovery mechanisms provide parochial employees with an opportunity early on in their careers to ascertain whether they might have an interest in international work. Recovery pertains to the organization's efforts to integrate repatriates when they return home. Developmental catalysts, such as feedback, reward systems and so on, help executives learn. Finally, business strategy refers to a firm's specific development needs, which are based on their particular strategic intent and organizational design. Strategy and structure will determine the number of international jobs, the types of global executives and their nationalities, and the skills they will need. Thus McCall and Hollenbeck (2002) view business strategy as a moderator in their global executive development framework. They confirm the findings of other scholars (Mendenhall et al., 2008) and practitioners (SHRM, 2010) that global experience is crucial to global leadership development.

Global Leadership Development: A 'Non-Linear' Perspective

The argument that global leadership is a process of personal transformation is an underlying theme in much of the literature. Assuming this thesis, it is likely that global leadership development is not a linear progression of adding competencies to an existing portfolio of leadership competencies, but rather a non-linear process whereby deep-seated change in competencies and world view takes places in the process of experiential overlays over time. This 'experiential crucible' includes experiences over which the company may have little or no control. Consequently traditional training cannot be the primary tool through which global leadership competencies are inculcated within individuals. This process is akin to phenomena that are studied within the emerging field of non-linear dynamics.

Traditional social scientific philosophy, methodology and understanding are based on a core assumption: that relationships between variables in social phenomena are linear in nature (Capra, 1983, 1996). This cognitive and perceptual bedrock, which has been the centre of socialization for thousands of doctoral students since the 1920s in North American universities, has produced the development of social scientific theories that are reductionistic, deterministic, and equilibrium-oriented in nature (Lichtenstein & Mendenhall, 2002). The superordinate goal of such social scientific theories is the prediction of human

behaviour (Capra, 1983, 1996; Hayles, 1991; Dooley, 1997; Lichtenstein & Mendenhall, 2002). This unconscious, ubiquitous paradigm is a lens through which managers, as well as academics, perceive reality. Wheatley (1992: 6) summarized the subtle effects of our socialization when she observed:

Each of us lives and works in organizations designed from Newtonian images of the universe. We manage by separating things into parts, we believe that influence occurs as a direct result of force exerted from one person to another, we engage in complex planning for a world that we keep expecting to be predictable, and we search continually for better methods of objectively perceiving the world. These assumptions... are the base from which we design and manage organizations, and from which we do research in all of the social sciences.

One reason for the sustained permanence of this core assumption is that linearity does exist in the world. Many systems and laws in the universe are inherently linear in nature. An understanding of linearity has allowed humankind to transport astronauts to the moon and, on a more mundane note, to know what time it is at any given moment of the day.

An overarching characteristic of linear, deterministic systems is their proportionality; that is, an input of x amount of force into a system results in a corresponding output which proportionately reflects the amount of force (x). Lichtenstein and Mendenhall (2002) note that the implicit belief that predictable, closed mechanical systems are the norm for natural and social science modelling (Harding, 1986; Turner, 1997) was the basis for virtually all models of biological and social process (Bateson, 1980; Berman, 1984).

Over the past two decades, however, discoveries of non-linearity in the natural sciences have led an increasing number of social scientists to explore the possibility that social phenomena have non-linear elements within them (Capra, 1996; Eylon & Giacalone, 2000). Some social scientists, such as George Herbert Mead, Joseph Schumpeter and Mary Parker Follett, saw and wrote about the relationship between non-linearity and social phenomena in the 1920s and 1930s, but their voices were drowned out by the tide of logical positivism that emerged at that time, and has continued to the present, to become the foundational philosophy of social science (Lichtenstein & Mendenhall, 2002).

The Nature of Non-Linearity

Lichtenstein and Mendenhall (2002: 8) describe non-linearity as 'a common state of dynamic systems in which events and their outcomes are non-proportional. In the simplest sense, non-linear system inputs are not proportional to the system's outputs; for example 140° F is not twice as pleasant as 70° F, and eight aspirin are not eight times as effective as one'. Another description of non-linearity was provided by Meiss (1995: 1):

Non-linear is defined as the negation of linear. This means that the result may be out of proportion to the input. The result may be more than linear, as when a diode begins to pass current; or less than linear, as when finite resources limit Malthusian population growth. Thus the fundamental simplifying tools of linear analysis are no longer available.

Some scholars have begun to theorize that global leadership development has non-linear aspects and that firms need to understand this process better than they currently do in order to develop global leaders.

The multitudes of daily experiences that are encountered in a dynamic, intercultural milieu are not linear. Certain intercultural experiences will trigger either functional or dysfunctional global competency development that is out of proportion to their importance to all other factors in the situation, or to the business context itself. Seemingly innocent or minor intercultural interactions can career out of control, causing global managers to internalize false or skewed intercultural understanding of 'why' the event occurred and 'what' the event means. In responding to these events, global managers continually create a new reality. Mary Parker Follett (1924: 62–3) argued that such social interaction was a non-linear process:

[an individual's] reaction is always reaction to a relating... I never react to you but to you-plus-me; or to be more accurate, it is I-plus-you reacting to you-plus- me... that is, in the very process of meeting, by the very process of meeting, we both become something different. It begins even before we meet, in the anticipation of meeting... It is I plus the-interweaving-between-you-and-me meeting you plus the-interweaving-between-you-and-me, etc., etc. If we were doing it mathematically we should work it out to the nth power.

Each intercultural situation that a global manager experiences—and there are myriad experiences like these occurring daily—consists of 'non-linear relatings'. That is, the creation of global leadership competencies is like a continuing dance with multiple partners. One is not independent of one's partners—the continual decisions and learning from decisions in response to continual behaviours enacted over time will transform someone into either a competent or an incompetent global leader—and all points in between. Lichtenstein and Mendenhall (2002) contend that components and behaviours in non-linear dynamical systems cannot be separated, so independent forces do not bring about dependent outcomes. All elements in such systems are 'mutually constituting': they arise and evolve as an interconnected network (Capra, 1996). A cause does not have one and *only* one effect; therefore the customary linear connection among antecedents and outcomes does not hold true. Instead the 'mutual causality' that characterizes this interdependence among variables constitutes a core principle of the new sciences (Briggs & Peat, 1989).

On the assumption that global leadership development in an individual is a non-linear, mutually causal, emergent process moderated by a variety of key variables across time, we would offer the following process model, depicted in Figure 37.1, as a first attempt to comprehend global leadership development through a non-linear, paradigmatic lens. The model is called, 'The Chattanooga model of global leadership development', as it was developed in a think-tank setting by global leadership scholars in Chattanooga, Tennessee, in 2001, at the Frierson Leadership Institute.

At the left of the model, in the corner, an individual enters a global/ cross-cultural context and is immersed in it (24/7) over a significant period of time. The person enters with basic, core immutable personality traits, which will include fairly immutable competencies (ambition, a desire to lead, sociability, openness, agreeableness, emotional stability, and so on) and cognitive processes (attribution flexibility, category width, tolerance for ambiguity, and so on). The individual also enters with existing levels of self-efficacy that are brought to bear on various aspects of living and working globally. The degree to which the individual perceives a 'call to do this', or, in other words, the degree to which people view themselves as global citizens and believe that this assignment fits 'who they really are' inside, is an important factor in their motivation to lead in a global situation. Finally the person enters the global context with existing levels of global managerial/leadership competencies.

Each individual will have a unique configuration of these variables and will bring this configuration to bear upon the multitude of daily experiences that are encountered in the new milieu. The 'folders' or 'pages' in Figure 37.1 represent the experiences, interactions and challenges the individual passes through over time. Each of these experiences differs in the degree to which they present the individual with complexity and the degree to which they are important to the individual, thus heightening the intensity of the experience for that individual. The combination of complexity and intensity contributes to the degree of emotional effect the individual experiences.

The recursive arrow in the model connotes the fact that a current experience can cause, through memory, an updating or reliving of past experiences. Thus the global leadership development process is not based on independent experiences; rather each experience is tied to past, multiple experiences and constitutes a sense-making process of learning and acquiring global leadership competencies, Bennis and Thomas (2002; 14) refer to the gestalt of these processes as constituting 'crucibles': situations 'characterized by the confluence of powerful intellectual, social, economic, or political forces' that severely test one's patience, and one's beliefs, and that produce a transformation in the individual, leaving him/her deeply different in terms of who they were before the crucible experience.

The nature of these various global crucible experiences is critical to the formation of global leadership. The degree to which these experiences are buffered by organizational policies or the individuals themselves, or the degree to which access to these experiences is curtailed by companies (for example, expensive housing that separates the global manager from interactions with the host society), moderates whether or not these potentially transforming experiences instead become shallow and non-catalytic in terms of global leadership development. Additionally educational support systems, culture novelty, job novelty, and spouse/family adjustment can each enhance or detract from global leadership development.

Thus a key factor in individual global leadership development is 'access to high-level challenges'. Access to these challenges may produce, in some cases, solid global leadership competency development over time, however such access holds the potential for failure as well. Individuals may have the right kind of experiences, but be unable to handle or learn from them because they are overwhelming. New mental models are indeed created within the individual; however those models may be dysfunctional. It is important to note that, although these mental models become apparent at the end of the process depicted in Figure 37.1, in actuality they are being created over and over again in response to each experience the individual has. Consequently the developing framework is malleable, but it may harden into a dysfunctional systemic framework if the experiences are not processed effectively.

In summary, the Chattanooga model depicts the global leadership development process as emergent in nature and constantly dynamic. If a person's competencies and access to powerful challenges are harmonious to working and learning in the global context, a functional global leadership process will ensue, and the individual will develop enhanced global leadership competencies. At any point in time, one's trajectory can rise, fall, or be moderated by the unique constellation of forces that will impinge upon any given experience.

Figure 37.1 A Non-linear Model of Global Leadership Development

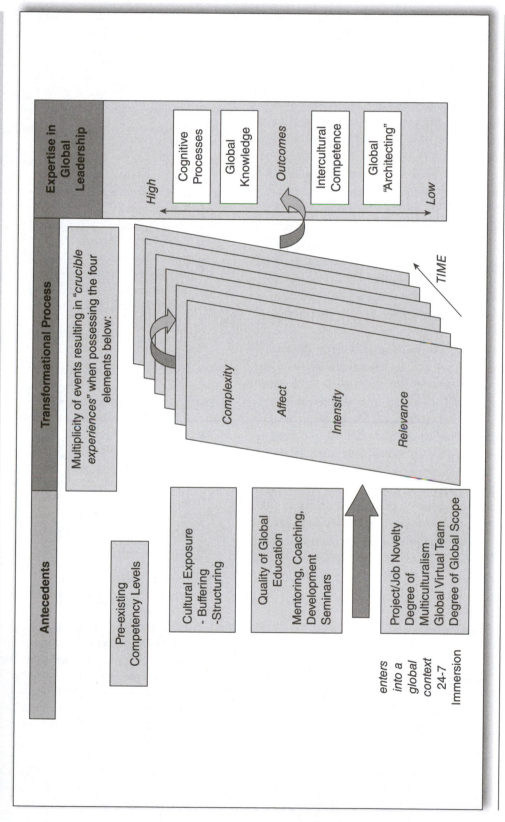

Source: Mendenhali, M., Osland, J. S., Bird, A., Oddou, G. & Maznevski, M. (eds) 2008. *Global Leadership: Research, Practice, Development.* London: Routledge.

Pless, Maak and Stahl (2011) conducted a study worthy of emulation that attempted to address the complex nature of global leadership development. 'Project Ulysses' was a service learning programme where participants were sent to developing countries to work in highly challenging environments. After going through this programme they found that participants increased in the following domains, all of which were important for global leadership: a responsible mindset, ethical literacy, cultural intelligence, a global mindset, self-development, and community building. They reported that the processes that facilitated the heightening of these competencies were paradox confrontation and resolution, the construction of a 'new life-world', and emotional sense-making. This study beckons other scholars in the field to dig beneath the surface of 'competency identification' and explore the processes that trigger competency development.

Much work remains to be done in the area of global mindset and leadership development. The Chattanooga model and others need to be tested, and the effectiveness and costs of different types of developmental methods need to be compared. The organizational aspect of development cannot be overlooked; the alignment of HRM and the organizational culture with a firm's efforts to develop global leadership and global mindset also requires more investigation. Also, systemic analyses of the processes that promote or impede global leadership and mindset development across multiple cultural contexts and cultural learning preferences will be necessary.

References

Adler, N. 2001. Global leadership: Women leaders. In M. Mendenhall, T. M. Kuhlmann & G. Stahl (eds), *Developing global business leaders: policies, processes, and innovations*: 73–97. Westport, CN: Quorum (also in *Management International Review*, 1997, 37(1): 171–96).

Adler, N. & Bartholomew, S. 1992. Managing globally competent people. *The Executive*, 6(3): 52–65.

Anastasi, A. & Urbina, S. 1997. *Psychological testing*. Seventh edition. Upper Saddle River, NJ: Prentice-Hall.

Arora, A., Jaju, A., Kefalas, A. G. & Perenich, T. 2004. An exploratory analysis of global managerial mindsets: A case of U.S. textile and apparel industry. *Journal of International Management*, 10: 393–411.

Ashby, W. R. 1956. *An introduction to cybernetics*. New York: Wiley.

Bartlett, C. A. & Ghoshal, S. 1989. *Managing across borders: The transnational solution*. Boston: Harvard Business School Press.

Bartlett, C. A. & Ghoshal, S. 1992. What is a global manager? *Harvard Business Review*, 124–31.

Bateson, G. 1980. *Mind and nature—a necessary unity*. New York: Bantam Books.

Beechler, S., Levy, O., Taylor, L. S. & Boyacigiller, N. 2004. Does it really matter if Japanese MNCs think globally? The impact of employees' perceptions on their attitudes. In T. Roehl & A. Bird (eds), *Japanese firms in transition*: 265–92. [*Advances in International Management*, 17], Amsterdam and Oxford: Elsevier JAI.

Begley, T. M. & Boyd, D. P. 2003. The need for a corporate global mind-set. *Sloan Management Review*, 44(2): 25–32.

Bennis, W. G. & Thomas, R. J. 2002. *Geeks and geezers: How era, values, and defining moments shape leaders*. Boston: Harvard Business School Press.

Berman, M. 1984. *The re-enchantment of the world*. New York: Bantam Books.

Bhagat, R., Triandis, H., Ram Baliga, B., Billing, T. & Davis, C. 2007. On becoming a global manager: A closer look at the opportunities and constraints in the 21st century. In M. Javidan, R. Steers & M. Hitt (eds), *The global mindset*: 191–213. [*Advances in International Management*, 19]. Amsterdam and Oxford: Elsevier JAI.

Bikson, T. K., Treverton, G. F., Moini, J. & Lindström, G. 2003. *New challenges for international leadership: Lessons from organizations with global missions*. Santa Monica, CA: Rand.

Bird, A. 2008. Assessing global leadership competencies. In M. Mendenhall, J.S. Osland, A. Bird, G. Oddou & M. Maznevski (eds), *Global leadership: Research, practice and development*: 64–80. London: Routledge.

Bird, A., Mendenhall, M., Stevens, M. & Oddou, G. 2010. Denning the content domain of intercultural competence for global leaders. *Journal of Managerial Psychology*, 25(8): 810–28.

Bird, A. & Osland, J. 2004. Global competencies: An introduction. In H. Lane, M. Maznevksi, M. E. Mendenhall & J. McNett (eds), *Handbook for Global Managers*: 57–80. London: Blackwell.

Black, J. S., Morrison, A. & Gregersen, H. 1999. *Global explorers: the next generation of leaders.* New York: Routledge.

Bouquet, C. 2005. *Building global mindsets: an attention-based perspective.* New York: Palgrave Macmillan.

Bouquet, C., Morrison, A. & Birkinshaw, J. 2003. Determinants and performance implications of global mindset: an attention-based perspective. *Academy of Management Journal.*

Bouquet, C, Morrison, A. & Birkinshaw. J. 2009. International attention and multinational enterprise performance. *Journal of International Business Studies,* 40(1): 108–131.

Bowen, D. E. & Inkpen, A. C. 2009. Exploring the role of 'global mindset' in leading change in international contexts. *The Journal of Applied Behavioral Science,* 45(2): 239–260.

Boyacigiller, N., Beechler, S., Taylor, S. & Levy, O. 2004. The crucial but illusive global mindset. In H. Lane, M. Maznevski, M. Mendenhall & J. McNett (eds), *Handbook of global management:* 81–93. Oxford: Blackwell.

Brake, T. 1997. *The global leader: critical factors for creating the world class organization.* Chicago: Irwin Professional Publishing.

Briggs, J. & Peat, D. 1989. *Turbulent mirror.* New York: Harper & Row.

Brownell, J. 2006. Meeting the competency needs of global leaders: a partnership approach. *Human Resource Management,* 45(3): 309–36.

Caligiuri, P. 2004. Global leadership development through expatriate assignments and other international experiences. Paper presented at the Academy of Management, New Orleans, August.

Caligiuri, P. & Di Santo, V. 2001. Global competence: what is it and can it be developed through international assignment? *HR Resource Planning,* 24(3): 27–36.

Calof, J. L. & Beamish, P. W. 1994. The right attitude for international success. *Ivey Business Quarterly,* 59(1): 105–10.

Calori, R., Johnson, G. & Sarnin, P. 1994. CEO's cognitive maps and the scope of the organization. *Strategic Management Journal,* 15: 437–57.

Capra, F. 1983. *The turning point.* New York: Bantam Books.

Capra, F. 1996. *The web of life.* New York: Anchor Books.

Clapp-Smith, R. 2009. Global mindset development during cultural transitions. Dissertation, University of Nebraska.

Clapp-Smith, R., Luthans, F. & Aviólo, B. J. 2007. The role of psychological capital in global mindset development. In M. Javidan, R. Steers & M. Hitt (eds), *Global mindset: advances in international management,* 19, 105-130

Cohen, E. 2007. *Leadership without borders.* Singapore: Wiley.

Conger, J. & Ready, D. 2004. Rethinking leadership competencies. *Leader to Leader,* 32: 41–8.

Dalton, M., Ernst, C, Deal, J. & Leslie, J. 2002. *Success for the new global manager: what you need to know to work across distances, countries and cultures.* San Francisco: Jossey-Bass and the Center for Creative Leadership.

Dooley, K. 1997. A complex adaptive systems model of organization change: nonlinear dynamics. *Psychology and the Life Sciences,* 3: 230–49.

Doz, Y. & Prahalad, C. 1991. Managing DMNCs: a search for a new paradigm. *Strategic Management Journal,* 12: 145–64.

Ernst, C. T. 2000. The influence of behavioral complexity on global leadership effectiveness. Unpublished dissertation, North Carolina State University.

Eylon, D. & Giacalone, R. 2000. Introduction: the road to a new management paradigm. *American Behavioral Scientist,* 43(Special issue): 1215–17.

Festing, M. 2001. The effects of international human resource management strategies on global leadership development. In M. Mendenhall, T.M. Kuhlmann & G. Stahl (eds), *Developing global business leaders: policies, processes, and innovations:* 37–56. Westport, CN: Quorum.

Follett, M. P. 1924. *Creative experience.* New York: Peter Smith.

Furuya, N., Stevens, M., Bird, A., Oddou, G. & Mendenhall, M. 2009. Managing the learning and transfer of global management competence: antecedents and outcomes of Japanese repatriation effectiveness. *Journal of International Business Studies,* 40: 200–15.

Goldsmith, M., Greenberg, C, Robertson, A. & Hu-Chan, M. 2003. *Global leadership: the next generation.* Upper Saddle River, NJ: Prentice-Hall.

Gregersen, H. B., Morrison, A. & Black, J. S. 1998. Developing leaders for the global frontier. *Sloan Management Review,* 40(1): 21–33.

Gupta, A. K. 2004. *Global strategy and organizations.* San Francisco: Wiley.

Gupta, A. K. & Govindarajan, V. 2002. Cultivating a global mindset. *Academy of Management Executive,* 16(1): 116–26.

Hall, D. T., Zhu, D. & Yan, A. 2001. Developing global leaders: to hold on to them, let them go! In W. Mobley & M. W. McCall, Jr (eds), *Advances in global leadership,* vol. 2. Stamford, CT: JAI Press.

Harding, S. 1986. *The science question in feminism.* Ithaca, NY: Cornell University Press.

Harveston, P. D., Kedia, B.L. & Davis, P.S. 2000. Internationalization of born global and gradual globalizing firms: the impact of the manager. *Advances in Competitiveness Research,* 8(1): 92–9.

Hayles, N. K. 1991. Complex dynamics in science and literature. In N.K. Hayles (ed.), *Chaos and order: complex dynamics in literature and science.* Chicago: University of Chicago Press.

Hind, P., Wilson, A. & Lenssen, G. 2009. Developing leaders for sustainable business. *Corporate Governance,* 9(1): 7–20.

House, R. J., Hanges, P. W., Javidan, M., Dorfman, P. & Gupta, V. (eds) 2004. *Culture. leadership and organizations: the GLOBE study of 62 societies.* Beverly Hills, CA: Sage.

IBM 2010. *Capitalizing on complexity: insights from the global chief executive officer study.* Somers, NY: IBM Global Business Services.

Javidan, M., Teagarden, M. & Bowen, D. 2010. Making it overseas. *Harvard Business Review,* April: 1–5.

Jeannet, J. 2000. *Managing with a global mindset.* London: Financial Times/Prentice-Hall.

Kedia, B. & Mukhcrji, A. 1999. Global managers: developing a mindset for global competitiveness. *Journal of World Business,* 34(3): 230–50.

Kefalas, A. G. 1998. Think globally, act locally. *Thunderbird International Business Review,* 40(6): 547–62.

Kets deVries, M. & Florent-Treacy, E. 1999. *The new global leaders.* San Francisco: Jossey-Bass.

Kets de Vries, M. & Mead, C. 1992. The development of the global leader within the multinational corporation. In V. Pucik, N.M. Tichy & C.K. Barnett (eds), *Globalizing management: creating and leading the competitive organization.* New York: John Wiley & Sons.

Kets de Vries, Vrignaud, M. P. & Florent-Treacy, E. 2004. The global leadership life inventory: development and psychometric properties of a 360-degree feedback instrument. *International Journal of Human Resource Management,* 15(3): 475–92.

Kobrin, S. J. 1994. Is there a relationship between a geocentric mind-set and multinational strategy? *Journal of international Business Studies,* 25(3): 493–512.

Kotter, J. 1990. What leaders really do. *Harvard Business Review,* 103–11.

Lane, H. W., Maznevski, M. L., Mendenhall, M. E. & McNett, J. (eds) 2004. *The Blackwell handbook of global management: a guide to managing complexity.* London: Blackwell.

Leslie, J. B., Dalton, M., Ernst, C. & Deal, J. 2002. *Managerial effectiveness in a global context.* Greensboro, NC: Center for Creative Leadership Press.

Levy, O. 2001. The influence of top management team global mindset on global strategic posture of firms.

Paper presented at the Annual Meeting of the Academy of Management, Washington, DC.

Levy, O. 2005. The influence of top management team attentional patterns on global strategic posture of firms. *Journal of Organizational Behavior,* 26(7): 797–819.

Levy, O., Beechler, S., Taylor, S. & Boyacigiller, N. A. 1999. What we talk about when we talk about 'Global Mindset'. Paper Presented at the Academy of Management Annual Meeting, Chicago, August.

Levy, O., Beechler, S., Taylor, S. & Boyacigiller, N. A. 2007. What do we talk about when we talk about 'global mindset'? Managerial cognition in multinational corporation. *Journal of International Business Studies,* 38 (2): 231–258.

Levy, O., Taylor, S., and Boyacigiller, N. 2010. On the rocky road to strong global culture. *MIT Sloan Management Review,* 61(4): 20–22.

Lichtenstein, B. & Mendenhall, M. 2002. Non-linearity and response-ability: emergent order in 21st century careers. *Human Relations,* 55(1): 5–32.

Maznevski, M. & Lane, H. 2004. Shaping the global mindset: designing educational experiences for effective global thinking and action. In N. Boyacigiller, R.M. Goodman & M. Phillips (eds), *Teaching and experiencing cross-cultural management: lessons from master teacher:* 171–184. London and New York: Routledge.

McCall, M.W. Jr & Hollenbeck, G. P. 2002. *Developing global executives.* Boston: Harvard Business School Press.

Meiss, J.D. 1995. Frequently asked questions about nonlinear science (version 1.0.9). Newsgroup sci.nonlinear: Department of Applied Mathematics at University of Colorado at Boulder, 1–31.

Mendenhall, M. 2001. Introduction: new perspectives on expatriate adjustment and its relationship to global leadership development. In M. Mendenhall, T.M. Kuhlmann & G. Stahl (eds), *Developing global business leaders: policies, processes, and innovations:* 1–16. Westport, CN: Quorum.

Mendenhall, M. & Osland, J.S. 2002. An overview of the extant global leadership research. Symposium presentation, Academy of International Business, Puerto Rico, June.

Mendenhall, M., Osland, J.S., Bird, A., Oddou, G. & Maznevski, M. 2008. *Global leadership: research, practice and development.* London: Routledge.

Mobley, W., Wang, Y. &M. Li Jr (eds) 2009. *Advances in global leadership,* vol. 5. Stamford, CT: JAI Press.

Murtha, T. P., Lenway, S.A. & Bagozzi, R.P. 1998. Global mind-sets and cognitive shift in a complex multinational corporation. *Strategic Management Journal,* 19(2): 97–114.

Ng, K.-Y., Van Dyne, L. & Ang, S. 2009. From experience to experiential learning: cultural intelligence as a learning capability for global leader development. *Academy of Management Learning & Education,* 8(4): 511–526.

Nummela, N., Saarenketo, S. & Puumalainen, K. 2004. A global mindset—a prerequisite for successful internationalization? *Canadian Journal of Administrative Sciences,* 21: 51–65.

Nunnaly, J. C. & Bernstein, I. H. 1994. *Psychometric theory.* Third edition. New York: McGraw-Hill.

Oddou, G., Mendenhall, M. & Ritchie, J. B. 2000. Leveraging travel as a tool for global leadership development. *Human Resource Management,* 39(2, 3): 159–72.

Ohmae, K. 1989. Managing in a borderless world. *Harvard Business Review,* 67(3): 152–61.

Osland, J. 2001. The quest for transformation. In M. Mendenhall, T.M. Kuhlmann and G. Stahl (eds), *Developing global business leaders: policies, processes, and innovations:* 137–56. Westport, CN: Quorum,

Osland, J. & Bird, A. 2006. Global leaders as experts. *Advances in Global Leadership,* 4: 125–145.

Osland, J. & Bird, A. 2007. Expert cognition in global leaders: what does it look like and how can it be developed? In M. Higano & A. Bird (eds), *Business Guide: Leadership:* 175–88. Tokyo: Nippon Hyoronsha.

Osland, J. & Taylor, S. 2001. Developing global leaders. *HR Com.* February.

Paul, H. 2000. Creating a mindset. *Thunderbird International Business Review,* 42: 187–200.

Perlmutter, H. V. 1969. The tortuous evolution of the multinational corporation. *Columbia Journal of World Business,* 4(1): 9–18.

Pless, N. M., Maak, T. & Stahl, G. K. 2011. Developing responsible global leaders through International Service Learning Programs: The Ulysses experience. *Academy of Management Learning and Education.*

Rhinesmith, S. 1993. *A manager's guide to globalization.* Alexandria, VA: Irwin.

Roberts, K., Kossek, E.E. & Ozeki, C. 1998. Managing the global workforce: challenge and strategies. *Academy of Management Executive,* 12(4): 93–106.

Rosen, R., Digh, P., Singer, M. & Philips, C. 2000. *Global literacies: lessons on business leadership and national cultures.* New York: Simon & Schuster.

Ruben, B. D. 1989. The study of cross-cultural competence: traditions and contemporary issues. *International Journal of Intercultural Relations,* 13: 229–39.

Sambharya, R. 1996. Foreign experience of top management teams and international diversification strategies of U.S. multinational corporations. *Strategic Management Journal,* 17(9): 739–46.

Srinivas, K. M. 1995. Globalization of business and the Third World: challenge of expanding the mindsets. *Journal of Management Development,* 14(3): 26–49.

Stahl, G. 2001. Using assessment centers as tools for global leadership development: an exploratory study. In M. Mendenhall, T.M. Kuhlmann and G. Stahl (eds), *Developing global business leaders: policies, processes, and innovations:* 197–210. Westport, CN: Quorum.

Stuart, D. K. 2009. Assessment instruments for the global workforce. In M. Moodian (ed.), *Contemporary leadership and intercultural competence: exploring the cross-cultural dynamics within organizations:* 175–190. Thousand Oaks, CA: Sage,

Suutari, V. 2002. Global leader development: an emerging research agenda. *Career Development International,* 7(4): 218–33.

The Society for Human Resource Management. 2010. *Research Quarterly: Global Leadership Development.* Fourth Quarter: 1–9.

Tichy, N., Brimm, M., Charan, R. & Takeuchi, H. 1992. Leadership development as a lever for global transformation. In V. Pucik, N. Tichy & C.K. Barnett (eds), *Globalizing management: creating and leading the competitive organization:* 47–60. New York: John Wiley & Sons.

Turner, F. 1997. Chaos and social science. In R. Eve, S. Horsfall & M.E. Lee (eds), *Chaos, complexity, and sociology.* Thousand Oaks, CA: Sage Publications.

Vanhoegaerden, J. 2010. Global mindset and decision making. Working paper, Ashridge Business School.

Von Glinow, M. A. 2001. Future issues in global leadership development. In M. Mendenhall, T.M. Kuhlmann & G. Stahl (eds), *Developing global business leaders: policies, processes and innovations:* 264–71. Westport, CT: Quorum.

Wheatley, M. 1992. *Leadership and the new science.* San Francisco: Barrett-Koehler.

Wills, S. & K. Barham. 1994. Being an international manager. *European Management Journal,* 12(1): 49–58.

Wilson, M. S. & Yip, J. 2010. Grounding leader development: Cultural perspectives. *Center for Creative Leadership, Industrial and Organizational Psychology,* 3: 52–55.

Yeung, A. & Ready, D. 1995. Developing leadership capabilities of global corporations: a comparative study in eight nations. *Human Resource Management,* 34(4): 529–47.

CHAPTER 38

Getting to "We"

Collective Leadership Development

Kristin L. Cullen[1]
Center for Creative Leadership

Charles J. Palus
Center for Creative Leadership

Donna Chrobot-Mason
University of Cincinnati

Craig Appaneal
Center for Creative Leadership

We agree with Yammarino, Salas, Serban, Shirreffs, and Shuffler (2012) that embracing collectivistic leadership approaches requires broadening leadership development beyond an exclusive focus on individuals. Over the last decade the leadership development community at the Center for Creative Leadership (CCL)—of which we are members—has shifted its view of leadership. We now approach leadership as an accomplishment of collectives rather than as the actions of individuals identified as leaders. This shift has led us to reconceptualize and evolve our practice of leadership development. In this commentary, we will expand on the focal article by offering examples that illustrate collective leadership development in action.

A Collectivistic View of Leadership

If leadership is a social process, what exactly does that social process produce? Our colleagues have argued that the outcomes of leadership are direction, alignment, and commitment within the collective (DAC; Drath et al., 2008). Direction is indicated by agreement on what the collective is trying to achieve. Alignment exists when activities are coordinated and integrated in service of the shared direction. Commitment is evident when individuals make the success of the collective a priority. Individual leaders' beliefs, competencies, and behaviors are but one part of this broader social process that produces DAC.

A focus on *collective outcomes* moves the goal of development beyond *only* individual leaders' competencies to the expansion of a collective's (e.g., team, organization, community, and nation) ability to produce DAC. The emphasis of development must now include *collective beliefs and practices for producing DAC*, the management of *identity-based boundaries* within the organization, and the *social network* connecting individuals. Further, this development process requires the adoption of a systems-based perspective to determine why a collective is succeeding or failing to produce DAC given the collective's environment and strategic objectives. This commentary expands the focal article by offering examples that illustrate collective leadership development in practice.

Leadership Culture: Developing Collective Beliefs and Practices for Producing DAC

Leadership culture is the collective's shared beliefs and practices for understanding and producing DAC (Drath et al., 2008; McGuire & Rhodes, 2009). Like broader culture, it is deeply embedded and difficult to change. Yet it is a change in the leadership culture that is often needed for organizations to continue producing DAC in an increasingly unstable, uncertain, and complex world. To help collectives improve their leadership, we needed to make culture change part of our leadership development practice.

The leadership culture transformation at KONE Americas illustrates this shift in practice. KONE, a long-time leader in the elevator-escalator and "people flow" industry, had grown comfortable in its historical success and was under-performing in a competitive market. It was clear to the new CEO and his core team that deep organizational change was needed. Through facilitated reflection and dialogue, they realized that a successful deep change would require their leadership culture to be aligned with, and a driver of, their new business strategy, which focused on customer-driven processes.

When changing the leadership culture in an organization, we have found that a core group of senior executives must first begin exploring and transforming their own beliefs and practices for creating DAC (McGuire & Rhodes, 2009). At KONE, our colleagues supported this process by coaching the executive team over a period of several years. This engagement was designed to create readiness, and then capability, for a broader transformation of the entire leadership culture. According to the CEO Vance Tang, "We had to appreciate that we had to change ourselves first in order to change the culture. We had to experience change together, with our team. We changed how we work together. We spent time on feedback, trust, and dialogue. Now we can challenge each other. Now we have better outcomes because we can all be on the same page and work much faster."

One of the key challenges in targeting the leadership culture for development is in getting people to "see" it and grasp it in various ways. Developing the leadership culture of a collective requires a discovery process of naming, exploring, assessing, and mutually reflecting on the various leadership cultures in the organization. We have found a framework that describes three basic stages of leadership culture to be useful in this work (Drath, Palus, & McGuire, 2010; Palus, McGuire, & Ernst, 2011). In the first, *dependent* culture, the responsibility of leadership belongs to those in formal positions of authority. In the second, *independent* culture, leadership is based on the expertise and formal position of individuals, personal influence, and the drive for individual achievement. In the third, *interdependent* culture, leadership is a collaborative activity of mutual inquiry and learning that can include the earlier stages as required to respond to emerging challenges.

Using a simple wall chart, each KONE executive team member made one mark indicating where he or she believed the stage of leadership culture was at present, and another mark for where the culture needed to be in the *future* to enact the business strategy. This provocative gap became the subject for sensemaking in an ongoing learning dialogue. Later, regional and senior managers completed a leadership culture survey, and the results helped the executive team check their initial assessment and extend the dialogue about the present and future desired leadership culture to a wider circle of leaders across all the regions. The executive team's message that "in order to reach our business goals of industry leadership, we are moving to a more interdependent leadership culture" gradually became believable and compelling to the wider organization, creating readiness for further collective leadership development. The later aspects of this development process took many forms, including team transformation work, large-group interventions, and an employee engagement tour, in which every employee at the branch level, including technicians, participated in creating DAC with senior leaders (see McGuire & Palus, 2013).

Boundary Spanning Leadership: Managing Identity-based Intergroup Divides

As with KONE, more interdependent, collaborative leadership cultures are required by organizations that seek to break down functional silos, integrate global offerings, and work closely with multiple stakeholders. These collaborations require groups with distinct identities to span boundaries and create DAC across groups. Although this may sound straightforward, it is often fraught with difficulties. When groups with significantly different values and priorities interact they often become more polarized and experience greater conflict (Chrobot-Mason, Ruderman, Weber, & Ernst, 2009). This polarization likely occurs because the security of the groups' identities is threatened during the process of collaboration (Fiol, Pratt, & O'Connor, 2009). Collective leadership development must balance the need for both intergroup differentiation and unity (Ernst & Chrobot-Mason, 2010; Fiol et al., 2009) by upholding subgroup differences in values, priorities, and skills while also promoting a common mission (Hogg, Van Knippenberg, & Rast, 2012).

Facilitating the production of DAC across boundaries is another practice that we have sought to add to our leadership development capabilities. For example, fifteen months prior to the departure of the United States military from Iraq, the Commanding General of U.S. Forces-Iraq and the Ambassador to Iraq partnered with CCL to work more effectively across the boundary between the Department of State and the Department of Defense. This boundary spanning leadership (BSL) initiative helped establish more interdependent leadership beliefs and practices for addressing the challenges of security and nation building in Iraq (Hughes, Palus, Ernst, Houston, & McGuire, 2011). The commanding general and ambassador understood the importance of collaboration for the transition of military operations to a sustainable diplomatic presence. They also recognized the distinct culture and priorities of their organizations and the potential these differences had to derail their collaborative effort.

In a day-long workshop, leaders from both departments joined together to apply the three strategies of the BSL model (Ernst & Chrobot-Mason, 2010) to their current leadership challenge—withdrawing troops, transferring responsibilities and equipment to the State Department, and negotiating with the Iraqi leadership about its future (Chrobot-Mason, Ernst, & Ferguson, 2012). The workshop began with both groups working separately with facilitators to *manage boundaries,* the first step in the BSL model. This step is designed to clarify and define differences that designate an intergroup boundary. Each group established their department's unique strengths and weaknesses and the outcomes they hoped to accomplish through a successful transition. Through this process subgroups experienced a sense of safety because the distinctiveness of their subgroup identity was emphasized.

During the second part of the workshop, leaders from Defense and State were brought together again. They shared with the other group, their own strengths and weaknesses and their vision for a successful transition. This step in the process fosters intergroup respect as it creates a space to discuss divergent perspectives, engage in conflict resolution, and share the unique challenges, skills, and knowledge of each group as well as the capabilities each lacks to resolve the challenges.

This step creates a path and desire to span boundaries and advance collaboration. What the Departments of Defense and State uncovered was both surprising and inspiring—their strengths and weaknesses were basically mirror images of each other. Instead of focusing on differences, they were able to see that the strength of one could offset the weakness of the other. At this point, leaders were encouraged to employ the second strategy of the BSL model—*forging common ground.* The goal became exploring their shared vision and their respective roles and responsibilities to learn how they might best collaborate. As the day progressed, leaders began to employ the final phase of the BSL model—*discovering new frontiers*—to craft a strategy for working more interdependently. Together they formed a shared vision, made personal commitments to creating unity of effort through collaboration, identified metrics to measure success, and developed plans to handle potential issues that might arise.

Follow-up interviews with the commanding general and ambassador (Chrobot-Mason et al., 2012) revealed how the work accomplished during this day-long retreat set the stage for a year-long commitment to interdependent leadership. The BSL model became a guiding framework for their future interactions. Diplomats and soldiers learned how to manage organizational boundaries and work more collaboratively. They recognized that their mission could only be accomplished through an interdependent leadership approach and the groups' identity shifted from one of "us versus them" to "we."

Expanding Our Capabilities to Facilitate Collective Leadership Development

Facilitating collective leadership development involves more than simply adopting best practices for developing individuals. Individual leader development is a necessary but insufficient part of collective leadership development. Further, as suggested in the focal article, this process requires new perspectives, methods, and interventions. Meeting this need requires expanding our capabilities as leadership development professionals, including adopting perspectives that traditionally resided outside of individual leader development (e.g., coaching teams from a systems perspective, drawing on knowledge regarding intergroup conflict).

We have also adopted a long-term perspective. Collective leadership development is an ongoing strategic effort that goes well beyond event-based training. This often means developing long-term relationships with groups and organizations to help them create the time and space to engage in developmental work before reaching their ultimate goal of more interdependent forms of leadership. In the first example, this occurred by helping the executive team fully explore and understand their assumptions, beliefs, and practices before taking actions to change the broader leadership culture. Similarly, we encourage clients engaging in BSL development to slow down by explaining that the natural tendency to focus first on creating a common mission and vision can actually lead to divisiveness and intergroup tension if differences are overlooked and devalued.

It is clear that the practice of collective leadership development is complex and challenging. There are many opportunities and needs for research and new development tools and techniques. For example, we are beginning to utilize network analysis to visualize identity-based boundaries within the organization, help collectives strategically span those divides, and track changes in cross-boundary activity. We are also developing new tools to measure and visualize leadership cultures and subcultures within collectives. We hope that by sharing our experiences we may spark additional research on collective leadership development and aid practitioners and organizations in transformations to "we."

Note

1. Correspondence concerning this article should be addressed to Kristin L. Cullen. E-mail: cullenk@ccl.org

Address: Center for Creative Leadership, One Leadership Place, Greensboro, NC 27410

We gratefully acknowledge the work of our colleagues at the Center for Creative Leadership in the Leadership Across Differences Research Group, the Boundary Spanning Leadership Community, and the Organizational Leadership

Practice. Special thanks to Bill Drath, Cindy McCauley, John McGuire, Chris Ernst, Ellen Van Velsor, Marian Ruderman, Kelly Hannum, Bill Pasmore, and Jennifer Martineau.

References

Chrobot-Mason, D., Ernst, C., & Ferguson, J. (2012). *Boundary spanning as a battle rhythm.* Greensboro, NC: Center for Creative Leadership.

Chrobot-Mason, D., Ruderman, M. R., Weber, T., & Ernst, C. (2009). The challenge of leading on unstable ground: Triggers that activate social identity faultlines. *Human Relations, 62,* 1763–1794.

Drath, W. H., McCauley, C. D., Palus, C. J., Van Velsor, E., O'Connor, P. M. G., & McGuire, J. B. (2008). Direction, alignment, commitment: Toward a more integrative ontology of leadership. *The Leadership Quarterly, 19,* 635–653.

Drath, W. H., Palus, C. J., McGuire, J. B. (2010). Developing interdependent leadership. In E. Van Velsor, C. D. McCauley, & M. N. Ruderman (Eds.), *The center for creative leadership handbook of leadership development* (pp. 405–428). San Francisco, CA: Jossey-Bass.

Ernst, C., & Chrobot-Mason, D. (2010). *Boundary spanning leadership: Six practices for solving problems, driving innovation, and transforming organizations.* New York, NY: McGraw-Hill Professional.

Fiol, C. M., Pratt, M. G., & O'Connor, E. J. (2009). Managing intractable identity conflicts. *Academy of Management Review, 34,* 32–55.

Hogg, M. A., Van Knippenberg, D., & Rast, D. E. (2012). Intergroup leadership in organizations: Leading across group and organizational boundaries. *Academy of Management Review, 37,* 232–255.

Hughes, R. L., Palus, C. J., Ernst, C., Houston, G. G. & McGuire, J. B. (2011). Boundary spanning across leadership cultures: A leadership strategy for the comprehensive approach (Chapter 8). In D. J. Neal, & L. Wells II (Eds.), *Capability development in support of comprehensive approaches: Transforming international civil-military interactions.* Washington DC: Center for Technology and National Security Policy, Institute for National Strategic Studies, National Defense University.

McGuire, J. B., & Palus, C.J. (2013). Case: Toward Interdependent Leadership Culture: Transformation in KONE Americas. In. D. Warrick, J. Mueller (Eds.), *Lessons in Changing Culture,* RossiSmith Academic Publishing.

McGuire, J. B., & Rhodes, G. (2009). *Transforming your leadership culture.* San Francisco, CA: Jossey-Bass.

Palus, C. J., McGuire, J. B., & Ernst, C. (2011). Developing interdependent leadership. In S. Snook, N. Nohria, & R. Khurana (Eds.), *The handbook for teaching leadership* (pp. 467–492). Thousand Oaks, CA: Sage Publications with Harvard Business School.

Yammarino, F. J., Salas, E., Serban, A., Shirreffs, K., & Shuffler, M. L. (2012). Collectivistic leadership approaches: Putting the "we" in leadership science and practice. *Industrial and Organizational Psychology: Perspectives on Science and Practice, 5,* 382–402.

CHAPTER 39

Generative Team Learning in Web 2.0 Environments

Manuel London[1]

State University of New York at Stony Brook

Organizations rely on work teams to conduct complex tasks that require a range of functional expertise and experiences. Electronic communications have for many years provided convenient means for team members to interact outside of face-to-face meetings. Web 2.0 technologies offer new opportunities for virtual teamwork and learning. These technologies and processes include social media, blogs, wikis, search engines, file and bookmark sharing sites, homemade videos, interactive webinars, a range of popular social media, crowd sourcing, virtual worlds, telepresence, voice and video over IP, and really simple syndication (RSS) for feeds of relevant websites, blogs, and posts. Combinations thereof, called mashups, integrate new software and advances in computer and wireless technologies. They provide a wide range of user initiated and self-directed applications for information search, knowledge management, interpersonal interaction, and task work. This chapter addresses the question of how individual team members and the teams as entities learn to be interpersonally sensitive,

develop virtual communities of practice, and produce innovative results. The chapter examines how Web 2.0 applications offer new ways of working and learning, and considers the value of Web 2.0 for generative interactions—those in which team members are open to new ideas, exploration, and reflection. It also considers barriers to virtual team learning and ways to overcome them.

The term "group" refers to a collection of individuals who are simply sharing information to improve individual performance. The term "team" implies a collection of individuals who develop a degree of mutual interdependence and modify their actions in response to the needs of the team. I use "team" throughout this chapter reflecting a focus on interdependence in a generative team process—one in which people work together to produce innovations and novel solutions to problems and issues that are complex and difficult. Other authors do not necessarily make this distinction, so I may use "group" when referencing various sources. This distinction between groups and teams raises the question of the extent to which on-line technologies affect how a group of individuals becomes a team. The term "group development" or "group learning" refers to individuals learning to work together, and the term "team learning" refers to the transformation of a group of individuals into a high-performing team (Hackman, 2002).

The chapter begins with an examination of teamwork and learning drawing on the group literature, defining generative teams and how they operate in Web 2.0 environments, and distinguishing between Web 2.0 and conventional, face-to-face team interactions. Cases are presented to describe different types of teams, show applications of Web 2.0 technologies, and demonstrate generative team inputs, processes, and outcomes, which are the basis for a model of team experiential learning. The model components and associated web-based activities and resulting team learning are described. The chapter concludes with implications for research and practice, particularly ways to improve team learning in Web 2.0 environments.

Teamwork and Team Learning

Organizations rely on teams to get work done because much work requires interdependent effort from people with diverse expertise and background (London and Sessa, 2006; Zaccaro et al., 2008). Team learning is important because organizations need work and project teams to be flexible systems that are reflective and continuously transforming in response to the pressures of today's competitive environment (Decuyper et al., 2010). Some work teams are ongoing. Others are temporary, formed to meet a specific task or objective. These teams may be composed of people who are co-located. However, individuals are often dispersed across departmental, geographic, and corporate boundaries. Communications technologies make this possible, but also impose dimensions of interaction that are different than teams working primarily face to face.

Teams engage in a variety of purposes and activities including knowledge management (seeking, sharing, and storing information), outcomes production (research and development, quality improvement,

production and supply-chain management, event planning committees, etc.), interest sharing (sharing common interests and goals in relation to the members' discipline, function, profession, avocation, health, family situation, etc.), and advocacy (promoting a political, social justice, human welfare, or environmental protection initiative). Teams may be local, national, or global. In companies, they occur across offices within and between regions. They may operate between institutions, such as a team of scientists from different laboratories and disciplines working on a common problem. They may be communities of interest focussed on society and community problems of local or broader concern, such as the BP oil spill and the earthquake in Haiti that engendered wide concern, participation in suggesting solutions, and fund raising to help the victims. As managers, functional experts, and those with vested interests participate in these on-line teams and communities, they learn how to interact and accomplish goals.

Teams vary in their scope and complexity of activity, number and involvement of members, time frame, members' roles, interactions, which may be one-to-one, one-to-many (e.g. the leader giving direction to everyone), or many-to-many (one team addressing another). Teams also vary in how they function and are managed/led (e.g. whether democratically, authoritatively). These features may change over time as the members share knowledge, search, make decisions, and develop a sense of identity and community.

Teams Learning

The concept of learning goes beyond individual learning to reflect the social organization as an entity dealing with creating, retaining, and transferring knowledge within and between teams (Argote et al., 2003). "Team learning is […] the acquisition of knowledge, skills, and performance capabilities of an interdependent set of individuals through interaction and experience" (Kozlowski and Ilgen, 2006, p. 86). Team learning can be conceptualized in terms of team processes and outcomes, "[…] the activities through which individuals acquire, share, and combine knowledge through experience with one another.

Evidence that [...] learning has occurred includes changes in knowledge, either implicit or explicit, that occur as a result of such collaboration" (Argote et al., 2001, p. 370). Team learning is a process that yields shared knowledge, shared mental models, and memories of ways to transact business successfully (transactive-memory structures) (Kozlowski and Ilgen, 2006). Team learning reflects collective knowledge, potential synergies between members, and unique member contributions. It is a holistic process in that all members of the team experience it together. They create effective social and work structures on their own or with varying degrees of direction from a team leader and/or facilitator. Given that members may come and go, team socialization and adjustment to changes in members are important processes that require attention from the leader and members (Chen and Klimoski, 2003). Team learning is facilitated by a climate of psychological safety—a shared perception that the team is a safe context for interpersonal risk taking (Edmondson, 1999).

There has been little research to specify the processes by which team learning happens (Kozlowski and Ilgen, 2006). Psychological safety, together with a supportive organization context and effective coaching by the leader contribute to perceptions of psychological safety (Edmondson et al., 2001). Decuyper et al. (2010) developed categories of team learning processes and outcomes for identifying learning improvement interventions. Processes include sharing ideas and information, the co-construction of a shared model (way of perceiving goals and interaction patterns, including how to resolve conflict constructively), discussions about team process, actually doing work, crossing team boundaries, and the storage and retrieval of team capabilities and information. Team processes occur through interpersonal behaviors such as sharing ideas and information, asking questions, seeking feedback, challenging assumptions, interpreting and re-interpreting perceptions and ideas, having discussions, seeking alternatives, and so forth. Team members enact different roles as the work progresses, learning what they are best at doing and what works best for the team (Fleishman and Zaccaro, 1992). Members engage in such roles and functions as orientation, resource-distribution, time monitoring and

control, response coordination, motivation, system monitoring, and procedure maintenance (Schiflett et al., 1982; in Kozlowski and Ilgen, 2006). Teams learn best by doing—practicing in ways that approximate, stimulate, or replicate their task. Members may be asked to learn each others' tasks, roles, and responsibilities (a process called "interpositional skills training"; Kozlowski and Ilgen, 2006).

Adaptive and Generative Learning

Team processes lead to adaptive and generative learning outcomes, which may be immediately observable or emerge slowly as the team acts adaptively or generatively, and sometimes transforms itself completely in membership, structure, goals, and methods of interaction (Sessa and London, 2008; London and Sessa, 2006). Adaptive learning includes minor changes or improvements in team operation, such as the development of shared mental models, the emergence of team psychological safety, or the establishment of shared habits or routines. Adaptive learning may also include how the team has been learning (using standard modes of operating or experimenting with new ways of working together), what the team has been learning, including learning about each other (social learning), and who has been learning—the individual team members, the team as an entity, and/or the organization or even society. Generative learning stems from members' openness to new ideas and processes, member self-initiated (not necessarily leader driven) exploration and experimentation, and new work structures, methods, and processes that produce novel outcomes (Senge, 1990; London and Sessa, 2006).

Team learning may be hampered by a variety of barriers, such as groupthink, diffusion of responsibility, free riding, or the Abilene paradox (not expressing true feelings so pursuing actions that members actually disagree with), and conflict escalation. The team may be influenced by such phenomena as feelings of safety (for instance, to express one's opinion in the team), team efficacy (members' belief that the team can accomplish it's goals), cohesion (identify and shared commitment with the team), team leadership, team structure and independence as well as member interdependence, and various dynamics that occur over time as the team develops (from setting goals, to doing work, to reflecting on process and outcomes) (London and Sessa, 2007).

Decuyper et al. (2010) emphasized that team learning occurs in complex, nonlinear ways with circular causality and so needs to be studied qualitatively, over time and in relation to structural elements such as team size, task, time constraints, etc. As in face-to-face teams, having needed talent on the team, a clear sense of goals and work processes, and a reasonable time line are key structural components for success. The team faces different demands as the work progresses, needing a leader, members, or facilitator who motivates members at the outset, helps to structure work as the team makes progress toward it's goals, and processes work methods and interactions once the teamwork is completed (Hackman and Wageman, 2005).

Team Learning and Operations in Web 2.0 Environments

"The term *virtual team* refers to a team that, for the most part, is linked through communication—for example, through Email, voice mail, telephone, videoconfereincing, and Internet-based forums—rather than face-to-face" (Harvard Business School, 2010, p. 4). Reviewing the effects of technological mediation on team performance, Driskell et al. (2003) concluded that negative effect on cohesiveness, block the transmission of status information thereby weakening the normative process that supports status-based behavior teams, and lead to more counter-normative behaviors, some of which may be desirable, but others of which may be dysfunctional, contributing to deindividuation, frustration, lack of accountability, confusion, and disruption of smooth interpersonal relations. However, Driskell et al. (2003) are addressing Web 1.0 technologies. Web 2.0 technologies go beyond one-way and centrally controlled technologies to user-controlled, self-regulated technologies. As such, Web 2.0 programs may overcome the dampening effects of technological communication on team member interaction and indeed expand opportunities for individual learning and team development.

Bell and Kozlowski (2002), formulating a typology of virtual teams, stated that virtual teams present the potential for real challenges to effective team development and performance management given that a team may be widely dispersed in space and spread across time. Web 2.0 provides opportunities for team members to take control and operate, in some if not large part, as if they were self-managing. This provides further challenges for maintaining focus on the team's purpose and goals (Manz and Sims, 1987). Bell and Kozlowski (2002) argued that virtual teams differ from conventional, face-to-face teams, not in their tasks, goals, and missions, but in the way they proceed to accomplish them and the constraints they face. They suggested several key features that distinguish virtual teams from face-to-face teams and that can be used to distinguish different types of virtual teams. These features are boundaries, time, roles, and membership across the team's life cycle. Specifically, first, virtual teams are flexible because the technology allows them to cross boundaries of space, organization, and culture, so members' locations and backgrounds are not an issue when forming a team, and the team's boundaries are likely to be permeable allowing for flow of members in and out of the team. Second, virtual teams can adopt synchronous and asynchronous communication media to facilitate collaboration, thereby not always dependent on all members availability at given times and allowing tighter interdependence when needed to carry out complex tasks. Third, virtual team leaders create structures and routines to distribute leadership roles across the team, thereby facilitating team self-management and allowing members to handle multiple roles which can be clearly defined for complex tasks and left looser and variable across members for less complex tasks. Finally, virtual teams can maintain a stable membership across their life cycle when handling complex tasks and can allow dynamic team membership when handling less complex tasks.

Mavromoustakos et al. (2004) presented a design model for e-learning corporate environments that drew on the social and collaborative aspects of the knowledge transfer process using Web 2.0 technologies. They argued that the use of social networks in e-learning improves learning outcomes. Collaborative learning and direct communication through various Web 2.0 systems provide an open source for learning and exchanging ideas. Tools such as weblogs, wikis, podcasts, and mashups provide interactivity that increases the learner's motivation, interest, and engagement blending the roles of content consumers and providers through peers' social interaction and collective intelligence. Information and ideas are combined from multiple sources and internet locations. Web site characteristics that enhance learning include: usability (understandability, friendliness, operability, and ethical use of information), functionality (accuracy, suitability, compliance, privacy, and other functions needed to accomplish the task), efficiency (response time, rapid access to information), reliability (fault tolerance, crash frequency, recoverability), and maintainability (analyzability, changeability, stability, testability—with data available to measure and track these factors).

Kraiger (2008) argued that we are on the cusp of a new generation of learning that places greater emphasis on the learner forming understanding through social negotiation that occurs on the job or in training programs. He suggested that this learner-controlled, social constructivist approach is facilitated by web-based networks that promote peer-to-peer mentoring and professional forums. Coleman and Levine (2008) identified trends that are pushing collaboration into more dynamic web modes: convergence of audio, video, and data; availability of communication technology everywhere through mobile hardware and wireless systems; merging synchronous and asynchronous collaboration; enterprise collaboration convergence and standardization; the push to the infrastructure for collaboration (the cloud for web access anytime anywhere); and various market forces—consolidation of software, distribution channels, and open source solutions (e.g., the ubiquitous and all-encompassing software and capabilities of "Ma Google").

There may be generational differences in the use of technologies for learning. For instance, Lancaster and Stillman (2003) compared age groups and offered the following observations: The GenY digital natives (ages 18–25) are used to and expect continuous learning. They engaged in collaborative networked learning through multiple channels. Gen Xers (ages 26–41) are more independent learners accessing sources in a one-to-many communication style (hub & spoke) compared to the Gen Yers' many-to-many use of social media. Baby boomers (ages 42–60) adapt to new technology as they encounter it and communicate and learn in a need-to-know basis facilitated by experts. Traditionalists (ages 61–84) learn the hard way. They expect formal classroom instruction with minimal technology and instructor-led, top-down communication.

A meta-analysis for the effects of organizational training on individual learning showed that methods of training determine effectiveness of learning for certain types of training and evaluation criteria. For instance, programmed instruction, audio visual, and discussion can be valuable for interpersonal skills training. Simulators can be effective for learning psychomotor skills (Arthur et al., 2003). A meta-analysis comparing the effectiveness of web-based and classroom instruction found that web- based instruction was 6 percent more effective than classroom instruction for teaching declarative knowledge. However, web and classroom instruction were equally effective when the same instructional methods were used on the web and in the classroom. Web- based instruction was 19 percent more effective than classroom instruction for teaching declarative knowledge when trainees practiced the training material and received feedback during training (Sitzmann et al., 2006).

Overall, Web 2.0 functionality provides new opportunities for team functioning and learning. Web 2.0 technologies give team members considerable opportunities for self- direction and regulation as they explore new ways of working together, form communities of practice, and innovate. Teams are likely to arise on their own and existing teams will become more collaborative when certain conditions are present, and Web 2.0 facilitates, and sometimes prompts, the emergence of teams and facilitates collaboration. So for instance, Wilkins (2009) suggested that Web 2.0 media will promote team emergence and learning when the organization is dependent on the creation of new ideas and work methods and products, is engaged in solving novel challenges or problems, relies on knowledge sharing among diverse teams either within or outside the organization, and the work involves synthesis, invention, or sense-making sorts of skills. Also, Web 2.0 media will improve team functioning when the task requires a diversity of perspective or expertise, leaders arise because of the admiration and esteem of peers, and issues are resolved through the ad hoc assembly of networked teams or individuals rather than formal hierarchies. Further, Wilkins (2009) suggested that teams will become more collaborate using Web 2.0 technologies when the organization depends on collaboration to drive key performance indicators, tasks depend on the sharing and coordination of distributed expertise, best practices will emerge from team consensus, members' value and influence are a result socially recognized expertise, and key performance indicators driven by socially-validated domain knowledge.

London and Hall (2011a) suggested that team learning occurs in Web 2.0 environments when the team has some direction, routine transactions are unfrozen, members try new ways to communicate, members value their diverse backgrounds and experiences, and there is lively participation (debate, conflict, negotiations, consensus). London and Hall (2011b) conceptualized generative learning processes in Web 2.0 environments in terms of Kolb's (1984) four modes of experiential learning (concrete experience, reflective observation, abstract conceptualization, and active exploration) produce generative learning experiences, as described below (adapted from London and Hall, 2011b).

Generative Teamwork and Learning Processes in Web 2.0 Environments

1. Goal is generative learning:
   * team members take advantage of interaction capabilities of social media;
   * team members represent different departments, functions, expertise, and/or companies; and
   * learning is integrated with work; learning occurs while searching for information and brainstorming novel ideas to solve real problems.

2. Concrete experience:
   * team member controlled—team members determine what they need to learn when in order to solve problems;
   * team members become observers of their own process as it unfolds;
   * group process is unstructured and fluid;
   * team members work with each other or contact others outside the team context to discuss a broad range of ideas and topics;
   * team members are uncertain about what needs to be done or learned; and
   * team members discuss the dimensions of the problems they are addressing.

3. Reflective observation:
   * leader and/or facilitator acts help team members deal with frustrations of uncertain and ambiguous problems;
   * team members are likely to disagree in their perceptions of the nature of the issues and problems addressed;
   * team members and leader and/or facilitator recognize the ambiguity of the problems they are addressing;
   * leader and/or facilitator helps team members recognize the possible synergies they can produce from interacting;
   * team members recognize their similarities and differences; they develop a mutual understanding of what each person can contribute to the learning and problem solving process; and
   * team members address and question their own and the leader and/or facilitator's assumptions and roles.

4. Abstract conceptualization:
   * the leader and/or facilitator and team members work together to generate theory (inductive learning);
   * they develop and try new behaviors and interaction patterns;
   * team members give each other formative (improvement oriented) feedback; and
   * the leader and/or facilitator helps team members recognize conflicts and nurture their resolution.

5. Active exploration:

- team members explore new ways of working together; through trial and error, they find effective work processes or solutions to problems;
- team members review what they learned and compare learning to expected outcomes; and
- team members examine unexpected outcomes, discuss their implications and needs for further exploration recognizing that learning and performance improvement are continuous processes.

Case Analyses

Five cases suggest how Web 2.0 technologies that are user-controlled and team-driven allow multiple modes of communication and team member active learning. The case analyses describe team web-based work processes and learning. Key events and observations about the cases are categorized according to the elements of generative experiential learning outlined above. The cases described in this section demonstrate different types of generative teams and how they use Web 2.0 technologies to form, transact business, and produce outcomes. Team members use Web 2.0 technologies to learn about each other, develop ways of getting work done, become learning communities, and produce innovations.

Company Task Force

1. Generative learning:

- A regional bank formed a task force of 12 representative branch managers who worked on methods to increase clients for new financial services. The task force examined facets of marketing and customer service that could make the new services attractive to more customers.
- They learned to work together, share their skills and experiences, express new ideas, and experiment with innovation.

2. Concrete experience:

- The technology provided methods for training and communication.
- Members met on-line through company-provided software that allowed anytime instant messaging, scheduling conference calls, and file sharing.
- Three members became core contributors, leading by suggesting direction, structuring events, and presenting results on-line to the bank's top leaders who were monitoring the task force's progress.

3. Reflective observation:

- During the course of the project, branch managers, who ordinarily would have had little contact with each other, learned about and from each other and shared the results more widely across the bank.
- Members learned to observe their team interactions and reflect on their meaning. Differences in talent, expressiveness, and motivation emerged.

4. Abstract conceptualization:

- team members developed norms of transaction that allowed them to express their ideas, apply their knowledge and experience, and understand different perspectives; and
- when a critical event occurred in a trial branch, the manage described the experience immediately after it occurred, allowing other branch managers to comment, present ideas for alternative actions, and avoid similar problems.

5. Active exploration:

- team members used the technology to learn about each other and develop ways of working together;
- occasionally, a manager discovered a useful self-paced training program or webinar in marketing and sales and shared its availability with the others, and they all agreed to participate;
- new sales and marketing methods were tried in local branches and the results were

shared quickly by posting descriptions on line; and

- the task force members developed employee training, trained themselves, and then described the process and outcome of training employees in their branches.

Hospital Quality Improvement Team

1. Generative learning:

- The emergency room team of a large urban hospital embarked on a quality performance improvement project to increase the speed and accuracy of lab tests and to reorganize the supply room and ordering process and reduce the cost of supplies. This had become a major problem with some unused supplies stockpiled, needed supplies on back-order, and delayed tests slowing responsiveness to patients. The emergency room chief learned of a similar situation at a similar hospital in another urban area, and felt that the two could join forces to learn from each other as they fine-tuned their operations. Also, there was an opportunity to partner with their prime suppliers and test analysis labs to design ordering and delivery methods.

- A team of 14 people was formed, five from each of the two hospitals. The team included an emergency room doctor, two nurses, and a lab technician from each hospital, two representatives from the supply house and two from the lab that served both hospitals, and two group facilitators, one from each of the hospital's organization development office.

2. Concrete experience:

- The team had weekly meetings using video conference calls. The members from each hospital met in a conference room at their facility and the two rooms with video connections. The representatives from the vendors participated from their computer desk tops with cameras and microphones so they could be seen and participate actively.

- As the work progressed, the teams within each hospital met separately to collect and analyze data reflecting operations at their respective hospitals. They needed to derive meaning from the data as they continued their exploration. This often entailed obtaining information from the vendors.

3. Reflective observation:

- Having to interact on-line with people from another hospital seemed to break down the status differences within their hospital team that might otherwise have hampered open discussion. However, this did not come easily. This was a leaderless team with the facilitators taking responsibility for setting the meeting schedules and agendas and taking minutes. One physician tended to dominate early conversations. The facilitators conferred and decided that they would facilitate a discussion among the members about their group process giving everyone equal time to express their views.

- The facilitators helped members overcome status differences among the members and take advantage of their different professional backgrounds.

- As the discussion evolved, members talked about the importance of everyone being equal and not overpowering the team. This was accomplished without pointing fingers. However, the physician in question got the message and was not happy. He withdrew from the group, and the chief assigned another doctor to the committee. Although this was awkward, it was a process that the team needed to work through. It seemed to strengthen their interaction. They welcomed the new member with relief, she, in turn, having been briefed on what the problem had been, was sensitive to her own contributions to the team and how others were reacting to her.

4. Abstract conceptualization:

- A common file sharing website was hosted by one of the hospitals. The data helped the group conceptualize major barriers in their operations and identify similarities and differences between the hospitals.
- A discussion board was established for each hospital but visible to all parties. As such, the team within each hospital could discuss the issues pertaining to their particular site, and the others could learn from this.
- Twice, on-line meetings were established to hear reports from hospitals.
- This allowed the team to conceptualize models of improvement.
- The hospital representatives learned that their facility was not unique and that they did not necessarily know best. The physicians learned to respect the opinions of other professionals.
- Members gained insight about each other as they produced innovative results.

5. Active exploration:

- Each hospital designed and tested new processes, tracking and sharing their results for six months.
- Several technologies were used for meetings. Members learned how to interact in-person and on-line, communicating viewpoints, resolving differences, generating, and reporting results of trials.
- The communication technologies developed new ways for hospital staff to cross-traditional organizational boundaries within and across hospitals and in relation to key partners.
- The vendors benefitted not only by providing better service to these clients but also improving their own operations generally, increasing their competitiveness and their bottom line.

International Fund Raising Committee

1. Generative learning:
   - a business unit of a multi-national nongovernmental organization (NGO) established

a 30-person committee with geographically dispersed employees and volunteers to raise money.

2. Concrete experience:

- The committee members established a web site on the agency's intranet.
- The site provided a calendar with a schedule for on-line meetings.
- The site also included a virtual thermometer for goal tracking progress, a list of examples of successful fund raising efforts, a motivational message from the organization's CEO, and vignettes from clients around the world who benefited from the NGO's services.
- The committee's appointed chair established a schedule for weekly on-line one-hour meetings.
- Members combined a dial-in toll free telephone number for multi-way audio combined with a website for visuals and posting questions.
- A discussion forum on the website allowed members to have an on-going dialogue outside of meetings.
- Subgroups of three to four members were established for regional initiatives. These groups communicated by on-line conference services with video and audio.

3. Reflective observation:

- the leader kept members on task and kept people informed of team progress while offering open discussion and providing a means for subgroups to form and contribute to overall goals;
- one subgroup established its own virtual room with members using avatars that reflected; and
- members recognized their differences, shared observations, and generated ways to raise funds, members' identity.

4. Abstract conceptualization:

- members identified and articulated multiple stakeholders;

- the conceptualized ways to describe the various needs for funds and express these needs to potential donors; and
- though a large, dispersed group, the discussion produced a clearer shared vision of the multi-pronged needs and ways the NGO helped, thereby providing stronger justification to donors.

5. Active exploration:

- the technology provided flexibility to explore different methods of communication and to generate and track members' experiences and contributions to the group; and
- members experimented by taking initiatives to express new ideas, try them out, and report results.

Interdisciplinary Research And Development Team

1. Generative learning:

- an interdisciplinary group of biologists, computer scientists, electrical engineers, and physicians formed a cross-institution and cross-national team to develop virtual scanning technology for diagnosis and treatment.

2. Concrete experience:

- The team established a file sharing website for posting and working on documents, software, and data analysis. Videos demonstrating techniques were posted on a password protected website hosted by one of the sponsoring scientific institutions. Members posted personal profiles to explain their expertise and prior discoveries related to the task at hand.
- A one-day virtual conference was planned using webinar technology during which posters of scientific papers were available, slide presentations with voice-overs were presented allowing Q&A and recording, and keynote presentations were given.

Scientists from around the world outside the task force were invited to participate as presenters and attendees.

3. Reflective observation:

- the group met virtually once a month in a virtual world room where members presented techniques and held discussions about thorny problems that needed to be solved as the work progressed;
- communities of practice developed, growing in number of participants and adding value in different ways; and
- participants learned from each other, shared their background, and worked together virtually.

4. Abstract conceptualization:

- ideas for new applications emerged from the conference;
- the original group sustained their effort through continuous on-line interaction in the forums including sharing files, data, on-line search results, and insights from researchers in different disciplines;
- computer scientists and engineers who knew little about medicine and biology added value in ways they would never have considered otherwise;
- physicians and natural scientists were drawing on technologies they would never have considered otherwise;
- often participants had to find ways to explain concepts and ideas in nontechnical terms so they could be understood across disciplines and then worked on within disciplines; and
- the participants developed meaning through interpretation of their experiences.

5. Active exploration:

- scientists and practitioners formed their own groups to develop these applications, sharing their concepts and drawing on the basic research, design, and implementation experience of the original group; and

- progress was rapid and novel applications emerged from new-found interdisciplinary synergies.

Political Action Committee (Pac)

1. Generative learner experience:
   - A PAC started as an on-line interest group on a social medium web portal.

2. Concrete experience:
   - Several members started blogs associated with the cause, providing their own opinions and sharing their experiences. On-line methods were used for surveys, petitions, collecting donations, announcing political events, and posts of testimonials and pictures from well-known supporters and short videos of speeches and reports of events.
   - A listserv for sending texts to mobile devises and e-mail addresses kept interested members up-to-date as events unfolded.
   - Participants felt close allegiance to the cause and fellow supporters.

3. Reflective observation:
   - participants felt part of the effort, more than if they had merely read about the initiative and possibly made a financial contribution with little additional involvement other than voting; and
   - these dynamic forums became ways of learning through on-going experiences of expressions, exploration and sharing of ideas, and development of mutual understanding.

4. Abstract conceptualization:
   - people with a common interest can interact in open, web-based forums for conveying a message and expressing vested interests; and
   - this was a dynamic, rapidly developing process that can be managed to maintain

focus while recognizing people's need to express their opinions.

5. Active exploration:
   - At one point, a rogue member began dominating the discussion forum with propaganda about a particular viewpoint on a regional issue. Other participants began expressing agreement in equally hot terms provoking confrontation with others who were similarly adamant about the opposite viewpoint. Still others expressed their feelings that the heated debate was inappropriate within the context of the PAC. The organizers quickly saw that the on-line forum was losing focus. Rather than alienate this interest group by denying team access, which would be technically difficult, or censoring discussion, they created a separate web site for the issue with a link from the PAC's home page, thereby learning on-line communication strategy and educating all participants about the purpose and etiquette of effective advocacy.

A Model to Promote Generative Learning in Web 2.0-Based Teams

The cases showed that Web 2.0 functionality is different than traditional, primarily face-to-face modes of work and learning. Web 2.0 technologies can promote generative learning processes in which team members are open to new ideas, explore new ways of interacting, and apply their learning. The cases demonstrated team and technology characteristics that are elements of generative team inputs, processes, and outcomes. The components outlined below suggest ways to design Web 2.0 communication technologies and facilitate on-line processes for generative actions and learning to produce interpersonal insights, communities of practice, and innovations.

Components of Web 2.0 Teamwork and Learning

1. Input:

   - Dynamic team characteristics: purpose (open to direction), functions within team (dynamic and unstructured trials of different structures), membership (enthusiastic/engaged/passionate, focussed), and substantive (skilled, knowledgeable):

   - Purpose: openness to new concepts and exploration, diffusion across boundaries, opportunity for engagement (dominance and role emergence).

   - Functions: structured through software (discussion boards, surveys, planned synchronous meetings) vs open to anyone anywhere anytime.

   - Member characteristics evident: enthusiastic/passionate; conscientious; extroverted, aggressive (conflict provoking)—open to new ideas; nonevaluative; self-driven and regulated; tech-savvy.

   - Interaction/technology interface: available, multi-modes of interaction, openness of interaction, role and task fluidity, control and structure, collaborative interdependence, and depth of interaction.

   - Leader's role: facilitator, guide, and technologist.

2. Processes:

   - Generative group behaviors, relationship emergence, and process evolution: members' descriptions of their knowledge and capabilities are related to the purpose and value of contribution, interaction rules and forums are established; networks emerge, members explore information and experiment with different transactions; depth and breadth of interaction; boundary spanning; members capture and retain work methods (cumulative learning).

3. Outcomes:

   - Interpersonal insight and transaction learning, community of practice, innovation.

Inputs

Consider three inputs: team characteristics, the Web 2.0 technologies, and leadership roles.

Team Characteristics

Generative teams are open to alternative goals and actions up to a point at least (the point at which alternative directions become dysfunction—see examples of the Hospital Improvement Team and the PAC above). Generative teams do not start with a fixed structure. They use the technology to express and explore alternative ideas. They are willing to go beyond their boundaries to search for resources and invite others' opinions. Opportunities for interaction in real time (synchronous) discussion forums and anytime (asynchronous) discussion threads provide opportunities for members to express themselves and take on different roles (e.g., functional expert) and voices (e.g., the voice of reason or restraint). Team functions may be enacted by the formal leader or other members as they engage in different roles and make contributions to the team. Their individual characteristics become evident as the interactions unfold, for instance, their enthusiasm and passion, conscientiousness, extroversion, aggressiveness, openness to new ideas without being evaluative, willingness to welcome and engage new members, and their technical expertise.

Web 2.0. The technologies adopted by the team are other forms of input, shaping the interaction to the degree that the media allow and facilitate free flowing interactions (one-to-one, one-to-many) in presentations and reactions. Multi-modes of communication range from structured opportunities (discussion boards, surveys, synchronous meetings) to internet sites that are open to anyone anywhere anytime and invite input. The more open the site, the more it creates opportunities for members to assume roles and volunteer for tasks, creating a fluid environment. This promotes generativity yet imposes the challenging of capturing accomplishments and avoiding tangents or dysfunctional interactions. The technology allows leaders to constrain or direct interaction (for instance, asking for responses to survey questions that limit response alternatives) and establish inter-dependent collaboration—members depending on each other to accomplish the team's goals. The technology allows increasing depth of interaction as members form separate discussion forums around work methods, exploration of resources, experiments, and issues.

Leadership

The leader's role in a virtual team can vary from directive and controlling to suggesting, facilitating, tracking, and reporting. Members quickly develop a sense of their own and others' identities within the team. They are likely to view each other similarly the more they have a chance to describe their backgrounds and experiences in relation to the task or purpose for the team. On the one hand, the technology can promote feelings of virtual proximity when members feel an affinity for other members and identify with the team (e.g. they feel pride in being a part of the enterprise). On the other hand, the technology can create virtual distance (Sobel-Lojeski and Reilly, 2008) with members feeling tangentially involved, unsure about the team's purpose and having difficulty understanding members' viewpoints and contributions. Technology and leadership interact to engage members in generative ways.

Web 2.0 technologies are more generative when the leader acts as facilitator by structuring forums for presentation and discussion, summarizing and integrating responses, commissioning subgroups for specific tasks and experiments, offering opportunities for learning (for instance, self-paced learning and information resources), and communicating and recognizing accomplishments, thereby retaining and motivating members and developing their sense that participating in the team is worthwhile and produces results. The technology allows spanning boundaries, opening chances for others beyond the team to participate. Generative on-line experiences include brainstorming for idea generation, critical thinking and analysis, exploration of the implications of alternative courses of action and decisions, reflecting on content and process, and conceptualizing the meaning of phenomena addressed to draw conclusions and create new applications. The technology also allows cumulating learning by posting accomplishments, continuing interactions processes that were effective and stopping others that were not, and communicating and evaluating the results of the team's efforts.

Processes

The section Generative teamwork and learning processes in Web 2.0 environments provides examples of how teamwork might be introduced, unfolds, is processed, and produces results in Web 2.0 on-line environments. Interpersonal processes emerging from Web 2.0 team interfaces include introductions so participants are aware of each other's talents and potential contributions, participants taking on different roles as needed, providing information, coordination, data and information analysis, recommendation of systems, processes, and methods as well as motivating others, encouraging involvement, and clarifying vision. As members participate actively and take turns with various roles, including elements of leadership, they gain a sense of involvement and cohesion, feelings of psychological safety (that they can contribute to the team without fear of being evaluated negatively), and valuing other team members' diverse contributions and perspectives. Transparent and data-driven work methods and systems allow tracking accomplishments and lead to members feeling a sense of efficacy and appreciation.

Processes are generative when they are open to dynamic, evolving interactions and relationships among the team members. Members describe themselves to clarify their potential value to the team. Their on-line, task-related identify and personality emerge. Interaction rules are stipulated by the leader or proposed by the leader or members. Networks emerge as members see common interests and begin interacting apart from the team (e.g. forming cliques or subgroups that get together through various modes of communication to explore common interests).

Outcomes

The model suggests three types of outcomes from Web 2.0-based generative interactions: interpersonal insight (this might also be called transaction learning or labeled emotional intelligence), communities of practice, and innovation.

Interpersonal Insight

Interpersonal insight refers to members learning about themselves and how others react to them; members learning about each other, their personality, expertise, and value to the team; and ways to communicate effectively through various social media. They test reactions to being open on-line as they witness others self-expression and express themselves. They seek affirmation for their identities and possibly learn something about their own capabilities that they did not realize before or grow in their interpersonal capability.

Communities of Practice

The team or subgroups may become on-going communities of practice or learning communities (Wenger *et al.*, 2009). These are members who have a common passion and interest and who remain in communication through a listserv, blog, on-line interest group, social network and microblogging service for regular updates, instant and text messaging, etc. The members recognize the value they provide to each other, asking and answering queries to help members solve problems and share solutions and experiences. The community may be open to new members, taking on a life of its own as members assume leadership roles and construct more formal means of staying in touch and sharing ideas and information (e.g. on-line conferences, webinars, virtual panel discussions, and such). The technology provides a virtual closeness for such affinity groups, promoting cohesiveness and a sense of belonging.

Innovation

The third major outcome of the model is innovation. A generative outcome is, by definition, innovative—novel, responsive to the problem at hand with possible spin-off benefits to other applications beyond those originally intended.

Implications for Practice

Overcoming Barriers to Effective Web 2.0 Learning Processes

Web-based teamwork imposes potential barriers of time, distance, culture (broadly speaking—reflecting a host of demographics, including differences from national, discipline/training, and demographics, such as gender) (Sobel-Lojeski and Reilly, 2008). Subgroups may form, going off on tangents, setting their own goals or work methods. The technology can constrain interaction—perspectives not clear or not fully expressed. Members experiment, taking on different roles on their own initiative. Participants can mislead others, deliberately or unwittingly, presenting false depictions of their background and capabilities. These may become evident after awhile, but perhaps after these individuals have influenced the team in negative ways.

The value of Web 2.0-based teamwork is to work generatively and produce generative outcomes. If the web needs to be structured and constrained to avoid dysfunctional processes and outcomes, then its value is diminished. Some dysfunction may be part of the cost of the hardware and software as well as the cost of members' time and energy and lost opportunity costs from not spending these resources on other endeavors. Reverting to traditional means of teamwork (e.g., holding in-person meetings, communicating by e-mail and scheduled telephone conference calls, saving and distributing electronic files in read-only modes) also imposes costs. Interventions are needed to maximize the value of Web 2.0 applications and avoid dysfunctional processes so that generative gains emerge that probably would not have been produced from more traditional means at least not as cheaply or as rapidly.

The team processes outlined in the section "Components of Web 2.0 team work and learning" and in Table 39.1 suggest interventions to

Table 39.1	Some Team Web-based Work Processes and Learning Outcomes	

Team work processes	*Web activities*	*What team learns*
Team is formed; work is introduced	Posts and reactions on discussion boards Sharing files, websites, and photos	How others see me
Talent appropriate for the task—self-initiated, appointed	Synchronous on-line discussions (video and audio) Email	How I want others to see me Interpretations and assumptions
Initial sharing of background and perceptions of the task	Emergence of theme, goals, concepts	Seeking feedback Testing self-insight
Leader structures process and outlines roles	Leader and/or members facilitate by summarizing and conceptualizing, test consensus through survey polls, ask for alternatives to unearth underlying conflicts, seek expressions of agreement sometimes votes or requests for feedback	Interpersonal congruence—agreement about how members see each other
Members consider own roles and test their perceptions and volunteer ways they can contribute		
Co-construction of shared model of membership, goals, and operation	Talent recognized, task elements recognized, time line established	
	Virtual work environment and on-line community spaces are established, explained, and explored (portals, wikis, doc sharing site, web tools, etc.)	
Work gets done through tools for virtual team and real time collaboration:	On-line meetings are held	Roles tackled and learned
	Information is sought (search and crowd sourcing) and posted and communicated (shared sites, pod casts)	Leadership roles Orientation of new members
Discussion and bulletin boards	Procedures are established and implemented (e.g., regular series of on-line meetings; virtual meeting spaces; virtual world avatars allow self-expression and personality emergence; iterating to revise documents and products	Saying good bye to members who are leaving
Content and document management sharing		Resource-distribution
Distributed project management tools		Timing (pacing)
E-rooms, team rooms, and e-collaboration tools		Response-coordination
Groupware	Norms of interaction (brainstorming procedures, instant messaging to entire group or between individual members for side-bars)	Motivational (balancing attention to individual and team goals)
Intra and extranets		
Knowledge management		
On-line community tools and spaces	Each member does a share of interdependent tasks	Systems monitoring (adjusting team and member activities in response to errors and omissions)
Portals	Outputs are shared and added to; progress and accomplishments are visible	
Wikis	Quality is reviewed, errors corrected	Procedure maintenance

(Continued)

Table 39.1   (Continued)

Team work processes	Web activities	What team learns
Reflecting group process Crossing boundaries	Group identity Side bar conversations create subgroup conflicts Trying new interaction applications; repeating productive methods (e.g. use of video on-line conferences; avoidance of instant messaging between members) Recognition of group and individual accomplishments Issues of distance (culture, demographics, time, professional background)	Feelings of cohesion—belonging, separation from other groups, and pride of membership Psychological safety (members feel free to express their opinions) Overcoming distance Valuing differences
Work and work methods are captured Collective knowledge management Storage and retrieval of information and team history Experiments and simulations used for testing products; results are communicated	Systems record events Repository for on-going products (document storage and sharing) High-fidelity simulations can be developed for realistic tests	Transparency (record of team activities and outputs readily available to team and others who are given access) Data are shared
Accomplishments	Innovations are generated New ideas emerge, products or systems developed Communities of practice emerge Goals met (outputs and timeline) Accomplishments are celebrated	Members gain insight about themselves and others in the Web 2.0 environment Group efficacy (members believe that the team can accomplish it's goals) Feeling appreciated as individuals and as a team

promote generativity and virtual closeness (team identity and efficacy, affinity, belonging, and member responsiveness to each other and the team as a whole). The composition, work structure, and time frame need to be appropriate for the task and clear to the members. This is true of any team, virtual or not. Moreover, coaching or facilitation can encourage members to share their stories and develop common frames about each other's value to the team. The operation of the team needs to be clear as it depends on various web-based means of discussion knowledge management, retrieval of work methods, and results of explorations, experiments, and simulations.

Promoting Virtual Proximity

The notion of virtual closeness or proximity is the idea that members can work in concert to promote the emergence of interpersonal insight, communities of practice, and innovation. Leading virtual teams, a publication of the Harvard Business School (2010), provided tips for fostering team identity and cultivating a sense of unity and commitment. The book recommends holding a launch meeting, establishing communication protocols (e.g., rules about using e-mail, blogs, wikis, and discussion boards), encouraging collaboration of subteam efforts, documenting expectations for the team and obligations of individual members, keeping everyone informed, and using on-line coaching and facilitation to clarify priorities and address performance problems.

Sobel-Lojeski and Reilly (2008) described ways to overcome virtual distance that occurs because of member differences in culture, education, work method familiarity, and geographic distance in teams that meet virtually and/or face to face. Operational discontinuities can be avoided by paying attention to holding meetings during critical times in the project, having the right technical support in place for virtual workers, reducing team sizes, and recognizing that using a variety of technologies and mutlitasking can produce diminishing returns. Cultural differences across virtual space can be overcome by social networking that includes assigning participants goals and responsibilities to ensure that people are connecting and not trying to force fit one cultural style or work ethic over another. Participants can be trained in team facilitation skills so that they understand how groups become cohesive teams with members having a common vision and operating interdependently.

Dr Tony Karrer is CEO/CTO of TechEmpower, a Los Angeles Web Development firm, and is considered one of the leading technologists in e-Learning. He recommends a series of steps to improve virtual team function using Web 2.0 applications. These include creating a wiki with a single shared password but allowing tracking back additions and edits to individual contributors. Then each team member creates a blog account and registers it on a common site. Relevant informational web and social networking sites as well as information and resource sites are identified by the team. One member sets up a team home page. Another member sets up a feed from them so that current information that will help the team do its work can be accessed instantly by any member at any time. All members subscribe to the home page (which could be a social media site, for instance, on Facebook or Twitter, or a standard server-based, web accessed home page) that may include the RSS blog and web feeds to remain current as well as contribute to the team.

Having technical and organizational support and facilitation are critical especially as the Web 2.0 applications become more functional and complex and when team membership becomes more diverse in distance, background, and skills, including communication and technical ability. So although the technologies can be self-driven and this is why they promote generative interaction and outcomes, as pointed out earlier, this can also create barriers and dysfunction that need to be managed. Small teams can emerge on their own. But as the members grow in numbers and depth of engagement, and as the members vary on a host of demographic, attitudinal, and behavioral dimensions, structure and guidance may be needed to orchestrate the experience and prompt reflection and abstract conceptualization. As suggested above, team members can learn to be their own facilitators just as they can enact other roles. This is likely to take some training, for instance, in resolving conflicts that emerge on-line, promoting openness to new ideas, designing and sharing the results of explorations, and capturing the learning.

Conclusion

Web 2.0 can promote generative team interaction and learning. This chapter presented a model for producing generative processes and outcomes that recognize the interpersonal/technology interface. As team members work, they learn about their individual and the team's interpersonal effectiveness in virtual environments. Communities of practice emerge, and the team produces innovative outcomes. However, the complexity and self-initiative, self-direction, and anything-goes potential of the applications can create barriers including misleading perceptions, tangents, and poor decisions. Interventions including facilitation and technical support can avoid these pitfalls and add value to Web 2.0 team functioning.

Recommendations to promote team learning using Web 2.0 include the following:

- Track interaction participation levels and content.
- Try different software structures to focus, avoid tangents, summarize results, and codify effective transactions; balance structure with fluidity, be open to exploring new systems.
- Provide guidelines to new members about how the team operates and how they can become productive members. Also provide guidelines to existing members about how to welcome and engage new members as well as recognize and say good bye to established members who are leaving the team.
- Analyze cost of software and on-line interaction in time, money, and other resources.
- Document and communicate the learning within the team and to other team.
- Maintain team openness to exploration and learning by providing access to the latest developments within and outside the team.

Next, consider directions for research to better understand Web 2.0-based team emergence and functioning:

- Measure involvement, process, and outcomes (measures for interpersonal awareness and sensitivity and mutual perceptions; community of practice—sustainable; innovation and impact) and directly measure changes in individual and team knowledge (as Kozlowski and Ilgen, 2006, called for).
- Assess reactions to and use of new software and team configurations.
- Measure the effects of diversity and the value that member differences bring to the team.
- Examine the effects of different modes of interaction on learning and outcomes, particularly

as new Web 2.0 applications become available and are integrated into team efforts. Measure how different mashups of technologies promote generative behavior, learning, and innovative outcomes. Assess the effects of different interventions on team processes and outcomes. Study possible configural relationships—the conditions under which Web 2.0 technologies are most effective and when they produce diminishing returns or create barriers to interaction and learning.

Note

1. Corresponding author: Manuel London can be contacted at: mlondon@notes.cc.sunysb.edu

References

Argote, L., Gruengeld, D. and Naquin, C. (2001), "Group learning in organizations", in Turner, M. E. (Ed.), *Groups At Work: Theory and Research*, Erlbaum, Mahwah, NJ, pp. 369–412.

Argote, L., McEvily, B. and Reagans, R. (2003), "Managing knowledge in organizations: An integrative framework and review of emerging themes", *Management Science*, Vol. 49 No. 3, pp. 571–82.

Arthur, W. Jr, Bennett, W. B. Jr, Edens, P. S. and Bell, S. T. (2003), "Effectiveness of training in organizations: a meta-analysis of design and evaluation features", *Journal of Applied Psychology*, Vol. 88 No. 2, pp. 234–45.

Bell, B. S. and Kozlowski, S. W. J. (2002), "A typology of virtual teams: Implications for effective leadership", *Group & Organization Management*, Vol. 27 No. 1, pp. 14–49.

Chen, G. and Klimoski, R. J. (2003), "The impact of expectations on newcomer performance in teams as mediated by work characteristics, social exchanges, and empowerment", *Academy of management Journal*, Vol. 46 No. 5, pp. 591–607.

Coleman, D. and Levine, St. (2008), *Collaboration 2.0: Technology and Best Practices for Successful Collaboration in a Web 2.0 World*, Happyabout.info. Cupertino, CA.

Decuyper, S., Dochy, F. and Van den Bossche, P. (2010), "Grasping the dynamic complexity of team learning:

An integrative model for effective team learning in organizations", *Educational Research Review*, Vol. 5 No. 2, pp. 111–33.

Driskell, J. E., Radtke, P. H. and Salas, E. (2003), "Virtual teams: Effects of technological mediation on team performance", *Group Dynamics*, Vol. 7 No. 4, pp. 297–323.

Edmondson, A. C. (1999), "Psychological safety and learning behavior in work teams", *Administrative Science Quarterly*, Vol. 44 No. 2, pp. 350–83.

Edmondson, A. C., Bohmer, R. M. and Pisano, G.P. (2001), "Disrupted routines: Team learning and new technology implementation in hospitals", *Administrative Science Quarterly*, Vol. 46 No. 4, pp. 685–716.

Fleishman, E. A. and Zaccaro, S. J. (1992), "Toward a taxonomy of team performance functions", in Swezey, R.W. and Salas, E. (Eds), *Teams: Their Training and Performance*, Ablex, Norwood, NJ, pp. 31–56.

Hackman, J. R. (2002), *Leading Teams: Setting the Stage for Great Performances*, Harvard Business Press, Boston, MA.

Hackman, J. R. and Wageman, R. (2005), "A theory of team coaching", *Academy of Management Review*, Vol. 30 No. 2, pp. 269–87.

Harvard Business School (2010), *Leading Virtual Teams: Expert Solutions to Everyday Challenges*, Harvard Business Press, Boston, MA.

Kolb, D. A. (1984), *The Experimental learning model as the Source of Learning and Development*, Prentice-Hall, Englewood Cliffs, NJ.

Kozlowski, S. W. J. and Ilgen, D. R. (2006), "Enhancing the effectiveness of work groups and teams", *Psychological Science in the Public Interest*, Vol. 7 No. 3, pp. 77–124.

Kraiger, K. (2008), "Transforming our models of learning and development: web-based instruction as enabler of third-generation instruction", *Industrial and Organizational Psychology*, Vol. 1 No. 4, pp. 454–67.

Lancaster, L. C. and Stillman, D. (2003), *When Generations Collide: Who They Are. Why They Clash. How to Solve the Generational Puzzle at Work*, Harper Business, Wheaton, IL.

London, M. and Hall, M. J. (2011a), "Support for individual, group, and organizational learning", *Human Resource Development International*, Vol. 14 No. 1, pp. 103–13.

London, M. and Hall, M. J. (2011b), "Unlocking the value of web 2.0 technologies for training and development: the shift from instructor-controlled, adaptive learning to learner-driven, generetive learning", *Human Resource Management*, Vol. 50 No. 6, pp. 751–75.

London, M. and Sessa, V. I. (2006), *Continuous Learning in Organizations*, Erlbaum, Mahwah, NJ.

London, M. and Sessa, V. I. (2007), "How groups learn, continuously", *Human Resource Management Journal*, Vol. 46 No. 4, pp. 651–69.

Manz, C. C. and Sims, H. P. (1987), "Leading workers to lead themselves: the external leadership of self-managing work teams", *Administrative Science Quarterly*, Vol. 32 No. 1, pp. 106–28.

Mavromoustakos, S., Papanikolaou, K., Leonidou, C. and Andreou, A.S. (2004), "The development of a quality e-learning environment based on human, social, and cultural factors", Information and Communication Technologies: From Theory to Applications, Proceedings, 2004 International Conference on Information and Communication Technologies, IEEE, Damaseus, April 19.

Schiflett, S. C., Eisner, E. J., Price, S. J. and Schemmer, F. M. (1982), *The Definition and Measurement of Team Functions (Rep. No. ARRO-2068-FR-R81-4)*, Advanced Research Resources Organization, Washington, DC.

Senge, P. M. (1990), *The Fifth Discipline: The Art and Practice of the Learning Organization*, Doubleday, New York, NY.

Sessa, V. I. and London, M. (2008), "Group learning: an introduction", in Sessa, V. I. and London, M. (Eds), *Work Group Learning: Understanding, Improving & Assessing How Groups Learn in Organizations*, Lawrence Erlbaum Associates, Mahwah, NJ, pp. 1–14.

Sitzmann, T., Kraiger, K., Stewart, D. and Wisher, R. (2006), "The comparative effectiveness of web-based and classroom instruction: a meta-analysis", *Personnel Psychology*, Vol. 59 No. 3, pp. 623–64.

Sobel-Lojeski, K. S. and Reilly, R. R. (2008), *Uniting the Virtual Workforce: Transforming Leadership and Innovation in the Globally Integrated Enterprise*, Wiley, Hoboken, NJ.

Wenger, E., White, N. and Smith, J. (2009), *Digital Habitats: Stewarding Technologies for Communities*, CPsquare Press, Portland, OR.

Wilkins, D. (2009), "Social media in learning", *Learning Solutions Magazine*, October 5, available at: www.learningsolutionsmag.com/articles/7/social-media-in-learning (accessed July 14, 2010).

Zaccaro, S. J., Ely, K. and Shuffler, M. (2008), "The leader's role in group learning", in Sessa, V.I. and London, M. (Eds), *Work Group Learning: Understanding, Improving & Assessing How Groups Learn in Organizations*, Lawrence Erlbaum Associates, Mahwah, NJ, pp. 15–44.

Further Reading

Dyer, J. C. (1984), "Team research and team training: state-of-the-art review", in Muckler, F. A. (Ed.), *Human Factors Review*, Human Factors Society, Santa Monica, CA, pp. 285–323.

Karrer, A. (2006), "How a group would work using Web 2.0—and learn in the process", available at: http:// elearningtech.blogspot.com/2006/09/personal-and-group-learning-using- web.html (accessed July 11, 2010).

International Standards Organization (2001), *IEC 9126-1, Software Engineering—Product Quality—Part 1: Quality Model*, International Standards Organization, Geneva.

CHAPTER 40

How Organizations Support Distributed Project Teams

Key Dimensions and Their Impact on Decision Making and Teamwork Effectiveness

Nathalie Drouin[1]
Université du Québec à Montréal

Mario Bourgault[2]
École Polytechnique de Montréal

1. Introduction

In the last decade, researchers have studied many different aspects of distributed project teams (Bourgault et al., 2008; Cramton and Webber, 2005; Gibson and Cohen, 2003; Lipnack and Stamps, 1997; Mortensen and Hinds, 2001). As proposed by Martins et al. (2004), distributed or virtual project teams are defined as:

> [...] teams whose members use technology to varying degrees in working across locational, temporal, and relational boundaries to accomplish an interdependent task (p. 808).

Researchers often seek to identify antecedents that affect output variables, such as team effectiveness and viability (Martins et al., 2004; Peters and Manz, 2007). Among the input factors that have been investigated are formal processes and communication infrastructure as a means to reduce the potentially negative impact of distance (Duarte and Snyder, 2001; Fink, 2007). In addition, the recent development of communication technologies has led to explorations of how these technologies contribute to and impact distributed work practices (Pick et al., 2008; Yu et al., 2009). Other researchers have considered individual and interpersonal dimensions of teamwork as success factors. Interpersonal processes have been strongly

Source: "How Organizations Support Distributed Project Teams: Key Dimensions and Their Impact on Decision Making and Teamwork Effectiveness," by Nathalie Drouin and Mario Bourgault in *Journal of Management Development,* Vol. 32, No. 8, pp. 865–885. Copyright © 2012, Emerald Group Publishing Limited. Reprinted with permission.

correlated with distributed team performance and member satisfaction (De Dreu and Weingart, 2003; Raver and Gelfand, 2005). The influential role of communication in teamwork effectiveness has also been examined (Mathieu et al., 2008; Tesluk and Mathieu, 1999). For instance, Geister et al. (2006) found a positive effect of feedback on motivation, interpersonal trust, and performance in virtual (i.e. distributed) teams. Balthazard et al. (2004) investigated personality traits as a specific variable affecting virtual team performance, while Kirkman and Rosen (1999) and Kirkman et al. (2004) concluded that empowering virtual team members (i.e. giving them more responsibility and decision-making authority) is positively related to team performance. Furthermore, Bourgault and Drouin (2008) and Bourgault et al. (2008) highlighted the need to build trust throughout the project life cycle, develop a common vision, and obtain clear support from top management at all site locations.

Taken together, these results cover a wide range of explanatory factors. However, the dimensions related to organizational support have received relatively little attention in empirical studies. Bissoonauth (2002) raised this issue, but did not conduct an in-depth investigation. Earlier studies reported that distributed teams need the support of a strong organizational infrastructure (Mohrman et al., 1995; Sundstrom, 1999; Townsley, 2001). More recently, studies in real-life teams have found that organizational support, in terms of team empowerment, standardized processes, and attention paid to individual competencies, may positively impact distributed team formation and management (Bourgault et al., 2008; Zwikael, 2008; Drouin et al., 2010a).

The decision-making process has also been underinvestigated in distributed project teams. Yet project conduct is generally very sensitive to organizational decisions. Due to the temporary and specific nature of projects, decisions can be critical and irreversible. In today's climate of technological and economic change, the decision-making process must be mastered for good project management. Nidiffer and Dolan (2005) explained the point view of practitioners and reported that:

The evolution toward distributed project management drives the need for improved processes, methods, and tools to input and share common data [y]. In our global economy, there's a growing need to decrease the time it takes to make an informed decision, to improve the team's decision velocity (p. 68).

The ability of a project team to take ownership for decisions that affect it is necessarily determined by the organizational environment in which it is situated (Hollenbeck et al., 1995). Far from being linear, decision making is a process that depends on a number of structural, environmental, and psychosocial factors, all of which can be difficult to grasp when projects are managed in uncertain or ambiguous environments. The quality of a distributed team's decision making could therefore provide a relevant measure of how it executes its mandates.

We explore these issues and attempt to identify the dimensions of organizational support that make the strongest contribution to the quality of the decision-making process and effective teamwork in distributed project teams. We begin by developing hypotheses about the dimensions of organizational support and their effects on the quality of decision making and effective teamwork. We then describe the research design and the data collection and hypothesis testing methods. The implications of our findings for practitioners and future research are then presented.

2. Background Literature

Drawing on organizational support theory (Eisenberger et al., 1986; Rhoades and Eisenberger, 2002) and the research on organizational support for distributed project teams (Drouin et al., 2010a; Mankin et al., 1996; Mathieu et al., 2008), we first consider the concept of organizational support.

Eisenberger et al. (1986) suggest that employees seek a balance in their social exchanges with organizations. That is, employees are committed to their organization insofar as they believe that the organization values and cares for them. The authors refer to these beliefs as "perceived organizational support" or POS, a term used in investigations of employee absenteeism and dedication to the organization (Shelton et al., 2010). POS has its roots in social exchange theory (Wayne et al., 1997), and stems from the norm of reciprocity: if one person does another a favour, there is a felt obligation to return the favour (Gouldner, 1960). Organizational support theory has been used to explain how employees personify the organization through social exchanges at work (Eisenberger et al., 1997). Levinson (1965) noted that actions taken by organizational agents are viewed as indications of the organization's intent, and not the agents' personal motives. This personification is abetted by the organization's legal, moral, and financial responsibilities.

In other words, organizational policies, norms, and culture provide continuity and prescribe role behaviours (Rhoades and Eisenberger, 2002). Rhoades and Eisenberger (2002) also conducted a meta-analysis and found that three main categories of beneficial treatment received by employees (fairness, supervisor support, and organizational rewards and favourable job conditions) were associated with POS. POS was in turn related to outcomes that were favourable to employees (e.g., job satisfaction, positive mood) and to the organization (e.g., affective commitment, performance, less withdrawal behaviour). These relationships depended on the psychological processes underlying the consequences of perceived organizational support. For instance, POS should produce a felt obligation by employees to care about the organization's welfare and to help it achieve its objectives. POS should also strengthen employees' beliefs that the organization recognizes and rewards performance. Shore and Shore (1995) noted that human resource practices such as recognition pay, promotions, autonomy, training, and recognition of employee contributions were positively related to POS. Rhoades and Eisenberger (2002) mentioned that:

> [...] organizational support theory supposes that employees personify the organization, infer the extent to which the organization values their contribution and cares about their well-being, and reciprocate such perceived support with increased commitment, loyalty and performance (p. 711).

Organizational support theory thus underscores the need to understand and identify the processes and practices underlying the organizational support that team members perceive.

Drouin et al. (2010a) studied two international high-tech firms and identified certain forms of organizational support and their effects on components of distributed teams. They found that senior management can support distributed teams with human resources, resource allocation, coordination, and communication support. These types of support foster enhanced project coordination and monitoring, information exchange and access, trust building, and team cohesion. They are manifest when systems are implemented to support operational activities, with specific mechanisms for each activity. Previous studies had identified similar supports that impact team performance. For instance, coordination and communication support oversight coordination among teams and departments (Denison et al., 1996; Sundstrom et al., 1990) and facilitate access to the information that teams need to accomplish their tasks (Hall, 1998; Mohrman et al., 1995; Sundstrom et al., 1990; West, 2004). Performance support enhances team performance in terms of the corporate mission and objectives, as measured by performance and individual achievement of objectives (Denison et al., 1996; Mankin et al., 1996; Mohrman et al., 1995; West, 2004). Human resource support refers to staffing, training, and career development (Hackman and Oldham, 1980; Mankin et al., 1996; Sundstrom et al., 1990; West, 2004). Resource allocation ensures that teams have the knowledge, skills, and competencies they need to perform their roles and accomplish tasks (Sundstrom et al., 1990; West, 2004). Reward systems ensure that the team's progress in achieving objectives is monitored (Hackman and Oldham, 1980), and technology support is used for distributing, implementing, and managing other support systems (Drouin et al., 2010a; Mankin et al., 1996; Mohrman et al., 1995).

A parallel can be drawn between organizational support as perceived by employees and team members and the organizational support that is provided to distributed project teams. In order to produce more effective teamwork and improved decision making, distributed team members must also perceive support as beneficial. However, some key aspects of organizational support have not yet been defined, especially for distributed project teams and based on concepts of organizational support theory (Bissoonauth, 2002; Eisenberger et al., 1986). In the next section, we provide an overview of these realities and develop a conceptual framework, and propose our hypotheses.

3. Conceptual Model and Hypothesis

This study investigates the dimensions of organizational support in distributed project teams that would contribute to improved decision making and more effective teamwork. Based on organizational support theory and the research on distributed project teams, four dimensions were identified: Strategic Staffing, Training and Tools, Team Autonomy, and Top Management Monitoring. These dimensions of

organizational support could impact decision-making quality and teamwork effectiveness in different terms (geographic dispersion; differences in culture, working practices, and experience) (see Figure 40.1). Below, we briefly discuss these concepts and develop our working hypotheses.

3.1 Dimensions of Organizational Support

Strategic Staffing

Staffing is a key dimension of the resource allocation support system. Proper staffing ensures that teams have the knowledge, skills, and competencies to perform effectively their roles and accomplish tasks (Sundstrom et al., 1990; West, 2004). Related to staffing are individual attributes that shape the distributed team and influence how it operates. Some

Figure 40.1   Theoretical Model

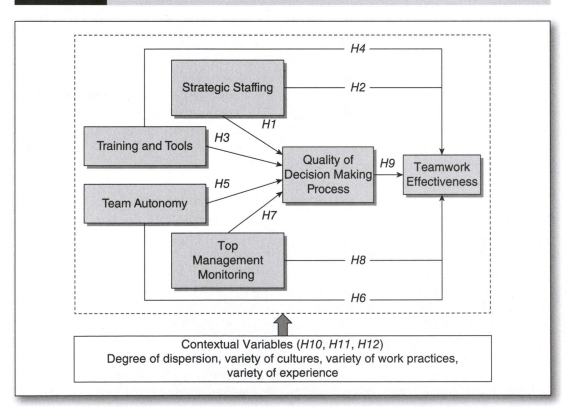

studies (e.g., Shin, 2004) indicate that certain combinations of personal attributes (e.g., flexibility and communicative skills) equip individuals to perform more effectively in virtual teams. Katzenbach and Smith (1993) noted that technical expertise, problem solving and decision-making skills, and relational qualities are key attributes that enhance team performance. It is also recognized that teams with members who have experience in distance collaboration are deployed more rapidly. Thus, Harrison and Klein (2007) found that team success depends on the resources that are made available to the team through the qualities and attributes of the individual team members. Hertel et al. (2005) grouped the key attributes into three categories: taskwork-related attributes (conscientiousness and integrity), teamwork-related attributes (cooperation and communication skills), and telecooperation-related attributes (self-management, interpersonal trust, intercultural skills, and expertise in new media and groupware technology). Some authors add that team members should possess a minimum amount of agreeableness and conscientiousness in order to prevent conflicts (Furst et al., 2004; Zakaria et al., 2004), while Rhoades and Eisenberger (2002) argue that conscientiousness might lead to enhanced job performance, which in turn leads to enhanced treatment by the organization and heightened POS. Distributed team members are selected for their professional and technical knowledge and expertise. In a virtual team, individual attributes appear to make a key contribution to decision-making quality and team performance. Beyond professional know-how, the influence of individual attributes depends on the team's degree of virtuality. In other words, individual characteristics become increasingly influential as the environment becomes more virtual (Drouin et al., 2010b). Leadership attributes are also considered input factors that influence team processes (coordination, creativity, knowledge sharing, empowerment, team commitment, and satisfaction) and teamwork effectiveness (Mathieu et al., 2008; Srivastava et al., 2006). In addition, Eisenberger et al. (1997) found that perceived competence was related to task interest.

We propose that team members can be strategically selected to provide certain key competencies,

and that through the team members' perceptions of these key competencies, both decision making and team effectiveness would improve:

H1. Strategic Staffing is positively related to the quality of decision making in distributed teams.

H2. Strategic Staffing is positively related to teamwork effectiveness in distributed teams.

Training and Tools

Training is a key dimension of the human resource support system (Hackman and Oldham, 1980; Mankin et al., 1996; West, 2004). Wayne et al. (1997) suggest that job training is a discretionary practice that communicates an investment in the employee and increases POS. Hyatt and Ruddy (1997) found that organizational factors such as training and rewards systems had both direct and indirect effects on group effectiveness. Vakola and Wilson (2004) recommend that a training programme be developed for distributed team members so that they can acquire the knowledge and competencies they need to work effectively in virtual mode. Schweitzer (2005) contents that providing effective tools, budgets, and methods (e.g. hardware and software, laptops, high-speed internet access, cell phones) as well as training in working effectively in a distributed team (e.g. use of tools, time management, long-distance management) can impact team effectiveness. It is therefore assumed that Training and Tools provided to team members will have a positive effect on the quality of decision making and on teamwork effectiveness. We therefore propose the following hypotheses:

H3. Training and Tools are positively related to the quality of decision making in distributed teams.

H4. Training and Tools are positively related to teamwork effectiveness in distributed teams.

Team Autonomy

Rhoades and Eisenberger (2002) argued that high autonomy, or the organization's trust that employees will make wise decisions about how to do their job, should increase perceived organizational support and consequently firm performance. Stewart (2006) also found that team autonomy and intrateam coordination corresponded with higher performance. Seibert et al. (2004) found that team empowerment influenced individual performance and job satisfaction. Mathieu et al. (2008) reviewed some of the "emergent states" (pp. 424-425) that have received much attention in the past decade, including team confidence, empowerment, team climate, cohesion, trust, shared mental models, and strategic consensus. Bourgault et al. (2008) identified team autonomy as a significant attribute of successful dispersed teams, regardless of the degree of distribution. We therefore propose the following hypotheses:

H5. Team Autonomy is positively related to the quality of decision making in distributed teams.

H6. Team Autonomy is positively related to teamwork effectiveness in distributed teams.

Top Management Monitoring

According to Simon (1994), top management can retain control through formal feedback systems used to monitor deviations from preset performance standards, by getting involved in subordinates' decisions, by setting limits on empowerment, and by instilling belief systems that incorporate core values and culture. Mahaney and Lederer (2010) mentioned the following:

> In project management, the purpose of monitoring is to collect three main classes of information about the progress of a project against a baseline and the anticipated outcome of the project. These classes include information that 1) assures managers that the project is progressing within acceptable budget, schedule, and quality expectations; 2) supports decisions to approve the movement of the project through its stages; and 3) confirms subjective assessments that benefits will be realised (p. 15).

Mahaney and Lederer (2010) further note that information about project progress (budget,

schedule, quality) constitutes feedback to team members, which can increase their accountability and motivate them to perform more diligently. Nath et al. (2008) concluded that the effect of controls such as project monitoring on the quality of offshored projects needs further study. We therefore propose the following hypotheses:

H7. Top Management Monitoring is positively related to the quality of decision making in distributed teams.

H8. Top Management Monitoring is positively related to teamwork effectiveness in distributed teams

3.2 Quality of the Decision-Making Process as an Antecedent of Effective Teamwork

Effective group decision making is an increasing concern for organizations, including decision making within projects (Brodbeck et al., 2007). Defining and understanding decision-making models is not an easy task (Pennings, 1985). Thanks to the seminal work of researchers such as Simon (1960) and March (1988), we can conceptualize the underlying decision-making processes and mechanisms. Bourgault et al. (2008), in their study of distributed teams, found strong support for the benefits of a good-quality decision-making process for distributed teamwork. Due to the numerous discontinuities that characterize such teams, an effective decision-making process is viewed as a way to surmount obstacles and produce successful outcomes. Compared to individual decision makers, groups have access to more information due to the individual knowledge of the constituent team members (Brodbeck et al., 2007; Hollenbeck et al., 1995). It is therefore assumed that, in project teams, the Quality of the Decision-Making Process is related to effective teamwork. We therefore formulated the following hypothesis:

H9. The Quality of the Decision-Making Process is positively related to teamwork effectiveness in distributed teams.

3.3 Effective Teamwork

Researchers have long examined various dimensions of effective teamwork in the field (e.g., Campion et al., 1993; Gladstein, 1984; Sundstrom et al., 1990). These dimensions relate to specific criteria such as productivity, team satisfaction, degree of task completion, and the accomplishment of project goals. In distributed teams, additional dimensions must be considered in order to assess the effectiveness of teamwork, such as the quality of decision making, team commitment, and cohesion between team members (Martins et al., 2004; Maznevski and Chudoba, 2000). Staples and Webster (2007) developed a self-efficacy teamwork measure based on virtual team best practices obtained from the literature and from six case studies. In the present study, Teamwork Effectiveness refers to the team members' perceptions of team performance in terms of task completion, goal achievement, information sharing, conflict resolution, problem solving, and the ability to create and sustain a good working environment. As proposed by Mathieu et al. (2008), the criteria for effective teamwork (e.g., productivity, team satisfaction, degree of task completion, and accomplishing project goals) should be appropriately related to the team's function and tasks. The proposed metrics are suitable for the distributed teams under study, and have been previously used by Bourgault et al. (2008).

3.4 Contextual Variables That Potentially Affect the Main Relationships in the Model

Studies have shown the effects of contextual variables, such as the degree of distribution, cultural differences, differing work practices, and experience, on various aspects of project management and teamwork. For instance, Hoegl et al. (2007) argue that teamwork affects team performance more strongly as members become increasingly distributed. This is because high-quality teamwork can leverage the increased knowledge potential of distributed teams, and team members in more distributed teams have

little possibility of compensating for low-quality teamwork through hands-on leadership. Thus, geographic proximity affects team processes and performance. Another contextual factor that affects the effectiveness of teamwork and the quality of decision making in distributed teams is the appropriate management of cultural and functional diversity among team members (Zakaria et al., 2004). Culturally diverse teams may have difficulty building trust, and extra time may be needed for such teams to work and communicate effectively (Corbitt et al., 2004). In addition, complex and interdependent tasks require synchronicity, communication, and coordination among team members, as each member plays a part in the overall team functioning. Moreover, when members of a distributed team come from different organizations, diverse work practices could impact the nature and intensity of interactions, communications, and operations (Drouin et al., 2010b). Harrison and Klein (2007) found that if the diversity attribute (e.g. different work practices or values) is vital for the completion of team tasks, then the team may bifurcate into two clusters or cliques, with few or no team members bridging the gap. This kind of behaviour may impede teamwork effectiveness and the quality of decision making. A variety of experience among team members broadens a team's cognitive and behavioural repertoire (Harrison and Klein, 2007). Teams with a range of knowledge, functional background, or experience can make more effective decisions and deliver more creative products (Jackson et al., 1995).

Thus, contextual variables may influence the impact of certain explanatory dimensions on outcome variables. We therefore formulated a final group of hypotheses:

H10. The context in which a distributed team operates (degree of distribution, variety of cultures, variety of work practices, variety of experience) moderates the power of organizational support to explain the Quality of the Decision-Making Process.

H11. The context in which a distributed team operates (degree of distribution, variety of cultures, variety of work practices, variety of experience) moderates the power of organizational support to explain Teamwork Effectiveness.

H12. The context in which a distributed team operates (degree of distribution, variety of cultures, variety of work practices, variety of experience) moderates the power of the decision-making process to explain Teamwork Effectiveness.

4. Methodology

In this section we outline the empirical procedure we used to test our hypotheses. Our initial aim was to test a theoretical model based on field data, or real-life situations. Methodologically speaking, the objective was to build on empirical studies conducted by practitioners rather than to repeat the approach of earlier studies, most of which have been limited to experiments in academic settings.

4.1 Measuring Instrument and Data Collection

The empirical work was conducted in several steps. At the outset of the project, we carried out several field studies (i.e. case studies) with the aim of gaining an in-depth understanding of the dimensions of organizational support for distributed teams. Our initial sample was highly diversified. For example, it included a multinational firm whose employees routinely work with colleagues around the world. It also included small- and medium-size companies that partake in international projects on an ad hoc basis. In this first step, we met with 13 project managers from ten different companies to discuss their positions and responsibilities and inquire about the issues and challenges they face when working with faraway colleagues and partners. The objectives were to gain as much information as possible and to identify the dimensions involved in managing distributed project teams, such as organizational support (see Bourgault et al., 2009 for more details). We then added case studies that addressed a single activity sector in order

to limit interorganizational differences. Two Canadian-based international high-tech companies were selected. Care was taken to select firms with experience in managing distributed project teams. Data were collected in Canada over a six-month period, using a combination of in-depth interviews and archival research to enhance accuracy. In-depth interviews were conducted with nine managers who had experience in distributed project team management, using a pretested interview guide. Each interview lasted from two to four hours and was conducted in French (for more details see Drouin et al., 2010a).

Based on the literature review and case studies, we developed a questionnaire as a measurement instrument. We opted for a customized web questionnaire, with the assistance of an expert programmer. The questionnaire was repeatedly reviewed by the research team and pretested by ten representative respondents from our sample (practising professionals). We then corrected certain interpretation errors, primarily related to the translation of the questionnaire (which was available in two languages: French and English).

Data were collected over a six-month period from project management practitioners who had experience with distributed teams. To identify potential respondents, we worked together with the local chapter of the Project Management Institute, an organization for project management professionals. With their support, invitations were emailed to 1,000 managers. Of this number, we obtained a total of 149 completed and usable questionnaires. The usable sample comprised a diversity of project manager and project profiles. The average project duration, project budget, and number of team members was, respectively, 16.5 months, C\$42.2 million, and 24.5 members. All respondents had experience working with distributed project teams. Although the amount of experience varied, the sample appeared highly suitable to test our hypotheses.

We primarily targeted the team manager, who was assumed to have the best overview of the project. In many cases, however, other influential project actors responded to the questionnaire. Respondents were asked to classify themselves into one of three main roles: project management oversight, administrative support for the project team, or technical expertise. Of the 149 completed usable questionnaires, these roles accounted for 60, 25, and 15 percent of respondents, respectively.

We are aware of the limitations of using a single responder per team. To control for a potential bias effect of the respondent's role, we began by running a means test (Kruskall-Wallis, 5 percent confidence coefficient) on all items to detect between-group differences for the three main roles. Of the 41 items (variables) considered in the analysis, a significant difference was found for only five items. We therefore concluded that the role bias was insufficient to affect the analysis results.

4.2 Data Analysis

The model in Figure 40.1 (12 hypotheses) was validated using structural equation models that are frequently used in similar studies (e.g. Isik et al., 2009; Mom et al., 2007; Chen et al., 2006). Models were run using SPSS 11.0 for Windows and EQS 6.1 for Windows. All analyses are presented in detail in appendices A, B, C, and D. We performed an initial principal components analysis (PCA) to aggregate the measures into factors that were correctly interpretable and coherent with the studied concepts (cut-off level of 0.5 for each loading). A confirmatory factor analysis (CFA) was also performed to verify the convergent and discriminant validity of the dimensions obtained (Hair et al., 1998). Three groups of factors were used in this model, with the same procedure repeated three times.

For the first group of factors (explanatory variables in the model), the PCA generated four clearly defined factors based on a number of questionnaire items. The factor Strategic Staffing is composed of four items (Cronbach's $\alpha = 0.69$ and variance = 20.1 per cent). It represents the team's competency as well as the team leader's authority and leadership. These characteristics are presumed to depend largely on the management's role in staffing the team. The factor Training and Tools is composed of two items (Cronbach's $\alpha = 0.60$ and variance = 15.94 percent). It represents the organization's support in terms of

preparing teams well and providing them with the tools they need to function in distributed mode. The factors Team Autonomy and Top Management Monitoring include two items each (Cronbach's $\alpha = 0.71$ and 0.73 and variance = 15.73 and 16.63 per cent, respectively). Here, autonomy refers to the team's ability to make decisions about the way it functions and how the project budget is used. The final factor represents management's presence in the project, both in the upstream phases (requirements specification) and during project conduct (monitoring). The unidimensionality and convergent validity of the factors were verified by CFA. According to the statistics provided by the model, the dimensions demonstrate strong convergent validity ($\chi^2 = 24.589$; $p = 0.372$; df = 23; $\chi^2/df = 1.069$; GFI = 0.959; IFI = 0.994; CFI = 0.993; RMSEA = 0.025).

The same procedure was applied to the model's two other principal dimensions Quality of the Decision-Making Process and Team Effectiveness. Quality of the Decision-Making Process refers to elements such as the assessment of different alternatives or options, time constraints (i.e. decisions were made within a reasonable timeframe), team cooperation and consensual support for decisions, and variations and changes in final decisions (i.e. once made, decisions did not usually change) (Bourgault et al., 2008). We used a two-item construct established by PCA (Cronbach's $\alpha = 0.87$ and variance = 28.8 percent) to measure whether the team was making decisions based on good practices (i.e. after collecting sufficient information and considering all possible options). Team Effectiveness refers to the team members' perceptions of activities such as setting common objectives, planning and organizing tasks, holding meetings, sharing information, resolving problems, and creating and sustaining a good working environment (Bourgault et al., 2008). The effectiveness of the team's work was therefore assessed with a six-item measure (Cronbach's $\alpha = 0.92$, variance = 46.87 percent) to determine the quality of traditional team tasks such as planning and organization of activities, appropriate distribution of information, problem solving and conflict resolution, and tracking and assessing task performance. The unidimensionality and convergent validity of these measures were verified in the same way as for the first group of factors ($\chi^2 = 17.593$; $p = 0.348$; df = 16; $\chi^2/$df = 1.100; GFI = 0.966; IFI = 0.998; CFI = 0.998; RMSEA = 0.029).

We also identified four contextual variables in the same way as described above. The variety of work methods measures within-team differences with respect to key functional factors such as task-related education and technical competencies the ways in which decisions are made and conflicts resolved (Cronbach's α = 0.84, variance = 33.05 percent). Our measure of cultural diversity captures the different nationalities and working languages within the team (Cronbach's α = 0.75 and variance = 17.20 percent). The measure of geographic distribution is a special case, because, as several authors have suggested, it can be measured in numerous ways (O'Leary and Cummings, 2007). We sought to establish an index that would capture the maximum variance in three respects: number of sites where the team is distributed, number of time zones between team members, and average distance between team members and the project leader.

The global distributedness index (GDI), proposed in Bourgault et al. (2008), is calculated as shown in Figure 40.2. Overall, this index provided the necessary variance for subsequent analysis (minimum = 2.00; maximum = 31.24). Once the variables of the model were established, we attempted to verify our hypotheses, as described in the next section.

5. Results

In this section, we present the results of the statistical analyses performed on the overall sample, as recommended by Joreskog and Sorbom (1993). We first analysed the behaviour of our variables based on the overall model (Model 1, Table 40.1) without distinguishing the contextual variables (control variables). As presented in Table 40.1, the overall model shows good explanatory power for both Quality of the Decision-Making Process ($R^2 = 26.38$ percent) and Team Effectiveness ($R^2 = 65.66$ percent). This means that the dimensions related to organizational support explain the variables in question well. Two explanatory variables stand out: Strategic Staffing (0.341 and 0.396) and Training and Tools (0.254 and 0.160).

In sum, these results confirm earlier studies that emphasized the importance of competent, carefully created teams to perform distributed teamwork. This type of team selection appears to impact Team Effectiveness more than all other aspects of organizational support considered in our study. The organization plays a major and visible role in the selection process: assigning people with appropriate profiles to distributed teams. In addition to the right people, organizations must provide teams with the necessary technical support, which wield a direct and highly significant effect on Team Effectiveness and decision making (high and significant b's). We also note the strong explanatory power of Quality of the Decision-Making Process (QDMP) on Team Effectiveness (TE), as predicted, according to Bourgault et al. (2008).

The dimensions Top Management Monitoring (TMM) and Team Autonomy (TA) show much lower (negligible) explanatory power in our model. Nevertheless, TMM and TA are not devoid of interest, as shown by the discriminant (intergroup) analyses presented below.

We next verified the effect of the contextual variables on the relationships in the initial model

| **Figure 40.2** | Global Distributedness Index |

$$GDI = NS + NZ + Log(AD)$$

Where NS is the number of sites; NZ the number of time zones between the most distant team members; AD the average distance between all team members and the project manager's site (log)

Table 40.1	Statistics for Initial Structural Model (Model 1)		
		β	R^2
H1	Strategic Staffing (SS) → Quality of DMP (QDMP)	*0.341*****	26.38
H3	Training and Tools (TT) → Quality of DMP (QDMP)	*0.254****	
H5	Team Autonomy (TA) → Quality of DMP (QDMP)	0.053ns	
H7	Top Management Monitoring (TMM) → Quality of DMP (QDMP)	0.092ns	
H2	Strategic Staffing (SS) → Teamwork Effectiveness (TE)	*0.396*****	65.66
H4	Training and Tools (TT) → Teamwork Effectiveness (TE)	*0.160****	
H6	Team Autonomy (TA) → Teamwork Effectiveness (TE)	0.075*	
H8	Top Management Monitoring (TMM) → Teamwork Effectiveness (TE)	−0.085*	
H9	Quality of DMP (QDMP) → Teamwork Effectiveness (TE)	*0.470*****	

(Tables 40.2 and 40.3). All the hypotheses addressing the moderating effects (*H10, H11, H12*) were tested. Thus, we reran the analyses on subsamples defined by the median for the control variable (Byrne, 1994): submodels 2A and 2B (effect of distribution), 3A and 3B (effect of cultural differences), 4A and 4B (effect of different working methods), and 5A and 5B (effect of different experience).

The results presented in Table 40.2 suggest that distribution has a strong influence when the explanatory power of Strategic Staffing (SS) on Quality of Decision-Making Process (QDMP) is considered (see Models 2A and 2B). Given that other variables play a role in the model, it appears that this dimension becomes more influential with increasing team distribution. Although this dimension has a different effect on Team Effectiveness (TE), the influence does not differ with the level of distribution (high and significant b's, but no difference across subgroups). The same holds true for the impact of Training and Tools (TT), which was significant in the first model: it is unaffected by distribution.

Table 40.2 shows the results of the effect of cultural differences on distributed teams (see Models 3A and 3B). TT is influential in teams with major cultural differences (b = 0.377). Training and Tools support would most probably mitigate interpretation and

communication problems in such cases. Similarly, TA shows a significantly higher effect on highly culturally diverse teams than on more homogeneous teams (0.181 vs −0.075).

Finally, the explanatory power of QDMP on TE is informative. The results differ significantly across subgroups for both control variables (dispersion and cultural differences), indicating a lower explanatory power of QDMP for TE. The difference is small but significant, and may be explained by the greater explanatory power of the other variables in the model, among others.

We now turn to the impact of the two other contextual variables (Table 40.3) intrateam differences in work methods (Models 4A and 4B) and common experience with teamwork (Models 5A and 5B). Contrary to expectation, differences in work methods, which are frequently mentioned in the literature on distributed teams, have only a moderate impact on the relationships in our model. Only the (QDMP-TE) relationship is influenced by this factor. QDMP therefore becomes a preponderant factor in explaining team success with large intrateam differences (b = 0.570) relative to the other dimensions of the model. The differences between subgroups are more significant when the impact of intrateam differences in experience is considered. Significant differences are found for five of the nine relationships studied.

Table 40.2 Statistics for Structural Models With Contextual Variables (I)

	Model 2A: Not very distributed	Model 2B: Very distributed	p/2	Model 3A: Few cultural differences	Model 3B: Large cultural differences	p/2
H1 SS → QDMP	0.149	0.445****	0.0770	0.323**	0.385****	0.2735
H3 TT → QDMP	0.321**	0.245**	0.4070	0.173	0.377****	0.0865
H5 TA → QDMP	0.077	0.051	0.4410	-0.075^{ns}	0.181**	0.0625
H7 TMM → QDMP	0.076	0.046	0.4425	0.099	0.034	0.3620
H2 SS → TE	0.364****	0.400****	0.3660	0.316****	0.376****	0.3765
H4 TT → TE	0.154*	0.152**	0.4860	0.199**	0.143*	0.3130
H6 TA → TE	0.039	0.095	0.3575	0.024	0.159**	0.1270
H8 TMM → TE	−0.178**	0.033	0.0440	−0.004	−0.133*	0.1590
H9 QDMP → TE	0.544****	0.409****	0.0730	0.583****	0.433****	0.0385

Table 40.3 Statistics for Structural Models With Contextual Variables (II)

	Model 4A: Few differences in work methods	Model 4B: Large differences in work methods	p/2	Model 5A: Few differences in experience	Model 5B: Large differences in experience	p/2
SS → QDMP	0.429****	0.255**	0.1185	0.236**	0.462****	0.0545
TT → QDMP	0.221**	0.252**	0.3545	0.257**	0.248**	0.4650
TA → QDMP	0.166*	−0.048	0.1210	0.163*	-0.072^{ns}	0.0790
TMM → QDMP	0.188**	0.056	0.2690	0.122	0.090	0.4970
SS → TE	0.521****	0.361****	0.1015	0.550****	0.244***	0.0345
TT → TE	0.220***	0.133*	0.3470	0.054	0.219***	0.0655
TA → TE	0.189**	0.055	0.1950	0.049	0.129**	0.2660
TMM → TE	0.003	−0.109*	0.1455	−0.002	−0.157**	0.0565
QDMP → TE	0.184**	0.570****	0.0015	0.413****	0.543****	0.1235

As with all the subgroups with marked differences in degree of distribution, SS plays a greater role in explaining QDMP with increasing intrateam differences in teamwork experience. This is attributable to the fact that TA does not have a significant impact on the same variable in the subgroup with the greatest difference in experience (b = −0.072). Thus, SS is more influential when a team contains large differences in experience. SS appears to act as a compensatory mechanism, showing greater intensity in teams with greater than less marked differences in experience. TT shows a similar effect on TE. The greater the difference in team members' experience, the greater the explanatory power of TT for Team Effectiveness. Note that the explanatory power of TT for QDMP remains considerable and significant in all subgroups, even though the difference between subgroups is not significant (b = 0.221, 0.252, 0.257 and 0.248).

Finally, it is noteworthy that the TMM dimension is not significant in any of the models. In fact, when b is significant, it is usually negative (models 1, 2A, 3B, 4B, and 5B). This result is counterintuitive. We initially assumed that management's involvement in monitoring projects would be useful for projects that were highly distributed, whether geographically, culturally, or in other senses. But the reverse appears to be true. This issue should be examined in more depth. In sum, we found empirical support for hypotheses *H1*, *H2*, *H3*, *H4*, *H9*, *H10*, *H11*, and *H12*. *H5*, *H6*, *H7*, and *H8* were not supported.

6. Conclusion

The aim of this study was to investigate four dimensions of organizational support that are related to superior decision-making quality and teamwork effectiveness in distributed project teams. Four main findings emerged.

First, strategic staffing is significantly associated with the quality of decision making and teamwork effectiveness. Strategic staffing is therefore a key dimension of organizational support that positively impacts distributed project team success. To conduct a successful distributed project, individuals with key attributes must be assigned to the team in order to enhance the quality of the team's decision-making process and its performance. As working environments become increasingly distributed, strategic staffing should become increasingly vital, particularly for the quality of decision making. These results are in line with previous findings by Drouin et al. (2010b), who found that the influence of individual

team member characteristics depends on the team's degree of virtuality. However, our results underscore that, for highly distributed teams, strategic staffing makes a greater contribution to the quality of decision making than to teamwork effectiveness. This supports the contentions of Clark and Stephenson (1989) and Hollenbeck et al. (1995), who view the team as a vehicle for combining and integrating a variety of knowledge, ideas, attributes, and perspectives in order to produce high-quality decisions. Compared to individual decision makers, groups have access to more information due to the wider range of knowledge contributed by the members.

Second, training and tools also constitute a key dimension of organizational support that positively impacts both teamwork effectiveness and the quality of decision making. These findings are consistent with studies that underscored the need to develop a training programme so that individuals can acquire the necessary competencies to work effectively in a virtual context (Duarte and Snyder, 2001; Mankin et al., 1996; Vakola and Wilson, 2004). Furthermore, by providing training, the organization demonstrates its recognition of employees' contributions. This perceived organizational support (POS) has a constructive influence on teamwork effectiveness and the quality of decision making (Shore and Shore, 1995). Consistent with Schweitzer's (2005) findings, we confirmed our hypothesis that providing effective tools and methods to distributed teams has a positive impact on teamwork effectiveness. Our results also underscore the importance of providing training and adequate tools to team members to enhance the quality of decisions in teams with wide cultural differences. Zakaria et al. (2004) also argued the need to manage cultural and functional diversities within virtual teams. Thus, training and tools constitute a dimension of organizational support that helps mitigate the impact of cultural diversity on team effectiveness and the quality of decision making.

Third, Bourgault et al. (2008) found that team autonomy is a critical dimension, regardless of the degree of distribution. In the present study, we found more specifically that team autonomy may be more salient and influential on the quality of decision making in a highly culturally diverse team. Our findings also support the association between the quality of decision making and team effectiveness, particularly in a highly distributed and culturally diversified context. Teams are perceived as vehicles for identifying and integrating individual viewpoints, knowledge, and backgrounds. It is therefore proposed that if the organization adequately equips and supports distributed project teams, they will be in a position to make decisions and conduct their work effectively.

This study contributes to the research on distributed project teams and on organizational support theory. The need to understand the dimensions that underlie the consequences of perceived organizational support (Rhoades and Eisenberger, 2002) is underscored. This conclusion is in line with competency-based management research (Draganidis and Mentzas, 2006), as it addresses the key knowledge that managers at the organizational level should possess in order to support both the quality of decision making and teamwork effectiveness in distributed project teams. According to recent research in competency-based management, this type of organizational support is directly related to personnel development plans (Draganidis and Mentzas, 2006; Beck, 2003), insofar as it involves dimensions such as strategic staffing, training and tools, team autonomy, and top management monitoring. Our findings confirm the need to implement practices designed to increase the recognition of team members' contributions (e.g., provide team autonomy) and treat them favourably (e.g., provide training and tools) in order to conduct successful distributed projects. Team members perceive such practices as beneficial treatment by top management. Consequently, decision-making quality improves and teamwork becomes more effective.

7. Limitations

This study has certain limitations: it examined firms and respondents based in North America, and therefore the results may not be transferable to other cultures, including European and Asian. Further research in other countries with multiple respondents per team is recommended to deepen our understanding of the influence of country on

the investigated relationships. Similarly, firms from different industries may show different relationships between variables. Future studies could also consider additional dimensions of organizational support, such as recognition pay and promotions, job security, and organization size, as proposed by authors such as Rhoades and Eisenberger (2002) and Shore and Shore (1995).

Much remains to be explored in terms of how corporate management can optimally support the work of distributed teams. However, it appears clear that managers cannot treat these teams in the same way as conventional teams. Several intervention and support methods show promise, and we believe that further studies in this area can contribute to identify the most appropriate applications for distributed teamwork.

Notes

1. Corresponding author: Nathalie Drouin can be contacted at: drouin.nathalie@uqam.ca

2. The authors wish to thank Mrs. Margaret McKyes for her very helpful comments during the various stages of this chapter.

References

Balthazard, P., Potter, R.E. and Warren, J. (2004), "Expertise, extraversion and group interaction style as performance indicators in virtual teams", *Advances in Information Systems*, Vol. 35 No. 1, pp. 42–64.

Beck, S. (2003), "Skill and competence management as a base of an integrated personnel development (IPD)- a pilot project in the Putzmeister, Inc/Germany", *Journal of Universal Computer Science*, Vol. 9 No. 12, pp. 1381–1387.

Bissoonauth, B. (2002), "Virtual project work: investigating critical success factors of virtual project performance", master's thesis, The John Molson School of Business, Concordia University, Montreal.

Bourgault, M. and Drouin, N. (2008), *How's Your Distributed Team Doing? Ten Suggestions from the Field*, Project Management Institute, Upper Darby, PA.

Bourgault, M., Drouin, N. and Hamel, E. (2008), "Decision-making within distributed project teams: an exploration of formalization and autonomy as determinants of success", *Project Management Journal*, Vol. 39 Nos S97–S110, pp. 97–110.

Bourgault, M., Drouin, N., Daoudi, J. and Hamel, E. (2009), *Understanding Decision-Making within Distributed Project Teams*, PMI Publications, Upper Darby, PA, p. 109.

Brodbeck, F.C., Kerschreiter, R., Mojzisch, A. and Schulz-Hard, S. (2007), "Group decision making under conditions of distributed knowledge: the information asymmetries model", *The Academy of Management Review*, Vol. 32 No. 2, pp. 459–479.

Byrne, B. (1994), *Structural Equation Modelling with EQS and EQS Windows*, Sage, Thousand Oaks, CA.

Campion, M.A., Medsker, G.J. and Higgs, A.C. (1993), "Relations between work group characteristics and effectiveness: implications for designing effective work groups", *Personnel Psychology*, Vol. 46 No. 4, pp. 823–850.

Chen, G., Tjosvold, D. and Liu, C. (2006), "Cooperative goals, leader people and productivity values: their contribution to top management teams in China", *Journal of Management Studies*, Vol. 43 No. 5, pp. 1177–1200.

Clark, N.K. and Stephenson, G.M. (1989), "Group remembering", in Paulus, P. B. (Ed.), *Psychology of Group Influence*, Lawrence Erlbaum Associates, Hillsdale, NJ, pp. 357–391.

Corbitt, G., Gardiner, L.R. and Wright, L.K. (2004), "A comparison of team developmental stages, trust and performance for virtual versus face-to-face teams", *Proceedings of the 37th Hawaii International Conference on System Sciences, IEEE Computer Society*, Hawaii, HI.

Cramton, C.D. and Webber, S.S. (2005), "Relationships among geographic dispersion, team processes, and effectiveness in software development work teams", *Journal of Business Research*, Vol. 58 No. 6, pp. 758–765.

De Dreu, C.K.W. and Weingart, L.R. (2003), "Task versus relationship conflict: team performance, and team member satisfaction: A meta-analysis", *Journal of Applied Psychology*, Vol. 88 No. 4, pp. 741–749.

Denison, D.R., Stuart, L.H. and Kahn, J.A. (1996), "From chimneys to cross-functional teams: developing and validating a diagnostic model", *Academy of Management Journal*, Vol. 39 No. 4, pp. 1005–1023.

Draganidis, F. and Mentzas, G. (2006), "Competency based management: a review of systems and approaches", *Information Management & Computer Security*, Vol. 14 No. 1, pp. 51–64.

Drouin, N., Bourgault, M. and Gervais, C. (2010a), "Effects of organizational support on components of virtual project teams", *International Journal of Managing Projects in Business*, Vol. 3 No. 4, pp. 625–641.

Drouin, N., Bourgault, M. and Gervais, C. (2010b), "Managing virtual project teams: recent findings", in Sherif, M.H. (Ed.), *Handbook on Enterprise Integration*, 3rd ed., Auerbach Publications, Boca Raton, FL.

Duarte, D.L. and Snyder, N.T. (2001), *Mastering Virtual Teams: Strategies, Tools and Techniques That Succeed*, 2nd ed., Jossey-Bass, San Francisco, CA.

Eisenberger, R., Cummings, J., Armeli, S. and Lynch, P. (1997), "Perceived organizational support, discretionary treatment, and job satisfaction", *Journal of Applied Psychology*, Vol. 82 No. 5, pp. 812–830.

Eisenberger, R., Huntington, R., Hutchison, S. and Sowa, D. (1986), "Perceived organizational support", *Journal of Applied Psychology*, Vol. 71, pp. 500–507.

Fink, L. (2007), "Coordination, learning, and innovation: the organizational roles of e-collaboration and their impacts", *International Journal of e-Collaboration*, Vol. 3 No. 3, pp. 53–70.

Furst, S.A., Reeves, M., Rosen, B. and Blackburn, R.S. (2004), "Managing the life cycle of virtual teams", *Academy of Management Executive*, Vol. 18 No. 2, pp. 6–20.

Geister, S., Konradt, U. and Hertel, G. (2006), "Effects of process feedback on motivation, satisfaction, and performance in virtual teams", *Small Group Research*, Vol. 37 No. 5, pp. 459–489.

Gibson, C.B. and Cohen, S.G. (2003), *Virtual Teams That Work: Creating Conditions for Virtual Team Effectiveness*, John Wiley & Sons, San Francisco, CA.

Gladstein, D. (1984), "Groups in context: a model of task group effectiveness", *Administrative Science Quarterly*, Vol. 29 No. 4, pp. 499–517.

Gouldner, A.W. (1960), "The norm of reciprocity: a preliminary statement", *American Sociological Review*, Vol. 25 No. 2, pp. 161–178.

Hackman, J.R. and Oldham, G.R. (1980), *Work Redesign*, Addison-Wesley, Reading, MA.

Hair, J.F Jr, Anderson, R.E., Tatham, R.L. and Black, W.C. (1998), *Multivariate Data Analysis*, 5th ed., Prentice Hall, Upper Saddle River, NJ.

Hall, C.A. (1998), "Organizational support systems for team-based organizations: employee collaboration through organizational structures", doctoral thesis, University of North Texas, Denton, TX.

Harrison, D. and Klein, K. (2007), "What's the difference? Diversity constructs as separation, variety, or disparity in organizations", *Academy of Management Review*, Vol. 32 No. 4, pp. 1199–1228.

Hertel, G., Geister, S. and Konradt, U. (2005), "Managing virtual teams: a review of current empirical research", *Human Resource Management Review*, Vol. 15 No. 1, pp. 69–95.

Hoegl, M., Ernst, H. and Porserpio, L. (2007), "How teamwork matters more as team member dispersion increases", *Journal of Product Innovation Management*, Vol. 24 No. 2, pp. 156–165.

Hollenbeck, J.R., Ilgen, D.R., Tuttle, D.B. and Sego, D.J. (1995), "Team performance on monitoring tasks: an examination of decision errors in contexts requiring sustained attention", *Journal of Applied Psychology*, Vol. 80 No. 6, pp. 685–696.

Hyatt, D.E. and Ruddy, T.M. (1997), "An examination of the relationship between work group characteristics and performance: once more into the breach", *Personnel Psychology*, Vol. 50 No. 3, pp. 553–585.

Isik, Z., Arditi, D., Dikmen, I. and Birgonul, M.T. (2009), "Impact of corporate strengths/ weaknesses on project management competencies", *International Journal of Project Management*, Vol. 27 No. 6, pp. 629–637.

Jackson, S.E., May, K.E. and Whitney, K. (1995), "Understanding the dynamics of diversity in decision-making teams", in Guzzo, R.A. and Salas, E. (Eds), *Team Effectiveness and Decision Making in Organizations*, Jossey-Bass, San Francisco, CA, pp. 204–261.

Joreskog, K.G. and Sorbom, D. (1993), *Lisrel 8 User's Reference Guide (Chapter 4: Causal Models for Directly Observed Variables)*, Scientific Software International, Lincolnwood, IL.

Katzenbach, J.R. and Smith, D.K. (1993), *The Wisdom of Teams: Creating the High Performance Organization*, Harvard Business School Press, Boston, MA.

Kirkman, B.L. and Rosen, B. (1999), "Beyond self-management: antecedents and consequences of team empowerment", *Academy of Management Journal*, Vol. 42 No. 1, pp. 58–74.

Kirkman, B.L., Rosen, B., Tesluk, P.E. and Gibson, C.B. (2004), "The impact of team empowerment on virtual team performance. The moderating role of face-to-face interaction", *Academy of Management Journal*, Vol. 47 No. 2, pp. 175–192.

Levinson, H. (1965), "The relationship between man and organization", *Administrative Science Quarterly*, Vol. 9 No. 4, pp. 370–390.

Lipnack, J. and Stamps, J. (1997), *Virtual Teams: Reaching across Space, Time and Organizations with Technology*, John Wiley & Sons, New York, NY.

Mahaney, R.C. and Lederer, A.L. (2010), "The role of monitoring and shirking in information systems project management", *International Project Management Journal*, Vol. 28 No. 1, pp. 14–25.

Mankin, D., Cohen, S.G. and Bikson, T.K. (1996), *Teams and Technology: Fulfilling the Promise of the New Organization*, Harvard Business School Press, Cambridge, MA.

March, J.G. (1988), *Decisions and Organization*, Blackwell, London.

Martins, L.L., Gilson, G.L. and Maynard, M.T. (2004), "Virtual teams: what do we know and where do we go from here?", *Journal of Management*, Vol. 30 No. 6, pp. 805–835.

Mathieu, J., Maynard, T.M., Rapp, T. and Gilson, L. (2008), "Team effectiveness 1997–2007: a review of recent advancements and a glimpse into the future", *Journal of Management*, Vol. 34 No. 3, pp. 410–476.

Maznevski, M.L. and Chudoba, K.M. (2000), "Bridging space over time: global virtual team dynamics and effectiveness", *Organization Science*, Vol. 11 No. 5, pp. 473–492.

Mohrman, S.A., Cohen, S.G. and Mohrman, A.M. Jr (1995), *Designing Team-Based Organizations: New Forms for Knowledge Work*, Jossey-Bass, San Francisco, CA.

Mom, T.J.M., Van Den Bosch, F.A.J. and Volberda, H.W. (2007), "Investigating managers' exploration and exploitation activities: the influence of top-down, bottom-up, and horizontal knowledge inflows", *Journal of Management Studies*, Vol. 44 No. 6, pp. 910–931.

Mortensen, M. and Hinds, P.J. (2001), "Conflict and shared identity in geographically distributed teams", *International Journal of Conflict Management*, Vol. 12 No. 3, pp. 212–238.

Nath, D., Sridhar, V. and Malik, A. (2008), "Project quality of off-shore virtual teams engaged in software requirements analysis: an exploratory comparative study", *Journal of Global Information Management*, Vol. 16 No. 4, pp. 24–45.

Nidiffer, K.E. and Dolan, D. (2005), "Evolving distributed project management", *IEEE Software*, Vol. 22 No. 5, pp. 63–72.

O'Leary, M. and Cummings, J.N. (2007), "The spatial, temporal, and configurational characteristics of geographic dispersion in work teams", *MIS Quarterly*, Vol. 31 No. 3, pp. 433–452.

Pennings, J. (1985), *Strategic Decision Making in Complex Organizations*, Jossey-Bass Publishers, San Francisco, CA.

Peters, L.M. and Manz, C.C. (2007), "Identifying antecedents of virtual team collaboration", *Team Performance Management*, Vol. 13 Nos 3/4, pp. 117–129.

Pick, J.M., Romano, N.C. and Roztocki, N. (2008), "Synthesizing the research advances in electronic collaboration: theoretical frameworks", *International Journal of e-Collaboration*, Vol. 5 No. 1, pp. 1–12.

Raver, J.L. and Gelfand, M.J. (2005), "Beyond the individual victim: linking sexual harassment, team processes, and team performance", *Academy of Management Journal*, Vol. 48 No. 3, pp. 387–400.

Rhoades, L. and Eisenberger, R. (2002), "Perceived organizational support: a review of the literature", *Journal of Applied Psychology*, Vol. 87 No. 4, pp. 698–714.

Schweitzer, L. (2005), "Understanding virtual team effectiveness: an exploration", doctoral thesis, Carleton University, Ottawa, ON.

Seibert, S.E., Silver, S.R. and Randolph, W.A. (2004), "Taking empowerment to the next level: a multiple-level model of empowerment, performance, and satisfaction", *Academy of Management Journal*, Vol. 47 No. 3, pp. 332–349.

Shelton, P.M., Waite, A.M. and Makela, C.J. (2010), "Highly effective teams: a relational analysis of group potency and perceived organizational support", *Advances in Developing Human Resources*, Vol. 12 No. 1, pp. 93–114.

Shin, Y. (2004), "A person-environment fit model for virtual organizations", *Journal of Management*, Vol. 30 No. 5, pp. 725–743.

Shore, L.M. and Shore, T.H. (1995), "Perceived organizational support and organizational justice", in Cropanzano, R. and Kacmar, K.M. (Eds), *Organizational Politics, Justice and Support: Managing Social Climate at Work*, Quorum Press, Westport, CT, pp. 149–164.

Simon, H.A. (1960), *The New Science of Management Decision*, Harper & Row, New York, NY.

Simon, R. (1994), "How new top managers use control systems as levers of strategic renewal", *Strategic Management Journal*, Vol. 15 No. 3, pp. 169–189.

Srivastava, A., Bartol, K.M. and Locke, E.A. (2006), "Empowering leadership in management teams: effects on knowledge sharing, efficacy, and performance", *Academy of Management Journal*, Vol. 49 No. 6, pp. 1239–1251.

Staples, D.S. and Webster, J. (2007), "Exploring traditional and virtual team members' best practices. A social cognitive theory perspective", *Small Group Research*, Vol. 38 No. 1, pp. 60–97.

Stewart, G.L. (2006), "A meta-analytic review of relationships between team design features and team performance", *Journal of Management*, Vol. 32 No. 1, pp. 29–54.

Sundstrom, E. (1999), "The challenges of supporting work team effectiveness", in Sundstrom, E. and Associates (Eds), *Supporting Work Team Effectiveness*, Jossey-Bass, San Francisco, CA.

Sundstrom, E., De Meuse, K.P. and Futrell, D. (1990), "Work teams: applications and effectiveness", *American Psychologist*, Vol. 45 No. 2, pp. 120–133.

Tesluk, P.E. and Mathieu, J.E. (1999), "Overcoming roadblocks to effectiveness: incorporating management of performance barriers into models of work group effectiveness", *Journal of Applied Psychology*, Vol. 84 No. 2, pp. 200–217.

Townsley, C. (2001), "Virtual teams: the relationship between organizational support systems and effectiveness", master's thesis, University of North Texas, Denton, TX.

Vakola, M. and Wilson, I. (2004), "The challenge of virtual organization: critical success factors in dealing with constant change", *Team Performance Management*, Vol. 10 Nos 5/6, pp. 112–120.

Wayne, S., Shore, L. and Liden, R. (1997), "Perceived organizational support and leader-member exchange: a social exchange perspective", *Academy of Management Journal*, Vol. 40 No. 1, pp. 82–111.

West, M.A. (2004), *Effective Teamwork: Practical Lessons from Organizational Research*, Blackwell Publishing, Oxford.

Yu, M.Y., Lang, K.R. and Kumar, N. (2009), "Internationalization of online professional communities: an empirical investigation of AIS-ISWorld", *International Journal of e-Collaboration*, Vol. 5 No. 1, pp. 13–31.

Zakaria, N., Amelinckx, A. and Wilemon, D. (2004), "Working together apart? Building a knowledge-sharing culture for global virtual teams", *Creativity and Innovation Management*, Vol. 13 No. 1, pp. 15–29.

Zwikael, O. (2008), "Top management involvement in project management: a cross country study of the software industry", *International Journal of Managing Projects in Business*, Vol. 1 No. 4, pp. 498–511.

PART VIII

Social Responsibility

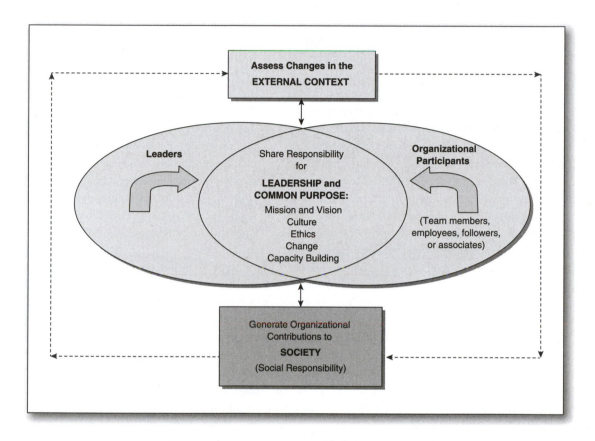

Overview

Part VIII provides insight into the actions new era organizations are pursuing in response to the complex global issues raised in Part I. A substantial and steadily growing number of leaders and members incorporate social issues and social activism as important components of their organizations' purpose, vision, mission, and values. Many organization leaders and members see their long-term viability as inextricably linked to the viability of society. This commitment to social responsibility has even resulted

in the creation of new organizational forms that connect social initiatives and profitability.

Robin Byerly (Chapter 41) builds on social contract theory to develop a collective notion of the role of business in global society. Social contract theory is an implied contract or covenant attributed to philosophers Hobbes, Locke, and Rousseau. It proposes that "human beings, as they have evolved to come together to live in communities and society, thus encountering interdependencies, must come to a common agreement regarding relationships and the responsibilities and rights of that society's member." Its basic intent throughout the centuries is to help individuals and social institutions understand their roles, relationships, and responsibilities to society's collective well-being.

While business has always been a part of the social contract, traditional market-based perspectives (espoused by economists such as Milton Friedman) promoted an isolated view of the firm that allowed businesses to relate to the larger community only through the marketplace. Byerly argues a more contemporary view of the firm recognizes that business is actually nested within a pluralistic, global community that does not allow it to exist in isolation from society. This perspective promotes a worldview of business as an institution *in* society, not above it. The new role for business in society is one of global corporate citizen with accompanying moral responsibilities to the environment, an array of stakeholders including workers, and the cultures and communities in which they are situated. These expanded responsibilities have generated new organizational forms, partnerships, and alliances that are explored in the next chapter.

Sandra Waddock and Malcolm McIntosh (Chapter 42) assert that human-induced causes—such as climate change or an increasing gap between the rich and poor, and misguided incentives in economic, business, and financial models—highlight the need for a new approach to capitalism. The emergence of new forms of enterprise is part of what the authors call *a change to a sustainable enterprise economy* (SEE Change). The Internet, especially Web 2.0 technology, has created transparency for any interested party so that social and ecological problems are readily visible.

The authors cite economist Joseph Schumpeter's theory of change that argues economies were never actually stable but change was always underway. Change takes place through "what he called 'creative destruction' by necessity because of the 'fundamental impulse' that 'comes from the new consumers, goods, the new methods of production or transportation, the new markets, the forms of industrial organization that capitalist enterprise creates." Waddock and McIntosh see this process of creative destruction occurring today where entrepreneurs are building new types of organizations to tackle wicked problems that are too complex to be handled by one organization or sector.

This movement toward a sustainable enterprise economy is generating new business enterprises whose purpose is to deliver social, human, and ecological benefit alongside profit. The authors examine several emerging forms of business enterprise intended to generate multiple bottom lines:

- The for-benefit corporation, similar to the B corporation, represents a convergence of for-profit money-making and non-profit mission.
- The B corporation uses business power to deal with complex social and ecological problems by building transparent social and environmental standards and values into its governing documents.
- The conscious capitalism movement advocates that companies incorporate three core principles: deeper purpose, which entails more than merely profit maximization; stakeholder model (delivering value to all stakeholders); and conscious leadership to serve as stewards of the company's deeper purpose and its stakeholders.

These types of organizations are characterized as the fourth sector because they blur the boundaries of different types of organizations to achieve the blended value proposition of making profits while simultaneously serving a social and/or ecological purpose. Many large corporations are already engaged in a range of activities—corporate social responsibility, environmental management and sustainability programs, cause-related marketing and purchasing, and carbon offset programs, among others—that have a social purpose and make profits. Waddock and McIntosh conclude that the process of creative disruption toward a sustainable enterprise economy creates hope for a better future.

While Waddock and McIntosh explore new forms of organizations to support the sustainable enterprise economy, Sander Tideman, Muriel Arts, and Danielle Zandee (Chapter 43) argue for a new type of leadership to guide these organizations through the transformation into a new way of creating and preserving a sustainable world. The authors contend that sustainability has become a business mega-trend that changes the demands placed on leadership, consequently creating the need for sustainable leadership.

They introduce the 6c Sustainable Leadership model, which incorporates a change in leadership mindset based on three Cs: *context*—recognizing interdependence, complexity, and ambiguity; *consciousness*—new or expanding mindsets and world-views; and *continuity*—long-term horizon, common purpose, and change processes. A complementary skill set consists of another three Cs: *connectedness*—serving the needs of all stakeholders; *creativity*—innovation for sustainable business models and sustainable shared value creation; and *collectiveness*—embedding sustainability in business structures and practicing sustainable consumption.

Tideman, Arts, and Zandee stress that this model contains some elements of Burns' transforming leadership and Bass' transformational model but goes beyond these models in scope and depth. They emphasize that tomorrow's leaders must change the way they think, create new practices, and develop new skills for the unprecedented journey ahead.

Ram Nidumolu, Jib Ellison, John Whalen, and Erin Billman (Chapter 44) provide insight into new partnership models that work to protect the environment and build value for the commons. The models have two defining characteristics: They engage carefully selected stakeholders, and they focus collaborative effort on innovation in operating process or business outcomes. Based on their practice, the authors present four models of sustainable collaboration that have produced effective results for participants and global citizens. These models encompass 1) corporate collaborations focused on processes, such as the Dairy Management's efforts to reduce milk's carbon footprint and produce renewable energy; 2) corporate collaborations focused on outcomes, including the sustainable Apparel Coalition's Higgs Index to measure and compare environmental performance outcomes such as material waste and energy efficiency; 3) extended collaborations with non-corporate participants focused on processes, such as the Action to Accelerate Recycling's to capture untapped value from recycling that could not be done by one company alone; and 4) extended collaborations with non-corporate participants focused on outcomes, such as the Latin American Water Funds' partnership to provide a steady, long-term supply of natural resources, including freshwater and forests.

Nidumolu et al. stress that many collaborative initiatives fail due to competitive self-interest, lack of a fully shared purpose, and a shortage of trust. They recommend Prahalad's concept of "next practices" to enable breakthroughs in innovation by collaborative partners: Start with a small, committed group; link self-interest to shared interest; monetize system values; create a clear path with quick wins; acquire independent project management expertise; build in structured competition; and nurture a culture of trust.

The chapters in this section emphasize that the economy, the environment, organizations, and society are interdependent and interconnected. A new worldview perceives business as firmly nested among the institutions in society that are responsible for the sustainability of our human, social, and ecological systems. Private, public, nonprofit, and fourth sector organizations must work in partnership to respond to the substantial issues raised in the Millennium Project's *State of the Future* report (Chapter 1) and the articles in this section. As stated early in the text, leaders and members of organizations may be in the most advantageous position to facilitate unprecedented advances for society and solve highly complex problems. It is imperative that we embrace this challenge and take action together.

Part VIII — Chapters

CHAPTER 41

Business *IN* Society

The Social Contract Revisited

Robin T. Byerly[1]

Appalachian State University

The problem is to find a form of association which will defend and protect with the whole common force the person and goods of each associate, and in which each, while uniting himself with all, may still obey himself alone, and remain as free as before. This is the fundamental problem of which the social contract provides the solution.

–Jean-Jacques Rousseau, The Social Contract and Discourses, 1988 (1762)

Introduction

In a rapidly and dramatically changing world marketplace where the whole of society, governments, and business are ever more closely connected, where old and new values compete (Friedman, 1999), where the power and influence of nation states is eroding while that of multinational corporations is growing exponentially, how can we find common ground and respond to fundamental concerns about the protection of human rights and responsibilities? Many suggest that we need a global ethic, a framework for defining right and wrong that knows no social, economic or political borders (Bruce et al., 2001; Kathrani,

2010). In the midst of this monumental challenge, some maintain that such is not possible without legal requirement and enforcement (Bishop, 2008; Sacconi, 2006). Yet a few offer hope and argument that a new normative global ethic and social contract is emerging that frames business activities in the global marketplace, includes recognition by businesses of their obligations to communities and citizenship, that acknowledges respect for fundamental human values, and that embraces partnerships with government and civil society (Cragg, 2000; Kathrani, 2010; Waddock, 2005). If indeed this is true, how can it be explained? Many theories of corporate social responsibility have emerged over the past 30-plus years to offer

Source: "Business IN Society: The Social Contract Revisited," by Robin T. Byerly in *Journal of Organisational Transformation & Social Change*, Vol. 10 No. 1, April, 2013, 4–20. Reprinted with permission from Maney Publishing.

instrumental, political, integrative, and ethical theories of normative persuasion (Garriga & Melé, 2004). All have sought to dismiss the common problem articulated by Votaw (1972: 25), who stated: 'Corporate responsibility means something, but not always the same thing to everybody.' In short, how can we find theoretical or principled agreement as to the concept and its practicality? It is argued here that the evolvement of social contract theory provides a solid basis for an increasingly collective understanding of our new world order and the role that business plays *in* it. The aim of this chapter is to build on that premise by developing additional moral and pragmatic arguments that support an increasingly collective notion of the role of business in a global society, business with government, and business with other institutional players—in short, an enlarged and more ratified notion of the social contract. The implications of this discussion are that the criticality of growing societal concerns and expectations in an increasingly interconnected and interdependent global environment, in combination with the growing power, influence, and presence of multinational corporations, is pushing us toward a paradigm shift in domestic and multinational corporate worlds. Its significance is profound as, in essence, such a paradigm shift may involve fundamental changes regarding the business corporation, its purpose, direction and process, and most particularly, the nature and extent of its involvement and participation with society and social issues.

This analysis will first explore historical theoretical development of social contract theory, then follow with more modern and Western applications of the theory, particularly developments in organization science that enlarge the contractual hypothesis to include business firms. Arguments follow to provide moral and pragmatic support for an evolving and strengthened notion of the social contract and its implications for business. Traditional roles of the firm in a firmly entrenched economic system are examined in light of the newer realities posed by global expansion and ecological and societal concerns. Differences, or paradoxes, are noted and indicate tensions that reflect new challenges to existing worlds of thought. Further, a conceptual model is offered that suggests a number of ways in which businesses are responding and how their roles are being redefined.

Social Contract Theory

The earliest proponents of the social contract, Socrates and Plato, sought to provide a rational perspective of what is good and necessary to achieve a state in which we, as members of a society, can depend upon to live well. Originally conceived as a normative theory of moral and political obligations determined by an understood contract and incumbent upon members of a society, this theory has been debated, critiqued, modified, even shunned over the centuries since. Nonetheless, it endures and, for more modern purposes, has been extended to include not only society and government, but also business. Although it has evolved over the centuries, its basic premise is still the same: to understand and determine what roles, relationships, and responsibilities each of us has relative to the whole of society and its collective well-being. Perhaps no theoretical perspective better supports evolving expectations of corporate social responsibility and an enlarged notion of the role that business plays *in* society.

The Historical Approach

The theory of a social contract emerged during the Enlightenment and is most notably defined by the work of Hobbes (1991 [1651]), Locke (1988 [1690]), and Rousseau (1988 [1762]). In brief, it is the hypothesis that human beings, as they have evolved to come together to live in communities and society, thus encountering interdependencies, must come to a common agreement regarding relationships and the responsibilities and rights of that society's members. Clearly hypothetical, it represents an implied contract or covenant by which individuals are said to have abandoned the 'state of nature' and its freedoms to form the society in which they now live.

The theory as initially formulated by Hobbes (in the *Leviathan*, 1991 [1651]) and John Locke (in *Two Treatises of Government*, 1988 [1690]) assumes that men at first lived in a state of anarchy in which there was no society, no government, and no organized coercion of the individual by the group. According to Hobbes, by the social contract, men had surrendered their natural liberties in order to enjoy the order and safety of the organized state. As society became organized and the role of government became instrumental, Locke used the social contract as the basis of his advocacy of popular sovereignty to champion the idea that the monarch or government must reflect the will of the people. Similarly, the French philosopher Jean Jacques Rousseau (in *Le Contrat Social*, 1988 [1762]) described the general will as a means of establishing reciprocal rights and duties, privileges, and responsibilities, thus serving as a basis of the state. In general, the position has held that the preservation of certain natural rights was an essential part of the social contract, and that 'consent of the governed' was fundamental to any exercise of governmental power. Further, of real significance to this theory is the premise that members of a society 'volunteer' and agree to be bound to the contract's terms because it is rational and in one's best interest to do so.

Some restrictions imposed by a social contract take the form of laws that society requires its members to follow. Indeed, many have emphasized the role of government and assert that obligation to adhere to the contract is strictly related to properly derived and promulgated laws—laws that both assist members of a society to live and flourish, as well as laws that punish those that fail to comply (Bishop, 2008). John Rawls (in *A Theory of Justice*, 1999b [1971]) attempted to generalize ideas of the social contract to yield truly common principles that could be used to assess the justice, or fairness, of political constitutions and of economic and social arrangements. Unlike earlier foundational assumptions, not being members of some society is simply not an option for us today. We have developed and exist as members of society and within its social framework and institutions. What makes these institutions and their arrangement the first subject for Rawls' principles of justice is his view that all are necessary to social cooperation and all have profound influences on the well-being of others. In the pursuit of justice, Rawls' emphasis is on political institutions that can fairly distribute rights, duties, opportunities, and powers; he recognizes other social institutions as being profoundly influential also but not generally necessary to society and social cooperation. Inherent in this reasoning is the notion that society could not long endure without

certain rules regarding property, transfer of goods and resources, regulation of economic production, trade, and consumption, and some political mechanism for enforcing economic and other cooperative norms. Such can only be achieved by a commonly accepted agreement on principles of justice, in other words, a social contract.

Modern Social Contract Theory and the Business Institution

In 1932, Harvard professor E. Merrick Dodd articulated an intellectual rationale for business responsibility toward society as a whole as being permitted and encouraged by law because it allowed business to exist as a service to the community and not primarily as a means of profit to its owners. McGuire (1963) suggested that the corporation take an interest in politics, in the welfare of the community, in education, in the well-being of its employees, and the whole social world about it. In 1978, William Frederick suggested a 'maturing' of this idea in that, given society's concerns, firms must pragmatically respond to certain social pressures. Business institutions were more definitively drawn into the social contract with the influential work of Freeman (1984) who conceptualized the modern corporation as a powerful force of large proportion, with the means of organizing economic life, and possessing significant attributes and powers to be dealt with as a major social institution—thereby having social obligations. Thus, the implied 'social contract' brought business into an acknowledged relationship with society and the view emerged that business organizations function by public consent. As so, the theoretical view then posits that businesses subscribe to the basic purpose of serving society by assuming broader responsibilities, serving a wider range of human values, and by contributing more to the quality of life than just supplying quantities of goods and services (Carroll, 1991).

A number of early theorists addressed the responsibility of business as larger than simply making a profit for its owners (Dodd, 1932; Frederick, 1978; McGuire, 1963), but also having an obligation to stakeholders, all parties who might be impacted or harmed by the firm's decisions and activities (Carroll,

1991; Freeman, 1984). While the social contract originally supposed business responsibility to all stakeholders, the legitimacy of many stakeholder claims, or their justification for corporate engagement, has traditionally been predicated on whether the stakeholder had the power to demand attention and, frequently, that power has not been enough. Stakeholder concerns may be weakened additionally by their competing nature. Attention to all stakeholder issues, many of which may conflict, may present overwhelming and distracting challenges to any business.

The legitimacy of many stakeholder concerns appears strengthened, however, in recent years as business firms operate within a larger ecosystem and global community whose stakeholders and audiences are more connected, more educated, and have changing expectations of companies (Henderson, 2010). Organizational philosophers suggest that, in today's global marketplace and society, the firm's social contract is pressing and binding. It is not to be construed as artificial or merely idealistically conceptual, held at bay until governing authorities make it official (Pestritto & West, 2003), or ruled out as complexities surround the international arena of economic activity. With stakeholders around the globe affected by the far reaching externalities of business activities, even if unintended, an even broader conceptualization emerges that parallels Davis' (1960) 'Iron Law of Responsibility'. In other words, the argument that the social responsibilities of businesses need to be commensurate with their social power becomes stronger than ever given the extraordinary reach, influence, and resource/ skill capabilities of modern multinational corporations.

In the previous half century, as business organizations increasingly became viewed as institutions of power, the need for good citizenship on the part of the corporation began to be recognized. As theory regarding the social contract has evolved, newer governmental and societal emphasis on citizenship has played an influential role in motivating corporations toward better local and global citizenship (Waddock, 2005). A civil society is attendant to the preconditions of culture, social morality, and character; further, citizenship requires that once educated to the pursuit of personal interests, individuals and organizations become turned to the service of the public good (Pestritto & West, 2003). The expectation has evolved that in corporate

worlds, once honest gain has been secured, good citizenship must follow. Glazebrook (2005) suggests that good corporate citizenship enables culturally significant social interactions and exchanges between individuals inside and outside of corporations that combine to breathe life into what is becoming a powerful social movement in shaping the direction of business operations. It can be noted that many modern corporations acknowledge the citizenship imperative in their mission statements, company reports, policies, and initiatives (e.g. Timberland) (Henderson, 2010).

Additional imperatives to enlarge and ratify the social contract include concern over individual rights and the moral and societal imperative to 'do no harm'. Characteristically, the governments of developed nations will strive to serve and protect the public by creating laws, regulations, and regulatory agencies dedicated to this very purpose. Multinational corporations doing business in a wide array of international markets (particularly in undeveloped markets) often find themselves without such guidelines and the potential for doing harm enlarges in scope and consequence. A proliferation of non-profits have assisted in providing guidance and oversight in this regard and several initiatives have emerged to both assess corporate social activity and to evaluate its merit (Papania et al., 2008). Where law and governance do not exist to protect society from harm, the social contract becomes paramount.

Moreover, formally granted individual rights have served to guide business behaviour in large measure within some specific business activities. Rights have been granted to employees regarding health, safety, wages, opportunity, etc. and consumers regarding product safety and integrity of information, etc. Yet, in many emerging markets, such granted rights are nonexistent. However, we are witnessing a revolutionary call for greater attention to human rights in all spheres of economic and political activity (Kolodziej, 2003).

Traditional Views and the Role of the Firm

Firm strategy has essentially been born of organizational purpose, economic goals, and a clear view of what the organization aspired to achieve for its own ends. Historically, the firm has been viewed as grounded in Friedmanite economics, a traditional market-based perspective in which a remarkable isolation of the firm was achieved, as businesses tended to relate to their broader communities only through the marketplace. Traditionally, government remained distant, seemingly acquiesced to its restrained role as an irrational intruder; and both firm strategy and political accommodation were primarily couched in economic self interest (Dixon, 2003; Friedman, 1962). The state, if it interfered for social purposes through coercion or compulsion, was considered destructive to the smooth operation of the market economy. Thus, the state created and preserved the business environment (von Mises, 1949).

Challenges to the Prevailing Paradigm and Role of Business

Several contemporary theorists suggest that, despite a general tenacity to cling to traditional philosophical notions, the reality of our modern social and economic environment suggests that traditional views are indeed being modified for the future (Buchholtz & Rosenthal, 2001; Dixon, 2003; Hedley, 2002; Slaughter, 2004; Tansey, 2000). Further, a more contemporary view of the firm recognizes that business is actually nested within a pluralistic community and does not allow firm isolation or a singular economic purpose. Thus, pragmatism guides business decisions and actions that reflect, not just profit concerns, but the multi-purpose concerns of the collective society and its ultimate good.

Newer approaches to the study of institutional organizations are increasingly drawn to a world view of the business institution with economic and social power, one that is more collaborative and networked, reflecting a holistic view of community, and a notion of the institution *in* society—not above it, serving the common good—not simply exercising authoritarian or commercial power (Dyrberg, 1997; Foucault, 1980; Scholte, 2007).

An increasingly globalized market and society, new and pressing social issues regarding human/labor rights, environmental sustainability, poverty,

education, modern slavery, etc. all serve to dramatically characterize the social environment of today's modern corporation. It is a world of serious concerns, pressing externalities, and larger societal expectations of modern corporations. Several modern day realities, both pragmatic and moral, present challenges to the prevailing paradigm and point to newer roles for business in today's society.

Economic Rationale and Resource Limits

The world we live in is shaped by a legacy of economic rationale that is anchored in: the championing of individualism; the principle of utility that manifestly honours the pursuit of personal gain; and a mechanistic approach to the purpose, structure, and activities of business organizations. By most accounts, this economic approach has served us well, particularly in that economic self-interest on the part of business has led to the collective economic interests of society. But society was more isolated in the past. Prior to the Industrial Revolution, lives tended to be separated with most working to sustain themselves, rarely travelling beyond limited borders (Whiteman & Cooper, 2000). Although our world has changed and moved extraordinarily since that time toward a global and pluralistic society and a world without borders, the theoretical views that shaped us early on still often pervade our 'understanding of contemporary individuals and groups, whether that group is a nation, society, or an organization such as a corporation' (Buchholtz & Rosenthal, 2001: 64).

The entrenched notion that the firm is justified by economic self-interest springs from a classical Western view of the individual as a basic building block of society or a community, endowed with certain constitutional rights, most notably those related to private property and the rights afforded by a capitalistic system of free enterprise. This is a system that implies separateness, no real bonds or meaningful relationships, and the absence of common goals and their pursuit. Embedded in such a system is the belief that, in the end, all are better served by it.

Economic theorists have sought for years to understand and explain how firms actually defy traditional economic logic to earn above average returns, and to grow to incredible size, power, and influence (Penrose, 1959; Rosenberg & Birdzell, 1986; Rumelt, 1974; Schumpeter, 1934). It must be recognized that theory regarding the growth of the firm has traditionally attached primary importance to *resources*, their limits, availability, use, deployment, etc. An implied assumption was that natural resources, the raw materials of production, were easily available and posed no real cost to others, i.e. society. Principles of capitalistic economic systems, including the powerful profit motive, provide incentives for businesses to create wealth, grow, innovate, and provide society with many goods and services, indeed creating a higher standard of economic living.

Nonetheless, such positive outcomes must be increasingly weighed against the ecological and societal consequences that unbounded global capitalism is spawning. The proliferation of global trade and production has created a number of negative externalities in the process, most particularly those associated with depletion and pollution of the earth's natural resources and harms related to economic development and human rights. Although economic theory could not have predicted such, in recent times, corporations have grown almost beyond comprehension in size, assets, revenue generation, and both economic and societal influence. It is highly unlikely that any early economists ever envisioned a world where corporations would become so large and powerful that they would become tantamount to private governments, indeed, more powerful than many national governments (Dixon, 2003; Slaughter, 2004; Tansey, 2000).

A New World and Social Order

If the economic rationale for business purpose, strategy, organization, and activity is based on past notions of individualism, how can it effectively serve a global society that no longer exists in isolation and is evermore affected by common issues regarding individual rights, ecological concerns, as well as increasingly shared economies? In short, the economic rationale that provides the infrastructure for modern business activity has been based on the historical reality of an aspiring, new

national world that was indeed characterized by a staunch cry for individualism and a fairly isolated, discrete manner of life. The motivation of self-interest that previously spurred a society to great heights now proves problematic in a new global world that is characterized by pluralism, a stronger cry for a larger society's collective interests to be served, and a more connected manner of life that is not at all isolated, in reality, increasingly interconnected and interdependent. Nonetheless, business self-interest does not have to suffer; many corporations are discovering that the market perceives (and rewards) social and ecological value creation (Harvie & Milburn, 2010).

That our social order has changed dramatically within the last 200 years and since the birth of Western democracy is without argument; indeed, today's global society appears to be the emergent form of social organization, representing social changes of incredible magnitude over past generations. Such changes are most characterized by innovations/development in technology, economics, the scale and complexity of integrated global systems, increasing populations, large urban centres, disparities between nations, and a strained global eco-environment (Hedley, 2002). Further, the unstoppable global march will surely result in economic gains for many and losses for others, but there is already evidence that it will weaken the capacity of nation states to shape their own economic destinies (Dyrberg, 1997; Soros, 1998; Thomson, 1999).

Old issues that dominated public discourse have been replaced by new issues of ecology, technology, developing nations. The economic historian Karl Polanyi (1944), argued that social and political institutions should regulate, stabilize, and legitimatize market outcomes for, without these supporting institutions, unfettered free markets would subject societies to a host of externalities (e.g. destabilizing boom and bust cycles, unfair competition, fraud, social problems, etc.) that would prove ultimately disastrous to the entire global market system. A proliferation of these negative outcomes is already being realized. Thus, at a minimum, we recognize the need of some evolution toward a social theory and system improvised to match our new world order and the collective concerns of a global civil society. While no one single country approach can deal with increased international interdependence, we see the questioning of the true meaning of 'nation-state' increasingly drawn to a world view. Further, many are realizing that we must collectively search for long-term principles to help guide political and economic actions; finding cooperative ways to align the collective interests of all will require bridging the gap between the instrumental institutions of government, business, and civil society (Dixon, 2003; Dyrberg, 1997; Saul, 1997; Slaughter, 2004; Tansey, 2000; Thomson, 1999).

Moral Persuasion

Moral arguments have been debated as to their relevance to the economic function of business, from Kantian, Aristotelian, Judeo-Christian, to the more practical, business-oriented utilitarian. The most rigid view, espoused by traditional economist Friedman (1962) and others (von Mises, 1949), holds that morality, while good in and of itself, if self-imposed by business organizations, is in essence wrong in that it detracts from their embedded economic purpose to increase profits for owners. But can we divorce ourselves from morality, on the basis of institutional purpose, or role within that institution? Dr Donald Schmeltekopf suggests not and entreats us thus:

> The economy is an institution alongside other institutions, such as the family, the church, government and law, hospitals and other health-related organizations, and cultural entities, such as the university, that God has established for the survival and flourishing of the human race. None of these institutions exists merely for itself. All exist for the good of mankind. (Schmeltekopf, 2003: 6)

In today's world, existing apart from one another is no longer possible, for as we are increasingly bound together in a web of global activities, we find ourselves inseparable parts of the whole of this planet's society. As the economic activities of business and government have brought us to this place, the moral argument can then be made that the purpose and meaning of business activity is enlarged to enhance a flourishing life for all, for we as individuals or as businesses must now co-exist in a state of mutual accountability (Schmeltekopf, 2003).

Moreover, in a moral sense, the social contract must extend well beyond any legal or prescribed condition. The reality is that we are not bound together by contract, nor limited in obligations; rather, we are bonded to each other by nature and by covenant. It is the calling of both business and of government to be good stewards of creation. Our collective moral priority is that which reflects stewardship of the earth, labor, wealth, and our neighbours, in other words, serves the common good (Drayton & Budinich, 2010; Schmeltekopf, 2003). Buchholtz and Rosenthal (2001) contend that what is now needed more than ever is a philosophy that recognizes the very social nature of humans and that incorporates the viewpoint of the other, developing ourselves to take the perspective of others as a whole. The collective will of a broad community is intrinsic to our very continued existence as social entities.

Moreover, it is becoming clear that society has increasing expectations and has imposed social obligations on the major institution of business. Given a stronger universal call to collective interests and the social compact, the question remains as to how business will continue to respond. Social values, though invisible, represent the indissoluble bonds that bind us together. The business corporation is not the only actor, but is, nonetheless, a very important one (Kolodziej, 2003; Slaughter, 2004). Indeed, it is a major institution that is becoming increasingly pressured by society to corroborate its self-interest with a recognition of shared humanity and its own role in society, and a serious dedication to embrace and respond to collective societal concerns.

As discussed, challenges to the old paradigm of business responsibility and activity suggest paradoxes between old and newer perspectives about business *in* society. Those are summarized in Table 41.1.

Table 41.1	Challenges to the Prevailing Paradigm: Traditional Versus Newer Perspectives

Traditional views of the role of the firm	*Paradoxes, newer perspectives*
• Championing of individualism and personal gain; a mechanistic approach to business purpose, structure, and activity; abundant resources; business size and influence within reasonable scope and size.	• Society much more pluralistic, globally connected and interdependent; limits to resources, negative externalities of production; business size and influence very powerful.
• Emphasis on individual property rights; social issues localized; slow and gradual social change; larger expectations of nation states to protect society as the institution of legitimate and effective power; business trepidation and self protection where government was concerned.	• Dramatic social change with pressing and significant social issues; increasing emphasis on global issues with larger effect and significance; larger expectations of powerful multinational business institutions to legitimately use power and influence for the common good.
• Moral persuasion limited in light of prevailing notions of free market (laissez faire) capitalism; limited notions of corporate social responsibility without government requirement and enforcement.	• Increasing acknowledgement of the social obligations of the major institution of business; greater education and awareness of society leading to greater expectations of business social responsibility and citizenship.

Institutional Reform: New Roles and Relationships for Business in Society

Abundant evidence suggests that many business organizations, large and small, are responding to societal and stakeholder expectations and embracing the notion of community at every level; in short, business corporations becoming an active participant in and contributor to society. Growing numbers of large organizations that operate within international markets and possess resources and power that rival those of many nations are representing a leap in humanity's capacity to organize for a shared purpose. A powerful momentum is being seen in the creative efforts of huge international companies to fundamentally transform themselves, stop destruction, and affirmatively address the effects of corporate activity on the planet and its people (Debold, 2005). In contrast to the adversarial relationships that characterized business behaviour in previous periods, many are now partnering and collaborating with agencies that are attendant to societal concerns, such as NGOs and interest groups (Van Huijstee & Glasbergen, 2010).

Citizenship: Global and Local

The institutionalized legitimacy of a global corporation may be defined as one developed in the climate of a truly global community, and one characterized by global citizenship, and moral responsibility to respect the cares of the various cultures and communities in which it operates (Buchholtz & Rosenthal, 2001). Schwab (2008) holds that a new imperative for business, best described as 'global corporate citizenship', must be recognized. This expresses the conviction that companies not only must be engaged with their stakeholders but are themselves stakeholders alongside governments and civil society. As good global citizens, international business leaders are encouraged to fully commit to sustainable development and address paramount global challenges, including climate change, the provision of public health care, energy conservation, and the management of resources, particularly water. Because these global issues increasingly also impact business, it can be self-damaging not to engage with them. Because global citizenship is in a corporation's enlightened self-interest, it is not merely ideological, it is sustainable, particularly at a time of increasing globalization and diminishing state influence. Tansey (2000) emphasizes that the influence of multinational corporations cannot be overestimated and compares their status to the state, with its control of vital resources and its networked infrastructure around the globe. With this mindset, political and business adjustments can be made through evolutionary change, as is inspired by the dynamics of global community that is constantly kept in focus. Although gradual, changes can be made as community is kept alive through an ongoing process of change through accommodating adjustments.

Transformational Organization Design

Rethinking the purpose of the organization can lead to a new public idea, new corporate design that builds upon shared principles built through a transformational process that translates those principles into institutional designs. Thus, a narrower focus of purpose gives life to that purpose by creating parity between social and financial considerations (Kelly & White, 2009). Corporation 20/20 (corporation2020.org) has drafted an international multi-stakeholder initiative called 'Principles of Corporate Design' that aims to shift the predominant corporate architecture to one whose mission is to envision and advocate new corporate designs that embed social mission into the heart of organizations. This organization challenges businesses to reconsider their core purpose and to find new ways to seamlessly blend sustainability into their design, ownership, governance, strategy, and practice.

Indeed, corporate founders, executives and managers appear to be converging in large numbers through human force and the dawning recognition that we are one humanity inhabiting one world. For the world to change, international business consultant Helen-Jane Nelson (of Cecara Consulting & Oxford Leadership Academy) argues that corporations must move from a profit-and-growth system to a more humanitarian whole systems perspective. Her consulting team works with business institutions to enact organizational transformations that embody whole systems change and a new focus and structure that encompasses the well-being of the entire global economic system. This

is indeed possible because corporations are extraordinarily influential institutions.

While transforming organizations from within is important, the Centre for Associative Economics (cfae.biz) advances the idea of 'associative economics', aimed at the creation of marketplaces with structures designed to optimize the whole—the consumer, the producer, and the distributor—so that money can be moved around for the benefit of the whole as opposed to the benefit of only one part. This organization takes into account the works of Milton Friedman and Rudolph Steiner, among others, and champions the role of leadership, a key capacity needed to enact new realities. This can be accomplished by bringing more parties into discussion, collaborating in social settings, finding solutions through shared leadership, and by creating organizational processes and models that shape moral development of both individuals in organizations and organizations themselves (Debold, 2005; Denis et al., 2001; Huxham & Vangen, 2000). Drayton and Budinich (2010) suggest that corporations and social entrepreneurs can reshape industries and solve the world's toughest problems through collaboration, innovation, and reaching new markets, in effect, providing both economic and social benefits for all parties.

The World Business Council for Sustainable Development (WBCSD) (wbcsd.org) is a CEO-led, global association of some 200 companies dealing exclusively with business and sustainable development. The Council provides a platform for companies to explore sustainable development, share knowledge, experiences and best practices, and to advocate business positions on these issues in a variety of forums, working with a variety of partners, including governments, non-governmental and intergovernmental organizations from around the globe. The Council also utilizes a global network of some 60 national and regional business councils and regional partners. This organization challenges business to redefine the appropriate boundaries of its new role in bringing solutions to global problems, and to manage societal expectations proactively. Within the WBCSD, the Business Role Focus Areas work to engage, equip and mobilize current and future business leaders to demonstrate business' evolving role in a sustainable society and to assist it to achieve this new vision.

Social Entrepreneurship

Many business observers have suggested that the criticality and vulnerability of our globalized, techno world requires urgent and collective action (Cragg, 2000; Hedley, 2002). Although there are many possible ways to organize societies, finding the best possible world is not easily selected, nor enacted. It has been suggested that modern capitalism need not necessarily exist only in the extreme free market form traditionally prescribed; instead, it could evolve into a variety of feasible forms that would differ in terms of institutional parameters (Hall & Soskice, 2001; Rosen & Wolff, 1999; Slaughter, 2004; Thomson, 1999). In recent years, a proliferation of social entrepreneurs have emerged in all sectors (nonprofits, non-governmental organizations, foundations, government, and for-profit business organizations, small and large). Many of these successfully straddle the civic, governmental, and business worlds, promoting and embracing ideas that were previously taken up by mainstream public services in welfare, schools, and health care but are now increasingly targeted by other business and institutional endeavours.

Others have proposed a new alliance for global change in which corporations and social entrepreneurs collaborate to create and expand markets with the goals of offering new products and services in diverse sectors that will reach those who have been economically and socially left out (Drayton & Budinich, 2010). Additionally, such transformative approaches create economic as well as social value by forming hybrid value chains to tackle large-scale problems, sharing expertise to lower costs, reach gains through social networking and bridge the imbalance between the business and social sectors of society. The implications are that we are witnessing a sea change in the way society's problems are being solved and businesses are growing.

New Business Partners: Government, NGOs International Agencies

Institutional reform is about; in many emerging markets we can see the work of the Business Roundtable, the Organization for Economic Co-operation and Development (OECD), the United Nations, the Worldwatch Institute, G7 and economic summit meetings, the World Bank, and commissioned reports on a variety of globalization scenarios, or problems (Hedley, 2002; Monks & Minow, 2004). Further, we are finding the paradigm by which not-for-profits have traditionally operated now moving in a revolutionary trend toward social entrepreneurship, a fundamentally new and powerful strategy for progressives to expand their power, their voice, and their social agenda (Drayton & Budinich, 2010; Shuman & Fuller, 2005). Despite the newsworthy proliferation of flawed corporate behaviour, many businesses still have potential virtues and can make positive contributions to people's lives and to social concerns with their goods and services and with their social agendas.

It is suggested by Van Luijk (2000) that the basic institutions of our social fabric, government, the market, and civil society are profoundly rearranging their mutual relations, power, and functions with new configurations, public/private partnerships and creative alliances emerging between governmental agencies and market parties, between market players and NGOs. In short, an institutional groundswell of multiple and collaborative approaches toward corporate responsibility and business ethics. Events have brought us here. No longer will codes of ethics, auditing systems, or moral climate be sufficient to ensure needed business ethics and social responsibility. Such will depend on the courage and commitment of all social players to take part in cooperative efforts to deliver higher standards of living and jobs, ensure protection of national identities, achieve environmental sustainability, and caringly cope with demographic developments. What Van Luijk (2000) is implying is an institutional revolution.

This analysis suggests that increasing evidence of institutional reform in response to driving social conditions and influences reflects a possible paradigm shift in which businesses recognize a much larger set of roles and responsibilities to the whole of society, reflecting a strongly enhanced notion and acceptance of the social contract evolved. Those dramatic shifts are summarized in Table 41.2.

Table 41.2	Business *IN* Society: Dramatic Shifts in Roles & Responsibilities

- Institutional legitimacy of businesses made more secure by good global citizenship, moral responsibility to cultures, workers' rights, sustainability, responsible use of resources; recognition of their power relative to the state and the embracing of greater responsibilities relative to their power, capability, proximity to, and the urgency of, social concerns.

- Business organizations transforming themselves not only in corporate responsibility actions and agendas but in organization design, sharing of principles, whole systems change; movement toward 'associative economics' with more social collaboration and shared leadership.

- An astonishing movement toward social entrepreneurship that reflects profit creation along with social solution creation, supported by many new institutional forms and connections; hybrid value chains tackling large-scale problems to create both economic and social value.

- New efforts at collaboration and cooperation on a grand scale, bridging old divides between business, government and society. A proliferation of creative alliances and partnering opportunities with international agencies, non-profits, and governments.

Conclusion

Two major arguments point to an enlarged purpose and role for business in today's global economic environment. First, the pragmatic, or practical: economic success has always depended on a multidimensional business model with business challenged to structure, collaborate and make coherent its various parts and adapt to the conditions without its borders. Students of business have seen organizational boundaries widen, even disappear, in recent years. While business behaviour has tended to remain most focused on the marketplace, increasingly it is being drawn to the very place it exists—in a larger world community. Businesses can no longer only relate through the marketplace, they must recognize their own citizenship in community, their relationship to humanity, and the enormous power they hold to solve problems and create solutions. A newer theoretical paradigm sees tomorrow's business organization as a truly social institution that can no longer isolate itself from society—it is pluralistic in nature and in presence. Indeed, it must change along with the social context in which it functions and thus honour in more stringent terms the social contract (Buchholtz & Rosenthal, 2001). The second argument is premised on morality and humanity. We all belong to this planet and we are all a part of the global village. We

must coexist and mutually prosper. Externalities related to the globalized economy and expanding spheres of trade present very serious concerns to present populations and to future generations. Further, we are all impacted. Living and working together as a global community means we all lose when damage or harm is done. The evolving social contract is now finding business organizations redefined in purpose; no longer economic only, they must increasingly attend to the effects of their size, power and influence. Playing a larger role in a larger world with more shared concerns requires a multipurpose business role with many non-economic functions.

Our foundational assumptions about the role of business have not altered dramatically. Society expects business to flourish and support quality of life with needed, affordable goods and services and to do so without harmful or illegal behaviours. Good governance continues to require trust, legitimacy, and the participation of societal members with attention to their interests. When the American democratic model was born, these principles guided its founders to establish an empowering government 'by the people and for the people'. While still adhered to in principle, many complain that in actual practice, political leaders have moved away from those original political ideals. However, not only are these principles more important than ever, given our globalized society and related concerns, philosophical theory must now be enlarged to empower and attend to the global village. Social contract theory, in its evolvement, lends a most feasible supporting hand. Future research may well consider the implications of associative economics, institutional change and transformation, and the linkages between social movements and business opportunity.

A shift in the social contract paradigm will most likely entail philosophical, political, structural, and interacting changes. Business organizations can only enjoy the autonomy of civil society if they, in fact, belong to it, if they cease to be self-serving at an expense and consequence to other members of that society, particularly those who have no voice in protecting their own interests (Dixon, 2003). Pragmatically, by moving to a new social paradigm that is multi-purposed, attentive to social justice issues, and proactively ordered to address the collective concerns of a global society, business organizations may truly serve their own interests as well.

Note

1. Correspondence to: Robin T. Byerly, Appalachian State University, Department of Management, P.O. Box 32089, Boone, NC 28608-2089, USA. Email: byerlyrt@appstate.edu.

References

Bishop, J. D. 2008. For-Profit Corporations in a Just Society: A Social Contract Argument Concerning the Rights and Responsibilities of Corporations. *Business Ethics Quarterly*, 28(2): 191–212.

Bruce, W., Menzel, D. & Erakovich, R. 2001. A Dialogue to Start a Dialogue: Impact of Globalization on Ethics. *PA Times*, 24(9): 3–4.

Buchholz, R. A. & Rosenthal, S. B. 2001. Pluralism, Change, and Corporate Community. *Business and Professional Ethics Journal*, 20(2): 63–83.

Carroll, A. B. 1991. The Pyramid of Social Responsibility: Toward the Moral Management of Organizational Stakeholders. *Business Horizons*, 34: 39–48.

Centre for Associative Economics. Website [accessed 15 March 2011]. Available at: http://www.cbae.biz.

Corporation 20/20. Website [accessed 15 March 2011]. Available at: http://www.corporation2020.org.

Cragg, W. 2000. Human Rights and Business Ethics: Fashioning a New Social Contract. *Journal of Business Ethics*, 27: 205–14.

Davis, K. 1960. Can Business Afford to Ignore Social Responsibilities? *California Management Review*, 2: 70–76.

Debold, E. 2005. The Business of Saving the World. *What is Enlightenment?* 28: 60–91.

Denis, J., Lamothe, L. & Langley, A. 2001. The Dynamics of Collective Leadership and Strategic Change in Pluralistic Organizations. *Academy of Management Journal*, 44(4): 809–37.

Dixon, J. 2003. *Responses to Governance: Governing Corporations, Societies and the World*. Westport, CT: Praeger.

Drayton, B. & Budinich, V. 2010. Can Entrepreneurs Save the World? A New Alliance for Global Change. *Harvard Business Review*, 88(9): 56–64.

Dyrberg, T. G. 1997. *The Circular Structure of Power: Politics, Identity, Community*. London: Verso.

Frederick, W. C. 1978. From CSR[1] to CSR[2]: The Maturing of Business-and-Society Thought. *Business & Society*. 33(20): 150–64.

Freeman, R. E. 1984. *Strategic Management: A Stakeholder Approach*. Boston: Pitman.

Friedman, M. 1962. *Capitalism and Freedom*. Chicago, IL: Chicago University Press.

Friedman, T. 1999. *The Lexus and the Olive Tree*. New York: Anchor Books.

Foucault, M. 1980. Two lectures. In: Colin Gordon, ed. *Power/Knowledge*. Brighton: Harvester Press, pp. 93–95.

Garriga, E. & Melé, D. 2004. Corporate Social Responsibility Theories: Mapping the Territory. *Journal of Business Ethics*, 53: 51–71.

Glazebrook, M. 2005. The Social Construction of Corporate Citizenship. *Journal of Corporate Citizenship*, 17: 53–68.

Hall, P. & Soskice, D. eds. 2001. *Varieties of Capitalism: The Institutional Foundations of Comparative Advantage*. Oxford: Oxford University Press.

Harvie, D. & Milburn, K. 2010. How Organizations Value and How Value Organizes. *Organization*, 17(5): 631–36.

Hedley, R. A. 2002. *Running Out of Control: Dilemmas of Globalization*. Bloomfield, CT: Kumarian Press.

Henderson, S. 2010. Corporate Citizenship in the Networked Marketplace. *MIT Sloan Management Review*, 22 July. Available at http://sloanreview.mit.edu/improvisations/2010/07/21/corporate-citizenship-in-the-networked-marketplace/.

Hobbes, T. 1991 [1651]. *Leviathan*. Cambridge: Cambridge University Press.

Huxham, C. & Vangen, S. 2000. Leadership in the Shaping and Implementation of Collaboration Agendas: How Things Happen in a (Not Quite) Joined-Up World. *Academy of Management Journal*, 43(6): 1159–75.

Kathrani, P. 2010. Social Contract Theory and the International Normative Order: A New Global Ethic?, *Jurisprudence* 1(119): 97–109.

Kelley, M. & White, A. L. 2009. From Corporate Responsibility to Corporate Design: Rethinking the Purpose of the Corporation, *The Journal of Corporate Citizenship*, 33: 23–28.

Kolodziej, E. A. ed. 2003. *A Force Profunde*. Philadelphia, PA: University of Pennsylvania Press.

Locke, J. 1988 [1690]. *Two Treatises of Government*. Cambridge: Cambridge University Press.

McGuire, J. W. 1963. *Business and Society*. New York: McGraw-Hill.

Monks, R. A. G. & Minow, N. 2004. *Corporate Governance*, Third Edition. Malden, Mass: Blackwell Publishing.

Nelson, Helen-Jane. Website [accessed 10 April 2011]. Available at: http://www.cecara.com & http://www.oxfordleadership.com/pool/helen-jane-nelson-profile.pdf.

Papania, L., Shapiro, D. M. & Peloza, J. 2008. Social Impact as a Measure of Fit between Firm Activities and Stakeholder Expectations. *International Journal of Business Governance and Ethics*, 4(1): 3–16.

Penrose, E. 1959. *The Theory of the Growth of the Firm*. Oxford: Oxford University Press.

Pestritto, R. J. & West, T. G. 2003. *The American Founding and the Social Compact*. New York: Lexington Books.

Polanyi, K. 1944. *The Great Transformation*. Boston, MA: Beacon Press.

Rawls, J. 1999b [1971]. *A Theory of Justice*. Cambridge, MA: Belknap Press.

Rosen, M. & Wolff, J. 1999. *Political Thought*. Oxford: Oxford University Press.

Rosenberg, N. & Birdzell, L.E. Jr. 1986. Excerpt from *How the West Grew Rich*. In: E.H., ed. *Morality and the Market*. Boston, MA: McGraw Hill, pp. 25–34.

Rousseau, J. J. 1988 [1762]. *The Social Contract and Other Discourses*. London: Everyman's Library.

Rumelt, R. P. 1974. *Strategy, Structure, and Economic Performance*. Boston, MA: Harvard Business School Press.

Sacconi, L. 2006. A Social Contract Account for CSR as an Extended Model of Corporate Governance (I): Rational Bargaining and Justification. *Journal of Business Ethics*, 168: 259–81.

Saul, J. R. 1997. *The Unconscious Civilization*. New York: The Free Press.

Schmeltekopf, D. D. 2003. The moral context of business. Inaugural lecture given to University community at Baylor University, 6 October 2003.

Scholte, J. A. 2007. Civil Society and the Legitimation of Global Governance. *Journal of Civil Society*, 3(3): 305–26.

Schumpeter, J. 1934. *The Theory of Economic Development*. Cambridge, MA: Harvard University Press.

Schwab, K. 2008. Working with Governments and Civil Society. *Foreign Affairs*, January/February, pp. 107–18.

Shuman, M. H. & Fuller, M. 2005. Profits for justice. *The Nation*, 24 January, pp. 13–22.

Slaughter, A. 2004. *A New World Order*. Princeton, NJ: Princeton University Press.

Soros, G. 1998. *The Crisis of Global Capitalism*. New York: Public Affairs.

Tansey, S. D. 2000. *Politics: The Basics*. London: Routledge.

Thomson, J. W. 1999. Globalization: Obsession or Necessity? *Business and Society Review*, 104(4): 397–406.

Van Huijstee, M. & Glasbergen, P. 2010. Business-NGO Interactions in a Multi-Stakeholder Context. *Business and Society Review*, 115(3): 249–366.

Van Luijk, H. J. L. 2000. In Search of Instruments: Business and Ethics Halfway. *Journal of Business Ethics*, 27 (1/2): 3–8.

Votaw, D. 1972. Genius Became Rare: A Comment on the Doctrine of Social Responsibility Pt. 1. *California Management Review*, 15(2): 25–31.

von Mises, L. 1949. *Socialism*. Indianapolis: Liberty Classics.

Waddock, S. 2005. Corporate Citizens: Stepping into the Breach of Society's Broken Contracts. *The Journal of Corporate Citizenship*, Autumn: 20–24.

Whiteman, G. & Cooper, W. H. 2000. Ecological Embeddedness. *Academy of Management Journal*, 43(6): 1265–82.

World Business Council for Sustainable Development (WBCSD). Website [accessed 20 February 2011]. Available at: <http://www.wbcsd.org>.

CHAPTER 42

Business Unusual

Corporate Responsibility in a 2.0 World

Sandra Waddock

Boston College

Malcolm McIntosh

Griffith University, Australia

Introduction

The imperatives of a growing consensus on human-induced causes of climate change, an increasing gap between rich and poor, and the misguided incentives in the economic, business, and financial models that dominated the last quarter of the twentieth century and first decade of the twenty-first century have highlighted the need for a new approach to capitalism. Combine these growing imperatives with the rapid growth in technology that has made large corporations "naked"[1] (highly transparent) and connected people almost instantaneously no matter what their location, and the world of 2020 looks different than anything humanity has seen before.

We have witnessed numerous dramatic events since 2008, for example, the global economic collapse that highlights the need to better regulate and control the financial services industry; the relatively limited success of COP15, the Copenhagen summit on climate change; in 2009, the massive oil spill resulting from the explosion BP's drilling apparatus in 2010; revolts in Egypt and other Middle Eastern nations; and the terrible earthquake and tsunami in Japan in 2011. We are also witnessing less dramatic but equally problematic effects of the current system: a growing global obesity crisis that is associated with lifestyle and the way we produce and consume food, collapsing ecosystems, growing concerns about privacy resulting from the growth of Web 2.0 media, and greater divides between rich and poor on multiple dimensions, to name only a few.

These shifts, among others, highlight the need for systemic change. In the highly connected world of the Internet—and the even more visible world of Web 2.0, which is dominated by social media that keeps people constantly connected—business as usual is becoming more difficult to sustain. After these and other events that have shocked the system, businesses may attempt to return to the "new normal" and hope that it looks at least something like the old normal. Chances are, however, that a real new normal will begin to emerge in which businesses themselves taken into consideration the ecological and social as well as the economic consequences of their business practices.

In the Web 2.0 and globally connected world of the Internet, where so much is readily visible to any interested party and where the social and ecological problems besetting the world have become more obvious even to steadfast deniers of reality, it is becoming increasingly clear that business as usual needs to change. But how? Economist Joseph Schumpeter's theory of change argued that economies were never actually stable because change was always underway. In Schumpeter's view, change occurs through what he called "creative destruction" by necessity because of the "fundamental impulse" that "comes from the new consumers, goods, the new methods of production or transportation, the new markets, the new forms of industrial organization that capitalist enterprise creates."[2] Noting that this process of creative destruction was the "essential fact about capitalism," Schumpeter pointed out that creative destruction comes, not from outside the system, but actually from inside. Indeed, he argued that this form of creativity was a product of the very entrepreneurial process that underpins the whole notion of capitalism.[3]

Wicked Problems

Today we see this same process of creative destruction occurring through what we are calling SEE Change—change to a sustainable enterprise economy—in our book by that title. In the process of creative destruction that is still occurring today, entrepreneurs of many stripes are building new types of enterprises, some based on the emerging "cloud" of connectivity that the World Wide Web has evolved into, others based on a multiple-bottom-line set of purposes from their inception. Still, others are premised on spanning traditional boundaries to find new solutions to what management theorist Russell Ackoff

once called "messes"[4] and what others call "wicked problems."[5] Messes are problems too complex to be solved by one organization or even organizations within one sector because of the inherently cross boundaries. Wicked problems, Churchman notes, are "that class of social system problems which are ill-formulated, where the information is confusing, where there are many clients and decision makers with conflicting values, and where the ramifications in the whole system are thoroughly confusing."[6]

In many respects, the whole movement toward a sustainable enterprise economy tackles one of these wicked problems, simply because moving in this direction necessitates that multiple considerations be built into enterprises of all sorts. Such enterprises go well beyond the simple single bottom line of maximizing shareholder wealth because many stakeholders' interests need to be taken into consideration and because the problems of society and ecology are difficult to resolve by any means.

We do not know whether the magnitude of change that will be brought by SEE will be sufficient or not. In many ways, we are pessimistic, given the enormous problems that the planet is facing that are complex and difficult to deal with using today's systems. As we think about what is needed, we are constantly reminded of Albert Einstein's famous saying that "You cannot solve a problem from the same consciousness that created it. You must learn to see the world anew." Whether SEE Change represents the sea change that is needed is still an open question. But given that we believe that new thinking *is* going into the design of enterprises that constitute SEE Change, we retain some optimism that we hope will come through in this brief exploration of SEE Change, which we examine more fully in our book by that title.

***

Enterprise Unusual: The For-Benefit Corporation, B Corporation, and Conscious Capitalism

Dematerialization and servicizing, along with corporate responsibility and sustainability initiatives that many, particularly large, companies have adopted, are only some of the moves toward SEE Change. In addition, there are many new and evolving business enterprises that take social, human, and ecological benefit alongside profit to be their purposes rather than focusing narrowly only on profits. To the extent that such enterprises use disruptive technologies like the electronic and dematerialized forms explored above—and incorporate multiple stakeholders into their statement of purposes, they may well represent new ways for people to express their humanity and their dreams—as well as new forms of enterprise that provide the basis of creative destruction that Schumpeter argued is how capitalism shifts.

Below, we will explore new forms of *business enterprise* that are now emerging and that are explicitly designed with a multiple bottom line imperative at their core, although we will not cover the initiatives of traditional corporations in adopting responsibility and sustainability initiatives as they are covered well elsewhere. Like the redesign of the corporate form, now under discussion in a group called Corporation 20/20 (see http://www.corporation2020.org), these SEE Change enterprises build in profits, society, and ecology to their business purposes and strategies. Three interesting developments in recent years are the for-benefit, the B corporation, and a nascent conscious capitalism movement. Both of these types of business enterprises explicitly take social and ecological considerations into account in their business strategies and purposes.

For-Benefit Corporations

A similar innovation to B corporations and perhaps a form of social entrepreneurship is the "for benefit corporation," a term apparently coined by the *New York Times* in talking about a company called Altrushare in 2007. Altrushare is a brokerage firm in which two charities jointly own a controlling interest. It is an example of what the *Times* called "the emerging convergence of for-profit money-making and non-profit mission."[23] The International Finance Corporation picked up the term, arguing that it had been supporting emerging "for-benefit" companies for years without the label, as a way of developing emerging markets.[24]

Although some economists, such as Michael Jensen, argue that companies (or any enterprise) can serve only one master, or what Jensen terms one objective function (typically profit maximizing),[25] the idea behind for-benefit, B corporations, and fourth sector enterprise more generally is that it is indeed possible for companies to successfully negotiate multiple bottom lines. A growing array of social entrepreneurs around the world is proving that assertion is incorrect as they are successfully navigating between the two worlds of doing well financially and doing good for the world.

B Corporations

In an interesting development aligned with the concept of the for-benefit corporation, a group of companies in the United States recently agreed to change their governance documents and become "B Corporations." A group of 81 pioneering, mostly relatively small, companies, including Seventh Generation, Trillium Asset Management, and White Dog Café founded B Corporation with the intent of trying to provide consumers with access to information about branded companies that are certified as actually having met specific criteria related to corporate responsibility. B Corporation at this writing had 255 members holding more than $1.1 billion in revenues and covering 54 industries.[26]

A B corporation attempts to use business' power to deal with complex social and ecological problems, live up to transparent, comprehensive social and environmental standards by building these values into companies' governing documents. They also incorporate stakeholders', not just shareholders', interests into their core governance structure and purposes.[27] By bringing together stakeholder interests, they hope to "build collective voice through the power of a unifying brand."[28]

B Corporation created what it calls a "Declaration of Interdependence" that frames its mission. In this declaration, the B Corporation companies state "That we must be the change we seek in the world. That all business ought to be conducted as if people and place mattered. That, though their products, practices, and profits, businesses should aspire to do no harm and benefit all. To do so requires that we act with the understanding that we are each dependent upon another and thus responsible for each other and future generations."[29] In 2009, *Business Week* published a list of 25 of what it termed "America's Most Promising Social Entrepreneurs." On that list were seven of the B Corporation companies.[30] Examples of B Corporation include King Arthur Flour, a Vermont, US-based flour company that is employee owned, and Seventh Generation, which provides natural and nontoxic household and personal care products.

Conscious Capitalism

Another development—deliberately designed as a movement—is the nascent conscious capitalism movement, which argues that a conscious business rests of three core principles:

1. *Deeper Purpose:* Recognizing that every business has a deeper purpose than merely profit maximization, a Conscious Business is clear about and focused on fulfilling its deeper purpose.

2. *Stakeholder Model:* A Conscious Business focuses on delivering value to all of its stakeholders and works to align and harmonize the interests of customers, employees, suppliers, investors, the community, and the environment to the greatest extent possible.

3. *Conscious Leadership:* In a Conscious Business, management embodies conscious leadership and fosters it throughout the organization. Conscious leaders serve as stewards to the company's deeper purpose and its stakeholders, focusing on fulfilling the company's purpose, delivering value to its stakeholders, and facilitating a harmony of interests rather than on personal gain and self-aggrandizement. Conscious leaders cultivate awareness throughout their business ecosystem, beginning with themselves and their team members, and moving into their relationships with each other and other stakeholders.[31]

C3, or Catalyzing Conscious Capitalism, was cofounded by Whole Foods CEO John Mackey, a leading company in natural and organic food retailing, to help create and deepen the conscious capitalism movement so that more enterprises could join Whole Foods, The Container Store, Joie de Vivre Hotels, and REI, among others, in achieving these goals.

On its website, C3 provides a rationale for choosing the term conscious capitalism: "The choice of the term 'conscious capitalism' has been made after considerable thought. We believe this term best captures the depth and complexity of the changes in the business-operating model that are needed. It reflects the fact that more people today are at higher levels of consciousness about themselves and the world around them than ever before. This is due in part to natural evolution, but also to the rapid aging of society, which has resulted in a higher proportion of people in mid-life and beyond, when consciousness is raised and higher-level needs predominate. The advent of the Internet has accelerated and cemented this trend, simultaneously connecting hundreds of millions of people and placing great demands for transparency on companies."[32]

Biomimicry

One emerging orientation for SEE Change is the evolution of biomimicry. Biomimicry is an "emerging discipline that studies nature's best ideas and then imitates these designs and processes to solve human problems" according to the Biomimicry website and emerging movement founded by science writer Jeanine Benyus.[33] According to Benyus, biomimicry focuses on designs based in nature to create products, processes, and even organizations and policies that are sustainable and adapted to nature's ways. The scientists work on the premise that nature "knows" what works, is appropriate, and lasts, that is, is sustainable, and that by imitating nature's ways, human enterprise can be created in a significantly more sustainable manner.

While companies actually producing things through biomimicry's techniques are still few in number, Benyus argues that such approaches, even though difficult to achieve, could produce results that avoid the toxic chemicals and resource-intensive manufacturing methods employed in much modern manufacturing.[34] Among products that have already been developed using biomimicry's approaches, reporting on a website entitled "the 15 coolest cases of biommimicry," however, are Velcro (which uses the way that burrs stick to things to create a zipper-like fastener), gecko tape (a tape covered with nanoscopic hairs like those on geckos to create a potent adhesive), and self-healing plastics (that use polymer composite hollow fibers filled with epoxy that is released if the fibers are stressed or cracked to reseal a tear). Another item, which helped US swimmer Mark Phelps achieve his Olympic triumph of eight medals in Beijing in 2008, is the Speedo "Fastskin FSII swimsuit," which is based on shark skin's ability to reduce drag.

Blurring Boundaries: Social Entrepreneurship and an Emerging Fourth Sector

The "wicked problems" of sustainability, climate change, poverty, economic and social development, food production, human security, and other ecological problems, to name a few, have created a glaring need for more organizations that reach across traditional sector boundaries and purposes. These entities, which are attempting to solve the messes or wicked problems, have resulted in the emergence of what is being called the "fourth sector."[35]

The fourth sector labeling recognizes the blurring of boundaries that has occurred in many types of enterprises, particularly around what Jed Emerson has called the blended value proposition[36] of making profits while simultaneously serving a social and/or ecological purpose. The fourth sector is a coalition of multi-sector leaders from a wide variety of enterprises focused on developing a fourth sector of society. Fourth sector's website and first report notes, as we have above, that boundaries between public and private enterprise are and have for some time been blurring.[37] In this context, fourth sector's founder Heerad Sabati points out that many companies are engaging in a wide array of activities that have social

purpose as well as profit-making potential, including numerous large corporations. Among the efforts that large companies are already engaged in are corporate social responsibility, cause-related marketing and purchasing, carbon offset programs, corporate philanthropy, environmental management and sustainability programs, community relations, socially responsible investment and triple bottom line approaches, stakeholder accountability, increasing transparency, and sustainability reporting, among others.[38]

Implicitly, following Schumpeter's theory of creative destruction, fourth sector highlights the surge in new types of enterprises that have begun—from inception or soon thereafter—to cross sector, goal, and organizational boundaries. Enterprises of the fourth sector go by many labels and involve many different types of what are called "hybrid" organizations and enterprises—hybrid because they do not neatly fit traditional categories of private, non-profit/NGO, or governmental organizations. Other labels for hybrid organizations include social enterprises, chaordic organizations, sustainable enterprises, blended value organizations, new profit companies, common good corporations, and social businesses.[39]

Because fourth sector enterprises blend purposes, their value proposition is by definition mixed. There are also numerous types of entities that can broadly be labeled social enterprises that arise initially from the perspective of other sectors, including non-profit enterprises, community wealth enterprises, ethical social institutions, faith-based enterprises, civic/municipal enterprises, community-interest organizations, and community development corporations.[40] Furthermore, there are numerous cross-sector partnerships, multi-sector collaborations, and related multiple sector enterprises working to achieve common good purposes, some of which are what Waddell and Khagram call global action networks (GANs).[41]

Many NGOs or CSOs are engaging in business-related practices to improve their performance, becoming more businesslike in the process. For example, NGOs frequently engage in defining measurable impact, use market discipline to harness their energy, employ efficiency and accountability methods developed in businesses. They also sometimes try to develop profit-making ventures to ensure that economic viability or engage in social investment activities.[42] Generally, as they attempt to become more efficient and effective in achieving their social mission, NGOs are finding that it is important to use more businesslike approaches, including, at times, profit-making activities that can bolster the bottom line.

The argument that fourth sector makes is that the blending of value in all of these enterprises is actually constructing a new—fourth—sector that differs from the traditional three sectors or spheres of business/economics, government/public policy, and civil society[43] because of the blended value proposition[44] integral to these different types of enterprise. In what it terms a convergence of organization into a "new landscape that integrates social purposes with business methods,"[45] these hybrid organizations are rapidly evolving and creating new ways of dealing with the wicked problems that our world is facing.

One example of a fourth sector enterprise is a new joint initiative by Grameen Bank of Bangladesh and Danone Foods of France called Grameen Danone Foods, which produces an enriched yogurt at a price that even very poor families can afford as a way of improving children's nutrition in Bangladesh.

Social Enterprise/ Social Entrepreneurs

There are also emerging enterprises that are largely business enterprises that are deliberately established for social benefit. Such enterprises are also sometimes labeled social enterprise—and they are started by individuals who are social entrepreneurs. Fourth sector enterprises of all sorts deliberately cross boundaries at their inception, while social enterprises frequently arise within a sector—and then cross boundaries as they evolve their purposes. Conceptually and in practice, however, there is a good deal of overlap among what might be labeled fourth sector enterprises and what have been called social enterprises or social entrepreneurial organizations.

Social Entrepreneurship— From Within Big Corporations

Social enterprises are often thought of as mission-driven businesses with multiple (at least dual) bottom lines: profitability and some social or ecological benefit. In social enterprise, the mission serves some social and/or sustainability purposes, typically in addition to generating enough profits to at least sustain the entity and often to make money much as traditional business enterprises do. Social enterprises can be for-profit or not-for profit, and they typically have at least the dual objectives of being profitable or balancing their budgets while seeking beneficial social change. They also tend to use business approaches to accomplish their objectives as opposed to the less structured "social good" approaches that many purely charitable organizations use.[46]

Many so-called "bottom of the pyramid" enterprises are social enterprises. The term "bottom of the pyramid" (BoP) comes from the work of the late C. K. Prahalad, who published a book by that name in 2005.[47] Corporate strategy and sustainability scholar Stuart Hart has also written extensively on how to solve the world's problems through social entrepreneurship.[48] Prahalad argued that there was a fortune to be made by companies who engaged in business with the four to five billion people at the "bottom of the pyramid" who are living in significant levels of poverty. He argues that, starting with respect for the poor as individuals, companies can and should use creative and innovative approaches, such as what Clayton Christensen and coauthors have called catalytic or disruptive innovations for social change.

The Christensen approach, which is based on his earlier work on disruptive innovative, suggests that catalytic *social* change has five qualities. Catalytic social entrepreneurs create systemic social change through scaling and replication. They meet a need that is either over-served (existing solution is more complex, expensive than some people need) or not served at all. They offer products and services that are simpler and less costly than existing alternatives and may have lower performance perception, too, but are perceived as good enough by their target customers. Furthermore, such catalytic social changes generate resources (donations, grants, volunteers, intellectual capital) in ways initially unattractive to incumbent competitors, and often are ignored, disparaged, or even encouraged by existing players (because the business model would be unprofitable for them).[49]

Not all social entrepreneurship, of course, is disruptive in the sense that Christensen discusses. Some of it is aimed simply at meeting previously unmet needs among poor or otherwise unserved populations. In his books and papers, C. K. Prahalad and his coauthors have argued that assumptions that people with low incomes do not spend money on goods and services or that barriers like corruption, illiteracy, and lack of infrastructure too frequently cause businesses to avoid the large population of people mired in poverty. He argues that this view is outdated. Prahalad points out that despite these assumptions, many corporations do, in fact, serve this population. Particularly in aggregate, the buying power of the bottom-of-the pyramid population is quite large, and that meeting the needs of this market for low-priced, reasonable quality goods could enhance revenues.[50]

Although some critics question whether the market is in fact nearly as large as Prahalad has argued and the consumption-oriented perspective Prahalad took,[51] nonetheless there has been an explosion of interest in social entrepreneurship. Similarly to Christensen's approach, Prahalad suggests that strategies for large corporations attempting to serve the bottom of the pyramid involve thinking more creatively, dealing with the assumptions that the market is fundamentally flawed, educating managers to the opportunities in the market, and focusing business development specifically at these markets. Making alliances with local entrepreneurs (especially, sometimes, women), changing internal structures to accommodate the differences in BoP markets, and dealing with local difficulties related to infrastructure, connectivity, corruption also need to be handled carefully.[52]

Social Entrepreneurship From Start-ups

The purposes of social enterprise tend to lean toward meeting some social or ecological need that the founding social entrepreneurs believe to be in the public interest or common good. Generally, they fit what might be characterized as progressive agendas. Many are focused on sustainability as well as positive social change, for instance, efforts to reduce poverty or create entrepreneurial activities among the poor through business activities can be viewed as social entrepreneurship, as can efforts to create businesses that serve otherwise unmet real needs or enhance sustainability. Unlike governmental bodies, however, social enterprises represent the entrepreneurs' notions about what the social benefit they intend is. They are in no way elected representatives of the public and in that sense their orientation toward the public good is based on whatever definition of the public good the entrepreneur applies.

Social Entrepreneurship and Enterprise

According to Ashoka, which over time has supported more than 2,000 social entrepreneurship through its Ashoka Fellows program with stipends, professional development, and networking, social entrepreneurs are "ambitious and persistent, tackling major social issues, and offering new ideas for wide-scale change."[53] Ashoka views social entrepreneurs as passionate system changers, who "often seem possessed by their ideas, committing their lives to changing the direction of their field. They are both visionaries and ultimate realists, concerned with the practical implementation of their vision above all else."[54]

The enterprises created by social entrepreneurs emerge in a variety of ways. Some, as discussed above, are divisions or initiatives that are created in large multinational corporations because the company believes it can "do well by doing good," that is, make a profit while serving some unmet social or ecological need or niche. Others are formed as entrepreneurial ventures and are designed from their inception to have the dual purpose of profits and social purpose. In some places, entities that serve social needs, like credit unions, associations, and cooperatives, are also considered to be social enterprises. Increasingly, non-profit organizations too are engaging in moneymaking activities that generate profits as a means of supporting their social goals, and sometimes these too are classified as social enterprises. Social enterprises are founded or initiated within larger entities by social entrepreneurs who have certain general characteristics.

Social Enterprise Within NGOs or as Nonprofit Enterprises

Social enterprise also takes place increasingly inside NGOs and civil society organizations, when they attempt to provide a stable source of income for their mission- or values-driven activities by developing an internal business model. David Bornstein, after documenting the impressive growth in NGOs in recent times, argues that these so-called independent, third, or not-for-profit sector enterprises should be labeled citizen sector enterprises.[55] Social entrepreneurs starting from the citizen sector increasingly need to adopt business models to sustain their businesses, even while they do not seek profits in the traditional sense.

To provide a steady source of income, for example, some social enterprises might create a business within the larger entity, for example, selling supplies or other goods so that they are bringing in money on a regular basis without having to rely on grants. Others create a business model that brings in resources but do not aim for profits, just an ability for the enterprise to survive. One interesting example of a social enterprise is called Invennovations. Invennovations is an NGO that bills itself as "putting the access puzzle together for the 'base of the pyramid.'"[56]

Micro-Enterprise and Microfinance

One of the important advances made in recent years has been the development of microfinance approaches to fund small businesses and entrepreneurs, particularly in developing countries where such approaches are used to try to bring people out of extreme poverty. Microfinance or micro-credit is premised on making quite small loans to entrepreneurs, frequently women, with little collateral, but who are willing to serve in a peer-based support and repayment network. The idea behind microfinance was pioneered by Mohammed Yunas, who, with Grameen Bank, won the Nobel Peace Prize in 2006 to provide small loans mostly to women so that they could fund small businesses from which they could earn enough to lift themselves and their families out of grinding poverty.

Grameen is perhaps the world's best known microfinance agency but its approaches have since been adopted by the United Nations and numerous other agencies to forward the entrepreneurship and small business efforts of people in poverty as well as some profit-making enterprises. In founding Grameen Bank,[57] Yunas understood that conventional banking practices would be too costly, so he created a system of local support based on the belief that credit is a basic human right that should foster human potential for growth, rather than relying on conventional thinking that fundamentally rests on the principle that "the more you have, the more you can get."[58]

As a leading microfinance bank, Grameen now serves more than eight million borrowers, of which 97% are women, has more than 2,500 branches, and serves more than 80,000 villages in Bangladesh. Grameen operates at the local level by providing very small loans to local entrepreneurs, organizing small groups of them into networks to ensure repayment. In contrast to conventional banking, Grameen's focus is on women, in the belief that they will use resources gained from their business to provide food, shelter, clothing, and opportunities for their children. It operates predominantly in small villages and rural areas, bringing the banking services to the people in their villages, and repayment occurs weekly in small installments. Combining social, antipoverty, and economic development objectives along with profitability goals, Grameen—and other microfinance entities—has a 97% repayment rate.

Today, there are many types of microfinance institutions, mostly supporting various forms of microenterprise. Most of these are microfinance institutions, founded like Grameen Bank to provide these very small, non-collateralized loans to the very poor. Sometimes, micro-finance institutions (MFIs) are run as for-profit entities because repayment rates tend to be very good, while others are organized as credit unions, financial cooperative, and even state-owned development agencies, and sometimes postal services.[59] Sometimes microloans and microcredit are criticized because of their high interest rates (which can range from as low as 4% to as much as 50%), and for lack of an actual ability to bring people totally out of poverty. Interest rates tend to be high because of the cost of administering numerous small loans, the need for loan officers to be present in many villages on a regular basis to ensure repayment, and because of related factors that mean that microfinance tends to be a costly service.

Despite criticisms and a good deal of uncertainty about whether microfinance actually alleviates poverty or changes lives,[60] there is evidence that access to microloans reduces the vulnerability of loan recipients to the ill effects of poverty, reduces financial insecurity, and enhances the consistency of their income flows.[61] Other studies suggest different benefits, articulated as more family income and quality of life, particularly since most loan recipients are women and spend on their families, promoting habits of saving among borrowers, raising awareness and empowering women, and motivating women, for example, in Bangladesh, to participate more actively in civic activities.[62]

Concluding Thoughts

Above, we have reviewed numerous types of enterprise that constitute the emergence of what we call SEE Change, the shift to a sustainable enterprise economy. Whether the types of enterprise briefly outlined above can actually help shift the momentum of the world toward a more socially equitable, responsible, and sustainable orientation remains to be seen. Business, of course, is only one sector, although its impact on the world has been profound. Although it is frequently claimed that much of job creation and certainly much of local economies rests in the small and medium-sized enterprise (SME) sector, it is the large multinational corporations that today dominate the world. It is their influence that has had the most problematic impacts on ecology and on some societies. Furthermore, of course, large businesses have also provided significant impetus for economic development and improvements in many parts of the world, including the provision needed goods and services as well as jobs. For businesses to shift toward SEE Change, and particularly for the relatively smaller, more socially conscious businesses discussed here to "disrupt" the current social order, they will need to gain in dominance and power. Yet, as is notable in today's economy, this type of creative disruption, as Schumpeter named it, happens constantly—and is evident in many of today's dominant enterprises. Just think of Google, eBay, and Facebook, to name a very few. It is in this process of creative disruption that we believe hope for a better future lies.

Notes

1. D. Tapscott, and D. Ticoll, *The Naked Corporation: How the Age of Transparency Will Revolutionize Business* (New York: Free Press, 2003).

2. J. A. Schumpeter, *Capitalism, Socialism and Democracy* (New York, Harper, 1975) (original publication, 1942), p. 82.

3. Schumpeter, cited above, pp. 82–84.

4. R. L. Ackoff, *Redesigning the Future* (New York: Wiley, 1975).

5. E.g., C. West Churchman, Wicked Problems, Guest Editorial, *Management Science* 14, 4(1967): B141–B142.

6. C. West Churchman, Wicked Problems, Guest Editorial, *Management Science* 14, 4(1967): B141.

7. H. Reingold, *Smart Mobs: The Next Social Revolution* (New York: Basic Books, 2003).

8. B. Appleyard, Sunday Times Online, February 15, 2009, http://technology.timesonline.co.uk/tol/news/tech_and_web/the_web/article 5725644.ece, accessed February 5, 2010.

9. This number comes from http://beerpla.net/2008/08/14/how-to-find-out-the-number-of-videos-on-youtube/, as of 2008, and is probably higher by now.

10. M. Arrington, YouTube Video Streams Top 1.2 Billion/Day, Tech Crunch, June 9, 2009, http://www.techcrunch.com/2009/06/09/youtube-video-streams-top-1-billionday/, accessed February 2, 2010.

11. J. Hagel, III, and J. F. Rayport, "The coming battle for customer information," *Harvard Business Review* 75, 1(1997): 53–65.

12. From Electronics Takeback Coalition, http://www.computertakeback.com/Tools/Facts_and_Figures.pdf, accessed February 4, 2010.

13. Electronics Takeback Coalition, cited above.

14. Electronics Takeback Coalition, cited above.

15. Electronics Takeback Coalition, cited above.

16. Conceptual information in this paragraph is from O. K. Mont, Clarifying the Concept of Product-service System, *Journal of Cleaner Production* 10(2002): 237–245.

17. A. L. White, M. Stoughton, and L. Feng, "The Quiet Transition to Extended Product Responsibility," submitted to US Environmental Protection Agency, Office of Solid Waste, May 1999, http://www.p2pays.org/ ref/17/16433.pdf, accessed February 4, 2010.

18. O. K. Mont, "Clarifying the concept of product-service system," *Journal of Cleaner Production* 10(2002): 237–245, p. 237.

19. A. Lovins, quoted on http://www.business.gov, http://www.business.gov/expand/green-business/product-development/servicizing.html, accessed February 4, 2010.

20. O. K. Mont, 2002, p. 238.

21. O. K. Mont, 2002, p. 238–239.

22. L. White et al., 1999.

23. A. S. Strom, "Businesses try to make money and save the world," *New York Times*, May 6, 2007, http://www.nytimes.com/2007/05/06/business/yourmoney/06fourth.html?_r=1&em&ex=1178769600&en=f898dbb3ee9240ab&ei=5087%0A, accessed April 30, 2009.

24. International Finance Corporation blog, http://ifcblog.ifc.org/ emergingmarketsifc/2007/06/forbenefit_corp.html, accessed April 28, 2009.

25. M. C. Jensen, "Value maximization, stakeholder theory, and the corporate objective function," *Journal of Applied Corporate Finance*, 14, 3(2000): 8–21.

26. B Corporation, http://www.bcorporation.net/, accessed February 4, 2010.

27. Certified B Corporation, http://www.bcorporation.net/about, accessed April 14, 2009.

28. B Corporation, about, http://www.bcorporation.net/about, accessed April 28, 2009.

29. B Corporation website, Declaration of Interdependence, http:// www.bcorporation.net/declaration, accessed April 28, 2009.

30. S. Perman, J. Tozzi, A. S. Choi, A. Barrett, J. Quittner, and N. Leiber, "America's most promising social entrepreneurs," *Business Week*, April 3, 2009, http://www.businessweek.com/smallbiz/content/mar2009/sb20090330_541747.htm, accessed April 28, 2009.

31. Conscious Capitalism website, http://consciouscapitalism.com/?page_id=59, accessed February 4, 2010.

32. Conscious Capitalism, Why Now, http://consciouscapitalism.com/?page_id=44, accessed February 4, 2010.

33. Biomimicry webpage, http://www.biomimicry.net/, accessed February 5, 2010.

34. J. Benyus, *Biomimicry: Innovation Inspired by Nature* (New York: Harper Perennial, 2002).

35. See http://www.fourthsector.net, accessed February 4, 2010.

36. J. Emerson, "The blended value proposition: integrating social and financial returns," *California Management Review* 45, 4(2003): 35–45.

37. Fourth Sector website, http://www.fourthsector.net/learn, accessed February 10, 2010.

38. See http://www.fourthsector.net/learn/fourthsector, accessed February 4, 2010.

39. Fourth Sector, http://www.fourthsector.net/learn, February 10, 2010.

40. Fourth Sector, http://www.fourthsector.net/learn, February 11, 2010.

41. Fourth Sector, http://www.fourthsector.net/learn, February 11, 2010.

42. Fourth Sector, http://www.fourthsector.net/learn, February 11, 2010.

43. See S. Waddock, *Leading Corporate Citizens: Vision, Values, Value Added*, 1st, 2nd, and 3rd editions (New York: McGraw-Hill, 2002, 2006, 2009), for an extended discussion of these sectors or spheres.

44. J. Emerson, "The blended value proposition: Integrating social and financial returns," *California Management Review* 45, 4(2003): 35–45.

45. H. Sabati with the Fourth Sector Network Concept Working Group, *The Emerging Fourth Sector: Executive Summary*, http://www.fourthsector.net, accessed February 11, 2010 (Washington, DC: Aspen Institute, 2009).

46. See K. Alter, 2009, "Social enterprise typology," http://www.virtueventures.com/setypology.pdf, accessed February 8, 2009.

47. C. K. Prahalad, *The Fortune at the Bottom of the Pyramid: Eradicating Poverty Through Profits* (New Delhi: Pearson Education/Wharton School Publishing, 2005). See also work by C. K. Prahalad, and A. Hammond, Serving the World's Poor Profitably, *Harvard Business Review* 80, 9(2002): 48–57.

48. S. Hart, *Capitalism at the Crossroads: The Unlimited Business Opportunities in Solving the World's Most Difficult*

Problems (Philadelphia: Wharton School Publishing, 2005); see also S. Hart, Beyond Greening: Strategies for a Sustainable World, *Harvard Business Review* 75, 1(1997): 66–76.

49. C. M. Christensen, H. Baumann, R. Ruggles, and T. M. Stadtler, "Disruptive innovation for social change," *Harvard Business Review* 84, 12(2006): 94–101.

50. C. K. Prahalad, *The Fortune at the Bottom of the Pyramid: Eradicating Poverty through Profits* (New Delhi: Pearson Education/Wharton School Publishing, 2005). See also work by C. K. Prahalad, and A. Hammond, Serving the World's Poor Profitably, *Harvard Business Review* 80, 9(2002): 48–57.

51. Notably, A. Karnani, Mirage at the Bottom of the Pyramid: How the Private Sector can Help Alleviate Poverty, *California Management Review* 49, 4(2007): 90–111.

52. C. K. Prahalad, and A. Hammond, "Serving the world's poor profitably," *Harvard Business Review* 80, 9(2002): 48–57. See also S. L. Hart, Innovation, Creative Destruction, and Sustainability, *Research Technology Management* 48, 5(2005): 21–27.

53. Ashoka website, http://ashoka.org/social_entre preneur, accessed February 11, 2010.

54. Ashoka website, http://ashoka.org/social_entre preneur, accessed February 11, 2010.

55. D. Bornstein, *How to Change the World: Social Entrepreneurs and the Power of Ideas* (Oxford, UK: Oxford University Press, 2007).

56. Invennovations, http://www.invennovations.com/, accessed February 15, 2010.

57. Information on Grameen Bank, the Grameen Bank website, various places, http://www.grameen.com/, accessed February 12, 2010.

58. Grameen Bank website, Is Grameen Bank Different? http://www.grameen-info.org/index.php?option=com_cont ent&task=view&id=27&Itemid=176, accessed February 12, 2010.

59. From http://www.microfinancegateway.org/p/ site/m/template.rc/1.26.9183/, accessed February 12, 2010.

60. E.g., T. Dichter, The Myth of Microfinance, *Banker* 157(July 2007): 10.

61. J. Murdoch, "Does microfinance really help the poor? New evidence from flagship programs in Bangladesh," Princeton University Working Paper No. 198, http://ideas. repec.org/p/pri/rpdevs/198.html, accessed February 12, 2010.

62. K. F. Ahmed, "Microcredit as a tool for women empowerment: The case of Bangladesh," Foreign AID Ratings, http://www.foreignaid.com/thinktank/microcre dit.html, accessed February 12, 2010, and N. Islam, "Can microfinance reduce economic insecurity and poverty? By how much and how?" DESA Working Paper No. 82, St/ESA/2009/DWP/ 82, 2009, http://www.un.org/esa/ desa/papers/2009/wp82_2009.pdf, accessed February 12, 2010.

CHAPTER 43

Sustainable Leadership

Towards a Workable Definition

Sander G. Tideman

Nyenrode Business University, The Netherlands

Muriel C. Arts

Nyenrode Business University, The Netherlands

Danielle P. Zandee

Nyenrode Business University, The Netherlands

Sustainable development is aimed at transforming the correlation between economic growth, the environment and society from negative to positive (World Bank 2012). This can be achieved when business organisations fully accept the challenges of sustainability as a business development opportunity and transform their business models. This is increasingly the case; leading companies are embarking on a transformational process with multi-stakeholders in their value chains and in doing so transform into sustainable business organisations. This is supported by a trend in science that places the human being in social context back at the centre of economic and business theory and practice. Sustainability has become a business mega-trend that changes the demands placed on business leadership in various fundamental ways, thus creating the need for a new type of leadership—sustainable leadership (SL).

By exploring the literature on trends in economics, organisational change, sustainability and leadership, and outcomes of a series of interviews with leading sustainability thinkers and practitioners, this chapter will identify a number of key features of SL. SL requires a redefinition of core concepts that underpin current mainstream business leadership practice. Foremost is the concept of creating value, which cannot be equated with mere profits or price. Profits are derived from shared value, which in turn is the result of a process of intentional collaboration and long-term interests with a collective purpose of stakeholders in a particular value chain. The features of SL can be divided into

Source: "Sustainable Leadership: Towards a Workable Definition," by Sander G. Tideman, Muriel C. Arts and Danielle P. Zandee in *Journal of Corporate Citizenship*, March 2013, 49, pp. 17–33. Reprinted with permission from Greenleaf Publishing.

six categories of leadership attributes, which all start with a C—context, consciousness, continuity, connected, creative and collective—hence these are referred to as the **6C-model**. This model will be compared with a number of other recent leadership models designed for sustainability.

The Changing Context Towards Sustainability

Sustainability as Mega-Trend

It is abundantly clear that profound changes are happening affecting business leadership, on all levels of society and on a global scale: global poverty, global disease, global violence, biodiversity decline and climate change continue unabated. The world's economic and political structures seem increasingly incapable of protecting our ecosystems, managing our resources or preventing rising social inequality. As a result, there is now a business imperative for rapid, non-linear change. Business leadership will need to take up the challenge of creating sustainable economic systems.

Milton Friedman (1970) famously said: 'the only business of business is business'. If this were true, business leadership would continue to operate with a mind-set that is predominantly geared towards creating short-term profit and value for their shareholders, employees and consumers, while ignoring social and ecological well-being. This mind-set, that was the cornerstone of the industrial age when resources seemed abundant and inexpensive, is now increasingly recognised as the prime driver behind the emerging 'tragedy of the commons', in which producers, consumers and financiers hold each other in a 'prisoner's dilemma', a race to the bottom of overproduction/consumption/borrowing and consequential ecological overshoot and social unfairness. Given the fact that we have finite common resources for a rapidly growing population, by continuing to focus primarily on our own short-term self-interests, we collectively end up as losers (Gilding 2011).

The 'business as usual' approach, in which the short-term financial interests of shareholders tend to take precedence over long-term interests of stakeholders, is no longer an option from a long-term survival viewpoint. Indeed, leading companies have recognised sustainability as the next business 'mega-trend', just like IT, globalisation and the quality movement earlier, determining their long-term viability as a business (Senge 2008; Lubin and Esty 2010). Or in the words of Frank Horwitz (Horwitz and Grayson 2010): 'The only business of business is *sustainable business*'.

The hypothesis in this chapter is that the global problems have been created (and persist) because political and economic leadership employs flawed and increasingly outdated economic and business systems, based on limited assumptions about the nature of economic, social and ecological reality and the drivers of human behaviour. These assumptions were derived from Newtonian physics and Darwinian biology, in which economy, society, environment and wildlife were seen as separate worlds that humans—the 'fittest' among competing species—hold dominion over in order to extract value from, against as low as possible cost, and utilise it for their human agendas (or liquidate it to maximise GDP or quarterly profit margins). In this worldview individuals and companies regard themselves as autonomous, individual agents who make their own rational choices—the image of *Homo clausus* or *Homo economicus* (Gintis 2000). But this worldview, which has left human psychology, sociology, biology and ecology outside the picture, is no longer fit for purpose.

The new world-view is one in which business, economy, environment and society are no longer separate worlds that meet tangentially, but a single, inseparable entity: as they are interconnected and interdependent, decisions need to be made with an eye to the complete picture. This matches with the view of sociologist Norbert Elias who said that humanity should see itself as *homines aperti*, so that people are in open connection with each other and their environment, being formed by and dependent on others and nature (Aya 1978). This view has meanwhile been confirmed by findings from psychology and social neuroscience (Seligman 2002; Siegel 2009).

Before exploring what this world-view shift means for business leadership—a change we refer to as from 'business leadership as usual' to 'sustainable leadership' (SL)—we will review some trends in economics and business thinking that form part of the changing context, while pointing to aspects of a new, more accurate world-view that could underpin efforts to create sustainable economic systems.

New Paradigm Economics

In order to explain the growing tension between economic theory and practice, the new field of behavioural and neuro-economics is increasingly called on to explain economic reality. This field has arisen over the last 30 years based on empirical findings from many experiments involving real people. It has gained considerable traction thanks to the financial crisis, which made it obvious that classical notions of rationality and equilibrium of markets were mere theoretical constructs and had little to do with how markets behave in reality (Taleb 2007).

Several recent publications have popularised these new insights (Akerlof and Schiller 2008; Ariely 2009, 2012; Sunstein and Thaler 2009). A central insight of behavioural economics is that of fairness and trust as prime human drivers (Camerer 2004). Neuro-economics, founded by Daniel Kahneman, who received the 2003 Nobel prize in Economics for his studies on intuitive judgement and decision-making, explores the same territory of real behaviour. The significance of this work lies in its ability—for the first time in the history of economics—to describe the neuro-biological basis of economic behaviour. This work is bridging the heretofore-distinct disciplines of psychology and economics (Kahneman 1979; Glimcher 2009).

The new neuro- and behavioural science is revelatory because it provides empirical evidence derived from a biological basis for the notion that human nature is *not* driven by greed and egoism alone; at least equally important are principles of fairness, cooperation and altruism, which can express themselves in non-rational behaviour, or 'bounded rationality' (Simon 1972; 1982; 1997; Kahneman 1979). Since neoclassical economics considers itself to be a science concerned with 'hard data', the fact that there is a hard biological basis for

these principles helps to uproot the long held yet untested assumptions of classical economics on selfishness, individuality and rationality (Beinhocker 2006; Gowdy 2009). The wiring of the human brain indicates that motives of fairness and degrees of altruism are more natural to the human mind than selfishness and individuality. Most significantly, neuro- and behavioural economics have established that the so-called 'rational self-regarding actor model' needs to be replaced by a framework that accounts for our irrational, emotional and prosocial behaviours (Gintis 2000; Beinhocker 2006; Gowdy 2008).

By extension, our view of markets as a neutral mechanism that efficiently processes our collective rational choices into collective well-being and a state of equilibrium has become obsolete. We now know that the minds of market players are continuously subjected to emotional and social influences (Zak 2008). Thus, the theory of market equilibrium needs to be replaced by a view of markets as a dynamic, evolutionary process that is both shaped by our choices and shaping our choices, mostly on an unconscious basis.

In summary, the economic theoretical paradigm is changing. Table 43.1 shows the existing and new theoretical principles.

In short, in new economic theory it is no longer only important to know what we produce and consume; equally important is the understanding of *the way we think* and *our awareness of the social context*. Given the central role of human thinking and interacting in the new economic paradigm, markets should be viewed as a community where stakeholders are engaged in a continuous interdependent process of dynamic co-creation of shared value fulfilling functional, rational, emotional and spiritual need, both short and long term.

Business Transformation Towards Sustainability

The field of organisational theory has seen similar shifts in paradigm, from the image of an organisation as a hierarchically structured machine (Taylor 1909) to one of a living network guided by purpose and values. Contributions to this shift came from Senge

Table 43.1	Economic Theoretical Paradigm

Existing	New
Supply and demand: The purpose of economics is to match material needs (demands) with material resources (supplies), which are scarce by nature	Economics belong to social science which has established that humans are driven by more than functional and rational needs; supply/demand laws do not apply to all facets of life
The theory of efficient markets: markets tend towards equilibrium	Markets are manifestations of social human behaviour, so they are constantly developing and evolve over time
The rational agent theory: people are rational and individualistic agents	People are more than rational and functional agents: they are also emotional, social and spiritual beings, with concordant needs

(1990), who took inspiration from psychology and introduced the field of organisational learning, De Geus (1997) with the notion of a 'living company', Collins and Porras (1997) who looked at firms 'built to last' and Sisodia et al. (2007) who created the term 'firms of endearment' to describe companies who create profits by following purpose and passion. Sustainability provides additional fuel to this shift.

The initial calls for sustainable development came from concerned environmentalists and visionary social and public leaders, such Carson (1962), Meadows et al. (1972) and WCED (1987), typically projecting a vision of sustainability as a desired utopian 'end point', while putting the business community on the defensive as they were perceived to be the major threat to this desired state of sustainability. In the years that followed, sustainability has been defined more as a change process in which business has gradually taken on a participatory role. The definition of sustainability evolved, in the words of Peter Senge (2008), from being 'a problem to be solved, to a future to be created'. When the bubble of financial capitalism burst in 2008, mainstream business leaders began to question the wisdom of the status quo. With the growing environmental resource crisis in the background, the creative search for sustainable economic models has intensified. In almost any sector one can now find leading companies engaged in sustainability initiatives that Eccles et al. (2012) has defined as 'high sustainability organisations' (HSOs).

Several are listed on the Dow Jones Sustainability Index and are earmarked by sustainability monitors and investors (Krosinsky 2012; Generation Investment Management 2012). They include Unilever (food), Akzo Nobel and DSM (chemicals), Puma and Nike (footwear), Ikea (furniture), Coca-Cola (refreshment) and Google (Internet).

This is not to say that these companies are sustainable in all aspects of their business. For example, Unilever, which is rated among peers as the leading sustainability company with regard to its food business, is still struggling with the transformation of various detergent categories. But most of these corporations are engaged in a process of *transforming themselves* into organisations that deliver sustainable value—beyond mere financial growth— and thus contribute to the larger process of sustainable development (WBCSD 2011; Nidumolu *et al.* 2012; Kiron et al. 2013).

In efforts to gain sustainability objectives such as reducing ecological footprint, energy inefficiency and waste, HSOs are redefining and restructuring their production process and supply chains. These changes typically imply a process of increased collaboration among stakeholders along the entire value chain, in order to meet existing and future needs. These needs are not merely material, but include social and environmental needs, specifically those of local communities in supplier countries who are particularly vulnerable to social and ecological pressures. Bob Doppelt (2003) speaks of a new production paradigm: from 'take-make-waste', which was common practice in the industrial era, to 'borrow-use-return', which respects both the cyclicality of nature and social equity needed for a truly sustainable production process.

Michael Porter and Mark Kramer (2006; 2011) have described this dynamic process as 'creating shared value' (CSV), a concept that emerged on the basis of transforming the coffee value chain of Nestlé, in which the various players in a value chain collaboratively create more value than they would do when pursuing individual financial objectives. Interestingly, HSOs have started to expand the value chain concept to include parties such as financiers and end-consumers. Without involving the financial industry, many sustainability investments that are critically needed cannot be made. Likewise, without changing consumer behaviour by stimulating sustainable consumption, with the projected population growth on this planet in the decades to come, sustainability efforts will fall short of reaching the necessary scale and impact. In any sustainability scenario, planetary boundaries will soon be crossed if we fail to adjust current consumption levels in developed nations downward. In other words, sustainability requires scale up and collective consumer participation (Gilding 2011). Importantly, this requires a shift in the marketing paradigm, where there is no longer exclusive focus on enhancing *demand* from consumers but instead a more balanced focus on serving their *needs*. Demand thinking tends to confuse needs with wants. While wants are limitless yet largely unnecessary for life satisfaction, needs tend to be more modest yet are critical for well-being and happiness. Unilever is actively experimenting with changing consumer behaviour: it has launched a new shampoo that can be used without taking a shower, thus substantially lowering water usage (Unilever Sustainable Living Report 2012). In this case Unilever distinguished between the *need* for hygiene and sustainable water and the *want* for daily showers.

Finally, leading HSOs are also actively creating new measurement models to capture sustainable value to complement standard business performance indicators, which on their own do not reflect a fair price for the value created or destroyed (Porter et al. 2012). Footwear company Puma, for example, is a pioneer in accounting for impacts on water supplies from its production process and has created an Environmental P&L (Nidumolu et al. 2012). Taken together, these sustainability changes present the expansion of the concept of value, which is expanding in both time (from short to long term) and space (from shareholders to stakeholders). While this chapter does not allow for exploring the sustainable business transformation in depth, it is fair to conclude that the sustainability challenges present a major transformation in business practice. Specifically, they present a challenge to traditional business concepts and thinking.

This is illustrated by a comment made by Paul Polman, CEO of Unilever, explaining how he put sustainability on top of his business agenda:

> Most businesses operate and say how can I use society and the environment to be successful? We are saying the opposite—how can we contribute to the society and the environment to be successful? So it starts with asking the right question to yourself, which will change the way you think (Forum for the Future 2011).

Business thinker Gary Hamel (Hamel and Breen 2007) goes one step further by specifically addressing the beliefs we hold in our minds:

> The biggest barrier towards the transformation of capitalism cannot be found within the observable realm of org charts, strategic plans and quarterly reports, but rather *within the human mind itself* ... The true enemy of our times is a matrix of deeply held beliefs about what business is actually for, who it serves and how it creates value.

Sustainability thinkers agree that sustainable development requires a change in the way we think (Marshall et al. 2011). In the words of David Orr: 'The crisis we face is first and foremost one of mind, perceptions and values' (Orr 1992: 27).

John Mackay (Mackay and Sisodia 2013), CEO of Whole Foods Market and one of the pioneers in sustainable business, recently launched a network on the principles of 'Conscious Capitalism'. He writes: 'Conscious [capitalism consists of] businesses [that] think caringly, creatively, and strategically about the environment. They consider it one of the company's key stakeholders and treat it with the same respect and attention they give to the others'.

These trends have put the mind—the way we think—back at the centre of our economic and business world-view. So we should also put the mind at the centre of business leadership. Our minds hold both the cause of the current unsustainable economic models and the key for transforming them.

Consequences for Leadership

New Mind-Sets and Skill Sets

The contextual changes on macro- and micro-levels imply that 'business leadership as usual' will not suffice in creating sustainable economic structures. In particular, as our review of best practices of HSOs indicates, the new leadership requires a shift in business thinking, mind-sets and awareness, hence an evolved type of consciousness, with an appropriate skill set derived from this consciousness.

These observations correspond to findings by a recent study undertaken by researchers from Ashridge University and EABIS on the mind-set and skill set of the global leaders of tomorrow (Gitsham 2009). This report is based on a global survey of 194 CEOs and senior executives at companies participating in the UN Global Compact meetings conducted in 2008, complemented by in-depth interviews with 33 individuals, including HR and sustainability executives and other thought leaders. We complemented this with 25 interviews with leading sustainability thinkers and practitioners in 2010–2011.

With regard to mind-sets, leaders of tomorrow need to understand the changing business context: 82% of those polled say senior executives need to understand the business risks and opportunities of social, political, cultural and environmental trends; 70% say the global leader of tomorrow needs to be able to factor social and environmental trends into

strategic decision-making. The challenges and opportunities that these issues and trends present tend, by definition, to be complex—there is often little certainty and little agreement both about their precise nature and about the response that is required. Leadership in these circumstances requires a range of discrete mind-sets: 88% of those polled say senior executives need the ability to be flexible and responsive to change; 90% the ability to learn from mistakes—in other words, they need to be open-minded—and 77% say the future leaders need to have the ability to balance shorter- and longer-term considerations. The global leader of tomorrow also needs to be able to understand the interdependence of actions and the range of global implications that local-level decisions can have and to understand the ethical basis on which business decisions are being made, according to the Ashridge/EABIS report. Mackay and Sisodia (2013) describe these leaders as follows: 'Conscious leaders are usually strong individuals who possess exceptional moral courage and are able to withstand constant scrutiny and criticism from those who view business in a more traditional and narrow manner'.

In short, the future leader's mind-set recognises the changing context with trends towards increasing complexity and interdependence among stakeholders. In addition, this type of leadership employs a long-term view, a sense of continuity, while exhibiting open-mindedness, moral courage and a high degree of self-knowledge. We summarise this mind-set as three Cs: **context**, **consciousness** and **continuity**.

With regard to the skill set that is associated with this mind-set, the Ashridge/ EABIS report refers to the ability of **connectedness**—the ability to understand the actors in the wider political landscape and to engage and build effective relationships with new kinds of external partners. For different businesses this can mean regulators, competitors, NGOs or local communities. To quote the report:

The mind-set with which our current leaders are groomed does not encourage productive engagement with partners outside the organisation—leaders receive plenty of training in negotiation skills, for example, but on the whole lack the skills for engaging for effective dialogue and partnership.

To survive in the future, 73% of senior executives say the leader needs to be able to identify key stakeholders that have an influence on the organisation; 74% say they need to understand how the organisation impacts on these stakeholders, both positively and negatively; 75% say senior executives need to have the ability to engage in effective dialogue; and 80% say they need to have the ability to build partnerships with internal and external stakeholders.

Another particular skill set that is required is referred to as **creativity**; 91% stress the ability to find creative, innovative and original ways of solving problems, according to the Ashridge/EABIS report. Our review of HSOs' best practices points to the importance of applying this skill towards value creation by meeting the present and future needs of all stakeholders in the value chain. Finally, all these efforts should be designed from the perspective of scaling up so as to achieve collective sustainable impact. This includes the creation of measurement models that account for sustainable, shared value and embedding sustainability practices in business structures and systems. This can be framed as an ability to create **collectiveness**, complementing the abilities of **connectedness** and **creativity**.

In other words, SL implies the development of three new mind-sets and three new skill sets, each starting with a C. We call this the 6C Sustainable Leadership model and summarise the key new leadership elements in Table 43.2.

Comparing Sustainable Leadership With Transformational Leadership

There are parallels to many schools, most specifically transformational leadership, which, like SL, is aimed at transforming systems. The theory of transformational leadership (TL) was developed by James Macgregor Burns (1978), who distinguished TL from transactional leadership. While the latter defines leadership as skills and knowledge aimed at making people work effectively within the current status quo, Burns defined transformational leadership as a process in which leaders and followers help each other advance to a stronger intrinsic motivation with a view of addressing unmet social needs by transforming the status quo. He found that transformational leaders offer followers something more than just working for self-gain; they provide followers

---

Table 43.2 Elements of Sustainable Leadership

SL elements	Concepts used in economics and business
Context	Recognising interdependence; complexity; ambiguity; interconnectedness; resource constraint; regulators; mega-trends
Consciousness	Mind-sets; world-views; beliefs; mental models; attitudes
Continuity	Long-term horizon; courage; strength; common purpose; centredness; change processes
Connectedness	Serving needs of all stakeholders; both long and short term influencing; collaboration; trust; fairness; altruism; relatedness; needs instead of wants
Creativity	Innovation for sustainable shared value creation; sustainable business models; new value measurement models; flow
Collectiveness	Scale up for collective impact; embedding sustainability in business structures; sustainable consumption

with an inspiring mission and vision and give them a renewed identity. In addition, this type of leader encourages followers to come up with new creative ways to challenge the status quo and to alter the environment to support people in successfully meeting their needs.

In an attempt to make TL more specific, in 1994 Bernard M. Bass further developed the concept. Bass discovered that transformational leaders consistently demonstrate four major skills and aptitudes (which correspond to various SL elements):

- **Individualised consideration.** Such leaders make their followers feel important, bringing about others' best efforts and fostering a sense of intrinsic motivation (**connectedness**)
- **Intellectual stimulation.** They are excellent at taking risks, challenging followers' assumptions about the world and fostering creativity by stimulating independent thought (**continuity/creativity**)
- **Inspirational motivation.** They communicate a vision that is appealing, hopeful and inspiring, instilling others with a deep sense of purpose and meaning (**consciousness/ connectedness**)
- **Idealised influence.** They have integrity. They consistently model the very changes that they seek to create, acting as solid, trustworthy and ethical role models for their followers (**consciousness**)

The definition of Bass corresponds to 4 of the 6Cs; context and collectiveness are not explicitly mentioned. Given the context shift presented by the mega-trend of sustainability, one can ask: is the Bass definition of TL enough? Is the TL model still relevant in today's context where the very cornerstones of capitalism are themselves being transformed? Will the current understanding of transformational leadership be sufficient to help us find and train leaders capable of creating the large-scale system change that sustainability calls for?

Our review concludes that the answer to these questions is negative. While the TL abilities can be found in the 6C Sustainable Leadership model, SL offers a framework that is somewhat broader in both scope (context shift, interdependency among multiple stakeholders, long term) and depth (serving needs of all stakeholders, shared value creation and collective scale-up). In order to determine the relevance of SL for solving tomorrow's challenges, we have compared SL attributes with a number of recent business leadership approaches developed from different backgrounds and disciplines.

Comparing SL With Recent Leadership Models Directed Towards Sustainability

In the context of this chapter, we have focused on those approaches that specifically orient themselves towards the challenge of sustainable transformation and development. These approaches are not exhaustive. They have been selected because of their apparent relevance for sustainability and systems change. Roberts (2012) has specifically attempted to upgrade transformational leadership skills to deal with the current crisis in capitalism. Likewise, Peter Senge (2008) has taken a holistic leadership view on the need for changing the larger economic system. Lueneberger and Goleman (2010) have looked at what it takes for leaders to drive sustainability initiatives in organisations. These three approaches represent different academic backgrounds—transformational leadership, systems thinking and emotional intelligence, respectively—which will enrich the comparison.

Marshall Roberts (2012)

According to Roberts, in order to be successful in the current context, transformational leaders typically exhibit the following five competences:

- **Holistic thinking.** They tend to see the 'whole' or big picture and avoid getting bogged down in siloed thinking
- **Systems thinking.** They see relationships between parts of the organisation that others miss, fostering breakthrough innovation

- **Humanistic thinking**. They are able to sense the emotions of others and connect on a 'heart' level when dealing with groups and teams
- **Social optimism**. They can authentically envision today's big problems being solved, and use this vision to overcome cynicism
- **Authentic filtering**. They quickly discern others' motives and react appropriately in complex social situations

Peter Senge (2008)

Senge, in his book *The Necessary Revolution: Working Together to Create a Sustainable World*, presents a new mind map that today's leaders must embrace. It has three core elements:

- **Systems thinking**. Yesterday's leaders thought in terms of parts and boxes.
- Today's leaders must be systems thinkers able to see the big picture relationships between parts of a system, and how these parts combine to create the emergent properties of the whole
- **Collaboration**—across boundaries. Yesterday's leaders embraced zero-sum thinking within the context of a scarcity-oriented, competitive framework. Today's leaders must be able to think from a larger, more expansive 'thrive and help thrive' mind-set, which allows them to collaborate across conventional business and social boundaries
- **Adaptivity**—through creating and adjusting. Yesterday's leaders focused on linear problem-solving and disciplined execution of detailed plans. Today's leaders must have a more creative orientation in which they re-contextualise old problems, allowing the inherent structural tension between their future vision and current reality to pull important goals into fruition According to Senge, who defines leadership as 'how we shape futures that we truly desire', these three parts work together to create an effective and selfreinforcing leadership paradigm for top learning organisations of tomorrow.

Goleman and Lueneberger (2009)

Goleman and Lueneberger have looked at how leadership within companies that are engaged in sustainability initiatives manifests and evolves. They found that sustainability initiatives could not be driven through an organisation the way other changes can. They have three distinct stages, and each requires different organisational capabilities and leadership competences.

- **Phase 1: making the case for change**. When an organisation is largely unprepared to address sustainability, the key challenge is to make a clear and compelling case for change. Because the organisation is at best reactive to the challenges of sustainability (and usually unaware of the opportunities), the sustainability leader must be adept at *collaborating and influencing* others in the course of the transition from unconscious to conscious reactivity. At the end of Phase 1, sustainability emerges as a powerful mandate that is pervasive throughout the organisation
- **Phase 2: translating vision into action**. When companies emerge from Phase 1, commercial orientation becomes the key competence in aligning sustainability initiatives and value creation, a point that cannot be emphasised strongly enough. Now the task is to translate high-level commitments into a comprehensive change programme with clearly defined initiatives and hard commercial targets. To make this happen, sustainability leaders in Phase 2 must excel at *delivering results, and they must have a strong commercial awareness*. At the end of this phase, the organisation is consciously proactive on sustainability across its footprint and tracks economic, environmental and social metrics over the business planning cycle
- **Phase 3: expanding boundaries**. The need for commercial orientation continues unabated but is now matched by a strong strategic orientation. As the organisation continuously raises the bar and leverages sustainability to create

competitive advantage, it increasingly views sustainability as a strategic opportunity and gauges its progress with metrics that reach beyond the short and medium term. As such, the sustainability leader must be *adept at anticipating and evaluating long-term sustainability trends*, spotting new opportunities and developing strategies to reposition the organisation to benefit from them. The goal is to embed sustainability in the organisation's DNA, much like quality or financial control, such that it is a core value and the organisation is unconsciously proactive about it

In short, sustainability leaders have the following six competences:

- Collaborating
- Influencing
- Delivering results
- Commercial awareness
- Anticipating long-term trends
- Evaluating long-term trends

Sustainable Leadership Attributes Framework

Taken together, the leadership attributes mentioned in the other sustainable leadership model systems generally correspond to the abilities of the 6C model. This is shown in Table 43.3.

Conclusion: Towards a Workable Definition of Sustainable Leadership

The leadership models reviewed in the context of this chapter confirm that while SL builds on TL, SL is broader in scope given the modern context of complexity and interdependence of stakeholder needs.

In particular, the review of sustainable business practices and the comparison of leadership theories confirm that tomorrow's leaders must fundamentally change the way they think, i.e. their mind-set or consciousness. The emphasis on consciousness corresponds with certain trends in economic science (such

Table 43.3 Sustainable Leadership Attributes Framework

6C SL	Roberts	Senge	Goleman and Lueneberger
Context	Holistic and systems thinking	Systems thinking	Evaluating long-term trends
Consciousness	Authentic filtering	Adaptivity	Anticipating long-term trends Commercial awareness
Continuity	Social optimism	Systems thinking	Anticipating long-term trends
Connectedness	Humanistic thinking	Collaboration	Collaborating Influencing
Creativity	Social optimism	Adaptivity	
Collectiveness		Systems thinking Collaboration	Driving results Anticipating long-term trends

as pointing to the shortcoming of classical economical thinking of supply/ demand, market equilibrium and rationality, which ignores psychological, social and ecological realities).

SL is distinct in that it starts with recognising the disruptive and transformational changes that occur in the context of business and society today, while many other leadership approaches start from the viewpoint of the leaders and/ or the current status quo of their organisation. By recognising the importance of worldviews, mind-sets and attitudes of both leaders and followers, SL implies the need for leadership transformation as the driver and necessary condition for sustainable transformation and development. From this it follows that future leaders will need to take up practices through which they can discover and adjust new mind-sets, beliefs and attitudes and develop the relevant skill set for the unprecedented transformational sustainability journey ahead.

In essence, success in sustainable business transformation rests on the interplay between leadership consciousness and contextual awareness, in both space and time. Therefore, among the 6Cs of sustainable leadership the mindset of context, conscious and continuity are the main drivers of sustainable leadership. Combined with the skills of connected and creative leadership, they enable the emergence of collective leadership necessary for sustainable value chain transformation and large-scale social sustainable impact. There is much research on the practices for connected and creative leadership that should form SL elements. However, SL recognises the relationship between context, consciousness and continuity as the fundament for sustainable leadership transformation and thus provides a new context and purpose for the connected, creative and collective leadership abilities.

More research will be needed to verify the SL model in business practice, while defining each SL leadership attribute in more detail. The next step is to determine the best way for leaders to develop these attributes. The ultimate aim of the 6C model lies in using it as a model for leadership development for those organisations intent on succeeding in sustainable business transformation and contributing to building sustainable economic systems.

References

Akerlof, G. A. and Schiller, R. J. (2008), *Animal Spirits, How Human Psychology Drives the Economy and Why it Matters for Global Capitalism*, Princeton University Press, Princeton, NJ.

Androff, J. and Waddock, S. A. (2002), 'Unfolding stakeholder engagement', in Andriof, J., Waddock, S. A., Husted, B. W. and Rahman, S. S. (Eds.), *Unfolding Stakeholder Thinking: Theory, Responsibility and Engagement*, Greenleaf Publishing, Sheffield, UK.

Ariely, D. (2009), *Predictably Irrational, the Hidden Forces that Shape our Decisions*, Harper Collins Publishers, New York.

Ariely, D. (2012), *The Honest Truth about Dishonesty*, HarperCollins, New York, p. 255.

Aya, R. (1978), 'Norbert Elias and "The Civilizing Process"', *Theory and Society*, Vol. 5, No. 2.

Bass, B. M. and Avolio, B. J. (Eds.) (1994), *Improving Organizational Effectiveness through Transformational Leadership*, Sage Publications, Thousand Oaks, CA.

Bass, B. M. (1998), *Transformational Leadership: Industrial, Military, and Educational Impact*, Erlbaum, Mahwah, NJ.

Beinhocker, E. (2006), *The Origin of Wealth*, Harvard Business School Press, Cambridge, MA.

Burns, J. M. (1978), *Leadership*, Harper & Row, New York.

Burns, J. M. (2003), *Transforming Leadership; A New Pursuit of Happiness*, Atlantic Monthly Press, New York.

Camerer, C. (2004), 'Behavioral economics: Past, present, future', in Camerer, C., Loewenstein, G. and Rabin, M. (Eds.), *Advances in Behavioral Economics*, Princeton University Press, Princeton, NJ, pp. 3–52.

Carson, R. (1962), *Silent Spring*, Mariner Books, New York (Houghton Mifflin, 2002).

Collins, J. and Porras, I. (1997), *Built to Last: Successful Habits of Visionary Companies*, Harper-Collins, New York.

De Geus, A. (1997), *The Living Company: Growth, Learning and Longevity in Business*, Longview Publishing, New York.

Doppelt, B. (2003), *Leading Change Toward Sustainability: A Change-Management Guide for Business*, Greenleaf Publishing, Sheffield, UK.

Doppelt, B. (2012), *The Power of Sustainable Thinking: How to Create a Positive Future for the Climate, the Planet, Your Organization and Your Life*, Earthscan, London.

Eccles, R., Ioannou, I. and Serafeim, G. (2011), 'The impact of a corporate culture of sustainability on corporate behavior and performance', Working Paper 12-035, Harvard Business School, Boston, MA.

Eccles, R. G., Miller Perkins, K. and Serafeim, G. (2012), 'How to become a sustainable company', *MIT Sloan Management Review*, Vol. 53, No. 4.

Forum for the Future (2011), 'Interview with Paul Polman', available at: www.forumforthefuture.org.

Friedman, Milton (1970), 'The Social Responsibility of Business is to Increase its Profits', *New York Times*, 13 September 1970.

Generation Investment Management Report (2012), 'Sustainable Capitalism', available at: www.generationim.com (accessed 9 May 2013).

Gilding, P. (2011), *The Great Disruption; Why the Climate Crisis Will Bring On the End of Shopping and the Birth of a New World*, Bloomsbury Press, New York.

Gintis, H. (2000), 'Beyond homo economicus: Evidence from experimental economics', *Ecological Economics*, Vol. 35, pp. 311–22.

Gitsham, M. (2009), 'Developing the Global Leader of Tomorrow', Ashridge University & EABIS Report, June 2009.

Glimcher, P. (2009), *Neuroeconomics: Decision Making and the Brain*, Academic Press, London.

Gowdy, J. (2009), *Economic Theory Old and New: A Students' Guide*, Stanford University Press, Palo Alto, CA.

Hamel, G. and Breen, B. (2007), *The Future of Management*, Harvard Business School Publishing, Boston, MA.

Horwitz, F. M. and Grayson, D. (2010), 'Putting sustainability into practice in a business school', *Global Focus*, Vol. 4 No. 2, pp. 26–29.

Kahneman, D. and Tversky, A. (1979), 'Prospect theory: An analysis of decisions under risk', *Econometrica*, Vol. 47 No. 2, pp. 313–27.

Kahneman, D. (1979), 'Prospect theory: An analysis of decision under risk', *Econometrica*, Vol. 47, pp. 263–91.

Kiron, D., Kruschwitz, N., Haanaes, K., Reeves, M. and Goh, E. (2013), 'The innovation bottom line', *MIT Sloan Management Review*, 5 February 2012.

Krosinsky, C. (Ed.) (2012), *Evolutions in Sustainable Investing; Strategies, Funds and Thought Leadership*, Wiley Finance, Hoboken, NJ.

Lubin, D. A. and Esty, D. E. (2010), 'The sustainability imperative', *Harvard Business Review*, May 2010.

Lueneburger, C. and Goleman, D. (2010), 'The Change Leadership Sustainability Demands', *MIT Sloan Management Review*, Vol. 51 No. 4 (Summer 2010).

Lutz, A., Greischar, L. L., Rawlings, N.B., Ricard, M. and Davidson, R. J. (2004), 'Longterm meditators

self-induce high-amplitude gamma synchrony during mental practice', *Proceedings of the National Academy of Sciences* 10116369-73.

Mackay, J. and Sisodia, R. (2013), *Conscious Capitalism: Liberating the Heroic Spirit of Business*, Harvard Business School Press, Boston, MA.

Marshall, J., Coleman, G. and Reason, P. (2011), *Leadership for Sustainability: An Action Research Approach*, Greenleaf Publishing, Sheffield, UK.

Meadows, D. H., Meadows, D. L., Randers, J. and Behrens, W.W. (1972), *The Limits to Growth: A Report for the Club of Rome*, Universe Books, New York.

Nidumolu, R., Kramer, K. and Zeitz, J. (2012), 'Leaders of Alcoa and PUMA, two forward-looking multibillion-dollar global companies, describe a framework for sustainable growth', *Stanford Social Innovation Review*, Winter 2012.

Orr, D. (1992), *Ecological Literacy: Education and the Transition to a Postmodern World*, State University of New York Press, New York.

Porter, M. E. and Kramer, M. C. (2006), 'Strategy and Society. The Link between Competitive Advantage and Corporate Social Responsibility', *Harvard Business Review*, December 2006.

Porter, M. E. and Kramer, M. C. (2011), 'The big idea: creating shared value', *Harvard Business Review*, January 2011.

Porter, M. E., Hills, G., Pfitzer, M., Patscheke, S. and Hawkins, E. (2012), 'Measuring shared value how to unlock value by linking social and business result', Conference Report available at: www.fsg.org

Roberts, M. (2012), 'Transformational Leadership', Worldview Thinking, www.worldviewthinking.com

Seligman, M. E. P. (2002), *Authentic Happiness: Using the New Positive Psychology to Realize Your Potential for Lasting Fulfillment*, Free Press/Simon & Schuster, New York.

Senge, P. M. (1990), *The Fifth Discipline: The Art and Practice of the Learning Organization*, Doubleday Currency, New York.

Senge, P. M. (2008), *The Necessary Revolution: How Individuals and Organizations Are Working Together to Create a Sustainable World*, Doubleday, New York.

Siegel, D. (2009), *Mindsight, the New Science of Personal Transformation*, Random House, New York.

Simon, H. (1972), 'Theories of Bounded Rationality', in McGuire, C.B. and Radner, R. (Eds.), *Decision and Organization*, North-Holland Publishing Company, Amsterdam.

Simon, H. (1982), *Models of Bounded Rationality, Vols. 1 and 2*. MIT Press, Cambridge, MA.

Simon, H. (1997), *Models of Bounded Rationality, Vol. 3.* MIT Press, Cambridge, MA.

Sisodia, R. S., Wolfe, D. B. and Sheth, J. N. (2007), *Firms of Endearment: How World-Class Companies Profit from Passion and Purpose*, Prentice Hall, Upper Saddle River, NJ.

Sunstein, C. R. and Thaler, R. H. (2009), *Nudge: Improving Decisions about Health, Wealth and Happiness*, Penguin Press, London.

Taleb, N. N. (2007), *The Black Swan: The Impact of the Highly Improbable*, Random House, New York.

Taylor, F. (1909), *The Principles of Scientific Management*, Harper and Brothers, New York.

Tideman, S. G. (2005), *Mind over Matter, Towards a New Paradigm for Leadership in Business and Economics*, Van Ede Publications, Amsterdam.

Unilever (2012), 'Unilever Sustainable Living Report', available at: www.unilever.com/sustainable-living/uslp/ (accessed 9 May 2013).

WBCSD (World Business Council for Sustainable Development) (2011), 'Collaboration, innovation and transformation, ideas and inspiration for accelerating growth: a value chain approach', December 2011, available at: www.wbcsd.org/Pages/EDocument/EDocument Details.aspx?ID=14257 (accessed 9 May 2013).

WCED (World Commission on Environment and Development) (1987), *Our Common Future*, Oxford University Press, Oxford, UK.

World Bank (2012), *Inclusive Green Growth*, World Bank, Washington, DC.

Zak, P. (2008), *Moral Markets: The Critical Role of Values in the Economy*, Princeton University Press, Princeton, NJ.

CHAPTER 44

The Collaboration Imperative

Ram Nidumolu

Innovastrat

Jib Ellison

Blu Skye

John Whalen

Blu Skye

Erin Billman

Blu Skye

"**B**USINESS COLLABORATION" IS the great oxymoron of corporate sustainability. Countless efforts by companies to work together to tackle the most complex challenges facing our world today—including climate change, resource depletion, and ecosystem loss—have failed because of competitive self-interest, a lack of a fully shared purpose, and a shortage of trust. To be sure, smart companies have embraced sustainability as a business imperative, and many have successful ongoing initiatives in areas they can address on their own–streamlining their manufacturing processes or reducing their fleet emissions, for instance. But when it comes to developing collaborative solutions to systemic problems, very little progress has been made.

The good news is that in our sustainability consulting to governments, NGOs, and global companies, we are seeing both a growing awareness of the critical need for improved collaboration and the emergence of innovative models that create value for companies and drive systemic change. Optimal collaborations focus on both business processes and outcomes. They start with a small group of key organizations, link self-interest to shared interest, encourage productive competition, and, above all, build and maintain trust.

In this chapter, we'll examine the most effective models for systemic sustainability collaboration, using case studies in dairy, apparel, waste reclamation, and municipal water management. But first, let's look more closely at why collaboration is critical in addressing global sustainability challenges.

Source: From "The Collaboration Imperative," by Ram Nidumolu, Jib Ellison, John Whalen, and Erin Billman, 2014, *Harvard Business Review, 92,* pp. 76–84. Copyright 2014 by Harvard Business Publishing. Reprinted with permission.

Systemic Solutions

The earth's natural commons—the atmosphere, natural resources, and biological ecosystems—provide enormous value to both business and society. However, much of that value is being destroyed through the suboptimal ways in which companies and other stakeholders use these complex and fragile systems. The next frontier of value creation for business, we believe, is to find ways to preserve and protect the natural commons while unleashing their vast untapped potential.

IDEA IN BRIEF

The Problem

Addressing global sustainability challenges—including climate change, resource depletion, and ecosystem loss—is beyond the capabilities of even the largest company.

The Analysis

To tackle these threats, and unleash new value, companies and other stakeholders must collaborate in new ways that focus on both processes and environmental impact.

The Solution

Optimal collaborations start with a small group, bring in project management expertise, link self-interest to shared interest, encourage productive competition, create quick wins, and, above all, build and maintain trust.

Consider the world's tropical forests. Spread over 1.9 billion hectares, they are among the most complex environmental systems in the world. They provide vital ecosystems services such as climate regulation, water filtration and supply, and nutrient cycling. They also provide natural resources, including food, fiber, freshwater, medicines, minerals, and other raw materials. The economic value of the forests (typically assessed by estimating the cost of replicating them through man-made means) is an estimated $4 trillion annually. Tropical forests also support 50% of the earth's terrestrial biodiversity. And, along with oceans, they are the world's most important global carbon sinks: natural reservoirs that capture and store more atmospheric carbon than they release.

Poor management has led to the disappearance of half of these forests in the past century, chiefly through their conversion to agricultural and commercial land. This is a classic case of sacrificing system value in favor of profits reaped by a few individual companies. Although business and society would ultimately benefit more in economic terms by preserving forests, shorter-term incentives for individual companies or sectors have led to their rapid destruction. Other vital natural commons—the atmosphere, oceans, watersheds, wetlands, coral reefs, and rivers—are experiencing similarly significant adverse impacts.

Preserving natural commons and tapping their full, long-term value require new collaboration models that consider ecosystems as a whole.

New Collaboration Models

In our work with global companies such as Walmart, Microsoft, Nike, Alcoa, and Waste Management, as well as with many NGOs and governmental organizations, we've identified four collaboration models that address systemic challenges and create systemwide value. These

Four Models for Sustainable Collaboration

Each square in this matrix represents a different model for collaboration, based on the breadth of organizations involved and the desired goals. Most collaborations will and should evolve over time, leveraging aspects of various models as needs and circumstances change.

FOCUS

Outcomes

Key Strategy
Develop *industry benchmarks* and *standardized systems* for measuring environmental performance across the value chain

Example
The Sustainable Apparel Coalition's Higg Index

Key Strategy
Institute "*payment for ecosystem services*" models in which firms invest in funds that compensate local communities for improving conservation and protection outcomes

Example
The Latin American Water Funds Partnership between Coca-Cola's larger bottler and upstream farmers and landowners

Operational Processes

Key Strategy
Identify and share *industrywide operational processes* that reduce emissions, natural resource consumption, and waste and protect the environment

Example
Dairy Management Inc.'s efforts to reduce milk's carbon footprint while producing renewable energy

Key Strategy
Initiate *extended collaborations* that engage the business community and noncorporate stakeholders in the pursuit of operational innovations and best practices that create shared value

Example
Action to Accelerate Recycling's collaboration to change consumer behavior

Companies Across the Value Chain

Companies and Nonbusiness Stakeholders

PLAYERS

models have two defining characteristics: (1) They engage carefully selected stakeholders and (2) they focus collaborative effort on innovation in either operating processes or business outcomes. (See the exhibit "Four Models for Sustainable Collaboration")

Stakeholder Inclusion

While sustainability collaborations typically engage a variety of players, including NGOs, academia, and governments, successful systemwide change requires participation by the right players. These are the key stakeholders that will be affected by sustainability initiatives and that, by changing their practices and other behaviors, can protect and capture system value. There are two such types of collaborations:

- *Corporate collaborations* include manufacturers, suppliers, distributors, retailers, and other players across the business value chain.

Non-corporate players such as NGOs, academics, and government may offer input, but they are not integral operational partners. It is the corporate players whose behavior must change to drive the requisite innovations.

- *Extended collaborations* are those in which both businesses and non-corporate partners—local governments and other stakeholder communities—are integral to the process.

Processes and Outcomes

The second dimension characterizing effective collaboration models is an explicit focus on improving either business processes or environmental impact outcomes.

- *Coordinated processes.* Stakeholders identify and share new operational processes that reduce resource consumption and waste and protect natural resources.
- *Coordinated outcomes.* Stakeholders work together to define desired outcomes, create standardized metrics for measuring environmental impacts, and benchmark performance.

Most sustainability collaborations will and should evolve over time, moving from one model to another or taking on features of multiple models. Let's look at each model in turn.

Corporate Collaborations Focused on Processes

Case Study: Dairy Management Inc.

Among the most effective ways companies can unlock the value in natural ecosystems is to collaborate on improving operations. Collaboration can focus on a particular node in the supply chain or address processes that span the value chain.

Consider the U.S. dairy industry. In 2007, key business leaders realized that the increasing pressure from NGOs, retailers, and consumers to reduce the industry's carbon footprint—especially from dairy operations and methane emissions—threatened the whole industry. In response, they began collaborating to identify inefficiencies and foster operational innovations across the value chain. For instance, they realized that manure, one of the biggest sources of carbon emissions, represented an untapped resource that could generate new revenue for farmers while reducing emissions.

However, the collaboration faced enormous barriers. Dairy farmers saw sustainability as a code word for government regulation and increased costs. The industry had no experience or skills in measuring or addressing its carbon footprint. In addition, there was no history of voluntary collaborative action among the farmers, processors, and retailers. To the contrary, the key players saw themselves as rivals in a zero-sum competition for profits.

Despite these challenges, Dairy Management Inc. (DMI), an industry group funded by dairy farmers, launched an initiative to reduce carbon emissions across the value chain by 25% by 2020. To govern this effort, DMI created the Innovation Center for U.S. Dairy, engaging CEOs of companies representing 75% of milk sales in the United States.

To overcome the skepticism of many industry leaders, DMI reframed the challenge by helping dairy farmers see that sustainability had long been a core value of the industry: In maintaining their family farms on the same land for generations, farmers had developed important capabilities that were directly relevant to the challenges ahead. DMI also pointed out that the farmers' biggest corporate customers were increasingly concerned about carbon emissions—a compelling reason to work together to reduce them. Finally, DMI promised the participants that only actions that were good for business would be considered.

With the farmers' support, DMI worked with the University of Arkansas's Applied Sustainability Center to develop a life-cycle analysis of milk's carbon footprint, which included primary research with hundreds of dairy farmers. This gave the industry a single shared knowledge base about carbon in the value chain. DMI also created a sustainability council, which convened 270 industry leaders and stakeholders in a three-day summit to identify opportunities for collaboration. An array of operational innovation projects were proposed, including initiatives to improve methods for growing feed crops, increase the use of methane digesters to turn manure into renewable energy, and

boost energy efficiency for farms and dairy processing plants. DMI estimated the potential business value of these projects at more than $250 million.

BUILDING AND MAINTAINING TRUST

Without trust, most collaboration efforts are unlikely to survive, however noble the cause and worthy the participants. Two practices can help organizations lay the groundwork of trust among stakeholders.

Practice appreciative inquiry. Pioneered by Blu Skye's academic partner David Cooperrider, from Case Western Reserve University, the appreciative inquiry method is based on research in the field of positive psychology. Appreciative inquiry helps focus attention in a specific direction.

If we focus on problems, we often find more problems. If we focus on strengths and possibilities, we become more inspired and innovative. The approach is designed to create in a short time a true spirit of collaborative innovation among participants.

We have adapted this model to address systemic sustainability challenges. Several projects described in this article employ the methodology in overall project management and in the ongoing facilitation of member communications and meetings. For example, the U.S. dairy industry's sustainability summit was focused on an inquiry that crystallized the promise of win-win solutions: "How might we work together to reduce the carbon footprint of the dairy value chain and create business value for our companies?"

Create deep meaning. To foster a strong sense of identity and belonging among members from different organizations, we suggest that individuals participate as a group in extended experiences that connect the head and the heart. Executive field trips such as white-water rafting, mountain climbing, and other wilderness trips, combined with storytelling and other shared experiences, strengthen bonds among collaborators and intensify their commitment to the group's goals.

The beauty of such deep engagement is that its effects persist even after the initial goals of the project are met. As Jason Kibbey, executive director of the Sustainable Apparel Coalition, put it, "What is unique about the SAC is the sense of personal mission and fulfillment among the individual members....This culture created the possibility for SAC's success and is continuing even after we've fulfilled our initial mission."

The corporate collaboration has strengthened trust and commitment among retailers, milk producers, and dairy farmers, and seven years later, it is going strong. A number of innovation projects have been fully implemented, and the industry continues to develop more-sophisticated tools for measurement and continuous improvement in farming, transport, and processing. The U.S. dairy industry has received millions of dollars in government grants from the USDA to support implementation of these projects. DMI was also recognized at the 2010 UN climate change summit in Copenhagen as a model for how the agriculture sector

can unlock system value by simultaneously addressing climate change and creating business value.

Corporate Collaborations Focused on Outcomes

Case Study: The Sustainable Apparel Coalition

One of the best ways to improve corporate sustainability is to set clear targets for desired outcomes and then measure progress. Likewise, one of the most effective ways to drive systemic collaboration is through the development of industry wide performance standards. In the highly competitive apparel industry, early innovator Nike invested years and many millions of dollars in developing internal tools for measuring the environmental impacts of apparel sourcing and manufacturing. However, Nike came to realize that as big as the company was, its measurement tools would have little systemic impact unless a critical mass of apparel brands and retailers adopted them as well.

In 2010 the unlikely pairing of behemoth Walmart and niche player Patagonia convened a group of 10 apparel companies in the belief that the adoption of a single, standardized index would drive efficiency and innovation across the apparel value chain and reduce environmental impact and supply chain risks.

The Sustainable Apparel Coalition, as the collaboration is known, developed a measurement tool called the Higg Index, which allows companies to compare environmental performance outcomes in areas such as energy efficiency, material waste, water use, and sustainable raw materials. It provides benchmarks at the company, product, and factory level. Drawing on work already done by Nike and the Outdoor Industry Association, the coalition quickly built a prototype and began testing it, in the fall of 2011, across more than 50 brands, retailers, and suppliers. The SAC's benchmarks have mobilized a "race to the top," in which companies that score lower than competitors on the index are motivated to improve their ratings.

The Higg Index is not just driving better outcomes; it is influencing capital investment decisions and changing operational behavior. Target and other major retailers have integrated the index into their supplier scorecard, using the measures to select suppliers. Apparel brands have used the index to help reduce fabric waste through improved product design. And manufacturers have used it to justify investments in new capabilities like wastewater recycling and improved energy efficiency. The index even improves performance within companies, as departments compare their scores and engage in productive competition.

More important, the Higg Index is enabling systemic collaboration on innovative practices that achieve desired outcomes, such as used-apparel recycling, are adopted across the industry. The SAC now includes well over 100 organizations, representing a combined 30% share of the global apparel market. The coalition has fostered a strong culture of trust, openness, and collaborative spirit among fierce competitors. As one member explained, the SAC is like a training camp for Olympic athletes. "Together we challenge each other to stretch and improve our performance. Then we go out and compete."

Extended Collaborations Focused on Processes

Case Study: Action to Accelerate Recycling

In extended collaboration models, non-corporate stakeholders—such as local communities (and the NGOs that represent them)—are integral partners in developing and implementing sustainability initiatives.

One such extended collaboration is the Action to Accelerate Recycling (AAR). AAR was formed, in 2012, to capture untapped value from recycling that no single company could on its own. Alcoa and other leading companies had been working for years to increase aluminum recycling rates but had achieved only incremental improvements. Every year in the United States, 54.3% of aluminum cans are recycled; the rest, worth $900 million, end up in landfills. The recycling rates for glass and PET plastic bottles are even lower (33% and 29%, respectively).

Boosting recycling clearly requires a systemwide collaboration. Recycling rates for aluminum depend heavily on the recycling of packaging and printed materials of all types, so the AAR initiative encompassed a spectrum of business stakeholders: Alcoa business leaders, consumer beverage brands, consumer packaged goods companies, materials manufacturers and packaging companies, retailers, and recycled content haulers and users. And because the success of recycling ultimately depends on consumer behavior, local municipalities, governments, and NGOs had to play a key role in developing AAR programs.

Six projects have been identified by this extended collaboration, including expanded curbside recycling programs; pilots for vending machines that accept consumers' returned cans; on-premise recycling at bars, restaurants, and workplaces; integrated awareness campaigns; and work with trade associations to collect key recycling data. The deliberately ambitious goal is to increase such "PPM" recycling—aluminum cans, glass and plastic bottles, paper and paper board, and steel—by 20% in three years. This stretch target was set to drive participants to seek significant system solutions, rather than solutions aimed at only one segment of the value chain. The increases called for in each of the PPM categories would produce an estimated $2.7 billion in recovered material value, reduce CO_2-equivalent emissions by 3.7 million metric tons, and create hundreds of thousands of green jobs.

The extended collaboration has reinvigorated efforts at the company level. For instance, Alcoa supplemented its AAR efforts with a $2 million commitment to expand education programs and improve recycling processes.

Extended Collaborations Focused on Outcomes

Case Study: Latin American Water Funds Partnership

Companies have always competed in their use of forests, watersheds, rivers, oceans, and other ecosystems. But an emerging class of collaboration models coordinates investment in and use of shared ecosystem services by focusing stakeholders' efforts on improving beneficial outcomes. The goal is to enable a steady supply of critical natural resources to corporations by working with local communities that affect, or are affected by, these businesses.

One of the most useful extended collaboration models is called payments for ecosystem services. PES models, as they're commonly known, maintain a steady flow of specific services (such as freshwater and timber from watersheds, forests, and other biodiversity habitats) in exchange for payments by corporations that use the services. Payments are made by corporations to local communities not simply as compensation for the use of the ecosystem services but as investments in their preservation and protection.

Consider the Latin American Water Funds Partnership (LAWFP), a PES initiative launched in June 2011. The partnership comprises corporations including Coca-Cola FEMSA (the world's largest bottler of Coca-Cola products), water utilities, NGOs such as the Nature Conservancy and the Global Environment Facility (the largest public funder of environmental projects), and the Inter-American Development Bank.

Together, the participants invest in a fund to pay upstream farmers and landowners, as well as local governments, to take actions that conserve the watersheds. Efforts include forest restoration, improvements in livestock grazing practices, sustainable agriculture to reduce soil erosion, and the shoring up of watershed boundaries to reduce sediments and improve water quality.

The LAWFP currently comprises 32 local funds totaling $27 million, based in Brazil, Colombia, Mexico, and other Latin American countries. The funds seek investments that will produce the highest returns (or eliminate the most cost) by increasing the quality and quantity of drinking and irrigation water, maximizing the efficiency of hydropower, and mitigating flood risks. The collaboration is expected to benefit 50 million people and improve 3 million hectares of natural ecosystems.

Funds of this type are typically trusts designed to provide long-term investment in sustainability over several decades. For corporate investors, the payoff takes several forms: The funds ensure both the quality and quantity of ecosystem services and reduce the need for expensive mitigation efforts in the future. A $1.5 billion New York City water fund, for example, supports farmers, landowners, and other upstream stakeholders in protecting and maintaining the Catskills-Delaware watershed, which supplies the city. Thanks to initiatives supported by the fund, the city has avoided the need to build a water filtration plant at an estimated cost of $8 billion to $10 billion—a 600% return on its investment.

To prevent logjams, start by convening a small "founding circle" of participants that share a common motivation and have mutual trust.

"Next" Practices

By design, many sustainability collaborations embrace a diverse array of stakeholders from the very beginning. Unfortunately, this approach dooms many efforts: By including participants with opposing intentions at the outset, progress is often stalled or killed before productive momentum can build. Even when the economic benefit to all participants is clear, these types of collaborations are difficult because of the complex human and organizational issues involved.

In particular, a deficiency of trust can undermine even the best-intentioned sustainability effort: Participants struggle to establish a shared vision and governance model, disagree on how investments and rewards are divvied up, and worry about the "free rider" problem, in which benefits accrue to nonparticipating actors. Making matters worse, many sustainability efforts suffer from a lack of independent, overarching project management capability.

The late C.K. Prahalad pioneered the concept of "next practices" as a way to enable breakthrough innovation in organizations. (See "Why Sustainability Is Now the Key Driver of Innovation," HER September 2009.) Let's look at seven next practices that enable successful sustainability collaborations.

Start With a Small, Committed Group

To prevent the logjams that can occur when many stakeholders with conflicting goals try to work together, start by convening a small "founding circle" of participants. The members must have a common motivation and have mutual trust at the outset. This group develops the project vision and selectively invites subsequent tiers of participants into the project as it develops. Ultimately, all stakeholders, including NGOs, governments, universities, and local communities, should be represented.

Careful selection of participants at each stage is critical. For example, in the dairy industry case, invitees were selected following a six-month interview process designed to identify participants who could bring the most knowledge, ability, and leadership skills. The nucleus of the Sustainable Apparel Coalition, which we advised, comprised a group of companies that had already demonstrated sustainability leadership in the industry. Walmart hosted the first meeting and invited the group (including several direct competitors) to tour its apparel offices and listen in as Patagonia's founder and CEO, Yvon Chouinard, talked about sustainability to the Walmart staff. This openness was so countercultural that some invitees wondered if the offer was genuine. As the initial group made progress in terms of both governance and action, the group reached out to more companies to participate. Then, as the SAC's vision, action orientation, and trust-based culture became more broadly recognized, it began to attract other industry players that wanted to drive change.

Link Self-interest to Shared Interest

To be successful, collaboration initiatives must ensure that each participant recognize at the outset the compelling business value that it stands to gain when shared interests are met. Such was the case with Coca-Cola FEMSA and its Latin America Water Funds partners. The bottler understood that the essential input into its operation—water—is best secured by investing in upstream efforts of farmers and other stakeholders at the river's headwaters to maintain a high-quality supply of water downstream.

Monetize System Value

The key to linking self interest and shared interest is to quantify how the collaboration reduces costs or generates revenue for each participant. FEMSA, for instance, reaps substantial financial benefits from its water-funds investment in the form of avoided costs; it won't need to build expensive water treatment plants to ensure the quality of its water supply.

Data analytics and business process analysis are also useful tools in monetizing system value at the group and individual level. In the case of the Latin American Water Funds Partnership, advanced analytics software helped identify which of the proposed protection and restoration activities would benefit the watershed and stakeholders the most. Projects were prioritized accordingly.

Create a Clear Path With Quick Wins

Successful collaborations convert a shared vision and individual passions into an action plan. However, many collaborative sustainability initiatives develop ambitious long-term goals that are only marginally relevant in the short term. To generate momentum and commitment, the action plan must also emphasize quick wins. Business thrives on visible and immediate results, and sustainability collaborations are no exception. Even if these wins are small initially, the cost savings or incremental revenues provide proof to other executives inside participants' organizations that the investment is worthwhile.

Large-scale sustainability collaborations must be structured to drive healthy competition among players.

The dairy industry summit led to a mix of projects that included longer-term initiatives, such as efforts to reduce cattle methane emissions, as well as ventures with immediate financial benefit, such as energy audits and energy-efficiency improvements that could lower operating costs for both farmers and processors in less than a year.

Acquire Independent Project Management Expertise

Sustainability collaborations can be complicated by participants' conflicting priorities of the various participants. Therefore, these partnerships should be designed and overseen by independent project-management specialists with demonstrated competence in trust building among diverse stakeholders. Additionally, the project management function must be seen by all participants as neutral and committed to the success of the project, rather than to any individual stakeholder. NGOs can often be quite effective in this role, but they must be committed to creating solutions that work for all participants, and the project managers must have the requisite skills.

Build in Structured Competition

The founding circle must find a way to sustain the focus on ambitious outcomes established at the outset. Healthy competition is often effective in generating long-term momentum. Unlike the self-interested competition that sinks many collaborative efforts, competition within large-scale sustainability collaborations must be explicitly structured to support shared goals. The Sustainable Apparel Coalition's Higg Index drove such structured competition, as players with low scores sought to improve while those at the top strove to remain there. The index also enabled transparency, which is central to most collaborations' success.

Nurture a Culture of Trust

Given the central importance of trust in successful collaborations, building and maintaining trust is an ongoing practice foundational to every other practice during the collaboration project. (See the sidebar "Building and Maintaining Trust" for two approaches to nurturing trust.)

ULTIMATELY, THE BEST WAY to scale collaboration is through markets that have the right incentives in place. We expect these markets to take off once the collaboration practices described here become widely adopted. When the full power of markets is brought to bear in unlocking environmental systems value, the good of the commons will truly become the common good of business.

Index

Figures, tables, boxes, and notes are indicated by *f*, *t*, *b*, or *n* following the page number.

About the Editor

Gill Robinson Hickman (Ph.D., University of Southern California) is currently Professor Emerita of Leadership Studies in the Jepson School of Leadership Studies at the University of Richmond. Her career has involved both administrative and academic appointments. Her expertise is in management, with an underpinning of organizational behavior, organizational theory, and human resource management. As an inaugural faculty member of the Jepson School, Dr. Hickman participated in the early structuring and formation of the program, a role for which her background as dean in the School of Health at California State University, acting associate dean in the School of Community and Public Affairs at Virginia Commonwealth University, and professor of public administration prepared her.

Dr. Hickman has presented at the China Executive Leadership Academy Pudong (CELAP), Shanghai, China; the Leadership in Central Europe Conference at Palacky University in Olomouc, Czech Republic; the Salzburg Seminar in Salzburg, Austria; and the University of the Western Cape in South Africa. She has presented at international conferences in Amsterdam, The Netherlands; Guadalajara, Mexico; and Vancouver and Toronto, Canada.

She is the author or editor of several books, including: *The Power of Invisible Leadership* (with Georgia Sorenson); *Leading Change in Multiple Contexts; Leading Organizations: Perspectives for a New Era; Leadership for Transformation* (with JoAnn Barbour); and *Managing Personnel in the Public Sector: A Shared Responsibility* (with Dalton Lee).

She has served as vice president and board member of the International Leadership Association and a member of several other professional, scholarly, and community organizations. Dr. Hickman is the recipient of several awards, including the University of Richmond Distinguished Educator Award.